The History of Legal Education in the United States

Commentaries and Primary Sources

The History of Legal Education in the United States

Commentaries and Primary Sources

Volume I

Editor
Steve Sheppard

Salem Press, Inc.
Pasadena, California   Hackensack, New Jersey

Frontispiece: Portrait of a Law Lecturer at the University of Pennsylvania. Oil painting by Mary Franklin. In 1998, Cynthia Arkin, Associate Director for Special Collections of the Biddle Law Library of the University of Pennsylvania Law School, physically compared this portrait to portraits of Penn faculty members of the nineteenth century and identified the lecturer in the portrait as strongly resembling the official portrait of Edward Coppee Mitchell (1836-1887), dean of the law school from 1872 to 1887. The portrait is believed to have been painted in 1879. (*Reproduction rights courtesy of the Honorable Morris Arnold. Duplication courtesy of Hugh Lauter Levin Associates.*)

∞ The paper used in these volumes conforms to the American National Standard for Permanence of Paper for Printed Library Materials, Z39.48-1992.

The history of legal education in the United States : commentaries and primary sources / edited by Steve Sheppard.
p. cm.
Includes index.
ISBN 0-89356-331-5 (set). — ISBN 0-89356-332-3 (vol. 1.). — ISBN 0-89356-333-1 (vol. 2)
1. Law—Study and teaching—United States—History. 2. Law schools—United States—History. I. Sheppard, Steve. 1963-
KF273.H535 1999 98-41481
340'.071'173—dc21 CIP

FIRST PRINTING

PRINTED IN THE UNITED STATES OF AMERICA

The History of Legal Education in the United States: Commentaries and Primary Sources

Edited by Steve Sheppard

VOLUME I

E. Nineteenth-Century Legal Scientists

VOLUME II

F. Nineteenth-Century Legal Science

G. The Twentieth Century

Contributing Authors

Abbott, Nathan
Adams, John
Ames, James Barr
Ballantine, Henry Winthrop
Beale, Joseph H.
Bruce, Jon W.
Carrington, Paul
Charles, Robert B.
Chase, George
Clark, Charles E.
Clark, David
Cohen, Morris L.
Cooley, Thomas M.
Coquillette, Dan R.
Corbin, Arthur L.
Dwight, Theodore
Eliot, Charles W.
Field, David Dudley
Finkelman, Paul
Frankfurter, Felix
Gould, James
Griswold, Erwin N.
Hand, Augustus
Herndon, William
Hoeflich, M. H.
Hoeflich, Michael
Hoffman, David
Holmes, Oliver Wendell
Hoover, James
Hunter, Thomas
Jarvis, Robert M.
Kennedy, Duncan
Kent, James
Klein, Stephen P., and Frederick M. Hart
Langbein, John H.
Langdell, Christopher C.
LaPiana, William P.
Lincoln, Abraham
Llewellyn, Karl N.
Marshall, John
Matile, M. G. A. (Gill, Brian, trans.)
Mayer, John
McMurray, Orrin K.
Minor, John B., and James P. Holcombe
Minor, Raleigh C.
Nicholson, Lowell S.
O'Connor, Sandra Day
Peden, James
Phelps, Edward J.
Pomeroy, John N.
Pound, Roscoe
Redlich, Josef
Reeve, Tapping
Rogers, Henry Wade, et al.
Roosevelt, Theodore
Rubin, Edward L.
Schlegel, John Henry
Schweber, Howard
Shapiro, Fred R.
Sheppard, Steve
Smith, George Harris
Staudt, Ronald
Stone, Harlan Fiske
Story, Joseph
Strauss, Peter L.
Sutherland, Edson B.
Swygert, Michael I.
Wambaugh, Eugene
Warren, Edward H.
White, James P.
Wigmore, John H.

Preface
A Message to the Reader

Steve Sheppard

The History of Legal Education in the United States: Commentaries and Primary Sources is unusual in its design, in that it presents not only writings by historians who have recently written in this field but also primary sources that are both important to the field as a whole and helpful for the reader of the more recent historical commentary. This division is hardly a clear one, and writings such as those of Paul Carrington on deans, Duncan Kennedy on students, Peter Strauss and Mike Swygert on teaching, Ed Rubin on scholarship, Jim White and Carl Monk on national organizations, and Ron Staudt, John Mayer, and Jim Hoover on technology are clearly both current commentary and future artifact.

The book is reasonably comprehensive of writings and artifacts in the history of legal education, but it is not meant to be truly exhaustive. There are, after all, already many other books that address particular questions or present certain archival material, and I saw no reason to reproduce much of this work.

Thus, for instance, the student of the history of law schools will recognize that few of the primary materials already published in Michael Hoeflich's excellent collection, *The Gladsome Light of Jurisprudence*, are reprinted here, nor are excerpts from certain important monographs, such as Alfred Z. Reed's reports for the Carnegie endowment, which are available in reprint editions to this day. Some work in the history of legal education, particularly the recent work of Paul Carrington and Bill LaPiana, is less fully represented here in the expectation that it will soon be printed in suitable volumes brought forth by the authors.

Another reason for occasionally spotty coverage of some issues considered in this book is simply the lack of recent scholarship in these fields. There is a paucity of scholarship in the history of law students, particularly of the changing class structure of students and of the long-delayed inclusion of women and racial minorities; of faculty and their working conditions; and of institutional histories of non-elite schools. Some of the scholarship that does exist in these fields is sufficiently skewed to present a false image of its subject. This is in part attributable to the scattered and damaged conditions of the archives for such work, but there are other reasons as well.

If we add to these limitations the limits that arise from my sometimes idiosyncratic emphases and curiosities, the reader is sufficiently on notice of the startling proposition that there is more to be found in the history of legal education than just between these covers, even if there are four of them. In any event, enough complaints regarding topics that are underserved in this collection might serve as grist for a sequel.

Still, as you, the reader, must have noticed, this is a large book. Large books are usually the product of many dedicated people, whose labor the editor may cheerfully accept and turn to his own advantage, and this book, which has been under development over many years, is no exception. Initially, I should note that without the initial encouragement of Michael Hoeflich, Mike Closen, and Chris Moose, I would never have undertaken this project, nor, without the dedication of Barbara Black would I have become interested in legal history.

I am grateful to Brian Gill, Jim Hoover, Tom Hunter, John Mayer, Jim Peden, Howard Schweber, and Ron Staudt, chapter authors who committed themselves to great labors as a favor. I am also thankful for the permissions of Jon Bruce, Paul Carrington, Robert Charles, David Clark, Morris Cohen, Dan Coquillette, Paul Finkelman, Michael Hoeflich, Bob Jarvis, John Langbein, Duncan Kennedy, William LaPiana, Carl Monk, Justice O'Connor, Ed Rubin, Fred Shapiro, John Schlegel, Peter Strauss, Mike Swygart, and Jim White, to reprint important works they had already written. My greatest thanks in this regard are reserved for Michael Hoeflich, whose work forms the backbone of several chapters here.

My selections of text to include were greatly improved in conversations with Whitney Bagnall, Paul Carrington, Morris Cohen, Dan Coquillette, Brian Gill, Michael and Karen Hoeflich, Wythe Holt, Tom Hunter, Mark Killenbeck, John Langbein, William LaPiana, Jim Peden, William Nelson, John Schlegel, Peter Strauss, Howard Schweber, and David Warrington. If by now you, the reader, have come to suspect that I really haven't had an original idea in compiling this book, you are probably nearer the truth than farther, but I am confident it is therefore a much better book.

The artwork that has found its way into these pages is largely here thanks to the kindness of Harvard Law School and the careful efforts of Steve Smith there. Although credits appear throughout, I am especially grateful to Judge Morris Arnold, who made possible the reproduction of *The Law Lecturer at the University of Pennsylvania*, which hangs in his chambers but graces all three of these volumes, to Columbia and Penn, which provided important portraits, and to Cynthia Arkin, who found the great picture of the tennis players and identified Judge Arnold's lecturer. The labor of production has fallen largely on the shoulders of the editorial and production teams at Salem Press as well as the diligent Kristin Keck, assisted by Jill Pullum and Cindy Hurst.

Finally, this book would not have been possible without the care of wonderful librarians. David Warrington, Steve Smith, and the staff at Harvard; Kent McKeever, Whitney Bagnall and the staff at Columbia; the staff of the Litchfield, Connecticut, Historical Society, and Cynthia Arkin at Penn were particularly kind and hospitable. Sharon Bradley and John Michaud at Thomas Cooley were miracle workers in tracking down my most obscure references at odd hours of the day and night.

By now it should be clear to the discerning reader that I not only had little to think about in this project, but little to do but bask in the glow of the warm efforts of my friends.

—*Steve Sheppard*

The History of Legal Education in the United States

Commentaries and Primary Sources

Introduction
Why Study the History of Law Schools?

Steve Sheppard

The author is currently a graduate fellow of Columbia University School of Law and a visiting associate professor in the law school of the University of Arkansas in Fayetteville.

When experience is not retained, as among savages, infancy is perpetual. Those who cannot remember the past are condemned to repeat it. —George Santayana[1]

The idea of a history of legal education appears at first blush to be one of the least exciting ideas one might have for a book. Certainly, the editor of this book has found it a perfect suggestion for moving along idle chatterers of the cocktail hour to more fertile topics elsewhere, leaving the editor free to while away the time with that small contingent of tolerant friends who never listen to the editor on any topic. (Indeed, the few idlers who feigned interest were routinely and finally dispatched with the news that the history would occupy two volumes.)

So, the question must be put of why a person of reasonable sanity would be attracted to such a study. The answers to this question are many, but resolve essentially into two groups: it's not really as boring as it sounds, and it's tremendously useful to anyone attempting to understand the law, let alone attempting to learn or teach it. Both sets of answers deserve explication.

First, the history is, really and truly, interesting as an intellectual enterprise in itself. As in many institutional histories, the record is not one of abstract labels so much as it is one of people, their ideas, their failures and successes, and, quite often, their outrageous idiosyncrasies. The stories of law schools have filled novels and movies, albeit without uniformly critical success, because law schools are scenes of drama, as teachers struggle to bring the students to the law, and the student struggles to understand it. The story of those stories inevitably unearths moments of pathos, triumph, conflict, humor, and the other tools of the story-teller's art. And, of course, many people are attracted to stories in which they or their kind are center stage, and so for many lawyers, the story of legal education has a nearly autobiographical quality to it.

The stories of law schools also offer the most effective method of understanding them. Whether for the teacher or the student, to know more about the idea of law teaching is to make some forms of it more comprehensible. Of course, this comprehensibility might suggest that the forms in which that idea is manifested are inadequate to the tasks of its pursuit, just as perfect comprehensibility might suggest that no task was particularly chosen. Even so, to understand surreality can be an odd comfort to those expecting the real.

Furthermore, the history of the law school is, effectively, the history of lawyers and, often, of the law. To attempt to fully understand the law, one must understand who creates, maintains, and changes it, and these people have only one common feature among them: a legal education.

Second, the history of legal education sets the stage for its future. Santayana likened human institutions to the individual, whose progress is only possible after moving from an easily distracted and ignorant youth, when all change is novel, and before reaching an age of forgetful repetition when adaptation is no longer possible. Only in the middle, when people are "docile to events, plastic to new habits and suggestions, yet able to graft them on original instincts" is progress possible.[2] Only then can we both discern some behaviors and ideas that deserve conservation and recognize new ones worthy of preference and substitution.

The modern American law school is a place of profound smugness. While there are occasional exceptions, the law schools are distant in thought, and sometimes in place, from universities and other centers of learning. Those who teach in law schools are usually intent upon narrow studies of narrow fields of teaching and research. For the most part the teachers of one age unwittingly copy the practices and habits of mind followed by the teachers of their youth, who were in turn copying the practices and habits of an even earlier age. The result can be, for some teachers, an unreflective repetition by the apprentice of the technique of long-removed masters in the law school guild. There are occasional struggles among the national professoriate to shake off the manacles of habit, but even these struggles recur with such cyclic repetition that one is tempted to find in them just more evidence of repetition. Thus, isolated from the currents of allied fields, as well as from the lessons of its own past, when changes occur in legal education, they are often the greatest surprise to those responsible for its leadership. Likewise, when unthinking stasis occurs in legal education, its corrosion is known to all but those who might reverse its invidious spread.

The dangers in such a condition are grave. Perhaps the greatest danger is that changes, when they inevitably occur, will obliterate past achievements. Like the leaders of cities that level architectural treasures in the blinding flash of money and progress, whose successor generations look back on the losses with nostalgia, law teachers who reject past methods of the academy without first understanding and valuing them risk replacing a noble edifice with one less attractive and less effective. On the other hand, a failure to understand the origins and limits of ideas may make an institution hidebound. A fear of change may retard progress that would have, in fact, strengthened the institution in realizing its aims as well as strengthened the roles of the individuals who labor within it. History is replete with leaders who protected their privileges and vassals from change, until the moment of the regicide.

Today, legal education may be on the brink of profound change. The reasons for this potential are numerous, and some are obvious, such as the technological shifts which already are evident in experimental forms. The reasons for others are less apparent but possibly more profound.

The most important reason for this potential is a change in cultural climate that is far greater than its effects in law schools. American culture is profoundly changing the personalities and talents of both law students and law teachers. In the latter fifty years of the twentieth century, notions of an ideal that was fundamental to an older ideal of law have declined. To suggest today that a professional class should represent an ideal of manners and aesthetics in which, most important for the law, fair play and civility are signal virtues, and that the idea of the right is distinct from the win or the profit is to open oneself to charges both of both elitism and of naïveté.

Of course, reality rarely met this ideal, but as the ideal has withered, reality seems to have moved even more distant from it, so that the professional is now seen as interested more in the self than in the client, and more interested that the client return for more business than that some notion of justice or any other goal be served. This degradation has, perhaps, sped the cultural inflation of the value of credentials, so that the ordinary phenomenon that the cachet of a credential will always devalue has been accelerated. New cultural elites have arisen based on fame and salary, which may be a more democratic affect than the old cultural system of elites based on manners and money, but which has had the effect of diminishing the significance of the professions, even at a time when they are more universally accessible for membership than ever before. Thus, the idea that a lawyer should have a particular manner and reflect a particular ideal of behavior or virtue is no longer current, and the idea that legal education should ensure such a personality in its graduates is in decline.

In the last three decades of the century, the role of legal education in the academic marketplace has reverted to something more like the university law school experience of the early nineteenth century, in which young students used the law as a finishing school and not necessarily as a preparation for an active practice of law. While an overwhelming percentage of law school graduates take licenses as lawyers, increasingly lawyers have moved from practice to alternative careers in publishing, arts, agriculture, management, and a host of other spheres. Thus while the preparation of new lawyers remains a defining element of legal education, law schools also deliberately provide an educational base that is not aimed toward the active practice of law but toward a particular intellectual experience and a concomitant cultural identity. That such an intellectual exposure is needed as a graduate experience is in part the product of another change, the decline of undergraduate education.

The American undergraduate at the close of the twentieth century, particularly in arts subjects, has been granted that most horrible of desires, unqualified empowerment. As universities have competed for students to support institutions defined by growth, students have been given a choice to spend their collegiate years either in the long hours studying alone in the pursuit of knowledge and understanding or in the short hours of searching with others for sexual experimentation and developed social standing. Colleges that provide profitable athletic spectacles while trimming reading lists and essay exams are not simply the more attractive; they are also the more cost-efficient. As a result, most students entering legal education at the close of the century are less likely than their predecessors to know the details of government and history, are less likely to have a developed ability to discern the meaning of text and context in a writing, and are far less likely to have a careful technique of prose writing and analytical argument. The product of a television-based, consumer society, the majority of students have come to expect that education should be entertaining, risk-free, and easily accomplished in twenty-minute segments. The product of a generation that challenged authority of all manners, they are unused to investing any source of information with authority and so have difficulty reconciling conflicts among information. On the other hand, these students are more technically adept, capable of using computers and computer networks with a facility that astonishes their elders, and more egalitarian.

Students who are anti-authoritarian consumers become purchasers of education, willing to buy only the minimum necessary and resisting the purchase of expensive additions to the product the student initially desires. To the degree law schools compete for such students, they are then faced with a classic marketing choice, either to sell what is first sought or to change the consumer's desire for the product on offer. The first choice usually being easier, the student consumer culture has created a considerable pressure for schools to lessen standards for both admission and performance. This pressure is offset, if only slightly, by other external market forces affecting student consumerism, the increased role of interschool ranking tables, which have had a marked influence on student application decisions, and increased costs and indebtedness, which seem to have had somewhat less influence. These forces have in turn led some schools to follow the student expectation of the school, measuring the value added by schools to the world not according to the contributions made by the student over a career, because these are seen not as the result of the student's training but of the student's preexisting will and personality, but merely according to whether the student has enjoyed the experience and received the license. Bar examination results have supplanted the achievements of the bar as a whole as the measure of success for many law schools. Thus, alumni donating aside, legal education has begun to turn from long-term returns to the short-term in its planning and self-image, an effect that has implications for scholars, whose work is no longer measured by content but by journal placement.

The result of the interaction of these and other forces of cultural change upon the legal academy is likely to be an end to a period of legal education and the beginning of a new one. If one accepts a model that there have been, roughly, three stages of American legal education thus far—a period of law office tutelage and proprietary schools, a period of text-taught university law schools and proprietary schools, and a period of university school and casebook dominance—it would then appear that the dominance of the university model of legal education and of the casebook is likely to decrease. The consequences of this change will be far-reaching, and how the institutions respond to it rather unpredictable.

The story of the stories of law schools not only foreshadows these changes but also helps to conserve that part of the institutional past that is beneficial and to identify that part of the past that is detrimental. It is thus not a great surprise that there is ongoing a quiet boom in the mining of libraries and archives to produce new histories of legal education. After a long period of disinterest, the past two decades have seen seminal articles by Michael Hoeflich, Paul Carrington, and John Schlegel; books by Robert Stevens, Michael Hoeflich, Laura Kalman, William LaPiana, and Michael Closen; and a greater flow of journal articles, and even Dan Coquillette's recently inaugurated Harvard course in the field. Part of this boom is attributable to the cycles of human endeavor, such as the massive work now under way by Dan Coquillette in celebration of yet another hundred years at Harvard, and part may be attributable to the invisible hand of the scholarly market. Even so, the last period to see such interest in the past of law schools was the period of Charles Warren and Alfred Reed, a time marked by great change, in which the university law schools and the casebook became the dominant features of the landscape.

The next stage in the metamorphosis of the institutions of legal education may be one of great improvement, in which an ideal of knowledge, analysis, and character may be made more truly accessible to a wider community of students who will more fully attain it. On the other hand, Santayana's tempered progressivism sounds something of a warning.

Not all readaptation is progress, for ideal identity must not be lost. The Latin language did not progress when it passed into Italian. It died. Its amiable heirs may console us for its departure but do not remove the fact that their parent is extinct. So every individual, nation, and religion has its limit of adaptation. So long as the increment it receives is digestible, so long as the organization already attained is extended and elaborated without being surrendered, growth goes on; but when the foundation itself shifts, when what is gained at the periphery is lost at the centre, the flux appears again and progress is not real. Thus a succession of generations or languages or religions constitutes no progress unless some ideal present at the beginning is transmitted to the end and reaches a better expression there; without this stability at the core no common standard exists and all comparison of value with value must be external and arbitrary.[3]

NOTES

1. George Santayana, *The Life of Reason: Or the Phases of Human Progress* (New York, Charles Scribner's Sons, 1953), p. 82.
2. *Ibid.*
3. *Ibid.* at 83.

I. Teaching Books and Methods in the Lecture Hall

1. George Wythe (1726-1806), the first law professor in the United States, was appointed Professor of Law and Police in the College of William and Mary, on the recommendation of his former pupil, Thomas Jefferson. (*Courtesy of The R. W. Norton Gallery, Shreveport, Louisiana.*)

Chapter 1

An Introductory History of Law in the Lecture Hall

1997

Steve Sheppard

A version of this article first appeared in 82 *Iowa Law Review* 547 (1997).

The pre-modern idea of teaching law as an academic discipline seems to have originated in Lombardy in the tenth and eleventh centuries. Scholars and judges in Bologna and nearby Pavia used the newly rediscovered Code of Justinian to organize both the laws of the province and the canon laws of the church using this complicated Roman tool.[1] The intricate relationships among provisions of the Code led Bolognese jurists to teach it as they taught science, requiring students to memorize and to apply Justinian edicts with precision. To aid in this task, the teachers added their own gloss on the subjects, annotating the texts. The students who flocked to the school of Bologna spread its method throughout Europe and to England in the wake of William the Conqueror.[2]

The American law school lecture and law book are the distant heirs to this tradition. In the few centuries of American law lecturing, the science of law has, itself, evolved. It is now routine to imagine the history of the American law lecture as methodological epochs framed by books and men. First were such commentators as William Blackstone, James Kent, and Joseph Story; then the organizers, Thomas Cooley, John Norton Pomeroy, and Theodore Dwight; then the scientists, Christopher Columbus Langdell and James Barr Ames. Lately have come the modernists, numerous and uncanonized, blazing paths with new theory and technology. Accepting that each age had its share of conservatives, just as each had unclassifiable eccentrics, such a chronicle is often followed, in the broadest sketch,[3] as it is here.

While this popular view is facially accurate, it is overly simple. The history is far subtler than this; the apparent conflicts between views were rarely so sharply defined as they may now seem. There is often as much in common as there is exceptional between various teaching modes, and preoccupation with the tools of pedagogies may obscure more fundamental agreements and quarrels ranging among all of the methods. One way to read both the commonalities and disagreements is to consider the following model.

I. Introduction: The Sciences of Legal Pedagogy

In general, the law professor brings order to a vast tangle of laws. To do so, the teacher must both educate the students in the generic methods of legal analysis and train them in the specific application of particular legal principles to a given cause. Even though pursuing one end may distract from the pursuit of the other, the two ends are interdependent; the rules are used to teach rationale, and the rationale is necessary to make sense of the rules.

There is an inevitable pattern to the order that is the end of each of these competing forms. The professor must encourage the student to grasp and recall certain ideas. While doing so, the professor must also inspire imagination and analysis, so that specific rules may be selected and applied to a particular question, new rules can be plausibly invented, and rules may be applied to the subtle facts of a given question. Thus, some part of law teaching is the promotion of memory of specific rules, and some part is the encouragement of new ideas related to those rules.

Given the reality that some students desire to avoid effort or to limit their efforts to no more than those calculated to prepare for evaluation, the professor must encourage a work ethic designed to accomplish the more essential ends. The goal in common to both professor and student is the student's exercise of memory, analysis, and imagination in employing the tools of law.

To realize this end, the law teacher must both instruct students in class and guide the students' use of time outside class. In both settings, and through a host of means, the teacher directs the students to accomplish this task in three steps:

(1) The student learns some body of law, either as historical rules or as reasons for decisions applied in resolving historical disputes;

(2) The student organizes this body of law into a scheme based on the relationships and distinctions among the applications and reasons;

(3) The student applies this body of law to a new situation, using the organization to pick the rules best suited to resolve the situation.[4]

Much in the materials below suggests that, at different times, the collective emphasis of legal educators has moved from one step to another. Thus, colonial and early federal teachers focused more upon the second step, and so treatises and copybooks were the norm. After the Civil War, concern shifted to the first step, leading to emphasis on cases and their criticism and thereby leading to the use, and abuse, of the casebook. Following the advent of legal realism, law teachers have paid increasingly more attention to the third step, leading to the popularity of the problem book and other approaches in which student involvement is more apparently necessary to ascertain the material's meaning. Still, preoccupation with one element has never led to complete disregard for the others. Instead, concern for one element has usually required incidental attention to the others.

Notably influencing these shifts of emphasis is the evolving conception of order. The lawyers who organized the legal materials were creatures of their age, at least so far as "order" had meaning in each age. The changing nature of this orderliness is particularly acute in the frequent description of the teaching of law as teaching "the science of law" and the changes of meaning represented by this description.

II. Treatises, Commentaries, and the Monologue Lecture

American law has been peculiarly influenced by its English colonial origins, owing in part to the common law's inherent preoccupation with its history and in part to American respect for her founding.[5] The simpler matter remains, however, that many concerns of the modern law school had predicates and parallels in earlier ages.

A. Foundations of Colonial Study

Law in the American colonies was English law, and to study law the American lawyer looked first to the English lawbook. These lawbooks initially came more often from the bar than from the academy.

The ancient universities in Oxford and Cambridge had been offering lectures in Roman and canon law, arguably, since Roger Vacarius lectured in twelfth-century Oxford and authored the first student text in England, the *Liber Pauperum*, a collection of extracts from the Emperor Justinian's Code and Digest.[6] But as medieval universities remained preoccupied with Roman law, instruction in the English common law devolved onto the Inns of Court, the organized colleges of barristers in London.[7] Only in 1756, when Charles Viner's legacy endowed a chair for the lecture of the common law in Oxford, did instruction in the common law become a university-sanctioned enterprise.[8]

So it was that the collegiate instruction of common law in England was not long established by the time Americans began to do the same. The primary textual influences from Britain in colonial law were case reports and a handful of treatises, especially the venerable Coke's *Institutes* and, arriving shortly before the revolution, Blackstone's *Commentaries.*

B. Eighteenth Century Law Study: Three Examples

The education of three colonial law students—Joseph Story, James Kent, and John Marshall—fairly represents the teaching practices of the age. Although there were periods of instruction from a lawyer, occasionally alongside a few other students, the bulk of their studies were in solitude, reading and copying from English law books.

Joseph Story graduated from Harvard College in 1798 and began reading the law, first in the office of Samuel Sewell. Away for months at a time as a member of Congress, Sewell was not the most attentive teacher. Story found himself

> left very much alone, and with no literary associate in my native town. I was driven, therefore, back upon my own resources, and I not unfrequently devoted for months more than fourteen hours a day to study. . . . [with] no opportunity to ask for any explanation of difficulties, and no cheering encouragement to light up the dark and intricate paths of the law.[9]

Sewell did give Story assignments, first setting him to read Blackstone. The *Commentaries* led Story to question the applicability of the common law to America. Sewell encouraged this query in his correspondence, urging Story to acquire "a knowledge of the laws of your country," which would be built on a broad foundation, for which a student must

> [e]xamine the theory & general doctrines & the origin of the municipal law, & descending from generals to particulars, to discover the partial applications & limits of the [English] system. In this last course you are engaged, & it is apparent that this must be the most scientific, & you need not fear that when you have the law of England as a system of political, moral & economic rules, you will find any difficulty in ascertaining the variations which our situation & difference of manners and general policy have required . . . [turning from English to Massachusetts law] and in them you will discover all the local and positive variations of the general system . . . . You are to view then, Blackst[one] & other books which you will be put to read, as affording you tenets & doctrines of which some are directly and plainly applicable & of full obligation in this country as well as in England; rules and principles of indirect effect & other parts tho[ugh] inapplicable, abrogated or disused, have a logical utility, seeming to connect the system and thereby aiding the memory in retaining the parts of it which have been adopted & serving also in may instances to explain & harmonize them.[10]

After Blackstone, Story was "hurried at once into the intricate, crabbed, and obsolete learning of Coke on Littleton,"[11] a task he found, initially, overwhelming. "I took it up, and after trying it day after day with very little success, I sat myself down and wept bitterly. My tears dropped upon the book, and stained its pages."[12] Only through tenacity did he begin "to see daylight, ay and to feel that I could comprehend and reason upon the text and the comments. . . . The critical period was passed; I no longer hesitated."[13]

He turned then to the King's Bench reports, particularly those of Edmund Saunders, from which he took a love of reporting, and to Fearne's treatise, *Contingent Remainders and Executory Devises*, which he condensed into a "manuscript abstract of all its principles."[14] This monasticism under Sewell was at last followed by a chance, during the few months that Story worked for Samuel Putnam, to talk about the law in his studies. Putnam later recalled, "He read much yet we talked more, and I believe in my heart, that even then, he did the greater part of it."[15]

James Kent began studying law as a fifteen-year-old, enrolling briefly in Ezra Stiles's courses at Yale, before the college was dispersed to evade British soldiers during the Revolution.[16] Over a summer's exile, Kent found a copy of Blackstone in a country village, which he read while waiting to re-enter college.[17] In 1781 after Kent graduated from Yale, he entered the law office of Attorney General Egbert Benson in Poughkeepsie, New York. His education there was based in part on work with fellow students in the office and in part on copying books at the farmhouse where he boarded.[18] He copied long passages from Grotius and Puffendorf, and "abridged Hales [*sic*] history of the common law, and the old books of practice, and read parts of Blackstone again & again."[19] After his admission to the bar in 1785, Kent continued his own schooling. He devoted his day to Greek and Latin in the morning, law practice and business in the afternoon, and French and English in the evening. From 1788 to 1789, his evening readings included Coke's commentary on Littleton.[20]

Unlike Story, Kent, and the mass of colonial students, John Marshall not only privately studied Blackstone before the Revolution,[21] but also, during a Revolutionary lull in the summer of 1780, studied in the academic cloister at the College of William and Mary. There he read under George Wythe, the newly installed Professor of Law and Police. Not that the benefit was as great as tradition suggests: the course lasted only a few months.[22] Still, Marshall found the school agreeable, both because of its democratic manner (students needed not wear shoes or coats in warm weather) and because of its proximity to his fiancé in Yorktown, twelve miles away. Wythe's law program included a mock assembly, which functioned according to the rules of Parliament, as well as a monthly moot court and twice-weekly lectures.[23] The lectures were more likely concerned with political theory than with the black-letter law, and Marshall also took detailed "commonplace" notes. These consisted of a typical index of entries forming a home-made law dictionary with illustrations of doctrines from cases. Marshall redacted his notes from a 1769 abridgement of Virginia statutes, Blackstone's *Commentaries*, Matthew Bacon's *Abridgement*, and a host of reports and treatises. All of these he arranged alphabetically into topics, beginning with entries on "abatement" and continuing through "libel."[24]

The notes are thorough, if liberally sprinkled with marginalia repeating the name Polly Ambler, his soon-to-be wife.[25] From these notes, the effect of Judge Wythe's lectures on Marshall's recordings of the law does not appear to be overwhelming: Polly notwithstanding, the commonplace notes reflect very little that scholars have not attributed to published sources,[26] and the completion of the already brief course of lectures was neither a sufficient desiderata to outweigh marriage nor a requirement for licensure.[27] Marshall was admitted to practice the year he left William and Mary.[28]

The commonplace books written by all three students drew from their readings of cases, topical treatises, and the general abridgements of law. None of these sources, however, were so influential in the particular or instructive in the whole as were the writings of the two great generalists, Coke and Blackstone.

C. Coke's and, of course, Blackstone's Books

Despite the constant complaints that students raised against Coke's comments on Littleton, Edward Coke's *First Institutes of the Laws of England* was, for over a century, the most accepted student text.[29] The *Institutes* succeeded partly because Coke wrote them primarily in English, rather than exclusively in Law French and Latin. Coke's long-lived success, however, was not for choice of tongue alone; there were other law books in English.[30] Rather, Coke's *First Institutes* was extraordinarily complete and succinct, and it long held first position as the textbook of the common law.[31]

Coke, famously, was a jurist, not an academic. As Chief Justice of Common Pleas and, later, of the King's Bench, he wrangled with James I, arguing that the King's prerogative and the Chancellor's writ did not extend to common-law cases. Instead, he asserted that they were governed by the "artificial logic of the law."[32] This position led, along with a tad of political intrigue and a few slights of protocol, to his dismissal in 1616.[33] Coke's earliest writings were small treatises on bail, copyholding, and pleadings, and in 1600, he began to publish his *Reports.*[34] In 1627 at the age of seventy-five, Coke embarked on a systematic discussion of the common law, beginning with a gloss, or commentary, on Sir Thomas Littleton's *Tenures.*[35] *Tenures* is a fifteenth-century treatise examining land tenures as construed in Year Book cases, which may be the earliest printed book on the English common law.[36] Coke had studied Littleton for years, referring to him in the *Reports* and occasionally defending him against critics.[37]

The whole of Coke's *Institutes* runs to four thick books, the last three of which generally discuss legal instruments and constitutional arguments for limiting the powers of the crown, criminal law, and the jurisdiction of courts.[38] The *Institutes* were, almost certainly, the first books that had enduring effect in English or American constitutional study.

Coke on Littleton is the hybrid product of two writers, working across a gulf of two centuries. Moreover, their projects were altogether different in scope. Littleton restricted his study to the rules of land tenures, but Coke's work was much broader, and sought the *ratio* of the law, for "if by your study and industry, you make not the reason of the law your own, it will not remain long in your memory."[39] The result is a rich but confusing trove of writings. It is filled with allusions to cases and obscure maxims in a variety of languages, as well as tangential scholarly enquiries dropped among fundamental points of law, and sprinkled throughout with homiletic statements. There is a slight ration of anachronistic and imaginative blunders, but the scholarship is generally sound.[40] In truth, the amalgam of the rich strains of scholarship on a host of matters is Coke's hallmark, even if the references are not all as clear as the reader might wish. The reader who first approaches *Coke on Littleton* without a well-stocked library for assistance embarks upon a truly formidable task.[41]

2. Sir William Blackstone (1723-1780), the first holder of Viner's chair for common law teaching at Oxford, wrote four volumes of *Commentaries* that held sway in American law schools for a century. Even so, arguments Blackstone presented in the *Commentaries* may have encouraged dubious decisions later made as a member of the Commons, before his elevation to the bench. (*Courtesy of Art & Visual Materials, Special Collections Department, Harvard Law School Library.*)

The difficulty of that task was a rite of passage for most early-American law students. It was a tedious affair, leading even a scholarly young Jefferson to send Coke to the Devil,[42] but its potential rewards were great, as when Joseph Story, upon conquering its mysteries, noted, "When I had completed the reading of this most formidable work, I felt I breathed a purer air, and that I had acquired a new power."[43] Nonetheless, the more common view was that of Daniel Webster, who resented the practice of assigning students to read such a sophisticated book. For an untutored boy of twenty to be set such an author, he said, was "folly."[44]

Student labors with *Coke on Littleton* were soon eased, in part because of new editions that reordered the text along Matthew Hale's more classical syllabus,[45] and in part because of another product of Hale's analytical tradition, Blackstone's *Commentaries.* The *Commentaries* almost immediately began to displace Coke from its pinnacle on their American publication. By 1810 a guide for students in law offices suggested that perusing Coke's "immethodological farago" was already a task "too often neglected."[46]

Serendipity brought William Blackstone to offer his lectures on the common law. Despite his prominence as a law lecturer for eight years in All Souls College, he was rejected by the patron of the ancient position of Regius Professor of civil (or classical Roman) law.[47] Thus barred from promotion to teaching the more elite civil law, Blackstone began unsanctioned lectures on the academically disregarded English common law. He began to outline the common law in his annual syllabi,[Analysis of the Laws of England, An] *An Analysis of the Laws of England*,[48i] which he then refined and delivered as the first holder of the chair newly endowed by Charles Viner's bequest of the copyright to his *General Abridgment of Law and Equity.*[49]

Thus, in 1758 Blackstone set out to deliver, as Vinerian Professor, a complete set of lectures that echoed his thwarted purpose of teaching the science of civil law. This he described as a "[s]cience . . . to be cultivated, methodized, and explained in a course of academical lectures" which would construct English law and constitution into "a species of knowledge, in which the gentlemen of England have been more remarkably deficient than those of all Europe besides."[50] For four years, he not only delivered the lectures but polished the four resulting volumes into his *Commentaries on the Laws of England.* These were printed in successive years, from 1765, at the Clarendon Press in Oxford University.[51]

The books were well received, even earning an uncharacteristically strong review from Edmund Burke's *Annual Register*, which noted that formerly "the law has been looked on, as the most disagreeable of all studies; and of so dry, disgusting, heavy a nature, that students of vivacity and genius were deterred from entering into it," but that Blackstone "has entirely cleared the law of England from the rubbish in which it was buried."[52]

Lord Mansfield recommended the *Commentaries* as a replacement for *Coke on Littleton*:

> Till of late I could never with any satisfaction to myself answer such a question [(recommending what books a young man should read for the bar)]; but since the publication of Mr. Blackstone's *Commentaries*, I can never be at a loss. *There* your son will find analytical reasoning, diffused into a pleasing and perspicuous style. *There* he may inhale imperceptibly the first principles on which our excellent laws are founded; and there he may become acquainted with an uncouth crabbed author, Coke upon Littleton, who has disgusted and disheartened many a Tyro, but who cannot fail to please in the modern attire in which he is now decked.[53]

The *Commentaries* were an immediate success in America. Robert Bell, a Philadelphia printer, sold subscriptions for fifteen hundred copies throughout America, even though Americans had already bought more than one thousand copies of English editions.[54] Still, Blackstone's own editions were not the sole basis for his enduring fame and influence on American legal education. For the next five decades, scores of annotated *Commentaries* poured forth.[55] Various authors annotated Blackstone's original text with the newly written law of England and, more particularly, of the American courts.[56] As if this were not enough, in America, Dane, Kent, and Story, and in England, Henry John Stephen, among others, conscientiously built their own commentaries and abridgements upon Blackstone's foundation.[57]

Blackstone's outline is derived in part from that of Matthew Hale's 1716 *The Analysis of the Law*, on which Blackstone had also modeled his syllabus.[58] The *Commentaries* are organized into four interdependent books, considering the rights of persons, the rights of things, private wrongs, and public wrongs.[59] The sections are broken into subheadings, each considering some particular subject in detail with surprisingly clear and readable prose. The sum of the work is so comprehensive that one might imagine there was little law left undescribed.[60] While the writing is liberally punctuated with Latin maxims, these are sufficiently rare that a reader lacking in the classics might have skipped them or guessed at them without too great a loss of comprehension. The text is sparingly annotated with references to *Coke on Littleton*, *Littleton's Tenures*, Bracton, and other writers as well as to statutes and opinions. Cases are rarely discussed in the text and, when they are, they serve essentially as illustrations rather than as sources of law.[61] Reading Blackstone in the late twentieth century is a bit like reading a current treatise; one is left with a reasonably, but not overly, detailed understanding of a host of related legal doctrines and their applications.

Even this brief description of Coke's and Blackstone's works requires a glimpse of their politics. Surely, much of Coke's life and writings were devoted to championing the law as a limit on the arbitrary acts of

King and council.[62] The *First Institute* has a predictably strong Whiggish overtone, protecting the jurisdiction of the courts and defending precedent from Parliamentary assault. In contrast, Blackstone presented a much more central role for the King and Parliament, even if this role is limited by the rights of citizens.

These biases tended to make the books into subtle mechanisms for political indoctrination. Jefferson complained of the ascendancy of Blackstone, and sought to have the legal instruction at the University of Virginia in a less Tory flavor.[63] On the other hand, Blackstone's influence may have fueled more Whiggish fervor than the often-partisan Jefferson was prepared to concede.[64]

In any event, the principles of law selected and presented by both authors surely had a real influence in the political ideals of students who absorbed them, and this nascent idealism was known to those who chose the works for student reading. Blackstone's American influence was long-lived. In the 1893 census of law schools performed by the American Bar Association and the U.S. Bureau of Education, twenty-six schools reported assigning Blackstone in their mandatory curricula.[65]

D. The Lectures of Litchfield

The first American *school* of law,[66] organized strictly to prepare students to be lawyers, and distinct from a general bachelor's degree course, was initially an overflow of students in Judge Tapping Reeve's law office in the quiet, backwater village of Litchfield, Connecticut.[67] Reeve served for sixteen years on the state supreme court and was well-regarded as a lawyer, even if he was prone to be a tad absent-minded.[68] Judge Reeve's first student was his bother-in-law, Aaron Burr, who began study with Reeve in 1775.[69] To instruct the young pupil, and the others who soon followed him, Judge Reeve began organizing instructional material into lecture notes, which he had somewhat standardized by 1782.[70]

The school was a great success, growing to fifty-five enrollees by 1813 before its decline a decade later. It had over a thousand graduates, many of whom were drawn from the social elite and led the young republic, including three U.S. Supreme Court members, fifty-six state supreme court judges, twenty-eight Senators, one hundred and one Congressmen, fourteen governors, six U.S. cabinet members, and eight professors, not counting educator Horace Mann.[71] Still, the school closed not long after the death of its founder, and the illness of his successor left it unable to compete with the newly opened law programs at Harvard, Columbia, Yale, and the other universities.

The course lasted fourteen months, including two one-month holidays.[72] Judge Reeve initially gave the lectures alone, although one of his students, James Gould, joined him as a lecturer in 1798, and ultimately became sole proprietor of the school.[73]

The Litchfield lectures established the framework for instruction in the professional law school. They ran the gamut of American private law and were eventually grouped into forty-eight distinct titles. The course was rooted in the practicalities of the common law governing private disputes, skipping public law topics of Constitutional government and politics, Roman civil law, and "stately lectures on the great principles of the Laws of Nature."[74] Instead, lectures included master and servant, actions for debt, evidence, trials, insurance, partnership, and the like.[75]

Lectures covered one topic at a time and described a pattern of principles punctuated by citations to cases and commentaries, occasionally referring to the facts of a given case.[76] Daily lectures lasted an hour and a half, during which students took notes for later transcription.[77] The students also used their notebooks for commonplace copying from treatises, with each week's work examined every Saturday morning.[78]

Both Reeve and Gould dictated detailed notes in treatise-like fashion. They would generally begin each topic with an overview of the scope of the topic and its general role in law, followed by an issue-by-issue treatment. They addressed each topic in general terms and punctuated their disquisitions with frequent references to Blackstone, Hale, and Coke, and the authors of topically more narrow treatises, making less frequent references to cases and statutes to guide the students' outside reading along with the lecture topic. The text of the lectures was essentially a narrative of the principles involved, although some topics were illustrated by brief discussions from cases.[79] They added case citations as string cites for later student review to illustrate particular points, and frequently referred to cases with very brief mention of their facts and a terse summary of their holdings.[80]

The lectures were given slowly, with deliberate repetition, "The practice of Judge Gould was to read the principles from his own [manuscripts] twice distinctly, pausing between, and repeating in the same manner the leading cases."[81] Gould sat on a huge, old-fashioned chair on a dais at the front of the room, from which he lectured each morning, beginning at nine o'clock, and where, students said, he "quaffs ice brandy in the afternoon."[82] Gould, particularly, employed venerable techniques of legal illustration, particularly the use of Blackacre and Whiteacre as illustrations,[83] a technique at least as old as the writings of Francis Bacon.[84] The systematic nature of the lectures became, in the end, somewhat frustrating to Gould; his students avoided work by cribbing from the numerous copies created in prior years,[85] and others benefitted from his lectures without payment.[86]

The success of the Litchfield program, as well as its inherently replicable structure, led to imitators and competitors. The independent law school became a mainstay of the young republic; by 1835, there were, or had been, eighteen other law schools independent of a university, each offering programs of instruction resonant with Reeve's and Gould's.[87] Even so, the real competition—the university law school—was only just on the horizon.

E. The University Lecturer: Round One

University law teaching had no easy birth. Although there were serious efforts to offer law classes in eighteenth-century American colleges, practically speaking, they nearly all failed. The only successful eighteenth-century university law programs were in the South, in Virginia and Kentucky. Thomas Jefferson appointed his old tutor, Judge George, to be the College of William and Mary's Professor of Law and Police in 1779. Wythe held the position for twelve years before resigning to devote more time to being Chancellor of Virginia, an office he held until his fatal poisoning in 1806.[88] Wythe was succeeded at William and Mary by St. George Tucker, who, despite Jefferson's dislike of Blackstone, not only arranged the lectures in a pattern following Blackstone's outline but also published his own annotated version.[89] Tucker, in the preface to his *Blackstone*, admitted that he had adopted the lectures because he had only three months to prepare his course, and that preparing "a regular course of *original lectures* would have required some years of study, and of labour, not only in collecting but in methodizing and arranging . . . materials. The exigencies of office did not permit this."[90] Legal instruction at the college in Williamsburg lasted unbroken until 1861, when the college briefly ended the professorship.[91]

The other successful law program was at

Transylvania University, in Lexington, Kentucky, which organized a law department in 1799.[92] George Nicholas, the founder of the law program at Transylvania, was a correspondent of Jefferson.[93] The school's early lectures were based on a model borrowed from Williamsburg and Charlottesville, particularly in the humanistic breadth of Jefferson's curriculum, designed to instill a Republican philosophy in western lawyers.[94] So it is no surprise that John Breckenridge and Henry Clay taught at the school, Clay lecturing there for two years.[95] Following Wythe's ideas, there were both lectures and a program of moot courts and moot legislatures.[96] Still, the lectures remained the essential means of instruction.[97]

The Transylvania lecture incorporated a mixture of sources from both treatises and cases, which were frequently consulted not just for their law but also for their facts. Thus, in a contracts class, a discussion of ten or so minutes of the legal disabilities of children was followed by a discussion for several minutes of *Cory v. Cory*, considering an agreement to settle disputes within a family.[98] Transylvania's law program lasted until 1858.[99]

The northern universities were less successful. In 1777 Yale refused Ezra Stile's plan to create a law professorship.[100] Dartmouth offered a haphazard smattering of law from 1796 to 1808, when a professorship of law was created, for which funds were never raised.[101] Little more than false starts occurred at Columbia, Philadelphia, Harvard, and Maryland.[102]

James Kent began offering lectures in Columbia College in 1793, holding a sinecure created for him by the Federalists among the college trustees after Kent lost a reelection bid in the state assembly.[103] Kent planned to deliver two one-hour lectures weekly throughout the winter,[104] during which he intended to cover

> a brief review of the history, the nature, the several forms, and the just ends of civil government... together with an examination of such parts of the civil and criminal codes of the federal jurisprudence . . . the courts of the several states . . . and the more particular examination of the Constitution of this state. The whole detail of our municipal law, with relation to the rights of property and of persons and the forms of administering justice, both civil and criminal, will then be treated fully and at large.[105]

Moreover, the "juridical education" he provided was meant to encourage the arts of close reasoning and public speaking, as well as an acquaintance with the doctrines of moral philosophy.[106] The program was a tad overambitious, and Kent managed to deliver only twenty-six lectures.[107] Although he thought the course tended to be "somewhat imperfect," he delivered his lectures to "seven students and thirty-six gentlemen, chiefly lawyers and law-students who did not belong to the college."[108] The next year, though, he had only two students, and the year after that, none.[109] Busy as a judge and assemblyman, he resigned his chair in 1797.

Over the two years, Kent had covered only federal and state constitutional law, the law of nations, and real property.[110] James Goebel's and Samuel Howard's history considered the causes of Kent's initial failures and noted that, while there is a "tradition that his students' patience was wearied by the dreariness of his style," his real problem was likely twofold: "Kent's lectures were too professional in content for undergraduate students of the arts, while too academic to attract apprentices at law steeped in the tradition of office study."[111] Moreover, for the law students, "one winter's lectures seem to have been enough to satisfy the demand."[112] Thus one might say that, committing two hours per week to the tasks of both training and educating, Kent did neither one well, and lost the audience that each goal attracted.

James Wilson, United States Supreme Court Justice from 1789 to 1797, began lecturing in the College of Philadelphia in 1790.[113] Like Kent, he lasted only two years. Wilson delivered a series of lectures that were meant to cover the whole of public and private law in a three-year program. After two winters, the College was merged into the University of Pennsylvania, and Wilson, never wholly engaged in the teaching post, chose not to join the new institution.[114] His successor, Charles Willing Hare was not appointed until twenty-five years later, in 1817. He lasted a year before being "afflicted with the loss of reason,"[115] and the school remained dormant until 1850, when it finally reopened under the hand of George Sharswood.

Wilson's lectures were narrative and often original in their consideration of the "Science of the Law."[116] His scope was essentially that set by Blackstone, beginning with a lecture on the study of law, and then moving to the general principles of law and obligation, the law of nature, the law of nations, municipal law, man as a member of a community and a state, and then the common law in general, evidence, corporations, judicial procedure, and property.[117] Philosophically, though, Wilson rejected Blackstone's views of sovereignty, arguing that legitimate government must protect the natural rights of its members.[118] Throughout the private law lectures, Wilson's style was that of the narrator of principles and champion of arguments, with only occasional references to statutes and judicial decisions.[119]

Matters were scarcely different at Harvard. Isaac Royall, an American Tory refugee, died in England in 1781, leaving a will endowing a professorship of laws, or of medicine, in Harvard College.[120] The position was unfilled until the end of the War of 1812, in 1815, when the last of the lands subject to the bequest finally sold and the estate successfully distributed subject to treaty. During that time, several attempts to establish a law chair had been made but failed owing either to disinterest of the appointee, poor finances, or disinterest by the trustees.[121]

One of the most ambitious early law programs was attempted in the University of Maryland by David Murray Hoffman.[122] Hoffman was one of six law professors appointed in 1816 to a professorship. Because financial troubles interfered with the opening of the school, Hoffman gave no lectures until 1822.[123] During the years that followed, he created a vast, nine-year program of study, based on a manual of lectures, which began wending its way to the public in the first edition of *A Course of Legal Study*.[124] The *Course* was both a treatise in itself and a collection of readings and references to other standard texts organized in topics similar to the Litchfield syllabus.

The Maryland course struggled, attracting between twenty and forty students from various states for several years. Because of delays in opening the school and sparse remuneration from the university, Hoffman opened a "Law Institute" on the side, which entailed a quizzer course of thirty lectures and a complicated moot court program, all priced to move at $120.[125] The institute fairly smothered under its own weight, completely unable to encompass the whole of the rapidly changing American and English law.

The course of lectures was impracticable for most students, and Hoffman was rarely capable of devoting himself fully to the lectures, which took longer to deliver than he had anticipated.[126] In 1832 Hoffman gave up lecturing and fled to Europe to evade his creditors,[127] although he made a later abortive effort to open a new "Legal Institution" in Philadelphia.[128] Even so, his detailed syllabus and bibliography had a continuing influence, and *Legal Study* was assigned reading at Harvard.[129]

With the exception of Hoffman, who designed, in essence, a program of independent study, the lectures of the early university were distinct, sometimes nearly divorced, from the student's reading, which was still generally designed to produce commonplace notebooks. The bulk of treatises were English treatises reprinted in the United States, occasionally with local annotations. Until Tucker published an American edition of Blackstone, there were very few general American legal materials. The few that did exist were the lectures of James Wilson, the works of two judges, Nathaniel Chipman's *Dissertations*[130] and H.H. Brackenridge's *Miscellanies*,[131] and Zephaniah Swift's Blackstonian work, used in Litchfield, *A System of Laws of Connecticut*.[132] Otherwise, there were constitutions, statutes, and reports, with a small but growing number of specialized treatises, particularly dealing with politics and property such as John Adams's 1765 *Dissertation on the Canon and Feudal Law*,[133] and Sullivan's later *Land Titles*.[134] This paucity of secondary discussion and elaboration affected the larger community of practitioners as much as law students, and the few books published were aimed distinctly at the professional market. These included two formbooks released in 1801[135] and in 1805, Joseph Story's first book, *A Selection of Pleadings in Civil Cases*.[136] Even so, American-authored books held only a small portion of the home market: Of the 282 law books sold at the 1814 auction of Massachusetts Chief Justice Theophilus Parsons's estate the American books amounted only to statutes and reports, plus three treatises, *Livermore on Agents and Factors*, *Lawes on Pleading with Story's Addition*, and *Story's Pleading*.[137]

F. The University Lecturer: Round Two

The United States began to awaken after the War of 1812. In the decades between the Treaty of Ghent and the fall of Fort Sumpter, industrial and geographic expansion caused a huge surge in the national economy, and a newly assertive Supreme Court became increasingly central to national affairs. It is little wonder that it was then that the first wave of major university law schools was formed. Not only did the earlier programs at Columbia and Pennsylvania revive, but Yale acquired a nearby independent school, Harvard filled its chairs, and a host of new university law programs were born.

Initially, these schools relied on English imports for texts. Blackstone's works were the most prominent migrants in a flood of law books from London that came ashore in reprints in Boston, Philadelphia, the city of New York, and the state capital at Poughkeepsie.[138] Dane, Kent, and Story soon followed Blackstone's model of a general commentary equally suited to the student attorney and to the practitioner, although the subject-area book meant primarily for law students was increasingly popular.[139]

James Kent returned to teaching in 1824, offering a comprehensive "plain and practical view of the principles of our municipal law."[140] In his first year, he offered a series of fifty public lectures delivered in one year, along with two private lectures for enrolled students.[141] The course was reduced to only private lectures the next year, after which he was "heartily tired of lecturing" and stopped doing it at all.[142] In the time thus freed, he devoted himself to publishing his *Commentaries on American Law*, the first volume of which appeared in 1826.[143]

Kent's *Commentaries* were both an American version of Blackstone and more. Following a theme he developed in his lectures,[144] he included significant sections on international law, as well as the history and government of the United States. There are six major sections: the law of nations, United States government, municipal law, personal rights, personal property, and real property.[145] Part I was innovative, as there seems to be no earlier treatise of international law originally in the English language. Although

Part II is largely a paraphrase of Supreme Court opinions, the remaining volumes are a clear narrative of commercial and property law, with a then-unusual emphasis on commercial transactions. The critical facet of the *Commentaries* was Kent's care to keep it updated in response to new opinions. He oversaw six editions between 1830 and his death in 1847, and each edition reflected state and federal opinions in each area up to that time.[146]

Harvard's law school, finally opened in 1815, had not developed as hoped under Isaac Parker and Asahel Stearns. Their program followed the Litchfield model, if in a slightly less taxing form. It included a mixture of student recitations from lawbooks, both Blackstone and treatises in specific legal topics,[147] as well as faculty delivery of written lectures; students also participated in moot courts and debating clubs.[148] The program, however, was not terribly rigorous, without required readings before lectures.[149] It averaged only nine students per year through the 1820s.[150]

Concerns for the school's management were resolved only with a gift from Nathan Dane. Dane, a Charles Viner for America, wrote a significant encyclopedia of American law, his eight-volume *Abridgement of American Law.*[151] Dane introduced each topic with a general narrative introduction, followed by a discussion of particular, leading cases. Several years of research yielded a rich layer of annotations to related cases.[152] Like Viner's work, Dane's result was too bulky for student use, although it influenced later treatise writers, whose books would greatly influence the class-room.[153] Moreover, Dane followed Viner's lead by endowing a chair of national law at Harvard, which was first held by Joseph Story.[154]

Story, by then already famous as Associate Justice of the U.S. Supreme Court, assumed the Dane Professorship in 1829, a position that was designed to take only such time for lecturing as he was inclined to give, but which allowed him to write. And write he did. From his first lecture, Story set out to advance the "science of law," which

> must be gradually formed by the successive efforts of many minds in many ages; that its rudiments seek deep into remote antiquity, and branch wider and wider with every new generation; that it seeks to measure the future by approximations to certainty derived solely from the experience of the past; that it must for ever be in progress. . . .[155]

Toward that end, Story proposed a series of treatises,[156] which ultimately included books on bailments, constitutional law, conflicts of law, equity principles, equity pleadings, agency, partnership, and bills and notes.[157] These commentaries, produced at a furious rate while Story was also serving on the Court, were taxing on Story, but eminently rewarding, reportedly bringing him royalties of ten thousand dollars a year.[158] The commentaries are narrative, but with numerous arguments and illustrations derived from cases and their facts, although cases were usually cited merely, if copiously, as authority for specific points in the narrative. He argued for particular points, notably in the constitutional law treatise, on which there was no case law or prior commentary. While Story certainly echoed the form of the works before his, the comprehensiveness of his books and his uniformity of treatment across a host of subjects were unusual and seem to have solidified the form of the modern subject-area treatise. Most later treatises, even into the twentieth century, have very much followed the same course.

Story's commentaries were, though, enterprises independent of his lectures. He spoke extemporaneously, threading stories of famous lawyers across particular principles of law and knitting copious instruction on the social and political obligations of the lawyer to the citizen.[159]

In contrast to Story's easygoing approach, the new holder of Harvard's Royall chair, Simon Greenleaf, presented a more focused lecture that demanded considerable student preparation and participation. Basing his lectures in part on the study of educational method,[160] Greenleaf required his students to prepare for class by reading his,[161] Story's, and others' books,[162] and then engaged them in spirited dialogue. The students seem to have found these two methods complementary. Future President Rutherford B. Hayes noted in his diary of 1843:

> We have no formal lectures. Professors Story and Greenleaf illustrate and explain as they proceed. Mr. G. is very searching and logical in examination. It is impossible for one who has

> not studied the text to escape exposing his ignorance; he keeps the subject constantly in view, never stepping out of his way for the purpose of introducing his own experience. Judge Story on the other hand, is very general in his questions, so that persons well skilled in nods affirmative and negative shakings of the head, need never more than glance at the text to answer his interrogatories. He is very fond of digressions to introduce amusing anecdotes . . . .[163]

Thus, an unspoken understanding was that Story gave students the presence of the law—the great man talking of great things—while Greenleaf actually taught the legal niceties, requiring the students to learn the details. Both styles were admirable, if for radically different qualities, owing more to the person than to the pedagogy.[164]

Neither Story's extemporaneous style nor Greenleaf's interrogations completely supplanted the earlier Litchfield style of rote dictation of principles. This method continued to be interwoven through their efforts, to be used by Greenleaf's predecessor, John Ashmun,[165] and to be employed by the next generation of Harvard professors, the triumvirate of Theophilus Parsons, Joel Parker, and Emory Washburn. As had Story and Greenleaf, both Parsons and Washburn wrote successful treatises, particularly Parsons's *Contracts*[166] and Washburn's *Property*.[167] Each lectured to classes of voluntary attendance, although their oratorical styles varied: Parker, philosophical but dull, reading from pages of assigned texts; Parsons, poet and story-teller, drawing students into the discussion around contemporary illustrations of his points; and Washburn, the father-confessor, reading from a lecture manuscript based on several treatises.[168]

Parsons's style displayed an interesting evolution. Initially, he employed hypothetical problems and invited questions from students in the audience, giving the students "a practical application of what he had read and heard."[169] Despite his initial success, he soon abandoned his interrogative method, finding it hard to obtain answers, both because of the time necessary to elicit a specific answer and because students so feared that the answer might be wrong that an erroneous answer became "a subject of dread."[170]

While these perennial difficulties sound familiar to a twentieth-century law teacher, part of the problem may have been that Parker was a "dry and uninteresting" conversationalist, a "mummy."[171] Parsons, too, had his moments. Rufus Choate grew so bored in his class as to write in his notes, "at this point, Parsons became Pathetic!"[172] Adding to the neglect of the courses, students could choose whether to be available to answer questions from treatises at the appointed hour, and the rightmost of three seating sections of the lecture halls was reserved for loafing students who were avoiding questions from the podium.[173]

Such student license became the rule in American law schools. Henry Booth, a Yale graduate, gave the first law lectures at Northwestern, beginning in 1859. He conducted his classes in monologue recitations. Students learned from lectures based on the standard readings, administered in a lax atmosphere,

> by reading assignments in a certain textbook which was supplemented by explanation by the professor and discussions by the students. . . . Students were at liberty to attend all classes and if they were able to pass the final examination, graduated. The main thing was to get through as quickly as possible.[174]

Despite the absence of any coordinating body or formal system of shared technique,[175] most American law schools at mid-century employed relatively similar lecturing styles, all more or less in the broad swathe of monologue styles. Timothy Walker, a student of Story at Harvard, not only lectured similarly at his law school in Cincinnati, but reprinted his lectures in a very successful general treatise.[176] At the University of Michigan, for example, David Walker, James Campbell, and Thomas Cooley lectured to students who studied from Cooley's annotated Blackstone and Story's commentaries,[177] as well as from Cooley's treatises.[178] Each presented a monologue discussion of general and specific principles, illustrated almost entirely by cases from the Michigan and U.S. reports, although with little discussion of the facts of the cases.[179] While there were differences in preparation—Campbell wrote his notes in detail, while Cooley wrote only an outline of points from which he presented a detailed analysis—their lecturing tended to be rather similar, at least in comparison to the variety among teachers at Harvard.[180]

There were schools, though, that reflected continental teaching techniques, both because of European influences in the training of their faculty and because of the legal and cultural histories of their locales. Albany reflected some of the Litchfield-style common-law lecture,[181] but it also employed a dialogue approach to discuss "two printed cases or questions . . . every week, after a reasonable time [for students] to examine them and prepare for the argument."[182] This mode was also employed at Buffalo.[183] William G. Hammond, discussed below, used a similar technique at Iowa in 1869 which he imported from Heidelberg, Germany.[184] Still, the dialogue was not a specifically continental device; in the civil code world of the University of Louisiana at New Orleans (now Tulane University) the Code Napoleon was taught alongside Coke and Blackstone in lectures of which Reeve and Story would have been proud.[185]

Not all lectures concentrated solely on the law of the cases. Story emphasized the duties of the lawyer to society in nearly every lecture, as did others.[186] Other such variations abounded, although within the common frame of lecture method, which persisted in most schools into the last quarter of the nineteenth century.

The University of Pennsylvania reopened its law department in 1850 under the leadership of the dour judge and Blackstone annotator, George Sharswood.[187] Lectures in the Penn school were provided by part-time lecturers, who generally followed the national pattern.[188] John Hare, though impressed by the new research in historical jurisprudence,[189] still conducted his lectures in the traditional fashion by illustrating his points with facts of cases and statements of jurists and drawing his points together in a broad context of law against the background of sociology and ethics.[190] He developed these contextual points over time, as his lectures in 1887 reflect his historical points in much greater detail than did his earlier notes.[191]

Neither Hare nor his colleagues, Algernon Sidney Biddle and James Parsons, however, would have found their teaching styles—in monologues of legal principles punctuated by cases chosen from England and America and interspersed with student quizzes[192]—to be incongruous with the Harvard of Parker and Washburn or with the Columbia of Theodore Dwight. Defending his lectures against the advancing spectre of the case method, Parsons argued as late as 1875 against the "delusive theory that the law is gradually developing itself into a science," by arguing that students must have a system of understanding before venturing into the cases.[193]

3. Sir Edward Coke (1557-1634) was a political scoundrel on behalf of the crown as Attorney General but his much-studied *Institutes* and *Reports* helped crystalize a notion of a comprehensive and apolitical common law that could encourage trade and limit tyranny, a view that led to his dismissal as Chief Justice. (*Courtesy of Art & Visual Materials, Special Collections Department, Harvard Law School Library.*)

The University of Virginia, ever happily in the shadow of its founder—and following strongly in his interdisciplinary tradition of the concurrent study of law, social science, and humanities,[194] had observed the stewardship of Tucker and John Minor on a course of relative pedagogical stability.[195] The professors lectured in monologues from Blackstone, Coke, and Madison, later adding Story and other course-specific textbooks, with a daily exam preceding each lecture, testing material from the previous lecture.[196]

G. The First American Legal Science

The organization of their materials, the "science" everyone seemed so concerned about, was a rather loose-knit idea. It seems, however, to have been very much in the tradition of Newtonian observation and organization: there is a place for everything, and everything would be in its place when sufficiently understood. The causal agent for this organization was either God or nature, and man merely needed to understand the whole of the system to work harmoniously in it. Thus, the system of laws, like systems of biology and geology, could be catalogued once all of the laws were discovered. Indeed, there is considerable similarity between Story's treatises and Linnaeus's classifications of plants.[197] All the science a student needed was to be exposed to the most complete articulation of the system of law and its catalogue of related principles, made to memorize it, and then taught to select the right principle for the right occasion. The archetype of such a program was that of Theodore Dwight.

H. Theodore Dwight: Acme of University Lecturers

In general, the university lecture given to students preparing from treatises assumed a variety of forms, occasionally including spontaneous questioning of students, but more often asking for no more than recitation of prepared readings from the treatises. This style of student preparation reached its personification in Theodore Dwight, Warden of Columbia Law School. Dwight was the model of the scientific lecturer, with a system of legal principles for dictation into the pages of carefully kept student manuscripts. Brought to Columbia from an established teaching career at Hamilton College, Dwight had already evolved a method of lecturing that was resonant of Tapping Reeve but distinctly more systemized following Dwight's maxim, "Principle before practice."

Dwight's lectures were highly programmatic, reflecting both his deliberate choice of a rote method to improve the "average student" and his view of legal science, which for him was necessary for the rule of law.

> It is essential to the due administration of justice that precedents should be followed unless there is some convincing reason to the contrary. It is only in this way that the law can be developed into a science. By means of this principle, a system of jurisprudence may be made to consist of a methodical collection of the principles involved in the decided cases.[198]

To encourage such a "methodical collection," Dwight recited lectures encompassing an outline of lists of principles and rules, illustrated with examples from cases,[199] all of which the students laboriously inscribed into manuscript books, which apparently served as a basis for catechismic recitation.[200] His lecture on statutory interpretation is typical. In it he presented five major rules necessary to affect "the great and leading rule of interpretation . . . that the meaning of the writing or text must be ascertained."[201] Each rule was lettered in an outline form:

A. The interpreter has a right to assume whatever is necessarily implied. . . .

B. Where there is nothing to lead to the contrary conclusion, language must be taken in its ordinary and popular sense, but words employed in any art, profession, trade, or religious sect must be taken in a special or technical sense.

C. The letter of the writing is not to be followed to the exclusion of the intent.

D. The meaning must be contained within the text, and the interpretation cannot add to it a sense which is not found therein by mere conjecture, supposition, or arbitrary interpretation.

E. The whole of the writing must be taken into account.[202]

Moreover, there were sixteen special rules which were generally amplifications of the broad concepts of the general rules, and ten more rules of greater detail for construing statutes that conflict with other laws or reason.[203] The lectures included more than lists alone, being punctuated not only with frequent cites to cases but also with relatively fact-laden examples to support various points.[204] All in all, there is thoroughgoing consistency in Dwight's lectures; once he established the lectures, his presentations to students varied only in occasional reflections of new law.[205]

With the rote approach of his dictated lectures, Dwight also employed a colloquial examination of students, testing their reading and understanding of assigned texts. He unwaveringly pursued the predetermined answer, although he seems to have been flexible in moving students from their errors.

> He never mortified a student; if an answer were manifestly wrong, he would say: "Would you not rather say it is so and so." Sometimes he would put to every student in turn the same supposed case and ask him his opinion upon it, and after each had answered, give the true solution. This afforded an opportunity to the clever ones to make a little proper display. We learned very much, too, by the questions which we asked of him in the classroom, and which he, like another Socrates, freely encouraged.[206]

Dwight used this technique to draw out understanding of the set texts, with at least an elementary analysis of them. It would seem he did not push overly hard for a sophisticated or imaginative understanding of the principles of law to be learned, although such efforts were applauded when found. "No student ever had his 'faculties tried in the highest degree,' or was ever driven to a standstill. Every student was 'encouraged.' Occasionally a student of ability or earlier training did discriminate or analyze: this was regarded with general favor."[207]

Dwight's hyper-didactic methods, however, were never universally accepted among law teachers, not even among the rest of the Columbia faculty. From 1857 until 1872, Francis Lieber conducted his lectures in jurisprudence and political theory in the manner of a traditional lecture.[208] John W. Burgess would fulfill this task even following the 1880 removal of his courses to the new graduate school of political science, and continuing until his retirement in 1913.[209]

Dwight, however, remained the headliner of the law school; in 1868, a trustee moved for the appointment of a junior lecturer in municipal law because Dwight's death or resignation would cause the whole school to "evaporate & evanesce the next day."[210] Indeed, he was still revered as a lecturer and paragon of legal education at Columbia when he was cast out in 1891 by Seth Low, Columbia's new president, and replaced with a young disciple of the "case method" of law teaching, William Keener.

Although Dwight had built the largest law school in America, Low considered it "moribund" and asked Keener, who had recently joined the faculty from Harvard, to design a new curriculum. Keener and Low's plan involved a closer relationship with the department of political science, which never materialized, and a greater reliance on the case method, which did.[211] Dwight's initial defense of the old school set out the benefits of the law school's employment of his version of the "Socratic method," the most distinct contrast to other approaches being clear:

> The method adopted in the Law School seeks to inculcate great principles of law, leaving to the Student to apply them by his own reasoning to special cases as they arise. It is thus truly educational by drawing out the powers of the Student and giving him comprehensive views. It is in sharp and as we think most favorable contrast with instruction by concrete cases, which leaves the Student without a guiding principle to connect them. Law is nothing without logic, and true logical methods should be pursued, and the Student trained not merely to think but to think on the spot, instead of acquiring his knowledge simply by absorption.[212]

Even so, Dwight was fighting in the rear guard. Low's plan was implemented, and Dwight retired. Keener and his casebooks thus had free rein, although some courses were still not fully converted. Keener's own jurisprudence course continued to use a selection of theoretical readings,[213] and in his contracts course, he initially assigned readings from treatises.[214]

The Columbia faculty prior to Dwight's fall—George Chase and Robert Petty—resigned from Columbia and moved across town, opening the New York Law School, where Dwight's principles were continued, although with a twist.[215] Dwight's method was followed religiously at first, even if with some concessions,

4. Asahel Stearns (1774-1839), along with Isaac Parker, presided over the first law classes of John Harvard's college in Massachusetts, although their program was then quite overshadowed by the school in Litchfield. (*Courtesy of Art & Visual Materials, Special Collections Department, Harvard Law School Library.*)

such as Chase's introduction of his own casebook.[216] The curriculum was based on a detailed syllabus of 145 pages, printing a summary of the topics and rules from Dwight's notes, albeit in slightly varied order. The syllabus was published in a single volume, then priced at a quite reasonable fifteen cents.[217] But the syllabus was also bound into larger notebooks, with four leaves of notebook paper inserted after each page of syllabus. Students then used these notebooks for transcribing the lectures into pages following the appropriate printed page.[218] The Dwight method seems not to have long survived the transplant, though, and is believed to have lost its prominence even before Professor Chase's death in 1924.[219]

Other schools continued the wholesale use of lectures and treatises. California Chief Justice Seranus Hastings's College of Law in San Francisco had long employed a system of lecturing similar to Dwight's comprehensive outline of the municipal law. Hastings College refined its lectures along the "scientific and practical" lines of John Norton Pomeroy's system.[220] The Pomeroy System was a framework of intensely detailed syllabi,[221] comprehensive treatises,[222] and recent case opinions in each subject with a discussion-based class lecture.[223] Pomeroy's system was rare among treatise-writers in that he placed considerable emphasis on statutes in both his texts and syllabi. The unforgettable bits of the system are Pomeroy's ponderous outlines, every law sketched in bracketed classifications and logical sets, a form seemingly borrowed from a seventeenth-century text by Serjeant Finch.[224]

Pomeroy's sketch of property rights as *Rights and Duties Relating to Things and Transactions as Their Object* is representative: Primary rights are in two categories, *in rem* and *in personam. In rem* rights are in three categories, relating to their objects, their essential nature, and their means of acquisition. *In personam* rights are in two categories, according to whether they arise from contracts or quasi contracts. Each of the categories of *in rem* rights established by a different relation then devolves into three to five more elements, each of which is, in turn, described by two more levels of subdivision.[225] It would be a mistake from such a list to believe, however, that Pomeroy's work was intrinsically unsubtle. For instance, while his consideration of the federal commerce power in constitutional law is compartmentalized, the treatment of each theory is thorough, relating points not only among the various theories but also to alternatives in the constitutional theory of England, France, and the United States.[226]

The similarity between Pomeroy's method and Dwight's is hardly random. Both were nearly fanatical in their use of categories and lists to present the doctrines of each area of law. Both men presented their lists in relationships moving from levels of great abstraction to great specificity. That such specific approaches could evolve on opposite coasts is not too difficult to explain—Pomeroy studied Classics in Hamilton College, New York, while Dwight was both tutor and professor there.[227]

The Pomeroy System prevailed at Hastings until the faculty expanded to the point that few of the teachers knew the comprehensive scheme or the subtle weights and emphases among the various facets of municipal law. 1894 was the last year in which a Pomeroy book was assigned, after which casebooks occupied the field.[228]

Other schools persisted to varying degrees in following the lecture method. The University of Virginia followed the view of John Barbee Minor, reflected in the words of William Minor Lile, who maintained the best lectures had no student discussion:

> Our theory is that a large part of the body of the law rests upon no particular reason, but is conventional, or may we not call it arbitrary? This cannot be deduced by any course of reasoning howsoever subtle or astute. The mere statement of the rule, with a practical illustration is its best exposition.[229]

Virginia followed its -based course of textbook and lecture and only adopted the casebook in the 1930s.[230]

Yale avoided the case method and employed a method based on treatise readings and oral quizzes until after the turn of the century.[231] The "Yale System" was adopted and advertised in contrast to Harvard's case method in the school's announcement of 1887-88.[232] The system was based on some lectures, but primarily on students' private study and recitation in response to questions posed by the instructor.[233] By 1892-1893, cases had been introduced as a source of study,[234] although the Yale System continued until 1903.[235]

While the lectures at Virginia, Yale, and other schools followed such traditions, there was experimental variation as well. Brooklyn Law School presented its entering students with a series of orientation lectures that were particularly well named, spending, as they did, much of their content describing development of legal systems from the ancient Egyptian and Japanese systems up to the jurisdiction of the New York municipal courts.[236]

Despite such innovations, the number of institutional holdouts for lectures became few, and the evolution of the University of North Carolina is more paradigmatic. Judge William Horn Battle's private law school in Chapel Hill was incorporated into the University of North Carolina in 1899.[237] Since 1844, Judge Battle had employed a lecture method based upon the standard commentaries, augmented with references to the thirty-seven volumes of state reports then available, and presented lectures for three hours each week. By 1893, the school required eight hours of lectures weekly, and, for roughly a decade, the case method "by gradual accretion" increased its profile, becoming the dominant tool by 1910.[238]

I. The Lecture and Treatise in the Twentieth Century

While the lecture method pervaded many schools well into the twentieth century, publishers, authors, deans, and professors increasingly moved student preparation from treatises to casebooks. Treatises became longer and more unwieldy, leading to a common bifurcation of the treatise—a multi-volume reference work with a single-volume student reference.[239] By mid-century, neither was commonly employed as a primary text for student course preparation.[240]

The assignment of treatises coupled with the delivery of monologue lectures is now a true rarity.[241] There remain a few classes in which the course is taught from a treatise, such as Philip Kissam's constitutional law course in the University of Kansas.[242]

It thus comes as no surprise that a survey conducted in conjunction with the writing of this Article in 1995 ("the 1995 survey") suggests that the treatise and the monologue have been nearly abandoned in the lecture hall.[243] The survey was distributed through the deans of the ABA-accredited schools to the 5,052 full-time law professors then teaching in those schools. There were 513 responses, of which 422 related to traditional lecture hall courses.[244] Of these respondents, only 3% (13) used a treatise as the "primary assigned text."[245] When asked how much of a class is spent in dialogue or monologue,[246] no respondent used monologue exclusively; 11% (46) were "mainly monologue"; 38% (160) were "roughly equal"; 45% (190) were "mainly dialogue"; 3% (13) responded "all dialogue." It would seem from this response that the treatise and the monologue are rare birds indeed. The few courses in which the lecture method has not utterly lost its hold tend to be in areas in which student readings are based on academic texts rather than cases, such as legal history and jurisprudence.[247] In the rest, the field has been occupied primarily by the casebook.

III. The Casebook and the Case Method

The most common texts for classroom instruction at the close of the twentieth century are casebooks. Although classroom methods have become increasingly diverse and despite a rise in the use of other text formats—particularly the problem book—the casebook has now held its prime place for a century.

Corresponding to the casebook is the dialogue as the principle mechanism of pedagogy, designed to elicit understanding of the cases from the students. The depth and focus of this discussion may vary widely, and yet the idea of dialogue continues, with its attendant benefits of continuous evaluation and correction and its corresponding detriments of less-discernable organization and student self-consciousness.

The essence of the case method, as created by its progenitor and promoters at Harvard, is to heighten student understanding of the nature of law, not just to train students in the content of the rules. Such a change was, perhaps, inevitable, as the understanding of law changed from Georgian certitude of Newtonian universalism to the Victorian conceptions of progress and system, promoted by the likes of Jeremy Bentham and Herbert Spencer. If man could be the measure of all things, then understanding the science of law meant to understand what men did with it, not merely cataloguing its rules.[248] The rules could be used to bring order on society and to interject rationalism toward scientific ends. That being the case, the rules could then be evaluated according to how well they accomplished those ends. The case, the moment the rule was applied in a court, was the best experimental result for both ascertaining the true meaning of a rule and measuring its effect.

There is doubt that the casebook is the best vehicle to accomplish this "scientific" end, which has nipped at the casebooks' heels from the start. The efficacy of case method teaching, even when done well, has often been disputed, and it is certainly not always done well.

A. The Casebook: Its Predecessors

The idea that students should learn the law from reading the cases is an idea far older than American legal education, and it has never been completely out of fashion. The *Year Books*, compilations of legal debates from the thirteenth century until 1535,[249] were initially copied manuscripts, first printed around 1480.[250] Long the essence of study for students of the Inns of Court,[251] the *Year Books* were not supplanted by reports until the 1500s.[252] The sixteenth century reports of Dyer,[253] Coke,[254] and Plowden[255] were originally written for the private use of the reporters and only later bound and published.[256] Even so, the reports soon became an essential tool for both lawyers and students,[257] remaining a focus of the young scholar's attention long after treatises and commentaries became widespread.[258] This is not too surprising as the lawyers who were the early reporters were not as much recorders as they were journalists and interpreters, sometimes presenting as much of their own views of both the cases and the cases' precedents as of the views of the judges. Their reports were likewise not exhaustive but were selective, representing many of the same editorial choices of significance and novelty that would later be made by casebook editors.

Students in the American colonies studied from the reports alongside institutes and commentaries.[259]

John Adams, for instance, read from English reports of Salkelds and Raymonds, along with the treatises of Wood, Coke, and Glanville.[260] The library at Litchfield was rich in American and English reports, to which students were constantly referred.[261] Many great lawyers, including James Madison, served as reporters in their youth.[262] Lecturers from Wythe to Dwight expected students to read cases from the reports and to link principles to cases, but the cases were still secondary to the more general principles and logical relationships between them.

The first "casebooks" were really specialized reporters for the consideration of a particular practice area.[263] In the nineteenth century, though, collections of cases, sometimes edited and annotated, were increasingly common methods of presenting the general state of the common law.[264] Lawyers might also collect cases as extended briefs of particular issues then pending before the courts, particularly the English courts considering taxation.[265] Such collections were common in America as well, such as that Dwight produced from the *Rose* case.[266]

Even so, between the death of Edward Coke and 1870, no author or teacher expected students to prepare for law lectures relying *exclusively* on readings of judicial cases. All of this changed with the advent of Christopher Columbus Langdell, the new Dean of Harvard Law School.

B. Langdell and His Science

Langdell was a Harvard student from 1851 to 1853. There he had been a poverty-blighted bookworm, found always wearing his green eye-shade in the library, usually at the center of a discussion of various points of law. His capability led to work both in the library and as Parsons's assistant in preparing his *Law of Contracts*.[267] For sixteen years after graduation, he practiced law in New York, living alone and unmarried in an apartment over the office of his firm, Stanley, Langdell, and Brown.[268]

In 1870 newly-appointed Harvard President Charles Eliot remembered having heard the student Langdell speaking with other students about the law:

> I remembered that when I was a Junior in College in the year 1851-1852, and used to go often in the early evening to the room of a friend who was in the Divinity School, I there heard a young man who was making notes to *Parsons on Contracts* talk about law. He was generally eating his supper at the time, standing up in front of the fire and eating with good appetite a bowl of brown bread and milk. I was a mere boy, only eighteen years old; but it was given to me to understand that I was listening to a man of genius.
>
> In the year 1870, I recalled the remarkable character of that young man's expositions, sought him in New York, and induced him to become Dane Professor.[269]

Eliot's decision was deliberate and informed. James Bradley Thayer had commended Langdell to Eliot.[270] So had George Shattuck, Oliver Wendell Holmes's future partner, although Shattuck did express some reservations concerning Langdell's "faults of manner and temper" and poor ties with the New York bar, owed in part to his "disgust with the New York courts and their general mode of doing things."[271] Eliot nonetheless pushed the appointment through the Harvard Boards.[272] Eliot later reflected:

> So he became Dane Professor. He told me, in 1870 . . . that law was a science: I was quite prepared to believe it. He told me that the way to study a science was to go to the original sources. I knew that was true, for I had been brought up in the science of chemistry myself; and one of the first rules of a conscientious student of science is never to take a fact or a principle out of second hand treatises, but to go to the original memoir of the discoverer of that fact or principle.[273]

Professor, and quickly Dean, Langdell's "science of law"[274] had an essential and quickly famous foundation: knowledge of the law is best derived from its sources, the cases.[275] A student would thus read and consider case opinions on a given topic, and then class discussion of that topic would develop the relationship of the principles of law reflected in the case to other points of law.

The other element of Langdell's lectures in the scientific manner was to exorcize the professor's recitation of prepared notes as the sole spirit of the law in class discussion. No longer would the professor deliver to uncritical mutes the essential ideas of cases and their relationship to the topics of the course. Instead, students were to discover the significance of the cases for themselves, to examine, analyze, and critique the cases they read by engaging professors in a colloquy.

The maiden flight of Langdell's case method was the first contracts class of the fall term of 1870. The lecture was delivered in a semi-circular auditorium, with a small platform holding the lecturer's desk. From the platform radiated rows of cushioned settees beside which students could rent a small writing table from the janitor.[276] The room was filled with an unusually large audience.[277] A student in the class, Samuel F. Batchelder, recalled the lecture:

> The class gathered in the old amphitheatre of Dane Hall—the one lecture room of the School—and opened their strange new pamphlets, reports bereft of their only useful part, the head-notes! The lecturer [Langdell] opened his.
> "Mr. Fox, will you state the facts in the case of *Payne v. Cave?*"
> Mr. Fox did his best with the facts of the case.
> "Mr. Rawle, will you give the plaintiff's argument?"
> Mr. Rawle gave what he could of the plaintiff's argument.
> "Mr. Adams, do you agree with that?
> And the case-system of teaching had begun.[278]

Langdell's method was not beloved. Batchelder continued, describing the course's reception over the term:

> His attempts were met with open hostility, if not of the other instructors, certainly of the bulk of the students. His first lectures were followed by impromptu indignation meetings.—"What do we care whether Myers agrees with the case, or what Fessenden thinks of the dissenting opinion. What we want to know is: What's the Law?"

But far from telling the students, "what is the law," Langdell doggedly refused to be their touchstone, making them take the measure of the cases for themselves, no matter how much they resented the lack of guidance. Batchelder continued:

> They were finding out how the law was made, and the reasons for it, and how it was applied in actual practice. The lecturer was working it out for himself with them. Every step of the reasoning was scrutinized and tested and re-examined till proved right or wrong. . . . The old professors called wholly for definitions and rules: . . . "What is the difference between an action of trespass and an action of trespass upon the case?" The new Dean presented actual problems for solution:—"If A contracts with B to serve him one year at so much per month, and at the end of six months' service he dies, will his representatives be entitled to recover against B for the six months' service; and if so, how much and upon what principle?"[279]

Of course, the students' change of role from receiver to thinker was also a great increase in student responsibility, an increase that was not much welcome, and in Batchelder's words, "dismay filled the school."[280] He wrote:

> Did the new lecturer himself know the law? He apparently took back in one lecture what he had said in the last. Young Warner, a keen logician (and one of the first converts to the new system) cornered him squarely one day, amidst a hurricane of derisive clapping and stamping. Would it be believed, "the old crank" went back to the same point next day and worked it out all over again! Most of the class could see nothing in his system but mental confusion and social humiliation. They began to drop away fast.[281]

5. Dane Hall Lecture Room. In this auditorium, in 1870, Dean Langdell asked Mr. Fox, "Will you state the facts of *Payne v. Cave*?" (*Courtesy of Art & Visual Materials, Special Collections Department, Harvard Law School Library.*)

And drop away they did. By the end of the first term, he had lost all but seven members of his contracts audience. Moreover, along with higher tuitions, a longer course, and newly instituted examinations of both applicants and students,[282] the grievous reputation of the method "undoubtedly" reduced enrollment,[283] if only briefly.[284]

Initially, Langdell circulated his pamphlets of cases to his students. In the following year, however, he bundled them together into his *Selection of Cases on the Law of Contracts.*[285] In his preface, Langdell made it clear that the quintessence of the casebook was merely to solve the logistical problems of access to a library of case reports. The practical difficulties of a student's access to cases, both while in a large class and in individual study afterwards, led him to publish "such a collection of cases as would be adapted to my purpose as a teacher."[286] This collection was "scientifically" culled from the rapidly increasing body of cases. The science involved, however, was rather like the cataloging organization of a treatise:[287]

> Law, considered as a science, consists of certain principles or doctrines. To have such a mastery of these as to be able to apply them with constant facility and certainty to the ever-tangled skein of human affairs, is what constitutes a true lawyer; and hence to acquire that mastery should be the business of every earnest student of the law. . . . Moreover, the number of fundamental legal doctrines is much less than is commonly supposed; the many different guises in which the same doctrine is constantly making its appearance, and the great extent to which legal treatises are a repetition of each other being the cause of much apprehension. If these doctrines could be so classified and arranged so that each should be found in its proper place, and nowhere else, they would cease to be formidable from their number.[288]

However he might derive or enumerate the principles, Langdell's book was still based on understanding not the principles alone but the principles in the light of the cases that reveal them. Langdell opined:

> Each of these doctrines has arrived at its present state by slow degrees; in other words, it is a growth, extending in many cases through centuries. This growth is to be traced in the main through a series of cases; and much the shortest and best, if not the only way of mastering the doctrine effectually is by studying the cases in which it is embodied. But the cases which are useful and necessary for this purpose at the present day bear an exceedingly small proportion to all that have been reported. The vast majority are useless and worse than useless for any purpose of systematic study.[289]

The cases that Langdell selected to represent these principles were not limited by time or jurisdiction, except that they were from courts of the common law or of equity. Instead, his selection method was broad indeed.[290]

Despite the cases' reflection of principles, the cases themselves were presented with few extrinsic hints of what principles those might be. The first edition of Langdell's book had no narrative beyond the three-page preface. There was only one student guide to the book's cases, an analytical index listing the principles in long narratives.[291]

In 1872 Langdell published a second casebook, *Cases on Sales*,[292] which was modeled rather closely after the first edition of the contracts book. Besides the bulk of unannotated cases, there was an analytical index, but no summary. A third volume as well, his *Cases on Equity*, followed the same pattern.[293] He also authorized the collection of his articles on equity into an essay book.[294]

Perhaps the strongest clues to Langdell's selection process are in the cases he retained or expunged in his second edition of the contracts book. In compiling the second edition, Langdell removed thirty-five of the "less important" cases from the original 346. He added twenty-four, including "several important cases which have been decided since the first edition,"[295] as well as beefed-up sections on consideration, including sources of consideration, forbearance as consideration, and moral consideration.[296] The majority of the cases removed relate to forbearance as consideration,[297] a response, perhaps, to criticism in the generally favorable review of the first edition by the *American Law Review*.[298] The bulk of the additional cases were clearly not added for their novelty, but for the introduction of principles that had been omitted from the earlier edition.[299] Langdell presented the ideas in each subject area through cases ordered in a way that generally reflected an evolution over time. Otherwise, Langdell did not often discriminate by age or jurisdiction.

Despite the changes in the cases selected, the most radical departure of the second edition was the addition of a brief summary at the end.[300] In a later edition of the summary, which Little, Brown also issued independently of the cases, Langdell made clear that the narrative was only a summary of the law reflected in the cases in the casebook, not a summary of the field of contracts as a whole.[301] The summary is, though, a small treatise, truncated to narrate the issues developed in the selected cases and meant for student reference.

Of course, just as the readings had matured, so had the reaction of the students to Langdell's classes. By the end of the decade, his circle of admirers had grown both larger and more tolerant. William Schofield described Langdell and his students in the 1880 Contracts class:

> He ascended the platform . . . and opened the course with a brief statement of the nature of a contract. Then he called upon some student to state the case of *Payne v. Cave*. . . . This fairly broke the ice, and the students soon learned what was expected of them under the Langdell System.
>
> . . . His dominant purpose seemed to be to bring out not only the decision of each case, but the reason for the decision. Students soon learned that any position they might advance was pretty soon to be followed by the question, "Could you suggest a reason?" This came with such frequent iteration that it was something of a by-word. . . .
>
> Another point upon which he laid stress was the correct use of terms. We were constantly speaking of "offer," "acceptance," "consent," "consideration." Occasionally Professor Langdell would rap impatiently upon the desk and say, "Gentlemen, I should like a little more precision

> in the use of terms." He was thoroughly fair and impartial in the discussions. If a student in explanation of a case made a point that was unusually good, Professor Langdell would remember it, and sometimes give credit to the student afterwards by name when he mentioned it,—a distinction of great importance in the law school world.
>
> It can hardly be said that Professor Langdell was a popular instructor. . . . Although he had collected a number of volumes of cases he never displayed any facility in recalling their names or in remembering the points decided in them or the facts. He seemed to take up each case in the class as if he had never seen it before. He went over all the steps in the reasoning as new work without any aid from or reliance upon memory. His method was a daily object lesson to students in thoroughness and accuracy. . . . His students soon began to feel that they were not only acquiring knowledge but developing new powers. . . .
>
> Professor Langdell was always willing to reconsider a conclusion in the light of new suggestions. Not infrequently in new courses with which he had not become thoroughly familiar, he would recant propositions which he had advanced as sound. A student recently informed me of a course in which Professor Langdell changed his opinion in regard to a case three times in the course of one week, each time advancing with positiveness a new doctrine. That he could do this without losing the respect or confidence of his students shows the esteem in which he was held.[302]

An interrogative approach to the classroom was certainly no innovation. Dwight and Hammond relied upon it, Parsons had experimented with it, and Greenleaf had exercised students with it. The differences, in a minor sense, were the portion of time spent on the colloquy and, in the major sense, the relationship of a student's preparation to the student's classroom performance.

Although exposing students to the organization of treatises, Langdell attempted to tear the students from rote memorization of principles set down for them by a treatise writer or professor. Instead, by providing them with the raw material from which the fine points of treatises are derived, Langdell led the students to make their own derivations. He did not so much force a particular view upon the student as force a journey of independent discovery.[303] For this reason, Langdell chose teachers from among able students, not merely from the ranks of practitioners.[304]

In 1870 Langdell alone employed the case method, using it exclusively in his courses in contracts and sales. His civil procedure course, however, revolved around a weekly moot court.[305] Emory Washburn continued teaching his property course from a treatise, as did Nathaniel Holmes in Equity, Agency, Corporations, Bailments, and Conflicts; Charles Bradley in Evidence; and Nicholas St. John Green in the first Harvard class devoted to Torts.[306] Indeed, Langdell remained sole practitioner of the case method until an influx of new faculty began to shift the tide.

James Bradley Thayer was appointed Royall Professor in 1873, adding to a faculty that then included Langdell and John Chipman Gray. Still, the most profound influence came from the 1873 appointment of Langdell student James Barr Ames as assistant professor. While the other professors continued to view Langdell's system with caution, Ames embraced it immediately. Ames, just twenty-seven years old, had taught history, German, and French in Harvard College before his appointment.[307] At the law school, he taught contracts and sales and, later, torts and procedure.[308]

Ames was initially an acolyte to Langdell, teaching courses Langdell had taught, and using Langdell's method and book. He soon became Langdell's champion against critics and, upon Langdell's retirement, his successor as Dean. He molded and refined the case system, producing a raft of casebooks including titles in torts, commercial law, partnership, and trusts.[309] Ames refined the composition of casebooks, jettisoning Langdell's method of including the cases necessary completely to describe the evolution of a legal principle, and choosing cases for interesting facts and crisp opinions to stimulate student engagement in the cases.[310]

One habit of Langdell's that Ames appears to have taken to greater heights was his willingness to criticize the results reached in the opinions he discussed.[311] While the students formed their own views of the merits of the cases, Ames expressed his views with sufficient force to guide student bias.[312]

Besides Ames, other converts to the case method were slow in coming, although there was less reluctance among the young. Louis Brandeis, a lecturer in evidence in 1882, used a combination of lecture and case dialogue.[313] Oliver Wendell Holmes, Jr., teaching from 1881 until 1883, adopted Ames's casebook for his torts class:

> With some misgivings, I plunged a class of beginners straight into Mr. Ames' collection of cases, and we began to discuss them together in Mr. Langdell's method. The result was better than I had ever hoped it would be. After a week or two, when the first confusing novelty was over, I found that my class examined the questions proposed with an accuracy of view which they never could have learned from the text books, and which often exceeded that to be found in the text books. I at least, if no one else, gained a good deal from our daily encounters.[314]

Eventually, Gray caved in to the new method. Although he continued to produce treatises, including his famous treatise on the Rule Against Perpetuities,[315] he also compiled a six-volume casebook on property.[316]

Thayer was the last Harvard teacher of the era to succumb to the case-method allure, moving toward it in the late days of the 1880s. He eventually conducted his constitutional law and evidence classes from cases and issued casebooks in both fields.[317] Thayer's books, particularly his constitutional law books, reverted to Langdell's approach, as modified by Ames. He emphasized a "genetic" approach by which one might "see a topic grow and develop," and which might aid a teacher in the one necessary attribute of good teaching—rousing the students to engage their "awakened, sympathetic, and co-operating faculties."[318] In promoting this "dephlegmatization," however, Thayer added brief narrative introductions to his sections of cases, sometimes drawn from histories or treatises.[319] By 1890 the casebook was deployed in every Harvard classroom.

Thayer's classes present something of an evolutionary model for the transit of information from professor to student. His own notes, initially written more or less for a monologue lecture, offer a straight history and list of the principles of his topic.[320] Over time, however, additions to the notes transform them into a collection of vignettes laced together into a whole.

The effect of the lecture delivered from Thayer's notes is evident from the class notes of his son, Ezra, who took his father's newly-restructured class in 1891.[321] The young Thayer's notes have many corrections, with large areas of each lecture marked over as initial impressions as the thrust of the discussion changed. There are marginal annotations in a later hand that suggest revisions and enlargements made during reviews. They are a mess. Still, they evidence personal involvement in the lectures and reflect the care with which the student was required to "fathom the depths of the subject before him."[322] This conclusion accords with a description of the lecture method offered by an anonymous Harvard student of the time to the Columbia law student newspaper:

> When a case has been stated to the class, discussion is freely encouraged under the direction of the instructor. The mere *ipse dixit* of the court is never accepted as final. In fact chief justices and chancellors are frequently overruled with surprising nonchalance. . . . [The student] has worked out legal principles in precisely the same way in which [text writers] have worked them out. He has studied law in the very sources of law. . . . If the student has done his work well he will not become a mere "case lawyer." This point needs to be carefully emphasized in order to dispel the usual charge against the Harvard method. Cases are not studied as if they were so much legal am[m]unition. The student may forget his list of authorities, but he will not be likely to forget the conclusion to which these authorities have led. He has gained an insight into the way law grows . . . when he has a case to handle, he approaches it at the right end.[323]

Even as Langdell's colleagues were converting to his approach, he was obliged to abandon his beloved case method. His health was weakening and his ever-troublesome eyesight had grown too poor to see the students; soon after 1880 he reverted from case discussions to a monologue.[324] By 1878 Langdell had already changed the classes somewhat, and he would sometimes introduce a case by posing a series of problems that the case might solve. His discussion commenced with principles from treatises before discussing the case at hand.[325] He would also present longer or more complicated cases by monologue, the method still preferred by at least one of his stronger admirers.

> Professor Langdell's sight was somewhat defective. . . . and, as it increased he gradually abandoned his method of instruction. He finally abandoned the Socratic method and stated and analyzed the cases himself. He occasionally did this in dealing with complicated cases long before he adopted it as a practice. . . . On such occasions Professor Langdell's students were treated to unrivaled exhibitions of analytical power. Everything pertaining to the case was laid bare, and all collateral and allied topics were fully discussed. This method of teaching by the Langdell System has advantages over the Socratic method. It enables the instructor to expound the whole case. . . . On the other hand, in a course . . . in which the students take part it is practically necessary to limit the consideration of each case to the point which is the subject of the particular course.[326]

In his last days, Professor Langdell's vision had left him sadly limited; he worked at a reserved library table, piled high with foolscap and an inkwell "at which he used to make desperate jabs with a pen, not always successfully. . . . The boy who renewed the ink was instructed to put very little ink in Prof. Langdell's inkwell."[327]

In many ways, Langdell was a thwarted messiah from whom later prophets built a religion. Ames, Gray, Williston, and other Langdell disciples quickly became the new standard-bearers, both articulating the strengths of case method instruction and subtly altering it in the process. Even if Langdell's parabolic career left him personally beyond the limelight, he often would be invoked by Ames and others in their proselytizing of the case method. Ames continued as dean until 1909, by which time the casebook was a fixture on the American landscape.

C. The Export of the Case Method

Casebooks and the case method swept through American law schools with rare speed. In one generation, they effectively supplanted the treatise and lecture as the dominant tools of law teaching. The prophets who spread the new religion were the students and faculty who traveled from Harvard across the land.

The case method immediately roused attention from other universities, although most of it was truly hostile. In 1872 Boston University opened a new law school under the direction of Harvard expatriate Nicholas St. John Green, as a refuge from the "particularly technical and historical" instruction across the river.[328] Langdell's emphasis on cases was not completely repudiated, however. Despite the vitriol from Boston's Kenmore Square, casework there remained an important part of the opposing pedagogy.[329] The centerpiece in B.U.'s treatise-driven curriculum was the treatises of its professor from Tennessee, Melville Bigelow. Bigelow's collection of books was meant both to give an understanding of concepts and to guide the student through the cases.[330] "[T]he student should therefore take [them] with him to his laboratory, the law library, and there carry on his work. He should [see] the cases given in the text as examples, and go as much further into the Reports as possible."[331]

The public hostility to Langdell's method shown in Boston, however, was not universal. One of the first migrations of the case method was to Iowa, in the bags of a young Harvard lawyer, Eugene Wambaugh. Wambaugh graduated from Langdell's school in 1880 and practiced in Cleveland, Ohio, until 1889. He then began his teaching career, using the case method at the State University of Iowa from 1889 to 1892. While at Iowa, Wambaugh wrote *The Study of Cases*, an introductory casebook which was sometimes constructed as a student workbook, an interleaved book alternating blank pages and pages of text.[332] Wambaugh left the following year to take up an appointment as Professor at Harvard, exercising considerable influence elsewhere in academic appointments.[333]

In 1905 North Dakota Professor Roger Cooley compiled *Brief Making* for West Publishing, including a section of Wambaugh's work from *Study of Cases*. *Brief Making* is a thorough, if dull, exploration of the process of redaction of elements from the cases of casebooks, as well as elementary legal research.[334] He advised students to read every case at least twice.

> The student should begin by reading the case rather rapidly from end to end, his purpose being to get a general idea of the purport of the case. He should then read the case again, looking up in a law dictionary or elsewhere the meaning of all abbreviations, technical words, and obscure expressions, not stopping until he is sure that he understands the whole case . . . . The chief things the student seeks are the points presented to the court whose opinion is reported and the propositions of law for which the decision is authority. Having made up his mind as to these matters, the student should next, with the book open before him, state the case orally, omitting none of those facts as to the pleadings, the evidence, or the procedure, which may be necessary to show what the points were and how they came before the court whose opinion is reported, and finally giving the result and the reasons upon which the court relied. He should then write a head-note containing the points of law for which the decision is authority, omitting *dicta*. He should then test the accuracy of his head-note in every possible way, attacking it as an enemy might. Finally, he should consider whether the decision is right and whether it conflicts with other decisions to which he has access.[335]

His instructions continue for forty pages, and the remainder of the book contains sample cases in contracts.

Another export from Iowa was William Gardiner Hammond, the compiler of the first Iowa Digest and, for a time, the only full-time teacher in a private law school, which became the law department of the State University.[336] Hammond was a student of history and classics at Amherst and of law at Heidelberg, Germany. He read for the law in the chambers of Brooklyn lawyer Samuel E. Johnson and was familiar with Langdell's case method, but was far from a slavish devotee. At the Iowa law school from 1869 to 1881, and then as dean at Washington in St. Louis until 1894, he used an independent style of teaching that was similar to Langdell's but also somewhat continental. He used lists of cases to be read in the library rather than casebooks, and he quizzed students and discussed their findings with them during class, as well as requiring that students pass an annual examination.[337] He apparently designed the dialogues to elicit considerable critical understanding, not merely rote recitation of principles, a characteristic of Hammond that paralleled his scholarship on the origins of law and its interpretation.[338]

Meanwhile, Columbia Law School in 1890 had hired away another Langdell student, William A. Keener, who had succeeded Holmes as the Story Professor.[339] He imported the method into the Kent Hall faculty and wrote his own casebooks,[340] as well as defending the case method's promotion of reasoning skills in arguments within the new Section of Legal Education of the American Bar Association.[341]

In 1895 Case Western Law School, then three years old, hired Evan Harry Hopkins as its first resident dean. Hopkins, a Langdell student, graduated from Harvard Law School in 1892, and imported the case method to Cleveland.[342] The Langdell influence grew strong even among Case's non-Harvard teachers. In 1921 the twelve faculty members all assigned readings from Harvard casebooks, except for the lecturer in bankruptcy, Austin V. Canon, who still required discussion of certain select cases.[343] At Wisconsin in 1895, a persistent associate dean and Wisconsin graduate, Charles Noble Gregory, convinced his recalcitrant superior, Dean Edwin E. Bryant, that the lecture, while easier on the professor, did not serve the student's needs.[344]

The University of Chicago Law Department reemerged from the Union College of Law as an independent program in 1902 amidst intense ideological struggles involving Langdell disciple Joseph Beale and Chicago scholar Ernst Freund.[345] After much wrangling, Beale was lent to Chicago from the Harvard faculty, bringing the case method to his courses at Chicago.[346] He was joined there by James Parker Hall, another Harvard graduate, who had taught at Stanford before becoming dean at Chicago in 1904.[347]

Of course, the case method coexisted in most schools for many years with the Dwight system, Pomeroy books, the Yale method, and other variations on the treatise and lecture method. In an 1893 law school census, only Columbia and Harvard thoroughly employed the case method.[348] Twelve schools reported study from both treatises and either casebooks or leading cases in the reports, and thirty-six schools reported using textbooks exclusively, either as the basis of lectures or of student recitation.[349] Even so, the spread of the case method was soon to gain pace.

Northwestern came under the sway of Nathan Abbott, a case method devotee who became dean at Stanford in 1895, and Harvard "legal missionary" Henry Wigmore, who served as Northwestern's dean from 1901 to 1929.[350] Wigmore imparted the Harvard method of casebooks, and although his influence was moderated throughout those years by the continuing influence of Freund's lecturing styles,[351] Wigmore reported that "all members of the faculty were believers" in the case method by 1902.[352]

Other holdouts persisted. At the University of Missouri, deans educated at Columbia, beginning with Christopher Tiedeman in 1879 and continuing in a succession until 1904, promoted Dwight's system. Even the 1904 decanal appointment of Eldon James, a casebook enthusiast from the University of Cincinnati, did not lead the case method to hegemony.[353]

The creation of new schools and the hiring of new deans were only two reasons for the spread of the case method. Some schools found it a natural transition, led by an ongoing national debate and the appointment of young professors. Notre Dame moved from an "eclectic" style, including dictated notes of digests, preparation of answers to questions, and recitation of briefs from cases, to the case method around 1905.[354] The 1906 return to Tulane of two New Orleans natives from schooling in the land of the casebook, Monte M. Lemmann from Harvard and Ralph Schwartz from Columbia, led to the adoption of the casebook as well as the introduction of Harvard courses, such as Torts and Agency.[355]

Still, at the turn of the century, decanal appointments were often the means of instilling case method teaching in any school. In 1909 the first Dean of Law at the University of Oklahoma at Norman, Julien C. Monnet, was a protégé of Eugene Wambaugh and a Harvard graduate. Unsurprisingly, he built the school around a Langdell curriculum.[356]

Similar stories describe the transition of most American law schools. All other factors being equal, the case method seems to have spread more quickly among schools that sought to identify themselves as elite, so that accredited schools were likely to adopt casebooks long before unaccredited schools in the same region.[357]

Of course, the spread of the case method like Kudzu through American law schools cannot be solely attributed to academic appointments or politics. As Paul Carrington has rightly mentioned, another particularly significant reason the case method was a resounding success was that it allowed for an exciting form of moral education.[358] In addition to its political draw, the case method quickly advanced across the landscape because with it, a skilled practitioner could deliver a memorable exercise in legal training and education.

The faster adoption of the case method at more exclusive schools led to concerns in the years after World War I that it was elitist. This charge, easily leveled at Harvard, Columbia, and other schools who early promoted the casebook, was crystallized in reports written for the Carnegie Foundation by Joseph Redlich in 1914[359] and Alfred Reed in 1928.[360] Redlich and Reed did not suggest that the case method was inherently unsuccessful. Rather they argued that the method was effective where employed, in better schools, and contributed to a perceived divorce between the best and the worst legal educations. As a result of these reports, and the debate that followed them in the American Bar Association and the Association of American Law Schools, greater uniformity of national standards evolved—uniformity premised on the acceptance of the case method.[361]

By the middle of the twentieth century, the casebook and case method dialogue were the dominant tools of the American law school. There were famous holdouts, such as New York Law School and the University of Virginia, and in most schools a fraction of the faculty used methods other than the case method. Even so, the books of the case method, especially casebooks in specialized fields, have persisted as the most common basis for student preparation even in courses not taught using the case method.

Much of the success of the case method system resulted from the rich library of casebooks that quickly became available. Printed casebooks made case method courses replicable: an able instructor could effectively copy the broad structure of a course already developed elsewhere, even if the later instructor had never seen the original course. All that was needed was an understanding of the law, the case method, and the proper books. Thus, a migrant professor from Harvard, armed with a bevy of casebooks in all disciplines, could quickly transform an entire curriculum.

Such a bevy there was. Within thirty years of Langdell's premiere casebook, casebooks had already come into being in nearly every course then offered, including contracts,[362] quasi contracts,[363] property,[364] trusts,[365] wills and decedents' affairs,[366] torts,[367] constitutional law,[368] municipal government,[369] criminal law,[370] equity,[371] suretyship, [372]pleading,[373] evidence,[374] damages,[375] transportation,[376] insurance,[377] agency,[378] corporations,[379] partnership,[380] commercial paper,[381] sales,[382] and admiralty.[383] Langdell's colleagues wrote the earliest casebooks, but authors were soon compiling casebooks across the country. Besides tapping into the increasingly national and international markets,[384] professors continued to develop and employ materials for use only in their own classes.[385] According to Joseph Redlich, eighty-six casebooks had been published by 1908.[386] Between the wars, the stream of casebooks flowed steadily and unceasingly. Nearly a hundred books per year were reviewed,[387] prompting concerns that there was no coordination of such a vast productive effort, and thus little progress of quality in either the law or its teaching.[388] The transition was so fast and thorough that West's casebooks issued in 1908 began with a defense of case study. West abandoned this practice in 1915 as unnecessary in the face of a friendly U.S. Bureau of Education report finding that "the case method forms the principal, if not the exclusive, method of teaching in nearly all of the stronger law schools of the country. Lectures on special subjects are of course still delivered in all law schools, and this doubtless always will be the case."[389]

While most of the new books followed Ames's modification of Langdell—delivering the gist of selected principles with the most engaging cases from American and English reports—concern grew that the principles were not presented in sufficient detail. In 1908 this concern led to West Publishing's American Case Book System,[390] designed to provide "training and knowledge" and to "cover the general principles of a given subject in the time allotted, even at the expense of a considerable sacrifice of detail."[391] Toward this end, the ABS books were long—property took four volumes—and included shorter excerpts from cases and occasional excerpts from treatises.

Taking the idea of more general coverage to logical extremes, schools began to promote casebooks directed to a complete rendition of the laws of given states,[392] a move forecast and supported by Albert Kales[393] and Arthur Vanderbilt.[394] The more common methods of increasing coverage were to reduce the percentage of a case reproduced, allowing more cases per book, to include more footnotes, annotations, and text notes, and to lengthen the book.[395] Many of these annotations were used not just to increase coverage, but to replace some of the structure of the treatises as a framework for student understanding of the cases.[396]

Langdell's disciples did not enthusiastically greet these transformations. A 1907 panel of the Association of American Law Schools fired the first salvos responding to Kales's article of that same year. Penn dean William Draper Lewis, Columbia dean George Kirchwey, and Harvard dean James Barr Ames all attacked the idea that law schools should provide "knowledge" rather than the "power of legal reasoning."[397] Roscoe Pound repeatedly blasted books promoting greater coverage stating, "the notion that the courses offered should include everything a student need know, that he need consider or will consider that is not gone over in class, is a mistaken one."[398]

Pound and others adopted still another method of promoting a comprehensive understanding of the principles of a topic—writing casebooks upon narrow, focused topics.[399] Dean Griswold, speaking later at the University of Michigan, lambasted the pursuit of comprehensive training in one of the more memorable defenses of educational emphasis on process.[400] He noted that the growth and complexity of legal materials taught in the same three years of law school has led to more hours in classrooms, more detailed and longer casebooks, and to more lectures and less class discussion. "All of these things, and more, are inescapable if we are going to try to cram all of the vast and growing complexity of American law into the three years which our students have in school."[401] Thus, Griswold argued, law professors

> should worry less about details and ramifications, and should concentrate more on method, technique, vocabulary, approach, arts, and the other things that go to make up a lawyer who will be qualified to dig into problems, learn their details, and handle them well when problems

> come before him in later years—for the most part, problems the details of which we could not possibly teach him now, no matter how hard we tried.[402]

He summarized his view of law teaching with Thomas Reed Powell's description of then-Professor Felix Frankfurter's teaching: "'Felix didn't teach the boys law. . . . He taught them lawyering. . . .' [W]e need concern ourselves less about teaching law; and we should focus our abilities and energies on teaching lawyering. They really are quite different things."[403]

Despite its impossible magnitude, the idea of comprehensive coverage—of teaching the law—lingers to this day.[404] Thus a tension remains between materials that promote education, using fewer examples to emphasize methods, and those that promote training, using more examples to emphasize content. From this tension, the modern casebook arises as a potentially dangerous compromise. In a 1967 speech, Dean Griswold noted a corporate ambivalence with the case method. While a "powerful device for inculcating a certain type of logical reasoning," the case method could easily be misused.[405]

> [T]he case method . . . is only a tool. It is not an end in itself, and it is fully as dangerous as it is useful. . . . It has often been said, for a smile, that legal education sharpens the mind by narrowing it. To my mind, there is more truth to this than we have been willing to admit. . . . I do not reject the case method. I only argue that we should be careful in its use.[406]

Such misuse was already so common as to amount to a wholesale change in the method itself, narrowing the class dialogue from lawyering to laws so completely as to awaken the ghosts of the commentators and lecturers.

D. The Case Method Reverts into the Class Quiz

Using a case *book* is one thing; using the case *method* is something else. Even as the casebook triumphed and became the national professoriate's unparalleled choice of text, the number of people engaged in the process led to considerable variation in how the books were used. In Herman Oliphant's 1927 study on legal education, the Columbia faculty carefully distinguished between using the cases as *"a method of investigation* for discovering new truth, and the study of cases *as a method of imparting knowledge* already acquired."[407]

In 1952 Edmund Morgan identified three prominent varieties of teaching from the casebook. First, it is a vehicle for imparting legal doctrine, at a level in which "the average student will seek for nothing more than the judicially approved generalization of the case."[408] Second, it is a mechanism for exactitude in understanding the facts and rationale of each case. Third, it is a basis for hypothetical extrapolation, a way in which to lead students to test the soundness of reasoning and to apply it to new situations. This third, most sophisticated approach is that closest to the views of Langdell and Ames, and Professor Morgan assumed that it was the method of "the majority of teachers in a modern law school." Concerns that this assumption was untrue in practice were even then being voiced.[409]

Despite the uniformity of schools' lauds of their own teaching, a suspicion had long lingered that Langdell's legacy had become not so much the exacting task of a case method discussion as the more predictable charade of a quiz game. Thus in the 1950s, the mammoth Survey of the Legal Profession was conducted, in which the inspectors' reports of the 160 schools suggested that the case method was weakly employed.[410] The report frequently stated, for example, that a particular "school uses the case method." Often, though, further information contained in the report cast doubt on the statement's accuracy. A not atypical report from the inspector for Pennsylvania suggested that the schools observed were not so much using the case method to learn analysis as they were using an older form of student recitation to test memory.

> The case system of teaching is in use, in the sense that casebooks are the teaching materials, but the teachers have not become accustomed to efficient use of the true case method of teaching. . . .

> [In Pennsylvania] . . . good case method instruction is a rarity. In this I do not think they are different from other law schools, including our most famous, for I am convinced there is a decline in the use of the case method as a whole. To avoid misunderstanding, it should be added that by 'the case method' I mean generally a method which involves a joint exploration of problems by instructor and class as contrasted with a method designed primarily to convey information from the instructor to the class.
>
> Even in classes where instruction proceeded in the form of an exchange between the professor and the student, often the object seemed not that of conducting a joint examination of issues but rather of testing the student's knowledge by a kind of quiz. In these 'quiz' sessions, the ratio of student talk to professor talk was high, but the student was there, not to analyze and think along with the instructor, but to demonstrate to his instructor and his classmates that he knew his way about the law. . . .
>
> At the hands of a good teacher instruction by the quiz method can be a very lively and entertaining thing, but it lacks the vital spark of genuine student participation. The student is in no sense helping to bring a solution into existence. He is demonstrating that he knows and understands the solutions that have been produced by other people: judges, legislators and professionals; restators of law. When he reads the case in the casebook, he reads it, not as a problem, but as an illustration of one of these solutions.[411]

Lest there be any doubt of the observations of the inspectors, the report offered as examples contrasts between the rare purveyors of case instruction with the more numerous quizzers.[412] Bad examples included professors' giving answers rather than trying to make the students think for themselves, "furnishing the key to the bar exam" rather than stimulating legal reasoning, and assigning questions or cases to recite to individuals in advance, freeing other students from a sense of imminent participation.[413]

Over the last half-century, some of these methods, such as advance selection of students to recite, have become common practice. Still, in the 1995 survey, sixty-nine percent of responding professors (290 of 513), gave no notice to students before calling upon them.[414]

The case method as Ames employed it, if these circumstances prevail generally, has become so eroded that it is fair to say that the modern case-based dialogue is not necessarily the case method but is really just the earlier form of class recitation, even if it is based on cases instead of treatises. At least in the eyes of these inspectors, the least significant of Professor Morgan's three modes, the unsophisticated use of casebooks as tools just for learning principles, was by the mid-1950s the dominant method of teaching in America.

In part because of the shift in casebook use, and in part because of the greater complexity of the law and perhaps a greater appreciation of the flaws of the case method, by the end of World War II, the drumbeat of criticism had reached a din. As early as 1944, the AALS Curriculum Committee report on legal education, written largely by one-time casebook defender Karl Llewellyn, found that the case method was "failing to do the job of producing *reliable professional competence* on the byproduct side *in half or more of our end-product*, our graduates."[415]

Criticism that the case method does not reach its goal of producing better novice practioners has grown increasingly intense as the century has progressed.[416] Many have also expressed the concern that a single method cannot work well in both upper-division and first-year courses.[417] Further, others have argued that the case method is too difficult for the average student,[418] which both increases student alienation[419] and has lasting effects on their socialization.[420]

Perhaps the oldest complaint against the case method is that it is inherently biased toward law issued from the bench, relegating the study of legislation and executive acts to the dim recesses of specialized courses and casebook footnotes. Langdell's supporters resisted the teaching of legislation from the beginning.[421] Accompanying this resistance was an unfortunate delay in moving from common law and equitable pleading courses to modern courses in civil procedure.[422]

The case method is sometimes thought to be conservative, and unresponsive to changes in the law, in part because of Langdell's hostility to changing views of the law.[423] In this regard the case method has been said to hinder the development of lawyers as makers of public policy.[424] These results, however, are not necessarily any more a concern for the casebook or case-method teacher than they are for the treatise writer or lecturer. One last, and hopefully purely historical, invidious effect of the casebook was its use as an excuse for the decline of libraries. At Hastings, for example, the 1920s were a period of frequent relocation of the school, and reliance on the abundance of specialized casebooks, each with its collection of "the right" cases, helped to delay the construction of a proper library until 1953.[425]

Of course, professors can obtain the benefits of the case method in ways that mitigate these concerns. One plausible development from a synthesis of the training and education missions is the hybrid case-textbook, a book combining treatise or digest-like information with example cases. While the form is hardly novel,[426] a demand remains for books that represent both the comprehensiveness of the treatise and the depth of selective case method analysis.[427] In a manner of speaking, the modern, note-laden, casebook is such a synthesis.

E. Current Use of the Casebook

In the later twentieth century, there have been experimental departures from the casebook, a growth in the use of the problem book, and occasional efforts to rely on treatises. Still, the case method remains so firmly entrenched in the law school that even the Massachusetts School of Law, a school that today loudly criticizes the American Bar Association for its claimed unresponsiveness to change, maintains that it "teaches the traditional courses in the traditional ways, including the use of casebooks and heavily Socratic class discussion."[428]

The 1995 survey suggests that the casebook and the dialogue are overwhelmingly the most popular devices in American law school lecture halls. Of the survey respondents, eighty-six percent use a casebook as the "primary assigned text."[429] Comparatively, a slightly higher percentage of teachers of predominantly common-law courses use casebooks than do their counterparts who teach statute-based courses. Casebooks were selected by ninety-three percent of respondents in common-law courses, and by seventy-nine percent of respondents in code courses.[430]

IV. The Problem Book

The science of the age of steam was quickly assaulted by new, chaotic visions of the physical world, in which theory and experiment could completely destroy the established order of prior understanding. As new views of realism in law displaced Victorian theories of authority and class, studying law as the result of thorough organization seemed inadequate.[431] The rules were no longer as important as the process by which the rules were understood. In law, the way to see the process of laws was to study the reasons and methods by which opinions are written and statutes are passed. This centerpiece of the original case method, displaced as the method eroded into the quiz-show class, not only remained essential to understanding the experimental scientific view of law but also became the foundation for critical assessments of the validity of the enterprise as a whole. To more clearly focus such efforts for teacher and student when examining the materials a third mode of instruction, and a third form of text, devotes the class to exercises in solving complex legal problems with predesignated, hypothetical questions in the legal materials. This is the problem method.

Law books in the form of a catechism—expositions in the form of questions and answers so that a student may learn and memorize rote answers—have been popular for centuries. Their use by law students, generally without faculty approval and in the current manifestation as "commercial outlines," is discussed below.[432] More sophisticated answers are usually suggested by the problem approach, however, and it too has its antecedents, primarily in the moot courts and secondarily in frequent examinations.[433]

There have long been efforts to encourage students to solve problems in class. Parsons seems to have required the solution to written hypothetical problems for solving pleading issues.[434] Wisconsin professor Henry Ballantine offered an early contrast between the case method dialogue and a problem approach to teaching large lectures as a method of ensuring that the student sees cases as problems and not as mere statements of law.[435] Such concerns were strategically, although not tactically, in keeping with Ames's views and those of other defenders of the casebook. The case method—when used precisely—is the presentation of a case as a problem, meant to be the foundation on which students are led to build various forms of structure. Even so, the decline of the case method into a quiz show quickly led to demands for more didactic approaches to problems that make clearer to the buyers of the books, whether professor or student, the problem-solving dimensions of the case. This demand was beginning to be met by the 1930s.

In 1927, and again in 1930, Jacob Landman, a professor at the College of the City of New York, wrote powerful criticisms of the case method, which he concluded was not really as "scientific" as had been suggested.[436] In Landman's view, scientific method required something scientific, namely the use of John Dewey's model of hypothesis and experiment, which usually requires five elements: "(1) the realization of a problem, (2) observation, diagnosis, definition, and classification of the data, (3) the entertainment of a tentative hypothesis, (4) the rejection or verification of the tentative hypothesis as a result of further deduction and induction, and (5) the formation of a belief."[437]

Landman, however, observed that the examination of a case is not as strictly inductive, because the student is given the judicial result as necessarily correct[438] (an observation that suggests the case method of his experience was very much the quiz show approach). Instead, he proposed the use of a new "Problem Method," in which a student is given a legal problem of factual complexity, a bibliography of cases and other legal materials to be taken into account, an outline of the various issues that must be resolved with the legal materials in order to solve the problem, and extra-legal information with which to round out understanding of the facts and the law.[439] From this, the student was to

> pass judgment in a pseudo-judicial fashion on the Problem. His tentative principle of law constitutes the inductive inference of law. . . . Deduction follows the inductive inference. . . . The student conducts [the provided materials] and applies his tentative principle of law to verify or to amend it. His inference or legal hypothesis may be wrong, but the prevailing rule of law may be wrong. For all that, the student has profited. Where the rule of law is fallacious, it places the student in the vanguard of legal enlightenment. . . . The law student terminated his scientific legal thought processes by arriving at a conclusion or principle of law, as the lawyer would refer to it.[440]

The problem method was a more structured means to the same end that Langdell and Ames had pursued.[441] It was precisely both Langdell's and Landman's point to teach cases as means not ends: the important goal was to teach the student how to use law, and teaching what the law is was only a secondary goal.

An important influence on the use of problems in law schools was the "case study" of the graduate business school. In the mid-1930s William O. Douglas, then at Yale, offered such instruction in joint law and business courses, observed by young Abe Fortas:

> A real-life factual situation which had been carefully compiled and completely documented by the Harvard Business School was presented for study; then the alternative avenues which one might consider for solution of its financing problems were explored. There was, by design, indiscriminate attention to and discussion of the business problems and considerations and their legal aspects.[442]

By 1940 the problem method was the basis for a successful Columbia seminar. Julius Goebel, Richard Powell, Walter Gellhorn, Elliot Cheatham, and several practitioners ran two sections of a Seminar in Selected Legal Problems. During the seminar, held once a week, the practitioners submitted a problem from their active files and students discussed the problem and later submitted memoranda suggesting solutions.[443]

David Cavers at Duke[444] and Karl Llewellyn at Columbia[445] both adopted the new method in the lecture hall, Cavers teaching conflicts of laws and Llewellyn using it in his upper-level commercial law courses.[446] Llewellyn also required problems to be solved by teams. Arthur Larson used a very similar technique at

Cornell, although his inductive element was interjected by requiring students to hypothesize solutions to the factual problem before being exposed to the legal materials.[447]

The problem method became a frequent experiment in the 1950s. The University of Pittsburgh created a mandatory summer problems course of eight weeks at the end of the second year. Pitt students were organized into "firms" of five, acting on problems brought to them by faculty clients, usually involving a commercial transaction leading to noncommercial problems.[448] In 1951 the problem method reached the University of Michigan, when L. Hart Wright and Paul Kauper integrated it into their tax courses and casebook.[449] Kauper also integrated problems into his privately printed constitutional law casebook,[450] although the problems were much less in evidence in his commercial revision two years later.[451] Harvard used problems in its government regulations course, Northwestern's Albert Cocourek used problems in secured transactions, and Colorado used them in constitutional law.[452] Notre Dame implemented the problem method in all of its upper-year courses; professors drafted problems of varying length and complexity and distributed them to students in advance of class discussions. The discussions were interrogative, with the professor asking questions and moderating students in their answers to the problem.[453] Kansas City offered problems courses for the third year.[454] With the increased interest in the pedagogy of problems, national faculty began to show greater interest in the methods of problem solving. By 1962 the idea of problem solving as an abstract skill was taught at the University of Buffalo in an elective "Creative Problem Solving Course."[455]

In addition to the creation of specialized courses to teach problem solving as a skill, the problem approach has strongly influenced traditional lecture-hall courses.[456] Early experiments using problems have led to changes in the modern casebook. Some current casebooks include brief problems like those promoted by Ballantine;[457] others are wholly organized around Landman's "problem cases" in which facts or authority were pared from cases, and the students were encouraged to work their way through an analysis using cases[458] or a bibliography provided by the instructor.[459]

The problem approach remains a popular framework for numerous pedagogical innovations.[460] Films and other media, team learning, hypotheticals, role plays, and narratives are often ancillary mechanisms for the solution of a problem.[461] In the 1995 survey, respondents teaching in all-lecture courses assigned problem books in nine percent of the courses surveyed. This number reflects higher use of problem books in code courses, for which thirteen percent of the teachers reported using problem books, as opposed to common-law courses, for which problem books were assigned only three percent of the time.

V. The Current Eclecticism

The casebook and the problem book were born of the nineteenth-century view of scientific laws as a means of improving the environment for humanity. This vision, along with its culture, has at least partially crumbled before a post-modern depiction of the universe as a complicated mess of forces that Einstein, Heisenberg, and company have shown to vary considerably according to whose eye is on them.[462] The American legal system has grown too complex to be singularly understood in every detail, and the commands and rationales of the multitudes of lawmakers are no longer thought to pursue coordinated goals according to a comprehensive philosophy. To bring order to this universe, the professor may rely on the cases to exhibit manifestations of law, but the cases may as easily be seen as acts of an official's will or as manifestations of rules binding the official.

The organization of law in this age is less often called scientific, even if it reflects contemporary views of science. Instead, the emphasis has perceptibly shifted from concern for the methods by which laws are made to the influence of the people who engage in those methods. Ironically, though, to study this influence, the artifacts from courthouses and legislatures, the stuff of the rules of law, remain the only benchmarks. To attempt to measure the accuracy of the benchmarks, the study of these rules remains a necessary pre-condition. Thus, in the midst of a continuing hegemony of the case method, there has been much experimentation in developing new mechanisms for teaching along two paths; one seeks to change the structure of student work out of class, and the other seeks to change the structure of class presentations.[463]

This section presents several of the divergent channels down which this current flows. While the first example, the use of anthologies and readers, is meant almost solely to provide information to students, the remainder of the examples demonstrate means to counteract student alienation. The numerous other pedagogical techniques in use, such as the teaching of ethical values and the critiquing of writing exercises, are discussed elsewhere.[464]

It is important to bear in mind that, despite the various means of accomplishing certain aims, the aims remain the same. In the 1995 survey, the largest groups of respondents devoted the bulk of class time to case discussion (75-99%), leaving considerably less time for elaborating principles (25-50%), solving problems (25-50%), and considering theory underlying the course (25-50%).[465]

A. Theory Readers and Anthologies

In the years following the essential triumph of the case method, concern has perennially been expressed that an unfortified diet of casebooks does not provide students with contextual and theoretical approaches to law that courts have not overtly adopted. Various supplementary schemes have evolved to remedy this perceived deficiency. Many casebooks and treatises now include social science materials as part of the readings, especially in problem-approach books.[466] Other approaches have been more radical.

In 1930 for instance, Columbia created a summer reading list of "Great Books" for first-year students.[467] A page-long list of questions concerning the ideas of the text and their application accompanied each book on the list.[468] The idea soon expanded, and the requirements included not only a short pre-entrance list of one book on the elements of law and one on logic, but also an optional second-year list including books in law, philosophy, ethics, logic, scientific method, and history.[469] While the course was initially popular, there were management problems from the start, such as occasional assaults on the books in the library.[470] More troublingly, students assembled outlines and cram courses which, even after a faculty ban in 1937, continued to bankrupt the original idea of individual study of great books in law. After several years of faculty dithering, the reading list was replaced by a required upper-class course in jurisprudence.[471]

A similar, if less pan-curricular, approach of assigning theoretical readers in particular courses has again become popular since the mid-1980s. While professors have long created their own collections of readings, West, Little Brown, and recently, Anderson Publishing, have begun producing large numbers of anthologies designed to augment casebooks in particular courses.[472]

In the 1995 survey, most respondents recommended some form of auxiliary reading, whether articles, anthologies, codes, treatises, or histories,[473] and this pattern was as true for courses based on the common law as it was for courses based on statutes. Seventy-nine percent of all respondents make such assignments, numbers which vary only slightly by form of course.[474] Although most respondents discussed some of this assigned material in class,[475] substantially fewer professors reported examining students on such material.[476]

B. Team Learning

Most nineteenth-century law schools were home to an array of clubs devoted to law, many of which hosted debates and moot courts. While a few of these clubs survive, and although there are practice-area specific organizations, few student organizations in law schools today are organized to promote understanding of the law taught in the classroom. On the other hand, students in nearly all law schools, especially first-year students, work together both informally and in relatively structured study groups. Professors are increasingly interested in encouraging such study and in assigning work, both in class and out of class, to such groups.[477] One such model of group work is that of the Oxbridge tutorial study group.[478]

Assigning students to opposing arguments of a case is, in a manner, the contrast to team learning.[479] This may be done with teams on either side, or with individuals, and it may be done either as a predesignation, or as a part of the surprise technique of daily examination.

C. Hypotheticals and Role Playing

Beyond the use of the problem approach as a mode of presenting an entire course, professors are increasingly augmenting problems with more detailed hypotheticals intended for use during several lectures or an entire semester. An extension of the hypothetical is a role play, in which students assume the persona of participants in the hypothetical problem, as lawyers, clients, witnesses, affected third parties, or legal officials.

One of the most successful recurring hypotheticals is *The Buffalo Creek Disaster*, a book used in civil procedure courses.[480] The book chronicles the causes and effects of a disastrous mining accident and flood in West Virginia, paying considerable attention to the litigation that followed. The students are thus exposed not only to the horrible circumstances in which the law must seek remedies, but also to the specific procedural choices made by the lawyers on all sides as the cases progressed through the courts. Civil procedure professors have made considerable use of the book and the case, both to illustrate actual pre-trial litigation and to challenge students for alternative approaches.[481]

Another approach to such hypotheticals is to simulate a legal situation, having students represent various views. The simulation may be brief, occupying only a small portion of one class, or it may last over an entire course.[482] Faculty members perform some simulations alone,[483] though most examples offered in the literature employ students as actors. Students may assume the role of lawyers, litigants, or judges.[484] Students in constitutional law courses at South Dakota, Iowa, and the University of Chicago, at the least, have taken the role of sitting Justices of the U.S. Supreme Court.[485] While most of these courses have been smaller seminars, the technique was employed at the University of South Dakota in an upper-level survey course, and aimed to develop understanding of recurrent themes, to emphasize the role of facts in adjudication, to encourage cooperative learning, and to reduce boredom.[486] Similar exercises have been used in administrative law[487] and in many of the traditional first-year courses.[488]

In the 1995 survey, most respondents reported using some form of role play, including mock arguments.[489] Twelve percent reported doing so "frequently," thirty-seven percent "occasionally," and twenty-four percent "rarely." Only twenty-three did not use any role play or mock argument at all.

D. Narratives and Stories

The narrative emphasizes a common element in the discussion of cases and other experiences of the law—stories of people's lives. Teaching as narrative is a tool used to tell the stories that matter, and to tell them so that students understand the law's effect on individuals.[490] Narrative is a mechanism for heightening student awareness of the recurrent occasions of harshness and injustice of the law. It may also serve to include students in the classroom teaching experience in an effort to defeat the hierarchical structure of the classroom.[491] Narrative as pedagogy is a direct offspring of the use of narrative in feminist jurisprudence,[492] although many of its promoters are not as closely identified with that school as with law and literature or law and society movements.[493] The form of the narrative may be storytelling, so long as the story is set in a personal frame, such as a biography or autobiography, and the stories may be recited or shown in film.[494] The narrative may illustrate human motivation or responses to legal or social stimuli. While the narrative forms a basis for understanding, as a hypothetical, it is sometimes also presented for its content, as a visceral criticism of law, or occasionally of lawlessness.[495]

Teaching as narrative is controversial. Narratives may take a long time to make a short point.[496] Moreover, a story may present itself as truth in statements with little reference to history of or extratextual reality. Thus, counterfactual stories may be presented as factual, the rare may be presented as common, and the unknown may be described as fully known. The added authority of an autobiographical or biographical claim need not affect these opaque attributes of the narrative, as self-referential stories are inevitably presented as perceptions.[497] Of course these claims may be as easily raised as criticism of most texts, including treatises and judicial opinions.

VI. Technology in the Classroom

One of the most powerful influences on the lecture is external to the lecture hall itself—the changes in opportunity posed by changes in technology. In a manner of speaking, technology entered the classroom long ago, with the use of manuscripts from the scriptorium, the printed book, and other forms of print duplication media. More recently, film, video, and computing technologies have made considerable progress into the lecture hall and into student preparation. This trend will likely accelerate in coming years.

A. Films, Tapes, and Television

Films and movies have long been a mechanism for comprehensively presenting hypothetical cases. As Irving Younger put it, "You can show any movie and relate it to the law in some way."[498] Films have also been used to instruct both in legal history and principles and in the social environment surrounding legal disputes.

While the first use of film in the law school classroom is still lost in the mists of time, the practice was widespread in collegiate instruction and military training by the mid 1920s, and it seems likely that some enterprising professor had begun using them in a law school.[499] By the end of World War II, professors had added film strips to their arsenal, and by the late 1960s, the ABA published a bibliography of eight hundred movies and film strips for law school use.[500] This bibliography included commercially produced movies, newsreels, and documentaries.

Perhaps the most notable of the documentary producers in the cross-over between hypothetical and history is the work of Frederick Wiseman, whose films *Titticut Follies*, *High School*, and *Law and Order* broke new ground in presenting chronicles of life in an asylum for the criminally insane, an urban high school, and a mid-sized city police department. These films, and their successors, have remained popular as demonstration pieces in law schools.[501]

Films are often shown out of class, particularly movies that provide particular legal and historical information. Buffalo has long held a Labor Law Film Festival for this purpose,[502] and Thomas Cooley offers a Constitutional Law Bijou.[503] Professors continue to use films in class as a catalyst for classroom discussion of hypotheticals.[504]

The use of tape recordings, particularly of oral arguments, seems to have dramatically increased with the public release of Supreme Court oral argument tapes in the series, *May It Please the Court.* Some use of such material has been common for years, particularly the integration of oral argument tapes already in the public domain.[505]

Television viewing, both via live broadcast and, more significantly, on videotape, has become a common event in recent years. Professors use television in the same manner as they have films—primarily as the basis for hypotheticals and sometimes as an instructional medium for its own content. As a source of hypotheticals, television shows about lawyers have been popular for both procedure and ethics courses.[506] Besides the reproduction of commercially produced tapes, video technology is also used in training for courtroom use and in student self-evaluation.[507]

In the 1995 survey, nearly a third of the responding professors use films in conjunction with their lectures, most of them using films during lectures.[508] Twenty-seven percent (113 respondents) use films during class. A small number (34 respondents) provide films out of class, either as required viewing, or as an option. Even so, sixty percent (255 respondents) reported using no audiovisual materials.

B. Computer-Aided Research and Communications

Computer assisted legal research began with an experimental system in Ohio, created as a result of a 1967 contract between Ohio Bar Automated Research, a division of the state bar association, and Data Corporation, a small information retrieval company soon thereafter acquired by the Mead Corporation.[509] The result was Lexis, operational in 1970 with a database holding the full text of Ohio's constitution, statutes, and judicial opinions, all indexed to be sorted by every word.[510] The system was quickly expanded, initially including the laws of Texas and Missouri, and eventually becoming international. Meanwhile, competition was quick to arrive from West Publishing Company, which introduced Westlaw in 1975, its national on-line service. As students and professors became more familiar with these systems and as technological advances made them more flexible, the national databases moved from a method of updating classnotes to a mechanism available for use in the classroom. Most significantly for the future, the availability of these services will allow students who were once dependent on physical access to a law school's library to retrieve much of their research at long distance.[511]

The use of computers in more direct pedagogy has fascinated many observers.[512] Numerous schools have invested resources in a consortium established in 1982 to develop CALI, or "computer assisted legal instruction," an interactive computer law teaching system now available with computer text files to explain and test basic rules in a multitude of core subjects.[513] Moreover, many schools have created departments for the development of educational technology. Harvard's Educational Technology Center publishes interactive videodiscs for law student training.[514] Cornell opened its Legal Information Institute in 1992, which has now published basic materials in civil procedure, administrative law, and evidence on its Web site.[515] The few months in which this Article has been in production over the winter of 1996-1997 have seen an explosion of both the number of law-related web sites and the quality of content available on them. Such growth of information provision and access augers much for teachers in the near future and demonstrates the finality of prediction over our horizon.

C. The Electronic Casebook

In the 1990s, considerable attention has been given to the production of computer-driven casebooks and treatises. Using Folioworks and other increasingly high-powered computer programs, law professors are creating computer-based class preparation materials that they integrate into their lectures. These materials are hybrids of casebooks and textbooks and are designed to communicate with national databases on the Internet, both through hypertext markup facilities on the world-wide web and through Westlaw and Lexis databases. Ron Staudt produced what is apparently the first electronic casebook—the Folioworks coursebook in computer law—in 1992 at Chicago-Kent's Center for Law and Computing.[516]

Along with these technological changes in course materials, telecommunications advances in the merger of cable television and telephone companies now allow a cable or satellite link between various sites, so that a class may occur simultaneously in several locations.[517] When these facilities are more complete, professors will be able to teach law courses to students at widely divergent sites, using materials that engage national databases and produce not only text but also images and sounds along with the text, both in programmed and user-designated formats. Later generations of electronic lawbooks will inevitably benefit from increasingly powerful and inexpensive animation, indexing, and accessing software, as well as more truly interactive hardware.[518]

In the 1995 survey, computer use as a part of instruction was rare, although there are signs it may increase.[519] A quarter of the 1995 survey respondents use CALI, four percent (18 respondents) requiring, and twenty-one percent (88 respondents) recommending it. On the other hand, sixty-four percent (268 respondents) do not suggest its use, and an honest seven percent (30 respondents) admitted to not knowing what CALI is. Very few respondents (six percent) use interactive computer programs in class.[520] On the other hand, when asked if one might use them if the availability were known, four percent (17 respondents) replied "certainly"; and thirty percent (123 respondents) replied "yes, if the content is pedagogically sound." Twenty-six percent (110 respondents) would use them "only as supplements to lectures." Twenty percent (86 respondents) replied probably not, and six percent (27 respondents) replied "no."

VII. The Student Initiative

The textual requirements set by the professor are not the only sources of study for the student. An important influence on what the professor accomplishes in the lecture hall are the tools the student employs outside of it.[521] Indeed, student use of extramural study aids is a venerable tradition. Whether encouraged, condemned, or ignored by the professor, students seem always to have looked away from the syllabus for help in understanding material and cramming for exams.

As one could see from the study of Marshall with Wythe, Story with Sewell, and Kent with Stiles and Benson, the student was expected to complete much of his own study with little guidance from his elders.

The books that were assigned, in particular the Reports, Coke, and Blackstone were jumbles of information that were difficult to understand. Furthermore, the information the student did understand needed to be committed to memory. The market for books with which to sort all this out was, and continues to be, immense.

As noted earlier, the legal catechism, or law student quizzer, was a popular means of both extracting information from various treatises and committing them to memory. In the 1800s, in addition to the quizzers for the book-by-book study of Blackstone[522] and Kent,[523] there were series of questions and answers developed for exams in particular courses.[524] Numerous quizzers were created for the use of students in particular schools.[525] One of these may well have been the name-sake of a familiar modern stepchild. *The Law in a Nut-Shell* was a quizzer developed for sale to Columbia students in 1878.[526] An important use of the quizzer was to prepare for bar exams in a jurisdiction, and a question-and-answer book existed for this purpose in Scotland by 1821.[527] The practice in America grew widespread, fueled in part by correspondence schools of law,[528] with numerous general law quizzers created for law student use.[529] There was even a national magazine of law school questions and tactics, *The Law Student's Helper*, published monthly from Detroit in the 1890s.[530] The life of the quizzer continues in one form in bar preparation materials sold commercially in the late twentieth century through companies who make it a primary product, such as BarBri, as well as the ubiquitous West Publishing Co. In its other form, the modern quizzer exists in both a few vestigial quiz books, such as *Ballantine's*[531] and in the frequent law school practice of maintaining files of old examinations for student review.[532]

Another favored study aid is the outline. Initially part of a student tradition of manufacturing copies of heralded outlines of former students, the outline became commercially institutionalized at least by the 1890s. The basic premise of an outline is to distill the details and examples in a book or lecture to their essence and arrange their ideas in a progressive order.[533] In many regards, the outline is the grandfather of two modern forms of study aids, the canned brief and the commercial outline.

Canned briefs seem, unsurprisingly, to have originated in the casebook creche at Harvard, where class notes and study materials appear to have been sold in the Harvard Coop by the turn of the century.[534] In the late twentieth century, several commercial vendors do land-office business selling distilled principles of cases, organized to correspond to successful casebooks in most courses. Every case is rendered and reduced into eight parts: the nature of the case, a fact summary, the concise rule of law, the facts, issue, holding and decision, the dissent (if there is one), and the editor's analysis.

Commercial outlines, on the other hand, are little more than student editions of treatises. Popular current products include some produced by young attorneys as well as others written by the same professors who write course books. Steven Emanuel published his first student outline in 1974, a typewritten review of Civil Procedure, and sold it to his first-year classmates at Harvard, who bought 112 copies at $6.00 each. Business has improved in the following decades, and Emanuel's company now sells more than 150,000 study aids every year, including books, flash cards, audio tapes, and computer software.[535] Harcourt Brace Legal & Professional Publications, Inc., provides Gilberts outlines, written by faculty members of various law schools, Legalines, which include case summaries with treatise-like notations, and audio tapes of famous lecturers on the most common large-lecture courses.[536] West Publishing produces a line of miniature treatises, known as "Nutshells," in so many courses, that they occasionally act as primary texts when few other materials are available.[537]

There are, of course, other providers of these materials, and one of the faster growing markets is for computer programs of questions and answers.[538] Law students seem not only to be a rich market for study aids, but also to be relatively constant consumers, regardless of their school's culture. The author of this Article compared student purchasing patterns at Harvard, a school of considerable admissions selectivity, and Thomas Cooley, a school with a liberal admissions policy, and found surprisingly similar levels of first-year consumption of these books. In 1995 book store managers at both schools estimated an average sale of three commercial study guides for each first-year casebook sold.[539]

Law professors react with a variety of degrees of support or resistance to student use of student study aids. In the 1995 survey, most professors either ignored them or discouraged their use, with a slightly greater displeasure shown toward canned briefs. Only one percent recommended the use of canned briefs, as opposed to thirty percent who discredited their use, and fifty-three percent who ignored them.[540] Slightly less harsh reactions were directed toward commercial outlines: five percent recommended them, only twenty-two percent discredited them, and fifty-eight percent ignored them.[541]

The fact remains that students have used, and will likely always use, a host of materials to order and truncate the course materials. Seemingly, the purpose of such use is less for general comprehension than for preparation for examinations. The pursuit of this singular purpose—getting desired grades—will almost certainly persist as a more significant goal for students than reconciling themselves to the pedagogical goals of the professor. Therefore, student reliance on these materials will inevitably alter the work promoted by the professor in the classroom.

VIII. Conclusions

The law schools of America exist with a fundamental purpose—to provide graduate education in the law and so to prepare their students to engage in the practice of law. This is an ambiguous goal, and yet over time it has become clear that schools have met these goals by the synthesis of two particular aims: to train students specifically to know the rules of the law and to educate them broadly and critically to understand the operation of those rules by and upon people. At different times and in different types of institutions, one emphasis has been more in vogue than the other, and these emphases may well have shifted in accord with shifts in the culture beyond the walls of law schools.

The books and teaching techniques used in law schools have varied over time, following a few general paths, but with remarkable variation and experimentation. Several of these techniques were popular at times when particular strategic emphases were popular (or were later thought to have been popular). Thus, the treatise was seen to have promoted training, and the casebook, initially, to promote education, each book doing so at the expense of the other's goals. Even so, arguments over the benefits of treatises and lectures over casebooks and dialogues tend to turn on matters of tradition and not of necessity. Each style is sufficiently similar to the other, and there is sufficient latitude within each style for dissimilarity allowing for a simple recognition: the choice of a means is not as important as the choice of the philosophical end of the person employing it. Thus, the choice of material is not what causes a choice of goal; they may be independent.

Returning to the three-step model of legal instruction suggested in the introduction, both training and education require success in all three tasks—learning law, organizing it, and applying it. Thus, it remains clear that these three steps are part and parcel of legal instruction, whether it is designed to train, educate, or both. The movements that might emphasize any one of the three stages or either one of the two goals are not tied to one or another step to pursue a particular goal. They are independent creatures of fashion.

That said, there is an historical relationship that suggests an emphasis of training is generally coupled with a focus on learning and organizing rules of law, and an emphasis of education is usually upon application. Thus, Dwight and the twentieth-century quizzers pursued training with an emphasis on rote memorization and recall. Langdell and his problem-method successors, preoccupied more with education, were keenly focused on application. These observations are rough-edged, but they may suggest an informal, if not a causal, relationship among methods and goals.

Looking beyond the current books of paper and cloth toward the age of computer-delivered lectures, the choice between training and education may become more stark. The computer can train, and it will be able to do so more exactly and more engagingly than most humans can aspire. The human may remain essential, however, in the provision of education; it may never be cost-effective to program a machine with the wherewithal to teach or demonstrate judgment or to respond to questions in which that judgment is manifest. If this limitation prevails, an economically forced division of labor seems imminent. The professor will be either a multimedia producer or an educator personally engaged with the student.

Whether tomorrow's Kingsfields could not accomplish over a cable hookup all that is today done in a lecture hall depends, then, on what we expect tomorrow's Harts to gain from the experience. The personal engagement, the emotional and chemical responses of real human dialogue, may be necessary to some part of training. Likewise, the ability to adapt the content of the class to the understanding and enquiry of the student may be necessary to the student's education. Or, maybe not.

Until then, should law schools use casebooks, dialogues, or problem solving in general? Llewellyn was right to say that asking whether the case system works is "like asking whether eating . . . [leads] to the Good Life."[542] In each case, the particular means is necessary to the end, but the terms are too broad to mean one thing, and neither is sufficient.[543] If the purpose of a law school is merely to stuff rules of law down the student gullet, then we should abandon the casebook. If the purpose is to prepare students to use reason to solve problems using the tools of law, then professors should continue to use cases as they were once employed—as problems and not just as quiz bait. This is not to say that some binary choice is required. Tomorrow's Kingsfield may accomplish both education and training, but only if both are deliberately pursued.[544]

In reality, numerous variations in pedagogy will continue. The danger will be in selecting or enshrining particular tools for reasons that thwart the underlying goals of education and training. Albert Kales suggested in 1918 that the casebook triumphed because the textbook "lent itself to lazy methods on the part of the student and teacher. It was likely, by its mere form, to degenerate into the student's learning generalizations by rote and the instructor merely quizzing the student perfunctorily about them."[545] Whatever the methods employed, such ghastly results as this must be ameliorated by the efforts of individual professors. The professor must remain a wellspring to inspire student work and make possible that work by providing order to the chaotic world of law.[546]

NOTES

1. An excellent general introduction to Lombard scholarship is in Charles M. Radding, *The Origins of Medieval Jurisprudence: Pavia and Bologna*, 850-1150 (New Haven, Yale University Press, 1988). A shorter and more classic description is given in Carlo Calisse, *Italy in American Association of Law Schools, A General Survey of Events, Sources, Persons, and Movements in Continental Legal History*, 95-107, 124-59 (Boston, Little, Brown, 1912).

2. The Pavian judge, Lanfranc, established a law school in Normandy before becoming advisor to William of Normandy and then Archbishop of Canterbury. Calisse, *Italy*, at 98-99. A fascinating, popular description of the revolutionary effect this development had upon European law and culture is given in James Burke, *The Day the Universe Changed* (Boston, Little, Brown, 1985).

3. See, e.g., William P. LaPiana, *Logic and Experience: American Legal Thought and Legal Education*, 1800-1920 (Harvard Ph.D. thesis 1987), Albert J. Harno, *Legal Education in the United States* (Westport, Conn., Greenwood Press, 1980), Alfred Z. Reed, *Training for the Public Profession of the Law: Historical Development and Principal Contemporary Problems of Legal Education in the United States with Some Account of Conditions in England and Canada* (New York, Carnegie Foundation for the Advancement of Learning, Bulletin Number 15, 1921). Of course, there are many valid heuristics that do not comport to this template view. See, e.g., William P. LaPiana, *Logic and Experience: The Origin of Modern Legal Education* (Oxford, Oxford University Press, 1994, an abbreviated version of the doctoral project cited above); and see also Robert Stevens, *Law School: Legal Education in America from the 1850s to the 1980s* (Chapel Hill, University of North Carolina Press, 1983). Indeed, with the exceptions of Reed's and LaPiana's earlier projects, historical discussions of classroom technique tend so often to center upon the adoption and effects of the case method that this chapter will attempt a greater weighting of the other steps along the path.

4. One component of the last step is nearly an additional step, in which the "best suited" rule is assayed by selected criteria of justice or utility or fairness, which may have been learned in the second step. Even so, these three steps are usually necessary to promote memory, analysis, and imagination in the law.

5. See William E. Nelson, *The Americanization of the Common Law: The Impact of Legal Change on Massachusetts 1760-1830* (2d ed. 1994).

6. There is some dispute regarding the actual connection of Vacarius, a Lombard canon who taught at Canterbury, to the Oxonian monastic studia of St. Frideswide, although there seems to be no doubt that King Stephen banned Vacarius from lectures on continental law, although Vacarius certainly produced a book on Roman law for the use of impoverished students, and although this treatise was universally used in Oxford by 1195. See J.L. Barton, "The Study of Civil Law Before 1380," in 1 *The History of the University of Oxford* 519, 523-24 (J.I. Catto ed., 1984); 1 William Blackstone, *Commentaries* 18-19; 2 William S. Holdsworth, *A History of English Law* 147-49 (Boston, Little, Brown, 1923); 1 Frederick Pollock & William Maitland, *The History of English Law Before the Time of Edward I* 118-119 (Cambridge, Cambridge University Press, 1903); R.W. Southern, "From Schools to University," in 1 *History of the University of Oxford, supra*, at 2-10 (J.I. Catto ed., 1984); Peter Stein & Francis DeZulueta, *The Teaching of Roman Law in England Around 1200* (1990); 44 *The Liber Pauperum of Vacarius*, Preface (Francis Zulueta ed., Selden Society, 1927). Still, he is traditionally credited with being the first law lecturer in an English university town, just as the study of Justinian jurisprudence is generally credited as the impetus for the growth of European universities. See Cecil Headlam, *Oxford & Its Story* 67-70 (London, J.M. Dent & Co., 1904).

7. Dean Harno exaggerated when describing the Inns of Court as "without parallel in history." Harno, *supra* note 3, at 5.

The College of the Faculty of Advocates of Scotland not only historically parallels the Inns in training litigators and promoting legal continuity and reform, but also boasts an illustrious history, meaningful to the American colonial era. While the English Inns never fully recovered from their dissolution during the Commonwealth, the seventeenth and eighteenth centuries saw a golden age of the writing and teaching of law and legal philosophy in Edinburgh. See David M. Walker, *The Scottish Legal System* 105, 437 (6th ed. 1993). Until recently, there has been little commentary on the Inns after the seventeenth century. This omission is partially remedied in David Lemmings, *Gentlemen and Barristers: The Inns of Court and the English Bar 1680-1730* (1990). For a brief discussion of instruction in the Inns, see the sources collected in Steve Sheppard, "An Informal History of How Law Schools Evaluate Students, with a Predictable Emphasis on Law School Exams," *U.M.K.C. L. Rev.* (reprinted as Chapter 60 of the present volume; hereinafter Sheppard, "Informal History").

8. The first holder of this professorship, William Blackstone, was elected in 1758. H.G. Hawbury, *The Vinerian Chair and Legal Education* (1958).

9. Joseph Story, *Autobiography*, in *The Miscellaneous Writings of Joseph Story* 1, 18 (William W. Story ed., Boston, Little, Brown & Co. 1852; hereinafter Story, *Autobiography*). See chapter 6. Law office instruction continued as a means of education for the next two centuries. See, e.g. chapters 30 and 31.

10. Letter from Samuel Sewell to Joseph Story (Feb. 12, 1799), in James McClellan, *Joseph Story and the American Constitution: A Study in Political and Legal Thought* 14 (1971).

11. Story, *Autobiography*, *supra* note 9, at 19.

12. *Id.* at 20.

13. *Id.*

14. *Id.*

15. R. Kent Newmyer, *Supreme Court Justice Joseph Story: Statesman of the Old Republic* 43 (1985; quoting Letter from Samuel Putnam to William W. Story, May 28, 1846).

16. A rather dramatic but well-documented summary of Kent's Yale years is in John Theodore Horton, *James Kent: A Study in Conservatism, 1763-1847*, at 3-13 (1939).

17. See Letter from James Kent to Thomas Washington (Oct. 6, 1828), in 1 *Select Essays in Anglo-American History* 837, 838 (American Association of Law Schools ed., 1907; hereinafter *Select Essays*, reprinted here in chapter 5).

18. See *id.*

19. *Id.* at 837-38.

20. See *id.* at 839-40.

21. See John Marshall, *An Autobiographical Sketch by John Marshall* 6 (John Stokes Adams ed., 1937; hereinafter Marshall, *Autobiography*).

22. There is some controversy as to how long Marshall studied in Williamsburg. Marshall's biographer Albert Beveridge believed it was six weeks. See 1 Albert J. Beveridge, *The Life of John Marshall* 154 (1916). Other evidence, including Marshall's own autobiography, suggests as long as three months. See Marshall, *Autobiography*, *supra* note 21; Charles Cullen, "New Light on John Marshall's Legal Education and Admission to the Bar," 16 *Am. J. Legal Hist.* 345, 348 (1972).

23. See Beveridge, *supra* note 22, at 155-60.

24. See John Marshall, "Law Notes," in 1 *The Papers of John Marshall* 40, 45 (Herbert A. Johnson ed., 1974; hereinafter Marshall, *Papers*, reprinted here in chapter 4).

25. *Id.* at 45-87.

26. See William F. Swindler, "John Marshall's Preparation for the Bar—Some Observations on His Law Notes," 11 *Am. J. Legal Hist.* 207 (1967).

27. See Marshall, Papers, *supra* note 24, at 37-41; Cullen, *supra* note 22, at 345.

28. See Marshall, *Autobiography*, *supra* note 21, at 6.

29. Edward Coke, *The First Part of the Institutes of the Laws of England; or A Commentary upon Littleton, Not the Name of a Lawyer only, but of the Law Itself* (London, Society of Stationers 5th ed. 1656; hereinafter *First Institute*). Coke's writings are collected in Steve Sheppard, ed. *Coke's Writings* (Liberty Fund, forthcoming 2001).

30. Indeed, in 1651 John Cowell's *Institutiones Juris Anglicani ad methodum institutionum Justiniani*, published in 1605, was translated into English by order of Parliament. The "Rump" Parliament ordered numerous Latin and French texts translated into English. See Daniel R. Coquillette, *Legal Ideology and Incorporation I: The English Civilian Writers, 1523-1607*, 61 *B.U. L. Rev.* 1, 71-76 (1981).

31. Although Blackstone was the first lecturer in Oxford to pursue a course dedicated to the common law, Thomas Wood, author of the 1720 *Institutes of the Laws of England*, had argued for such lectures in 1708, based mainly on Coke's works. Thomas Wood, "Some Thoughts Concerning the Study of the Laws of England in the Two Universities," in *The Gladsome Light of Jurisprudence* 34 (Michael H. Hoeflich ed., 1988).

32. *Prohibitions del Roy*, 77 *Eng. Rep.* 1342-43 (1608).

33. See *id.*; see also Catherine D. Bowen, *The Lion and the Throne: The Life and Times of Sir Edward Coke* 297-306 (1957) (discussing Coke's view of government which differed with his superiors); 1 John, Lord Campbell, *Lives of the Chief Justices of England* 284 (Jersey City, Linn & Co. 1881), describing events which ultimately led to the removal of Coke as Chief Justice; Hastings Lyon & Herman Block, *Edward Coke: Oracle of the Law* 198-208 (1929), describing actions by Coke which led to his dismissal from the King's Bench; Humphry W. Woolrych, *The Life of the Right Honourable Sir Edward Coke, Knt.* 80-128 (1826; South Hackensack, N.J., Rothman Reprints, Inc. 1972), providing a sympathetic account of his chief justiceship. One of the causes of regal concern, found after some investigation by Coke's opponents, was that Coke had allowed his coachman to ride

without a hat. Coke remained sporadically active in Parliament following his dismissal, leading the opposition in 1620, and among his last official acts was support of the Petition of Right of 1628. A fine recount of Coke's contributions to the Petitions debate, particularly his opposition to hobbling amendments, is in Stephen D. White, *Sir Edward Coke and the Grievances of the Commonwealth, 1621-1628* (1979), particularly Chapter 7. Even so, the twentieth century's most significant study of Coke's life and contributions to the law will almost certainly be that now being written by Allen Boyer for Stanford Press.

34. Edward Coke, *Les Reports de Edward Coke, Jades Chiefe Justice de Bank le Roy* (1600-1615; London, John Streater, 1672). The reports were initially in Law French, with an English translation. Edward Coke, *The Reports of Sir Edvvard Coke, Late Lord Chief-Justice of England* (London, W. Lee, M. Walbanck 1658). The published reports were only a portion of the case reportage that Coke compiled between 1579 and 1616. See J.H. Baker, "Coke's Note-books and the Sources of His Reports," 30 *Cambridge L.J.* 59 (1972).

35. Thomas Littleton, *Tenures* (London, Lettou & Machlinia, 1481). Eugene Wambaugh, discussed below, reprinted a copy of Littleton in 1903. Littleton's *Tenures in English* (Eugene Wambaugh ed., 1903).

36. See Frederick C. Hicks, *Men and Books Famous in the Law* 86 (1921); David M. Walker, *The Oxford Companion to Law* 772 (1980). Of course, earlier books on English law existed, notably de Glanville's *Treatise*, written circa 1188, Bracton's *Tractatus*, circa 1250, and Britton, as well as the *Speculum Justiciriorum*, circa 1290, and Fortescue's *De Laudibus Legum Angliae*, of about 1466, but these were manuscripts produced before the arrival of the printing press. For some of the reasons why Littleton's treatise was so hard to emulate, see A.W.B. Simpson, "The Rise and Fall of the Legal Treatise: Legal Principles and the Forms of Legal Literature," 48 *U. Chi. L. Rev.* 632, 634-41 (1981).

37. See Hicks, *supra* note 36, at 91-95.

38. See Edward Coke, *The Second Part of the Institutes of the Lawes of England, Containing the Exposition of Many Ancient, and Other Statutes* (London, M. Flesher, R. Young 1642; hereinafter Coke, *Second Institute*); Edward Coke, *The Third Part of the Institutes of the Lawes of England, Concerning High Treason and Other Pleas of the Crown, and Criminal Causes* (London, M. Flesher, R. Young 1642; hereinafter Coke, *Third Institute*); Edward Coke, *The Fourth Part of the Institutes of the Lawes of England: Concerning the Jurisdiction of the Courts* (London, M. Flesher 1644; hereinafter Coke, *Fourth Institute*). The *Second, Third,* and *Fourth Institutes* were published posthumously by Parliamentary decree.

39. Coke, *First Institute, supra* note 29, 394(b).

40. Samuel Thorne gives a sympathetic but clear-eyed appraisal of Coke's scholarship in the inaugural Selden Society Lecture. Samuel E. Thorne, *Sir Edward Coke 1552-1952* (1957).

41. The modern reader is aided considerably, however, by the recent reproduction of a well-annotated 1824 edition, along with superb modern notes by Professor Thomas Barnes. Edward Coke, *The First Part of the Institutes of the Laws of England; or, A Commentary upon Littleton, Not the Name of a Lawyer Only, but of the Law Itself* (Thomas Barnes, ed., Legal Classics Library, 1985) (1656).

42. On Christmas Day 1762, Jefferson wrote his friend John Page of a number of minor disasters that had befallen him and of the feminine distractions that preoccupied him "too often, I am sure, to get through old Coke this winter; for God knows I have not seen him since I packed him up in my trunk in Williamsburg. Well, Page, I do wish the Devil had old Coke, for I am sure I never was so tired of an old dull scoundrel in my life. What! Are there so few inquietudes tacked to this momentary life of ours, that we must be loading ourselves with a thousand more?" Letter from Thomas Jefferson to John Page (Dec. 25, 1762), in 4 *The Writings of Thomas Jefferson* 1 (Albert Ellery Bergh ed., Washington, D.C., Thomas Jefferson Memorial Association 1905; hereinafter *Jefferson Writings*).

43. Story, *Autobiography, supra* note 9, at 20.

44. According to Webster, "There are propositions in Coke so abstract, and distinctions so nice, and doctrines embracing so many distinctions and qualifications, that it requires an effort not only of a mature mind, but of a mind both strong and mature, to understand him. Why disgust and discourage a young man by telling him he must break into his profession though such a wall as this?" 1 *The Works of Daniel Webster* xxviii (Edward Everett ed., 1974). The biographer went on to describe Webster's preference for the study of titles of law "of greater importance in this country than the curious learning of tenures, many of which are antiquated, even in England." *Id.*

45. See J.H. Thomas, *Systematic Arrangement of Lord Coke's First Institute of the Laws of England* (1836, 3 vols.). Hale's book was more deliberately based upon the outlines of the Roman law masterpiece, the *Institutes* of Justinian. See Thomas Collett Sandars, *The Institutes of Justinian; with English Introduction, Translation, and Notes* (7th ed. 1941). While Coke's whole *Institutes* is also clearly patterned on Justinian, this influence is weakest in the only volume to find fame or wide circulation, which was based on Littleton.

46. *A General Course of Preparatory Study for the Duties of the Bar by Counsellor at Law of the City of New York* (New York, S. Gould, 1810).

47. See James Clitherow, *Preface to William Blackstone, Reports of Cases Determined in the Several Courts of Westminster-Hall, from 1746 to 1779* (London, S. Sweet et al., 2d ed. 1828). Lord Campbell relates the interview between Blackstone and the Duke of Newcastle, who passed over Blackstone for the talentless but politically reliable Dr. Jenner. Campbell, *supra* note 33, at 378-79.

48. William Blackstone, *Analysis of the Laws of England* (1756; London, J. Sharpe, 1821). Blackstone published a preliminary analysis based on his lectures for those who attended his classes in 1756, 1757, and 1758. William Blake Odgers, "Sir William Blackstone," 27 *Yale L.J.* 599, 605 (1918).

49. Viner's immense project was an unwieldy, 23-volume "encyclopedia of legal lore," on which Viner labored for nine years. The value of the bequest, which included other property, was about £12,000 and was to support not only a chair but other scholars as well. Indeed, Blackstone resigned the chair in 1766 when the university convocation refused to adopt his scheme

of creating a school of English law in New Inn Hall, of which he was then principal. See William Blake Odgers, "Sir William Blackstone," 28 *Yale L.J.* 542 (1918); Odgers, *supra* note 48, at 610-12.

50. William Blackstone, "A Discourse on the Study of Law" (1758) in 1 William Blackstone, *Commentaries on the Laws of England* (1765-69, facsimile edition, Univ. of Chicago Press, 1979). There seems to be a clear effort in Blackstone's writing to relate this "scientific" view of the common law to the contemporary description of the civil law as a "science," a label it had held from its Roman roots. See generally Tony Honoré, *Ulpian* (1982). Certainly, the *Commentaries* follow the structure then long associated with the Code of Justinian. See generally Sandars, *supra* note 45. For a contrast between the scientific and the mysterious in Blackstone's work, see Daniel Boorstin's classic essay, "The Mysterious Science of the Law: An Essay on Blackstone's Commentaries" (1996). John Langbein emphasizes the point that a critical influence in Blackstone's great clarity is that his work comes at the end of the worst confusions of the writ system, allowing a more substantial set of categories. Telephone Conversation with John Langbein (Nov. 18, 1996).

51. See Stanley N. Katz, "Introduction," in 1 Blackstone, *Commentaries on the Laws of England*; *supra* note 50. That Clarendon Press published his Commentaries was all the more natural as Blackstone had been a delegate to the press for several years, instituting reforms in its management. Odgers, *supra* note 48, at 605.

52. Albert V. Dicey, "Blackstone's Commentaries," 4 *Cambridge L.J.* 286, 286 (1932, quoting Annual Register, 1767).

53. Dicey, *supra* note 52, at 287 (quoting Lord Mansfield). The *Commentaries* would not long remain so popular in England. Dicey sets out John Austin's influential criticisms of 1826, that Blackstone was more apologist than anything else, adopting numerous errors, having "swallowed the matter of his reading, without choice and without rumination." *Id.* Austin's criticisms echo Jeremy Bentham's, first published in *A Fragment on Government* in 1776. See Jeremy Bentham, *A Fragment on Government* (J.H. Burns & H.L.A. Hart eds., 1990). But see Richard A. Posner, "Blackstone and Bentham," 19 *J.L. & Econ.* 569 (1976), a view of Blackstone's contributions shared by Harold J. Berman & Charles J. Reid, "The Transformation of Legal Science: From Hale to Blackstone," 45 *Emory L.J.* 437 (1996).

54. See William Blackstone, *Commentaries on the Laws of England* (Philadelphia, R. Bell 1771). I am indebted to Whitney Bagnall at the Columbia Law Library for her descriptions of her ongoing research into the disposition of the various orders on Bell's subscription list.

55. Dr. Lockmiller and those who have followed him may somewhat underrepresent the number of English printings as "at least twenty-one," in part because Dr. Lockmiller relied almost exclusively on Dean William Hammond's bibliographic survey, which ends in 1844. Compare David Lockmiller, *Sir William Blackstone* 157 n.41 (1938), delineating the books as published from the first in 1765 to the twenty-first in 1844, with Dennis R. Nolan, "Sir William Blackstone and the New American Republic: A Study of Intellectual Impact," 51 *N.Y.U. L. Rev.* 731, 736 n.34 (1976), stating that twenty-one editions were published in England, twelve in the United States, three in Ireland, and other foreign translations, with William G. Hammond, "Bibliography of the *Commentaries*," in William Blackstone, *Commentaries on the Laws of England* xxi-xxv (San Francisco, Bancroft-Whitney Co., William G. Hammond ed., 1890). But Dean Hammond did not consider later English editions, such as Maxwell's various printings. *Id.* See William Blackstone, *Commentaries on the Laws of England* (Herbert Broom & Edward Hadley eds., London, W. Maxwell, 1869).

56. Of the many American editions of Blackstone, three seem to have had the greatest academic influence: St. George Tucker's in 1803, Sharswood's in 1859, and Cooley's in 1870. There were of course many other editions, some specifically meant for use in particular schools, such as the one George Chase edited in 1890 for use at Columbia. See Lockmiller, *supra* note 55, at 171 n.7; Nolan, *supra* note 55, at 761-64. The Lawbook Exchange has recently issued a facsimile of St. George Tucker's edition. Blackstone's *Commentaries: With Notes of Reference to the Constitution and Cases of the Federal Government of the United States and of the Commonwealth of Virginia* (1803; Paul Finkelman & David Cobin eds., 1996).

57. See Henry J. Stephen, *New Commentaries on the Laws of England* (New York, Halsted & Voorhies, 1st Am. ed. 1841; London, Butterworths, 8th English ed. 1880), relying partially upon Blackstone). The remaining works are discussed below.

58. See Lockmiller, *supra* note 55, at 42. Compare at *id.* app. V, at 253-59, with *id.* app. V, at 260-64, and references in n.18.

59. Lockmiller reprints Blackstone's outline at Lockmiller, *supra* note 55, app. V, at 253-59. The classical influence of Hale, already noted, largely accounts for Blackstone's four essential topics and their order. See Thomas G. Barnes, "Notes from the Editors," *Commentaries on the Laws of England* 16-24 (1994).

60. Jefferson noted his respect but typical criticism of Blackstone in 1812: "Blackstone . . . although the most elegant and digested of our law catalogs, has been perverted more than all others, to the degeneracy of legal science. A student finds there a smattering of everything, and his indolence easily persuades him that if he understands that book, he is master of the whole body of the law. The distinction between these, and those who have drawn their stores from the deep and rich mines of Coke and Littleton, seems well understood even by the unlettered common people, who apply the appelation of Blackstone lawyers to these ephemeral insects of the law." Letter from Thomas Jefferson to John Tyler (June 17, 1812), 13 *Jefferson Writings*, *supra* note 42, at 165, 166-67. This seemingly perfect comprehensiveness was integral to Blackstone's efforts to systematize a "science of the law." See Berman & Reid, *supra* note 53.

61. See, e.g., 2 William Blackstone, *Commentaries* *143 (discussing a case establishing a lease as for a term of years).

62. See Glenn Burgess, *Absolute Monarchy and the Stuart Constitution* 152-57 (1996); R.A. MacKay, "Coke—Parliamentary Supremacy or the Supremacy of the Law?," 22 *Mich. L. Rev.* 215 (1923); Ruth Mertz, "Sir Edward Coke in the Parliament of 1621" (1942; unpublished Ph.D. dissertation, Washington University Dept. of History). Although, just as surely, much of his career, particularly his term as Solicitor General, was spent in slavish devotion to the increased prerogative of the crown. Woolrych, *supra* note 33, at 50-74.

63. Jefferson wrote: "In the selection of our Law Professor, we must be rigorously attentive to his political principles. You

will recollect that before the Revolution, Coke on Littleton was the universal elementary book of law students, and a sounder Whig never wrote, nor of profounder learning in the orthodox doctrines of the British constitution, or in what were called English liberties. You remember that our lawyers were then all Whigs. But learning got out of fashion, and the honeyed Mansfieldism of Blackstone became the students' hornbook, from that moment, that profession (the nursery of our Congress) began to slide into toryism, and nearly all the young brood of lawyers now are of that hue. They suppose themselves, indeed, to be Whigs, because they no longer know what Whigism or republicanism means. It is in our seminary that that vestal flame is to be kept alive; it is thence it is to spread anew over our own and the sister States." Letter from Thomas Jefferson to James Madison (Feb. 17, 1826), in 16 *Jefferson Writings, supra* note 42, at 155.

64. See Beverly Zweiben Rowsome, *How Blackstone Lost the Colonies* (1990). More recently, deeper ideological criticism has been echoed by Duncan Kennedy. See Duncan Kennedy, "The Structure of Blackstone's Commentaries," 28 *Buff. L. Rev.* 205 (1979). Other works have considerably outshone and strongly criticized Kennedy's ahistorical work. See John W. Cairns, "Blackstone, an English Institutionalist: Legal Literature and the Rise of the Nation State," 4 *Oxford J. Legal Stud.* 318 (1984); Alan Watson, "The Structure of Blackstone's *Commentaries*," 97 *Yale L.J.* 795 (1988). Watson examined the resonances and dissonances between Blackstone's *Commentaries* and Justinian's *Institutes* and concluded that the civilian influence in Blackstone's work was strong, but that it is difficult to conclude he had a "particular and precise political ideological motivation." *Id.* at 810-12. Such a conclusion, of course, does not refute Kennedy's argument of Blackstone's ideology, even if it does deny its claims of Blackstone's intent. A more detailed consideration of the political influence in the early Republic is in Paul D. Carrington, "Legal Education for the People's Populism and Civic Virtue," 43 *U. Kan. L. Rev.* 1 (1994).

65. Only half of the schools surveyed reported titles of assigned books. Of those that did, Alabama, Columbian (D.C.), Cornell, DePauw, Emory, Georgetown, Georgia, Hastings, Howard, Illinois Wesleyan, Iowa College of Law, Kansas, Louisville, McKedree (Ill.), Michigan, Mississippi, North Carolina, Northwestern, Oregon, South Carolina, Texas, Tulane, Virginia, Washington and Lee, West Virginia, and Willamette (Or.) reported assigning at least one volume of Blackstone (usually that edited by William G. Hammond). U.S. Bureau of Education, *Report on Legal Education* 44-62 (Washington D.C., Government Printing Office 1893, reprinted here in chapter 38).

66. Emphasis on the nature of a "school of law" is meant strictly to deflect loyalists of other claimants to such a title, according to differing definitions.

67. See Lawrence M. Friedman, *A History of American Law* 319 (2d ed. 1985). The isolated character of the town was later credited as one reason for the school's enormous success as a training center. "The Litchfield Law School," 20 *Albany L.J.* 72, 73 (1879).

68. Reeve would sometimes fail to notice that his horse slipped its bridle, leaving Reeve dragging the empty leather in the dirt behind. See Marian C. McKenna, *Tapping Reeve and The Litchfield Law School* 160 (1986).

69. See Samuel H. Fisher, "The Litchfield Law School, Address Delivered at the Tapping Reeve House, Before the Litchfield Historical Society, Aug. 29, 1930" (Harvard pamphlet US 907 CON FIS). See also chapters 11, 12, and 13 of this book.

70. McKenna, *supra* note 68, at 60. See also chapter 15.

71. *Id.* at xvi, 175.

72. See *id.* at 63.

73. Gould later became a judge of the Connecticut Supreme Court of Errors. See Reed, *supra* note 3, at 130.

74. See McKenna, *supra* note 68, at xvi. This framework, of course, has some similarity to that of the more liberal university approach, but remained distinct for some time during their mutual developments. See note 87 below.

75. For a full list of subjects, see *id.* at 64, reprinting Theodore D. Woolsey, *Historical Discourse at the Semi-Centennial of the Yale Law School* 8 (New Haven, 1874). That Reeve's interests are to advise the practicing lawyer is clearly seen in his writings, such as Tapping Reeve, *The Law of Baron and Femme* (Albany, W. Gould & Son, 3d ed. 1862), although his contributions to law reform are part and parcel of such projects. See Tapping Reeve, *A Treatise on the Law of Descents* (New York, Collins & Hannay, 1825; hereinafter Reeve, *Descents*), employing uniform meanings for terms in various state's descent statutes.

76. See Lonson Nash, "Tapping Reeve's Lectures on Various Legal Subjects" (1803; unpublished manuscript, Harvard Law Library no. MS 2011); C(aleb) Stark Jr., "Lectures upon Law by Hon. James Gould, Litchfield Con., 1824," at 566 (unpublished manuscript, Harvard Law Library no. 2016). See also chapter 13, for a view of life as a Litchfield student.

77. According to one student: "The lectures were taken in the following way. By an abbreviation of each word, I followed the lecturer in the lecture as he delivered it, and afterwards copied the lecture in full at my own room. So . . . I got in this way a very good transcript of the lecture. I would suggest this mode to the law students at Cambridge." Letter from William S. Andrews to Emory Washburn, in "Lectures upon the Various Branches of Law by Messrs, Reeves & Gould at the Law School in Litchfield Connecticut Taken in 1812-1813" (unpublished manuscript, Harvard Law Library no. 2010). Andrews was a graduate of Harvard College in 1812; his dedicatory note declares, "Presented to the Law School at Cambridge Oct. 12, 1859, through the Hon. Emory Washburn Professor at the Law School by William S. Andrews, with his respect. The current price for a set of these Lectures at Litchfield was $100." A transcription of Yale Law School's copy of Aaron Burr Reeve's notebook is currently being produced by Tracy Thompson. Telephone conversation with John Langbein (Nov. 8, 1996).

78. See Reed, *supra* note 3, at 41. See also chapters 10 and 13 of this book.

79. See "Contracts by J. Gould, Esq." (unpublished manuscript, Harvard Law Library no. 2138).

80. See James Gould, "Of Agreements Between Husband and Wife, in James Gould, Lectures 1824" (unpublished manuscript, Harvard Law Library no. MS 2015).

81. McKenna, *supra* note 68, at 166-67.

82. *Id.* at 170-71 (quoting Letter from Augustus Hand to Samuel Hand, Nov. 12, 1827).

83. See Charles Samuel Stewart (Farand Stewart Fanshaw), "Notes of the Lectures Delivered at the Law School at Litchfield Connecticut by the Honorable Judges Reeve & Gould (1818)" (unpublished manuscript, Harvard Law Library no. MS 2131, 2 vols.). This habit was shared by Reeve. See Reeve, *Descents, supra* note 75, at vi-vii. The role of other proprietary law schools of the succeeding era is described in the case of North Carolina in chapter 29.

84. Francis Bacon, "Maxims," in 4 Francis Bacon, *The Works of Francis Bacon, Baron of Verulam, Viscount St. Albans, and Lord High Chancellor of England* (London, W. Baynes and Son, 1824).

85. Clearly the bulk of the library of student notebooks from Litchfield is marked by consistency from one lecture to the next. Augustus Hand remarked that he preferred the infallibility of copying from older notes to the recopying of his own lecture shorthand. See McKenna, *supra* note 68, at 171, quoting Letter from Augstus Hand to Samuel Hand (Nov. 12, 1827). Gould's sole publication was a very successful book on pleadings, which ran to numerous editions. See James Gould, *A Treatise on the Principles of Pleading in Civil Actions* (Boston, Lilly and Wait, 1832); James Gould, *A Treatise on the Principles of Pleading in Civil Actions* (New York, B. & S. Collins, 1836); James Gould, *A Treatise on the Principles of Pleading in Civil Actions* (George Gould ed., Albany, William Gould, 4th ed. 1861).

86. See McKenna, *supra* note 68, at 171, quoting Letter from George Catlin to George C. Woodruff (Nov. 16, 1826).

87. See Reed, *supra* note 3, *Training* app. I, at 443-44. There is much cause to suggest that this influence of Litchfield on the university instruction of its time is, at least, indirect. Probably more influential was the syllabus prepared and distributed by David Hoffman, which is discussed below. Even so, the practicality of the order of instruction, and the limited focus on the elements of pleading and their substance, has been a recurrent emphasis of the practical, independent law school.

88. See chapter 8 of this book. See also Robert B. Kirtland, *George Wythe: Lawyer, Revolutionary, Judge* 11, 166 (1986). Wythe is routinely described as America's first law professor, a title that is in some sense true, even if it overlooks earlier college courses that included law, Bernard Schwartz, *The Law in America* 37 (1974); Stevens, *supra* note 3, at 4, taught by Ezra Stiles, as well, of course, as the ongoing practices of self-tutelage and apprenticeship. See *supra* note 16 and accompanying text.

89. *Blackstone's Commentaries: With Notes of Reference, to the Constitution and Laws, of the Federal Government of the United States, and of the Commonwealth of Virginia* (St. George Tucker ed., Philadelphia, William Young Birch & Abraham Small, 1803). See also chapter 9 of this book.

90. *Id.* at vi.

91. See Reed, *supra* note 3, at 116-17.

92. See Paul D. Carrington, "Teaching Law and Virtue at Transylvania University: The George Wythe Tradition in the Antebellum Years," 41 *Mercer L. Rev.* 673, 678 (1990).

93. See *id.*

94. See generally *id.*

95. See *id.* at 682; 1 Charles Warren, *History of the Harvard Law School and of Early Legal Conditions in America* 177 (1908).

96. See Carrington, *supra* note 92, at 679.

97. Dr. Holley, the University's president, argued the benefits of law lectures, noting: "The great object of a course of public lectures is to produce excitement in the teacher and the pupils, to furnish all the well known benefits of competition, to call up the most important subjects of inquiry, to point out and solve difficulties, to increase the appreciation of the mind for knowledge and its power of digestion, to lead the student to a proper method of investigation, and thus enable him to conduct his own studies with success." Charles Kerr, "Transylvania University's Law Department, 31 *Americana* 1, 31 (1937), quoting Transylvania University's 1823 catalog. See also chapter 8 of this book.

98. See Jesse Bledsoe, "A Course of Lectures upon Contracts within the Jurisdiction of Courts of Law as well as of Equity by Jesse Bledsoe, Professor of Law in T[ransylvania] University" (unpublished manuscript, Harvard Law Library no. LMS 4036).

99. See Carrington, *supra* note 92, at 699.

100. Stiles's plan is set out in full in 1 Warren, *supra* note 96, at 166-68.

101. See James Fairbanks Colby, *Legal and Political Studies in Dartmouth College, 1796-1896*, at 6 (Hanover, New Hampshire, Dartmouth Press, 1896).

102. See Reed, *supra* note 3, at 45-46, 120-27.

103. The position was even funded by the Federalist-controlled state assembly. Julius Goebel, Jr., & Samuel F. Howard, *A History of The School of Law, Columbia University* 13 (Columbia University Press 1955), quoting Resolution of the Columbia Board of Trustees, Dec. 2, 1793, 1 Kent Papers 187.

104. See *id.* at 13 (quoting Letter from James Kent to M. Kent, Jr., Jan. 7, 1794, 2 Kent Papers 191).

105. *Id.* at 14, quoting *The Present State of Learning in the College of New York* 10 (1794).

106. See James Kent, *An Introductory Lecture to a Course of Law Lectures, Delivered Nov. 17, 1794* 16-17 (New York, Francis Childs 1794). See also chapters 16 and 17 of this book.

107. Goebel & Howard, *supra* note 103, at 16 (quoting Letter from James Kent to M. Kent, Jr., March 1, 1795, 2 Kent Papers 281).

108. *Id.* at 16 (quoting *Memoirs and Letters of James Kent, LL.D.* 77 [William Kent ed., 1898]).

109. See *id.* at 17.

110. See *id.* at 16 (quoting Letter from James Kent to M. Kent, Jr., Mar. 1, 1795, 2 Kent Papers 281).

111. *Id.* at 17.

112. Goebel & Howard, *supra* note 103, at 18.

113. See Reed, *supra* note 3, at 122; 1 Warren, *supra* note 95, at 172.

114. See Hampton L. Carson, *An Historical Sketch of the Law Department of the University of Pennsylvania* (Philadelphia, Times Printing House, 1882); C. Stuart Patterson, "The Law School of the University of Pennsylvania," 1 *The Green Bag* 99 (1899).

115. Carson, *supra* note 114, at 19.

116. Wilson admonished his students to pursue in the manner of John Fortescue's advice of law study to the Prince of Wales: "whoever knows the principles and elements of any science, knows the science itself—generally, at least, though not completely. . . . In the same manner when you shall become acquainted with the principles and elements of law, you may be denominated a lawyer." James Wilson, *Of the Study of the Law in the United States*, in Bird Wilson, *The Works of the Honourable James Wilson, LL.D.* 1, 15 (Philadelphia, Lorenzo Press, 1804; hereinafter *Wilson Works*), quoting John Fortescue, *De Laudibus Legum Angliae* (1470).

117. *Wilson Works, supra* note 116, at xv-xvi.

118. See *id.* at 466.

119. A close reading of the three volumes of his lectures suggests agreement with the contemporary view Fisher Ames took of the introductory lecture, "Whether there are not many parts that discretion and modesty . . . would have expunged you will be at liberty to judge." 1 Warren, *supra* note 95, at 173, quoting Letter from Fisher Ames to Thomas Dwight (Jan. 6, 1791); see also 2 Seth Ames, *Works of Fisher Ames* 845 (William B. Allen ed., 1983), reprinting entire letter. Ames, however, was more concerned with Wilson's criticism of English government than with the distance of his love for the common law.

120. See 1 Warren, *supra* note 95, at 281-82, quoting Isaac Royall's will (May 26, 1778) and codicil (Nov. 31, 1779).

121. See *id.* at 283-87. For summaries of similarly short-lived experiments in the teaching of law at Brown, Princeton, Dartmouth, North Carolina, and Vermont, see generally Paul D. Carrington, "The Revolutionary Idea of University Legal Education," 31 *Wm. & Mary L. Rev.* 527 (1990).

122. David Hoffman, *Syllabus of A Course of Lectures on Law; Proposed to be Delivered in The University of Maryland; Addressed to the Students of Law in the United States* (Baltimore, Edward J. Coale, 1824) reprinted in part in chapter 20 of this book. See also M. H. Hoeflich, "Plus Ça Change, Plus C'est la Même Chose: The Integration of Theory and Practice in Legal Education," 66 *Temp. L. Rev.* 123 (1993), placing Hoffman's theory in context with Butler's at New York University, Maye's at Pennsylvania, Hoggin's at Philadelphia, and Field's at Chicago.

123. See Reed, *supra* note 3, at 123-25; David M. Hoffman, *A Lecture, Introductory to a Course of Lectures, Now Delivering in the University of Maryland* (Baltimore, J.D. Toy, 1823), reprinted as chapter 18 of the present volume.

124. David M. Hoffman, *A Course of Legal Study* (Baltimore, Joseph Neal, 2d ed. 1836). The course was slow to find interest, and there are some indications that Joseph Story may have assisted in its promotion. See Letter from David M. Hoffman to Joseph Story, reprinted in Michael Hoeflich and Steve Sheppard, *Justice Story and Nineteenth Century Law Publishing: Two Examples.*

125. David Hoffman, *An Address to Students of Law in the United States* (Baltimore, John D. Toy, 1824).

126. See Reed, *supra* note 3, at 124. The lectures at Maryland are chronicled in Thomas L. Shaffer, "David Hoffman's Law School Lectures, 1822-1833," 32 *J. Legal Educ.* 127 (1982).

127. See *id.* at 125. Hoffman attempted a brief return, opening a short-lived law school in Philadelphia in the 1840s. He returned to Britain and began a history of the world, which he had completed to the year a.d. 573 when he died in 1854. *Id.*

128. See David Hoffman, *Circular to Students at Law in the United States* (Baltimore, Barrett & Jones, 1844).

129. See Edmund H. Bennet, *General Syllabus of Law Studies Prepared and Arranged by Edmund H. Bennet and Printed by and for the Students in Harvard Law School.*

130. Nathaniel Chipman, *Reports and Dissertations, in Two Parts* (Rutland, Vermont, Anthony Haswell, 1793). This paucity of materials for the law school must be seen, however, in the light of the growing number of American law books for the nonspecialist. See M. H. Hoeflich, "Law in the Republican Classrooms," 43 *U. Kan. L. Rev.* 711 (1993).

131. Hugh H. Brackenridge, *Law Miscellanies: Containing an Introduction to the Study of the Law; Notes on Blackstone's Commentaries, Shewing the Variations of the Law of Pennsylvania from the Law of England, and What Acts of Assembly Might Require to be Repealed or Modified; Observations on Smith's Editions of the Laws of Pennsylvania; Strictures on Decisions of the Supreme Court of the United States, and on Certain Acts of Congress, with some Law Cases, and a Variety of Other Matters, Chiefly Original* (Philadelphia, P. Byrne, 1814).

132. See Zephaniah Swift, *A System of Laws of the State of Connecticut* (2 vols.; Windham, John Byrne, 1796); *A Revision of Swift's Digest of the Laws of Connecticut* (Henry Duton ed., New Haven, Durrie & Peck, 1851).

133. John Adams, "A Dissertation on the Canon and Feudal Law," in 3 *The Works of John Adams* 448 (Charles F. Adams ed., Boston, Little, Brown, 1851).

134. James Sullivan, *The History of Land Titles in Massachusetts* (Boston, I. Thomas & E.T. Andrews, 1801).

135. *American Precedents and Declarations* (Salem, Barnard B. Macanulty, 1801); Thomas Harris, *Modern Entries, Adapted to the American Courts of Justice, Being a Complete System of Approved Precedents* (Annapolis, F. Green, 1801).

136. Joseph Story, *A Selection of Pleadings in Civil Actions; Subsequent to the Declaration; with Occasional Annotations on the Law of Pleading* (Salem, B. Macanoltry, 1805).

137. See 1 Warren, *supra* note 95, at 213.

138. A wonderfully thorough bibliography of colonial lawbooks and their origins is available in Jenni Parrish, "Law Books and Legal Publishing in America, 1760-1840," 72 *L. Libr. J.* 335 (1979).

139. See, e.g., Asahel Stearns, *A Summary of the Law and Practice of Real Actions* (Boston, Cummings, Hilliard & Co., 1824) (discussing the law and practice of ancient remedies as a practical tool for students).

140. James Kent, *A Lecture, Introductory to a Course of Law Lectures in Columbia College, Feb. 2, 1824,* at 1 (New York, Clayton & Van Norden, 1824; hereinafter Kent, *Lectures*).

141. See Goebel & Howard, *supra* note 103, at 20.

142. James Kent, "American Law Student," in 3 *Select Essays, supra* note 17, at 846.

143. James Kent, *Commentaries on American Law* (4 vols; New York, O. Halsted, 1826-30; hereinafter Kent, *Commentaries*).

144. See James Kent, *A Summary of the Course of Law Lectures, in Columbia College* (New York, Clayton & Van Norden, 1824); see also Kent, Lectures, *supra* note 140, at 13.

145. See Kent, *Commentaries, supra* note 143. Kent's *Commentaries*' place in the tradition of the classical institute is well considered in John H. Langbein, "Chancellor Kent and the History of Legal Literature," 93 *Colum. L. Rev.* 547 (1993), reprinted as chapter 16 in this book.

146. For a chronicle of the various editions, see Goebel & Howard, *supra* note 103, at 24.

147. Indeed, Stearns wrote a property treatise from his lecture notes. See Stearns, *supra* note 139.

148. See Asahel Stearns, *Report to Overseers of Harvard College* (Jan. 9, 1826).

149. See Arthur E. Sutherland, *The Law at Harvard* 52-53 (1967). The forms of student examinations and evolutions for the era at Harvard are discussed in Sheppard, "Informal History," *supra* note 7.

150. Sutherland, *supra* note 149, at 62 (quoting Harvard College Catalogue, 1820-30).

151. Nathan Dane, *A General Abridgment and Digest of American Law* (Boston, Cummings, Hilliard & Co., 1823).

152. See Nathan Dane, "Manuscript of Dane's Abridgment of American Law" (unpublished manuscript, Harvard Law Library no. AKN 0553).

153. See *infra* notes 160-162 (citing Butler's syllabus and Greenleaf's schedule).

154. See Andrew J. Johnson, *The Life and Constitutional Thought of Nathan Dane* 10-11 (1987).

155. Joseph Story, *A Discourse Pronounced upon the Inauguration of the Author, as Dane Professor of Law in Harvard University, on the Twenty-Fifth Day of August, 1829,* at 8-9 (Boston, Hilliard, Gray, Little & Wilkins, 1829).

156. See *id.* at 47-59.

157. *Commentaries on the Constitution of the United States: with a Preliminary Review of the Constitutional History of the Colonies and States, Before the Adoption of the Constitution* (Boston, Hilliard, Gray & Co., 1833); *Commentaries on the Conflicts of Laws, Foreign and Domestic: In Regard to Contracts, Rights, and Remedies and Especially in regard to Marriages, Divorces, Wills, Successions, and Judgments* (Boston, Hilliard, Gray & Co., 1834); *Commentaries on Equity Jurisprudence: As Administered in England and America* (Boston, Hilliard, Gray & Co., 1836); *Commentaries on Equity Pleadings, and the Incidents Thereof: According to the Practice of Courts of Equity, of England and America* (Boston, Little & Brown, 2d ed. 1840); *Commentaries on the Law of Agency: as a Breach of Commercial & Maritime Jurisprudence, with Occasional Illustrations from the Civil and Foreign Law* (Boston, Little & Brown, 1839); *Commentaries on the Law of Bailments: With Illustrations from the Civil and Foreign Law* (Cambridge, Hilliard & Brown, 1832); *Commentaries on the Law of Bills of Exchange, Foreign and Inland, as Administered in England and America: With Occasional Illustrations from the Commercial Law of the Nations of Continental Europe* (Boston, Little & Brown, 1843); *Commentaries on the Law of Partnership: As a Branch of Commercial and Maritime Jurisprudence, with Occasional Illustrations from the Civil and Foreign Law* (Boston, Little & Brown, 1841); *Commentaries on the Law of Promissory Notes, and Guaranties of Notes and Checks on Banks and Bankers: With Occasional Illustrations from the Commercial Law of the Nations of Continental Europe* (Boston, Little & Brown, 1845).

158. See *Little, Brown and Company, 1837-1987: One Hundred and Fifty Years of Publishing* 19 (1987).

159. See McClellan, *supra* note 10, at 274-80 (collecting narratives of lawyers); 2 Warren, *supra* note 95, at 47-69 (collecting narratives of lawyers).

160. Greenleaf hand-copied these notes from Amos's lectures. See Andrew Amos, *An Introductory Lecture upon the Study of English Law* (London, T. Davison, 1829): "Law should be studied—not as a collection of arbitrary rules & maxims & antiquated usages, retained, perhaps, long after their value has ceased—but as a liberal science—a harmonious arrangement of principles essential to the well being of society—not as an instrument of litigation—but as the great mean of preserving the peace & order & happiness of individuals & states and nations. . . . Mode of instruction—public lectures—notes taken authorities examined Public questions proposed answered in writing private motto adopted by each student answers exam. By counsell prizes and certificates awarded at close of each term. Class meets in comtt. of the whole professor with them—for purpose of free conversation on doubts & misapprehensions—Principles illustrated by recent trials—at which students may have been present."

Simon Greenleaf, "Mr. Amos's Introd. Lecture. Nov. 2, 1829" (unpublished manuscript, Harvard Law Library Special Collections, Simon Greenleaf Papers).

161. E.g., Simon Greenleaf, *A Treatise on the Law of Evidence* (Boston, C.C. Little & J. Brown, 1842).

162. At one point, the bulletin for Greenleaf's second year lectures announced: "The Exercises in the law School during the ensuing term will be as follows: —with Professor Greenleaf—On Mondays, Wednesdays & on every other Friday, commencing with Friday, Sept. 3d—At 10 A.M. in Story on Bills of Exchange, to be followed by Story on Promissory Note & the Conflict of Laws—At 11 A.M. in Story on Equity Jurisprudence vol. 1 to be followed by Story on Equity Pleading." Simon Greenleaf, "Exercises" (unpublished manuscript, Harvard Law School Special Collections, Simon Greenleaf Papers). Even so, the syllabus of Edmund Bennet frequently assigned readings from Story on commercial law, but more often assigned Kent than any other writer, followed closely by Blackstone. Edmund H. Bennet, *General Syllabus of Law Studies.*

163. 2 Warren, *supra* note 95, at 49 (quoting Rutherford B. Hayes's diary).

164. Perhaps the best contrast in styles was offered by former student Daniel Saunders, who described the professors' responses to fire alarms, a constant threat, and distraction, of the time: "It was reported to me that a fire alarm was sounded during a class examination by Professor Greenleaf; and when the class began to show more interest in the fire than in class work, the Professor quietly said, 'Young men, the fire department will attend to the fire and we will attend to the subject before

us. . . .' After a similar alarm had been sounded during a class recitation under Judge Story, at which I was present, as the engines went clanging by, we began to peer out of the windows, and our interest was so plainly shown in the matter of the fire rather than our class work the Judge took a look out of the window himself, just as a large volume of smoke burst up from a near-by building, and said, 'Run, boys, run! Inter ignes, silent leges.' We ran, and the Judge followed." 2 Warren, *supra* note 95, at 55 (quoting letter from Daniel Saunders).

165. Ashmun presented a straightforward lecture, with general principles of equity, punctuated with references to both statutes and treatises. His lectures were frequently organized into lists, illustrated with long discussions of cases, which he apparently enlarged and updated in later years. See John H. Ashmun, "Lectures in Equity and Medical Jurisprudence" (unpublished manuscript, Harvard Law Library no. MS 2008).

166. Theophilus Parsons, *The Law of Contracts* (Boston, Little, Brown & Co., 7th ed., with additions by William V. Kellen, 1883).

167. Emory Washburn, *Real Property* (Boston, Little, Brown & Co., 1860). Although he continued actively to write, no other book of his attained the same stature. For an example of Washburn's other writing, see Emory Washburn, *A Manual of Criminal Law, Including the Mode of Procedure by Which It Is Enforced: Especially Designed for the Use of Students* (Chicago, Callaghan & Co., 1878). Washburn resigned from Harvard in 1876. 2 Warren, *supra* note 95, at 401.

168. See Sutherland, *supra* note 149, at 140-61; Warren, *supra* note 95, at 302-18.

169. Joel Parker, *The Law School of Harvard College* 17-19 (New York, Hurd & Houghton, 1871).

170. *Id.* at 19-20.

171. "Professor Parker . . . made Chitty's Pleadings about as interesting as Webster's Dictionary—But then Professor Parsons made ample amends by making the Law of Contracts almost as fascinating as a dime novel." Letter from James Carmical to Charles Warren (Oct. 10, 1907), in Charles Warren Papers, Harvard Law School Special Collections.

172. LaPiana, *Logic and Experience*, *supra* note 3, at 51 (quoting Joseph Choate, Harvard Lectures, box 22, Joseph Choate papers, Manuscript Division, Library of Congress, Washington, D.C.).

173. See *id.* (citing various sources discussing their teaching methods); 2 Warren, *supra* note 95, at 317 (stating that this section of the hall became known as "Oregon," for its distance from class affairs).

174. James A. Rahl & Kurt Schwerin, *Northwestern University School of Law—A Short History to Commemorate Its Centennial, 1859-1959*, at 11 (1960), quoting "Reminiscences of Thomas M. Hoyne," 16 *The Alumni Journal* 28-31 (June 30, 1916). Student readings were based on Blackstone, Greenleaf, Parsons, Washburn, Chitty, and Stevens. See *id.*

175. See George-Auguste Matile, "A Letter Written by Him to M. Edouard LaBoulaye, Collège de France, Les Écoles de droit aux États-Unis [Law Schools in the United States]." Extrait de *La Revue historique de droit français* numéro de novembre-décembre 1863 (Paris, A. Durand, 1864). See chapter 22 of this book.

176. *Golden Age of American Law* 51-52 (C. Haan ed., 1965); Timothy Walker, *Introduction to American Law, Designed as a First Book for Students* (Derby, Bradley & Co., 2d ed. 1846).

177. William Blackstone, *Commentaries on the Laws of England* (Thomas Cooley ed., Chicago, Callaghan & Co., 2d ed. 1876-79); Joseph Story, *Commentaries on the Constitution of the United States: With a Preliminary Review of the Constitutional History of the Colonies and States Before the Adoption of the Constitution* (Thomas M. Cooley ed., Boston, Little, Brown & Co., 4th ed. 1873).

178. Thomas M. Cooley, *The Elements of Torts* (Chicago, Callaghan & Co., 1895); Thomas M. Cooley, *General Principles of the Constitutional Law of the United States* (Boston, Little, Brown & Co., 1880); Thomas M. Cooley, *A Treatise on the Constitutional Limitations Which Rest upon the Legislative Powers of the States of the American Union* (1868; Legal Classics Reprint, 1987); Thomas M. Cooley, *A Treatise on the Law of Taxation, Including Local Assessments* (Chicago, Calaghan & Co., 1876); Thomas M. Cooley, *A Treatise on the Law of Torts or the Wrongs Which Arise Independent of Contract* (Chicago, Callaghan & Co., 1879). See also chapter 27 of this book.

179. See Harrison Hume, "Law Notes, University of Michigan, Ann Arbor, 1867" (unpublished manuscript, Harvard Law Library No. 5310).

180. See chapter 27 of this book. See also Elizabeth Gaspar Brown, *Legal Education at Michigan* 183 (Ann Arbor, University of Michigan Law School, 1959), excerpting Thomas M. Cooley, *To Wit: Department of Law, University of Michigan, Class of '94.* Cooley's career and teaching are discussed in contrast to the approaches at Harvard and in the context of Cooley's intellectual climate in Paul D. Carrington, "Law as 'The Common Thoughts of Men': The Law-Teaching and Judging of Thomas MacIntyre Cooley," 49 *Stan. L. Rev.* 495 (1997).

181. M.E. Barlow, "Notes from Professor Dean's Lectures, Albany, 1862" (Harvard MS 5251, 6 vols.). Barlow's notes are of a typical dictation lecture, with various principles enumerated, and carried in this style from one lecture to the next. Case annotations were made in the margins. Class notes were clearly not to be missed, and in the week of Sept. 16, 1863, the student seems to have asked someone else to take his dictation for him. See *id.* at 30-43.

182. Henry Strong McCall et al., Albany *Law School: A Historical Sketch* 2 (reprinted from Albany Argus, Albany, May 1, 1877).

183. Judge Charles Daniels lectured the first students in Buffalo Law School, then in Niagara University in 1887. The course was a hybrid of lectures from treatises and law-office clerking. The course of lectures was said to be those of "a practical school. It does not go deeply into the history or theory of law; but it points out to its students the things they most need to know in successfully practicing their profession and making a living. It explains the practical bearing of principles that are most useful to clients in ordinary affairs, so that its students may give sound advice in common business matters. . . . In a word, it aims to inform its pupils concerning the principles and methods which every lawyer must know to be a valuable man to those who employ him, whether in consultation or in court." Gilbert J. Pedersen, *The Buffalo Law School: A History* 34 (1962), quoting *Albany Law Journal*, Jan. 7, 1899.

184. See, e.g., William G. Hammond, "American Law Schools in the Past and in the Future: An Address Delivered Before the Law Department of the State University of Iowa (June 20, 1881)" (Iowa City, 1881).

185. See Lamar C. Quintero, "The Law School of the Tulane University of Louisiana," 2 *The Green Bag* 116 (1890); John Minor Wisdom, "A Piquant History of the Tulane Law School," 1 *Tulane Lawyer* 2-10 (1979).

186. See *supra* note 159 and accompanying text; see also Paul D. Carrington, "Legal Education for the People: Populism and Civic Virtue," 43 *U. Kan. L. Rev.* 1 (1994); Michael Hoeflich, "Virtue in the Nineteenth Century Law Lecture" (forthcoming 1998).

187. See Gary B. Nash, "The Philadelphia Bench and Bar 1800-1861," 7 *Comp. Stud. in Soc'y & Hist.* 203, 208 (1965). A glimpse of Sharswood's character and time is provided in marginalia of a copy of Sharswood's *Blackstone*, owned by Williams Carter and discussed by University of Pennsylvania librarian Cynthia Arkin: "This day—May 31st 1883 I went at 10 a.m. to the funeral of Judge Sharswood. Who died at a quarter before seven o'clock on the morning of last Monday, May 28. The Judge looked better & happier in his coffin than I ever saw him look out of it.

May God rest his soul in spite of the damned officiating presbyterian Parson." Marginalia in William Blackstone, *Commentaries on the Laws of England* (George Sharswood ed., Philadelphia, J.B. Lippincott Co., 1890; copy owned by Williams Carter Sharswood, University of Pennsylvania Biddle Law Library Special Collection).

188. See *The History of the Law School/The 1916 Class Report, University of Pennsylvania Law School*, at 85-88.

189. One of Hare's students restated in his class notes: "To consider the growth of jurisprudence and law we must go back to the times when man lived in tribes. . . . It is evident that the growth of jurisprudence closely followed and was closely allied to this extension of relations between the various nations of the world. Law is also a moral science, and thus legal principles draw largely on ethics." Henry Hoyt, Jr. "John Hare's Law Lectures, University of Pennsylvania" 1 (Harvard Law School manuscript MS 2151). These notes are duplicates, probably produced by planograph, for distribution to later students by their transcriber. The bulk are in blue paste ink. The last two lectures are in black paste.

190. The same student's notes later included the following statements: "Parol contracts are now divided into two heads, viz: 1. Promises in consideration of promises.— 2. Promises in consideration of performance. It is a rule of law that the right of action must begin with the party from whom the consideration flows. In *Blymin v. Boisllte* 6th Watts 182 it was decided by Sergeant, J. 'That if one pay money to another for the use of a third person, or having money belonging to another, agree with that other to pay it to a third, action lies by the person beneficially interested.'" In *Edmunson v. Penny for Use of MaCaudless* 1st Barr 334. It is held that "a parol promise to bestow to A for B's services as preacher twenty-five dollars, and to cease at this date, will support an action in the name of B." In this case *Chief Just. Gibson* says, "Whatever may be the conflict of opinion in the earlier cases, it is now settled that a parol promise to one for the benefit of another, can support an action on it only by him from whom the consideration moved, or who was the meritorious cause of it." *Id.* at 5.

191. See George Wharton Pepper, *Lectures on Contracts by Prof, Jos. Clarke Hare, LL.D.* (Lect. 1, 10-4-87, University of Pennsylvania, Biddle Law Library, Special Collections manuscripts). These notes also appear to be planographed.

192. George Wharton Pepper, *Lectures on Evidence by Prof. Biddle* (University of Pennsylvania, Biddle Law Library, Special Collections manuscripts); George Wharton Pepper, *Lectures on Partnership by Prof. James Parsons* (University of Pennsylvania, Biddle Law Library, Special Collections manuscripts). These notes may be duplicates as well.

193. James Parsons, *"Law as a Science": The Introductory Lecture Delivered at the University of Pennsylvania at the Annual Opening of the Annual Course in the Law Dept. (Oct. 1, 1875)* (Philadelphia, King & Baird, Printers, 1875).

194. See Thomas Jefferson, "Education for a Lawyer," in *The Complete Jefferson* 1043-45 (Saul K. Padover ed., 1943); see also Letter from Thomas Jefferson to John Tyler (May 26, 1810), in 12 *Jefferson Writings, supra* note 42, at 391; Letter from Thomas Jefferson to Dabney Terrel (Feb. 16, 1821), in 15 *Jefferson Writings, supra* note 42, at 318-22. For arguments that Jefferson and other early federal humanists presaged the modern movement of law and social science, see Brainerd Currie, "The Materials of Law Study," 3 *J. Legal Educ.* 331 (1951).

195. John Ritchie, *The First Hundred Years: A Short History of the School of Law of the University of Virginia for the Period 1826-1926*, at 17-53 (1978).

196. See University of Virginia, *Law School of the University of Virginia (July 10, 1851)* (college catalog).

197. See Carl von Linné, *Philosophia Botanica: In qua explicantur fundamenta botanica cum definitionibus partium, exemplis terminorum, observationibus rariorum, etc.* (Stockholm, Apud Godfr. Kiesewetter, 1751). For a more detailed study of science as a metaphor for law in the early nineteenth century, see Berman & Reid, *supra* note 53; I. Bernard Cohen, *Science and the Founding Fathers: Science in the Political Thought of Thomas Jefferson, Benjamin Franklin, John Adams, and James Madison* (1995). See also chapters 44, 45, and 46 of this book.

198. Theodore W. Dwight, *Commentaries on the Law of Persons and Personal Property, Being an introduction to the Study of Contracts* 17 (Edward F. Dwight ed., Boston, Little, Brown & Co., 1894). True to his idiom, Dwight articulated seven rules by which to determine cases worthy of such treatment. Dwight's conception of "legal science" is particularly resonant with that earlier expressed by Silas Jones. See Silas Jones, *An Introduction to Legal Science: Being a Concise and Familiar Treatise on such Legal Topics as Are Earliest Read by the Law Student* 50-57 (New York, John S. Voorhies, 1842).

The treatise is a traditional march through personal and real property. A narrative of general principles is accompanied by references and notes to primarily American, but also significant numbers of older English, cases, treatises, and commentaries, and American and English statutes. He was prone to some discourse concerning particular cases in his text, particularly facts of cases illustrative of his principles of law, but the larger portion of the text is narration of these principles. Dwight had no reluctance to distribute his lectures for the use of his students, having earlier authorized a distribution of copies of his own notes among the students. See Theodore Dwight, *Lectures on Municipal Law* (typescript, 1881; Columbia Law School treasure room CU D961mb): "The secretary of the Law School has been authorized to issue thirty copies hereof, and for the use of Columbia Law College School only." Moreover, *The Columbia Law Times*, a monthly magazine for students in law and political science, often printed Dwight's lecture notes, beginning in 1887, with his lectures on Blackstone, "[o]fficially revised," for nine pages, and his lectures on Parsons on Contracts was printed for five more. *Columbia Law Times*, vols. 1-2, 53-57. For the place of the *Law Times* and its predecessor in the development of student-edited law reviews, see Michael I. Swygert & Jon. W. Bruce, "The Historical Origins, Founding, and Early Development of Student-Edited Law Reviews," 36 *Hastings L.J.* 739, 764-58 (1985), reprinted as chapter 73 in this book.

199. Dwight described his method as "the inculcation of the elementary rules of law applicable to its leading branches, by presenting them in the clearest form, under a carefully studied and logical arrangement, and fixing them in the mind by apt illustration and the drill of recitation and review." Theodore Dwight, "Columbia College Law School," 1 *The Green Bag* 152 (1889); see also George C. Austin, "The Dwight Method of Legal Instruction," 9 *Q. L. Rev.* (1893).

200. The notes of nineteenth-century students were meticulous. The bound copies of some are models of calligraphy, organization, and completeness. Most include tables of contents or indexes, lecture by lecture. While some of Dwight's students marked the lectures by date, all used his method of organizing the lectures by chapter headings. Dwight clearly preferred *vide* to "see." The habit not only is reflected universally in student notes but also led to some rather curious marginalia. See Henry S. Davis, *Lectures of Columbia College Law School (cont.) Junior Year, 1867* (Columbia Law School treasure room CU D96 Lda); Samuel Greenbaum, *Law Lectures by Theo. Dwight, L.L.D., Book First*, 47 (1872) (Columbia law School treasure room CU D 96 Lec). See chapters 23, 24, and 26. A study of Theodore Roosevelt's notebooks from Dwight's lectures is presented in Robert B. Charles, "Legal Education in the Late Nineteenth Century, Through the Eyes of Theodore Roosevelt," 37 *Am. J. Legal Hist.* 233 (1993), reprinted as chapter 26 of this book.

201. There are numerous student notebooks containing this lecture practically without change. The quotations above are from Theodore Dwight, *Dwight's Lectures*, 1876 (Columbia Law School treasure room CU D 961d; hereinafter *Dwight's Lectures*).

202. *Id.* at 15-16.

203. The sixteen rules: "(1) The language of the statute must be taken in its popular sense . . . [with a railroad case illustration]. (2) The court must not go beyond the statute in search of a supposed sense. (3) The whole of a statute must be taken into account. . . . (4) . . . regard must be had to the old law, the mischief, and the remedy. (5) Remedial statutes should have a large and liberal interpretation. (6) Penal statutes must have a close and strict interpretation. (7) When statutes appear to contradict each other they must be construed, if possible, so that both will stand. (8) There is a distinction between an exception and a proviso. . . . (9) The opinion of the legal profession is of great importance in interpreting a statute. There is a maxim that contemporaneous exposition is very strong influence. (10) A statute must in general be assumed to act prospectively, the court does not give it a retrospective effect unless the language imperatively requires it. (11) When the meaning of a statute is doubtful, the preamble may be resorted to and even the petition which led to its enactment. (12) There is a difference in regard to a statute between words that are mandatory and those that are directory. (13) Any authority which is given in derogation of a private right, must be strictly followed, and closely construed . . . [case cite]. (14) When an act is prohibited by a statute it is a misdemeanor or a crime of an inferior grade, unless some penalty is affixed. (15) A person may waive a statutory provision intended for his benefit unless it be a provision conferring jurisdiction on a court [case cite]. (16) When a statute gives a new remedy for a right already existing at common law, resort may be had either to the common law or the statutory remedy, unless the common law be repealed expressly or by implication. . . ." *Ibid.* 16-20.

The ten subsequent rules: "(1) A statute becomes a rule of law for the future. (2) Where words in the same statute contradict each other, the last are to be preferred. (3) Legislation cannot be rendered irrepealable. . . . (4) When a statute is repealed all proceedings under it must cease. . . . (5) When a repealing statute is itself repealed the former law revives by implication. . . . (6) As a general thing, the statute is confined to the territory of the state or county which enacts it. . . . (7) When a statute requires an act to be done within a given time the first day is excluded from the count. . . . (8) Any statute which is contrary to the constitution, binding the legislative power is void at least when declared so by the courts. (9) There is a class of cases where the act is not opposed to any particular clause of the constitution, but is contrary to the general theory of republican government and institutions. In this class of cases a proper court has power to declare an act void [NY case cite]. (10) Any statute contrary to reason or absurd in principle is of course *inoperative*." *Ibid.* 20-26.

Dwight's Lectures, *supra* note 201, at 20-26.

204. One of his favorites, the rejection of *mitior sensus*, was invariably rolled out in each year's torts class in municipal law: "In interpreting the alleged slanderous words, the practice formerly was to give them the meaning most favorable to the slanderer. This was the so-called *mitior sensus* and an instance or two will suffice. In one case, the words were, 'Thou art a thievish rogue, and hast stolen bars of iron out of other men's windows.' It was held that the words must be taken to mean bars of iron fastened in the windows and not loose. In this view, there was no slander, for the bars were then real estate, and one cannot steal real estate. So where a person said that 'Sir Thomas Holt struck his cook on the head with a cleaver and cleaved his head, so that the one part lay on one shoulder and the other on the other,' it was held that there was no cause of action, since though Sir Thomas might have cleaved the head into parts, the wound might not have been mortal. This absurd doctrine has long since been exploded. The correct rule is to take that meaning which the supposed utterer to convey." Dwight's Lectures, *supra* note 201, at 41-42 (citations omitted).

205. Indeed, the "thievish rogue" story is repeated with no variation year after year. See, e.g., 1 George Baker, *Law Lectures Delivered to the Junior Class of Columbia College Law School by Prof. Theo. W. Dwight, LL.D. During the Junior Term of 1869-70*, at 42-43 (Columbia Law School treasure room CU D961); 1 Towson Caldwell, "Dwight's Lectures," *Municipal Law* 64-63 (1877; Columbia Law School treasure room CU D961a); John B. Fine, *Lectures on Municipal Law by Theodore Dwight, L.L.D., Columbia Law School,*

83-87 (1878-79; Columbia Law School treasure room CU D 96 Lma); 1 Herbert L. Satterlee, *Municipal Law* 29-30 (1884; Columbia Law School treasure room D96 L); Alfred P. Thorndike, *Municipal Law* 29 (no date; Columbia Law School treasure room D96 Lb); 1 T.H. Walser, *Lectures of Municipal Law by Theodore Dwight, '76 "Love's Labor Lost"* 113-15 (1876; Columbia Law School treasure room D 961e).

206. Goebel & Howard, *supra* note 103, at 37, quoting Richards, in *Swift's Tribute* 18 (1891).

207. *Id.*, quoting Beekman, in *Swift's Tribute* 25 (1891). For a sketch of the reverence and popularity in which Dwight was held, see Whitney S. Bagnall, "The Poet and the Professor: Scenes from the Early Law School," 44 *Colum. Libr. Columns* 26 (1995).

208. See Goebel & Howard, *supra* note 103, at 46-48.

209. See *id.*

210. *Id.* at 64, quoting George Templeton Strong Diary, May 13, 1868 (housed in Columbiana Library, Columbia University).

211. See *id.* at 124-26.

212. Letter from Theodore Dwight to Seth Low (Jan. 28, 1891), in Goebel & Howard, *supra* note 103, at 127.

213. For an example of the theoretical readings used by Keener, see William A. Keener, *Selections on the Elements of Jurisprudence* (St. Paul., West Publishing Co., 1896).

214. For an example of a treatise Keener assigned, see William A. Keener, *Selections from Leake's Elements of the Law of Contracts and Finch's Cases on Contracts: Arranged as a Text-book for Law Students* (New York, Baker, Voorhis & Co., 1895). His "purer" casebook was published three years later. William A. Keener, *A Selection of Cases on the Law of Contracts* (New York, Baker, Voorhis & Co. 1898).

215. See George Chase, The Dwight Method of Legal Instruction as Compared with Other Methods (1894; Harvard pamphlet S US 907 CHA). See also chapter 43 of this book.

216. See George Chase, *Preface to Leading Cases on the Law of Torts* (St. Paul, West Publishing Co., 1891). In his preface, Chase noted that the book was "intended to supplement and illustrate the statements of legal principles which are set forth in the various treatises upon this subject. Object lessons, showing the application of principles, are as efficacious in the study of law as in the study of other branches of learning." *Id.*

217. See New York Law School, Law Syllabus, New York, 1904.

218. See Law Syllabus of William van Wyck (Columbia Law School treasure T 16167).

219. Telephone interview with Professor William LaPiana, New York Law School (July 15, 1995).

220. John Norton Pomeroy, *The Hastings Law Department of the University of California: Inaugural Address by John Norton Pomeroy, Aug. 8, 1878*, at 1 (San Francisco, A.L. Bancroft & Co. 1878), reprinted here as chapter 28. Pomeroy's standard biography, is John N. Pomeroy, Jr., *John Norton Pomeroy*, in William D. Lewis, 8 *Great American Lawyers* 91 (1909; hereinafter *Pomeroy Biography*); see also C.W. Slack, "Hastings College of the Law," 1 *The Green Bag* 522 (1889).

221. See, e.g., John Norton Pomeroy, *Syllabus of Lectures on Remainders and Executory Interests* (Hastings College of the Law, University of California; Yale Law School Library pamphlet); John Norton Pomeroy, *Syllabus of Lectures on Remedies* (Hastings College of the Law, University of California; Yale Law School Library pamphlet); John Norton Pomeroy, *Syllabus of Lectures on Uses and Trusts* (Hastings College of the Law, University of California; Yale Law School Library pamphlet).

222. See, e.g., J.F. Archbold, *A Complete Practical Treatise on Criminal Procedure, Pleading, and Evidence, in Indictable Cases* (John Norton Pomeroy ed., New York, Banks & Bros., 8th ed. 1880); John Norton Pomeroy, *Code Remedies* (Thomas A. Bogle ed., Boston, Little, Brown, & Co., 4th ed. 1904); John Norton Pomeroy, *An Introduction to the Constitutional Law of the United States* (New York, Hurd and Houghton, 8th ed. 1885); John Norton Pomeroy, *An Introduction to Municipal Law* (San Francisco, Bancroft-Whitney Co., 2d ed. 1886); John Norton Pomeroy, *An Introduction to Municipal Law, Designed for General Readers, and for Students in Colleges and Higher Schools* (New York, D. Appleton & Co., 1864); John Norton Pomeroy, *Lectures on International Law in Time of Peace* (New York, Houghton, Mifflin & Co., 1886); John Norton Pomeroy, *Remedies and Remedial Rights by the Civil Action According to the Reformed American Procedure: A Treatise Adapted to Use in All the States and Territories Where That System Prevails* (Boston, Little, Brown, & Co., 3d ed. 1894); John Norton Pomeroy, *A Treatise on Equitable Remedies; Supplementary to Pomeroy's Equity Jurisprudence* (San Francisco, Bancroft-Whitney, 1905); John Norton Pomeroy & Carter Pitkin Pomeroy, *A Treatise on Equity Jurisprudence, as Administered in the United States of America Adapted for All the States, and to the Union of Legal and Equitable Remedies Under the Reformed Procedure* (San Francisco, Bancroft-Whitney, 1892); John Norton Pomeroy, *A Treatise on the Law of Water Rights: Being a Rev. and Enl. Ed. Of "Pomeroy on Riparian Rights," with Several Additional Chapters by Henry Campbell Black* (St. Paul, Minnesota, West Publishing Co., 1893); John Norton Pomeroy, *A Treatise on the Specific Performance of Contracts as It Is Enforced by Courts of Equitable Jurisdiction in the United States of America* (New York, Banks & Brothers, 2d ed. 1897); see also Theodore Sedgwick, *A Treatise on the Rules Which Govern the Interpretation and Construction of Statutory and Constitutional Law* (John N. Pomeroy ed., New York, Baker, Voorhis & Co., 2d ed. 1874).

223. It is unclear now exactly how much of Pomeroy's discussion was designed to elicit a predeterminable, "correct" answer, and how much was designed to spark original thought. Thomas Barnes was convinced that the discussions were toward the latter end, but this conclusion seems drawn from a rather ambiguous description. Henry McPike recalled that, during his class under Pomeroy, Pomeroy would "pause and quiz the class, passing questions around indiscriminately, and treating all answers with gravity, no matter how far off any of them might be. He corrected errors in the most kindly spirit. . . ." Thomas Garden Barnes, *Hastings College of the Law, The First Century* 113 (Hastings College of the Law Press, 1978), quoting *The Golden Jubilee Book, 1878-1928*, at 41. Anthony Chase asserts that Pomeroy's classes at the Law School of the University of the City of New York may have been the first case method classes. See Anthony Chase, "The Birth of the Modern Law School," 23 *Am. J. Legal Hist.* 329, 333 n.18 (1979).

224. Serjeant Henry Finch, *Law, or a Discourse Thereof* (1759; W.S. Hein, 1992). Barnes states that Pomeroy "had read" the book, although no attribution for this knowledge is provided. See Barnes, *supra* note 223, at 102.

225. Pomeroy's chart from which this is drawn is reproduced in part in Barnes, *supra* note 223, at 103.

226. See generally John Norton Pomeroy, *An Introduction to the Constitutional Law of the United States, Especially Designed for Students, General and Professional* 269 (Boston, Houghton Mifflin, 1886). Pomeroy's constitutional thought is explored in Stephen A. Siegal, "Historicism in Late Nineteenth-Century Constitutional Thought," 1990 *Wis. L. Rev.* 1431 (comparing and contrasting Cooley and Tiedeman).

227. See *Catalog of the Corporation, Officers & Students of Hamilton College, 1846-47* (Utica, R.W. Roberts, 1846). Pomeroy studied at Hamilton from 1843 until "a short time before the graduation of his class." *Pomeroy Biography, supra* note 220, at 92. Hamilton College records confirm that he graduated in 1847, being conferred a degree with his class. Telephone conversation with Frank Lorenz, Archivist of Hamilton College (July 28, 1995).

228. See Barnes, *supra* note 223, at 128.

229. John Ritchie, *The First Hundred Years: A Short History of the School of Law of the University of Virginia for the Period 1826-1926*, at 57 (1978), quoting Centennial of the University of Virginia 1922; Thomas J. Michie, "John Barbee Minor," 7 *The Green Bag* 401 (1895), admiring portrait of Minor by a former student on the occasion of his death.

230. See Ritchie, *supra* note 229, at 58-59.

231. A depiction of the early use of lectures at Yale can be found in Frederick C. Hicks, *Yale Law School: From the Founders to Dotton* 49-55 (Yale Library Publication No. 3, June 1936).

232. Frederick C. Hicks, *Yale Law School: 1869-1894, Including the County Court House Period* 32 (Yale Library Publication No. 4, 1937).

233. A Yale Law School Announcement stated: "The method of instruction, especially in the undergraduate course, is mainly that of recitations. It is the conviction of the Faculty of this Department, as well as the tradition of the University, that definite and permanent impressions concerning the principles and rules of any abstract science are best acquired by the study of standard textbooks in private, followed by the examinations and explanations of the recitation room. Hence, although certain subjects are separately taught by lectures, . . . care is taken that the same topics shall be covered by recitation work. . . . The recitation hours, however, are not devoted entirely to the questioning of the student. While this is done with sufficient thoroughness to hold him up to his work of preparation, ample opportunity is afforded for a free colloquial discussion of the subject of the less and for the presentation and solution of the difficulties which he may have encountered in his private study." Hicks, *supra* note 232, at 33 (quoting Yale Law School's Announcement 1887-1888); see also Leonard M. Dagget, "The Yale Law School," 1 *The Green Bag* 239, 249-50 (1889).

234. See *id.* at 34.

235. See Frederick C. Hicks, *Yale Law School: 1895-1915, Twenty Years of Hendry Hall* 43-44 (Yale Law Library Publication No. 7, Sept. 1938).

236. See William B. Carswell, *Outline of Orientation Lectures* (Brooklyn 1952; Harvard Pamphlet US 907 CAR).

237. See Albert Coates, *A Task of Legal Education in North Carolina* 11 (1938; Harvard Pamphlet US 907/mc COA); see also Albert Coates, "The Story of the Law School at the University of North Carolina," 47 *N.C. L. Rev.* 1 (1968). See also chapter 29.

238. See *id.*

239. See, e.g., *McCormick on Evidence* (Edward W. Cleary ed., 3d ed. 1984), a student hornbook; *McCormick on Evidence* (Edward W. Cleary ed., 2d ed. 1972), a multivolume reference.

240. See *infra* notes 348-369 and accompanying text.

241. The effect of the treatise's decline on scholarship is significant, particularly in areas of law in which "learned treatises" are recognized sources of positive law. See A.W.B. Simpson, "The Rise and Fall of the Legal Treatise: Legal Principles and the Forms of Legal Literature," 48 *U. Chi. L. Rev.* 632 (1981); Thomas M. Franck, "Review Essay: The Case of the Vanishing Treatises," 81 *Am. J. Int'l L.* 763 (1987), a book review.

242. See Philip C. Kissam, "Teaching Constitutional Law Differently," 9 *Const. Commentary* 237 (1992). Professor Kissam's students study primarily from Laurence H. Tribe's treatise, *American Constitutional Law* (2d ed. 1988).

243. The results of the study are on file with the author.

244. The inferential utility of the survey is limited by imprecision in distribution through third parties and the allowance of professors to submit multiple responses when one professor teaches different courses. As a practical matter, few professors did submit two forms and fewer still submitted more than two. Even so, the responses are considered by the author to be suggestive.

245. Question 43: "Is your primary assigned text best described as a—(1) Casebook (2) Treatise (3) Problem book."

246. Question 87: "Is your average class primarily monologue lecture or dialogue with students? (1) all monologue (2) mainly monologue (3) roughly equal (4) mainly dialogue (5) all dialogue."

247. See, e.g., Steve Sheppard, "The Case for Expanding the Jurisprudential Tent," *The Law Teacher* 5 (October 1996).

248. See Simpson, *supra* note 241, at 677. For a view that the pursuit of such an understanding by the core method is inherently modern, see Thomas L. Grey, "Langdell's Orthodoxy," 45 *U. Pitt. L. Rev.* 1 (1983).

249. See, e.g., *Les Reports des Cases Argue & Adjudge in le temps del' Roy Edward le Second, et auxy Memoranda del' Exchequer en Temps le Roy Edward le Primer* (Richard de Winchedon ed., London, George Sawbridge, William Rawlins & Samuel Roycroft, 1678). English translations are in the Selden Society series. See, e.g., *Year Books of Edward II*, Vol. XXVI (Part I), *The Eyre of London, 14 Edward II, a.d. 1321*, Vol. I (Helen M. Cam ed., Selden Society, 1968).

250. See William C. Bolland, *The Year Books: Lectures Delivered in the University of London at the Request of the Faculty of Laws* (1921); Charles C. Soule, "Year-Book Bibliography," 14 *Harv. L. Rev.* 557 (1901).

251. See Lemmings, *supra* note 7, at 102.

252. Bacon was so accustomed to the year books, and so unlikely to commend the work of his rival, Coke, that he declared, "[T]he Common Law of England, it appeareth, is no text law, but the substance of it consisteth in the series and succession of Judicial Acts from time to time which have been set out in the books which we term Year Books." Bolland, *supra* note 250, at 22.

253. See Thomas Ireland, *An Exact Abridgment in English of All the Reports of That Learned and Reverend Judge Sir James Dyer, Knight* (London, Matthew Walbancke and John Place, 1651).

254. Edward Coke, *Les Reports de Edward Coke . . . de dieurs resolutions & iudgements* (London, The Company of Stationers, 1619); Thomas Ireland, *An Exact Abridgment in English, of the Eleven Books of Reports of the Learned Sir Edward Cook Knight &tc., Wherein Is Briefly Contained the Very Substance and Marrow of All These Reports, Together with the Resolutions on Every Case Also a Perfect Table for the Findings of the Names of All Those Cases, and the Principal Matters Therein Contained* (London, G. Dawes, 1666).

255. Edmund Plowden's *Commentaries* were published in 1571 and 1579.

256. See Holdsworth, *supra* note 6, at 364. This tradition would appear to have been copied in America. Thomas Jefferson seems to have begun collecting case reports for his own use, these being bound posthumously into a volume of reports. Thomas Jefferson, *Reports of Cases Determined in the General Court of Virginia; From 1730 to 1740; and from 1768 to 1772* (Charlottesville, F. Carr & Co., 1829).

257. See Holdsworth, *supra* note 6, at 355-79.

258. See William Wright (attrib.), *Advice on the Study of Law, with Directions for the Choice of Books, Addressed to Attorneys' Clerks with Additional Notes for the American Student* 65 (1811; Fred Rothman, 1994).

259. This point is the opening salvo of Simeon Baldwin's consideration of the casebook in 1900. See Simeon E. Baldwin, "Teaching Law by Cases," 14 *Harv. L. Rev.* 258, 258 (1900). For Baldwin's exposition on the need of principles prior to cases, see Simeon E. Baldwin, "The Study of Elementary Law: The Proper Beginning of a Legal Education," 13 *Yale L.J.* 1 (1903).

260. See John Adams, *Autobiography of John Adams*, in 3 *The Adams Papers: Diary and Autobiography of John Adams* 253, 271 (L.H. Butterfield ed., 1962).

261. See McKenna, *supra* note 68, at 111.

262. Madison's reporting of *Paxton's Case* on the Writs of Assistance became the basis for the Fourth Amendment warrant requirement. See, e.g., the opinion of Judge William Barbour in *American Civil Liberties Union v. Mabus*, 719 F. Supp. 1345, 1353 (S.D. Miss. 1989).

263. See, e.g., John W. Willis Bund, *A Selection of Cases from the State Trials: Trials for Treason (1327-1681)* (Cambridge, Cambridge University Press Warehouse, 1879); W. Hunt, *Cases on the Annuity Act (London 1794)* (Harvard Law School unclassified); Henry Nicholl, *Cases Relating to Railways and Canals, Argued and Adjudged in the Courts of Law and Equity: 1835 to 1854* (7 vols.; London, A. Maxwell, 1840-55); Anson V. Parsons, *Select Cases in Equity Argued and Determined in the Court of Common Pleas of the First Judicial District of Pennsylvania* (Philadelphia, T. & J.W. Johnson, 1859-88).

264. For an example of such a casebook, see John I.C. Hare, *American Leading Cases: Being Select Decisions of American Courts in Several Departments of Law; with Especial Reference to Mercantile Law, with Notes* (Philadelphia, T. & J.W. Johnson, 2d ed. 1851).

265. See, e.g., *Cases of Appellants Relating to the Duties on Houses, Windows, or Lights, with the Opinion of the Judges Thereon* (London, Office for Taxes, 1786); *Cases of Appellants Relating to the Duties on Male and Female Servants, on Horses and Carriages and on Shops; with the Opinions of the Judges Thereon* (London, Office for Taxes, 1787); *Cases of Appellants Relating to the Tax on Servants, with the Opinion of the Judges Thereon* (London, Office for Taxes, 1781); Edward Griffith, *Cases of Supposed Exemption from Poor Rates, Claimed [by the Inns of Court] on the Ground of Extra-Parochiality, with a Preliminary Sketch of the Ancient History of the Parish of St. Andrew, Holborn* (London, H. Butterworth, 1831); George Sweet, *Cases on a Wife's Separate Estate and Equity to a Settlement out of Her Equitable Property, viz. Scarborough v. Borman, Tullett v. Armstrong, Dixon v. Dixon, Nedby v. Nedby, Stead v. Nelson, Newlands v. Holmes, and Sturges v. Champneys: With Notices of the Earlier Decisions* (London, S. Sweet, 1840); Thomas George Western, *Cases Relating to the Tithes of the City of London* (London, H. Butterworth, 1823). For an Irish example, see *Cases with Opinions of Eminent Counsel, in Matters of Law, Equity, and Conveyancing* (Philip John Kennedy Burton ed., Dublin, H. Watts, 1791-93).

266. See, e.g., *Cases of Appellants Relating to the Duties on Houses, Windows, or Lights, with the Opinion of the Judges Thereon* (London, Office for Taxes, 1786); *Cases of Appellants Relating to the Tax on Servants, with the Opinion of the Judges Thereon, [1778-81]* (London, Office for Taxes, 1781); *Cases of Appellants Relating to the Duties on Male and Female Servants, on Horses and Carriages and on Shops; with the Opinions of the Judges Thereon* (London, Office for Taxes, 1787); Thomas George Western, *Cases Relating to the Tithes of the City of London* (London, H. Butterworth, 1823); Edward Griffith, *Cases of Supposed Exemption from Poor Rates, Claimed [by the Inns of Court] on the Ground of Extra-parochiality, with a Preliminary Sketch of the . . . History of the Parish of St. Andrew, Holborn* (London, Butterworth, 1831); George Sweet, *Cases on a Wife's Separate Estate and Equity to a Settlement out of Her Equitable Property, viz. Scarborough v. Borman, Tullett v. Armstrong, Dixon v. Dixon, Nedby v. Nedby, Stead v. Nelson, Newlands v. Holmes, and Sturges v. Champneys: With Notices of the Earlier Decisions* (London, S. Sweet, 1840). For an Irish example, see Philip John Kennedy Burton, ed., *Cases with Opinions of Eminent Counsel, in Matters of Law, Equity, and Conveyancing* . . . (Dublin: H. Watts, 1791-93). Areas of administrative regulation garnered the greatest case book and specialized reporter publication, particularly railroads. See, e.g., *Cases Relating to Railways and Canals, Argued and Adjudged in the Courts of Law and Equity: 1835 to 1852* (Boston, Little, Brown & Co., 1854); *Cases Relating to the Law of Railways Decided in the Supreme Court of the United States & in the Courts of the Several States* (Boston, Little, Brown & Co., 1854-56).

267. Rufus Choate, Langdell's contemporary, remembered him as a student: "Professor Langdell was at that time the

Librarian and was assisting Mr. Parsons in getting out the notes of his work upon contracts, of which I have often thought the notes were the most valuable part. He was a tremendous student, following the system of studying the cases and not caring much about text books, which are generally of a very evanescent character. Many years afterwards he established this system at the law school as the standard one. . . ." Letter from Rufus Choate to Charles Warren, Oct. 18, 1907 (Harvard Law School, Charles Warren Papers).

268. See James Barr Ames, *Christopher Columbus Langdell*, in William D. Lewis, 8 *Great American Lawyers* 465, 472-75 (1909).

269. 2 Warren, *supra* note 95, at 360-61 (quoting Charles W. Eliot, Speech at the Dinner of the Harvard Law School Association, Nov. 5, 1886). See also a later version of this speech reprinted as chapter 33.

270. See Letter from James B. Thayer to Charles Eliot (Nov. 13, 1869), in LaPiana, dissertation, *supra* note 3, at 211.

271. Letter from G.O. Shattuck to Charles Eliot (Dec. 17, 1869), in LaPiana, dissertation, *supra* note 3, at 211.

272. See Charles W. Eliot, "Langdell and the Law School," 33 *Harv. L. Rev.* 518, 518 (1922).

273. Warren, *supra* note 95, at 360-61 (quoting Charles W. Eliot, Speech at the Dinner of the Harvard Law School Association, Nov. 5, 1886).

274. The idea of law as a science was by then already centuries old, but it had taken yet another turn in keeping with contemporary conceptions of the meaning of "scientific." Lon Fuller noted that Professor, later Justice, Oliver Wendell Holmes, Jr., used the term "legal science" in a manner derived from Karl Pearson's, *The Grammar of Science*, more closely than any other work. Pearson's description of the scientific method is "to marshal facts, to examine their complex mutual relationships, and predict upon the result of this examination their inevitable sequences—sequences which we term natural laws and which are as valid for every normal mind as for that of the individual investigator." Lon L. Fuller, "Notes on Oliver Holmes" (Harvard Law School, Lon L. Fuller Papers), quoting Karl Pearson, *The Grammar of Science* 9 (2d ed. 1900).

275. Langdell's most specific recorded consideration of law as science are brief remarks delivered in an after-dinner speech. See Christopher C. Langdell, "Teaching Law as a Science," 21 *Am. L. Rev.* 123 (1887), reprinted as chapter 34. Michael Hoeflich has considered the roots of Langdell's conception of science as empirical in M.H. Hoeflich, "Law & Geometry: Legal Science from Leibniz to Langdell," 30 *Am. J. Legal Hist.* 95 (1986). The similarity and contemporaneousness between this view and Holmes's view are seen in Grey, *supra* note 248 and in William P. LaPiana, "Victorian from Beacon Hill: Oliver Wendell Holmes's Early Legal Scholarhip," 90 *Colum. L. Rev.* 809 (1990), reprinted as Chapter 76 of the present volume. Its antecedents are depicted in chapters 32 and 46 and its significance discussed in chapters 44 and 45.

276. See Franklin G. Fessenden, "The Rebirth of the Harvard Law School," 33 *Harv. L. Rev.* 493, 498 (1920).

277. See *id.*

278. Samuel F. Batchelder, "Christopher C. Langdell," 18 *The Green Bag* 437 (1906).

279. *Id.* at 440.

280. *Id.* at 441.

281. *Id.* at 440.

282. For a discussion of these exams, see Sheppard, "Informal History," in chapter 62.

283. See 2 Warren, *supra* note 95, at 382. The number of students enrolled for the year's course fell from 138 in 1868-1869 to 117 in 1871-1872, which was the lowest enrollment since the mobilization for the Civil War. See *id.* at 348, 520.

284. By 1884-1885, enrollment had reached 156, helping to bring the law school back into a fiscal surplus. See *id.* at 438.

285. Christopher C. Langdell, *Selection of Cases on the Law of Contracts. With References and Citations* (Boston, Little Brown & Co., 1871; hereinafter Langdell, *Contracts* 1st ed.).

286. *Id.* at vi.

287. For continental antecedents, see chapters 32, 44, 45, and 46. See also Mathias Reimann, "Nineteenth Century German Legal Science," 31 *B.C. L. Rev.* 837 (1990). The idea of the "science of law" was taken to lengths far removed from the structure of education, befitting its long-standing role as a metaphor for jurisprudence. A series of expositions in this vein can be found in Sheldon Amos, *The Science of Law* (New York, D. Appleton, 1874); Karl Gareis, *The Science of Law* (Boston, Boston Book Co., 1911; AALS Modern Legal Philosophy Series, Vol. 1); Benjamin N. Cardozo, *The Paradoxes of Legal Science* (1928); Huntington Cairns, *The Theory of Legal Science* (1941); J.W. Harris, *Law and Legal Science: An Inquiry into the Concepts of Legal Rule and Legal System* (1979).

288. Langdell, *Contracts* 1st ed., *supra* note 286, at vi.

289. *Id.* at vi-vii.

290. Langdell stated: "It seemed to me, therefore, to be possible to take such a branch of the law as Contracts, for example, and arrange all the cases which had contributed in any important degree to the growth, development, or establishment of any of its essential doctrines; and that such a work could not fail to be of material service to all who desire to study that branch of law systematically and in its original sources." *Id.* at vii.

291. See *id.* at 1009-22. Of course, if the future hints of the prologue, many of Langdell's students might have remained somewhat clueless to the value of the indexes as a tool. There seem to be remarkably few references to it in his student's notes and reminiscences.

292. Christopher Columbus Langdell, *Select Cases on Sales of Personal Property: With References and Citations* (Boston, Little, Brown, 1872).

293. Christopher Columbus Langdell, *Cases in Equity Pleading Selected with Special Reference to the Subject of Discovery* (Cambridge, Printed for the Author, 1878).

294. Christopher Columbus Langdell, *A Brief Survey of Equity Jurisdiction: Being a Series of Articles Reprinted from the Harvard Law Review* (1905).

295. Christopher C. Langdell, *Select Cases on Contracts with a Summary of the Topics Covered by the Cases* (Boston, Little, Brown, 2d. ed. 1879; hereinafter Langdell, *Contracts* 2d ed.).

296. Compare Langdell, *Contracts* 2d ed., *supra* note 295, at xii-xvi, with 1 Langdell, *Contracts* 1st ed., *supra* note 285, at xv-xvii.

297. See *id.*

298. See Oliver Wendell Holmes, "Book Notices: A Selection of Cases on the Law of Contracts," 5 *Am. L. Rev.* 340, 353 (1871), in 1 *The Collected Works of Oliver Wendell Holmes* 243 (Sheldon M. Novick ed., 1995; hereinafter Holmes, *Collected Works*). The second edition prompted a sharper response, however: "We do not agree with [Langdell), however, in his seemingly exclusive belief in the study of cases. We should not shut our eyes to a rapid and continuous view of the principles deduced from them. And this can only be got in the text-books." Oliver Wendell Holmes, "Book Notices: A Selection of Cases on the Law of Contracts," 6 *Am. L. Rev.* 353 (1871), in 1 Holmes, *Collected Works*, *supra*, at 273. The review of Langdell's book on sales, unsigned but perhaps by Gray, was much more charitable: "We have dealt on this second book of Professor Langdell's more than we intended, because we have observed in some quarters a disposition to depreciate his former book. . . . To understand fully how good these books are, the reader must be a pretty good lawyer himself." "Book Notices: A Selection of Cases on the Sales of Personal Property," 6 *Am. L. Rev.* 145, 146 (1872).

299. A detailed discussion of the particular cases added or redacted is too complicated for this article, although work along these lines may be found in LaPiana, dissertation, *supra* note 3; Oliver Wendell Holmes, "Book Notices: A Selection of Cases on the Law of Contracts," 6 *Am. L. Rev.* 353, 353-54 (1871); see also LaPiana, *Logic and Experience*, *supra* note 3, at 58-78.

300. Langdell, *Contracts* 2d ed., *supra* note 289, at 985.

301. See Christopher C. Langdell, *A Summary of the Law of Contracts* iii (Boston, Little, Brown & Co., 2d ed. 1880).

302. William Schofield, "Christopher Columbus Langdell," 55 *Am. L. Rev.* 273, 274-77 (1907).

303. Bill LaPiana points out that one of Langdell's greater achievements was to lead a transition from the essentially sacral view of the law as received to the secular view of law as produced. See William LaPiana, "Honor Langdell," 20 *L. & Soc. Inquiry* 761, 762 (1995).

304. Langdell once stated: "What qualifies a person . . . to teach law is not experience in the work of a lawyer's office, not experience in dealing with men, not experience in the trial or argument of causes—not experience, in short, in using law, but experience in learning law; not the experience of the Roman advocate or of the Roman praetor, still less of the Roman procurator, but the experience of the jurisconsult." 2 Warren, *supra* note 95, at 361, quoting Christopher C. Langdell, Speech at the Dinner of the Harvard Law School Association (Nov. 5, 1886).

305. See 2 Warren, *supra* note 95, at 375, 383-84, quoting Christopher C. Langdell's report as dean.

306. See *id.* at 375-76.

307. See *id.* at 388; Sutherland, *supra* note 149, at 183-84.

308. See 2 Warren, *supra* note 95, at 386-90; Sutherland, *supra* note 149, at 183-84.

309. See, e.g., James Barr Ames, *Cases on Bills & Notes & Other Negotiable Paper* (Boston, Soule & Bugbee, 2d ed. 1894), with a summary of the law appended; James Barr Ames, *Cases on Suretyship* (Cambridge, Harvard Law Review Publishing Association, 1896); James Barr Ames, *A Selection of Cases on the Law of Partnership* (Cambridge, John Wilson & Sons, 1881-87); James Barr Ames, *A Selection of Cases on the Law of Trusts* (Cambridge, Harvard Law Review Publishing Association, 1893); James Barr Ames, *A Selection of Cases on Pleading at Common Law* (Cambridge, John Wilson & Sons, 1875). His first book was on torts, which he had initially published privately. See James Barr Ames, *A Selection of Cases on the Law of Torts* (Cambridge, 1875). Several later editions of that book were also published. See James Barr Ames & Jeremiah Smith, *A Selection of Cases on the Law of Torts* (Cambridge, Harvard Law Review Publishing Association, 2d ed. 1893); James Barr Ames & Jeremiah Smith, *A Selection of Cases on the Law of Tort* (Roscoe Pound ed., 1917).

310. A brief survey of the books themselves will prove this point, but it is made by others. See, e.g., Edmund M. Morgan, "The Case Method," 4 *J. Legal Educ.* 379, 381 (1952), quoting James Barr Ames, 31 A.B.A. Rep. 1025 (1907); Rosamond Parma, "The Origin, History and Compilation of the Casebook," 4 *Am. Law S. Rev.* 741, 742-43 (1922). See also chapters 38 and 39.

311. See 2 Warren, *supra* note 95, at 456-57.

312. Louis Brandeis, a student of Ames, was displeased by this habit. Sutherland, *supra* note 149, at 186. Ames's lectures began with brief introductory comments and moved quickly to case discussions of various lengths. One student frequently noted Ames's remarks in the third person, such as "Ames thinks," "Ames says," or even "Ames does not think that" in describing Ames's analysis of the rules of law in the cases. R.W. Gifford, "Notes on Contracts 1898-99 Professor Ames" (Columbia Law School treasure CU G36 noc).

313. W.H. Wade, "Notes from Brandies's Lectures on Evidence (1882-1883)" (unpublished manuscript, Harvard Law Library no. 5008). Wade was an industrious note taker. In preparing for class, he tabulated not only the cases cited but also all of the references made to treatises in the lectures, including Best, Greenleaf, Stephen, Taylor, and Wharton, at length, on evidence, as well as Dana on international law, Halleck's international law, Cooley's constitutional limitations, Benjamin on sales, Proffat on jury trials, Broom's legal maxims, Holmes's common law, Blackstone (but only for modes of trial), and eight law review articles. The 275 pages of class notes are followed by another 250 of annotations to these references.

314. Oliver Wendell Holmes, Jr., "The Use of Law Schools," reprinted in this book as chapter 41. 2 Warren, *supra* note 95, at 431 (quoting Oliver Wendell Holmes, "Oration at the Law School Day, Nov. 5, 1886, at the Commemoration of the 250th Anniversary of the Founding of Harvard College"). Notes from a student in Holmes's suretyship lectures suggest a similar story. Holmes drew his lectures directly from the cases. Many of the cases are introduced by comments and questions, as well as treatise references. See Alfred Mack (1882-83) "Suretyship, Prof. O.W. Holmes Monday 3 to 4 p.m." (unpublished

manuscript, Harvard Law Library no. 4090, vol. 4). Holmes was more accepting then of the casebook than during his first encounter with it in 1872. See Carrington, *Hail! Langdell!*, *supra* note 1, at 731.

315. See, e.g., John Chipman Gray, *Restraints on the Alienation of Property* (Boston, Boston Book Co., 2d ed. 1895). Numerous editions were produced of Gray's famous treatise. John Chipman Gray, *The Rule Against Perpetuities* (Boston, Little, Brown & Co., 1886). See also chapter 38 of this book.

316. Gray continued both to produce treatises and to defend the case method in his property case book through a simple criticism of the sole study of treatises: "To thrust before the eyes of a student of law the answer to the problem contained in a case is like telling a student in arithmetic the answer to his sum before he does it. . . ." John Chipman Gray, *Select Cases and Other Authorities on the Law of Property* v (Cambridge, Charles W. Sever 1888).

317. See James Bradley Thayer, *Cases on Constitutional Law for the Use of the Class in Constitutional Law at the Harvard Law School, 1892-3* (Cambridge, Massachusetts, n.d.); James Bradley Thayer, *Cases on Constitutional Law: With Notes* (Cambridge, Charles W. Sever, 1895; hereinafter Thayer, *Constitutional Law*); James Bradley Thayer, *Cases on Evidence* (Cambridge, 1890, for the use of the class in evidence at the Harvard Law School); James Bradley Thayer, *Select Cases on Evidence at the Common Law with Notes* (Cambridge, C.W. Sever, 1892). Thayer's work is generally considered in Jay Hook, "A Brief Life of James Bradley Thayer," 88 *Nw. U. L. Rev.* 1 (1993). See also chapter 38 of this book.

318. Thayer, *Constitutional Law*, *supra* note 317, at v-vii.

319. See, e.g., *id.* at 1783-86 (quoting Marshall's *Life of Washington* for historical context in the introduction to the chapter on regulation of commerce). Thayer continued, of course, to produce treatises for student use, such as his evidence manual. James B. Thayer, *A Preliminary Treatise on Evidence at the Common Law* (Boston, Little, Brown & Co., 1898).

320. James Bradley Thayer, *Lecture Notes* (James B. Thayer Papers, Harvard Law School Special Collections).

321. See Ezra Thayer, *Constitutional Law (1890-91)* (Ezra Thayer Papers, Harvard Law School Special Collections).

322. Samuel Williston, "James Bradley Thayer," 15 *Harv. L. Rev.* 599, 607 (1902).

323. M. Letter to the Editors, 1 *Colum. L. Times* 24, 25 24-25 (1888).

324. See Schofield, *supra* note 303, at 55.

325. See generally Eugene Wambaugh, Langdell's notebooks (Harvard Law School manuscript 4074).

326. See Schofield, *supra* note 303, at 55.

327. Letter from Robert Anderson (Librarian at Harvard) to Dean Landis, Feb. 24, 1938 (Harvard Law School, Papers of Robert B. Anderson).

328. George R. Swasey, "Boston University Law School," 1 *The Green Bag* 55, 55 (1889). Chronicles of the polemical resistance against Langdell's method can be found in Carrington, *Hail! Langdell!*, *supra* note 2, at 739.

329. One method of the B.U. instructors was to print syllabi including lists of cases along with citations to treatises. See Jabez Fox, *A Syllabus of the Course in Evidence Prepared for the Use of Students in the Boston University Law School* (Boston, Boston University Press, 1899).

330. Bigelow wrote treatises and casebooks, as well as scholarly monographs. See, e.g., Melville M. Bigelow, *Elements of Equity* (Boston, Little, Brown & Co., 1879); Melville M. Bigelow, *Elements of the Law of Torts: For the Use of Students* (Boston, Little Brown, 4th ed. 1891; hereinafter Bigelow, *Elements of Torts*); Melville M. Bigelow, *History of Procedure in England from the Norman Conquest 1066-1304* (Boston, Little, Brown & Co., 1880); Melville M. Bigelow, *The Law of Bills Notes and Cheques* (Boston, Little, Brown & Co., 1880); Melville M. Bigelow, *The Law of Estoppel* (Boston, Little, Brown & Co., 1872); Melville M. Bigelow, *Law of Fraud* (Boston, Little, Brown & Co., 1890); Melville M. Bigelow, *The Law of Torts* (2d ed. 1903); Melville M. Bigelow, *Leading Cases on the Law of Torts* (Boston, Little, Brown & Co., 1875); Melville M. Bigelow, *Placita Anglo-Normannica* (Boston, Soule & Bugbee, 1879).

331. Bigelow, *Elements of Torts*, *supra* note 330, at v.

332. See Eugene Wambaugh, *The Study of Cases: A Course of Instruction in Reading and Stating Reported Cases, Composing Head-Notes and Briefs Criticizing and Comparing Authorities, and Compiling Digests* (Boston, Little, Brown and Co., 1891), reprinted in part in chapter 42 of this book. This construction is similar to that used in the New York Law School syllabi. See *supra* note 216. An important legacy of Wambaugh's work, both at Iowa and at Harvard, was the greater methodization of student use of casebooks. See, e.g., Emlin McClain, "Law Department of the State University of Iowa," 1 *The Green Bag* 374, 384 (1889).

333. See 2 Warren, *supra* note 95, at 448. For a biographical look at Professor Wambaugh, see Felix Frankfurter, "Eugene Wambaugh," 54 *Harv. L. Rev.* 1 (1940).

334. See Roger W. Cooley, *Brief Making and the Use of Law Books* (5th ed. 1926).

335. *Id.* at 1-2.

336. See William G. Hammond, *Digest of the Decisions of the Supreme Court of the State of Iowa: From the Close of the Year 1859 to the June Term, 1866* (Des Moines, Mills & Co. 1866); Emlin McClain, "William Gardiner Hammond," in William D. Lewis, 8 *Great American Lawyers* 191 (1909). Professor McClain, himself a fixture in Iowa, noted in Hammond-like terms in a brief treatise that "lectures alone constitute a very unsatisfactory method of imparting elementary instruction in law. . . . This outline then is intended to enable the student to acquire by collateral study of a fuller, more accurate and systematic knowledge than he could get from oral lectures and hasty notes." Emlin McClain, *Outlines of Criminal Law and Procedure for the Use of Students* (Iowa City, Published by the Author, 1883; hereinafter McClain, *Outlines*). For further examples of this outline approach, see Richard, Lord Acton & Patricia Nassif Acton, *To Go Free: A Treasury of Iowa's Legal Heritage* (1995); Emlin McClain, *Synopsis of the Law of Bailments and Pledges* (Iowa City, University of Iowa, 1890); Emlin McClain, *Synopsis of Lectures on Remedial Law* (Iowa City, University of Iowa, 1889).

337. See McClain, *Outlines*, *supra* note 336, at 220. Hammond's exam, which is one of the earliest annual exams in the country, is described in Sheppard, "Informal History," *supra* note 7.

338. See, e.g., William Blackstone, *Commentaries on the Laws of England* (William G. Hammond ed., San Francisco, Bancroft-Whitney, Co., 1890); William G. Hammond, *The System of the Roman Institutes in Its Relation to That of Hale and Blackstone, Prepared as an Introduction to the First American Edition of Sander's Institutes of Justinian* (Chicago, Callaghan & Co., 1876); Francis Lieber, *Legal and Political Hermeneutics, or Principles of Interpretation and Construction in Law and Politics, with Remarks on Precedents and Authorities, with the Author's Last Corrections and Additions, and Notes by William G. Hammond* (St. Louis, F.H. Thomas & Co., 3d ed. 1880); Thomas C. Sandars, *The Institutes of Justinian; with English Introduction, Translation, and Notes* (Chicago, Callaghan & Co., 1st American, from the 5th London ed. 1876, with an introduction by William G. Hammond). For a careful discussion of Hammond's study of Lieber's work, and his role in sustaining the study of hermeneutics, see Paul D. Carrington, "William Gardiner Hammond and the Lieber Revival," 16 *Cardozo L. Rev.* 2135 (1995). Lieber's work is chroniced at Johnathan S. Henes, "A Lieber Bibliography, with Annotations," 16 *Cardozo L. Rev.* 2321 (1995). Perhaps as a result of the studies, Hammond introduced a new course devoted solely to torts, as opposed to municipal law or personal actions. See Helen S. Moylan, "Note: A Manuscript Record of the Early Days of the Iowa Law School," 22 *Iowa L. Rev.* 108, 110 (1936).

339. See Goebel & Howard, *supra* note 103, at 136-58; 2 Warren, *supra* note 95, at 444.

340. See, e.g., William A. Keener, *A Selection of Cases on Equity Jurisdiction* (New York, Baker, Voorhis & Co., 1895-98); William A. Keener, *A Selection of Cases on the Law of Contracts* (New York, Baker, Voorhis & Co., 1898); William A. Keener, *A Selection of Cases on the Law of Private Corporations* (New York, Baker, Voorhis, & Co., 1898); William A. Keener, *Selection of Cases on Quasi-Contracts* (New York, Baker, Voorhis & Co., 1898).

341. See William A. Keener, "The Inductive Method in Legal Education," 17 *Am. L. Rev.* 487 (1894).

342. See C.H. Cramer, *The Law School at Case Western Reserve University: A History 1892-1977*, at 38 (1977).

343. Albert M. Kales, *Legal Education in Cleveland* 5 (1921). Another program that opened in the dawning days of the casebook, which quickly embraced it, was Cornell's. See Rudolf B. Schlesinger, "The Cornell Law School's Birth and Its March to Greatness: A Rambling Centennial Tribute," 73 *Cornell L. Rev.* 1262, 1267 (1988); see also material collected and cited at *id.*, n.2.

344. Bryant's opinion on the topic was that "[l]ectures upon a topic of law are admirable when delivered to old, trained lawyers. They can take it all in, and perceive the treatment of the subject. The mere beginner, however, but little read in legal principles and untrained in legal methods of thinking carries away but little from the best and clearest thinking. . . . The lecture system alone is of aid to the reading, thinking, eager student, with a habit of perfect attention; but with the majority of law students it is of comparatively small value." William Robert Johnson, "The University of Wisconsin Law School, 1868-1930," at 134-40 (1972; unpublished Ph.D. dissertation, University of Wisconsin), quoting Edwin E. Bryant, "Legal Education," 2 *Reports of the Wisconsin Bar Assoc.* 141 (1895). A detailed treatment of Wisconsin's transition to the Socratic method is in William R. Johnson, *Schooled Lawyers: A Study in the Clash of Professional Cultures* 83-179 (1978).

345. See Frank L. Ellsworth, *Law on the Midway: The Founding of the University of Chicago School of Law* 74-77 (1977).

346. See Ellsworth, *supra* note 345, at 74-77.

347. See Howard Bromberg, "Legal Legacies: A Brief History of the Stanford Law School," *Stanford Mag.* (Sept. 1993); John Henry Schlegel, "Between the Harvard Founders and the American Legal Realists: The Professionalization of the American Law Professor," 35 *J. Legal Educ.* 311, 314 (1985).

348. See U.S. Bureau of Educ., *supra* note 65.

349. See *id.*

350. See *id.*

351. See Rahl & Schwerin, *supra* note 174, at 20.

352. Henry Wigmore, Letter of Transmission to the President of the University (Sept. 15, 1927).

353. See William F. Fratcher, *The Law Barn: A Brief History of the School of Law, University of Missouri-Columbia* 51, 57, 92 (1978).

354. See Philip S. Moore, *A Century of Law at Notre Dame* 24-27 (1969).

355. See Wisdom, *supra* note 185, at 7. A similar story is told at Indianapolis, which moved to the case method between 1899 and 1916, under the influence of faculty secretary James Rohbach. See Ronald W. Polston, "History of the Indiana University School of Law-Indianapolis," 28 *Ind. L. Rev.* 161, 175 (1995), citing 2 *Courts and Lawyers of Indiana* 482-83 (1916).

356. See generally Dave R. McKown, *The Dean: The Life of Julien C. Monnet* (1973).

357. See Herschell W. Arant, "A Survey of Legal Education in the South," 15 *Tenn. L. Rev.* 179 (1938). Indeed, unaccredited and part-time schools were likely to avoid the case method, and were encouraged to avoid it by the voices of the elite schools, because the case method required greater time in student preparation and skill in the instructor than did treatise-based lectures. See Reed, *supra* note 3, at 382.

358. Letter from Paul Carrington to Steve Sheppard (April 8, 1996).

359. Joseph Redlich, *The Common Law and the Case Method*, Carnegie Found. Rep. for the Advancement of Learning No. 8 (1914).

360. Reed, *supra* note 3, at 382.

361. See Stevens, *supra* note 3, at 112-30.

362. See, e.g., Langdell, *Contracts*; Samuel Williston, *A Selection of Cases on the Law of Contracts* (Boston, Little, Brown & Co., 1894); William a. Keener, *A Selection of Cases on the Law of Contracts* (New York, Baker, Voorhis, 1898).

363. See, e.g., William A. Keener, *A Selection of Cases on the Law of Quasi-Contracts* (Cambridge, Massachusetts, C.W. Sever, 1888-89).

364. See, e.g., John D. Lawson, *Select Cases in the Law of Personal Property with Analysis and References to Other Cases* (Columbia, Missouri., E.W. Stephens, 1896); Christopher G. Tiedeman, *Cases on Real Property, Selected and Arranged for Use in Connection with the Author's Treatise on Real Property* (St. Louis, Missouri, Thomas Law Book Co., 1925; 2d ed. Guy M. Wood, rev.). Jasper Calvin Gates, *Cases on the Law of Real Property* (St. Paul, Minnesota, West Publishing Co., 1898); Elmer E. Barrett, *Cases on the Law of Real Property* (St. Paul, Minnesota, West Publishing Co., 1898)

365. See, e.g., James B. Ames, *A Selection of Cases on the Law of Trusts: With Full References and Citations* (Cambridge, Massachusetts, J. Wilson, 1881-82).

366. See, e.g., Floyd Russell Mechem, *Cases on the Law of Succession to Property after the Death of the Owner* (St. Paul, Minnesota, West Publishing Co., 1895).

367. See, e.g., [James B. Ames], *Select Cases on Torts* (Cambridge, Massachusetts, 1874); [James B. Ames] *Harvard Law School. Cases on Torts; for the Use of the Class in Torts at the Harvard Law School, 1892-93* (Cambridge, Massachusetts, 1892?); James B. Ames & Jeremiah Smith, *A Selection of Cases on the Law of Torts* (Cambridge, Harvard Law Review Publication Association, 1893-1900); [] *Cases on Torts Selected and Arranged for the Use of Law Students in Connection With Pollock on Torts* (New York: Banks & Brothers, 1891); Melville Madison Bigelow, ed., *Cases on Torts to Accompany the Editor's Work on That Subject* (Boston, Little, Brown and Co., 1895).

368. See, e.g., John Day Smith, *Cases on Constitutional Law* (St. Paul, Minnesota, West Publishing Co., 1896).

369. See, e.g., Jeremiah Smith, comp., *Cases on Selected Topics in the Law of Municipal Corporations* (Cambridge, Massachusetts, The Harvard Law Review Publishing Association, 1898).

370. See, e.g., Joseph H. Beale, *A Selection of Cases and Other Authorities upon Criminal Law* (Cambridge, J. Wilson and Sons, 1893-94); Herman W. Chaplin, *Cases on Criminal Law: A Collection of Reported Cases on Some of the Leading Heads of the Criminal Law Prepared for Use in the Law School of Harvard University* (Boston, Little, Brown, 1891).

371. See, e.g., Seth Shepard, comp., *Cases on Equity Jurisprudence* (St. Paul, West Publishing Co., 1895). (The following cases have been printed at the request of Hon. Seth Shepard, lecturer before the Georgetown University school of law, for use in connection with his lectures. . . . They have been chiefly selected from Fetter's Cases on equity jurisprudence and Pattee's Cases in equity.)

372. See, e.g., James B. Ames, A Selection of Cases on the Law of Suretyship (Cambridge, Massachusetts, H.O. Houghton and Co., 1901?).

373. See, e.g., James B. Ames, *A Selection of Cases on Pleading at Common Law: With References and Citations* (Cambridge, Massachusetts, J. Wilson, 1875); Charles M. Hepburn, *A Selection of Cases and Statutes on the Principles of Code Pleading* (Cincinnati, W.H. Anderson and Co., 1899).

374. See, e.g., Austin Abbott, *Select Cases on the Law of Evidence as Applied During the Examination of Witnesses* (New York, The Diossy Law Book Co., 1895).

375. See, e.g., Floyd R. Mechem, ed., *Cases on the Law of Damages* (St. Paul, Minnesota, West Publishing Co., 1895). The following cases have been printed at the request of Professor Mechem, of the Law Department of the University of Michigan, for use in connection with his lectures in that law school.

376. See, e.g., Simeon E. Baldwin, *Cases on Railroad Law* (St. Paul, Minnesota, West Publishing Co., 1896); Emlin McClain, *A Selection of Cases on the Law of Carriers of Goods and of Passengers* (Iowa City, Iowa, The Author, 1894); Joseph Beale, Jr., *A Selection of Cases on the Law of Carriers* (Cambridge, Massachusetts, Harvard Law Review Publication Association, 1898).

377. See, e.g., Eugene Wambaugh, *A Selection of Cases on Insurance* (Cambridge, The Harvard Law Review Publishing Association, 1899); Edwin H. Woodruff, *A Selection of Cases on the Law of Insurance* (New York, Baker, Voorhis & Co., 1900).

378. See, e.g., Eugene Wambaugh, *A Selection of Cases on Agency* (Cambridge, Massachusetts, Harvard University Press, 1896).

379. See, e.g., Jeremiah Smith, *Cases on Corporations* (undated, 1894?; Harvard Law School Library unclassified, for the use of the class in corporations at the Harvard Law School); William A. Keener, *A Selection of Cases on the Law of Private Corporations* (New York, Baker, Voorhis & Co., 1899).

380. See, e.g., James B. Ames, *A Selection of Cases on the Law of Partnership: With Notes and Citations* (Cambridge, Massachusetts, The Riverside Press, 1881-87).

381. See, e.g., James B. Ames, *A Selection of Cases on the Law of Bills and Notes and Other Negotiable Paper: With Full References and Citations, and Also an Index and Summary of the Cases* (Boston, Soule and Bugbee, 1881).

38C: See, e.g., Christopher C. Langdell, *A Selection of Cases on Sales of Personal Property: With References and Citations* (Boston, Little, Brown and Co., 1872); Samuel Williston, *A Selection of Cases on the Law of Sales of Personal Property* (Cambridge, Massachusetts, The Harvard Law Review Publishing Association, 1894?); Frank A. Erwin, ed. *Cases on Sales of Personal Property* (New York, Banks, 1898).

383. See, e.g., Henry B. Brown, *Cases on the Law of Admiralty* (St. Paul, Minnesota, West Publishing Co., 1896); James Barr Ames, *A Selection of Cases on the Law of Admiralty, with Notes and Citations* (Cambridge, Massachusetts, Harvard Law Review Publication Association, 1901).

384. The earliest English example of a casebook for student use seems to be Gerard B. Finch, *A Selection of Cases on the English Law of Contract, Prepared as a Text-book for Law Students in the Universities* (London, C.J. Clay & Son, 1886).

385. See, e.g., James Barr Ames, *A Selection of Cases on the Law of Trusts with Notes and Citations* (Cambridge, Harvard Law Review Publishing Association, 2d ed. 1893); Yale Law School, *Cases on Wills* (n.d., Harvard Law School Library unclassified); University of Minnesota Law School, *Cases on Wills and Descent* (1923); *A Selection of Cases for Study in the Course in Contracts, with Parallel Citations: For Use of Students in the Boston University Law School* (Boston, Boston University, 1899).

386. See Redlich, *supra* note 359, at 49.

387. See Albert Ehrenzweig, "The American Casebook: 'Cases and Materials,'" 32 *Geo. L.J.* 224 (1944).

388. See, e.g., Karl Llewellyn, "On the Problem of Teaching 'Private Law,'" 54 *Harv. L. Rev.* 775 (1941); Roscoe Pound, "Taught Law," 37 *Rev. of the A.B.A.* 975 (1912). See also chapter 51.

389. William R. Vance, preface to 1 Harry A. Bigelow, *Cases on the Law of Property* v (1917).

390. See, e.g., William E. Mikell, *Cases on Criminal Law* (1908).

391. Parma, *supra* note 310, at 743 (quoting James Brown Scott, general editor of the American Case Book Series, in the prefaces to the casebooks from 1905 to 1908).

392. See, e.g., Roscoe Pound, *Cases on Practice: Select Cases and Other Authorities on Procedure in Civil Causes with References to the Code and Decisions of Nebraska* (Lincoln, T. North, 1904); University of Minnesota Law School, *Cases on Extraordinary Legal Remedies* (1914); University of Minnesota Law School, *Cases on Mortgages* (Minneapolis, University of Minnesota Law School, 1921); George Vaughan, *Cases on Land Titles* (Fayetteville, University of Arkansas, 1938); Sam Bass Warner, *Cases on Forms of Action in Oregon* (undated; Harvard Law School Library unclassified); Sam B. Warner, *Cases on Oregon Pleading* (1925?; Harvard Law School Library unclassified).

393. See Albert M. Kales, "The Next Step in the Evolution of the Casebook," 21 *Harv. L. Rev.* 92, 92 (1907).

394. Judge Vanderbilt's argument is persuasive, if based on a somewhat thin representation of case-method instruction: "I wonder if [students) realize that the body of law which they evolve from their casebooks with decisions drawn from many states, is not the law of any single jurisdiction at all. I am not criticizing the casebooks which provide the materials to aid the search for the true principles of law. . . . I am venturing to suggest, however, that some day the student will be called upon to practice in a particular jurisdiction and that he will then have to know the law of that jurisdiction. If eventually, why not now? There is no sound reason why the graduates of our law schools should spend the first three or four years of their practice, which might be devoted to more pressing matters, in discovering for the first time wherein the law of their state differs from the law of their classroom. . . . I am unalterably opposed to having the instructor spoon-feed the law of a particular state to him. I would have the student do this comparative work privately. On the other hand, the instructor must be prepared . . . to learn many new things . . . [h]e will no longer be able to pontificate. The effect of this widened discussion on the work of the classroom is electric. Instructor and pupil inevitably become fellow students searching together for the true principle of the law. It is the best antidote that I know of for the evil practice, current, I fear, in too many law schools, of bequeathing the professor's notes from one generation of law students to another." Arthur Vanderbilt, "Trends in Pre-Legal and Legal Education," in *Proceedings of the Symposium on Legal Education at Vanderbilt University, Held at the School of Law in Connection with the Inauguration of Oliver C. Carmichael as Chancellor, Feb. 4, 1938*, at 19-20. See also chapter 48 for then-professor Frankfurter's similar views.

395. A vast array of examples of each method is given in Ehrenzweig, *supra* note 366, at 244.

396. The process of this particular evolution is discussed by one of its progenitors. William A. Keener, "Methods of Legal Education (Part II)," 1 *Yale L.J.* 139, 148 (1892). See also chapter 37.

397. The debates are reprinted in *Proceedings of the Seventh Annual Meeting of the Association of American Law Schools* (1907), reprinted at 2 *Amer. L. Sch. Rev.* 116 (1907), and discussed in Schlegel, *supra* note 347, at 324. See also chapters 37 and 45.

398. Roscoe Pound, "Book Review," 4 *Ill. L. Rev.* 150 (1909), reviewing William E. Mikell, *Cases on Criminal Law* (1908).

399. See Roscoe Pound, *Cases on Equitable Relief Against Defamation and Other Injuries by Writing and Speaking: Supplementary to Ames's Cases in Equity Jurisdiction* (Cambridge, 1915); Zechariah Chafee, *Cases on Insurance Supplementary to Wambaugh's Cases* (Cambridge, 1917).

400. See Erwin Griswold, *Some Thoughts About Legal Education Today, in Frontiers in Law and Legal Education: Addresses Given at the University of Michigan Law Centennial, Oct. 22-24, 1959* (1961). See also chapter 53.

401. *Id.* at 77.

402. *Id.* Other scholars have often expressed similar views. For example, E. Blythe Stason stated: "When Sir Edward Coke argued with King James about the supremacy of law over the crown (circa 1600), he read law in a library containing not more than 5,000 reported judicial decisions. Today there are nearly 2,000,000. . . . [T)he postwar student of legal institutions finds himself confronted both with an endless and ever increasing array of legal problems—some old and many new, some unsolved, many insoluble—and by a virtually insurmountable mass of legal material of which he must become the master. No one mind can encompass all, or even a major fraction. Only the ablest minds can make a real dent in it. That is a significant thought and one not a little appalling. . . . Are we going to be able to produce the geniuses to solve the major problems of the future? Or is the profession so utterly inundated by the hosts of workday details that its members cannot 'see the forest for the trees'? . . . Much depends upon the answer to these questions." E. Blythe Stason, introduction to Arthur T. Vanderbilt, *Men and Measures in the Law: Five Lectures Delivered on the William W. Cook Foundation at the University of Michigan, Apr. 1948*, at xii-xiii, xiv (1949).

403. Griswold, *supra* note 379, at 79.

404. See Reed, *supra* note 3, at 371; Ehrenzweig, *supra* note 366, at 245-46.

405. Erwin Griswold, "Intellect and Spirit," in *The Path of the Law from 1967: Proceedings and Papers at the Harvard Law School Convocation Held on the One Hundred Fiftieth Anniversary of Its Founding* 149-150 (Arthur E. Sutherland ed., 1968).

406. *Id.*

407. Faculty of Law of Columbia University, *Summary of Studies in Legal Education* 44 (1928).

408. Morgan, *supra* note 310, at 383.

409. *Id.* Professor Morgan was a member of the Survey of the Legal Profession, and his 1952 article was a preliminary report. He had taught at Harvard and was then at Vanderbilt. *Id.* at 379.

410. See Lowell S. Nicholson, *The Law Schools of the United States: A Statistical and Analytical Report Based on 136 Completed*

Questionnaires and on Inspections of 160 Law Schools, Prepared for the Survey of the Legal Profession (1958), reprinted in part in chapter 54 of this book.

411. *Id.* at 33-35.

412. See *id.*

413. See *id.* at 37.

414. Question 88: "If you use dialogue, do you give students whom you will call upon notice beforehand? (1) yes, before class; (2) yes, at the start of class; (3) yes, occasionally; (4) no. Responses: (1) = 50 (12%); (2) = 5 (1%); (3) = 40 (10%); (4) = 290 (69%).

415. Stevens, *supra* note 3, at 214 (quoting AALS Proceedings, 1944, at 168).

416. See generally Deedra Benthall-Nietzel, "An Empirical Investigation of the Relationship Between Lawyering Skills and Legal Education," 63 *Ky. L.J.* 373, 393 (1975); Thomas F. Bergin, "The Law Teacher: A Man Divided Against Himself," 54 *Va. L. Rev.* 637, 648-49 (1968). This complaint is echoed by many practitioners. See Leonard I. Baird, "A Survey of the Relevance of Legal Training to Law School Graduates," 29 *J. Legal Educ.* 264, 278 (1978). A current summary of implementary criticisms of the case method, with recommendations for keeping the books nonetheless is in Russell L. Wearer, "Langdell's Legacy: Living with the Case Method," 36 *Vill. L. Rev.* 517 (1991).

417. Practically the only useful research in this regard is that in Charles J. Senger, "Learning Legal Reasoning in Law School: The Differences Between First and Third Year Students" (unpublished Ph.D. dissertation, Michigan State University, 1989). For a more general discussion of cognitive styles in torts students, see Alfred G. Smith, Cognitive Styles in Law Schools (1979). For a study of shifts in student attitudes toward pedagogy over the three years, see Ronald M. Pipkin, "Legal Education: The Consumer's Perspective," 1976 *Am. B. Found. Res. J.* 1161.

418. These concerns for the "average" or "C" student have cyclicly been raised, even at Harvard and Columbia, but changes of pedagogy to mitigate these limits have been routinely rejected. See generally Faculty of Columbia University, *supra* note 386; Harvard Law School, *Report to Faculty (Committee on Legal Education)* (1947).

419. While this effect is clear to anyone who has even walked near to law school buildings in this century, useful data toward proving this point, and details in understanding it in a more useful context, are provided in Paul D. Carrington & James J. Conley, "The Alienation of Law Students," 75 *Mich. L. Rev.* 887 (1977), explaining the results of a study of alienated law students and examining the impact of these feelings on their lives.

420. See Duncan Kennedy, "Legal Education and the Reproduction of Hierarchy," chapter 64 of this book. Paul N. Savoy, "Toward a New Politics of Legal Education," 79 *Yale L.J.* 444, 449 (1970).

421. Frank Grad places this dispute into the context of the rise of legislation as both a source of law and a focus of instruction in Frank Grad, "The Ascendancy of Legislation: Legal Problem Solving in Our Time," 9 *Dalhousie L.J.* 228 (1985). Columbia offered a course in legislation beginning in 1928. Goebel & Howard, *supra* note 103, at 315-16; Milton Handler, "What, If Anything, Should Be Done by Law Schools to Acquaint Law Students with the So-Called New Deal Legislation and Its Workings," 8 *Am. L. Sch. Rev.* 164 (1935).

422. Columbia, influenced by Redfield's work at the turn of the century, adopted a civil procedure course in 1926. See Goebel & Howard, *supra* note 103, at 177, 319. For a fuller consideration of the history of procedure courses, see Mary Brigid McManomon, *The History of the Course on Civil Procedure* (forthcoming 1997); Paul D. Carrington, *A History of Civil Procedure* (forthcoming 1998).

423. See Samuel Williston, *Life and Law: An Autobiography* 200 (1940); Jacob Henry Landman, "Anent the Case Method of Studying Law," 4 *N.Y.U. L. Rev.* 139 (1927).

424. See generally Harold Lasswell & Myres S. McDougal, "Legal Education and Public Policy: Professional Training in the Public Interest," 52 *Yale L.J.* 203, 232 (1943).

425. See Barnes, *supra* note 223, at 149.

426. Zephaniah Swift's evidence book followed essentially this form in 1810. See Zephaniah Swift, *A Digest of the Law of Evidence in Civil and Criminal Cases and a Treatise on Bills of Exchange with Promissory Notes* (1810; New York, Arno Press, 1972).

427. The argument for the case-textbook is put forth at length in Ehrenzweig, *supra* note 366, at 241-46. See also chapter 45.

428. Massachusetts School of Law, *The Deeply Unsatisfactory Nature of Legal Education Today: A Self Study Report on the Problems of Legal Education and On the Steps the Massachusetts School of Law Has Taken to Overcome Them* 4 (1992). See also *Massachusetts Sch. of Law of Andover v. American Bar Assoc.*, 65 USLW 2587 (3d Cir. 1991—ABA accredition process not antitrust violation). Likewise, a recent study of legal education by the ABA, strongly emphasizing the need for enhanced skills training, pursues this good by promoting distinct skills courses, making little mention of change or concern for the case method in the lecture hall. American Bar Association, Section on Legal Education and Admission to the Bar, *Legal Education and Professional Development-An Education Continuum* (The McCrate Report, 1992).

429. Question 43: "Is your primary assigned text best described as a—(1) Casebook (2) Treatise (3) Problem book."

430. Teachers of code courses selected treatises in four percent of responses and problem books in thirteen percent.

431. See Laura Kalman, "Legal Realism at Yale, 1927-1960," at 98-144 (1986); John Henry Schlegel, *American Legal Realism and Empirical Social Science* (1995).

432. See *infra* notes 502-521 and accompanying text.

433. For a detailed consideration of the quizzes of the nineteenth-century law school, see chapter 58.

434. An 1848 notebook of cases on declarations sets out twelve problems for declarations of a debt. Unpublished manuscript, Harvard Law Library no. MS 5009.

435. See Henry W. Ballantine, "Teaching Contracts with the Aid of Problems," 4 *Am. U. L. Rev.* 115 (1916). See also chapter 42 of this book.

436. See Landman, *supra* note 402, at 139; Jacob H. Landman, *The Case Method of Studying Law: A Critique* (1930; hereinafter Landman, *Case Method*). It is plausible that there might be earlier defenders of the problem method than Landman, although none were found in the research for this article. Professor Stevens begins his brief discussion of problem instruction with the writings of David Cavers, which are fifteen years later. See Stevens, *supra* note 3, at 215.

437. Landman, *Case Method, supra* note 436, at 36.

438. See *id.* at 65-77.

439. There is little necessity for Landman's criticism of the case method as inductive rather than deductive. Legal reasoning uses both tools, and both tools are necessary to successful use of the case method, or even of the quiz show approach to the casebook. Still, the difference between the two approaches can be usefully highlighted in the problem method. See Charles Richard Calleros, "Variations on the Problem Method in First-Year and Upper-Division Classes," 20 *U.S.F. L. Rev.* 455, 457-58 (1986). For a professional philosopher's view of the matter, see Peter Suber, "Analogy Exercises for Teaching Legal Reasoning" 17 *J.L. & Educ.* 91 (1988). Chicago-Kent Professor Dan Hunter is now deeply engaged in exciting research on these lines in a Cambridge doctoral thesis.

440. Landman, *Case Method, supra* note 436, at 91-92.

441. The place of Langdell's case method as a problem-based pedagogy is considered in Tom L. Beauchamp, *Case Studies in Business, Society & Ethics* (1989).

442. Abe Fortas, "The Training of the Practitioner," in *The Law School of Tomorrow: The Projection of an Ideal* 179, 182 (David Haber & Julius Cohen eds., 1968). For a discussion of the development of problems and teaching styles generally at Yale, see Kalman, *supra* note 432.

443. See Goebel & Howard, *supra* note 103, at 338-39.

444. See David F. Cavers, "In Advocacy of the Problem Method," 43 *Colum. L. Rev.* 449, 455 (1943).

445. See Karl Llewellyn, "The Current Crisis in Legal Education," 1 *J. Legal Educ.* 211, 217 (1948-49). See also chapter 51.

446. According to Llewellyn: "The course would promote skills in '(1) Statutory Construction (2) Reading, absorption, analysis and application of text material (3) Organization of case material plus the foregoing, for counseling and for appellate argument (4) simple commercial drafting.' Students were to 'make heavy use of the *text* material, of three kinds: Uniform statutes, and other statues as needed, in both the present and the proposed Revised form . . . (2) The 'Legal' text: notably the Comments on the Revised Acts . . . [and] (3) 'Background' text which sets a picture of business problem and business practice.

"The key to his course was to center work and discussion around 'Problem Materials selected to *cumulate* practice in techniques, but to *range* in point of the requisite legal information.' His plan for the course, which was partly built on problems created by Soia Mentschikoff, expected the students to solve '8 problems properly chosen and somewhat intensively developed. This gives as an average of 6 hours per problem (which is a squeeze) plus 4 hours introduction while the students seek to learn to read, and 4 hours general leeway.' In creating the problems, he attempted to occupy available student time, measured by the number of students in the course, their likely teamwork, and the availability of teaching assistants. In general, his aim was to 'consume 2½ hours outside time per class hour,' or ten hours weekly." Karl Llewellyn, *Memorandum, A Commercial Law Course of 4 Semester Hours, Spring, 1948* (Karl Llewellyn Papers, Columbia Law School treasure room). Paul Carrington has suggested that Llewelyn's commitment to case-based instruction remained strong throughout his life, despite such experiments. Letter from Paul Carrington to Steve Sheppard (April 8, 1996).

447. See Arthur Larson, "An 'Inductive' Approach to Legal Instruction," 1 *J. Legal Educ.* 287, 287-88 (1948-49).

448. See Charles W. Taintor, "Required Summer Term and 'Problem' Course," 2 *J. Legal Educ.* 347 (1950).

449. See Paul G. Kauper & L. Hart Wright, *Cases and Materials on Federal Income Taxation* (1951; prepared for the use of students in the University of Michigan Law School); Elizabeth Gaspar Brown, "The Law School of the University of Michigan: 1859-1984: An Intellectual History," 18 *J.L. Reform* 341, 349-50 (1985).

450. See Paul G. Kauper, *Cases on Constitutional Law* (1952, 2 vols.; prepared for the exclusive use of students in the University of Michigan Law School).

451. See Paul G. Kauper, *Constitutional Law: Cases and Materials* (1954).

452. See sources collected in Stevens, *supra* note 3, at 228 nn.83-84.

453. Moore, *supra* note 354, at 112; Bernard J. Ward, "The Problem Method at Notre Dame," 11 *J. Legal Educ.* 100, 107 (1958).

454. Marlin M. Volz, "The Legal Problems Courses at the University of Kansas City," 7 *J. Legal Educ.* 91, 91 (1954). Kansas City students were offered three courses totaling seven hours. See *id.* at 93.

455. Gordon A. MacLeod, "Creative Problem Solving—For Lawyers?!," 16 *J. Legal Educ.* 198, 198 (1963). Numerous models of problem-solving technique have been presented, a representative model of which is presented in H.F.M. Crombag et al., "On Solving Legal Problems," 27 *J. Legal Educ.* 168 (1975).

456. See Stephen Nathanson, "The Role of Problem Solving in Legal Education," 39 *J. Legal Educ.* 167 (1989); Leo H. Whinery, "The Problem Methods in Legal Education," 58 *W. Va. L. Rev.* 144 (1955).

457. See, e.g., Jesse Dukeminier & James E. Krier, *Property* (2d ed. 1988).

458. See, e.g., Edward H. Rabin, *Fundamentals of Modern Real Property* (2d ed. 1982).

459. See Ehrenzweig, *supra* note 366, at 236. Materials for use in teaching with problems have recently been summarized. Myron Moskovitz, "Beyond the Case Method: It's Time to Teach with Problems,' 42 *J. Legal Educ.* 241 (1992).

460. See Gregory L. Ogden, "The Problem Method in Legal Education," 34 *J. Legal Educ.* 654 (1984).

461. See *infra* section V.

462. See, e.g., Werner Heisenberg, "The Copenhagen Interpretation of Quantum Theory," in Werner Heisenberg, *Physics and Philosophy: The Revolution in Modern Science* (1958).

463. For a recent guided tour of trendy classroom techniques, see the materials collected in Association of American Law Schools 1995 Conference: New Ideas for Experienced Teachers, Conference Materials, particularly the reprint of Arturo L. Torres & Karen E. Harwood, "Moving Beyond Langdell: An Annotated Bibliography of Current Methods for Law Teaching," 1994 *Gonz. L. Rev.* 1. For the antecedent in bibliography, see chapter 56.

464. These topics are described throughout the rest of this two-volume work.

465. There is an obvious error in the construction of this question, and the interpretation of any validity in the answers is left to the reader. For the interpretative and comparative reconstruction of this data, see Sheppard, "State of the Art," chapter 57 in the present volume.

Question 89: "In a week, how much time of your class is spent discussing cases representative of your field? (1) none (2) 1-25% (2) 25-50% (3) 50%-75% (4) 75-99% (5) all."

Responses: (1) = 7 (2%) (2) = 99 (24%) (3) = 96 (23%) (4) = 169 (40%) (5) = 25 (6%).

Question 92: "In a week, how much time of a class is spent elaborating the 'black letter law' in your field? (1) none (2) 1-25% (2) 25-50% (3) 50%-75% (4) 75-99% (5) all."

Responses: (1) = 27 (6%) (2) = 322 (76%) (3) = 42 (10%) (4) = 12 (3%) (5) = 0 (0%).

Question 95: "In a week, how much time of your class is spent solving problems illustrating the law in your field? (1) none (2) 1-25% (2) 25-50% (3) 50-75% (4) 75-99% (5) all."

Responses: (1) = 28 (7%) (2) = 293 (70%) (3) = 63 (15%) (4) = 21 (5%) (5) = 5 (1%)."

Question 98: "In a week, how much time of your class is spent considering theoretical underpinnings of your field? (1) none (2) 1-25% (2) 25-50% (3) 50%-75% (4) 75-99% (5) all."

Responses: Survey 98 (1) = 10 (24%) (2) = 337 (80%) (3) = 49 (12%) (4) = 7 (2%) (5) = 2 (0%).

466. See David Reisman, "Law and Social Science: A Report on Michael and Wechsler's Classbook on Criminal Law and Administration," 50 *Yale L.J.* 636 (1941).

467. Announcement of School of Law 1930-31, Memorandum, First Year Assigned Readings, in Columbia University School of Law Faculty Reports and Studies, 1928-31 (Columbia treasure CU C7135 F13).

468. The list included Aristotle's *Politics*, Pollock's *Maine's Ancient Law*, Hobbes's *Leviathan*, Lowie's *Primitive Society*, Sumner's *Folkways*, Gray's *Nature and Sources of the Law*, Jhering's *Law as a Means to an End*, Pound's (initially) *Introduction to the Philosophy of Law* (and later) *Introduction to Legal History*, Holmes's *Collected Papers*, Cardozo's *Nature of the Judicial Process*, and Llewellyn's "A Modern Law School, and Four Further Articles, Including Francis M. Burdick, Is Law the Expression of Class Selfishness?," 25 *Harv. L. Rev.* 349 (1911). These works were assigned at the beginning of the first year, and an examination was given on them in September of the second year.

469. See Memorandum, Optional Readings for Second and Third Year Students (Columbia Law School treasure CU C735 Op).

470. "Library facilities for his enterprise are not easy to arrange. The Committee has placed ten copies of each book or periodical . . . on reserve. . . . The Committee casts its curse of unchastity upon any knight who mutilates the book! May his name be Vandal and his bones bleach unshriven!" Memorandum, First Year Assigned Readings Foreword: The Play of Ideas 3 (Columbia Law School treasure, Karl Llewellyn papers).

471. Goebel & Howard, *supra* note 103, at 340.

472. Anderson has positioned itself as a market leader in this field. Its publication list includes more than forty anthologies in most commonly taught fields. See, e.g., publisher's advertisement in *A Property Anthology* (Richard H. Chused ed., 1993).

473. Question 47: "Do you recommend auxiliary readings, such as articles, anthologies, codes, treatises, or histories? (1) yes (2) no."

474. In common-law courses, 78% (222) answered "yes"; 21% (60) answered "no." In code courses, 80% (164) answered "yes," and 17% (35) answered "no."

475. Question 48: "Do you discuss auxiliary readings in class? (1) yes (2) no." Answers for (1) were 215 (51%) and for (2) were 193 (46%). These answers were again consistent when the response pool was divided into common law and code courses: Common Law: (1) = 52% (148) (2) = 46% (130). Statute: (1) = 50% (102) (2) = 48% (97).

476. Question 49: "Do you examine the students on auxiliary readings? (1) yes (2) no." Answers for (1) were 133 (32%) and for (2) were 270 (64%). These answers were again consistent when the response pool was divided into common law and code courses:

Common Law: (1) = 32% (91) (2) = 66% (186). Statute: (1) = 30% (61) (2) = 66% (135).

477. See John M. Burnam, "Out-of-Class Assignments as a Method of Teaching and Evaluating Law Students," 42 *J. Legal Educ.* 447 (1992); David F. Cavers, "The First Year Group Work at Harvard," 3 *J. Legal Educ.* 39 (1950); David Dominguez, "Beyond Zero-Sum Games: Multiculturalism as Enriched Law Training for All Students," 44 *J. Legal Educ.* 175 (1994).

478. See Clive Parry, "The Cambridge Supervision System," 7 *J. Legal Educ.* 1 (1954).

479. See Howard L. Oleck, "The 'Adversary Method' of Law Teaching," 5 *J. Legal Educ.* 104 (1952). A superb, and sophisticated, example of paradoxical teamwork both in transactional and litigious settings is illustrated in Phyllis G. Coleman and Robert M. Jarvis, "Using Skills Training to Teach First-Year Contracts," 44 *Drake L. Rev.* 725 (1996).

480. See Gerald M. Stern, *The Buffalo Creek Disaster* (1976).

481. I am grateful to my colleague Mark Kende for introducing me to Buffalo Creek several years ago. Good illustrations

of its use are in Charles A. Rees, "A Calendar of Buffalo Creek Hypotheticals for the Civil Procedure Course," 18 *Ohio N.U. L. Rev.* 233 (1991).

482. For an example of a long-playing simulation, see Stacy Caplow, "Autopsy of a Murder: Using Simulation to Teach First Year Criminal Law," 19 *N.M. L. Rev.* 137 (1989).

483. See, e.g., John Barkai, "The Lecture-in-Disguise," 19 *N.M. L. Rev.* 117 (1989).

484. See, e.g., Denton Moore & Jerry Tomlinson, "The Use of Simulated Negotiation to Teach Substantive Law," 21 *J. Legal Educ.* 579 (1969); Charles W. Taintor, "Required Summer Term and 'Problem' Course," 2 *J. Legal Educ.* 347 (1950).

485. See David S. Day, "Teaching Constitutional Law: Role Playing the Supreme Court," 36 *J. Legal Educ.* 270 (1986).

486. See *id.* at 269; see also Robert P. Davidow, "Teaching Constitutional Law and Related Courses through Problem-Solving and Role Playing," 34 *J. Legal Educ.* 527 (1984), finding that role playing helps early law school learning of substantive law and results in proficient lawyering.

487. See, e.g., Michael S. Botein, "Simulation and Role Playing in Administrative Law," 26 *J. Legal Educ.* 234 (1974).

488. See, e.g., Kenny Hegland, "Fun and Games in the First Year: Contracts by Roleplay," 31 *J. Legal Educ.* 534 (1981); Joseph W. Little, "Skills Training in the Torts Course," 31 *J. Legal Educ.* 614 (1981). See also Coleman and Jarvis, *supra* note 479.

489. Question 110: "Do you have students or others 'role play' in your classes, including mock arguments? (1) frequently (2) occasionally (3) rarely (4) no."

490. See Peter Brooks & Paul Gewirtz, *Law's Stories: Narrative and Rhetoric in the Law* (1996).

491. In this way, narrative may move beyond Duncan Kennedy's criticism that a primary effect of law schools is to prepare students for roles in hierarchies. See Catherine W. Hantzis, "Kingsfield and Kennedy: Reappraising the Male Models of Law School Teaching," 38 *J. Legal Educ.* 155, 162-63 (1988), arguing that narratives are part of the process by which old pedagogies are superseded. See, e.g., Shauna Van Praagh, "Stories in Law School: An Essay on Language, Participation, and the Power of Legal Education," 2 *Colum. J. Gender & L.* 111, 140-44 (1992), discussing how storytelling expands learning potential in law schools.

492. For an example of narrative discussed with reference to feminist jurisprudence, see Robin West, "Jurisprudence and Gender," 55 *U. Chi. L. Rev.* 1, 61-67 (1988).

493. See Paul Gewirtz, Introduction, in *Law's Stories: Narrative and Rhetoric in the Law* 2, 3-4 (1996), using "law as literature" to describe the law and literature movement in its relationship with narrative.

494. See John Batt, "Law, Science, and Narrative: Reflections on Brain Science, Electronic Media, Story, and Law Learning," 40 *J. Legal Educ.* 19, 26-29 (1990). See also *infra* notes 479-489 and accompanying text.

495. See Teresa Godwin Phelps, "Narratives of Disobedience: Breaking/Changing the Law," 40 *J. Legal Educ.* 133, 134-35 (1990).

496. See David O. Friedrichs, "Narrative Jurisprudence and Other Heresies: Legal Education at the Margin," 40 *J. Legal Educ.* 3, 5 (1990), pointing out the potential conflict between well-developed narratives and our cultural predisposition to be easily bored.

497. But see H. Jefferson Powell, "Transparency, Opacity, and Openness in Narrative," 40 *J. Legal Educ.* 161 (1990).

498. Robert Stein, "A Tribute to Irving Younger," 73 *Minn. L. Rev.* 815, 816 (1989).

499. A good candidate for the first law film may be the film of the Dreyfus affair produced in 1898 by Doublier. See Erik Barnouw, *Documentary: A History of the Non-Fiction Film* 25-26 (1974).

500. American Bar Association, *Films and Film Strips on Legal and Law-Related Subjects* (rev. ed. 1974).

501. Telephone interview with Frederick Wiseman (July 25, 1995); Letter from Karen Konicek, Zipporah Films, to Steve Sheppard (July 27, 1995, on file with author), noting that Wiseman's films have been ordered for use in Harvard, Yale, Dickinson, Michigan, Bridgeport, and Boston University, among others.

502. Telephone conversation with Buffalo professor John Henry Schlegel (Aug. 1, 1995).

503. The author of this article does so.

504. A collection of discussions of films for this purpose is Reynard Strickland, *Screening Justice* (forthcoming 1998). See Justin Brook's use of *Beverly Hills Cop* in criminal procedure, in *Will Boys Just be Boyz 'n the Hood? African American Directions Portray a Crumbling Justice System in Urban America, in Screening Justice* (forthcoming 1998).

505. See Paul R. Baier, "What Is the Use of a Law Book Without Pictures or Conversations?," 34 *J. Legal Educ.* 619, 626 (1984).

506. See, e.g., Steven P. Gillers, "Popular Legal Culture: Taking *L.A. Law* More Seriously," 98 *Yale L.J.* 1607 (1989); Lee Stuesser, "The Need for Change in Teaching Law," 38 *U. New Brunswick L.J.* 55, 72 (1989). The bulk of recent sources and references are collected in Christine Alice Corcos, "Columbo Goes to Law School: Or, Some Thoughts on the Uses of Television in the Teaching of Law," 13 *Loy. L.A. Ent. L.J.* 499 (1993). This material has yet to include the wealth of attention given to the trials of O.J. Simpson, although such an inclusion is probably certain to occur.

507. See Vincent Robert Johnson, "Audiovisual Enhancement of Classroom Teaching: A Primer for Law Professors," 37 *J. Legal Educ.* 97 (1987). A glance at use of audiovisual recordings earlier in the age of video recording is given in New York Law School's 1974 survey of videotape use, which found most video use in law schools was then in clinics. Michael Botein, *Videotape in Legal Education* (Communications Media Center, New York Law School 1989).

508. Question 109: "Do you use films or other audiovisual material with your course? (1) during class (2) required outside of class (3) optional outside of class (4) no."

509. See William G. Harrington, "Computers and Legal Research," 56 *A.B.A. J.* 1145, 924 (1970).

510. See William G. Harrington, "What's Happening in Computer Assisted Legal Research?," 60 *A.B.A. J.* 924 (1974).

511. For several visions of the future under such a system, see chapters 88-91 of this book. See also Ronald W. Staudt, "Does

the Grandmother Come With It? Teaching and Practicing Law in 21st Century," 44 *Case W. Res. L. Rev.* 499 (1994); James L. Hoover, "Legal Scholarship and the Electronic Revolution," 83 *L. Libr. J.* 643 (1991); Charles D. Kelso & J. Clark Kelso, "How Computers Will Invade Law School Classrooms," 35 *J. Legal Educ.* 507 (1985).

512. For a current depiction of computer-aided teaching, see Richard A. Matasar & Rosemary Shiels, "Electronic Law Students: Repercussions on Legal Education," 29 *Val. U. L. Rev.* 909 (1995). For early visions of the merger between computers and writing programs, see Layman E. Allen & Charles S. Saxon, "One Use of Computerized Instructional Gaming in Legal Education: To Better Understand the Rich Logical Structure of Legal Rules and Improve Legal Writing," 18 *J.L. Reform* 383 (1985). For a more general forecast, see Roger Park & Russell Burris, "Computer Aided Instruction in Law: Theories, Techniques, and Trepidations," 1978 *Am. B. Found. Res. J.* 1.

513. *4th Annual Conference for Law School Computing Professionals: Conference Materials* (Chicago-Kent & CALI Project ed., 1994; hereinafter *Computing Conference Materials*).

514. Jeremy Seeger, The Educational Technology Center at Harvard University Law School, in Computing Conference Materials, *supra* note 493, at 445.

515. See Peter Martin, "The Legal Information Institute at Cornell University Law School, in Computing Conference Materials, *supra* note 493, at 440, 442. Similar work is done at Villanova. See Henry H. Perritt, Jr., The Center for Law, Information & Policy & Villanova University School of Law, in Computing Conference Materials, *supra* note 513, at 299.

516. See Ronald Staudt, "The Center for Law and Computers: The Electronic Publishing Initiative," in *Computing Conference Materials, supra* note 513, at 292, 293.

517. 1995 Conference on Distance Learning.

518. For a moving discussion of these developments, see Matasar & Shiels, *supra* note 512, at 909.

519. "Do you suggest students perform supplemental computer assisted legal instruction (CALI)? (1) yes (2) no (3) I have no idea what this is."

520. "Do you use interactive computer programs in presenting any of your course material in class? (1) yes (2) no."

521. As one of the author's colleagues describes student use of commercial study aids: "The students prefer the Europeans to us—the French scholar Gilbert, the Italian Legalines, the Israeli Emanuel, even the Englishman Nutshell."

522. See, e.g., Barron Field, *An Analysis of Blackstone's Commentaries on the Laws of England, in a Series of Questions, to Which the Student Is to Frame His Own Answers by Reading That Work* (London, T. Cadell and W. Davies, 1811); Asa Kinne, *The Most Important Parts of Blackstone's Commentaries Reduced to Questions and Answers* (New York, W.E. Dean, 1838); John C. Devereux, *The Most Material Parts of Blackstone's Commentaries, Reduced to Questions and Answers: Upon the Plan and in the Place of Kinne's Blackstone* (New York, Baker, Voorhis & Co., 1875); William Sprague, *Blackstone Quizzer D . . . Being Questions and Answers on Book 4 of Blackstone's Commentaries, for Students Preparing for Examination for Admission to the Bar* (Detroit, Michigan, Collector Publishing Co., 3d ed. 1896).

523. See, e.g., Asa Kinne, *The Most Important Parts of Kent's Commentaries, Reduced to Questions and Answers* (New York, W.E. Dean, 2d ed. 1840).

524. See, e.g., George Gardiner Fry, *Questions and Answers on Municipal Law: Containing About One Thousand of the Most Important Questions Propounded to Law Students, Both at the New York Supreme Court and Columbia College Law School Examinations* (New York, Baker, Voorhis & Co. 1895).

525. See, e.g., Walter Smith Cox, *Questions for the Use of Students in the Junior Law Class of Columbian University* (Washington, D.C., W.H. Morrison, 1886).

526. See Morris F. Dowley, *The Law in a Nut-Shell, Comprising Concise and Lucid Answers to Five Hundred Leading Legal Questions, Including All Questions Propounded to Law Students at the Prize Examinations of Columbia College, A Synopsis of the Laws Governing Husband and Wife, the Rates of Interest, and the Statutes Against Usury in the Several States; and A Miniature Dictionary of Law Terms Culled from Standard Legal Authors* (New York, Ward & Peloubet 1878). After such a loquacious title, the publisher noted on the cover, "Be brief, be pointed. . . ."

527. See *A Summary of the Law of Scotland, by Way of Question and Answer, in the Order of Mr. Erskine; Chiefly Adapted to the Use of Gentlemen on the Eve of Trial as Advocates, Writers to the Signet, and Solicitors or Agents, Either Before the Supreme of Inferior Courts* (Edinburgh, Bell & Bradfute, 1821).

528. The role of correspondence legal education seems to have been quite significant at the dawn of the century, although it has since radically declined. See generally Elridge B. Pierce, "Correspondence Law Schools," *J. Legal Ed.* 160 (1951). The earliest of these programs appears to be the Blackstone School of Law, the 1890 creation of William C. Sprague, who appears to have had a close relationship with the major producer of quizzers. See, e.g., Griffith O. Ehlis, *Quizzer No. 10, Being Questions and Answers on Bills, Notes, and Cheques for Students Preparing for Examination for Admission to the Bar or for Advanced Standing in Law Schools or for Review in Connection with Text Books and Lectures* (Detroit, Michigan, The Collector Publishing Co., 1897); Emil W. Snyder, *Quizzer No. 7. Being Questions and Answers on Equity, Pleading, and Practice for Students Preparing for Examination for Admission to the Bar or for Advanced Standing in Law Schools or for Review in Connection with Text Books and Lectures* (Detroit, Michigan, The Collector Publishing Co., 1900); William C. Sprague, *Quizzer No. 13, Being Questions and Answers on Partnership for Students Preparing for Examination for Admission to the Bar or for Advanced Standing in Law Schools or for Review in Connection with Text Books and Lectures* (Detroit, Michigan, The Collector Publishing Co., 1899). Further discussion of the Blackstone College curriculum is in its false advertising defense. See Pierce, *supra*, at 165-67, discussing *In re Blackstone College of Law, Inc.*, 44 F.T.C. 756 (1948). The scheme of competing programs is depicted in James P. Downs, *Introductory Lecture to a Series of 26 Lecture-Lessons Embodying William Raymond Board's Principles of American Law, which Constitute a Course of Study at the New York Correspondence School of Law* (Harrisburg, J.H. McFarland, 1892), as well as the massive *Cyclopedia of Law Produced for the American Correspondence School of Law*

(12 vols.; Charles E. Chadman ed., 1908). For a more general account of correspondence schools, see Harry W. Ballantine, "The Place in Legal Education of Evening and Correspondence Law Schools," 4 *Am. L. Sch. Rev.* 369 (1919).

529. See, e.g., Edwin Baylies, *Questions and Answers for Law Students* (Albany, New York, W. Gould & Co., 1888); Russell Whitman, *Law Students' Review and Quiz Book in the Form of Questions Which Supply Concrete Statements of Facts and of Answers Which Set Forth the Legal Principles Involved* (1916).

530. See Griffith Ogden Ellis, "Questions Answered and Difficulties Met for Students of Law: Being Questions and Their Answers That Appeared During One Year," in *The Law Student's Helper: A Monthly Magazine for Law Students* (Detroit, Michigan, The Collector Publishing Co., 1899).

531. *Problems in Law for Law School and Bar Examination Review: A Collection of Concrete Problems with Solutions Covering Principle Topics* (Henry W. Ballantine ed., 1927). This is truly the most massive of the quizzers, running to nearly 1,500 pages in each edition.

532. For a short chronicle of the printing of exams for distribution, see chapter 58.

533. See W.C. Bates, *Exponential Outline with Definitions of Blackstone's Commentaries* (Columbus, London Printing & Publishing Co., 1893).

534. A mimeographed, bound copy of Williston's lectures, running 118 pages of legal-sized paper, is testament both to the thriving industry of out-of-class shortcutting and to the method by which Williston ran his courses. The notes, bound and apparently sold in later years of Williston's lecturing through the Harvard Cooperative Bookstore, are thorough recitations of Williston's classes, including long discussions of general principles, hypothetical questions and answers, and case discussions. The typical notation of a case is brief, only a few lines of facts, followed by a holding and a paragraph-length rationale. "Williston Lectures on Contracts, 1894-'95" (unpublished manuscript, Harvard Law Library no. 5602). Reproduced class notes are, of course, older than this, as seen in Judge Gould's complaints of lecture piracy at Litchfield, in the text near notes 86 and 87 above, and as demonstrated by the Penn. planographs described above in notes 190-193.

535. Steven Emanuel, *Some Thoughts About the First Year of Law School* (1994).

536. Gilbert Law Summaries Product Catalog (1994).

537. Telephone conversations between the author and Brett Arnold, July 1995 and January 1997. For instance, the *Nutshell on Art Law, Leonard DuBoff, Art Law* (2d ed. 1993), is an assigned coursebook in law and the arts at Boston University, John Marshall, and Georgia State. *Id.*

538. See, e.g., *The Law in a Flash Study Series* (1995).

539. Telephone interviews with Andy Metheny, the store manager of the Harvard Coop, Law School Branch, and with Fred Puffenberger, the director of the Thomas Cooley Bookstore (May 1996).

540. Question 53. "How do you react to student use of commercial briefs of cases? (1) Recommend (2) Discredit (3) Ignore."

541. Question 53. "How do you react to student use of commercial outlines of your course? (1) Recommend (2) Discredit (3) Ignore."

542. Karl N. Llewellyn, "The Current Crisis in Legal Education," 1 *J. Legal Educ.* 211 (1948). See also chapter 51.

543. See *id.*

544. Of course such a path is absolutely essential if law schools are to develop, in any way, toward again becoming the forges of civic virtue. See, e.g., Carrington, *supra* note 186; Hoeflich, *supra* note 130. The satisfaction of a teacher's moral obligation to do so, to teach in the grand manner as did Story, is dependent on such an approach. See Michael I. Swygert, "Striving to Make Great Lawyers—Citizenship and Moral Responsibility: A Jurisprudence for Law Teaching," 30 *B.C. L. Rev.* 803 (1989), reprinted in chapter 74.

545. Kales, *supra* note 343, at 23.

546. See Peter L. Strauss, "The Metamorphosis of Legal Education," 30 *N.Y.L. Sch. L. Rev.* 637, 637-38 (1985), reprinted in chapter 73, discussing the reforms proposed by Professor Gorman and arguing that law professors should be more than just vocational instructors.

A. The Early Experience

Chapter 2

Justinian in Braintree

John Adams, Civilian Learning, and Legal Elitism, 1758-1775

1984

Daniel R. Coquillette

Daniel R. Coquillette was Dean of Boston College Law School from 1985 to 1993 and is Professor at Boston College and Visiting Professor at Harvard Law School, for which he is writing the bicentennial history. This article first appeared in Volume 62 of the *Publications of the Massachusetts Historical Society*, 1984; reprinted here are sections I through IV of the original article.

Author's Note: To Professors Charles Donahue, Samuel Thorne, Harold Berman, and Andrew Kaufman at Harvard Law School, my teachers and friends, and to Catherine Menand, Theodore Chase, and Professor John Leubsdorf, who carefully examined this text, I owe a special debt.

I have read about 10 pages in Justinian and Translated about 4 Pages into English. This is the whole of my Days Work. I have smoaked, chatted, trifled, loitered away this whole day almost. . . . But I am resolved to translate Justinian and his Commentators Notes by day light and read Gilberts Tenures by Night till I am master of both. . . . [Diary, 5 October 1758[1]]

But, it is my Destiny to dig Treasures with my own fingers. No Body will lend me or sell me a Pick axe. [Diary, 18 December 1758[2]]

I. Introduction: The Influence of Civilian Learning in Early American Jurisprudence

What influence did continental European jurisprudence, the civilian learning of the Roman-based civil law and of the European Enlightenment, have on the English colonies in America? Much ink has flowed on aspects of this topic, over issues as disparate as whether the characteristic American "district attorney" derived from the Dutch institution of the "schout" and whether Cicero was a "role model for early American lawyers."[3] Masterful studies have been done by Peter Stein on "The Attraction of Civil Law in Post-Revolutionary America" and by Herbert Alan Johnson on the law merchant in colonial New York. I certainly do not intend to make outrageous claims for civilian influence[4] or to populate the rural courthouses of America with Ulpians, Justinians, and home-spun Montesquieus. I put forward only one such "barn yard Justinian," and a very atypical one at that, John Adams.

Young Adams, sitting in Braintree as a neophyte lawyer in 1758, certainly saw himself as something of a classical Roman character. In his mind's eye an invisible toga often descended over his young shoulders, at least when he was not chasing the attractive Hannah Quincy in "Cupid's Grove."[5] Adjusting the imaginary folds of this toga, he wrote in his new diary: "Few of my Contemporary Beginners, in the Study of the Law, have the Resolution, to aim at much Knowledge in the Civil Law. Let me therefore distinguish my self from them, by the Study of the Civil Law, in its native languages, those of Greece and Rome."[6]

Adams was ever eager to put distance between his young self, humble in origin but Harvard educated, and what he perceived to be the rabble of "common" colonial lawyers, whom he characterized as "Petty foggers" and "dirty Dablers in the Law."[7] And he was ambitious. Even before he had met his role-models in the elite of the Boston bar, such as Jeremiah Gridley, James Otis, Benjamin Pratt, Benjamin Kent, and Oxenbridge Thacher, Adams felt the pressing need to be one of a select few.[8] A direct corollary, at least in his aspiring young mind, was the need to master the classics of both the civilian and the common law literature.

Adams started out his legal career in rural Worcester. He had gone there after Harvard to teach school. Teaching school was one way to avoid the family pressure to become a minister, but Worcester was dull. The best source of intellectual and social excitement was the occasional visits of the circuit judges to the local courthouse.[9] In 1756 Adams signed up for the usual legal apprenticeship. His master was James Putnam, a Worcester attorney.

Life with Putnam was not all roses. Adams would later lament that "[n]ow I feel the Disadvantages of Putnams Insociability, and neglect of me. Had he given me now and then a few Hints concerning Practice, I should be able to judge better at this Hour than I can now."[10] Nevertheless, Putnam had a good library. It was, according to Adams, "not large: but he had all the most essential Law Books: immediately after I entered with him however he sent to England for a handsome Addition of Law Books and for Lord Bacons Works."[11] And Adams read. By his contemporary account he did, while at Worcester, read "Wood. Coke. 2 Vols. Lillies Ab[ridgemen]t. 2 Vols. Salk[eld's] Rep[orts]. Swinburne. Hawkins Pleas of the Crown. Fortescue. Fitzgibbons. Ten Volumes in folio I read, at Worcester, quite thro—besides Octavos and Lesser Volumes, and many others of all sizes that I consulted occasionally, without Reading in Course as Dictionaries, Reporters, Entries, and Abridgements, Etc."[12]

On completion of his Worcester apprenticeship, Adams returned to his native Braintree to seek his fortune in law practice. But he had a problem. His primary need was to gain admission to the Suffolk bar, and that would require being put forward by some influential Boston lawyers. What to do? His first act, the day after arriving from Worcester, was to go to the Harvard College Library and take out "Justinians Institutions with Arnold Vinnius's Notes."[13] Why? "I shall gain the Consideration and perhaps favour of Mr. Gridley and Mr. Pratt [patriarchs of the Boston bar] by this means."[14]

He was not far from the mark. In Adams' fateful call on Gridley three weeks later, to obtain Gridley's crucial support for his bar application, Gridley cross-examined him on his education, emphasizing the need to study the "civil Law, and natural Law, and Admiralty Law."[15] Adams particularly recalled being asked if he had read Grotius and Pufendorf, whom Gridley described as "great writers."[16] Adams had to make lame excuses. "I cannot say I have Sir. Mr. Putnam read them, when I was with him, and as his Book lay on the Desk in the office for the most part when he had it not in his hand, I had generally followed him in a cursory manner, so that I had some very imperfect Idea of their Contents. . . ."[17] "[B]ut," Adams hastily added, it was his "intention to read them both as soon as possible."

Fortunately, because of his cram efforts with Vinnius on his arrival from Worcester, Adams was better able to answer another question. What, Gridley inquired, had Adams "lately read" in Latin? Adams answered proudly, "Cicero's Orations and Epistles, and the last Latin I read was Justinians Institute with Vinnius's Notes."[18] Gridley, at that point, took Adams to his library and lent Adams a copy of Van Muyden's *Compendiosa Institutionum Justinian Tractatio In Usum Collegiorum.*[19] In Gridley's opinion this text was better for Adams, Vinnius being "a Commentator more suitable for Persons, of more advanced Age and longer research, than yours."[20] Adams recalled, years later, how he was utterly dumbfounded by Gridley's "handsome library of the civil and Cannon Laws and Writers in the Law of Nature and Nations."

Adams next dutifully called on Benjamin Pratt and James Otis. They also cross-examined Adams on his classical training and asked him why he had omitted being sworn in the Worcester Inferior Pleas Court and had failed to get the usual letter of recommendation from Putnam.[21] But, nevertheless, "Mr. Otis received me more like a Brother than a father, and began to descant on Homer and Horace and Latin and Greek Prosody."[22]

As a result of his efforts Adams was routinely sworn in at the Suffolk bar on 6 November 1758. He had no formal legal education and only a two years' apprenticeship in the countryside.[23] But he could talk about Cicero. As Gridley put it to the Court, on moving Adams' application, "I take it he is qualified to study the Law by his scholarship. . . ."[24]

So Cicero and Justinian helped Adams get sworn at the bar. But what practical use did civilian learning—the civil law jurisprudence of the neoclassicists and the European Enlightenment—have in Braintree or Boston in 1758? Was it just an elite affectation? Or was it a device for restricting practice to an educated few and controlling the "pettyfogger" competition? Could it have influenced, in any demonstrable way, the fundamental jurisprudence of important colonial lawyers such as Adams?

One thing is certain. The civil law and Roman law books were here, and in surprising numbers. Recent research by Herbert Johnson and others has clearly established that.[25] But, as Maxwell Bloomfield has recently queried, were these books really read?[26] Did the serious study of contintental jurisprudence and civilian learning predate the Revolution? Was it part of the Revolution's background, or was it a result of the Revolution? Or both? Was it applied in practice? Any kind of complete answer is far beyond the scope of this paper, but, fortunately, the tireless labors of the editors of the *Adams Papers*, particularly the editors of *The Legal Papers of John Adams*, Kinvin Wroth and Hiller Zobel, and the editors of the first two volumes of the *Papers of John Adams*,[27] together with the work of Julius Goebel, Jr. on *The Law Practice of Alexander Hamilton*[28] have begun to shed some light on these problems. Most particularly, we now can know more about the application of civilian learning in early American legal practice and the influence of neoclassicism on the self-image of the legal profession.[29]

Again, I intend to concentrate solely on the legal career of John Adams from 1758 to 1775. Why? I certainly do not intend to imply that Adams was a typical lawyer of the period, or that anything that was true of his knowledge, his legal education, or his practice was necessarily true for anyone else. But Adams was in at the beginning of a formal structure for the Suffolk County bar in 1770 and at the initiation of requirements for legal education in Massachusetts. His extraordinary papers give us a "candid" view of the pre-revolutionary legal elite that he knew intimately and whose values he shared. Furthermore, the scope and nature of Adams' legal learning are just plain interesting. Adams was the man sent in 1784 to negotiate the crucial five million guilder loan from the Dutch bankers in the dark hours for America.[30] What did he know about the civil law of Europe?

II. Young John Adams and His "Pick Ax": Early Legal Training (1756-1761)

The young Adams frequently felt sorry for himself. This was particularly so when his first writ was abated, a crisis for any adolescent attorney. He lamented: "[I]t is my Destiny to dig Treasures with my own fingers. No Body will lend me or sell me a Pick axe."[31] And, to an astonishing degree, Adams really was self-taught.

Adams' *Diary* indicates almost exactly what he read in the period from 1756 to 1758 in Worcester and in the period from 1758 to 1760 in Braintree.[32] During the earlier period Adams was technically a student and apprentice, but Putnam was an indifferent teacher.[33] During the later period Adams was technically a full-fledged practitioner, but, in fact, business was slow starting. Under the informal tutelage of Jeremiah Gridley, a great teacher, Adams filled the empty hours between clients with an extensive course of study.

There was quite a difference between the books read in Worcester, which were largely common law classics and abridgements, and Adams' Braintree reading under Gridley's influence. In Adams' words: "I have read no small Number of Volumes, upon the Law, the last 2 Years [1758-1760]. Justinians Institutes I have read, thro, in Latin with Vinnius's perpetual Notes, Van Muydens Tractatio Institutionum Justiniani, I read thro, and translated, mostly into English, from the same Language. Woods Institute of the Civil Law, I read thro. These on the civil Law; on the Law of England I read Cowells Institute of the Laws of England, in Imitation of Justinian, Dr. and Student, Finch's Discourse of Law, Hales History, and some Reporters, Cases in Chancery, Andrews Etc. besides occasional searches for Business. Also a general Treatise of naval Trade and Commerce, as founded on the Laws and Statutes."[34]

This is quite a list, with a strong civilian flavor. In particular, not only was there a heavy emphasis on Roman Law, but Dr. Cowell's *Institutes of the Laws of England* exposed Adams to England's leading civilian propagandist.[35] Cowell's *Institutes* laid out the entire English common law on the framework of Justinian's *Institutes*.[36] Furthermore, St. Germain's *Doctor and Student*, Mathew Hale's *History of the Common Law of England*, and the "general Treatise of the naval Trade," almost certainly Charles Molloy's *De Jure Maritime et Navali*, incorporated many references to civil and canon law.[37]

But did Adams really absorb this learning? By his own account, "All this series of Reading, has left but faint Impressions, and [a] very Imperfect system of Law in my Head."[38] First, Adams doubted his own grasp of common law principles. "I must form a serious Resolution of beginning and pursuing quite thro, the Plans of my Lords Hale, and Reeve. Woods Inst[itutes] of common Law I never read but once, and my Ld. Coke's Com[mentary] on Lit[tleton] I never read but once. These two Authors I must get, and read, over and over again. And I will get em too, and break thro, as Mr. Gridley expressed it, all obstructions."[39] Gridley clearly would have made a great football coach!

Adams was equally concerned about his civilian learning. "Besides, I am but a Novice in natural Law and civil Law. There are multitudes of excellent Authors, on natural Law, that I have never read, indeed I never read any Part of the best authors, Pufendorf and Grotius."[40] This is consistent with Adams' awkward admission to Gridley, during Adams' interview for the bar, that he hadn't really read Grotius or Pufendorf.[41] "In the Civil Law, there are Hoppius, and Vinnius, Commentators on Justinian, Domat, Etc. besides Institutes of Cannon and feudal Law, that I have to read." Adams concluded by vowing, "Thus let me, every night before I go to bed, write down [in my diary] what Book of Law, I have read."[42] Alas, the next entry reads, "I have not read one Word of Law, this Day."[43] Was it the distraction of Hannah Quincy again?

In addition to the listed volumes, Adams' *Diary* indicates that, during the 1759 to 1760 period, he did further reading in the Enlightenment authors, particularly Montesquieu's *Spirit of the Laws*,[44] and in 1761 Adams did indeed carry out his resolve to read canon law. "I borrowed of Mr. Gridley, the second Volume of the Corpus Iuris Canonici Notis illustratum. Gregorii 13 Iussi editum. . . . Mr. Gridley about 15 months since, advised me to read an Institute of the Cannon Law—and that Advice lay broiling in my Head, till Last Week, when I borrowed the Book."[45]

But that canon law book was borrowed by a very prejudiced man. Adams remarked: "I am very glad, that he gave, and I took, the Advice, for it will explain many Things in Ecclesiastical History, and open that system of fraud, Bigotry, Nonsense, Impudence, and Superstition, on which the Papal Usurpations are founded, besides increasing my skill in the latin Tongue, and my Acquaintance with civil Law, for in many Respects the Cannon Law is grafted on the civil."[46] One might have hoped that, on actually reading the book, Adams would change his good Congregationalist mind-set. Alas, no. Two weeks later Adams remarked, "This Institute is a curious Monument of Priestly Ambition, Avarice and sublety. Tis a system of sacerdotal Guile."[47] As will be seen, Adams' "A Dissertation on the Canon and Feudal Law," written in 1765, reflected the same knee-jerk prejudice.

Was all of Adams' civilian reading a facade to conceal such preconceived views of the world? Fortunately, we have more concrete evidence of how much he learned. The most important evidence will be analyzed in Parts III, IV, and VI of this paper. That was Adams' actual application of canon and civil law authority in his legal practice and political writing.

6. John Adams (1735-1826) was an important colonial lawyer before becoming a statesman and ambassador of revolutionary America. He served as the second President of the United States. Etching by H. B. Hall, after a portrait by Gilbert Stuart. (*Courtesy of Art & Visual Materials, Special Collections Department, Harvard Law School Library.*)

And there is other evidence. In Adams' *Earliest Diary* there are his laborious notes on Justinian's *Institutes* 2.1.12 and 3.14.3 through 3.18.pr.[48] The notes are clearly based on the Van Muyden *Tractatio* . . . 3d ed. Utrecht, 1707. This book, again, was an abridgement of Justinian's *Institutes*, and almost certainly the copy lent to Adams by Gridley.[49] While these notes are hardly polished, they demonstrate serious effort. The editors of the *Earliest Diary*, doubtless in despair over Adams' "cramped" writing, allege that Adams, in abstracting and translating, "seems to have been satisfied at times with gibberish."[50] How true, but the notes bear a striking resemblance to my own painful efforts as a student of Roman law at Oxford, and, I am sure, the same could be said of countless other law students. Furthermore, as will be seen, Adams actually applied *Institutes* 2.1.12 in a famous case, *Doane* v. *Gage* (Court of Vice Admiralty 1768-1769),[51] and his understanding of the Roman *jus naturale* and *jus gentium* concepts in *Institutes* 2.1.12 and 3.14.3 *ff.* appears to have had a direct influence on his famous *Novanglus* letters.[52]

We also have Adams' student "Commonplace Book" and a fragment of his "Student Notes."[53] The "Notes" reveal that Adams was well aware of the passages in *Coke on Littleton*, folio 11b (E. Coke, *The First Part of the Institutes of the Lawes of England*, London, 1628), which set out the use of civil law in the ecclesiastical, Constable and Marshal, and Admiralty jurisdictions. There is also mention of the Laws of Oleron, the early sea laws, which would continue to fascinate Adams.[54] Questions over the proper choice of civil law in key jurisdictions, particularly in Admiralty, probate, and divorce cases, would later be a feature of Adams' law practice.[55] Adams' "Commonplace Book" also demonstrated a good knowledge of Roman contract and bailment principles, and had at least one reference to Christopher St. German, the pioneer of English comparative law studies.[56]

Adams' *Diary* itself contained crabbed passages that were evidence of painful agony over Wood's *New Institutes of the Imperial or Civil Law* and Van Muyden's *Tractatio*.[57] Again, the editors of the *Adams Papers* were not impressed with Adams' accuracy, suggesting that "the diarist's mind was not on his books when he made these memoranda, but was 'roving from Girls to friends' and other matters not closely related to law."[58] But there can be no doubt that Adams was actually *reading* the books. And, again speaking as one who has also studied the *Institutes* as examination set texts, it *is* agony. As Adams later recalled: "At this time October 1758 the Study of the Law was a dreary Ramble, in comparison of what it is at this day [1802]. The Name of Blackstone had not been heard, whose Commentaries together with Sullivans Lectures and Reeves's History of the Law, have smoothed the path of the Student, while the long Career of Lord Mansfield, his many investigations and Decisions . . . have greatly facilitated the Acquisition of it."[59]

Blackstone and Mansfield might "smooth the path" for law students, but in his later career, both legal and political, Adams found reason to distrust both. On several occasions he used the knowledge he had gained by a hard slog through original sources to contradict what Jefferson called "the honeyed Mansfieldism of Blackstone."[60] Indeed, in both "The Clarendon Letters" and "The Novanglus Letters," Adams attacked the principles of parliamentarianism that Blackstone held most dear.[61] Proximate to the "gibberish" so taxing to Adams' editors are also some gems of insights, most particularly that the ultimate justification of all law is human reason and that principles of government must be adapted to new conditions.[62]

Adams had some rivals in this early period, and he was terribly sensitive about competition. One was Robert Treat Paine. "Bob Paine is conceited and pretends to more Knowledge and Genius than he has."[63] Adams once told Paine that he, Adams, was reading Vinnius, a "Dutch Commentator" on the *Institutes.* Paine was not suitably impressed and retorted, "Vinnius . . . you cant understand one Page of Vinnius."[64] Adams did not take this lightly. "He must know that human Nature is disgusted with such incomplaisant Behaviour. Besides he has no Right to say I dont understand every Word in Vinnius . . . for he knows nothing of me."[65] Both Adams' law practice and his political writing will demonstrate that he did understand a little Vinnius and perhaps even more Van Muyden.[66]

Adams had another rival, Peter Chardon. "He has a sense of the Dignity and Importance of his Profession, that of the Law. . . . He talks of exulting in an unlimited field of natural, civil, and common Law. . . . This fellows Thoughts are not employed on Songs and Girls. . . . He will make something."[67] Adams wanted to be like him, "exulting in an unlimited field of natural, civil, and common Law" and filled with the dignity and importance of being a lawyer.

III. The Sodalitas Club: The Intellectual Elite at the Pre-Revolutionary Boston Bar (1761-1765)

"Last Monday [prior to 8 January 1761], had a passionate Wrangle, with Eb Thayer, before Major Crosby. He called me a *petty* Lawyer. This I [Adams] resented."[68] And so he should. Adams was making steady progress at the bar by 1761. In November 1761 he was "admitted an attorney in the Superior Court," the highest step then available.[69] In 1762 as a result of Chief Justice Thomas Hutchinson's desire "to add dignity to the proceedings of that [the Superior] Court, all members of its bar were formally called as barristers at the August term."[70] "Adams was among those who thereafter appeared in 'Gowns and Bands and Tye Wiggs.'"[71]

Great was the difference that Adams perceived between his bewigged self and "petty Lawyers." Indeed, the period of Adams' first success corresponded with a new offensive, at least in his diary, attacking his more "base" rivals. "Looking about me in the Country, I found the practice of Law was grasped into the hands of Deputy Sheriffs, Petty-foggers and even Constables, who filled all the Writts upon Bonds, promissory notes and Accounts, received the Fees established for Lawyers and stirred up many unnecessary Suits. I mentioned these Things to some of the Gentlemen in Boston, who disapproved and even resented them very highly. I asked them whether some measures might not be agreed upon at the Bar and sanctioned by the Court, which might remedy the Evil?"[72]

The answer, even in 1761, was the "Association" and "the Club." Civilized professional men could join together and set down the standards of decent behavior and practice. "A Meeting was called and a great Number of regulations proposed not only for confirming the practice of Law to those who were educated to it and sworn to fidelity in it, but to introduce more regularity, Urbanity, Candour and Politeness as well as honor, Equity and Humanity, among the regular Professors. Many of these Meetings were the most delightfull Entertainments, I ever enjoyed. The Spirit that reigned was that of Solid Sense, Generosity, Honor and Integrity: and the Consequences were most happy, for the Courts and the Bar instead of Scenes of Wrangling, Chicanery, Quibbling and ill manners, were soon converted to order, Decency, Truth and Candor."[73] When Adams' colleague and Gridley's friend, Benjamin Prat, rode away to New York in November of 1761, "to take his Seat as Chief Justice of that State," his final words to his comrades were "Brethren above all things forsake not the Assembling of yourselves together."[74]

But there were Clubs and, then, there were *Clubs*. On 24 January 1765 Adams was approached in court by Samuel Fitch. The news was electrifying: "[T] hat Mr. Gridley and he had something to communicate to me, that I should like, in Sacred Confidence however."[75] Adams went to Gridley's office "after many Conjectures what the secret might be" and heard the news:

> That He and Mr. Fitch had proposed a Law Clubb—a private Association, for the study of Law and oratory.—As to the Bar, he thought of them, as he did think of them—Otis, Thatcher, Auchmuty. He was considering, who was for the future to support the Honour and Dignity of the Bar. And he was determined to bring me into Practice, the first Practice, and Fitch too. He could easily do it, by recommending. And he was very desirous of forming a Junto, a small sodality, of himself and Fitch and me, and Dudley if he pleased might come, in order to read in Concert the Feudal Law and Tullies orations. And for this Purpose he lent me, the Corpus Juris Civilis in 4 Partes distinctum, eruditissimis Dionysii Gothofredi J.C. clarissimi notis illustratum, at the End of which are the Feudorum Consuetudines Partim ex Editione vulgata partim ex Cujaciana vulgata, appositae, as also the Epitome Feudorum Dionysio Gothofredo Authore.[76]

The Club was called the "Sodalitas, A Clubb of Friends." Adams was thrilled. Regular meetings were arranged; reading projects were designed, with a heavy emphasis on legal classics:

> We accordingly agreed to meet the next Evening [10 January 1765?] in one of Ballards back Chambers and determine upon Times, Places, and studies. We accordingly met the next Evening, Mr. Gridley, Fitch and I, and spent the whole Evening. Proposals were to read a Reign and the statutes of that Reign, to read Hurds Dialogues and any new Pieces. But at last we determined to read The Feudal Law and Cicero only, least we should loose sight of our main Object, by attending to too many. Thursday Nights were agreed on, and to meet first at Mr. Gridleys office. There we accordingly met on the Thurdsday Night [17 January 1765] following, and suffered our Conversation to ramble upon Hurds Dialogues, the Pandects, their Discovery in Italy by Lotharius in 1127, in the Reign of Stephen, upon Lambard de priscis Anglorum Legibus, in Saxon and Latin, upon Ld. Kaims [Kames], Mr. Blackstone &c. But we agreed to meet the next Thursday night at Mr. Fitch's, and to read the Three first Titles of the feudal Law, and Tullies oration for Milo.[77]

The next meeting was at Samuel Fitch's on 24 January 1765. "We read the 3 first Titles of the feudal Law, and We read Gothofreds Notes and We looked into Strykius for the Explanation of many hard Words in those 3 Titles—The Valvasors, Capitanii, Guardia and Guastaldi. This Strykius wrote an Examen Juris feudalis, by Way of Question and Answer. His account of the original of the Consuetudines Feudorum is, that they were collected and written by Gerardus Niger, and Obertus, the Consulls of Milan.—We read also Part of Tully's Milo—and are to read the 4th. and 5th Title of The Feudal Law, and the rest of that oration next Thurdsday night [31 January 1765]."[78]

Adams was in seventh heaven. "I expect the greatest Pleasure from this sodality, that I ever had in my Life—and a Pleasure too, that will not be painfull to my Reflections."[79] How unlike his memories of other "Pleasures," particularly with Hannah Quincy![80] Adams missed the next Sodalitas meeting at Joseph

Dudley's on 31 January 1765,[81] but the following meeting, on 21 February 1765, was his turn to be host. He entertained the Club "at Blodgets":

> We were never in better Spirits, or more Social. We began the 13th. Title of the feudal Law De Alienatione Feudi and read three Titles. Gridley proposed that we should mark all those Passages, which are adopted by the English Law, that when we come to read Ld. Coke we may recur back upon Occasion, to the originals of our Law.[82]

This was an important meeting in the development of Adams' political thought and jurisprudence. The topic of conversation was the feudal system, and Adams had brought up Rosseau's hostility to feudal institutions. This sparked a lively analysis of the merits and defects of feudalism.[83] Later, in writing "A Dissertation on the Canon and Feudal Law," Adams would reflect on this conversation and recall the writing of Strykius on the *ius gentium* and the function of the feudal law as a component of the *ius gentium.*[84] In Adams' opinion there was no "absurdity" in the institutions of the feudal law taken by themselves. At certain times such institutions had served a necessary purpose. It was the survival of these laws and institutions into different times and conditions which made them unjustifiable. Laws and institutions, Adams reflected, must continue to justify themselves, by reason or consensus, or they become oppressive.[85]

Gridley returned the conversation to self-improvement by producing "a Book intituled in Herennium Commentarius, as an Introduction to Tully De Oratore":

> *Gridley.* Our Plan must be, when we have finished the feudal Law, to read Coke Littleton, and after him a Reign and the Statutes of that Reign. It should also be a Part of our Plan, to improve ourselves in Writing, by reading carefully the best English Writers, and by Using ourselves to writing—for it should be a part of our Plan to publish Pieces, now and then. Let us form our Style upon the Ancients, and the best English Authors.[86]

Adams concluded: "I hope and expect to see, at the Bar, in Consequence of this Sodality, a Purity, an Elegance, and a Spirit, surpassing any Thing that ever appeared in America. Fich [Fitch] said that he would not say he had Abilities, but he would say he had Ambition enough to hope for the same Thing."[87]

Ironically, this is the last account of the Sodalitas in Adams' *Diary.* Gridley died shortly thereafter, in 1767, as did Joseph Dudley, the same year at the age of only thirty-five.[88] Samuel Fitch and Adams alone survived. Fitch chose royal preferment as Advocate General in Admiralty from 1770 to 1776, and as Solicitor to the notorious American Board of Customs Commissioners.[89] In 1776 Fitch sailed to Halifax and then to England.[90] Adams took the other fork in the way and became President of the United States.

IV. Dead Whales, Smuggled Madeira, and Applied Civilian Learning in Adams' Legal Practice (1766-1774)

After the question of whether a lawyer like Adams ever read his civil law books, the next logical question is whether they ever did him any good.

Of course, there are many conceivable ways such legal learning might do a lawyer like Adams some "good." It might be of direct help in his practice, with immediate application to certain kinds of legal problems. Or it could assist in his definition of himself as a professional, or in his conception of what should characterize the best features of any lawyer or association of lawyers. Or it could influence his fundamental *ideas* about the operation of the legal system, such as his ideas about the ways in which law and lawyers ought to relate to political society as a whole. The latter I will call "legal ideology."

Regrettably, even with the splendid edition of the *Legal Papers of John Adams,* we still do not know as much about Adams' legal Ideas as we would like.[91] But we do know something. The obvious place to start would be to see if there was any evidence that Adams' study of Roman or Enlightenment civilian sources had a direct application in his law practice.

In England, as Adams carefully noted in his "Student Notes," civil law was applied "in certain Cases, not only in Courts Ecclesiastical, but in the Court of the Constable and Marshal, and of the Admiralty."[92] There is clear evidence that he read, in his travails with *Coke upon Littleton*, the famous section defining—perhaps a bit narrowly—the scope of civil law authority in English Courts.[93] He must have been at least aware of the existence of Doctors' Commons in London—the last stronghold of English civilian practice.[94] Was civil law applied in Massachusetts in analogous cases? Did Adams at least attempt it? The first sensible places to look would be the Admiralty cases, as well as any cases touching on the traditional ecclesiastical jurisdictions of domestic law and non-realty probate.[95]

A. The Case of the Whale: *Doane* v. *Gage* (1766-1769)[96]

The colonial vice-admiralty courts were "primarily to provide a forum for enforcement of the Acts of Trade and Navigation, with which England sought to control colonial commerce for the benefit of the Mother Country."[97] Most admiralty cases in Adams' Massachusetts were smuggling and revenue cases. But Adams did have one classic civil jurisdiction (i.e. non-revenue or non-criminal) admiralty case, *Doane* v. *Gage*, the "Case of the Whale."

This was a truly fabulous squabble over which whale ship was entitled to a dead whale. The whale had been hit by a harpoon from a boat launched by a ship captained by Adams' client, a Captain Doane. The whale, quite sensibly, took off for the bottom. At some later point he returned to the surface and was hit by another harpoon. This harpoon came from a boat launched by a rival ship, commanded by a Captain Gage. At some other point—either before or after Gage's "iron" hit—Doane's boat's line came free. Under the custom of the whalers, a whale "belonged" to the boat that first struck it, even if another struck it later, *if* the first harpoon's line was attached to its boat at the time of the second hit. But "if the whale became 'loose' without having been struck a second time," the new harpoon gained full possession.[98]

So the key issue was simply whether Doane's boat was attached to the whale when Gage struck it, or whether the whale was a "loose" whale. No less than seventy-four witnesses, thirty-four for Doane and forty for Gage, would testify. John Adams represented Captain Doane and Robert Treat Paine and James Otis represented Captain Gage.[99] Never was a dead whale given such posthumous dignity. He was fought over by seventy-four eyewitnesses, two signers of the Declaration of Independence—one a future President of the United States—and the great James Otis!

For this case Adams prepared a truly remarkable "Notes of Authorities," with lengthy quotations on ownership of wild animals from Grotius' *De Jure Belli ac Pacis* and Justinian's *Institutes*. Adams' key point—rather contrary to the whalers' custom—was that once a wild animal was acquired by possession (presumably by being hit with his client's harpoon) that "Property acquired by Possession does not cease with the Loss of Possession." This proposition came directly from Grotius.[100] But Adams' notes contained a contrary rule from the Roman law sources themselves. "Ferae igitur Bestiae et Volucres, et Pisces, et omnia animalia, quae mari, Coelo, et Terra nascuntur: simulatque ab aliquo capta fuerint, jure gentium, statirn illius esse incipiunt. Quod enim ante nullius est, id, naturali Ratione, occupanti conceditur." "Wild animals, birds, and fish, that is to say all the creatures which the land, the sea, and the sky produce, as soon as they are caught by any one become at once the property of their captor by the law of nations; for natural reason admits the title of the first occupant to that which previously had no owner."[101] (Justinian's *Institutes*, 2:1:12). But the *Institutes* add: "[c] um vero tuam evaserit Custodiam, et in Libertatem naturalem sese receperit, tuum esse definit, et rursus occupantis fit," "An animal thus caught by you is deemed your property so long as it is completely under your control; but so soon as it has escaped from your control, and recovered its natural liberty, it ceases to be yours, and belongs to the first person who subsequently catches it."[102] This, of course, was a rule more in keeping with the whalers' custom.

Adams did not leave it there. He checked the *Institutes'* passage against the *Digest*, thus demonstrating both a degree of sophistication about the Roman law and access to a copy of the entire *Corpus Juris Civilis*. There he located the section *(Digest* 41:I:5) describing a controversy between Trebatius and Justinian's compilers. Trebatius was of the opinion that one who wounded a wild beast immediately became owner, and that "he must be held to retain the ownership so long as he kept on following the animal up, but that, if he relinquished the pursuit, his ownership ceased . . . so that if, at any moment while the pursuit lasted, some other person should capture it . . . he must be held to have committed a theft on the person first mentioned."[103] This was certainly a view which would appeal to Captain Doane. Justinian's compilers, however, indicated that "[a] good many authorities hold that the party does not become owner unless he captures it, because there is a considerable chance of the capture not being made; and this is a better view to take."[104] Here was a view that would surely appeal to Captain Gage!

Regrettably, no one seems to have recorded who won. There is only Paine's cryptic note on 27 October 1769, "Whale case finished."[105] Lengthy depositions survive, however, and they tend to indicate more concern with whalers' customs, such as "mateship," than with Roman law. There is no indication that Adams' classical learning was ever brought to bear. This result would have amused Herman Melville—who described the unwritten law of whaling as "a system which for terse comprehensiveness surpasses Justinian's Pandects and the By-laws of the Chinese Society for the Suppression of Meddling with other People's Business . . .

I. A Fast-Fish belongs to the party fast to it.

II. A Loose-Fish is fair game for anybody who can soonest catch it."[106]

But Adams certainly did get his Roman law books out for the case, and doubtless would have tried to see if the Court of Vice Admiralty would have listened to those arguments, even in Boston in 1768. This would have been particularly true if the Roman law had clearly cut his way. Equally significant, the lengthy testimony and depositions that definitely did take place were all in the form of written interrogatories, a civilian practice adopted "in deference to the civil law procedure followed in the High Court of Admiralty in England, or for convenience in a hearing four years after the event. . . . "[107]

B. The Case of John Hancock's Remarkable, Vanishing Madeira: Sewall v. Hancock (1768-1769)[108]

John Hancock, according to the sworn testimony of His Majesty's Commissioners of Customs, claimed that he could land wine from his vessel, the good sloop *Liberty*, without, alas! actually paying His Majesty's customs. The wine seemed to disappear between the point of arrival and the subsequent inspection by royal officers. This maneuver legally was known as "landing goods before entry."[109]

On 9 May 1768 the *Liberty* arrived at Boston from Madeira and made entry of "twenty-five pipes of madeira wine, upon which the duties were paid."[110] Cynics that they were, almost nobody in authority around the Boston waterfront took this declaration seriously. The case of the vanishing Madeira was on.

The revenue officers' problem was getting witnesses. It was not easy. To make a long story short, one Thomas Kir, a tidesman who at the time of the *Liberty*'s arrival had reported nothing, became willing to testify that he had been locked in the *Liberty*'s steerage while Hancock's men illegally unloaded wine. There was no corroborating testimony, as his fellow tidesmen were "variously reported as asleep or drunk."[111] But the Commissioners of Customs, with the help of the powerful H.M.S. *Romney*, seized the *Liberty* in Boston harbor.

Adams represented Hancock. A lengthy and complex case followed in the Court of Admiralty, "and a painfull Drudgery I had of his [Hancock's] cause":

> There were few days through the whole Winter, when I was not summoned to attend the Court of Admiralty. It seemed as if the Officers of the Crown were determined to examine the whole Town as Witnesses. Almost every day a fresh Witness was to be examined upon Interrogatories. They interrogated many of his [Hancock's] near Relations and most intimate Friends and threatened to summons his amiable and venerable Aunt, the Relict of his Uncle Thomas Hancock, who had left the greatest Part of his Fortune to him. I was thoroughly weary and disgusted with the Court, the Officers of the Crown, the Cause, and even with the tyrannical Bell that dongled me out of my House every Morning.[112]

The litigation featured the in-chamber examination and interrogatory procedure of the civil law, rather than common law procedures. Further, Adams at least twice employed extensive civilian authorities to advance his client's cause, and used them to illuminate two separate questions of legal principle. First,

Adams stated that "[w]e are here to be tryed by a Court of civil not of common Law."[113] This meant that "we are therefore to be tryed by the Rules of Evidence that we find in the civil Law, not by those that We find in the Common Law."[114] In the absence of a jury trial right at civil law, the civil law insisted on certain strenuous rules of proof. One such rule was:

> "The Number of Witnesses ought to be two at the least to make a full Proof, and these must be free from all Exceptions, Either as to their Persons or their Depositions. For the Testimony of a single Witness is of no Validity, tho the Person is of a great Character," &c. "For one Witness may mistake or lie, and be corrupted, and yet be consistent with himself, and so remain undiscovered; whereas two or three Witnesses may more easily be found in a Conspiracy by a prudent Judge if they are separately examined."

Adams quoted this key rule, which would destroy the Crown's single witness case, from Thomas Wood, *A New Institute of the Imperial, or Civil Law*, a book he had studied as a student.[115] Adams backed up this argument with an abundance of civilian authority, quoting the classic *Codex* maxim, "Simili modo sanximus, ut unius testimonium nemo Indicum, in quacunque causa facile patiatur admitti. Et nunc manifeste sanximus, ut unius omnino testis responsio non audiatur. . . . " *(Codex* 4:20:9:I). He also included some slightly inconsistent passages from the *Digest*, further sections from Wood's *New Institute of the Imperial, or Civil Law*, sections from Johannes Calvinus' *Lexicon Juridicum Juris Caesarei Simul et Canonici*, and references to the account of civil law procedures in Fortescue's *De Laudibus Legum Angliae.*[116]

Adams' second key argument was that in cases where the laws inflict specially severe penalties—as in the case of the smuggling laws invoked against Hancock—these laws should be strictly construed. For this argument he cited Jean Domat's *The Civil Law In Its Natural Order* (Strahan trans., 1722):

> Domat. V. I. Page 13. Preliminary Book. Tit. I. Sect. 2 N. 15. "The Laws which restrain our natural Liberty, such as those that forbid any Thing that is not in itself unlawfull or which derogate in any other manner from the general Law, the Laws which inflict Punishments for Crimes and offences, or Penalties in civil matters; those which prescribe certain Formalities; *the Laws which appear to have any Hardship in them"* &c. "are to be interpreted in such a manner, as not to be applied beyond what is clearly expressed in the Law," &c. "We ought to give to such Laws all the Temperament of Equity and Humanity, that they are capable of." Notae: "Interpretatione Legum Poenae molliendae sunt, potius quam asperendae. In Poenalibus Causis benignius interpretandum est. In levioribus Causis proniores at Lenitatem Judices esse debent, in gravioribus Poenis, Severitatem Legum, cum aliquo temperamemto benignitatio subsequi."[117]

The last three sentences, as the editors of the *Legal Papers* observed, are quoted from a note in Domat from *Digest* 48:19:42; 50:17:155; 48:19:11. Adams also cited again, for the same proposition, Wood's *A New Institute of the Imperial, or Civil Law.*[118]

Adams concluded his analysis with an eloquent plea. He held that the Admiralty judge, his erstwhile dining partner Robert Auchmuty, could not have "his cake and eating it too" by choosing the worst from the common and civil law systems, at his discretion:

> Shall We say that We are to be governed by some Rules of the common Law and some Rules of the civil Law, that the Judge at his Discretion shall choose out of each system such Rules as please him, and discard the rest. If so Misera Servitus est. Examinations of witnesses upon Interrogatories, are only by the Civil Law. Interrogatories are unknown at common Law, and Englishmen and common Lawyers have an aversion to them if not an Abhorrence of them. Shall We suffer under the odious Rules of the civil Law, and receive no advantage from the beneficial Rules of it? This, instead of favouring the Accused, would be favouring the Accuser, which is against the Maxims of both Laws.[119]

Adams' arguments were not, in the end, successful,[120] but his knowledge of civilian authorities was certainly used directly to the aid of his client, John Hancock, and to the preservation of Hancock's excellent, but remarkably elusive, Madeira wine.

C. Divorces, Wills, and Harpooned Officers of the Royal Navy: Applications of Civil Law in *Broadstreet* v. *Broadstreet* (1771-1774); Clap's Will (1767-1768); and *Rex* v. *Corbet* (1769)

Adams' application of civil law was not limited to spectacular or unusual cases. His background proved useful in ordinary will and divorce problems. A good example is *Broadstreet* v. *Broadstreet* (1771-1774).[121] Poor Abigail Fuller married Dr. Joseph Broadstreet in February 1770. Within a few months, Broadstreet was making not-so-loving statements, such as "'he was a damned fool for having of her and that he should rather have married a Negro if She had money!'"[122] Domestic bliss diminished.

Abigail eventually sought a divorce before the Governor and Council, who had jurisdiction under the *Province Act of 3 Nov. 1692,* c. 25.[123] Represented by Jonathan Sewall, and probably by Adams as well, Abigail sought a divorce *a mensa* ("from Bed and Board"—the equivalent of a separation and maintenance decree) and "'thereby be intitled to the separate and sole use and improvement of her own Estate for the maintenance of herself and Child.'" Joseph, represented by Josiah Quincy, Jr., denied Abigail's "libel"—the civil law writ—and alleged that "'dark and mercenary Enemies to his household'" had by "'insinuating arts [withdrawn] the affections of his Wife.'" Two justices of the peace were assigned to take testimony . . . , depositions were read and the parties heard.[124]

The critical issues were whether a separation should be ordered and whether alimony was due. Adams' notes, as carefully analyzed by the editors of the *Legal Papers,* make it clear that "the canon law, as applied in the ecclesiastical courts in England, was an important source of the Massachusetts law of divorce."[125] The key sources examined were a treatise by a distinguished English civilian, John Godolphin's *Repertorium Canonicum* (London, 3d ed., 1687), Richard Burn's famous *Ecclesiastical Law* (London, 2nd ed., 1767), and, again, Thomas Wood's *A New Institute of the Imperial, or Civil Law* (4th ed., 1730).[126] Abigail, incidentally, won. She got a separation, plus costs and 25 pounds sterling alimony a year.

The Governor and Council also sat as the Supreme Court of Probate.[127] *Clap's Will* (1767-1768) was a case about one Samuel Clap, who allegedly "had not been himself for the last year of his life."[128] The issue was whether Clap, during his last year, was capable of making a will which disinherited his eldest living son, William. Evidence was taken according to the procedure and form of civil law interrogatories. Adams, who appeared in defense of the will and Clap's sanity, referred in his case notes to William Nelson's *Lex Testamentaria* (London, 2d ed., 1724) and John Godolphin's *The Orphan's Legacy* (London, 4th ed., 1701), both basic civil law texts of Doctors' Commons.[129] Adams apparently relied on Godolphin's statement of presumptions in favor of sanity when "the testator is known to have intervals of lucidity, or if the will is 'wisely and orderly made.'"[130] He also referred to both Godolphin and another leading English civilian, Henry Swinburne, in making notes of the case of *Gardiner* v. *Purrington* (1763) in his *Diary.*[131] Swinburne's leading treatise, *A Treatise of Testaments and Last Wills, compiled out of the laws ecclesiastical, civil and canon . . .* (5th ed., 1728) was a great civilian text and was in Adams' law library.[132]

Even more striking examples of applied civilian learning were provided by Adams'cases on the criminal side of the Admiralty. The statute of 28 Hen. 8. c. 15 (1536) established a "criminal jurisdiction" for the Admiralty, encompassing various criminal offenses committed at sea. Provision was included for jury trial. During the days of Adams' practice in Massachusetts,such trials were held before a Special Court of the Admiralty under a commission issued on 14 January 1762.[133]

On 22 April 1769 the British warship, H.M. Frigate *Rose,* intercepted the brig *Pitt Packet* off Marblehead. The brig was boarded, apparently to press sailors. The crew hid in the forepeak, and, when confronted by the British lieutenant, Henry Panton, one sailor, Michael Corbet, drew back a harpoon and impaled the British officer, killing him instantly.[134] Lieutenant Panton is now in a King's Chapel, Boston, grave.

Adams, with James Otis, was hired to represent the seaman.[135] The key issue was whether the killing was justifiable homicide and, if so, was there any appropriate punishment at civil law. In his preparation for the case Adams scoured the civil law authorities on self-defense and provocation. Among the sources listed in his "notes of Authorities" and/or quoted in his "Argument and Report" are John Calvin's *Magnum*

Lexicon Juridicum, title "culpa" (Geneva, 1734); Jean Domat's *The Civil Law in its Natural Order: Together with the Public Law* (1st ed. Strahan trans., 1722); Thomas Wood's *A New Institute of the Imperial, or Civil Law* (3d ed., 1721); Robertus Maranta's *Praxis, sive de ordine judiciorum . . . vulgo speculum aureum et lumen advocatorum* (Cologne, 1614); and Andreas Gail's *Practicarum observationum tam ad processum judiciarum praesertim imperialis camerae quam causarum decisiones pertinentium* (Cologne, 1721).[136]

At trial, on 14 June 1769, Adams came prepared to argue that the homicide was a justified response to the threat presented by press gang officers to an innocent seaman, who only wished to stay with his ship:

> In these Circumstances what could he do? but defend himself, as he did? In these Circumstances what was his Duty? He had an undoubted Right, not merely to make a push at Lt. Panton, but to have darted an Harpoon, a dagger thro the Heart of every Man in the whole Gang.[137]

Adams invoked the *Codex*, 9:16:2, for the right to kill in self-defense. "'De eo, qui salutem suam defendit. Is qui *aggressorem* vel quemcunque alium, in dubio vitae discrimine constitutus occiderit, nullum ob id factum, calumniam metuere debet.'"[138] He also invoked the Scottish civil law authority, Barrington's *Observation upon the Statutes* (London, 2nd ed., 1766). "'By the Law of Scotland there is no such Thing as Man Slaughter, nor by the civil Law; and therefore a criminal indicted for Murder, under the Statute of Henry the Eighth, where the Judges proceed by the Rules of the civil Law, must either be found guilty of the Murder or acquitted.'"[139]

Furthermore, reasoned Adams, if the governing law was civil law, then the killing was punishable by death only if it were murder, there being no civil law death penalty for unjustifiable homicide without malice. The equivalent common law crime of manslaughter was more risky, as it might be argued that the seamen were not entitled to benefit of clergy before a Special Admiralty Court.[140] Adams also discovered a statute forbidding impressment of American seamen and moved for jury trial.[141]

The result was dramatic. Adams had only just begun his closing argument to the Special Court of Admiralty when, suddenly, Lieutenant Governor Hutchinson called for an adjournment. Four hours later the Special Court returned. A verdict of justifiable homicide was announced. The seamen were set free.[142]

D. Conclusion

There are many other examples of Adams' use of civil law authorities in his practice. In the bizarre criminal admiralty case, *Rex* v *Nickerson* (1772-1773), Adams invoked the *Codex*, Maranta, Domat, Gail, Wood, and Francis Bacon in a brilliant and successful defense against a charge of piracy. There he obtained an acquittal on the grounds that the evidence against his client was either wholly circumstantial, or inadmissible under the applicable civil law.[143] And there were cases on slavery, where Gridley cited the *Institutes*[144] and Adams cited Voltaire and Montesquieu.[145] There were also routine Admiralty revenue cases where Adams cited civilian sources.[146] A close examination of the record would find many more.[147]

True, some of Adams' accounts were nearly comic searches for authority. "I went upon the first Appeal that has been yet made and prosecuted before Judge Auchmuty, and as it is a new Thing the Judge has directed an Argument, and a Search of Books concerning the Nature of Appeals by the civil Law. I found Time to look into Calvins Lexicon Title Appellatio and Provocatio, and into Maranta, who has treated largely of Appeals. Borrowed Ayliff, but there is no Table and could find nothing about the Subject. Domat I could not find."[148]

At other times, Adams clearly evaded the issue of choice of law between common law and civil law jurisdictions. "I shall not enter into any enquiry, how far the Admiralty sessions in England, or a Special Court of Admiralty in America ought to proceed by the rules of civil law, though it is a question of immense importance to Americans."[149] But Adams certainly did employ his civil law books and his civilian learning in the "trenches" of active practice, and he employed them effectively. Of that there can be no doubt.

Notes

1. *Diary and Autobiography of John Adams*, L. H. Butterfield ed., 4 vols. (Cambridge, Mass., 1964), I, 45. (Hereafter cited as *Diary*.) The Diary is to be found in chapter 3, following these notes.

2. *Ibid.*, I, 63.
3. See W. Scott Van Alstyne, Jr., "The District Attorney—A Historical Puzzle," *Wisconsin Law Review*, CXXV (1952); Stephen Botein, "Cicero as Role Model for Early American Lawyers: A Case Study in Classical 'Influence,'" *Classical Journal*, LXXIII (1977-1978), 313; Peter Stein, "The Attraction of the Civil Law in Post-Revolutionary America," *Virginia Law Review*, LII (1966), 403; Herbert A. Johnson, *The Law Merchant and Negotiable Instruments in Colonial New York 1664 to 1730* (Chicago, 1963).
4. Cf. Charles P. Sherman, *Roman Law in the Modern World*, I (Boston, 1937), 344-413.
5. As to Adams' infatuation with Hannah Quincy, which occurred simultaneously with his first serious legal study, see *Diary*, I, 72-74. "And by Reason of my Inattention my mind is liable to be called off from Law, by a Girl. . . ." *Ibid.*, I, 72. See also below, page 380, note 80.
6. *Ibid.*, I, 44-45.
7. *Ibid.*, I, 137-138.
8. *Ibid.*, I, 44-46, 54. See the helpful biographical register of Adams' contemporaries in *Legal Papers of John Adams*, L. K. Wroth and H. B. Zobel, eds. (Cambridge, Mass., 1965), I, xcv-cxiv, (hereafter cited as *Legal Papers*) ; and the useful biographical list of lawyers practicing in Massachusetts in 1775 attached as Appendix IV to C. R. McKirdy's "Massachusetts *Lawyers* on the Eve of the American Revolution: The State of the Profession," above, 339-358.
9. See *Legal Papers*, I, ii-liii. "Moreover, amidst rural boredom, the law was hardly an arid study but the principal entertainment after church-going. . . ." *Ibid.*, liii. Braintree was hardly a "hot spot." As Adams wrote to his friend John Wentworth, "Here, no Idea of a Lady, of Diversions . . . or of Pleasure ever enters . . . Old Roman Lawyers, and dutch Commentators are my constant Companions." *The Earliest Diary of John Adams*, L. H. Butterfield, ed. (Cambridge, Mass., 1966), 64. (Hereafter cited as *Earliest Diary.)*
10. *Diary*, I, 63.
11. *Diary*, III, 264. Adams recalls that he brought with him to Worcester "Lord Bolingbrokes Study and Use of History, and his Patriot King," which made Putnam "so well pleased" that they were added to Putnam's book seller order. *Ibid.*, III, 264.
12. *Ibid.*, I,173.
13. *Diary* 1, 44. This was probably the Leyden 1730 edition. See *ibid.*, I,45, note 3.
14. *Ibid.*, I, 45.
15. *Ibid.*, I, 55.
16. *Ibid.*, III, 272.
17. *Ibid.*, III, 271-272. According to Adams' recollection in his *Autobiography*, he had been able to mention that he had read "Burlamaqui . . . and Heineccius in Turnbulls Translation, and Turnbulls Moral Phylosophy" as books "upon the Law of Nature and Nations." *Ibid.*, III, 271. There are substantial differences between the *Diary* and the *Autobiography* accounts of the meeting with Gridley. Cf. *ibid.*, I, 54-56; III, 270-272, but the emphasis on neoclassical learning was present in both accounts.
18. *Ibid.*, III, 271.
19. *Ibid.*, I, 56.
20. *Ibid.*, III, 271.
21. *Ibid.*, I, 56; III, 272-273.
22. *Ibid.*, III, 273.
23. This was not atypical, although the "normal" education of colonial lawyers could reward further study. Some were educated at the Inns of Court in London, if a gentleman's life in those institutions in the eighteenth century could be described as a "formal legal education." See W. Holdsworth, *A History of English Law* (London, 1938), XII; C. R. McKirdy, "Massachusetts Lawyers on the Eve of the American Revolution: The State of the Profession," Appendix IV, "Biographical Sketches of Lawyers Practicing in Massachusetts in 1775," above, 339-358. Very few Massachusetts lawyers were educated in the Inns of Court after 1733. See G. W. Gawalt, *The Promise of Power: The Emergence of the Legal Profession in Massachusetts, 1760-1840* (Westport, Conn., 1979), 31-32, note 17; E. A. Jones, *American Members of the Inns of Court* (London, 1924), xviii-xx.
24. *Diary*, I, 58. Gridley went on, "and that he has made a very considerable, a very great Proficiency in the Principles of the Law, and therefore that the Clients Interest may be safely intrusted in his Hands."
25. See H. A. Johnson, *Imported Eighteenth Century Law Treatises in American Libraries 1700-1799* (Knoxville, Tenn., 1978), xxiii-xxiv. (Hereafter cited as Johnson, *Law Treatises.)* As to the substantial collection of books on Roman and civil law in the early Harvard catalogue, see J. Quincy, *The History of Harvard University* (Cambridge, Mass., 1840), II, 424-425, 586; A. Sutherland, *The Law at Harvard* (Cambridge, Mass., 1967), 68. As a result of the bequest of a New Orleans practitioner, Samuel Livermore, in 1833, Harvard Law School received a "whole library of foreign law, consisting of the works of leading civilians . . . amounting in numbers to upwards of three hundred costly volumes." J. Quincy, *History*, II, 425. See also *ibid.*, I, 586. These books were actively used in a curriculum, as designed by Joseph Story and Nathan Dane, which emphasized "Law of Nature, the Law of Nations, Commercial and Maritime Law," II, 375. Quincy paid Story the compliment of describing him as an "eminent lawyer and civilian." *Ibid.*, II, 377. In 1917 Roman law was still required for an advanced law degree at Harvard. See *The Centennial History of the Harvard Law School, 1817-1917* (Boston, 1918), 77.
26. See M. Bloomfield, *Book Review, American Journal of Legal History*, xxv, 79 (1981). By 1756 the College of Philadelphia (now the University of Pennsylvania) was offering a course which included the "civil laws" and assigned Grotius' *De Jure Belli ac Pacis* and Pufendorf's *De jure Naturae et Gentium.* A-H Chroust, *The Rise of the Legal Profession in America* (Norman, Oklahoma, 1965), II, 176. See Johnson, *Law Treatises*, 27, 46. By 1763 both Grotius and Pufendorf were part of the fourth-year curriculum at King's College (Columbia). Johnson, *Law Treatises*, xxiv. But were they part of a professional legal education, or just thought of as treatises on ethics and philosophy? Much later, during the enthusiasm of the codification movement, anonymous writers

in the *North American Review* would state that "The common, civil, and customary law of Europe have each precisely the same force with us in this branch [the law merchant and maritime law]. . . . [O]ur courts study them all, and adopt from them whatever is most applicable to our situation, and whatever is on the whole just and expedient, without considering either course obligatory. . . . In fact, all eminent lawyers in this country sooner or later find it necessary to study the law books of the continent. . . . [T]he continental law ought to be made an important, it might also be said the most important, branch of elementary legal education." Anonymous, *North American Review*, XL (October 1820), 412; *North American Review*, XXI (October 1825), 387-388; quoted in Chroust, *Rise of Legal Profession*, II, 55-56. "In our courts of justice the writings of the [French] civilians are referred to freely and fearlessly. The Institutes of Justinian and the commercial treatises of Pothier, Emerigon and Roccus are naturalized among us." Anonymous, *North American Review*, XXI (October 1825), 387-388, quoted in Chroust, *Rise of Legal Profession*, II, 55. As to the practical reality of these statements, which is more doubtful, see Peter Stein's article "The Attraction of Civil Law in Post Revolutionary America," *Virginia Law Review*, LII (1966), 403, and A. W. B. Simpson's "The Rise and Fall of the Legal Treatise Legal Principles and the Form of Legal Literature," *Chicago Law Review*, XLVIII (1981), 632. See also Alan Watson's illuminating *The Making of the Civil Law* (Cambridge, Mass., 1981), 27-38.

27. *Papers of John Adams*, R. J. Taylor, M. Kline, G. L. Lint, eds. (Cambridge, Mass., 1977). (Hereafter cited as *Papers.*)

28. See *The Law Practice of Alexander Hamilton*, J. Goebel, Jr., ed., 2 vols. (New York, 1964, 1969). (Hereafter cited as *Law Practice.*)

29. Hamilton was "profoundly" learned in the law, and this included "basic Roman law texts" and contemporary civilian sources. See *Law Practice*, 1, 6-7. Goebel's edition of Hamilton's legal papers provides detailed evidence of how European civil law sources were used in maritime and law merchant cases during the early eighteenth century in New York. *Ibid.*, II, 48-231. These papers also show that questions of "incorporation," *ibid.*, II, 20-21, and "universal principles of custom," *ibid.*, II, 1-28, were very much afoot, encouraged by the rapid expansion of New York trade from 1775 to 1800. There were regular citations to the civilian law merchant treatises, *ibid.*, II, 215, 428, and to French law, *ibid.*, II, 224-227. This evidence backs up other contemporary documents stressing the value of civil law as it pertains to *ius gentium*, including the lectures of President Stiles at Yale in 1777 on Montesquieu, Vattel, Pufendorf, and "modern continental civil law." See *The Literary Diary of Ezra Stiles*, Dexter, ed. (New York, 1901), 166-168. See also the lectures by Justice James Wilson in Philadelphia in 1790. *The Works of James Wilson*, R. C. McCloskey, ed. (Cambridge, Mass., 1967), I, 76, 85, 149-150, 257, 279.

30. See *Diary*, III, 154.

31. *Diary*, I, 62-63, 64-65.

32. *Ibid.*, I, 173-174.

33. *Ibid.*, I, 63.

34. *Ibid.*, I, 173-174. As to Gridley's career and famous pupils, such as William Cushing, James Otis, Benjamin Pratt, and Oxenbridge Thacher, see *Legal Papers*, I, ci.

35. See D. R. Coquillette, "Legal Ideology and Incorporation I: The English Civilian Writers, 1523-1607," *Boston University Law Review*, LXI (1981), I, 71-81. (Hereafter cited as "Legal Ideology I.")

36. *Ibid.*, 71-73.

37. See D. R. Coquillette, "Legal Ideology and Incorporation II: Sir Thomas Ridley, Charles Molloy, and the Literary Battle for the Law Merchant, 1607-1676," *Boston University Law Review*, LXI (1981), 315, 363 ff. (Hereafter cited as "Legal Ideology II.") Molloy's treatise was present in Adams' library. See Johnson, *Law Treatises*, 40.

38. *Diary*, I, 174.

39. *Ibid.*

40. *Ibid.*

41. Cf. *ibid.*, III, 271-272.

42. *Ibid.*, I, 174.

43. *Ibid.*, 175.

44. See *ibid.*, 115-117, 142, 123, note 19. Adams referred to Montesquieu as "Secondat," that being the baron's family name. Adams owned Nugent's translation, "Second Edition corrected and considerably improved" (London, 1752), a copy of which is still in the family. *Ibid.*, 123, note 19.

45. lbid., 199.

46. *Ibid.*

47. *Ibid.*, 200.

48. *Earliest Diary*, 53-59.

49. *Ibid.*, 58, note 2. See the Illustration above, 365.

50. *Ibid.*, 58-59, note 2.

51. See *Legal Papers*, 11, 73 *ff.*

52. See below, 408-416.

53. *Legal Papers*, 1, 2 *ff.*

54. Adams enjoyed a chance to see the Island of Oleron, although from a distance, during his first trip to Europe. See *Diary*, II, 291.

55. See *Legal Papers*, II, 173 *ff.*, 275 *ff.*, 335 *ff.*; *Legal Papers*, I, 228-230, 245-247, 280-285.

56. See *ibid.*, 6, 7, 10, 11, 18, 24. As to St. German, see Coquillette, "Legal Ideology I," 39-49.

57. See *Diary*, I, 104-106.

58. *Ibid.*, 122, note 4.

59. *Diary* , III, 273-274.

60. See Richard B. Morris, "Legalism versus Revolutionary Doctrine in New England," in *Essays in the History of Early American Law*, D. Flaherty, ed. (Chapel Hill, N.C., 1969), 431. See also below, 415-416, note 5. Adams wrote that he "had a low Opinion of the Compilers, Abridgers, and Abstract makers. We had better draw science from its fountain in original Authors." *Diary*, I, 177. Nevertheless, Adams did find Wood's *New Institute of the Imperial or Civil Law* and Van Muyden's *Tractatio* to be useful. "Have this moment finished Woods new Institute of the Imperial or civil Law. It is a great Help in the study of Van Muyden and Justinian. I understand Wood much better for having read Van Muyden, and shall now understand Van Muyden much better for having read Wood." *Ibid.*, 103.

61. See below, 408-416.

62. Thus Adams wrote in his diary: "Law is human Reason. It governs all the Inhabitants of the Earth; the political and civil Laws of each Nation should be only the particular Cases, in which human Reason is applied." Adams continued: "Let me attend to the Principle of Government. The Laws of Britain, should be adapted to the Principle of the british Government, to the Climate of Britain, to the Soil, to its situation, as an Island, and its Extent, to the manner of living of the Natives as Merchants, Manufacturers and Husbandmen, to the Religion of the Inhabitants." *Diary*, I, 117.

63. *Ibid.*, 59. See Stephen T. Riley's fine essay "Robert Treat Paine and John Adams: A Colonial Rivalry" in *Sibley's Heir*, vol. 59, *Publications*, Colonial Society of Massachusetts (1982), 415-429.

64. *Diary*, I, 59.

65. *Ibid.* Robert Treat Paine became a signer of the Declaration of Independence, Attorney General of Massachusetts, and a Justice of the Supreme Judicial Court. See *Legal Papers*, I, cvi.

66. "[S]et down to Van Muyden in Earnest. His latin is easy, his deffinitions are pretty clear, and his Division of the subject, are judicious." *Diary*, I, 57.

67. *Ibid.*, 47. Peter Chardon died young in Barbadoes in 1766. See *ibid.*, 48, note 2.

68. *Diary*, 1, 189 (emphasis added).

69. *Legal Papers*, I, lviii, *Diary*, I, 224.

70. *Legal Papers*, I, lviii.

71. *Ibid.*; *Diary*, III, 276.

72. *Diary*, III, 274.

73. *Ibid.*

74. *Ibid.* As to Benjamin Pratt (1711-1763) see *Legal Papers*, I, cvi.

75. *Diary*, I, 251.

76. *Ibid.*

77. *Ibid.*, 251-252. Adams' copy of Richard Hurd's *Moral and Political Dialogues* (3d. ed., London, 1765) is in the Boston Public Library. At one point Hurd describes the kind of person who is "[i]n a word, both in mind and person the furthest in the world from any thing that is handsome, gentlemenlike, or of use and acceptance in good company!" Besides this description, Adams later wrote: "An exact description of a Dartmouth educated Schollar." *Ibid.*, 252, note 5.

78. *Ibid.*, 252-253.

79. *Ibid.*, 253.

80. Adams had bittersweet memories of Hannah. See *ibid.*, I, 72-74. Hannah married Bela Lincoln, not a happy match. *Ibid.*, 176-177.

81. Joseph Dudley (1732-1767) married Gridley's daughter. See *Legal Papers*, I, c.

82. *Diary*, I, 253.

83. *Ibid.*, 254.

84. See the full analysis of this debate in connection with Adams' "A Dissertation on the Canon and Feudal Law," below, 401-403.

85. *Diary*, I, 254-258.

86. *Ibid.*, 255. Gridley's suggestion that it "should be a part of our plan to publish Pieces, now and then . . ." may well have inspired Adams' "A Dissertation on the Canon and Feudal Law."

87. *Ibid.* The Sodalitas Club was not unique. In Boston many lawyers certainly dined together during this period as informal groups. These included James Otis (1725-1783), Robert Auchmuty (1723-1788), and Oxenbridge Thacher (1719-1765), who often ate with Adams, Gridley, and the others. Indeed Richard B. Morris lists them as members of the Sodalitas Club. See R.B. Morris, "Legalism versus Revolutionary Doctrine in New England," in *Essays in the History of Early American Law*, D.H. Flaherty, ed. (Chapel Hill, N.C., 1969), 425. Cf. Page Smith, *John Adams* (Garden City, N.Y., 1962), I, 77-78. Thacher died in 1765. Otis was a great patriot, but plagued by madness. He was killed by lightning in 1783. Auchmuty, like Fitch, became Advocate General in Admiralty and Judge of the Vice Admiralty Court, a post held by his father. He was a leading loyalist and fled to Halifax and England in 1776. See *Legal Papers*, I, xcvi.

In New York the prestigious "Moot" Club, copied from the famous afterdinner moot association at Gray's Inn, met regularly in the eighteenth century. So did New Jersey's Institutio Legalis. See A-H Chroust, *Rise of the Legal Profession*, II, 130, note I. The descendants of these associations, the famous "library companies," such as the Library Company of Philadelphia (1802), and Boston's Social Law Library (1804), did much lasting practical good. *Ibid.*, 130, note 1.

88. *Legal Papers*, I, c. According to Adams' Autobiography the "little Clubb" met "once a Week," but for how long is unclear. Diary, III, 285. On Gridley's death, Adams characteristically wrote, "He was a great Admirer of Barbeyrac: thought him a much

more sensible and learned Man than Puffendorf. I admired the facility with which he translated and criticised the Greek Passages in the Notes." *Diary*, III, 286.

89. *Ibid.*, I, c.

90. *Ibid.*

91. See *Legal Papers*, I, xciii-xciv.

92. *Ibid.* 3.

93. See E. Coke, *The First Part of the Institutes of the Lawes of England* (London, 1628), *11b. Indeed, Adams' notes are a paraphrase, as the editors point out.

94. For a list of the standard scholarly sources on English civilian specialists, monopolies, and a brief description, see Coquillette, "Legal Ideology and Incorporation I," 19-22.

95. See *ibid.*, and Coquillette, "Ideology and Incorporation II," 346-363.

96. *Legal Papers*, II, 68-97 (Case No. 43).

97. Ibid., 68. See the excellent account by L. Kinvin Wroth, "The Massachusetts Vice Admiralty Court," in *Law and Authority in Colonial America: Selected Essays*, G. Billias, ed. (Barre, Mass., 1965), 32 *ff.* See also L. Kinvin Wroth, "The Massachusetts Vice Admiralty Court and the Federal Admiralty Jurisdiction," *American Journal of Legal History*, VI (1962), 250-268, 347-367.

98. *Legal Papers*, II, 71-72.

99. Ibid., 71.

100. Ibid., 73.

101. Ibid., 74, note 23.

102. Ibid., 73, 74, note 24.

103. Translation of *Digest* 41:1:5 from *De Adquirendo: Translation of Justinian's Digest, Book 14, Title* I, 3 (Cambridge, trans. C. H. Monro, 1900), set out in *Legal Papers*, II, 75, note 26.

104. Ibid.

105. Ibid., 73. The parties agreed to arbitration in April, 1769.

106. H. Melville, *Moby Dick* (1950 ed.), 393-394, quoted by the editors of the *Legal Papers*, II, 72, note 27.

107. *Legal Papers*, II, 72.

108. Case No. 46, Legal Papers, II, 173-210.

109. See *ibid.*, 174-177.

110. Ibid., 174.

111. *Ibid.*, 175. A riot had driven the commissioners to Castle William.

112. *Diary*, III, 306.

113. *Legal Papers*, II, 203. In another context Adams was not so sure. "But disregarding order, for the present let me record the Controversy We had last Week, Concerning the Rules of Law which were to govern this Case. The Court of Admiralty is originally a Civil Law Court. Jurisdiction of a Crime, is given to it in this Case by Act of Parliament. The Question is whether it is to proceed by the civil Law?" *Legal Papers*, II, 206. As to the early choice-of-law doctrine in the colonies, see William E. Nelson, "The American Revolution and the Emergence of Modern Doctrines of Federalism and Conflict of Laws," below, 419-467.

114. *Ibid.*, 203.

115. *Ibid.*, 206. As the editors of the *Legal Papers* alertly noticed, Adams omitted language from Wood making key exceptions from this rule: "unless he swears of his own Fact, and where there are other Circumstances to concur or corroborate, or unless he is a publick Officer; as a Notary, &c. deposing by Vertue of his Office. This is founded upon very good reason." Wood, *New Institute of the Civil Law*, 361 (2d ed. 1712). *Legal Papers*, II, 203, note 107.

116. See *Codex* 4:20:9:1; *Digest* 22:5:12; Thomas Wood, *New Institute of the Imperial, or Civil Law*; J. Calvinus, *Lexicon Juridicum Juris Caesarei Simul et Canonici* (Cologne ed., 1622), 905; J. Fortescue, *De Laudibus Legum Angliae* (London, 1741, ed.), 38. See also *Legal Papers*, II, 203-204, notes 109, 116, 117. As the editors of the *Legal Papers* observe, Fortescue was, ironically, "pointing to" the rule "as a defect in civil-law procedure." *Legal Papers*, II, 205, note 117.

117. Jean Domat, *The Civil Law in its Natural Order* (Strahan Trans., 1722), I:13-14, as set out in *Legal Papers*, II, 205.

118. T. Wood, *A New Institute of the Imperial, or Civil Law* (3d ed., 1721), 310. See *Legal Papers*, II, 205.

119. *Ibid.*, 207.

120. Robert Auchmuty's Interlocutory Decree (probably 1 March 1769), which rejected Adams' arguments, also referred extensively to the *Digest.* See *Legal Papers*, II, 207-209.

121. Case No.22, *Legal Papers*, I, 280-285.

122. *Ibid.*, 280.

123. *Ibid.*, 281, note 6. For an excellent discussion of the colonial Massachusetts law of divorce, see the editorial note at *ibid.*, 280-284.

124. *Ibid.*, 283.

125. *Ibid.*

126. *Ibid.*, 284-285. See W. Holdsworth, *History of English Law*, V (London, 3d ed., 1945), 12-15; *ibid.*, XII (1st ed., 1938), 425-427.

127. See *Legal Papers*, I, 245-247 for another excellent editorial note.

128. Case No.15, *ibid.*, 245-254.

129. *Ibid.*, 254. At least according to the editors of the *Legal Papers*, the notation by Adams "in a heavier hand" suggests that "these are authorities for his position." *Ibid.*, 254, note 17.
130. *Ibid.*, 254, note 20.
131. See *Diary*, I, 243-244. As to Henry Swinburne's distinguished career as an English civilian, see J. Duncan M. Derrett, *Henry Swinburne* (?1551-1624), *Civil Lawyer of York* (York, England, 1973), a useful piece for biography and bibliography.
132. See Johnson, *Law Treatises*, 52.
133. See "Editorial Note," Legal Papers, II, 275-276.
134. *Ibid.*, 276-279.
135. *Ibid.*, 278.
136. *Ibid.* 283 (Calvin) *ibid.*, 283, 326 (Domat); *ibid.*, 283, 326 (Wood); *ibid.*, 283, 329-330 (Maranta); *ibid.*, 330, note 118; *ibid.*, 283, 327-329 (Gail); *ibid.*, 328, note 116.
137. *Ibid.* 330-331. See also *ibid.*, 280.
138. *Ibid.* 326 (emphasis Adams'). "Of those who defend their own safety. He who, when in danger of his life, kills his aggressor or anyone else, should have no fear of prosecution on this account." *Ibid.*, 326-327, note 115.
139. *Ibid.* 334. Adams had a copy of Barrington's book in his library. See Johnson, *Law Treatises*, 5.
140. *Legal Papers*, II, 278-279, 331.
141. *Ibid.*, 278, 323-324.
142. *Ibid.*, 280. Later, Hutchinson would write that the Special Court believed the homicide to be justified. *Ibid.*, 280.
143. Case No. 57 (1772-1773), *ibid.*, 335-351. For the importance of Francis Bacon as a conduit for civilian learning into the common law, see D. R. Coquillette, "Legal Ideology I," 9-10.
144. *Slew* v. *Whipple*, Case No. 38 (1766), *ibid.*, 52-55 (Whether "Jenny Slew" was wrongfully kept in "Servitude as a Slave" by "John Whipple Jnr. of . . . Ipswich.").
145. *Newport* v. *Billing*, Case No. 39 (1768), *ibid.*, 55-57 (Plaintiff claims he was capable of bringing "Trespass and false Imprisonment" action, as he was "no slave but a freeman.").
146. *Ibid.*, 104.
147. See, for example, *ibid*, iii, 257-258, in the context of the famous case of *Rex* v. *Wemms* (Case No.64), the "Boston Massacre" case (1770).
148. *Diary*, II, 56, quoted in *Legal Papers*, II, 104.
149. *Ibid.*, III, 258, note 218.

Chapter 3

Experiences as a Law Student

1758

John Adams

John Adams (October 19, 1735 - July 4,1826), an important colonial lawyer, was a framer of the Declaration of Independence, the first Vice President and second President of the United States. These excerpts are taken from *Diary and Autobiography of John Adams*, edited by L. H. Butterfield, Leonard C. Faber, and Wendell D. Garrett, Volume I, *Diary, 1755-1770* (New York: Atheneum Press, 1964). The entries reprinted here are from the year 1758. Adams began his studies in 1756, although the diaries for the first two years are now known to exist after his entry for August 23, 1756. See also chapter 2.

Conscience and confirmed Piety. If I could but conform my Life and Conversation to my Speculations, I should be happy.—Have I hardiness enough to contend with omnipotence? Or have I cunning enough to elude infinite Wisdom, or Ingratitude enough to Spurn at infinit Goodness? The Scituation that I am in, and the Advantages that I enjoy, are thought to be the best for me by him who alone is a competent Judge of Fitness and Propriety. Shall I then complain? Oh Madness, Pride, Impiety.

15 Sunday.

If one Man or Being, out of pure Generosity, and without any Expectation of Returns, is about to confer any Favour or Emolument upon Another, he has a right and is at Liberty to choose in what manner, and by what means, to confer it. He may convey the Favour by his own Hand or by the Hand of his Servant, and the Obligation to Gratitude is equally strong upon the benefited Being. The mode of bestowing does not diminish the kindness, provided the Commodity or good is brought to us equally perfect and without our Expence. But on the other Hand, If our Being is the original Cause of Pain, Sorrow or Suffering to another, voluntarily and without provocation, it is injurious to that other, whatever means he might employ and whatever Circumstances the Conveyance of the Injury might be attended with. Thus we are equally obliged to the Supream Being for the Information he has given us of our Duty, whether by the Constitution of our Minds and Bodies or by a supernatural Revelation. For an instance of the latter let us take original sin. Some say that Adams sin was enough to damn the whole human Race, without any actual Crimes committed by any of them. Now this Guilt is brought upon them not by their own rashness and Indiscretion, not by their own Wickedness and Vice, but by the Supream Being. This Guilt brought upon us is a real Injury and Misfortune because it renders us worse than not to be, and therefore making us guilty upon account of Adams Delegation, or Representing all of us, is not in the least diminishing the Injury and Injustice but only changing the mode of conveyance.

22 Sunday.

Yesterday I compleated a Contract with Mr. Putnam, to study Law under his Inspection for two years.[1] I ought to begin with a Resolution to oblige and please him and his Lady in a particular Manner. I ought to endeavour to oblige and please every Body, but them in particular.

Necessity drove me to this Determination, but my Inclination I think was to preach. However that would not do. But I set out with firm Resolutions I think never to commit any meanness or injustice in the Practice of Law. The Study and Practice of Law, I am sure does not dissolve the obligations of morality or of Religion. And altho the Reason of my quitting Divinity was my Opinion concerning some disputed Points, I hope I shall not give Reason of offence to any in that Profession by imprudent Warmth. Heard Crawford upon the Love of God. The Obligation that is upon us to love God, he says, arises from the Instances of his Love and Goodness to us. He has given us an Existence and a Nature which renders us capable of enjoying Happiness and of suffering Misery. He has given us several senses and has furnished the World around us with a Variety of Objects proper to delight and entertain them. He has hung up in the Heavens over our Heads, and has spread in the Fields of Nature around about us, those glorious Shows and Appearances, by which our Eyes and our Imaginations are so extremely delighted. We are pleased with the Beautyful Appearance of the Flower, we are agreably entertaind with the Prospect of Forrests and Meadows, of verdant Field and mountains coverd with Flocks, we are thrown into a kind of transport and amazement when we behold the amazing concave of Heaven sprinkled and glittering with Starrs. He has also bestowed upon the Vegetable Species a fragrance, that can almost as [agreeably?] entertain our sense of smell. He has so wonderfully constituted the Air that by giving it a particular Kind of Vibration, it produces in us as intense sensation of Pleasure as the organs of our Bodies can bear, in all the Varieties of Harmony and Concord. But all the Provision [s] that he has [made?] for the Gratification of our senses, tho very engaging and unmerited Instances of goodness, are much inferior to the Provision, the wonderful Provision that he has made for the gratification of our nobler Powers of Intelligence and Reason. He has given us Reason, to find out the Truth, and the real Design and true End of our Existence, and has made all Endeavours to promote them agreable to our minds, and attended with a conscious pleasure and Complacency. On the Contrary he has made a different Course of Life, a Course of Impiety and Injustice, of Malevolence and Intemperance, appear Shocking and deformed to our first Reflections. And since it was necessary to make us liable to some Infirmities and Distempers of Body, he has plentifully stored the Bowells and the surface of the Earth with Minerals and Vegetables that are proper to defend us from some Deseases and to restore us to health from others. Besides the Powers of our Reason and Invention have enabled us to devize Engines and Instruments to take advantage of the Powers that we find in Nature to avert many Calamities that would other wise befall us, and to procure many Enjoyments and Pleasures that we could not other wise attain. He has connected the greatest Pleasure with the Discovery of Truth and made it our Interest to pursue with Eagerness these intense Pleasures. Have we not the greatest Reason then, yea is it not our indispensible Duty to return our sincere Love and Gratitude to this greatest, kindest and most profuse Benefactor. Would it not shew the deepest Baseness and most infamous Ingratitude to despize or to disregard a Being to whose inexhausted Beneficence we are so deeply indebted.

23 Monday.

Came to Mr. Putnams and began Law. And studied not very closely this Week.

29 Sunday: Braintree Octr. 5th. 1758.[2]

Yesterday arrived here from Worcester.[3] I am this Day about beginning Justinians Institutions with Arnold Vinnius's Notes. I took it out of the Library at Colledge.[4] It is intituled, D. Justiniani Sacratissimi Principis Institutionum sive Elementorum Libri quatuor, Notis perpetuis multo, quam hucusque, dilligentius illustrati, Cura & Studio, Arnoldi Vinnii J.C. Editio novissima priori Progressu Juris civilis Romani, Fragmentis XII. Tabularum & Rerum Nominumque Indice Auctior, ut ex Praefatione nostra patet.—Now I shall have an opportunity of judging of a dutch Commentator whom the Dedicat[ion] calls celeberrimus suâ Etate in hac Academiâ Doctor.—Let me read with Attention, Deliberation, Distinction. Let me admire with Knowledge. It is low to admire a Dutch Commentator m[erely] because he uses latin, and greek Phraseology. Let me be able to draw the True Character both of the Text of Justinian, and of the Notes of his Commentator, when I have finished the Book. Few of my Contemporary Beginners, in the Study of the Law, have the Resolution, to aim at much Knowledge in the Civil Law. Let me therefore distinguish my self from them, by the Study of the Civil Law, in its native languages, those of Greece and Rome. I shall gain the Consideration and perhaps favour of Mr. Gridley and Mr. Pratt by this means.[5]—As a stimulus let me insert in this Place Justinians Adhortationem ad Studium Juris. "Summa itaque ope et alacri Studio has Leges nostras accipite: et vosmet ipsos sic eruditos ostendite, ut Spes vos pulcherrima foveat, toto legitimo Opere perfecto, posse etiam nostram Rem publicam in Partibus ejus vobis credendis gubernari." Data Constantinopoli XI. Kalendas Decembris, Domino Justiniano, perpetuo Augusto tertium Consule.—Cic. I. deOrat-Pergite, ut facitis, Adolescentes, atque in id Studium in quo estis incumbite ut et vobis honori, et Amicis Utilitati, et Reipublicae emolumento esse possitis.—Arnoldus Vinnius in Academia Leidensi Juris Professor fuit celeberrimus.

I have read about 10 Pages in Justinian and Translated about 4 Pages into English. This is the whole of my Days Work. I have smoaked, chatted, trifled, loitered away this whole day almost. By much the greatest Part of this day has been spent, in unloading a Cart, in cutting oven Wood, in making and recruiting my own fire, in eating nuts and apples, in drinking Tea, cutting and smoaking Tobacco and in chatting with the Doctor's Wife[6] at their House and at this.[7] Chores, Chatt, Tobacco, Tea, Steal away Time. But I am resolved to translate Justinian and his Commentators Notes by day light and read Gilberts Tenures by Night till I am master of both, and I will meddle with no other Book in this Chamber on a Week day. On a Sunday I will read the Inquiry into the Nature of the human Soul, and for Amusement I will sometimes read Ovids Art of Love to Mrs. Savel.—This shall be my Method.—I have read Gilberts ist Section, of feuds, this evening but am not a Master of it.

Fryday. Oct. 6.

Rose about sun rise. Unpitched a Load of Hay. Translated 2 Leaves more of Justinian, and in the afternoon walked to Deacon Webbs, then round by the Mill Pond home. Smoaked a Pipe with Webb at the Drs. and am now about reading over again Gilberts section of feudal Tenures.

Saturday [7 October].

Read in Gilbert. Rode with Webb to Mr. Cranche's. Dined and drank Tea with him, and then home. Saturday night.

Sunday [8 October].

Read a few Leaves in Baxters Enquiry into the Nature of the human Soul. He has explaind with great Exactness, the Resistance, which Matter makes to any Change of its State or Condition, whether of motion or of Rest. The Vis Inertiae, the positive Inactivity of matter not barely its Inactivity, but its AntiActinty. For it not only is destitute of a Power of changing its state from Rest to motion or from motion to Rest, but it has the possitive Power, each single Particle has a Possitive Power of Resisting any force that attempts to change its state. But a leaden Ball, held between my fingers, as soon as I withdraw my fingers, will of itself for ought I see change its State from rest to motion and fall suddenly to the floor. This Phenomenon is not Vis Inertiac, 'tis by no Reluctance or Aversion to motion that it moves, but it seems to be a Tendency to motion, an Active Principle. If it is passive the Agent that presses it downwards is invisible. But because matter in all the Experiments I have tried, resists a Change from rest to motion upwards will it follow, that all matter essentially resists a Change from rest to motion, downwards. Is it a Posteriori from Experiments, that he deduces this Proposition, that all matter essentially resists any Change of State, or is it a Priori from some Property that is essentially included in our Idea of Matter that he demonstratively [argues?] this Vis Inertiae. Is Inactivity, and AntiActivity, included in our Idea of Matter? Are Activity, Perceptivity &c. Properties that we by only comparing Ideas can see to be incompatible to any Properties of matter.

If nothing is Matter which has not this antiactive Principle, then human Minds are not matter for they have no such Principle. We are conscious, that we can begin and end motion of ourselves. If he argues a Posteriori from Experiments, he can pretend only to Probability. For Unless he was certain that he had made the Experiment and found the Property in every Particle of Matter that ever was created, he could not be certain, that there was no Particle in the World, without this Property, tho he had tried all but one and found that they had it. We have tried but a few Parcells of Matter. The Utmost we can say is, that all we have tried are inactive. But for Argument sake I will deny, that all the Parcels that we have tried, have this Property. On the Contrary I will say that all have a motive Power downwards. Powder has an Active Power springing every Way &c. Thus Experiment is turned against the Doctrine. I cant yet see how he will prove all matter Anti inactive a Priori from Properties of matter before known essential, with which he must shew this to be necessarily connected.

Monday Octr. 9.

Read in Gilberts Tenures. I must and will make that Book familiar to me.

Tuesday [10 October].

Read in Gilbert. I read him slowly, but I gain Ideas and Knowledge as I go along, which I dont always, when I read.

Wednesday [11 October].

Rode to Boston. Conversed with Ned Quincy and Saml.,[8] Peter Chardon &c. By the Way Peter Chardon is a promising Youth. He aspires, and will reach to a considerable Height. He has a sense of the Dignity and Importance of his Profession, that of the Law. He has a just Contempt of the idle, incurious, Pleasure hunting young fellows of the Town, who pretend to study Law. He scorns the Character, and he aims at a nobler. He talks of exulting in an unlimited field of natural, civil and common Law, talks of nerving, sharpening the mind by the Study of Law and Mathematicks, quotes Locks Conduct of the Understanding and transcribes Points of Law into a Common-Place Book on Locks Modell.[9] This fellows Thoughts are not employed on Songs and Girls, nor his Time, on flutes, fiddles, Concerts and Card Tables. He will make something.[10]

Thurdsday [12 October].

Examined the Laws of this Province concerning Pads,[11] Cattle, fences &c. and read in Gilbert. This small volume will take me a fortnight, but I will be master of it.

Fryday [13 October].

Read Gilbert. Went in the Evening to Coil. Quincys. Heard a Tryal before him, as a Justice between Jos. Field and Luke Lambert.[12] The Case was this. Lamberts Horse broke into Fields Inclosure, and lay there some time, damage feasant. When Lambert found that his Horse was there he enters the Inclosure and altho Feild called to him and forbid it, waved his Hat, and Screamed at the Horse, and drove him away, with[out] tendering Feild his Damages. This was a Rescous of the Horse, out of Feilds Hands, for altho Lambert had a Right to enter and take out his [Horse] tendering the Damages, yet, as [the] Words [of] the Law are "that whoever shall rescous any Creature out of the Hands of any Person about to drive them to pound, whereby the Party injured shall be liable to lose his Damages, and the Law be eluded, shall forfeit &c.," and as Feild was actually about to drive them to Pound, and Lambert offered him no Damages, this was compleatly a Rescous. Feild, after the Rescous, went to Coll. Quincy, made Complaint against Lambert and requested and obtained a Warrant. The Warrant was directed to the Constable, who brought the Offender before the Justice, attended with the Complainant, and the Witnesses ordered to be summoned. Quincy, for Defendant, took Exception on the Warrant, to the Jurisdiction of the Justice, because the sum originally sued for, consisting of the forfeiture of 40S. to the Poor, and the Parties Damages estimated at 9d. which was 40S. 9d., was a greater sum than the Justice can take Cognisance of, and because the Words of this Act of the Province are, that this 40S. to the Poor, and these Damages to the Party injured shall be recovered, by Action &c., in any of his Majesties Courts of Record. Now as the Court of a single Justice is not one of his Majesties Courts of record the forfeiture and Damages prayed for in this Complaint, cannot be recovered in this Court. The Justice adjourned his Court till 8 o'clock monday morning, in order to jnform himself, 1st. Whether the Court of a single Justice of the Peace was one of his Majesties Courts of Record? 2. Whether a single Justice can take Cognisance of any Matter, in which the sum originally prosecuted for is more than 40s.? If upon Examination the Coil. shall find, that, a single Justice has no Authority to hear and determine such a Rescous, at the Adjournment the Proceedings will be quashed, and, the Complainant must begin de Novo, but if he finds, that a single Justice has Authority, to determine the matter, he will proceed to Judgment.—The Questions that arise, in my mind, on this Case are these.

1. What is the true Idea, and Definition of a Court of Record? What Courts in England and what in this Province are Courts of Record and what are not? Wood, Jacobs, &c.

2. Whether a Justice has Authority, by Warrant, to hear and determine of any offence the Penalty of which, or the forfeiture to the K[ing], the Poor, the Informer &c. is more than 40s.?

3. Whether a Court is denominated a Court of Record from its keeping Records of its Proceedings? Whether every Court is a Court of Record, whose President is a Judge of Record? For it seems plain in Dalton that a Justice of the Peace is a Judge of Record?

4. On supposition the Warrant should be quashed, who should pay the Cost of the original Warrant, of the Defendants attendance, and of Witness[es'] Oaths and attendance? The Complainant, who was mistaken thro Ignorance in going to the Justice for a Remedy, or the Justice who was mistaken, in the same manner, in Acting upon the Complaint beyond his Authority?

5. What are the Steps of prosecuting by Information? Is not a motion made in Court, that the Information may be amended or filed? Are Informations ever filed, but by Attorney General? When the Penalty sued for by the Information is half to the King or half to the Poor and the other half to the Informer, is the Defendant committed till he discharges the Penalty? Or is an Execution ever issued?

6. Tis said Courts of Record alone have Power to impose a fine, or Imprison. Q[uery] which?

7. A Rescous is a Breach of Law and a Breach of the Peace, and Remedy for it may be by Action of Trespass, which is always contra Pacem.

8. Are not Justices Warrants confined to criminal matters? May a Warrant be issued for a Trespass Quare Clausum fregit?[13] It may for a Trespass of assault and Battery. Justices may punish by fine, Imprisonment, Stripes &c.

The Coll. inquired, what Punishment he could inflict on a Constable for Disobedience to his Warrant, for not making Return of his Doings? And he found a Case ruled in K[ing]'s Bench that a Constable is a subordinate officer to a Justice of the Peace and is indictable at common Law for neglect of Duty. The

Malefeasance or Nonfeasance of officers are Crimes and offences that may be inquired of, indicted or presented by the grand Jury at Common Law.

Feild took Lamberts Horses Damage feasant in his Close once before and impounded them, and gave him verbal Notice, that his Horses were in Pound, but neglected to give either Lambert or the Pound keeper an account of the Damages the Horses had done him. Lambert went to the Pound keeper and demanded his Horses, tendering the Poundkeepers fees, and the Pound keeper delivered them up.

Now Q. Whether Feild is injoined by any Law of the Province, to get his Damages appraised and to lodge an account of them with the Pound keeper?

2. Whether as he neglected this, the Pound keeper cant justify his resigning of them to the owner?

3. If Feild had lodged an Estimation of his Damages with the Pound keeper, and the Pound keeper had nevertheless resigned the Creatures up, without taking the Damages, would not an Action lay against him as an Action lies against a Prison keeper for a voluntary Escape? And Quere what Action would be proper. I want a form of an Action of Escape, now.

4. It cant be called an indirect Way of delivering his Creatures out of Pound, to pay or tender the Poundkeeper his fees and demand and receive his Cattle of him, when he has unlocked and opened the Pound Gate and turned the Creatures out? So that it will not admit a Quere whether Lambert is liable to an Action for receiving his Horses of the Pound keeper. Tis plain I think he is not.

Monday [16 October].

Read a few Pages in Gilbert. I proceed very slowly.

Tuesday [17 October].

Read in Gilbert. Went to Monatiquot to see the Raising of the new Meeting House.[14] No Observations worth noting.

I have not Spirits, and Presence of mind, to seek out scenes of Observation, and to watch critically the Air, Countenances, Actions and Speeches of old men, and young men, of old Women and young Girls, of Physicians and Priests, of old Maids and Batchelors. I should chatter with a Girl, and watch her Behaviour, her answers to Questions, the workings of Vanity and other Passions in her Breast. But objects before me dont suggest proper Questions to ask, and proper Observations to make, so dull and confused at present is my mind.—Betsy Niles affects to trip lightly across the floor, to act with a Sprightly Air, and to be polite. But she is under Restraint, and awe, from her Unacquaintance with Company. Saw Lawyer Thachers Father,[15] at Mr. Niles's. He said old Coll. Thatcher of Barnstable was an excellent man. "He was a very holy man. I used to love to hear him pray. He was a Counsellor, and a Deacon. I have heard him say, that of all his Titles, that of a Deacon, he tho't the most honourable."[16]—Q[uery] is he a new Light? Old Age has commonly a sense of the Importance and Dignity of Religion. I dare say, he is not well pleased with his son's professing the Law. He had rather have him a Deacon.

Wednesday [18 October].

Went to Boston.

Bob Paine. I have ruined myself, by a too eager Pursuit of Wisdom. I have now neither Health enough for an active Life, nor Knowledge enough for a sedentary one.

Quincy. We shall never make your great fellows.

Thus Paine and Quincy both are verging to Despair.

Paine. If I attempt a Composition, my Thoughts are slow and dull.

Paine is discouraged, and Quincy has not Courage enough to harbour a Thought of acquiring a great Character. In short, none of them have a foundation that will support them. P. Chardon seemed to me in the directest Road to Superiority. Pains Face has lost its Bloom, and his Eye its Vivacity and fire. His Eye is weak, his Countenance pale and his Attention unsteady. And what is worse, he suffers tyis decline of Health to retard, almot to Stop yis studies. And Q's dastard soul is afraid to aim at great Acquisition.

Paine (to me). You dont intend to be a Sage, I suppose.

Oh! P. Has not Penetration to erach the Bottom of my mind. He dont know me. Next time I will answer him, A Sage, no. Knowledge eno' ti keep out of fire and Water, is all that I aim at.

Thursday [19 October].

I borrowed yesterday of Quincy, the 1st Volume of Batista Angeloni's Letters,[17] and a general Treatise of naval Trade and Commerce as founded on the Laws and Statutes of this Realm in which those (Laws and Statutes I suppose) relating to his Majesties Customs, Merchants, Masters of Ships, Mariners, Letters of Marque, Privateers, Prizes, Convoys, Cruizers &c. Are particularly considered and treated with due Care under all the necessary Heads from the earliest time down to the present, 2d Edition in 2. Volumes.[18] Read Angeloni thro I believe, and studied, carefully, about a dozen Pages in mercantile Law. Angelonis Letters are all of a Piece. He has an odd System of Faith, viz. That Utility is Truth and therefore that Transubstantiation is true, and Auricular Confession is true because they are useful, they promote the Happiness of mankind. Therefore Rain is true because it is useful in promoting the Growth of Herbs, and fruits and flowers, and consequently of Animals for mans Use. This is very different from Mathematical Truth, and this Explanation of his meaning gives Room to suspect that he disbelieves a Revelation, himself, tho he thinks it useful for the World to believe it.

He reasons, who can conceive that a Being of infinite Wisdom, Justice and Goodness, would suffer the World to be governed 2000 [years] by a Religion that was false. But may not this Question be asked of the Mahometan, the Chinese, in short of every Religion under the sun, and will not the Argument equally prove them all to be true?

What Passion is most active and prevalent in Dr. Savel's mind?[19] The Desire of Money. He retails Sugar by the Pound, [. . .] by the bunch, Pins, Pen knifes, to save these Articles in his family, and neat[20] a few Shillings Profit. He makes poor People who are in his Debt pay him in Labour. He bargains with his Debtors in the 2 other Parishes for Wood, which he sends to the Landing Place, and to Dr. Marshes. Thus by practice of Physick, by trading and bargaining and scheming he picks up a Subsistance for his family and gathers very gradually, Additions to his Stock. But this is low. The same Application, and scheming in his Profession, would raise and spread him a Character, procure him profitable Business and make his fortune. But by this contemptible Dissipation of mind, among Pins, Needles, Tea, Snuff Boxes, Vendues, Loads of Wood, day labour &c. he is negligent of the Theory of his Profession, and will live and die unknown.—These driveling souls, oh! He aims not at fame, only at a Living and a fortune!

Saturday [21 October].

Rose with the sun. Brot up the Horse and took a Ride over Penns Hill, as far as John Haywards in a cold, keen, blustering N. Wester. Returned and breakfasted. I feel brac'd, as if the cold clear Air had given a Spring to the System.—I am now sett down to the Laws relating to naval Trade and Commerce. Let me inquire of the next Master of a Ship that I see, what is a Bill of Lading, what the Pursers Book. What Invoices they keep. What Account they keep of Goods received on Board, and of Goods delivered out, at another Port, &c.

Sunday [22 October].

Conversed with Capt. Thatcher about commercial affairs.—When he receives a freight of Goods on board his Vessell, he signs 3 Bills of Lading (a Bill of Lading, by the Way, is a List of the several Articles, and the Receipt of them signed by the Master) two of which the Merchant keeps, and the other he incloses in a Letter to his Correspondent to whom he sends the Goods and sends it by the Vessell. When the Master arrives at the Port he is destined to, he delivers the Letter, and then the Goods to his Employers Correspondent, who upon Receipt indorses the Bill of Lading, and delivers it up to the Master, and this Bill thus endorsed, will [. . .] the other two in the Merchants Hands. The Receiver of Goods pays the freight.

Some Voyages, We have nothing to do, but receive Goods on board, keep them safely on the Voyage and deliver them safely to the Merchant to whom they are directed. But sometimes we make Trading Voyages. We carry a Cargo of Goods, to sell for money or exchange for other Goods, in the most profitable manner we can. Here we keep a regular Account, make the owners Debtors for Goods that we buy or receive, and give them Credit for Goods that we deliver out.

Monday [23 October].

Tuesday [24 October].

Rode to Boston. Arrived about 1/2 after 10. Went into the Court House, and sett down by Mr. Paine att the Lawyers Table. I felt Shy, under Awe and concern, for Mr. Gridley, Mr. Prat, Mr. Otis,[21] Mr. Kent,[22] and Mr. Thatcher were all present and looked sour. I had no Acquaintance with any Body but Paine and Quincy and they took but little Notice. However I attended Court Steadily all Day, and at night, went to Consort with Samll. Quincy and Dr. Gardiner.[23] There I saw the most Spacious and elegant Room, the gayest Company of Gentlemen and the finest Row of Ladies, that ever I saw. But the weather was so dull and I so disordered that I could not make one half the observations that I wanted to make.

Wednesday [25 October].

Went in the morning to Mr. Gridleys, and asked the favour of his Advice what Steps to take for an Introduction to the Practice of Law in this County.[24] He answered "get sworn."

Ego. But in order to that, sir, as I have no Patron, in this County.

G. I will recommend you to the Court. Mark the Day the Court adjourns to in order to make up Judgments. Come to Town that Day, and in the mean Time I will speak to the Bar for the Bar must be consulted, because the Court always inquires, if it be with Consent of the Bar.

Then Mr. Gridley inquired what Method of Study I had pursued, what Latin Books I read, what Greek, what French. What I had read upon Rhetorick. Then he took his Common Place Book and gave me Ld. Hales Advice to a Student of the Common Law, and when I had read that, he gave me Ld. C[hief] J[ustice] Reeves Advice [to] his Nephew, in the Study of the common Law. Then He gave me a Letter from Dr. Dickins, Regius Professor of Law at the University of Cambridge, to him, pointing out a Method of Studying the civil Law. Then he turned to a Letter He wrote himself to Judge Lightfoot, Judge of the Admiralty in Rhode Island, directing to a Method of Studying the Admiralty Law. Then Mr. Gridley run a Comparison between the Business and studies of a Lawyer or Gentleman of the Bar, in England, and that of one here. A Lawyer in this Country must study common Law and civil Law, and natural Law, and Admiralty Law, and must do the duty of a Counsellor, a Lawyer, an Attorney, a sollicitor, and even of a scrivener, so that the Difficulties of the Profession are much greater here than in England.

The Difficulties that attend the study may discourage some, but they never discouraged me. [Here is conscious superiority.][25]

I have a few Pieces of Advice to give you Mr. Adams. One is to pursue the Study of the Law rather than the Gain of it. Pursue the Gain of it enough to keep out of the Briars, but give your main Attention to the study of it.

The next is, not to marry early. For an early Marriage will obstruct your Improvement, and in the next Place, twill involve you in Expence.

Another Thing is not to keep much Company. For the application of a Man who aims to be a lawyer must be incessant. His Attention to his Books must be constant, which is inconsistent with keeping much Company.

In the study of Law the common Law be sure deserves your first and last Attention, and He has conquered all the Difficulties of this Law, who is Master of the Institutes. You must conquer the Institutes. The Road of Science is much easier, now, than it was when I sett out. I began with Co. Litt.[26] and broke thro.

I asked his Advice about studying Greek. He answered it is a matter of meer Curiosity.—After this long and familiar Conversation we went to Court. Attended all Day and in the Evening I went to ask Mr. Thatchers Concurrence with the Bar. Drank Tea and spent the whole Evening, upon original sin, Origin of Evil, the Plan of the Universe, and at last, upon Law. He says He is sorry that he neglected to keep a common Place Book when he began to study Law, and he is half a mind to begin now. Thatcher thinks, this County is full.[27]

Thursday [26 October].

Went in the morning to wait on Mr. Prat. He inquired if I had been sworn at Worcester? No. Have you a Letter from Mr. Putnam to the Court? No. It would have been most proper to have done one of them things first. When a young Gentleman goes from me into another County, I always write in his favour to the Court in that County, or if you had been sworn, there, you would have been intitled to be sworn here. But now, no Body in this County knows any Thing about you. So no Body can say any Thing in your favour, but by hearsay. I believe you have made a proper Proficiency in science, and that you will do very well from what I have heard, but that is only hearsay. [How different is this from Gridleys Treatment? Besides it is weak, for neither the Court nor the Bar will question the Veracity of Mr. Gridly and Mr. Prat, so that the only Uncertainty that can remain is whether Mr. Putnam was in Earnest, in the Account he gave of my Morals and Studies to them Gentleman, which cannot be removed by a Line from him, or by my being sworn at Worcester, or any other Way than by getting Mr. Putnam sworn.][28] After this, he asked me a few, short Questions about the Course of my studies which I answered, and then came off as full of Wrath as [I] was full of Gratitude when I left Cridley the morning before. Prat is infinitely harder of Access than Gridley. He is ill natured, and Gridley is good natured.—Attended Court all Day, and at night waited on Otis at his office where I conversed with him and he, with great Ease and familiarity, promised me to join the Bar in recommending me to the Court. Mr. Gridley lent me Van Muydens Compendiosa Institutionum Justiniani Tractatio in usum Collegiorum. Editio tertia prioribus Auctior et emendatior. Pax Artium Altrix.[29]—After I have mastered this, I must read Hoppius's Commentary on Justinian. The Design of this Book is [to] explain the technical Terms of the civil Law, and to settle the Divisions and Distributions of the civil Law. By the Way this is the first Thing a student ought to aim at, viz. distinct Ideas under the terms and a clear apprehension of the Divisions and Distributions of the science. This is one of the principal Excellences of Hawkins's Pleas of the Crown,[30] and it is the very End of this Book of Van Muyden's.

Let me remarke here one important neglect of the last Week. I omitted minuting the Names of the Cases at Trial in my Ivory Book, and I omitted to keep Pen, Ink and Paper at my Lodgings, in order to comitt to Writing, at Night, the Cases and Points of Law that were argued and adjudged in the Day.

Let me remember to mark in my Memorandum Book, the Names of the Cases, and the Terms and Points of Law that occur in each Case, to look these Terms and Points in the Books at Otis's, Prats or any other office, and to digest and write down the whole in the Evening at my Lodgings. This will be reaping some real Advantage, by my Attendance on the Courts, and, without this, the Observations that I may make will lie in total Confusion in my mind.

Friday, Saturday, Sunday, Monday [27-30 October].

All Spent in absolute Idleness, or what is worse, gallanting the Girls.

Tuesday [31 October].

Set down, and recollected my self, and read a little in Van Muyden, a little in naval Trade and Commerce.

Wednesday [1 November].

Read a little in Van Muyden, and a little in naval Trade and Commerce.

Thurdsday [2 November].

Rode as far as Smelt Brook. Breakfasted, made my fire and am now set down to Van Muyden in Earnest. His latin is easy, his deffinitions are pretty clear, and his Divisions of the subject, are judicious.

Sunday [5? November].

Drank Tea at Coll. Quincy's. He read to me a Letter Coll. Gouch[31] wrote him in answer to his Questions, whether a Justices Court was a Court of Record? and then concluded, "So that Sammy was right, for he was all along of that Opinion. I have forgot what your Opinion was?" [This must be a Lye, or else Partiality and parental affection have blotted out the Remembrance that I first started to his son Sam and him too, the Doubt whether he had Jurisdiction as a Justice—and made him really imagine, what he wished had been true viz. that Samll. had started it. If he did remember he knew it was insult to me. But I bore it. Was forgetfulness, was Partiality, or was a cunning Design to try if I was not vain of being the Starter of the Doubt, the true Cause of his saying, He forgot what my Opinion was.] [32]

Sam has the utmost Reason to be grateful to Mr. Pratt. He will have an opportunity 100 times better than Mr. Prat had of rising into the Practice and Reputation of the Law. I want to see and hear Sam at the Bar. I want to know how he will succeed. I am concerned for him. The Govr.[33] likes Sam much better than Ned. He has seen or heard some of Neds freaks. This is a Partiality in favor of one Child and against another quite indecent in a father. Tis great Weakness to expose himself so before Strangers.

Monday [6? November].[34]

Went to Town. Went to Mr. Gridleys office, but he had not returned to Town from Brookline. Went again. Not returned. Attended Court till after 12 and began to grow uneasy expecting that Quincy would be sworn and I have no Patron, when Mr. Gridly made his Appearance, and on sight of me, whispered to Mr. Prat, Dana,[35] Kent, Thatcher &c. about me. Mr. Prat said no Body knew me. Yes, says Gridley, I have tried him, he is a very sensible Fellow.—At last He rose up and bowed to his right Hand and said "Mr. Quincy," when Quincy rose up, then bowed to me, "Mr. Adams," when I walked out. "May it please your Honours, I have 2 young Gentlemen Mr. Q. and Mr. Adams to present for the Oath of an Attorney. Of Mr. Q. it is sufficient for me to say he has lived 3 Years with Mr. Prat. Of Mr. Adams, as he is unknown to your Honours, It is necessary to say that he has lived between 1 and 3 Years with Mr. Put[nam] of Worcester, has a good Character from him, and all others who know him, and that he was with me the other day several Hours, and I take it he is qualified to study the Law by his scholarship and that he has made a very considerable, a very great Proficiency in the Principles of the Law, and therefore that the Clients Interest may be safely intrusted in his Hands. I therefore recommend him with the Consent of the Bar to your Honors for the Oath." Then Mr. Prat said 2 or 3 Words and the Clerk was ordered to swear us. After the Oath Mr. Gridley took me by the Hand, wished me much Joy and recommended me to the Bar. I shook

Hands with the Bar, and received their Congratulations, and invited them over to Stones to drink some Punch. Where the most of us resorted, and had a very chearful [Chat?].

Tuesday. December 3 or 4 [i.e. 5?].[36]

Bob Paine is conceited and pretends to more Knowledge and Genius than he has. I have heard him say that he took more Pleasure in solving a Problem in Algebra than in a frolick. He told me the other day, that he was as curious after a minute and particular Knowledge of Mathematicks and Phylosophy, as I could be about the Laws of Antiquity. By his Boldness in Company, he makes himself a great many Enemies. His Aim in Company is to be admired, not to be beloved. He asked me what Duch Commentator I meant? I said Vinnius.—Vinnius, says he, (with a flash of real Envy, but pretended Contempt,) you cant understand one Page of Vinnius.—He must know that human Nature is disgusted with such incomplaisant Behaviour. Besides he has no Right to say that I dont understand every Word in Vinnius, or even in [. . .] for he knows nothing of me. For the future let me act the Part of a critical spy upon him, not that of an open unsuspicious friend.—Last Superiour Court at Worcester he dined in Company with Mr. Gridly, Mr. Trowbridge,[37] and several others, at Mr. Putnams, and altho a modest attentive Behaviour would have best become him in such a Company, yet he tried to ingross the whole Conversation to himself. He did the same, in the Evening, when all the Judges of the Superiour Court with Mr. Winthrop, Sewall, &c. were present, and he did the same last Thanksgiving day, at Coll. Quincies, when Mr. Wibirt, Mr. Cranch &c. were present. This Impudence may sett the Million a Gape at him but will make all Persons of Sense despize him, or hate him. That evening at Put[nam]s, he called me, a Numbskull and a Blunder Buss before all the Superiour Judges. I was not present indeed, but such expressions were indecent and tended to give the Judges a low Opinion of me, as if I was despized by my Acquaintance. He is an impudent, ill-bred, conceited fellow. Yet he has Witt, sense, and Learning, and a great deal of Humour, and has Virtue and Piety except his fretful, peevish, Childish Complaints against the Disposition of Things. This Character is drawn with Resentment of his ungenerous Treatment of me, and Allowances must therefore be made, but these are unexaggerated facts.

Lambert setts up for a Witt and a Humourist. He is like a little nurley[38] ill natured Horse that kicks at every Horse of his own size, but lears and shears off from every one that is larger. I should mind what I say before him for he [is] always watching for wry Words to make into a droll story to laugh at. He laughs at John Thayer, for saying, "Lambert, I am sorry [I] am your good Friend I am sorry. This will cost you between 2 and 3 hundred Pounds."[39] And it was a silly, [. . . impertinent?], ignorant Speech. He laughs at Field for being nettled at his laughter. Field complained that he laughed at him. Lambert said, I will laugh when I please. If you carry me to the Rat hole I will laugh all the Way, and after I get there.—Such fellows are hated by all mankind, yet they rise and make a figure, and People dred them.

Altho men of better witt, are hated and feared, yet they are respected, by the World.

Quaere, was there ever a Witt, who had much Humanity and Compassion, much Tenderness of Nature? Mr. Congreve was tender, extreamly tender of giving offence to any man. Dr. Arbuthnot was a[s] great a Wit and Humourist, yet he was tender, and prudent. Mr. Cranch has Witt, and is tender and [gentle?].[40]

The other Night I happened to be at the Drs., with Ben. Veasey. He began to prate upon the Presumption of Philosophers in erecting Iron Rods to draw the Lightning from the Clouds. His Brains were in a ferment with strong Liquor and he railed, and foamed against those Points and the Presumption that erected them, in Language taken partly from Scripture and partly from the drunken Disputes of Tavern Philosophy, in as wild mad a manner as King Lear raves, against his Daughters Disobedience and Ingratitude, and against the meaness of the Storm in joining with his Daughter against him in Shakespears Lear. He talked of presuming upon God as Peter attempted to walk upon the Water, attempting to controul the Artilry of Heaven, an Execution that Mortal man cant Stay—the Elements of Heaven, fire, Heat, Rain, Wind, &C.

Let me search for the Clue, which Led great Shakespeare into the Labyrinth of mental Nature! Let me examine how men think. Shakespeare had never seen in real Life Persons under the Influence of all those Scenes of Pleasure and distress, which he has described in his Works, but he imagined how a Person of such a Character would behave in such Circumstances, by analogy from the Behaviour of others that were most like that Character in nearly similar Circumstances, which he had seen.

[Marginalia in Winthrop's *Lecture on Earthquakes*, December 1758?][41]

"O! there is no getting out of the mighty hand of GOD!"[42]

This Exclamation was very popular, for the Audience in general like the rest of the Province, consider Thunder, and Lightning as well as Earthquakes, only as Judgments, Punishments, Warnings &c. and have no Conception of any Uses they can serve in Nature. I have heard some Persons of the highest Rank among us, say, that they really thought the Erection of Iron Points, was an impious attempt to robb the almighty of his Thunder, to wrest the Bolt of Vengeance out of his Hand. And others, that Thunder was designed, as an Execution upon Criminals, that no Mortal can stay. That the attempt was foolish as well as impious. And no Instances, even those of Steeples struck, where Iron Bars have by Accident conveyed the Electricity as far as they reached without damage, which one would think would force Conviction, have no weight at all.[43]

This Invention of Iron Points, to prevent the Danger of Thunder, has met with all that opposition from the superstition, affectation of Piety, and Jealousy of new Inventions, that Inoculation to prevent the Danger of the Small Pox, and all other usefull Discoveries, have met with in all ages of the World.

I am not able to satisfy myself, whether the very general if not universal apprehension that Thunder, Earthquakes, Pestilence, Famine &c. are designed merely as Punishments of sins and Warnings to forsake, is natural to Mankind, or whether it was artfully propagated, or whether it was derived from Revelation.

An Imagination that those Things are of no Use in Nature but to punish and alarm and arouse sinners, could not be derived from real Revelation, because it is far from being true, tho few Persons can be persuaded to think so.

Monday. December 18th. 1758

I this Evening delivered to Mr. Field, a Declaration in Trespass for a Rescue.[44] I was obliged to finish it, without sufficient examination. If it should escape an Abatement, it is quite indigested, and unclerk-like. I am ashamed of it, and concerned for it. If my first Writt should be abated, if I should throw a large Bill of Costs on my first Client, my Character and Business will suffer greatly. It will be said, I dont understand my Business. No one will trust his Interest in my hands. I never Saw a Writt, on that Law of the Province. I was perplexed, and am very anxious about it. Now I feel the Dissadvantages of Putnams Insociability, and neglect of me. Had he given me now and then a few Hints concerning Practice, I should be able to judge better at this Hour than I can now. I have Reason to complain of him. But, it is my Destiny to dig Treasures with my own fingers. No Body will lend me or sell me a Pick axe. How this first Undertaking will terminate, I know not. I hope the Dispute will be settled between them, or submitted, and so my Writt never come to an Examination. But if it should I must take the Consequences. I must assume a Resolution, to bear without freting.

Heard Parson Wibirt exert his Casuistry to J. Spear.[45] Warned him against selling his [drowned?] Sheep for merchantable Mutton. It was not so nutritive nor palatable as Mutton butchered and dressed, and therefore, was not worth the same Price, and it would be an Imposition and a Cheat that his Conscience must disapprove to describe it and sell it as good Mutton. He could not [sentence unfinished]

Wednesday [20 December].

I am this forenoon, resuming the Study of Van Muyden. I begin at the 99th Page.

THURSDAY [21 DECEMBER].

Yesterday and to day I have read loud, Tullius 4 Orations against Cataline. The Sweetness and Grandeur of his sounds, and the Harmony of his Numbers give Pleasure enough to reward the Reading if one understood none of his meaning. Besides I find it, a noble Exercise. It exercises my Lungs, raises my Spirits, opens my Porr[s], quickens the Circulations, and so contributes much to Health.

NOTES

1. The terms were that JA would continue to keep the Worcester school, the town paying Mrs. Putnam for Ms Board, and that JA would pay Putnam "an hundred dollars, when I should find it convenient" (JA, Autobiography).

2. First entry in JA's booklet "No. 2," as numbered by CPA (our D/JA/z). Actually this is a collection of loose leaves, not a stitched gathering, and many of the leaves are badly chipped and worn at the edges. Where illegible or partly missing words or phrases can he reconstructed from the early transcripts prepared for JQA and carefully corrected by CPA, the editors have not ordinarily used square brackets, reserving them for very doubtful readings.

3. JA had recently finished his two-year period of legal studies under the "Inspection" of James Putnam. He kept no diary during that period and wrote almost no letters that have been preserved. A few incidents of his life in Worcester, 1756-1758, are recorded in his Autobiography, q.v. On sq July 1758 he had attended commencement in Cambridge and argued, for his master of arts degree, the affirmative side of the quaestio, *An Imperium civile, Hominibus prorsus necessarium, sit* (Harvard *Quaestiones*, 1758, broadside).

4. This copy of Vinnius' Justinian, which was probably of the edition published at Leyden, 1730, is no longer in the Harvard College Library.

5. Jeremiah (or Jeremy) Gridley (1702-1767), Harvard 1725, and Benjamin Prat (1711-1763), Harvard 1737 and later chief justice of New York Province, were at this time the two leading lawyers of Boston.

6. Mrs. Elisha Savil; see entry of 17 March 1756 above, and note 3 there.

7. This sentence, falling at the foot of one page of the MS and the top of the next, is partly worn away. The present text follows the early transcript as corrected by CFA.

8. Samuel Quincy (1735-1789), son of Col. Josiah Quincy; Harvard 1754; lawyer; loyalist.

9. A self-indexing commonplace book or collection of quotations arranged under topical headings. Locke's explanation of his plan is in a letter to M. Toignard (*The Works of John Locke. A New Edition, Corrected*, London, 1823, 3:331-349). Among CFA's papers is such a book, partly filled up by him, with a printed titlepage and the imprint of Cummings and Hilliard, Boston, 1821 (Adams Papers, Microfilms, Reel No. 312).

10. This prophecy was not borne out, as CFA points out in a note on this passage; Chardon, Harvard 1757, admitted barrister in the Superior Court, March term, 1763, died in Barbadoes in 1766 (JA, *Works*, 2:39, note; Superior Court of Judicature, Minute Book 79).

11. Pad: "A path, track; the road, the way. Orig. *slang*, now also *dial.*" (OED).

12. Field V. Lambert (or Lambard), in which JA served as counsel for the plaintiff, was evidently JA's first case as a practicing lawyer. As later entries show, it caused him great concern and vexation because his writ proved defective. The cause was heard by Justice Josiah Quincy, whose son Samuel was the defendant's counsel.

13. "Because he has broken the close" (Bouvier, *Law Dictionary*, 2:610)

14. Monatiquat (variously spelled) was an ancient name freqÃ_ntly used by JA and others for the settlement on the Monatiquot River in present Braintree—at that time the Middle Precinct of Braintree. The "new Meeting House" was that of the Second Parish, to which Rev. Samuel Niles, Harvard 1699, had long ministered. See Pattee, *Old Braintree and Quincy*, p.7, 56, 285-286; also map in CFA2, *Three Episodes*, vol. 2: following p. 578.

15. Oxenbridge Thacher the elder (1681-1772), Harvard 1698, father of the eminent Boston lawyer of the same name who will be frequently mentioned in these pages.

16. Quotation marks supplied, here and above, around what is certainly a direct quotation from old Mr. Thacher.

17. *Letters on the English Nation*, London, 1755, 2 vols., purporting *to* be "by Batista Angeloni, a Jesuit," were actually the work of John Shebbeare (see *DNB*), a British political writer whose identity *JA had discovered by the time of his next reference to this book; see 19 March 1759, below. JA's own copy of the Letters,* now in the Boston Public Library contains a few marginal notes in his hand and some underscoring, though none in Letter IX, on religion, from which the paraphrase below is largely derived.

18. The first volume of JA's own copy of this edition survives, as does the first volume of his copy of the first edition, London, 1740 (*Catalogue of JA's Library*, p 101).

19. The present paragraph is separated from the preceding ones by a line across the page in the MS; it may therefore have been written on either 19 or 20 Oct.

20. Neat, vb.: to clear or net (a sum of money) (OED).

21. James Otis Jr. (1725-1783), Harvard 1743, the celebrated lawyer and pamphleteer.

22. Benjamin Kent (1708-1788), Harvard 1727, another leading lawyer and later attorney general of the Province.

23. Silvester Gardiner (1707-1786), Boston physician and druggist; founder of Gardiner, Maine; one of JA's early law clients.

24. The account of this momentous interview in JA's Autobiography differs so widely in details from this contemporary record of it as to suggest that JA did not consult his Diary in composing the later account.

25. Brackets in MS.
26. Coke upon Littleton, the famous *Institutes of the Laws of England*, London, 1628-1644, in four parts, which consisted of Sir Thomas Littleton's treatise on tenures with an elaborate commentary by Sir Edward Coke, long the standard authority on real property in England and America.
27. Of lawyers.
28. Brackets in MS.
29. JA later acquired this book (as he did others) from Gridley's library, and it survives among JA's books in the Boston Public Library.
30. JA's copy of William Hawkins, *A Treatise of the Pleas of the Crown*, 4th edn., London, 1762, 2 vols. in I, is in the Boston Public Library. It bears his autograph and that of his son Charles.
31. Joseph Gooch, on whom see further the entry of 9 Aug. 1760, below.
32. Initial bracket in MS; closing bracket supplied.
33. Evidently a sobriquet for Col. Josiah Quincy; possibly an inadvertence for "the Colonel."
34. In his Autobiography JA twice says, in varying language, that his admission as attorney to the Suffolk bar (which is to say his swearing-in before the Inferior Court of Common Pleas for Suffolk County) occurred on the last Friday (i.e. the 27th) of October 1758. Since the records of the Suffolk Inferior Court for this period have been lost, the date cannot be finally established, but there can be little doubt that the present Diary entry has been correctly dated as 6 Nov. even though this date has had to be assigned, and, accordingly, that the swearing-in occurred on that day. Note again how widely the account in the Autobiography varies from that written at the time.
35. Richard Dana (1700-1772), Harvard 1718, often called "Father Dana" by JA to distinguish him from his son Francis, who also became a lawyer and, later, JA's secretary in Europe, a diplomat, and a judge.
36. If JA was correct in giving the day of the week as Tuesday, this entry should he dated 5 Dec.
37. Edmund Trowbridge (1709-1793), of Cambridge; Harvard 1728; attorney general and later a justice of the Superior Court. JA sometimes calls him Goffe, a Trowbridge used in college and for a time thereafter because his guardian was a great-uncle named Edmund Goffe.
38. Dwarfish, gnarled (OED, under "knurly").
39. The point of this anecdote is now lost, perhaps owing to JA's punctuation, which stands here as in the MS except for moving back the closing quotation mark to this point from its original position after the first use of the word "sorry" in the preceding sentence.
40. The following two paragraphs are separated from the present entry and from each other by lines drawn across the page in the MS; they may have been written at any time between 5 and 8 Dec.
41. The two following paragraphs were written, without indication of date, in JA's copy of John Winthrop, *A Lecture on Earthquakes; Read in the Chapel of Harvard-College in Cambridge, N.E. Notember 26th* 1755, Boston, 1755, the first at p.37 and the second on a blank final leaf. This copy is in the Boston Public Library, and Mr. Zoltan Haraszti has published the marginalia, with a helpful commentary, in "Young John Adams on Franklin's Iron Points," *Isis*, 41:11-14 (March 1950). See also entries of 18 Nov. 1755, above, and 12 March 1761, below.
42. This sentence is quoted in Winthrop's text from Rev. Thomas Prince's *Earthquakes the Works of God*, Boston, 1755, a sermon first published in 1727 and reissued with a new appendix after the earthquake of 18 Nov. 1755. In the appendix Prince took a very dim view of the recent invention by "the sagacious Mr. Franklin." "The more *Points of Iron* are erected round the *Earth* to draw the *Electrical Substance* out of the *Air;* the more the *Earth* must needs be charged with it," and consequently the more earthquakes. "In *Boston* are more erected than any where else in *New England;* and *Boston* seems to be more dreadfully shaken. Oh! there is no getting out of the mighty Hand of God! If we think to avoid it in the *Air*, we cannot in *Earth:* Yea it may grow more fatal." To this Winthrop replied in an appendix of his own: "I should think, though with the utmost deference to superior judgements, that the pathetic exclamation, which comes next, might well enough have been spared. 'O! there is no getting out of the mighty hand of GOD!' For I cannot believe, that in the whole town of Boston, where so many iron points are erected, there is so much as one person, who is so weak, so ignorant, so foolish, or, to say all in one word, so atheistical, as ever to have entertained a single thought, that it is possible, by the help of a few yards of wire, to 'get out of the mighty hand of GOD.'" JA's comments are attached to this paragraph of Winthrop's.
43. JA's faulty grammar is retained as in MS.
44. In the case of Field v. Lambert.
45. This detached paragraph may have been written on 19 December.

Chapter 4

Entries in a Commonplace Book

1780

John Marshall

John Marshall (September 24, 1755-July 6, 1835) was Chief Justice of the United States from 1801 to 1835. These excerpts are taken from John Marshall's commonplace book, which was reprinted in Volume 1 of *The Papers of John Marshall*, Charles Cullen, editor (University of North Carolina Press, 1974).

Abatement

Abatemt. is a plea put in by the Deft. in which he shews cause to the Ct. why he should not be impleaded or if impleaded not in the manner & form he then is.

I.B.2.; [Gil.] His. of the crown 186.

A plea in Abatemt. to the jurisdiction of the Ct. [must] be put in by the Deft. in person & before any imparlance. He must make but half defence.

I.B.2.; Gil. H. crown 187.; Show. 386.; C.L. 127.

There are several pleas to the person of the Pf. Outlawry does not entirely abate the writ but only suspends it.

I.B. 2.; G.H.C. 196.

This disability is not pleadable when the action is brought in Auter droit.

Excommunication, Premunire & popish recusancy are pleas in abatement.

C.L. 128.

An Alien Enemy can bring no action. 4. Mod. 285. An Alien in Lague may bring personal actions.

Secus Ld. R. 282.

Officers of a court are privileged in actions brought in their own right.

I.B.5.

If a writ vary materially from that in the register or be defective in point of substance the party may [take] advantage of it; so if the declaration varies from the writ.

I.B. 6; 12 Mod. 273; Fitz. B. 219, 231.

Tis a genl. rule that where any party dies & the plea [*is in*] the same condition as if such party [*were living*] death makes no abatement of the writ.

I.B.7; G.H.C. 242; 12 MOD. 251.

Two Exrs. bring debt—one dies—the writ does not abate. Secus if one was dead when the writ was brought.

Action agt. several Defts. one dies—the writ does not abate.

I.B.8.

Actions originally maintainable by & against Exrs. etc. not to abate after interlocutory judgmt.

Death of either party between verdict & judgemt. not to be pleaded in abatement.

22.G.2; CH. 5, 180, 181.

Process agt. one returnd, no inhabitant shall abate.

DO. 184.

Coverture is a good plea in Abatement & may be either before the writ sued or pending the writ. By the first the writ is abated de facto, by the second tis only abateable. Coverture pending the writ must be pleaded since the last continuance. If a feme sole takes out a writ & after marries the deft. may plead in Abatemt. or in chief.

I.B.9; DOCT. P1. 3, SID. 140; LEON. 168, 169

If a writ is false when sued out it shall abate.

FITZ. B. 476.

If a writ is de facto a nullity & destroyed so that judgmt. thereupon would be erroneous there the writ is de facto abated. As if an action be brought agt. a feme covert as sole, or where the Plaintiff by his own shewing had no cause of action at the time the writ was brought.

I.B. 10; DOCT. P1. 3; CR. EL. 121, 185, 193, 330; CART. 172, THE CT. GAVE [*leave to*] A[*mend*].

Where the writ is only abateable it must be abated by pleading in time; for matters in & before the writ cannot be taken advantage of in error.

SAL. 2. P1. 5; LD. R. 853.

Tis a good plea that a stranger in tenant in common with the Plaintiff.

CR. EL. 554; I.B.10.

Whenever it appears on record that the Plaintiff has sued out two writs against the same Defendants for the same thing the second writ shall abate.

7. John Marshall (1755-1835) was a student of Wythe at the College of William and Mary, which he enjoyed particularly because its lax dress code allowed him to go barefoot and without a vest in the summer. As Chief Justice of the United States, his opinions fundamentally altered the role of the courts in U.S. constitutional law and strengthened the central government. (*Courtesy of Art & Visual Materials, Special Collections Department, Harvard Law School Library.*)

I.B.13; 12. Mod. 418; 5 Coke. 6I.

Whatever destroys the Plfs. action & disables him forever from recovering may be pleaded in bar but the Deft. may sometimes plead it in Abatemt. As in Replevin the Deft. may pl[e]ad property in himself or in a stranger either in bar or in Abatemt.

I.B. 14; Vent. 249; 2. Ld. R. 984.

If a Deft. pleads matter in bar & concludes in abatemt. or matter in abatemt. & concludes in bar this shall be deemed a plea in bar.

I.B. 14; 2. Mod. 64; Ld. R. 593; 6. Mod. 203; Con. 2. Ld. R. 1019.

Where the matter of Abatemt. appears on the face of the record the plea shall begin & end with a petit judicium de brevi but where the matter is dehors the Deft. shall only end his plea with a petit judicium.

I.B. 15.; Moor. 30; 5 Mod. 136.

Pleas in abatemt. are not to be recd. but on oath.

Suits shall not abate for want of form if there be matter sufficient in the Declara [tion.]

Account

Account, at common law, lay only agt. a Guardian in socage, Bailiff or Receiver, or by one in favor of trade & commerce. The statutes on that subject have given this action to the Execrs. of Merchants, the Exrs. of Exrs. & to Administrators.

I.B. 17 C.L. 90.

Action of account is by the laws of Virga. given agt. the Exrs. or Admrs. of every Guardian Bailiff or Receiver & also to one joint tenant or tenant in common his Exrs. or Admrs. against the other as Bailiff for receiving more than comes to his proportion, or agt. his Exrs. or Admrs.

22.G. 2, Ch. 3, p. 166.

An infant appointed Factor etc. not accountable in law or equity but by his sureties.

I.B. 17; 4. Leon 32.; Sec. I. Vern. 208.

If I make J.S. my Bailiff etc. who appoints a Depy. I cannot have account against his Deputy.

Do.

An apprentice by the name of an apprentice is not chargeable in account.

II.Co. 89.

To maintain an action of account there must be a privity either in law or by the provision of the parties.

I.B. 18; Co. L. 172.

Equity will make all persons account for the profits of lands they have received to such as have the equitable title.

I.B. 18; The case of coventry vers. Hall.

A Bailiff cannot be charged as receiver—whether the same person may be charged as Bailiff & Receiver. Quere.

I.B. 19.

No action of account lies for a thing certain.

I.B. 19.

If a man by obligation acknowleges that he has recd. money ad proficiendum & computandum the obligee may either sue the bond or bring account.

I.B. 19; Cr. El. 644.

Where account would lie Assumpsit may be brought on an express promise. Wherever one acts as Bailiff he promises to render an account.

I.B. 19, 20; Sal. 9. Pl. 1.

A release or submission to an award are good pleas in bar of account. It is no good plea that the Deft, has paid the money.

I.B. 20; Cr. Ch. 116; Br. 48.

In an action of account the first judgment is quod computet after which the Ct. assigns Auditors armed with authority to convene the parties before them from day to day at any day & place that they shall appoint till the account be settled: the time by which the account is to be settled is prefixed by the Ct. but may be enlarged. Either of the parties on injustice may apply to the Court. If the Deft. denies any article or demurs to any demand it is to be tried in court.

I.B. 21; Mod. 42; Co. Ent. 46.

Whatever may be pleaded to the action shall never be allowed of as a good discharge before the Auditors.

I.B. 21; Cr. Ch. 116.

Accord and Satisfaction

Accord can not be pleaded in bar unless satisfaction be actually made.

I.B. 22; Ray. 450.

An accord must appear to be advantageous to the party otherwise it can be no satisfaction.

I.B. 22; 9 Ed. 419; Rol. Ab. 128.

An accord with satisfaction is no good plea to an action real.

I.B. 22; 4 Co. 1.

When a duty in certain accrues by a deed tempore confectionis scripti it ought to be avoided by matter of as high a nature.

I.B. 22; 6 Co. 43; Cr.Ja. 254.

If an accord be pleaded by way of accord a precise execution thereof in every part must be pleaded, if by way of satisfaction, the Deft. need plead no more but that he paid the Plf. 10/in full satisfaction of the action which he received. Accord cannot be plead without satisfaction.

I.B. 25; 9. Co. 80; Rolls Abr. 129.

Actions in General

It is clear that for every injury a man shall have an action & for every right he has a remedy—where a person has several remedies he may chuse which he pleases, but in this he must follow the rules of that society of which he is a member, for though a man has a right & is barred by the Statute of limitations yet he can have no remedy.

I.B. 28; Co. L. 145; Stile 4.

Also in cases where there may be damnum absque injuria the party can have no action.

Roll. Abr. 107; 1 Mod. 69.

None are excluded from bringing an action except on account of their crimes or their country.

Co. L. 128.

A man that hath a special property in goods shall have an action agt. a stranger who takes them away because he is answerable in damages to the absolute owner.

Mod. 30.

A man who has cause of action agt. two may bring it agt. which he pleases.

Dyer. 98.

In real actions in those writs which contain the time place & demand particularly several lands by several titles cannot be demanded in the same writ. Secus where there is only a genl. complaint as in the writ of trespass quare clausum fregit.

8. Co. 87; F.N.B. 209; Dyer 145.

In personal actions several wrongs & trespasses may be joined. Fraud & warranty may be joind.

I. Ba. 30; 8 Co. 87; Ray. 233.

But actions founded on a tort & a contract cannot be joined as Assumpsit & trover.

Ld. Ray 58.

Where one hath a right to recover in the same kind of action though he derives his right from difft. titles, yet being conjoined in him he may recover in one action.

I.Ba. 31; Yel. 63; Cro.Ja. 68.

But one cannot in the same action join a demand in his own right & one which he hath in right of another.

Cro. El. 486.

Several persons may join in an action where their interest is joint.

Roll. Ab. 31.

Actions Local & Transitory

All actions real or mixd must be laid in the county where the lands lie.

I.Ba. 34.

All personal actions may be brought in any Cty. & laid in any place & the Deft. cannot traverse it.

I.Ba. 35; Co. L. 282; 7. Co. 3.

The Deft. cannot by his plea oblige the Plf. to lay his action in a dift. Cty. unless the matter pleaded be local. The motion must be on affadavit.

2 Sal. 66g pi. 6.

Actions Qui Tam

Wherever a statute prohibits a thing as being an immediate offence agt. the publick good, under a certain penalty the whole or part of which is given to him who will sue for it, any person may bring such action or information & lay his demand with a qui tam. Also where a Statute prohibits or commands a thing the doing or omission of which is both an immediate damage to the party & also highly concerns the good of the publick, the party may & some say ought to bring his action with a qui tam.

Co. En. 375; 4. Co. 13; 2. Haw. [P]C. 265.

An action on a publick stat, need not recite the stat. But if the prosecutor recites the Stat. & materially varies from a substantial part this is fatal.

Cro. El. 236; 2 Haw. P.C. 246.

If an information contain several offences & be well laid as to some but defective as to others the informer may have judgt. for such as are well laid.

Cr. Ja. 204.

An action or information need not conclude contra pacem or in contemptum as an Indictment must.

Cr. Ja. 529.

Every informer on any penal statute shall exhibit his suit in person & pursue it by himself or attorney.

18. El. Ch. 5.

The Deft. cannot plead specially & the genl. issue either to the whole or to part of the charge.

Rol. rep. 49, 134.

If there be more than one deft. they ought not to plead jointly.

2 H.P.C. 276.

Where a Stat. gives a certain penalty to the party grieved he is entitled to his costs.

2. Hawk. P.C. 274.

Any informer (not grieved) who willingly delays his suit etc. shall pay costs charges & damages to be assigned by Ct. & no informer shall compound without leave of Ct. under penalty of standing in the pillory, of being disabled to sue in any popular or penal statute & of forfeiting ten pounds.

18. El. Ch. 5.

Actions on the Case

If A delivers goods to B to deliver to C & B does not deliver them but converts them to his own use either A or C may have an action agt. B. They cant join.

Bulster 68.

If a servant is cozened of his Masters money the Master may have an action agt. the cozener.

Cr. Ja. 223.

No action lies by a Master agt. his sert. for the bare breach of his comd. but if a Servt. does any thing falsely & fraudulently to the damage of his Master an action lies.

Sid. 298.

No master is chargeable with the acts of his Servant but when he acts in execution of the authority given by his Master & then the act of the Sert. is the act of the Master.

Sal. 282 Pl. 11.

If I deliver goods to A who delivers them to B to keep to the use of A who wastes them I may have an action against B.

Though an injury happens to a Man in his property by the neglect of another yet if by law he was not obliged to be more careful no action lies.

If a man uses or abuses the thing he finds he shall answer for it.

Cr. El. 219.

If by the wrongful act of A, B. becomes chargeable to C B may have his action against A before he is sued by C.

Cr. Ja. 474; Cr. El. 53.

If a man forges a bond in my name' tis possible I may be injured by it, but' till it be put in suit agt. me I have no action agt. the forger.

Hob. 267; vide 6 Mod. 46.

Where a man has the possession of any personal chattel & sells it, the bare affirming it to be his amounts to a warranty & gives an action.

Sal. 210. pl. 2; Ld. Ray. 284; Cr. Ja. 474.

If on a treaty for the purchase of a house the Deft, affirms the rent of the house to be £30 whereas it was but £20 & thereby the Plf. is induced to give so much more than the house is worth an action lies.

Sal. 211. pl. 3.

If I sell unsound goods & knowing them to be unsound affirm them to be sound, or not knowing them to be unsound warrant them to be sound an action lies.

Cr. Ja. 469.

If a man rides an unruly horse in places much frequented & the horse breaks from him & runs over B & hurts him, B shall have an action. For an injury accruing to a Man in his real estate of freehold or inheritance the action lies.

Vent. 295; Ld. Ray. 38.

If a Man lend or hire anothers horse & for want of safe keeping the horse dies an action lies.

Cr. El. 777.

If A obtains a judgt. in debt agt. B as Exr. to his Father, & thereupon A takes out a Fi. Fa. but before the sheriff can execute it B removes & disposes of all the Testators goods so that the sheriff is forced to return nulla bona an action on the case lies agt. B for the sheriff could not return a devastavit & if this action does not lie the party is without remedy.

Godb. 285, 2. Rol. Rep. 322, vide con. Mod. 286.

In genl. where by the covin of a third person a man loses his debt an action on the case lies agt. him.

Also for injuries done to a man with respect to his wife his child or his servant an action lies.

Carth. 3, 4.

If a minister of justice have a warrant to attach the goods of another & can do it & does it not an action lies against him.

3. Bul. 212; Cr. El. 873.

If a smith refuses to shoe my horse or if he pricks him; if a farrier kills my horse with bad medecine or by neglect in curing him; or if a client receives an injury by the neglect or fraud of his attorney an action lies.

San. 312; 2 Bulster 373; Cr. Ja. 395.

If by a common nusance I suffer a particular damage an action lies, so too for continuing a nuisance.

Cr. Ja. 446; Ld. Ray 370.

It seems agreed that for a false & malicious prosecution for any crime whether capital or not by which a man may be endangered of his life, suffer in his liberty reputation or property an action on the case in nature of a writ of conspiracy lies whether an indictment was exhibited or not.

Cr. El. 70; 134, Sal. 15.

If a stranger brings an action in the name of J. without consulting J. an action lies.

Ray. 503; Cr. El. 629.

If an action on the case is brought for a civil action special grievance must be shewn.

Style 379; Sand. 228.

It seems the better opinion that a person guilty of felony & pardoned or burnt in the hand[6] may be proceeded agt. at the suit of the party injurd.

Stile 346; Yel. 99.

Action lies for a virgin of good fame married by a man who had a wife.

Skin. 119.

Affadavit
Agreements

A person non compos, an infant & a feme covert are generally incapable of entering into agreements.

See Eq. ca. ab. 25. pl. 6.

The ancestor seised in fee may by his agrt. bind his Heir.

2. Ver. 215.

Tis a genl. rule that wherever the matter of the bill is merely in damages the remedy is at law, but if there be matter of fraud mixt with the damages the remedy is in chancery. So where the agreemt. is to do something in specie.

Ab. Eq. 16; chan. rep 158; Ch. ca. 42.

A court of equity has decreed a performance of covenants & directed a trial in a quantum damnificat."

Ver. 189 Pl. 190; 2 Ch. ca. 146.

Agreemts. out of which an equity can be raised for a decree in specie ought to be obtaind with all imaginable fairness & without any mixture tending to surprise or circumvention and that they be not unreasonable in themselves.

Ab. Eq. 17; 2. Ch. ca. 17; Ver. 227 Pl. 225.

A ct. of eqty. will much sooner dismiss a bill which prays a specific execution of an unreasonable agrt. than set aside an agrt. though not strictly fair on a bill for that purpose and when such agreements are set aside it must be on refunding what was paid, making reasonable allowances for improvemts. etc.

2. Ch. Ca. 136; Ver. 271; Rep. in Eq 155; 2 Ver. 227.

In law & equity voluntary conveyances are good agt. the parties & cannot be revoked, nor will the Ct. interpose in behalf of one volunteer agt. another. But if they affect creditors purchasers or younger children the Ct. will set them aside.

Ver. 100, 464.

If there be a defective conveyance without an equitable consideration equity will not oblige the party to make it good though there be a covenant for farther assurances.

2. Ven. 365; 2 Ver. 40.

If the agreemt. be to quit the possession of lands the Ct. will not decree a conveyance.

VER. 121.

If one is bound to transfer £300 Stock before such a time which he does not do, & the stock is much risen he shall transfer the stock in specie & account for dividends since the time.

2 VER. 394, PRECED. IN CH. 533.

No estate for life or any higher estate shall be made to take effect, nor shall an use thereof be created unless it be by deed indented sealed & recorded in the Genl. Ct. or the Ct. of that coty. where the land lies. The deed of residents to be recorded in 8 months of non residents in 2 Years.The Deed to be acknowleged by the grantor or proved by three witnesses before it can be admitted to record. Deeds of inheritance, for term of years, or for marriage settlement; all deeds of trust & Mortgages whatsoever not recorded etc. to be void as to subsequent purchasers & creditors but binding between the parties & their heirs.

19. G. 2 CH. 1 P. 142, 143.

The foregoing act is very similar to the stat. of frauds & perjuries on which the following determinations have been made by the Judges in England.

NOTE THE STAT. OF FRAUDS ETC. DOES NOT REQUIRE RECORDING.

If the Deft. in his answer confesses the substance of a bill setting forth a parol agrt. & demanding a specific execution the Ct. will decree it.

AB. E.19 P1.3; VER. 151, 159.

A parol agreemt. which is intended to be reduced to writing but is prevented by fraud may be decreed in specie.

AB. EQ. 20.

A letter from a father promising a portion & a marriage had in consequence thereof has been deemed sufficient.

2. VER. 322; 2 VENT. 361; PREC. IN CH. 361.

It seems to be admitted that if an agreement be made concerning lands etc. though not in writing & the whole or part of the money is recd. by the party equity will decree a specific execution. The doubt is what evidence shall be admitted as proof of the receipt. If the Deft. confesses it in his answer 'tis sufft. if he denies it the Plaintiff must prove it by written evidence.

2 VER. 151; 2. CH. CA. 135; STR. 426; GIL. HIS. CH. 239, CONTRA, 2. CH. CA. 36, GIL. HIS. CH. 231.

If a man on the promise of a lease lays out money on improvements he shall oblige the lessee to execute a lease. Secus if he has been at no expense.

VER. 159; 2. VENT. 361.

If a man purchases lands in anothers name & pays the money it shall be a trust for him.

VER. 366.

AMENDMENT AND JEOFAIL
ANNUITY AND RENT CHARGE

Whenever the remedy by way of charge for the rent is not commensurate to the rent, the rent is called seck & the charge is only appurtenant.

CO. L. 247; 7 CO. 151.

If I bind my land & goods for the payment of a rent, or if I grant that if such a rent be arrear B may distrain for it in the manor of C. This is a good rent charge.

CO. L. 149; BROKE RENT. 14.

If an original grant be made of a rent charge to commence after the death of J.S. it is good, secus of a rent in being.

BROKE GRANT 86; 2 VENT. 204; B. GRANT 86.

If a man grants by his deed an annual rent out of certain lands with distress & does not provide that the grant shall not charge his person, the grantee may distrain for the rent or have a writ of annuity.

Lit. Sec. 219, 220; 6 Co. 58.

If a rent be granted out of lands in which the grantor has no interest, or in which the grantee cannot by the deed distrain, with a proviso that it shall not charge his person the proviso is void.

Co. L. 146; 6. Co. 41; 6. Co. 58.

A grant that a man may distrain in certain lands if a certain sum be unpaid does not charge the person.

Co. L. 146.

A rent is granted out of an inheritance & term for years. The grantee may distrain in both but must avow for a rent issuing out of the inheritance.

Co. L. 147; Cr. Ja. 390.

If such power is given in the deed the grantee may when rent is arrear enter & hold the lands till he is satisfied by the perception of the profits.

Ray. 135; San. 112.

An action of debt does not lie for the arrearages of an annuity if the grantee be seised of it for life or in fee, secus if for years.

Co. L. 162; 4 Co. 49; Cr. El. 268.

If the grantee distrains & avows or brings a writ of annuity and declares he has determined his election & shall ever after be confined to the remedy he has adopted.

Lit. S. 219; Co. L. 145.

If the grantee of a rent charge before he has made his election purchases a part of the land he is without any remedy.

C.L. 148; see 2. Ver 143-4.

Arbitrament & Award

A right of freehold cannot be transferd, an Annuity determind, partition made by award. But if the parties are bound in mutual obligations to stand to the award & a transfer etc. is awarded the party refusing forfeits his obligation.

9. Co. 78.

Debt certain & fixed cannot be discharged by naked award, nor causes criminal or matrimonial decided.

6. Co. 44; Cr. Ja. 99; 2 Vent. 109.

Chattels & actions personal may be determined by arbitrament & transfered by award without deed. The submission is to be taken largely & according to the intent of the parties, where tis made by word the remedy to enforce a performance of the award is by reciprocal actions on the case. An action of debt will lie if money be awarded.

9 Co. 78.

Ex nuda submissione non oritur actio, but notice must be given. If the submission be by deed tis still revocable but the party forfeits his obligation. Marriage of a feme sole is a revocation.

8 Co. 81; 8. Co. 82; 2 Keb. 845.

In debt on a bond to perform an award if non submisit must be pleaded no breach need be alledged.

Sid. 290.

An award must be made according to the submission. It ought to be certain, equal, & mutually satisfactory. It must be lawful & possible. It must be final.

If the award is good as to one party & void as to the other party tis void in the whole.

If money be awarded & not paid the party may either have his first action or action of debt.

8 Co. 98.

In pleading a man should set forth the award & therein how he hath performed it.

Moor. 3. pl 9.

Where any thing is awarded in satisfaction the award is a bar, but where releases are awarded 'tis no bar till performance.

CARTH. 378; LD. RAY. 247.

Not necessary to lay time & place of the award.

2. BROWNL. 137.

ASSAULT & BATTERY

Any injury whatever actually done to the person of a man, in a angry revengeful, rude or insolent manner is a battery.

6 MOD. 149; LD. RAY. 62; SALK. 407 PI. 2.

The least touching of anothers person wilfully or in anger is battery.

3. BL. 120.

A Parent may moderately chastise his child, a Master his servt. or his scholar. An officer having a warrant agt. one who will not be arrested may beat or wound him in the attempt to take him. A man may beat wound or maim one who makes an assault on his person or on that of his wife parent child or master, or who attempts to kill a stranger.

I may justify an ass[aul]t in defense of my land or goods. In an action on the case the Deft, must plead the matter of justification specially.

HAWK. P.C. 830; 3. BL. 120; 6 MOD. 272.

Every ass[aul]t will not justify every beating.

2 INST. 316; 2 HAW. P.C. 159.

ASSIGNMENT

In assignments of a lease for life or years a man parts with his whole property & the assignee stands in the place of the Assignor.

2.BL. 326-7.

Assignment of lease etc. to be recorded etc.

19. G. 2. CH. I. 143.

To avoid maintenance a possibility, right of entry thing in action, cause of suit or title for a condition broken cannot be granted or assignd over. Assignee of bond or note for money or tobacco may sue in his own name allowing all discounts the Deft, can prove either agt. the Plf. himself or the first obligee before notice of assignment.

A personal trust not assignable.

CO. L. 214; 27. G. 2. 249.

ASSUMPSIT

In assumpsit damages are recovered in proportion to the loss sustaind by the violation of the contract. Indebitatus will lie in no case but where debt woud lie.

4 CO. 92.

Obligor in a bond witht. any new considn. promises to pay the Money Ass[umpsi]t will not lie but debt.

HUTT. 34; CR. EL. 240 CONT.

Neither debt nor a genl. Ind. ass. will lie agt. the acceptor of a bill of exchange but action on the case.

HARD. 485; SAL. 23. PI. 3.

But debt or a genl. Ind. may be brought agt. the drawer.

LD. RAY. 175.

An Ind. lies for money won at play, paid by mistake.

2 Vent. 175.

An indet. lies for money recd. to the P1. use on an implied contract. Lies agt. sheriff for money levied on a Fi. Fa.

All promises are to be taken most strong agt. the promisor & are not to be rejected if they can be reduced to certy.

Salk. 27. pl. 14.

Wherever a person promises without a benefit arising to the promisor or loss to the promissee tis a void promise as being without sufft. consideration.

2 Buls. 269.

If the father of A & B lying sick declares his intention of devising a rent to his younger son during life & the elder in consideration his father will not charge the lands promises to pay the rent in consequence of which the land is not charged, this is a good consideration.

A consideration altogether executed & past, unless moved by a precedent request will not maintain ass [umpsi]t.

Leon. 192; Cr. El. 163.

Where the consideration is agt. law promise void.

Cr. Ja. 103.

The Plf. must set forth every thing essential to the Gist of the action with such certainty that it may appear there was cause of action. But the law requires no greater certainty than the nature of the thing requires.

The Deft. must shew there was no contract, or that the contract was void & without consideration or that he has performed it.

An entire promise cannot be apportioned.

March 200.

The Deft. cannot plead that he has revoked the promise.

Cr. Ja. 483.

Attachment

Attachmt. is a process that issues at the discretion of the Judges Of a Ct. of record agt. a person for some contempt for which he is to be committed & may be awarded by them upon a bare suggestion or on their own knowlege.

All courts of record have a discretionary power over their own officers & will punish them for disobeying their commands for executing them oppressively or otherwise misdemeaning themselves in their office.

Dyer. 218; 2 Haw. P.C. 142, 145.

Attachmts. have been granted for speaking contemptuous words concerning the rules of Ct., for disobedience of those rules & for the abuses of the process.

Sal. 84. pl. 4; Mod. 21; 2 Haw. P.C. 154.

Audita Querela

An Audita querela is a writ to be releived against an unjust judgement or execution by setting them aside for some injustice of the party that obtaind them which could not be pleaded in bar to the action.

If A being within age becomes bail for B & Judgement is given against him he may avoid it by Audita querela.

AUTHORITY

A naked authority must be strictly executed. Several persons named in a will to sell lands, one dies, the survivors cannot sell.

Co. L. 181, 113.

Deed not delivered till after the day of date, attorney makes livery on the delivery of the deed good.

Cr. Ja. 153.

Letter of Attorney to make livery absolutely, he delivers on condition good. Secus if to make livery on condi[ti]on & he delivers absolutely.

Co. L. 258.

Feofment made to A & B, livery by attorney to one in name of both good. Authority cannot be transfered. 9. Co. 77.

Co. L. 49.

Must be executed during the life of the person that gives it.

Co. L. 52.

BAIL IN CIVIL CAUSES

When the Shf. arrests anyone he is obliged to take bail otherwise an action on the case lies agt. him.

Vent. 55; 3. Bl. 290.

Deft, failing to appear, or give special bail when ruled thereto, the bail returned shall be subject to the same judgement & have the same liberty of defense as Deft. would have had.

No bail to be taken after judgement.

22. G. 2.ch. 4, 171; 27. G.2. ch.1, 296.

In suit on a penal stat, the Deft, not held to Bail.

22. G. 2.ch. 4. 172.

Heir, Exr., or Admr. not held to special bail

2. Brown. 293.

Bail subject to judgement of Genl. Ct. in appeals.

The Bail liable to judget. etc. agt. Deft. unless he render his body in execution. If the Bail plead a render of the principal he must plead prout patet per recordum.

22. G. 2. ch. 4. 178.

Chapter 5

Experiences as a Law Student

1828

James Kent

James Kent (July 31, 1763-December 12, 1847) was Chancellor of New York from 1814 to 1823 and professor at Columbia College (later Columbia University) from 1793 to 1795 and 1824 to 1826. His *Commentaries on American Law* are described in chapter 1. See also chapter 17. Reprinted here is a letter to a correspondent in Tennessee, printed in *The Green Bag*, vol. IX (Boston: Boston Book Co., 1897), pp. 206-211, with the following note: "This letter was recently found in the old Capitol at Jackson, Miss. There is no record showing how it got there. The Thomas Washington to whom it was addressed was a lawyer of some note who lived at Nashville, Tenn." Further biographical and bibliographical data appear in the letter.

New York, October 6th, 1828

Dear Sir:—Your very kindly & friendly letter of the 15th ult. was duly received, and also your argument in the Case of *Ivey vs. Pinson*. I have read the Pamphlet with much interest & pleasure. It is composed with masterly ability, of this there can be no doubt, & without presuming to give any opinion on a great case, still *Sub Judice*, & only argued before me on one side, I beg leave to express my highest respect for the law reasoning & doctrine of the argument, & my admiration of the spirit, & eloquence which animate it. My attention was very much fixed on the perusal, & if there be any lawyer in this State who can write a better argument in any point of view I have not the honor of his acquaintance.

As to the rest of your letter concerning my life & studies, I hardly know what to say, or to do. Your letter & argument, & character & name have impressed me so favorably, that I feel every disposition to oblige you, if it be not too much at my own expense. My attainments are of too ordinary a character, & far too limited, justly to provoke such curiosity. I have had nothing more to aid me in all my life than plain method, prudence, temperance & steady persevering diligence. My diligence was more remarkable for being steady & uniform, than for the degree of it, which never was excessive, so as to impair my health or eyes, or prevent all kinds of innocent & lively recreation. I would now venture to state briefly but very frankly & at your special desire, somewhat of the course & progress of my studious life. I know you cannot but smile at times at my simplicity, but I commit myself to your indulgence & honor.

I was educated at Yale College & graduated in 1781. I stood as well as any in my class, but the test of scholarship at that day was contemptible. I was only a very inferior classical scholar, & we were not required,

& to this day I have never looked into a Greek book but the New Testament. My favorite studies were Geography, History, Poetry, bellesletter, &c. When the College was broken up & dispersed in July 1779 by the British, I retired to a country village & finding Blackstone's com. I read the 4th volume, parts of the work struck my taste, & the work inspired me at the age of 16 with awe, and I fondly determined to be a lawyer. In November 1781 I was placed by my father with Mr. (now called Judge) Benson, who was then attorney general at Poughkeepsie on the banks of the Hudson, & in my native County of Dutchess. There I entered on law, & was the most modest, steady, industrious student that such a place ever saw. I read the following winter *Grotius & Puffendorf* in huge folios, & made copious extracts. My fellow students who were more gay and gallant, thought me very odd and dull in my taste, but out of five of them four died in middle life drunkards. I was free from all dissipation, and chaste as pure virgin snow. I had never danced, or played cards, or sported with a gun, or drank anything but water. In 1782 I read *Smollets* history of England, & procured at a farmers house where I boarded, *Rapins History* (a huge folio) and read it through; and I found during the course of the last summer among my papers, my M. S. abridgment on *Rapins* dissertation on the laws and customs of the Anglo Saxons. I abridged Hales history of the common law, and the old books of practice, and read parts of Blackstone again & again. The same year I procured *Humes* History and his profound reflections & admirable eloquence struck most deeply on my youthful mind. I extracted the most admired parts and made several volumes of M. S. S. I was admitted to the bar of the Supr. Court in January 1785, at the age of 21, and then married without one cent of property; for my education exhausted all my kind father's resources and left me in debt $400.00, which took me two or three years to discharge. Why did I marry? I answer that.

At the farmers house where I boarded, one of his daughters, a little modest, lovely girl of 14 generally caught my attention & insensibly stole upon my affections, & I before I thought of love or knew what it was, I was most violently affected. I was 21. and my wife 16 when we married, & *that charming lovely girl has been the idol & solace of my life,* & is now with me in my office, unconscious that I am writing this concerning her. We have both had uniform health & the most perfect & unalloyed domestic happiness, & are both as well now & in as good spirits as when we married. We have three adult children. My son lives with me and is 26, & a lawyer, & of excellent sense, & discretion, & of the purest morals. My eldest daughter is well married, & lives the next door to me, with the intimacy of our family, my youngest daughter is now of age, she lives with me, & is my little idol.

I went to housekeeping at Poughkeepsie, 1786, in a small, snug cottage, & there I lived in charming simplicity for eight years. My practice was just about sufficient to redeem me from debt, & to maintain my wife & establishment decently, and supply me with books about as fast as I could read them. I had neglected & almost entirely forgotten my scanty knowledge of the Greek & Roman classics, & an accident turned my attention to them very suddenly. At the June Circuit in 1786, I saw Ed. Livingstone[1] (now the codifier for Louisiana) & he had a pocket Horace & read some passages to me at some office & pointed out their beauties, assuming that I well understood Horace. I said nothing, but was stung with shame & mortification, for I had forgotten even my Greek letters. I purchased immediately Horace and Virgil, a dictionary & grammar, and a Greek Lexicon & grammar and the testament, & formed my resolution promptly and decidedly to recover the lost languages.

I studied in my little cottage mornings and devoted an hour to greek and another to latin daily, I soon increased it to two for each tonge in the 24 hours, my acquaintance with the languages increased rapidly. After I had read Horace and Virgil I ventured upon Livy for the first time in my life, & after I had completed the Greek Testament I took up the Iliad, & I can hardly describe at this day[2] with which I progressively read and studied in the original *Livy* & the Iliad. It gave me inspiration, I purchased a French Dictionary & grammar & began French & gave an hour to this language daily. I appropriated the business part of the day to law, & read Co. Litt, & made copious notes. I devoted evening to English literature in company with my wife. From 1788 to 1798 I steadily divided the day into five portions, & alotted them to *Greek, Latin, law and business, French & English.* I mastered the best of the *Greek, Latin* and *French* classics, & as well as the best English & law books at hand & read Machiavel & all collateral branches of English history, such as Libeletines H. 2nd Bacons H. 7th. Lord Clarendon on the great Rebellion, &c. I even sent to England as early as 1790 for Warbertons divine legation Lusiad.

My library which started from nothing grew with my growth, & it has now attained to upwards of 3,000 volumes, & it is pretty well selected, for there is scarcely a work, authority or document referred to in the 3 volumes of my commentaries but what has a place in my own library, next to my wife, my library has been the solace of my greatest pleasure & devoted attachment.

The year 1793 was another era in my life, I removed from Poughkeepsie to the city of New York, with which I had become well acquainted, & I wanted to get rid of the incumbrance of a dull law partner at P, but though I had been in practice nine years, I had acquired very little property. My furniture & library were very scanty, & I had not $500 extra in the world. But I owed nothing, & came to the City with good character & with a scolar's reputation. My newspaper writings, & speeches in the assembly had given me some notoriety. I do not believe any human being ever lived with more pure and perfect domestic repose & simplicity & happiness than I did for those nine years.

I was appointed professor of law in Columbia College late in 1793 & this drove me to deeper legal researches. I read that year in the original Bynkersheek Quinctillion & Ciceros rhetorical works, besides reports and digests, & began the compilation of law lectures. I read a course in 1794 & 5 to about 40 gentlemen of the first rank in the City. They were very well received, but I have long since discovered them to have been slight & trashy productions. I wanted Judicial labors to teach me precision. I dropped the course after one term, & soon became considerably involved in business, but was never fond of, nor much distinguished in the contentions of the bar.

I had commenced in 1786 to be a zealous Federalist & read everything on politics. I got the Federalist almost by heart, and became intimate with Hamilton. I entered with ardor into the federal politics against France in 1793, & my hostility to the French democracy, & to French power beat with strong pulsation down to the battle of Waterloo, now you know my politics.

I had excellent health owing to the love of simple diet, & to all kinds of temperance, & never read late nights. I rambled daily with my wife on foot over the hills, we were never asunder. In 1795 we made a voyage through the lakes George & Champlain. In 1797 we run over the 4 New England States. As I was born and nourished in boyish days among the highlands East of the Hudson, I have always loved rural & wild scenery, & the sight of mountains & hills, & woods & streams always enchanted me, and do still. This is owing in part to early associations, & it is one secret of my uniform health & chirfulness.

In 1796 I began my career of official life. It came upon me entirely unsolicited & unexpected. In Feby 1796 Governor Jay wrote me a letter stating that the office of *Master in Chancery* was vacant, & wished to know confidentially whether I would accept. I wrote a very respectful but very laconic answer. It was "That I was content to accept of the office if appointed." The same day I received the appointment, & was astonished to learn that there were 16 professed applicants all disappointed. This office gave me the monopoly of the business of that office, for there was but one other master in N York. The office kept me very busy in petty details and outdoor concerns, but was profitable. In March 1797 I was appointed *Recorder of N. York.* This was done at Albany, & without my knowledge that the office was even vacant or expected to be. The first I heard of it was the appointed announced in the papers. This was very gratifying to me, because it was a judicial office. I thought that it would relieve me from the drudgery of practice & gave me a way of displaying what I knew; & of being useful entirely to my taste. I pursued my studies with increased appetite & enlarged my law library very much. But I was encumbered with office business, for the governor allowed me to retain the other office also, & with these joint duties & counsel business in the Sup. Court, I made a great deal of money that year. In Feby 1798 I was offered by Gov Jay & accepted the office of youngest *Judge of the Supreme Court.* This was the summit of my ambition. My object was to return back to Poughkeepsie, & resume my studies, & ride the circuits, & inhale country air, & enjoy *otium cum dignitate.* I never dreamed of volumes of reports & written opinions. Such things were not then thought of. I retired back to P in the Spring of 1798 & in that Summer rode all over the Western wilderness & was delighted. I returned home and began my Greek & Latin, & French, & English, & law classics as formerly, & made wonderful progress in books that year.

In 1799 I was obliged to remove to Albany, in that I might not be too much from home, & *there I remained stationary for 24 years.* When I came to the bench there ([3]) no reports or State precedents. The opinions from the bench were delivered *ore tenus.* We had no law of our own, & nobody knew what it was. I first introduced a thorough examination of cases & written opinions. In Jany T 1799 the 2d case reported in 1st Johnsons cases, of *Ludlow vs. Dale*[4] is a sample of the earliest. The judges when we met all assumed that foreign sentences were only good prime facie. I presented and read my written opinion that they were conclusive & they all gave up to me & so I read it in court as it stands.[5] This was the commencement of a new plan, & then was laid the first stone in the subsequently erected temple of our jurisprudence.

Between that time & 1804 I rode my share of circuits, attended all the terms, & was never absent, & was always ready in every case by the day. I read in that time ([6]) and completely abridged the latter, & made copious digests of all the English new reports and treatises as they came out. I made much use of the *Corpus Juris, &* as the Judges (Livingston excepted) knew nothing of French or civil law I had immense advantage over them. I could generally put my Brethern to rout & carry my point by mysterious want of French and civil law. The Judges were republicans & very kindly disposed to everything that was French, & this enabled me without exciting any alarm or jealousy, to make free use of such authorities & thereby enrich our commercial law.

I gradually acquired preponderating influence with my brethern, & the volumes in Johnson after I became Ch. J in 1804 show it. The first practice was for each judge to give his portion of opinions when we all agreed, but that gradually fell off, but for the two or three last years before I left the bench, I gave the most of them. I remember that in 8th Johnson all the opinions one Term are *per curiam.* The fact is I wrote them all, & proposed that course to avoid existing jealousy & many a per curiam opinion was so inserted for that reason.

Many of the cases decided during the 16 years I was in the Supr. Court were labored by me most unmercifully, but it was necessary under the circumstances in order to subdue opposition. We had but few American precedents. One judge was democratic, and my brother *Spencer* particularly of a bold, vigorous, dogmatic mind, & overbearing manner. English authorities did not stand very high in those feverish times, & this led me a hundred times to attempt to bear down opposition, or flame it by exhausting research & overwhelming authority. Our Jurisprudence was probably on the whole improved by it. My mind certainly was roused, & was always kept ardent and inflamed by collision.

In 1814 I was appointed Chancellor. The office I took with considerable reluctance. It had no claims. The person who left it was stupid, & it is a curious fact that for the nine years I was in that office, there was *not a single decision, opinion or dictum of either of my two predecessors (Ch. Livingston & Ch.* ([7])) from 1777 to 1814 cited to me or even suggested. I took the court as if it had been a new institution, & never before known to the U. S. I had nothing to guide me, & was left at liberty to assume all such English chancery powers and jurisdiction as I thought applicable under our constitution. This gave me great scope, & I was only checked by the revision of the Senate & court of Errors. I opened the gates of the court immediately, & admitted almost gratuitously the first year 85 counsellors, though I found there had not been but 13 admitted for 13 years before. Business flowed in with a rapid tide. The result appears in the seven volumes of Johnson's Ch. reports.

My study in Equity jurisprudence was very much confined to the topics elicited by the cases. I had previously read, of course, the modern Equity reports, down to the time, & of course I read all the new ones as fast as I could procure them. I remember reading Pear Williams as early as 1792 and made a digest of the leading doctrines. The business of the court of chancery oppressed me very much, but I took my daily exercise, & my delightful country rides among the Catskill or the Vermont mountains with my wife, & kept up my health and spirits. I always took up the cases in their order, & never left one until I had finished it. This was only *doing one thing at a time.* My practice was first to make myself perfectly & accurately (mathematically accurately) master of the facts. It was done by abridging the bill, & then the answers, & then the depositions, & by the time I had done this slow tedious process I was master of the cause & ready to decide it. I saw where justice lay and the moral sense decided the cause half the time, & I then sed down to search the authorities until I had exhausted my books, & I might once & a while be embarrassed by a technical rule, but I *most always found principles suited to my views of the case,* & my object was to discuss a point ([8]) as never to be teared with it again, & to anticipate an angry & vexatious appeal to a popular tribune by disappointed counsel.

During those years at Albany, I read a great deal of English literature, but not with the discipline of my former division of time. The avocations of business would not permit it. I had dropped the Greek as it hurt my eyes. I persevered in Latin, & used to read Virgil, Horace, Juvenal, Lucan, Salust, Tacitus, &c & Ciceros offices, & some of them annually. I have read Juvenal, Horace & Virgil eight or ten times. I read a great deal in Pothiers works and always consulted him when applicable. I read the Ed & Q reviews & Annl register *ab initio* & thorougly, & voyages & travels & the Waverley novels &c, as other folks did. I have always been excessively fond of voyages and travels.

In 1823 a solemn era in my life arrived. I retired from the office at the age of 60, & then immediately with my son visited the Eastern States. On my return the solitude of my private office & the new dinasty did not please me. I besides would want income to live as I had been accustomed. My eldest daughter was permanently settled in N York, & I resolved to move away from Albany, & I ventured to come down to N. Y. & be Chamber Counsel, & the trustees of Columbia College immediately tendered me again the old office of professor which had been dormant from 1795. It had no salary, but I must do something for a living, & I undertook (but exceedingly against my inclination) to write & deliver law lectures. In the two characters of Chamber Counsellor and College lecturer, I succeeded by steady perseverance beyond my most sanguine expectations, & upon the whole the five years I have lived here in this City since 1823 have been happy & prosperous, & I live aside of my daughter, & I take excursions every Summer with my wife & daughter all over the country. I have been twice with he ([9]) Canada & in every direction. I never had better health. I walk the battery uniformly before breakfast. I give a great many written opinions, & having got heartily tired of lecturing I abandoned it, & it was my son that pressed me to prepare a volume of lectures for the press. I had no idea of publishing them when I delivered them. I wrote over one volume & published it as you know. This led me to remodel & enlarge, & now the 3rd volume will be out in a few days, & I am *obliged to write a 4th to complete my law.*

My reading now is as you may well suppose, quite desultory, but still I read with as much zeal and pleasure as ever, I was never more engaged in my life than during the last Summer. I accepted the trust of receiver to the Franklin (insolvent) Bank, & it has occupied, & perplexed, & vexed me daily, & I had to write part of the 3rd volume, & search books a good deal for that very object, and I have revised the proof sheet.

If I had a convenient opportunity (though I do not see how I can have one) I would send the 3rd volume out to you, & another to our excellent friend, Governor Carroll, to whom I beg you will be so good as to present my best respects & the expression of my great esteem.

Your suggestion of an Equity treatise contains a noble outline of a great & useful work, but I cannot & will not enter on such a task I have much more to lose than to gairi & I am quite tired of Equity law. I have done my part, & choose to live more at my ease, & to be prepared for the approaching infirmities of age.—On reviewing what I have written, I had thoughts of burning it, I speak of myself too entirely, & it is entirely against my habit or taste, but I see no other way fairly to meet your desires.

I am with great respect and good wishes,

JAMES KENT.

Thomas Washington, Esq.

NOTES

1. For the work of Edward Livingstone in American law, see Essay No. 15, *ante* (Dillon: *Bentham's Influence in the Reforms*, etc.).—EDS.

2. Words omitted in original.

3. Words omitted in the original.

4. Probably January, 1806, 1st Case in 1 John. Ludlow v. Bowne.

5. For a note indicating an error of memory in Chancellor Kent's allusion to the tenor of this decision, see Professor Schofield's article in 1 *Illinois Law Rev.* p.257.—EDS.

6. Blank in the original.

7. Blank in original.

8. "So" omitted.

9. So in original.

Chapter 6

Experiences as a Law Student

1851

Joseph Story

Joseph Story (September 18, 1779-September 10, 1845) was associate justice of the U.S. Supreme Court, from 1811 to 1845, and the first Dane Professor at Harvard, from 1829 to 1845. His commentaries and his influence are described in chapter 1. See also his lecture, chapter 20. These excerpts are taken from Story's *Autobiography*, which was reprinted in William Story's *Miscellaneous Writings of Joseph Story* (Boston: Little, Brown) in 1851.

Just as I was fifteen years of age, in the autumn of 1794, an event occurred, which had some influence upon my character and destiny. I was preparing to enter Harvard College the next year, and having mastered the usual preparatory studies in Latin, and that most discouraging book, the Westminster Greek Grammar, I was beginning to study the Gospel of John, with a view to make an easy transition into Greek. Some boyish affair, I have quite forgotten what, induced me to chastise a lad belonging to the school, who boarded with my instructor, and this reaching the ears of the after, he determined, under another preference, to seek an occasion in school to punish me for the transaction. It is very easy to find such an occasion when we are determined on it. Some very slight peccadillo occurred on my part. I was, called up in the presence of the whole school and beaten very severely with a ferule on my hands. I bore it without shrinking, and submitted without resistance, being at that time too old to cry like a little boy, and having some pride to meet the punishment manfully. The schoolmaster was a man of violent and irascible temper when aroused, and seeing my calmness and firmness he struck me in his rage, I believe, as many as a hundred blows on my hands, until the agony was so great that I could no longer restrain myself from crying aloud. I was then ordered to my seat, and remained there suffering much pain until the school was dismissed. I never can think of this brutal and coarse treatment by this man, who was a clergyman, without a feeling of resentment and disgust. A few years after, when I had arrived at manhood, he took occasion to express his regret at the transaction, his consciousness, that he was in the wrong, and my total guiltlessness of anything to justify the punishment. He admitted that it was a retaliation for this chastisement I had inflicted on his boarder, and that his passions had carried him beyond the bounds of moderation. I forgave him, heartily forgave him. But though in other respects a deserving man, I never desired to have any communion with him beyond the mere formalities of common respect.

With the approbation of my father, I immediately left the academy. But it was a case full of embarrassment. There was no other school in the town in which the learned languages were taught; and with so large a family the expenses attendant upon an education at a distance were not to be overlooked. Fortunately, the principal town schoolmaster (whom I shall always remember with gratitude and respect) was acquainted with Latin, and the Greek of the New Testament, and he undertook to superintend my studies in those languages in the common books. It was in the autumn, and I formed the sudden resolution to prepare myself so as to be offered for admission at Harvard College in the ensuing January vacation as a Freshman. To do this was no small labor, and required extraordinary diligence and exertion. My master had not much time to assist me, and undertook little beyond merely hearing my recitation. My pride was roused, and my ambition stimulated. I determined to go through the labor: and though I was then but just in the beginning of Greek, and had considerable in Latin as well as in other departments to master, I was not discouraged. In the course of two short months, I had not only gone over all these studies with care, but I had several times reviewed them, and I felt confident that I could pass the necessary examinations.

8. Joseph Story (1779-1845), the first Dane Professor of Law at Harvard, presided over that institution's rise to national significance, while writing a shelf-ful of innovative legal treatises and serving as justice on the U.S. Supreme Court. In his spare time, he judged moot courts, entertained students, and saw to the appointment of Simon Greenleaf to the faculty. Portrait engraving by M. Rosenthal, 1890. (*Courtesy of Art & Visual Materials, Special Collections Department, Harvard Law School Library.*)

Accordingly, just as the winter vacation was about to commence (it was then a vacation of six weeks) I was taken by my uncle to Cambridge for examination, and I felt the flush of hope play on my cheeks. Great was my disappointment upon being told by the president on my arrival there, that I must be examined, not merely in the previous preparatory studies, but in all the studies which the freshman class had been pursuing for the last six months. I was completely overwhelmed. I was dumb, disconsolate, and mortified. In one moment, at a single blow, all my hopes were demolished and my labors lost. I scarcely spoke a word during my whole homeward journey. My uncle, however, had taken a precaution to ascertain to what extent the class had gone, and what were the books which I must study.

I returned home in my great dejection. My father asked me what I intended to do? I replied, after some hesitation, that there were six weeks of vacation, and if he pleased, I would try to fit myself in that period for examination in the prescribed studies. I told him I could but fail, and if so, I must wait patiently until the next morning with a determination to go on. All the books were obtained that day, by purchase or borrowing. But here a new difficulty presented itself. I had no knowledge of the Greek dialects, and unluckily my master was in the same predicament; while the Iliad (which was one of the books to be studied) was full of them. All he could promise was, that he would hear me recite in Homer as well as he could. But he promised no aid in mastering these difficulties.

My task was now before me. I have a distinct recollection of the main parts. Sallust was to be read through, the Odes of Horace, two books of Livy, three books, I think, of Nenophon's Anabasis, and two books of Homer's Iliad, besides English Grammar and Rhetoric, and, I think, Logic, and some other studies. I sat down boldly to the task, reciting every morning five lessons, which I mastered during the preceding evening, and five or six more in the course of the day. It was intense labor, but I found no great difficulty except in Homer. The dialects puzzled me exceedingly, and my treacherous memory failed in preserving them accurately, so that I was often obliged to go over the same ground. For my first lesson in Homer I got five liens well; for my second, ten; for my third, fifteen; and then the mystery dissolved apace. In the course of the first three weeks I had gone through all the requisite studies. I could look back upon my past labors with the silent consciousness of victory. There is nothing to a young mind, unaccustomed to the exercise of its powers, so gratifying as this. The hero who conquers in battle, the orator who triumphs in the senate or the forum, feels not a more intense delight, than the youth first perceiving, that though born of the dust he is not altogether earth, but that there is something within him of an ethereal and intellectual nature. The remaining three weeks I passed in reviewing all these studies, which I did in the most difficult, more than once, and could say without a boast, at the end of the time, that I could go through two hundred lines of Homer at a recitation. At the end of the vacation I was again offered for examination, and without difficulty obtained my matriculation.

I have forgotten to mention a circumstance which occurred at an earlier period of my life, and which had wellnigh proved fatal to me. I slept in a small chamber over the front entry of my father's house, and the bed had curtains to it. I went to bed at my usual hour, and set the candle on a chest, which was at the bottom of the bed, and so near that it touched it. From carelessness, I placed the candle close by the curtains, and being very sleepy I forgot to put it out. By some accident it afterwards fell over and the curtains and bed caught fire. I was asleep. The family were not yet retired to rest. My door was shut; but my mother, sitting in a distant room, smelt something burning. Immediate search was made in that room and in those adjoining, but nothing was found. It then occurred to her that I had gone to bed about half an hour before with a light, and she instantly exclaimed that it must be in my chamber. My father ran up over one flight of stairs, and my mother over another. My father arrived first, opened the door, and the smoke was so intense and suffocating that he fell back breathless. My mother at this moment arrived, rushed in, and with that intrepidity and presence of mind which never desert a woman on such occasions, she caught me from the blazing clothes and carried me down stairs in her arms. I was not sensible of anything until I was below, and then found myself in my mother's arms. She was very severely burnt. I suppose that I was nearly suffocated when I was seized. The fire was stopped, and thus my life, when in the most imminent jeopardy, was saved. This admonition was sufficient to guard me at all times from indulging in that most dangerous practice of reading by candlelight in bed.

My entrance into Harvard College gave an entirely new course to my thoughts. Every thing was new to me. I seemed to breathe a higher atmosphere, and to look abroad with a wider vision and more comprehensive powers. Instead of the narrow group of a village, I was suddenly brought into a large circle of young men engaged in literary pursuits, and warmed and cheered by the hopes of future eminence.

It was considerable time, however, before I could acquire any familiar acquaintance with my classmates. One of the disadvantages of entering at an advanced standing is, that the associations of your class are already selected and fixed; and that you enter as a mere stranger, without rights and without sympathy. Your rank is not fixed; your scholarship is not known; your character is not ascertained; and you are viewed with a coldness and reserve peculiarly painful to the frankness of youth. I had the good fortune to chum with a young man who saw my embarrassment and gave me a kind welcome. From the first moment of my acquaintance up to this hour there has been a most unreserved friendship between us. Not a shadow has ever obscured it; not a chill has ever passed over it. I owe him much. He is one of the best and worthiest of men, and the lapse of thirty-five years enables me now to speak of him as a bosom friend, in whom I repose unlimited confidence and to whom I owe much of the truest happiness of life. My God preserve the blessing to me even to the close of my life.

Of course, on entering my class, I had no rank, and therefore silently stood at the fag-end of it. It was for me to prove that I had a title to a better place in the estimate of my judges, who were also my peers. It was some time before my classmates were inclined to form a favorable judgment, but by degrees I began to rise, and before I left college I had attained a high rank (it is not for me to say how high) for scholarship. Indeed, I was most thoroughly devoted to all the college studies, and scarcely wasted a single moment in idleness. I trace back to this cause a serious injury to my health. When I entered college I was very robust and muscular, but before I left I had become pale and feeble and was inclining to dyspepsia.

From my early years I had an inclination for poetry. I wrote verses, when I was not more than twelve years old, though I cannot say with Pope, "I lisped in numbers, for the numbers came." On the contrary, it was an exercise of skill with me, not as I imagine very successful or very attractive. One of my earlier efforts in college was a translation of an ode of Horace: of which I have now no other remembrance, than that it was thought well of by those about me. I received the usual rewards of good scholarship at the public exhibitions; delivering a poem at one exhibition; and a mathematical exercise at another in my senior year; and at the commencement at which I was graduated, I delivered the poem immediately before the closing English oration. It was received with much applause; but I burned it with some other early efforts a few years afterwards; and my memory retains no traces of it.

My college life was to me very delightful as well as instructive. I there formed several intimate friendships, which have been continued with unabated sincerity down to the present day. I believe that those friendships were highly useful to me, not merely as sources of private gratification and social intercourse; but they gave a vigor to my moral feelings, and strengthened those religious impressions of duty and those sentiments of honor, which are so important at the critical moment when a lad is passing from the feverish restlessness and unbridled passions of youth to the verge of manhood. I have some pride in saying, that I passed through this dangerous period, without a stain or reproach. I quitted college with regret; and shed many bitter tears in parting from scenes which I could never revisit with the same familiar pleasure, and classmates, whom in the future I could never expect to see again gathered in the same groups, with the buoyancy of hope, and the vivacity of unsuspecting confidence about them. I have never since read Gray's beautiful Ode on a Distant View of Eton College, without having my thoughts called back to the associations of those days with a deep and saddening feeling. I am now again an inhabitant of Cambridge; and I never pass the walls within which I spent so many happy hours, without a mixed sensation of tenderness and melancholy; for they speak to me in the voice of departed times, "departed never to return," and in the spirit of admonition of the sad inroads made by death among those who then graced its hall and guided the instructions of our Alma Mater.

Upon quitting college I returned to Marblehead, and began the study of law, under Mr. Samuel Sewall, then a distinguished counsellor at the bar, and a member of Congress, and afterwards a Judge, and finally Chief Justice of the Supreme Court of Massachusetts. With him I remained until his appointment as a Judge; and in December, 1801, I entered the office of Mr. Putnam, now Mr. Justice Putnam, in Salem, with whom I completed my preparatory studies, and was admitted to the bar at July term of the Common Pleas in Essex County, 1801.

From the causes to which I have already alluded, during my professional studies in Mr. Sewall's office, I was left very much alone, and with no literary associate in my native town. I was driven, therefore, back upon my own resources, and I not unfrequently devoted for months more than fourteen hours a day to study. Mr. Sewall's absence in Congress for about half the year also was a serious disadvantage to me, for I had no opportunity to ask for any explanation of difficulties, and no cheering encouragement to light up the dark and intricate paths of the law.

Beginning my studies in this recluse and solitary manner, I confess that I deeply felt the truth of Spelman's remarks, when he was sent to the Inns of Court for a similar purpose; my heart, like his, sunk within me, and I was tempted several times to give up the science from the firm belief that I could never master it. The case was very different then from what it is now, in respect both to the plan of studies and the facilities to acquire the elements. Then there were few elementary books; now the profession is inundated with them. Then the student, after reading that most elegant of all commentaries, Mr. Justice Blackstone's work, was hurried at once into the intricate, crabbed, and obsolete learning of Coke on Littleton. Now there are many elementary works which smooth the path towards the study of this great master of the Common Law. Then, there were scarcely any American Reports (for the whole number did not exceed five or six volumes) to enable the student to apply the learning of the Common Law to his own country, or to distinguish what was in force here, from what was not. Now, our shelves are crowded with hundreds.

Hitherto my pursuits had been wholly of a literary and classical character. I loved literature, and indulged freely in almost every variety of it to which I had access, from the profound writings of the great historians, metaphysicians, scholars, and divines, down to the lightest fiction, the enticing novel, the still more enticing romance, and the endless pageantries and imaginings of poetry. You may judge, then, how I was surprised and startled on opening works where nothing was presented but dry and technical principles, the dark and mysterious elements of the feudal system, the subtle refinements and intricacies of the middle ages of the Common Law, and the repulsive and almost unintelligible forms of processes and pleadings, for the most part wrapped up in black-letter, or in dusty folios. To me the task seemed Herculean. I should have quitted it in despair, if I had known whither to turn my footsteps, and to earn a support. My father had often told me, in the sincerity of his affection, that he should leave little property; that the most I could expect would be my education; and that I must earn my livelihood by my own labors. I felt the truth of the admonition; and it was perpetually whispered into my secret soul whenever I felt the overpowering influence of any discouragement. My destiny was to earn my bread by the sweat of my brow; and I must meet it or perish.

I shall never forget the time, when having read through Blackstone's Commentaries, Mr. Sewall, on his departure for Washington, directed me next to read Coke on Littleton, as the appropriate succeeding study. It was a very large folio, with Hargrave and Butler's notes, which I was required to read also. Soon after his departure, I took it up, and after trying it day after day with very little success, I sat myself down and wept bitterly. My tears dropped upon the book, and stained its pages. It was but a momentary irresolution. I went on and on, and began at last to see daylight, ay, and to feel that I could comprehend and reason upon the text and the comments. When I had that I breathed a purer air, and that I had acquired a new power. The critical period was passed; I no longer hesitated. I pressed on to the severe study of special pleading, and by repeated perusals of Saunders's Reports, acquired such a decided relish for this branch of my profession, that it became for several years afterwards my favorite pursuit. Even at this day I look back upon it with a lingering fondness, although many years have elapsed since I ceased to give it an exclusive attention. It is, in my judgment, the best school for the discipline of an acute and solid lawyer. While in Mr. Sewall's office, I also read through that deep admirable work upon one of the most intricate titles of the law, Fearne on Contingent Remainders and Executory Devises, and I made a manuscript abstract of all its principles. I am not quire sure that it may not yet be found among my manuscripts.

Upon my admission to the bar I was at a loss where to open an office, and indeed sat down in Salem, rather because I knew not where to go, than because I thought there was any real prospect of success. To young men with my political opinions the times were very discouraging. My father was a Republican, as contradistinguished from a Federalist, and I had naturally imbibed the same opinions. In Massachusetts, at that period, an immense majority of the people were Federalists. All the offices (with scarcely an exception, I believe,) were held by Federalists. The governor, the judges, the legislature, were ardent in the same cause. It cannot be disguised, too, that a great preponderance of the wealth, the rank, the talent, and the civil and literary character of the state, was in the same scale. Almost all of the profession of the law were of the party. I scarcely remember more than four or five lawyers in the whole state who *dared* avow themselves Republicans. The very name was odious, and offensive epithets (such as Jacobins) were familiarly applied to them. The great struggle was just over between Mr. Jefferson and Mr. Adams, and the former had been chosen to the Presidency. The contest had been carried on with great heat and bitterness; and the defeated party, strong at home, though not in the nation, was stimulated by resentment, and by the hope of a future triumph. Under such circumstances, there was a dreadful spirit of persecution abroad.

The intercourse of families was broken up, and the most painful feuds were generated. Salem was a marked battle ground for political controversies, and for violent struggles of the parties. The Republican party was at first very small there; and its gradual growth and increasing strength, so far from mitigating, added fuel to the flame.

Chapter 7

The Study of Law

1852

Joseph Story

Joseph Story (September 18, 1779-September 10, 1845) was associate justice of the U.S. Supreme Court, from 1811 to 1845, and the first Dane Professor at Harvard, from 1829 to 1845. His commentaries and his influence are described in Chapter 1. See also his lecture in chapter 20. These excerpts are taken from *Life and Letters of Joseph Story* by William Story (Boston: Little, Brown) in 1852.

Enters Mr. Sewall's Office at Marblehead—Feelings of Regret on quitting College—Difficulties in the Study of the Law—"Restless State 'twixt Yea and Nay"—Raptures on Rousseau—Disgust on first entering into the World—Praise of his Friends—Opinion of Southey, Junius, Kotzebue, Schiller, and the German Drama—Delivers a Eulogy on General Washington—Writes "The Power of Solitude"—Removes to Salem—Anecdote illustrating his Self-forgetfulness and Kindness—Society in Salem—His Political Views and Position—Cabals against Him—Letter containing Anecdotes and Reminiscences of Him—Letter stating his Political and Religious Opinions.

The brief years of college life having ended, it became necessary for him to choose a profession. His ambitious hopes as well as the constitution of his mind soon determined him to the study of the law. Accordingly, upon leaving Cambridge he immediately returned to Marblehead, and there opened his first law books in the office of Mr. Samuel Sewall, then a distinguished advocate at the Essex bar, and a member of congress; and afterwards Chief Justice of the supreme court of Massachusetts. It was not, however, without many a lingering look at the happy days which he had just past, that he returned to the dreariness of Marblehead. He felt with a pang the gates of youth shut down behind him as he entered the narrow task-room of professional manhood. For a time he seems to have desired a literary career, and to have resigned these hopes reluctantly. He, who had dallied with the muses in the gardens of classic and English literature,

> "And played with Amaryllis in the shade,
> Or with the tangles of Neæra's hair,"

shuddered as he embraced the common law. In a letter to his friend, Mr. Fay, dated September 6th, 1798, immediately after quitting Cambridge, he says,

"Conceive, my dear fellow, *what* is my situation, doomed to spend at least ten years, the best of my life, in the study of the law,—a profession whose general principles enlighten and enlarge, but whose minutiæ contract and distract the mind. Ambition is truly the food of my existence, and for that alone life is desirable. Yet, hard lot! Those favorite studies, those peculiar pursuits by which I have fondly (however vainly) hoped to attain celebrity, are ravished from me, and I must consent to be *a plodder* in order to be what the world calls a *man.* Yet it is the part of cowardice to shrink, and of imbecility to hesitate. I have determined, and will execute."

In another letter, dated September 8th, 1798, addressed to Mr. Charles P. Sumner, one of his early friends with whom he particularly sympathized in matters of literature, and father of one of his pupils and most intimate friends in later life, he says,

"I have begun the study of the law, and shall continue it with unremitting diligence; but a sigh of regret often accompanies my solitary moments,—a sigh, expressive of my ardent love of literary fame, and the impossibility of devoting all my attention to the object of my wishes. I candidly confess, that the hope of 'immortality' alone buoys me up, and if this hope should be destroyed, even should I remain unaffected by the meanness of mankind, all pleasure will have flown, and this world will appear 'a dreary waste, a wild without a flower.'"

This feeling however, soon wore away, and no sooner was his decision to pursue the law as a profession perfectly fixed, and his mind occupied in mastering its principles, than he began to be enamored of its harsh and crabbed forms and rules. Accordingly, in a letter to Mr. Fay, dated September 15th, 1801, we find his tone changed, and he says,

"You well know my love for my profession. The science claims me as a fixed devotee;—it rules me, and with my studious inclination, binds me more firmly to literary pursuits. Would to God this were my only ruling passion. But Love, like the pestilence, walketh in darkness and wasteth at noon-day."

The difficulties against which every student at law was forced to contend, at that day, as well as the peculiar disadvantage under which my father commenced his study of the law, will appear from a passage in the Autobiography in which he describes his position. He says,

"During my professional studies in Mr. Sewall's office, I was left very much alone, and with no literary associate in my native town. I was driven, therefore, back upon my own resources, and I not unfrequently devoted for months more than fourteen hours a day to study. Mr. Sewall's absence in congress for about half the year was also a serious disadvantage to me, for I had no opportunity to ask for any explanation of difficulties, and no cheering encouragement to light up the dark and intricate paths of the law.

"Beginning my studies in this recluse and solitary manner, I confess that I deeply felt the truth of Spelman's remarks, when he was sent to the Inns of Court for a similar purpose,1 my heart like his sunk within me; and I was tempted several times to give up the science from a firm belief that I could never master it. The case was very different then from what it is now, in respect both to the plan of studies and the facilities to acquire the elements. Then there were few elementary books; now the profession is inundated with them. Then the student, after reading that most elegant of all commentaries, Mr. Justice Blackstone's work, was hurried at once into the intricate, crabbed, and obsolete learning of Coke on Littleton. Now there are many elementary works which smooth the path towards the study of this great master of the common law. Then, there were scarcely any American Reports (for the whole number did not exceed five or six volumes,) to enable the student to apply the learning of the common law to his own country, or to distinguish what was in force here, from what was not. Now our shelves are crowded with hundreds.

"Hitherto my pursuits had been wholly of a literary and classical character. I loved literature, and indulged freely in almost every variety of it to which I had access, from the profound writings of the great historians, metaphysicians, scholars, and divines, down to the lightest fiction, the enticing novel, the still more enticing romance, and the endless pageantries and imaginings of poetry. You may judge, then, how I was surprised and startled on opening works, where nothing was presented but dry and technical principles, the dark and mysterious elements of the feudal system, the subtle refinements and intricacies of the middle ages of the common law, and the repulsive and almost unintelligible forms of processes and pleadings, for the most part wrapped up in black-letter, or in dusty folios. To me the task seemed Herculean. I should have quitted it in despair, if I had known whither to turn my footsteps, and to earn a support. My father had often told me, in the sincerity of his affection, that he should leave little property; that the most I could expect would be my education; and that I must earn my livelihood by my own labors. I felt the truth of the admonition; and it was perpetually whispered into my secret soul whenever I felt the overpowering influence of any discouragement. My destiny was to earn my bread by the sweat of my brow; and I must meet it or perish.

"I shall never forget the time, when having read through Blackstone's Commentaries, Mr. Sewall, on his departure for Washington, directed me next to read Coke on Littleton, as the appropriate succeeding study. It was a very large folio, with Hargrave and Butler's notes, which I was required to read also. Soon after his departure, I took it up, and after trying it day after day with very little success, I sat myself down and wept bitterly. My tears dropped upon the book, and stained its pages. It was but a momentary irresolution. I went on and on, and began at last to see daylight, ay, and to feel that I could comprehend and reason upon the text and the comments. When I had completed the reading of this most formidable work, I felt that I breathed a purer air, and that I had acquired a new power. The critical period was passed; I no longer hesitated. I pressed on to the severe study of special pleading, and by repeated perusals of Saunders's Reports, acquired such a decided relish for this branch of my profession, that it became for several years afterwards my favorite pursuit. Even at this day I look back upon it with a lingering fondness, although many years have elapsed since I ceased to give it an exclusive attention. It is in my judgment the best school for the discipline of an acute and solid lawyer. While in Mr. Sewall's office, I also read through that deep and admirable work upon one of the most intricate titles of the law, Fearne on Contingent Remainders and Executory Devises, and I made a manuscript abstract of all its principles. I am not quite sure that it may not yet be found among my manuscripts."

I cannot help remembering, in this connection, the remark which Lord Eldon made to Wilberforce, when he was consulted as to the best mode of study and discipline for the young Grants to adopt in the law: "I know of no rule to give them," said he, "but that they must make up their minds to live like hermits and work like horses."[2]

During this period of his life, my father's mind was passing through that phase of struggle and vague aspiration, which lies between the manhood and youth of every man of genius.

"A restless state 'twixt yea and nay,
His heart all ebb and flow."

He is full of indefinite yearning. What he desires, he can never distinctly state. He continually quotes Rousseau in his letters, and the peculiar doctrines of this great enthusiast seem to have deeply affected him. In a letter to Mr. Fay, dated September 6th, 1798, he says,—

"I perceive by a hint in your letter, that you have read Emilius. Pray write me your folio opinion of it. I know you admire it. Read his Eloisa and be crazy. Oh, Fay! conceive me in Marblehead, and you must know that I am wretched."

He is passionate, enthusiastic, at times greatly depressed, always very sentimental, and often morbid. He vaults from the deepest glooms into the highest hopes; for his natural vivacity and morbid sensibility alternately reacting upon each other, push him to as great extravagancies of joy as of grief. In the loneliness of Marblehead, with no companions of his own age to sympathize with him, and to conduct away the electrical currents of feeling which agitate him, he becomes surcharged with nervous excitement. He sighs constantly for the presence of friends, and in one letter he says,—

> "I have not here a single companion, so that I am completely isolated. You may judge, therefore, how far my situation is susceptible of happiness. Solitude is enchanting, but it requires at intervals the society of friends."

Again, he says in a letter to Mr. C. P. Sumner, dated September 8th, 1798,—

> "Fate condemns me to a solitary situation, while all my companions with whom in pleasant converse I have spent the midnight hours, are far distant. Life has no independent charms; in reciprocity consists all enjoyment."

This last thought, thus early expressed, affords a key not only to my father's social nature, but to that long series of generous labors for others, by which his life was so much distinguished.

In a letter to Mr. Fay, dated January 6th, 1801, he says,—

> "My hours are alternately divided between the difficulties of study, and the intercourse of friendship, and are never passed in dull *emnui* or idle folly. Yet, my dear fellow, with the craving inanity of the human mind, I still exclaim, I am not happy. My throbbing heart can never be at rest. The visions of the future have not yet been discolored by the disappointments of the past, and I am alternately the veriest knight-errant in romance, and the most despondent monk in Christendom."

This is the chafing of a young, sensitive nature when it first feels the stern limitations of life. Like every spirited youth, he stepped across the threshold of manhood, eager to realize that visionary future, which his imagination had painted in such enchanting colors. Pure in heart, rich in affection, and sanguine in fancy, he had looked forward to life as to an Eldorado paved with the golden sands of Romance. He found on it prosaic dust. The world encountered him as the cynic does the poet. He asked for bread, and it gave him a stone. His dreams of perfectibility were met by the cold sneer of criticism. His lofty hopes were opposed by the hard maxims of policy and experience. Where he had expected heroic friendships and generous self-sacrifice, he found worldly policy and competitive selfishness wrangling and appropriating all within their reach. He saw that the real and the ideal were two quite different things. The sentiments of poetry did not walk up and down the avenues of business, but lurked in happy secluded valleys. Practical Christianity, he perceived, was considered as wholly visionary; while theoretic Christianity (the ghost,) went about preaching in pulpits, and in the market-place. In his impatience he frets at the limitations and meanness of life. Like every generous youth, he would be a reformer, and tear from society its odious mask of hypocrisy, and its armor of selfishness. In letters written during the year 1799, the following, among many other similar passages, occur:—

> "In life—good heavens what a word—how I fear lest like the crowd, I shall become an apostate from generosity and nature; 'for man is naturally good.' In life,—for we are yet on the threshold of existence,—I shall anticipate little pleasure, except in the participations of my friends. Let me with seriousness say, that I shall ever, I hope, be open in heart and action."

Again,—

> "I have long ceased to admire the world. Its manners and its sentiments are equally objects of my disgust and my detestation. I would fain indulge the delusion that youth is uninfluenced by its maxims, and that old age sometimes revolts from them. Though I had theorized on its depravity, and ought not to have expected pleasure, yet the mind fondly cherishes even in its despondency a latent hope that some glorious exception might justify its hopes."

Yet again, in a letter dated June 21st, 1800, he writes,—

> "I am told that the tinge of romance yet discolors my ideas, and that *real life* is a picture widely different from the imagery that now bewitches my fancy. What is all this but the calculating meanness of individual experience, which content to walk in the common road, knows not that flowers as well as thorns could blossom in the paths of life. The truth is, man may be what he will, and consequently when ideas of the delusiveness of love, and the vanity of friendship, stamp the mind, the heart becomes regulated by other impulses than those of nature, and an artificial system assumes the aspect of infallible truth."

The following passage also occurs in a letter to Mr. Fay, dated January 6th, 1801:—

> "I know not how it is, but the shackles of the world and its customs become every day more insupportable to me. Instead of viewing men merely as madmen, I perceive with too veritable an aspect that they are knaves or dupes. Scarcely any thing like principle can be discerned in their general conduct. If formerly the intimacies of friendship awakened my warmest feelings, they now are the end of all my hopes. I despair to advance among the crowd, when at every instant I must sacrifice integrity and falsify principle. The petty chicanery of worldly cunning is so detestable to my soul, that the doom of poverty is preferable to its guilty attainments."

The strong coloring which his mind received from Rousseau at this period, shows itself in every word he wrote. Disgust at the artificiality of life, and raptures on the claims of friendship and love, fill half his letters. He pours out his affection with a lavish heart, and indulges in the warmest expressions of it. It seems to intoxicate his brain. In him this was neither affectation nor flattery, but a natural exaggeration of the estimable qualities of those to whom he was attached, which was always a beautiful trait of his nature. He always overrated. He never believed in a base motive when he could avoid it. The constant dupe of designing persons, he was quick-sighted only to virtues.

On this subject he says, writing to his friend Mr. Fay, April 15, 1799:—

> "Reading St. Pierre the other day, I was extremely affected with the justness and candor of an observation, which will meet sympathy in your bosom. 'Flattery is not my vice,—if I use it, it is only to those I love,' says that eloquent author. This has afforded me much matter for reflection. I have been sometimes told that I adulate; but it was only the overflow of my feelings, and only to those I loved with ardent sympathy. Susceptible minds can scarcely avoid the expressions of friendship and esteem, and in such what is generally a vice and the tribute of hypocrisy becomes a radiant virtue."

The following extracts from letters written at this period, exhibit some of the young student's views of poets and politics. Speaking of Southey and his early opinions, he says:—

> "The friend of man and of humanity, he has disdained to cloak his feelings under general observations. He perceives cruelty in its detail, and unmasks the monster in the spirit of righteousness. He has been denounced as the friend of anarchy, but to me his sentiments bear the stamp of truth, liberty, justice, and native integrity. Our degeneracy alone prevents us from perceiving his merit. As a poet he is *inter magnates;* as a politician (as far as works speak,) equitable

and humane in his principles; as a man, benevolent. I should say that the predominant qualities of his poetry were picturesqueness, sweetness of sentiment, and purity of diction. When I first heard of his epic, I was vehemently prejudiced against it. A modern epic, thought I (such was the influence of early prejudice,) must necessarily he tame and jejune. But I read, and the change was instantaneous. *Veni, vidi, victus fui.* He is now my favorite. His miscellaneous poems are full of various excellence."

In another letter, he says,—

"I have lately perused the masterly writings of Junius. A statesman who professes the principles of freedom, the legislator who contemplates the benefit of mankind, and the philosophic citizen of the world ought to make this a *vade mecum.* Yet because he has attacked the English administration with equitable violence, he has been branded as a disorganizer; and because he disdained the versatility of popular sentiment, he has been declared an apostate. Such, my dear fellow, are the epithets bestowed by partisans on the moderate and just, who think with coolness and decide with alacrity. You shall have an instance of public prejudice in a confined circle—and I the little hero of the tale. A gentleman in Boston, asking in company what were my political sentiments, Federal or Jacobinical, was answered,—Neither, but that I was a person *sui generis.* 'He that is not with us, is against us,' replied he, and I was accordingly dubbed a political heretic."

It is proper here, to say, that his opinion of the letters of Junius became entirely changed in after life. The next letter was addressed to a friend and classmate, who was then studying at Berlin:—

To Thomas Welsh, Esq.,
Marblehead, October 19, 1799.
My Dear Friend:

I have lately heard much, and read more of the praise which has been bestowed on the literati of Germany. Wieland, Schiller, and Goethe, are not unknown to me in their works. Kotzebue is the presiding deity of our theatre. The rage for his plays is unbounded. The development of the bolder and fiercer passions alone seems now to command the attention of an American audience. All must be "wrapt in clouds, in tempest tost"; alternately chilling with horror, or dazzling with astonishment. This mania, however, is not peculiar to us. The polished Cumberland and the masterly Sheridan have already been driven from the London theatres by the northern poets. Shakspeare himself might tremble for his supremacy, had not he fortunately created the sportive "Ariel" and the ghost of hamlet's father. From the translations of Schiller and Kotzebue, which I have read, I do not hesitate to declare the former infinitely superior in poetic conception and delineation to his applauded rival. The German plays acquire their effect from the strength, more than the justness, of their execution; from their power to excite surprise, rather than their expression of the tender passions. Indeed, they are by no means my favorites. Their plots are for the most part ill-contrived and irregularly supported. As a whole, they fail in effect; but I could select passages which are sublime and pathetic.

I regret exceedingly my ignorance of the German tongue. Translations seldom convey the spirit of the original, and it is only through them that I can acquire any knowledge of your Northern planets. At some future period, I hope to remove this disability; yet I perceive, that "*hoc opus, hic labor est.*" Indeed, except with an independent inheritance, no American can spare time for the cultivation of those literary pursuits, which are the delight of a superior intellect. When I view the immensity of science, which yet remains wholly unexplored by me, I confess my resolution is staggered; and it requires all my philosophy to overcome my despondency.

Last winter several pieces appeared in the poetic department under the signature of "A***" and "Henry." To confess the truth they excited much attention and more surprise. You will not be alarmed when you learn, that it was continued with some interruption for six months. The fact was, that an "Address to Winter" appeared over the signature of "A***," which, from the peculiarity of style and sentiment I presumed was the production of Miss S. M., a young lady whose merits you may have heard me mention, and whose attainments are equalled by her genius. With this idea and the persuasion that I might remain wholly unknown, I addressed her in return. The correspondence was continued, and after six months experience I remain in greater doubts than ever of the real author of the female pieces. In my leisure hours I still continue to soothe my languor and melancholy with the sportings of the Muse, and the fictitious "Henry" often usurps the poet's corner with the real effusions of Story. In the mean time I have composed a poem of about fifteen hundred lines, on the "Power of Solitude." As the *cacoëthes scribendi* is not more catching than that of publication, this may possibly not expire in manuscript.

I am now engaged with the avidity of a man who relies on law for his livelihood, yet with the *sang froid* of one to whom it is a secondary consideration, in the perusal of Coke and the Reporters. Law I admire as a science; it becomes tedious and embarrassing only when it degenerates into a trade. I regret the necessity of any profession, because it infringes on those studies which a citizen of the world would like to pursue. If you are not satiated with the prominence of my egotism and vanity already, you must at least possess in a high degree one great qualification of friendship,—patience. You shall not, however, have one word of politics from my pen. It is a subject which, in its present details, is too important to arrest attention and to excite curiosity.

By the way, Mrs. Morton has lately published a work called, "The Virtues of Society." It is certainly superior to her "Beacon Hill," and worthy of her former reputation. The Virtues of Society are illustrated in the tale of the heroic Lady Harriet Ackland, a woman whose conduct in the American war has received universal applause.

I am, my dear Welsh,
Your unaltered Friend,
Joseph Story

In February, 1800, General Washington died. My father was deputed by the town of Marblehead to deliver a eulogy on the occasion, in pursuance of the recommendation of Congress and the General Court of Massachusetts, that eulogies should be delivered in all the towns. This was somewhat of an honor for so young a man, and shows the consideration in which he was held by the town. The Columbian Centinel called this production "an elegant Address," but my father condemned it as "poor and in bad taste." It was printed, and though written in the bombastic style of the time, was considered as a very creditable performance. Judge Sewall, in acknowledging the receipt of a copy, says,—

"I have read it with a great deal of pleasute. I doubt not it will give you reputation, and it by no means needs an apology for haste or inconsiderateness."

During this period he composed a poem, entitled, "The Power of Solitude," which was afterwards published, and which, in one of his letters, dated December 26th, 1798, he calls, "the sweet employment of my leisure hours." I shall have occasion to refer to it hereafter.

After remaining in Mr. Sewall's office a little more than a year, he removed to Salem in January, 1801, upon the appointment of Mr. Sewall as one of the Justices of the Supreme Court of Massachusetts, and entered the office of Mr. Samuel Putnam, who afterward occupied a seat upon the same Bench.

"While he was in my office," says Mr. Justice Putnam, in a letter dated May 28th, 1846, "although he read much, yet we talked more; and I believe in my heart, that he even then did the greater part of it. I had a pretty full practice, and his regular course of reading was frequently interrupted by the examination of the books, touching the cases which were offered for my consideration, and I have no doubt that my clients were greatly benefited by his labors in my service.

> "My office was then in my dwelling-house, and he was in the daily and familiar intercourse with my family, always manifesting the most lively interest in our concerns. 'Mair by token,'—one of my daughters got a piece of Chinaware in her throat, and seemed to be in imminent danger of suffocation. We could do nothing for her relief. He rushed out of the house and ran bareheaded through the streets with the speed of a race-horse, nearly half a mile, for a physician, who arrived in a few moments after the child was happily relieved by a strong effort of nature. Your father was at the doctor's house with the tale of her distress in about the time that some men (who always consult their own appearance and convenience) would have taken to put on their hat and gloves. The event was of thrilling interest to us; and you may imagine that the *race*, which was at midday, attracted much attention from those who saw it. In point of fact, your father was as much distinguished by never-failing kindness as by his legal attainments."

No anecdote could better illustrate that entire self-forgetfulness and *abandon* of action, which was a conspicuous trait in his character. Thus energetic, impulsive, and careless of appearances, whenever any worthy object was to be gained or any kindness to be conferred, lie continued throughout his life. He was thoroughly simple and genuine in all his actions, and I do not believe that a consideration of "what the world would think" ever influenced him.

NOTES

1. The passage alluded to will be found in the preface to Sir Henry Spelman's Glossarium Archaiologicum. It is as follows:—"Emisit me tamen sub anno altero (1579) Londinum; juris nostri capescendi gratiâ: cujus cum vestibulum salutassem, reperissemque linguam peregrinam, dialectum barbaram, methodum inconcinnam, molem non ingentem solum, sed perpetuis humeris sustinendam: excidit mihi (fateor) animus."
2. *Life of Wilberforce.* Entry in Journal, April 17th, 1801.

Chapter 8

The Teaching of George Wythe

1998

Thomas Hunter

Thomas Hunter is a sometime law professor and a doctoral candidate in history at The Johns Hopkins University.

Author's note: When George Wythe died in 1806, his most famous student, Thomas Jefferson, stated, "He was my antient master, my earliest & best friend; and to him I am indebted for first impressions which have had the most salutary influence on the course of my life."[1] Likewise, nearly half a century later another famous Wythe pupil, Henry Clay, noted that, "to no man was I more indebted, by his instructions, his advice, and his example, for the . . . intellectual improvement which I made, up to . . . my twenty-first year."[2]

For many years George Wythe was a major political figure, representing Virginia in the Continental Congress and the Constitutional Convention, serving as Speaker of the Virginia House of Delegates, and signing the Declaration of Independence. His judicial career was equally impressive, for he was on Virginia's High Court of Chancery for nearly three decades, including fourteen years as the Commonwealth's sole Chancellor. Such accomplishments, however, while impressive, do little to differentiate Wythe from several of his contemporaries, and his true claim to fame lies not in the law or politics, but as a teacher.

For four decades, Wythe instructed the most promising youth of Virginia in both the law and classics, and in 1779 he became America's first university law professor, and only the second in the English-speaking world, when he was appointed Professor of Law and Police at the College of William and Mary. From Jefferson's entrance into the Continental Congress in 1774 until Clay's resignation from the Senate in late 1851, Wythe's students played crucial roles in the nation's legislative chambers. They were equally important in shaping this nation's jurisprudence, for he taught such noted federal and state jurists as John Marshall, Bushrod Washington, and Spencer Roane. Wythe instructed so well that most of his students assumed leading positions very soon after leaving his counsels, many while still in their twenties.

Despite his role in developing several generations of national leaders, not to mention the high political and judicial stations in which he served, George Wythe has not received the scholarly attention bestowed upon many of his contemporaries or students. It was not until 1970 that the first book-length portrait of

9. George Wythe (1726-1806) influenced legal education throughout the South, as his students carried his ethics and methods from school to school. (*Courtesy of Art & Visual Materials, Special Collections Department, Harvard Law School Library.*)

Wythe was published, and in the ensuing decades none of the works which have appeared could in any way be termed close to definitive.[3]

Thus, after briefly describing his legal and political career, this essay will examine Wythe's role as Revolutionary Virginia's foremost teacher of both the law and the political process, focusing especially on his seminal ten-year professorship at the College of William and Mary.

* * * * *

George Wythe was born in 1726 or 1727 at his family's home, Chesterville, in Elizabeth City County, Virginia.[4] His parents were Margaret Walker and Thomas Wythe (III), whose grandfather, the first Thomas, emigrated to Virginia in 1680. The first three Thomas Wythes all died quite young, although two lived long enough to serve in the Virginia House of Burgesses.

As for George Wythe's mother, she was the granddaughter of noted teacher, preacher, and controversialist George Keith. The Scottish Keith was "a promising mathematician and student of Oriental languages" before becoming a Quaker and joining the ministry.[5] Coming to America in 1685, Keith was headmaster of a Quaker school until he fell out with the sect because of doctrinal differences. After returning to England, he eventually joined the established church, and in 1702 Keith became the first Anglican missionary sent to America under the auspices of the Society for the Propagation of the Gospel in Foreign Parts. It appears that George Wythe inherited both his Christian name and much of his intelligence from his great-grandfather Keith, although he did not have the minister-teacher's "unbearable temper and carriage."[6]

George Wythe was the second of three children, and when his father Thomas (III) died young, an older brother, Thomas (IV), through primogeniture, inherited the family's Chesterville plantation; their other sibling was a sister, Anne, who married Charles Sweeney, and, as is noted below, a grandson of this union, George Wythe Sweeney, perpetrated one of the foulest deeds in Virginia history.

Because he was not in line to inherit the family plantation, it was determined to situate George in one of the professions, with the law being the eventual choice. His earliest schooling, however, was at the hands of his mother, who, because she was raised a Quaker, was unusually educated for a woman of the day. Besides the traditional basics, Margaret Walker Wythe's tutelage of her son included Latin and Greek. At some point Wythe also briefly attended William and Mary, although it is thought that it was only the college's grammar school.[7]

Wythe's professional instruction began in the mid-1740s, when he began an apprenticeship in the Prince George County law office of his uncle Stephen Dewey. As a leading attorney, Dewey's instructions could have proved quite valuable, yet Wythe later told a friend that his uncle "treated him with neglect, and confined him to the drudgeries of his office, with little, or no, attention to his instruction in the general science of law."[8] One commentator has opined that posterity should maybe thank Dewey for his inattentions, for he may "have sharpened Wythe's appetite for learning in the deeper and richer historical basis of legal institutions[, and a]bove all, he seems to have given Wythe a thorough grounding in how *not* to teach!"[9]

After completing his legal apprenticeship, Wythe received his law license in 1746 and initially settled in Spotsylvania County. There he began a wide-ranging practice which included the counties of Caroline, Orange, and Augusta, and he also became married to attorney Zachary Lewis' daughter Anne. The young Mrs. Wythe died less than a year later, however, and several months after, in October 1748, Wythe returned to the Tidewater region, accepting an offer to become clerk of the two most important committees of the House of Burgesses.

These legislative responsibilities did not preclude the practice of law, so once in Williamsburg Wythe resumed his profession and was soon representing members of such influential Virginia families as the Blairs and Custises. In 1750, the young attorney was elected a Williamsburg Alderman, yet a much higher honor came four years later when he was appointed the colony's Attorney General. Wythe, the youngest attorney general in Virginia history,[10] was chosen to succeed Peyton Randolph, who was visiting England, and he resigned the position once Randolph returned to the colony. While serving as attorney general, another honor came to Wythe when he was elected to the House of Burgesses from Williamsburg.

In 1755, Thomas Wythe (IV) died without an heir and his brother George inherited the Chesterville plantation in Elizabeth City County. It was also at this time that Wythe again married, to Williamsburg heiress Elizabeth Taliaferro, who, being fourteen or fifteen years old, was half of her husband's age. Despite the age difference, theirs was an extremely happy thirty-two year marriage, although their only child died in infancy.

Wythe, who suddenly found himself with his own substantial holdings as well as being married into a wealthy family, could at last "borrow time from his busy professional life for [the] study of the classics and early English literature and law." Such an opportunity was extremely welcomed, for one author has opined that the attorney "thirsted like a living Tantalus for the refreshing springs of the ancient authors."[11] These pursuits had their obvious results, for Thomas Jefferson later called his law teacher "the best Latin and Greek scholar in the State."[12]

Wythe, while pursuing such academic subjects, did not neglect his professional responsibilities, for he continued his rapid assent into Virginia's highest legal and political circles. His law practice continued to prosper, and at some early time he became admitted to practice before the colony's highest court, the General Court. The attorneys who practiced before the appellate General Court were a highly select group, usually no more than ten in number, and included such names as Peyton and John Randolph, Robert Carter Nicholas, and Wythe's lifelong rival, Edmund Pendleton. Wythe soon had one of the most notable practices before the court, and Jefferson later noted that Wythe "held without competition the first place at the bar of our general court for 25 years."[13]

As for public service, Wythe lost a race for the House of Burgesses in 1756 when he ran for one of the two seats allotted to his native Elizabeth City County. Two years later, however, he was returned to the House by being elected to the William and Mary seat, for which the electorate was only the college's President and its Masters. In 1761 Wythe received another connection to the college when he was appointed to its Board of Visitors; by this time, however, he was no longer representing the college in the Burgesses, for overcoming his previous defeat he had won election to one of the Elizabeth City County seats.

Wythe was elected Clerk of the House of Burgesses in 1768, a position he would hold for six years, and that year also saw him selected as Mayor of Williamsburg. In addition, his growing influence led to his 1765 appointment to a committee, along with Peyton Randolph, John Randolph, Benjamin Waller, and Robert Nicholas, to collect, edit, and publish the colony's statutes, with the resulting collection being known as the "Code of 1769."

As the Revolution approached, Wythe became known as an ardent rebel, and Jefferson later recalled that "instead of higgling on half-way principle, as others did . . . [Wythe] took his stand on the solid ground that the only link of political union between us and Great Britain, was the identity of our Executive; that that nation and its Parliament had no more authority over us, than we had over them."[14] An early example of these feelings came in the 1760s, when Wythe's "remonstrance against the Stamp Act was very bold and strong."[15] Thus, with such sentiments added to his superb qualifications, it was no surprise when, on August 11, 1775, Wythe, along with Jefferson, Peyton Randolph, Richard Henry Lee, Richard Bland, Benjamin Harrison, and Thomas Nelson, was elected to the Second Continental Congress.

Wythe served in Congress until December 1776, and despite making few speeches he cultivated many friendships and wielded much influence. John Adams was much impressed by Wythe's legal abilities, while Dr. Benjamin Rush of Philadelphia thought him "[a] profound lawyer and able politician. He seldom spoke in Congress, but when he did his speeches were sensible, correct and pertinent. I have seldom known a man [to] possess more modesty, or a more dove-like simplicity and gentleness of manner."[16]

By February 1776 Wythe was strongly arguing for independence, yet he did not initially sign the Declaration of Independence in July, for the Virginia delegation had earlier selected Wythe and Richard Henry Lee to travel back to Virginia to attend the convention then drafting a state constitution. The two men left Philadelphia on June 13, yet by the time they arrived in Virginia the drafting, led by George Mason, was well in hand. Wythe, however, was appointed to a small committee to design a state seal, and it is thought that he played a decisive role in choosing the final design.

Wythe returned to Philadelphia in August, and he signed the Declaration in a space his colleagues had specifically left blank in his honor at the top of the delegation's signatures. Wythe remained in Congress until late that fall, returning to Virginia because he, Jefferson, Pendleton, George Mason, and Thomas Ludwell Lee had been appointed to a committee to revise the state's laws. Earlier, there had been several collections of the laws, such as the Code of 1769 produced by Wythe and his colleagues, but this was to be the first thorough revision of all the Commonwealth's statutes. The committee eventually consisted of only three members, Wythe, Jefferson, and Pendleton, and they divided the work such that Jefferson's area of responsibility would be the common law up to 1619, Wythe was to study the British statutes enacted since 1619, and Pendleton was to look at all Virginia-based law.

The work of the revisors was complete in June 1779, when they sent 126 bills to the General Assembly. The legislature, however, dragged its feet in enacting the proposals, and it was only six years later in 1785 that through the efforts of future President James Madison many of the revisors' suggestions were adopted. One reason for this delay might have been that while the majority of the 126 proposed statutes only reiterated the existing law, minus arcane or inappropriate language, under Jefferson's lead the revisors had suggested several profound alterations. Among the suggestions eventually approved were the abolishing of primogeniture, transforming estates in fee tail to fee simple, and establishing religious freedom. Other suggestions equally audacious, however, such as bills promoting public education, a public library, and enlightened penal policies, did not win approval.[17]

While on the revision committee in 1777, Wythe was chosen as Speaker of the House of Delegates (as it was now termed under the new Constitution). An even greater honor came the following year upon the restructuring of Virginia's court system, when the General Assembly created three different superior courts which would have appellate jurisdiction in their specialties. A five-member General Court would hear cases at law, while a three-man High Court of Chancery would examine suits in equity, and a Court of Admiralty would make decisions involving maritime law. In addition, the judges of all three courts would, together, form a supreme Court of Appeals.

Of the three separate superior courts, it was considered that the Chancery court, which would meet in April and September, was the most important, and only the foremost attorneys in Virginia were considered in filling the three slots. According to Nathaniel Beverly Tucker, few attorneys of the day had all of the qualifications necessary for the position, for "*Integrity* and *talent* were abundant, but a *learned* lawyer was indeed a *rara avis.*" George Wythe, however, was "the one man in the state who had any claims" to meeting all of these qualifications.[18] The members of the General Assembly obviously agreed, for on January 14, 1778, the names of Wythe, Edmund Pendleton, and Robert Carter Nicholas, were placed in nomination for the new court, and they were elected unanimously.

Thus, by the fall of 1779 Wythe was well ensconced on the High Court of Chancery. By filling this high judicial station, however, he could no longer practice law, nor could he serve in the state or national legislature. Thus, it is likely that Wythe was looking for a new challenge, and such was soon offered by his former student Thomas Jefferson.

* * * * *

During his first fifty years, George Wythe did not solely devote himself to politics and the law, for he also gained an enviable reputation as a teacher of young men. Although there likely were earlier students,[19] the first known person to study law under Wythe was Thomas Jefferson (1743-1826). After attending William and Mary for two years, Jefferson began his legal apprenticeship in 1762, and he spent three years reading under Wythe's supervision, although the majority of the first year was spent at home in Albemarle county. As was traditional, Jefferson first read *Coke on Littleton,* and his later readings touched on both the theoretical and practical sides of the law; among the law books he purchased at this time were several volumes on pleading as well as collections of Virginia and British statutes.

Wythe also had Jefferson read widely in the humanities, for the latter purchased and read various works on history, literature, philosophy, religion, and science. As for his routine, shortly after he was admitted to practice Jefferson advised an aspiring lawyer to study such subjects as science, ethics, and religion before breakfast, devote the hours between eight o'clock and noon solely to the law, and then spend the afternoon and evening reading history and literature. While Jefferson could have followed such a rigorous reading schedule while at home, it is known that part of his time in Williamsburg was also spent attending sessions of the General Court and following the legislature; in addition, the young student frequently dined at the

Governor's Palace with Wythe, William and Mary professor William Small, and Governor Francis Fauquier, and he also spent much time practicing the violin.[20]

Jefferson, of course, would go on to author the Declaration of Independence, serve as Governor of Virginia, Minister to France, Secretary of State, Vice President, and our nation's third President, and, in his retirement, found the University of Virginia. Throughout this impressive career, the bond between Jefferson and his legal mentor remained extraordinarily strong, and in later years Jefferson would refer to Wythe at his "second father,"[21] while Wythe "often said that [Jefferson was] dearer to him than any relation he had."[22]

While Wythe undoubtedly taught other law students in the 1760s besides Jefferson, his next known student is James Madison (1749-1812), who studied law during 1772-1773.[23] Madison was a second cousin to the man of the same name who would follow Jefferson in the Presidency, and despite being admitted to the bar he never practiced law. Instead, Madison, in 1773, became professor of natural philosophy and mathematics at William and Mary, and two years later he was ordained in the Church of England. In 1777, the Reverend Madison was elected President of William and Mary, a position which he held for the remainder of his life, and in 1790 he also became the first Episcopal Bishop of the Diocese of Virginia.[24]

Following Madison as a Wythe pupil was St. George Tucker (1752-1827), a native of Bermuda who came to Virginia specifically to study under Wythe. Tucker had also been formally enrolled at the Inner Temple in London, but his father, upon learning about Wythe's instruction, wrote that with "so good a tutor," Tucker should stay in Williamsburg. Tucker studied under Wythe from 1773 to 1775, and he later succeeded his teacher as Professor of Law and Police at William and Mary (1790-1804). In addition, Tucker served on the Virginia Court of Appeals, was the United States Judge for the District of Virginia, and edited the first American edition of Blackstone's *Commentaries*.[25]

Another early Wythe pupil was James Innes (1754-1798), a one-time attorney general of Virginia who was known for his both great oratory and legal ability. Although forgotten today, Innes would have achieved greatness but for ill-health and an untimely death.[26] His brother Harry Innes (1752-1816), a Federal judge in Kentucky from 1789 until his death, has been listed by one historian as an early Wythe student, although another scholar states that this teaching was "not likely."[27]

A handful of other prominent attorneys have also been mentioned as possible Wythe students before he assumed the professorship at William and Mary. The foremost among these is Edmund Randolph (1753-1813), the first Attorney General of the United States, Governor of Virginia, and United States Secretary of State. Three twentieth-century sources cite Randolph as an early Wythe student,[28] although it has traditionally been assumed that he received his legal education under his father John, a one-time Virginia Attorney General;[29] the latest colonial Williamsburg pronouncement is that it is currently unknown with whom Randolph studied law.[30] Other possible students include Samuel Jordan Cabell (1756-1818), who served in Congress from 1785 to 1803,[31] as well as four additional delegates to Virginia's Ratifying Convention, Thomas Read (c. 1735-1817),[32] James Mercer (1736-1793),[33] Andrew Moore (b. 1752),[34] and Warner Lewis (ca. 1747-1791).[35]

While Wythe's pre-Revolutionary teaching undoubtedly encompassed more students than just Jefferson, Madison, Tucker, and Innes, his reputation as a great teacher rests principally on his connection to the College of William and Mary, through which his teaching would become available to a much wider audience.

* * * * *

Founded in 1693, the College of William and Mary was where the sons of the Virginia gentry went to be educated when they did not go abroad. While normally a staid institution that saw little controversy, this changed dramatically at the start of Revolution, for at that time the student-body was "staunchly rebel," while the faculty was dominated by Tories, the most notorious being the school's President, John Camm. When student, and private Wythe pupil, James Innes raised a company during the first days of the War, he was condemned by the faculty, and this raised the ire of the school's Visitors, one of whom was George Wythe. The Visitors responded to the faculty's Toryism by forcing out both the Master of the Indian School and the Professor of Divinity, and when President Camm disagreed with the Visitors' authority for such actions, he too was suspended.[36]

To replace Camm, the Visitors in the Spring of 1777 selected Wythe's former law pupil James Madison as the College's new President; although only twenty-eight, the Reverend Madison was already known for both his great intellect and his republican sympathies.[37] A more sweeping attempt to alter the college occurred two years later, when Thomas Jefferson proposed to drastically change the structure of his *alma mater* through the revised laws that he, Wythe, and Pendleton were then formulating.

Jefferson wished to lessen the ties of the school to the established church, increase its public support, and totally revamp its curriculum. As for the latter, in bill number 80 of the revisal, Jefferson proposed the creation of eight professorships at William and Mary: moral philosophy, fine arts, and the laws of nature and nations; law and police; history, civil and ecclesiastical; mathematics; anatomy and medicine; natural philosophy and natural history; ancient languages, oriental and northern; and modern languages. The professor of law and police would be responsible for teaching municipal law, which included the common law, equity, and merchant, maritime, and ecclesiastical law, as well as economical law, defined as politics and commerce.[38]

Professorships in law, history, medicine, and modern languages would be new to the faculty, and Jefferson proposed to delete the chair in divinity as well as the Indian/grammar school. He later wrote that his purpose was "to enlarge [William and Mary's] sphere of science, and to make it in fact an University."[39]

Ironically, despite Jefferson's purpose of changing the institution from a church-based into a public-based institution, revisal bill 80 was killed in the General Assembly by religious dissenters; Jefferson later wrote, "the religious jealousies . . . of all the dissenters took alarm lest this might give an ascendancy to the Anglican sect and refused acting on that bill."[40]

This defeat did not deter Jefferson from his goal of restructuring the college, however, for after his election as Governor of Virginia in 1779 he also became a member of the William and Mary Board of Visitors, and through this body he succeeded in seeing through most of the changes which had been blocked by the General Assembly. On December 3, 1779, the Board of Visitors gave the professors and president of the college, acting collectively as "the Corporation," the power to revise the institution's statutes and by-laws, and the following day the Corporation followed Jefferson's instructions by making numerous changes in the school's structure.[41] The Sage of Monticello later recalled: "I effected . . . a change in the organization of [William and Mary] by abolishing the Grammar school, and the two professorships of Divinity and Oriental languages, and substituting a professorship of Law and Police, one of Anatomy, Medicine and Chemistry, and one of Modern languages."[42] The college's charter, which could only be changed by action of the General Assembly, limited the school to six professorships, so Jefferson's initial plans had to be altered by the deletion of both the traditional professorship of oriental languages and the proposed professorship of history.

The chair in law was the first of its kind at an American university, and second in the English-speaking world, only antedated by Oxford's Vinerian chair of law, first held in 1758 by Sir William Blackstone.[43] As for the seemingly strange name, "law and police," the latter word "did not refer to enforcement of the criminal law but was a transliteration of the Greek word for *state*. In the context of the William and Mary curriculum it meant government or political science."[44]

While certainly revolutionary, that the first institutionalization of legal education in America happened in Virginia should come as no surprise. In most of the colonies the bar had come into much disfavor by generally siding with the crown, but in Virginia the opposite was true, for the revolution had been spearheaded by the colony's lawyers. Jefferson saw a professorship in law and politics as a way to teach not only the legal profession, but also republicanism, and in Virginia this idea was met with "enthusiastic approval."[45]

As for who would fill the new chair of law, the obvious choice, in fact the only choice, was George Wythe. The Chancellor had a profound knowledge of the law, he had already demonstrated great skill in imparting such knowledge to intelligent young men, and, just as important, he was a zealous republican. W. Hamilton Bryson has stated that "It is difficult to conceive that anyone more acceptable, more appropriate, more competent, or more scholarly could have been found; no one else was considered."[46]

On December 4, 1779, the Visitors appointed three men to fill the new chairs, all of whom "were thoroughly in sympathy with the visitors" regarding the ongoing struggle with Great Britain.[47] Charles Bellini was named Professor of Modern Languages, Dr. James McClurg was selected as Professor of Anatomy and Medicine, and Wythe became the Professor of Law and Police.[48] These three, plus President Madison, who would also hold the Chair of Natural Philosophy and Mathematics, and the Reverend Robert Andrews, who was Professor of Moral Philosophy, the Laws of Nature and of Nations and of the Fine Arts, would comprise the institution's faculty.[49]

Besides the addition and deletion of various subjects, another change made by the faculty was the adoption of the elective system. No longer would the school have any mandatory subjects; rather, students could decide which subjects and under which professors they wished to learn. Accordingly, at the first faculty meeting after the reorganization, held on December 29, 1779, Wythe and his colleagues resolved that out of the courses offered by Wythe, Madison, and Andrews, "a Student on paying annually one thousand Pounds of Tobacco shall be entitled to attend any two . . . and that for fifteen hundred Pounds he shall be entitled to attend the said three Professors."[50] With the changes in structure, "William and Mary now became a university, the first such in the new nation,"[51] and it became known as "The University of William and Mary."[52]

* * * * *

George Wythe entered into his duties as Professor of Law and Police at William and Mary immediately after his December 1779 appointment, and such alacrity was necessary, for the school year was scheduled to begin on January 17.[53] As for the yearly schedule, the month of April was designated as the school's spring vacation, and the term following would last from the first of May into July. A fall term would then begin around October first.[54]

Undoubtedly drawing on his previous teaching, Wythe quickly designed an innovative, rigorous, and enjoyable curriculum for his students. He continued the tradition of having students read major legal treatises and then systematically forming the notes they took into an alphabetized legal notebook/dictionary that would summarize the current common law of the jurisdiction—a process typically called "commonplacing" because the notebooks were known as "commonplace books."[55] Although he only finished commonplacing legal subjects through the letter "L," John Marshall's notebook is one of the best sources in determining the readings Wythe assigned his pupils, and most of the future Chief Justice's information apparently came from three works: Bacon's *New Abridgement of the Law*; Blackstone's *Commentaries*; and the 1769 *Acts of Assembly . . . of Virginia.*[56]

In addition to assigning readings, Wythe also lectured twice a week.[57] No one knows the exact contents of Wythe's lectures, although some modern commentators state that Wythe intricately discussed the substantive and procedural details of the law, while others posit that the material was more theoretical in nature.[58] In reality, Wythe likely touched upon the major legal points of Blackstone and other sources,[59] paying especial attention to how Virginia's law was different from England's. It seems likely that Wythe also discussed materials more akin to political science, and since the first written constitutions in the English-speaking world had just been produced in various colonies, Wythe has been called the first commentator on constitutional law.[60]

The best evidence of the nature of Wythe's lectures comes from 1810, when Governor John Tyler asked Thomas Jefferson to edit and publish Wythe's lecture notes. Tyler noted:

> Judge Roane has read them, or most of them, and is highly pleased with them, thinks they will be very valuable, there being so much of [Wythe's] own sound reasoning upon great principles, and not a mere servile copy of Blackstone, and other British commentators,—a good many of his own thoughts on our constitutions and the necessary changes they have begotten, with that spirit of freedom which always marked his opinions.[61]

In response, Jefferson declined this task, noting that he had not practiced law for thirty-seven years. For posterity's sake, this decision was extremely unfortunate, for the lecture notes were never published, and the manuscript's whereabouts has been unknown for over a century.

In addition to the lectures and readings, for his students Wythe designed two institutions which were new to North America. The first was a moot court, the concept for which likely came from the London Inns of Court, which, a couple of centuries previous, had held "mootings." These earlier exercises had seen the member-barristers deliver arguments on both sides of set cases;[62] however, Wythe reversed the process by having the students themselves do the arguing.

Wythe decided to hold the moot courts in the courtroom of the Capitol, which was empty after the government moved to Richmond at the end of April 1780,[63] and he and some of his colleagues acted as judges while the citizens of Williamsburg attended as spectators. Wythe student John Brown reported to his uncle in July 1780 that the "Moot Court [is] held monthly or oftener in the place formerly occupied by the Genl Court in the Capitol. Mr Wythe & the other professors sit as Judges[.] Our Audience consists of the most respectable of the Citizens, before whom we plead Causes given out by Mr Wythe [—] Lawyer like I assure you."[64]

Thomas Jefferson thought highly of the moot court concept, stating that in addition to teaching legal procedure, such an institution gave "opportunities to students of practicing their lessons in Rhetoric, of habituating themselves to think and to speak with method, and lessens the shock of the premier debut at the bar: so terrible is the first essay of strength before the public."[65] Of course it is now a universal practice in American law schools to have both a moot court program and classes in trial advocacy.

Wythe's second institutional innovation was the moot legislature. This too was held in the old Capitol, in the legislative chamber last used by the General Assembly on Christmas Eve 1779, and Wythe served as Speaker while his students debated the merits of proposed legislation. John Brown reported that Wythe "form'd us into a Legislative Body, consisting of about 40 members[.] Mr Wythe is speaker to the House, & takes all possible pains to instruct us in the Rules of Parliament. We meet every Saturday & take under our consideration those Bills drawn up by the Com[mit]tee appointed to revise the laws, the[n] we debate & Alter . . . with the greatest freedom."[66]

Wythe designed his moot legislature to prepare his students for the leading roles that he anticipated them soon taking in the state and national legislatures, and his ultimate goal was to create a class of ardent, well-prepared republicans. Through an exercise that they very much enjoyed, his students learned both the intricacies of legislative maneuvering as well as the substance of important, relevant issues. While the students in 1780 debated the laws proposed by the recent revisal, the material used in Wythe's later classes included proposals then under consideration in both the General Assembly and Congress. For example, Tommy Shippen in 1784 wrote that an Impost measure recommended by Congress was then under debate in the moot legislature, and that he was attempting to have it defeated by severely altering it in committee.[67]

As would be expected, Wythe's students thought highly of both the moot court and the moot legislature, and John Brown noted: "These Exercises, serve not only as the best amusement after severer studies, but are very usefull & attended with many important advantages."[68] Wythe's law class was undoubtedly the school's most popular, for even during its first year approximately half of William and Mary's eighty students enrolled to study under the law professor.[69]

While the students obviously enjoyed the moot courts and moot legislatures, there were other things at William and Mary to add to a student's law studies as well. For example, the Phi Beta Kappa Society had been formed at William and Mary several years earlier, and one historian has stated that membership in this was "an essential part of law study at the College because of the opportunity to participate in its debates."[70] In addition, there were the other courses offered at the college, and it has been suggested that Professor Andrews' course on moral philosophy was an important supplement to Wythe's because of its treatment of natural law.[71] Wythe undoubtedly expected that the law students who came to Williamsburg without any prior collegiate training would also enroll in some of these other courses, for he "never wished to see young men [at William and Mary] who meant to stay but two years,—at least, unless they had made a considerable progress before."[72]

At the end of their studies, Wythe's students could receive the degree of Bachelor of Law, although because of the requirements it is likely that few did. For the degree, one would have to "have the requisites for [the] Bachelor of Arts [degree, and] must moreover be well acquainted with civil History, both Ancient and Modern, and particularly with municipal Law and police." As for what it would take to earn the Bachelor of Arts, "the Student must be acquainted with [the various] branches of the Mathematics, both theoretical and practical, . . . Natural Philosophy[,] . . . Logic, the Belles Lettres, Rhetoric, Natural Law, Law of Nations, . . . Geography and of Ancient and Modern languages."[73] In short, to earn the LL.B., one would have to successfully complete the courses offered by Professors Wythe, Madison, Andrews, and Bellini, as well as show knowledge in other subjects.

As for a student's daily routine, Tommy Shippen, who in 1784 was attending the lectures of Wythe and Madison, told his father:

> [B]efore Breakfast, I generally read an hour and a half, some times two hours in Blackstone or else am employed in compositions, which by the advice of my instructors I pay a great deal of attention to. From breakfast to dinner, I read Blackstone, Hume or Montesquieu. After dinner If I dine at home . . . I play a piece of music on the violin, or read some entertaining book in French or . . . some favorite Roman author Horace, Virgil or Terrence. . . . At night . . . read . . . until 10, 11, or 12 o'clock. . . . But as Mr. Wythe lectures every Tuesday and Mr. Madison every Thursday and Saturday . . . I can read very little on those days between breakfast and Dinner, as we are at College from 10 to 12.[74]

Undoubtedly, the readings, lectures, moot courts, and moot legislatures were all important in Wythe's goal of educating the next generation to be skilled in both the law and public service. What should also not be overlooked, however, is the moral tone that Wythe set for his students. One biographer has stated that "Wythe's incorruptibility even in the smallest matters became legendary,"[75] another has called Wythe's integrity "truly stunning,"[76] and a contemporary minister stated that Wythe was "the only honest lawyer he ever knew."[77] While practicing law, if Wythe ever doubted the truth of what a client told him, he would either drop the case or require the client to swear an oath.[78] Many compared Wythe to Aristides the Just,[79] while Thomas Jefferson made a different classical allusion:

> No man ever left behind him a character more venerated than George Wythe. His virtue was of the purest tint; his integrity inflexible, and his justice exact; of warm patriotism, and, devoted as he was to liberty, and the natural and equal rights of man, he might truly be called the Cato of his country, without the avarice of the Roman; for a more disinterested person never lived.[80]

As would be expected, Jefferson was quite proud of Wythe's law class, and in July 1780 he told his future successor James Madison, "Our new institution at the college has had a success which has gained it universal applause. Wythe's school is numerous. They hold weekly courts and assemblies in the capitol. The professors join in it; and the young men dispute with elegance, method and learning." Jefferson then revealed what he saw as the true mission of Wythe's teaching by stating: "This single school by throwing from time to time new hands well principled and well informed into the legislature will be of infinite value."[81]

* * * * *

While Wythe's classes got off to a splendid start, the simmering conflict with Britain caused much concern by the latter months of 1780. Much of this centered on the fear of an enemy invasion into Virginia, the threat of which greatly affected the work of the college. At the end of October, Wythe student John Brown wrote that the "Invasion of the English" was "expected daily," and the college therefore had been "intirely deserted by every Stud[en]t but one or two who are sick." He also added that "it is more than probable that College will be suspended for some time[.] Mr Madison [is] talking of resigning his Professorship, & the Stud[en]ts [have] all turned Soldiers & everythin[g is] in the utmost Confusion."[82]

These fears were fully realized on January 5, 1781, when troops under Benedict Arnold occupied Williamsburg, and although they did not stay long, the raid disrupted the college's winter session. Despite the interruption, Wythe advertised that his classes would reconvene on May 1, 1781, yet if such happened the session lasted only a few weeks. This was because Cornwallis and his British troops entered Williamsburg in June of 1781, after which William and Mary remained closed for approximately eighteen months.[83]

On July 4, 1781, Cornwallis evacuated Williamsburg on his way to Yorktown, but shortly thereafter

Lafayette and the French occupied the college town, followed by Washington and the Americans in the middle of September. Upon the invitation of Wythe, Washington set up his headquarters in the law professor's residence,[84] and after the British surrender at Yorktown, the French encamped in Williamsburg for nine months, with Rochambeau staying in the Wythe house. The French leaders appear to have been quite taken with the still-closed William and Mary, for Chastellux wrote: "The beauty of the building is surpassed by the richness of its library, and still farther by the distinguished merit of . . . its professors, such as the Doctors Madison, Wythe, Bellini . . . who may be regarded as living Books." The French general then noted that these professors "have already formed many distinguished characters, ready to serve their country in the various departments of government."[85]

Unfortunately, the average French soldier was less inclined to honor the college and its vicinity, and this caused Wythe, only six days after the surrender at Yorktown, to write Washington concerning the institution's protection. Wythe mentioned that "until the british invasion, the university was in a prosperous state. A respectable number of young gentlemen in it were pursuing their studies with such assiduity, and some of them had made such progress, as I venture to say, would have given you pleasure." The professor of law was confident that such success would continue after peace was restored, but he wished Washington to ask Rochambeau to make sure that his officers protected the college, especially its "costly library [and] a valuable apparatus for making philosophical experiments."[86]

Wythe's fears proved prescient, for a couple of months later the carelessness of the French caused the Governor's Palace and a wing of the College to be destroyed by fire, including the much prized library and scientific equipment. Thus, there likely was much relief when the French finally began evacuating Williamsburg on July 1, 1782, a process which took the remainder of the summer. It is unknown when, exactly, Wythe was able to restart his classes, although it obviously took some time to get the college back in the condition in which it could regain its former functions.[87]

It appears, however, that Wythe was able to restart his classes sometime in 1783, and late that year he told his friend John Adams that he was once again settled in Williamsburg, "assisting, as professor of law and police in the university there, to form such characters as may be fit to succeed those which have been ornamental and useful in the national councils of America."[88]

Earlier that year, Richard Henry Lee wrote Wythe that Lee's son Ludwell was again going to study law under Wythe, and this letter is notable for giving evidence that young men from neighboring states would be venturing to Williamsburg to study under Wythe. Lee wrote: "I am happy to be informed that sensible men in the neighboring Countries, entertain a proper sense of the benefits to be derived from your benevolent attention to the instruction of youth; as I understand that young gentlemen now of Philadelphia propose to *finish* their studies with you."[89]

Within a short period Wythe's classes regained their former size, and the teacher's methods and purposes remained as before, especially the nurturing of future state and national leaders through such devices as the moot legislature. In February 1784, Wythe student Tommy Shippen wrote his father: "Last Saturday was the day of my political birth, if I may call so, the day on which I first assumed the character of a Legislator; for then I delivered an oration for the first time in our grand and august Assembly." Shippen noted that "very lately Mr. Wythe has [had] a lofty presidential Seat erected [in the legislative chamber], which adds very much to his dignity and may with great propriety be called his hobby horse. . . . This throne has a greater effect in throwing a damp upon the spirits of the speaker, than you can imagine." Despite being extraordinarily nervous, after delivering his first speech Shippen felt amply rewarded, by both the experience gained and the applause he received from his fellow students.[90]

Not only the students but also various visitors to the college thought quite highly of Wythe's program. In 1784, for example, Walker Maury, who had just moved from Orange county to become the headmaster of Williamsburg's grammar school, wrote Thomas Jefferson:

> As to the university, I cannot conceive an institution better planned, or more judiciously managed for the forming, either the lawyer, or the statesmen. You can judge better than I can, what advantages youth must reap from meeting twice a week in Mr. Wythe's school, and going thro all the forms of pleadings of a court of judicature, with the utmost exactness and decorum,

> and from assembling once a fortnight, as a body of Legislators, in whom you see our assembly in miniature debating, at least many of them, extempore, on important questions of state. Some of their harrangues wou'd be heard with pleasure in any house of representatives; and the whole is conducted with, perhaps, more spirit than was ever display'd in any institution of this nature.[91]

Jefferson also continued to take great pride in Wythe's law program, and in late 1787 South Carolinian Ralph Izard wrote him: "I have heard you speak of the University of Williamsburgh, and of the abilities of Mr. Wyth, which make me desirous of [my eldest son Henry] being placed for two, or three years under the tuition of that Gentleman."[92] To this proposition, the Virginian sent his ardent approval: "I cannot but approve your idea of sending your eldest son, destined for the law, to Williamsburgh." After briefly noting the excellent instruction offered by Professors Madison and Bellini, Jefferson wrote, "But the pride of the Institution is Mr. Wythe, one of the Chancellors of the state, and professor of law in the college. He is one of the greatest men of the age, having held without competition the first place at the bar of our general court for 25 years, and always distinguished by the most spotless virtue." As for Wythe's methods, his early student continued, "He gives lectures regularly, and holds moot courts and parliaments wherein he presides and the young men debate regularly in law, and legislation, learn the rules of parliamentary proceeding, and acquire the habit of public speaking." Jefferson then added his ultimate praise when he stated, "I know no place *in the world, while the present professors remain,* where I would so soon place a son."[93]

* * * * *

An early twentieth-century historian has commented that "If the test of the teacher is the ability and character of the students he turns out into the world and the respect which they retain for him in the more mature years . . . , Wythe must have been one of the greatest of instructors."[94] While only a handful of Wythe's students at William and Mary have been identified, a brief perusal of this small roster conclusively shows the truth of this comment.[95]

If judged by his future impact, Wythe's most notable student at William and Mary was undoubtedly John Marshall (1755-1835), the most important jurist in American history. Marshall, who was already somewhat familiar with Blackstone, spent only three months in Williamsburg, for he was eager to start a law practice. During that time, however, he was able to compile a commonplace book of nearly 200 pages, containing over seventy subject headings, from "Abatement" to "Limitation of Actions."[96]

One of Marshall's classmates, William Short, remembered that the future Chief Justice went "to the bar, as I well know, with little even general knowledge of law, & less particular & practical law learning." Short also recalled that "[t]he most important cause w[hic]h was argued before [Wythe's moot court] was one with four of us on each side. Marshall led one side & I the other. . . . The auditory at that time certainly considered my speech far superior to his."[97]

Despite the brevity of Marshall's formal legal education, Short would be the first to admit that "No man has ever had in this country a more successful & more brilliant career."[98] Marshall developed a strong law practice, and later served in Congress, as Secretary of State, and, for his last thirty-four years, as Chief Justice of the United States. Although Wythe's influence was greater on some of his other students, especially Jefferson, one commentator has opined that Marshall's decision in *Marbury v. Madison* was likely influenced either by Wythe's teaching or the Professor's reasoning in a 1782 decision, *Commonwealth v. Caton,* discussed below.[99]

One of Marshall's classmates at William and Mary, Bushrod Washington (1762-1829), would be the Chief Justice's leading friend and supporter on the U.S. Supreme Court, not to mention an eminent jurist in his own right. George Washington's "favorite nephew," Bushrod graduated from William and Mary in 1778 and then returned to Williamsburg in early 1780 to attend Wythe's lectures. Unlike Marshall, Washington stayed through the fall, and after service in the army he furthered his training by apprenticing in James Wilson's Philadelphia law office. Clearly one of the new nation's best-educated attorneys, Washington maintained an impressive law practice until his 1798 appointment to the U.S. Supreme Court. Although largely forgotten today, Washington was an influential and stabilizing force on the Court for three decades, serving until his death in 1829.[100]

During the decades when Marshall and Washington were championing a strong national government through their work on the federal Supreme Court, a former classmate, Spencer Roane (1762-1822), was the nation's leading jurist embracing the doctrine of states' rights. Roane, who was considered "a prodigy of his generation," was one of Wythe's "most brilliant pupils." Like Washington, he continued his legal education in Philadelphia, after which he won election to the House of Delegates at age twenty-one, became a judge of the General Court six years later, and was a member of the Court of Appeals at age thirty-two. Roane served on Virginia's highest court the last twenty-eight years of his life, and he quickly became the nation's most noted strict-constructionist judge. Had Jefferson, instead of Adams, been able to appoint a Chief Justice to replace Oliver Ellsworth, he would have chosen his friend and supporter Roane, rather than Marshall, and such a choice clearly would have changed this nation's history.[101]

Another famous Virginian, the nation's fifth President, James Monroe (1758-1831), may have attended Wythe's classes in 1780, although this has yet to be conclusively proved. Monroe attended William and Mary from 1774 until he left to fight in the Revolution in 1776, and disappointed in his failure to receive a proper command, he was advised by Jefferson to study law. Thus, according to his leading biographer, Harry Ammon, "Monroe re-entered William and Mary early in 1780 and joined William Short and [John F.] Mercer in reading law under Jefferson's direction."[102] It is unknown if his association with William and Mary, which Ammon thinks "was probably nominal,"[103] included the studying of law under Wythe, although it is clear that Monroe at least contemplated attending the professor's lectures—and this caused him some uncertainty about following Jefferson to the new capital in Richmond. Monroe's dilemma is clear from a March 7, 1780, letter he received from his uncle Joseph Jones:

> If Mr. Wythe means to pursue Mr. Blackstone's method, I should think you ought to attend him from the commencement of his course, if at all . . . indeed I incline to think Mr. Wythe under the present state of our laws will be much embarrassed to deliver lectures with that perspicuity and precision which might be expected from him under a more established and settled state of them. The undertaking is arduous and the subject intricate at the best. . . . Whichever method he may like, or whatever plan he may lay down to govern him, I doubt not it will be executed with credit to himself and benefit to his auditors.[104]

The uncle went on to say that were he Monroe, he would follow whatever suggestions Jefferson made, and, in the end, Monroe followed Jefferson to Richmond. This letter and Monroe's eventual actions, however, in no way prove whether or not he attended Wythe's lectures while still in Williamsburg. It seems intuitive that Jefferson would recommend to any aspiring attorney the advantages offered by attending Wythe's lectures. In addition, it is known that William Short was a Wythe pupil while also reading law with Jefferson, and most importantly, there is no other good reason why Monroe would re-enroll in William and Mary. Still, while every author seems to know the definitive answer to this question—of thirteen sources consulted, eleven list Monroe as a Wythe student, while two emphatically deny the association[105]—the fact remains that there is no conclusive proof one way or the other.

While Monroe's attendance is uncertain, another student who definitely did attend Wythe's lectures in 1780, after facing the same sort of dilemma, was John Brown (1757-1837); and his letters to an uncle give us our best picture of Wythe's law class that year. Brown, the son of a prominent Presbyterian minister in the Shenandoah Valley, attended Princeton until it was captured by the British, and he then travelled south to William and Mary to continue his collegiate education. While in Williamsburg, Brown determined to study law, and in the fall of 1779, Virginia's Attorney General Edmund Randolph, upon the recommendation of college president Madison, took Brown as an apprentice, "without a fee, provided I would assist him in writing."[106]

Several months after Brown began this tutelage, the Professorship of Law and Police was established, and on December 9, 1779, the young apprentice wrote his uncle:

> William & Mary has undergone a very considerable Revolution; The Visitors met on the 4th Instant & form'd it into a University; annul'd the old Statutes, abolish'd the Grammar School[;] continued Mr Madison President, & Professor of Mathematics[;] Appointed Mr Wyth Professor

> of Law, Dr McClurg of Physick[,] Mr Andrews of Moral Philosophy, & Monsr Belini of modern Languages. Each of these Professors have an Annuity of eight Hogsheads of Tobacco. The Students have to . . . pay a Hd of Tobacco to each Professor, they shall attend.

At this time, Brown hinted that he would like to attend Wythe's lectures, but he did not know how to quit his apprenticeship with Randolph. With the removal of the government to Richmond, Randolph, as Attorney General, would necessarily have to move to the new capital, and Brown noted that "if I continue with him I shall have to move there also." This he did not want to do, yet he realized that because Randolph was "a Gentl[ema]n of great delicacy perhaps it might be improper to q[u]it him & attend Mr Wyth's Lectures."[107]

For many weeks Brown remained unsure of his plans, until Randolph, in late January 1780, recommended that he stay in Williamsburg and attend Wythe's lectures, for the Attorney General saw this choice "as the best opportunity . . . for Study [and] Instruction [in law] that this Country affords."[108] Brown began to study under Wythe almost immediately, and in the middle of February he reported to his uncle: "I apply closely to the Study of Law and find it to be a more difficult Science than I expected, though I hope with Mr Wythes assistance to make some proficiency in it; those who finish this Study in a few months either have strong natural parts or else they know little about it."[109]

Brown continued to study under Wythe for most of the year, and in July he reported that "the Advantages of my situation, . . . of late have been greatly augmented; for Mr Wythe[,] ever attentive to the improvement of his Pupils, founded two Institutions for that purpose," the Moot Court and the Moot Legislature. As quoted above, Brown went on to describe both institutions, and he then noted, "I take an active part in both these Institutions & hope thereby to rub off that natural Bashfulness which at present is extremely prejudicial to me."[110]

Wythe's institutions must have worked their magic, for after his 1782 admission to the bar Brown moved to what is now Kentucky and quickly became one of that region's most noted politicians. He was elected to the Virginia Senate in 1784, and three years later he began service in the Continental Congress. After the adoption of the Constitution, Brown served in the first two sessions of Congress as a Representative from Virginia, and in 1792 when Kentucky received her statehood, he was elected one of the Commonwealth's first United States Senators, serving until 1805.[111]

Brown was not the only person in his family to study law under Wythe, for evidence suggests that a brother and two first cousins did likewise, all of whom also became known for their public service. The brother, James Brown (1766-1835), eventually settled in New Orleans, and twice represented Louisiana in the U.S. Senate (1813-1817, 1819-1823), as well as serving as Minister to France (1823-1829).[112]

As for the cousins, the most famous was John Breckinridge (1760-1806), who at age nineteen while a student at William and Mary was elected to the Virginia legislature by the citizens of Botetourt county. In 1792, Breckinridge was elected to Congress from the district surrounding Charlottesville, but shortly thereafter he resigned the seat and settled in Kentucky. There, the young attorney flourished, serving as state Attorney General and speaker of the state House. In 1801 he was elected to the U.S. Senate, serving alongside his cousin John Brown, and four years later he was appointed United States Attorney General by his friend Thomas Jefferson. Breckinridge was serving in this position when he died prematurely at the age of forty-six.[113] John's younger brother, James Breckenridge (1763-1833), who served in thirteen sessions of the Virginia legislature in addition to four terms in Congress (1809-1817), has also been listed as a Wythe pupil.[114]

The Kentuckian who in 1805 replaced John Brown in the U.S. Senate, Buckner Thruston (1764-1845), was also a Wythe student at William and Mary. Thruston resembled his legal mentor, for he was "a scholarly man" who did not care for "the rough-and-tumble of Washington politics." Accordingly, he resigned his Senate seat in 1809 to become judge of the U.S. Circuit Court for the District of Columbia, a position in which he served for thirty-six years until his death.[115]

While many Wythe students moved west, especially to Kentucky, a noted politician who studied under Wythe at William and Mary and then stayed in Virginia was William Branch Giles (1762-1830). Giles had earlier graduated from Princeton, and during his career he represented Virginia in the U.S. House

(1790-1798, 1801-1803) and the U.S. Senate (1804-1815), as well as serving as the state's Governor (1827-1830).[116]

A Wythe student who possibly could have achieved even more than Giles was Samuel Hardy (c. 1758-1785). Like John Breckinridge, Hardy was elected to the General Assembly while still a student in Williamsburg, and in 1783, when about twenty-five, he won election to the Continental Congress. There, Hardy impressed all with whom he came into contact, but unfortunately he died in Philadelphia two years later; despite failing to reach his thirtieth birthday, the General Assembly named a county in Hardy's honor.[117]

As detailed below, Wythe tutored many students in the classics, and among those who also studied law with the great teacher were William Munford and Jefferson's nephew Peter Carr.[118] Another Wythe law student with a close association to Jefferson was William Short (1758-1849), whom the third President considered his "adopted son."[119]

Short, who attended Wythe's lectures in 1780 and then studied under Jefferson, recalled: "In point of general knowledge I am sure I may say without vanity that I [was] prepared more than most of the Lawyers who then were practicing at the bar. I had read and made copius notes on Coke [on] Lyttleton. I had done so with Blackstone, of course." In addition, "I had plead causes . . . in a simulated court, where our professor presided, & I was considered able and eloquent, &c."[120] Thus, Short "went to the bar . . . full of all the general principles & erudite knowledge of the sources of law. The law of nature, the law of the land, viz. England, for all our books were of English law; such things had occupied me. . . . I was full of myself and of my own superiority."[121]

Short, however, soon realized that his "mere theoretical study" under Wythe and Jefferson would, by itself, be "deficient" for a successful law practice, and he later told a nephew that "collegiate courses under celebrated professors are more the luxury of [legal] education than the solid utility of the thing. The success of a lawyer must essentially & intrinsically depend on the course he pursues after he has entered the field of practice. It is then that the real education begins."[122] Short specifically mentioned two areas in which Wythe's instructions did not prepare him for a life at the Virginia bar; Short was not sufficiently acquainted with the acts of the Virginia legislature, and he was not thoroughly grounded in the forms of pleading.

Less than a month after leaving Wythe's classroom, Short was hired by a visiting South Carolinian who was accused of murdering one of his slaves, and the young attorney "was immediately for showing all of my law learning to the court," and began "preparing for a most elaborate & scientific speech." For that purpose, he "sent to a gentleman of the bar in Williamsburgh to lend me certain reports of criminal cases. From his answer I perceived that these reports w[oul]d not bear on the case in question & that it w[oul]d depend entirely on the act of the Virginia Assembly." While attending Wythe's lectures, Short "had never read or condescended to think of the acts of the assembly of Virginia," and the "information as to [the dispositiveness of] the act of the Assembly operated on me as the moves of his legs does on the Peacock when he is strutting. It showed me my own ignorance & real unfitness for the defence of my client."[123]

Shortly thereafter, Short, who intended to confine his practice to the highest courts in the state, had the only occasion in his career to appear before a county court, and in one particular he was quite unprepared. He later explained: "Scientific students [of the law] are apt to despise the mere technical & practical part of the business—that is the process or forms of pleading. . . . I had read the best reporters, but I was miserably ignorant of the mere technical forms. These were known to the clerks of court, & to every pettifogger, & I despised them." Thus, when Short, in the process of defending his county court client, was asked what plea he was entering, he was at a complete loss: "Had I been asked a most obstruse metaphysical question I w[oul]d not have been more completely put at a *non plus*. . . . Now this plea any underclerk w[oul]d have known, & I who had followed courses, &c, &c, did not know. I had never the less read the books of practice & thought I understood the subject." Thus, Short's "experience convinced me that this technical & practical part [of the law] is to be learned only in an attorney's office. My advice therefore always would be to everyone to pass one year in this way previous to the commencement of the practice."[124]

It is interesting to note, however, that in Short's career he likely benefitted a great deal more from

Wythe's "theoretical" learning than he would have from the knowledge gained by apprenticing in an attorney's office. Shortly after beginning his practice, Short became Jefferson's private secretary in Paris, and he later was a noted diplomat himself.

Jefferson was not the only important revolutionary leader to send those close to him to study law under Wythe, for another was Richard Henry Lee. In April 1780, while Lee's son Ludwell Lee (1760-1836) was in Europe attending his diplomat uncle Arthur Lee, Richard Henry wrote his brother: "Our worthy & learned friend, Geo. Wythe esquire is now Professor of Law in Wm & Mary College—his lectures are greatly admired; and it deserves your attention whether your nephew Ludwell would not be greatly benefitted by attending his lectures whilst he is reading the laws of Virginia . . . his father thinks so. . . ."[125] Arthur and Ludwell were scheduled to return to America, and four months after his first letter Richard Henry wrote Arthur to the same effect: "I think [Ludwell] may benefit himself by repairing to Williamsburg and finishing his law studies under Mr. Wythe, who is now most worthily employed in the character of Law professor at Willi[a]m & Mary College." Lee then added that Wythe "discharges the duty of [his professorship] with wonderful ability both as to the theory and practise. The sooner therefore that Ludwell gets under his tuition the better!"[126] Following his father's advice, Ludwell Lee began his studies at Williamsburg soon thereafter, and after the Revolution he returned to Williamsburg to complete his legal education.[127]

One of Lee's classmates during his later sojourn at the college was his first cousin, Thomas Lee Shippen (1765-1798), of Philadelphia. Shippen, the son of Dr. William Shippen, Professor of Anatomy at the University of Pennsylvania, studied with Wythe from 1784 to 1786, and he spent an additional two years at the Inner Temple. Despite displaying great talent and having arguably the best legal education of anyone in America, Shippen never aimed for, or achieved, greatness.[128]

Shippen was not the only Wythe student to come from out of state. Noted South Carolina patriot Ralph Izard, for instance, sent his eldest son Henry (b.1771) to be educated by Wythe,[129] and a North Carolinian who ventured north was Kemp Plummer (1769-1826), later a member of the "Warren Junto" which controlled North Carolina politics for several decades.[130] The great majority of Wythe's students, however, appear to have been Virginians.

Another son of the Virginia aristocracy who attended Wythe's lectures was Richard Randolph (1770-1796), the eldest brother of John Randolph of Roanoke and step-son of Wythe's pupil and successor St. George Tucker. Besides his familial connections, Randolph is most famous for being falsely accused of adultery and infanticide. Through the efforts of Patrick Henry and John Marshall, Randolph was acquitted on murder charges, yet he died shortly thereafter at the age of twenty-six. In his will, Randolph named as his executors his stepfather, two brothers, and "the most virtuous and incorruptible of mankind, and next to my father-in-law my greatest benefactor, George Wythe, Chancellor of Virginia, the brightest ornament of human nature."[131]

Another noted father whose sons may have attended Wythe's lectures was Robert Carter Nicholas, Wythe's colleague on the High Court of Chancery. Although their attendance is questionable, several sources list Wythe's students as including George Nicholas (c. 1754-1799), a noted Virginia attorney,[132] and his younger brother Wilson Cary Nicholas (1761-1820), a Virginia Governor who also represented the state in both houses of the federal legislature.[133]

Other men alleged to have been Wythe pupils include: Archibald Stuart (1757-1832), a legislative leader who later served on the General Court for three decades;[134] noted Richmond attorney John Wickham (1763-1839);[135] William Cabell, Jr.;[136] John Minor III (1761-1816), a Fredericksburg attorney and member of the Virginia General Assembly;[137] Jacob Walker, a distant relative of Wythe's whom the teacher thought showed "great promise";[138] and Daniel Call (c. 1765-1840), John Marshall's brother-in-law and a long-time Reporter of the Virginia Court of Appeals.[139]

One person has estimated that Wythe instructed fewer than 200 pupils in the law,[140] yet it is amazing what these students accomplished in later life. Students taught by George Wythe occupied almost every office this young nation had to offer, including President, Vice President, Secretary of State, Attorney General, U.S. Senator, Speaker of the U.S. House, Chief Justice, Associate Justice, federal District Judge, foreign Minister, Governor of Virginia, President of the Virginia Court of Appeals, member of the Virginia, Kentucky, and North Carolina legislatures, President of William and Mary, Professor of Law at both William and Mary and Transylvania, and Episcopal Bishop of Virginia.[141] While some of the men who occupied such stations were taught by Wythe in a private capacity, it is also true that "no law school in America has since sent from its class rooms into public life, in the same length of time, if at all, an equal number of men of such amazing ability."[142]

Wythe felt exceptionally close to "his boys," and it has been said that "[a]ll of his students entertained for him a veneration that was almost a religion."[143] There is little doubt that Paul Carrington is correct when he states that "Wythe's teaching career may be assessed . . . as consequential beyond comparison to that of any successor in American university law teaching."[144]

* * * * *

It has been said that one special advantage Wythe had as an instructor was that he "remained an active participant in both judicial and governmental activities and, as such, could bring much more vitality to his classroom."[145] During his tenure at William and Mary, Wythe travelled to Richmond during the months of April and September to hear cases on the High Court of Chancery as well as the Court of Appeals.

Wythe's most notable case, *Commonwealth v. Caton,* occurred on the latter court in 1782, when he, in *dicta,* became one of the first American jurists to espouse the doctrine of judicial review, stating:

> if the whole legislature . . . should attempt to overleap the bounds prescribed to them by the people, I, in administering the public justice of the country, will meet the united powers at my seat in this tribunal, and, pointing to the constitution, will say to them, "here is the limit of your authority; and hither shall you go, but no further."[146]

In another important case, Wythe defied public opinion when he became the first judge after the Revolution to hold that Virginians had to pay the previous debts they owed to British merchants.[147]

On several occasions in the 1780s Wythe was also pressed into other forms of government service. Having done nothing to enact the laws earlier drafted by the revisers, in 1783 the Virginia General Assembly decided that the state needed a new collection of its laws, and for this task it appointed the Commonwealth's three Chancellors, Wythe, Pendleton, and John Blair II. These men completed the work the following year, and ever since it has been known, incorrectly, as the "Chancellors' Revisal."[148]

In 1785, it was the national government that sought Wythe's service, for the Continental Congress named him to a jury of national leaders, including Jefferson, Monroe, John Rutledge, and William Patterson, to negotiate a settlement between New York and Massachusetts over the ownership of a vast tract of land in what is now western New York State. Not finding himself able to leave Williamsburg, Wythe refused this appointment.[149]

The one appointment he was unable to refuse, however, was to the Constitutional Convention in 1787. One authority has stated that "Wythe's eminence as a judge and his long legal and parliamentary experience made him an almost inevitable choice as a delegate to the Philadelphia convention of 1787."[150] In October 1786, the Virginia General Assembly chose seven delegates for the Philadelphia convention: Wythe, George Washington, James Madison, George Mason, John Blair, Edmund Randolph, and Patrick Henry—who declined to serve and was replaced by Wythe's former colleague on the William and Mary faculty, Dr. James McClurg.

In Philadelphia, Wythe's greatest service was as chairman of the rules committee,[151] and as in the Continental Congress, he was highly respected for his knowledge of both the law and classical literature. Delegate William Lee Pierce wrote that "Mr. Wythe is the famous Professor of Law at the University of William and Mary. He is confessedly one of the most learned legal characters of the present age." Pierce continued his description by noting that the Virginian had "acquired a compleat knowledge of the dead languages and all the sciences" and "[n]o man, it is said, understands the history of government better than Mr. Wythe." About the only thing Pierce could write against Wythe was that "from his too favorable opinion of men, he is no great politician."[152]

Wythe had been extremely reluctant to leave Virginia because of the health of his wife, who was gravely ill back in Williamsburg, and after only three weeks in Philadelphia he sought and was given permission to return home. Wythe found his wife's situation so serious that he formally resigned from the Convention on June 16, 1787, and two months later, on August 18, Elizabeth Taliaferro Wythe succumbed to her illness.[153]

Wythe's service in establishing a national constitution was not complete, however, for the following year he was elected to Virginia's ratifying convention. Wythe's selection by his fellow citizens came as a complete surprise, and a student remembered that upon being informed, "tears flowed down [Wythe's] cheeks in copious streams."[154]

The convention was held in Richmond during June 1788, and Wythe was called to the chair when the delegates went into the committee of the whole; the site of Wythe presiding over a legislative assembly must have seemed quite familiar to the not insubstantial number of delegates who had been his students at William and Mary. The "Father of the Constitution," James Madison, later listed Wythe, Pendleton, Blair, Innes, and Marshall as the five most important delegates, and Wythe was chosen to present the resolution calling for ratification.[155]

The following year, in recognition of his over-forty years of service to the Commonwealth, the Virginia General Assembly, on December 1, 1789, named a county in Wythe's honor. It is also interesting to note that at least five Virginia counties (all of them now in West Virginia) were named for Wythe's students: Jefferson, Hardy, Marshall, Roane, and Clay.[156]

As if his judicial and teaching duties were not enough to keep him busy, during the 1780s Wythe also began instructing young men in the classics. As noted above, William and Mary's grammar school had been closed in 1779, and at that time the college also stopped teaching the ancient languages. At some point an independent grammar school was formed in Williamsburg, yet its most notable master, Walker Maury, quit the school in 1786 when he moved to Norfolk.[157] Thus, Wythe likely saw it as a public duty to instruct intelligent youth in the classics, and it is noteworthy that he would not accept any payment for this service.[158] Of course in addition to his great sense of public duty, Wythe probably began instructing young men in the classics simply because teaching gave him great enjoyment. The Reverend Maury once told Jefferson that "Mr. Wythe . . . seems to enjoy himself no where, so much as with his pupils."[159]

During this period, Wythe's first classics pupil was Littleton Waller Tazewell (1774-1860), the precocious grandson of one of Wythe's best friends. Tazewell, who at age twelve was the youngest boy Wythe ever taught,[160] began studying Greek, Latin, Arithmetic, and other subjects under Wythe in 1786. Tazewell later recalled:

> I attended him every morning very early, and always found him waiting for me in his study by sunrise. When I entered the room, he immediately took from his well-stored library some Greek book, to which any accidental circumstance first directed his attention. This was opened at random, and I was bid to recite the first passage that caught his eye. Although utterly unprepared for such a task, I was never permitted to have the assistance of a Lexicon to a grammar but whenever I was at a loss, he gave me the meaning of the word or structure of the sentence which had puzzled me. . . . Whenever in the course of our reading any reference was made to the ancient manners, customs, laws, superstitions or history of the Greeks, he asked me to explain the allusion, and when I failed to do so satisfactorily (as was often the case) he immediately gave full clear and complete account of the subject to which reference was so made. Having done so, I was bidden to remind him of it the next day, in order that we might then learn from some better source, whether his explanation was correct or not; and the difficulties I met with on one day, generally produced the subject of the lesson of the next.[161]

In this way, Wythe tutored Tazewell in Greek from sunrise until breakfast, and the same method was employed from noon until two p.m. to teach the young pupil Latin. From four in the afternoon until dark, Wythe and Tazewell studied mathematics using French texts, and in the evenings Wythe had his young pupil read to him from both major works of English literature and current periodicals.[162]

Tazewell studied under Wythe for approximately five years, during most of which time he lived in the Wythe home. The young prodigy later compiled an impressive record at William and Mary and then read law under John Wickham. Becoming one of the nation's foremost attorney-statesmen, Tazewell served in both houses of the federal legislature (House, 1800-1801; Senate, 1824-1832) and as Governor of Virginia (1834-1836). He was likely the last-surviving student of George Wythe when he died in 1860 at the age of eighty-six.[163]

Another Wythe pupil for most of this period was Peter Carr (1770-1815), Thomas Jefferson's nephew. Jefferson sent his kinsman to be educated in Williamsburg, and after attending Maury's grammar school Carr enrolled in William and Mary in the fall of 1786, taking classes in natural and moral philosophy, mathematics, and modern languages (French and Spanish). Carr, however, also "enjoy[ed] the advantage of Mr. Wythe's valuable patronage and instructions," for at this time the law professor began privately tutoring Jefferson's nephew in Latin and Greek, with Carr reading, among other authors, Herodotus, Sophocles, Cicero, Horace, and Lucretius.[164] Jefferson was highly pleased that his nephew was studying under Wythe, telling the young man, "I am sure you will find this to have been one of the most fortunate events of your life, as I have ever been sensible it was of mine."[165]

In early 1788 Carr also began the study of law under Wythe. As for his routine at this time, he wrote his uncle, then in Paris, that he was following Wythe's suggestion of "reading [law] two or three hours every day, and devoting the rest of my time to languages, history and Philosophy." More specifically, the young student would "rise about day, and take a walk of half an hour to shake off sleep, read law till breakfast, then attend Mr. Wythe till 12 oclock in the languages, read philosophy till dinner, history till night and poetry till bedtime."[166] Jefferson thoroughly approved of this education, telling his nephew, "I like well the distribution of your time mentioned in your letter . . . and the counsels of Mr. Wythe so kindly extended to you, leave it necessary for me to add nothing of that kind."[167]

The following year Carr told his uncle, "Your sentiments with regard to Mr. Wythe, and the attention which ought to be paid to his precepts perfectly coincide with mine." Showing a streak of independent thinking, however, Carr questioned the emphasis his tutor put on the classics, stating: "The mode of education which he pursues, and to which he is so much attached, is in a measure fallen into disuse, and for my own part I think not entirely without reason." Carr then asked, "Might not a great part of that time which he bestows on the dead languages, be better employed on the modern languages, natural history, and the Mathematics?"[168]

As noted above, Elizabeth Wythe died in August 1787, and likely fearing the loneliness that might overtake him, Wythe determined to open a grammar school at his house, which would include the boarding of the students. Wythe was making plans for this even before his wife died, for he placed an advertisement for the school in the *Virginia Gazette* on August 2, 1787:

> I purpose in October, when the next course of lectures in law and police will commence, to open a school for reading some of the higher Latin and Greek classics and the approved English poets and prose writers, and also for exercises in Arithmatic.
>
> George Wythe[169]

Unfortunately, the boarding of a number of boisterous youths did not work out, for as was remembered by Tazewell, Wythe found the plan "much more trouble than he could sustain." The teacher "was irritated and vexed by a thousand little occurrences he had never forseen," and the "necessary domestic duties occupied . . . much of his time, broke in upon his pursuits, and interrupted even his business and his amusements." Thus, while continuing to give board to Tazewell, Wythe found suitable lodgings for the other students and began teaching them as day students.[170]

As previously mentioned, all of Wythe's students benefitted not only from his academic instructions, but also from their teacher's profound sense of morality. Peter Carr told his uncle that Wythe "adds advice and lessons of morality, which are not only pleasing and instructive now, but will be (I hope) of real utility in the future."[171] Along these lines, one of Wythe's special interests was the abolition of slavery, and it is interesting to note that his great-grandfather Keith had been the first Quaker to take a stand for emancipation.[172]

In 1785, noted British abolitionist Dr. Richard Price asked Thomas Jefferson about Virginia's sentiments on slavery, and this caused Jefferson to think of Wythe. The then Minister to France responded: "The college of William and Mary in Williamsburg, since the remodeling of it's plan, is the place where are collected together all the young men of Virginia under preparation for public life." He then continued, "They are there under the direction (most of them) of a Mr. Wythe one of the most virtuous of characters, and whose sentiments on the subject of slavery are unequivocal." Jefferson then suggested to Price how he might be able to affect sentiment on the issue: "I am satisfied [that] if you could resolve to address an exhortation to those young men, with all that eloquence of which you are master, that its influence on the future decision of this important question would be great, perhaps decisive."[173]

While a one-time owner of at least seventeen slaves himself, over the last two decades of his life Wythe managed to divest himself of this burden. Wythe's views on slavery obviously had an effect on many of his students, one example being John Minor III, who, not too many years after he left Wythe's classroom, introduced a bill in the Virginia General Assembly which would have led to a gradual emancipation of the Commonwealth's slaves.[174] In addition, former student Richard Randolph in his will freed all of his slaves and left provisions so that they might be set up as landed farmers. Randolph named Wythe as one of his executors, but, unfortunately, this experiment never proved successful.[175]

* * * * *

Despite the great success of Wythe's law program throughout the 1780s, at the end of the decade he voluntarily relinquished his professorship, never again to teach in an institutional setting. Several events likely combined to force this situation, including the death of his wife, a reorganization of Virginia's court system, and a religious controversy at William and Mary.

As noted above, Elizabeth Wythe died in August 1787, and Wythe thereafter almost completely withdrew from society. Nathaniel Beverly Tucker, son of Wythe's early pupil St. George Tucker and himself the Chair of Law and Police at William and Mary in later years, recalled that during Wythe's last years in Williamsburg, "a morbid sadness came over him, which disqualified him for social enjoyment"; the great teacher was "silent and grave; his whole air and manner betokening a gentle sadness."[176] Others, too, recalled Wythe's reluctance to engage in conversation; Wythe "sometimes politely bowed in persons calling on business, attended to it and then politely bowed them out of the house, without speaking a word," and when he visited a neighborhood bakery early each morning to buy his bread, he would "put down his money and t[ake] his loaf without uttering a word."[177] At this time the only person Wythe visited was a relative, Mrs. Taliaferro,[178] and he "became more and more immersed in a life of books," with his writings and conversations becoming "ever more pedantic and obscure."[179]

Shortly after his wife's death, another major change occurred in Wythe's life when, in 1788, the Virginia General Assembly reorganized the state's court system. The legislature made the Court of Appeals a separate, five-judge, court, and two of the five judges chosen for the new court were Wythe's colleagues on the chancery court, Pendleton and Blair. In addition, the legislature reduced the number of judges on the High Court of Chancery to one, with Wythe being the only member.

Serving as the Commonwealth's sole chancellor very much appealed to Wythe, for the following year Edmund Randolph informed President Washington that far from desiring a federal judgeship, Wythe "sits in a kind of legal monarchy, which to him is the highest possible gratification."[180] One downside, however, was that Wythe's decisions could now be reviewed by the new Court of Appeals, including its Chief Justice Pendleton, a situation which would cause friction in the coming years.[181] For Wythe, the reorganization also meant that he would now have to travel to Richmond four times a year to hold court, and this likely caused him to rethink his commitment to teaching at William and Mary; Peter Carr wrote in May 1789 that Wythe's "public avocations have lately taken up much of his time[,] so that my attendance on him has not been such as I could have wished."[182] The court reorganization has traditionally been assigned as the one reason why Wythe stopped teaching and removed to Richmond, and while it was certainly a major factor, Wythe was also led to this decision by a controversy then brewing at William and Mary.

Over the course of the 1780s, "the new impetus given to the College by Jefferson's reforms slowly yielded to the weight of resistance, tradition, and habit . . . [and] the conservatives and the Church slowly fought their way back into control of the institution."[183] The leader of the conservative forces was John Bracken, rector of Bruton Parish in Williamsburg since 1773, and master of the college's grammar school and professor of humanity from 1777 until the 1779 reorganization. In 1787, Bracken sued the College to regain his former position, arguing that the 1779 reorganization was illegal, and one historian who has studied the matter says that the plaintiff's plea was "a religious protest against the secularism which the Jeffersonian reform had introduced." In court, Wythe's former student John Marshall represented the college and was able to defeat Bracken's suit, yet the college determined to reinstate the Reverend as a professor, and he later served as President of William and Mary for two years after Madison's death in 1812.[184]

The situation involving Bracken must have upset Wythe greatly, for on September 14, 1789, Jefferson informed William Short:

> Mr. Wythe has abandoned the college of Wm. & Mary, disgusted with some of the conduct of the professors, and particularly of the ex-professor Bracken, and perhaps too with himself for having suffered himself to be too much irritated with that. The visitors will try to condemn what gave him offence and press him to return; otherwise it is over with the college. . . . Hampden Sidney . . . too, . . . is going to nothing, owing to the religious phrensy they have inspired into the boys young and old, which their parents have no taste for.[185]

The William and Mary Board of Visitors was unable to change Wythe's mind, so the law professor's resignation was reluctantly accepted; at the same time the school conferred on Wythe an honorary Doctor of Laws degree.[186] The changes at William and Mary upset Jefferson greatly, for when recommending a college for his nephew in 1790, Jefferson told a brother-in-law, "I know there is nobody left at [William and Mary] to render his return there an object"; instead, Jefferson suggested Princeton or, possibly, the University of Pennsylvania.[187] Disheartened that his plans for his *alma mater* had gone awry, Jefferson in his retirement founded the University of Virginia.

As for what occurred at William and Mary after Wythe's resignation, in March 1790 the Visitors named Wythe's former pupil St. George Tucker as his replacement in the chair of law and police. Tucker, who would serve in this position until his own disagreement with the faculty in 1804, continued to assign readings and deliver lectures, the latter of which he later incorporated into the first American edition of Blackstone's *Commentaries.* Tucker, however, unlike Wythe, did not come from a legislative background, and although he regularly lectured on the state and national constitutions, he abandoned the idea of teaching practical politics through a moot legislature.[188] Tucker student Joseph C. Cabell in 1801 wrote a friend that "You may remember that a notion formerly prevailed here that a student of law should make the study of his profession subservient to that of politics. This opinion however seems not to prevail here" under Tucker.[189]

Beyond Jefferson's letter to Short, the best evidence that Wythe's decision to quit William and Mary was not based solely on the reorganization of the Virginia court system is that he did not immediately move to Richmond; but, rather, waited two-and-a-half years after the court reorganization, and two years after Jefferson noted that Wythe was resigning from his professorship. During this transitional period, the Chancellor, in a private capacity, continued to instruct a number of young men in the law and classics, including Tazewell, Carr, John Coalter, William Munford, and John Wayles Eppes.

John Coalter (1771-1838), who later served for many years on the Virginia Court of Appeals, began the study of law under Wythe in the fall of 1789, at which time he told his father:

> I have just begun to attend Mr. Wythe on Law to which I shall do with pleasure and alacrity. The exalted character and tried abilities of that Gentleman promise the apt & diligent Student a certain noble source of instruction; and his attentions and willingness to inform flatters me that even my improvement is not to be doubted.[190]

Coalter's friend William Munford (1775-1825) also studied the law and classics with Wythe, and he told Coalter in June 1790, "My great resource is Mr. Wythe." Munford thought that he might be asked to live with Wythe, and he noted that "If so, your friend['s] fortune is made. Nothing could advance me faster in the world than the reputation of having been educated by Mr. Wythe, for such a man as he casts a light upon all around him."[191] Munford was correct in his prediction about living arrangements, for in April 1791 he was writing Coalter that "thro' the surprising friendship and generosity of Mr. Wythe, I live in his house, and board at his table, at the same time enjoying the benefit of his instructions without paying a farthing. My esteem for this man, together with my love, increase every day."[192]

Next to Jefferson, it is likely that Munford was the student who had the closest relationship with Wythe, and he shared his teacher's love of both the law and classical literature. Munford later served in the General Assembly and as Reporter of the Virginia Court of Appeals, yet he is best known for his magnificent translation of the *Iliad*.[193]

One of the "old" students, Peter Carr, left Wythe's tutelage in late 1789 or early 1790,[194] although at this time Jefferson sent another of his nephews, John Wayles Eppes (1773-1823), to study under Wythe. In December 1789, Jefferson wrote Wythe that Eppes' father desired that his son quit William and Mary and instead attend Wythe, studying mathematics, natural philosophy, and history before learning the law.[195] It is assumed that Wythe agreed to such,[196] although ten months later Eppes was no longer in Williamsburg.[197] Thereafter, Eppes followed Jefferson to Philadelphia, where he studied law under his uncle's direction, and still later he married Jefferson's daughter Maria and was a strong supporter of his father-in-law's party while serving five terms in Congress (1803-1811, 1813-1815) and two years in the U.S. Senate (1817-1819).[198]

* * * * *

George Wythe finally moved to Richmond in September 1791, where he would live the final fifteen years of his life. As he aged, Wythe became a figure of veneration and awe, and his erudition caused persons to refer to him as "the learned" or "the famous" judge.

This erudition was in full view in Wythe's written opinions on the court of chancery, and one historian has stated that "his learning was so extensive and so lavishly spread upon the pages of his opinions that these opinions appear somewhat pedantic and cumbersome."[199] For example:

> In the eight pages of one opinion with its footnotes, Bracton and Justinian, Juvenal's Satires, and Quintilian, Euclid, Archimedes and Hiero, hydrostatic experiments and Coke on Littleton, Tristam Shandy and Petronius, Halley and Price and Prometheus, Don Quixote and Swift's Tale of a Tub, Locke's Essay on Human Understanding, and Turkish travellers, chase one another up and down to the bewilderment of all but the universal scholar.[200]

Wythe was obviously intensely proud of the effort he put into his opinions, and in his later years one of the major vexations in his life was that there was a higher court, led by his chief nemesis Edmund Pendleton, which could review, and reverse, his decisions. In the fourteen years between the formation of the separate Court of Appeals and the 1803 death of Pendleton, over 150 of Wythe's cases were appealed to the higher court, and of these, more than half were reversed or in some way modified by Pendleton. This enraged Wythe, who in 1795 "took the unprecedented step of writing a volume of reports on chancery cases reviewed by the Court of Appeals in which he attacked his superior judge at times with bitter sarcasm."[201] Pendleton was initially inclined to respond in like manner, but the elderly judge was finally convinced that this would serve no purpose.

Wythe served as the Commonwealth's sole Chancellor until 1802, when his judicial lode was somewhat lightened by the General Assembly. The legislature divided the state into three Chancery districts, each with its own chancellor, with sessions to be held in Williamsburg, Richmond, and Staunton. Wythe was given the Richmond district.[202]

Besides his judicial position, other forms of public service continued to attract Wythe during his Richmond years. In 1795, the Chancellor was named chairman of a committee appointed by the General Assembly to compile and publish the state's laws on lands, tenements, and hereditaments. What is most interesting about this committee is that it appears probable that all of the other members were former Wythe students: John Marshall, John Wickham, John Brown, and Bushrod Washington.[203] In addition, Wythe presided over two meetings of Virginia's electoral college, in 1800 and 1804, both of which cast its votes for Wythe's most famous student, Thomas Jefferson.

As he had throughout his life, Wythe continued his own education while in Richmond, for he engaged the local spiritual leader of the Richmond Jewish community to teach him Hebrew.[204] This was his seventh language, for he already could read English, French, Italian, Spanish, Latin, and Greek.

As would be expected, Wythe also continued his teaching of young men, in both the law and classics. Although Littleton W. Tazewell stayed in Williamsburg to complete his studies at William and Mary, Wythe had William Munford move with him to Richmond, and this student later remembered that "for three years, at all spare moments, he devoted himself without reward to my instruction, giving me the best and most excellent advice, and imparting knowledge which I never could have acquired otherwise."[205] Munford was one of Wythe's last law students, and he distinctly recalled his teacher's instructions on learning the subject: "Don't skim it; read deeply, and ponder what you read; they begin to make lawyers now without the *viginti annorum lucubrationes* of Lord Coke; they are mere skimmers of law and know little else."[206]

At this time, one of Wythe's students in the classics was John Thomson (1777-1799), who "would have been one of the ablest of Virginia's scholars and lawyers" had he not died very young.[207] The most notable Wythe student during his Richmond years, however, and next to Jefferson and Marshall the most famous person Wythe ever taught, was Henry Clay.

Clay (1777-1852) was a sixteen-year-old clerk in the chancery office when, in 1793, he was asked by Wythe to serve as his amanuensis. For nearly four years, Clay painstakingly wrote out Wythe's judicial opinions and private correspondence, and in return Wythe instructed Clay in history, law, and the classics. Wythe had his young pupil read "Harris's *Homer*, Tooke's *Diversions of Purley*, Bishop Lowth's *Grammar*, Plutarch's *Lives*, and [other] books of law and of history," including Coke on Littleton.

Clay's foremost biographer, Robert V. Remini, has stated that "the chancellor's society and assistance became an extended seminar in the law, the classics, literature, history, and social refinement and grace." He continues, "Wythe took a bright, eager, talented, attentive, promising, and courteous sixteen-year-old student, and by the time Clay reached the age of twenty-one, the chancellor had molded him into an educated, cultivated, urbane, and articulate gentleman, with considerable knowledge of the law."[208]

Wythe saw that Clay finished his legal education by studying for a year under the Commonwealth's Attorney General, Robert Brooke, and after passing the bar the young man settled in Kentucky. Clay, of course, went on to become the most notable American politician never elected to the Presidency, serving, over his fifty-year public career, as Speaker of the U.S. House, Secretary of State, and "dictator" in the U.S. Senate. One source has stated that "[t]hroughout his long life, Clay's position on public issues reflected the teachings of Wythe," and Clay gave his first-born son the middle name of Wythe.[209]

George Wythe's beliefs in liberty and the importance of education also led him to teach his black servants to read and write,[210] the most noted of whom was Michael Brown, a young mulatto who was freed by Wythe. The Chancellor also taught Latin and Greek to Brown, and in his will Wythe both left a legacy for Brown and asked President Jefferson to continue the young man's education.

It was partially because of this legacy to the servant that both Wythe and Brown were murdered by Wythe's grandnephew, George Wythe Sweeney; a dissipated, spendthrift young man, Sweeney was the residual legatee of Wythe's will. Long the beneficiary of Wythe's generosity, in 1806 the ungrateful Sweeney began to steal from his great-uncle, including the forging of at least six checks. These crimes were discovered, yet before Sweeney could be charged, he placed arsenic in the food or drink of the Wythe household. Brown died shortly thereafter, but Wythe lingered in agony for two weeks, during which he disinherited Sweeney. Unfortunately, on June 8, 1806, the poison finally led to the venerable Chancellor's death.[211]

Because of his nearly sixty years of service to the Commonwealth, as well as the manner of his death, the public was greatly grieved by Wythe's passing; one historian has determined that "more column inches of eulogy [were devoted to Wythe] than had been elicited in Virginia newspapers by the death of George Washington or by that of any other person."[212] The *Richmond Enquirer*, for instance, opined that "Kings may require mausoleums to consecrate their memory; saints may claim the privileges of canonization; but the venerable GEORGE WYTHE needs no other monument than the services rendered to his country, and the universal sorrow which that country sheds over his grave."[213]

There could be no more fitting eulogy for Wythe, however, than the realization that upon his death in

1806, the nation's President (Jefferson), its Chief Justice (Marshall), an Associate Justice (Washington), the Attorney General (Breckinridge), U.S. Senators from Virginia (Giles) and Kentucky (Thruston), and the most influential state judge in America (Roane) all were former students of George Wythe.

NOTES

1. Thomas Jefferson to William DuVal, June 14, 1806, quoted in Dice Robins Anderson, "The Teacher of Jefferson and Marshall," 15 *South Atlantic Qtly.* 327, 343 (1911). While mispronounced by some, in Virginia the name "Wythe" rhymes with "Smith"; according to one commentator, it is "[p]ronounced 'With' by the *cognoscenti* for the same reason that they pronounce Coke as 'Cooke'; the linguistic explanation in these cases is perhaps more persuasive than any that might be found for the Virginia practice of pronouncing Talliaferro as 'Tolliver.'" William F. Swindler, "America's First Law Schools: Significance or Chauvinism?," 41 *Conn. B.J.* 1, 2 n.4 (1967).

2. Henry Clay to Benjamin B. Minor, May 3, 1851, in *The Papers of Henry Clay*, ed. Robert Seager II et al. (11 vols., 1959-1992), X, 888-89.

3. The four book-length biographies of Wythe are William Clarkin, *Serene Patriot: A Life of George Wythe* (1970); Joyce Blackburn, *George Wythe of Williamsburg* (1975); Alonzo Thomas Dill, *George Wythe, Teacher of Liberty* (1979); Imogene E. Brown, *American Aristides: A Biography of George Wythe* (1981). Of these, Dill's is by far the best, although it is quite short. Clarkin and Brown include much interesting material, but their works also contain a number of errors and, worst of all, they fail to give citations to much of their information.

The best source on Wythe's life up to 1776 remains W. Edwin Hemphill, "George Wythe, the Colonial Briton: A Biographical Study of the Pre-Revolutionary Era in Virginia" (unpublished doctoral dissertation, University of Virginia, 1937). A published dissertation, Robert B. Kirtland, *George Wythe: Lawyer, Revolutionary, Judge* (1986), contains some useful information.

Articles or published speeches on Wythe include Lyon Gardiner Tyler, "George Wythe," in *Great American Lawyers*, ed. William Draper Lewis (1907), I, 51-90; Oscar L. Shewmake, *The Honorable George Wythe: Teacher, Lawyer, Jurist, Statesman* (1950); "George Wythe," *Dictionary of American Biography*, eds. Allen Johnson, Dumas Malone, et al. (1929-1936), XX, 586-89 (hereinafter referred to as *DAB*); E. Lee Shepard, "George Wythe," in W. Hamilton Bryson, *Legal Education in Virginia, 1779-1979: A Biographical Approach*, 748-55; Hugh Blair Grigsby, *The Virginia Convention of 1776* (1855), 119-30; John Sherman, "George Wythe, the Neglected Patriot: A Bibliography," 34 *Bull. Biblio. & Mag. Notes* 185 (1977). An excellent source on Wythe's death is *The Murder of George Wythe: Two Essays* (1955).

On Wythe's teaching, see also Anderson, "Teacher of Jefferson and Marshall," *supra* note 1; W. Edwin Hemphill, "George Wythe, America's First Law Professor and Teacher of Jefferson, Marshall, and Clay" (unpublished master's thesis, Emory University, 1933); Paul D. Carrington, "The Revolutionary Idea of University Legal Education," 31 *Wm. & Mary L. Rev.* 527 (1990); Swindler, "America's First Law Schools," *supra* note 1; Robert M. Hughes, "William and Mary, the First American Law School," 2 *Wm. & Mary Qtly.*, 2d ser., 40 (1922); Fred D. Devitt, Jr., "Note: William and Mary, America's First Law School," 2 *Wm. & Mary L. Rev.* 424 (1960).

Oscar Shewmake states that a biography of George Wythe "is not an assignment for a potboiler, ghost-writer or rapid-fire biographer of eminent men . . . nor can it be done by some immature doctor of philosophy, suddenly 'come from the nowhere into the here,' who knows only what he had read." Instead, Shewmake writes that the biographer has to be "a Virginian whose ancestors had some part, however small, in the stirring events of the times in which [Wythe] lived." In addition, "he will be one who has himself labored in the several fields in which Wythe wrought so well. He will have been a teacher . . . of the type exemplified by Wythe. He will of necessity be a lawyer and, preferably, a member of the judiciary . . . [and] will have had experience in legislative work. . . . Finally, he will be a man of scholarly attainments with an understanding heart, in short, a gentleman." Shewmake, *Honorable George Wythe*, at 23-24. It is almost impossible that anyone today could meet all of these qualifications; the late U.S. senator and dean of the William and Mary Law School William B. Spong seems to have satisfied all of the requirements except that he never served on the judiciary. Of course Shewmake's comments are in some respects silly, for in noting the two foremost Virginia biographers of this century, Dumas Malone was neither a lawyer nor a politician (unlike Jefferson), and Douglas Southall Freeman was not a soldier (unlike Robert E. Lee and George Washington).

4. Unless otherwise noted, all information in this subsection, which briefly recounts Wythe's life from 1726 until 1779, comes from Dill, *Wythe, Teacher of Liberty*, *supra* note 3, at 3-41.

5. *Id.* at 4.

6. Tyler, "George Wythe," *supra* note 3, at 52; Dill, *Wythe, Teacher of Liberty*, *supra* note 3, at 5.

7. One source, Shewmake, *Honorable George Wythe*, *supra* note 3, at 8, states that Wythe entered William and Mary in 1740 at age fourteen, yet he does not cite to any evidence proving this assertion.

8. Daniel Call, quoted in Dill, *Wythe, Teacher of Liberty*, *supra* note 3, at 9.

9. *Id.* at 9 (emphasis in original).

10. Shewmake, *Honorable George Wythe*, *supra* note 3, at 10; Clarkin, *Serene Patriot*, *supra* note 3, in the Forward.

11. Dill, *Wythe, Teacher of Liberty*, *supra* note 3, at 19.

12. Thomas Jefferson, "Notes for the Biography of George Wythe," enclosed in Jefferson to John Saunderson, August 31, 1820, in *The Writings of Thomas Jefferson*, ed. Andrew A. Lipscomb (1903), I, 167.

13.Thomas Jefferson to Ralph Izard, July 17, 1788, in *The Papers of Thomas Jefferson*, ed. Julian P. Boyd et al. (27 vols. to date, 1950-1997), XIII, 372.

14. Jefferson, "Notes of Wythe," *supra* note 12, at I, 167-68.

15. Tyler, "George Wythe," *supra* note 3, at 59.

16. Quoted in Dill, *Wythe, Teacher of Liberty, supra* note 3, at 30.

17. For the text of, and commentary about, the proposed laws coming out of the revisal, see the *Jefferson Papers, supra* note 13, at II, 303-665.

18. Quoted in Anderson, "Teacher of Jefferson and Marshall," *supra* note 1, at 334-35. According to Tucker, "Without ambition, without avarice, taking no pleasure in society, [Wythe] was by nature and habit addicted to solitude, and his active mind found its only enjoyment in profound research." Wythe devoted himself to "[t]he language of antiquity, the exact sciences, and the law," and "he became a profound lawyer for the same reason than he was a profound Greek scholar, astronomer and mathematician." *Id.*

19. William Clarkin, *Serene Patriot, supra* note 3, at 142, states that Jefferson was Wythe's first pupil, while W. Edwin Hemphill believes that Wythe's first educational service may have come several years earlier, in 1757-58, when he served as guardian of a Lockey Collins, who was a student at the grammar school at William and Mary. Hemphill, "Wythe, America's First Law Professor," *supra* note 3, at 37. Several sources, however, suggest that Wythe was tutoring students well before Jefferson, including William F. Swindler, who states that "Wythe's reputation as a teacher and lawyer was established by the time Jefferson turned to him in 1762." Swindler, "America's First Law Schools," *supra* note 1, at 6. Likewise, one of Wythe's own students, Littleton Waller Tazewell, stated that to the best of his knowledge, "there was no period of [Wythe's] life . . . after he attained to manhood, during which he did not superintend the education of several young men." Quoted in Kirtland, *George Wythe, supra* note 3, at 120. Lyon G. Tyler also leaves the impression that Wythe was known for his teaching before tutoring Jefferson, for he states, "there is something curious in a young law student like Thomas Jefferson choosing Mr. Wythe as his instructor, when Peyton and John Randolph, sons of his great-uncle, Sir John Randolph, were also living in Williamsburg, and were eminent lawyers and his attached friends." Tyler, "George Wythe," *supra* note 3, at 67.

20. Frank L. Dewey, *Thomas Jefferson, Lawyer* (1986), 9-17; Dumas Malone, *Jefferson, the Virginian* (1948), 62-87.

21. Quoted in Brown, *American Aristides, supra* note 3, at 226; Carrington, "University Legal Education," *supra* note 3, at 533.

22. William DuVal to Thomas Jefferson, 1806, quoted in Julian P. Boyd, "The Murder of George Wythe," in *The Murder of George Wythe: Two Essays* (1955), 24.

23. Dill, *Wythe, Teacher of Liberty, supra* note 3, at 42.

24. On Madison, see "James Madison," *DAB, supra* note 3, at XII, 182-84.

25. Henry Tucker to St. George Tucker, August 1, 1772, quoted in Swindler, "America's First Law Schools," *supra* note 1, at 6; Dill, *Wythe, Teacher of Liberty, supra* note 3, at 42; Charles T. Cullen, "St. George Tucker," in Bryson, *Legal Education in Virginia, supra* note 3, at 657-86.

26. On Innes, see "James Innes," *DAB, supra* note 3, at IX, 486-87. Sources listing Innes as a Wythe student include Bryson, *Legal Education in Virginia, supra* note 3, at 21; Brown, *American Aristides, supra* note 3, at 228; Tyler, "George Wythe," *supra* note 3, at 72; Hugh Blair Grigsby, *The History of the Virginia Federal Convention of 1788* (1890), I, 75 n.90, and *Convention of 1776, supra* note 3, at 123; and Hemphill, "Wythe, America's First Law Professor," *supra* note 3, at 2.

27. On Innes, see "Harry Innes," *DAB, supra* note 3, at IX, 485-86. Hugh Blair Grigsby, the Commonwealth's leading historian during the middle decades of the nineteenth century, lists Innes as a Wythe student, although A.T. Dill states that it is "not likely [that he] received private training under Wythe." Dill, *Wythe, Teacher of Liberty, supra* note 3, at 99 n.319.

28. Shepard, "George Wythe," in Bryson, *Legal Education in Virginia, supra* note 3, at 754; Shewmake, *Honorable George Wythe, supra* note 3, at 17; Devitt, "William and Mary," *supra* note 3, at 429. W. Edwin Hemphill, however, could find no evidence of this relationship. Hemphill, "Wythe, America's First Law Professor," *supra* note 3, at 2.

29. See, e.g., Moncure Daniel Conway, *Omitted Chapters of History Disclosed in the Life and Papers of Edmund Randolph* (1888), 14; "Edmund Randolph," *DAB, supra* note 3, at XV, 353-55.

30. Stated in the Colonial Williamsburg Foundation's online *Historical Almanack.*

31. Hugh Blair Grigsby lists Cabell as an early Wythe student. *Virginia Federal Convention, supra* note 26, at I, 75 n.90. This relationship, however, has been labeled "not likely" by A.T. Dill. *Wythe, Teacher of Liberty, supra* note 3, at 99 n.319.

32. Grigsby, *Virginia Federal Convention, supra* note 26, at I, 75 n.90. In another work, Grigsby states that Read, "though not a lawyer by profession, was well versed in the law." *Convention of 1776, supra* note 3, at 105. Unlike for several other names, Dill does not question this relationship, *Wythe, Teacher of Liberty, supra* note 3, at 99 n.319, although it seems more unlikely than the others he does doubt.

33. Kirtland, *George Wythe, supra* note 3, lists a James Mercer as one of Wythe's students. On Mercer, see "James Mercer," *DAB, supra* note 3, at XII, 542. It is possible that James Mercer has been confused with his younger half-brother, John F. Mercer (1759-1821), a onetime governor of Maryland.

34. Hugh Blair Grigsby states that Moore attended in about 1772 a course of lectures at William and Mary given by Wythe, *Virginia Federal Convention, supra* note 26, at II, 32, although this date, of course, is far too early for Wythe's institutional teaching. Of course Moore could have apprenticed in Wythe's law office.

35. Hugh Blair Grigsby lists as one of Wythe's pupils a "Lewis" who attended Virginia's ratifying convention, and there were two delegates by that name, Thomas Lewis (b. 1718) of Rockingham, and Warner Lewis (ca. 1747-1791) of Gloucester. The former, of course, would have been too old to study under Wythe. See Grigsby, *Virginia Federal Convention, supra* note 26, at I, 75 n.90, and II, 20, 374 n.349.

36. Clarkin, *Serene Patriot, supra* note 3, at 141.

37. *Id.* at 142.

38. For the text of bill 80 as well as commentary, see the *Jefferson Papers, supra* note 13, at II, 535-42.

39. Thomas Jefferson's 1821 "Autobiography," in *The Writings of Thomas Jefferson*, ed. Paul L. Ford (1892), I, 66.
40. *Id.* at I, 67. James Madison again brought the bill up in the General Assembly in 1785, but it was again not acted upon.
41. Kirtland, *George Wythe, supra* note 3, at 114-15.
42. Jefferson's "Autobiography," in *Writings of Jefferson, supra* note 39, at I, 69-70.
43. Dill, *Wythe, Teacher of Liberty, supra* note 3, at 42.
44. Bryson, *Legal Education in Virginia, supra* note 3, at 22. Another source has stated that the word police "meant civil order or administration." Dill, *Wythe, Teacher of Liberty, supra* note 3, at 42.
45. Bryson, *Legal Education in Virginia, supra* note 3, at 22. Many other sources agree that having disposed of the royalist faculty, the Visitors saw the college as "a training ground for republican citizenship." See, e.g., Brown, *American Aristides, supra* note 3, at 200; Hemphill, "Wythe, America's First Law Professor," *supra* note 3, at 44.
46. Bryson, *Legal Education in Virginia, supra* note 3, at 22.
47. Lyon G. Tyler, "A Few Facts from the Records of William and Mary College," 4 *Papers of the Amer. Hist. Assn.* 129, 132 (1890).
48. Brown, *American Aristides, supra* note 3, at 201.
49. See, e.g., Clarkin, *Serene Patriot, supra* note 3, at 142; Brown, *American Aristides, supra* note 3, at 201.
50. Faculty resolution quoted in Tyler, "Records of William and Mary," *supra* note 47, at 133.
51. Clarkin, *Serene Patriot, supra* note 3, at 142; see also Tyler, "Records of William and Mary," *supra* note 47, at 135.
52. See, e.g. Clarkin, *Serene Patriot, supra* note 3, at 183; Brown, *American Aristides, supra* note 3, at 217; Anderson, "Teacher of Jefferson and Marshall," *supra* note 1, at 334; Tyler, "Records of William and Mary," *supra* note 47, at 134-35; Shewmake, *Honorable George Wythe, supra* note 3, at 16.
53. Clarkin, *Serene Patriot, supra* note 3, at 143.
54. It is interesting to note that William and Mary would not be in session during the entire months of April and September, the two months during which Wythe would have to hold court. See Charles T. Cullen, "New Light on John Marshall's Legal Education and Admission to the Bar," 16 *Am. J. Legal Hist.* 345, 345 (1972).
55. *Id.* at 348.
56. William F. Swindler, "John Marshall's Preparation for the Bar—Some Observations on His Law Notes," 11 *Am. J. Legal Hist.* 207, 208 (1967). Without citing any sources, Jean Edward Smith in his *John Marshall: Definer of a Nation* (1996), 78, states, "Every morning the students read law under Wythe's supervision: first Blackstone, then the traditional treatises, abridgements, and statutes. Wythe believed that mental vigor was greatest in the mornings, and he assigned the tough work early." As for the afternoons, they were supposedly "devoted to reading in related fields, particularly political philosophy," including Montesquieu and Hume.
57. Smith, *John Marshall, supra* note 56, at 78, without giving a source, states that Wythe's lectures were at noon on Tuesdays and Thursdays. It is known, however, that in 1784 Wythe was giving a law lecture on Tuesdays from 10:00 a.m. to noon. Thomas Lee Shippen to Dr. William Shippen, February 5, 1784, quoted in Clarkin, *Serene Patriot, supra* note 3, at 156.
58. See, for example, the discussion on different interpretations of John Marshall's commonplace book in Cullen, "New Light," *supra* note 54, at 347-48. Many commentators, such as Brown, *American Aristides, supra* note 3, at 202-03, and Clarkin, *Serene Patriot, supra* note 3, at 154, have suggested that John Marshall's commonplacebook detailing Virginia's substantive law were notes taken from Wythe's lectures. Cullen, however, is of the opinion that "Wythe's lectures probably dealt more with political theory than with substantive or procedural law," and in regard to the readings Wythe assigned, "The most Wythe seems to have done in his lectures in 1780 was to question his students on passages in these works." *Id.* at 348. See also Shepard, "George Wythe," in Bryson, *Legal Education in Virginia, supra* note 3, at 753: "In the lectures [Wythe] stressed political theory and surveyed the rapidly developing realm of constitutional law, always striving to reach beneath the surface to the ideas which had shaped the common-law tradition."
59. Yale president Ezra Stiles wrote in his diary on June 8, 1784, that "Blacston the Basis of Law Lectures in Wm & Mary Coll." Quoted in *Jefferson Papers, supra* note 13, at VII, 302-03.
60. Tyler, "George Wythe," *supra* note 3, at 68.
61. Quoted in Brown, *American Aristides, supra* note 3, at 225.
62. Dill, *Wythe, Teacher of Liberty, supra* note 3, at 44.
63. Cullen, "New Light," *supra* note 54, at 346 n.5.
64. John Brown to William Preston, July 6, 1780, in "Glimpses of Old College Life," 9 *Wm. & Mary Qtly.*, 1st Ser., 18, 80 (1900).
65. Quoted in Shepard, "George Wythe," in Bryson, *Legal Education in Virginia, supra* note 3, at 753.
66. *Id.*
67. Brown, *American Aristides, supra* note 3, at 204-05.
68. *Id.*
69. Among other sources, see Dill, *Wythe, Teacher of Liberty, supra* note 3, at 43. The source for the forty students claim was a letter from student John Brown in July 1780 stating that forty students were participating in Wythe's moot legislature. John Brown to William Preston, July 6, 1780, in "Glimpses of Old College Life," *supra* note 64, at 80. It is conceivable that the number of students attending Wythe's lectures was actually less, for one source, without giving any citations, states that the moot legislature was "open to any college student" and consisted of "virtually the entire student body." Cullen, "New Light," *supra* note 54, at 346. What evidence there is, however, suggests that Wythe's law course was the most popular at the school.
70. Cullen, "New Light," *supra* note 54, at 346.

71. *Id.* at 346.
72. William Nelson to St. George Tucker, February 2, 1787, quoted in Brown, *American Aristides, supra* note 3, at 230 n.39.
73. Hughes, "The First American Law School," *supra* note 3, at 42-43. Although the college statutes quoted date from 1792, two years after Wythe's resignation, Hughes states that they were likely enacted "very soon after the organization of the law department." *Id.* at 43.
74. Quoted in Clarkin, *Serene Patriot, supra* note 3, at 156.
75. Dill, *Wythe, Teacher of Liberty, supra* note 3, at 59.
76. Carrington, "University Legal Education," *supra* note 3, at 534.
77. Anderson, "Teacher of Jefferson and Marshall," *supra* note 1, at 331, quoting Bishop William Meade, *Old Churches, Ministers, and Families in Virginia*, who was, in turn, quoting a Reverend Lee Massey.
78. Tyler, "George Wythe," *supra* note 3, at 73.
79. Tyler, "George Wythe," *supra* note 3, at 81; Boyd, "Murder of Wythe," *supra* note 22, at 6. In fact, the latest biography of Wythe is entitled *American Aristides, supra* note 3.
80. Jefferson, "Notes of Wythe," *supra* note 12, at I, 169-70.
81. Thomas Jefferson to James Madison, July 26, 1780, in *Jefferson Papers, supra* note 13, at III, 507.
82. John Brown to William Preston, October 27, 1780, in "Glimpses of Old College Life," *supra* note 64, at 83.
83. Brown, *American Aristides, supra* note 3, at 208; Clarkin, *Serene Patriot, supra* note 3, at 145-46.
84. Clarkin, *Serene Patriot, supra* note 3, at 147; Brown, *American Aristides, supra* note 3, at 211.
85. Quoted in Clarkin, *Serene Patriot, supra* note 3, at 149.
86. George Wythe to George Washington, October 25, 1781, quoted in Brown, *American Aristides, supra* note 3, at 211-12.
87. Dill states that upon the evacuation of the French, "it was several years before the buildings were rehabilitated." *Wythe, Teacher of Liberty, supra* note 3, at 54. The date when Wythe was able to restart his classes is unknown, although one source states that "By early 1782 at the latest, Wythe's classes were in full swing once more." Kirtland, *George Wythe, supra* note 3, at 118. This, however, seems far too early, for the French had not even left Williamsburg at that point, and all available evidence points to 1783.
88. George Wythe to John Adams, December 5, 1783, quoted in Clarkin, *Serene Patriot, supra* note 3, at 156.
89. Richard Henry Lee to George Wythe, February 28, 1783, in *The Letters of Richard Henry Lee*, ed. James Curtis Ballagh (1911), II, 279.
90. Thomas Lee Shippen to Dr. William Shippen, February 5, 1784, quoted in Clarkin, *Serene Patriot, supra* note 3, at 156; Brown, *American Aristides, supra* note 3, at 204.
91. Walker Maury to Thomas Jefferson, ca. April 29, 1784, in *Jefferson Papers, supra* note 13, at VII, 112.
92. Ralph Izard to Thomas Jefferson, November 10, 1787, in *id.*, at XII, 338-39.
93. Thomas Jefferson to Ralph Izard, July 17, 1788, in *id.*, at XIII, 372 (emphasis in original).
94. Anderson, "Teacher of Jefferson and Marshall," *supra* note 1, at 341.
95. Although Wythe likely taught 200 or more men while at William and Mary, no class rosters are now available, so the vast majority of his students are currently unknown. To muddy the picture further, those who have written on Wythe have been in the habit of listing his students without giving the source from which their information comes, thus leading to the inevitable conclusion that some names may be only conjecture. Thus, below when discussing Wythe's students it will be noted when the teaching relationship has not been conclusively proved. It is hoped that the future publication of the multivolume *Dictionary of Virginia Biography* will clear some of the confusion and provide a much longer list of Wythe pupils.
96. Cullen, "New Light," *supra* note 54, at 347; Swindler, "Marshall's Preparation," *supra* note 56, at 208. See also chapter 4.
97. William Short to Greenbury W. Ridgely, November 10, 1817, in "To Practice Law: Aspects of the Era of Good Feelings Reflected in the Short-Ridgely Correspondence, 1816-1821," ed. George Green Shackelford, 64 *Md. Hist. Mag.* 342, 367 (1969). Jean Edward Smith confuses this moot court argument with a speech Marshall made during a Phi Beta Kappa meeting. Smith, *John Marshall, supra* note 56, at 554 n.67.
98. William Short to Greenbury W. Ridgely, November 10, 1817, in "Short-Ridgely Correspondence," *supra* note 97, at 368.
99. Dill, *Wythe, Teacher of Liberty, supra* note 3, at 62.
100. On Washington, including his attendance of Wythe's lectures, see "Bushrod Washington," in *The Supreme Court Justices*, ed. Clare Cushman (2d ed. 1995), 51-55; G. Edward White, *The Marshall Court & Cultural Change: 1815-1835* (abr. ed. 1991), 344-54; Smith, *John Marshall, supra* note 56, at 75, 554 n.66.
101. On Roane, see *DAB, supra* note 3, at XV, 642-43; Dill, *Wythe, Teacher of Liberty, supra* note 3, at 51.
102. Harry Ammon, *James Monroe: The Quest for National Identity* (1971), 30.
103. *Id.* at 30.
104. Joseph Jones to James Monroe, March 7, 1780, quoted in *id.*, at 31.
105. Those sources listing Monroe as a Wythe student are: Grigsby, *Convention of 1776, supra* note 3, at 123, and *Virginia Federal Convention, supra* note 26, at I, 75 n.90; Shepard, "George Wythe," in Bryson, *Legal Education in Virginia, supra* note 3, at 754; Brown, *American Aristides, supra* note 3, at 207; Tyler, "George Wythe," *supra* note 3, at 68; Anderson, "Teacher of Jefferson and Marshall," *supra* note 1, at 327; Devitt, "William and Mary," *supra* note 3, at 429; Carrington, "University Legal Education," *supra* note 3, at 538; Kirtland, *George Wythe, supra* note 3, at 116; and Hemphill, "Wythe, America's First Law Professor," *supra* note 3, at 2. In addition, William and Mary's law school, now known as the Marshall-Wythe School of Law, claims Monroe as an alumnus. Those denying the relationship are Clarkin, *Serene Patriot, supra* note 3, at 144; and Dill, *Wythe, Teacher of Liberty, supra* note 3, at 43.

106. John Brown to William Preston, October 20, 1779, in "Glimpses of Old College Life," *supra* note 64, at 21.

107. John Brown to William Preston, December 9, 1779, in *id.*, at 22-23.

108. John Brown to William Preston, January 26 and March 7, 1780, in *id.*, at 75, 77.

109. John Brown to William Preston, February 15, 1780, in *id.*, at 76. At this time Brown also reported that he had had to give up the study of French, because of the expense of attending Wythe's lectures.

110. John Brown to William Preston, July 6, 1780, in *id.*, at 80.

111. "John Brown," *Biographical Directory of the American Congress: 1774-1949* (1950), 900; "John Brown," *DAB, supra* note 3, at III, 130-31.

112. On Brown, see "James Brown," *DAB, supra* note 3, at III, 126. Carrington, "University Legal Education," *supra* note 3, at 558, states that Brown was a Wythe pupil, while Hemphill, "Wythe, America's First Law Professor," *supra* note 3, at 48, mentions it as a possibility.

113. On Breckinridge, see "John Breckinridge," *DAB, supra* note 3, at III, 6. Among the sources listing Breckinridge as a Wythe pupil are Clarkin, *Serene Patriot, supra* note 3, at 144; Devitt, "William and Mary," *supra* note 3, at 429; Carrington, "University Legal Education," *supra* note 3, at 538; Swindler, "America's First Law Schools," *supra* note 1, at 12; and Kirtland, *George Wythe, supra* note 3, at 116. Dill, *Wythe, Teacher of Liberty, supra* note 3, at 51, notes that Breckinridge attended William and Mary in 1780 and states that he "may" have attended Wythe's lectures.

114. On Breckenridge, who, unlike his brother, maintained the traditional spelling of his last name, see "James Breckenridge," *DAB, supra* note 3, at III, 5. This source states that he attended the "academic and law courses in the College of William and Mary, graduating in 1785," *id.*, and other sources listing Breckenridge as a Wythe pupil are Brown, *American Aristides, supra* note 3, at 228; Tyler, "George Wythe," *supra* note 3, at 72; and Hemphill, "Wythe, America's First Law Professor," *supra* note 3, at 2.

115. On Thruston, see Robert V. Remini, *Henry Clay: Statesman for the Union* (1991), 37, 47, 58; *Biographical Directory of the American Congress, supra* note 111, at 1919. Sources listing Thruston as a Wythe pupil include Hemphill, "Wythe, America's First Law Professor," *supra* note 3, at 2; Tyler, "George Wythe," *supra* note 3, at 72; Brown, *American Aristides, supra* note 3, at 228. It is interesting to note that in the U.S. Senate, Thruston replaced a Wythe pupil (John Brown), for part of his tenure his colleague from Kentucky was also a Wythe pupil (Henry Clay), and he was succeeded by a Wythe pupil (again, Clay).

116. "William Branch Giles," *DAB, supra* note 3, at VII, 283-84. This sketch, written by Dumas Malone, states that Giles studied law under Wythe, as does Clarkin, *Serene Patriot, supra* note 3, at vii, 155; and Brown, *American Aristides, supra* note 3, at 213.

117. *Encyclopedia of Virginia Biography*, ed. Lyon G. Tyler (1915), II, 10-11 (hereinafter referred to as *EVB*); see also Clarkin, *Serene Patriot, supra* note 3, at 159.

118. See below for descriptions of these students' educations under Wythe.

119. On Short, see George Green Shackelford, "William Short, Jefferson's Adopted Son, 1758-1849" (unpublished doctoral dissertation, University of Virginia, 1955); "William Short," *DAB, supra* note 3, at XVII, 128-29.

120. William Short to Greenbury W. Ridgely, December 11, 1816, in "Short-Ridgely Correspondence," *supra* note 97, at 349.

121. William Short to Greenbury W. Ridgely, November 10, 1817, in *id.*, at 368.

122. William Short to Greenbury W. Ridgely, January 30 and November 10, 1817, in *id.*, at 352, 366. Short gave John Marshall as an example of one whose formal legal education was scanty, yet who developed an impressive practice.

123. William Short to Greenbury W. Ridgely, November 10, 1817, in *id.*, at 368. Short went on to note that "such was the aversion of a bench of white men to condemn one of their own color for killing a black, that I found no difficulty & he was acquitted." *Id.*

124. William Short to Greenbury W. Ridgely, December 11, 1816, and November 10, 1817, in *id.*, at 349-50, 369.

125. Richard Henry Lee to Arthur Lee, April 24, 1780, in *Lee Letters, supra* note 89, at II, 177.

126. Richard Henry Lee to Arthur Lee, August 31, 1780, in *id.*, at II, 199.

127. See Richard Henry Lee to George Wythe, February 28, 1783, in *id.*, at II, 279.

128. Paul C. Nagel, *The Lees of Virginia: Seven Generations of an American Family* (1990), 124, 145-52.

129. See Thomas Jefferson to Ralph Izard, July 17, 1788, in *Jefferson Papers, supra* note 13, at XII, 372. Brown misidentifies Izard's son by stating that it was the younger George Izard. *American Aristides, supra* note 3, at 213.

130. Daniel M. McFarland, "Kemp Plummer," in *Dictionary of North Carolina Biography*, ed. William S. Powell (6 vols., 1979-1996), V, 104.

131. Clarkin, *Serene Patriot, supra* note 3, at 158, 198; Brown, *American Aristides, supra* note 3, at 214. On Randolph's trial, see, among other sources, Smith, *John Marshall, supra* note 56, at 148-53.

132. On Nicholas, see "George Nicholas," *DAB, supra* note 3, at XIII, 482-83. At least eight sources list Nicholas as a Wythe pupil, including Grigsby, *Convention of 1776, supra* note 3, at 123, and *Virginia Federal Convention, supra* note 26, at I, 75 n.90; Carrington, "University Legal Education," *supra* note 3, at 557; Shepard, "George Wythe," in Bryson, *Legal Education in Virginia, supra* note 3, at 754; Hemphill, "Wythe, America's First Law Professor," *supra* note 3, at 2; Brown, *American Aristides, supra* note 3, at 213, 228; Tyler, "George Wythe," *supra* note 3, at 72; and Shewmake, *Honorable George Wythe, supra* note 3, at 17. A.T. Dill, however, disputes this teacher-pupil relationship by stating that Nicholas, as well as his brother Wilson Cary Nicholas, "undoubtedly read law under their father." Dill, *Wythe Teacher of Liberty, supra* note 3, at 99 n.319. This also appears to be the conclusion of Victor Dennis Golladay, who in his dissertation on the Nicholas family wrote that George "probably could not have found a better lawyer to guide his studies than his father." Golladay, "The Nicholas Family of Virginia: 1722-1820" (unpublished doctoral dissertation, University of Virginia, 1973), 220. Golladay also shows that George Nicholas received his

law license in September 1778, more than a year before Wythe began his lectures, yet realizing that various sources, especially Grigsby, assert the Wythe teaching, he also adds that Nicholas "perhaps" did additional reading under Wythe. *Id.* at 220, 228.

133. On Nicholas, see "Wilson Cary Nicholas," *DAB, supra* note 3, at XIII, 486-87. Sources listing Nicholas as a Wythe pupil include Grigsby, *Virginia Federal Convention, supra* note 26, at I, 75 n.90; Clarkin, *Serene Patriot, supra* note 3, at 184; Blackburn, *Wythe of Williamsburg, supra* note 3, at 108. Again, A.T. Dill suggests that like his brother George, Wilson Cary Nicholas also studied under his father. Dill, *Wythe, Teacher of Liberty, supra* note 3, at 99 n.319. As for Golladay, all he says is that "Wilson allegedly had legal training." Golladay, "Nicholas Family," *supra* note 132, at 233 n.9.

134. On Stuart, see "Archibald Stuart," *DAB, supra* note 3, at XVIII, 161-62. Sources listing Stuart as a Wythe pupil include Hemphill, "Wythe, America's First Law Professor," *supra* note 3, at 2; Tyler, "George Wythe," *supra* note 3, at 72; Brown, *American Aristides, supra* note 3, at 228. Stuart's son, Congressman Alexander H.H. Stuart, wrote that his father studied at William and Mary from 1777 to 1781, and that after the Revolution he spent an additional two years reading law with Thomas Jefferson. Grigsby, *Virginia Federal Convention, supra* note 26, at II, 386.

135. On Wickham, see "John Wickham," *DAB, supra* note 3, at XX, 181-82. Sources listing Wickham as a Wythe pupil include Grigsby, *Convention of 1776, supra* note 3, at 123; Hemphill, "Wythe, America's First Law Professor," *supra* note 3, at 2; Tyler, "George Wythe," *supra* note 3, at 72; Shepard, "George Wythe," in Bryson, *Legal Education in Virginia, supra* note 3, at 754; and Brown, *American Aristides, supra* note 3, at 213, 228. Although it does not in any way preclude Wickham's attending Wythe's classes—for many of Wythe's William and Mary students, such as Washington, Roane, and Short, also apprenticed with a private attorney—it is known the Wickham also read law with Henry Tazewell. See Hugh Blair Grigsby, *Discourse on the Life and Character of the Hon. Littleton Waller Tazewell* (1860), 11; Norma Lois Patterson, *Littleton Waller Tazewell* (1983), 7.

136. Clarkin, *Serene Patriot, supra* note 3, at 144, states that William Cabell, Jr., treasurer of Phi Beta Kappa, studied under Wythe in 1780, and this source also states that William H. Cabell (1772-1853), a three-term governor of Virginia (1805-1808) and member of the Virginia Court of Appeals for forty years (1811-1851), was also a Wythe pupil. *Id.* at 209. The *Dictionary of American Biography* states that William H. Cabell "attended Hampden Sidney College, 1785-89, and then entered the College of William and Mary, from which he received his law degree in 1793," *DAB, supra* note 3, at III, 390, while another source states that he studied law under St. George Tucker at William and Mary in 1790. *EVB, supra* note 117, at II, 47.

137. Clarkin, *Serene Patriot, supra* note 3, at 157.

138. Brown, *American Aristides, supra* note 3, at 213-14.

139. *EVB, supra* note 117, at II, 178.

140. Carrington, "University Legal Education," *supra* note 3, at 537.

141. Among the positions occupied by known Wythe students: President (Jefferson), Vice President (Jefferson), Secretary of State (Jefferson, Marshall, and Clay), Attorney General (Breckinridge), U.S. Senator (John Brown, James Brown, Breckinridge, Thruston, Giles, Eppes, Clay, Tazewell), Speaker of the U.S. House (Clay, with many other students serving in the House), Chief Justice (Marshall, with Washington serving as an Associate Justice), federal District Judge (Tucker, Thruston), foreign (or treaty) Minister (Jefferson, Short, Marshall, Clay), Governor of Virginia (Jefferson, Giles, Tazewell), and President of the Virginia Court of Appeals (Roane, with Tucker, Coalter, and others serving on the court, and Munford acting as its Reporter; it has been said that "During the existence of the William and Mary law course [1779-1861] twenty-five out of forty-three judges of the Virginia Court of Appeals received their legal education there." Devitt, "William and Mary," *supra* note 3, at 426, quoting a Robert M. Hughes 1920 letter to the *New York Times*). Wythe's pupil St. George Tucker was his replacement as Professor of Law and Police at William and Mary, and it has been stated that the first three law professors at Transylvania University (George Nicholas, James Brown, and Henry Clay) were all Wythe students. See Carrington, "University Legal Education," *supra* note 3, at 537. Of course only about ten percent of Wythe's students are currently known, and the foregoing lists would be even more impressive if one included the accomplishments of the supposed students whose attendance cannot be readily proved (Monroe and Wilson Cary Nicholas being two prime examples).

142. Shewmake, *Honorable George Wythe, supra* note 3, at 16.

143. Sallie E. Marshall Hardy, "Some Virginia Lawyers of the Past and Present," 10 *The Green Bag* 12, 18 (1898), quoting an unidentified source.

144. Carrington, "University Legal Education," *supra* note 3, at 538.

145. Brown, *American Aristides, supra* note 3, at 216-17.

146. See Dill, *Wythe, Teacher of Liberty, supra* note 3, at 60-62; Tyler, "George Wythe," *supra* note 3, at 78-79.

147. Boyd, "Murder of Wythe," *supra* note 22, at 5.

148. Dill, *Wythe, Teacher of Liberty, supra* note 3, at 57-58.

149. Clarkin, *Serene Patriot, supra* note 3, at 162.

150. Dill, *Wythe, Teacher of Liberty, supra* note 3, at 63.

151. *Id.* at 64.

152. Quoted in Brown, *American Aristides, supra* note 3, at 217; Dill, *Wythe, Teacher of Liberty, supra* note 3, at 64-65.

153. Dill, *Wythe, Teacher of Liberty, supra* note 3, at 65.

154. Littleton Waller Tazewell, quoted in *id.*, at 67.

155. Clarkin, *Serene Patriot, supra* note 3, at 180; Dill, *Wythe, Teacher of Liberty, supra* note 3, at 67-69.

156. See Clarkin, *Serene Patriot, supra* note 3, at 184. In addition, three other counties were named for statesmen who have been listed as possible Wythe students: Edmund Randolph, James Monroe, and Wilson Cary Nicholas. Kentucky named a county in honor of Wythe student John Breckinridge. Clarkin states that a West Virginia county honors Littleton Waller

Tazewell, but this county is actually in Virginia, and it was named for Tazewell's father Henry; a county in Illinois, however, is named for the younger Tazewell.

157. Clarkin, *Serene Patriot, supra* note 3, at 164.

158. *Id.* at 164; Kirtland, *George Wythe, supra* note 3, at 121-22.

159. Quoted in Dill, *Wythe, Teacher of Liberty, supra* note 3, at 56.

160. Brown, *American Aristides, supra* note 3, at 220.

161. Quoted in Swindler, "America's First Law Schools," *supra* note 1, at 10-11.

162. See Dill, *Wythe, Teacher of Liberty, supra* note 3, at 55-56; Brown, *American Aristides, supra* note 3, at 220-21; Clarkin, *Serene Patriot, supra* note 3, at 164-66.

163. On Tazewell, see Grigsby, *Discourse on Tazewell, supra* note 135; Peterson, *Littleton Waller Tazewell, supra* note 135; White, *The Marshall Court, supra* note 100, at 214-29; "Littleton Waller Tazewell," *DAB, supra* note 3, at XVIII, 355-57.

164. See James Madison to Thomas Jefferson, November 25, 1786, in *Jefferson Papers, supra* note 13, at X, 549; George Wythe to Thomas Jefferson, December 13, 1786, in *id.*, at X, 592-93; Peter Carr to Thomas Jefferson, December 30, 1786, in *id.*, at X, 648. Wythe was following a plan designed by Jefferson for Carr's education.

165. Thomas Jefferson to Peter Carr, August 10, 1787, in *id.*, at XII, 14. In this letter, Jefferson told his nephew to begin the study of sciences under Wythe, to study Spanish instead of Italian, and not to study moral philosophy. He also laid out a long list of readings for Carr, although for law and politics he told his nephew to study whatever works Wythe suggested. *Id.* at XII, 14-19.

166. Peter Carr to Thomas Jefferson, March 18, 1788, in *id.*, at XII, 677.

167. Thomas Jefferson to Peter Carr, August 6, 1788, in *id.*, at XIII, 470.

168. Peter Carr to Thomas Jefferson, May 29, 1789, in *id.*, at XV, 156.

169. *Virginia Gazette and Weekly Advertiser*, August 2, 1787, quoted in Clarkin, *Serene Patriot, supra* note 3, at 174; Brown, *American Aristides, supra* note 3, at 219; and Dill, *Wythe, Teacher of Liberty, supra* note 3, at 65.

170. Clarkin, *Serene Patriot, supra* note 3, at 174; Dill, *Wythe, Teacher of Liberty, supra* note 3, at 66.

171. Clarkin, *Serene Patriot, supra* note 3, at 157-58, 185.

172. Dill, *Wythe, Teacher of Liberty, supra* note 3, at 5.

173. Thomas Jefferson to Richard Price, August 7, 1785, in *Jefferson Papers, supra* note 13, at VIII, 357. Price chose not to write to the William and Mary students.

174. Clarkin, *Serene Patriot, supra* note 3, at 157.

175. *Id.* at 158.

176. Quoted in *id.*, at 173.

177. Benjamin Blake Minor, quoted in *id.*, at 186. At a coffee-house that he would visit, persons would wonder whether Wythe would make a sound. *Id.*

178. *Id.* at 186, quoting Benjamin Blake Minor.

179. *Id.* at 186.

180. Edmund Randolph to George Washington, December 15, 1789, in *The Papers of George Washington*, ed. W.W. Abbot et al. (1983-present), Presidential Series, IV, 415.

181. Clarkin, *Serene Patriot, supra* note 3, at 182; Dill, *Wythe, Teacher of Liberty, supra* note 3, at 71.

182. Peter Carr to Thomas Jefferson, May 29, 1789, in *Jefferson Papers, supra* note 13, at XV, 156.

183. Kirtland, *George Wythe, supra* note 3, at 133.

184. *Id.* at 134-35; Dill, *Wythe, Teacher of Liberty, supra* note 3, at 72.

185. Thomas Jefferson to William Short, September 14, 1789, *Jefferson Papers, supra* note 13, at XVI, 25-26. Beyond the Jefferson letter, one person has written that the traditional reason for Wythe's move, the change in court structure, could not have been the real reason, for "the Chancery and the Supreme Court of Appeals had by then been sitting in Richmond for nearly ten years." Kirtland, *George Wythe, supra* note 3, at 143 n.105. Of course travel likely became harder for Wythe as he aged, and under the reorganization the court now met four times a year in Richmond instead of just twice.

As for Wythe's dissatisfaction with the actions of others, Imogene Brown has written, "Beneath the dignified exterior, Wythe was critical, perhaps too critical, of others, demanding of them the same high standards he set for himself. He was proud, almost to the point of being self-righteous, and personal and professional criticism hurt him deeply." This source continues, "Wythe was aware of his tendency to fret and brood, and impatient with himself because of it. Yet he was never able to master it and indeed, as he grew older, the characteristic became more pronounced." Brown, *American Aristides, supra* note 3, at 223.

186. Tyler, "George Wythe," *supra* note 3, at 71.

187. Thomas Jefferson to Francis Eppes, October 8, 1790, in *Jefferson Papers, supra* note 13, at XVII, 581.

188. On Tucker's tenure at William and Mary, see Charles T. Cullen, "St. George Tucker," in Bryson, *Legal Education in Virginia, supra* note 3, at 657-686. After Tucker's resignation, the reputation of William and Mary's law program declined significantly, although the seventeen-year tenure of Tucker's son Nathaniel Beverly Tucker (1834-1851) helped revive part of its good name. The school continued teaching law until 1861, and in 1922 the law program, currently under the name of the Marshall-Wythe School of Law, was reestablished. See generally Bryson, *Legal Education in Virginia.*

Compared to the William and Mary of St. George Tucker's tenure and later years, Wythe might have had a larger impact on law teaching at Kentucky's Transylvania University, where the first three law professors were supposedly Wythe students and where moot courts and moot legislatures were part of the law and politics curriculum. See Paul D. Carrington, "Teaching Law and Virtue at Transylvania University: The George Wythe Tradition in the Antebellum Years," 41 *Mercer L. Rev.* 673 (1990).

189. Cullen, "St. George Tucker," in Bryson, *Legal Education in Virginia, supra* note 3, at 668.

190. John Coalter to Michael Coalter, November 24, 1789, quoted in "Glimpses of Old College Life," 8 *Wm. & Mary Qtly.* 153, 157 (1900); see also Clarkin, *Serene Patriot, supra* note 3, at 183. Brown, *American Aristides, supra* note 3, at 221, also uses this quote, although she states that it comes from a letter William Munford sent to John Coalter on April 24, 1789.

191. William Munford to John Coalter, June 13, 1790, in "Glimpses of Old College Life," *supra* note 190, at 153-54.

192. William Munford to John Coalter, April 23, 1791, quoted in Brown, *American Aristides, supra* note 3, at 270.

193. On Munford, see "William Munford," *DAB, supra* note 3, at XIII, 326-27. Munford was chosen to give the eulogy at Wythe's funeral.

194. By March 1790, Carr was residing in Goochland County, reading law books recommended by Jefferson. See Thomas Jefferson to Peter Carr, March 28, 1790, in *Jefferson Papers, supra* note 13, at XVI, 276-77.

195. Thomas Jefferson to George Wythe, December 17, 1789, in *id.*, at XVI, 37.

196. The very careful A.T. Dill, *Wythe, Teacher of Liberty, supra* note 3, at 54-55, states that Wythe was agreeable to this and actually designed a specific course of study which Eppes undertook, although no evidence for this statement is given.

197. See Thomas Jefferson to Francis Eppes, October 8, 1790, *Jefferson Papers, supra* note 13, at XVII, 581.

198. On Eppes, see "John Wayles Eppes," *DAB, supra* note 3, at VI, 170-71.

199. Anderson, "Teacher of Jefferson and Marshall," *supra* note 1, at 335. Many persons have accused Wythe of pedantry, including William Cabell Rives (Wythe "sometimes wore the air of pedantry"), quoted in Clarkin, *Serene Patriot, supra* note 3, at 150; and William Wirt (Wythe "carried his love of antiquity rather too far; for he frequently subjected himself to the charge of pedantry"), quoted in Dill, *Wythe, Teacher of Liberty, supra* note 3, at 19.

In addition, it has been said that Wythe's own will was "strongly marked by eccentricity. The language was scarcely that of orthodox legal phraseology and was interspersed with Greek and Latin phrases and pious verse." Boyd, "Murder of Wythe," *supra* note 22, at 21.

200. Anderson, "Teacher of Jefferson and Marshall," *supra* note 1, at 335.

201. Dill, *Wythe, Teacher of Liberty, supra* note 3, at 74.

202. Clarkin, *Serene Patriot, supra* note 3, at 206.

203. Hemphill, "Wythe, America's First Law Professor," *supra* note 3, at 79. The work of this committee was never completed. Hemphill states that all of the members were Wythe students except for Bushrod Washington, *id.* at 79 n.2, yet as is shown above, Washington did study under Wythe at William and Mary in 1780. The one student for whom there might be any question is Wickham.

204. Dill, *Wythe, Teacher of Liberty, supra* note 3, at 78.

205. Quoted in Brown, *American Aristides, supra* note 3, at 227.

206. Quoted in Clarkin, *Serene Patriot, supra* note 3, at 188; and Brown, *American Aristides, supra* note 3, at 227. The Latin has been translated as "twenty years of reflection."

207. Clarkin, *Serene Patriot, supra* note 3, at 174; *EVB, supra* note 117, at II, 246. The sources do not state where Thomson studied with Wythe, although because of his age it almost had to be Richmond rather than Williamsburg. Another classics student was a Charles Turnbull. Clarkin, *Serene Patriot*, at 174.

208. Remini, *Henry Clay, supra* note 115, at 9-12; Clarkin, *Serene Patriot, supra* note 3, at 192; see also Henry Clay to Benjamin B. Minor, May 3, 1851, *Clay Papers, supra* note 2, at X, 886-89.

209. Carrington, "Transylvania," *supra* note 188, at 680-85. As suggested above in the text, the best biography of Clay is Remini, *Henry Clay, supra* note 115. Although Remini does not mention this, it has also been stated that Clay studied law under Wythe's pupil Bushrod Washington. See Cushman, *Supreme Court Justices, supra* note 100, at 53.

210. In July 1791, for instance, William Munford was surprised to discover that Wythe was teaching one of his servants, Jimmy, to write. See, e.g., Clarkin, *Serene Patriot, supra* note 3, at 188-89.

211. On Wythe's poisoning, his death, and the trial of Sweeney, see the two essays in *Murder of Wythe, supra* note 3.

212. W. Edwin Hemphill, "Examinations of George Wythe Swinney for Forgery and Murder: A Documentary Essay," in *The Murder of George Wythe: Two Essays* (1955), 35.

213. Richmond *Enquirer*, June 10, 1806, quoted in Boyd, "Murder of Wythe," *supra* note 22, at 20.

Chapter 9

Thomas Jefferson Recommends a Course of Law Study

1971

Morris L. Cohen

Morris Cohen is Librarian Emeritus of Yale Law School. This article first appeared in 119 *University of Pennsylvania Law Review* 823 (1971).

Author's note: I would like to acknowledge the kind help and advice of Dr. Julian P. Boyd, distinguished editor of The Papers of Thomas Jefferson, and, as always, the assistance of my colleagues at the Biddle Law Library.

On September 18, 1970, Morris Wolf, Esq., a distinguished senior member of the Philadelphia bar, presented to the University of Pennsylvania Law School an important manuscript letter by Thomas Jefferson which outlined a proposed course of legal education. The full text of the manuscript, given in honor of the Law School's new Dean, Bernard Wolfman, is set forth following this introductory note.

The letter was written by Jefferson at Monticello on August 30, 1814, and was addressed to General John Minor.[1] The date and place of writing are set out at the top of the first page, General Minor's name appears at the foot of that page, and the letter is signed by Jefferson at the end of the text on the last page. The manuscript consists of six sides on three leaves, written clearly and legibly in Jefferson's own hand. It incorporates a course of law study and readings which Jefferson had prepared "near fifty years ago for the use of a young friend" and which was contained in an earlier letter to Colonel Bernard Moore.[2] In fact only the first and last paragraphs of the 1814 letter are specifically directed to its recipient, John Minor.

Both Minor and Moore were Virginia friends of Jefferson and both letters were apparently intended for the guidance of their respective sons. Colonel Moore had, among other children, a son Bernard who apparently did study law and was undoubtedly the intended beneficiary of Jefferson's earlier letter. John Minor's eldest son, also named John, was born in 1797 and would have been about 17 years of age in 1814. He in fact studied law, practiced for a short time, and lived until 1862. The younger John Minor seems to be the object of the suggestions in this letter.

The letter itself outlines a program of reading and study in a variety of subjects, which constituted a well-rounded education for a gentleman of the period. In addition to standard works in law, it includes readings in fields designated by Jefferson as follows: mathematics, astronomy, natural philosophy, agriculture, chemistry, anatomy, zoology, botany, ethics and natural religion, sectarian religion, politics, political economy, history (divided into ancient, modern, English, and American), belles lettres, criticism, rhetoric, and oratory. After a general discussion of recommended legal writers, he makes specific suggestions, separately listed, for readings in the common law and chancery.

A large part of the letter is devoted to an allocation of the hours of the day to various areas of study, with readings for each time segment. The following periods are mentioned: until eight in the morning for "Physical studies, Ethics, Religion natural and sectarian, and Natural law"; eight to twelve noon for law; twelve noon to one for politics; the afternoon for history; and "From Dark to Bed-time" for belles lettres, criticism, rhetoric and oratory.

In 1814, Jefferson was leading a rather quiet life at Monticello, although still somewhat involved in public affairs. His second term as President of the United States had ended in 1809, five years before. In addition to his private business and the improvement of Monticello, he was already involved in the planning of the new University of Virginia, which was later to be established at Charlottesville in 1819. He consulted frequently with his immediate successors to the Presidency, James Madison and James Monroe, who were also friends and neighbors. He served as President of the American Philosophical Society, entertained extensively, maintained a wide correspondence, and pursued his varied scientific interests. He was also involved in negotiating the sale of his large book collection to the Library of Congress, which was completed in 1815.

The extent of Jefferson's correspondence throughout his life is noteworthy.[3] He wrote letters almost every day, both to friends and to strangers who made inquiry of him. In addition to the original manuscripts, many of which have survived, Jefferson also made copies for his own file, first by a copy press, and later by the polygraph copying machine of that time.[4] Most of Jefferson's retained copies are in the Manuscript Division of the Library of Congress.

He frequently complained to his friend and long time correspondent, John Adams, about the pressures of that correspondence. The following excerpts from three different letters to Adams are interesting in that regard:

> Instead of writing 10. or 12. letters a day, which I have been in the habit of doing as a thing of course, I put off answering my letters now, farmer-like, till a rainy day, & then find it sometimes postponed by other necessary occupations.[5]

> From sunrise to one or two o'clock, and often from dinner to dark, I am drudging at the writing table. And all this to answer letters into which neither interest nor inclination on my part enters; and often from persons whose names I have never before heard. Yet, writing civilly, it is hard to refuse them civil answers. This is the burden of my life, a very grievous one indeed, and one which I must get rid of.[6]

> I do not know how far you may suffer, as I do, under the persecution of letters, of which every mail brings a fresh load. They are letters of inquiry, for the most part, always of good will, sometimes from friends whom I esteem, but much oftener from persons whose names are unknown to me. . . . I happened to turn to my letter-list some time ago, and a curiosity was excited to count those received in a single year. It was the year before the last. I found the number to be one thousand and sixty-seven, many of them requiring answers of elaborate research, and all to be answered with due attention and consideration. Take an average of this number for a week or a day, and I will repeat the question. Is this life? At best it is but the life of a mill-horse, who sees no end to his circle but in death. To such a life, that of a cabbage is paradise.[7]

In this correspondence, Jefferson frequently wrote to young men with advice about their education and reading. Typical of these letters is one written to Thomas Mann Randolph, Jr., on July 6, 1787, recommending a general course of study leading to a career in politics.[8] In this letter, Jefferson suggested a year's study in Williamsburg with his friend and preceptor, George Wythe, and proposed the study of law for Randolph, noting:

> Every political measure will for ever have an intimate connection with the laws of the land; and he who knows nothing of these will always be perplexed and often foiled by adversaries having the advantage of that knolege over him.[9]

Jefferson's letter to Robert Skipwith, dated August 3, 1771,[10] is more bibliographic. In it, he responds to Skipwith's request for a catalogue of books (presumably to be purchased for the latter's library) amounting in value to about thirty pounds sterling. After a delightful literary discussion, Jefferson provides a long list of titles, arranged by subject, including three law titles.[11] Having initially indicated his dissatisfaction with the thirty pound limit, Jefferson concludes by calculating the total cost of the collection at £107/10.

Jefferson's two letters (August 19, 1785,[12] and August 10,1787[13]) to Peter Carr, the son of his beloved friend and brother-in-law, Dabney Carr, are among the best statements of his thinking about general education. In the 1785 letter, he recommends a series of readings in the classics and then offers a strong plea for physical activity to relieve the pressure of study:

> In order to assure a certain progress in this reading, consider what hours you have free from the school and the exercises of the school. Give about two of them every day to exercise; for health must not be sacrificed to learning. A strong body makes the mind strong. As to the species of exercise, I advise the gun. While this gives a moderate exercise to the body, it gives boldness, enterprize, and independance to the mind. Games played with the ball and others of that nature, are too violent for the body and stamp no character on the mind. Let your gun therefore be the constant companion of your walks. Never think of taking a book with you. The object of walking is to relax the mind. You should therefore not permit yourself even to think while you walk. But divert your attention by the objects surrounding you. Walking is the best possible exercise. Habituate yourself to walk very far.[14]

Young Carr went on to study law under Jefferson's guidance, although there are no specific recommendations for law readings in these two letters. The letter of August 10, 1787, does refer to the fact that Carr was already studying with Jefferson's mentor, George Wythe, and in a letter to John Garland Jefferson, dated June 11, 1790, Jefferson makes mention of Carr's law study and of having lent Carr his own books for that purpose.[15]

Perhaps most relevant for comparison with the John Minor letter, however, are those letters which Jefferson wrote to prospective law students, specifically on law study—particularly that noted above to John Garland Jefferson, and another to Dabney Terrell.[16] Both of these are considerably shorter than the Minor letter, but include many of the same recommended readings.

The letter to John Garland Jefferson again evidences Jefferson's concern with a well-rounded education and recommends readings in history, politics, economics, grammar, rhetoric, literature, and style—in addition to over thirty legal titles. Although he outlined a division of the day into study segments similar to (but less rigorous than) that in the Minor letter, as in the Carr letter Jefferson emphasized physical activity—a concern which was not apparent in the letter to John Minor. He urges John Garland Jefferson to leave open "all the afternoon for exercise and recreation, which are as necessary as reading; I will rather say more necessary, because health is worth more than learning"[17]

In contrast to Thomas Jefferson's own good experience in studying law in the office of George Wythe of Williamsburg from 1762 to 1767,[18] this letter reveals a general skepticism about study in a lawyer's office. He wrote to John Garland Jefferson in that regard as follows:

> It is a general practice to study the law in the office of some lawyer. This indeed gives to the student the advantage of his instruction. But I have ever seen that the services expected in return

> have been more than the instructions have been worth. All that is necessary for a student is access to a library, and directions in what order the books are to be read.[19]

Although heartening to law librarians, that attitude is surprising in view of Jefferson's warm feeling toward Chancellor Wythe, with whom he studied. In his Autobiography, Jefferson refers to Wythe as follows:

> Mr. Wythe continued to be my faithful and beloved mentor in youth, and my most affectionate friend through life. In 1767, he led me into the practice of the law at the bar of the General court, at which I continued until the Revolution shut up the courts of justice.[20]

Charles Warren, in *A History of the American Bar* (1913),[21] offers a number of varied accounts of the experience of famous lawyers in reading law in the office of a practitioner. These include Patrick Henry, William Livingston, John Quincy Adams, John Adams, Joseph Story, Daniel Webster, James Kent, and Roger Taney, as students; and George Wythe, James Wilson, James Alexander, Theophilus Parsons, Joshua Atherton, and Christopher Gore, as lawyer-teachers. There is considerable overlapping between the various reading lists described by Warren and most include titles recommended by Jefferson in his letter to Minor.

Jefferson's letter to Dabney Terrell of February 26, 1821,[22] contains a good discussion of the major legal commentators and offers a reading course similar to that in the Minor letter. Although part of the Terrell letter seems to be missing from both the published versions and from the copy at the Library of Congress,[23] it does suggest a full program in general education, in addition to a typical Jeffersonian law course. The former is recommended in these words:

> Besides these six hours of law reading, light and heavy, and those necessary for the repasts of the day, for exercise and sleep, which suppose to be ten or twelve, there will still be six or eight hours for reading history, politics, ethics, physics, oratory, poetry, criticism, etc., as necessary as law to form an accomplished lawyer.[24]

In addition, Jefferson enclosed with his letter to Terrell a copy of a letter which he had written to Thomas Cooper several years before, on January 16, 1814.[25] That letter contained a long review of English legal history and of the early law writers. Although a Professor of Chemistry at Carlisle, Cooper was a legal scholar of considerable stature, having prepared an important edition of the Justinian Institutes.[26] Jefferson's comments on the law to Cooper would have been quite useful to a beginning student like Terrell.

Although the present letter begins, "I have at length found the paper of which you requested a copy," there is no record of a written request from Minor to Jefferson for it. Presumably it was requested in person, perhaps after hearing Jefferson describe the Moore letter, or through an intermediary who might have heard of it from Jefferson. There is no request letter from Minor in the Manuscript Division of the Library of Congress, nor in the files of the Princeton project on the Papers of Thomas Jefferson. There is also no reference to such a letter in Jefferson's copious register of his correspondence.

We do have, on the other hand, the text of John Minor's acknowledgement of having received Jefferson's letter of August 30, 1814. The Princeton project has a copy of a note from Minor to Jefferson, dated September 8, 1814, about a week after Jefferson's letter, and bearing Jefferson's endorsement that he had received it on September 9. Minor began that letter from Fredricksburg as follows: "Accept, Dear Sir, my thanks for your kind Letter. I shall give it to my Son as the most valuable present I can make him." Minor then goes on to discuss the military and political situation in the vicinity. Although that may seem a weak response to Jefferson's long letter, the rest of Minor's letter indicates a preoccupation and deep anger with the British military inroads into Virginia. The War of 1812 was in full progress and British troops had burned the public buildings in Washington, a short distance away, only two weeks earlier.

There is an almost identical copy of Jefferson's letter of August 30, 1814, to John Minor in the Manuscript Division of the Library of Congress.[27] The only difference is that one additional reading suggestion, that of "Geography. Pinkerton.,"[28] was inserted by Jefferson near the bottom of the first page of the Library of Congress copy, presumably after the letters were executed. Since both the original and the copy were

10. Thomas Jefferson (1743-1826), third President of the United States, was instrumental in laying the foundations not only of the nation but also of the form that legal education would take within that nation. (*Library of Congress.*)

apparently made simultaneously by similar pens with the same ink and on the same quality paper, a polygraph must have been used, and it is difficult to determine from the letters themselves which was the product of Jefferson's own pen and which was made by the attached pen of the polygraph. The Library of Congress copy having been in Jefferson's retained files, it seems certain that the Biddle Law Library manuscript was the one sent to General Minor. Neither, however, bears any endorsement by Minor, nor does either bear an address cover or delivery direction. Both letters can be considered holographs, signed by Jefferson.

There is considerable uncertainty about the dating of the letter to Bernard Moore on which the Minor letter is based. There is, unfortunately, no available independent text of Jefferson's original letter to Moore. The Library of Congress does not have one, the Jefferson publication project at Princeton has not been able to locate one, and the only published versions are based on the text incorporated in the later letter to Minor. Jefferson's dating of the Moore letter in his letter to John Minor as "near fifty years ago" is indefinite and there is consequent disagreement as to the actual date.

The Library of Congress dates it as circa 1784.[29] That seems most improbable. It would be thirty rather than fifty years earlier, in a busy year when Jefferson completed his service in Congress (May 7) and then left for France (July 5) to serve with Benjamin Franklin and John Adams in negotiating commercial treaties with various European states.[30] Since 1784 would also be more than forty years after Moore's marriage, it is unlikely that he would have had a student son at so late a date. To choose Jefferson's own estimate—"near fifty years ago," i.e. 1764, would be equally unsatisfactory, since at that time Jefferson was himself still studying law with George Wythe in Williamsburg and was three years away from the start of his own law practice. Although in the last paragraph of our letter Jefferson refers to the "juvenile date" of the Moore letter, his sophisticated comments on legal literature and law study seem to evidence a somewhat older man and a later date. Based in part on Bernard Moore's purchase of the books in the estate of Dabney Carr, who died in 1773,[31] a date in the early 1770's would seem to be a more likely estimate. Jefferson would have been thirty years old, married, in practice for several years, a member of the Burgesses, and a significant figure both in the legal profession and in public life. In addition, the purchase of the Carr library would seem to be a likely consequence of the reading program outlined by Jefferson.

Since Jefferson did not date the Moore letter separately and left no copy, we can only guess as to the basis of his recall of its contents. The use of rough notes, a partial copy, or even a complete, undated copy, which may have been subsequently discarded or lost, are all possibilities. In any case, it is clear that he must have made several changes from the original Moore text, particularly to update the recommended readings. Jefferson indicated this to Minor in the opening paragraph of our letter:

> I shall give it to you without change, except as to the books recommended to be read; later publications enabling me in some of the departments of science to substitute better, for the less perfect publications which we then possessed. in this the modern student has great advantage.

As a result, there are several references in the Minor letter which would be anachronistic for the original Moore version. The *Federalist*, first published in a collected form in 787,[32] is included, and Tracy's work on political economy is cited as "*now* about to be printed. (1814.)"[33] In addition, among the law books, the following editions are cited, all of which post-date the latest possible date of the Moore letter: Tucker's edition of Blackstone, published in Philadelphia in 1803;[34] Fonblanque's edition of Ballow's Treatise of Equity, whose first edition was published during 1793 and 1794;[35] and the third edition of Lord Kames' (Kaims') Principles of Equity, published in Edinburgh and London in 1778.[36]

As to the nature of the legal education proposed by Jefferson to Minor, we can say that it was similar to the best programs described by other American law students and teachers of the time.[37] It was liberal, well-rounded in both its legal and general aspects, and supported by well-chosen readings from the available literature of the time. Despite the rather strenuous daily regimen set out, the suggested study methods are sensible and some are still considered good practice for today's law student. The breadth of learning and quality of readings in the program describe a more cosmopolitan and sophisticated level of education than a modern lawyer undertakes. However, the plan reflects a far simpler and more easily circumscribed legal system and legal literature. The absence of any serious concern with behavioral sciences related to the law bespeaks, at least in that respect, the less enlightened quality of a good lawyer's education in Jefferson's day. But perhaps that also reflects a simpler society in which the study of man could be subsumed in the writers of "Ethics, Religion, natural and and sectarian, and Natural law. . . ."

This introduction has been slow in reaching its real goal—Jefferson's letter of August 20, 1814, to John Minor. The complete text of that manuscript is now set forth in full,[38] with the hope that it has been placed in a context helpful to the reader.

* * * * *

Monticello Aug. 30th

Dear Sir

I have at length found the paper of which you requested a copy. it was written near 50. years ago for the use of a young friend whose course of reading was confided to me; and it formed a basis for the studies of others subsequently placed under my direction, but curtailed for each in proportion to his previous acquirements and future views. I shall give it to you without change, except as to the books recommended to be read; later publications enabling me in some of the departments of science to substitute better, for the less perfect publications which we then possessed. in this the modern student has great advantage. I proceed to the copy.

'Th. Jefferson to Bernard Moore.

Before you enter on the study of the law a sufficient ground-work must be laid. for this purpose an acquaintance with the Latin and French languages is absolutely necessary. the former you have; the latter must now be acquired. Mathematics and Natural philosophy are so useful in the most familiar occurrences of life, and are so peculiarly engaging & delightful as would induce every person to wish an acquaintance with them, besides this, the faculties of the mind, like the members of the body, are strengthened & improved by exercise. Mathematical.reasonings & deductions are therefore a fine preparation for investigating the abstruse speculations of the law, in these and the analogous branches of science the following elementary books are recommended.

Mathematics. Berout, Cours de Mathematiques. the best for a student ever published. Montucla or Bossu,' histoire des Mathematiques.

Astronomy. Ferguson, and Le Monnier, or de la Lande.

Nat. Philosophy. Joyce's Scientific dialogues. Martin's Philosophia Britannica. Mussenbroek's Cours de Physique.

This foundation being laid, you may enter regularly on the study of the Law, taking with it such of it's kindred sciences as will contribute to eminence in it's attainment. the principal of these are Physics, Ethics, Religion, Natural law, Belles lettres, Criticism, Rhetoric and Oratory. the carrying on several studies at a time is attended with advantage, variety relieves the mind, as well as the eye, palled with too long attention to a single object. but with both, transitions from one object to another may be so frequent and transitory as to leave no impression. the mean is therefore to be steered, and a competent space of time allotted to each branch of study. again, a great inequality is observable in the vigor of the mind at different periods of the day. it's powers at these periods should therefore be attended to in marshalling the business of the day. for these reasons I should recommend the following distribution of your time.

Till VIII. aclock in the morning employ yourself in Physical studies, Ethics, Religion natural and sectarian, and Natural law, reading the following books.

Agriculture. Dickson's husbandry of the antients. Tull's horse-hoeing husbandry. Ld. Kaim's Gentleman farmer. Young's Rural economy. Hale's body of husbandry. De-Serres Theatre d'Agriculture.

Chemistry. Lavoisier Conversations in Chemistry.

Anatomy. John and James Bell's Anatomy.

Zoology. Abrege' du Systeme de Linnée par Gilibert. Manuel d'histoire Naturel par Blumenbach. Buffon, including Montbeillard & La Cepede. Wilson's American Ornithology.

Botany. Barton's elements of Botany. Turton's Linnaeus. Persoon Synopsis Plantarum.

Ethics. & Natl. Religion. Locke's Essay. Locke's Conduct of the mind in the search after truth. Stewart's Philosophy of the human mind. Enfield's history of Philosophy. Condorcet, Progrès de l'esprit humain. Cicero de officiis. Tusculana. de Senectute. somnium Scipionis. Senecae Philosophica. Hutchinson's Introduction to moral Philosophy. Ld. Kaim's Natural religion. Traite' elementaire de Morale et Bonheur. La Sagesse de Charron.

Religion, sectarian. Bible. New Testament. Commentaries on them by Middleton in his works, and by Priestley in his Corruptions of Christianity, & Early opinions of Christ. Volney's Ruins, the Sermons of Steine, Massillon & Bourdaloue.

Natural law. Vattel Droit des Gens. Reyneval, Institutions du droit de la Nature et des Gens.

From VIII. to XII. read Law, the general course of this reading may be formed on the following grounds. Ld. Coke has given us the first view of the whole body of law worthy now of being studied: for so much of the admirable work of Bracton is now obsolete that the student should turn to it occasionally only, then tracing the history of particular portions of the law. Coke's institutes are a perfect Digest of the law as it stood in his day. After this, new laws were added by the legislature, and new developments of the old laws by the judges, until they had become so voluminous as to require a new Digest. This was ably executed by Matthew Bacon, altho' unfortunately under an Alphabetical, instead of Analytical arrangement of matter. the same process of new laws and new decisions on the old laws going on, called at length for the same operation again, and produced the inimitable Commentaries of Blackstone. In the department of the Chancery, a similar progress has taken place. Ld. Kaims has given us the first digest of the principles of that branch of our jurisprudence, more valuable for the arrangement of matter, than for it's exact conformity with the English decisions. the Reporters from the early times of that branch to that of the same Matthew Bacon are well digested, but alphabetically also in the abridgment of the Cases in Equity, the 2d volume of which is said to have been done by him. this was followed by a number of able reporters, of which Fonblanque has given us a summary digest by commentaries on the least of the earlier work ascribed to Ballow, entitled 'a Treatise of equity.' the course of reading recommended then in these two branches of law is the following.

Common law. Coke's institutes.

select cases from the subsequent reporters to the time of Matthew Bacon.

Bacon's abridgment.

select cases from the subsequent reporters to the present day.

select tracts on law, among which those of Baron Gilbert are all of the first merit.
the Virginia laws. Reports on them.
Chancery. Ld. Kaims Principles of Equity. 3d edition.
select cases from the Chancery reporters to the times of Matthew Bacon.
The Abridgment of Cases in Equity.
select cases from the subsequent reporters to the present day.
Fonblanque's Treatise of Equity.
Blackstone's Commentaries (Tucker's edition) as the last perfect
Digest of both branches of law.

In reading the Reporters, enter in a Commonplace book every case of value, condensed into the narrowest compass possible which will admit of presenting distinctly the principles of the case. this operation is doubly useful, inasmuch as it obliges the student to seek out the pith of the case, and habituates him to a condensation of thought, and to an acquisition of the most valuable of all talents, that of never using two words where one will do. it fixes the case too more indelibly in the mind.

From XII. to I. read Politics.

Politics general. Locke on government. Sidney on Government. Priestley's First principles of Government. Review of Montesquieu's Spirit of laws. Anon.
De Lolme sur la constitution d'Angleterre. De Burgh's Political disquisitions.
Hatsell's Precedents of the H. of Commons. select Parliam'y debates of England & Ireland.
Chipman's Sketches of the principles of government.
the Federalist.

Political Economy. Say's Economie Politique. Malthus on the principles of population.
Tracy's work on Political Economy. *now* about to be printed. (1814.)

In the *Afternoon.* read History.

History. Antient. the Greek and Latin originals.
select histories from the Universal history. Gibbon's decline of the Rom. Empire.
Histories Ancienne de Millot.

Modern. Histoire moderne de Millot. Russel's History of Modern Europe.
Robertson's Charles V.

English. the original historians. to wit. the Hist. of E.II. by E.F.—Habington's E.IV. More's R.III. Ld. Bacon's H.VII. Ld. Herbert's H.VIII. Goodwin's H.VIII. E.VI. Mary. Cambden's Eliz. & James. Ludlow. Mc.Cauley. Fox. Belsham. Baxter's History of England. (Hume republicanised & abridged.) Robertson's Hist. of Scotland.

American. Robertson's History of America. Gordon's History of the independence of the US. Ramsay's Hist. of the Amer. revolution. Burke's Hist. of Virginia. Continuation of do. by Jones & Girardin. nearly ready for the press.

From Dark to Bedtime. Belles letters. Criticism. Rhetoric. Oratory. To wit.

Belles letters. read the best of the Poets, epic, didactic, dramatic, pastoral, lyric etc but among these Shakespear must be singled out by one who wishes to learn the full powers of the English language. of him we must advise, as Horace did of the Grecian models, 'vos exemplaria Graeca Nocturnâ versate manu, diversate duirnâ.'

Criticism. Ld. Kaim's Elements of criticism. Tooke's Diversions of Purley. of Bibliographical criticism the Edinbg Review furnishes the finest models extant.

Rhetoric. Blair's lectures on Rhetoric. Sheridan on Elocution. Mason on Poetic and Prosaic numbers.

Oratory. this portion of time (borrowing some of the afternoon when the days are long and the nights short) is to be applied also to acquiring the art of writing & speaking correctly by the following exercises. Criticize the style of any books whatever, committing your criticisms to writing.—translate into the different styles, to wit, the elevated, the midling, and the familiar. Orators and Poets will furnish subjects of the first, historians of the second, & epistolary and Comic writers of the third.—undertake, at first, short compositions, as themes, letters etc. paying great attention to the correctness and elegance of your language.—read the Orations of Demosthenes & Cicero. analyse these orations, and examine the correctness of the disposition, language, figures, states of the cases, arguments etc.—read good samples also of English eloquence, some of these may be found in Small's American speaker, and some in Carey's Criminal Recorder, in which last the defence of Eugene Arum is distinguishable as a model of logic, condensation of matter, & classical purity of style.—exercise yourself afterwards in preparing orations on feigned cases. in this observe rigorously the disposition of Blair into Introduction, Narration etc. adapt your language & figures to the several parts of the oration, and suit your arguments to the audience before whom it is supposed to be spoken. this is your last and most important exercise, no trouble should therefore be spared. if you have any person in your neighborhood engaged in the same study, take each of you different sides of the same cause, and prepare pleadings according to the custom of the bar, where the pl. opens, the def. answers, and the pl. replies.—it would farther be of great service to pronounce your orations (having before you only short notes to assist the memory) in the presence of some person who may be considered as your judge.

Note, under each of the preceding heads, the books are to be read in the order in which they are named. these by no means constitute the whole of what might be usefully read in each of these branches of science. the mass of excellent works going more into detail is great indeed. but those here noted will enable the student to select for himself such others of detail as may suit his particular views and dispositions. they will give him a respectable, an useful, & satisfactory degree of knolege in these branches, and will themselves form a valuable and sufficient library for a lawyer, who is at the same time a love of science.'

So for the paper; which I send you, not for it's merit, for it betrays sufficiently it's juvenile date; but because you have asked it. your own experience in the more modern practice of the law will enable you to give it more conformity with the present course; and I know you will recieve it kindly with all it's imperfections, as an evidence of my great respect for your wishes, and of the sentiments of esteem and friendship of which I tender you sincere assurances.

Th. Jefferson

Notes

1. Minor was born in Caroline County, Virginia, in 1761, served in the Revolution, and later studied law under George Wythe as had Jefferson. He practiced law in Virginia for many years and died in 1821.

2. Moore was born about 1720, was a Colonel of Militia, a Justice of King William County, and a member of the House of Burgesses.

3. For a general discussion of Jefferson's correspondence, see 1 *The Papers of Thomas Jefferson* xi-xiii, xxv-xxix (J.P. Boyd ed. 1950) [hereinafter cited as *Papers*]. This definitive edition of Jefferson's papers is still being published. Citations to material appearing in the already published volumes of the Papers will be given only to that collection. The other editions are fully described in the leading biography, 1 D. Malone, *Jefferson and His Time, Jefferson the Virginian* 459-61 (1948) [hereinafter cited as *Malone*]. Other references will be made to *The Writings of Thomas Jefferson* (P.L. Ford ed. 1892-99) (10 vols.) [hereinafter cited as *Ford*]; and *The Writings of Thomas Jefferson* (A.A. Lipscomb & A.E. Bergh eds. 1903-04) (20 vols.) [hereinafter cited as *Lipscomb & Bergh*].

4. The polygraph was a device having one or more additional pens connected to a writer's pen to produce extra copies by simultaneously tracing the same course as the primary pen. In an 1805 letter to C.F. Volney, Jefferson describes it as follows: "A Mr. Hawkins of Frankford, near Philadelphia, has invented a machine which he calls a polygraph, and which carries two, three, or four pens. That of two pens, with which I am now writing, is best; and is so perfect that I have laid aside the copying-press, for a twelvemonth past, and write always with the polygraph." XI *Lipscomb & Bergh* 62, at 67-68. Then in 1806, in a letter to James Bowdoin, he noted further, "It is for copying with one pen while you write with the other, and without the least additional embarrassment or exertion to the writer. I think it the finest invention of the present age. . . ." XI *Lipscomb & Bergh* 118. Jefferson himself made several improvements in his own version of the polygraph.

5. Apr. 25, 1794, in VI *Ford* 505.

6. Jan. 11, 1817, in X *Ford* 72.

7. June 27, 1822, in X *Ford* 218.

8. 11 *Papers* 556.

9. *Id.* 557-58.

10. 1 *Papers* 76.

11. Ld. Kaim's Principles of equity. fol. £1.1
Blackstone's Commentaries. 4 v. 4to. £4.4
Cuningham's Law dictionary. 2 v. fol. £3
Id. 80.

12. 8 *Papers* 405.
13. 12 *Papers* 14.
14. 8 *Papers* 407.
15. 16 *Papers* 480, at 481.
16. Letter from Thomas Jefferson to Dabney Terrell, Feb. 26, 1821, in XV *Lipscomb & Bergh* 318.
17. June 11, 1790, in 16 *Papers* 480, at 481.
18. For a good discussion of Jefferson's own legal education, see 1 *Malone* 65-74.
19. June 11, 1790, in 16 *Papers* 480.
20. I *Lipscomb & Bergh* 4. See also Jefferson's letter to John Saunderson, Aug. 31, 1820 (with an attached biographical note on Wythe), in I *Lipscomb & Bergh* 165.
21. See ch. VIII (entitled *A Colonial Lawyer's Education*).
22. XV *Lipscomb & Bergh* 318.
23. Library of Congress, Manuscript Division, folio 39219.
24. XV *Lipscomb & Bergh* 318, at 322.
25. XIV *Lipscomb & Bergh* 54.
26. See Letter from Thomas Jefferson to Dabney Terrell, Feb. 26, 1821, in XV *Lipscomb & Bergh* 318, at 321; 4 *Dictionary of American Biography* 414-16 (A. Johnson & D. *Malone* eds. 1930).
27. Library of Congress, Manuscript Division, vol. 202, folios 35940-35942.
28. This is undoubtedly John Pinkerton's *Modern Geography* (1804), which is listed and described in IV *Catalogue of the Library of Thomas Jefferson*, No. 3827, at 90 (E.M. Sowerby ed. 1955). It is interesting to note that many of the other books cited by Jefferson in the Minor letter were also in his own library and are listed in the published catalogue.
29. See L.C. Manuscript Division Card Catalog entry for letter from Thomas Jefferson to General John Minor, August 30, 1814.
30. 1 *Malone* ch. XXVIII.
31. See Letter from Thomas Jefferson to Martha Jefferson Carr, July 25, 1787 (in regard to the sale), in 11 *Papers* 623.
32. See VI J. Sabin, *A Dictionary of Books Relating to America*, No. 23979, at 376 (1868) (first collected edition of Federalist published in two volumes, on Sept. 17, 1787).
33. D. Tracy, *A Treatise on Political Economy* (J. Milligan transl. & ed. 1817). XXV J. sadin, *supra* note 32, No. 96415, at 352-53, indicates 1818 as the date of publication of Tracy's work and notes that Jefferson had revised the translation.
34. W. Blackstone, *Commentaries* (St. G. Tucker ed. 1803) (5 vols.).
35. H. Ballow, *A Treatise of Equity* (J. Fonblianque ed. 1793-95) (2 vols.).
36. H.H. Kames, *Principles of Equity* (3d ed. 1778).
37. See, e.g., II A. Chroust, *The Rise of the Legal Profession In America* ch. IV (entitled *Training for the Practice of Law*); P. Hamlin, *Legal Education in Colonial New York* (1934); C. Warren, *A History of the American Bar* (1913).
38. A copy of the handwritten manuscript is provided first. Following that is a printed copy, set forth to aid the reader in deciphering parts of the letter which may be difficult to read. Jefferson's spelling, capitalization, and punctuation have been retained.

B. The Litchfield Law School

Chapter 10

Advertisement of the Litchfield Law School

1828

The Litchfield Law School is discussed in chapter 1. This advertisement from the school's 1828 catalog is in the Harvard Law School Library Department of Special Collections.

The Committee, to whom has been referred the publication of this catalogue, deem it proper to prefix a few observations in relation to the institution, and the course of instruction therein prescribed.

This Law School was established in 1782 by the Hon. Tapping Reeve, late Chief Justice of this State, and continued under his sole direction until the year 1798, when the Hon. J. Gould was associated with him. These gentlemen continued their joint labours until 1820, since which period Judge Gould has lectured alone. From its commencement, it has enjoyed a patronage, which distinguished talent combined with great legal attainment justly merited. It has been composed of young men from every section of the Union, many of whom have since been eminently conspicuous, both as Jurists and as Statesmen. And indeed even now, notwithstanding the numerous legal seminaries which have been established throughout our country, this school maintains its proud pre-eminence. This, it is believed, is to be attributed to the advantages, which the mode of instruction here prescribed, possesses over the systems usually adopted in similar institutions.

According to the plan pursued by Judge Gould, the Law is divided into forty-eight Titles, which embrace all its important branches, and of which he treats in systematic detail. These Titles are the result of thirty years severe and close application. They comprehend the whole of his legal reading during that period, and continue moreover to be enlarged and improved by modern adjudications. The Lectures, which are delivered every day, and which usually occupy an hour and a half, embrace every principle and rule falling under the several divisions of the different Titles. These principles and rules are supported by numerous authorities, and generally accompanied with familiar illustrations. Whenever the opinions upon any point are contradictory, the authorities in support of either doctrine are cited, and the arguments, advanced by either side, are presented in a clear and concise manner, together with the lecturer's own views of the question. In fact, every ancient and modern opinion, whether over-ruled, doubted, or in any way qualified, is here systematically digested. These lectures, thus classified, are taken down in full by the students, and after being compared with each other, are generally transcribed in a more neat and legible hand. The remainder of the day is occupied in examining the authorities cited in support of the several rules, and in reading the most approved authors upon those branches of the Law, which are at the time the subject of the lectures. These notes, thus written out, are, when complete, comprised in five large volumes, which constitute books of reference, the great advantages of which must be apparent to every one of the slightest acquaintance with the comprehensive and abstruse science of the Law. The examinations, which are held

11. Litchfield Law School. The structure built by Tapping Reeve to house his law school still stands in the yard of his house in Litchfield, Connecticut, where it is maintained by a diligent historical society. (*Photograph by Stephen Sheppard.*)

every Saturday, upon the lectures of the preceding week, consist of a thorough investigation of the principles of each rule, and not merely of such Questions as can be answered from memory without any exercise of the judgment. These examinations are held by Jabez W. Huntington, Esq., a distinguished gentleman of the bar, whose practice enables him to introduce frequent and familiar illustrations, which create an interest, and serve to impress more strongly upon the mind the knowledge acquired during the week.

There is also connected with this institution, a Moot Court for the argument of law questions, at which Judge Gould presides. The questions that are discussed, are prepared by him in the forms in which they generally arise. These courts are held once at least in each week, two students acting as Counsellors, one on each side, and the arguments that are advanced, together with the Opinion of the Judge, are carefully recorded in a book kept for that purpose. For the preparation of these questions, access may at all times be had to an extensive library. Besides these courts, there are societies established for improvement in forensic exercises, which are entirely under the control of the students.

The whole course is completed in fourteen months, including two vacations of four weeks each, one in the spring, the other in the autumn. No student can enter for a shorter period than three months. The terms of instruction are $100 for the first year and $60 for the second, payable either in advance or at the end of the year.

This Catalogue extends only as far back as 1798. Previous to that period, it is believed that the whole number exceeded four hundred; no record, however, has been preserved. The names of the students are placed in the order in which they entered, without any regard to the length of time they continued members of the institution. The committee have endeavored to notice those who have distinguished themselves; but as this has been done merely from recollection, they have no doubt passed by many, who have conferred honor upon their country and their profession.

Litchfield, Jan. 1, 1828.

Chapter 11

Rules of the Debating Society of Law Students in Mr. Reeve's Office

1794-1798

The original manuscript of the rules of the Debating Society are in the Tapping Reeve Papers of the Litchfield Historical Society.

The Students at Law in the Office of Mr Reeve agreeing to form themselves into a Society for the purpose of disputing Questions establish these rules & regulations which follow—

Art. 1st The meetings of this Society shall be weekly, on Thursday evening, for the discussion of Questions of Law.

Art. 2^{d} The officers of the Society shall be a President, Vice-President & Clerks who shall be chosen by ballot, by a simple plurality of votes and shall hold their respective offices for the term of four weeks.

Art.3^{d} It shall be the duty of the President to preside in the meetings of the Society & preserve order & decorum in the same.

Art. 4th The Vice President, in the absence of the President, and when the President shall take a part in the debate of the evening, shall preside and perform his duties.

Art. 5th It shall be the duty of the Clerk to open and adjourn all meetings of the Society receive & count the votes at elections, and report such cases as shall be brought before the Society with the decisions thereon and the grounds of those decisions; and these if the President so direct he shall shew to Mr Reeve & request his opinion thereon.

Art. 6th The President shall be ex officio Chief Justice & with him there shall sit two members of the Society, appointed in alphabetical rotation. These three Judges shall decide on such Questions as shall be discussed at the meetings of the Society & give the reasons of their actions.

Art. 7th At each meeting the Clerk shall name, in alphabetical rotation, four persons, who shall be disputants for the next succeeding meeting & the first & fourth thus named shall be for the P^{ff} & the intermediate one for the Deft.

Art. 8th All Questions shall come before the Society, with writs, pleadings, &c. In the same manner as a suit for the like question would be brought before a regular Court.

Art. 9th In case the same person be at any time both Disputant and Judge he shall not sit as Judge, & the President shall nominate a person to supply his place.

Art. 10th Whenever it shall happen that the same person shall be both Judge & Disputant, & in consequence thereof (by the provision of the last article) loses his set as Judge for the evening on which he becomes a Disputant, he shall not eventually lose his seat as Judge, but shall on the succeeding meeting succeed to that office.

Art. 11th Whenever the disputants cannot agree upon a subject of dispute, for the next ensuing evening, the Society at large shall determine it.

[Signed:] Geo. Lord, Elijah Adams, Timy Burt, Cyrus Swan, Dan Sheldon, Allen Stevens, Elijah Hubbard, Benj'm Hall, E.W. Bull, Samis Blakely, M Curtis, Mr Jonn Attwater, Rufus Adams, Walter Mitchell, BGardenier

12. Tapping Reeve (1744-1823) began teaching as an office practitioner, with Aaron Burr as his first pupil. He systematized his lectures, built a hut on the lawn to house books and classes, and opened the first law school in the United States devoted to preparing students for the practice of law. (*Engraving reproduction courtesy of the Litchfield Historical Society, Litchfield, Connecticut.*)

Chapter 12

Laws of the Office and Library Catalogue

1800-1810

Tapping Reeve

The original manuscript of the laws and the library list is in the Tapping Reeve Papers of the Litchfield Historical Society.

Laws of the Office

I Any person that takes down a volume and neglects to return it to its proper place on the same day, shall be fined.

II Any person who writes upon the cover or pages of a book, or upon paper lying upon an open volume, shall be fined.

III Any person who takes from the office any books except those which are privileged, shall be fined. The privileged books are: Blackstone's Commentaries, Powell's Elementary Treatises, Woodeson's Lectures, Epinasse's Nisi Prius, Kyd on Awards, Jones on Bailments, [St.Germain's] Doctor and Student, Lovelass on Wills, Fearne on Remainders, Gilberts Laws of Evidence, Swift's System, Lawyers Magazine, Cooke's Bankrupt Laws, Gilbert on Devises, Wilson on Awards, Sullivan's Lectures, Baron and Femme, Boots' Historical treatises, Cunningham on Bills of Exchange, Jacob's Introduction, Law of [illegible]. Bacon's Abridgement, Law of Costs, Haines Law Tracts, Instituti Legalis, Institutes, Tracts of the English Constitution, Gilbert's Common Pleas.

IV If a book not privileged, be found in the room of any gentleman, it shall be deemed prima facie evidence of his having taken it from the office.

V There shall be a standing chairman, whose duty it shall be to preside and keep order in the office, and when it shall be necessary for him to vote, he shall vote according to Law.

VI There shall be an Attorney General whose duty it shall be to prosecute all offenses against the laws of the office.

VII There shall be a committee of three gentlemen, members, whose duty it shall be to arrange the books and if any be left out of their places to replace them within 3 days after information of the same has been lodged in the office.

VIII There shall be a Secretary whose duty it shall be to keep a book and to record in it all the laws and Resolutions of the office now made, or to be hereafter made, together with a catalogue of the names of the members of the same.

IX There shall be a Treasurer whose duty it shall be to receive and account for all fines imposed by the office. [in pencil: Dmn . . . who observe not these rules and regulations]

X No member shall leave the office without leave first obtained by the Chairman.

XI All fines arising from the Breach of any of the articles shall be . . . to be paid into the hands of the Treasurer within 3 days from the time of its being imposed.

XII It shall be the duty of the members of the office to inform the Chairman of all breaches of these articles within two days after their knowledge of the same.

XIII The consciences of gentlemen may be appealed to in all cases to discover testimony where sufficient testimony to convict one cannot be procured from any other quarter.

XIV No person who has once subscribed to these Laws shall be at Liberty to withdraw his name under a penalty of Ten Dollars, and if he does not pay the fine, he shall be excluded from the festivals of the office.

XV Any person who shall tear, deface, or in any way alter these laws shall be fined.

XVI . . . Majority of the office shall have power to . . . all orders . . . and necessary a proper . . . to carry the aforesaid. . . .

XVII . . . sign these

XVIII . . . down a book or misplace it . . . to its proper place the same day

List of Books for Law Library

Bacon's Abridgment	8vo	5 vols.	Hobart's Rep.		1 vol.
Comyn's Digest	Do	5 vols.	Shower's Rep.	8vo	2 vols.
Co.Litt. Harg. D.	Folio	1 vol.	Powell on Debt & Mortgages	Do	2 vols.
Rolle's Abridgment	Do	1 vol.	Lovelass on Wills	Do	1 vol.
Hawkins' Pleas of Crown	8vo	2 vol.	Kyd on Bills of Exch. & Awards	Do	2 vols.
Coke's Rep.	Do	7 vols.	Fonblanque	Do	2 vols.
Croke's Rep.	Do	3 vols.	Buller's Nisi Prius	Do	1 vol.
Modern Rep.	Do	12 vols.	Gilbert's Law of Evidence	Do	1 vol.
Strange's Rep.	Do	2 vols.	Woodesow's Lect.	Do	4 vols.
Willes' Rep.	Do	3 vols.	Equity Cases Abridged	Do	3 vols.
Burrow's Rep.	Do	5 vols.	Precedents in Chy.	Do	1 vol.
Cowper's Rep.	Do	1 vols.	Vernon's Rep.	Do	2 vols.
Douglas's Rep.	Do	1 vol.	Talbot's Cases	Do	1 vol.
Term Rep.	Do	5 vols.	P.Wms' Rep.	Do	3 vols.
Salkeld's Rep.	Do	3 vols.	Atkyns's Rep.	Do	3 vols.
Ld.Raymond's Rep.	Do	3 vols.	Vesey's rep.	Do	2 vols.
Blackstone's Rep.	Do	2 vols.	Ambler's Rep.	Do	2 vols.
H. Blackstone's Rep.	Do	1 vol.	Brown's Chancery Rep.	Do	2 vols.
Comyn's Rep.		1 vol.	Mitford's Chanc'y.	Do	2 vols.
Ventris's Rep.		2 vol.	Morgan's Equity and Trials		
Carthew's Rep.		1 vol.			

Chapter 13

Description of the Law School

1823

James Gould

This article was initially published as "Law School at Litchfield" in 3 *United States Law Journal* 400 (January, 1823).

[Editor, 1823]: The fame of the Law School at Litchfield, was, long since, diffused over the nation; and the seminary has been viewed for many years, by legal tribunals, as the fertile source of elemental knowledge, and the nursery of eminent men. We do not hesitate to say, that the system of instruction which has been adopted in this school, is the most perfect of its kind, of any than has yet been established; and that it enables the law student to acquire more in one year, than is gained in three years, if not in five, in the ordinary method of securing an acquaintance with legal principles. We recommend it to the American Union; and we do this with a full conviction, that if our approbation can give it additional claims to patronage, we are contributing to the respectability of the American Bar. We speak with safety, when our humble tribute of praise is subsequent to the eulogiums of such men as Chancellor Kent, Chief Justice Spence, Judge Story, and in accordance with those of a great man who has departed from this world . . . the late Chief Justice Parsons, of Massachusetts.

The following letter from James Gould . . . was written in answer to several inquiries addressed to him, by one of the editors of this Journal.

Litchfield, Nov. 17, 1822

Sir:

Yours of October 30th has been received. . . .

At the commencement of my professional life, I entered upon the task of digesting, with my own hand, the several titles of the law, in a prescribed order. This undertaking I pursued by taking a memorandum, or abridged note, of each definition, principle, and substantive rule, falling under the several heads, or divisions, of the respective titles. . . .

From these notes I deliver a course of lectures, upon the several titles, in succession: a lecture, (varying in length, from an hour and a quarter to an hour and a half,) being given every day, Sundays excepted. The length of the whole course has, usually, been somewhat more than a year—in general, about 14 months; but, by extending the time of each lecture, to a full hour and a half, as I have now once done, for the first time, and by a supernumerary evening lecture, once a week, on criminal law, I have been able to bring the course within about the compass of a year, including in the computation, the usual vacations. Of these there are two, of four weeks each; one in the spring, the other in autumn.

Of the objects, proposed in my lectures, the first is, of course, to possess my pupils of all the principal rules, or doctrines, of the law; to each of which I add a collection of references. And all such rules as are not, in my judgment, too simple to require it, I illustrate, by one or more brief examples.

But a higher object, and (if the remark, as coming from myself, may be excused,) one, which I regard, as in some measure peculiar to my plan of instruction, is to teach the law—the common law, especially—not as a collection of *insulated positive rules*, as from the exhibition of it, in most of our books, it would appear to be; but, as a *system of connected, rational principles:* for such the common law unquestionably is, not only in its fundamental and more comprehensive doctrines; but also, generally speaking, in its subordinate, and more artificial provisions. In this view of the common law I regard our books, in general, as extremely defective. They treat it, rather, as a code of arbitrary, but authoritative rules and dogmas, than as a science. They are conversant, too exclusively, about doctrines, to the neglect of principles. They deal much in rules, but little in reasons. But we have Lord Coke's assurance that "the law is unknown to him, who knoweth not the reason thereof." . . .

I thus endeavor to assist [my pupils], not only in understanding the science, but also, in making analogical, as well as direct applications of its rules and principles.

All the principal rules and distinctions, given out in the lectures, together with the references intended to support them, are taken down, in full, as delivered, by the students, in notes of their own. In doing this, they find, after a few days' practice, no difficulty: my delivery being studiously adapted to their convenience, in this particular. My reasonings and illustrations, they take down, or omit, at their discretion—as they deem the noting of the one, or the other, to be essential, nor not, to their own future correct understanding, or recollection, of the doctrines or principles advanced.

The notes, which the students take of the lecture, in the morning, they correct, and generally transcribe, after they have left the lecture-room; and are expected to employ the residue of the hours of study, each day, in reading, in the most approved digests, abridgements, or treatises, on the title of which the lecture treats, and in comparing their notes with some of the references in it. The course of reading, which I recommend to be pursued by my pupils, while they remain in the school, is confined, chiefly, to works of the description just mentioned: so that they read reports, generally speaking, only by way of reference, as a test to the lectures, or for the purpose of studying particular questions, given out to them for discussion, in their forensic exercises. I always dissuade them from reading reports, in course.

The future use, for which the pupil designs his own notes, is that of a manual, or commonplace book, (including a repository of references) to aid him in his professional practice: and I am persuaded, that a given individual can, in no other way, acquire so ready and accurate a knowledge of the law, as by digesting it in his own hand-writing. Whatever he has once read, he thus makes his own, in a sense, in which, I believe, no other scheme of study can make it so; and subject all its parts to his more ready use and command; because they are arranged and distributed, according to landmarks of his own rearing. It is, indeed, for a time, an arduous plan of study; but it becomes comparatively easy, by practice, and is, ultimately, I think, the best mode of economizing professional labour. "Writing," says Lord Bacon, with his usual strength and discrimination of thought, "makes the correct" and I am persuaded, that the remark will be found to hold true, as well, (though not, perhaps, in the same degree,) of compilation, as of original composition. I have learnt, from very many of my former pupils—from all indeed, who have given me any information on the subject—that, in their practice, their notes have proved invaluable.

To assist the students in investigating, for themselves, as in forensic exercises, there is kept up, in my lecture-room, a Moot-Court, in which they, once in each week, argue before me, questions of law, on a case given out by myself, for the purpose. The questions are raised, either upon issues in law, formally joined, or upon facts found in a special verdict, or specially stated, as in regular courts of justice,—two students being heard, as counsel, on each side. This exercise, however, is not compulsory, and is principally confined to those, who have made considerable progress in legal studies. It is permitted, however, to all the pupils, without distinction. . . . The emulation, excited by this sort of competition, is very strong; and it is but justice to the young gentlemen, to say, that they usually acquit themselves very respectably.

I have endeavored thus to give you a faithful sketch, of the kind you requested.

Chapter 14

Letters Home

1827-1828

Augustus Hand

Augustus Hand enrolled in the Litchfield Law School in 1827 at the age of twenty-four. He stayed one year before leaving to open a practice in New York, across Lake Champlain from his father's house in Shoreham, Vermont. Hand became a congressman, a trial judge, and a judge of the highest court in New York. Learned Hand, one of the most influential judges of the Twentieth Century, was Augustus's grandson. All of these letters are reproduced from the Archives of the Litchfield Historical Society. Commentary appearing in square brackets is that of the editor.

James Gould to Augustus Hand

Litchfield, Aug 9th, 1827

Sir,

Your letter of July 28th was received last evening. In reply to your inquiries respecting the Law School under my care, I state that the Summer term begins in June, usually near the middle of the month, and closes near the last of September, or the first of October. There is then a vacation of four weeks. The next term continues till about the middle of May—when there is another vacation of four weeks. The title of Universal Law will, probably, come on at the commencement of the next term, or very soon after that time. It would be difficult to make an estimate of the probable time when the principle title will come on. The whole course occupies about fifteen months. The first title is that of Municipal Law. Then follows the Domestic Relations—Bailments—Contracts—Actions &c—Pleadings—Evidence—Law Merchant—and Real Property—which concludes the course. These are the principal titles in my course; and you may form some idea of the time when a particular title will be taken up, from the order of the titles, and the beginning of the course. It would be difficult for me to be more explicit. As to your inquiry respecting studies preparatory to my lectures; I can only say that my lectures are intended to systematize and simplify the science of the Law, in order that the Student, on entering upon his studies, may begin with ease and advantage to himself. Any Preparatory study is of course unnecessary.

Your obedt.
Sevt. James Gould

Edgar Leonard Ormsbee to Augustus Hand

Rutland July 19, 1827
Dear Sir
I received your letter on Saturday last. I should have answered it by Tuesdays mail—but I had intended to have sent by Mr. Power—but when he passed through Rutland on his return I was too busy to write. In answer to your inquiries—First there are two terms and two vacations. One of the vacations begins I think about the middle of May and continues five weeks—the other begins about the last of September and continues also four weeks. A full course of the lectures requires a few weeks more time than the two terms: of course it is impossible for any one not acquainted with the present state of the school to tell at what time a person should go in order to commence with the beginning of the course—which is municipal law. I commenced at the fall term with lectures on the subject of real property. For me I should not deem it very important at what particular part of the course a Student commences provided he begin with some important title—or at least did not begin when some important title had been partly finished. It would be advisable to begin with municipal Law. A person can stay there any time he chooses. The fee for a year is one hundred dollars—and a proportionate sum for any [illegible] or longer time. The lectures are delivered one on each day (excepting the Sabbath) commonly commencing at nine in the morning in winter and at eight in the summer—occasionally the time of commencing is altered to suit the convenience of the Students. There was when I was there a weekly examination on Saturday afternoon and an occasional discussion held on some other afternoon on some mooted point. The examination was by Huntington. The discussion was by the students before Judge Gould who delivered an opinion on the point argued. The other expenses aside from the fee for instruction are about one fourth higher than is usual in villages of the like size of Litchfield in New England—or at least in Vermont. To conclude I know of no place where I [illegible] warmly recommend a person to go who wished to acquire legal knowledge—than the law school at Litchfield.

I am Respectfully
Your Obedient Servant
Edgar L. Ormsbee

Augustus C. Hand to Richard Hand [his brother]

Litchfield Jan 7 - 1828
Dear Brother,
"sans cue mouie"
I thank you for your kind letter indeed it came very [illegible] I had the horrors very bad—but there are [ilegible] like to our house home—Indeed business has completely dismissed all [illegible]—You ask the number & of our professors—As for numbers there [missing] in to singular numbers—ages about 30— Ability [missing] completely circumscribed by a law book acquirements [missing]

Lecture subjects *law law law*—To be serious brother [missing] meet nine o'clock a.m. in a kind of whited [illgeble] where we find a white headed bluff looking old man (who quaffs brandy well in the afternoon) seated in a great old fashioned chair on a little eminence & [illegible] & from this delivers his lectures which are composed of "Rules" of Law indeed forming a complete digest of that Study. The Rule is given & then [illegible] how the authorities i.e. principles & precedents. This has been his morning seat for 30 years as you well see by a catalogue which I shall send you as soon as they are struck off which is published by the students containing names & residence of all the students for the last 30 years. These morning lectures are delivered everyday (homis Sun—) & constitute the principal part of his labors. It is the duty of the scholar if he pleases to seek the authorities referenced & prove the rule—On Friday p.m. we have an extra lecture on Criminal Law—& also a Moot Court—where two persons argue a moot question (taking their turns in alphabetical order) which is [missing] by to Judge with his [missing] On Saturday p.m. we [missing] examined by Huntington Esq who is probably prep [missing] himself to tread in the footsteps of Judge Gould. He is about nearly 40 arooting himself entirely to the Study of Law & arguing cases caring apparently nothing for money. This is indeed as Judge Skinner told us a Legal [illegible] This Judge Gould is a man who succeeded Judge Reeve—He manages the school entirely on his own footing—is completely absorbed in the Law—of Strong gigantic mind—a cold headed [ ] mortal perhaps I may say almost without any good qualities of the heart. The school consists of a sociable number from 10 to 40.

As to your advice about securing a future M's[1] good but I believe useless brother—I have just counted my numbers & found the pages to account 944 that I have written since I came to this place (Entre nous) [Illegible] selfish [illegible, but what ever it is, it isn't nice] old fellow would charge [missing] for these when I have if he knew it—& a Law would [TORN] hear our in that—so—put your finger on your mouth for this & [ ] to me—By the[illegible] is the very[i]of cash [illegible]so say[i]the[i]places it is impossible to evade twice—But [illegible] are all [illegible] & genteel people [i] aim really high

Their presbyterian minister Mr. Carrol a powerful young man has just left for the south in—There is great difference of opinion here about lay preaching—Mr. Stone is the Epis[l] Priest to the by high for this [illegible: six or seven words] may preach like fine fellows—using the most clear [illegible] original & forcible language without [illegible] or fury

The Sheet on which I write is the kind used in taking lectures—which are covered when complete [illegible] in 2 vol containing 600 pp each—Were I accustomed to "brag" I would say I take the best lectures in the office—or any [missing] often referred to for correction by my fellows [illegible three words] My Society is very companionable here not withstanding we have [i] combustible [missing]—having by the age a knock down scape over us [illegible] while—*all* for my *friends* (popular speaking)

We have on Monday night a Debate to try a powers of elocution—If Sister A is with you give her a kiss & thank her for her "word" God bless her—& God bless you my Dear Brother farewell—

Augustus C. Hand

Augustus Hand to his father

Litchfield Jan 30th 1829

My Dear Father—

I set down to write you a long letter I hope a good one—But as Shakespeare says "there 'is a rub" & this shall come first that when it is disposed of, you may read the other with better appetite- as- we say my dear father no notion of giving you a "pill" in molasses, but the pill & then the molasses—It is about cash!—I have received a letter from my friend Mr Waller informing me that our course does not commence till *June* Now our vacation here does not commence till May. Which you will observe gives me about five weeks longer than I anticipated—Will you lend me 40 dol. to continue to use my present privileges till that time? In the support of the negative I will myself remark I am not ignorant of the toil & trouble with which a farmer of [illegible] commands cash Nor am I ignorant of these [illegible] of this place area the total inadequacy of farmers sons to hear them. I have [illegible] this matter will if I devote my life to usefulness it is but a trifle, if not, a fathers labor shall not be wasted On this point I need advice but no *information.*

Now a word on the affirmative On this part of the subject I can say noting more persuasive to a father than to detail my present advantages Let me tell how I spending times. I rise between 7 & 8, make a fire & send for breakfast From there to Lecture where I remain until between 10 & 11—there to my room & copy Lectures till 5 pm I have dinnertime at 1 pm thence to tea thence to O.S. Seymour's office with whom I read Law till ½ past 9 pm. then again to my room & write till between 12 & 1 o'clock—then [I on my night cap & "turn in." Exceptions—Monday Eve spend from 6 to 9 in the Law School Debating Society over which I have the honor-[illegible] (I never brag)—Friday 3 pm attend an extra Lecture on Criminal Law & also hear an argument in the "Moot Court" & decision by the judge—On Saturday at 2 pm attend a Severe 3 hour examination on the Studies of the week Jabez W. Huntington Esq. Aside from these exceptions the first day is a correct Specimen—As to the Lectures & their utility I will refer you to the Preface of the Catalogue mailed with this- I can only say that this daily practical use to a lawyer can only be appreciated by those who have enjoyed thence- without any doubt they give the same [illegible] a powerful superiority—The whole course is completed in between 2500 & 3000 pages of the sheet on which I am now writing (some small spaced margins occasionally for future additions) of these I have written between 1200 & 1300 & Shall remain here till May & enjoy my present excellent health there will be no difficultly in copying the whole-having access to Seymour's volumes (for what I do not take in the office) who has attended two courses & has them complete This however is business between ourselves for these Lectures are Sacred to the Judge being the labor of his life in the same manner as a patent might So we take use I [illegible] faster—This Seymour with whom I study is the son of the Sheriff of this County nephew of our W S^{r}.—a graduate of Yale—a bachelor of about 26 or 27 of most sterling mind & manners with a brain completely identified with the Study of Law in its most theoretical & scientific part—From a natural weak use of his eyes he does not allow himself to study evenings & therefore invited me to read with him—This offer knowing his fame &c I readily accepted—his office being next door to mine he being altogether such a man as "studies learning to use it"—We take up a title in the Lectures & progress with it till its finished reading (about) between 10 & 20 pages an evening he giving me a thorough incite in to it as we proceed-allowing me without reserve to tease him with as many questions as I prepare & Then & now reading a report of some case adapted to the subject—before the [illegible] commences he examines me in the proceeding upon memory—

This my dear father is a brief outline on the privileges I enjoy It is for you to say whether they shall continue till May—My great desire is to obtain a complete set of Lectures the bare *copying* of which costs *those* who are too lazy to write of course I am my own [illegible] about $130. If you decide against me I shall regret but not blame I have no claim—Should you send me the remittance I will not offend you by puffing gratitude-children no doubt have no difficulty about this when *paid* for it—I can only remark that it will add obligation to the many inducements which already urge me on in this [illegible five words]—I see when I can [illegible] what a [illegible] I there is in my life-what a blank there is in my Spring that the Law is the Study & business of a man's life not the mere smattering to "be admitted" it must be agreed that inducements are not wanting—But this is digressing the "rub" unless I have care with Spread all over myletter—a beggar surely does not want for words—To this point shall you or shall younot my Dear Father grant my request I wish to know it immediately that I may calculate according—Not that I am in immediate want of money by any means—On this point—know exactly how my wealth stands to a [illegible]. I hardly think I shall spend $40 but I dare not [illegible] without it—I have already informed you something of the expense of this place—You may be surprised at this call—but I believe father if you stood at my elbow many times, you would say "I *was* a *Yankee* for a bargain"—I face them to it—but they have the advantage, they can keen & I *must have*—Just think how my horse shakes-journey—suit of clothes—already written over $8 worth of paper—*fuel* almost a dol. per week. From $600 to 1000 is the usual expense per annum—but this is no rule for me & you will say without hesitation [illegible] I am my own Servt &c. &c. & I believe a solitary instance best Judge to this—there *is* a *spot* where I too am ever with them—

There are two subjects my dear father which I desire to call your attention in your last 1st When I passed through Albany Renney the son in law of Mr. Gager & junior Editor of the Argus press we had to join him in a paper at Midd'y Vt.—We can establish a very good paper for 600 $ (crt) I consider it rather below the real Law but it is best to begin as Editor—2nd A Gentleman here by the name of Russel M.D. has called upon me for information respecting Shore Vt. as a location for a physician—For a year or two past he has been the junior partner of Dr. Abbe a man of this place who charges about $5000 per an. He was at the Hospital at Phila sometime & received his diploma at that School—a young man of about 27 years a bachelor & a finished physician & surgeon without doubt—Shall he go to Shore—For certain reasons I felt very delicate on the subject notwithstanding I believe it to be a chance for Sh—He has an idea of *mediocrity*—I promised him I would desire my father to consult with the mighty of Shore—which I beg you do just as your own best judge dictates—please to be cautious as to me—The Law here is a *Study*—There are one or two Lawyers in this vicinity who make 4 or $5000 a year—I pass every day by the door of one worth $150,000 about ½ of which he made in Law.—This "Huntington" who [illegible] arraives is a bachelor rather about 40 who studies, thinks & talks Law sleeping & waking—He never "pettifogs" but pleads in the higher courts & writes opinions for other lawyers in every section of the country. He will sometimes become so active in directing questions which arising on the law of nations that he can hardly keep his seat—Friday the first it came my turn for the second time to come on to the "Moot Court" (See Pref to Cat.) A short time after my admission My name came on oppos[d] to Mr. Halsted of N.J. (in alphabetical order) who was an old student—I tried to crop the Rubieau but like an hoor—stuck in the wind—I could not [illegible] Frightened out of my wits surrounded by a *literary fog*—in the midst of my "*nothing*" I quoted from an author (Swift) with whom the judge had a personal quarrel My compeers began to "snicker" this with being on the wrong side of the question now fix[d] me—This time I resolved to retrieve—A most intricate question on the doctrine of relation & estoppel was handed M. Brown of N.Y. & myself by Sg. Sanford of this place. Having nothing to lose I omitted the matter till Thursday Eve & then "stuck up" nearly all night-"Now Caesar I *win* or you lose [illegible] we "appeared" & I beat upon the "tympanum" of his honors ear about 210 minutes with all sorts of sounds. Mr. B. succeeded —Yesterday we had a very learned answer highly in my favor—Nor my dear father then I could have you think a pedagogue would be edified or influenced by hearing his urchins read "Baker" But then Mr B's views never were individually different & so it may go for what it will fetch.

The little circumstance gave me a little pleasure You would hardly [illegible] that with so. The business on hand I should meddle with politics—I have so done over only which I believe was well enough though I begrudged the time then—When Clay's famous Vindication came out & Sg. Sanford a mess mate of mine & the widowed son in law of Hon. M. Merwin in Congress from this state politely but with triumph requested me to read it I did so It gave him the advantage a little (I'm a Jack. man) I could not for fear letting off *my* big guss in the paper of this place—It was blasphemy—Who dare do it? Suspicion fell on me by the booksellers recognizing the paper which he sold me. I was not ashamed of the [illegible] by any means so [ilegible] the fun-ha-ha Well father have I bragged enough. Now I do not believe it is a mortal sin to tell [illegible: Uteri?] little successes to a [illegible: har cut? father?]—at any rate no [father?] is likely to be elated with a begging letter—

I received brother N's letter & have [illegible] an answer to Govr.—I am in a state & anxiety about Sis. Agnes. I hope my friends will not forget that I can know only what is written to me—What are Br R's feelings on the prospect—I still hope for the best—I send Br R a catalogue & Stanton's Sermon a dead [illegible] "Lay Preaching" wish you to read it if you wish father & then forward it to him if he has left which I suppose he has is Sister A's health would admit—as Sister Mercy says he has a substitute till February only--As to Col Howes case the fault was his for not giving timely notice—they probably know by this time—God bless you my dear father & mother & sisters & brother (wherever he is) God bless you farewell

My dear father Your aff. son Augustus C. Hand

P.S. Should you send money further I think you had better send it in two different letters at least at two different times—Write with [illegible]

NOTE

1. Editor's note: Correspondence from Litchfield students often mentions the prospects of marriage, thanks to a very successful academy for young ladies located only a few hundred yards away. A typically candid letter includes the following: "Litchfield appears to be a very pretty place and I think I shall like it well, I attended an evening or two ago an exhibition of the young ladies seminary at this place of which you speak in your letter. There were several very handsome & interesting young demoiselles. The court room in which it was held was excessively crowded, and two or three fainted, 1 young lady upon receiving her premium. At one end of the room men, boys & girls were all heaped up together, and ever and anon, you would hear some sturdy bum, resounding against the floor, its luckless owner having incautiously pushed it out beyond the line of equilibrium. I understand from Mrs. Reeve that all the marriagable young ladies have been married off, and that there is at present nothing but young fry in town, consequently that it will not be as gay as usual. The young ladies, she tells, me, all marry law students, but as it will take 2 or 3 years for the young crop to become fit for the harvest, you need apprehend no danger of my throwing up my batchelorship." Letter from Cornelius Dubois, Jr. to Edgar VanKonkle, October 28, 1830.

Chapter 15

Litchfield Law Students

1790-1830

The following list of names of students who attended the Litchfield Law School has been compiled by the Litchfield Historical Society, under the direction of Tess Reismeyer, Curator of Library Collections. The Society has discovered several new students in recent years and invites any reader with information about a student not listed below to contact it. Readers seeking information about a particular student are invited to inquire at the Litchfield Historical Society's Ingraham Memorial Research Library, located in our building at the corner of East and South Streets, Litchfield, Connecticut 06759.

Abbott, Nehemiah, 1823
Abeel, George, 1823
Adams, Charles, 1812
Adams, Elijah, 1794
Adams, John Frink, 1823
Adams, John Turvill, 1833
Adams, Joseph Thornton, 1820
Adams, Rufus, 1796
Aiken, Charles, 1832
Albro, John Adams, 1821
Alden, Cyrus, 1808
Alden, Hiram Orlando, 1823
Allen, Alexander M., 1801
Allen, John, 1784
Allen, Zimri Enos, 1811
Allyn, Joseph Tyler, 1821
Alston, William Jeffreys, 1824
Alston, William Williams, 1818
Ames, Samuel, 1824
Anderson, Franklin, 1813
Anderson, John, 1815
Andrews, Edward Warren, 1831
Andrews, William Stutson, 1812
Andrews, William Turell, 1812
Andrews,? 1797
Ashley, Chester, 1814
Aspinwall, Thomas Sowers, 1810
Atwater [Attwater?], Frederick, 1814
Atwater [Attwater?], Jonathan, 1797
Atwater [Attwater?], Nathan, 1790
Atwater [Attwater?], Russell C, 1815
Austin, Charles, 1812
Austin, Ralsaman C., 1801
Austin, Seneca, 1820
Averell, William Holt, 1817
Averill, Elisha, 1814
Ayer, Zacheus, 1817
Babbitt, Roswell, 1833
Bacon, Asa, 1794
Bacon, David, 1806
Bacon, Ezekiel, 1794
Bacon, William Johnson, 1823
Baker, Joshua, 1821
Baker, Walter, 1812
Balcom, Everett, 1818
Baldwin, Birdsey, 1806
Baldwin, Charles, 1801
Baldwin, Charles, 1810

Baldwin, Ebenezer, 1810
Baldwin, Henry, 1797
Baldwin, Roger Sherman, 1812
Baldwin, Samuel Sacket, 1800
Banks, William Crawford, 1818
Barclay, David, Jr., 1832
Barnes, Enos H., 1826
Barnes, Jonathan c. 1784-1785
Barnes, Joseph, 1801
Barnes, Laurens, 1806
Barnwell, William Wigg, 1817
Barnwell, William Hazzard Wigg, 1826
Bartram, Daniel Starr, 1799
Bates, Anson, 1820
Bates, Elijah, 1794
Battell, Josiah B., 1798
Battell, Philip, 1828
Baxter, Eli Harris, 1818
Baxter, Horace, 1812
Beach, Erasmus Darwin, 1832
Beach, Jesse, 1789
Beebe, Levi Swift, 1830
Beecher, Truman, 1816
Beers, David Booth, 1829
Beers, Frederick, 1809
Beers, Seth Preston, 1803
Belden, Hezekiah, 1797
Bell, Harvey, Jr., 1812
Bell, James, 1824
Bellamy, Joseph Hart, 1808
Benedict, Amos, 1802
Benedict, Noah Bennet, 1789
Benedict, William, 1797
Bennett, Milo Lyman, 1811
Beverly, James B., 1813
Beverly, William C., 1813
Bigelow, Horatio, 1810
Bigelow, Silas, 1814
Billings, Noyes, 1820
Bingham, Flavel White, 1830
Birch/Burch, Heman, 1798
Bird, John, 1787
Bishop, Jonathan P., 1814
Bissell, Edward, 1828
Bissell, John, Jr., 1826
Bixby, Alfred, 1821
Blackman, Samuel Curtis, 1796
Blackwell, David, 1813
Blake, Ephraim W., 1817-, 1818
Blake, Francis Arthur, 1817
Blake, Eli Whitney, 1817
Blakeley, Samuel C., 1796
Boardman, David Sherman, 1793
Boardman, George Sherman, 1819
Boardman, William Whiting, 1816
Bolles, Job Samuel Taber, 1822
Bond, Nathaniel P., 1819
Bond, William Key, 1811
Bonesteel, Virgil Dryden, 1830
Bonnell, Joseph, 1815
Booth, James, Jr., 1810
Bosson, Charles Thompson, 1811
Bostwick, Charles, 1798
Boyle, James, 1833
Brace, John Pierce, 1812
Brace, Thomas Kimberly, 1802
Bradley, Abraham, 1790
Bradley, Benjamin H., 1818
Bradley, Edwin D., 1827
Bradley, Jesse Smith, 1801
Bradley, Stephen Row, 1775
Brainerd, Hezekiah, Jr., 1793
Brayton, George Arnold, 1825
Breckenridge, John, 1821
Brinsmade, Daniel Bourbour, 1803
Bronson, Frederick, 1824
Brooks, Whitefield, 1814
Broome, Jacob Pierce, 1809
Brown, Charles R., 1813
Brown, Franklin, 1827
Brown, George, 1814
Brown, Nicholas, Jr., 1811
Bruyn, Andrew DeWitt, 1811
Buchanan, William S., 1824
Buffet, William Platt, 1813
Bulkeley, Joseph, 1810
Bull, Epaphras Wadsworth, 1796
Bull, Epaphras We, 1826
Bullard, Royal, 1810
Bunker, Charles, 1822
Bunnell, James Fitch, 1827
Burgess, Welcome Arnold, 1821
Burnet, Jacob pre-1796
Burr, Aaron, 1774
Burrall, William Porter, 1828
Burt, Timothy, 1794
Butler, Chester Pierce, 1818
Butler, David B., 1825
Calhoun, John Caldwell, 1805
Cambreling, Stephen, 1813

Camp, Ralph Garwood, 1824
Campbell, Colin, 1809
Campbell, George Lindsay, 1826
Campbell, John, 1820
Canfield, Ezra, 1801
Canfield, Henry Judson, 1808
Canfield, Joseph, Jr., 1785
Cantelou, Peter Louis, 1813
Cantelou, William Bernard, 1813
Cardwell, John W., 1823
Carroll, Charles Hobart, 1817
Carroll, William Thomas, 1823
Castor, Dyre [not Dyer], 1825
Catlin, George, 1817
Catlin, George Smith, 1827
Catlin, Grove, Jr., 1806
Chamberlain, Mellen, 1819
Chambers, Benjamin Lee, 1822
Chambers, Joseph, 1820
Champion, Epaphroditus, 1805
Champlin, Christopher, 1810
Chandler, Anson Gansello, 1818
Chandler, Hannibal, 1832
Chandler, John Alfonzo, 1818
Channing, Henry William, 1809
Chapin, Moses, 1813
Chapman, Asa, 1794
Chapman, Charles, 1818
Chase, Harvey, 1800
Chase, Moses, 1798
Chase, Samuel, 1818
Cheever, Samuel, 1812
Chester, Henry, 1815
Chester, Stephen Mitchell, 1813
Chester, Stephen Mitchell, 1813
Childs, Timothy, Jr., 1814
Chittenden, Frederick, 1824
Church, Aaron M., 1800
Church, Samuel, 1806
Clarke, Gibson, 1804
Clark, James, 1804
Clark, Archibald Bellinger, 1800
Clarke, Henry L., 1826
Clark, Peter Imlay, 1811
Clarke, Robert, 1832
Clayton, John Middleton, 1817
Cleaveland, Stephen, 1815
Cleaveland, William Pitt, 1794
Clifton, William Clisby, 1815
Clinton, George William, 1828
Cockburn, William, 1818
Coggeshall, Josiah Haydon, 1809
Cole, John L., 1810
Cole, Sands G., 1825-26
Coleman, John Jay, 1827
Collier, John Allen, 1805
Collins, Augustus, 1804
Collins, Josiah III, 1826
Condit, Jacob A., 1813
Conkling, Thomas L., 1817
Converse, Porter, 1804
Cooke, James Clarke, 1813
Cooke, Roger W., 1817
Cooke, Oliver Dudley, Jr., 1818
Cooley, James, 1799
Cooper, Benjamin F., 1821
Cowles, Henry Booth, 1817
Cowles, Samuel, 1802
Cowles, Sands G., 1812
Crawford, James, 1832
Crawford, Joel, 1806
Croghan, William, Jr., 1815
Crosby, Platt Hiram, 1813
Cruger, Henry Nicholas, Jr., 1821
Cumming, Edward Hamilton, 1826
Cumming, William Clay, 1806
Cunningham, Robert, 1810
Curtis, Medad, 1789
Cushman, Charles Chaplin, 1828
Cushman, John Paine, 1808
Cuthbert, Alfred, 1804
Cuthbert, John Alfred, 1807
Cutler, George Younglove, 1819
Cutting, Frances Brockholst, 1823
Dart, John Sanford, 1821
Davidge, Francis Hathorn, 1815
Davies, Henry, 1809
Davis, John Brazer, 1815
Davis, John H., 1817-, 1818
Davis, Israel Woodberry, 1811
Davis, James, 1816
Davis, John, 1811
Davis, John H., 1817
Dawson, Lawrence Edwin, 1822
Dawson, William Crosby, 1817
Day, Edgar Burr, 1826
Day, Thomas, 1797
Deas, Henry, 1818
Delafield, John, 1830
Delamotta, Jacob, 1821

DeMenou,Count Charles Julius, 1808
Deming, Buel Hunt, 1825
Denny, Thomas, 1825
Devereux, George Pollock, 1817
Devereux, Thomas Pollock, 1813-, 1815
Dexter, Christopher Champlin, 1813
Dickinson, Daniel Stephen, 1827
Doan, Guy William, 1814
Doolittle, Amos B., 1806
Downes, Appleton, 1811
Downman, John Bartholomew, 1813
Doyle, Francis, 1822
DuBois, Cornelius, Jr. [1830]
Dunbar, Daniel, 1798
Dunbar, Miles, 1809
Dwight, Henry William, 1809
Dyer, Eliphalet, 1790
Dyer, Thomas, 1799
Eastman, Ahira G., 1833
Edwards, Henry Pierrepont, 1828
Edwards, Henry Waggaman, 1798
Edwards, John Starke, 1796
Edwards, Jonathan Walter, 1794
Edwards, Moses Ogden, 1801
Eichelberger, Louis, 1810
Elgin, Hezekiah R., 1815
Ellis, Grindall R., 1809
Ellmaker, Amos Stanhope, 1806
Eworth, Henry Leavitt, 1811
Eworth, William Wolcott, 1811
Elmendorf, Edmund B., Jr., 1826
Ennis, William, 1820
Erwin, Isaac H., 1828
Esten, James Christie, 1792
Everest, Sherman, 1800
Fairchild, Robert, 1794
Fairlie, Frederick, 1818
Felder, John Myers, 1806
Fenn, Linus, 1793
Fine, John, 1813
Fisher, Isaac, Jr., 1811
Fisher, Samuel, 1810
Fleming, Matthew, 1815
Flourney, Thomas, 1797-1798
Follett, Timothy, 1812
Folsom, Joshua, 1811
Foot, John Alfred, 1824
Foot, Samuel Augustus, 1797
Foote, Ebenezer, 1795
Footman, William Caldwell, 1816
Ford, William H., 1826
Foster, George, 1812
Foster, James, 1812
Foster, Thomas Flourney, 1816
Fowler, James, 1808
Fowler, John Douglass, 1813
Francis, John Brown, 1813
Franklin, Walter S., 1818
Frazier, Alexander Gardner, 1810
Frisbie, Samuel, 1809
Fuller, Henry Holton, 1812
Fuller, Rufus, Jr., 1835
Fuller, William Williams, 1814
Fullerton, Alexander Norton, 1826
Fullerton, Thomas Stearns, Jr., 1822
Gansevoort, Peter, Jr, 1810
Gantt, Samuel, 1817
Gardenier, Baren [?], 1796
Gardner, Philip S., 1826
Gibbs, David, 1808
Gibbs, Henry William, 1808
Gibbs, William Channing, 1810
Gibson, William, 1823
Glover, Samuel, 1820
Gold, Thomas Ruggles, 1786
Gold, Thomas Augustus, 1808
Goodwin, Edward, 1823
Goodwin, Hiram Gould, 1823
Gould, George, 1827
Gould, James, 1795
Gould, James Reeve, 1824
Gould, William Tracy, 1818
Graham, Henry, 1804
Graham, John Lorimer, 1812
Grant, William A., 1823
Grant, William Joshua, 1823
Graves, Thomas C., 1808
Gray, Thomas, 1817
Green, Caleb, Jr., 1830
Greene, Albert Collins, 1812
Greene, Benjamin Daniel, 1813
Green, Henry Woodhull, 1823
Greene, Richard Ware, 1812
Greene, William, 1817
Griffin, George, 1798
Griswold, Shubael Flagg, 1809
Groome, John Charles, 1824
Gunn, Frederick, 1812
Gustin, Alpheus, 1819
Gwathmey, Isaac R., 1813

Hadnall, William B., 1819
Hall, Ambrose, 1802
Hall, Benjamin, 1796
Hall, Gideon, Jr., 1829
Hall, Horace, 1803
Hall, Willis, 1826
Halsey/Holsey, Hopkins, 1819
Halsted/Halstead, Robert W., 1827
Halsted, William, Jr., 1814
Hamilton, Thomas Napier, 1810
Hand, Augustus Cincinnatus, 1827
Harrison, Tipton B., 1818
Harvey, Leroy, 1821
Hasbrouck, Abraham Bruyn, 1812
Hasell, Bentley, 1825
Hatch, Moses, 1801
Hawkes, Benjamin B., 1821
Hawks, Francis Lister, 1818
Hawkins, Samuel, 1798
Hawley, Charles, 1813
Hawley, William, 1788
Hayden, Moses, 1804
Head, George Edward
Hepburn, Joseph L., 1819
Heyward, Benjamin, 1795
Hicox, Guy, 1806
Hill, Joseph Alston, 1819
Hill, William R., 1821
Hillhouse, Augustus Lucas, 1812
Hine, Homer, 1800
Hines, Richard, 1814
Hinman, Royal Ralph, 1806
Hitchcock, Samuel Johnson, 1809
Hitchcock, Samuel, 1828
Hodges, William Franklin, 1812
Holabird, William S., 1815
Holcomb, Chauncey Pettibone, 1824
Holley, Mr., 1820
Holley, John Milton, Jr., 1823
Holmes, Uriel, 1785
Holt, George B., 1812
Holt, Thaddeus Goode, 1816
Hooker, James, 1810
Hoopes, W.L., 1812-, 1813
Hopkins, Abiathar, 1808
Hopkins, Samuel Miles, 1791
Hotchkiss, Minor, 1813
Houghton, Josiah, 1817
Houston, Patrick, 1798
Howard, Benjamin Chew, 1812
Howard, John H., 1813
Howe, Samuel, 1805
Hoyt, Henry Sheaff, 1829
Hubbard, Elijah, 1796
Hubbard, Elizur, 1799
Hubbell, James, 1802
Hudson, Jonathan Trumbull, 1826
Huffington, William, 1823
Hull, Hezekiah T., 1813
Humphrey, Joseph Drake, 1812
Hunt, Hiram P., 1817
Hunt, Jonathan, 1808
Hunt, Nathaniel, 1797
Hunt, R., 1813
Hunt, Ward E., 1830
Huntington, Jabez Williams, 1808
Hyde, John Jay, 1829
Ingersoll, Charles Medifer, 1812
Ingersoll, David Bryan, 1792
Ingham, Alpheus, 1825
Ives, Henry C., 1831
Ives, Moses Brown, 1812
Ives, Thomas, 1778
Jackson, Ebenezer, Jr., 1814
Jackson, John Peter, 1824
Jackson, Joseph Webber, 1817
Jackson, Oliver P., 1823
Jackson, Thomas L., 1823
Jacobs, Cyrus H., 1832
Jacobs, George Washington, 1819
Jacobs, William Charles, 1820
James, Edward N., 1805
Janvier, Thomas, Jr., 1828
Jarvis, Russel, 1815
Jenkins, Charles M., 1831
Jesup, Ebenezer, Jr., 1825
Jewell, Ezra, 1809
Johns, Kensey, Jr., 1812
Johnson, Charles Frederick, 1824
Johnson, Edwards, 1826
Johnson, James Slidell, 1816
Johnson, William Samuel, 1816
Johnston, James T., 1816
Joline, John E., 1796
Jones, Ebenezer, 1817
Jones, Henry, 1810
Jones, Joel, 1819
Jones, John Quentin, 1817
Jones, Rice, 1807
Jones, Robert, 1813

Judson, Noah, 1799
Kellogg, Edward, 1823
Kelso,Charles William, 1828
Kerr, Joseph C., 1817
Key, Philip Barton, 1829
Keys, Eleazer W., 1795
Kilbourn, Austin, 1821
King, Edward, 1813
King, George Gordon, 1826
King, James Gore, 1810
Kingsbury, John, 1788
Kingsbury, John, 1809
Kingsbury, Sanford, 1801
Kinnicutt, Thomas, 1823
Kirby, Abraham, 1780
Kirby, Reynold Marvin, 1809
Kirkland, Charles Pinckney, 1818
Knight, Frederick, 1812
Lake, Joseph, 1820
Lamar, Lucius Quintus Cincinnatus, 1817
Langdon, Benjamin F., 1821
Langdon, Chauncey, 1787
Lansing, Leviness S., 1830
Larned, George, 1795
Lashels, John, 1810
Latham, Allen, 1814
Law, Lyman, 1791
Law, Samuel Andrew, 1793
Lawrence, Augustine N., 1813
Lawrence, Philip Kissic, 1814
Lawrence, William Beach, 1819
Leavenworth, Elias Warner, 1825
Leavenworth, Nathan, 1813
Leavenworth, William Curtiss, 1822
Leavitt, Harvey Freegrace, 1816
Ledyard, Henry, 1830
Leonard, Cornelius Van Vechten, 1810
Lewis, Daniel Wadsworth, 1791
Lewis, John Lawson, 1825
Lewis, Robert H., 1821
Lewis, William, 1817
Lide/Lyde, Mr. pre-, 1800
Livingston, Carrol, 1827
Livingston, Henry Walter, 1820
Livingston, James Kane, 1818
Livingston, John R, 1823
Livingston, Robert Cambridge, 1829
Livingston, Walter C., 1820
Livingston, William, 1817
Lloyd, Joseph Ross, 1818
Lockwood, Ephraim, 1798
Long, Richard Harrison, 1813
Longstreet, Augustus Baldwin, 1813
Loring, Charles Greely, 1813
Loring, Edward Greely, 1822
Lothrop, Cyrus H., 1810
Lott, Adrian, 1831
Low, Cornelius F., 1812
Lowery, Romeo, 1819
Lowndes, Benjamin, 1825
Lucas, William, 1817
Ludlow, Alfred Gulian, 1822
Lundy, Ethelred H., 1818
Lyman, Darius, 1811
Lyman, Samuel Fowler, 1819
Lyman, Theodore, 1811
Mc Cawley, Robert, 1822
Mc Clean, James G., 1822
Mc Elhenny, James, 1822
Macfarland, William H., 1818
McKaleb, Joseph A., 1829
McKaleb, William, 1827
Mack, Elisha, 1805
Mackie, Peter, Jr., 1813
Maer/Mayer, Abraham, 1817
Magruder, Enoch, 1816
Mallery, Garrick, 1810
Man, George Flagg, 1826
Mann, Horace, 1822
Mansfield, Edward Dering, 1823
Marbury, John, 1813
Markley, Benjamin A., 1806
Marsh, Charles, 1787
Marsh, Charles, Jr., 1813
Marsh, Samuel, 1787
Martin, Joseph Foster, 1818
Martin, William Dickinson, 1810
Marvin, Ebenezer, Jr., 1799
Mason, Hezekiah Day, 1822
Mason, John Young, 1817
Mason, William Alexander, 1811 or 1814?
Mason, William, 1821
Mather, Nathaniel, 1811
Maxcy,Virgil, 1805
Maxwell, Joseph, 1817
Maxwell, Robert, 1817
Mayer, John B., 1823
Mayo, Harman B., 1821
Mayson, Charles C., 1814
Merwin, Elijah Bottom, 1801

Metcalf, Theron, 1806
Middleton, Henry, 1817
Middleton, Henry Augustus, 1815
Miller, Fleming Bowyer, 1817
Miller, Charles, 1818
Miller, Joseph, 1801
Miller, Morris, 1798
Miller, Rutger Bleecker, 1824
Miller, Solomon Samuel, 1811
Mi, Michael Frederick, 1801
Mi, Roger, 1798
Miner, Phineas, 1796
Minor, Alexander, 1797
Minturn, Thomas R., 1826
Mitchell, Charles, 1804
Mitchell, Donald Grant, 1792
Mitchell, Henry A., 1826
Mitchell, Lewis C., 1807
Mitchell, Louis, 1813
Mitchell, Stephen Mix, 1800
Mitchell, Walter, 1796
Moffit, Thomas, 1816
Moore, Robert, 1822
Morris, Henry, 1826
Morris, James E., 1803
Morrison, James, 1809
Morse, Sidney Edward, 1814
Morson, Arthur Alexander, 1823
Morton, Marcus, 1806
Moseley, Charles, 1806
Mumford, William Woolsey, 1815
Munger, Warren, 1811
Nash, Losson/Lonson, 1803
Neill, George B., 1829
Nelson, Armistead, 1814
Newcomb, Isaac Mead, 1828
Nicoll, Edward, 1813
Nichols, Joseph Hulbert, 1827
Nicoll, John C., 1814
Nisbet, Eugenius Aristides, 1823
Nixon, Henry George, 1820
North, Theodore, 1808
Norton, James Clinton, 1819
Nutall, William B., 1823
Oakley, Jesse, 1814
Ogden, Matthias B., 1813
O'Hara, Arthur Harper, 1814
Olcott, Theophilos, 1801
Oliver, Henry, 1821
Oliver, Samuel White, 1820
Olmsted, Charles Goodrich, 1810
Ormsbee, Edgar Leonard, 1824
Orne, Henry Harvey, 1811
Overton,Thomas Bleasdale, 1813
Page, Benjamin, 1805
Page, Henry, 1816
Paine, Elijah, Jr., 1815
Painter, Alexis, 1817
Parker, Amasa, 1809
Parker, Aurelius Dwight, 1826
Parker, Charles Tarbell, 1828
Parker, William M., 1820
Parrott, Abner B., 1821
Parsons, Anson Virgil, 1825
Pasteur, Edward Griffith, 1823
Patton, Robert Bridges, 1814
Patterson, Christopher Stuart, 1821
Payson, Charles, 1811
Pearce, Amos, 1786
Peck, William Virgil, 1824
Pell, Duncan Campbell, 1826
Penny, Samuel, Jr., 1828
Perkins, Charles, 1813
Perkins, Thomas Shaw, 1812
Petit/Pettet, Joel T., 1800
Petit, William W., 1815
Pettibone, Augustus, 1788
Pettibone, Sereno, 1802
Phelps, Charles B., 1806
Phelps, Edward Arah, 1828
Phelps, Elisha, 1801
Phelps, Jedediah, 1810
Phelps, Oliver Leicester, 1794
Phelps, Samuel Shethar, 1811
Pickett, Reuben, 1825
Pickett, William Dickson, 1826
Pierce, James, 1798
Pierce / Peirce/ Pearce, Levi, 1815
Pierce, William Leigh, 1809
Pierpont, John, 1809
Pierpont, John, 1825
Pierson, George, 1830
Pibury, William, 1813
Pitcher, John, 1815
Pitcher, Philip E., 1828
Pitt, John Robbins, 1816
Plant, David, 1804
Player, Thompson Trezevant, 1826
Poe, Washington, 1823
Polk, Thomas Gilchrist, 1811

Porter, George Bryan, 1812
Porter, Peter Buell, 1791
Porter, Timothy Hopkins, 1807
Porteous, John, 1800
Post, Alfred L., 1832
Potter, Ansel, 1805
Potter, Asa, 1826
Prentice, Henry Epaminondas, 1832
Preston, Isaac Trimble, 1812
Price, Benjamin, 1820
Pumpelly, George James, 1826
Putnam, Austin, 1828
Putnam, Charles Samuel, 1814
Rankin, Robert Gozman, 1827
Raymond, Daniel, 1810
Raymond, David Hillhouse, 1812
Raymond, James, 1820
Rayner, Benjamin Lester, 1824
Read, George 3rd, 1808
Read, John Dickinson, 1823
Read, John Harleston, 1809
Read, William Thompson, 1812
Rees, William James, Jr. prior to, 1801
Reeve, Aaron Burr, 1802
Reynolds, Walter, 1822
Richards, George Hallam, 1809
Richards, Henry Smith, 1826
Richards, Robert Kerr, 1829
Ridgate, Benjamin C., 1814
Ridgely, Greenberry William, 1816
Ridout, Addison, 1813
Robbins, Samuel Hinkley, 1817
Robbins, Silas Webster, 1808
Robert, Daniel, 1811
Rogers, Archibald Gracie, 1823
Rogers, Artemas, 1811
Rogers, Charles William, 1829
Rogers, Edward, 1810
Rogers, Henry, 1823
Rogers, Henry Augustus, 1821
Rogers, Henry Bromfield, 1823
Rogers, Henry William, 1810
Rogers, John, 1813
Rogers, Moulton Cropper, 1807
Rogers, William M. Horsey, 1829
Ross, Thomas, 1827
Ruggles, Heman, 1803
Ruggles, Henry Joseph, 1832
Ruggles, Philo, 1790
Rutherford, John, 1829
Rutherford, Robert Walter, 1806
Rutledge, Benjamin Huger, 1817
Saltonstall, Dudley, 1791
Sampson, John Philpot Curran, 1817
Samuel, Beverly, 1819
Sanford, Nathan, 1798
Sanford, Rollin, 1831
Sankey, Joseph S., 1826
Sargent, William FitzWinthrop, 1817
Saunders, Curtius H., 1833
Savage, Thomas, 1792
Schell, Augustus, 1831
Schley, John Thomas, 1828
Schuyler, Robert Sands, 1818
Scott, Jessup W., 1822
Scott, John Ray, 1807
Scudder, Philip Johnston/Johnson, 1813
Sedgwick, Henry Dwight, 1807
Sedgwick, Philo Collins, 1831
Selden, Ulysses, 1802
Sewall, William Henry Brent, 1816
Seymour, Henry, 1829
Seymour, Horatio, 1798
Seymour, Isaac Gurdon, 1825
Seymour, Origen Storrs, 1824
Seymour, Ozias, 1821
Shaffer, Joseph L., 1825
Shaumburgh, Charles W., 1827
Shaw, Henry, 1810
Sheldon, Daniel, Jr., 1798
Sheldon, Isaac, 1810
Sheldon, William, 1822
Shelton, Stephen T., 1799
Shepherd, Samuel, 1799
Sherman, Elkanah C., 1825
Sherman, Roger, Jr., 1792
Sherman, Roger Minott, 1794
Sherrill, Joseph, 1815
Sill, Theodore, 1798
Simkins, Eldred, 1803
Simons, Edward Peter, 1815
Simons, Moses, 1810
Sims, John Green, 1812
Skinner, John Burr, 1820
Skinner, Oliver, 1800
Skinner, Richard, 1798
Skinner, Roger Sherman, 1815
Sloan, Douglass Wheeler, 1804
Slosson, Barzillai, 1830
Smallwood, William A., 1824

Smith, Aaron, 1791
Smith, Archibald, 1814
Smith, Charles, 1810
Smith, Henry Barney, 1809
Smith, Ira E., 1809
Smith, James H., 1818
Smith, John Cotton, 1788
Smith, Joseph Lee, 1800
Smith, Junius, 1802
Smith, Lemuel, 1817
Smith, Levi Bull, 1825
Smith, Nathan, 1790
Smith, Nathaniel, 1786
Smith, Nathaniel Benedict, 1817
Smith, Perry, 1807
Smith, Truman, 1817
Southmayd, Samuel W., 1793
Spaight, Charles George, 1822
Sparks, William Henry, 1820
Spaulding, Richard B., 1809
Speed, Robert H., 1827
Spencer, Alexander O., 1818
Spencer, Charles, 1817
Spencer, Oliver M., 1829
Spires, Brancey T., 1832
Spooner, William Jones, 1813
Sprague, Peleg, 1813
Stagg, Peter P., 1823
Stanley, Henry, 1801
Stansbury, George Alexander, 1827
Staples, Seth Perkins, 1798
Stark, Caleb, Jr., 1823
Starke, Wyatt Waites, 1811
Starr, Ephraim, Jr., 1803
Starr, Henry, 1809
Steele, William F., 1814
Stephens, John Lloyd, 1822-, 1824
Sterling, Elisha, 1789
Sterling, Micah, 1804
Sterret,William P., 1821
Sterrett, John A., 1822
Stevens, Henry Wilburne, 1811
[Stevens, Allen?]
Stevens, James, 1796
Stevens, Thomas, 1823
Stewart, Charles Samuel, 1817
Stiles, Joseph Clay, 1817
Stites, Richard Wayne, 1822
Stoddert, John Truman, 1813
Stone, Gregory D., 1823
Storrs, Juba, 1806
Strobel, Martin, 1806
Strong, Elisha Beebe, 1810
Strong, Martin, 1801
Strong, Moses McCure, 1830
Strong, Theron Rudd, 1822
Stuart, Francis Henry, 1809
Stuart, Josephus B., 1812-, 1813
Sullivan, James, 1822
Sutherland, Josiah, Jr., 1825
Swan, Cyrus, 1796
Sweezy, Thomas, 1811
Swift, Benjamin, 1801
Swift, George, 1816
Swift, Milton Homer *** c. 1837
Swift, William, 1817
Tabor, William J., 1813
Taliaferro, William Francis, 1813
Tallmadge, Frederick Augustus, 1811
Tatnall, Edward Fenwick, 1810
Taylor, Edwin Mygatt, 1832
Taylor, Hubbard, 1810
Taylor, James Simon, 1818
Taylor, John Gilman, 1803
Taylor, William Jesse, 1828
Teackle, James Henry Dennis, 1817
Telfaire, Josiah, 1804
Telfaire, Thomas, 1806
Tenney, William, 1809
Terry, Alfred, 1823
Thayer, James, 1815
Thomas, Alexander, 1810
Thompson, Charles, Jr., 1799-, 1800
Thompson, Charles, 1812
Thompson, James, 1790
Thompson, Henry, 1814
Thorndike, Larkin, 1809
Thweatt, Uriah, 1802
Tod, George, 1796
Todd, Charles Scott Stewart, 1810
Tolman, Thomas William, 1813
Torrey, Charles, 1814
Tracy, George H., 1830
Tracy, Uriah, 1778
Treat, Selah B., 1825
Trescot, Henry, 1816
Trotter, James Gabriel, 1809
Troup, Robert R., 1809
Tucker, George Joseph, 1824
Turner, Bates [1780]

Tuthill, Cornelius, 1815
Twining, Stephen, 1796
Twining, Thomas, Jr., 1814
Tyler, Nathan, 1820
Upson, Stephen ca., 1804-5
Vanderheyden, Samuel D., 1820
VanDeursen, William, 1803
Van Dyke, Kensey Johns, 1818
Vanmeter, John Inskeep, 1821
Van Wagenen, Gerritt, 1823
Verplanck, James Delancy, 1827
Wadhams, Noah, 3rd, 1791
Wager, John William Stem, 1823
Wakeman, Jonathan, 1807
Walburg, George M., 1815
Waldo, William Besley, 1828
Walker, Charles, 1822
Walker, George Josiah Sturges, 1826
Wallace, James Wilson, 1829
Ward, Isaac, 1813
Ward, Richard Ray, 1817
Ward, Solomon, 1802
Ware, Nicholas, 1792
Waring, Nathaniel F., 1827
Warner, Ely, 1808
Warner, Thomas, 1809
Waterhouse, Andrew Oliver, 1811
Waterman, Thomas Glasby, 1806
Watkins,George Claiborne, 1833
Watson, Henry, 1817
Watson, John Bliss, 1815
Watson, Samuel, 1826
Watson, William, 1831
Webber, Sumner Allen, 1823
Weeks, Alfred Augustus, 1823
Weems, James J., 1820
We, Ralph, 1812
We, Thomas Lawrence, 1823
Wetmore, William Courtney, 1815
Wheeler, Justus Perry, 1804
White, John Phillips, 1799
White, Thomas, 1816
White, William, 1818
Whiting, John C., 1823
Whitman, John, 1808
Whitman, Lemuel, 1805
Whittlesey, Elisha Dana, 1813
Whittlesey, Frederick, 1819
Whittlesey, Roger, 1788
Whittlesey, Thomas Tucker, 1818
Wight, John L., 1824
Wilkins, Edmund, 1817
Wilkins, John Limbrey, 1820
Wilkins, William Wyche, 1793
Williams, David, 1816
Williams, Elisha, 1792
Williams, Henry F., 1815
Williams, Jared Warner, 1820
Williams, Lemuel, 1806
Williams, Thomas Scott, 1796
Williams, William Gillett, 1799
Wilson, Andrew Porter, 1825
Winship, John Cravath May, 1810
Winslow, Edward D., 1831
Wittich, Lucius L., 1824
Wolcott, Frederick, 1787
Wolcott, Oliver, Jr., 1778
Wolcott, Oliver Stoughton, 1818
Wood, Bradford Ripley, 1825
Wood, James, 1798
Woodbridge, William, 1802
Woodbury, Levi, 1809
Woodruff, Ezekiel? c. 1779 / or, 1809??
Woodruff, George Catlin, 1825
Woodruff, Lewis Bartholomew, 1830
Wooldridge, Thomas, 1815
Worthington, Perry, 1831
Wright, Augustus Romaldus, 1833
Wright, John Crafts, 1808
Yates, Metcalf, 1821
Yates, William, 1824
Young, Charles Clark, 1827
Young, Ebenezer, 1809

C. The Commentators

Chapter 16

Chancellor Kent and the History of Legal Literature

1993

John H. Langbein

John Langbein is Chancellor Kent Professor of Law and Legal History at Yale Law School. This article first appeared in 93 *Columbia Law Review* 547 (1993).

Author's note: I am indebted to several archivists for helping me use their collections, especially Billy Aul at the New York State Library in Albany; Whitney Bagnall at Columbia Law Library; and Nancy Lyons at Yale University, Sterling Library, Manuscripts and Archives. I am grateful for references and suggestions from John Cairns, Morris Cohen, Robert Gordon, Fred Konefsky, Klaus Luig, William E. Nelson, Mark Ouweleen, Donald Roper, Fred Shapiro, Peter Stein, Alan Watson, and Ruth Wedgwood. Regarding the citation practices used in this article for manuscript and other antiquarian sources, see *infra* note 14.

Those of us who live much of our lives in or near law libraries tend to take our law books for granted. If, however, we pause to look, we find that our law reports, statute books, treatises, practice manuals, encyclopedias, legal periodicals, and the rest are the products of a long and fascinating history. The forms of legal literature undergo ceaseless cycles of innovation, maturation, and decay.

We are living through an age of extreme flux in the character of American legal literature. The genre of legal literature that epitomized the later nineteenth and early twentieth centuries, the treatise, is in propitious decline. The law school casebook, which a century ago was a pristine collection of appellate cases, has metastasized into what is sometimes called the coursebook, a cross between casebook and treatise. The law reviews, which originated to serve practicing lawyers and judges, are now largely directed inward toward the greatly expanded audience in legal academia. New forms of literature have burst upon us—in particular, the loose-leaf services and electronic databases—that are transforming our ideas about law reporting and legal research. These changes in the character of our legal literature are intimately connected to changes in the practice and administration of the law, to changes in legal education and legal theory,[1] and to the astonishing advance of new information technologies.

13. James Kent (1763-1847), twice professor at Columbia College, as well as Chancellor of New York. His later lectures became the basis for his *Commentaries on American Law,* essential for American lawyers and students for the rest of the century. (*Courtesy of Art & Visual Materials, Special Collections Department, Harvard Law School Library.*)

This Article is devoted to an earlier cycle of the history of American legal literature, the period that Roscoe Pound aptly called "the formative era."[2] My purpose is to examine the role of that legendary figure, Chancellor Kent, in the origins of American legal literature. James Kent has long been a figure of renown, especially at Columbia, where his appointment as professor of law in 1793 inaugurated legal education at the University. Kent reworked his second set of lectures, presented at Columbia in the 1820s, into the Commentaries on American Law,[3] the most influential American law book of the antebellum period. Columbia derived enormous luster from the success of Kent's Commentaries, and the Columbia Law School has ever since burnished its link to Kent, for example, through the school's former seat in Kent Hall, the designation of outstanding students as Kent Scholars, Columbia's Kent professorship, and the archival holdings of Kent's books and papers that figure centrally in this Article.

Long before Kent put pen to paper for the Commentaries, however, he was already a famous figure in American law. Indeed, writing the Commentaries was a project that Kent undertook in his mid-sixties after a quarter-century on the New York state bench. His reputation then rested upon what we continue to regard as the most characteristic genre of Anglo-American legal literature, the printed law report. In ways that I shall explain in Part III of this Article, Kent had much to do with establishing what has become the vibrant tradition of law reporting in America.

As for Kent's book, the *Commentaries*, I shall ask you to see it in an unconventional light. I shall link it to another type of legal literature, called institutional writing. This genre came to its highest expression on the European Continent in the seventeenth and eighteenth centuries, but its roots stretch back almost two thousand years to the Institutes of Gaius. I shall explain in Part IV of this essay why I think it is illuminating to understand Kent's Commentaries as one of—indeed, perhaps the last of—the great institutionalist works.

I. Who Was Chancellor Kent?[4]

James Kent was a vigorous person. Although physically small, he was blessed with good health and immense energy. He was long-lived in an age when few people were. Kent was born in 1763 in the tiny village of Doanesburg, New York, in what is now Putnam County, near the Connecticut border in the Poughkeepsie region of the Hudson Valley.[5] His life spanned the French and Indian War, which was concluded by the Treaty of Paris in the year of his birth; the American Revolution, whose military engagements disrupted his youth; the formation of the Union, from which he emerged an ardent Federalist; the War of 1812, a war that he bitterly opposed; the organizing jurisprudence of John Marshall's Supreme Court, which Kent largely supported; the Jacksonian Age, which he detested; the opening of the American West; and the drift toward Civil War.[6] Kent died in 1847, vigorous into his eighties.[7] Across his long life, he tried his hand at a dazzling array of legal careers—attorney, state legislator, trial and appellate judge, master in equity, chancellor in equity, statutory compiler, law professor, and juristic writer.

A. Family and Schooling

Kent's grandfather, the Rev. Elisha Kent, was a Presbyterian clergyman who graduated Yale College in the Class of 1729.[8] Kent's father, Moss Kent, who graduated Yale College in the Class of 1752,[9] was a marginal lawyer [10] and farmer.[11] James Kent's mother died when he was seven years old.[12] Kent had a younger brother, Moss Junior (1766-1838), to whom he remained devoted throughout his life. Moss Junior became an upstate New York lawyer and later a Congressman.[13] James and Moss Junior corresponded in candor for fifty years, and much of what we know about Kent's personal life comes from their letters, which survive in the Kent Papers in the Library of Congress.[14]

At age five, Kent was boarded with his maternal grandfather in Norwalk, Connecticut, where he attended school for four years. Thereafter, he studied for several years at a Latin School in Danbury and privately with tutors.[15] Kent entered Yale College in September 1777 at the age of 14. There were 27 men in Kent's class of 1781, including Simeon Baldwin (1761-1851),[16] grandfather of the better known Simeon E. Baldwin (1840-1927).[17] Kent maintained a lifelong friendship with the elder Simeon Baldwin; the two corresponded for 65 years, and they were the last survivors of the Class of 1781.[18] When Kent looked back on his education at Yale from a distance of about 50 years, he remembered that he stood at the top of his class, but he deprecated that achievement on the ground that "the test of scholarship at that day was contemptible."[19]

Long Island Sound was a major theater of military operations during the first years of the Revolutionary War, and the war repeatedly interrupted Yale College during Kent's undergraduate career.[20] During Kent's freshman year, classes were relocated for safety to towns in the center of the state, away from the war zone along Long Island Sound.[21] Back at Yale for his junior year, Kent witnessed British troops land in West Haven and capture New Haven on July 5, 1779. During the same campaign, British forces burned the house of Kent's grandparents in Norwalk. Speaking at his fiftieth college reunion in 1831, Kent was still indignant about this torching of his childhood home.[22]

B. Legal Education

In the eighteenth century, organized legal education for the common law scarcely existed, either in England [23] or in America.[24] The Regiuschairs at Oxford and Cambridge were dedicated to Roman law.[25] Blackstone devised his course of lectures on English law for Oxford undergraduates in the 1750s, but more with a view toward giving civics lessons than training legal professionals. American university law schools were, for all practical purposes, nineteenth century foundations.[26] Thus, on either side of the Atlantic in the eighteenth century, if you meant to become a lawyer, you did it by combining personal study with some form of apprenticeship.[27]

Kent entered upon the study of law the way most Americans of his time did, by reading Blackstone. He later recalled: "When the College was broken up and dispersed in July 1779 by the British, I retired to a country village, and finding Blackstone's *Commentaries*, I read the 4th volume. . . . [T]he work inspired me at the age of 16 with awe, and I fondly determined to be a lawyer."[28] In November of 1781, a few months after leaving Yale, Kent commenced an apprenticeship in Poughkeepsie with Egbert Benson, a prominent lawyer who was then serving as the state attorney general.[29] Benson's next-door neighbor in Poughkeepsie was John Jay, the future Chief Justice of the United States and Governor of New York.[30] Jay would figure prominently in advancing Kent's career. Through his clerkship with Benson, Kent made his first acquaintance of the great figures of the day, including Jay, Alexander Hamilton, Aaron Burr, George Clinton, and even George Washington.[31]

Kent's clerkship with Benson lasted somewhat more than three years. During this time, Kent studied the standard English legal literature—Coke, Hale, and various "old books of practice"; he read parts of Blackstone "again and again."[32] Flailing around these raw materials without the guidance of organized legal education was a frustrating way to learn, even for somebody as clever and ambitious as Kent. A few months into his studies he complained to his friend Simeon Baldwin about having to sort through this "voluminous rubbish."[33]

C. Early Career

Kent was admitted to the bar in 1785 at the age of 21.[34] He promptly entered a partnership in Poughkeepsie with Gilbert Livingston, who was related to the great New York landowning family. The partners' law practice emphasized conveyancing and collecting debts, the staple work of country lawyers.[35] Kent also married in that year, to Elizabeth Bailey (1768-1851),[36] who was then 16. She was the daughter of the house in which he had lodged while clerking for Benson. Kent's papers are full of expressions of his devotion to her.[37] When Kent died in 1847, their marriage was in its sixty-third year. They had four children, of whom three survived to adulthood. Their son William (1802-61) became a New York lawyer and judge, and in 1846, the year before Kent died, William briefly succeeded Joseph Story as professor of law at Harvard.[38]

Kent had a life-long knack for turning disappointment to advantage. When the disruptions of the Revolutionary War shut down Yale College, Kent curled up with Blackstone and found himself a career. During his law partnership in Poughkeepsie, this pattern of profiting from adversity recurred. The partners' practice was only modestly successful, and Kent had time on his hands throughout the later 1780s and into the 1790s. Kent seized upon this underemployment to develop himself as a man of letters,[39] launching upon a prodigious and disciplined program of self-instruction that covered not only English and Continental law, but also classical and modern literature. Kent divided his day into an early morning session for Greek and Latin, then he attended to "law and business," and he concluded the day by reading French and English literature.[40] Kent would in due course bring this immense learning to bear on his judicial work and in the writing of his *Commentaries*. He observed in 1828 as he was completing the Commentaries that his personal library had come to number above 3,000 volumes, and that almost every book cited in the *Commentaries* "has a place in my own library."[41]

D. The Federalist Connection

During the period that Kent was underemployed in his law practice in Poughkeepsie, he seized the opportunity to forge personal and political links to the great figures of the Federalist Party in New York, above all Jay and Hamilton. These relationships resulted in his rapid preferment to the New York bench a decade later. Kent recalled that he "commenced in 1786 to be a zealous Federalist and read everything on politics. I got the Federalist [Papers] almost by heart, and became intimate with Hamilton."[42] Kent survived Hamilton by four decades and revered him all his life.[43]

In 1787 the Constitution makers in Philadelphia promulgated their wondrous text and sent it to the states for ratification. The New Yorkers met in convention at Poughkeepsie in June and July of 1788. Decades later Kent recalled the convention in a letter to Alexander Hamilton's widow:

> It formed the most splendid constellation of the sages and patriots of the Revolution which I had ever witnessed, and the intense interest with which the meeting of the Convention was anticipated and regarded can now scarcely be conceived and much less felt. As I then resided in that village, I laid aside all other business and avocations, and attended the Convention as a spectator, daily and steadily, during the whole six weeks of its sessions, and was an eye and an ear witness to everything of a public nature that was done or said.[44]

Soon Kent tried his hand at elective politics on behalf of the Federalists. In April 1790 and again in 1792, he won a seat in the New York State Assembly from Dutchess County.[45] Kent sided with the Federalists in the bitterly disputed gubernatorial election of 1792 between Clinton and Jay. The contest was thrown into the legislature and decided for Clinton on a shabby pretext that effectively reversed the electoral will,[46] but the future would be kinder to Jay, and Jay would repay Kent's support. The Federalists nominated Kent for a seat in Congress, but in January 1793 the anti-Federalist candidate, who was in fact Kent's wife's brother, defeated him at the polls.[47]

E. The Columbia Professorship

It was at this point that Kent made the riskiest decision of his life. He decided to throw over his life in Poughkeepsie and start again in New York City, dissolving his partnership with Livingston.[48] The move began disastrously. Kent did not attract law business,[49] and like many another newcomer to New York City he found the expenses of city life, even for staples, to be ruinous.[50] As he was struggling to establish his career, his firstborn child, a two-year-old daughter whom he adored, died of small pox. In a grieving letter, Kent told his brother: "I have been visited with a most dreadful calamity. My precious lovely daughter was buried yesterday. It has almost broke [her mother's] heart, and mine also. I feel myself bereft of all human comfort. . . . I have lost all consolation."[51]

It was at this juncture, undoubtedly the ebb tide of his life, with his family devastated and his career in seeming tatters, that Kent's fortunes began to revive. In December 1793, the trustees of Columbia College, a strongly Federalist lot that included Alexander Hamilton and John Jay,[52] appointed Kent to be the first incumbent of a new professorship of law.[53] Kent later attributed the appointment to his Federalist connections.[54] The post brought with it a secure annual income of £200, which came as a financial godsend.[55]

Kent prepared a course of lectures for delivery in the 1794-95 academic year. He presented the lectures twice a week for 13 weeks. Since university law schools did not yet exist, the intended audience for Kent's lectures would have been the undergraduate youths of Columbia College, together with auditors from among the practicing bar and their apprentices.[56] Blackstone's course for the young gentlemen at Oxford was doubtless an important model. The full text of Kent's lectures appears not to have survived,[57] but we do have the text of the first four lectures and a syllabus for the rest.[58] Kent's course commenced with some generalities of civics, including the law of nations, then advanced to the federal and state constitutions, and then took up property law.[59] Kent's initial lectures of the 1790s strike the modern reader as simplistic,[60] and that seems to have been the contemporary judgment as well. Kent initially thought that the lectures were a success,[61] but he soon learned that they were a flop. He later recounted the saga of this first teaching career:

> I read that season twenty-six lectures (two a week) and was honored by the attendance throughout the [1794-95] course of seven students and thirty-six gentlemen, chiefly lawyers and law students who did not belong to the college.[[62]] During my second course, commencing November, 1795, I read thirty-one lectures, in my office, and had only two students besides my clerks. The next season I attempted another course, but no students offering to attend, I dismissed the business, and in May, 1797, sent a letter of resignation to the trustees.[63]

In the light of hindsight, it seems that the failure of Kent's first undertaking in legal education was a failure in concept, perhaps in aspiration. University legal education was still a novelty in the Anglo-American world, and Kent had few models beyond Blackstone for what the enterprise might be about. Kent's instinct in 1794 was to simplify and popularize, but he aimed too low. Three decades later, when Kent next undertook a course of lectures, they were more substantial. The trustees of Columbia may have thought that the failure lay more with the idea of university legal education than with Kent's course, for when he resigned, Columbia let the professorship expire.

F. Path to the Bench

However badly Kent flopped in his maiden voyage as a law professor, the appointment to Columbia was the turning point in Kent's career. It bestowed legal-professional distinction upon him at a time when his law practice was not well-established. The stipend gave him financial security and freed up his other resources for real estate speculation, an endemic activity of the age.[64]

During the mid-1790s, events were occurring that propelled Kent to the New York bench. John Jay made a second, and this time successful, run for the Governorship of New York, and thereupon resigned the Chief Justiceship of the United States in 1796. As Jay was taking office in New York, there broke out the celebrated controversy over the unpopular "Jay Treaty" with Britain that Jay had negotiated on behalf of the United States. Kent actively defended Jay in the public prints.[65]

No sooner did Jay take office in New York than the spoils of gubernatorial favor descended upon Kent. In 1796 Jay appointed Kent to the office of master in chancery. This post was sufficiently remunerative to allow Kent to escape private law practice, which, he later confessed, "I always extremely hated."[66] The following year Jay appointed Kent to a part-time municipal court judgeship, as the Recorder of New York City. Jay intervened to see to it that Kent was able to keep both offices,[67] with the result that, as Kent happily wrote years later, "I made a great deal of money that year."[68]

A year later, in 1798, Jay appointed Kent, who was then 35 years old, to a vacancy on the New York Supreme Court. As Kent prepared to move back to Poughkeepsie and then to Albany to take up the judgeship, he reflected with evident satisfaction upon his five-year career in New York City, a career that had begun so disastrously:

> [S]o rapid a change in so short a space of time few persons have met with. I went to New York poor, without patronage [sic; "patrimony"?]. . . . In five years I had run through several honorable offices and attained [in the Supreme Court judgeship an office] of the highest respect in the community. I had collected not only a large and valuable library, and a neat and valuable stock of furniture, but I returned say at least £1000 richer than when I went.[69]

The judgeship, he wrote, had been "the grand object of my ambition for several years past," and would allow him, he hoped, to "display . . . my knowledge, talents and virtue. . . ."[70] He could not have known that he was embarking upon a 25-year judicial career that would change American law forever.

G. The New York Courts

The New York Supreme Court that Kent joined closely resembled the English common law courts of the day.[71] The Supreme Court was a collegial court of five judges, that although based in Albany, also sat in full session twice each year in New York City.[72] The court discharged routine trial work outside those cities by having the individual judges of the court ride circuit around the vast extent of New York State. Statute required these circuit courts to be convened in each county at least once a year.[73] The Kent Papers contain letters from Kent to his family describing his travels by stage or on horseback as he rode circuit.[74] These circuit tours could endure for several months at a stretch.[75]

Unlike the New England states and Pennsylvania, New York emerged from the American Revolution with a separate court of equity.[76] In New York, as in England, Chancery was a one-judge court. The Chancellor had his permanent seat in Albany but convened the court twice a year in New York City.[77] Appeal lay from either the Supreme Court or the Chancery to the Court of Errors, which was composed of the New York Senate together with the judges of the Supreme Court and the Chancellor. Combining upper-house legislators and judges into an appellate court imitated the English system of appellate review to the House of Lords.[78]

The Supreme Court judges and the Chancellor sat with the Governor of New York on a remarkable body known as the Council of Revision. The Council was responsible for reviewing bills enacted by the state legislature and for rejecting not only those that were constitutionally deficient, but also those that were, in the words of the Constitution of 1777, "inconsistent with the public good."[79] The Council of Revision thus enmeshed the judiciary in state legislative politics. Appointive judges, holding office until the constitutional retirement age of 60, exercised veto-like powers.[80] This messy confusion of legislative and judicial functions endured almost to the end of Kent's judicial career. The New York Constitutional Convention of 1821 abolished the Council.[81]

H. Judge and Jurist

Kent served on the New York Supreme Court for sixteen years, from 1798 to 1814. Six years into his term, in 1804, he became chief justice of the court. A decade later, in 1814, Kent left the Supreme Court to accept an appointment as Chancellor of New York.[82] Not much is known about why the appointment was offered or why Kent accepted it. Part of the attraction for Kent, who was then 50 years old, may have been the opportunity to escape the rigors of riding circuit in the wilderness. Kent served as Chancellor of New York for nine years. He left office against his wishes in July 1823 on his sixtieth birthday.[83] For reasons to be discussed, Kent's tenure in Chancery was particularly influential, and he continued to be known as Chancellor Kent throughout his life.

Like many other involuntary retirees, Kent resented being forced from office and fretted about what to do with himself. He toyed with the idea of setting up a proprietary law school in Albany modelled on Tapping Reeve's school in Litchfield.[84] Once again, Columbia intervened at a down moment in Kent's life, inviting him to be professor of law in Columbia College, a post that had not been filled since Kent resigned in 1797.[85] Kent leapt at the job.

Kent moved back to New York City and began lecturing in February 1824.[86] He also set up a consulting law practice that flourished.[87] Within a few months, Kent was mulling the idea of publishing his lectures in the work that became Kent's *Commentaries on American Law*.[88] He revised the lectures, presented them once more in the 1825-1826 academic year,[89] and never again lectured at Columbia. In the published *Commentaries*, Kent emphasized in the preface that the work originated as lectures at Columbia, and he numbered his units in "lectures" rather than "chapters."[90]

Volume One of the *Commentaries* appeared in 1826, Volumes Two, Three, and Four in 1827, 1828, and 1830.[91] The work was a huge commercial success. Kent took the book through five revisions in his own lifetime, and various editors updated it after his death.[92] Oliver Wendell Holmes prepared the twelfth edition in 1873.[93] The fourteenth and last edition appeared in 1896.[94] Kent had a variety of abridged editions produced for the student market.[95] In the 1840s, Kent's *Commentaries* was generating royalties of $5,000 per year, stupendous sums in those days. Contemporary opinion had it that no American book had ever earned so much money,[96] and Kent died rich enough to be included by the tax assessor on the list of New York's wealthiest persons.[97]

II. The Struggle for Learned Law

In the first decades of American independence there occurred a titanic struggle about the character of American law, especially at the state level. Arrayed on one side were people who were hostile to lawyers and legal doctrine. They viewed the legal system as serving an essentially arbitral function: Ordinary people, applying common sense notions of right and wrong, could resolve the disputes of life in localized and informal ways.[98] Opposing this vision of folk law were those who understood that the intrinsic complexity of human affairs begets unavoidable complexity in legal rules and procedures. With legal complexity comes legal professionalism. Specialists accumulate knowledge and skill in applying the law, and they assist clients both in the conduct of litigation and in the shaping of transactions to avoid litigation. The legal professionals insisted that law had to be, in this special sense, *learned.*

We know from the light of hindsight that the professionals won this contest between nostalgia and professionalism. The professionals had to make some concessions, such as popular election of judges and the entrenchment of civil juries.[99] In the end, however, American law came to be learned law, a body of law so strongly patterned on the learned English law that we still for many purposes think of the English and American legal systems as comprising an inseparable entity called Anglo-American law.

Chancellor Kent's reputation arises from this epoch in which legal professionals succeeded in defining the character of American legal institutions.[100] Kent and his contemporary and friend, Joseph Story, were the largest figures in this triumph of the learned law. Their triumph was all the more remarkable for having been achieved largely during the period—culminating in the Jacksonian age—in which the temper of American politics was hostile to their enterprise.

When Kent joined the New York Supreme Court in 1798, he found that the other judges were, in his view, "very illiterate as lawyers."[101] At least, however, the New York judges were lawyers, for not all American high court judges were.

> Two of the three justices of the highest court of New Jersey during the Revolution were not lawyers. Of the three justices in New Hampshire after independence, one was a clergyman and another a physician. A blacksmith sat on the highest court of Rhode Island from 1814 to 1818, and a farmer was chief justice of that state from 1819 to 1826.[102]

There was an occasion in which one of the farmer justices of the New Hampshire Supreme Court, sitting as a trial judge, instructed a jury that whereas the lawyers in the pending case "want to govern us by the common law of England . . . , common sense is a much safer guide for us. . . . A clear head and an honest heart are worth more than all the law of the lawyers."[103]

Mixed in with this belief in the legal capabilities of the common citizen was a strong sentiment of hostility to things English. The Americans had just fought the Revolutionary War to defeat English rule. Why, then, should Americans obey those pronouncements of English judges that were called the common law? The clearest expression of this sentiment came in various state statutes, such as a New Jersey act of 1799 that prohibited lawyers from citing in court any legal decision, opinion, commentary, digest, or lecture made or written in Great Britain since July 4, 1776.[104]

Kent devoted much of his career to overcoming populist impulses in legal administration [105] and to justifying the continued validity of the English common law in the new republic. Kent subscribed to the standard caveat that American courts should not apply English law in circumstances in which American conditions rendered it inappropriate. For Kent and persons of his persuasion, however, the presumption lay strongly with the inherited English law.[106] Writing to Simeon Baldwin in 1786, the youthful Kent disclosed that he had "a much higher veneration for [the English common law] than for our own decisions because . . . [the English decisions] were pronounced by Judges of vastly higher erudition and skill in the knowledge of the common law."[107]

Nearly thirty years later, sitting in the New York Court of Chancery, Kent took the same tack: "[T]he dignity or independence of our Courts is no more affected by adopting [English judicial precedents], than in adopting the English language. . . ."[108] For Kent, therefore, English law was as free of imperial taint as English grammar. Kent maintained that the common law of England should apply in America because the principles it embodied were universal. Kent's universalism was, of course, a natural-law theory,[109] and in the *Commentaries* he said as much, characterizing judicial decisions as "the application of the dictates of natural justice, and of cultivated reason, to particular cases."[110]

Both in his judicial opinions and in the *Commentaries*, Kent resorted incessantly to foreign law, especially to the French and Dutch juristic writers, and to the Code Napoleon.[111] Kent's impulse to consult foreign law is commonly mentioned as evidence of his great learning,[112] but the use of Continental legal materials served a strategic role in Kent's campaign to legitimate the English common law. Kent invoked foreign examples primarily to show that the foreign source was congruent with the result that the English common law reached.[113] This argument was another way of justifying the use of English judicial precedents. If the French and the Dutch and the Germans reached the same result, the result must flow from natural justice rather than from any peculiarly English circumstances or from English political authority.[114] Indeed, Kent was so enamored of this idea that it led him to assert a serious historical error: He repeatedly contended that English law was derived from Roman law.[115]

III. Kent and the Law Reports

In the campaign to make American law a "learned law" rooted in the English common law, Kent and his friend Story were artists who worked in three media—the published judicial opinion, juristic writing, and legal education.[116] Whereas legal education was a weak suit for Kent, he was hugely influential with his opinions and his *Commentaries*.

Kent left a memoir of sorts, written in 1828, in which he described the conditions that prevailed on the New York Supreme Court at the time of his appointment in 1798. "When I came to the bench there [were] no reports or State precedents. The opinions from the bench were delivered [orally],"[117] and thus largely lost to recollection, although in some states opinions were recorded in manuscript reports that were copied and circulated at the bar.[118] Early in his judicial career, Kent set out to overcome these features of New York law. He wanted to produce written opinions and get them reported.

A. Written Opinions and Law Reports

Because we are today so accustomed to the written opinion as the authoritative version of a judicial decision, we need to remind ourselves that the written opinion was a novelty in the later eighteenth century. In the English courts of that day, judicial decisions were rendered extemporaneously—indeed, modern English courts continue to render oral opinions at the close of the evidence. The great difference between the English and the American courts of 1798 was that in England there were systematic arrangements for law reporters to be present to record what the judges were saying.[119] The English reports were published under the names of the reporters,[120] hence the term "nominate reports," and were available as precedents in later cases. The nominate reports circulated in America as well as in England.[121]

Kent insisted upon preparing written opinions in every case that came before the full Supreme Court of New York.[122] His opinions were emphatically "learned," in the special sense that I have been using that word. When New York and American authorities were unavailable, as was frequently the case, Kent drew mainly upon English law reports and juristic literature, but also, as I have explained, on Continental sources. Kent recollected in a memoir that one of the reasons that he undertook to produce written opinions was to intimidate the other judges into acquiescing in his views.[123] Obviously, Kent had only one vote out of five, and it was easy enough for him to be outvoted in circumstances in which other members of the court genuinely differed with him. What Kent wanted most was to get control of the business of stating New York law on issues that were not particularly divisive. New York was the premiere American commercial jurisdiction, yet it had almost no reported case law of its own. Kent saw a golden opportunity to formulate a body of learned precedent.

Kent needed to do more than merely produce written opinions. He had to arrange for his opinions to be preserved and circulated. In short, he needed a series of law reports. In colonial America "the reporting of any decision was unusual,"[124] and this state of affairs lasted well into the early national period. When Kent ascended the bench in 1798, there existed only a few volumes of American law reports.[125] Ephraim Kirby published a volume of Connecticut reports in 1789 [126]—the first American reports—and a trickle of further Connecticut reports appeared in the 1790s.[127] Alexander Dallas put out a volume of Pennsylvania reports in 1790,[128] and another in 1799.[129] When the United States Supreme Court commenced operations in Philadelphia, Dallas included some of its decisions in his Pennsylvania series—and by this happenstance became the first Supreme Court reporter.[130] George Wythe published a volume of Virginia chancery reports in 1795,[131] and Bushrod Washington produced two further volumes of Virginia civil cases in 1798.[132] William Coleman published a volume of New York cases from the 1790s in the year 1801;[133] the work is rare and it may not have been well-marketed or well-received.

Thus, at the time Kent joined the New York bench, the impulse toward law reporting was traceable in several of the American states, but the individual state legal professions were small and the market for reports was relatively uninviting. A quarter-century after the outbreak of the American revolution, most American jurisdictions still depended almost exclusively on English law reports.[134] The Americans had not been able to organize an indigenous system of law reporting.

In 1804 New York and Massachusetts hit upon what was to become the American solution. The state legislatures provided for the designation of official reporters, who were paid stipends that effectively subsidized the reports.[135] Although this was a period in which Kent had close relations with the New York legislature, we are unable to say whether Kent had a hand in provoking the New York legislation. He had held a Federalist seat in the Assembly as late as 1797, on the eve of his judgeship. In 1800-1801 the legislature commissioned Kent and his fellow Supreme Court judge, Jacob Radcliff, to undertake a recompilation of all the New York State statutes, which the legislature enacted in 1801.[136] Moreover, the judges of the Supreme Court sat with the members of the New York Senate in the Council of Revision.[137] Hence, it is a good surmise, but only a surmise, that Kent used his legislative connections to arrange for the creation of the reportership he desperately wanted.

In 1804 a lawyer named George Caines won the new post of official law reporter for the New York Supreme Court. He published a three-volume set entitled *Caines' Reports*.[138] Kent's copies of *Caines' Reports* survive in the New York State Library in Albany. By the time Caines' first installment of 107 pages appeared, Kent had concluded that Caines was incompetent. Kent wrote on his copy of the advance sheets that "the work is too full of mistakes."[139]

B. The Role of the Law Reporter

The idea that a law report can be full of errors may not strike the modern lawyer as particularly likely. Among the things lawyers worry about in the study and practice of the law, the fidelity of law reports is not included. It is hard to see how a law reporter can botch. Today's American reporter is a ministerial entity, an organization that scoops up whatever the judges drop in the reporter's in-basket. The reporter usually adds headnotes, such as those in the West Key Number system, but otherwise the reporter does little more than supervise publication of a product that has emerged in final form from the judge's chambers.

In the eighteenth century, however, the reporter had a much larger role than we now expect in the production of the reported opinion. Consider, for example, the most influential law reports of the years when Kent joined the New York bench, the King's Bench Reports of Charles Durnford and Edward Hyde East.[140] Durnford and East's so-called *Term Reports* display a number of striking differences from modern reports. The West Publishing Company exercises virtually no discretion in the selection of its cases. By contrast, in the age of the nominate reporters like Durnford and East, it was the reporter and not the judges who had the final say about which cases would be reported.

A reported English case from the end of the eighteenth century has a format nearly as stylized as the movements of an eighteenth-century concerto: facts, argument, opinion. The report begins with a statement of the facts of the case. The reporter, not the judge, supplied this statement—based on what the reporter heard in court and what he read in the pleadings. Next comes the reporter's account of the arguments of counsel—something we have ceased to care about in our modern American reports. Part of the explanation for the interest in counsel's arguments is that, in a procedural system in which pleading could still be of decisive importance, the lawyers' courtroom moves were potentially more consequential than in modern litigation.

Finally, after the facts and the arguments comes the opinion. Because judges were still rendering their opinions orally, the reporter quite literally wrote the report. Accordingly, the reporter needed shorthand or other note-taking skills to capture accurately what the judges said, as well as considerable legal knowledge in order to decide which of the judges' observations to preserve. The nominate reporter supplied what today would be called headnotes, often printed in the margins, identifying the main questions being discussed in the case. The reporter also felt free to insert additional annotations in footnotes or in marginalia, supplying references or authorities beyond those mentioned by the court.

In a style of law reporting that remitted so much discretion to the reporter, it mattered desperately that the reporter be competent. The various English nominate reporters from the seventeenth and eighteenth centuries have reputations as distinctive as Bordeaux vintages, ranging from the widely admired to the greatly disparaged.[141]

Perhaps the attribute of the nominate law reports that the modern lawyer finds most striking is that, even after judges assumed responsibility for writing their own opinions, it was still the reporter rather than the judges who formulated the published statement of facts. By contrast, in modern practice we regard the statement of facts as a critical part of the judge's opinion. Edward Levi's famous account of the dynamic of the common law starts with the insight that our notion of precedent depends on the court's control of the fact statement.[142] A modern court carefully matches its legal rationale to its version of the facts.[143] How, then, could our judicial ancestors have relegated this vital work to reporters?

The answer, I think, has to do with the origins of the reporting tradition at common law. Judicial opinions began as extemporaneous oral explanations rendered immediately at the close of proceedings. When the opinion was addressed to the parties and to the lawyers who had just presented the facts to the court, there was no point in the judges restating the facts to people who were already fully conversant with them. The reported statement of facts was originally produced for readers who came to know the case only as a result of the reporter's intervention; telling them what the case was about was the reporter's job.

It was well into the nineteenth century, as the quantity of law reports mushroomed and other attributes of the system of large-scale administration of justice fell into place, that the modern conception of the law report came to prevail. The function of the judicial opinion changed. The modern judge addresses an opinion only incidentally to the parties and to the lawyers who argued the case. Especially for appellate judges, the primary audience is the readership of the published report. The main job is not explaining the outcomes to the immediate participants, but rather, generating precedents to guide future conduct and adjudication. Across the nineteenth century, Anglo-American judges came to sense this change, and they reacted to it by taking over from reporters the job of stating the facts.[144] That stage of development had not been reached during Kent's quarter-century on the bench. In Kent's day, the reporter remained a figure of great consequence—the person who selected the cases, stated the facts, summarized the views of counsel, summarized the views of those judges who gave oral opinions, and supplied annotations of his own.

C. William Johnson

Within about a year of his appointment as the first official law reporter for New York State, George Caines was out of the job. Just how Kent got rid of Caines we do not know, but it was Kent who arranged in 1805 for the appointment of Caines' successor, William Johnson.[145] Johnson held office throughout the remainder of Kent's judicial career, and the collaboration of Kent and Johnson had a deep influence on antebellum American law. As reporter for the New York Supreme Court, Johnson produced the 20 volumes of *Johnson's Reports* that cover the period from 1806 to 1823;[146] Kent ceased to appear in this series after Volume 11, when he left the Supreme Court to become Chancellor in 1814. In 1808 Johnson cobbled together a three-volume retrospective series of Supreme Court cases, known as *Johnson's Cases,*[147] which cover the years 1799 to 1803, roughly the period from Kent's accession to the bench until the start of *Caines' Reports.* Apparently as part of the deal by which Kent moved to Chancery in 1814, the legislature authorized the creation of an official Chancery reporter,[148] and Johnson assumed that position in addition to the Supreme Court reportership. He produced seven volumes of *Johnson's Chancery Reports* covering the years 1814-1823.[149] Kent was the only judge in Chancery in this period, and the Kent-Johnson collaboration reached its zenith in the Chancery Reports.

As Johnson's stream of New York reports grew, there arose a market for a reference work that would allow the legal researcher to locate relevant authority within the many volumes of reports. To meet this need, Johnson, in 1815, published a one-volume *Digest* of his and Caines' Supreme Court case reports;[150] in 1825 he produced a two-volume *Digest* that updated the work to 1823 and incorporated material from the *Chancery Reports* as well.[151] Johnson's *Digest* is in the abridgment tradition, those subject-indexed law finders that trace back to Statham's *Abridgment* in the 1480s and Fitzherbert's *Abridgment* in 1514.[152] The book served as a crude encyclopedia of New York decisional law, with titles in alphabetical order covering the major doctrinal and procedural topics, from "accords" to "writs."

Johnson's *Digest* was a tangible marker of how far Kent's campaign to create a state decisional law had progressed. Recall Kent's claim that when he went on the bench, "we had no law of our own, and nobody knew what it was."[153] Kent took immense pride in the accretion of precedents reflected in Johnson's *Digest.* He wrote in the flyleaf of his copy of the 1815 edition: "I was on the bench and took a part in every case and point decided in this volume. . . ."[154] Contemporaries such as Joseph Story understood and remarked upon the importance of the Kent-Johnson collaboration.[155] Kent felt himself so deeply in Johnson's debt that he dedicated the *Commentaries* to Johnson.[156]

Because Johnson was a central figure in the early history of American law reporting and in the saga of Chancellor Kent, I have struggled to learn more about Johnson. It has, alas, been tough going. Johnson left no memoirs, and he appears to have destroyed his papers.[157] Scattered correspondence to and from Johnson survives in the Kent Papers and in a few other manuscript collections, but on balance it seems unlikely that much will ever be known about Johnson. He was born in 1769, six years after Kent. He graduated Yale College in the Class of 1788.[158] He came from Middletown, Connecticut, but settled in New York City. He became a practicing lawyer,[159] but he was not particularly successful. He seems to have had enough time on his hands in the year before his appointment to the reportership that he was able to translate from the French and publish an 800-plus-page edition of Azuni's treatise on *The Maritime Law of Europe.*[160]

By 1794 Johnson was sharing lodgings in New York City with Elihu Hubbard Smith, a physician who graduated Yale College two years before Johnson.[161] Smith moved in a circle of cultured New York professional and business people, many of them Yale alumni, and Johnson may have found access to this world through Smith. A dozen or so of these people, including Smith, Johnson, and James Kent, had, by 1794, coalesced into a group that called itself the Friendly Club and met at each other's homes on Saturday nights to discuss literature and public affairs.[162] Two of the Friendly Club members, Smith and the dramatist and theatrical producer William Dunlap, kept diaries during these years.[163] These diaries establish that Kent and Johnson were in constant association from the mid-1790s, a decade before Kent summoned Johnson to the Supreme Court reportership.[164]

Judging by the diary entries, Johnson was a very self-effacing person. He is mentioned hundreds of times, yet neither diarist finds anything of note to say about him—no reflections, no adventures, no bon mots.[165] Kent clearly knew what he was doing when he installed Johnson as his law reporter. Johnson was learned and genteel, diligent but unambitious, a Federalist by disposition[166] and hence politically congenial, yet recessive in the extreme—in short, an ideal minion. Kent had found his Boswell, happily named Johnson.

As their working relationship developed across the years, Kent placed ever greater trust in Johnson, yielding to his criticisms and soliciting his advice about what to say in his opinions.[167] The two men were so closely identified that when Kent retired in 1823 in some political disfavor,[168] Johnson fell with him. Kent tried to protect Johnson from being replaced but could not. Kent wrote him on this occasion that "you retire with my gratitude, love, and admiration. If my name is to live in judicial annals, it will be in association with yours."[169]

Of Johnson's three series of reports that chronicle Kent's judicial work, the Chancery Reports were undoubtedly the most influential. Because Chancery was a one-judge court, Kent had the stage to himself. His judicial style was fully mature. Equity courts had emerged from the American revolution under a taint for several reasons, including their association with unpopular colonial governors and their jury-free civil procedure.[170] Even in England, much of the detail of equity law, including trusts and succession, had only recently developed.[171] Kent relished the opportunity to lay down the law on a fresh slate. He later recollected that when he was appointed Chancellor in 1814 there was no indigenous equity law: "*[N]ot a single decision, opinion or dictum of either of my two predecessors* . . . from 1777 to 1814 [was] cited to me or even suggested. I took over the court as if it had been a new institution, and never before known to the U.S."[172] Kent remarked that his object in preparing his Chancery opinions "was to discuss a point so as never to be teased with it again."[173]

Kent's Chancery decisions exemplify his campaign to entrench English decisional law as the foundation of American law. Within his first year on the Chancery bench, Kent trumpeted this theme anew: "The system of equity principles, which has grown up and matured in England . . . is a scientific system, being the result of the reason and labors of learned men for a succession of ages."[174] Accordingly, Kent says, it is his duty to "endeavor to transplant and incorporate all that is applicable in that system into [American law]."[175] Johnson's *Chancery Reports* were the only specialized American equity reports of their time, greatly enhancing their influence in other American states.[176]

IV. The Commentaries and the Institutionalist Tradition

Kent's *Commentaries* is a work that is commonly lumped together with Story's treatises and thereby placed at the relative beginnings of the grand nineteenth-century tradition of American treatise writing.[177] There is, indeed, a treatise-like depth to some portions of the *Commentaries*, and as a consequence, certain segments of the work were stripped out and sold as freestanding topical treatises. Kent's chapters on the law of nations, for example, were peddled in England under the title of Kent's *Commentary on International Law*.[178] Kent's chapters on American constitutional law were packaged as a one-volume work in North America and also translated for German,[179] Argentinean,[180] and Mexican editions.[181] Most remarkably, a selection of Kent's chapters on partnership, agency, contract and commercial law, insurance and maritime law, bailments and servitudes was published in Scotland in 1837 under the title, *A Practical Treatise on Commercial and Maritime Law*.[182] This Scottish edition supplies a wonderful demonstration of the point that Kent's *Commentaries on American Law* was at least as much a commentary on English law,[183] consistent with Kent's lifelong mission to entrench English law as the basis of a learned American law.

A. The Institutionalist Tradition

Notwithstanding the evident connections between Kent's *Commentaries* and the dawning treatise tradition, I think that the *Commentaries* is a work that is better understood as belonging to a different genre of legal literature, called the *institutes of national law*. This genre flourished on the European Continent in the seventeenth and eighteenth centuries.[184] Most of the European legal systems produced one or two prominent institutional writers. My suggestion is that the American legal system also produced an institutionalist work, namely Kent's *Commentaries*. In other words, it is instructive to see Kent's *Commentaries* not so much as an early treatise, but as a late institutionalist.

There are four major attributes of institutionalist legal literature. The most prominent feature is the breadth of subject matter. The distinguishing trait of institutionalist writing is the effort to be comprehensive, to describe the private law of an entire legal system in a single work. This breadth of field contrasts sharply with the treatise writer's effort to delimit a single topic in exhaustive depth.

Second, the institutes of national law are devoted to the task of defining national legal systems. The impulse to write these works in the seventeenth and eighteenth centuries came from the breakup of the European *ius commune* and the rise of the national legal systems.[185] The institutional writers identified the main elements of the private law of the particular state. They frequently struggled with the task of articulating the relations between older customary law, primarily the Roman law of the European *ius commune*, and the law of the nation-state. In countries such as France, the Netherlands, and Spain, the institutionalists were also attempting to unify divergent bodies of customary law. You will perhaps recall Voltaire's remark that, in journeying through France by stagecoach, the traveller was obliged to change laws as often as he changed horses.[186] Institutionalist writers undertook to unify divergent local customs in a variety of ways, most importantly by finding reasons for treating one body of regional law as presumptively superior. The French institutionalists gave this sort of primacy to the *coutume de Paris*, the Dutch used Holland, the Spanish writers used the law of Castille.[187] Thus, the institutionalist works commonly served the purpose of helping to create and to unify national legal systems.

Third, the institutes of national law have a pronounced didactic purpose. They are works of instruction, introducing neophytes to the law.[188] They speak not only to intending legal professionals, but to the educated classes in general. Sometimes these works arose in connection with formal university education, but commonly they were meant to serve in place of organized university education or in advance of it. The institutionalist writers often worked in the vernacular, whereas Latin had been the ordinary language of European law into the seventeenth century;[189] the use of the vernacular greatly enhanced the didactic power of these books.

Fourth, the institutes of national law are systematic works, and in a special way. Decisional law and legislation get accreted in bits and pieces as circumstances call them forth, but one cannot learn the law exclusively from the raw sources. The law has to be organized around categories and principles. This need to systematize was not a novel one, even in the seventeenth and eighteenth centuries. Rather, it had been faced in classical Roman law, in the textbook called the *Institutes of Gaius*,[190] which was written about the year 160 A.D.[191]

Gaius hit upon a scheme of organization that worked. Although his scheme was flawed, it proved adequate and became immensely influential. Gaius divided the law into three grand categories: persons, things, and actions. Under "persons" fell questions of status, including guardianship and family law. Under "things" Gaius dealt with property, succession, contracts, and tort. And under "actions" Gaius treated civil procedure. In 533 the emperor Justinian arranged for the publication of a comparable work, known as the *Institutes of Justinian*, which served as the officially authorized schoolbook companion to Justinian's compilation of Roman sources in the Digest.[192] Justinian's *Institutes* carried forward Gaius' system of organization—persons-things-actions—prefacing it with some observations about natural law and about the law of nations.[193]

From the time that Roman law began to be recovered and employed as the basic raw material of European private law in the eleventh century, Justinian's *Institutes* was the elementary text that was studied everywhere in Europe. It is not, therefore, surprising that Justinian's *Institutes* should have supplied a model to the learned writers of the seventeenth and eighteenth centuries who were undertaking to do for their legal systems what Justinian's *Institutes* had done for Roman law. These European writers did not imitate every attribute of Justinian's *Institutes*, but the basic format of persons-things-actions prevails through this body of literature.

B. The Later European Institutionalists

The burst of institutional writing began in France with Guy Coquille's *Institution au droit francais* in 1607.[194] There were several subsequent French works, including Gabriel Argou's *Institution au droit francais* in 1692 [195] and Claude Serres' *Les institutions du droit francais* in 1753.[196] In Holland, Grotius published his *Introduction to the Law of Holland* in 1631.[197] Other Dutch works of this character were published by Simon van Leeuwen in 1652, and Ulrich Huber in 1686.[198] In Scotland, where the law was deeply influenced by association with the Dutch, there appeared the three famous works,[199] Lord Stair's *Institutions of the Law of Scotland*, published in 1681;[200] Sir George Mackenzie's *Institutions of the Law of Scotland*, published in 1684;[201] and John Erskine's *Institutes of the Law of Scotland* in 1773.[202]

Within the German states there were many works that qualify as national institutes—Sebastian Khraisser's *Institutes* of Bavarian law in 1644[203] is an early example.[204] The works by Georg Beyer in 1718[205] and Johann Gottlieb Heineccius in the 1730s[206] were especially influential. In the Italian states, where resentment of Roman law was not so pressing, the institutionalist tradition was less prominent, but one can find examples: for Venice, in 1697, the work of de Pozzo;[207] for Naples, the works by Francesco Rapolla in 1746[208] and Oronzio Fighera in 1766.[209] In Scandinavia there was a comparable work on Swedish law by David Nehrman in 1729[210] and on Danish and Norwegian law by Laurids Norregaard in 1784-99.[211] In Spain the major work was the *Institutions of the Civil Law of Castille* by Asso and Manuel, published in 1771.[212] Perhaps the last of the acknowledged institutionalist books was one written for Hispanic America by Jose Maria Alvarez, under the title *Institutes of the Royal Law of Castille and the Indies*. The first edition appeared in Guatemala in 1818-1820;[213] further editions were published in Cuba, Mexico, and elsewhere as the young nation states of Latin America took shape.[214]

C. Blackstone's *Commentaries*

Recent scholarship has come increasingly to the view that Blackstone's *Commentaries on the Law of England*, which appeared in the years 1765-1769,[215] deserves to be seen as part of the institutionalist tradition.[216] Blackstone differs from the Continental and Scottish writers in important respects. English law did not need to be disentangled from antecedent Roman law, having developed since the Middle Ages on a path separate from the European *ius commune*. Moreover, English law did not require national unification.[217] The English traveler did not change laws when changing horses. Thanks to the precocious development of the medieval English monarchy and its administration, customary law in England had the character of national law, rather than the regional or provincial law that prevailed in France and elsewhere in Europe.

Blackstone did, however, have an organizational job to do that at least echoes the structural work of the Continental institutional writers. Blackstone wrote at a time when English law required redefinition. The medieval common law had been organized around the writs—that is to say, organized procedurally—but by the later seventeenth century the writ of trespass had captured most of private law, making the inherited writ-based scheme of organization obsolete. Much of what Blackstone achieved was a reorientation of the categories of English law away from the writs and toward modern notions of substantive law.[218] In the substantive categories he used, Blackstone was strongly influenced by the institutionalist tradition. Blackstone was deeply versed in Roman law, and the first three volumes [219] of Blackstone's *Commentaries* adhere straightforwardly to the persons-things-actions format. Contemporaries understood Blackstone's debt to the institutionalist tradition. Thomas Jefferson, for example, thought that Blackstone's *Commentaries* "rightfully tak[es] its place by the side of the Justinian Institutes."[220]

D. Kent's *Commentaries*

Blackstone supplied the inspiration both for the title of Kent's *Commentaries* and for the organization, although Kent made major departures from Blackstone in coverage. Kent was well-acquainted with Blackstone: Kent's Damascus, his conversion to a legal career, came about through his reading of Blackstone's *Commentaries*.[221] Across his lifetime Kent had also studied many of the Continental institutional writers, especially the French and the Dutch. In 1813 Kent wrote his brother Moss, the Congressman, who had some pending contact with a traveler to Europe, seeking Moss's help in obtaining a copy of Heineccius.[222] Kent prepared a list of his library in the 1840s that survives among the Kent manuscripts at Columbia.[223] Among the Continental institutes of national law that Kent owned were those of Argou, Huber, Heineccius, and Erskine, as well as many of the European works on natural law and the law of nations.[224]

If you are sensitive to the traits of institutionalist legal writing, you will have no difficulty detecting the main attributes in Kent's *Commentaries*. First, Kent's *Commentaries* has the characteristic breadth of an institutionalist work. It purports to treat American law in its entirety, although Kent in fact excluded many topics, as had the European writers. In Volumes Two, Three, and Four of the *Commentaries*, Kent started down the path toward the conventional persons-things-actions format, but, because he declined to cover procedure, he never got to actions. Kent also replaced the label "things" with the categories of "personal property" and "real property."

Volume One of Kent's book will throw you off the scent slightly if you are looking for the institutionalist tradition. Volume One contains a unit of just under 200 pages on the law of nations, and another 200-page unit on American constitutional and federal law. There was, of course, a vibrant European tradition of writing about the law of nations, beginning with the sixteenth-century Spaniards and continuing with the Dutch and other writers of the seventeenth and eighteenth centuries.[225] Kent merged his account of this subject within an otherwise institutionalist work. Recall, however, that the institutionalist tradition was not without precedent for this step. The preface to Justinian's *Institutes* touches on the law of nations, although quite perfunctorily,[226] as do various later institutional writers.[227]

Kent's inspiration to include a substantial account of American constitutional and federal law may have come from Blackstone's Volume One.[228] Half of Blackstone's book on the law of persons is devoted to the monarch, parliament, and executive powers.[229] This confusion of governmental functions with the law of persons may have suggested to Kent the further refinement of placing a unit on the structure of government in the front of an institutionalist work. Kent's treatment of constitutional law is not particularly insightful; and Story's three-volume treatise on the Constitution, published in 1833,[230] effectively superseded Kent's account for serious students. However, Kent's decision to cover the Constitution in an institutionalist work for the United States was clever, because it allowed him to root his *Commentaries* in a topic that was unmistakably American. The coverage of federal law offsets to some extent Kent's determined reliance upon English law.

The case for treating Kent's *Commentaries* as the last of the institutes of national law rests upon a host of features. Like the Continental institutes, Kent's book arose in close proximity to legal education—as lectures given at Columbia.[231] Kent's book exhibits the characteristic breadth of the institutionalists. As the title proclaims, the work purports to cover "American Law." Kent's *Commentaries* shares, even though it does not wholly replicate, the distinctive persons-things-actions format of the institutionalist works. And like many of the European institutes, Kent's book is centrally concerned with the relationship between the law of the new nation-state and the older customary law. The difference is that the European writers were trying to sort out the relationship between the national law and the Roman law, while Kent was working mainly on the relationship between American law and English common law. Above all, what Kent's *Commentaries* shares with the European institutes of national law is the auspicious enterprise of giving character and definition to the law of a newly self-conscious nation. The United States was among the last of the nation-states to emerge from the breakup of the *ancien régime*, and appropriately, Kent's *Commentaries* was among the very last of the institutionalist books.

The institutionalist tradition is today extinct. As a genre, the institutional book on national law was an inherently transitional form. Once the job was done, it did not bear much repeating. The concept that there was a unified and well-delimited national legal system passed into the political and cultural consciousness of the people, and, therefore, did not require fresh elaboration. As for the didactic purpose of institutional writing, these do-it-yourself books were no match for the power of specialist legal education. University instruction in national law spread everywhere in the wake of the institutionalist tradition. Finally, within the realm of doctrinal writing—that is, for the work of ordering and explicating the continuing life of the national law—the institutionalist genre could not withstand the competition from later forms of legal literature. Doctrinal writing can be done better when it is separated from the need for schoolbook simplicity that characterizes the institutionalist tradition. Breadth is the enemy of depth, and when breadth is no longer needed, depth will prevail. As a result, everywhere in the Western legal systems, the institutes gave way to the treatise, and that is what happened in the United States. Nobody ever again wrote a book like Kent's *Commentaries*, because nobody needed one. Kent gave way to the treatises of Story and Greenleaf in his own day, and in the next century, to the megatreatises [232] of Corbin, Powell, Scott, Wigmore, and Williston.

Conclusion

The year 1993 marks the two hundredth anniversary of Kent's appointment as professor of law at Columbia, effectively the bicentennial of legal education at Columbia. The connections between the history of legal education and of legal literature are often intimate, as Kent's career illustrates. His enduringly influential *Commentaries*, which emerged from Columbia's lecture hall, paved the way to the legal treatise. The treatise became the characteristic medium of juristic writing in the United States during the century or so after Kent's death, as the new legal professorate took up the enterprise.

Kent's other great contribution to the history of legal literature was his role in instigating the system of official, state-supported law reporting in New York in the early nineteenth century. Versions of this system spread widely among the other American states. Judicial decisions, mainly appellate decisions, were methodically preserved. The growth of American law reporting contributed the raw materials for the treatise tradition. Part of what drove the enterprise of treatise writing was the felt need to systematize the ever-growing corpus of reported decisions.

By the end of the nineteenth century, the flow of American law reports altered the character of American legal education. The restless youths who heard Kent deliver his first lectures at Columbia in the 1790s were college students. By the later nineteenth century the university law schools were training intending professionals. The main medium of instruction became what it has remained, the study of reported appellate decisions, selected and republished for the purpose in casebooks.

Kent embarked upon his legal career at a time when professionalism in the administration of justice was still derided. Kent made his career stand for the learned law. His involvement with law reporting, with juristic writing, and with legal education should be seen as common manifestations of his hugely successful campaign to make American law a learned law.

Notes

1. On the connections between legal theory and legal literature, see A.W.B. Simpson, The Rise and Fall of the Legal Treatise: Legal Principles and the Forms of Legal Literature, 48 U. Chi. L. Rev. 632 (1981).

2. Roscoe Pound, The Formative Era of American Law 3 (1938) [hereinafter Pound, Formative Era]. See especially Pound's chapter on "doctrinal writing," id. at 138-72.

3. James Kent, Commentaries on American Law (New York, O. Halsted 1826-30) [hereinafter Commentaries] (4 vols.). Kent's lectures at Columbia are discussed *infra* notes 56-63, 86-90 and accompanying text.

4. See generally 10 Dictionary of American Biography 344-47 (Dumas Malone ed., 1933) (brief biographical sketch of James Kent). Kent is about due for a serious biography, something with the range of Newmyer's life of Story. See R. Kent Newmyer, Supreme Court Justice Joseph Story: Statesman of the Old Republic (1985). The closest we have is the adulatory narrative by John T. Horton, James Kent: A Study in Conservatism 1763-1847 (photo. reprint 1969) (1939). Horton's narrative biography is based upon the Kent Papers in the Library of Congress. That collection is discussed *infra* note 14. Horton overlooked important sources. For example, he did not locate the trove of Kent's papers and diaries that Kent's descendants held until 1964, when the materials were deposited in Columbia University, Butler Library, Rare Book and Manuscript Library. Horton seems also to have been unaware that much of Kent's law library survived in Albany and at Columbia, see *infra* note 41; these books contain manuscript material and marginalia. Quite apart from shortcomings in Horton's sources, the major drawback to his book is that, because it is insensitive to the main currents of American legal history, it does not relate Kent's work to the doctrinal issues and institutional developments of the time.

The work by Kent's great-grandson, William Kent, Memoirs and Letters of James Kent, LL.D. (Boston, Little, Brown & Co. 1898) [hereinafter William Kent, Memoirs], remains quite valuable. It reprints a number of the most interesting documents contained in the Kent Papers collected in the Library of Congress.

Valuable biographical detail about Kent appears in George Goldberg, James Kent, The American Blackstone: The Early Years, *in* Law-Making and Law-Makers in British History: Papers Presented to the Edinburgh Legal History Conference, 1977, at 157 (Alan Harding ed., 1980).

5. See William S. Pelletreau, Birthplace of Chancellor James Kent: His Interesting Letter of Reminiscence, 17 Mag. of Am. Hist. 245 (1887); see also Horton, *supra* note 4, at 10 n.31 (Kent's birthplace was part of Dutchess County prior to the formation of Putnam County in 1812).

6. An autobiographical chronology in the Kent Papers in the Library of Congress is reproduced in Macgrane Coxe, Chancellor Kent at Yale, 17 Yale L.J. 311, 330 n.3 (1908) [hereinafter Coxe; document hereinafter Coxe, Chronology]. Kent's opposition to the War of 1812 is discussed in Horton, *supra* note 4, at 196. On his opposition to the Mexican War, see Letter from James Kent to Simeon Baldwin, New York City (Sept. 18, 1847) (Yale Univ. Manuscripts and Archives, Baldwin Family Papers, General Correspondence, Group 55, Series I, Box 26, Folder 300). As early as 1830-31 Chancellor de Saussure of South

Carolina wrote to Kent about the temper toward disunion on account of tariff policy: "I fear for the safety of the Union." See, e.g., letters reprinted in William Kent, Memoirs, *supra* note 4, at 223-26.

7. Writing in his eightieth year, Kent told a correspondent in 1842 that "I get hold of every law report in the U.S. that I can and read it and make notes to be used in the 5th edition of my Commentaries if ever I should issue one." (He did.) Letter from James Kent to Ambrose Spencer, New York City (Mar. 21, 1842), reprinted in Hampton L. Carson, James Kent, 7 A.B.A.J. 662, 668 (1921). Carson compiled a massive collection of legal literature, manuscripts, and illustrations, including various items of correspondence from Kent that are reproduced in the 1921 article. Carson's collection is now housed in the Free Library of Philadelphia. For the 1842 letter quoted above, see 2 Catalog of the Hampton L. Carson Collection 1769 (1962). Kent weakened in the last months of his eighty-fifth year. See Horton, *supra* note 4, at 325-26. Kent kept diaries in the last years of his life, which survive in Columbia University, Butler Library, Rare Book and Manuscript Library. The deterioration of Kent's handwriting at the end of his life is apparent in the last volume.

8. See 1 Franklin B. Dexter, Biographical Sketches of the Graduates of Yale College 384-85 (New York, Henry Holt & Co. 1885-1912).

9. See 2 id. at 287-88.

10. See Horton, *supra* note 4, at 10 & n.29, 15. A volume of colonial New York legislation, 2 Laws of New-York from the 11th Nov. 1752 to 22d May 1762 (W. Livingston & W. Smith, Jr., eds., New York, William Weyman 1762), inscribed "Moss Kent his book" at the flyleaf is shelved with the portion of James Kent's law library that came to rest in the New York State Library, Manuscripts and Special Collections, Albany. The work may have passed from father to son. The Albany holdings of James Kent's law books are described *infra* note 41.

11. Moss Kent's finances never recovered from the dislocations of the Revolutionary War. See Horton, *supra* note 4, at 15.

12. See 2 Dexter, *supra* note 8, at 288.

13. See Biographical Dictionary of the United States Congress 1774-1989, at 1303 (Bicentennial ed. 1989).

14. Kent's son, William (1802-1861), discussed *infra* note 38, assembled the collection, according to Kent's great-grandson, also William (1858-1910). See William Kent, Memoirs, *supra* note 4, at viii. The younger William and others deposited the collection in the Library of Congress during the years 1904-14. See Typescript Guide, in 1 The Papers of James Kent (Library of Congress, Manuscript Division) (1974). The Kent Papers have been microfilmed and copies are held at the Columbia and Yale law libraries. Yale also holds a multi-volume bound positive photocopy from the microfilm.

I continue in this Article certain conventions that I have established in prior work for adapting law review citation practices to the difficulties of antiquarian and manuscript sources. In quotations from manuscripts as well as from published antiquarian sources, I modernize and Americanize the spelling. Words that are abbreviated in the originals, or rendered in part in superscript, have been written out. Obvious misprints or misspellings in the originals are corrected without mention. When the original source uses a colon, semicolon, or dash to end a sentence, as was common in manuscript material of the time, I render the terminal punctuation as a period. In citing printed works I have left archaic orthography in the titles unaltered, which makes it easier for researchers to locate works cataloged under the original spellings. I have, however, applied modern conventions of initial capitalization to titles. When citing printed sources that may be exceptionally rare, I disclose the library and shelfmark of the exemplar that I consulted.

15. The school in Danbury was operated by the Rev. Ebenezer Baldwin (1745-76), a former tutor at Yale College. See 3 Dexter, *supra* note 8, at 4-8; Horton, *supra* note 4, at 12-13. Among Kent's fellow students at Baldwin's little academy was Ebenezer Baldwin's younger brother, Simeon, see *infra* text accompanying notes 16-18, who became Kent's college classmate and lifelong friend. See William Kent, Memoirs, *supra* note 4, at 9-10. Ebenezer Baldwin died of disease while serving as a chaplain in the revolutionary army in 1776. See James Kent, An Address Delivered at New Haven Before the Phi Beta Kappa Society, September 13, 1831, at 31-34 (New Haven, Hezekiah Howe 1831) [hereinafter Kent, Phi Beta Kappa Address]. Years later Kent recollected that Ebenezer Baldwin had buried Kent's mother. See Letter from James Kent to Ebenezer Baldwin, [son of Simeon Baldwin], New York City (Nov. 24, 1834) (Yale Univ. Manuscripts and Archives, Baldwin Family Papers, General Correspondence, Group 55, Series I, Box 19, Folder 217). After Ebenezer Baldwin's death Kent studied for another year with other tutors in Danbury and Stratfield until he entered Yale.

16. See 4 Dexter, *supra* note 8, at 178-80.

17. Professor of Law at Yale, Governor of Connecticut, Justice of the Connecticut Supreme Court, a founder of the American Bar Association. See 1 Dictionary of American Biography, 544-47 (Allen Johnson ed., 1928).

18. Kent lamented "the Devastation that time has made in the wide circle of my collegiate Friends and acquaintances. You and I are the only spared monuments of God's Providence in our class. . . ." Letter from James Kent to Simeon Baldwin, New York City (Sept. 18, 1847) (Yale Univ. Manuscripts and Archives, Baldwin Family Papers, General Correspondence, Group 55, Series I, Box 26, Folder 300).

19. Letter from James Kent to Thomas Washington, New York City (Oct. 6, 1828). Although this document has been reprinted in several places, I cite what I think is the most convenient version, published under the title, "An American Law Student of a Hundred Years Ago," in 1 Association of American Law Schools, Select Essays in Anglo-American Legal History 837, 838 (Boston 1907) [hereinafter Kent, 1828 Letter].

In fairness to Yale, let it be said that Kent was a tough critic. Late in life, Kent recollected that United States Supreme Court Justice Smith Thompson, who had apprenticed under Kent in Poughkeepsie in the 1790s, had been "nominally educated" at Princeton. See Donald M. Roper, Justice Smith Thompson: Politics and the New York Supreme Court in the Early Nineteenth Century, 51 N.Y. Hist. Soc'y Q. 119 (1967). The passage from Kent regarding Thompson is extracted in William Kent, Memoirs, *supra* note 4, at 56.

20. "[T]he College was not open and in regular exercise more than half the usual time." Kent, Phi Beta Kappa Address, *supra* note 15, at 41.

21. See Letter from Simeon Baldwin to William Kent [Kent's Son] (Feb. 1848), reprinted in William Kent, Memoirs, *supra* note 4, at 10, 12 [hereinafter Baldwin Letter].

22. See Kent, Phi Beta Kappa Address, *supra* note 15, at 40-41 n.

23. See 12 William Holdsworth, A History of English Law 77-91 (1938) [hereinafter Holdsworth, H.E.L.].

24. Regarding late eighteenth-century stirrings toward legal education, notably under George Wythe at the College of William and Mary and James Wilson at the University of Pennsylvania, see Paul D. Carrington, The Revolutionary Idea of University Legal Education, 31 Wm. & Mary L. Rev. 527, 533-38, 546-50 (1990). Wilson's course of lectures, presented at the forerunner of the University of Pennsylvania in 1790-91, has been published in The Works of James Wilson (Robert Green McCloskey ed., 1967) (2 vols.).

25. See Harold G. Hanbury, The Vinerian Chair and Legal Education 5-6 (1950).

26. See Robert Stevens, Two Cheers for 1870: The American Law School, *in* Law in American History 405, 407-16 (Donald Fleming & Bernard Bailyn eds., 1971) [volume hereinafter Fleming & Bailyn].

27. See Paul M. Hamlin, Legal Education in Colonial New York 35-55 (1939) (apprenticeship); *id.* at 56-72 (recommended curricula).

28. Kent, 1828 Letter, *supra* note 19, at 838. Blackstone's Volume Four is devoted to criminal law and procedure. See 4 William Blackstone, Commentaries on the Laws of England (Oxford 1765-69) (4 vols.).

29. See Kent, 1828 Letter, *supra* note 19, at 838. Benson was then 35 years old. If we are curious about how a 35-year-old could have ascended to the attorney generalship of New York, part of the answer is that the Revolution just ending in 1781 had decimated the bar. Many members of New York's pre-Revolutionary bar had bet on the British to win the war and were in consequence unwelcome at the post-colonial bar. It is said that when Kent began his clerkship, there were ten lawyers still admitted in good standing before the New York Supreme Court; Benson was one. See Goldberg, *supra* note 4, at 161.

Benson and Kent remained life-long friends. See Donald Roper, The Elite of the New York Bar as Seen from the Bench: James Kent's Necrologies, 56 N.Y. Hist. Soc'y Q. 199, 218 (1972) [hereinafter Roper, Necrologies]. Kent owned a copy of Egbert Benson's Memoir Read Before the Historical Society of the State of New York. Kent recorded on the title page overleaf, "Judge Benson died at Jamaica on Long Island August 24, 1833, aged 87. . . . I attended his funeral." See Egbert Benson, Memoir Read Before the Historical Society of the State of New-York (New York, 1817) (Columbia Univ., Butler Library, Rare Book and Manuscript Collection).

30. See Goldberg, *supra* note 4, at 162.

31. See William Kent, Memoirs, *supra* note 4, at 20 (quoting a letter written by Kent in 1847).

32. Kent, 1828 Letter, *supra* note 19, at 838-39.

33. Letter from James Kent to Simeon Baldwin, Poughkeepsie (Oct. 10, 1782) (Yale Univ. Manuscripts and Archives, Baldwin Family Papers, General Correspondence, Group 55, Series I, Box 2, Folder 30); see Goldberg, *supra* note 4, at 161-62. "Law I must frankly confess is a field which is uninviting and boundless, notwithstanding it leads forward to the first stations in the state. The study is so encumbered with voluminous rubbish and the baggage of folios that it requires uncommon assiduity and patience. . . ." *Id.* Expression of frustration with the apprenticeship made of legal education were commonly voiced in the eighteenth and nineteenth centuries. For comments by William Livingston, Josiah Quincy, and Daniel Webster, see 1 The Papers of Daniel Webster: Legal Papers 1, 3, 6-7 (Alfred S. Konefsky & Andrew J. King eds., 1982).

34. See Kent, 1828 Letter, *supra* note 19, at 839.

35. See Goldberg, *supra* note 4, at 163. The Library of Congress is said to possess the partners' account book, "which is valuable as illustrating [Kent's] early professional practice." Horton, *supra* note 4, at 328.

36. See *id.* at 326.

37. See, e.g., William Kent, Memoirs, *supra* note 4, at 263; Kent, 1828 Letter, *supra* note 19, at 839.

38. In 1846 Kent wrote Simeon Baldwin that his son "has accepted the appointment of law professor at Cambridge, made vacant by the death of Judge Story." Letter from James Kent to Simeon Baldwin, Summit, New Jersey (Aug. 3, 1846) (Yale Univ. Manuscripts and Archives, Baldwin Family Papers, General Correspondence, Group 55, Series I, Box 25, Folder 291). Story had been the Dane professor at Harvard. On Story's death Greenleaf moved from the Royall chair to the Dane chair, and William Kent became the Royall Professor. See Arthur E. Sutherland, The Law at Harvard 149 (1967).

A year later, in James Kent's last letter to Baldwin, he reported: "My son has resigned his office of professor of law in Cambridge" and returned to New York to help the declining father. Letter from James Kent to Simeon Baldwin, New York City (Sept. 18, 1847) (Yale Univ. Manuscripts and Archives, Baldwin Family Papers, General Correspondence, Group 55, Series I, Box 26, Folder 300). After Kent's death in 1847, William took over the job of publishing updated editions of the *Commentaries*, publishing the 6th (1848), 7th (1851), 8th (1854), 9th (1858) and 10th (1860) editions. William died in 1861 at the age of 59.

39. For the story of how contact with Edward Livingston, later the Louisiana codifier, stimulated this course of study, see Kent, 1828 Letter, *supra* note 19, at 839-40. Kent corresponded with Livingston in later life, when Livingston was producing the Louisiana codes. Irritated by a section of Livingston's projected penal code, Kent wrote him:

> I beg leave to question the necessity of laws making it penal to attack the liberty of the Press in any way not already provided by the comprehensive provisions of the common law. I have lived long enough to believe that the Press flourishes sufficiently in all the vigor of wantonness, without any new stimulus to its action.

Letter from James Kent to Edward Livingston, New York City (Feb. 17, 1826), at 2 (Princeton Univ. Library, Edward Livingston Papers).

40. See Kent, 1828 Letter, *supra* note 19, at 840. Kent recalled having "mastered the best of the Greek, Latin and French classics, as well as the best English and law books at hand." *Id.* On the tradition of high culture and literary accomplishment among the leaders of the bar in Kent's generation, see generally Robert A. Ferguson, Law and Letters in American Culture (1984). On Kent's place in this tradition, see *id.* at 27-28, 66-68.

41. Kent, 1828 Letter, *supra* note 19, at 840. Kent compiled a manuscript "Catalogue of my library made November 1842," which survives in Columbia Univ., Butler Library, Rare Book and Manuscript Collections [hereinafter Kent, 1842 Library Handlist]. Kent bequeathed his library to his son, William. See Will of James Kent, Aug. 22, 1846 (with Surrogate's office probate certificate dated Dec. 24, 1847 attached) (Columbia Univ., Butler Library, Rare Book and Manuscript Collections) [hereinafter Kent, Last Will].

Portions of Kent's library are divided between two Columbia libraries. The Columbia Law Library holds most of Kent's law books, about 750 volumes that "were donated to the Law Library by Edwin C. Kent, a great-grandson of James Kent," in 1911. Letter from Whitney S. Bagnall, Librarian for Special Collections in Law, Columbia Law School Library to John H. Langbein (Jan. 9, 1992) (on file with author).

The Butler Rare Book and Manuscript Collections hold several hundred volumes from Kent's library on topics of foreign and domestic travel, geography, antiquities, history, politics, theology, poetry, foreign affairs, Latin classics, and English literature. There are half a dozen law titles mixed in. These works also appear to have come to Columbia from Edwin C. Kent. See New York Historical Society Library, "Inventory of the Library of Chancellor James Kent, 1938" at 1 (n.d.) (typescript) (shelfmark Z997/ .K37) (title page records: "This library was sold to Columbia University").

The University of Michigan's Clements Library holds a fuller copy of this typescript inventory. The Michigan version includes a section listing 2,051 political and other pamphlets from the 1780s through the 1840s. It appears from a note filed with the Michigan typescript that the collection of Kent's books and pamphlets passed through the hands of Edward Eberstadt, a New York bookseller, in 1940. A photocopy of the Clements Library typescript inventory is now on deposit in the Yale Law Library. (I wish to acknowledge the help of Margaret Leary, University of Michigan Law Librarian, in arranging for the deposit.)

The New York State Library in Albany holds a further 200 or so volumes from Kent's law library, including Kent's copies of the New York law reports, especially Caines and Johnson, that are discussed in Part III of this article. The Albany holdings are described in John T. Fitzpatrick, Chancellor Kent's Law Library, 21 L. Libr. J. 9, 9-11 (1928). The Kent collection in Albany includes another 100 or so volumes that were added by Kent's son, William. See *id.*

The Harvard Law School Library owns five books from Kent's library, acquired between 1889 and 1938. Letter from David Warrington, Librarian for Special Collections, Harvard Law School Library to John H. Langbein (Jan. 17, 1992) (on file with author).

I infer from this pattern of holdings that Kent's library was dispersed piecemeal after the death of his son.

42. Kent, 1828 Letter, *supra* note 19, at 841. Elsewhere Kent wrote that he began to watch Hamilton in action in court while Kent was an apprentice and a young lawyer and that he was first introduced to Hamilton at a dinner at the home of Hamilton's father-in-law, General Schuyler, in Albany, on the occasion of the October 1787 term of the Supreme Court. See William Kent, Memoirs, *supra* note 4, at 281, 301 (quoting Letter from James Kent to Elizabeth Hamilton (Dec. 10, 1832)). Hamilton was then writing the Federalist Papers. See *id.* at 301-02.

Kent wrote his friend Simeon Baldwin excitedly in September 1787 that "I am what we understand here to be a *federal man* and God grant that no demon may ever rescind the Union of these states, or prevent *a firm and equal compact. . . .*" Letter from James Kent to Simeon Baldwin, Poughkeepsie (Sept. 7, 1787) (Yale Univ. Manuscripts and Archives, Baldwin Family Papers, General Correspondence, Group 55, Series I, Box 4, Folder 56).

43. A quarter-century later, writing the *Commentaries*, Kent digressed from his account of the progress of maritime law to reminisce about what a learned and effective commercial lawyer Hamilton had been. See 2 Commentaries, *supra* note 3, at 527-28. Kent figured personally in the slur that provoked the duel between Burr and Hamilton in 1804 that cost Hamilton his life. See Letter from Alexander Hamilton to Aaron Burr, New York (June 20, 1804), reprinted in 26 The Papers of Alexander Hamilton 247-48 (Harold C. Syrett ed., 1979); William Kent, Memoirs, *supra* note 4, at 33-36.

44. William Kent, Memoirs, *supra* note 4, at 303.

45. See Coxe, Chronology, *supra* note 6, at 330-31 n.3.

46. See Goldberg, *supra* note 4, at 169-71.

47. See Coxe, Chronology, *supra* note 6, at 330-31, n.3; Goldberg, *supra* note 4, at 171.

48. Political and personal tensions had developed between the two men, and Kent later recalled: "The partnership with Mr. Livingston had by this time become a heavy and mortifying burden, and this was my principal inducement to quit Poughkeepsie and remove to New York, the last of April, 1793." William Kent, Memoirs, *supra* note 4, at 50-51 (quoting Kent).

49. "My first summer in New York was very gloomy. I was poor and had but little business and lived in a narrow, dirty street, and a thousand times recalled with eagerness the country beauties and domestic pleasures of the preceding year." *Id.* at 52 (quoting Kent). "I have as yet scarcely any business," he wrote to his brother in July 1793. Goldberg, *supra* note 4, at 173 (quoting Kent).

50. Later in that year Kent complained to his brother about the "great and uncommon expenses since I have been here, and the total stop to business which my removal occasioned. . . ." William Kent, Memoirs, *supra* note 4, at 54 (quoting Kent). For Kent's alarm at the cost of staples, see *id.* at 54-55. "He managed to pay his first year's rent by accepting a clerk, whose father paid the £100 fee in advance." Julius Goebel, Jr., A History of the School of Law Columbia University 12 (1955) [hereinafter cited as Goebel, Columbia].

51. Letter from James Kent to Moss Kent, New York City (May 29, 1793), in 1 The Papers of James Kent (Library of Congress, Manuscript Division).

52. See Goldberg, *supra* note 4, at 175; Goebel, Columbia, *supra* note 50, at 13—14.

53. For a succinct account of Kent's efforts at Columbia and of the refounding of the Columbia Law School under Theodore Dwight, see Goebel, Columbia, *supra* note 50, at 3-29. On the background to the creation of the professorship, which was funded with state money paid in partial reparation for war losses, see *id.* at 11. The trustees' certificate reciting Kent's nomination to the position is preserved in Meeting of the Trustees of Columbia College (Dec. 2, 1793), in 1 The Papers of James Kent (Library of Congress, Manuscript Division). Goebel reprints the certificate in Goebel, Columbia, *supra* note 50, at 13. Kent's actual appointment was effected on December 24, 1793. See *id.*

54. See William Kent, Memoirs, *supra* note 4, at 58.

55. Kent wrote his brother, exulting that the salary would commence at once, whereas his lectures would not be due until November 1794. Furthermore, Kent hoped that the professorship might brighten his prospects in the consulting markets. "[T]he appointment [is] not only honorable and profitable," he wrote his brother, "but will even aid my professional practice at the Bar." Letter from James Kent to Moss Kent, New York City (Jan. 7, 1794), in 1 The Papers of James Kent (Library of Congress, Manuscript Division). It is difficult to get a picture of the kind of law practice Kent had in New York in the 1790s. Isolated documents survive, for example, a letter from Kent to Charles E. Genet (1763-1834), on behalf of Kent's client, Cornelius Read, threatening suit for the loss of a vessel caused by the negligence of Genet's pilot, and offering to arbitrate. See Letter from James Kent to Citizen Genet, New York (July 7, 1795) (New York State Library, Albany, Manuscripts and Special Collections, James Kent Collection, single accession 20231, No. 1140); see also Goebel, Columbia, *supra* note 50, at 12-13 (Kent on retainer for a real estate speculator in the future Washington, D.C., in 1793-94).

56. When Kent's lectures proved unsuccessful, his friend of this period, Elihu Hubbard Smith, discussed *infra* text accompanying notes 161-164, complained of the failure of "the principal lawyers, in this city" to encourage their apprentices to attend Kent's course. Letter from Elihu Hubbard Smith to John Allen (Jan. 24, 1796), *in* The Diary of Elihu Hubbard Smith (1771-1798), at 126, 127 (James E. Cronin, ed., American Philosophical Society 1973) [hereinafter Smith Diary]. Smith may have been reflecting Kent's own disappointment at the low turnout of clerks.

57. Years later Kent deprecated the lectures as "slight and trashy productions," Kent, 1828 Letter, *supra* note 19, at 841, which invites the surmise that he destroyed them. By contrast, from Kent's second professorship at Columbia in the 1820s, we have both the *Commentaries* and some sets of student notes. See *infra* notes 89-90.

58. See James Kent, An Introductory Lecture to a Course of Law Lectures Delivered Nov. 17, 1794 (New York, Francis Childs 1794), reprinted in 3 Colum. L. Rev. 330 (1903) [hereinafter Kent, Introductory Lecture]; James Kent, Dissertations: Being the Preliminary Part of a Course of Law Lectures (New York, George Forman 1795) (next three lectures, outline of projected course). The pamphlets reprinting the lectures bombed on the marketplace as thoroughly as the original lectures. Regarding the difficulty that Kent's friend Elihu Hubbard Smith had in helping Kent sell the pamphlets, see Smith Diary, *supra* note 56, at 126-27; *id.* at 102.

59. These same subjects would hold the center stage three decades later in the new lectures that Kent would prepare for his *Commentaries*. Writing to his brother in March 1795, Kent explained that he had hoped to cover personal property but ran short of time; he hoped to add that subject for the next course in November. See Letter from James Kent to Moss Kent, New York City (Mar. 1, 1795), in 2 The Papers of James Kent (Library of Congress, Manuscript Division).

60. See Goldberg, *supra* note 4, at 176-80. "The second lecture dealt with elementary American history in a manner which might have been all right for young children or immigrants. . . . [T]he third lecture, on international law, was even worse." *Id.* at 179-80. Julius Goebel was more forgiving about the lectures. "Probably the difficulty was that Kent's lectures were too professional in content for undergraduate students of the arts, while too academic to attract apprentices at law steeped in the tradition of office study." Goebel, Columbia, *supra* note 50, at 17. James Wilson's course of lectures, delivered a couple of years earlier in Philadelphia, exhibits a similar proclivity for generalities of civics, and Wilson also slights the detail of the legal doctrine and legal administration of his day. See 1 Wilson, *supra* note 24, at 42.

61. Kent wrote his brother that the lectures "meet with as much encouragement as I could have expected." Letter from James Kent to Moss Kent, New York City (Jan. 12, 1795), *in* 2 The Papers of James Kent (Library of Congress, Manuscript Division). Kent wrote his brother several weeks later that "I am satisfied that my Lectures have been well received. . . ." Letter from James Kent to Moss Kent, New York City (Mar. 1, 1795), *in* 2 The Papers of James Kent (Library of Congress, Manuscript Division). This letter is substantially reprinted in William Kent, Memoirs, *supra* note 4, at 74.

62. Columbia was then located on lower Broadway, hence close to legal New York. Kent lectured "in the College Hall at the corner of Murray Street and West Broadway. . . ." Goebel, Columbia, *supra* note 50, at 14.

63. William Kent, Memoirs, *supra* note 4, at 77 (reproducing the text of a note that Kent penned in the flyleaf of his copy of the pamphlet edition of his first lecture).

Kent was forthright with the trustees of Columbia about the failure of his course. When resigning the professorship, he told them how steeply the attendance had declined in his second year and that, for his third course, "no student appeared to countenance the attempt. . . ." William Kent, Memoirs, *supra* note 4, at 77-78 (reprinting Kent's letter of May 2, 1797). Kent concluded with the hope that Columbia's experiment with legal education would be renewed "under abler professors. . . ." *Id.* at 78. Kent's friend Elihu Hubbard Smith also spoke freely about the failure of Kent's lectures, blaming the bar for not encouraging young lawyers to attend. See Smith Diary, *supra* note 56, at 126-27.

The trustees waited a year to accept the resignation, and Kent did read the lectures in his office to a group of "six or eight" students in the winter of 1797-98. See William Kent, Memoirs, *supra* note 4, at 77 (quoting Kent); Goebel, Columbia, *supra* note 50, at 17.

64. Kent wrote his brother that:

I am very considerably engaged in new land speculations. This, however, is a circumstance to be kept private. You know of the success of my former ones. . . . I expect great profit from what I am now concerned in. If I am lucky I shall be able in two or three years to retire into the country.

Letter from James Kent to Moss Kent, New York City (Mar. 1, 1795), in 2 The Papers of James Kent (Library of Congress, Manuscript Division). This letter is substantially reprinted in William Kent, Memoirs, *supra* note 4, at 74, 75; see also Goldberg, *supra* note 4, at 189 (Kent speculating on Dutchess County lands with income from his mastership in chancery). The mastership is discussed *infra* note 66 and accompanying text.

65. See Vindication of the Treaty of Amity, Commerce and Navigation with Great Britain (New York 1795) (authored by James Kent & Noah Webster); Goldberg, *supra* note 4, 182-83. On the politics of the treaty see Alfred F. Young, The Democratic Republicans of New York: The Origins 1763-1797, at 445-67 (1967). Kent was also carrying Federalist legislative baggage at this time. In 1796 the Federalists arranged to have Kent elected from New York City to a safe seat in the New York State Assembly, which he reluctantly accepted. See Roper, Necrologies, *supra* note 29, at 209. Kent sat in the legislature's winter 1797 session. See Goebel, Columbia, *supra* note 50, at 17.

66. Goldberg, *supra* note 4, at 187 (quoting Kent). "This office promised me a more steady supply of pecuniary aid (of which I stood in need), and it enabled me in a degree to relinquish the practice of an attorney which I always extremely hated." *Id.*

67. See William Kent, Memoirs, *supra* note 4, at 98-99.

68. Kent, 1828 Letter, *supra* note 19, at 842.

69. William Kent, Memoirs, *supra* note 4, at 109 (quoting Kent).

70. *Id.* at 108.

71.

> The various powers exercised by the three great courts for the administration of justice in England, viz. the king's bench, the common pleas, and the plea side of the court of exchequer, are all, in this state, united together, and reposed in one tribunal, called from its extensive jurisdiction, the supreme court of judicature.

William Wyche, A Treatise on the Practice of the Supreme Court of Judicature of the State of New-York in Civil Actions 1 (New York, T. &. J. Swords, 2d ed. 1794).

72. See *id.* at 2, 10.

73. See *id.* at 11.

74. See Horton, *supra* note 4, at 123-39. Kent reckoned that he rode circuit for 16 years and tried 1,755 cases, of which 8 were murders. See *id.* at 135 n.43 (citing William Kent, Memoirs, *supra* note 4, at 123). For a pamphlet account of one of the murders, see The Trial of Stephen Arnold for the Murder of Betsy Van Amburgh, a Child of Six Years of Age; Before the Court of Oyer and Terminer and General Gaol Delivery, for the County of Otsego, at the Court-House in Cooperstown: June 4th, 1805 (Cooperstown, n.d. [1805]) (Yale Law Library shelfmark Closed S/Trials B/Ar 65).

75. See William Kent, Memoirs, *supra* note 4, at 128. "Appeals from the [circuit] courts were taken to the court *en banc.*" John H. Moore, One Hundred Fifty Years of Official Law Reporting and the Courts in New York, 6 Syracuse L.Rev. 273, 278 (1955). As with the English assize system on which it was patterned, New York's circuit system facilitated local processing of fact disputes before local juries while reserving matters of legal consequence for the full Supreme Court. "The result . . . was to funnel any question of moment to the full court." Donald Roper, The New York Supreme Court and Economic Development: 1798-1823, at 58, 61 (1979), in Law and Economic Development: Papers from the Fall 1979 Regional Economic History Conference (Eleutherian Mills-Hagley Foundation) [hereinafter Roper, Courts]. Roper's study may also be found in 3 Working Papers from the Regional Economic History Research Center No. 3 (1980).

76. See 1 The Law Practice of Alexander Hamilton: Documents and Commentary 167-83 (Julius Goebel, Jr. ed., 1964) [hereinafter Goebel, Hamilton]; Henry W. Scott, The Courts of the State of New York: Their History, Development and Jurisdiction 259-62 (1909); Stanley N. Katz, The Politics of Law in Colonial America: Controversies over Chancery Courts and Equity Law in the Eighteenth Century, *in* Fleming & Bailyn, *supra* note 26, at 257, 273-82.

77. To his copy of 1 Johnson's Chancery Reports (1816), Kent appended an undated manuscript "Memorandum of the length of my New York Terms," in which he recorded the dates of all his sittings in New York City from 1814 when he became Chancellor through 1823 when he left office. The pattern was two sessions of approximately three weeks each, the first held sometime between May and July, and the second occurring between October and December. See Kent, Manuscript entry at iii (n.d.), located in Kent's copy of 1 William Johnson, Reports of Cases Adjudged in the Court of Chancery of New-York (Albany, E.F. Backus 1816) (New York State Library, Albany, Manuscripts and Special Collections, James Kent Law Book Collection).

78. In an appeal against a judgment of the Supreme Court, its judges did not vote in the Court of Errors; likewise, the Chancellor did not vote when his decision was the subject of the appeal. See Roper, Courts, *supra* note 75, at 61, 80 n.20. The proper title of the court was Court for the Trial of Impeachments and the Correction of Errors of the State of New York.

79. Donald Roper, James Kent and the Emergence of New York's Libel Law, 17 Am. J. Legal Hist. 223, 224 (1973) (quoting Article II of the 1777 Constitution).

80. See Roper, Courts, *supra* note 75, at 59-60.

81. The verbatim transcript of the 1821 convention was published as Reports of the Proceedings and Debates of the

Convention of 1821, Assembled for the Purpose of Amending the Constitution of the State of New-York (Nathaniel H. Carter et al. eds., Albany, E. & E. Hosford 1821). The 1821 convention dealt with many other topics, including the extension of suffrage, which Kent opposed, see *id.* at 219-22. Kent's copy of this work survives in Columbia Univ., Butler Library, Rare Book and Manuscript Collections. Kent pasted in a newspaper clipping that reports the outcome of the 1832 federal presidential election in New York. The Jacksonian candidates for the electoral college defeated Kent and the other anti-Jacksonians by a margin of about two to one. Kent writes in ink, "This Election in 1832 is a Sample of what I anticipated in my Speech, *supra* page 221, under the operation of universal Suffrage in the City of New York."

82. On Kent's dates of judicial service, see Kent, 1828 Letter, *supra* note 19, at 842-45.

83. See Horton, *supra* note 4, at 260-62.

84. See Letter from James Kent to William Johnson, Albany (Sept. 27, 1823), in 5 The Papers of James Kent (Library of Congress, Manuscript Division). On Reeve's remarkable proprietary law school, see generally Marian C. McKenna, Tapping Reeve and the Litchfield Law School (1986).

85. There survives in the Kent Papers a wonderful document, an extract from the minutes of the trustees of Columbia dated November 3, 1823. It recites not only Kent's election to the professorship, but also a particular inducement, for which I surmise Kent negotiated strenuously: "that the Professor be not obliged to attend the meetings of the [Columbia] Faculty. . . ." Meeting of the Trustees of Columbia College (Nov. 3, 1823), *in* 5 The Papers of James Kent (Library of Congress, Manuscript Division) (filed immediately after the letter to William Johnson cited *supra* note 84).

86. See Goebel, Columbia, *supra* note 50, at 20.

87. See Kent, 1828 Letter, *supra* note 19, at 846, describing himself as "Chamber Counsellor." A number of his opinions to clients from the 1830s and 1840s survive in Columbia Univ., Butler Library, Rare Book and Manuscript Collections.

88. Kent wrote Joseph Story about the project in January 1825. He reckoned that the first 20 lectures treating "the law of nations and the constitutional jurisprudence of the United States . . . would fill a large volume of 700 pages." Letter from James Kent to Joseph Story (Jan. 17, 1825), *in* 14 Proc. Mass. Hist. Soc'y (2d ser.) 398, 415 (Charles C. Smith ed., 1901) (emphasis omitted) [hereinafter Kent/Story Letters]. These subjects did indeed comprise the first 21 chapters (called "lectures") of Kent's *Commentaries* and required just over 400 printed pages.

89. See Goebel, Columbia, *supra* note 50, at 20. Two sets of student notes survive from Kent's lectures: Charles R. Alsop, Preliminary Drafts of Notes of Lectures Delivered by Chancellor James Kent in Columbia College, 1824-25 (unpublished notes) (Yale Law Library, Mss B/C72/1824 and C72/1824a), and Charles McVean, Notes of Lectures Delivered at the City of New York by James Kent Esquire Commencing Oct. 24th 1825 (New York State Historical Ass'n Library, Cooperstown) [hereinafter McVean's Notes].

90. McVean's Notes, *supra* note 89, allow one to reconstruct some of the stages through which the lectures became the *Commentaries.* The student notes and the *Commentaries* have mostly identical chapter ("Lecture") headings, with the revisions resulting in a variation of one or two lecture numbers. Thus, Lecture 31 on corporations in the student notes becomes Lecture 33 in the *Commentaries.* See 2 Commentaries, *supra* note 3, at 215. The final lecture in McVean's notes, Lecture 35, primarily on fisheries, becomes Lecture 51 in Volume Three of the *Commentaries.* See *id.* at 321. Thus, Kent's course at Columbia appears to have lapsed with the material on persons (status) that extends into Volume Two of the *Commentaries.* The material on contract and maritime law (personal property) in Volumes Two and Three and on real property in Volumes Three and Four was written expressly for publication, and was not part of the Columbia lecture series, although Kent continued to call his chapter divisions "lectures." The preface to the later volumes of the *Commentaries* corroborate that Kent was writing as he was publishing—he twice predicted wrongly that the next volume would be the last. See 2 *id.* at iii; 3 *id.* at iii.

Not only did the book grow beyond the lectures in the first edition, it grew in later editions. See, e.g., Alan Watson, Joseph Story and the Comity of Errors: A Case Study in Conflict of Laws 27-37, 87-89 (1992) (discussing Kent's increased coverage of conflicts in second edition).

91. See *supra* note 3.

92. For editions and abridgments see 293 American Library Ass'n, National Union Catalogue: Pre-1956 Imprints, at 475-78 (1973) [hereinafter NUC]. Kent's son prepared the early posthumous editions. See *supra* note 38.

93. James Kent, Commentaries on American Law (Oliver W. Holmes, Jr. ed., Boston, Little, Brown & Co. 1873). For brief accounts of Holmes' work on the twelfth edition, see Liva Baker, The Justice from Beacon Hill: The Life and Times of Oliver Wendell Holmes 209-12 (1991); 2 Mark De Wolfe Howe, Justice Oliver Wendell Holmes: The Proving Years 1870-1882, at 10-23 (1963).

94. James Kent, Commentaries on American Law (John M. Gould ed., Boston, Little, Brown & Co. 1896).

95. Kent sought Story's advice on whether to prepare "a cheap and abridged edition for our Western schools, academies, and colleges," adding that he has been warned that if he does not do it others might. Letter from James Kent to Joseph Story (May 29, 1839), in Kent/Story Letters, *supra* note 88, at 418. Story encouraged him. See Letter from Joseph Story to James Kent (June 1, 1839), *in id.* at 423. For examples of the genre, see J. Eastman Johnson, An Analytical Abridgment of Kent's Commentaries on American Law: With a Full Series of Questions for Examination (New York, Halsted & Voorhies 1839); Asa Kinne, The Most Important Parts of Kent's Commentaries Reduced to Questions and Answers (New York, W.E. Dean 2d ed., 1840).

96. See 2 The Diary of Philip Hone 1828-1851, at 645-46 (Allan Nevins ed., 1927); Horton, *supra* note 4, at 303-04 (citing Hone Diary). Kent's forerunner, Blackstone, had a somewhat comparable financial success in England. At Blackstone's death, it was reckoned that he had made £14,000 from his *Commentaries.* See Gareth H. Jones, Introduction, The Sovereignty of the Law: Selections from Blackstone's Commentaries on the Laws of England ix (1973). Kent knew that his book was a gusher,

and in his last will and testament, which was written the year before he died, he made careful provision for his son to manage the copyright and to divide the proceeds among Kent's three children. See Kent, Last Will, *supra* note 41, at 2-3.

97. "In 1845 Kent's taxable wealth in New York City was assessed at between $45,000 and $100,000." Donald M. Roper, The Elite of the New York Bar as Seen from the Bench, 56 N.Y. Hist. Soc'y Q. 199, 204 n.9 (1972) (citing Edward Pessen, The Wealthiest New Yorkers of the Jacksonian Era: A New List, 54 N.Y. Hist. Soc'y Q. 145, 168 (1970)).

98. This theme is richly developed in Perry Miller, The Life of the Mind in America 99-116 (1965).

99. Although the civil jury was preserved, the scope of its authority would be cut back during the nineteenth century, in the direction of the English fact/law distinction. For a discussion of the law-finding powers of eighteenth- century American civil juries, see William E. Nelson, The Eighteenth-Century Background of John Marshall's Constitutional Jurisprudence, 76 Mich.L.Rev. 893, 904-17 (1978). Regarding the later trend to remove the jury from law-finding, see Note, The Changing Role of the Jury in the Nineteenth Century, 74 Yale L.J. 170, 173-85 (1964) (civil and criminal jury practice).

100. As early as 1785, when Kent was just arriving at the New York bar, we find him explaining in a letter to Simeon Baldwin that the affairs of free and commercial societies require numerous and subtle distinctions in the law, which is why the law "must become a *distinct* Science. . . ." Letter from James Kent to Simeon Baldwin, Poughkeepsie (Feb. 1, 1785) (Yale Univ. Manuscripts and Archives, Baldwin Family Papers, General Correspondence, Group 55, Series I, Box 3, Folder 43). Kent speaks again of "the Science of American Jurisprudence" when writing to Baldwin in July, 1786. Letter from James Kent to Simeon Baldwin, Poughkeepsie (July 18, 1786) (Yale Univ. Manuscripts and Archives, Baldwin Family Papers, Group 55, Series I, Box 3, Folder 48).

101. William Kent, Memoirs, *supra* note 4, at 58 (quoting Kent).

102. Pound, Formative Era, *supra* note 2, at 92 (footnotes omitted).

103. Richard E. Ellis, The Jeffersonian Crisis: Courts and Politics in the Young Republic 115 (1971) (quoting John Dudley).

104. See Pound, Formative Era, *supra* note 2, at 32 n.5 (citing Act of June 13, 1799, § 5, Patterson's Laws of the State of New Jersey 436 (Newark, Matthias 1800)); see also David W. Raack, "To Preserve the Best Fruits": The Legal Thought of Chancellor James Kent, 33 Am. J. Leg. Hist. 320, 334 (1989) (noting a similar Kentucky statute); Ellis, *supra* note 103, at 115 (noting that "[o]ther states" had passed similar laws).

105. When publishing the *Commentaries*, Kent rebuked a proofreader for suggesting that ordinary readers would be helped if the Latin phrases were rendered in English. "[W]e don't want every man to be his own lawyer, and he could not be, even if all the Latin was in the plainest possible English. What kind of legal protection would you have if every man could be a lawyer?" William Kent, Memoirs, *supra* note 4, at 199-200 (quoting Kent).

Professional financial interests also motivated Kent's concern to restrict the practice of law to the elite. Writing Simeon Baldwin from Poughkeepsie on February 1, 1785, the youthful Kent broods lest

> popular prejudice . . . penetrate into the legislature and control them. I mean the notion of either so far restricting the profits of the practice or of rendering the admittance to the bar so easy that the pursuit will not be alluring to men of genius and education, it will then fall into the hands of needy and ignorant persons and become a *contemptible profession.*

Letter from James Kent to Simeon Baldwin, Poughkeepsie (Feb. 1, 1785) (Yale Univ. Manuscripts and Archives, Baldwin Family Papers, General Correspondence, Group 55, Series I, Box 3, Folder 43).

106. In Goix v. Low, 1 Johns. Cas. 341 (N.Y. Sup. Ct. 1800), Kent bristled at counsel's argument that the principle expressed in a certain line of English case law should be disregarded as the manifestation of mere British state interests: "The dignified character of their courts of justice, (I speak of their higher courts of law and equity) which have maintained their integrity, and protected right to a degree never before witnessed in the history of civil society, is sufficient to repel the force of such an unfounded insinuation." *Id.* at 345.

Kent undertook to instruct his friend Simeon Baldwin, an intending law student, about the force of English law in immediate post-colonial New York:

> [T]he English common law is part of the law of this State and can only be discovered and known by searching into the decisions of the English courts, which are the only evidence of the common law, and these decisions are regarded with us as authentic evidence of the common law and therefore are cited as precedents binding with us even down to the year 1776.

Letter from James Kent to Simeon Baldwin (n.p.) [Poughkeepsie] July 18, 1786) (Yale Univ. Manuscripts and Archives, Baldwin Family Papers, General Correspondence, Group 55, Series I, Box 3, Folder 48). Portions of this document are reproduced in Goebel, Hamilton, *supra* note 76, at 50 n.50.

107. Letter from James Kent to Simeon Baldwin (n.p.) [Poughkeepsie] (July 18, 1786) (Yale Univ. Manuscripts and Archives, Baldwin Family Papers, General Correspondence, Group 55, Series I, Box 3, Folder 48).

108. Manning v. Manning, 1 Johns. Ch. 527, 531 (N.Y. Ch. 1815) (emphasis omitted). For further discussion of this well-known passage, see James Brown Scott, James Kent: 1763-1847, *in* 2 Great American Lawyers 491, 511-14 (William Draper Lewis ed., 1907); see also Raack, *supra* note 104, at 344 (citing passages from *Manning* tending to indicate that Kent felt bound by English common law).

109. On the natural-law propensities of the nineteenth century American treatise tradition see A.W.B. Simpson, *supra* note 1, at 671-74.

110. I Commentaries, *supra* note 3, at 439.

111. See, e.g., Gardner v. Trustees of Newburgh, 2 Johns. Ch. 162 (N.Y. Ch. 1816). Kent read French but neither Dutch nor German; he knew the Dutch and German authors from Latin originals, or in a couple of instances, from English or French translations. As of 1842, Kent owned works by Argou, Domat, Grotius, Heineccius, Hubner, Kames, Montesquieu, Pothier, Puffendorf, Vattel, and Vinnius, as well as the modern French codes. See Kent, 1842 Library Handlist, *supra* note 41.

112. See, e.g., Scott, *supra* note 108, at 516.

> "The most casual reader of Johnson's Chancery Reports has doubtless observed that Chancellor Kent received his inspiration from the juridical writings of almost every nation in Europe, ancient and modern; the compilations of the Justinian era, the French jurists, Domat, D'Aguesseau, Fournel, Emerigon, Pothier, and Valin; the Swiss publicists, Burlamaqui and Vattel; the Dutch juridical writers, Grotius, Vinnius, Voet, and Bynkershoek; the German writers, Puffendorf, Heineccius, and Strykius. From these, and many like sources in addition to the English jurists, Chancellor Kent illustrated the true scope and province of equity tribunals."

Id. (extracting Fowler, Observations on the Particular Jurisprudence of New York, 23 Alb. L.J. 285, 288 (1881)).

In a recent paper, however, Alan Watson has shown that Kent's references to foreign law are frequently "inaccurate, and one is forced to wonder whether he has always consulted the sources he cites." Alan Watson, Chancellor Kent's Use of Foreign Law, in Studies in Continental Influence on American Law (Mathias Reimann ed., forthcoming 1993). Watson tracks some of Kent's citations. He shows in one instance, in which Kent cites the Justinianian Digest, that Kent "took his references at second hand from the articles he cites from Pothier." See *id.* Watson shows in another instance that Kent took his Roman law from Blackstone rather than from the cited Roman-law texts. *Id.* Watson concludes that while Kent "usually shows a firm knowledge of the foreign law he uses, . . . he sometimes cites works that he has either not consulted or, at least, not on that occasion. And it is possible for him at times to make almost unbelievably egregious mistakes." *Id.* Some years ago Peter Stein reprinted a letter that Kent wrote late in life, in which Kent deprecated research into the "'logical minutiae of the German Philosophers and Jurists. . . . I find sufficient in the texts of the Institutes and the Pandects for all the illustrations of the principles of the Roman jurisprudence that I care for. . . .'" Peter Stein, The Attraction of the Civil Law in Post-Revolutionary America, 52 Va. L. Rev. 403, 433-34 (1966) (quoting Kent in 1841).

113. See Watson, *supra* note 112 ("Many of [Kent's] citations are mere window dressing when there was already sufficient English or American authority.").

114. Kent may have been the most prominent figure pushing this idea, but he was hardly alone. Professor Richard Helmholz recently read virtually the entirety of American reported decisions from the period 1790-1825, with a view to detecting the influence of Roman and European law. See Richard Helmholz, Use of the Civil Law in Post-Revolutionary American Jurisprudence, 66 Tul. L. Rev. 1649, 1651-52 (1992). He found that civilian sources were most often cited in areas in which the English common law was relatively primitive, especially maritime law, marine insurance, and other topics of commercial law. See *id.* at 1657-58. Occasionally, the civilian sources filled outright gaps in the common law, but "[n]umerically at least, such cases were dwarfed by those in which common law and civil law were basically the same, but in which authorities from both were adduced to support a rule or a decision." *Id.* at 1677.

115. Kent told the Law Association of the City of New York in 1836:

> The writings of Bracton afford decisive proof that [the English common law] had also been nurtured and strengthened by touching the living fountains of the Roman law. We are then at liberty fondly to trace its descent in the collateral line, from the great civilians of the Roman forum, whose writings compose the immortal Pandects, the grandest monument extant of ancient wisdom, applied to the business of civil life.

James Kent, An Address Delivered Before the Law Association of the City of New York (New York, G. & C. Carvill & Co. 1836), extracted in 16 Am. Jurist 471, 474 (1837).

We can trace the wishful idea that common law was Roman law back into Kent's youth. Writing to Simeon Baldwin in 1786, as a 25-year-old starting lawyer, Kent links the scientific quality of English law to Roman law.

[T]he Science of the Law is a Study of prodigious extent & requires proportionable talents & application as well as the most—[illegible] Perseverance. The English Lawyers I find too were equally masters of the Civil Law and the Law of Nations. They [that is, the civil law and the law of nations] are interwoven in fact with the Body of the English Law.

Letter from James Kent to Simeon Baldwin, Poughkeepsie (July 18, 1786) (Yale Univ. Manuscripts and Archives, Baldwin Family Papers, General Correspondence, Group 55, Series I, Box 3, Folder 48). Kent does, however, admit that Roman law had less influence in England than in the Continental systems. See *id.*

116. Kent and Story were primarily judges and writers, but their connection to legal education is far from incidental. A main reason that Kent at Columbia and Story at Harvard (as well as James Wilson at the University of Pennsylvania, George Wythe at William and Mary and David Hoffman at the University of Maryland) wanted to place legal education in the universities was for the purpose of associating the law with other recognized bodies of learning. That is also one reason why Kent, Story, and the others speak incessantly about law as a science.

117. Kent, 1828 Letter, *supra* note 19, at 842-43. Kent further claimed that "We had no law of our own, and nobody knew what it was." *Id.* at 843. Donald Roper quite correctly calls that a "distortion," pointing to the works of Julius Goebel and others, which depict the sophistication of colonial New York law and the substantial continuity of colonial law into the early national period. See Roper, Necrology, *supra* note 29, at 209-10 & n.18 (1972). Goebel was also unamused at this line of Kent's. See 1 Goebel, Hamilton, *supra* note 76, at 7-8.

118. See, e.g., Miscellaneous Virginia Law Reports 1784-1809 (W. Hamilton Bryson ed., 1992) (recently published collection

of manuscript reports of Virginia cases); William E. Nelson, Americanization of the Common Law: The Impact of Legal Change on Massachusetts Society, 1760-1830, at 180-81 (1975) (citing Massachusetts sources).

119. On the history of law reporting in England in the eighteenth century see 12 Holdsworth, H.E.L., *supra* note 23, at 116-17. See generally, John W. Wallace, The Reporters (Boston, Soule & Bugbee, 4th ed. 1882) (surveying English law reports up until the late nineteenth century).

120. For a convenient listing of the nominate reports, see Sweet & Maxwell's Guide to the Law Reports 39-66 (4th ed., 1962).

121. See generally Herbert A. Johnson, Imported Eighteenth-Century Law Treatises in American Libraries 1700-1799 (1978) (cataloguing law reports and treatises).

122. The idea that American judges ought to produce written opinions was current at the time. In 1785, Connecticut enacted legislation that required the judges to write and retain their opinions on law matters. See Erwin C. Surrency, A History of American Law Publishing 42 (1990).

123. See Kent, 1828 Letter, *supra* note 19, at 843.

124. 1 Julius Goebel, Jr., History of the Supreme Court of the United States: Antecedents and Beginnings to 1801, at 6 (Oliver Wendell Holmes Devise History of the Supreme Court of the United States 1971) [hereinafter Goebel, Antecedents]; Raack, *supra* note 104, at 346 n.131.

125. See Wallace, *supra* note 119, at 561-91; see also Note, American Reports and Reporters, 22 Am. Jurist 108, 110 (1839) [hereinafter American Reports] (providing bibliographical accounts of American reports, beginning with United States Supreme Court's February 1790 term reported by James Dallas).

126. See Wallace, *supra* note 119, at 571 n.2 (discussing Reports of Cases Adjudged in the Superior Court of the State of Connecticut (Litchfield, Collier & Adam 1789) and noting that another reporter may have predated Kirby by a few months). See generally Alan V. Briceland, Ephraim Kirby: Pioneer of American Law Reporting, 1789, 16 Am. J. Legal Hist. 297 (1972) (discussing life of Ephraim Kirby and his contribution to American law). In 1784 Connecticut enacted legislation requiring judges to supply written reasons for their decisions. See Craig Joyce, The Rise of the Supreme Court Reporter: An Institutional Perspective on Marshall Court Ascendancy, 83 Mich. L. Rev. 1291, 1297-98 (1985); American Reports, *supra* note 125, at 118.

127. See Wallace, *supra* note 119, at 571.

128. See Reports of Cases Ruled and Adjudged in the Courts of Pennsylvania Before and Since the Revolution (Philadelphia, T. Bradford 1790).

129. Kent recorded that he read Dallas' volume two immediately in 1799. See Horton, *supra* note 4, at 147 n.73 (reproducing Kent's legal reading list for the years 1799-1805).

130. On Dallas, see Joyce, *supra* note 126, at 1294-1306. The story of the Supreme Court reportership continues in G. Edward White, The Marshall Court and Cultural Change, 1815-35, at 384-426 (3-4 Oliver Wendell Holmes Devise History of the Supreme Court of the United States 1988).

131. See Decisions of Cases in Virginia, by the High Court of Chancery (Richmond, Thomas Nicolson 1795).

132. See Reports of Cases Argued and Determined in the Court of Appeals of Virginia (Richmond, Thomas Nicholson 1798-99) (2 vols.). See generally W.H. Bryson, Law Reporting and Legal Records in Virginia, 1607-1800, *in* Judicial Records, Law Reports, and the Growth of Case Law 319-29 John H . Baker ed., 1989) (5 Comparative Studies in Continental and Anglo-American Legal History) (describing early legal recordkeeping in Virginia).

133. See Cases of Practice Adjudged in the Supreme Court of the State of New York (New York, I. Collins 1801).

134. Goebel remarks upon the Americans' "utter dependence upon English case law. The reason for this dependence was not alone the availability of published abridgments and reports, but also the deference colonial lawyers were ready to pay to the opinions of courts regarded as peerless." Goebel, Antecedents, *supra* note 124, at 6. Kent's letter to Baldwin in 1786, extracted *supra* note 106, exemplifies this attitude.

135. See Moore, *supra* note 75, at 273-74 & n.1. William Johnson, discussed *infra* text accompanying notes 145-169, acknowledges the importance of the subsidy in the preface to I Johns. v (1807). Other states came to emulate this practice; the unsigned note on American law reporting in the American Jurist for 1839 identifies on a state-by-state basis the date when subsidies were instituted. See American Reports, *supra* note 125, passim.

136. Kent describes this event in a manuscript note to his copy of the edition of New York statute law that his work rendered obsolete. Kent recalls that by an act of March 28, 1800, the legislature empowered Kent and Radcliff to revise the statutes. The two judges

> were allowed two years and their compensation was to each $1,000. They commenced the work in August 1800, and transmitted to the legislature the completion of their revision on the 12th March 1801. They drew but 115 revised acts, and which were taken from and comprise the substance of about 400 statutes. They left 76 public acts unrevised, as they had never been altered or amended by any subsequent law, and made a list of a great number of acts relating to particular subjects and to corporate rights, and which being partly executed could not be properly reenacted. A long list of acts deemed obsolete or private was also made. The most laborious and difficult part of their task was to abridge and improve the style, and to note imperfections on the former acts, and especially in those, which in the preceding revision, had been taken from the old English Statutes. The laws thus revised they were directed by another act of 8th April 1801 to publish, and were allowed each $850 for superintending the press, making index, etc. They were published in 2 volumes octavo and the first volume appeared in January 1802 and the second volume in April following.

Kent, Manuscript entry at flyleaf (n.d.), located in Kent's copy of 1 Laws of the State of New-York (Samuel Jones & Richard

Varick eds., New York, Hugh Gaine 1789) (New York State Library, Albany, Manuscripts and Special Collections, James Kent Law Book Collection). The Kent/Radcliff recompilation of New York statute law was published as Laws of the State of New-York (Albany, Charles R. & George Webster 1802-1812) (2 vols.).

Kent soured on Radcliff. Political differences at the 1821 Constitutional Convention put them at cross purposes, and Kent came to view Radcliff as "a sad example of bad temper and perverted ambition. . . ." Roper, Necrologies, *supra* note 29, at 236-37 (quoting Kent).

137. See *supra* text accompanying note 78.

138. See George Caines, New-York Term Reports of Cases Argued and Determined in the Supreme Court of That State (New York, Isaac Riley & Co. 1804-06) (3 vols.) [hereinafter Caines' Reports].

139. Caines' Reports were probably issued in pamphlet installments, at least to the judges, and then bound up when all the installments of a volume had been published. Kent identifies the contents of the first installment as running "From May Term 1803 to February Term 1804, both inclusive." Kent, Manuscript entry at title page (n.d.), located in Kent's copy of 1 Caines' Reports, *supra* note 138 (1804) (New York State Library, Albany, Manuscripts and Special Collections, James Kent Law Book Collection). At the end of the installment, page 107 of the volume, Kent wrote:

I think the reporter does not take notes very correctly and that the work is too full of mistakes. The decisions of the Court when in writing, as most of them are, appear correct and this source of accuracy stamps the whole value on the book, for without that aid, I should have no reliance on the reporter. His own annotations in the margin might well be spared. However, as the first essay, the work deserves great indulgence.

Kent, Manuscript entry (n.d.), located in *id.* at 107.

Kent's annotations on his copies of *Caines' Reports* indicate that Caines managed to blunder in every aspect of the reporter's work. Kent wrote in his copy of the second volume of the second edition of Caines' Reports that Caines had botched the report of Alexander Hamilton's argument in the case of Vandervoort v. Smith, 2 Cai. R. 155 (N.Y. Sup. Ct. 1805): "General Hamilton spoke for 4 hours, and made a most forceful argument, and it is very imperfectly reported. It was the last argument he ever made at the Bar of the Supreme Court. . . ." Kent, Manuscript entry at flyleaf (n.d.), located in Kent's copy of 2 George Caines,' New-York Term Reports (New York, Isaac Riley & Co., 2d. ed. 1814) (3 vols.) [hereinafter Caines' Reports 2d] (New York State Library, Albany, Manuscripts and Special Collections, James Kent Law Book Collection). In his copy of Caines' Reports, Kent writes in the margin alongside the report of Spencer v. Webb, 1 Cai. R. 118 (N.Y. Sup. Ct. 1803): "This case is very badly reported," and he explains why. Kent, Manuscript entry at flyleaf (n.d.), located in Kent's copy of 1 Caines' Reports 2d, *supra* (New York State Library, Albany, Manuscripts and Special Collections, James Kent Law Book Collection).

Kent was scathing about Caines even after Caines was in his grave. Kent wrote in his copy of Caines' revised edition that Caines died poor in 1825, "and since he ceased to be Reporter in 1805, he had never been prosperous nor greatly respected either for sound judgment or pure morals." Kent, Manuscript entry at flyleaf (n.d.), located in Kent's copy of 1 Caines' Reports 2d, *supra* (New York State Library, Albany, Manuscripts and Special Collections, James Kent Law Book Collection). This passage is reproduced in full in Roper, Necrologies, *supra* note 29, at 212-13. Roper observes that Caines may have raised Kent's ire by having attempted to regain the reportership in 1823, when Johnson left office along with Kent. See *id.* at 213 n.23. On Johnson's dismissal, see *infra* notes 168-169 and accompanying text.

140. See Term Reports in the Court of King's Bench (London, J. Butterworth 1794-1802). (8 vols.). There was a successor series by East alone, for the years 1801 to 1812, which numbered 16 volumes. See Reports of Cases Argued and Determined in the Court of King's Bench (London, J. Butterworth 1801-18) (16 vols.). Of Durnford & East, Wallace writes: "None of the modern Reports exceed these for the care and accuracy of finish, including great propriety of style, which they everywhere maintain." Wallace, *supra* note 119, at 529-30 n.2. Kent records having read "7th Durnford" in 1799 and "8th Durnford" in 1801, doubtless the last two volumes of Durnford & East. See Kent, "Books read in 1799," etc. (n.p.) (n.d.), in 3 The Papers of James Kent (Library of Congress, Manuscript Division) (filed after letter from Elizabeth Kent to James Kent, Albany, Nov. 16, 1806). In the same source Kent records reading the first seven volumes of East's Reports as they appeared, one or more a year, in the years 1802-06. See *id.* Horton purports to reproduce the legal entries from this document, but deletes without disclosure Kent's entries for "Durnford," that is, for Durnford & East's Reports. See Horton, *supra* note 4, at 147 n.73.

William Johnson commences the preface to 1 Johnson's Reports (1807) by locating his New York reports in what he reckons as the five-hundred-year tradition of law reporting in England. "If works of this nature have been found so indispensable in that country, they are far more necessary in our own, where new questions every day arise, in the decision of which English adjudications cannot always afford a certain guide." 1 Johns. iii. Johnson discloses that, "[w]ithout bestowing much thought on the best possible plan for a work of this kind, I have adopted the manner of the most approved English Reporters, because it was familiar to every lawyer, and possessed the authority of experience in its favour." *Id.* at vii.

141. Wallace's dissection of the multi-volume, multi-reporter series entitled Modern Reports provides an example. See Wallace, *supra* note 119, at 347-90.

142.

> [T]he scope of a rule of law, and therefore its meaning, depend upon a determination of what facts will be considered similar to those present when the rule was first announced. The finding of similarity or difference is the key step in the legal process. . . . [T]he judge in the present case may find irrelevant the existence or absence of facts which prior judges thought important.

Edward H. Levi, An Introduction to Legal Reasoning 2 (1949).

143. Lord Halsbury's account in Quinn v. Leathem, 1901 App. Cas. 495, 506 (H.L.) (appeal taken from Ir.), is prominent:

> [E]ver y judgment must be read as applicable to the particular facts proved, or assumed to be proved, since the generality of the expressions which may be found there are not intended to be expositions of the whole law, but governed and qualified by the particular facts of the case in which such expressions are to be found.

144. In the preface to the second edition of his Reports, George Caines discloses that it was his practice sometimes "to discard from the opinions of the judges the statements of facts, by which they were, when delivered, in general preceded." 1 Caines' Reports 2d, *supra* note 139, at v.

145. In the preface to the final volume of Johnson's Chancery Reports, Johnson recalls that it was at Kent's "friendly solicitation [that Johnson] undertook to report the decisions of the Supreme Court, in which [Kent] then presided. . . ." 7 William Johnson, Reports of Cases Adjudged in the Court of Chancery of New-York 3 (Philadelphia, E.F. Backus, 2d ed. 1816-1824) [hereinafter Johnson's Chancery Reports] (7 vols.). Correspondence survives in which Johnson thanks Kent for Kent's "attention to my pecuniary interest in this appointment." Letter from William Johnson to James Kent, New York City (Dec. 23, 1805), in 3 The Papers of James Kent (Library of Congress, Manuscript Division). This letter is partially reproduced in William Kent, Memoirs, *supra* note 4, at 125-26.

146. See William Johnson, Reports of Cases Argued and Decided in the Supreme Court of Judicature . . . in the State of New-York (New York, Isaac Riley & Co. 1807-24) (20 vols.) [hereinafter Johnson's Reports].

147. William Johnson, Reports of Cases Adjudged in the Supreme Court of Judicature of the State of New-York from January Term 1799 to January Term 1803 (New York, Isaac Riley & Co. 1808-12) (3 vols.). Johnson explains in the preface how he compiled these reports:

> [T]he facts in each cause are stated from the *cases* and *paper-books* delivered to the judges on the argument, and from the affidavits and records filed with the clerks of the court. The opinions of the judges are taken from their own manuscripts, and, in almost every case, are given exactly as they were pronounced. . . . For obvious reasons, the arguments of counsel, except in a very few instances, are not inserted.

1 *id.* at iv.

148. See Act of Apr. 15, 1814, ch. 193, 1814 N.Y. Laws 243.

149. See Johnson's Chancery Reports, *supra* note 145.

150. See William Johnson, A Digest of the Cases Decided and Reported in the Supreme Court of Judicature and the Court for the Correction of Errors, in the State of New-York, from January Term 1799 to October Term 1813, Inclusive (Albany, E.F. Backus 1815) [hereinafter Johnson, 1815 Digest].

151. See William Johnson, A Digest of the Cases Decided and Reported in the Supreme Court of Judicature, the Court of Chancery, and the Court for the Correction of Errors, of the State of New-York from 1799 to 1823 (Albany, E.F. Backus 1825) (2 vols.).

152. See generally John D. Cowley, A Bibliography of Abridgments, Digests Dictionaries and Indexes of English Law to the Year 1800 (Selden Society) (1923) (tracing history of case law abridgments from late 14th century to late 17th century). On the abridgment tradition in the eighteenth century, see 12 Holdsworth, H.E.L., *supra* note 23, at 162-75. The great American exemplar was published just before Johnson's second edition. See Nathan Dane, A General Abridgment and Digest of American Law with Occasional Notes and Comments (Boston, Cummings, Hilliard & Co. 1823) (8 vols.).

153. Kent, 1828 Letter, *supra* note 19, at 843. This portion of the letter is also quoted *supra* note 117.

154. Kent, Manuscript entry at flyleaf (n.d.), located in Kent's copy of Johnson, 1815 Digest, *supra* note 150 (emphasis omitted) (New York State Library, Albany, Manuscripts and Special Collections, James Kent Law Book Collection).

155. Joseph Story wrote to Johnson in 1821 that "you have conferred the highest honor on [New York] State; and [] its judicial character abroad has been greatly elevated by your excellent Reports." Letter from Joseph Story to William Johnson (Nov. 11, 1821), in 1 Life and Letters of Joseph Story 405, 407 (William W. Story ed., 1851) [hereinafter Story Letters]. In 1824, on Johnson's retirement, Story wrote him: "your thirty volumes of Reports will form an era, not merely in the jurisprudence of New York, but of America." Letter from Joseph Story to William Johnson (May 16, 1824), in Story Letters, *supra*, at 428, 429. These sources are noticed in G. Edward White, *supra* note 130, at 106 & nn.129-30. In a correspondence stimulated by Daniel Webster, Story wrote Kent in 1819, when Kent was still sitting in the New York Court of Chancery and Story was riding circuit for the U.S. Supreme Court:

> At an early period of my professional life, I read the New York Reports with zeal and care, and I felt how much you had contributed to enlarge our commercial law, by liberal drafts from the civil law and foreign jurists; and our common law, by a habit of tracing every principle to its original foundations, through all the shifting authorities.

Letter from Joseph Story to James Kent (Aug. 21, 1819), *in* Story Letters, *supra*, at 330, 330.

156. "You have reported every opinion which I gave . . . during the five and twenty years that I was a Judge at Law and in Equity, with the exception of the short interval occupied by Mr. Caines' Reports." 4 Commentaries, *supra* note 3, at iii.

157. See Letter from William Johnson to William Wetmore Story, son of Joseph Story (June 6, 1846) (New York, Massachusetts Hist. Soc'y) ("[H]aving previous to my removal to my present residence destroyed all letters and papers the preservation of which was not deemed necessary in regard to the interests or affairs of others or of myself."). I acknowledge the kindness of Ruth Wedgwood, who brought this document to my attention.

158. See 4 Dexter, *supra* note 8, at 607-08.

159. The dramatist William Dunlap, mentioned *infra* text accompanying note 163, records in his diary for January 29, 1798,

that he was employing Johnson to defend him in a piece of commercial litigation. 1 Diary of William Dunlap (1766-1839): The Memoirs of a Dramatist, Theatrical Manager, Painter, Critic, Novelist, and Historian 215 (N.Y. Hist. Soc. 1930) (3 vols.) [hereinafter Dunlap Diary].

160. Domenico Alberto Azuni, Droit maritime de L'Europe (Paris 1805) (2 vols.), translated as The Maritime Law of Europe (William Johnson trans., N.Y., Isaac Riley & Co., 1806) (2 vols.) [hereinafter Azuni]. The French edition from which Johnson worked was itself a translation of Domenico Alberto Azuni, Dizionario universale ragionato della giurisprudenza mercantile (Nice, Presso de la Societa tipografica 1786-88) (4 vols.). In the same letter in which Johnson writes to thank Kent for arranging for the terms of the reportership, *supra* note 145, Johnson tells Kent that he prepared the translation the previous summer. See Letter from William Johnson to James Kent, New York City (Dec. 23, 1805), in 3 The Papers of James Kent (Library of Congress, Manuscript Division). Johnson did not identify himself as the translator on the title page of the English-language edition, but he disclosed his hand in the work by identifying himself as the copyright owner. See 1 Azuni, *supra*, at iv. Kent refers to Johnson as the translator when citing Azuni in 2 Commentaries, *supra* note 3, at 512 n.e.

161. See 4 Dexter, *supra* note 8, at 508-11.

162. Kent's membership in the Friendly Club is noted in Goldberg, *supra* note 4, at 184. "[T]he Friendly Club was organized some time during the twelve months following September, 1793." James E. Cronin, Elihu Hubbard Smith and the New York Friendly Club, 1795-1798, 64 Publications of the Mod. Language Ass'n of Am. 471, 472 (1949). For a description of a similar institution in Boston, the Friday Evening Club, see Alfred S. Konefsky, Law and Culture in Antebellum Boston, 40 Stan. L. Rev. 1119, 1155-56 (1988) (book review). Cronin observes that in New York City "during this period there were clubs without number," and he lists a dozen. James E. Cronin, Introduction to Smith Diary, *supra* note 56, at 15.

163. Regarding Dunlap, see 5 Dictionary of American Biography 516-18 (Allen Johnson & Dumas Malone eds., 1943). The diaries are Dunlap Diary, *supra* note 159; Smith Diary, *supra* note 56.

164. See, e.g., Smith Diary, *supra* note 56, at 161 (entry for May 1, 1796) ("Kent, Johnson and I took a long and very pleasant walk into the country.").

165. James E. Cronin, who edited the Smith Diary for publication, noticed that Johnson's "relationship with Smith is strange in that, although he is mentioned scores of times in the 'Diary,' he does not appear to have expressed his opinion on much of anything, at least nothing that Smith felt like recording." Smith Diary, *supra* note 56, at 44 n.59 (note of James E. Cronin, ed.).

166. In a letter written in 1806, Johnson makes passing mention of his Federalist disposition. "We have had a very contested election here; although the federalists have lost it, they have shown that much may be done by exertion. They drove the democrats so hard, that many of them really despaired of success. . . ." Letter from William Johnson to William P. Beers, New York City (May 2, 1806) (Columbia Univ., Butler Library, Rare Book and Manuscript Collections, X973/C72/vol. 7, at 114).

167. Because Johnson was based in New York City and Kent in Albany, their collaboration required correspondence, and some of it has survived in the Kent Papers in the Library of Congress.

Writing Johnson to enclose opinions for the first volume of the Chancery reports, Kent tells him that "I am only afraid of reporting too much, and I shall stand in need of your judgment on that point, seeing I am alone in my Court and have no other aid, and I shall place more reliance on your judgment than my own." Letter from James Kent to William Johnson, Albany (Apr. 8, 1815), in 4 The Papers of James Kent (Library of Congress, Manuscript Division).

Toward the end of his chancellorship, Kent writes Johnson in response to a letter from Johnson that has not survived, in which Johnson questioned something Kent had written about the Roman law of Societas.

I subscribe entirely to all that you say, and I am satisfied on a moment's reflection that what I wrote was unnecessary, and that I was contesting a shadow. The observations in my opinions respecting incestuous marriages, and that a surety cannot have recourse even against his principal before a default, are self evident, and the learning I had collected was misplaced and ostentatious, and I will request that these opinions be entirely suppressed unless there be something in the cases separate from these points. . . . The opinions now sent I—[illegible] are true Business opinions and I am not too much hurried. I should like to revise and prune them, and you would gratify me if you would strike out in every case any thing that does not conform to the model I have suggested.

Letter from James Kent to William Johnson, Albany (Mar. 2, 1821), in 5 The Papers of James Kent (Library of Congress, Manuscript Division).

168. Regarding Kent's involvement on the losing side in the politics of constitutional revision in New York State in 1821, events which appear to have led to his downfall in 1823, see Horton, *supra* note 4, at 245-63. At a banquet held in Kent's honor at Harvard shortly after his retirement in 1823, someone led a toast with the observation that "[t]he Athenians banished Aristides for excess of virtue. . . . It was reserved for an American state to banish a great man for the excess of learning." *Id.* at 266.

169. Letter from James Kent to William Johnson, Albany (Apr. 29, 1823), in 5 The Papers of James Kent (Library of Congress, Manuscript Division).

170. See Katz, *supra* note 76, at 262-84 (discussing association of unpopular colonial governors with equity courts); Perry Miller, *supra* note 98, at 171-72 (1965) ("Popular distrust arose first of all from the fact that it dispensed with juries.").

171. See 12 Holdsworth, H.E.L., *supra* note 23, at 257-85 (discussing the development of substantive equity under Lord Hardwicke (1737-1756)). Roscoe Pound observed of the early period of American independence: "The system of equity was not yet complete in England and absorption of the law merchant was still going forward. . . . Our courts had to complete the development of equity and the taking over of the law merchant concurrently with the English courts." Pound, Formative Era, *supra* note 2, at 20. Regarding Lord Mansfield's use of civilian sources in building the English commercial and maritime law,

see Christopher P. Rodgers, Continental Literature and the Development of the Common Law by the King's Bench: c. 1750-1800, in The Courts and the Development of Commercial Law 161-94 (Comparative Studies in Continental and Anglo-American Legal History) (Vito Piergiovanni ed., 1987).

172. Kent, 1828 Letter, *supra* note 19, at 844.

173. *Id.* at 845. He explains that he worked very hard on his opinions in Chancery in order to forestall review and reversal in the "Senate & court of Errors." *Id.* at 844. "[M]y object was . . . to anticipate an angry and vexatious appeal to a popular tribune by disappointed counsel." *Id.* at 845.

174. Manning v. Manning, 1 Johns. Ch. 527, 529 (1815).

175. *Id.*

176. Story wrote Kent in 1819 that

I read your Chancery decisions with the greatest pleasure and instruction. This is a branch of law in which, as you may well suppose, from the want of State Chancery Courts in my Circuit to aid my studies and reduce my investigations to practice, I must necessarily be very deficient. . . . I make it a rule in my circuit to adopt the practice of your Court wherever it can be applied; and I hope hereafter to build up, if I can awaken the ardor of the Bar, a system of Chancery Jurisprudence for the States included in my circuit. To you we shall be most deeply indebted, and from your Reports we shall draw most amply.

Letter from Joseph Story to James Kent (Aug. 21, 1819), *in* Story Letters, *supra* note 155, at 331. With Story's protestations of naivete regarding equity, contrast Roscoe Pound's judgment of Story's ultimate influence on American equity. See Pound, Formative Era, *supra* note 2, at 156-57.

It was said in the 1830s that "'no English books of chancery decisions are more frequently or more respectfully cited in the courts of South Carolina than the seven volumes of Mr. Johnson's reports of Kent's decisions.'" Horton, *supra* note 4, at 211 n.38 (quoting 6 London Law Magazine 132 (1831)).

Hampton Carson thought that Kent's influence was immensely buttressed by the fact that his opinions as Chancellor were published and bound in exclusively Equity Reports and not mixed as they were in Pennsylvania, where no separate Chancery existed, with common law matters. Kent's administration of Equity forms an epoch in the judicial history of New York and the seven volumes of Johnson's Chancery Reports are classics of the profession.

Carson, *supra* note 7, at 670.

177. See, e.g., Pound, Formative Era, *supra* note 2, at 140-41.

178. Kent's Commentary on International Law (J.T. Abdy, ed., Cambridge, Deighton, Bell & Co. 1866) (2d ed. 1878).

179. Friedrich Bissing, Das Verfassungsrecht der Vereinigten Staaten Nord-Amerikas nach James Kent (Heidelberg, G. Reichard 1836).

180. James Kent, Del gobierno y jurisprudencia constitucional de los Estados Unidos (Alejandro Carrasco Albano, trans., Buenos Aires, Imprenta de Buenos Aires 1865).

181. James Kent, Comentarios a la constitucion de los Estados Unidos de America (J. Carlos Mexia, trans., Mexico City, Imprenta Poliglota de Carlos Ramiro 1878).

182. James Kent, A Practical Treatise on Commercial and Maritime Law, with a Chapter on Incorporeal Hereditaments (Edinburgh, Thomas Clark 1837). This work is quite scarce. I have used University of Virginia Law Library, shelfmark T/. K374p/1837. The book was published during Kent's lifetime, and he owned a copy of it. See Kent, 1842 Library Handlist, *supra* note 41, at 52.

183. On the relative recency of the absorption of commercial and maritime law into the English common law of the day, see *supra* note 171. For extensive recent discussion, see generally 1 James Oldham, The Mansfield Manuscripts and the Growth of English Law in the Eighteenth Century (1992).

184. There are three superb modern studies of Continental institutionalist writing: Alan Watson, Roman Law and Comparative Law 147-81 (1991) [hereinafter Watson, Roman Law], a portion of which derives from Alan Watson, The Making of the Civil Law 62-82 (1981); John W. Cairns, Institutional Writings in Scotland Reconsidered, 4 J. Legal Hist., Dec. 1983, at 76 [hereinafter Cairns, Institutes]; and Klaus Luig, The Institutes of National Law in the Seventeenth and Eighteenth Centuries, 17 Jurid. Rev. (n.s.) 193 (1972) [hereinafter Luig, Institutes], an English-language version of Klaus Luig, Institutionenlehrbucher des nationalen Rechts im 17. und 18. Jahrhundert, 3 Ius Commune 64 (1970).

185. See Luig, Institutes, *supra* note 184, at 194-98.

186. 7 Francois M.A. de Voltaire, Oeuvres de Voltaire 5 (Paris 1838).

187. See *id.* at 201-02.

188. See Watson, Roman Law, *supra* note 184, at 147-50.

189. See Cairns, Institutes, *supra* note 184, at 77-78.

190. The Institutes of Gaius (Francis de Zulueta, trans. 1946-53) (Latin text and English translation) (2 vols.). A recent translation is The Institutes of Gaius (W.M. Gordon & O.F. Robinson trans., 1988). The full text of Gaius was rediscovered in Kent's lifetime. This event caused great excitement in legal intellectual circles; Kent refers to it in 1 Commentaries, *supra* note 3, at 501.

191. See H.F. Jolowicz & Barry Nicholas, Historical Introduction to the Study of Roman Law 386-90 (3d ed. 1972).

192. See Watson, Roman Law, *supra* note 184, at 15. For an English translation of the work, see The Institutes of Justinian (J.B. Moyle trans., Oxford, Clarendon Press 1883) [hereinafter Justinian]. For discussion of the continuity from Gaius to Justinian and the importance of Justinian's Institutes, see Watson, Roman Law, *supra* note 184, at 147-49.

193. See Justinian, *supra* note 192, at 3-6.

194. Guy Coquille, Institution au droit francais (1st ed. Paris 1607), republished in 2 Les Oeuvres de Maistre Guy Coquille (Paris 1665). Regarding Coquille, see Luig, Institutes, *supra* note 184, at 204-06; Watson, Roman Law, *supra* note 184, at 150-51.

195. Gabriel Argou, Institution au droit francais (Paris 1692). Regarding Argou, see Cairns, Institutes, *supra* note 184, at 87-88. Kent's copy of the 1773 edition is in the Columbia Law Library. Kent wrote on the flyleaf of his copy of the 1773 edition of Volume 1: "Chancellor D'Aguesseau speaks of . . . the Institutes of M. D'Argou as a proper introduction to the study of the droit francois." Kent, Manuscript entry at flyleaf located in Kent's copy of Gabriel Argou, Institution au droit francais (Paris 1773) (2 vols.) (Columbia Law Library, Special Collections).

196. Claude Serres, Les institutions du droit francais (Paris, Caveller 1753).

197. Hugo Grotius, Inleidinge tot de Hollandsche rechtsgeleerdheyd (s'Gavenhage, Hillebrant 1631).

198. Ulric Huber, Heedensdaegse rechtsgeleertheyt (Leuwarden 1686) (rough translation: "contemporary legal learning"); Simon van Leeuwen, Paratitula juris novissimi, dat is, een kort begrip van het Rooms-Hollandtsreght (Leyden, P. Leffen 1652) (roughly: "Titles of the new law, that is, a short version of Roman-Dutch law"). I follow Watson, Roman Law, *supra* note 184, at 153, in directing attention to these Dutch works.

199. For an extensive discussion, see Cairns, Institutes, *supra* note 184, at 88-98.

200. James Viscount of Stair, The Institutions of the Law of Scotland (Edinburgh, Anderson 1681). There is a modern scholarly edition: James D. Stair, The Institutions of the Law of Scotland (David M. Walker ed., 1981) [hereinafter Stair, 1981].

201. George Mackenzie, Institutions of the Law of Scotland (Edinburgh, John Reid 1684). On Mackenzie, see Alan Watson, Some Notes on Mackenzie's *Institutions* and the European Legal Tradition, 16 Ius Commune 303 (1989).

202. John Erskine, Institutes of the Law of Scotland (Edinburgh, J. Bell 1773).

203. Sebastian Khraisser, Institutiones iuris Romano-Bavarici electoralis (Augsburg, Weh 1644).

204. See Watson, Roman Law, *supra* note 184, at 160.

205. Georg Beyer, Delineatio juris Germanici [Outline of German Law] (Halle, Gribner 1718). Beyer is cited in Luig, Institutes, *supra* note 184, at 209; Watson, Roman Law, *supra* note 184, at 162.

206. Johann Gottlieb Heineccius, Elementa iuris Germanici [Elements of German Law] (Halle, Orphanotrophei 1736-37). Gottlieb is discussed in Luig, Institutes, *supra* note 184, at 209; Watson, Roman Law, *supra* note 184, at 163. Regarding the renown of Heineccius in the eighteenth century, see M.H. Hoeflich, Edward Gibbon, Roman Lawyer, 39 Am. J. Comp. L. 803, 807-08 (1991).

207. Julius Marchio de Pozzo, Paraphrasis Institutionem italica cum legisbus Venetis collata [Summary of Italian Law Collated with the Venetian Statutes] (Venice 1697). This work is noticed in Luig, Institutes, *supra* note 184, at 223 n.227.

208. Francesco Rapolla, Commentaria de iure regni Neapolitani [Commentaries on Royal Neapolitan Law] (Naples 1746). Rapolla is cited in Luig, Institutes, *supra* note 184, at 225 n.235.

209. Oronzio Fighera, Institutiones iuris Regni Neapolitani [Institutions of the Royal Neapolitan Law] (Naples 1766). Fighera is cited in Luig, Institutes, *supra* note 184, at 225 n.236.

210. David Nehrman, Inledning til den Swenska jurisprudentiam civilem [Introduction to Swedish Civil Law] (Lund, Decreaux 1729). Nehrman is discussed in Luig, Institutes, *supra* note 184, at 219-20.

211. Laurids Nørregaard, Forelaesinger over den danske og norske private Ret [Lectures on Danish and Norwegian Private Law] (Copenhagen 1784-99). Nørregaard is discussed in Luig, Institutes, *supra* note 184, at 217-19.

212. Ignacio Jordan de Asso y del Rio & Miguel de Manuel y Rodriguez, Instituciones del Derecho Civil de Castilla (Madrid, Francisco Xavier Garcia 1771). See also Cairns, Institutes, *supra* note 184, at 82-83 (briefly describing the work of Asso and Manuel and noting their "determination to distinguish Castilian law from the Roman"). There is an English translation, Institutes of the Civil Law of Spain (Lewis F.C. Johnson trans., London, J. Butterworth & Son 1825). The translation was reprinted in the United States. See Joseph M. White, A New Collection of Laws, Charters, and Local Ordinances of the Governments of Great Britain, France, and Spain . . . To Which Is Prefixed Judge Johnston's Translation of Azo [sic] and Manuel's Institutes of the Civil Law of Spain (Philadelphia, T. & J.W. Johnson 1839).

213. José Maria Alvarez, Instituciones de derecho real de Castilla y de Indias [Institutes of the Royal Law of Castille and the Indies] (Guatemala City, I. Beteta 1818-20). Alvarez is discussed in Watson, Roman Law, *supra* note 184, at 164.

214. See *id.*

215. See Blackstone, *supra* note 28.

216. See, e.g., Michael Lobban, The Common Law and English Jurisprudence: 1760-1850, at 19-26 (1991); Watson, Roman Law, *supra* note 184, at 165-81; John W. Cairns, Blackstone, An English Institutist: Legal Literature and the Rise of the Nation State, 4 Oxford J. Legal Stud. 318 (1984). An earlier version of Watson's argument can be found in Alan Watson, The Structure of Blackstone's Commentaries, 97 Yale L.J. 795 (1988).

217. It should, however, be observed that a variety of local and special-purpose courts had survived into Blackstone's day outside the main common-law courts. Blackstone devotes Chapter 6 of Book 3 to these courts. His theme is that they are archaic, and that the main common-law courts "have a concurrent jurisdiction with these, or else a super-intendency over them. . . ." 3 Blackstone, *supra* note 28, at 81. Further, purporting to follow the views of Sir Edward Coke, Blackstone urges hostility to these enclave courts: "[T]hese particular jurisdictions, derogating from the general jurisdiction of the courts of common law, are ever taken strictly, and cannot be extended farther than the express letter of their privileges will most explicitly warrant." 3 *id.* at 85.

218. See S.F.C. Milsom, The Nature of Blackstone's Achievement, 1 Oxford J. Legal Stud. 1, 9-12 (1981).

219. Volume Four is devoted to criminal law. See 4 Blackstone, *supra* note 28.

220. Quoted in Cairns, *supra* note 216, at 340. Cairns discusses the relation of Blackstone's Commentaries to the

institutionalist tradition, see *id.* at 340-52, and cites, among others, Wood's civil law Institute as an influence on Blackstone's work. See *id.* at 343. On Wood, see Robert B. Robinson, The Two Institutes of Thomas Wood: A Study in Eighteenth Century Legal Scholarship, 35 Am. J. Legal Hist. 432 (1991) (discussing place of Wood's work in civil and common law traditions of English legal scholarship in the eighteenth century). Regarding the early seventeenth-century institutional works by Cowell and Finch, see David J. Seipp, The Structure of English Common Law in the Seventeenth Century, *in* Legal History in the Making: Proceedings of the Ninth British Legal History Conference Glasgow 1989, at 61 (W.M. Gordon & T.D. Fergus eds., 1991).

221. See *supra* text accompanying note 28; text accompanying note 32 (Kent recalls that as a student he read Blackstone "again and again").

222. See Letter from James Kent to Moss Kent, Albany (Feb. 6, 1813), in 4 The Papers of James Kent (Library of Congress, Manuscript Division).

223. Kent, 1842 Library Handlist, *supra* note 41.

224. See *supra* note 111.

225. See generally James B. Scott, The Spanish Origins of International Law (1934).

226. See *supra* text accompanying note 193.

227. See, e.g., Stair, 1981, *supra* note 200, at 79-80.

228. Another influential forerunner was Swift's treatise on Connecticut law, whose citations acknowledge its debt to Blackstone. Swift's Book 2 (persons) and Book 3 (things) are preceded by Book 1 on powers of government. See Zephaniah Swift, A System of the Laws of the State of Connecticut (Windham, John Byrne 1795) (2 vols.).

229. 1 Blackstone, *supra* note 28, at 142-326.

230. See Joseph Story, Commentaries on the Constitution of the United States (Boston, Hilliard, Gray & Co. 1833) (3 vols.).

231. Recall that Kent titles the chapters of the Commentaries "lectures," and that the preface to Volume One identifies the work as the fruit of Kent's appointment as professor of law at Columbia. On the connection between lectures and Commentaries, see *supra* text accompanying notes 86-90 and note 90.

232. See Simpson, *supra* note 1, at 674 (discussing main American treatise writers).

Chapter 17

A Summary of the Course of Law Lectures in Columbia College

1824

James Kent

James Kent (July 31, 1763-December 12, 1847) was Chancellor of New York from 1814 to 1823 and professor at Columbia College (later Columbia University) from 1793 to 1795 and 1824 to 1826. His *Commentaries on American Law* are described in chapter 1. See also chapter 5. Reprinted from James Kent, *A Summary of the Course of Law Lectures in Columbia College: Commenced November 8, 1824* (New York: Clayton and Van Norden, Printers, 1824).

LECTURE I.

History of the American Union.

LECTURE II.

History of the Law of Nations.

The foundations of the law of nations considered, and its connexion with ethical jurisprudence. It is composed, (1) of the principles of natural law; (2) of usages and customs; (3) of conventional or instituted law—The reasons why the Christian powers of Europe have a law of nations peculiar to them and to us—The very imperfect state of international law among the ancient Greeks both as to intercourse in peace, and as to the rules and maxims of war—The better condition of public law with the Romans—The ferocity and cruelty of the laws of war even among them—Efforts of Cicero and the Roman civilians to meliorate the character of their public law—Its great defects even under the Roman system—Deplorable state of national law under the dominion of the northern nations who overturned tho Roman empire—The several institutions which contributed to improve the law of nations in the middle ages—The favourable influence of Christianity, of chivalry, of the civil law of treaties, and of resident ministers, upon the improvement of the law of nations—The great merit and influence of Grotius, and the merit of his principal successors, considered—The influence of judicial decisions and commercial ordinances in bringing the law of nations to its present state of perfection.

Lecture III.

The Rights and Duties of Nations in a State of Peace.

Right of every people to choose its own form of government—The equality and independence of the nations—Instances of the flagrant violation of this right—How far one nation may assist another in distress, and under oppression—Precedents on this point cited—Obligation of nations to perform their contracts—The extent of the domain of a nation, and its jurisdiction over the adjoining seas, extensively and historically considered. The right of every nation to regulate its own foreign as well as domestic commerce, and no nation has a right to interrupt the commerce between other nations—Instances of the violation of this right mentioned and condemned—Every nation has a right to regulate its own colonial trade—The allowance of an innocent passage to foreigners over the waters and territories of other powers, and without any unreasonable exactions, is a duty—Every nation is bound to deliver up atrocious fugitives from justice—Ambassadors are not responsible to the municipal law of the government to which they are deputed—When and how far a government is bound by the act of its ambassador—The legality and effect of consular establishments.

Lecture IV.

On the Commencement and Incipient State of War.

The just causes of war—How far we are bound by a previous treaty to assist in war—A view of the power to declare war, and in what department of the government it is or ought to be vested—Whether a previous declaration of war be necessary—History of the practice on this subject—How far the persons and property of the enemy, found in the country at the commencement of war, are entitled to protection—A view of the provisions in the conventional law of nations on this point—The settlement of the question judicially in this country—The question on the right to confiscate debts due to the enemy considered, and the authorities reviewed—The illegality of all commercial intercourse with the enemy examined—The great authority and excellence of English and American judicial decisions in prize cases, and on the whole doctrine of maritime capture.

Lecture V.

Of the Various Descriptions of Property Impressed with a Hostile Character.

A hostile character attaches to property,

1. As being the produce of a hostile soil, though owned by a neutral; or,
2. Belonging to a person concerned in a commercial establishment in the enemy's country; or
3. Belonging to a person residing or domiciled there—Residence the test of national character by the modern law of maritime capture—The circumstances constituting a residence.
4. Being employed in a trade specially allowed to the party by the enemy, or going under his flag or passport.
5. History, nature and authority of the rule of 1756.
6. Character of property while *in transitu* between the belligerent and the neutral.

Lecture VI.

The Rights of Belligerent Powers in Relation to Each Other.

The violence and ferocity of the old laws of war, and the modern improvement of them—The limitations imposed to warfare on land—The law of retaliation, and the restrictions upon it—The necessity of commission, or special authority, to justify offensive hostilities, discussed—The law of nations on the subject of privateering extensively considered—Prohibitions imposed upon assistance afforded to one foreign nation against another with whom our country is at peace—When property captured at sea vests in the captor—The necessity of a judicial condemnation—To what Courts, and in what cases, the jurisdiction of prizes appertains by the law of nations—The doctrine of ransom bills discussed, and the authorities reviewed—The right of *postliminium*, when, and to what extent it applies—Of the effect of recapture of property captured on the high-seas, and the allowance of salvage.

Lecture VII.

The Rights and Duties of Neutrality.

A neutral may furnish a stipulated succour consistent with a general neutrality—His property on board an enemy's vessel is free, and not liable to confiscation—Belligerent property inviolable while within neutral territory—No hostile acts can originate in a neutral country—It is in the discretion of a neutral to grant or refuse a passage to belligerent forces—A belligerent cannot pursue his enemy within neutral territory—A belligerent may be allowed, or denied, in the discretion of the neutral, the privilege of bringing his prizes into a neutral port—Enemy's property may be seized on the high seas on board a neutral vessel—How far the neutral is entitled to freight in such cases—The history of the fruitless efforts to make free ships free goods—Neutral property may even be safely laden on board an armed belligerent cruiser—A critical review of the decisions on this point.

Lecture VIII.

Restrictions Imposed by War on Neutral Trade.

The law of contraband of war considered, and the questions which have been in dispute on this point—Penalties inflicted on a trade in contraband of war—The rights of blockade, and the violation of these rights, and the penalty for such violation, considered—Penalties for breach of neutral duty in carrying despatches for the enemy—The belligerent right of visitation and search examined, and the penalty for illegally resisting search even by an armed neutral convoy—The effect of a spoliation of papers by a neutral.

Lecture IX.

On the Termination of Hostilities.

The nature and effect of truces, and passports, and safe conducts, considered, and the various obligations which arise out of them—To whom is intrusted the power to make truces, and grant safe conducts, and conclude treaties of peace—Whether it be competent for the treaty-making power to alienate any part of the national territory—The obligation of negotiating peace in concert with allies—The operation of a treaty of peace upon conquered territory, and upon the causes of the war, and upon previously acquired rights—The construction of treaties of peace as to the time of operation—The moral and political obligation of treaties, and the rules of construction of acts touching the violation of them.

Lecture X.

Offences Against the Law of Nations.

The violation of safe conducts—The violation of the privileges of ambassadors—Tho crime of piracy, and the crime of being concerned in the slave trade—in what manner, and to what extent, these offences are punished.

[*To be continued as the Lectures advance.*]

Part II: The Government and Constitutional Jurisprudence of the United States

Lecture XI.

Of Congress.

The division of the legislature into two branches—The policy and utility of such a division—President Adams' work on this subject recommended—Erroneous theories and vicious examples, in Europe and in this country, on that point, corrected by experience—The constitution of the senate—Its structure, mode of appointment, and term of office, intended for stability in legislation—The election, qualifications, and characteristic features of the house of representatives considered—Their number, and rule of apportionment—The efficacy and great value of popular representation—The powers and privileges of each house—Sketch of the powers of congress—The order and course of passing laws—Policy and utility of the qualified negative of the president.

Lecture XII.

Judicial Construction of the Powers of Congress.

The United States can lawfully give themselves a right to priority of payment over private creditors—Such an implied power declared constitutional—Congress can lawfully institute banks for national purposes—The discussions on this subject in congress, and in the executive cabinet, reviewed—Decision of the supreme court in favour of the power—Congress can lay a duty on carriages, without following the rule of apportionment—The decision on this point considered—Supreme power of taxation in congress over all the unrepresented territories of the United States declared—Absolute title and exclusive right of pre-emption in the United States, over the Indian lands within the bounds of the United States, asserted and adjudged—The effect of judgments of one state in the courts of other states declared and ascertained—Difference of opinion between the federal government and the governments of some of the states, on the power of calling out the militia—How far the state authorities can lawfully punish the militia who are delinquent under the call into the service of the United States—The decision on this point examined.

Lecture XIII.

Of the President.

The unity of the executive department, and the utility of this principle—Qualifications of the president—His mode of appointment—The wisdom of the provision examined—His duration and support—A particular consideration of his power over the national force, his power of pardon, and his power of making treaties with the consent of the senate—The discussions on the obligation of treaties upon congress reviewed—The power of appointment to office, and the wisdom of its disposition—His other general duties and responsibility.

Lecture XIV.

Of the Judicial Department.

The mode of appointment of the judges—The tenure of their office—The provision for their support—The pre-eminence of the constitution of the United States in all these respects—A general sketch of the judicial power—The organization and jurisdiction of the Supreme Court, both original and appellate—The organization and jurisdiction of the circuit courts—The organization and jurisdiction of the district courts—The officers of the courts, as attorneys and counsel, clerks and marshals, with their appropriate distinctions, and their regulations under the laws of the United States.

Lecture XV.

The Powers of the Supreme and Circuit Courts.

The appellate jurisdiction of the supreme court over the state courts extensively considered—The case of *Fairfax v. Hunter*, asserting that jurisdiction, examined at large—Limitation of the power of that court on the subject of *mandamus*—When a state can be considered a party, so as to give the court original jurisdiction—Its appellate jurisdiction from circuit and territorial courts construed strictly—Limited also to matter appearing on the face of the record—Its appellate jurisdiction, though a state be a party, explained and enforced in an examination of the case of *Cohens v. Virginia*—The jurisdiction of the court over state officers, acting under state laws which were unconstitutional, how far vindicated by the case of *Osborn v. The Bank of the United States.*

Lecture XVI.

Subject Continued.

The common law, to what extent it is a part of the jurisprudence of the United States, examined—The case of the *United States v. Worrall* considered—The doctrine to be deduced from that case, and the cases of the *United States v. Hudson and Goodwin*, and the *United States v. Coolidge*, on the subject of the existence and application of the common law in the federal courts—The merit of *Duponceau's* view of this point—A review of the whole series of decisions respecting the jurisdiction of the federal courts, in controversies where an alien was a party, or between citizens of different states, and notice taken of the various distinctions on that subject.

Lecture XVII.

The Powers of the District and Territorial Courts.

When the district court acts as a court of admiralty and maritime jurisdiction, and when as a court of common law—The questions and cases, arising on its admiralty jurisdiction examined and discussed at large—The peculiar mode of proceeding in the admiralty—Jurisdiction of the district judges as claimed in bankruptcy—The character of the jurisdiction of the territorial courts.

Lecture XVIII.

Restrictions on State Powers.

In what cases the powers of congress are to be deemed exclusive, and in what cases concurrent with the exercise of like power in the states—No state can pass an *ex post facto* law, and the case of *Calder v. Bull* examined—No state can by law control or obstruct the judgments or authorities of the United States, and several cases on this point examined—No state legislature can repeal a state law, or revoke or alter a legislative grant or charter, in the nature of a contract, vesting rights either in individuals, or in private, corporations, or do any act impairing the obligation of contracts—The several cases and decisions on this subject reviewed and considered at large.

Lecture XIX.

Subject Continued.

The power of naturalization exclusive—Cases considered—The states may pass bankrupt laws under certain limitations, but not insolvent laws discharging the debtor from his pre-existing debts—The judicial doctrine on this subject examined—No state can tax, or otherwise impede or control, the bank of the United States, or other lawful means employed by the government of the union to execute its powers—The cases on this point reviewed—The effect of a cession by a state of lands to the United States, as to local jurisdiction—How far the right of congress to regulate commerce, controls the power of the states over navigable waters within its jurisdiction—The case of *Gibbons v. Ogden* considered—Reflections on the progress and influence of national jurisprudence.

Lecture XX.

On the criminal jurisprudence of the United States, and the various crimes and misdemeanors cognizable in the federal courts.

[*To be continued as the Lectures advance.*]

Part III: On the Sources of Municipal Law, and the Law Concerning Personal and Domestic Rights

Lecture XXI.

Statute Law.

English statutes held to be absolute and uncontrollable—statutes in the United States must be constitutional—duty of the judicial power to set them aside, if they are not so—history of state and federal decisions on this point—from what time statutes take effect—injustice of the former English rule—the rule in the United States not correct—rules in the construction of statutes—how far the title and preamble can be resorted to—effect of a saving clause, and a proviso—a statute to be construed by the rules of the common law—operation of statutes, when amended, continued, and revived—vain attempts to exempt written law from doubt and commentary.

Lecture XXII.

Common Law.

Common law to be found in reports of adjudged cases—the multiplication of reports—examination of the doctrine of *stare decisis*—a review of the most important books of reports—the Year Books, Dyer, Plowden, Coke, Hobart, Croke, Yelverton, Saunders, Vaughan, &c.—ancient mode of arguing causes—a summary of the best modern reports—how far precedents govern in Chancery—character of the English Court of Chancery prior to the reign of Charles I.—when the reported cases begin—a short view and character of the English Chancery reports.

Lecture XXIII.

Same Subject Continued.

The principal treatises on law summarily examined—Glanville, Bracton, Fleta, Fortescue, Littleton's Tenures, Perkins, Doctor and Student, Bacon's Tracts, Coke's Institutes, Fitzherbert and Brooke's Abridgments, Finch's Treatise, Shepherd's Touchstone, Rolle's Abridgment, the modern abridgments of Bacon, Comyn, Viner, and Cruise, Wood's Institutes, Blackstone's Commentaries, Wooddeson's Lectures, Baron Gilbert's works, Wright on Tenures—notice of the best modern and contemporary treatises on law.

Lecture XXIV.

The Civil Law.

Its great influence in matters of contract—history of the Roman law—substance of the twelve tables—vast accumulation of the civil law—attempts at reform—revision under Justinian, and the manner of effecting it, and its result—subsequent history of the civil law—the Institutes of Justinian particularly examined.

Lecture XXV.

Absolute Personal Rights.

Bills of rights, and how far valuable in a constitution—power of the law over personal liberty—how far punishment by death is admissible—protection against personal violence, and against calumny and libel—remarks on the law of slander and libel—remedy by *habeas corpus* against unlawful imprisonment—a review of the cases on the *habeas corpus* act—on the writ of *ne exeat.*

Lecture XXVI.

Natives and Aliens.

How far citizens of one state have immunities in all, under the constitution of the United States—

allegiance indefeasible under the English law—the doctrine of expatriation examined, and the adjudged cases reviewed—English rule of perpetual allegiance modified by commerce—when a person is to be deemed a citizen, though born abroad—how far an alien can purchase or transmit by descent—privileges of resident aliens—sketch of the law of naturalization—policy of other countries on the subject of aliens—how far the state legislatures can confer privileges on aliens—limitation of the power of naturalization to whites.

Lecture XXVII.

Marriage and Divorce.

Who may marry—marriage, when valid, and between whom—laws of other countries as to unlawful and incestuous marriages—effect of marriages made abroad *in fraudem legis*—cases on this subject examined—law of divorce considered—the doctrine of divorce in other states, and in foreign countries—a foreign divorce, how far binding—the effect of Scotch divorces on English marriages, and the cases reviewed—effect of divorce *a mensa et thoro.*

Lecture XXVIII.

Husband and Wife.

Right of the husband in the property of the wife, whether it be an estate in fee, or for life, or in terms for years, or *choses in action*—right of survivorship as to the wife's property—the wife's equity to a reasonable provision—how far the husband is responsible for the debts of the wife, and for her maintenance—the cases on this subject reviewed—when, and how far, the wife may act as a feme sole—history of the English law on this subject.

Lecture XXIX.

Same Subject.

How far a wife may be regarded in equity as a feme sole as to her separate property—how far she may contract with her husband—when she may devise by will—nuptial settlements considered, and the doctrines of equity on this subject—how far husband and wife may be witnesses for or against each other—the law of France, Holland, &c. on this subject.

Lecture XXX.

The Remaining Domestic Relations.

The rights and duties of parents in respect to the person, and property, and maintenance, and education, of their children—the laws of other nations on the subject of parental and filial power and duty—the rights and duties of guardians—their mode of appointment and responsibility—the different kinds of guardians under the English law—the control of Chancery over the relation of guardian and ward—the privileges and disabilities of infants—what acts of infants are void, and what only voidable—the general protection afforded them by Chancery, and the jurisdiction of that Court also over idiots and lunatics—of illegitimate children, and their disabilities—the duties of the putative father, and his liability—statute provisions on this subject—a general survey of the rights and duties growing out of the relation of master and servant—historical sketch of the law of personal slavery, as it formerly existed in this state.

Lecture XXXI.

Of Corporations.

How corporations are created—the history and policy of these institutions—their essential properties, capacities, and disabilities—the distinctions between sole and aggregate, public and private, civil and eleemosynary corporations—where the right of visitation resides, and how it is to be exercised—when and how corporations may be dissolved—effect of such dissolution.

Part IV: The Law Concerning Real Property

Lecture XXXII.

Absolute Rights of Property.

The foundation of the rights of property—feeble sense of the right in early ages, illustrated by the Roman law, and the English law concerning wrecks and stolen goods—history of the growth of the right of property—progress of real property from occupancy to permanent inheritance—right of alienation—right of inheritance—right of enjoyment of property without restraint, without sumptuary laws, and without unequal taxation or legislative interference—examination of the question concerning the claim of a wrongful occupant to payment for his improvements—when, and upon what terms, private property may be taken for public uses.

Lecture XXXIII.

Of Real Property; and, First, of Incorporeal Hereditaments.

Title to real property derived from the grant of government—priority of discovery gives title—the extent and equity of the *Indian title* to occupancy—the incorporeal hereditaments known to our law—the *right of common*, to what extent, and in what variety it exists here, and the American cases on the subject examined—the *right of fishery* in navigable waters considered—remedy for disturbance of these rights.

Lecture XXXIV.

Of Incorporeal/Hereditaments Continued.

The *right of way* over another's land, in what cases it may exist, and to what extent—the distinctions on this subject considered—whether the banks of navigable rivers afford a tow path, considered—distinction between public and private streams—remedy for disturbance in a right of way—*offices* and franchises examined—the doctrine of *rents* examined at large, as to the different kinds of rent—when due, and to what extent—how far calamity excuses the non-payment of rent—of apportionment of rent—history of the remedy by distress for rent unpaid—statute regulations on the subject of the remedy.

Lecture XXXV.

Of Feudal and Allodial Estates.

History of the feudal tenures—their oppression—their abolition—socage tenures under our statute, and the theory of them, with the incidents belonging to them—allodial estates—history of that species of property, and the reasons why it was converted into feudal.

Lecture XXXVI.

Of Estates in Fee, and for Life and Years.

An estate in fee explained, and how created—of qualified fees—history, policy, and fate of entailments—leases for life—tenant by the curtesy, and tenant in dower—these two last estates fully considered, and the questions thereon which have arisen in our Courts—incidents which belong to estates for life—of estates for years, and at will.

Lecture XXXVII.

Of Estates upon Condition, and with Respect to the Time of Enjoyment and the Number of Owners.

Estates upon conditions in law—estates upon condition in deed—of precedent and subsequent conditions—distinction between a condition and a limitation—distinction between a pledge and mortgage—different kinds of mortgage—how considered at law—how in equity—of the operation of the registry acts—equity of redemption, when and how barred—estates in remainder, and the principles which govern them, stated and illustrated—contingent remainders, and the qualities of them—executory devises, and the limitations controlling them—the doctrine of joint tenancy, and of tenancy in common.

Lecture XXXVIII.

Of Title by Descent, and by Operation of Law.

History of title by descent—the five canons of inheritance under the statute successively stated, and each of them illustrated by examples and the usages of other nations—the common law rules of inheritance applicable to all cases not embraced within the five statute rules—maxims of law applicable to the doctrine of descent—title by escheat and by forfeiture.

Lecture XXXIX.

Of Title by Deed.

The right of alienation of land—sale of pretended titles—requisites to a valid transfer of land by deed—escrows—seal—sample of a good deed in the fewest words—the consideration requisite—the covenants to insure title—rule of damages on eviction—foreign rules on this subject—record of deeds—a view of the several forms of conveyance under our laws, and their distinct properties explained.

Lecture XL.

Of Title by Devise.

History of the right of devising land by will—who can devise—what may be devised—the solemnities requisite to a valid devise, and the cases on this point examined—revocations of a devise by implication examined—nature of codicils—rules of construction of devises—view of the discussions on the rule in Shelley's case.

Part V: The Law Concerning Personal Property and Commercial Contracts

Lecture XLI.

Of Personal Property, and Title Thereto.

Distinctions between chattels real and personal—what things are considered as attached to the freehold, and what not—qualified property in wild animals, and how far it extends—qualified property in goods pledged—joint tenancy in chattels—limitation of chattels in remainder—title to chattels by capture in war—*by accession,* and by *confusion* of goods, and the laws of other nations on this subject considered—property acquired by literary labour and mechanical invention—the law respecting copyrights and patents examined.

Lecture XLII.

Same Subject.

Title to personal property by act of law, as by succession, judgment, insolvency, and intestacy—the subject of insolvent laws, and of the administration of intestates' estates, considered—title to personal property by will—the doctrine of bequests to charitable uses examined.

Lecture XLIII.

The Contract of Sale.

A valid consideration to a contract considered—the effect of a partial failure of the consideration—when and how far the seller is responsible for failure of title, or for defects in the quality of the article sold—how far the seller is bound to disclose defects—remedy for false affirmation by a third person—the question considered, how far the parties, in dealing with each other, may be silent on material facts known to one party, and not to the other—the time when the property in a chattel is deemed in law to pass to the vendee—the place of delivery of articles in bulk—what is a sufficient delivery to take the case out of the statute of frauds.

Lecture XLIV.

Bailment.

The duty and the responsibility of the bailee, in the case of a naked deposit of goods—the duty and the responsibility of a mandatory, who undertakes to do a thing for another gratuitously—the duty and responsibility of a person who borrows for use a chattel of another—the duty and responsibility of a creditor or pawnee, who receives goods in pledge for a debt—the leading cases and authorities, foreign and domestic, on each of these heads, considered—the duties and responsibilities of persons who hire articles for use, or carry goods for hire, and the extraordinary liability of common carriers and innkeepers, &c. particularly considered.

Lecture XLV.

An historical view of the origin, progress, cultivation, and present improvement, of maritime law.

Lecture XLVI.

Law of Shipping.

The steps requisite to a valid sale, and to a valid mortgage of a vessel—what is necessary to give a vessel American privileges—rights and duties of part owners of vessels—the power and duty of the master of the vessel, and his power over the ship, cargo, and freight—how and when a lien on a vessel may be created, for repairs, &c.—the rights and duties of seamen, acts of congress on the subject—the doctrine as to seamen's wages extensively considered.

Lecture XLVII.

Same Subject.

The rights of parties under charter parties—duties of the master as to the carriage and delivery of the goods—the rights and duties of the parties growing out of disasters occurring on the voyage—when the entire freight is earned, and when a rateable freight is allowed—when a loss is to be settled by a general average—the doctrine of contribution examined—when and to what extent salvage is allowed—the events which will dissolve the contract of affreightment.

Lecture XLVIII.

Principal and Agent.

When an agency is duly constituted—when the authority of an agent will be presumed, so as to stop the principal from questioning it—the authority of agents considered, and how far a partial performance, or one varying in extent or degree, will bind—powers of a general and special agent differently construed—power of a factor or commission merchant to bind his principal by sales on credit—restrictions on his power as to pledging—the doctrine of lien in favour of factors, attorneys, innkeepers, common carriers, &c. extensively considered—the right of the vendor to stop goods in their passage to the vendee, in case of his insolvency, and particularly when the goods have been so far delivered as to destroy the right, considered—the subject of the negotiability of bills of lading examined—what acts amount to a valid sale at auction—how far the owner of goods sold at auction may employ persons to bid for him.

Lecture XLIX.

Negotiable Paper.

Origin of bills of exchange—the essential qualities of a negotiable bill or note—how far the holder has an indefeasible title—what amounts to a valid acceptance of a bill—of the endorsement, its nature and extent—of the demand and protest, and of the steps requisite to free the drawer and endorsers—the cases in which the acts of the holder amount to a discharge of the drawer and endorsers—a review of the several treatises on the subject of bills and notes.

Lecture L.

Policies of Insurance.

What are lawful subjects of insurance—the law concerning wager policies examined—the case of a double insurance, and the principle upon which losses in that case are adjusted—the difference between a representation and a warranty, and the rules which apply to each—the usual kinds of warranty examined—when deviation will affect the policy—a view of the usual perils by which loss is produced—the doctrine of abandonment considered—the principles upon which policies are adjusted—when the assured is entitled to a return of premium—observations on maritime loans.

[To be continued as the Lectures advance. But, to avoid advancing into the summer season, and to accelerate the course, it will be respectfully proposed, some weeks hence, to the gentlemen who attend, that the number of Lectures in a week be increased. In order to complete the plan of the present course, it will be requisite to add two more general divisions, viz. Part VI. *On the remedies at law and in equity for the recovery and protection of private rights*; and, Part VII. *On the criminal code of the United States, and this state, and including criminal prosecutions.*]

Chapter 18

Syllabus of a Course of Lectures on Law

1821

David Hoffman

David Hoffman (December 24, 1784-November 11, 1854) was a lawyer and professor of law in the University of Maryland from 1816 to 1832. His works and their influence are described in chapter 1. The Syllabus is reprinted from David Hoffman, *Syllabus of a Course of Lectures on Law: Proposed to Be Delivered in the University of Maryland, Addressed to Students of Law in the United States* (Baltimore: E. J. Coale, 1821).

Title I.

Lecture I. Of the origin and nature of man, his physical and moral constitution.

(1) Of the propriety of treating of Man's nature previously to the consideration of the science which unfolds his rights and duties. (2) Idea of some antient Philosphers as to a triple nature of the soul. (3) Man not merely a *gregarious* but a *social* animal. (4) Man endued with reason, and progressive in knowledge. (5) Man a religious animal. (6) Man's free agency. (7) His actions imputable or not. (8) Society, Government, Religion, and Knowledge congenial to man, and essential to his happiness. (9) What is meant by the natural equality of Man.

Lecture II. Of man in a state of nature.

(1) Why the state of nature is treated of. (2) Its various meanings. (3) Merely theoretical and metaphysical. (4) Its real and only useful meaning. (5) Whether this supposed state of nature be one of war or peace; and herein of.the opinions of Hobbes, Puffendorf, Grotius, Montesquieu, &c. &c. (6) Of the inconveniencies and miseries of this state of nature.

Lecture III. Of the rights of nature.

(1) Various meanings of the word *right.* (2) Rights perfect, imperfect, natural, adventitious, alienable, unalienable. (3) In what the rights of nature consist; as,—to life and the integrity of our body; to the fruits

of mental an bodily labour; to reputation; to liberty, and herein of *natural* liberty, as distinguished from *savage* liberty, &c. (4) Liberty subject by natural law to three species of restriction.

LECTURE IV. OF THE ORIGIN OF PRIMARY SOCIETY, AND OF CIVIL GOVERNMENT.

(1) Of primary society as distinguished from political or civil society. (2) Of the motives which indowed men to establish civil society and government, and herein, *First*, of the theory which ascribes the origin of government to Divine command. *Secondly*, of the theory which supposes man originally a solitary animal, and that society and government sprung from various causes, such as

1. The social principle.
2. Sense of impotency.
3. Natural hostility.
4. Wants.
5. Sexual passion.
6. Desire for knowledge.

(3) Political science more indebted to authentick history, and a knowledge of man's physical and moral nature, than to systems.

LECTURE V. OF THE RIGHT OF CIVIL GOVERNMENT.

(1) Division of this right into original and subsequent. (2) Of the original right arising. *First*, from Divine command. *Secondly*, from the consent of the governed. (3) Of the subsequent right of civil government, and herein *First*, of the opinion that all government, original and subsequent, rests on *consent. Secondly*, of the opinions that the subsequent right of government rests either on

1. Possession.
2. Inheritance.
3. Prescription.
4. Antient consent of governed.
5. Virtues of political rulers.
6. Expediency.

LECTURE VI. OF THE EFFECTS OF SOCIETY OR JURISDICTION ON THE NATURAL RIGHTS OF MAN.

(1) Jurisdiction and law the necessary result of the change from a state of nature to that of civil union. (2) Men not reduced to a *state of nature* by a dissolution of the government. (3) Effects of civil union on the right of personal security. (4) Effects of civil union on the right to the fruits of mental and bodily exertition. (5) Effects on the right to reputation. (6) Effects of the union as to personal liberty, and herein

1. Of social, as distinguished from natural liberty.
2. Of civil, as distinguished from political liberty.
3. Of that liberty which consists in simple freedom from confinement.
4. Of relative liberty.
5. Extent to which liberty is alienable.

LECTURE VII. OF LAW IN THE *ABSTRACT*, OR THE SIGNIFICATION OF THE TERM "LAW"—OR "THE LAW." OF LAW IN THE *CONCRETE*, ITS FOURFOLD DIVISION INTO DIVINE, NATURAL, NATIONAL, AND CIVIL OR MUNICIPAL LAW. THE PRESENT COURSE TO EMBRACE THE THREE LAST DIVISIONS, THE FIRST BELONGING EXCLUSIVELY TO THE CHAIR OF THEOLOGY.

(1) Of the various definitions of Law as a *genus*, and herein, of the errour of most authors in defining the *species* when tbe *genus* was intended.

(2) Professor's definition of Law, as a *genus* and *species*.

(3) Of the general properties.of Law, as applied to the regulation of human conduct, and herein

1. How Law is distinguished from contract; how from counsel or advice.
2. Whether permissions, in any respect, can be regarded as laws.

3. That Laws should speak a general language, and not attempt to comprehend all possible cases.
4. That Laws should not only be general in their phraseology, but universal in their operation.
5. That Laws should be of a legal nature, and their language simple and perspicuous.
6. That Laws should have a possible, reasonable, and useful object.
7. That Laws should not be needlessly multiplied, but be as few in number as the genius of the government, and the state of society will admit.
8. That Laws should contain a sanction.
9. Obligation essential to laws, and herein
   1. Meaning of the word obligation.
   2. Various definitions of obligation.
   3. Division into *perfect, imperfect, external, internal.*
   4. Cause, or origin of obligation, and
      1. Of the obligation of moral Law.
      3. Of the obligation of civil Law.
      5. How obligation differs from sanction.
10. Laws should operate *in futuro.* [This property of law will be hereafter fully considered, when we come to examine the Constitution of the United States, Art. 1. Sec. 9—10. relative to *ex post facto laws.*]

LECTURE VIII. OF THE LAWS OF NATURE, APPLIED TO MAN INDIVIDUALLY, WHETHER IN A STATE OF NATURE, OR OF SOCIETY AND GOVERNMENT.

(1) This subject partly treated in the previous Lectures. Foreign to the design of this course to dwell on these topicks; but shall endeavour to combine all that is really valuable on this extensive learning, in a small compass.

(2) Definitions of the Law of nature. Best definition.

(3) Opinion of those who consider the Laws of nature common to man and brute; and how far the Law is common to God and man.

(4) Difference between the Laws of nature, and divine positive Law.

(5) Of the opinion that this Law is derived from the consent of mankind, and herein of the doctrine of Aristotle.

(6) Of the idea of those who maintain that we are to look for this Law in the manner and customs of nations, and of those, on the other hand, who contend that the Law relates exclusively to actions intrinsically good or evil, independent of all positive Law.

(7) Whether Hobbes' doctrine, that nature did not institute *society*, but *discord* among men, justifies the conclusion of his criticks, that society is against the design of nature.

(8) Laws of nature the dictates of right reason, and herein of the opinion of Hobbes, that these dictates should not be regarded as *laws*, only so far as they have been enacted by God, in his scriptures.

(9) Of the matters referred to the Laws of nature *reductively*, and of the distinction between those things which are commanded or prohibited, and those which are merely permitted by, or are consentaneous to, the laws of nature.

(10) Division of the laws of nature into laws relative

1. *To man's duty to himself*, which consists principally, *first*, in the cultivation of his moral and religious character; *Secondly*, in the improvement of the intellectual faculties by the aquisition of all useful knowledge; *thirdly*, in the preservation of his health of body and mind; *fourthly*, in the acquisition of property; *fifthly*, in the pursuit of salutary pleasure.

2. *To man's duty to his fellow-creatures*, which may be considered, *first*, ABSOLUTE, or such as oblige all men; in all countries, and independently of all human institutions.

Secondly, HYPOTHETICAL or such as arise after the establishment of society, and which are nevertheless founded on the condition of mankind, considered in general, and herein of the difference between this hypothetical natural law, and positive or civil law.

Lecture IX. Of political, as distinguished from civil law, and of the various forms of civil government.

(1) Of Political Law, what it is, and how distinguished from Civil Law. Political state, how different from Civil state.

(2) Of the exercise of governmental power, relative, or not, to the constitutional and fundamental laws of a state, and herein

First, Definition of a *Constitution.*

Secondly, That the constitution and laws should have reference to the natural and constitutional character of the governed, as no one form of government would answer for every nation; and herein of the errour of Montesquieu in carrying this doctrine too far.

Thirdly, That the constitution and laws should vary according to the *great and radical* changes in the genius and disposition of a people, effected by the gradual development and expansion of the energies of the nation, due veneration, however, being had at all times for existing laws, and a wholsome jealousy of innovatons.

(3) Of the various forms of Government.

First. Form of Government defined, and how different from Constitution.

Secondly. Of the influence of Government on individual and national character.

Thirdly. Various divisions of the forms of government, and herein of the division

1. Of Plato.
2. Of Socrates.
3. Of Aristotle.
4. Of Machiavel.

(4) Division of Civil Governments into

1. Pure and simple, as
    1. Simple Monarchy.
    2. Simple Aristocracy.
    3. Simple Democracy.
2. Pure and mixed, as,
    1. Monarchy combined with Aristocracy.
    2. Monarchy combined witb Democracy.
    3. Aristocracy combined with Democracy.
    4. Monarchy, Aristocracy, and Democracy combined.
    5. Single Republic.
    6. Confederate Republic.
3. Corrupt and Simple, as,
    1. Despotism, or Tyranny.
    2. Oligarchy.
    3. Ochlocracy.

(5) Of Patriarchal Government. The Theocracy of the Jews, and herein of the former, as referred to simple monarchy, and the latter, as referred by Sidney to Aristocracy, and by Filmer, to Monarchy.

(6) The above forms of government illustrated and exemplified.

Lecture X. Of the elementary and constitutional principles of the municipal law, and herein.

I. Of the Feudal Law.

Lecture XI.

II. Of the Instititutes of the Municipal Law generally.

Title II. Of the law of real rights and real remedies.

I. Of real rights.

Lecture XII.

Introductory observations. (1) On the study of the Real Law. (2) On the propriety of treating first of the *jura rerum.* Justice Blackstone's method, when unfolding the Institutes merely, being proper, but Mr. Sullivan's and lord Hale's opinion preferable, when the science is to be studied in detail. (3) Real Remedies, why nearly obsolete. (4) Whether the change from real to personal and mixed remedies, be advantageous (5) Of the Real Law in this country; why much studied in the United States; why formerly more than at present, particularly in the Atlantic states. (6) Ejectment law on *location,* nearly peculiar this country, and why. (7) Little of this law to be found in our Books of Reports; traditionary; important that it should be reduced to system, and no longer remain *Lex non scripta.* (8) Some account of distinguished writers on the doctrines of the *Realty;* and of some eminent real lawyers of this Country.

(9) Things Real we shall consider in order and in detail, in *five* points of view, viz.

I. As regards the *Objects,* or several kinds of real property.
II. The *Estate,* or interest which may be had in real property.
III. The *Time of Enjoyment* of estates in real property.
IV. The *Number* and *Relation* of owners of real property.
V. The *Modes* of *Acquiring* title to real property.

(10) In a minute exposition of the various learning of the Realty, the present division of our subject preferable to that of Sir William Blackstone, and why.

(11) The *Tenures* by which Estates may be holden, need not be further treated than has been done in our observations on the Feudal Law. (Vide Lecture X.)

Lecture XIII. I. Of the objects of real property, viz. lands, tenements, hereditaments, corporeal and incorporeal.

Lecture XIV. Of Incorporeal Hereditaments—Ten in number. Six only worthy of particular notice, viz.

1. Rents.
2. Annuities.
3. Offices.
4. Franchises.
5. Ways.
6. Common.

Lecture XV. II. Of the estate or interest which may be had in real property.

(1) Why prefer to to treat of *all* the objects of real property, corporeal and incorporeal, prior to the consideration of the estate or interest which may be had in them, and reasons for departing from the method adopted by Mr. Cruise.

(2) Under the subject of estates we shall treat in order,

1. Estate in fee simple.
2. Estate tail.
3. Estate tail after possibility, &c.
4. Estate for life.
5. Estate for life, and occupancy.
6. Estate for years.
7. Estate from year to year.
8. Estate at will.

9. Estate at sufferance.
10. Estate by courtesy.
11. Estate in dower and jointure.
12. Estates upon condition.
13. Mortgage.

(3) Of an Estate in Fee simple.

LECTURE XVI. OF AN ESTATE TAIL, ITS ORIGIN AND VARIOUS KINDS.

LECTURE XVII. HISTORY OF THE TENANT IN TAIL'S POWER OVER THE ESTATE, AND THE VARIOUS DEVICES FOR DEFEATING THE DONOR'S INTENTION. SOME ACCOUNT OF THE ESTATE TAIL IN THIS COUNTRY, STATUTORY MODIFICATIONS IN DIFFERENT STATES, AND IMPORTANT DECISIONS IN AMERICAN COURTS.

LECTURE XVIII. OF THE ESTATE TAIL AFTER POSSIBILITY OF ISSUE EXTINCT.

LECTURE XIX. OF ESTATES FOR LIFE, POUR AUTER VIE, OCCUPANCY.

LECTURE XX. OF AN ESTATE FOR TERM OF YEARS.

LECTURE XXI. SAME SUBJECT CONTINUED.

LECTURE XXII. OF ESTATES AT WILL, FROM YEAR TO YEAR, AND AT SUFFERANCE.

LECTURE XXIII. OF AN ESTATE BY COURTESY.

LECTURE XXIV. OF AN ESTATE IN DOWER.

LECTURE XXV. SAME SUBJECT CONTINUED.

LECTURE XXVI. SAME SUBJECT CONTINUED.

LECTURE XXVII. OF JOINTURES.

LECTURE XXVIII. OF ESTATES UPON CONDITION, AND OF THE ORIGIN AND VARIOUS KINDS OF MORTGAGE.

LECTURE XXIX. OF THE ESTATE OF THE MORTGAGOR AND MORTGAGEE AT DIFFERENT TIMES.

LECTURE XXX. OF THE EQUITY OF REDEMPTION, AND THE MANNER IN WHICH THE MORTGAGE IS TO BE SATISFIED.

LECTURE XXXI. OF THE ORDER IN WHICH MORTGAGES SHALL BE PAID. AND OF THE DOCTRINE OF TACKING.

LECTURE XXXII. HOW MORTGAGES ARE ENFORCED IN LAW, AND IN EQUITY.

LECTURE XXXIII. III. OF THE TIME OF ENJOYMENT OF ESTATES IN REAL PROPERTY.

Introductory observations. (1) On Estates in *possession*, and *expectancy.* (2) On the origin of remainders. (3) Of the distinction between vested and contingent remainders. (4) Certain rules relating to remainders.

LECTURE XXXIV. OF VESTED REMAINDERS.

(1) General division of estates into *vested* and *contingent*; further division necessary, viz. into *executed* and

executory; as there are some executory estates, which are neither vested nor contingent, and herein of the defect of Mr. Fearne's division, and of Mr. Preston's view of the subject. (2) Various instances of Vested Remainders.

LECTURE XXXV. OF CONTINGENT REMAINDERS.

(1) General observations. (2) Mr. Fearne's division of Contingent Remainders into *four* kinds, each stated *generally*. (3) Exceptions to the *third* kind. Exceptions to the *fourth* kind—these touched on, as they will be hereafter particularly considered. (4) Of Conditional Limitations, as distinguished from the *first* class of contingent Remainders.

LECTURE XXXVI. OF THE EXCEPTIONS TO THE THIRD CLASS OF CONTINGENT REMAINDERS.

LECTURE XXXVII, XXXVIII. XXXIX. OF THE *FIRST* EXCEPTION TO THE *FOURTH* CLASS OF CONTINGENT REMAINDERS, OCCASIONED BY THE CELEBRATED RULE IN *SHELLEY'S* CASE AND HEREIN.

(1) Statement of the rule. (2) Origin of the rule. (3) Policy of the urle. (4) Cases within the rule, where conveyance is by deed. (5) Cases out of the rule, where conveyance is by deed. (6) Cases within the rule, where conveyance is by devise, &c. (7) Cases out of the rule, in devises, &c. (8) Mr. Butler's view of this celebrated rule. (9) Mr. Blackstone's view of it. (10) Mr. Hargrave's admirable exposition of the rule. (11) American cases on this doctrine.

LECTURE XL. OF THE *SECOND* EXCEPTION TO THE FOURTH CLASS OF CONTINGENT REMAINDERS.

LECTURE XLI. OF THE *THIRD* EXCEPTION TO THE *FOURTH* CLASS OF CONTINGENT REMAINDERS.

1. This not generally treated of as a distinct exception to the fourth class of contingent Remainders, and why.

2. As much so as either of the others, and why.

LECTURE XLII. OF THE SPECIES OF UNCERTAINTY WHICH CHARACTERIZES A CONTINGENT REMAINDER.

LECTURE XLIII. OF THOSE CONDITIONS ANNEXED TO A PRECEDING ESTATE WHICH *ARE*, OR ARE *NOT*, CONDITIONS PRECEDENT TO GIVE EFFECT TO ULTERIOR LIMITATIONS.

LECTURE XLIV. OF THE NATURE OF THE CONTINGENCY ON WHICH REMAINDERS MAY BE LIMITED; AND OF THE ESTATE REQUIRED TO SUSTAIN CONTINGENT REMAINDERS.

LECTURE XLV. WHEN CONTINGENT REMAINDERS MUST VEST AND HOW THEY MAY BE DESTROYED.

LECTURE XLVI. OF TRUSTEES TO PRESERVE CONTINGENT REMAINDERS; AND OF OTHER MATTERS RELATING TO THEM.

LECTURE XLVII. OF CROSS REMAINDERS.

(1) Express or implied. (2) Raised *first* by deeds at common law. *Secondly* by limitations of an use. *Thirdly*, by limitations by will. (3) Of cross remainders between two, three, or four persons.

LECTURE XLVIII. OF EXECUTORY DEVISES.

(1) Origin and history of executory devises. (2) This subject more properly considered under the third head, which treats of *"The time of enjoyment of estates in real property"* than under the fifth, which speaks of the *"modes of acquiring title to real property."* Mr. Cruise's method therefore departed from. (3) Executory devise defined. (4) Executory devises either vested in interest, contingent in interest, or neither vested nor contingent in interest. (5) Errour of Mr. Fearne in classing such executory devises with *contingent estates*, as are dependent on an uncertain event, they being executory, but neither vested nor contingent estates.

(6) Division of executory devises into *three* classes. (7) Mr. Fearne's phraseology in defining the *second* Class of executory devises, departed from.

LECTURE XLIX. OF THE *FIRST* CLASS OF EXECUTORY DEVISES.

LECTURE L. OF THE *SECOND* CLASS OF EXECUTORY DEVISES.

LECTURE LI. OF THE *THIRD* CLASS OF EXECUTORY DEVISES.

LECTURE LII. OF THE DISTINCTIONS BETWEEN AN EXECUTORY DEVISE, AND A CONTINGENT REMAINDER; OF THE GENERAL QUALITIES OF, AND OTHER MATTERS RELATING TO, EXECUTORY DEVISES.

LECTURE LIII. OF ESTATES IN REVERSION.

LECTURE LIV. IV. OF THE NUMBER AND RELATION OF OWNERS OF REAL PROPERTY.

(1) Of an estate in joint tenancy.

LECTURE LV. OF THE SEVERANCE AND DESTRUCTION OF A JOINT TENANCY.

LECTURE LVI. (2) OF AN ESTATE IN COPARCENARY.

LECTURE LVII. (3) OF TENANCY IN COMMON.

LECTURE LVIII. V. OF THE MODES OF ACQUIRING TITLE TO REAL PROPERTY.

Introductory observations. (1) On the nature of *title* to things real in general. (2) Of the four degrees of title. (3) Of the different kinds of title, viz. by *descent and purchase.*

LECTURE LIX. OF DESCENT.

(1) Natural law of descent. (2) Descent among the Jews, Greeks, Romans, Lombards, &c. &c. generally considered. (3) Common law of descent.

LECTURE LX. OF THE CANONS OF DESCENT.

LECTURE LXI. OF THE DESCENT OF REMAINDERS, REVERSIONS, AND ESTATES TAIL.

LECTURE LXII. OF THE DESCENT OF REAL PROPERTY BY THE LAWS OF MARYLAND.

LECTURE LXIII. OF PURCHASE.

Introductory observations. (1) On the distinction between descent and purchase. (2) Of the *five* modes of acquiring title to real property by purchase, viz *escheat*; *occupancy*; *prescription*; *forfeiture*, *alienation*, of four kinds, viz. by deed, record, custom, devise.

LECTURE LXIV. OF TITLES BY ESCHEAT, PRESCRIPTION, OCCUPANCY AND FORFEITURE.

LECTURE LXV. OF TITLE BY ALIENATION.

(1) History of the Potestas alienandi. (2) Of the different modes of alienation.

LECTURE LXVI. OF TITLE BY DEED, AND HEREIN.

(1) Of the essentials to a deed.

LECTURE LXVII.
(2) Of the Orderly Parts of a Deed.

LECTURE LXVIII.
(3) Of the Covenants in a deed, and herein particularly of the covenant of Warranty.

LECTURE LXIX.
(4) Of the different kinds of deed, and herein of Foeffment, Gift, Grant.

LECTURE LXX. OF EXCHANGE, RELEASE, CONFIRMATION.

LECTURE LXXI. OF PARTITION, SURRENDER, ASSIGNMENT, DEFEASANCE.

LECTURE LXXII.
(5) Of deeds deriving their efficacy wholly or in part from the statute of uses, and herein
I. OF THE ORIGIN OF USES.

LECTURE LXXIII. II. OF THE NATURE OF USES PRIOR TO THE STATUTE 27TH HENRY 8TH CH. 10.

LECTURE LXXIV. III. OF THE NATURE OF USES BY THE STATUTE 27TH HENRY 8TH CH. 10.

LECTURE LXXV. IV. OF THE VARIOUS MODIFICATIONS OF USES ARISING FROM THE CONSTRUCTION OF THE STATUTE OF USES.

LECTURE LXXVI. OF THE ORIGIN OF TRUSTS, AND THE RULES WHICH GOVERN TRUST ESTATES OF *FREEHOLD*.

LECTURE LXXVII. OF THE RULES WHICH GOVERN TRUST *TERMS*.

LECTURE LXXVIII. OF THE ESTATE AND DUTY OF TRUSTEES.
[Having fully investigaged the nature of *Uses* and *Trusts*, we may now proceed to the consideration of such Deeds as derive their operation wholly, or in part, from the statute of uses.]

LECTURE LXXIX.
(6) Of the deed of bargain and sale.

LECTURE LXXX.
(7) Of the deed of covenant to stand seized to uses.

LECTURE LXXXI.
(8) Of a lease and release.

LECTURE LXXXII.
(9) Of deeds to lead and declare uses.

LECTURE LXXXIII.
(10) Of powers of revocation and appointment; and of the execution of powers.

LECTURE LXXXIV.
(11) Of powers to jointure and lease, and of the extinguishment of powers.

[Where the defective execution of a power will be aided in equity, will be hereafter considered under Title IV.]

LECTURE LXXXV.

(12) Of registering and inrolling deeds, and of the laws of Maryland on this subject.

LECTURE LXXXVI.

(13) Of avoiding deeds, and of the interpretation, or the construction of deeds. [We now proceed to the *second* species of alienation, viz. by matters of record, of which there are four kinds, by *Act of Parliament, King's Grant, Fine, Recovery,* and shall close our inquiry into the "modes of acquiring title to real property" by an

LECTURE XXXVII. OF PARLIAMENT, AND BY KING'S GRANT.

LECTURE LXXXVIII. OF TITLE TO REAL PROPERTY BY FINE.

LECTURE LXXXIX. OF TITLE TO REAL PROPERTY BY RECOVERY.

LECTURE XC. OF TITLE BY DEVISE.

(1) Of tbe origin and nature of devises. (2) Who may devise, and to whom real property may be devised.

LECTURE XCI. WHAT THINGS AND INTERESTS MAY BE DEVISED.

LECTURE XCII. OF THE SOLEMNITIES REQUIRED IN A DEVISE.

LECTURE XCIII. OF THE REVOCATION AND REPUBLICATION OF DEVISES; AND OF VOID DEVISES.

LECTURE XCIV. OF THE MODES OF CONSTRUING DEVISES.

LECTURE XCV. OF THE WORDS REQUISITE TO CREATE A DEVISE; TO DESCRIBE THOSE WHO ARE TO TAKE; AND THE INTEREST AND THINGS TO BE TAKEN.

II. OF REAL REMEDIES.

LECTURES XCVI, XCVII.

(1) Of real actions in former times, and at present. (2) Division of real actions. (3) Of droitural actions, writs of right, properly so called, and writs, in the nature of writs of right. (4) Of writs of entry upon disseisin, intrusion, alienation. (5) Of the various kinds of auncestral possessory actions. (6) Of real actions in the United States.

[Having finished the abstruse and extensive doctrine of the Realty, in which the student, though he may find some obsolete law, will discover most of the important principles and analogies of the entire system of municipal jurisprudence, we shall now proceed to an equally minute investigation into the learning of what has been denominated the Personalty.]

TITLE III. OF THE LAW OF PERSONAL RIGHTS, AND PERSONAL REMEDIES

LECTURE XCVIII.

Introductory. (1) Of the rights of persons. (2) Of persons in freedom, or in slavery. (3) Commentaries on some of the chapters of Magna Charta. (4) Commentaries on some of the sections of the Maryland Declaration of Rights.

LECTURE XCIX. OF MARRIAGE AND DIVORCE, AND OF BASTARDY.

LECTURE C. OF BARON AND FEME.

LECTURE CI. OF GUARDIAN AND WARD, AND OF INFANCY AND AGE.

LECTURE CII. OF IDIOTS AND LUNATICKS.

LECTURE CIII. OF ALIENS, OF AMBASSADORS, OF PREROGATIVE.

LECTURE CIV. OF CORPORATIONS.

LECTURE CV. OF BY-LAWS; AND OF STATUTES.

LECTURE CVI. OF WILLS AND TESTAMENTS.

LECTURE CVII. OF EXECUTORS AND ADMINISTRATORS.

LECTURE CVIII. SAME SUBJECT CONTINUED.

LECTURE CIX. OF LEGACIES.

LECTURE CX. SAME SUBJECT CONTINUED.

LECTURE CXI, CXII, CXIII. OF CONTRACTS OR AGREEMENTS.

LECTURE CXIV. OF OBLIGATIONS, ASSIGNMENT, AUTHORITY.

LECTURE CXV. OF FRAUD, OF DURESS.

[The law of personal rights being thus far unfolded, we shall, before we inquire into the various remedies and actions to enforce these rights, examine into the organization of the tribunals, or courts of judicature, which have been constituted to ascertain, define, and execute such rights, and also into the peculiar *powers* of these courts.]

LECTURE CXVI. OF COURTS AND THEIR JURISDICTION IN GENERAL; AND OF THE COURT OF PARLIAMENT.

LECTURE CXVII. OF THE COURTS OF KING'S BENCH AND COMMON PLEAS.

LECTURE CXVIII. OF THE COURT OF EXCHEQUER; THE COURT OF THE JUSTICES OF ASSISE AND NISI PRIUS, AND OF ECCLESIASTICAL COURTS.

LECTURE CXIX, CXX. OF THE OFFICERS OF COURTS.

(1) Attorney. (2) Sheriff. (3) Coroner. (4) Constable.

LECTURE CXXI, CXXII. OF THE POWERS OF COURTS OF JUDICATURE.

(1) Attachment. (2) Fine. (3) Amercement. (4) Habeas Corpus. (5) Prohibition. (6) Certiorari. (7) Mandamus.

OF THE LAW OF PERSONAL REMEDIES.

LECTURE CXXIII. OF ACTIONS IN GENERAL, AND OF THE ACTION OF ACCOUNT.

Lecture CXXIV. Of the actions of debt and covenant.

Lecture CXXV. Of the actions of detinue and trover.

Lecture CXXVI. Of the action on replevin.

Lecture CXXVII. Of the action on the case.

Lecture CXXVIII. Of the action of assumpsit.

Lecture CXXIX. Same subject continued.

Lecture CXXX. Same subject continued.

Lecture CXXXI. Of the action of trespass.

Lecture CXXXII. Of the action of ejectment.

Lecture CXXXIII. Of the actions for slander and libel.

Lecture CXXXIV. Of the action of assault and battery.

Lecture CXXXV. Of arbitrament and award.

Lecture. CXXXVI. Of accord and satisfaction.

Lecture CXXXVII. Of actions local and transitory, of venue, of abatement, of misnomer and addition.

Lectures CXXXVIII, CXXXIX, CXL, CXLI. Of pleading.

Lecture CXLIL. Of amendment and jeofail, of nonsuit, of summons and severance.

Lecture CXLIII. Of escape in civil cases, of rescue, of bail in civil cases, of juries.

Lectures CXLIV, CXLV, CXLVI. Of evidence.

Lecture CXLVII. Of trial, verdict, damages, costs.

Lecture CXLVIII. Of bills of exception, of errour, of supersedeas.

Lecture CXLIX. Of scire facias, of audita querela, of injunction.

Lecture CL. Of execution.

[The student having attended us through the important and interesting topicks of *personal rights* and the *ordinary remedies* for their enforcement, We shall close the subjects embraced by our *Third Title*, by an inquiry into that *extraordinary* remedy founded on the customs of London, Exeter, &c. and established in most of the states of our union by statute, under the denominations of foreign and domestic attachment.]

Lectures CLI, CLII. Of foreign and domestick attachments.

Title IV. Of the law of equity.

Lecture CLIII. History of chancery jurisdiction; equity defined; four great divisions of chancery jurisdiction.

1. Common law jurisdiction.
2. Equity jurisdiction.
3. Statutory jurisdiction.
4. Delegated jurisdiction.

Lecture CLIV. Of the common law jurisdiction of the chancellor; and the general objects of equity jurisdiction; viz.

(1) Accident. (2) Mistake. (3) Account. (4) Fraud. (5) Infants. (6) Specifick performance of agreements. (7) Trusts *express, first,* Marriage Settlements. *Second,* Conveyances to purchasers. *Third,* Mortgage, &c. for payment of debts. *Fourth,* Choses in action. *Fifth,* Trusts created by will. (8) Trusts *implied, first,* from the office of executor or administrator, and herein of the administration of assets, and payment of legacies. *Second,* from purchases in the name of another. *Third,* Purchases with notice of trust.

Lecture CLV. Of the statutory jurisdiction of the chancellor.

(1) Admiralty jurisdiction. (2) Bankrupts. (3) Charitable uses. (4) Habeas corpus. (5) Arbitration. (6) Infant trustee.

Lecture CLVI. Of the delegated jurisdiction.

(1) Idiots and Lunaticks. (2) Petition of right.

[The four cardinal divisions of chancery powers having been summarily treated, we shall proceed to a more minute examination of the subjects embraced in the second head, viz. "*Equity jurisdiction,*" this being, by far, the most extensive and important branch of our subject.

Previously to this, however, we shall speak of the organization of the court in which chancery law is administered.]

Lecture CLVII. Of the court of chancery in England, and in the state of Maryland. Equity jurisdiction of the chancellor.

Lecture CLVIII. Of accident and mistake.

Of *accidents* in case (1) Of deeds and bonds lost. (2) Unsettled boundaries. (3) Penalties and Forfeitures.

Of *mistakes.* (1) In the execution of deeds. (2) Execution of Powers. (3) In Settlements. (4) In Bonds. (5) In Policies of insurance. (6) In Judgements. (7) In Pleadings. (8) In Arbitrators. (9) In settled accounts. (10) In Wills. (11) As to Law.

Lecture CLIX. Account.

(1) Origin of this jurisdiction. (2) Between tradesman and customer. (3) Landlord and tenant. (4) Felling timber, &c. (5) Factor. (6) Partnership dealings. (7) Opening stated accounts.

Lecture CLX. Fraud.

(1) Prolifick source of jurisdiction. (2) Definition of fraud. (3) *Suppressio veri,* and *Suggestio falsi.* (4) Of purchases made by persons in fiduciary relation—Trustee and *Cestui que Trust*—dealings between Attorney arid Client—Guardian and Ward—Sales by expectant heirs.

Lecture CLXI. Of avoiding deeds, fines, letters patent &c. when obtained by fraud.

Lecture CLXII. Of avoiding contracts for fraud, deduced from the *intrinsick* nature of the agreement.

LECTURE CLXIII. OF AVOIDING CONTRACT FOR FRAUD, APPARENT FROM THE *CIRCUMSTANCES* OF THE CONTRACTING PARTIES.

LECTURE CLXIV. OF AVOIDING CONTRACTS MADE IN FRAUD OF CREDITORS; AND OF COMPOSITION DEEDS.

LECTURE CLXV. OF AVOIDING CONTRACTS MADE IN FRAUD OF PURCHASERS.

LECTURE CLXVI. OF AVOIDING CONTRACTS MADE IN FRAUD OF MARITAL RIGHTS; AND OF MARRIAGE AGREEMENTS.

LECTURE CLXVII. OF AVOIDING CONTRACTS WHOSE NULLITY ARISES RATHER FROM *PUBLICK* POLICY, THAN FROM FRAUD, AND HEREIN.

(1) Of marriage and office brocage contracts. (2) Of contracts founded on the consideration of unlawful sexual intercourse. (3) Contracts for money won at play, &c.

LECTURE CLXVIII. OF OTHER MATTERS OF FRAUD COGNIZABLE IN EQUITY.

LECTURE CLXIX. OF THE AUTHORITY OF THE CHANCELLOR OVER INFANTS, AND OF THE LIGHT IN WHICH EQUITY VIEWS THEIR CONTRACTS.

LECTURE CLXX. OF THE POWER OF CHANCERY TO DECREE THE SPECIFICK EXECUTION OF CONTRACTS.

(1) Origin of this power. (2) What kind of contracts will be thus executed. (3) Of the specifick performance of contracts out of the statute of frauds and perjuries. (4) Specifick performance of other contracts.

LECTURE CLXXI. WHEN EQUITY WILL REFUSE TO DECREE SPECIFICK PERFORMANCE, AND OF OTHER MATTERS RELATIVE TO THE EXERCISE OF THIS POWER.

LECTURE CLXXII. OF CHANCERY JURISDICTION IN CASES OF EXPRESS TRUST.

(1) General observations. (2) Of marriage settlements. (3) Of trust terms, or conveyances to purchasers in bar of dower. (4) Conveyances or trusts for payment of debts. (5) Of the assignment of choses in action.

LECTURE CLXXIII. OF EXPRESS TRUSTS CREATED BY WILL, AND HEREIN OF THE DISTINCTION BETWEEN *EXECUTED* AND *EXECUTORY* TRUSTS.

LECTURE CLXXIV. OF IMPLIED TRUSTS, AND HEREIN OF THE ADMINISTRATION OF ASSETS, &C.

LECTURE CLXXV. OF IMPLIED TRUSTS, AND HEREIN.

(1) Of the origin of chancery jurisdiction in case of Legacies. (2) Various kinds of legacies. (3) Other matters relative to legacies.

LECTURE CLXXVI. OF IMPLIED TRUSTS RESULTING.

(1) From a conveyance made to A. of an estate purchased with the money of B. (2) From purchase of property bound, by a *trust* known to the purchaser. [The powers of chancery being fully considered, we shall finish the subjects of our *Fourth Title*, with a few Lectures on the practical proceedings in chancery courts.]

LECTURE CLXXVII. OF CHANCERY PRACTICE.

(1) General Observations. (2) Institution of a suit. (3) Analysis of a bill in equity. Mode of compelling appearance. (5) Analysis of answer to a bill in equity. (6) Necessary parties to a bill. (7) Amendment of bills. (8) Mode of procuring evidence. (9) Defense to a suit.

LECTURE CLXXVIII.

(1) Of publication. (2) Of bringing the cause to hearing. (3) Of the decree. (4) Of rehearsing and review. (5) Of enforcing the decree.

LECTURE CLXXIX. OF THE VARIOUS KINDS OF BILLS IN EQUITY.

LECTURE CLXXX. OF VARIOUS PETITIONS, MOTIONS, ORDERS &C. AND OF THE STATUTORY PROVISIONS RELATIVE TO CHANCERY PROCEEDINGS IN THE STATE OF MARYLAND.

TITLE V. OF THE LAW OF CRIMES AND PUNISHMENTS.

LECTURE CLXXXI.

Introductory observations. (1) Of the words *Crime, Misdemeanour, Offence, Transgression; Sin, Guilt.* (2) Origin and right of punishment. (3) Ends of punishment. (4) Measure of punishment. (5) Right, and necessity of capital punishment. (6) Of the criminal jurisprudence of various nations.

LECTURE CLXXXII. ANALYSIS OF THE WORK OF MR. BENTHAM, ENTITLED,
"Theorie des Peines, et des Urcompenses."

LECTURE CLXXXIII. I. OF CRIMES AGAINST RELIGION AND PUBLICK MORALS, AND PARTICULARLY OF THE STATUTES OF MARYLAND ON THIS HEAD.

LECTURE CLXXXIV. II. OF CRIMES AGAINST SOVEREIGNTY; AND HEREIN CHIEFLY OF TREASON AGAINST THE UNITED STATES, AND THE STATE OF MARYLAND.

LECTURE CLXXXV. III. OF CRIMES AGAINST THE PERSON.

(1) Of Homicide in general, and *first* of *Murder*, and herein of the *degrees* of Murder, by the law of Maryland. *Secondly*, of *Manslaughter* and *Suicide.*

LECTURE CLXXXVI. OF JUSTIFIABLE AND EXCUSABLE HOMICIDE.

LECTURE CLXXXVII. OF MAYHEM, ASSAULT, BATTERY, RAPE.

LECTURE CLXXXVIII. OF FALSE IMPRISONMENT, KIDNAPPING, &C. &C.

LECTURE CLXXXIX. IV. OF CRIMES AGAINST PROPERTY.

(1) Of Arson. (2) Of Burglary.

LECTURE CXC. OF LARCENY AND ROBBERY.

[The law of Piracy, will be fully considered under Title X.—"Laws of the United States."]

LECTURE CXCI. OF CHEATS.

(1) At common law. (2) Under the statutes.

OF FORGERY.

(1) By the laws of England. (2) In Maryland. (3) A general view of the Penal Code of Maryland.

LECTURE CXCII. V. OF PRACTICAL PROCEEDINGS IN CRIMINAL CASES.

(1) Arrest. (2) Bail. (3) Presentment and Indictment. (4) Arraignment and standing mute. (5) Pleas. (6) Evidence. (7) Judgment. (8) Reversal of Judgment. (9) Reprieve and Pardon. (10) Execution.

Title VI. Of the lex mercatoria.

Lecture CXCIII.

Introductory observations. (1) Every branch of this extensive subject will *not* be treated by us with our usual minuteness, *first,* because not equally interesting to the students of every state; *Secondly,* as the doctrines are simple, and sufficiently attractive to induce the student to bestow an ample portion of his time on them; *Thirdly,* as this law is so much practised in some of the states, as necessarily to insure a minute acquaintance with it, and the design of these Lectures being to dwell on, and to enforce such portions of the law as are apt to be in some degree neglected, either from their *abstruseness,* or the infrequency of occasion to investigage them. (2) The present course, however, will exhibit a full analysis of the principles, enforced by all of the important decisions of the Lex Mercatoria. (3) Definition of Lex Mercatoria. (4) History of the progress of this law in England, France, and the United States. (5) Grand divisions of the Lex Mercatoria—viz. into law.

1. Of Principals, Agents, Factors, and Brokers.
2. Of Bills of Exchange.
3. Of Promissory Notes.
4. Of Partners and Joint Traders.
5. Of Marine insurance.
6. Of Owners and Masters of ships.
7. Of Mariners, and their Wages.
8. Of Bills of Lading, and Stoppage in Transitu.
9. Of Freight, Charter Party and Demurrage.
10. Of Average and Salvage.
11. Of Bankruptcy.

(6) The above eleven divisions will embrace every topick of this varied and useful system of law.

Lecture CXCIV. Of the law of principal, agent, &c.

Lecture CXCV. Same subject continued.

Lecture CXCVI, to CCII. Of the law of bills of exchange and promissory notes.

Lecture CCIII. Of the law of partnership.

Lecture CCIV. Same subject continued.

Lectures CCV, CCVI, CCVII CCVIII. Of the law of insurance.

Lectures CCIX, CCX, CCXI, CCXII. Of owners and masters of ships.

(1) Of Vessels of the United States. (2) Of foreign vessels. (3) General duties of the master. (4) His powers of Hypothecating, &c. (5) Owner's interest in vessel. (6) Duty of Owner or Owners. (7) Responsibilities of Owner. (8) Of Clearance, Manifest, Report, Entry, &c.

Lecture CCXIII. Of mariners.

(1) How employed. (2) American and foreign. (3) Their duties. (4) Common law remedy for wages. (5) Other matters relative to Seamen. [The subject of Mariners' wages will be fully considered under Title VIII. of "Admiralty and Maritime Law."]

Lecture CCXIV. Of bills of lading, and stoppage in transitu.

LECTURE CCXV. OF FREIGHT, CHARTER PARTY, AND DEMURRAGE.

LECTURE CCXVI. SAME SUBJECT CONTINUED.

LECTURE CCXVII. OF AVERAGE AND SALVAGE.
[The latter subject will be more particularly considered under Title VIII.]

LECTURE CCXVIII. OF BANKRUPTCY AND THE INSOLVENT LAWS OF THE STATE OF MARYLAND.

TITLE VII. OF THE LAWS OF NATIONS.

LECTURE CCXIX.

(1) History of the Law of Nations as a science. (2) Various definitions of the Law of Nations. (3) Professor's Deftnition. (4) Division of the Law of Nations into

1. Universal, Necessary, or Natural Law of Nations.
2. Voluntary, or Presumed Law of Nations.
3. Customary, or Tacit Law of Nations.
4. Conventional, or Express Law of Nations.

(5) Of the different views of Grotius and Puffendorf as to a Positive Law of Nations.

LECTURE CCXX.

(1) Of the Laws of Nations as they respect the threefold relations of states with each other, viz.

1. Of Peace.
2. Of War.
3. Of Neutrality.

(2) Of Peace, and herein, *first* definition of Peace. *Secondly* of certain rights and duties appertaining to nations in a state of peace, and herein

1. Of the right of sovereignty, and absolute equality and independence in all matters of self government.
2. The extent of national jurisdiction.
3. Of commercial and other intercourse between nations.
4. Of the reciprocal right of Embassy.

LECTURE CCXXI. OF *WAR*, AND HEREIN

(1) Definition of War. (2) To whom the right of making war appertains. (3) War perfect, imperfect, offensive, defensive. (4) Of the justifying causes of war. (5) Of the time and modes of commencing war, and herein

1. Declaration of War.
2. Manifestoes.
3. Warlike Embargoes.
4. General Reprisals.
5. Commencement of Hostilities.
6. Belligerant's treatment of enemies found in the country when war commences, or is declared by or against the country.

LECTURE CCXXII. OF THE MEANS TO BE USED IN CONDUCTING THE WAR.

1. Of killing, or enslaving an enemy.
2. Of quarter.
3. Of confiscation by belligerant of enemy's property taken within his dominions.

4. Of conquest.
5. Of capture of moveables.
6. Of recapture and the *jus postliminii.*
7. Of the use of Privateers.
8. Of Persons exempted.
9. Of Things exempted.

LECTURE CCXXIII.

(1) Of the illegality of commerce between alien enemies, &c. (2) Exceptions and qualifications of this rule. (3) Of those who are deemed alien enemies, as to certain purposes, by acquiring a *hostile character,* and of the various modes in which this character may be impressed.

LECTURE CCXXIV. OF TERMINATING THE WAR.

(1) In case of conquest, and herein,

1. Of exterminating the inhabitants.
2. Of enslaving them.
3. Of subjecting them to the laws of the conqueror.
4. Of simply annexing them to the conqueror's dominion.

(2) Without conquest, and herein,

1. Of Mediation.
2. Of Negotiation.
3. Of Amnesty.
4. Of Arbitration.
5. Of Conferences, Congresses, &c.

LECTURE CCXXV. OF *NEUTRALITY.*

(1) Definition of neutrality. (2) Of the right of remaining neutral. (3) General duties of neutrality. (4) Different kinds of neutrality. (5) The consideration of nautrality leads us to inquire.

1. As to the conduct of neutrals towards either of the belligerants.
2. As to the conduct of belligerants towards neutrals.

(6) Enumeration of the rights and duties of neutrals. (7) Enumeration of the rights and duties of belligerants.

LECTURE CCXXVI. OF THE CONDUCT OF NEUTRALS TOWARDS BELLIGERANTS.

(1) Of the strict impartiality required by neutrals. (2) Of the right of neutrals to carry on their accustomed trade, with the exceptions *to blackaded places;* in *contraband* articles, and of liability to *visitation* and *search.* (3) Of the commerce of neutrals with belligerants in contraband articles. (4) Of the universal and positive law of nations with respect to contraband, and of the three classes of contraband articles.

LECTURE CCXXVII. OF TRADE BY NEUTRALS WITH A PLACE BLOCKADED OR BESIEGED.

LECTURE CCXXVIII. OF THE TRADE OF NEUTRALS, ALLOWED BY EITHER BELLIGERANT IN TIME OF *WAR,* BUT WHICH IS FORBIDDEN IN TIME OF *PEACE.* OF THE RULE OF THE WAR OF 1756, AND THE RELAXATIONS THEREOF.

LECTURE CCXXIX. OF THE CONDUCT OF BELLIGERANTS TOWARDS NEUTRALS.

(1) Of the conduct of a belligerant in passing through a neutral country. (2) Of the respect due from belligerants to neutral limits. (3) Of the exception, contended for by some jurists, as to the right to consummate a capture within neutral limits, which had its inception beyond them. (4) Of the exemption

of *neutral* property from seizure when found in enemy's vessel. (5) Of the seizure of *enemy's* property on board a neutral vessel, and of the doctrine that "Free ships make free goods."

LECTURE CCXXX. SAME SUBJECT CONTINUED.

(1) History of the right of visitation and search. (2) Of this right *first*, where neutral vessel has *contraband* property; *secondly*, where vessel is proceeding to a or place, *thirdly*, for *enemy's goods.* (8) Of the right of belligerants to carry their prizes into neutral ports for sale.

[Various doctrines of international law will necessarily be considered under Title VIII. viz. of "Maritime and Admiralty Law."]

TITLE VIII. OF THE MARITIME AND ADMIRALTY LAW.

LECTURE CCXXXI. ORIGIN OF THE ADMIRALTY, AND ITS COURTS; AND OF THE GENERAL PRINCIPLES OF ADMIRALTY AND MARITIME LAW.

LECTURE CCXXXII. OF THE CIVIL AND PRIZE DROITS, OR PERQUISITES OF THE ADMIRALTY.

LECTURE CCXXXIII. OF THE CRIMINAL JURISDICTION OF THE ADMIRALTY.

(1) Murder. (2) Treason. (3) Piracy. (4) Felonies. (5) Violations of Truce aud Safe Conduct.

LECTURE CCXXXIV. OF CONTRACTS COGNIZABLE IN THE INSTANCE COURT OF THE ADMIRALTY.

LECTURE CCXXXV. OF TORTS COGNIZABLE IN THE INSTANCE COURT.

LECTURE CCXXXVI. OF THE JURISDICTION OF THE PRIZE COURTS.

LECTURE CCXXXVII. OF THE JURISDICTION AND LAW OF THE DISTRICT COURT OF THE UNITED STATES IN CIVIL CAUSES, OF AN ADMIRALTY AND MARITIME NATURE, AS,

1. Or Maritime capture.
2. Of Maritime torts or injuries to the person or property of citizens, or foreigners.
3. Of Ransoms.
4. Of Salvage.
5. Of Derelict.
6. Of Seaman's Wages.

(1) Of Maritime capture. (2) Of Maritime Torts, &c.

LECTURE CCXXXVIII. OF RANSOM, OF SALVAGE, AND OF DERELICT.

LECTURE CCXXXIX. OF SEAMAN'S WAGES.

LECTURE CCXL. OF THE PRACTICE OF THE PRIZE AND INSTANCE COURTS OF ENGLAND, AND OF THE DISTRICT COURTS OF THE UNITED STATES, AND HEREIN OF *PROCEEDINGS IN REM.*

(1) Libel. (2) Attachment. (3) Monition. (4) Appearances, *absolute* or *under protest.* (5) Caution. (6) Claim, by *Counsel, Agent, Owner.* (7) Answer. (8) Receiving the property on stipulation, (9) Of the power of the court to order stipulators to give further security when they become incompetent or *lapsi facultutibus.* (10) Default. (11) Sales under perishable monition. (12) Appraisement and sale for other reasons. (13) Publication. (14) Disposition of proceeds. (15) Libel for wages. (16) Libel on Hypothecation and Bottomry Bonds. (17) Other Libels *in rem.*

Lecture CCXLI. Of proceedings *in personam.*

(1) Of Injuries to tbe *person.* Libel for Assault and Battery; Answer to such Libel. (2) Injuries to *property,* as, *first,* Libel for collision, *secondly,* Libel for recovery of damages for injuries, or illegal seizures of property at sea; *thirdly,* Libels by Ambassadors or Consuls, for recovery of damages where seizure was *jure belli,* but by persons violating the neutrality or laws of that nation in whose court jurisdiction is claimed. (3) Answer and Defence to these Libels. (4) Decree. (5) Mode of enforcing decree. (6) Of Appeals and Writs of Errour, and herein of the distinction between these modes of removing causes. (7) Of the extent of the further security to be given on appeals, after the property claimed has been given to the claimant on stipulation.

[The above is necessarily a very imperfect enumeration of the interesting and various topicks of Maritime aod Admiralty Law. The subject is so extensive and diversified, that the bare mention of all the items of consideration, with the subjects yet to be stated, would swell this Syllabus much beyond its contemplated size.]

Title IX. Of the civil or Roman law.

Lecture CCXLII.

Introductory observations. (1) On the excellence of the Civil Law. (2) Its intimate connexion with many of the most important branches of the Common, National, Admiralty and Maritime Law. (3) Of the *Corpus Juris Civilis,* as reduced by the order of the Emperor Justinian. (4) Of the *Basilica.* (5) Of the *"Pandectae Justinianae in novum ordinem digestae,"* of M. Pothier. (6) Of the modes of citing the *Institutes, Digest, Code,* and *Novels.* (7) Of the most distinguished works on the Civil Law. (8) Of the study of the Civil Law in Europe and America, and of the chief schools in which it has been taught in Europe; and of the vast importance and extent of the subject, and the necessity of distinct Professorships in this country.

Lecture CCXLIII. I. Of the state of persons.

[*De Statu hominum.*]

(1) In what the state of persons consists. (2) Division into natural and civil state. (3) The *status naturalis* as it regards persons, either *to be born* (*nascituri,*) or *born* (*nati.*) (4) Natural state founded on *sex, age, birth.* (5) The *status civilis,* or civil state, had relation to the person's *Liberty, Country,* or *Family.* (6) The *first* as it regarded persons in freedom or in slavery. (7) The *second,* as Roman citizens, or strangers. (8) And the *third,* as fathers of a family, and children subject to their authority. (9) The first and third only considered, which give rise to the great relations in civil life, of *Husband and Wife, Parent and Child, Master and Slave or Servant.*

Lecture CCXLIV. Of husband and wife.

(1) General observations. (2) Of Marriage, and herein of *Matrimonium, Nuptiae, Connubium, Conugium, Consortium, Contubernium,* each explained. (3) Definition of *matrimonium,* and how distinguished from *nuptiae;* sometimes used indiscriminately. (4) Regarded only as a civil contract. (5) The subject but little noted in the Institutes.

Lecture CCXLV. Of contracting marriage.

(1) Of matters essential to the contract, and herein of the *will* and *ability* to contract. (2) Of temporal disabilities, and herein of *infancy, want of consent of parents or guardians, alienage.* (3) Of the disability arising from *turpitude,* which may be *incestuous, indecorous, noxious,* [included in the last.] (4) Of consanguinity and affinity, and of *natural* and *civil* incest. (5) Of the degrees of proximity. (6) Mode of computing degrees by the *Civil, Canon, English* and *American* Laws. (7) Of the disability flowing from what was considered *indecorum.* (8) Of noxious disabilities, and herein of marriage between Christian and Jew; Guardian and Ward; of Clergy or others after vow; of Polygamy.

LECTURE CCXLVI. SAME SUBJECT CONTINUED.

(1) Of the *actual consent*, in concurrence with *will* and *ability*, requisite in marriage; and herein of Precontract, *per verba de prasenti, and per verba de futuro*, and of the doctrines of the *canonists* in regard to these contracts. (2) Of consent founded in Errour, and herein of errours *de substantia*, and *de qualitate*. (3) Of the *forms*, &c. sometimes required to be added to *willingness*, *ability*, and *consent*, and herein, of marriages either solemn (*solennes*,) unsolemn, or less solemn (*minus solennes*,) the former contracted by Confarreation (*confarreatione*,) Coemption (*coemptione*,) or by use (*usu*.) (4) Of unsolemn marriage, and herein of the marriage *ex usu*, why classed with solemn marriages. (5) Of certain ceremonies which attended Roman marriages. (6) Of inducements to marry, and of restraints on marriage.

LECTURE CCXLVII. OF THE EFFECTS RESULTING FROM MARRIAGE.

(1) Husband and Wife *not* considered as one person, having one will, but as distinct individuals who might enjoy separate property, rights, &c. and be subjected to correspondent duties. (2) Of suits by Husband against Wife, and *e converso*. (3) Of suits by or against them individually. (4) Not responsible for each other's debts, injuries, or illegal acts. (5) Of Husband and Wife inheriting each other's property. (6) Of the *Dos adventitia*, and *Dos profectitia*. (7) Of their disability to testify for or against each other, though distinct persons. (8) Of the Husband's power over his Wife.

LECTURE CCXLVIII. OF DIVORCE AND REPUDIATION.

(1) History of the right of Divorce among the Romans. (2) Of the distinction between *Divortium* and *Repudium*, though sometimes confounded. (3) Causes of divorce of Husband from Wife, and of Wife from Husband. (4) Of the ceremonies attendant on Divorces. (5) Distinction between Divorces *a vinculo matrimonii*, and a *mensa et thoro*, unknown to the Civil Law, and herein of the causes of the present distinction.

LECTURE CCXLIX. OF PARENT AND CHILD.

(1) History of parental power among the Romans how acquired, and its extent, *first* over the person of the child, *secondly* over his property. (2) Of the son's *peculium*. (3) of the obligations of parent and child to each other. (4) Of the termination of parental authority, and herein of the *death*, *relegation*, *deportation*, *punishment*, and *captivity* of the father. (5) Of Emancipation.

LECTURES CCL, CCLI. OF MASTER AND SLAVE.

(1) Division of Persons into *freemen* and *slaves*. (2) Of freemen who are *sui juris*, and such as are not, and of those who are *ingenui* or *libertini*. (3) Definitions of slavery and of freedom, and of classing slaves under the head of *Homo*, but not of *Persona*. (4) Of slavery arising from captivity. (5) Of slavery arising from birth, and herein of the maxim *Partus sequitur ventrem*. (6) Of slavery arising from consent. (7) Of slavery, the consequence of crimes and offences. (8) Of the master's power over the *person* of his slave. (9) Of the master's power over the property of his slave. (10) Of the slave's *peculium*. (11) Of the slave's general condition. (12) or the manumission of slaves, either *solemn* or *less solemn*; the former, as by enrolment (*census*,) the Lictor's Wand, (*vindicta*,) by *Will*, (*Testamentum*,) in the face of the Church, (*in ecclesiis*.) The less solemn, as by Letter, (*per epistolam*,) before Friends, (*inter amicos*,) by being constituted Heir or Tutor, by Nomination, by Admission to his master's table, (*per convivium*,) &c. (13) Emancipation not to be made in fraud of creditors. (14) Of other matters relating to manumission. (15) Of the Laws made to ameliorate the slave's condition.

LECTURE CCLII. OF TUTELAGE AND CURATION.

(1) Tutelage defined. (2) Distinguished from curation. (s) Who were subject to tutelage, as Infants, Idiots, Lunaticks, Women, Prodigals. (4) Of the modes of appointing tutors, by law or by the Magistrate (5) Of Testamentary tutors. (6) Of Legal tutors. (7) Of tutors appointed by Magistrates or Bishops. (8) Of the duties and powers of the tutor. (9) Of the obligations of the minor to his tutor. (10) When and how tutelage terminates.

Lecture CCLIII. Of curation.

(1) Of the office of curators. (2) Mode of their appointment. (3) Who are subject to curation (4) Of the duty and power of curators. (5) Of the duties of those under curation. (6) Of the causes excusing those nominated curators or tutors from serving. (7) Of suspected curators and tutors.

[Having treated of individuals or *natural* persons, we shall finish this branch of our subject with an examination of the Law relative to those *artificial* bodies composed of several individuals, denominated Universities, Communities, or Corporations, considered as [text lost].]

Lecture CCLIV. Of communities, corporations, or universities.

(1) Origin of artificial persons. (2) Several kinds of corporations. (3) All corporations are aggregate. (4) How corporations were constituted. (5) Of the capacities and incapacities of corporations. (6) Of their power of self government by by-laws. (7) Of their contracting and being contracted with. (8) Of their power to receive donations. (9) Of their power to elect members to fill vacancies. (10) Of their suing or being sued. (11) Of their acting by syndics. (12) By what kind of majority corporations were obligated. (13) Of the dissolution of corporations. (14) University a word of generical import, comprehending every species of corporation or community, and herein of Universities for the advancement of the Sciences and Liberal Arts.

[The material doctrines under the head "*De statu hominum*," or as we might express it, *The Rights of Persons*, having been considered; we now proceed to investigate the Law or *Things*, a learning more extensive and important, and in *some respects* bearing a nearer similitude to the *jura rerum* of the Common Law, though on the doctrines of the *realty* often very dissimilar.]

II. Of Things.

Lecture CCLV. (1) Civil Law doctrine as to the origin of property. (2) Of things in *patrimonio*, or *extra patrimonium*. (3) Of things extra patrimonium, in *common*, *publick*, *universitatis*, [or belonging to some community,] lastly *nullia*, the property of no one, comprehending things either *sacred*, *religious*, or *holy*. (4) The division of things by *Caius*, followed by Taylor and other civilians, preferable.

Lecture CLCVI. Of things in patrimonio.

(1) Of things considered as corporeal moveable, corporeal immoveable, and incorporeal. (2) Of things incorporeal *lato sensu*. (3) Of usus fruct. (4) Of use and *res fringibiles*. (5) Of habitation. (6) Of Prædial services, *rural* and *city*.

Lecture CCLVII. Of the estate or quantity of interest in things.

(1) The numerous and refined distinctions of the Common Law, between *real* and *personal* estates, unknown to the Civil Code. (2) Of the *dominum eminens*, and the *dominium vulgare*. (3) Of the *dominium directum*, *dominium utile*, *dominium plenum*, *dominium minus plenum*. (4) Of substitution, Papillary, Quasi Papillary, and Fiduciary. (5) Of the Fidei Commissary Substitution, and herein of their resemblance to the Common Law estates in *Tail*, *Remainder*, and *Trust*. (6) Courtesy and dower, unknown to the Civil Law—Estates for life very unusual. (7) Of *Emphyteusis*, perpetual or long *leases*; how Emphyteuis may be created, and the obligations of the Emphyteuta.

Lecture CCLVIII. Of the acquisition of things jure naturae.

(1) Of Occupancy. (2) Of Accession. (3) Of Delivery.

[These are subjects of considerable extent and nicety, and will be minutely examined and compared, in all material respects, with the doctrines and decisions of the Common Law. The subject of *Delivery*, however, will be more particularly examined in the 6th section of the ensuing Lecture.]

LECTURE CCLIX. OF THE ACQUISITION OF THINGS JURE CIVILI.

(1) Of Prescription. (2) Of *Caduca*, or devolutions of property to the Exchequer. (3) Of the *Cessio Bonorum*. (4) Who might alien, what could not be aliened. (5) Of the modes of alienating. (6) Of Proper Gifts, or *donatio inter vivos*.

LECTURE CCLX.

(1) Of Improper Gifts, first *propter nuptias*, secondly *causa mortis*. (2) Of inheritance, first by Testament; secondly by Law, or Right of Descent; thirdly the *Bonorum Possessio* of the Praetor; these three now briefly considered.

LECTURE CCLXI. OF INHERITANCE OR SUCCESSION BY TESTAMENT.

(1) Whether the right of disposing of property by will be the creature of positive law. (2) Definition of Testament, and of the four kinds of Testament. (3) Of solemn testaments, Common to all. (4) Of unsolemn, particular, or privileged testaments. (5) Of Codicils.

LECTURE CCLXII.

(1) By whom testaments could be made. (2) Of things devisable or not. (3) Of testamentary heirship, who might become heirs, and of the rights and duties of such heirs. (4) Of executors, as distinguished from testamentary or instituted heirs. (5) Of Legacies.

LECTURE CCLXIII.

(1) Of annulling testaments, first *by law*, as by implication, cancellation, express revocation, subsequent testament; secondly *by the judge*, for inofficiousness, for fraud in their acquisition, arrogation, &c. (2) Of the constructions of wills. (3) Of the proof of wills.

LECTURE CCLXIV. OF LEGAL INHERITANCE, OR SUCCESSION AB INTESTATO.

(1) Definition of heirship. (2) Difference between the legal heir and the hæres factus. (3) Of the ideal unity of ancestor and heir, and consequences flowing from this doctrine. (4) Division of heirs into *necessarii, sui et necessarii, and extranei*. (5) Succession to moveable and immoveable property the same; the common law distinction between real and personal estate being unknown.

LECTURE CCLXV.

(1) Of the rules of descent of property, and of the order of heirship. (2) Of the computation of degrees. (3) Of succession *per capita* and *per stirpes*. (4) Of succession in the descending line. (5) Of succession in the ascending line. (6) Of succession in the collateral line. (7) Comparison of the canons of descent with those of the common law, and the rules of descent in Maryland. (8) Of the Bonorum Possessio. (9) Of the Collatio Bonorum.

LECTURE CCLXVI. OF HYPOTHECA (MORTGAGE) AND OF PIGNUS (PAWN.)

(1) Hypotheca and Pignus defined and distinguished. (2) Three species of mortgage. (3) Of conventional hypothecation, as a security only for debt, interest and costs, and herein of the several respects in which the Roman Hypotheca differes from the common law mortgage. (4) Of the modes in which the creditor satisfied himself out of the hypothecated property. (5) Of matters common to hypotheca and pignus. (6) Of the various kinds of pledges. (7) Of Subrogation, the various kinds, and consequences resulting from such assignments.

LECTURE CCLXVII. OF JOINT ESTATES.

(1) General observations. (2) Of the *jus accrescendi*. (3) Of *communio Bonorum*, and the actions *communidividudno et familiae erciscundæ*. (4) Of services charged, in case of unequal division, similar to the common law rent charge, for *owelty* of partition.

Lecture CCLXVIII. Of obligations, contracts, and pacts.

(1) Of obligations, natural, civil, and mixed. (2) Obligation distinguished from contract or covenant. (3) Definition of covenant, either *nude* or a *contract.* (4) Definition of contract—contracts either *nominate* or *innominate.* (5) Nominate contracts enumerated. (6) Innominate contracts explained, and divided into classes. (7) Of obligations arising *ex contractu, quasi ex contractu, ex delicto,* and *quasi ex delicto,* generally explained.

Lecture CCLXIX. Of obligations arising ex contractu.

(1) Of Nominate or true contracts, proceeding *ex ve,* from a thing done; *ex verbis,* from words; *ex literis,* from writing; *ex consensu,* from consent. (2) Of nominate contracts, *ex re,* viz. Mutuum, Commodatum, Depositum, and Pignus, fully treated of, except the last, which has been considered in Lecture CCLXII. (3) Of nominate contracts *ex verbis,* viz. *stipulation* and *surety.* (4) Of nominate contracts *ex literis.*

Lecture CCLXX. Of nominate contracts ex consensu.

(1) General observations. (2) Of the distinction between consensual and real contracts. (3) Division of consensual contracts, and *first* of the contract of sale, *emptio-venditio, secondly* of the contract of hiring, *locatio-conductio,* which has been in part considered in Lecture CCLIII. *thirdly* of the contract of partnership, *societas; fourthly* of the contract of commission or authority, *mandatum.*

Lecture CCLXXI. Of innominate contracts, and of obligations arising quasi ex contractu.

(1) General observations. (2) Of the *actio in factum,* and the *locus pæniteutiæ.* (3) Of improper or quasi contracts. (4) Of the *negotiorum gestio,* and how different from *mandatum.* (5) Of the *Tutelae Administratio, Judicium, figum regundorum, Aditio hæreditatis, Solutio indebiti.* (6) Of obligations proceeding from accidents and frauds.

Lecture CCLXXII.

(1) Of contracts *bona fidei,* and *stricti juris.* (2) Of the interpretation of contracts. (3) Of the termination of contracts, and herein of Payment, Consignation, Acceptilation, Confusion, Novation, Compensation, Mutual Consent, and Oblation.

Lecture CCLXXIII. Of obligations arising ex delicto.

(1) Of the nature of' the obligation occasioned by the commission of publick and private offences, and of the difference, in this respect, between the civil and common law (2) Of private crimes, or rather offences, *delicta et quasi delicta,* as distinguished from publick crimes, *crimina.* (3) Of delicta or proper offences, viz. Theft, *furtum,* Robbery, *rapina,* Damage, *damnum,* lnjury, *injuria.*

Lecture CCLXXIV. Of obligations arising quasi ex delicto.

(1) Of private, improper offences, or *quasi delicta.* (2) Of the seven species of *quasi* torts, and herein *first,* of an erroneous Judgment of a Judge, through ignorance; *secondly,* of carelessly throwing any thing out of a house, &c. whereby another suffers harm; *thirdly,* of loss of property committed to innkeepers or or masters of a vessel; *fourthly,* of placing or suspending any thing on high; near a house, so that persons may be injured; *fifthly,* of harm contemplated from a work about to be erected; *sixthly,* of harm expected to arise from a work already built, and herein of the *nuntiatio, cautions,* and proceedings of the Praetor in the two last cases; *seventhly,* of harm from beasts.

Lecture CCLXXV. Of obligations arising from crimes, properly so called.

(1) Preliminary observations on the Penal Laws of the civil code. (2) Of Blasphemy. (8) Of Treason, *læsa majestas.* (4) Of Adultery and Stuprum. (5) Of Bigamy. (6) Of Incest. (7) Of Sodomy. (8) Of Homicide. (9) Of Parricide. (10) Of Witchcraft (11) Of Banishment. (12) Of House-burning (13) Of Theft, after it became criminal. (14) Of the Crimen Falsi. (15) Of Robbery, after it became criminal, and herein of *effractores, latrones, pirates,* and *expilatores.* (16) Of the Crimen Peculatus. (17) Of the Crimen Residui. (18)

Of Bribery, *crimen repetundarum.* (19) Of the Crimen Ambitus. (20) Of Plagium, or man-stealing, Saccularii, Abigei, Balnearii. (21) Of Forestaling and Monopolizing, Crimen Fraudatæ Annonæ.

Lecture CCLXXVI.

(1) Of the division of crimes into ordinary and extraordinary. (2) The ordinary crimes having been fully considered, we now proceed to the latter, viz. Procuring Ahortion. (3) Threatening death or bodily harm, *scopelisinus.* (4) Violating tombs. (5) Prostration of the dams of publick rivers. (6) Concussion, or extortion of money &c. by various illegal devices. (7) Prevarication, of collusion between Informer and Defendant. (8) Abigeatus, or stealing a specifick number of cattle. (9) Harhouring criminals. (10) Enticing and harbouring bondmen, &c. (11) Exposure of infants. (12) Stellionate, or undefined cheats and frauds. (13) Removing landmarks. (14) Unauthorised Universities or communities. (15) Perjury. (16) Breaking prison. (17) Desertion by soldiers. (18) Taking unlawful pledges or distresses. (19) Purchasing silks and purple. (20) Attempts on chastity. (21) Polluting publick waters.

Lecture CCLXXVII. Of the organization of the roman courts of judicature, and forms of practice.

(1) Of the office and power of a Judge. (2) Of contentious and voluntary jurisdiction. (3) Of exceptions to the jurisdiction, and of challenging the Judges. (4) Of the Assessor to the Judge. (5) Of the distinct duties of the Judge and Magistrate, and of the modes of appointing them. (6) Of the Parties to an action, Actor, *plaintiff,* Reus, *defendant,* and herein, who may sue or be sued. (7) Of the oath of calumny. (8) Of taking the complaint *pro confesse.* (9) Of the duties of the Advocate and Proctor. (10) Of Apparitors and Notaries.

Lecture CCLXXVIII. Of actions.

(1) Definition of action. (2) Division of actions into Civil, Criminal, Real, Personal, Mixed, Petitory, Possessory, Prejudicial, Persecutory, Noxal, Bonæ fidei, Stricti juris, &c. each explained. (3) Of Real actions or Vindications. (4) Of Personal actions, or Condictions. (6) Of Mixed actions. (6) Of the Cession of actions. (7) Of the Cumulation of actions. (8) Of Interdicts.

Lecture CCLXXIX. Of actions (continued).

(1) Of Citation. (2) Of the Libel (3) Of the Litis Contestatio. (4) Of the Answer. (5) Of Exceptions, dilatory and peremptory. (6) Of the Replication. (7) Of the *fidejussory, pignoratitious, juratory,* and *promissory* Cautions. (8) Of intervention, Laudation, Nomination, Transaction, and Arbitration. (9) Of Trials *pro tribunali* and *deplano.*

Lecture CCLXXX. Of actions (continued.)

(1) Of the Evidence or Proof; and herein of General, Particular, Plena, and Semi.plena proof, and the topicks of argumentation. (2) Of Particular proof arising from Confession, Presumptions, either *juris,* or *juris et de jure.* (3) Of Witnesses, and herein of their number, qualification, and mode of giving their testimony. (4) Of Instruments, and herein of Publick and Private instruments, *cautio, apocha, antipocha, syngraphia, chirographia, litera,* Merchants and Tradesmen's *books,* and herein of the Suppletory Oath. (5) Of Oaths, how, and to whom administered, when and how far proof. (6) Different kinds of Oaths, as *decisive, ad litem, suppletory, juramentum calumnie,* of *expenses,* of *truth* &c.

Lecture CCLXXXI. Of actions (continued.)

(1) Of the submission, or argument of the cause. (2) Of the Decree, interlocutory or final. (3) Of Appeal and stay of Execution. (4) Of Supplication. (5) Of *Restitutio in integrum.* (6) Of Remedium Syndicatus, and Appeals from a *nullity.* (7) Of Rebearsing. (8) Of Executions.

TITLE X. Of the constitution and laws of the United States of America.

Lecture CCLXXXII. Of a confederation, a constitution, and of the division of governmental powers.

(1) Of the objects of confederation, deduced from an historical view of national associations. (2) Of a Constitution, its true meaning, and advantages. (3) Of the rule requiring the Legislative, Judicial, and Executive functions to be distinct and separate.

Lecture CCLXXXIII. Of the constitution of the United States, and first of the national legislature.

(1) All Legislative power vested in Congress, consisting of a Senate, and House of Representatives.

(2) *House of Representatives,* how composed, its Duration, Qualifications of Electors and of Representatives, Apportionment of Representation, Vacancies how filled up, Powers of the House in the choice of Officers, in Impeachments, in originating Revenue Bills, &c.

(3) *Senate,* of whom composed, how chosen, its Duration, Division into three classes, and Mode of voting, Vacancies how replenished, Qualifications of Senators, Powers of the Senate in the choice of its Officers; as a Court for the trial of Impeachments; in relation to Revenue Bills; in making Treaties, Appointment of Ambassadors, &c.

(4) Of Powers, Duties, and Privileges common to both houses, or the members thereof, and herein of holding elections for senators and representatives, and of the power of Congress herein. Of the assembling of Congress. Of the Power of either house to decide on the election of its own members. Of the quorum required in certain cases. Of the Power of each house to regulate its internal government, and of the power of adjournment, &c. Of the compensation of members. Of exemption from arrest, and of certain incapacities of members. Of enacting Laws, after the dissent of the Executive.

Lecture CCLXXXIV. Of the powers expressly delegated to Congress by the Constitution.

Lecture CCLXXXV. Of the powers expressly denied to Congress by the Constitution and amendments thereto.

Lecture CCXXXLVI. Of matters obligatory on the several States of the Union.

(1) Of the articles for the preservation of the rights of the several States and of the People. (2) Of the amendments to the Constitution proposed by Congress, but not ratified by the States.

Lecture CCLXXXVII. Of the executive power.

(1) President and Vice President, how chosen. (2) Duration of office. (3) Qualifications of President; his compensation; oath of office; when his powers devolve on the Vice-President. (4) Commander in chief of the Army, Navy, and Militia in actual service of the United States. (5) Powers of the President in making Treaties, appointment of Ambassadors, filling up vacancies in the Senate which occur during the recess; to pardon or reprieve. (6) When he may convene or adjourn Congress.—Of his duty to inform Congress of the state of the Union—to propose measures for their consideration—to receive Ambassadors and Publick Ministers—to see that the Laws are executed—to Commission all the officers of the United States. (7) Of the removal from office of the President, Vice-President and other civil officers.

Lecture CCLXXXVIII. Of the judicial power.

(1) Judicial Powers how distributed. (2) Tenure of office. (3) Compensation of the Judges. (4) Extent of the Judicial powers.

Lecture CCLXXXIX. Of other provisions in the Constitution.

(1) Of Trial by Jury. (2) Of the Guarantee from the United States of a Republican form of government to every State, and their protection against invasion or domestick violence. (3) Of the debts and

engagements prior to the adoption of the Constitution. (4) The Constitution, Laws, and Treaties the Supreme Law of the Land. (5) Of excessive Bail, Fine, and Cruel and unusual Punishments.

Of the laws of the United States.

[In our Commentaries on the *Constitution* of the United States, much has necessarily been said of those laws, enacted in virtue of the powers delegated by the Constitution to Congress. This, however, is not sufficient. We shall, therefore, proceed to treat of the most important of these Laws, and in our observations thereon, shall introduce all of the leading decisions wbich have occurred in our courts of Judicature in exposition of the Laws. In treating of the *Laws* of the United States, we shall generally adopt a very simple method, viz. the *Alphabetical*, as we presume that the student, who has proceeded thus far with us in our inquiries, which have been as regardful of *method* as practicable, stands no longer in need of a more philosophical arrangement.]

Lecture CCXC. Of aliens, and herein

Of the Laws enacted under Art. 1. Sec. viii. 4. of the Constitution, by which "Congress shall have power to establish an uniform rule of Naturalization."

Lecture CCXCI. Of the Bank of the United States.

(Art. 1. Sec. viii. 2. 17.)

(1) Of the constitutionality of the Acts, 5th of February, 1791, ch. 84, and 10th of April, 1816, ch. 44. (2) Of the establishment of Branches, or Offices of Discount and Deposite within any state. (3) Of the State's right to tax such Branch or Office. (4) In what courts the Bank of the United SLates, or its Branches, may sue or be sued.

Lecture CCXCII. Of copy right and patent.

(Art. 1. Sec. viii. 8.)

[In the foregoing Lectures we have purposely omitted to treat of the rights of Authors and Inventors, and shall, therefore, at this time fully consider the English and American Law on these subjects.]

Lecture CCXCIII. Of crimes and punishments.

(Art. 3. Sec. 2. ch. 3. Sec. 3. ch. 1. 2. Art.4. Sec. 2. ch. 2.)

Lecture CCXCIV. Of duties on imports and tonnage, and of drawbacks.

[On this numerous class of Laws, nothing more will be attempted than to present the important decisions which have been made on any of them, and to bring to the student's notice such of the laws on this subject as may be deemed material.]

Lecture CCXCV. Of the judicial system of the United States.

(Art. 3. Sec. 1. ch. 1. Sec. 2. ch. 1. 2. 3. Art. 4. Sec. 1. ch. 1. Art. 11. Amendments.)

(1) Division of the United States into Districts. (2) Division of the United States into Circuits. (3) Division of the Judicial Power and herein

1. Of the *Supreme Court*; its Organization, Powers and Jurisdiction, *first* Original and exclusive; *secondly* Original but not exclusive; *thirdly* Appellate.

2. Of the *Circuit Courts*, their Organization, Powers, and Jurisdiction, *first* Original exclusive, *secondly*, Original concurrent, *thirdly*, Appellate.

3. Of the *District Courts*, their Organization, Powers, and Jurisdiction, *first*, exclusive Original; *secondly*, concurrent.

[In treating of the Organization, Powers and Jurisdiction of the courts of the United States, we shall embrace the entire Judiciary system, and present to the student the material decisions thereon.]

LECTURE CCXCVI. OF THE LAWS RELATIVE TO NAVIGATION, POST OFFICES, AND POST ROADS.

LECTURE CCXCVII. OF THE LAWS RELATIVE TO SEAMEN.

[Under the Titles of "*Lex Mercatoria*," and "*Admiralty and Maritime Law*," we have spoken fully of Seamen's Wages, and incidentally of several other matters, growing out of the various acts of Congress relating to Seamen. Many Laws, however, have not been mentioned, which, together with some important Judicial decisions yet remain for the present Lecture.]

LECTURE CCXCVIII. OF SHIPS OR VESSELS, AND OF THE SLAVE TRADE.

LECTURE CCXCIX. OF THE STATE, TREASURY, NAVY, AND WAR DEPARTMENTS.

TITLE XI

LECTURE CCC. OF LEGAL BIOGRAPHY AND BIBLIOGRAPHY.

LECTURE CCCI. OF PROFESSIONAL DEPORTMENT.

Chapter 19

A Lecture, Introductory to a Course of Lectures

1823

David Hoffman

David Hoffman (December 24, 1784-November 11, 1854) was a lawyer and professor of law in the University of Maryland from 1816 to 1832. His works and their influence are described in chapter 1. The Lecture is reprinted from David Hoffman, *A Lecture, Introductory to a Course of Lectures, Now Delivering in the University of Maryland* (Baltimore: J. D. Toy, 1823).

Author's note: I would embrace the present occasion, to correct a misapprehension, which has partially prevailed, that the engagements into which I am about entering, may interfere, in some degree, with my avocations as Counsellor and Attorney. No impression can be more unjust, as the studies in which the prosecution of these lectures will engage me, would have been pursued, had the present enterprise never been attempted—and as my scheme thus far, has been prosecuted only in leisure hours. I therefore desire to state, emphatically, that my duties here, can never, in any way, be permitted to interfere with those due to my Clients—but, on the contrary, that I do not contemplate the relinquishment of any portion either of my professional zeal, or of my practice.

The science of jurisprudence, as it concerns the topicks most interesting to human understanding, and human happiness, is also that of the widest extent, and most numerous particulars. As it relates to the conduct of man, it is a moral science of great sublimity; as its object is individual and national prosperity; as its object is individual and national prosperity, it must be, of all others, the most important; as it regards the actions, both of communities and individuals, it is infinitely various; and as it concerns all the rights and obligations derived from, or due to God, our country, and ourselves, it is a science endlessly diffusive, whose "seat is," indeed, "the bosom of God, and whose voice is the harmony of the world."

Lawgivers have, in all ages, been esteemed the largest and most transcendent benefactors of the race; not only because their institutions have obviously promoted the tranquillity and elegance of societies, but because it was equally obvious how large a share of observation, how clear a discernment of causes and effects, and how judicious an adjustment of various principles, were requisite to the success of any form of policy. Scarcely less accurate or admirable, too, is that perspicacious talent by which the expositor of laws is led to the recognition of these general principles,—to use them in the interpretation of old, and in the framing of new enactments; or that steady, and liberal understanding by which general consequences are regarded, instead of particular, and general justice is distributed, without reference to private or partial inconvenience.—These are, or, ought to be the characteristicks of the three great classes of lawyers.—Legislators, who make, Jurisconsults, who expound, and Judges, who both interpret and distribute, the laws of policed societies.

We are not then to expect, and far be it from me to inculcate the opinion, that such a science requires no extraordinary powers of genius, of application, or of both. That which has been aptly described by Burke, as the "*pride of the human intellect, and the collected wisdom of ages, combining the principles of original justice with the boundless variety of human concerns,*" cannot be acquired, but by the steady, and methodical application of a well regulated mind.

You will doubtless find, in the very largeness of the career on which you are entering—in the difficulties by which it is environed—in the strong thought, and assiduity which it enforces, additional motives of admiration, and (to bold and generous minds) additional causes of ambition, and of emulation. Were your profession of vulgar and easy attainment, there would be no just reason for the high veneration with which we regard the great masters, and luminaries of the science; nor should I have any motive for proffering the aids, which, among others, I have proposed for the progress of the student; or for stimulating your industry and emulation. I am earnestly of opinion that few, perhaps none, have ever attained "*unto the depths of learning,*" in any science, without industry and talent, regulated by method, and accompanied by a love of study, bordering on enthusiasm. To use the strong language of Gesner, in relation to knowledge in general, and which is emphatically applicable to law, "He who would be learned, must cry after knowledge, and lift up his voice for understanding: he must seek her as silver, and search for her as for hidden treasures."—Yet when I use this language, which may, perhaps, seem discouraging, I must be understood to speak of students who desire to study and practise law, as one of the most *honourable, profitable,* and *laudable* professions, and not of such as desire to rank the knowledge of its general principles, among the number of their elegant accomplishments; between whom, and professional men, there is as wide a difference, as between the polite man of science, who in his closet, studies the philosophy of mechanicks, and the learned mechanician, who applies them to the erection of complex machinery, or the edification of perfect models of architecture. To the professional student, then, we must be understood to address ourselves, when we discourse of the largeness of the science enveloped in his profession, and of the zeal, the method, and enduring perseverance with which it is essential to pursue it.

Students of law, in common with others, partake of those obstacles which science (in this age) herself erects to the followers of science. Not only are the boundaries of legal, as well as other learning, greatly enlarged, and its topicks equally multiplied, but the literature of the age, even that which solicits your regard, as kindred to your legitimate studies, are vastly extended, and diversified. To these allurements of polite, and general learning, it is necessary to oppose the greatness, and importance of your own particular science, and to urge you to the remembrance of the maxim, now more just than ever, "*non omnia possumus omnes.*" Of this point I presume, I shall not be misunderstood—as in a work, some time since, addressed by me to American students of law, I insisted on the necessity of preparing their mind for its legal studies, by imbuing it with general and liberal learning, thus previously acquiring information on subjects, which the study of their profession will seldom permit to be extensively, and minutely inquired into afterwards; and at the same time of framing their minds to habits of research and diligence. This is not, however, designed to exclude altogether the study of other sciences, or of polite literature, *cotemporaneously* with that of law: the most indefatigable student has either from external circumstances, or from mental exhaustion, many intervals of time, in which he revolts from his immediate pursuit through he would gladly fill them with less laborious avocations. The mind is unwilling to be forever contending with difficulty, or excited to the full measure of its strength: the most diligent require some relaxation of employment, some change to diversify the rugged track of investigation. The sage Ascham, the erudite Erasmus, the deeply thinking Montesquieu, and the sublime Newton, were accustomed to unbend the mind, in the moments stolen from their intellectual toils, by the perusal of the fancies of Dante, or of Tasso, or of some of the voluminous tales and romances of the times.

The student who desires to economise time, should therefore indulge these variations of the mental appetite, and tempt this intellectual satiety with every modification with which genius has adorned literature, or disguised the harshness of science. Such an occupation of the fragments of time, often idly and unprofitably thrown away, under the plea of mental exhaustion, would enable the law student to accomplish himself in the principles of universal science, without, in any degree breaking in upon those hours which should be sacred to the study of his profession. It is fortunate that the instruction which the mind rejects in one shape it will often receive in another.

Like a chemical *menstruum*, it may be saturated with one species of matter, and imbibe a different, even with avidity. In this nice art of supplying it with various food, and at suitable times, of courting, or commanding it, consists the principal difficulty of study. But whilst a law student should endeavour previously to treasure up a fund of general and diversified knowledge, and aim during his professional studies, to fill its occasional intervals by the pursuits of analogous or elegant science, he should beware of an overweening attachment to the *literae humaniores*, and more especially avoid the jejune, though fashionable trifles which modern literature pours perpetually from the press, no less than the noisy verbiage and the speculative and passionate vituperation of the day. These considerations are the more important at this time, when not only the *delicioe* of letters are served up in innumerable attractive shapes, but, as I have intimated, the fashion of the age, in knowledge and reading, is excursiveness and generality, rather than system and correctness;—a method of reading no less destructive of taste than of time, and which has the additional disadvantage of loosing, in the crowd, the pure and ancient standards of literary excellence. Leave then to the Reviewers, the too often unprofitable labour of skimming the wide surface of ephemeral literature, and reserve for the acknowledged models of thought and the true fountain of science, the brief and precious hours of occasional leisure. It is the peculiarity, however, of a long habit of research into a science, however vast and various, that the mind acquires, in no small degree, powers of methodising, of selecting, and investigating, which every day renders its labours less fatiguing, and its search less perplexing. Thoughts and topicks arrange themselves insensibly; the scientifick, and technical divisions suggest themselves with little effort; what is known, becomes so, not more from memory, than from system; and what is unknown is speedily found, because we have learned towards what point to direct our search. In this respect the adept in a science resembles the captain of a host; where the vast number is weilded without disorder, because it is symmetrically classified; and every thing takes, or is found in its proper place, because it is arranged there by an invariable system.

There have been times in which learning was chiefly measured by the mere knowledge, or rather multiplicity of facts, treasured up by the *memory*. Before the invention of printing, it was extremely difficult, and scarcely possible, to become learned in the science and literature of the age, without a retentive memory. This was considered a faculty admirable in itself, and, in consequence of its utility, was then allowed to hold a more dignified position among the intellectual powers, than modern metaphysicians are willing to grant it. In those days of primitive knowledge, we hear of the most surprising instances of the cultivation of this faculty. We read of *Portius Latro*, who remembered every word of every oration he ever spoke. We are told that *Seneca* could repeat two thousand words after once hearing them, and strictly preserve their order, though they had no dependence whatever on each other. Demagogues, also, who were desirous to please the people, often knew the names of all their fellow citizens, as *Cyrus* knew that of every soldier in his numerous army. We likewise read of an ambassador from *Pyrrhus* to the Romans, who in one day learnt the names of his spectators, and on the following, saluted the Roman senate, and all the assembled populace, each by his name! An incredible story, certainly, unless the crowd were less moved than in our own day, by vulgar curiosity. In more modern times, but prior to the revival of letters in Europe, a man who had read a few manuscripts, and committed them to memory, was deemed learned, and regarded as a national treasure. He could travel from place to place, and by repeating from Aristotle, Plato, Homer, Eusebius, or St. Jerome, not only live, but thrive by his learning.

Knowledge, however, which is deposited in the memory, is not necessarily valuable. Natural, and even acquired memory, are not frequently accompanied by the higher mental endowments; by the power of philosophical arrangement, of analysis, and synthesis; and we find that the most able and learned philosophers have not relied on this species of knowledge, or on the arduous cultivation of this faculty, as is forcibly illustrated in the history of Bacon, of Voltaire, Franklin, Montaigne, and others, and remarkably, in the case of Sir Isaac Newton, who, of all philosophers, perhaps, thought most deeply, and in an eminent degree possessed the power of arranging his extensive knowledge to useful purposes; yet, he, according to Doctor Pemberton, was often at a loss, even when conversation turned on his own discoveries, and excellent writings.

A consciousness of his own inventive powers, of his perfect ability again to analyze and arrange, prevented his taking much pains in treasuring in his memory the details of his knowledge. On this subject Dugald Stewart has a pertinent remark. "A man of original genius," says he, "who is fond of exercising his reasoning powers anew, on most points as they occur to him, and who cannot submit to rehearse the ideas of others, or to repeat by rote the conclusions which he has deduced from previous reflection, often appears to superficial observers to fall below the level of ordinary understandings; while another, destitute both of quickness, and invention, is admired for that promptitude in his decisions, which arises from the inferiority of his intellectual abilities." Who now regards with veneration the astonishing memory of the *Abbé de Longuerue,* whose erudition was said to be so vast as to have been called terrible—who spoke all languages, knew all facts of history—had recorded in his memory all the places and times of geography and chronology, and who actually wrote a history of France, purely from memory, and without consulting a single volume! Or, who delights to remember the learning of the Florentine Librarian, *Magliabechi,* who is said to have read six large rooms full of books! Both of these prodigies of the erudition of the memory, were however, remarkably deficient in the powers of induction, of philosophical analysis, and arrangement, and of all those qualities, which, at the present day, are considered as really valuable, and indicative of mental ability. The Abbé admired an antiquarian commentator on Homer, more than Homer himself, and the learned librarian left, for the benefit of posterity, but one line of his own composition, and that was round a medal of his own likeness, and contained neither sentiment, knowledge nor wit. Fortunately for the jurisprudent, his attainments do not depend exclusively on a faculty which ranks so low among the intellectual powers; and I cannot but express, on this occasion my disapprobation of the mode recently recommended by an able lawyer of a neighbouring state, who insists, (strange as it may appear) on students actually getting by rote the whole of Blackstone's Commentaries, and some other elementary works. I would urge you, on the contrary, to study the general and pervading principles of the science. Treasure up its maxims, their meaning, and application. Cultivate it in all its bearings and analogies. Search into its philosophy with care, and be sure that you understand what you read. Study much but all with *method.* Let your inquiries be censorial, as well as expository; and trust to your knowledge of the reasons and grounds of law, added to your recollection of the sources of information, rather than to the vain hope of treasuring up its *particulars.* Should these rules be regarded, the entire science may be open to your view, though nearly all of its facts be but imperfectly remembered by you. If your mind be deeply imbued with its philosophy, your acquaintance with the paths and sources of knowledge will soon enable you to obtain, with certainty, the special information you desire.

To your profession you must devote yourself as the industrious merchant to his gains, and with a zeal and steadiness the greater, as your pursuit is more laborious, more noble and more profitable in all that enriches and adorns life. Nor can I but confess, as I have just remarked, that your task is a great one, if you design to complete it as you should; and it requires certainly the steadfast application of all the high powers, which attract dignity and respect to the human understanding. And while I thus speak my candid sentiments on this point, I trust you will only be incited by them to a higher, and more earnest emulation; to a respect for the profession itself, and an admiration for those illustrious sages, who have bent almost the whole splendour, and force of their genius, to the most profound, as well as the most excellent of human sciences.

It is fortunate, indeed, that the study of the law has a nearer alliance than any other with the business of the world, and all the high concerns of human life. Its collateral topicks, also, fit him better for the business and conversation of men, amidst which his vocation lies than those which engage the divine and the physician.

The lawyer, then, it particularly behoves to be uninfected with those prejudices and peculiarities of mind, those excentricities of manner and expression, which often arise from men's avocations, which colour and too frequently circumscribe the operations of their talents, and which the illustrious Bacon has quaintly, but forcibly placed under the general head of *idola specus.*—He should studiously guard against the little remaining pedantry of his science, and endeavour to soften the strong impressions made on his mind by his chief and favourite pursuit, by mingling them with such as are derived from his intercourse with other men, and other books. This consideration is still more important in America, where the lawyer and the politician pass into each other by so easy a transition; more easy at least, than is found by the votaries of other pursuits.

And as it is from those who have been *students* of this profession, if not from its *practitioners,* that the nation draws the largest portion of its legislators and statesmen, there is an obvious reason for somewhat enlarging the circuit of the law student's acquirements, arising from this probable combination of the counsellor with the politician. The studies of these two, their habits of extemporaneous discipline, their converse with society resembles each other; and as there is, with us, no privileged class, the maker is often found in the expositor or distributor of laws. This circumstance exerts a happy influence on our profession, first, as it offers its members the chance of advancement in two roads of life; and secondly, as it cannot fail to unfetter them from the technical narrowness, too often the result of an exclusive devotion to a single science: and hence a lawyer without materially diverting his mind from the topicks of his profession, has a field, abundantly large, and various for the active and pleasing employment of his intellectual powers.

The sedentary and studious have, indeed, to contend with obstacles peculiar to themselves. Secluded of necessity, for the larger portion of their time, from the business and bustle of men, their ideas insensibly assume a monotonous aspect, and receiving little ventilation from the constant current of novelties, which refresh those who are engaged in active and crowded scenes, are apt to stagnate into languor and melancholy.—It is little wonderful that intellectual exertion should become irksome, when thus accompanied by despondency; and that the student should find the lapse to indolence and relaxation so easy, and the return to his solitary avocations so painful—a painfulness most generally augmented by a consciousness of neglect of duty, which he is happy to drown in the pleasures or bustle of society, rather than brood over in the stillness of his study.—Instead of attempting to remedy this tendency by total seclusion, it is better, gentlemen, to indulge it with moderation; and to mingle business and pleasure in those proportions, which will equally prevent the fatigue of too much exertion, and the satiety of too much enjoyment. Hermits, whether in religion or in science, have generally found their scheme of exclusive and solitary devotion to a single pursuit, to issue in lassitude and indolence. But with occasional relaxation from society; with exact and uniform attention, and strict economy in the occupation of your time, together with a rigid adherence to method in your studies, and the devotion of your leisure time to the pursuit of miscellaneous literature, or general science, you will find your chief study, that of law, to be not only easy, but pleasing. There is no difficulty in cultivating even a passion for this study; and though a lawyer should be, in some degree, acquainted with the whole circle of human science, so that he, may be as occasion may require, a philosopher to detect, a logician to reason, a poet to describe, and an orator to persuade, yet, believe me, that excellence in a single scientifick profession, is all that our reasonable expectations should embrace.

> "One science only can one genius hit,
> "So vast is art, so narrow human wit."

A student, who is animated by a just zeal to attain the summits of professional learning and renown, is not to be surprised, or discouraged by the prospect of a thousand nights devoted to research, and a thousand days employed in the practical application or its results.—No eminence, that is worth having, is attainable *per saltum;* nature has included in steady application the seeds both of mental sanity and pleasure; and while, to the pursuit of amusement, she has destined a sickly appetite, inevitably and speedily cloyed, business and study, on the contrary, not only reap a reward in themselves, but quicken the relish of unaccustomed relaxation. Science, if not like the well, which my lord Coke quaintly describes, is perhaps, like the grotto, or the mine,—to which the access is uninviting and fatiguing, but which often rewards him who is content to groupe awhile with pains and patience, with the view of unexpected beauties, wealth and wonders. It is true, indeed, that to taste the pleasures which spring from legal research, we must have entered into the principles, discovered the harmonies, and arranged with method and curiosity the innumerable topicks of the science; as in the caverns of the earth the accomplished and inquisitive mineralogist and geologist reap a satisfaction, and an interest unknown to the uninformed spectators.

With these views of the science, to which you are pledged to devote yourselves, the number and variety of its subjects, instead of alarming your patience, should animate your enterprise.

A profession so liberal and extended, so sublime and important, should be cultivated by those only who are actuated by principles of the purest, and most refined honour. Regarding law as a science equally venerable from its objects, and noble from the ingenuity and mental expansion employed and excited in its acquisition and practice, it should be the ardent desire of its votaries to see its shrine unprofaned by knavery and ignorance, and its retainers not more eminent, from the importance of their functions, than from the honesty and skill with which they discharge them. It is true, we cannot reasonably expect that this can ever be fully accomplished: it is incident to the best things to be the most perverted; and while we may admire and emulate the portraiture which the sincere lovers of this science have been fond to appropriate to its professors, we must be content to see its dignity sometimes debased by the ignorant, and its liberality by the mercenary. We believe that, in most cases, enlarged knowledge, and noble studies exercise, in themselves, a happy influence on those who have pursued them. The very acquisition of liberal knowledge, supposes the acquisition of liberal ideas; so that, in most cases, the possession of intellectual power begets correctness in its application to the purposes of life; and the complexion of its pursuits seems to be, almost necessarily, accompanied by more sound, more enlarged, and more honourable views, than we find in those whose knowledge has been circumscribed. But, if the intrinsick excellence of the profession, and its natural tendency to beget elevated and honest dispositions, be not sufficient to check the wayward proclivity of some men's minds towards vice and dishonour, it is fortunate that our profession has a powerful control over its members, in the authority possessed by courts of justice (whose officers lawyers are, and under whose commission alone, are they competent to act) to suspend them, or wholly to deprive them of the privilege of practice; and, if this be once done, by any court of judicature, all others, by courtesy, would, at once, adjudge them unworthy members, and close every hope of amending their condition, by a change of residence.

You have then, every motive for exerting the utmost assiduity in your studies, and the most sacred honour in the practice of your profession. Respect and influence in society, professional reputation, the highest stations of honour and profit, in a great and enlightened republick, and all the goods of intellectual and worldly wealth are proffered to you. The character of a lawyer who does justice to his profession, and to the important station he holds in life, is, indeed, truly excellent and dignified. He is one, whom early education has imbued with the principles of probity, and habituated to labour and research; in that which enlarges, and refines the mind. He desires to impart lustre to the utility of his learning, by fostering every honourable and amiable affection. The fountains of liberal science and polite letters he has tasted of, before he enters on the pursuit of his more technical studies, and has thus protected himself from pedantry and narrow views.

Versed in the sciences most necessary to the purposes of society, he naturally obtains over it a large and legitimate control, which he exercises only that he may become in it a more useful member. He is the asserter of right, the accuser of wrong, the protector of innocence, and the terror of crime. He labours not for those alone who can afford the *honorarium*, but the widow, the fatherless, and the oppressed are ever in his mind. No prospect of gain will ever induce him to advise the pursuit of law against right, or sober judgment; nor will any man's greatness be a shield against the justice due to his client. If he assist in the enaction of laws, which he may afterwards be called on to vindicate, it is done with an eye solely to his country's good, and whilst he respects its legislature and judiciary, he learns to reverence the constitution more than either.—History is his field, as he learns in it the rudiments and revolutions of his science. Rhetorick and logic are the weapons by which he imparts to his oratory warmth and grace, force and clearness. From his knowledge of man he learns truth, and he cultivates rectitude for the more useful exercise of his powers. Destitute of these, he is either unprofitable, or mischievous to society, and endued with them, he is one of its *chiefest ornaments* and *firmest safeguards.*

Most of you, gentlemen, are no doubt apprised of my intention to deliver a course of Lectures in this University, on every branch of jurisprudence, in any degree applicable to this country, or which may be useful to the American student of law.—The actual execution of this laborious enterprise has been delayed, in part, by the extensiveness of the scheme of instruction, of which the Syllabus, which I sometime since addressed to you, and the course of Legal Study, previous to that, contain the outline; and in part, by the imperfect state and deficient funds of the University, which have prevented those accommodations which are essential. This wide subject has hitherto, either been partitioned out to several professors, or the *institutes* only have been taught; but the object of the course; now to be delivered in this University, is to treat all of its branches, and to investigate every important one in detail: and though this be perhaps the first attempt of the kind in England or in this country, the enterprise, however laborious and responsible, will certainly be prosecuted with all the industry and zeal which I can command; relying on such encouragement from students of law throughout the Union, as may compensate me for the sacrifice inevitable to my undertaking.

Though law has been publickly taught in Great Britain, it is a little remarkable that no attempt has been made to go beyond the institutes of the science. *Sir William Blackstone's* immortal work presents only a bird's eye view of this various, extensive, and complicated science: and though it be admitted, by so competent a judge as Sir William Jones, to be "the most correct and beautiful outline that was ever exhibited of any human science,"—yet this accomplished scholar unites with Hargrave, Redesdale, Brown, Story, Tucker, and, others, in the decided opinion that it presents nothing beyond the mere rudiments of English law; and, to use the well known language of Sir William Jones, "these beautiful commentaries will no more form a lawyer, than a general map of the world, how accurately and elegantly soever it may be delineated, will make a geographer."

The lectures of the second Vinerian Professor, *Dr. Wooddeson*, have prosecuted some of the topicks more at large; but still the whole work is strictly rudimental.

Doctor Sullivan's Lectures, which are comprised in one volume, are solely on feudal learning, and the first principles of the English constitution, and some of its laws; and those of *Doctor Brown*, delivered in the University of Dublin, do not aspire to any thing beyond the presentation of a well arranged contour of the Roman Civil Law, and the law of the Admiralty; and it cannot, with justice, be said, that even this design has been accomplished, as there are several, even important branches, in no way alluded to, and others, which are merely named.

There have been several elementary courses delivered in this country, with what success, and how far meritorious, I regret I have not the means of judging, as they have never been published, with the exception of Lectures by the late Doctor Wilson, of Philadelphia, which, even as a course of elementary *legal* instruction, are extremely imperfect, and better suited (from their general and indefinite legal information, embellished by the ornaments of literature) for polite scholars, or students, in the course of their collegiate inquiries, than for the regular student of law. We entertain great respect for the character and learning of this gentleman, and had his scheme been more extensive, his lectures, no doubt, would have proved highly valuable to American law students.

The lectures which for many years past have been delivered at Litchfield, in the state of Connecticut, by the venerable Judge Reeves, and his able associate, Judge Gould, we are persuaded, are well entitled to the high reputation they have ever maintained. The eminence of many lawyers who now adorn our country, and who were students in that institution, are the best proofs of the excellence of the scheme of instruction which is there pursued. Massachusetts and Virginia also, have not been inactive in the laudable endeavour to promote our favourite science through the medium of lectures: and the state of New-York possesses, in the genius, learning, and highly embellished mind of its late Chancellor, an inestimable resource, could that able lawyer and civillian be induced to devote a portion of his time in this way.[1] As far, however, as my acquaintance with these various enterprises extends, I believe that no attempt has yet been made to embrace even the rudiments of the *entire science.*

The enterprise, then, in which I am now engaged, has been hitherto unessayed: the experience of others, if it afford me no cause of very flattering expectation, at least gives me no anticipation of disappointed efforts. Inclination, and judgment, bid me proceed; and I am unwilling to believe, what diffidence sometimes whispers to me, that my design may not meet an adequate encouragement. As long as this is the case, I shall endeavour to enliven and sustain myself, in the many hours of exhaustion incident to this enterprise, with the confident hope and belief of receiving sufficient to gratify my ambition, as well as all other reasonable expectation. Should all this fail, I am not vain, in hoping that the failure may be softened by the remark, *"Magnis tamen, excedit ausis."*

But let us now proceed to other topicks:—

The tendency of science, as she enlarges her acquisitions, is to methodize and arrange them. As want is the obstacle to the first steps of her progress, so abundance is that of her later stages. If in the gradual accessions to human learning, the base could be accurately separated from the precious—the certain from the obscure and the impenetrable, the task of the modern scholar were comparatively easy; and if his *memory* were burdened, his *judgment* would be relieved and anticipated. Such, however, are the revolutions of human opinion, such the motive for reverting often to systems and doctrines deemed to be exploded—that scarcely any thing which has been written can be thrown entirely aside, as having been tested to be false, or unfit for the purposes of instruction. Scarcely any, so to speak, of the *old furniture of the mind,* is to be thrown entirely out of doors.

If such is the case in regard to the sciences more metaphysical and theoritick, it is manifestly more so in such as are positive and arbitrary. In them, as in municipal law, for example, it is not sufficient to establish only general principles, whose application is left for the individual, in each particular case as it occurs. As these principles are continually compared with the emergencies of life, as their seeming collision, in particular cases, is explained and reconciled, and as it is important to know distinctly their operation on our interests and conduct, cases decided on analogous principles are carefully sought; the records of expository jurisprudence are perpetually swelled, and the general maxim comes attended in the books by a host of corroborative instances of its application. Hence the voluminous books of reports, from which the inquirer is to seek his principles, his maxims, his precedents—scarcely more from the cases which have *established,* than from those which have sought to *impeach* them.

Hence too the importance, nay, necessity as adjudicated cases multiply, of arranging them in classes, and extracting their spirit in treatises. This method subserves a double purpose: it gives the student a comprehensive view of the subject, and collects under his eye the cases from which it has been extracted, to which he may, and often should refer for confirmation or correction. It is true, that while a student has the power to inquire at the fountains themselves; while the amount of collected knowledge is not yet so great but that within the usual legal novitiate, he may himself survey the whole ground, it is all important, for correct and certain knowledge, that he mark, learn, and digest for himself. Such, however, is the vast extent of most of the branches of *legal* science, that such a mode of study would be nearly impossible. But should he pursue this course to the greatest extent, the methodized treatises, especially of our own time, are of infinite use: they give the natural order of inquiry, they show what is to be sought, and where it is to be found—with such aids, if we inquire for ourselves, it is of little importance that our conclusion shall be exactly the same.

The common law has in it a feature somewhat peculiar; or at least it has this in a peculiar degree. We find that it has survived many ages, and many revolutions of manners, and has yet been accommodated to them all. Hence, in many cases, it has retained its *form,* while it has altered its *spirit,* and the student, astonished sometimes at the principles, and more frequently at the forms which it presents, can only discover their reason in an antiquated system. It is scarcely necessary to say how valuable is a guide through these mazes of blackletter learning, where so much is dark, some is useless, and some perhaps, even absurd. How, necessary, if not brilliant, the *industry,* which, content to groupe, like a Belzoni among the catacombs, brings from amidst dust, oblivion, and darkness, some scattered but valuable relicks!

These considerations may serve to show the usefulness and true province of a *lecturer*—to collate and select with diligence and discernment—to trace his doctrines from their first germ to their final growth, through all the variations of judicial opinions—to mark the accordance of decided cases with general principles, or the exceptions and deviations—to declare what has been said, not *merely* and *indiscriminately,* but with a view to general results, and with an examination of its consistency with legal analogy and reason—and finally, to refute, or fearlessly to combat error, without regard to mere authority, remembering with the philosophick Boyle, that although *authority* be a long-bow, the effect of which generally depends on the strength of the arm which draws it, reason is a cross-bow of equal efficacy in the hands of the dwarf and the giant.

These, I apprehend, are the chief features of such a method of instruction, and thus united, they present the subject in the fullest manner, and most obvious light, stripped at the same time of the too frequent incumbrance of pedantick learning, or of false reasoning. The student, informed of the *sources* of the knowledge which is imparted by the professor, has ample opportunity, in the intervals [ ] his instruction, to examine, to reason, and to criticize for himself; and his attention, in the mean while, is directed with particular force to what is presented in condensed form, and becomes therefore the theme of solitary inquiry, or of ardent discussion with other learners. We march more patiently forward, when a pioneer thus opens the way; and we add emulation to patience when thus accompanied in the march by companions, who are sometimes aids and sometimes competitors.

However we may acknowledge in general the force of habit, we do not always sufficiently weigh its power in selecting, and in the manner of pursuing our avocations. The interests, the topicks of these around us, affect us insensibly, and almost determine the bent of our emulation, whatever abstract opinions we may entertain of the comparative excellence and importance of things. We all remember, and sometimes with a smile, when the immediate excitement is past, the importance which we have attached to successive objects and pursuits—to the feats of boyhood—the scholastic exercises of our *alma mater*,—and even the trifles of the drawing room, or the turf—a feeling, which though it springs in some degree, from the natural changes wrought by years, and the progress of life, is no doubt, prodigiously spread and heightened by sympathy with such as happen to surround us. If, therefore, *similarity of pursuits* did not naturally determine us in the choice of companions, *policy* should lead us to select those, who animated by the same views as ourselves, perpetually start topicks of inquiry akin to our studies, and minister the spirit of emulation.

The peculiarity of collegiate manners has been often noticed: The members of such institutions, separated in some degree from every day pursuits, gather topicks, and objects of emulation peculiar to themselves. A metaphysical distinction shall make as obstinate *parties* as ever divided a parliament or a cabinet; and youths naturally become scholars where nothing but scholarship is an object of dictinction—such a spot has been aptly called by a giant scholar *"an atmosphere of learning;"* and it strikes me that, if the habits of our country had not established a different system in this matter, a Law Seminary, would be eminently useful if conducted under a similar discipline, where all that should be seen and heard, all that would interest, and emulate, and distinguish, is connected with an expanded and enlightened study of jurisprudence, where, to vary the phrase, the very *air* should be *legal.*

In the pursuit of studies so harsh as those of law are apt at first to appear, where the mind must be fashioned by habit, and impelled by strong motive, to its daily task, where some stimulus more poignant than the remote and somewhat uncertain prospect of emolument or honour is required to rouse the flagging attention—the advantage of such an institution may seem extremely obvious. In this country it has been usual to pursue these studies not only without these aids, but amidst a vortex of opposite feelings, and seductive pleasures; for the years, at which young men begin their legal studies are generally those which are most eagerly devoted to society, fashion and pleasure. Separated into groups, over the country, under instructors of every kind (if the busy, and more often inattentive advocates, whose offices they frequent, can be called such)—and having little or no close association with fellow students, or, with an ambition diverted into more agreeable paths than that of arid and fatiguing research; students, thus situated, have on the one hand few incitements from emulation, and that inborn love of eminence which when strongly indicated points to future greatness, and is generally first shown in communion with many; but on the other hand they are strongly solicited by idleness, by pleasure, by a notoriety, pleasing to the inexperienced, and more easy of attainment—by all the amiable seductions, in fine which attend the first essay in society.

It is, perhaps, a fault in the manners of our country, that the young are introduced too early into the circles of the gay; and it is a question of some consequence in the education of young men whether that partial *separation* of them from the world, which obtains at colleges, while they are in pursuit of *philosophy* and the classicks, might not be extended with advantage through the period during which they receive the elements of *professional learning*. At all events, if they are at that period to taste of the first allurements of gaiety, they should not be deprived of the advantages of collegiate association: they might still, with benefit, be collected into *studious communities*, where emulation might be propagated from mind to mind, where talents and success in professional acquirements might be the sole reason of distinction, and where the topicks of professional learning, being constantly discussed, might still excite them to inquiry, and urge them forward in the race of competition.

However inadequate the talents which I could bring to the accomplishment of so desirable a scheme, it would be a matter of pride and satisfaction to me to collect around me some portion of the large fund of talent which is annually devoted by the *rising hopes* of the country to the *first profession in it*. Baltimore, in a central position from north to south, is conveniently located for such an object. It is salubrious, populous and refined; its libraries and publick institutions comparatively good; its manners auspicious to strangers; it is near to the seat of the national government; and it already draws annually into its bosom some hundreds of young gentlemen devoted to another of the liberal professions. A Law Seminary established here under such circumstances, beside the direct instructions of the professor, would be fraught, therefore, with numerous indirect advantages. Its members, as I have just said, would form a kind of *studious republick*, employed in the same subjects, and animated by the same emulation; the spirit of research would be kindled and increased among members; friendships would be formed (at years more mature than those which are usually spent at colleges) which while fraught with as much advantage as pleasure to individuals, would foster the *esprit du corps* among the members of a profession which largely contributes its talent to the most conspicuous stations of the government. The mind of the student amidst such a nursery of scientifick curiosity and spirit, would be withdrawn, in some measure, from the influence of pleasure and dissipation. It matters little to the gratification of the mind, what is the object of interest, while it is of much moment to its profit to fasten that interest on pursuits of grave and substantial benefit. These reflections will receive some weight from the recollection how long, even in the thoughtlessness of boyhood, the notions and sentiments abide by us, which have grown up in the scholastic retirement of colleges and universities. I would add to this the advantage (and in time it may become an important one) of prosecuting your *legal* studies under the auspices of a university, and of obtaining from it the honours awarded to those who have complied with its requisitions. These will be stated to you at another time.

I forbear to say any thing of what benefit may be derived to you from the lectures I am about to pronounce, or from those which will be *annually added*, until my course is complete—except, that so far as much zeal and industry in a pursuit, which has ever been with me a very favourite one, can give assurance, I feel that I have not been wanting to myself or to you.

The Syllabus, which has been submitted to you, presents the outline of a very extensive course of legal instruction. This has been with me, and will continue to be, our mutual guide,—with no deviations, except those which will lead to a deeper research into particular topicks, than was originally intended. The whole course, when finished, will embrace three hundred and one lectures, and will occupy at least eighteen months, and more probably two years in the delivery. As the whole scheme, however, is divided into thirteen titles, students may commence their attendance at any of them, as they may be more or less advanced in their studies. By a lecture, however, is not meant that portion which may be delivered at a particular time, but the *integral* portions or divisions of my subject. Thus, on some occasions, perhaps two lectures will be delivered on the same day; and at others, a lecture may occupy, in its delivery, the allotted time of two or more days. Those which I am about to commence will demand of us at least an hour, generally more, four times a week, during four months. The first title, as it is the *prolegomina* of a course which is designed to treat the principal topicks, not only of local but universal law, of censorial, no less than of expository jurisprudence, may be found to occupy more of our time than is indicated by the Syllabus. Some may also be inclined to the opinion, that as the instruction embraced in this first division of my subject is initiatory to a scheme so much more extensive than what is *at once* to be entered on, it will be found disproportioned to that which is immediately to follow. This, indeed, is true: but it is to be remembered that this course is to be regularly augmented, until the whole design be complete, which will certainly be the case should life and health be allowed me: and farther, the objection loses all weight, if the course now to be delivered be valuable in itself.—The subjects themselves are obviously so; nor could any other plan be consistently adopted. I shall, therefore, proceed in my undertaking, without any material deflexion from the outline which I have prescribed to myself.

The ensuing course of lectures, then, will be introduced with various *metaphysical and ethical* dissertations; with discussions on most of the interesting topicks of natural jurisprudence, and the philosophy of legislation; with the elements of political law, and with occasional biographical and bibliographical information, as it may be suggested by the subjects under consideration. I have commenced the course with the metaphysicks and ethicks of the law, from a profound conviction of their particular serviceableness to the lawyer, as well in disciplining his mind to logical accuracy, as in opening to him the foundations of all municipal law. Metaphysical science is invaluable to him to whom habits of abstract thought, of accuracy, of subtlety, of scrupulous precision of language, are among the first requisites to success, whether in acquiring the learning, or conducting the argumentative war of his profession.

It may be laid down as a fundamental truth, that all sound legislation must have relation both to the moral and physical nature and condition of man. Such is the intimate relation between *mind* and *matter* as to render it impossible to proceed far in the philosophy of natural and political jurisprudence, without some acquaintance even with man's physical nature, and certainly with the phenomena of mental philosophy. Hence was it that the great German metaphysicians, Leibnitz and Kant, were not content to study the georgicks of the mind—they cultivated the laws of *matter* with equal zeal—so Descartes, Clarke, Cudworth, Locke, Reid, Stewart, and others, have acknowledged the intimate connexion between physicks and metaphysicks, on the one hand and ethicks and jurisprudence, on the other. The judicious remarks of Dugald Stewart on the aid which metaphysicks have lent to inquirers into sciences, seemingly remote from its pursuits, have a particular force as regards the jurisprudent. To the lawyer the ready perception of distinctions, the scrupulous and determined definition of terms, the analytical powers, and the habit of sifting the combinations established in the fancy, and the casual associations which warp *common* understandings, are of utility every day, and must be made *habits* of the mind, because their exercise is for the most part extemporary.—"The connexion between metaphysics and ethicks," says Stewart, "is more particularly close, the theory of morals having furnished several of the most abstruse questions which have been agitated concerning the general principles (both intellectual and active) of the human frame,"—and, we may add, what is ethicks, moral philosophy, and natural jurisprudence, but different *names* for essentially the same system of rules, all dependent on the laws of the human mind? But, without pressing further this alliance between the laws of matter and of mind, and the close connexion between Ethicks and Natural Law, it must be admitted that ethical and political considerations are nearly akin to the proper studies of the accomplished lawyer. Even municipal law (in its most restricted signification) is not a system of merely positive and arbitrary rules. It has its deep foundations in the universal laws of our moral nature, and, all its positive enactments, proceeding on these, must receive their just interpretation with a reference to them. Would it be possible (for instance) to interpret justly a law, or explain a contract, without knowledge of the general principles on which they are promulgated or entered into? Whence proceeds the rule that laws should not be retrospective, but from the principle of natural law, or ethicks, that associations are bound only by rules to which they may be supposed to have consented? What are the rules of evidence, but metaphysical and ethical modes of investigating truth on the one hand, and limiting our deductions by a regard to human rights and feelings, and to our moral constitution, on the other? How else is the great point of expatriation (on which there have been so many positive enactments) to be settled but by reference to the universal principles on which political association at first arose? In these and infinite other cases, nay, in all modifications of positive institutions, there can be no just design on the part of legislators, nor correct interpretation on those who administer their provisions, without knowledge of the true principles of moral and political philosophy. Nay, the very obedience of the governed proceeds, doubtless, from an apprehension, however imperfect, of the great and obvious principles of moral justice. As in the construction of the most elaborate machine, no law of physical nature can possibly be transgressed, so in the great scheme of government, provisions seemingly the most arbitrary, and the most connected with an artifical state of society, cannot violate, with impunity, the great moral law—and therefore, whether as legislators or expounders of legislative institutions, you must be sure that you understand justly their true principles. Metaphysicks, ethicks, and politicks, then, are the appropriate studies of the jurisprudent—on these repose, as solid foundations, all sound legislative enactments; and, as these apply to the conduct of a being composed of body, as well as soul or mind, the physical and moral nature of this being should be known to those who presume to minister, in any way, in the temple of justice. I have deemed these observations proper for those (should there be any such) who may erroneously incline to regard with indifference the ethicks and metaphysicks of the law, and would wish to vindicate the propriety of bestowing much attention on these too much neglected portions of our science.

After we have dwelt, somewhat in detail, on the important doctrines to which we have just alluded, we shall conclude the *first title* of our subject with an inquiry into the elementary and constitutional principles of the *municipal* law, and shall investigate, with some minuteness, the origin, progress, and influence of that remarkable polity which, during many centuries, pervaded Europe; affected all her political and civil institutions; diminished the lustre even of the imperial law; impressed on the international law of Europe some bold and enduring features, which the refinements even of the present age have not entirely obliterated; and finally, which by reason of its universality has been denominated the *Jus Gentium* of the western world, but is known to us all, under the more appropriate name of the *Feudal Law.* No one can study the history, language, or jurisprudence of England, without at once perceiving their miscellaneous character. The history of that country shows the mixed and even discordant materials which compose its population: the *language* is Celtic, Teutonic, Greek, and Latin: the *laws* are British, Saxon, Feudal, Roman—but nearly every portion of this vast system of jurisprudence is somewhat tinctured with feudalism, and the laws affecting *real* property in particular, have their foundations deeply laid in the rules, customs, and principles of the dark and feudal ages.

In order, therefore, to acquire a comprehensive view of the laws of our parent country, we must study her history, and that of Europe generally—we must explore feudal institutions and laws, which are the very sources and springs whence our jurisprudence originated. Should this be neglected, what student can repose with confidence on the certainty, or fixity of his legal attainments? Whose memory will be adequate to retain the numerous refined distinctions which appear so arbitrary and even absurd, without this key to their true import? How numerous are the rules of this description, which perplex students, who have not previously laid a sure foundation in the learning of the feudists? The operation of *common law conveyances,* so called, in contradistinction to those deriving their efficacy from the statute of uses, and which were introduced with no other design than to supplant the more rigid and subtle doctrines of the feudal law—most of the rules affecting *remainders,* whether vested or contingent—nearly all of the rules or canons of *descent;* the learning of *Conditions,* of *Entails*—the doctrines of *Abeyance,* of Merger, of *Forfeiture,* of *Rents,* properly so called—of *Releases,* of *Warranty,* and of the well known *Rule* in *Shelly's Case,* are all essentially of feudal origin, and of feudal modification; and never can be comprehended to any useful extent, without a competent acquaintance with that extraordinary code, which for a time maintained *divisum imperium* with the Roman Civil Law, but which finally gained a decided ascendancy.

Passing from these topicks, we shall then proceed to the *second* division of our subject—the extensive and important learning of the *Realty.* This we shall delight to dwell on, as, we trust, before we leave it, we shall redeem this portion of our jurisprudence from the unmerited charge of exhaustive abstruseness, of unphilosophical arrangement, and of useless subtleties. We hope to show that, of all the branches of the vast and multifarious system of Common Law, none is entitled to more of your admiration, and respect, and studious attention, than this, whether we regard its own intrinsic excellence and importance, the numerous useful analogies furnished by it, or the happy influence which it exercises in fashioning the mind to close and systematick investigation.

Having thus briefly stated to you, gentlemen, an outline of the ensuing *commencement* of my professorial engagement—there are some auxiliary modes of instruction, to which I now claim your attention; as they enter into the views of that scheme of legal education, which I have selected, and which, whilst they confirm you in the knowledge derived from *books,* will serve to illustrate and familiarize the *practice* of a profession, so often beset with difficulties to the young practitioner, and which, not unfrequently are the cause of much anxiety, and even despondency, to those who have studied the science with no little care and industry.

The auxiliaries, to which I allude, are the organization of a tribunal for the argument of supposed cases, brought before it with a strict regard to *all the forms of good Pleading*, and the rules of *Evidence*, and prosecuted with a rigid attention; to all the decorums of forensick disputation. This tribunal will have the name of *Moot Court*, the history and nature of which I shall presently explain.

There is also much advantage to be received from the discussion of such general doctrines (of a legal nature) as cannot well be introduced through the ordinary forms of judicature. Such points will be argued in a distinct association, denominated *The Rota*. In regard to the "Rota," I would merely observe that it is an appellation derived from the celebrated Harrington, whose debating society, under that name, is too well known to need further mention, in order to justify our adoption of the word. Added to these, (which we trust will prove themselves powerful provocatives to the acquisition of legal learning) we shall propose annually four topicks, for prize essays, not to exceed sixty, or to fall short of thirty printed pages. For the two best essays, (the merit of which will be decided on by the Faculty of Law) a golden medal will be awarded to each author—and for the successful candidates for the remaining two, a silver medal will be adjudged, in the same manner. These written discussions will be open to all of the members of the Law Institute, the Moot Court, the Rota and those who attend lectures, if they be students of law. There is still another auxiliary to which we would direct your attention. Too little regard, we think, has been paid, in all countries, to the comfort and convenience of those engaged in the toils of a long and arduous course of study. The law student, in common with those of divinity and medicine, cannot be too strongly invited to constancy in his pursuits; and this, can hardly be expected, unless the *locus studiorum* be in itself inviting. When the numerous days and nights, perhaps, of many years, are to be spent in intellectual toil, it is fit that some attention be paid to physical comfort; and likewise that students should have at hand, all that may be requisite to facilitate their progress. With this design an establishment has been opened, which we have named the Law Institute. In this a limited number of students, of industrious habits, and who are actuated by the honourable ambition of becoming enlightened lawyers, are admitted. The advantages of this institution are, in brief, a *course of methodical study: colloquial examinations: union of practical, with theoretical knowledge: oral and written discussions of legal subjects: frequent presentation of questiones vexatæ: and resort to an extensive library, in every department of legal science.* Under the auspices of these several means of facilitating your studies, we cherish a hope of your certain, speedy, and solid advancement in the knowledge of your profession.

It can scarcely be necessary to dwell on the advantages of instruction by *lectures*, over any other mode: for though it be not indispensable in the *moral*, as it certainly is, in most *physical* sciences, where reasoning requires the aid of *experiment*, or other occular demonstration, yet it cannot be questioned that law, perhaps, more than any other moral science, may be most beneficially communicated by lectures orally delivered. The prominent advantages of this mode are, first, the *greater liveliness* with which knowledge may be impressed by oral instruction, than by the silent and retired labours of the closet; secondly, the *compendious views* which may be given by lectures, after researches which were found by the student, either difficult or unprofitable; thirdly, the familiarity of example, and the illustration, in which they are allowed to indulge; which cannot be exercised by an author in his printed works, lest they should be too voluminous, and perhaps, too colloquial; fourthly, the opportunity which is afforded of solving, by private study, doubts which have arisen during the lecturers; fifthly, the necessity students are under, of daily adding to their store of legal knowledge; sixthly, the advantage they possess in receiving this knowledge simultaneously through the medium of two, and in some degree, three of the senses, (if we are to trust the notions of metaphysicians on this point) viz. in hearing the professor; seeing the motion of his lips, and the other natural and impressive actions of his body; and lastly, through the touch or feeling consequent on noting down the substance of the lectures as they are delivered; all of which circumstances, no doubt, add strength and vividness to those impressions which are made by the subject alone. To these we may add, the advantages students have in the discourses of a lecturer, whose constant aim is to study, and anticipate their various doubts and perplexities; to offer a simple solution of them; and to encourage students, in their moments of despondency, by some appropriate history of the triumph of industry and method over the most appaling combination of difficulties. These advantages are certainly too manifest to require illustration: the most important, however, is, that the professor can give greater latitude to his illustrations and examples, and can present his subject in a greater variety of aspects than is consistent with the condensed language of books—and besides this advantage, (which will be much valued by those who have pursued their law studies, unaided and solitary,) the lecturer can combine, in one view, points and principles which can be sought only in many books, and which are mingled with much matter, that is either useless in itself, or darkly and barbarously set forth.

This mode of instruction is particularly convenient, nay necessary, to *American* students. The laws of *England*, with some exceptions, are to be studied as much in detail by them, as by English students; to which must be added the laws of the United States; those of the state in which they design to practice; and also, such of the laws of the other states as relate to topicks of universal concern. If they would keep pace, too, with the growth of the science, as it is measured by the numerous volumes which emanate from English and American presses, they must have some acquaintance with a mass of books, which they have neither time to study, nor, perhaps, the means of procuring; for, scarcely a week passes, which does not usher to light some new treatise of law, or a former one, with such amendments and additions, as render the old one of little utility. A complete law library, at present, consists of many thousand volumes, requiring nearly a fortune to procure them, in addition to the judgment and time necessary for their selection. In this point of view, the utility of lecturing is strongly displayed, as thereby most of the difficulties would be solved, and most of what is valuable in these voluminous works, advantageously set forth.

That law is a proper subject for university instruction, through the medium of lectures, appears to have been the opinion of jurists and publicists as early as the first reduction of law into a systematick science. As far back as history gives us any knowledge of a regular code, we find jurisprudence taught, as one of the most important branches of learning, in publick seminaries, colleges, and universities. In Egypt, Rome, Constantinople, Berytus, Bagdad, Bologna, Cæsarea, Laodicea, Carthage, and more recently in most of the European countries, law has been taught by lectures; and in many of them degrees have been conferred in this, as in other departments of knowledge.

Irnerius, Bartolus, Cujacius, Baldus, Voetius, Accursius, Heineccius, Gentilis, Gothofrede, Lampredi, Buddæus, Gravina, Imola, Zouch, Pothier, Blackstone, Wooddeson, Brown, and *Sullivan*, all members of universities, are great and imposing names, as professors in this august science: and the reasons which have made it to be thus taught, are of yet greater weight in this country, whose fundamental principles of government invite all, without distinction of rank, to the participation of political power, and to the administration of its laws.

The advantages of *social* over *solitary* study have been in no way, perhaps, more strikingly manifested than in the history of the *Inns of Court*, and of *Chancery*, those seminaries of common law, established in England many centuries since; to whose influence the judicious Spelman attributes most of what is regular, scientifick and excellent in English jurisprudence. A short examination into the origin and designs of these institutions, will not (we trust) be deemed digressive; as it will be found confirmatory of the views we have endeavoured to inculcate, in regard to the benefits we would hope from assembling in our own country the dispersed students, or *apprentitii ad legem*, and forming them into an associated body, incited and stimulated by the noble ambition of continually honouring, and being honoured by a profession, whose aim is the preservation of every valuable right of nations, no less than of individuals.

We are to date the establishment of these *Inns of Court*, and of *Chancery* from the reign of the third Henry. Prior to that period the courts of judicature were ambulatory; and were holden in such of the king's palaces, as the royal personage happened to reside in. It is obvious, and so history informs us, that the professors and students of law would not be likely to have a *fixed* abode, or to assemble in such numbers as to accomplish any useful design of self-improvement, or of the melioration of a science, then extremely rude and chaotic. When it was ordained however, by *magna charta*, that the "Common Pleas should no longer follow the king's court, but be held in some certain place," the fixation of this important tribunal in Westminster, at once induced those learned in the *common* law, to assemble in London. Students at law, from all parts of the kingdom, attracted by this talent and knowledge, also convened.—A little republick was almost immediately formed; they all addicted themselves to closer, and more methodical study; and finally they constituted themselves into a collegiate body, no less beneficial to the experienced or learned, than to students; who previous to this, had been used to no guide whatever, amidst the barren mazes of the then common law. The extensive dwelling houses of several noblemen, then called *Inns*, (meaning the same as the French word *Hotel,*) were purchased, and fitted up for their reception. They were organized as colleges for instruction in the *common law*—the universities of Oxford and Cambridge having adopted the Roman civil law as the basis of their lecturing.

The colleges thus established were of two kinds, one denominated *Inns of Court,* the other Inns of Chancery.

Inns of *Court* are for a higher order of instruction, and are supposed to have derived the *adjunct* name, from the necessity their students were under of attending the *courts* of judicature; or, as some contend, because, on their first establishment, these students were chiefly the sons of noblemen qualified to serve the king in his court.

Inns of *Chancery* derive their adjunct name from the fact that their students were mainly employed in the study of the forms of the various writs emanating from Chancery. These Inns were preparatory colleges for younger students, prior to their admission into the Inns of Court. Very little, however, is known of any of these Inns during the reign of Henry III. In that of Edward II. four of them were established; viz: *Johnson's, Fetter's, Pater Noster,* and *Lincoln's* Inns. Several others were established in the reign of Edward III. viz: *Thaive's, Gray's, Clifford's* and *The New Temple;* some of which were Inns of Court, and others of Chancery. But it was during the reign of the sixth Henry, that these law societies most flourished. There were then not less than ten Inns of Chancery, for elementary studies, and particularly, as we have stated, for instruction in the *forms* of original and judicial writs; which in those days was esteemed the very *substratum* of a good legal education. There were also four Inns of Court. We are informed by Fortescue, that these various Inns accommodated no less than two thousand students of law; that *"in them all vice was discouraged and banished, and every thing good and virtuous taught."* He further states, that *"in addition to* LAW, *musick, singing, dancing, history, (sacred and profane,) were taught; and divers other accomplishments."*

These juridical universities, as my Lord Coke denominates them, received the royal protection; by all persons being inhibited from teaching law, except members of the Inns of Court and Chancery.

The *exercises* established in these Inns, were various, and admirably adapted to promote emulation, and to advance the student in the practical as well as theoretick knowledge of his profession. After a long novitiate, and many ordeals, students were admitted to the honours of these grave institutions. Degrees were conferred on them in the common law, similar to those conferred in the more ancient universities, in the canon and civil law. The degrees were those of *Barrister,* equivalent to Bachelor of Law; and *Sergeant,* which corresponds to that of Doctor in the Civil and Canon Law. These barristers were styled Apprentices; now more usually Counsellors at Law. They may be called, by the king's mandate, to the degree of Sergeant at Law, after they have been of sixteen years standing as Barristers. The ceremonies, used in the creation of these dignified law officers, were very curious, and conducted with much expensive pomp and festivity. Sergeants at law, however, are of greater antiquity than the institution of these Inns, and are supposed, by Dugdale and others, to have been known even prior to the Conquest; certain it is, that this dignity existed in the reign of the first Edward.

Formerly, students were obliged to study in these Inns eight years, prior to their admission to the degree of Barrister—it is now, however, reduced to five years. The gentlemen of the Inns of Court are of three degrees, viz. 1. *No Utter Barristers,* or Students, properly so called; 2. *Utter or Outer Barristers,* and 3. *Inner Barristers,* or *Benchers.* These three compose the company of what are called *Masters* Commons. There is still, however, a class of inferior, or rather, junior students who compose the company of *Clerks* Commons. This is formed of students during their two first years of standing; or rather, until they are called to the society of the *Masters* Commons.

The degrees of progression, from the commencement of a student's course, to that of his taking the coif, appear to have been eight, viz.

1st. *Admission into the Clerks Commons,* in which students generally continued two years, or until admitted members of the company of *Masters* Commons.

2d. *No Utter Barrister,* or Students, properly so called, when first admitted into fellowship with the Masters Commons. They generally continued such three or four years.

3d. *Utter Barristers,* who had been of five or six years standing, that is, about two years as Clerks, and three or four as No Utter Barristers. They were then called on to argue at the mootings; they wore a bar-gown, and practised their profession after a certain number of mootings.

4th. *Cupboard Men*, who were such Utter Barristers, as had taken the oath of supremacy at the cupboard, and had performed certain moots, and given an expensive feast, declaring their intention of accepting the duties of Reader, should they be appointed to that station.

5th. *Inner Barristers*, or *Benchers*, who had been in these Inns fourteen or fifteen years, having passed through the previous degrees.

6th. *Readers*, chosen from the Benchers, to read or expound the law openly to the society and Students in the Inns of Chancery. Benchers were generally chosen Readers after they had been Cupboard Men two years. When appointed a second time, they were called Double Readers, which was regarded a high honour.

7th. *New Sergeants*, those, who having been called to this honourable degree, had not yet taken the coif.

8th, and lastly. *Coifed* or *perfect Sergeants* at law, who had then assigned to them chambers in the Sergeant's Inn. They took a formal and solemn leave of the Inn of Court, on which occasion the treasurer of the Inn presented each with a purse of gold, value ten pounds, as a present from the whole society.

The internal regulations of these institutions were often very minute, and we are inclined to believe, sometimes equally absurd. Were it not too particular, we might here notice the silly regulations in regard to the *costume* of their members; who, among other things, were not allowed to wear cut or pansied hosen, or pansied doublets, on pain of expulsion; and the sin of wearing *long beards*, could be expiated by nothing less than being excommoned, or by what we now understand, being put in coventry, or under the ban. But these Inns not being corporations, had no judicial power over their members—all was conventional—the laws were preserved and enforced by no other sanction than an honourable *esprit du corps*—a sacred respect for a plight given by students on their admission. If the rules were violated, the offenders were, by universal acclamation, either excommoned, that is, not permitted to eat or commune in any way with the rest; or their chambers were closed. This being notified, comity excluded them from admission into any of the other Inns.

The various and continued learned exercises in these institutions, could not fail to produce the happiest results. We find, accordingly, that most of the enlightened jurists of that country received in them their legal education.

The great commentator on Littleton owed, in great part, his rapid promotion, to the solid learning, and merited honours, which he had received in the *Inner Temple*. Lord Chancellor Audly, Sir Heneage Finch, Manwood, and Anderson—all students, and subsequently Benchers and Readers in this Inn of Court—are names too well known, in the common law, to need further mention.

To the *Middle Temple* are we indebted for the names of Plowden, Dyer, Doddridge; the Lord Chancellors, Rich, Yorke, Cowper, and Eldon; Lord Chief Justice Kenyon, Mr. Justice Blackstone, and numerous others.

From *Gray's Inn* we hear of the illustrious Bacon, and the Lord Keeper, Nicholas Bacon; and *Lincoln's Inn* is honoured by the names of Fortescue, Sir Thomas More, Spelman, Sir Matthew Hale—a splendid constellation, on which every student must delight to gaze.

In fine, nearly all who have been eminent, and learned, and virtuous in this most distinguished profession, had their morals, their studies, and their habits fashioned, and established in these illustrious seminaries of the common law.

The Inns of Court at present existing, are four, viz. the Inner Temple, and Middle Temple, Lincoln's Inn, and Gray's Inn. The two Temples are so called, from their being anciently the dwelling houses of the Knights Templars, and by them leased, in the reign of the third Edward, to certain professors, who established Inns of Court. In the reign of Henry VIII. these Temples (on the dissolution of the religious houses) fell to the crown, and were granted by King James I. in fee simple, to these collegiate bodies, for the reception of the professors and students of the common law.

Lincoln's Inn, and Gray's Inn, were so called from the Earls of those names, in the reigns of Edward II. and III. when they were founded.

The Inns of Chancery existing at present, are nine; viz. *Clifford's* and *Thavie's*, established in the reign of Edward III.; *Clement's* and *Furnival's*, in the reign of Henry IV.; *Staple's* and *Lyon's*, in the reign of Henry V.; *Bernard's*, in that of Henry VI. and *New Inn*, in the reign of Henry VIII.

These Inns of Chancery belong to, or are attached to the four Inns of Court; viz, to the *Inner Temple*, Clifford's, Clement's, and Lyon's Inns are subordinate. To the *Middle Temple*, New Inn. To *Lincoln's Inn*, are attached Furnival's and Thavie's Inns; and to *Gray's Inn*, belong Staple's and Bernard's Inns. These Inns of Chancery, however, can now scarcely be considered in their former light, as students are no longer entered in them, with a view of subsequent admission into the Inns of Court; and these Inns of Court do not regard the time spent in the Inns of Chancery as a portion of the student's legal novitiate.

Having (tediously we are apprehensive) explained the origin, organization, and general views of these Inns of Court and of Chancery; and alluded to the very beneficial influence exerted by them, in forming accomplished scholars in the law, and thereby adding dignity and lustre to the science; we shall now explain more particularly, the *means* adopted by them for the advancement of students in their legal education. We trust that this inquiry will strongly evince the probable utility of the several auxiliaries which we (in humble imitation) have already proposed.

The exercises practised by students of law in these Inns, were principally in attending the various *readings*, and in arguing *moot cases* before the Benchers, and also among themselves.

The *readings* consisted of lectures on any subject of the common law, delivered by Benchers, specially appointed as Readers. These Benchers were such as had been *Utter* Barristers for many years, and having been made *Inner* Barristers, or Benchers, were, occasionally appointed Readers, to treat and expound any statute or doctrine to the students of the Inns of Chancery, or to their society at large.

Whilst their appointment lasted they were called Readers, but when it terminated, they again took the name of Bencher. "During the time of his readings," says Stowe, (which lasted nearly two months in the year) "the Reader kept a constant and splendid table, feasting the nobility, judges, bishops, and sometimes the king himself, at a cost of about one thousand pounds."

There were two great periods assigned for these readings, called the *grand vacations*; one during Lent, the other late in summer. During these "Learnings," as they were also called, the elementary students, or No Utter Barristers, were obliged to attend every reading, under the penalty of twenty shillings for each default.

When the vacation readings were closed, the students, attended their Reader with great state to his residence, and invited him at night, to partake of a sumptuous repast, at their own charge.

Readings were also given, during what was called Term time; when each of the Inns of Court sent two Readers to each of the Inns of Chancery. Students were also employed in various other exercises during these vacations and term time.

The most important of them all was that of mooting. The word *moot* is supposed, by some, to be derived from the French *mot*, (word) and by others, with more likelihood, from the Saxon *metan*, *gemetan*, or *gemot*, (meeting,) because at appointed meetings or assemblings of students, questions, fit for grave disputation, were argued by them, and determined by the Benchers. This deduction is highly probable, as there are many compound words with similar termination, which are universally allowed to import an *assemblage*. As for example; *reevemote*, *shiremote*, *folkmote*, *wettena-gemot*, which last means an assembly of wise men. Be this, however, as it may, the points argued by students in the Inns of Court and Chancery, were called moot cases; the students who argued them, moot men; the place where they convened, moot hall; the disputations, mootings; and the Benchers, before whom they usually argued, a moot court. Students who thus argued, were the Utter or Outer Barristers; in contradistinction to those, on the one hand, whose inexperience ordinarily excluded them from these exercises; and who, as I have already stated, were called No Utter Barristers, Tyros, or Elementary Students; and to the Benchers, on the other hand, who, from superior knowledge, were raised from Utter to the degree of Inner Barristers; and, as such, entitled to sit as Judges at these mootings.

These Benchers annually appointed an officer, called the Bailiff, or *Surveyor of the Moots*; whose duty it was, to keep an accurate account of all matters argued; by whom discussed; and all other proceedings in these mock forensick encounters. These mooting's were of two kinds, *grand* and *petty*. The former occurred during the grand vacations, of which I have spoken; that is, during the Readings. When the Reading had terminated, any Utter Barrister was at liberty to oppose some point advanced by the Reader; and thus was the grand mooting commenced. At these vacations, the elementary students, also, were entitled to open points, before three of the Benchers; they were then followed by the Utter Barristers; and the case was decided by the Benchers. All this was done in that barbarous dialect, the Law French, of which Sir Henry Spelman so feelingly complains, when sent by his mother to commence his studies in the common law, at Lincoln's Inn.

"Emisit me mater Londinum," (says he) *"juris nostri capessendi gratia; cujus cum vestibulum salutassem, reperissemque linguam peregrinam, dialectum barbarum, methodum inconcinnam, molem non ingentem solum, sed perpetuis humeris sustinendam, excedit mihi fateor animus."*

The *petty mootings* were those which occurred in term time before the Readers, or Benchers of the respective Inns. There were also other mootings, called *mean vacation* moots, or chapel moots: these were performed by the younger students after the term, and grand vacations were over. There were likewise *private* mootings, which are thus described by one of the black-letter law writers:

"Furthermore, after dynner and supper, the students and lerners in the house sit together, by *three* and *three* in a company; and one of the three putteth forth some doubtful question in the law, to the other two of his company; and they reason and argue unto it in English; and at last, he that putteth forth the question declaryth his own minde, also showing unto them the judgment, or better opinion of his boke, where he had the same question—and this do the students observe every day through the yere, except *festivall* days."

It is reasonable to suppose that these various exercises, publick and private, must have been attended with the most salutary consequences; and that they largely contributed to the ascendency of the Common over the Civil Law, which for ages has maintained an angry jealousy between their numerous professors and retainers.

The detail, which I have now brought to a close, I fear has been too minute, and proved tedious to my auditors. But we had, in this investigation, several objects to gratify: otherwise we should not have introduced it, as it has been one of no easy accomplishment, amidst the many dark and conflicting statements of various dull and dusty authors. We supposed, that a minute account of what has been done for students, in the land whence we have derived most of our law; together with an exposition of the admirable results, could not fail to stimulate the young jurisprudents of this country, favourably to receive and foster an attempt to introduce among us, not the *same*, but *similar* institutions, adapted to the more refined state of our manners and jurisprudence.

From what has been stated, we perceive how important it has been deemed in England, not only that students of law should be *assembled*, and *associated* in their studies, but that they should be disciplined in regular and methodical exercises.

Were this matter, however, open to doubt, after the example we have just furnished; and, indeed, were it not obvious in itself, we might appeal to the views and practice of the ancient Romans, among whom similar methodical studies were deemed essential; and students were assembled from all parts of the empire, to receive instruction at appointed places. We are informed that in their law schools, over which the *Antecessor*, or professor presided, students were divided into five classes; viz—*Dupondii, Edictales, Papinianistœ, Lytœ, and Prolytœ.* Four years were occupied by them before they were expected to engage in the study of the Code, or Imperial Constitutions.

The *Dupondii* were such elementary students as were engaged during the first year of their novitiate, in the study of the Institutes, and the first four books of the Digests. They were called *dupondii*, or students of small consideration, from the most common coin known in the Roman empire, about the value of a penny sterling, and as they were then admitted only "*ad limina legitimœ scientiœ.*" The emperor Justinian, however, whose parental regard for students induced him to attend even to such small matters, changed the name of this first class, to *Justinianei novi*; this being a more flattering designation.

The *Edictales* occupied the second year, in the study of the Digests, from the fifth to the twentieth book, inclusive; which contain the *Edicta Magistratuum.*

The *Papinianistœ* were such students, as during the third year, were employed in reading the Digests, from the twenty-first to the twenty-eight book, inclusive; which contain the opinions of Papinian, justly styled the "living voice, and oracle of Roman jurisprudence"—arriving at this stage of their studious career, they were regarded as having accomplished more than the passage of the *pons assinorum.* "*Quo nomine,*

Papinianistæ," says Heinecceus, "*adeo sibi placebant, ut diem quo ejus doctrina primum fuerant initiati, festum solennemque haberent.*" And this rejoicing, and festivity are not to be considered as mere juvenile gaiety—for it was a festival not only countenanced but instituted, by imperial authority, evincive of the deep respect for the learning, virtues and talents of one of the most accomplished of Roman jurists.

The *Lytæ* finished the Digests during the fourth year; and were then regarded as competent to the solution of the most difficult points. But still, those "*qui juris nodos, legumque ænigmata solvunt,*" were then put to the study of the Code, and other works, *ad libitum*: at this time they assumed the name of *Prolytæ*, and usually completed their studies at the end of the fifth year.

The quinquennial term of study appears to have obtained in most ages. In the reign of Queen Mary, a famous civilian styled himself "*Magister Artium, et Prolyta juris.*"—and in most of the universities of the continent, this period has been adopted as the time of legal study. By a statute of the University of Oxford, it is provided, "*Quodque per* BIENNIUM *in Academia, Dialecticæ, Morali Philosophiæ et Politicæ aliisque Humanioribus Literis incumbat, priusquam* QUINQUENNIUM *in studio juris ponere incipat*"; and the statute of Cambridge ordains, that "a *year* be devoted by students in their chambers, to the study of the institutes, after which they shall hear, during *five years*, the publick prælector of law."

The provisions made at various times by the Roman Emperors, were admirably adapted to produce enlightened lawyers: and to repress those ignorant pretenders in the science, those *leguleii*, whom Cicero so much censures and ridicules, as being versed only in numerous unmeaning forms, and an unceasing flow of forensick jargon. We might here detail the wise institutions of the Emperor Valentinian, in his celebrated constitution, "*De Studiis,*" &c. We might dwell on the discipline and studies of the ancient seminaries of learning—a topick full of interest and profit; to this we might add, an inquiry into many important regulations in various modern universities, in regard to law students—but these would demand a further call on your time—already too freely occupied.

In conclusion—May we not emphatically ask, are not like institutions and regulations essential in this country? Is it not of first importance, that American students of law should have *prescribed studies* and *stated exercises*; and, in order to incite a suitable emulation, that they should be brought, as far as may be practicable, to *associate* in their studies? Is there any system of law, of any age or country, more various, complicated, and extensive than our own? We admit there are in our, as in other professions, degrees of knowledge suited to different capacities, and fitted to the particular, ultimate views of individuals. But those who are ambitious of fame, and an elevated standing in their profession; those who would honour and be honoured by their vocation; and, in fine, those who desire to minister as high priests at the altar, and give their opinions as oracular, must regard the study of the law, as the assiduous and methodized labour of a *life*—full of toils, but likewise full of encouragements and auspicious promises—ever realized to the truly zealous and persevering.

NOTE

1. We are happy to learn that our wishes in this respect are about to be realized, Chancellor Kent having removed to the city of New-York with the view of delivering a course of lectures in the University of that state.

Chapter 20

The Inauguration of the Author as Dane Professor of Law

1829

Joseph Story

Joseph Story (September 18, 1779-September 10, 1845) was associate justice of the U.S. Supreme Court from 1811 to 1845 and the first Dane Professor at Harvard, from 1829 to 1845. His commentaries and his influence are described in chapter 1. See also chapter 6. This address is reprinted from *A Discourse Pronounced upon the Inauguration of the Author, as Dane Professor of Law in Harvard University on the Twenty-fifth Day of August, 1829* (Boston: Hilliard, Gray, Little, and Wilkins, 1829).

It has been customary in this university, for professors, upon their induction into office, to deliver a public discourse upon some topics suitable to the occasion. Upon the establishment of a new professor it may also be expected, that he, who for the first time fills the chair, should give some account of the foundation, and of the studies, which it proposes to encourage. I shall endeavour not wholly to disappoint the just expectations of my audience in both respects; premising, however, that much reliance must be placed upon their indulgence, since the subject affords little scope for elegant disquisition, and almost forbids those ornaments, which gratify the taste, and warm the imagination of the scholar.

My plan is, in the first place, to lay before you some considerations touching the general utility of the study of the law; and to address them with more pointed application to those, who propose to make it the business of their lives. In the next place, I shall briefly unfold the nature and objects of the professorship, which I have now the honor to occupy, and the particular studies, which it comprehends; so that the noble design of the founder may be amply vindicated, and receive, as it deserves, the public approbation. In proportion, however, to the value and importance of these studies, I cannot but feel a diffidence, lest they should fail under my care of becoming as attractive and interesting as they ought; and that my own imperfect execution of duty should cast a shade upon the bright prospects, which the founder is opening to our view. In the present state of knowledge, such a diffidence might well become the teacher of any science; but the remark applies with augmented force to a science so vast, so intricate, and so comprehensive, as that of jurisprudence. In its widest extent it may be said almost to compass every human action;

and, in its minute details, to measure every human duty. If we contemplate it in the highest order of subjects, which it embraces, it can scarcely be surpassed in dignity. It searches into and expounds the elements of morals and ethics, and the eternal law of nature, illustrated and supported by the eternal law of revelation. It is in this sense, that it has constituted the panegyric of philosophers and sages in almost every age. It is in this sense that Cicero has spoken of it, in a passage, which is upon the lips of every scholar: *"Est quidam vera lex, recta ratio, naturæ congruens, diffusa per omnes, constans, sempiterna, quæ vocet ad officium jubendo, vetando a fraude deterreat, quæ tamen neque probos frustra jubet, aut vetat, nec improbos jubendo, aut vetando movet. Huic legi nec abrogari fas est, neque derogari ex hac aliquid licet; neque tota abrogari potest. Nec vero, aut per senatum aut per populum solvi hac lege possumus."*[1] It is in this sense, also, that the genius of Sir William Jones, rising into poetical enthusiasm, has proclaimed, that

"Sovereign law, the state's collected will,
O'er thrones and globes elate
Sits empress, crowning good, repressing ill."

But if we contemplate it in a narrower view, as a mere system of regulations for the safety and harmony of civil society; as the instrument of administering public and private justice; as the code, by which rights are ascertained, and wrongs redressed; by which contracts are interpreted, and property is secured, and the institutions, which add strength to government, and solid happiness to domestic life are firmly guarded;—if, I say, we contemplate it in this narrower view, its dignity may in some measure be lessened, but its design will yet appear sufficiently grand, and its execution sufficiently difficult, to have strong claims upon the gratitude and admiration of mankind.

The common law purports to be such a system of jurisprudence. By the *common law* is sometimes understood that collection of principles, which constitutes the basis of the administration of justice in England, in contradistinction to the maxims of the Roman code, which has universally received the appellation of the *civil* law. The latter has been adopted, or, if I may so say, inosculated, into the juridical polity of all continental Europe, as a fundamental rule. The former is emphatically the custom of the realm of England, and has no authority beyond her own territory, and the colonies, which she has planted in various parts of the world. It is no small proof of its excellence, however, that where it has once taken root, it has never been superseded; and that its direct progress, or silent sway, has never failed to obliterate the attachment to other codes, whenever the accidents of conquest or cession have brought it within the reach of popular opinion. But there is another sense (which is the most usual sense), in which it is called the *common* law, to distinguish it from the *statute* law, or the positive enactments of the legislature. In this sense the common law is the *lex non scripta*, that is, the unwritten law, which cannot now be traced back to any positive text, but is composed of customs, and usages, and maxims, deriving their authority from immemorial practice, and the recognitions of courts of justice. Thus, the right of primogeniture, which is a fundamental rule of inheritances in England, does not depend upon any known statute, but upon the simple custom of the realm, of such high antiquity, that history does not reach its exact origin. Much, indeed, of this unwritten law may now be found in books, in elementary treatises, and in judicial decisions. But it does not derive its force from these circumstances. On the contrary, even judicial decisions are deemed but the formal promulgation of rules antecedently existing, and obtain all their value from their supposed conformity to those rules.

When our ancestors emigrated to America, they brought this common law with them, as their birthright and inheritance; and they put into operation so much of it as was applicable to their situation. It became the basis of the jurisprudence of all the English colonies; and, except so far as it has been abrogated or modified by our local legislation, it remains to this very hour the guide, the instructer, the protector, and the ornament of every state within this republic, whose territory lies within our boundaries by the treaty of peace of 1783. May it ever continue to flourish here; for it is the law of liberty, and the watchful and inflexible guardian of private property and public rights.

It is of this common law, in its largest extent, that the Law Institution in this university proposes to expound the doctrines and diversities; and thus to furnish the means of a better juridical education to those, who are destined for the profession, as well as to those, who, as scholars and gentlemen, desire to learn its general principles.

Nor let any scholar or gentleman imagine, that the study is little worthy his attention, unless he is to engage in it for professional objects. I do not exaggerate its value, when I express the deliberate opinion, that there is not, within the compass of human attainment, any science, which has so direct a tendency as this, to strengthen the understanding, to enlarge its powers, to sharpen its sagacity, and to form habits of nice and accurate discrimination. Sir James Mackintosh, an elegant scholar, as well as a very competent judge, has said,[2] "that more understanding has perhaps been in this manner exerted to fix the rules of life, than in any other science; and it is certainly the most honorable occupation of the understanding, because it is the most immediately subservient to general safety and comfort." If this were a question dependent upon mere authority, perhaps testimony more unexceptionable to the general scholar might be drawn from other sources. Dr. Johnson, with his accustomed vigor of expression has stated, that "law is the science, in which the greatest powers of the understanding are applied to the greatest number of facts." And Mr. Burke, himself an orator and statesman of the most enlarged research, has not hesitated to declare, that it is "one of the first and noblest of human sciences; a science, which does more to quicken and invigorate the understanding, than all other kinds of learning put together."[3]

But there is little need to appeal to the testimonies of the living or the dead upon such a topic. Whoever will take the trouble to reflect upon the vast variety of subjects, with which it is conversant, and the almost infinite diversity of human transactions, to which it applies; whoever will consider, how much astuteness and ingenuity are required to unravel or guard against the contrivances of fraud, and the indiscretions of folly, the caprices of the wise and the errors of the rash, the mistakes of pride, the confidence of ignorance, and the sallies of enterprise, will be at no loss to understand, that there will be ample employment for the highest faculties. If he will but add to the account, that law is a science, which must be gradually formed by the successive efforts of many minds in many ages; that its rudiments sink deep into remote antiquity, and branch wider and wider with every new generation; that it seeks to measure the future by approximations to certainty derived solely from the experience of the past; that it must for ever be in a state of progress, or change, to adapt itself to the exigencies and changes of society; that even when the old foundations remain firm, the shifting channels of business must often leave their wonted beds deserted, and require new and broader substructions to accommodate and support new interests.[4] If, I say, he will but add these things to the account, it will soon become matter of surprise, that even the mightiest efforts of genius can keep pace with such incessant demands; and that the powers of reasoning, tasked and subtilized, as they must be, to an immeasurable extent, should not be absolutely overwhelmed in the attempt to administer justice.

From its nature and objects the common law, above all others, employs a most severe and scrutinizing logic. In some of its branches it is compelled to deal with metaphysical subtilties and abstractions, belonging to the depths of intellectual philosophy. From this cause it has sometimes been in danger of being enslaved by scholastic refinements, by the jargon of the old dialectics, and the sophisms of over-curious minds. It narrowly escaped shipwreck in the hands of the schoolmen of the middle ages; and for a while was almost swallowed up in the quicksands of the feudal system. If it had not been, that it necessarily dealt with substances instead of shadows, with men's business, and rights, and inheritances, and not with entities and notions, it would have shared the fate, or justified the satire, upon metaphysical inquiries, that those, who attempted to sound its depths,

"In that unfathomable gulph were drown'd."

But common sense has at all times powerfully counteracted the tendency to undue speculation in the common law, and silently brought back its votaries to that, which is the end of all true logic, the just application of principles to the actual concerns of human life. One cannot but smile in the present times at some of the reasoning and some of the fictions, which spread themselves, here and there, in small veins in the system. We are gravely told, for instance, by Bracton, in which he is followed by Lord Coke, that the true reason why by the common law a father cannot inherit real estate by descent from his son, is, that inheritances are heavy, and descend, as it were, by the laws of gravitation, and cannot reascend.[5] We are again told, that, when the title to an estate is suspended upon future contingencies, in the mean time the inheritance is in abeyance, that is, (as we are taught by the accompanying explanations,) the inheritance is *in gremio legis*, or *in nubibus*, in the bosom of the law, or in the clouds, which seems to mend the matter exceedingly in point of plainness. And, again, when an estate is conveyed to trustees to serve existing uses, and future contingent uses also, we are told, that though a seisin is necessary to feed them, and it be now exhausted, yet happily for us, there remains a possibility of seisin, a *scintilla juris*, which kindles at the very moment the new uses spring into being, and by its vital power executes at once the possession of the estate to those uses, by some sort of legal legerdemain.[6] Shakspere has immortalized by his genius the report of a case in that book of painful learning, Plowden's Commentaries,[7] in which Lady Margaret Hales, by the suicide of her husband, lost an estate by forfeiture to the crown, which she held jointly with him. One of the learned judges upon that occasion, in order to establish the legal conclusion, that the party killed himself in his lifetime, reasoned in this manner: "The felony is attributed to the act, which act is always done by a living man, and in his lifetime; for Sir James Hales was dead, and how came he to his death? It may be answered, By drowning. And who drowned him? Sir James Hales. And when did he drown him? In his lifetime. So that Sir James Hales, being alive, caused Sir James Hales to die; and the act of the living man was the death of the dead man. And then for this offence it is reasonable to punish the living man, who committed the offence, and not the dead man. But how can he be said to be punished alive, when the punishment comes after his death?" &c. &c.

But apart from a few blemishes of this sort, which belong, indeed, rather to the studies of the age, than to the law, and are now so harmless, that they serve little more than to give point to some sarcasm upon the profession, it is certain, that the common law follows out its principles with a closeness and simplicity of reasoning, which approach, as near as any artificial or moral deductions can, to the rigour of demonstration.

How, indeed, can it be otherwise? It is not employed in closet speculations, in the silence of the monastery, or in the seclusion of private life. Every cause is heard in the presence of men, whom practice and study have made singularly acute and discriminating. The advocate is stimulated, not merely by the hope of reward, and devotion to his client, but by the love of fame, to exert all his talents in order to detect fallacies, and answer objections. He is not at liberty, from mere courtesy or kindness, from private respect, or popular feeling, to gloss over the mistakes, or conceal the blunders, or suppress the inconsistencies of the argument of his adversary. In such places and on such occasions the law expects every man to do his duty, and his whole duty. He must search the dark, explore the weak, clear the doubtful, or confirm the strong points of his cause, as its exigencies may require. In such contests victory is rarely to be won, victory, I had almost said, is never won, without an arduous struggle. Mere fanciful analogies, and set phrases, and fine turns of expression, and plausible statements will not do. They are but shadows or mists, which hover over the pathways to truth, but do not impede them. They may blind the novice, or betray the ignorant; but they do not deceive the wary and experienced traveller. There must be a firmer and closer grapple with realities. The contest is fit for men of strong sinews, and deep thoughts; and such men in all ages have been found foremost in the ranks of the bar, and eager for its distinctions. To the inquisitive scholar and gentleman, therefore, the law will be found a study full of instruction, and admirably adapted to brace his mind to a wholesome discipline. He will thus avoid what Lord Bacon considers some of the greatest obstacles to knowledge. For, says he, "facility to believe, impatience to doubt, temerity to answer, glory to know, doubt to contradict, end to gain, sloth to search, seeking things in words, resting in part in nature; these, and the like, have been the things, which have forbidden the happy match between the mind of man, and the nature of things."[8]

I might commend the study of the law to American citizens generally upon considerations of a broader cast. From the structure of our institutions, there is much to provoke the vigilance, and invite the leisure of all, and especially of educated men. Our government is emphatically a government of the people in all its departments. It purports to be a government of laws, and not of men—and yet beyond all others it is subject to the control and influence of public opinion. Its whole security and efficiency depend upon the intelligence, virtue, independence, and moderation of the people. It can be preserved no longer than a reverence for settled, uniform laws constitutes the habit, I had almost said the passion of the community. There can be no freedom, where there is no safety to property, or personal rights. Whenever legislation renders the possession or enjoyment of property precarious; whenever it cuts down the obligation and security of contracts; whenever it breaks in upon personal liberty, or compels a surrender of personal privileges, upon any pretext, plausible or otherwise, it matters little, whether it be the act of the many, or the few, of the solitary despot, or the assembled multitude ; it is still in its essence tyranny. It matters still less what are the causes of the change; whether urged on by a spirit of innovation, or popular delusion, or state necessity, (as it is falsely called,) it is still power, irresponsible power, against right; and the more to be dreaded, when it has the sanction of numbers, because it is then less capable of being resisted or evaded. Unfortunately, at such times the majority prevail by mere numbers, and not by force of judgment; *numerantur, non ponderantur.* I do not, therefore, overestimate its value, when I say, that a knowledge of the law and a devotion to its principles are vital to a republic, and lie at the very foundation of its strength.

An American citizen has many political duties to perform, and his activity is constantly demanded for the preservation of the public interests. He must watch the exercise of power in every department of government, and ascertain, whether it is within the prescribed limits of the constitution. He is to study deeply and thoroughly the elements, which compose that constitution; elements, which were the slow results of genius, and patriotism, acting upon the largest views of human experience. The reasons, on which every part of this beautiful system is built (may it be as durable, as it is beautiful) are to be examined and weighed. Slight inconveniences are not to overturn them; slight objections are not to undermine them. Whatever is human is necessarily imperfect; whatever is practical necessarily deviates from theory; whatever works by human agency works with some inequality of movement and result. It is easier to point out defects, than to devise remedies; to touch blemishes, than to extract them; to demolish an edifice, than to erect a convenient substitute. We may not say of forms of government, that 'that which is best administered is best.' But we may say, that that, which generally works well, should rarely be hazarded upon the chances of a better. It has been observed by a profound statesman, that the abstract perfection of a government with reference to natural rights may be its practical defect. By having a right to do every thing, men may want every thing.[9] Great vigilance and great jealousy are therefore necessary in republics to guard against the captivations of theory, as well as the approaches of less insidious foes. Governments are not always overthrown by direct and open assaults. They are not always battered down by the arms of conquerors, or the successful daring of usurpers. There is often concealed the dry rot, which eats into the vitals, when all is fair and stately on the outside. And to republics this has been the more common and fatal disease. The continual drippings of corruption may wear away the solid rock, when the tempest has failed to overturn it. In a monarchy, the subjects may be content to trust to the hereditary sovereign and the hereditary nobility the general superintendence of legislation and property. But in a republic, every citizen is himself in some measure entrusted with the public safety, and acts an important part for its weal or woe.

Our government also opens the widest field for talents and exertion to every rank of life. Few men, comparatively speaking, may not indulge the hope, if they covet the distinction, at some time to have a seat in the public councils, and assist in the public legislation. What can be more important or useful in such a station, than a knowledge of those laws, which the legislator is called upon to modify, amend, or repeal? How much doubt may a single injudicious amendment introduce. One would hardly trust to an .unskillful artisan the repairs of any delicate machine. There would be an universal exclamation against the indiscretion of such an attempt. But yet it would seem, that we are apt to think that men are born legislators; that no qualifications beyond plain sense and common honesty, are necessary for the management of the intricate machine of government; and above all of that most delicate and interesting of all machines, a republican government. To adjust its various parts requires the skill of the wisest, and often baffles the judgment of the best. The least perturbation at the centre may transmit itself through every line of its movements; as the dip of a pebble on the calm surface of a lake sends its circling vibrations to the distant shore.

It is a fact well known to professional gentlemen, that more doubts arise in the administration of justice from the imperfections of positive legislation, than from any other source. The mistakes in the language of a deed, or a will, rarely extend far beyond the immediate parties to the contract or bounty. And yet innumerable questions of interpretation have arisen from these comparatively private sources of litigation, to perplex the minds, and exhaust the diligence of the ablest judges. But what is this to the sweeping result of an act of the legislature, which declares a new rule for a whole State, which may vary the rights, or touch the interests, or control the operations of thousands of its citizens? If the legislation is designedly universal in its terms, infinite caution is necessary to prevent its working greater mischiefs than it purports to cure. If, on the other hand, it aims only at a single class of mischiefs, to amend an existing defect, or provide for a new interest, there is still great danger, that its provisions may reach beyond the intent, and embrace what would have been most sedulously excluded, if it had been foreseen or suspected. An anecdote told of Lord Coke may serve as an appropriate illustration. A statesman told him, that he meant to consult him on a point of law. "If it be common law," said Lord Coke, "I should be ashamed if I could not give you a ready answer; but if it be statute law, I should be equally ashamed, if I answered you immediately."[10] What an admonition is this! And how forcibly does it teach us the utility of a knowledge of the general principles of law to persons, who are called upon to perform the functions of legislation.

But to gentlemen, who contemplate public life with higher objects, who indulge the ambition of being, not silent voters, but leaders in debate, and framers of laws, and guides in the public councils, every consideration already urged applies with ten-fold force. I will not speak of the disgrace and defeat, which must in such stations follow upon the exposure of ignorance; nor of the easy victory achieved by those, who bring to the controversy a ready knowledge, over those, who grope in the dark, and rely on their own rashness for success; nor of the intrinsic difficulty, in times like the present, of commanding public confidence without bringing solid wisdom in aid of popular declamation. But I would speak to the consciences of honorable men, and ask, how they can venture, without any knowledge of existing laws, to recommend changes, which may cut deep into the quick of remedial justice, or bring into peril all that is valuable in jurisprudence by its certainty, its policy, or its antiquity. Surely they need not be told, how slowly every good system of laws must be in consolidating; and how easily the rashness of an hour may destroy, what ages have scarcely cemented in a solid form. The oak, which requires centuries to rear its trunk, and stretch its branches, and strengthen its fibres, and fix its roots, may yet be levelled in an hour. It may breast the tempest of a hundred years, and survive the scathing of the lightning. It may even acquire vigour from its struggles with the elements, and strike its roots deeper and wider, as it rises in its majesty; and yet a child, in the very wantonness of folly, may in an instant destroy it by removing a girdle of its bark.

It has been said, that a spirit of innovation is generally the result of a selfish temper and confined views.[11] Perhaps this is pressing the reasoning too far. It is more often the result of a strong imagination and ardent temperament, working upon the materials of the closet. But it is well in all cases to remember the wise recommendation of Lord Bacon, "that men in their innovations would follow the example of time itself, which, indeed, innovateth greatly, but quietly, and by degrees scarce to be perceived."[12] And nothing can introduce more sobriety of judgment than the experience derived from the history of jurisprudence, and thus check what has been so happily termed too great a fluidness, lubricity, and unsteadiness in the laws.[13]

It is not, therefore, from mere professional pride or enthusiasm, that I would urgently recommend to gentlemen, ambitious of public life, some devotion to the study of the law, or suggest to scholars, that their education still wants perfection and polish, unless they have mastered its elements, In doing so, I do little more than adopt the precept of Mr. Locke, who says it is so requisite, that he knows of no place, from a justice of the peace to a minister of state, that can be well filled without it.[14] And in the days of Fortescue it was esteemed almost a necessary accomplishment for a gentleman of rank.[15]

But my principal object in this discourse is, to address myself to those, who intend to make the law a profession for life. To them it seems almost unnecessary to recommend the study, or press the ancient precept,

> "Versate diu, quid ferre recusent,
> Quid valeant humeri."

To them the law is not a mere pursuit of pleasure or curiosity, but of transcendent dignity, as it opens the brightest rewards of human ambition, opulence, fame, public influence, and political honours. I may add, too, that if the student of the law entertains but a just reverence for its precepts, it will teach him to build his reputation upon the soundest morals, the deepest principles, and the most exalted purity of life and character. One of the beautiful boasts of our municipal jurisprudence is, that Christianity is a part of the common law, from which it seeks the sanction of its rights, and by which it endeavours to regulate its doctrines. And, notwithstanding the specious objection of one of our distinguished statesmen, the boast is as true as it is beautiful. There never has been a period, in which the common law did not recognise Christianity as lying at its foundations.[16] For many ages it was almost exclusively administered by those, who held its ecclesiastical dignities. It now repudiates every act done in violation of its duties of perfect obligation. It pronounces illegal every contract offensive to its morals. It recognises with profound humility its holidays and festivals, and obeys them, as *dies non juridici.* It still attaches to persons believing in its divine authority the highest degree of competency as witnesses; and until a comparatively recent period, infidels and pagans were banished from the halls of justice, as unworthy of credit. The error of the common law was, in reality, of a very different character. It tolerated nothing but Christianity, as taught by its own, established church, either Protestant or Catholic; and with unrelenting severity consigned the conscientious heretic to the stake, regarding his very scruples as proofs of incorrigible wickedness. Thus, justice was debased, and religion itself made the minister of crimes by calling in the aid of the secular power to enforce that conformity of belief, whose rewards and punishments belong exclusively to God.

But apart from this defect, the morals of the law are of the purest and most irreproachable character. And notwithstanding the sneers of ignorance, and the gibes of wit, no men are so constantly called upon in their practice to exemplify the duties of good faith, incorruptible virtue, and chivalric honour, as lawyers. To them is often entrusted the peace and repose, as well as the property, of whole families; and the slightest departure from professional secrecy, or professional integrity, might involve their clients in ruin. The law itself imposes upon them the severest injunctions never to do injustice, and never to violate confidence. It not only protects them from disclosing the secrets of their clients, but it punishes the offenders, by disqualifying them from practice. The rebuke of public opinion, also, follows close upon every offence; and the frown of the profession consigns to infamy the traitor, and his moral treason. Memorable instances of this sort have occurred in other ages, as well as in our own. Even the lips of eloquence breathe nothing but an empty voice in the halls of justice, if the ear listens with distrust or suspicion. The very hypocrite is there compelled to wear the livery of virtue, and pay her homage. If he secretly cherishes a groveling vice, he must there speak the language, and assume the port of innocence. He must feign, if he does not feel, the spirit and inspiration of the place.

I would exhort the student, therefore, at the very outset of his career, to acquire a just conception of the dignity and importance of his vocation. Let him not debase it by a low and narrow estimate of its requisites or its duties. Let him consider it, not as a mere means of subsistence, an affair of petty traffic and barter, a little round of manœuvres and contrivances to arrest some runaway contract, to disinter some buried relic of title, or to let loose some imprisoned wrong from the vengeance of the law. Let him not dream that all is well, if he can weave an intricate net of special pleadings, to catch the unwary in its meshes; or hang a doubt upon a subtile distinction; or quibble through the whole alphabet of sophisms. Let him not imagine, that it is sufficient, if he be the thing described by Cicero in his scorn;—"jurisconsultus ipse per se nihil, nisi leguleius quidem, cautus et acutus, præco actionum, cantor formularum, auceps syllabarum";[17] "a sharp and cunning pettifogger; a retailer of lawsuits; a canter about forms, and a caviller upon words ; "—or one of the tribe, defined by a master spirit of the last age, as the ministers of municipal litigation, and the fomenters of the war of village vexation.[18] God forbid, that any man, standing in the temple, and in the presence of the law, should imagine that her ministers were called to such unworthy offices. No. The profession has far higher aims and nobler purposes.[19] In the ordinary course of business, it is true, that sound learning, industry, and fidelity are the principal requisites, and may reap a fair reward, as they may in any other employment of life. But there are some, and in the lives of most lawyers, many occasions, which demand qualities of a higher, nay of the highest order. Upon the actual administration of justice in all governments, and especially in free governments, must depend the welfare of the whole community. The sacred rights of property are to be guarded at every point. I call them sacred, because, if they are unprotected, all other rights become worthless or visionary. What is personal liberty, if it does not draw after it the right to enjoy the fruits of our own industry? What is political liberty, if it imparts only perpetual poverty to us, and all our posterity? What is the privilege of a vote, if the majority of the hour may sweep away the earnings of our whole lives, to gratify the rapacity of the indolent, the cunning, or the profligate, who are borne into power upon the tide of a temporary popularity? What remains to nourish a spirit of independence, or a love of country, if the very soil, on which we tread, is ours only at the beck of the village tyrant? If the home of our parents, which nursed our infancy and protected our manhood, may be torn from us without recompense or remorse? If the very graveyards, which contain the memorials of our love and our sorrow, are not secure against the hands of violence? If the church of yesterday may be the barrack of to-day, and become the gaol of to-morrow? If the practical text of civil procedure contains no better gloss than the Border maxim, that the right to plunder is only bounded by the power?

One of the glorious, and not unfrequently perilous duties of the bar is the protection of property, and not of property only, but of personal rights, and personal character; of domestic peace, and parental authority. The lawyer is placed, as it were, upon the outpost of defence, as a public sentinel, to watch the approach of danger, and to sound the alarm, when oppression is at hand. It is a post, not only full of observation, but of difficulty. It is his duty to resist wrong, let it come in whatever form it may. The attack is rarely commenced in open daylight; but it makes its approaches by dark and insidious degrees. Some captivating delusion, some crafty pretext, some popular scheme, generally masks the real design. Public opinion has been already won in its favor, or drugged into a stupid indifference to its results, by the arts of intrigue. Nothing, perhaps, remains between the enterprise and victory, but the solitary citadel of public justice. It is then, the time for the highest efforts of the genius, and learning, and eloquence, and moral courage of the bar. The advocate not unfrequently finds himself, at such a moment, putting at hazard the popularity of a life devoted to the public service. It is then that the denunciations of the press may be employed to overawe or intimidate him. It is then, that the shouts of the multitude drown the still, small voice of the unsheltered sufferer. It is then, that the victim is already bound for immolation; and the advocate stands alone to maintain the supremacy of the law against power, and numbers, and public applause, and private wealth. If he shrinks from his duty, he is branded as the betrayer of his trust. If he fails in his labour, he may be cut down by the same blow, which levels his client. If he succeeds, he may, indeed, achieve a glorious triumph for truth and justice, and the law. But that very triumph may be fatal to his future hopes, and bar up for ever the road to political honours. Yet what can be more interesting, than ambition thus nobly directed? that sinks itself, but saves the State? What sacrifice more pure, than in such a cause? What martyrdom more worthy to be canonized in our hearts?

It may be that his profession calls him to different duties. He may be required to defend against the arm of the government a party standing charged with some odious crime, real or imaginary. He is not at liberty to desert even the guilty wretch in his lowest estate; but he is bound to take care, that even here the law shall not be bent or broken to bring him to punishment. He will at such times, from love of the law, as well as from compassion, freely give his talents to the cause, and never surrender the victim, until the judgment of his peers has convicted him upon legal evidence. A duty, not less common, or less interesting, is the vindication of innocence against private injustice. Rank, and wealth, and patronage may be on one side; and poverty and distress on the other. The oppressor may belong to the very circle of society, in which we love to move, and where many seductive influences may be employed to win our silence. The advocate may be called upon to require damages from the seducer for his violation of domestic peace; or to expose to public scorn the subtle contrivances of fraud. The ardour of youth may have been ensnared by cunningly devised counsels to the ruin of his estate. The drivelling of age may have been imposed on to procure a grant or a will, by which nature is outraged, and villany rewarded. Religion itself may have been treacherously employed at the side of the death-bed to devour the widow's portion, or plunder the orphan. In these, and many other like cases, the attempt to unravel the fraud, and expose the injury, is full of delicacy, and may incur severe displeasure among friends, and yield a triumph to enemies. But it is on such occasions, that the advocate rises to a full sense of the dignity of his profession, and feels the power and the responsibility of its duties. He must then lift himself to thoughts of other days, and other times; to the great moral obligations of his profession; to the eternal precepts of religion; to the dictates of that voice, which speaks within him from beyond the grave, and demands, that the mind given by God shall be devoted to his service, without the fear, and without the frailty of man.

But whatever may be the dignity and the brilliancy either of fame or fortune, which the profession holds out to those, who strive for eminence in the law, the student should never imagine that the ascent is easy, or the labour light. There cannot be any delusion cherished more fatal to his ultimate success than this. Young men of gay and ardent temperaments are apt to imagine, that little more is necessary than to read a few elementary books with reasonable diligence, and the rewards are already within their grasp. They fondly indulge the belief, that fluency of speech, a kindling imagination, ready wit, graceful action, and steady self-confidence will carry them through every struggle. If they can but address a court or jury without perturbation, and state their points with clearness and order, the rest may fairly be left to the workings of their own minds upon the excitements of the occasion. That because the hour is come and the trial is come, the inspiration for the cause will come also.

Whoever shall indulge in such visionary views, will find his career end in grievous disappointment, if not in disgrace. I know not, if among human sciences there is any one, which requires such various qualifications and extensive attainments, as the law. While it demands the first order of talents, genius alone never did, and never can, win its highest elevations. There is not only no royal road to smooth the way to the summit; but the passes, like those of Alpine regions, are sometimes dark and narrow; sometimes bold and precipitous; sometimes dazzling from the reflected light of their naked fronts; and sometimes bewildering from the shadows projecting from their dizzy heights. Whoever advances for safety must advance slowly. He must cautiously follow the old guides, and toil on with steady footsteps; for the old paths, though well beaten, are rugged; and the new paths, though broad, are still perplexed.

To drop all metaphor, the law is a science, in which there is no substitute for diligence and labour. It is a fine remark of one, who is a brilliant example of all he teaches, that "it appears to be the general order of providence, manifested in the constitution of our nature, that every thing valuable in human acquisition should be the result of toil and labour."[20] But this truth is nowhere more forcibly manifested than in the law. Here, moderate talents with unbroken industry have often attained a victory over superior genius, and cast into shade the brightest natural parts.

The student, therefore, should, upon his first entrance upon the study, weigh well the difficulties of his task, not merely to guard himself against despondency on account of expectations too sanguinely indulged; but also to stimulate his zeal, by a proper estimate of the value of perseverance. He, who has learned to survey the labour without dismay, has achieved half the victory. I will not say with Lord Hale, that "the law will admit of no rival, and nothing to go even with it"; but I will say, that it is a jealous mistress, and requires a long and constant courtship. It is not to be won by trifling favours, but by a lavish homage.

Many causes combine to make the study of the common law, in the present day, a laborious undertaking. In the first place, it necessarily embraces the reasoning and doctrines of very remote ages. It is, as has been elegantly said, "The gathered wisdom of a thousand years ";[21] or, in the language of one of the greatest of English judges, it is not "the product of the wisdom of. some one man, or society of men, in any one age; but of the wisdom, counsel, experience, and observation of many ages of wise and observing men."[22] It is a system having its foundations in natural reason; but at the same time built up and perfected by artificial doctrines adapted and moulded to the artificial structure of society. The law, for instance, which governs the titles to real estate, is principally derived from the feudal polity and usages, and is in a great measure unintelligible without an intimate acquaintance with the peculiarities of that system. This knowledge is not, even now, in all cases easily attainable; but must sometimes be searched out amidst the dusty ruins of antiquity, or traced back through black-lettered pages of a most forbidding aspect both in language and matter. The old law, too, is not only of an uncouth and uninviting appearance; but it abounds with nice distinctions, and subtile refinements, which enter deeply into the modern structure of titles. No man, even in our day, can venture safely upon the exposition of an intricate devise, or the effect of a power of appointment, or of a deed to lead uses and trusts, who has not, in some good degree, mastered its learning. More than two centuries ago Sir Henry Spelman[23] depicted his own distress upon entering upon such studies, when at the very vestibule he was met with a foreign language, a barbarous dialect, an inelegant method, and a mass of learning, which could be borne only upon the shoulders of Atlas; and frankly admitted, that his heart sunk within him at the prospect. The defects of a foreign tongue, and barbarous dialect, and inelegant order, have almost entirely disappeared, and no longer vex the student in his midnight vigils. But the materials for his labour have in other respects greatly accumulated in the intermediate period. He may, perchance, escape from the dry severity of the Year Books, and the painful digestion of the Abridgments of Statham, Fitzherbert, and Brooke. He may even venture to glide by the exhausting arguments of Plowden. But Lord Coke, with his ponderous Commentaries, will arrest his course; and faint and disheartened with the view, he must plunge into the labyrinths of contingent remainders, and executory devises, and springing uses, and deem himself fortunate, if after many years' devotion to Fearne, he may venture upon the interpretation of that darkest of all mysteries, a last will and testament. So true it is, that no man knows his own will so ill, as the testator; and that over-solicitude to be brief and simple, ends in being profoundly enigmatical. Dum brevis esse labero, obscurus fio.

In the next place, as has been already hinted, every successive age brings its own additions to the general mass of antecedent principles. If something is gained by clearing out the old channels, much is added by new increments and deposits. If here and there a spring of litigation is dried up, many new ones break out in unsuspected places. In fact, there is scarcely a single branch of the law, which belonged to the age of Queen Elizabeth, which does not now come within the daily contemplation of a lawyer of extensive practice. And all these branches have been spreading to an incalculable extent since that period by the changes in society wrought by commerce, agriculture, and manufactures, and other efforts, of human ingenuity and enterprise.

We are, therefore, called upon at this moment to encounter, ay, and to master the juridical learning of the three last centuries, during which the talents of the bar, and the researches of the bench are embodied in solid and enduring volumes. Fortescue[24] has told us, that in his age the judges did not sit in Court but three hours in the day; and that when they had taken their refreshments, they spent the rest of the day in the study of the law, reading of the holy Scriptures, and other innocent amusements at their pleasure; so that it seemed rather a life of contemplation than of much action; and that their time was spent in this manner free from care and worldly avocations. The case was greatly changed in the succeeding century; and we need but examine the ample reports and commentaries of Lord Coke, to perceive what a prodigious influx of learning bore down the profession in his day. At the distance of another century Lord Hale was compelled to admit the heavy and almost overwhelming burthens of the law. And we in the nineteenth century may well look with some apprehension upon the accumulations of our own times. It is not an over-statement to declare, that the labours of the profession now are ten times as great, as they were in the days of Lord Coke; and that they have been quadrupled within the last century. The whole series of English Reports down to the Revolution of 1688, scarcely exceeds one hundred volumes; while those since that period fall little short of three hundred. To this goodly mass America has added within the short space of twenty years more than two hundred volumes. If to these we add the excellent elementary treatises, which have filled our libraries during these latter periods, we shall find, that not merely the lucubrations of twenty years, but a long life will scarcely suffice to attain the requisite learning.

In truth, the common law, as a science, must be for ever in progress; and no limits can be assigned to its principles or improvements. In this respect it resembles the natural sciences, where new discoveries continually lead the way to new, and sometimes to astonishing results. To say, therefore, that the common law is never learned, is almost to utter a truism. It is no more than a declaration, that the human mind cannot compass all human transactions. It is its true glory, that it is flexible, and constantly expanding with the exigencies of society; that it daily presents new motives for new and loftier efforts; that it holds out for ever an unapproached degree of excellence; that it moves onward in the path towards perfection, but never arrives at the ultimate point.

But the student should not imagine, that enough is done, if he has so far mastered the general doctrines of the common law, that he may enter with some confidence into practice. There are other studies, which demand his attention. He should addict himself to the study of philosophy, of rhetoric, of history, and of human nature. It is from the want of this that enlarged view of duty, that the profession has sometimes been reproached with a sordid narrowness, with a low chicane, with a cunning avarice, and with a deficiency in liberal and enlightened policy. Mr. Burke has somewhat reluctantly admitted the fact, that the practice of the law is not apt, except in persons very happily born, to open and liberalize the mind exactly in the same proportion, as it invigorates the understanding; and that men too much conversant in office are rarely minds of remarkable enlargement.[25] And Lord Bacon complains, that lawyers have never written as statesmen.[26] The reproach is in some measure deserved. It is, however, far less true in our age, than in former times; and far less true in America, than in England. Many of our most illustrious statesmen have been lawyers; but they have been lawyers liberalized by philosophy, and a large intercourse with the wisdom of ancient and modern times. The perfect lawyer, like the perfect orator, must accomplish himself for his duties by familiarity with every study. It may be truly said, that to him nothing, that concerns human nature or human art, is indifferent or useless. He should search the human heart, and explore to their sources the passions, and appetites, and feelings of mankind. He should watch the emotions of the dark and malignant passions, as they silently approach the chambers of the soul in its first slumbers. He should catch the first warm rays of sympathy and benevolence, as they play round the character, and are reflected back from its varying lines. He should learn to detect the cunning arts of the hypocrite who pours into the credulous and unwary ear his leperous distilment. He should for this purpose make the master-spirits of all ages pay contribution to his labours. He should walk abroad through nature, and elevate his thoughts, and warm his virtues by a contemplation of her beauty, and magnificence, and harmony. He should examine well the precepts of religion, as the only solid basis of civil society, and gather from them not only his duty, but his hopes; not merely his consolations, but his discipline and his glory. He should unlock all the treasures of history for illustration, and instruction, and admonition. He will thus see man, as he has been, and thereby best know, what he is. He will thus be taught to distrust theory, and cling to practical good; to rely more upon experience, than reasoning; more upon institutions, than laws; more upon checks to vice, than upon motives to virtue. He will become more indulgent to human errors; more scrupulous in means, as well as in ends; more wise, more candid, more forgiving, more disinterested. If the melancholy infirmities of his race shall make him trust men less, he may yet learn to love man more.

Nor should he stop here. He must drink in the lessons and the spirit of philosophy. I do not mean that philosophy described by Milton, as

> "a perpetual feast of nectared sweets,
> Where no crude surfeit reigns ";

but that philosophy, which is conversant with men's business and interests, with the policy and the welfare of nations; that philosophy, which dwells not in vain imaginations, and Platonic dreams; but which stoops to life, and enlarges the boundaries of human happiness; that philosophy, which sits by us in the closet, cheers us by the fireside, walks with us in the fields and highways, kneels with us at the altars, and lights up the enduring flame of patriotism.

What has been already said, rather presupposes than insists upon the importance of a full possession of the general literature of ancient and modern times. It is this classical learning alone, which can impart a solid and lasting polish to the mind, and give to diction, that subtile elegance and grace, which colour the thoughts with almost transparent hues. It should be studied, not merely in its grave disquisitions, but in its glorious fictions, and in those graphical displays of the human heart, in the midst of which we wander as in the presence of familiar, but disembodied spirits.

It is by such studies, and such accomplishments, that the means are to be prepared for excellence in the highest order of the profession. The student, whose ambition has measured them, if he can but add to them the power of eloquence, (that gift, which owes so much to nature, and so much to art,) may indeed aspire to be a perfect lawyer. It cannot be denied, indeed, that there have been great lawyers, who were not orators; as there have been great orators, who were not lawyers. But it must be admitted at the same time, that when both characters are united in the same person, human genius has approached as near perfection, as it may. They are kindred arts, and flourish best in the neighborhood of each other.[27]

The eloquence of the bar is far more various and difficult, than that which is required in the pulpit, in the legislative hall, or in popular assemblies. It occasionally embraces all that belongs to each of these places, and it has, besides, many varieties of its own. In its general character it may be said to be grave, deliberative, and earnest, allowing little indulgence to fancy, and less to rhetoric. But as it must necessarily change its tone according to its subject, and the tribunal, to which it is addressed, whether the court or the jury, there is ample scope for the exercise of every sort of talent, and sometimes even for dramatic effect. On some occasions it throws aside all the little plays of phrase, the vivid touches of the pencil, and the pomp and parade of diction. It is plain, direct, and authoritative. Its object is to convince the understanding, and captivate the judgment by the strength and breadth of its reasoning. Its power is in the thought, and not in the expression; in the vigour of the blow from the hand of a giant; in the weight of the argument, which crushes in its fall, what it has not levelled in its progress. At other times it is full of calm dignity and persuasiveness. It speaks with somewhat of the majesty of the law itself, in strains of deep, oracular import. It unfolds its results with an almost unconscious elegance, and its thoughts flash like the sparkles of the diamond. At other times it is earnest, impassioned, and electrifying; awing by its bold appeals, or blinding by its fiery zeal. At other times it is searching, and acute, and rigorous; now brilliant in point, now gay in allusion, now winning in insinuation. At other times it addresses the very souls of men in the most touching and pathetic admonitions. It then mingles with the close logic of the law those bewitching graces, which soothe prejudice, disarm resentment, or fix attention. It utters language, as the occasion demands, which melts to pity, or fires with indignation, or exhorts to clemency.

But whatever may be the variety of effort demanded of forensic eloquence, whether to convince, or captivate, or persuade, or inflame, or melt;—still its main character must for ever be like the "grave rebuke," so finely sketched by our great epic poet, "severe in youthful beauty," that it may possess an "added grace invincible."[28] It may not stoop to ribaldry, or vulgar jests, or sickly sentimentality, or puerile conceits. It forbids declamation, and efflorescence of style. There is no room for the loquacity of ignorance, or the insolence of pride. If wit be allowable, it must be chaste and polished. The topics discussed in courts of justice are too grave for merriment, and too important for trifling. When life, or character, or fortune hangs on the issue, they must be vindicated with dignity, as well as with force.

But I forbear. I seem, indeed, when the recollection of the wonders wrought by eloquence comes over my thoughts, to live again in scenes long since past. The dead seem again summoned to their places in the halls of justice, and to utter forth voices of an unearthly and celestial harmony. The shades of Ames, and Dexter, and Pinkney, and Emmett pass and repass, not hush as the foot of night, but in all the splendour of their fame, fresh with the flush of recent victory. I may not even allude to the living. Long, long may they enjoy the privilege of being nameless here, whose names are every where else upon the lips of praise.

Enough has been said, perhaps more than enough, to satisfy the aspirant after juridical honours, that the path is arduous, and requires the vigour of a long and active life. Let him not, however, look back in despondency upon a survey of the labour. The triumph, if achieved, is worth the sacrifice. If not achieved, still he will have risen by the attempt, and will sustain a nobler rank in the profession. If he may not rival the sagacity of Hardwicke, the rich and lucid learning of Mansfield, the marvellous judicial eloquence of Stowell, the close judgment of Parsons, the comprehensive reasoning of Marshall, and the choice attainments of Kent;—he will yet, by the contemplation and study of such models, exalt his own sense of the dignity of the profession, and invigorate his own intellectual powers. He will learn, that there is a generous rivalry at the bar; and that every one there has his proper station and fame assigned to him; and that, though one star differeth from another in glory, the light of each may yet be distinctly traced, as it moves on, until it is lost in that common distance, which buries all in a common darkness.

Having spoken thus much upon the dignity, the qualifications, and the duties of the profession, I trust it will not be supposed, that we have the rashness to indulge the belief, that the Law Institution here, under the guidance of its present Professors, can fill up the outline, which has thus been traced. My learned brother will, indeed, bring to the task of instruction, the ardour, the attainments, and the experience, which elsewhere have given him such an elevated reputation. Little, indeed, of what has been sketched out in this discourse, can be attained by any academical instruction during the usual period assigned for the preparatory studies for the bar. And of that little, we have not the presumption to believe, that our method or efforts can reach even our own wishes and opinions. What we propose is no more than plain, direct, familiar instruction; something to assist the student in the first steps of his studies; something to cheer him in his progress; something to disencumber him of difficulties by the way-side; and something to awaken a sincere ambition for professional excellence.

For myself, I am but too conscious, how little I can bring to the task, worthy of the occasion. The perpetual round of judicial duties, full of anxious thoughts, and anxious vigils, might, even at an earlier period of life, have repressed the elasticity of hope. But in entering upon new duties at the present time, I confess myself more fearful of failure, than ambitious of distinction. I may not say, with the enviable self-satisfaction of an eminent judge, now reposing in leisure sustained with dignity, that "long absence from the bar, the consequent want of practice, age, the enjoyment of repose, and the indolence, which that repose often produces, have increased *my* unwillingness to undertake a work of labour."[29] But I may say, in the language of a kindred mind to his, that "after a certain age and portion of experience, the sense of duty becomes a stronger principle of action, than the love of reputation."[30] I shall be content, therefore, if, able to meet the duties of the office, I shall not wholly disappoint the expectations of the Founder, by whose kind solicitude I have been advanced to this chair. Indeed, I may say, that but from a desire to justify his early friendship (as welcome, as it was then unexpected), and to express my own sense of his liberal donation, I should have declined a post, which others might fill with more undivided attention, though not, perhaps, with more sincere zeal. Under such circumstances, I hope that I may be permitted to occupy a few moments more, in expounding the objects of this professorship, and thus demonstrate the wisdom and munificence of the Founder.

The duties assigned to the Dane Professorship are, in the first instance, to deliver lectures upon the Law of Nature, the Law of Nations, Maritime and Commercial Law, Equity Law, and, lastly, the Constitutional Law of the United States. No reflecting man can hesitate to admit the importance of these branches of jurisprudence, and their intimate connexion with the best interests of civilized society. To comment on either of them, fully and worthily, might well employ the diligence of a long life, without exhaustion or repetition. A course of lectures, therefore, which embraces them all, must necessarily treat them in a brief, summary, and imperfect manner. It must suggest matter for inquiry, rather than expound principles with copiousness. It must create, rather than satisfy curiosity. It must illustrate by examples, rather than exhaust by analysis. It must display the foundations, rather than the size or exact proportions of the edifice. It must, if I may venture upon such a metaphor, conduct the inquirer to the vestibule of the temple of jurisprudence; and leave to his future curiosity the survey of its magnificent halls, its decorated columns, its splendid porticos, its harmonized orders, its massive walls, its varied crypts, its lofty domes, its "ever-during gates, on golden hinges moving."

And first, the Law of Nature. This lies at the foundation of all other laws, and constitutes the first step in the science of jurisprudence. The law of nature is nothing more than those rules, which human reason deduces from the various relations of man; to form his character, and regulate his conduct, and thereby ensure his permanent happiness. It embraces a survey of his duties to God, his duties to himself, and his duties to his fellow men; deducing from those duties a corresponding obligation. It considers man, not merely in his private relations as a social being, but as a subject and magistrate, called upon to frame, administer, or obey laws, and owing allegiance to his country and government, and bound, from the protection he derives from the institutions of society, to uphold and protect them in return. It is, therefore, in the largest sense, the philosophy of morals; what Justinian has defined justice to be, "constans et perpetua voluntas jus suum cuique tribuendi "; or what may be denominated national jurisprudence, as expounded in the same authority; "divinarum atque humanarum rerum notitia, justi atque injusti scientia." With us, indeed, who form a part of the Christian community of nations, the law of nature has a higher sanction, as it stands supported and illustrated by revelation. Christianity, while with many minds it acquires authority from its coincidences with the law of nature, as deduced from reason, has added strength and dignity to the latter by its positive declarations. It goes farther. It unfolds our duties with far more clearness and perfection than had been known before its promulgation; and has given a commanding force to those of imperfect obligation. It relieves the mind from many harassing doubts and disquietudes, and imparts a blessed influence to the peaceful and benevolent virtues, to mercy, charity, humility, and gratitude. It seems to concentrate all morality in the simple precept of love to God and love to man. It points out the original equality of all mankind in the eyes of the Supreme Being, and brings down the monarch to the level of his subjects. It thus endeavours to check the arrogance of power, and the oppression of prerogative; and becomes the teacher, as well as the advocate of rational liberty. Above all, by unfolding in a more authoritative manner the doctrine of the immortality of the soul, it connects all the motives and actions of man in his present state with his future interminable destiny. It thus exhorts him to the practice of virtue, by all, that can awaken hope, or secure happiness. It deters him from crimes by all, that can operate upon his fears, his sensibility, or his conscience. It teaches him, that the present life is but the dawn of being; and that in the endless progress of things the slightest movement here may communicate an impulse, which may be felt through eternity. Thus Christianity becomes, not merely an auxiliary, but a guide to the law of nature, establishing its conclusions, removing its doubts, and elevating its precepts.

In this manner it is, that the law of nature involves a consideration of the nature, faculties, and responsibilities of man. From his intellectual powers, and the freedom of his will, it deduces his moral perceptions and accountability. From his love of happiness, as the end and aim of his being, it deduces the duty of preserving that happiness. From his dependence upon the Supreme Being, whose will has indissolubly connected virtue with happiness, it deduces the primary duty of obedience to that will. From these simple elements it proceeds to consider him in the various relations of life, in which he may be placed, and ascertains in each his obligations and duties. It considers him as a solitary being, as a member of a family, as a parent, and lastly as a member of the commonwealth.

The consideration of this last relation introduces us at once to the most interesting and important topics; the nature, objects, and end of government; the institution of marriage; the origin of the rights of property; the nature and limits of social liberty; the structure of civil and political rights; the authority and policy of laws; and indeed all those institutions, which form the defence and the ornament of civilized society.[31]

Upon many of these topics, of which a very imperfect sketch can here be given, I shall speak with much brevity and reserve, for two reasons. In the first place, in the course of the academical instruction in this University already provided for, the subjects of ethics, natural law, and theology, are assigned to other professors. In the next place, in the elementary education, every where passed through, before entering upon juridical studies, they are usually taught with sufficient fulness and accuracy.

In the next place, the Law of Nations. By this we are to understand not merely that portion of public law, which is generally recognised among nations, as seems to have been the prevailing sense of the phrase in the Roman code; but that portion of public law, which regulates the intercourse, adjusts the rights, and forms the basis of the commercial and political relations of states with each other. Perhaps the most appropriate name would be, International Law, *jus inter gentes*. It has in this view been very correctly subdivided into three sorts ; first, the natural or necessary law of nations, in which the principles of natural justice are applied to the intercourse between states; secondly, the customary law of nations, which embodies those usages, which the continued habit of nations has sanctioned for their mutual interest and convenience; and, thirdly, the conventional or diplomatic law of nations, which embraces positive compacts by treaties and conventions between nations, and derives its sole obligation from the same sources as other contracts. Under this last head many regulations will now be found, which at first resulted from custom, or a general sense of justice, and are now made of positive obligation for the purpose of preventing national disputes and collisions.

Upon the general theory of the law of nations much has been written by authors of great ability and celebrity. At the head of the list stands that most extraordinary man, Grotius, whose treatise *de Jure Belli et Pacis* was the first great effort in modern times to reduce into any order the principles belonging to this branch of jurisprudence, by deducing them from the history and practice of nations, and the incidental opinions of philosophers, orators, and poets. His eulogy has been already pronounced in terms of high commendation, but so just and so true, that it were vain to follow, or add to his praise.[32] Puffendorf in a dry, didactic manner, has drawn out, in the language of the times, much to strengthen the conclusions of his master upon natural law; and the sagacity of Barbeyrac, in his luminous Commentaries, has cleared away many obscurities, and vindicated many positions. Wolfius, who is better known among us in his elegant abridger, Vattel, has more elaborately discussed the theory, with the improved lights of modern days. And Ward, in his unpretending, but exact Inquiry into the Foundation and History of the Law of Nations in Europe from the time of the Greeks and Romans to the age of Grotius, has afforded ample materials for illustration and profound reflection. Bynkershoeck is a writer of a very different cast; and in a clear, bold, and uncompromising manner, lays down his principles, as practical results, with a brevity and vigour, which give them almost the authority of a text-book. He is not, however, a mere apologist, or collector of usages; but he insists with an animated vehemence, that reason is the very soul of the law of nations. "Ratio ipsa (inquam) ratio juris gentium est anima.[33]

But I know not, if there be in existence any treatise on this subject, which in point of fulness and accuracy of principles, or copiousness of detail, is adapted to the exigencies of modern society, or is calculated in any moderate degree to satisfy the expectations of a scholar or a publicist. There is yet living a man,[34] whose character as a philosophical moralist, enlightened statesman, and liberal jurist, commands universal respect, who taught us in his early performances, that to his genius we might thereafter owe such an invaluable donation. But the lapse of thirty years, and the seductive influence of other studies lead us now to fear, that our hopes will end in disappointment. Such a treatise should embrace, among other things, a general view of the sovereignty, equality, and independence of nations; the rights of public domain, and territorial jurisdiction in rivers, bays, lakes, and streams, and the ocean; the intercourse of nations in times of peace, in respect to commerce and navigation; the immunities, and liabilities, and privileges of foreigners; the rights and duties of ambassadors and other ministers; the grounds of just war; the rights and duties of belligerents and neutrals, and the limits of just hostilities; the rights of conquest; the nature of piracy; the nature and effect of alliances, armistices, passports, and safe-conducts; and the negotiation, interpretation, and obligation of treaties of peace and other treaties. My object will be, in the discussion of these topics, to expound the general theory with as much conciseness, as the nature of the case will admit; and to devote my principal labour to the developement of those practical results, which are of perpetual application in the common business of life, and regulate the daily concerns of individuals and nations in peace and in war. For this purpose, I shall adventure far more, than has been usual with publicists, into an examination of those general principles of jurisprudence, which affect the contracts, govern the titles, and limit the remedies of the subjects of independent powers, who acquire rights, or contract obligations, or succeed to property, or are in any measure subjected to the municipal law in a foreign country. This will include a variety of delicate and interesting topics belonging to the operation of foreign jurisprudence, or, as it is sometimes called, *the lex fori et lex loci*. Among these are the law of foreign domicil and expatriation; of foreign marriages, divorces, and crimes; of foreign testaments and successions *ab intestato*; of foreign grants and agreements; of foreign prescriptions, limitations, presumptions, discharges, and judgments; of foreign asylum to deserters and fugitives; and as incidental, the nature and extent of the jurisdiction exercised by courts of law in enforcing rights between foreigners, or giving effect to the municipal prohibitions of foreign countries. I shall also adventure upon an ample discussion of the law of prize, including therein the law of captures, and recaptures, and reprisal, the law of postliminy, and the law of contraband, and blockade, and illegal trade. And as a fit conclusion of such a discussion, I shall give a summary view of the practice and jurisprudence of those tribunals, emphatically called courts of the law of nations, which in every country are ordained to administer this important branch of public law. In England and America, this jurisdiction is vested in the courts of Admiralty. In this part of my labours I shall freely use the materials, which have been furnished by those distinguished civilians, who have from time to time adorned the English and American courts of Admiralty. And, above all, I shall endeavour to avail myself of those masterly judgments, full of wisdom, and learning, and captivating eloquence, which have been pronounced within the last thirty years by a man,[35] to whom, in my deliberate opinion, the world is more indebted for a practical exposition of the law of nations, upon the eternal principles of justice and reason, than to all the jurists of all former ages.

In the next place, Equity Jurisprudence. This is a very comprehensive head of our municipal law, and in its actual administration, probably embraces as great a variety and extent of learning, as the aggregate of all those, which now fall within the jurisdiction of the courts of common law, in the strict sense the terms. The jurisdiction in equity is sometimes concurrent with courts of common law, as in matters of account, partition, and dower; and sometimes it is exclusive and paramount. Its exclusive jurisdiction covers an immense mass of doctrines, relative to truths, frauds, mistakes, and accidents, and other cases, which the remedial justice of the common law courts cannot reach. It is a common, but groundless notion, that equity consists in the administration of a sort of discretionary justice; and is not, like the common law, built upon exact principles and settled rules; that it is a transcendental power, acting above the law, and superseding and annulling its operations, and resting in an undefined and arbitrary judgment, at best the *arbitrium boni viri*, rather than *boni jurisconsulti*. There is, therefore, among those, who have not cultivated it, as a science, a spectral dread of it, as if some unquiet spirit walked abroad to disturb the repose of titles, and revive forgotten and dormant claims. It is strange, that such a delusion should find countenance, even within the pale of the profession itself. There is not, at the present moment, a single department of the law, which is more completely fenced in by principle, or that is better limited by considerations of public convenience, both in doctrine and discipline, than equity. It is an intricate, but an exquisitely finished system, wrought up with infinite care, and almost uniformly rational and just in its conclusions. Indeed, that portion of the common law, which is now most admired for its sound policy, derives its principal attraction from its being founded in a large and liberal equity, and therefore is assumed as a rule equally at Paris and at London, at Rome and at Washington. If it would not occupy too much space in an introductory discourse, I might vindicate these assertions against every objection. But this is not the time, or the occasion.

In the next place, Commercial and Maritime Law. By commercial law, we are accustomed to understand those branches of jurisprudence, which regulate the operations of trade at home and abroad; and by maritime law, those, which concern navigation, shipments, commerce, and other transactions on the sea. In truth they are perpetually running into each other, as the streams of many rivers flow into the ocean, and form a part of its mass of waters, and are almost incapable of an absolute separation. There can be little need to descant upon the value and importance of this part of our jurisprudence. It is the golden chain, which connects the nations of the earth, and binds them together in the closest union. It comes home to every man's business and bosom, and is as captivating by the philosophy of its doctrines, as it is commendable for its sound morals, its flexible adaptations, and its enlightened policy. Much of its excellence, it must be admitted, is the growth of modern times. Its history may be easily traced back to the classical shores of the Mediterranean, where maritime enterprise upon the revival of letters spread itself with wonderful rapidity and success. It succeeded the age of chivalry; and by blending the common interests of nations, it softened the manners, and subdued the barbarous spirit of rivals and adversaries. The customs of trade and navigation soon acquired the authority of law; and assisted by the persuasive equity of the Roman law of contract, (then much studied and admired, and still entitled to profound admiration,) it silently pervaded all Europe, from the farther Calabria to the frozen Baltic. The *Consolato del Mare*, which still instructs us by the wisdom of his precepts, is but a collection of the rules and maxims of this voluntary international code. The celebrated Ordinance of Louis the Fourteenth (which will be gratefully remembered, when his ambitious projects shall be lost in the dimness of tradition,) is little more than a text gathered from the civilians, and the customs of commerce, by the genius of a minister, whose life seemed devoted to the interests of posterity. England was almost the last to receive into her bosom this beautiful effort of human reason. Little more than a century has elapsed, since she could scarcely be said to possess any commercial jurisprudence. The old common lawyers repelled it with a sullen inhospitality and indifference. And though it cannot be doubted, that the spirit of commerce would, first or last, have forced it into the courts of England, and compelled them to protect the interests, which the enterprise of her subjects idern had created; it may be reasonably questioned, whether, but for the extraordinary genius of Lord Mansfield, she would not have been, at this very moment, a century behind continental Europe in adopting its doctrines. He was in a great measure the author of the law of insurance; and he gave to the other branches of commercial law, a clearness and certainty, which surprise us more and more, as we examine and study his decisions. That he borrowed much from foreign jurisprudence is admitted; but he more than repaid every obligation to these sources. He naturalized the principles of commercial law, when he transplanted them into the soil of England, and they have flourished with new vigour in her genial climate. It is her just boast, that having been once a tributary, she has now in turn laid the whole Continent under contribution. Her commercial law has attained a perfection, order, and glory, which command the reverence of the whole world. It is almost universally followed and obeyed; not, indeed, as of positive institution; but as wisdom, practical wisdom, acting upon the results of a large experience, in a government, where opinion is free, and justice is administered without favour and without reproach.

A treatise upon this branch of law must necessarily comprehend a wide range of subjects. It must discuss, among other things, the law of principals and agents, brokers, factors, and consignees; of partnerships, and other joint ownerships; of negotiable instruments, such as bills of exchange, promissory notes, checks, and bills of lading; of contracts of bailment, shipments, and affreightment; and, as incidents, of charter-parties, freight, demurrage, and stoppage *in transitu*; of navigation and shipping, and, as incidents, the rights and duties of owners, masters, and mariners; and of insurance, bottomry, respondentia, salvage, and general average. My object will be to deal as fully with these topics, as may consist with the limits, by which every system of lectures must be circumscribed.

In the last place, the Constitutional Law of the United States. In the correct exposition of this subject, there is not a single American citizen, who has not deep stake and permanent interest. "In questions merely political," says Junius, "an honest man may stand neuter. But the laws and constitution are the general property of the subject. Not to defend is to relinquish; and who is so senseless as to renounce his share in a common benefit, unless he hopes to profit by a new division of the spoil?"[36] The existence of the union of these States, does, (as I think,) mainly depend upon a just administration of the powers and duties of the national government; upon the preservation of that nice, but ever changing influence, which balances the State and General Governments, and tends, or should always tend to bring them into a due equilibrium. There is no safety to our civil, religious, or political rights, except in this union. And it is scarcely too much to affirm, that the cause of liberty throughout the world is in no small measure suspended upon this great experiment of self-government by the people. I shall endeavour, in my commentaries upon this important branch of political law, to discuss it with all the delicacy and reserve becoming my official station, and with all the sobriety appertaining to the fundamental law of organization of a free government. My object will be to unfold its divisions, and explain its principles, as far as practicable, by the lights of those great minds, which fostered into being, and nourished its infancy. I shall deal little with speculative discussions, and still less with my own personal opinions. But I shall rely with undoubting confidence upon the early commentaries of its framers, upon the legislative recognitions of authority and duty, and the judicial decisions of the highest courts, as safe guides for interpretation. Above all, I shall freely use the doctrines of the admirable production[37] of Hamilton, Madison, and Jay, (patriots as pure, and statesmen as wise, as any, which have graced our country,) which has already acquired the weight of an authority throughout America. If by such means I shall contribute to fix in the minds of American youth a more devout enthusiasm for the constitution of their country, a more sincere love of its principles, and a more firm determination to adhere to its actual provisions against the clamours of faction, and the restlessness of innovation, my humble labours will not be without some reward in the consciousness of having contributed something to the common weal.

I have thus sketched a general outline of the course of lectures, which the Founder of the Dane Professorship has in the first instance assigned to this chair, for the encouragement of juridical learning. Imperfect as this outline is, it must strike the most superficial observer, how rich and various are the topics, which it proposes to examine; how extensive is the learning, and how exhausting the diligence, to accomplish the design. While it does honour to the public spirit, and the sagacity and enlightened zeal of the Founder; while it testifies his enthusiasm for the science, in which he has so deservedly attained eminence; it at the same time admonishes us, that he, who matured the plan, seems alone to possess the courage and ability to execute it with complete success. In truth, the venerable Founder has measured the strength of others by his own; and scarcely seems to have suspected the difficulties of the task, from the consciousness of his own power to subdue them. The skilful guide in the Alps walks with fearless confidence in the midst of dangers, which appal the traveller, who has never made trial of his strength. Lord Coke, himself a prodigy of professional learning, has somewhere laid down, for the benefit of students, the various employments for every day, and has assigned six hours for the pursuit of the law.[38] Lord Hale has limited his exactions to the same period;[39] and Sir William Jones, whose early ambition thought, that all the departments of law might be mastered by a single mind in satisfactory Commentaries, has not ventured upon a different assignment of labour.[40] I feel justified in saying, that for more than fifty years our generous patron has daily devoted to his favourite studies of politics and jurisprudence more than double that number of hours.

I trust, it will not be deemed an intrusion, if upon this occasion I venture to speak somewhat of the public services of this distinguished lawyer, which are already matter of notoriety, and, considering his age and character, may almost be deemed matter of history.

It is now more than fifty years since Mr. Dane first came to the bar, and brought to its practice his varied stores of knowledge. He was almost immediately engaged in the duties of legislation in this, his native State; and to him we are chiefly indebted for the first general revisal of our Provincial Statutes; as well as for other improvements in our code of positive law. At the distance of thirty years, he was again called upon by the voice of the legislature to a similar duty; and to him, in a great measure, we owe the valuable collection of our Colonial and Provincial Statutes, which now adorns our libraries. In the intermediate period he served many years in the Continental Congress during some of its most difficult operations, and there maintained a high reputation for sound judgment, and an inflexible adherence to the best principles of political polity. His advancement to public life was always unsought for by himself; and his retirement from it has always been matter of public regret. To him belongs the glory of the formation of the celebrated Ordinance of 1787, which constitutes the fundamental law of the states northwest of the Ohio. It is a monument of political wisdom, and sententious skilfulness of expression. It was adopted unanimously by Congress, according to his original draught, with scarcely the alteration of a single word. After his retirement from public life, he devoted himself with matchless assiduity to the duties of the bar; and gradually arriving to the first rank, he became the guide, the friend, and the father of the profession in his own county. In the midst of an extensive practice, he found leisure to compile his Digest and Abridgment of American Law, which, in eight large octavo volumes, comprehends a general survey of all our jurisprudence, and attests the depth of his learning, his unwearied industry, and his independent, but cautious judgment. It is now some years since he bade farewell to the bar, but not to his favourite studies.[41] In contemplating his professional character one is perpetually reminded of the fine portrait of Lord Chief Justice Rolle, drawn by Lord Hale, in his preface to Rolle's Abridgment of the Law, which has so close a resemblance, that it seems another, and the same. "He argued frequently and pertinently," says Lord Hale; "his arguments were fitted to prove and evince, not for ostentation; plain, yet learned; short, if the nature of the business permitted, yet perspicuous. His words few, but significant and weighty. His skill, judgment, and advice in points of law and pleading were sound and excellent.—In short, he was a person of great learning and experience in the common law, profound judgment, singular prudence, great moderation, justice, and integrity." Mr. Dane has nobly educated the whole proceeds of his great work to the establishment of this professorship; and thus has become to our parent University, in the highest sense, the American Viner. I am but too sensible, that here the parallel must stop; and that to pursue it farther would cover with humiliation him, who now addresses you. To the liberal donation of Mr. Viner the world is indebted for the splendid Commentaries of Sir William Blackstone, a work of such singular exactness and perspicacity, of such finished purity and propriety of style, and of such varied research, and learned disquisition, and constitutional accuracy, that as a text-book it probably stands unrivalled in the literature of any other language, and is now studied as a classic in America, as well as in England. Perhaps when we are gathered in the dust, some future Blackstone, nursed and reared in this school, may arise, and by a similar achievement blend his own immortality with the fame of the Founder. Would to God, that it may be so! And thus this fair seat of science become the pride of the law, as it now is the pride of the literature of our country.

When we look around us, and consider, how much has been done by this University for the glory and safety of the Commonwealth; when we recollect, how many distinguished men have been nourished in her bosom, and warmed by her bounty, and cheered by her praise;[42] it is impossible to suppress the wish, the earnest wish, that this last triumph may yet crown her matron dignity. What consolation could be more affecting to her grateful children, than that in these academical shades their should arise a temple, sacred to the majesty of the law, where our future orators, and jurists, and judges, and statesmen, might mature their genius, and deepen their learning, and purify their ambition. Where future generations may approach, and read the wisdom of the law, as it is personified in the glowing sketch of Algernon Sidney.

"It is void of desire and fear, lust and anger. It is *mens sine affectu*, written reason, retaining some measure of the divine perfection. It does not enjoin that, which pleases a weak, frail man; but without any regard to persons, commands that, which is good, and punishes evil in all, whether rich or poor, high or low. It is deaf, inexorable, inflexible."[43]

NOTES

1. Cic. Fragment. de Repub. 17 Ernesti. Cic. op. 185 (Wells & Lilly). See also, Cic. de Legg. Lib. I. § 6.
2. Introductory Discourse on the Study of the Law of Nature and Nations. p. 62, (3d edition.)
3. Speech on American Taxation, 1774.
4. See Lord Hale's noble Discourse on the Amendment of the Law, ch. 3.
5. "Descendit itaque jus, quasi ponderosum quid cadens deorsum rectâ lineâ, vel transversali, et nunquam reascendit eâ viâ quâ descendit." Bracton, lib. 2. ch. 29; Co. Litt. 11; 2 Bl. Com. 212.
6. Chudleigh's case (1 Co. Rep. 120) contains some curious reasoning on this subject.
7. Plowden's Com. 258, 262.
8. Praise of Knowledge, 2 Bacon's Works, 125.
9. Burke on the French Revolution. The whole passage is worthy of commendation. It begins thus: "Government is not made in virtue of natural rights, which may and do exist in total independence of it, and exist in much greater clearness and in a much greater degree of abstract perfection. But their abstract perfection is their practical defect."
10. Teignmouth's Life of Sir W. Jones, 268.
11. Burke on the French Revolution.
12. Bacon. Essays, 2 vol. Essay 24, p. 311.
13. Lord Hale in Harg. Tracts, 255.
14. Locke on Education, p. 84.
15. Fortescue De Legg. ch. 49.
16. See the remarks of Mr. Justice Park, in *Smith* v. *Sparrow*, 4 Bing. R. 84, 88.
17. Cicero, De Orat. Lib. I. § 55. p. 87.
18. Burke's Reflections on the French Revolution.
19. I would commend to students the perusal of Mr. [now Judge] Hopkinson's Address before the Law Academy of Philadelphia, in 1826. It abounds with just remarks, chaste diction, and unpretending eloquence. Its matter and its style are excellent.
20. Chancellor Kent's Introductory Discourse, p. 8. Why has this finished discourse been withdrawn from his Commentaries?
21. Teignmouth's Life of Sir W. Jones, 100.
22. Lord Hale in preface to Rolle's Abridgment, 1 Coll. Jurid. 266.
23. Preface to his Glossary. The passage is partially quoted in 1 Blackstone's Com. 31, note.
24. Fortescue, De Laud. Legum Angliae, ch. 51.
25. See Burke's Reflections on the French Revolution, and Speech on American Taxation.
26. Lord Bacon on the Advancement of Learning, 1 Bacon's Works, 218.
27. "Præclaras duas artes," says Cicero, "atque inter se pares, et ejusdem socias dignitatis." Cic. de Oratore, Lib. I. § 55.
28. Paradise Lost, Book iv. line 844.
29. Lord Redesdale.
30. Chancellor Kent.
31. Mr. Hoffman's Legal Outlines, of which the first volume only is yet published, contains some very interesting and valuable disquisitions upon several of the topics belonging to this branch of law. I trust the learned author will soon favour the public with the residue of his work.
32. Sir James Mackintosh, in his Introductory Discourse.
33. Bynker. Quest. Pub. Jur. ch. 2. Mr. Du Ponceau's Translation of this work is a most valuable present to the profession. Indeed, when one considers the liberal and acute spirit, which pervades all the juridical publications of Mr. Du Ponceau, it is matter of universal regret, that he has not exclusively devoted his life to the exposition of law, and particularly of the civil law.
34. Sir James Mackintosh.
35. Lord Stowell (late Sir William Scott).
36. Letter 41, to Lord Mansfield.
37. The Federalist.
38. Co. Litt. 64 b.

> "Sex horas somno, totidern des legibus æquis,
> Quatuor orabis, des epulis duas.
> Quod superest ultro sacris largire camœnis."

39. Boswell's Life of Johnson, iii. 398.
40. Teignmouth's Life of Sir William Jones, p. 257.

"Six hours to law, to soothing slumber seven,
Ten to the world allot, and all to Heaven."

See also, Law of Bailments, p. 122, 123.

41. At this very moment there is in the press a ninth supplementary volume by Mr. Dane to his Digest and Abridgment, which contains a full abstract of thirty volumes of Reports published since his original work.

42. The members delegated from Massachusetts to serve in the Revolutionary Congress between 1774 and 1789, (when the new Constitution was adopted,) were in number twenty-one. Of these seventeen were educated in Harvard University. Their names are as follows: Samuel Adams, Thomas Cushing, John Hancock, John Adams, Robert T. Paine, Francis Dana, Elbridge Gerry, John Lowell, Samuel Osgood, Jonathan Jackson, Artemas Ward, George Partridge, Rufus King, James Lovell, Samuel A. Otis, George Thatcher, and Nathan Dane. Mr. Dane is the only survivor.

43. Works of Algernon Sidney, sect. 15, p. 69.

Chapter 21

Law-School of the University of Virginia

1851

Reprinted from the catalogue of the University of Virginia Law School, 1851, courtesy of the Harvard Law School Library Department of Special Collections.

The Board of Visitors of the University of Va., anxious to enlarge the sphere of legal instruction therein, have appointed an Adjunct Professor of Law, to whom will be assigned the duty of teaching more extensively than has hitherto been practicable, the subjects of Equity, and of Commercial law.

The object will be to acquaint the student familiarly and practically with the practically with the principles of his profession. With this view, instruction, (which is designed to be as thorough as possible,) will be given as heretofore, partly through text books, and daily examinations upon the subjects taught, partly by comments intended to supply what is deficient, and explain what is obscure in the text, and partly also, by independent lectures.

A Moot-Court is instituted in connection with the school, upon a plan which experience has shown to be well calculated to perfect the student in the details of practice. Under the immediate superintendence of the Professors he is required to pronounce opinions upon supposed cases; to devise and to institute remedies, by suit or otherwise; to conduct suits at Law, and in Chancery, from their inception, through all their stages; to draw wills, conveyances and other assurances; and in short to perform most of the functions of a practicing lawyer.

A course of lectures upon the civil law, and a detailed exposition of the most important leading cases in Law, and in Equity, will constitute, it is believed, a valuable addition to the system of instruction heretofore pursued in this school.

The school will be divided into three classes, viz: the *Junior* class, embracing such studies as are at once essential to the professional student, and form a highly useful branch of general education;—the *Intermediate* class, which will be occupied exclusively, with the theory and practice of law, as a profession, being adapted to the occasions of those who have time or inclination to push their elementary attainments beyond the most absolute necessity;—and the *Senior* class in which efforts will be made to impart a professional cultivation as liberal as the growing wants of the county shall demand, or allow.

The degree of Bachelor of Laws is conferred upon those, who upon examination, manifest a familiar acquaintance with the subjects taught in all the classes; and to those who exhibit a competent knowledge of International and Constitutional law, and of the science of Government, a certificate of Proficiency is awarded.

The Session begins on the 1st day of October, and ends on the 29th day of June following.
The course of study in the several classes is as follows:

Junior Class.	Intermediate Class.	Senior Class.
Vattel's International Law.	Stephen on Pleading.	Story's Equity.
Lectures on Government.	Barton's Suit in Equity.	Chitty on Contracts.
Federalist.	Coke on Littleton.	Mitford's Equity Pleadings.
Madison's Report, 1799.	Smith's Mercantile Law.	Lomax on Executors, &c.
Blackstone's Commentaries.	Greenleaf's Evidence.	Byles on Bills and Notes.
	Holcombe's Equity.	White and Tudor's Leading Cases.
		Smith's Leading Cases.
		Lectures on Civil Law.

The student is recommended to be provided with the following books for reference, viz: Gordon's Digest of laws of U. States, Virginia code of 1849, and Broom's maxims.

All the books required can be procured at the book stores near the University, on reasonable terms.

The expenses, for a session of nine months, are as follows:

Board and Lodging \$100; *Washing* \$8 to 10	\$108.00
Room rent. Of entire dormitory \$16; if two students occupy one room,	8.00
Fuel and Candles—Supposing two to occupy one room,	15.00
Matriculation fee,	15.00

Fees—Junior Class—If two other schools, besides the School of Law, be attended: \$25; if one other, \$35; no other, \$50.
Intermediate Class, \$60
Senior Class, \$75
The higher fee, in each instance, gives admission to any lower class.

July 10, 1851

Chapter 22

Law Schools in the United States

1863

G. A. Matile
Brian J. Gill, translator

Brian J. Gill is an attorney with the New York law firm of Davis Polk & Wardwell, assigned to its London and Paris offices. This translation is of *Les Écoles de Droit aux États Unis, Un Lettre Adressée à M. Édouard Laboulaye, Professeur au College de France*, first published in the *Revue historique de droit française et étranger* (novembre-décembre 1863).

Translator's note: Matile was born in Switzerland in 1807 and was a professor of law at the University of Neufchatel, before emigrating to the United States in 1849. He was professor of French at Princeton and practiced law in Philadelphia before joining the States Department during the Civil War. He ended his career as a translator in the Department of the Interior. I am grateful for the invaluable assistance of Michael S. Gill.

Washington,
October 26, 1863.
Monsieur Edouard Laboulaye,
Professor at the College of France
Dear Sir,

I am happy to be able without delay to give you the information that you ask me for in your letter of September 25, about law schools in my country; for this is a subject dear to my heart. In fact, for almost six years now I have been collecting materials for a work which I began with the idea of introducing reforms into our system of legal education. My idea, among other things, was to tell my fellow citizens how law schools in Europe are organized and describe the resources that they offer to their students. (When I talk of Europe, I mean the Continent. I leave to one side law schools in the United Kingdom, which have the same problems and the same failings as ours.)

Finding out about law schools in continental Europe, and obtaining details of courses and statistics, is easy because of your centralized system (which is a good thing, when it is no more centralized than is absolutely necessary) and the close academic links among the better schools. In contrast, in this country, as you know—and who knows better than you?—there is no recognizable central point. Schools function individually, with no coordination among them. One university is almost completely ignorant of what another is doing, no matter how close to each other they may be. Relationships between one school and another are only, so to speak, accidental, or the result of personal acquaintance. This isolation can be explained partly by the fact that these schools are more or less private—the state has no responsibility for them—and partly by the fact that they are so small. For example, I could only point you to a single law school which has as many as four professors. The others have only three, two or even one. It is common to see a law school open up only to close down again quickly, whether for the lack of a professor or a lack of students. Unlike the schools you have, these law schools have no secretarial offices, which is what makes it difficult to get information. In order to get the information that I needed I had to write out a questionnaire containing all my questions and send it round to all of our schools. But barely half of them replied and even among those very few were satisfactory or complete. Almost all showed a complete indifference to that subject which I find so important. Nevertheless, I persevered, and I had almost managed to complete my task when the civil war, and a task of an altogether greater order, made me break it off. But I hope to be able to return to it later, if my public duties allow.

There is no denying the fact that it is extremely difficult to achieve any reforms in this country, because even if you succeed in convincing your opponents that they are necessary, there still remains the problem of seeing how to fit a new cog into the larger machine. Even the best-intentioned often give up in the face of such a difficult task. In order for any institution to take root in this country it has to be popular, but generally speaking the people are not at all interested in higher education. It will take quite some time before our higher education reaches the level of our middle and even our lower schools, which are so rightly famous and which are available to all citizens. In fact, we could not claim that there is a single branch of higher studies in which our best is as good as what we need. Nevertheless I must point out that the system is improving, thanks in particular to those generous men (and there are more than a few of them) who give a part of their wealth to help the advancement of learning.

I have looked in vain in England for an effort comparable to that which I had set myself concerning our law schools. And yet such a task would be no less useful there than here. Let us hope that it will happen some day and that we will have an overall picture of how law is taught in Oxford, Cambridge, London, Edinburgh and Dublin, and in law offices. That is the only way that we will be able to have a clear idea of what is needed in the United Kingdom and to consider how to meet that need. However, there too the task is difficult, because of the respectable but too often disproportionate attachment of its people to whatever already exists, because everything in that society is intimately bound in with that strange political structure which is less the work of man than the work of time.

The English, as a people, are even less theoretical than the Americans; and they have the right idea. What they prize above all is their liberty. After that, they worry very little about the forms of the society in which they live, and even less about what other people think about it. In 1855, at the instigation of Parliament, the Queen appointed a Commission whose task was to propose such reforms as would seem to it appropriate in the interests of the practice and the learning of law. The Commission began its task by an inquiry into the current state of studies in England. It then heard evidence from several foreign legal experts about how law was taught in their respective countries, including France, Germany, Italy and the United States (which was represented by Mr. Thomas and Mr. Binney of the New York and Philadelphia bars). Although the Commission's main concern was legal studies as conducted in the Inns of Court and Chancery, it also revealed valuable information about other schools in the United Kingdom. What were its findings? That is for your English correspondents to tell you. But the seriousness with which this important task was approached and the good intentions which inspired it are good grounds for believing that it will not have been fruitless.

The universities of Oxford and Cambridge drag along slowly and listlessly, weighed down by their wealth and their monastic traditions. Roman Law is hardly to be found there (other than in their syllabuses), unlike the new University of London, where it is undergoing a renaissance, and in Edinburgh, where it is cultivated carefully. The English believe that this study of Roman Law is the reason why the Scottish bar is better than the English.

But I realize that I am wandering onto English ground, when I should be staying on American. In this country too an inquiry like the one I have just mentioned (which the European law journals, I am sure, will have been keeping their readers informed about as it has gone on) is greatly needed. But here there is nothing that might inspire the idea. Law schools are not in the jurisdiction of the federal government; and the state governments take hardly anything to do with them, other than authorizing their existence by incorporating them when individuals or companies request it. If the task of such an inquiry is ever undertaken, it will be the work of one person. I started it, and I hope to be able to continue it.

We have eighteen incorporated law schools, either independent or attached to other educational institutions, in the following twelve states:

Massachusetts	Cambridge, Harvard College, founded in 1817
Connecticut	New Haven, Yale College, 1820
New York	Albany, 1851
	New York University, 1859
	Columbia College, New York City, 1859
	Clinton, Hamilton College, 1853
	Poughkeepsie, 1853
Pennsylvania	Philadelphia, 1850
Virginia	Williamsburg, 1782
	Charlottesville, 1825
North Carolina	Chapel Hill, 1845
Louisiana	New Orleans, 1852
Kentucky	Louisville, 1852
Tennessee	Lebanon, 1847
Ohio	Cincinnati, 1833
Indiana	Bloomington, 1840
	Green Castle, 1853
Michigan	Ann Arbor, 1859

This means that not one of the other twenty-four states and territories, which together have a population of 24 million, has a law school—even though several of them (like Georgia, Illinois or Missouri) have populations of between one and two million. As well as the schools listed above, we have also had the following, which did not survive long: Baltimore, Maryland; Lexington, Kentucky; Franklin Springs, Kentucky; Albemarle, Virginia; Fredericksburg, Virginia; Nashville, Tennessee; Oxford, Mississippi; Carlisle, Pennsylvania; Raleigh, North Carolina; Mockville, North Carolina; Tuscaloosa, Alabama; and Princeton, New Jersey.

The general idea in the United States, as in England, is that law is a trade, to be learned in the office of one's pupil master by reading Blackstone and Kent and doing errands and clerical work for him. Nothing suggests that it will be anything other than a long time before law becomes a science rather than an art. And yet both the bar and the bench are full of lawyers and judges of the highest caliber. The judges are elected by the people, which means that they are liked and their decisions are willingly accepted. I have never known a country where lawyers forget each of their cases so quickly, which may explain why there is so much litigation—but I must add that cases are dealt with quickly and cheaply. So the people are satisfied with their judicial system, and, more than in other countries, laws are the work of the people. They do not have any sense that it could be improved, or that another judicial system might allow them more freedom. They are content with what they have; they listen solemnly and politely (but no more) to the doctrines of foreign theorists, before hurrying back to their work. They have too many real problems to deal with to allow others to create illusory ones.

According to the most recent census, the total number of young persons enrolled in the eighteen law schools mentioned above was 1,002. In a total population in the United States of 35 million, that makes one law student for every 35,000 inhabitants. What is more, their studies in law school never last more than two years, and often only 18, 12 or even 6 months. After 18 months, without having to pass any examinations, the student becomes a Bachelor of Laws. This title alone is enough to be admitted to the roll of practicing lawyers. There is no such thing as a Doctor of Laws in North America. Those who are not Bachelors of Laws must sit examinations to join the bar—at least, in some states. In others, the candidates are presented to the court by a colleague, usually the lawyer with whom they served their apprenticeship. The court hears the petition and decides; I have not seen one candidate be rejected. In those states where examinations are required, they are conducted in public, all in one sitting. I have seen some examinations where there were hundreds of candidates. One student would be finished in a few minutes; for another the examination would last between fifteen and twenty minutes, though never longer. The examination is carried out by three lawyers delegated on an *ad hoc* basis by the Supreme Court, who take it in turn to ask questions. The questions are set in advance in such a way that the examiners do not know which student will be asked which question. Once the test is over, they report to the Court and a few days later the successful candidates are invited to the courthouse to receive their diploma and to swear the oath of office. Very few candidates ever fail the examination. Those who do are invited to present themselves again at another session (there are two each year), and with perseverance they eventually succeed. Once the lawyer is sworn in, he can plead before all the courts, of any type or jurisdiction, in the state. If the occasion requires, he will even be admitted (although purely as a courtesy) to practice before the courts of other states, by producing his diploma. In order to plead before the Federal Courts, a lawyer must have been presented to them by a colleague in the same way as I have described above, and have been admitted by them.

As I have said, the number of professors in each law school is very small. I know hardly any, or even none, for whom teaching is their sole occupation; almost all also practice at the bar or sit on the bench. Connections among professors are much less frequent than in Europe (especially Germany). There are different reasons for this, particularly the facts that that there are so few of them, that faculty meetings (when there is such a thing as a "faculty") are rare, and that they do not work together on scholarly projects. We do have a few legal journals, but the part that the professors play in them is very small. If they do publish anything other than books, it is in literary and not legal journals. Even the most highly regarded legal journals contain almost nothing but case reports, and only rarely have theoretical articles. For every volume of legal analysis, you will find twenty volumes of reports. This last type of book, always bound in the same way, in tan leather with a red title on the spine, and always the same size, is the main component of the American lawyer's library. Only in extremely exceptional cases will you find foreign-language works. Out of the 1,500 lawyers in New York City, there are not twenty who have a copy of the *Corpus Iuris.* Finding myself one day in the library of one of the most important institutions in the state, I asked to see the *Corpus Iuris.* "The what?" asked the gentle librarian. I repeated my question; then, on my prompting, he went off to consult the catalog under the word "Justinian." And that was the *Corpus Iuris*! I do not know a single person here who could translate even ten lines of it correctly. This is understandable, for it is a book that they have never opened, because they do not study Roman Law; and moreover, it is suspect because it is foreign. Nevertheless, Roman Law has a reputation for great wisdom. Lawyers cite it (always from Domat's recent translations and very rarely from Pothier)—but studying it, or teaching it, is out of the question.[1] In the entire United States today there is not to be found a single chair of Roman Law.

In an article that I published recently in the *Boston Law Review*, entitled "Common Law Roman Law," I tried to show how useful and necessary the study of Roman Law is, even from the point of view of the common law. Whether this will change anything in the future, I do not know. Our most eminent legal scholars read it with approval; but, as I said at the beginning of this letter, nothing is more difficult than trying to introduce a new branch of the law into teaching—especially Roman Law. In any case, for a professor to be able to teach it properly, he needs an audience with a strong grounding in classics. Another problem is the shortness of the studies. Here it is generally accepted that a lawyer will start practice and earn his living at the age of 21 or 22. In another article, I explained to the Americans what is required in your country from the young man who wishes to study law and go to the bar. The classics are taught better in Europe than here; with you they start earlier, they are more focused and they last longer, so they leave an indelible mark on the young man. When he enters law school, he is ready to tackle Roman law, to study it in the original language and in its historical and doctrinal development. In this country, any exegesis would be barely understood or attempted. But by no means does this mean that we should abandon the idea of introducing Roman Law into our teaching. The first steps, no doubt, will be hard and slow. I picture the first professor of Roman Law (in the sense that you and I understand), surrounded at first by a very small number of students, perhaps two or three. If he has some spark of the sacred fire, he will pass it on to them; after a few years, he will have turned them into men capable of teaching it themselves. They will each have pupils of their own, and in no time Roman Law will be taught in all our schools. Those who know what a great and beneficial influence it has had on the legislation of continental Europe will understand how much we could draw from Roman Law ourselves, even if only to give our laws a better form. (My remarks about the United States on this subject apply equally to England.)

So far I have been discussing the state of our law schools in general, and have given you a glimpse of what they leave to be desired. I will finish this letter by telling you about the University of Cambridge in the state of Massachusetts, which together with Yale College occupies perhaps the foremost position in education in the United States, and about its law school, which with good reason is renowned as one of the best. The Faculty of Law of this university, established partly on the English system, has three professors.

"The aim of the school," according to the syllabus, "is to present a complete legal education to those young men aiming to go to the bar in one or other states of North America, and a course in commercial law to those aiming to go into commerce."

The "complete" course, for the bar, covers the various branches of common law and equity, admiralty law, commercial law, constitutional law and Federal Court practice. Those young persons aiming to go into commerce are given a more limited instruction. The principal classes in this course are: agency, corporations, security, bills of exchange, notes, insurance, [bailment], navigation, general maritime affairs and sales.

The school's library, which has 15,000 volumes, is made up exclusively of legal works. It is particularly well provided with reports, both from the United States and from England. The large number of English works to be found in our libraries can be explained by our common language and common legal foundations. The English, on their side, value our publications just as highly, and find them indispensable. The Law School library in Cambridge also contains a number of works that have been noteworthy in the history of legal theory in continental Europe, which come from various collections of libraries acquired by purchase or bequest. But the modern jurisprudence of Europe is very poorly represented. The University also possesses a magnificent library of 120,000 volumes, which is maintained to the highest standards of modern science, both American and European.

In private law subjects, the teaching focuses essentially on the common law and equity, although the professors often quote legislation and noteworthy decisions of the courts of the various states of the Union and the Federal Courts. Teaching is oral, and is accompanied by questions addressed to the students. Custom allows them to interrupt the professor to ask for explanations. Students are admitted to classes without any preliminary examination; all that is required, if they do not possess a Bachelor's degree, is to be at least nineteen and to present a certificate of good morals. This naturally opens the door to many young persons who are not sufficiently prepared for analytical classes, which is unfortunate for them and inconvenient for the others, because the professor has to try to make himself understood by all. Tuition fees for the complete course, which lasts two years, are $200 (around 1,000 francs). The students are free to enter classes at any time and follow only those that they want to. Two prizes, one of $50 and the other of $40, are awarded each year to the authors of the two best dissertations on subjects set by the Faculty. The judges, who are always external, are nominated by the Faculty. Today there are 90 law students at Cambridge. As I said above, there are a total of 1,002 students enrolled in the eighteen law schools, an average of 56 per school. The university with the most law students is Lebanon, Tennessee, with 188; then Ann Arbor, Michigan, 129; Poughkeepsie, New York, 119; Charlottesville, Virginia, 109; etc. Several schools have only four students. (These statistics are taken from *The American* and the *National Almanac*.) The academic year is divided into two semesters, each of which is between four and five months long. I list here the full titles of the classes given by the three law professors at Cambridge.

FIRST YEAR

First Semester

First Professor (Dean of Faculty)	Agency. Equity.
Second Professor	Insurance. Evidence.
Third Professor	Real Property. Arbitration.

Second Semester

First Professor	Moot Court. Constitutional Law.
Second Professor	Evidence.
Third Professor	Real Property. Wills. Administration of Estates. Criminal Law.

SECOND YEAR

First Semester

First Professor	Pledge and Security. Law of Corporations. Equity.
Second Professor	Notes and Bills of Exchange. Navigation and Admiralty Law. Criminal Law.
Third Professor	Real Property. Family Law. Insolvency. Bankruptcy.

Second Semester

First Professor	Constitutional Law. Jurisprudence of the Federal Courts. Proceedings in Equity. Evidence.
Second Professor	Bills of Exchange. Corporate securities.
Third Professor	Real Property. Sales. Conflict of Laws.

This syllabus, so different in every way from those of the European schools, is a good illustration of what legal instruction in the United States is like. You have so many classes that we lack! We have no class that is an introduction to the study of law—a class that is given in every law school in your continent and generally recognized as useful. I published an article on this subject in the *Boston Law Review* last year. There again my views were received with approval. But that is not all that we lack. If necessary, we could get by without Canon and Ecclesiastical Law (if we did not wish to give a complete course in legal science). But we also lack a Feudal Law class, which would have the benefit of explaining land tenure. And, as I have said, there is no Roman Law course, and consequently no exegesis or hermeneutics. And there is no course designed to introduce the young man to consular and diplomatic matters. The English common law is taught and studied thoroughly, but without being treated and understood as a branch of Germanic Law. There is no Legal History course. There is a course in Criminal Law at Cambridge, but that is a rare exception—which is not surprising, when you consider that Chancellor Kent used to like to observe that a few hours were enough to learn that subject thoroughly. If you search in his commentary—which purports to embrace the whole of legal science—it is only with great difficulty that you will find, here and there, a paragraph or two relating to a topic of Criminal Law.[2]

Kent attempted to do for the United States what Blackstone had done for England. Your readers have long been familiar with Blackstone and know what a deservedly great and honored place his work has in every library. His writing is still read with pleasure, both in England and in this country. His style is flawless, and he was the first to give his country a work of synthesis. However, it is regrettable that his book does not have a more systematic plan, and is written for the amateur rather than the professional. It is far too long to be suitable to give to the new student as a first book.

Kent's work in four volumes was written with the same aim as Blackstone's, and it has the same weaknesses. Be that as it may, it is enormously popular here. Blackstone and Kent are the two pivots around which the studies of the young American turn. Since Kent's death his work has been through a dozen editions, each time revised and enlarged, to the extent that soon there will be almost nothing of the original left. It will be of interest to reproduce the plan of Kent's commentary designed to provide a full legal course. The first volume covers the Law of Nations, Constitutional Law, the History of the Sources of Law; the second, the Absolute Rights of Persons and Personal Property; and the third and fourth, Real Property. I am the first to acknowledge the great merit of these two works; but in the present state of jurisprudence we need something better, and this type of work could be done better.

I would like to point out again that, however great the deficiencies of legal education in this country may be, it must be acknowledged that the United States has a great number of extremely skilled lawyers, even though many of them have never set foot in a law school. This skill can be attributed to their natural ability; but also to the direct and practical common sense that an American education produces, to the freedom of their society and to the political system in which they live.

But to return to Cambridge. The three chairs of law each owe their existence to a founder, three wealthy men who at different times gave a part of their fortune to establish a chair: Royall, Dane and Bussey. This is how, in the Middle Ages, many schools which later became the centers of great academic institutions were founded. Still in existence today, these three chairs have all been occupied by several professors, almost all of whom have found the time, on top of the time that they spent on their own studies, to write truly valuable works. I could give you a long list, but I will merely mention *Real Actions* by Stearns[3] and *Evidence, or A Treatise on Proof* by Greenleaf.[4] The latter is a famous name in Europe, almost as famous as Judge Story, the author of a number of works, who was also a professor of law at Cambridge.

The three current professors, Mr. Joel Parker, Dean of Faculty, Mr. Theophilus Parsons and Mr. Emory Washburn, are distinguished successors. Mr. Parker has spent most of his career concentrating on Constitutional Law. His numerous articles on this subject in our literary journals, including the *North American Review*, are notable for their wit, and bear witness to their author's great political independence. Again, it is regrettable that we do not have at least one journal specializing in legal theory in which our jurists could publish. We urgently need one. All the necessary elements are here in Cambridge and Boston, which is only three miles away. The Cambridge Law Faculty should have its own journal, as several faculties in Europe do. Its important position in public opinion would allow it to exercise a beneficial influence, and its example would quickly be followed by other schools. Not only that, but a publication of this type, which is entirely lacking in this country, would also have the great benefit of bringing legal scholars from all over the country into contact with each other. Mr. Parsons has published several highly regarded works, including *Law of Contracts*, *Laws of Business*, and *Maritime Law*.[5] Mr. Washburn has written a substantial treatise on *Real Property*[6] and has recently published a monograph on *Servitudes*. The latter work is especially interesting for its demonstration of how servitudes have developed in Anglo-Saxon cultures, and how Roman Law, where the theory of servitudes is so developed, has been introduced and has partly taken the subject over. Seeing the author draw so much from Roman Law again makes me wonder why this subject, which everyone cites and praises, is nevertheless not taught in a single one of our schools. Mr. Washburn previously held the highest office of the State of Massachusetts, that of Governor. He took up the chair upon leaving public life when his term of office expired.

Our university system has no equivalents to the supply teachers (extraordinary professors or "docents") that are found in continental Europe. That is another large deficiency that must be pointed out, although it is partly filled by those eminent men who are occasionally invited to give a limited number of classes. This is how, for example, Mr. Wheaton, author of *International Law*,[7] and Mr. Luther S. Cushing, who has published an important work on *Parliamentary Law*[8] and an edition of Domat, came to Cambridge.

The University of Cambridge, or rather of Harvard (from the name of its founder, who after graduating from Cambridge in England emigrated to America in 1637), is made up of the Faculties of Theology, Law and Medicine and Sciences, as well as other preparatory schools. Each of the special schools owes its existence to legacies, and to gifts from individuals or corporations. These similar institutions duplicate each other in many ways, with the result that they are not properly coordinated and there is much repetition. This is the old English system, which has its advantages, for it is evidence of the fact that the citizens act freely and spontaneously. In this country, we do not expect the State to provide everything, and when we can get by without it, we do so. We found our establishments out of our own pockets and ask nothing more of the State than that it recognize their existence as legal persons, with the ability to own property. That is all the State does—it is not concerned with the internal management of our institutions, for it realizes that the people are enlightened enough to choose those responsible for looking after its interests properly. The State is not greedy to extend its power; far from it; and it would not be able to even if it was.

Nevertheless, we cannot deny that the current system is not as efficient as it might be; there is repetition, and strengths are duplicated instead of being combined to produce better results. We recognize this, and our leading men are at the moment taking care of making the necessary changes to the system. But, of course, nothing will happen suddenly, and no one's rights will be infringed. Any changes will be the result of an amicable agreement among the interested parties. I think you will be grateful to me for reproducing here the following extract from a speech on this subject made before the Massachusetts legislature by Mr. John A. Andrew, the honorable Governor of that state, on January 9 of this year. Your statesmen, especially those in charge of the department of public education, will have something to learn from it.[9]

> [Model farms and experimental culture in all the varieties of soil our lands present, and also branches or subordinate schools are not to be discouraged.] Neither are the schools and colleges for academic study already provided or contemplated, nor any gifts or grants thereto, to be less favored in the future. Nor does unity of plan and cooperation in method, of necessity imply confinement of all the departments of an institution to one place. The object should be to centralize and economize means and power, while distributing and popularizing education and its fruits.
>
> But, in order to fulfill the highest functions of a University adopted to the wants and developments of modern society, to an intellectual and free people, its professorships, libraries and apparatus should be so combined and distributed as to include the faculties of Divinity, of Law, or Medicine, of Military instruction, of Letters and Natural Science, all of them organized and represented in their highest perfection. The faculty of Divinity should have, as its basis, a strong corps of scholars in Hebrew, literature and history, in ecclesiastical history, and in dogmatic theology, admitting as professors members of every church competent to teach. The teaching of the law school should include the civil law, comparative jurisprudence, political economy and diplomacy. The faculty of letters should combine the deepest scholars in ancient literature, including Sanskrit, and the other oriental languages, as well as Greek and Latin; and in antiquities proper, history in all its manifestations, the modern languages and their literature, philosophy in all its branches with its history. For the faculties of medicine and of natural sciences, should be combined mathematicians, astronomers, physicists, chemists, minerologists, botanists, zoölogists, geologists, devoting themselves chiefly to the scientific pursuit of their study; and also men distinguished for their eminence in the application of the sciences to the useful arts, civil engineers, architects, mining engineers, military engineers, and agriculturalists.
>
> That we should continue to build on the foundation our fathers laid, endeavoring to make actual in the life of our society their ideal, I religiously believe. Let us plan to concentrate here the "gladsome light" of universal science. Let learning be illustrated by our most brilliant luminaries, and let the claims of every science be vindicated by its bravest champion. Two-thirds of an amount equal to the sum we annually and wisely expend in public and private instruction, would found professorships and furnish the fund which would give to Massachusetts a University worthy of the dreams of the fathers, the history of the state, and the capacity of her people.

This speech was extremely favorably received. It may surprise Europeans because it shows that the United States is on the verge of entering a broader scientific path, a path which our other preoccupations will not prevent us from taking soon. Governor Andrew's recommendations have already begun to be put into effect, and there is no doubt that the rest will come. And then especially Cambridge will deserve to be called the leading university in the United States, and its law school will be the equal of any in Europe.

On the subject of Roman Law, I forgot to mention that I have translated the *Institutes* by Marezoll.[10] This excellent manual is, of all those that I am familiar with, the most suitable for study and teaching. In our language we have very few works on this subject, as you know, and none that is better than this. I hope to have it published. My translation is already out of my hands, and will be published as soon as the war is over. (Mr. Marezoll, who agreed to my translating his work, will be pleased to read this.)

Mr. Grellet-Dumazeau's work on the Roman bar, which I found here, is the sort of work likely to be well received. In other circumstances, I would gladly have translated it; but I had to be content with a long analysis, which the *North American Review* published last year. I understand from the newspapers that the article was read with pleasure and interest. The honour is all Mr. Grellet-Dumazeau's.

But I realize, dear Sir, that my letter has become very long, perhaps longer than you would wish. I have spoken to you at length about my country, because I know that it is a country that you love, and you love it because you have thoroughly studied it. You have recounted its political history and drawn its customs so well that an American can hardly believe that you have never visited this country, let alone spent a long time studying it here. The fact that you are a foreigner has allowed you to show us both overall points and points of detail which we did not notice, because we see them too closely, without any frame of comparison. In an earlier letter, I told you about the high opinion that our most eminent men hold of your most recent publication, *Paris in America.*[11]

We really should have more frequent contact between the jurists of the Old and the New Worlds. In matters of theoretical learning, we have much to learn from you; and in matters of practical science and freedom, you have much to learn from us. Germany, Switzerland and perhaps other countries already have their congresses of legal experts. I am sure that this example will soon be followed in other states, and then one day you will have a European congress. Make it a Universal congress, and invite America.

Yours etc.

George A. Matile

NOTES

1. Translator's note: See Jean Domat (1625-1696), *The Civil Law in Its Natural Order.* Translated from the French by William Strahan and edited from the second London edition by Luther S. Cushing (Boston: 1850).

2. Translator's note: See James Kent (1763-1847), *Commentaries on American Law* (New York: O. Halsted, 1826-1830).

3. Translator's note: See Asahel Stearns (1774-1839), *A Summary of the Law and Practice of Real Actions: With an Appendix of Practical Forms* (Boston: Cummings, Hilliard, 1824).

4. Translator's note: See Simon Greenleaf (1783-1853), *A Treatise on the Law of Evidence* (Boston: C. C. Little & J. Brown, 1842-53).

5. Translator's note: See Theophilus Parsons (1797-1882), *The Law of Contracts* (Boston: Little, Brown, & Co., 1853-55); *The Elements of Mercantile Law* (Boston: Little, Brown, 1856); *Law of Promissory Notes and Bills of Exchange* (Philadelphia, 1863); *The Laws of Business for Business Men, in All the States of the Union: With Forms for Mercantile Instruments, Deeds, Leases, Wills, &C.* (Boston: Little, Brown, 1857); *A Treatise on Maritime Law. Including the Law of Shipping; the Law of Marine Insurance; and the Law and Practice of Admiralty* (Boston: Little, Brown and Co., 1859).

6. Translator's note: See Emory Washburn (1800-1877), *A Treatise on the American Law of Easements and Servitudes* (Philadelphia: G.W. Childs, 1863); *A Treatise on the American Law of Real Property* (Boston: Little, Brown, 1860-1862).

7. Translator's note: See Henry Wheaton (1785-1848), *Elements of International Law* (2d annotated ed. by William Beach Lawrence; Boston: Little, Brown & Co., 1863).

8. Translator's note: See Luther Stearns Cushing (1803-1856), *Lex Parliamentaria Americana: Elements of the Law and Practice of Legislative Assemblies in The United States of America* (2d ed.; Boston: Little, Brown, 1863); *Manual of Parliamentary Practice Rules of Proceeding and Debate in Deliberative Assemblies* (Boston: Brown & Taggard, 1862).

9. Editor's note: The following text is reproduced directly from *Address of His Excellency John A. Andrew to the Legislature of Massachusetts, January 9, 1863* (Brown Wright & Porter, State Printers, 1863; Senate Publication #1).

10. Translator's note: See Gustav Ludwig Theodor Marezoll (1794-1873), *Lehrbuch der Institutionen des Romischen Rechtes* (Leipzig: J. A. Barth, 1857).

11. Translator's note: See Edouard Laboulaye (1811-1883), *Paris in America: By Dr. Rene Lefebvre.* Translated by Mary L. Booth (New York: Scribner, 1863).

Chapter 23

Our Municipal Law, and the Best Mode of Acquiring a Knowledge of It

1858

Theodore W. Dwight

Theodore Dwight (July 18, 1822-June 29, 1892) was founder and Professor in the law school of Hamilton College, and was Professor and Warden of Columbia Law School, from 1858 to 1891. His lectures and influence are described in chapter 1. See also his lecture notes in chapter 24 and student notes of his lectures in chapter 26 and dean's letter in chapter 81. This address is reprinted from *Inaugural Addresses of Theodore W. Dwight, Professor of Law, and of George P. Marsh, Professor of English Literature, in Columbia College, New York* (New York: Trustees of Columbia College, 1859).

Gentlemen of the Law Class:

The subject to which we invite your attention is the science of Municipal Law. This science, although special in its character, has relations to law in general, and cannot be comprehensively studied without tracing those relations or connections. Most writers upon special subjects of Jurisprudence, as, for example, Blackstone in his commentaries upon our Municipal Law, or Hooker in his "Ecclesiastical Polity of England," introduce their theme to the reader by a general disquisition upon law in the abstract—upon the divine law as revealed in the Bible, upon the law of nature and of reason—and thus deduce their own topic from the wider principle. Hooker, by a bold personification, represents all nature as actually rendering a voluntary and a glad devotion to the Supreme Lawgiver, as it yields an unswerving obedience to appointed laws. "What if," says he, "nature should leave for a while the observation of her own laws; if the frame of that heavenly arch erected over our heads should *loosen, and dissolve itself*; if celestial spheres should forget their wonted motions, and turn themselves any way, as it might happen; if the prince of the lights of Heaven, which now as a giant doth run his unwearied course, should through a languishing faintness begin to stand and to rest himself; if the moon should wander from her beaten way, the winds breathe out their last gasp, and the clouds yield no rain—if all this present joyous obedience of nature should be intermitted, what would become of man himself," &c. He then proceeds to speak of the law of reason, of the law of nations and of civil society, until he comes by easy gradations to his immediate subject.

Such a view would carry us too far from the theme immediately before us, and, while we recognize the connection thus indicated, we will at once apply ourselves to our own municipal law.

By one, the term law is briefly defined to be "a rule of action"; by another, it is said, "that which doth assign to each thing the kind of work, that which doth moderate the force and power, that which appoints the form and measure of working, we call law."[1]

By municipal law we mean the rule that governs us in our civil conduct, under the fundamental law of the State. This is divided into common and statute law; the first rests upon general usage as its basis, and is *ascertained* by judicial decision; the other is directly originated by the Legislature.

I shall not attempt on this occasion to give a detailed account of the principles of our Municipal law. In the short hour allotted to me, I could present but a barren outline of its provisions. I shall have accomplished my purpose, if I sketch its origin, some of its vital, distinctive principles, the mode of its growth, and its present condition.

It is to be stated at the outset that Americans did not lay the foundations of American Jurisprudence. These were built by other hands. Our forefathers found the common law complete in its essential parts. They adopted it without shrewd inquiry into its origin. They even claimed it as an indefeasible right under the sacred law of descent. Whether induced to leave their homes by persecution, or allured by the persuasive voice of ambition, or charmed by the prospects of immediate wealth—whether they came with their fortunes or destitute of means—whatever else they brought with them, or whatever they abandoned, they claimed the law of England as their own; as part of their own persons; as inhering essentially in the very notion of their property. The very term was, doubtless, dear to them. It was the *common* law. It was like the common sun that lighted them, the common air they breathed. They no more thought of criticising or questioning the legitimacy of the one than of the other. Here, without class distinctions, it sheltered the evil and the good. It had in part originated in the forest; it protected the hardy sons of our forest, expanded with their growth, and still continued to govern them as their once uncultivated wastes were organized into States and blossomed with imperial cities.

The Roman law, which is the basis of the legal codes of Continental Europe, had been termed the *civil* law. It treated the individual as an incident to the State, and regarded him in the main as a citizen. To it we owe our city corporations, and our now sacred right of local self-government. The common law, however, regards the person more strictly in his individual nature, and bears proudly on its front personal freedom, considering the State as the means for individual protection and development. The flame of liberty which we can perceive, through the vistas of history, gleaming from the morasses of the German forests, was carried to England, where it burned with a purer light. No rude blast was allowed to quench its virgin fire. The early Englishmen covered it, while it kindled, with their shields, till Magna Charta, in every line, grew ruddy with its glow.

The exact source of the common law no one can trace. It was formed at the confluence of many separate streams. Undoubtedly the Roman law contributed largely to its formation. Mr. Spence has shown this at large, and with elaborate research, in his work called "the Equitable Jurisdiction of the Court of Chancery."[2]

The Anglo-Saxons contributed invaluable results; above all, in the respect for personal freedom, and in the love of order, and perhaps in a rudimentary trial by jury. It may be that relics of the old Briton law may remain,[3] though Gibbon's remark is unquestionably true, "that before the irruption of the Saxons, England had been moulded into the elegant and servile form of a Roman province," while some of Rome's greatest jurists sat there in the seat of judgment. With other points of resemblance between the development of England and the United States, they are strikingly alike in this respect, viz.: that each is a composite nation. In the beginning, England was a prize for the valiant; in later times, an asylum for the persecuted and the outcast. "All such have crossed the sea, and made the great island their country. Thus England has thriven on misfortunes, and grown great out of ruins." These various races who have struggled there for the mastery, or have resorted thither as a refuge, have had a powerful effect on the development of the law. Like the composition of forces in mechanics, the combination of the contending powers has contributed to a resultant force in a new direction.

Thus, while we may admit that the English law incorporated into itself many of the doctrines of the civil jurisprudence of Rome, and while it may have no claim to compare with that splendid code for scientific precision, breadth and comprehensiveness of view, and while the English language may not express legal formulæ with the rigorous accuracy of the Latin tongue, yet we may with pride remember that this plain common law contained within itself, that potential and vital element so lamentably deficient in the former—legal protection for individual freedom. "The political law of Rome is moulded," says one, "in its later forms in an oriental seraglio, and was fit only for a debased and servile population."

Although the early English law writer, Bracton, copied in his treatise that courtly and submissive maxim of the Roman code, "what pleases the prince has the force of law,"[4] it did not become an admitted principle in jurisprudence. This exotic could not be made to flourish upon British soil.

The true theory of trial by jury is peculiar to the common law. This mode of trial was not created by the great charter, but was secured by it. It was so well known then as to be described by mere formulary words. The freeman was not to forfeit his life, liberty, or property, except by the judgment of his peers, and by the *law of the land.*[5] Though the Roman law recognized the selection of a body of men to whom legal questions might be submitted, somewhat analogous to a jury, yet it did not make the grand and capital distinction which has preserved our theory so long, and has incorporated it so fully into the fundamental law of our States, that a criminal on trial cannot dispense with its full number, even if he will. The select body, in the Roman procedure, in its later development, pronounced both the law and the fact.[6] They ultimately needed assistants, or assessors who knew the law. These associates were usually wily and subtle men, who were conversant with the intricacies of jurisprudence. They gradually elbowed out their unlearned companions, until all the questions were decided by a body of judges who had no sympathy with the people at large. The law became more scientific, but the arbitrary maxims borrowed from the Roman codes were thus introduced into the laws of most of the nations of Continental Europe. In France, justice became not a duty, but an inheritance. The right of judicature was used as a means of personal gratification. The bar, as Stephen tell us, "formed not a *profession,* but a *caste;* a distinct noblesse, in favor of aristocratic rights, and the rights of the King. The aristocracy of the robe had no alliance with the democracy of the jury box."[7]

But with the great and distinctive idea of English jurisprudence, that the Jury are to take the law from the court, it cannot disappear from our tribunals. Nor ought it to fall into disuse; for, aside from the protection furnished to the individua1, its value as a means of education to the people at large cannot be overestimated. The humblest citizen is taught to think, to analyze, to compare evidence; while, if he be at all thoughtful, he cannot fail to perceive that a new dignity is conferred upon him, as he wields one of the greatest powers exercised by the Supreme Being over man—the power of judging of his acts. Although this principle has been grafted on to the law of some of the countries governed by the civil code, it has seemed to grow like a scion on an alien stock.[8]*

So, too, the bold maxim, that "Every man's house is his castle," though evidently the product of an age when private wars were in vogue, and men defended themselves by their own arm, breathes the free spirit of the forest and the fastness. It is not the polished phrase of a Cicero or Hortensius, nor can its equivalent be found in the pages of any Roman jurist. The Roman lawyer Gaius says a man's house is his *refuge.* So is the sheepfold for the lamb; but what cares the wolf for that when he enters. The common law declares that a man's house is his *fortress,* which he may defend against all assailants, even the chief magistrate himself; unless the intruder comes armed with a legal mandate in a proper case. I barely notice those delicate theories of the common and statute law, in regard to personal security and personal liberty, so delicate that the most sensitive lady could not wall herself around with a protection more complete than the law itself furnishes, as well as the theory that each individual who violates the rights of others is personally responsible, and cannot shield himself by proving the mandate of a superior officer. In these respects our law may claim a proud pre-eminence, as long as man is of more consequence than the property which he possesses.

In fine, speaking in general terms, but two systems of civil jurisprudence have challenged the attention of the world: the civil law of Rome and the common law of England. The first drew the most refined and philosophical distinctions in regard to property. The more it is studied, the more its truly symmetrical and majestic proportions strike the beholder with astonishment. Its penal code was in many respects equitable, but in the matter of personal rights it had yielded to absolutism. It was like an accomplished gentleman, who had every grace except that he lacked independence and personal freedom. The common law, on the other hand, was in many respects rude and unphilosophical; it was, in its early forms technical to the last degree; its discussions were often puerile, and its solutions worthless, but it had in most vigorous life precisely that element which the other system lacked. It was not ashamed to borrow of the civil code many of its best provisions, for it had vigor enough to assimilate them, and incorporate them into its own growth. It was the rude man of the country, capable, by contact with civilization, of receiving the highest polish, and it was free. The one has aided to produce continental Europe, the other, England and the United States.

In the next place the English law has a history parallel with English progress. The great epochs in the history of the nation are eras in the history of constitutional and municipal law. These two are so closely connected together, that it is almost impossible to separate them. When William the Norman, in the year 1066, conquered, or, as Sir William Blackstone in more polished terms expresses it, acquired England, he with rough hand repressed the murmurs of a discontented people, and laid upon them all the heavy burdens of the feudal system. After him England had its rulers who legalized oppression, and systematized rapine. So far had this gone, that in Stephen's reign men openly inveighed against Providence, crying aloud that "Christ and his saints were asleep."

The great progress of England has consisted in protecting the person, and in shaking off the fetters from the law of her landed property. I do not mean that she has abandoned feudal theories, for these are so entwined with the growth of the law, that to pluck them out would be to root up the law itself; but I speak of the feudal clogs on transfer, the exactions and tyrannous burdens of the system. Even her wars have been but of little consequence, except so far as they have effected legal and constitutional alterations. The sea-girt isle has always been too firmly anchored to feel sensibly any shock from without. The surface of English society has not been disturbed by exterior storms, but by internal volcanic eruptions. Their wars, when not civil, have been fought on foreign soil. Her citizens may have been allured by the visions of glory, but they have not been compelled to summon all their energies for the exercise of the sacred right of self-defense. If you ask them where are the events of interest in their national life, they do not point to Agincourt or Blenheim, or even to Waterloo, but to Magna Charta, the Petition of Rights, the Habeas Corpus Act, and the Bill of Rights. Magna Charta itself contains provisions of a strictly legal nature—such as the one which secures a widow's right of dower with her quarantine. The members of the bar and the judges sprang from the people, and by means of the jury were always in contact with them. In fact, the bar formed one of the ties by which the middle and lower classes were bound up with the aristocracy. Many of the Chief Justices, like Lord Chief Justice Hale, had the advantage of being born in the middle ranks of life, of receiving a liberal education, and of being obliged to depend on their own exertions for distinction. Those who were descended from the aristocratic classes were almost all younger sons of younger brothers, and had their fortunes to make and their fame to achieve. They sympathized with the progress of society. When the legislature endeavored to establish entailed estates, the judges by a pious fraud defeated them; when a further attempt was made to introduce perpetuities, under the subtle doctrine of contingent uses, Lord Bacon, in his character of lawyer, suggested the general principles of that happy medium, by which estates can be locked up in families for a well-ascertained, and limited period. When Charles the First needed to be checked in the undue exercise of his prerogative, "our great master," Lord Coke, framed and carried the "petition of right" with such lawyers as Selden and Pym to advocate it. When the old writ of Habeas Corpus, which sprang out of Magna Charta, needed to be fortified and strengthened by new provisions and penalties, Shaftesbury, once Lord Chancellor, promoted it. When the House of Stuart was driven from the throne and the English constitution was to be secured for all time, the draft of the substance of the great state paper of that period made the name of the distinguished lawyer, Somers, immortal. To a prominent member of that profession, Sir S. Romilly, it was left to suggest the principles of reforms in the criminal law, while the recent great changes in the administration of the civil code have been fostered by such men as Lords Brougham, Campbell and others, although due credit should be given to the philosopher Bentham, for the suggestion of fruitful ideas. It is true, that leading lawyers have opposed many of these changes, and that others, not lawyers, have been greatly instrumental in the introduction of some or all of them. I do not deny that, in the progress of the law, individual members of the bar have been oppressive and unjust, and that bad monarchs have found among them pliant, expert and unprincipled servants. Still it is also true that, in every crisis where a bold patriot and statesman from their body was needed, he could readily be found. In no one instance, as in France before the Revolution, have the whole profession abandoned the people.

The influence of the legal profession can also be traced in the cautious and conservative character of all the changes in the common law. From the earliest state paper down to the latest, the plan of the patriot lawyers has been, to retain, so far as practicable, the old; to add, by way of amendment, the new. In the same spirit was our own United States Constitution formed. When the old Confederation was found to be illogical in principle, and utterly inefficient in action, it was not resolved to discard it, but only to form a *more perfect* Union—to *establish* justice—to *insure* domestic tranquillity. There have been more elegantly devised schemes of government, both in this country and abroad, than either of these constitutions—logically faultless—beautiful in their mechanism—their only possible defect was, that, when an effort was made to put them in motion, they would not go. On the other hand, the English constitution, largely framed by lawyers, full of contradictions and absurd legal fictions, has been practical and effective, and in its development has made rich and free one of the greatest nations of the earth.

This historical progress of the law is important in another point of view—it greatly complicates its study. There is a large class of questions in the English law which ought to have no place in a truly philosophical system of jurisprudence. These may in general terms be called questions of *forum—the* inquiry is not what a person's rights are, but where they must be enforced. So that rights which are denied in one court are granted in another. The Roman theories of jurisprudence admitted no such view. Her law, in its full development, was as comprehensive as her empire. When she had conquered a nation, she annexed it, incorporated it, assimilated it, while important legal questions arose which could only be settled by a true philosophy.[9]

Although, down to the destruction of the empire, there was a distinction between cases of ordinary and extraordinary jurisdiction, analogous to our distinction between law and equity, they were both examined by the same judicial officer. Great Britain was insular and isolated. If she had gained territory, she would have governed it as a mere dependency, and would have applied to the colonists the narrow rules of the common law. She had no great legal questions with which to deal in the early periods of her history. Her courts were created by accident, or gained jurisdiction by quarreling for it, or by filching it under the guise of some subtle legal fiction. The higher clergy had the care of testaments, and of the administration of estates, and the court of admiralty of certain questions arising at sea.[10]

The common law courts dealt with crimes, personal actions, and questions in regard to land, while their views in some respects were so narrow that the Court of Chancery was obliged to supply the defects in their administration of justice. The Court of Chancery grew out of the practice of appealing to the king's prerogative for redress in cases where the positive law was deficient. The king, being unable personally to decide the cases that sprang up, heard the cause in council or delegated the duty to his officer, the Chancellor, then always an ecclesiastic. The Chancellor, in the early history of the courts, proceeded without adherence to rule. He would direct the parties to go before arbitrators, or he would mediate between them himself; or he said to them that he would talk with some great man in regard to the case. Some of the early decrees are sufficiently singular. Thus in one case the court say, "Considering the honorable dealings of the plaintiff during her whole course of life, and of the good opinion had of her counsel, the Court thinks well of her title, notwithstanding the allegations and *proofs* to the contrary." It was emphatically a court *of good feeling.* A plaintiff had failed in his suit, and had been condemned to pay costs. The court say, "Considering that he is a poor boy, in very simple clothes, and under twelve years, the costs shall be remitted." The costs for dismissing a bill were as remarkable as any part of the case—only twenty shillings. As the Court advanced, although it disregarded form, and took for its guide general jurisprudence, and looked for substantial justice, it became bound down to a set of rules and was governed by precedents. These must now be studied as a science, and are not to be discovered, as many suppose, by the plain, common sense of a layman.

Many have supposed that this very division of remedies among separate courts has conduced to greater precision in the law, and that different rules can be adopted therein to meet the public convenience and promote real justice. Without enter-ing upon that question, it is only our purpose to show how much the labor of the student is increased. Nothing is more distressing to the learner in jurisprudence, in the outset, than the apparently conflicting views taken in the different Courts. In his common law books he finds it positively laid down that husband and wife are one, that they cannot sue each other—that they cannot contract together, and that all the wife's personal property belongs to the husband. Having treasured this up, he learns in his equity books, that they may be in that Court two closely contending litigants, pursuing each other with rancor, not necessarily veiled even under the forms of courtesy—that they may contract together in a proper case, and that the wife's *separate* property does *not* belong to her husband. In his common law books he learns that a mere finder of goods upon land has no lien upon them, even if he has rescued them from injury; in the Admiralty books he learns that a finding or saving at sea, or under the jurisdiction of that Court, is "highly meritorious," and that the salvor is carefully protected in his rights—so that, if he should save a sunken or abandoned boat, with its contents, in the Hudson River, where the tide ebbs and flows, he would have a lien upon the property, which would be recognized even in the common law courts; if above tide-water, he would have no lien on the goods, even though he had used the same exertion, and perhaps would receive no compensation at all, unless the act was done with the knowledge or consent of the owners. In studying the law in regard to wills, their proof and validity, he finds that a decision of the Surrogate (who represents the Ecclesiastical Courts of England in one branch of their jurisdiction), in regard to the validity of a will of *personal* estate, if not appealed from, or reheard in a limited period, is conclusive; but that, if the will includes both real and personal estate, so far as the real estate is concerned, an appeal from the Surrogate's decision is wholly unnecessary, and that for a long series of years the question may be raised anew in the common law courts; or, if the case has been appealed from the Surrogate to the highest Court on one branch of the property, and has been decided after the appeal, still he may bring a new suit in regard to the real estate, without any reference to the decision of the appellate Court. Thus it may happen that on the same will, and precisely the same state of facts, it may be decided that the testator is sane enough to make a will as far as his personal property is concerned; and that he is so insane that he *cannot* make the will when the real estate is considered. The only possible reason for this latter theory is the one given by Ch. Baron Yelverton, in the House of Lords,[11] that the cases are heard by different jurisdictions! The anomaly does not exist from the fault of the judges, for they have regarded it as an absurdity, and recommended its abolition, from Lord Hardwicke's time down to the present day.[12]

The importance, then, of studying the law historically cannot be too strongly inculcated. Some of the leading questions of our time have been fully illustrated only by the industry of those who have traced the whole course of legal history. For instance, the question, in what cases dispositions by will to charitable uses are valid, was thus carefully examined "in the Girard College case" by Mr. Binney, and the means furnished to the Court for a discussion of the true doctrine upon that involved and intricate subject. *Adhus sub judice lis est.* While, then, the student is mastering the present law, he must descend through all the strata of centuries, hammer in hand, till he comes to the hard granite of the feudal system. It would in general be useless to seek to get any lower, or to chip away much of its substance. He may look and pass on. In the secondary and other formations he will find many rare things of value, not merely fit to be laid away in the cabinets of the curious, but which can be polished and fitted for immediate use.

This historical examination may in part accompany, and in part succeed, the systematic study of the present law.[13]

It is another prime feature of the common law that it has not been the mere deduction of theorists, reasoning from certain admitted principles, but that it has been slowly worked out by actual experience, announced by the judges, and formed into binding precedents. The Anglo-Saxon mind cannot admit the idea that a judge may originate law. He can only *pronounce* it, and that after argument, and when the precise point is involved. Everything else is a dictum—a mere saying—a bright scintillation, perhaps, from the judicial mind, but expiring with the occasion which gave it birth. Thus, in developing the law, sharp contests have arisen over tangible facts. Judicial discussions have been animated by the fierce passions of the parties to the suit. The questions of slander have not grown out of hypothetical cases, but have been actual charges, envenomed by party rancor or personal enmity. The ejectment suits were not mere mooted questions, but arose when the true owners had been turned out of possession with the strong hand. Here, under color of judicial decision, have been great battles fought. Here have been struggles for wealth and power, and contests for the prizes of party ambition. All that talent, learning, subtle disquisition, and nice analysis could do, has been done. The lawyers have at times contended so desperately as to arouse the monarch's sceptre. Thus, the development of our law has been a great drama of centuries—a romance in its circumstances—a drama in its action.

As a general rule, where the government was not concerned, and in later times where it was, the judges perceived the excitement without sharing in the passion, and have had a solemn consciousness that they were elaborating rules for the use of future ages. A high English authority, Chief Baron Pollock,[14] has recently stated, from the bench, that he whom we only know as "the infamous judge Jeffries" was no bad judge when the rights of the king were not in question. Roger North, also, in his admirable life of Lord Keeper Guilford, tells us in what round terms and with what virtuous indignation the same judge berated from the bench the magistrates of the city of Bristol, for an evil practice into which they had fallen.[15]

It is remarkable with what slowness—intolerable slowness it would be in our time—the early judges proceeded to a decision on an important point—how they had it argued and re-argued—through how many appeals and re-arguments on each appeal the case went, how long they kept it under consideration, until they, perhaps, forgot the argument, while the interests of the client were lost sight of in their anxiety not to jeopard the integrity of the law. This theory, adopted from good motives, was a mistaken one, and was shorn of its defects at the opening of the career of Lord Mansfield. A well-known and competent authority, after an examination of all the evidence, is clearly of the opinion that Shakespeare was once a clerk in a lawyer's office. As this was during the period spoken of, if he copied all the papers, and waited on the arguments, he had good reason to know what was meant by "the law's delay."[16]

The great father of modern philosophy, profoundly versed in our jurisprudence, though disliking professional practice, adhered closely to precedent, directing Justice Hatton, when he was made Judge, to draw his learning out of his books, and not out of his brain. It would be interesting to trace how Lord Bacon's legal studies acted on his philosophical speculations, and how much his caution, in reaching conclusions in philosophy, depended on the care which he used in sifting evidence, and in weighing conclusions at the bar.

By the process the municipal law of England has gained a steady and fixed character. The principle, having been settled after the most exhaustive discussion, and the most careful examination, assumes the binding force of a precedent. Judges have sometimes struggled in a mental conflict between precedent and principle. Lord Mansfield used to say that he ought to be drawn placed between the two, like Garrick between Tragedy and Comedy. And yet this very Judge, in a great case, in which there was a difference of opinion on the bench, says, "This is the first instance of a final difference since I have been here—thirteen years. That unanimity could never have happened if we did not communicate our sentiments with great freedom; if we did not form out judgments without prepossessions; if we were not open to conviction, and ready to yield to each other's reasons." Although it is usual to account for this unanimity by stating that the master intellect of Lord Mansfield overshadowed the other judges, yet, wehen we consider their ability[17] and this declaration, it is fair to presume otherwise.

How different is this from the condition of parts of the Roman law. A distinguished jurist of our own country, Judge Story, has collected the opinions of the leading civilians on the subject of the conflict of laws. The wide and comprehensive research of the author has only displayed its uselessness, for, from the discordant views of the writers cited, scarcely any intelligible principle can be extracted. Instead of presenting us the conflict of laws, our ears are stunned by the conflict of opinions. Of course, large portions of that law are definite and certain, but the fact that, since its codification by Justinian, its progress as a system has been largely due to text writers, reasoning without an actual case discussed before them, while the progress of the common law has been mainly due to judicial decision, based on actual cases and discussions, forms a marked difference in the two theories of jurisprudence. Countries govered by the civil law have felt the difficulty of this theory. Spain resolved, in 1713, that it was a great inconvenience that her tribunals had followed foreign jurists and authors, to the depreciation of her own, and forbade the quoting of foreign opinions in antagonism to the views of Spanish jurists. What was this but establishing in an indirect way the rule of following precedents.[18]

When law is developed in the English mode, it is not theoretical—an object of speculation or criticism; it is practical, and becomes at once a rule of action. It will be generated slowly as cases arise, and may be submitted to the tests of experience. If it appears that a wrong step is taken, it can be retraced, and the mischief corrected before the vice has permeated the entire system. It is known that Lord Mansfield almost created our commercial law, and the law of insurance. It is a sagacious remark of Lord Campbell's, that when the former had to grapple with the great questions that came before him, instead of proceeding by legislation, and attempting to codify, he wisely thought it more according to the genius of English institutions to introduce improvements, gradually, by way of judicial decision, while, he not only settled the particular case, but established with precision, and on sound principles, a rule to be afterwards quoted and recognized as governing similar cases.

Doubtless, the judges have sometimes assumed the duty of the legislator, but even then judge-made law is better than text law. In this manner the common law has been accommodated to the advancing spirit of each age. This has been especially true in the law of personal property, contracts and commercial law. The spirit of the old scholastic philosophy had so pervaded the law of real estate that few organic changes could be made. The law of fixtures, however, is an instance of a modification made to meet the changing circumstances of the times, while a court of equity, "that rib," as Bentham says, "taken out of the side of the law in the dark ages," the younger, and in some respects the comelier sister, has so treated it, in the law of partnership and otherwise, as to meet the exigencies of an advancing trade and commerce.

If any new product or invention is introduced, the common law establishes rules in analogy to similar cases.[19] Thus, it attches itself to the railroad, and soon there are worked out bulky volumes on the common law in regard to railroads. It applies itself to the electric telegraph, and adds that subtle and incorporeal agent, electricity, the very Ariel of jurisprudence, to the list of common carriers, laying down the rules for its guidance in the transmission of messages.[20] In this manner the law is everywhere present, either active, or, if dormant, ready to spring into life when the occasion arises.

Side by side with the study of the history and principles of law, you are also to examine legislation and its history. The statute-making power has been, in modern times, continually on the alert, changing the rules of the common law, and adopting new provisions to meet the altered conditions of society. It will be necessary to examine the principles that guide the courts in the interpretation and construction of statutes, especially in the case of their conflict with the fundamental law of the State or of the United States. Legislation has a history which has also to be studied, for one statute cannot be understood without the examination of others on the same subject, and sometimes not without a more or less minute examination of the general history of legislation. The knowledge of this enacted law grows in importance every year.

In our own State, we have made great changes in the common law, especially regarding real estate, while, as every person knows, we have abolished the old forms of procedure. It may be remarked in passing, that by a singular coincidence we have gone through with the same process, in respect to pleadings, as the Romans. They had technical forms of actions; so had we. They had actions, analogous to our chancery suits. They consolidated the two, and proceeded without form. This we have done. In proceeding without form, they found, after a long experience, that it was necessary to pass a rule which we have not yet adopted. The Justinian code required that a case should not be in court more than three years. The reason given was, that suits were likely to outlast the life of man, and to become immortal. We may yet find it necessary to complete the parallel, by adopting a similar provision.

By constitutional provisions from the beginning, such parts of the common law and amendatory statutes as were in use during our colonial period, down to April, 1775, were adopted as the law of this State. Taking, as we did, an entire system of law from another country, it is surprising that it could be so readily adapted to our institutions. Whatever we found unsuited to our condition, we rejected, either by judicial decision or by legislation. Thus we discarded the English theory of the descent of land to the eldest son. So the theory of ancient lights or windows, if it ever had any solid foundation in the law, to the extent to which it was carried, was rejected or modified, so as to suit our circumstances. So we dealt with the ecclesiastical law, in regard to the effect of future promises to marry, and with some of the rules of law in regard to the dead. A branch of the latter doctrine has been recently shown, with elaborate research, to rest on false theories, fanciful etymologies, and in its details to be wholly alien to our most cherished sentiments, and was pronounced no part of our law.[21]

How readily will the conclusion be acquiesced in, when we learn that, in this last year, it was decided in the high Court of Criminal Appeal, in England,[22] that a son might, by the common law, be indicted and convicted of a misdemeanor, who openly, and in the light of day, removed from a dissenting burialground the remains of his own father, although he was prompted by the most filial sentiments, and although he had reason to believe that the trustees of the cemetery were about to devote the ground to secular purposes. The son had not asked the permission of the trustees. The judge, who pronounced the opinion, said, "the common law recognizes no property in the remains of the dead." He then gave a singular reason for his decision, stating that if the conviction were not sustained, there would be no mode of protecting the remains of deceased persons, interred in the burial-grounds of dissenters. As if the best way to protect them was not to decide that the sone had a property in the remains of a deceased parent. Be it said, to the honor of the Bench, that they exercised a humane discretion in inflicting only a nominal fine. Doctrines like these we ought to reject at once, wthout waiting for legislative action. They are the result of circumstances peculiar to English history, and ought to be regarded as no part of our law. It is evident, too, to any one, who watches the development of the law of the two nations, and the course of legislation, that their jurisprudence diverges from the common point more widely every year.

The common law is to be learned in a great variety of reports, and in some authoritative treatises. Among the good cases will be found many that are mistaken and worthless. They were either badly argued or miserably reported, or the "Judge mistook rapidity for the due administration of justice, and made decrees which ought to serve not as examples to be imitated, but as land-marks to be avoided by all future judges." Many of these cases have been explained, limited, criticised, or overruled in other decisions. They are declared counterfeit coin; but the inexperienced eye is in great danger of receiving them as genuine. Other cases have their authority diminished because a bare majority of the judges concurred in the decision, although, as it has been happily expressed by Justice Coleridge, late of the Queen's Bench, English judges, as a whole, "have had so much of general agreement as served to give authority to their judgments, with so much occasional difference as served to show their individual responsibility and independence." This crowd of volumes urges upon us a systematic study of the law. One must be guided by the principle rather than by the case. Even abolished law must be studied carefully, both because it governs all acts done while it was in force, and because it is often explanatory of what is introduced in its place. After Chancellor Kent had given in his commentaries an extended discussion of a legal rule known among lawyers as "the rule in Shelley's case," he appended a note to his text, in which he spoke in eloquent language of the fact that this rule was abolished by our Revised Statutes, and remarked that, so far as this State is concerned, all he had written is but a monument to the memory of departed learning. Yet, since that note was written, scores of cases have occurred in our courts, in which the abolished rule was examined, with its qualifications and limitations. Every real estate lawyer meets it, from time to time, in deducing a chain of title to land. The fact that it exists in full force in other States makes it necessary to know it. Changes in the law only complicate the lawyer's studies. He must be alike familiar with the old rule and the new. Janus-faced, he must look both forward and backward. Notwithstanding the vital alterations that have been made in the law of husband and wife, and the more comprehensive changes that are threatened, no competent lawyer supposes that a full knowledge of the old rules will not be necessary at least during this generation.

Thus, in free countries, like England and the United States, the studies of the ripest jurist are never at an end; rather, just beginning. A great German poet, if he had lived here, would not have made one of his well-known characters say that legal rights are transmitted from grandsire to grandson, like an hereditary disease.[23] They seem, sometimes, more like the fabrics of which the English poet speaks, "they rise like an exhalation."

We will be asked if all this complexity of laws be necessary? We reply, so long as the variety of human events is so great; while men seek wealth with energy, and compass sea and land to obtain it; while pride and vanity influence testators; while trust and confidence are reposed by man in his fellow; while fraud assumes its Protean shapes; while the family exists, and absolute rights are regarded, so long will jurisprudence be obliged to adapt itself to these important facts in all their details. The complexity and intricacy of legal principles, I do not say of legal forms, is the price we pay for our free, advancing and refined state of society—an intricacy only to grow more intricate, and a complexity to grow more complicated. Yet it is safe to say that he, who is thoroughly familiar with the fundamental principles of law, has the thread in his hand by which he can be guided through the labyrinth. The science of pure mathematics has its settled and determined principles, which can be mastered by patience and application; when these principles are applied to celestial mechanism and the perturbations of the planets, the problems which grow up need the intellect of a La Place and a Plana to compass them. The principles are few; the objects to which they can be applied are almost infinite. Yet, through all these complicated movements and action and reaction of matter, the master mind goes with certainty, sounding the abysses with his well-known principles, and carrying the torch of exploration steadily before him. The mechanism of the heavens is none the less scientific, because it is difficult in some cases to apply right principles in the examination of its intricacies. Yet how many regard jurisprudence, with the same difficulties to contend with, as having little claim to a scientific character! Goethe opens his great tragedy of Faust by introducing the future arch-magician in a rhapsody on the worthlessness of law and the sister sciences. He says:

> "I've now, alas! Philosophy,
> Medicine and Jurisprudence too,
> And, to my cost, Theology,
> With ardent labor studied through.
> And here I stand, with all my lore,
> Poor fool! no wiser than before;
> Master, ay, Doctor, styled indeed,
> Already these ten years I lead
> Up, down, across, and to and fro,
> My pupils by the nose, and learn
> That we, in truth, can nothing know."[24]

After more to the same purpose, and a determination to look into the very essence of things, and no more to busy himself with words, he abandons these sciences in despair, betakes himself to magic and kindred subjects, and ends, as was natural, in a close and altogether disagreeable intimacy with Mephistopheles.

There is a floating opinion somewhat similar to this in the minds of many, the more difficult to meet, because undefined, that the science of law is no science, but that it is mere hap-hazard and chance. If this be so, it is not due to the subject itself, but to the way in which it is administered. No science known among men is more strictly deductive than the science of a true Jurisprudence. If the conclusions arrived at be uncertain and unreliable, it is due to the bar who argue, or to the Judiciary who decide, the cases as they arise. If the charge be true against them, it only shows the necessity of a more thorough apprehension of legal principles. If the bar be ignorant, no amount of learning on the part of the Judiciary will save the science from the infusion of false principles; if the bar be highly educated and accomplished, they will, in a measure, elevate even an incompetent Judiciary. The argument only goes to show that, unless juries are honest and intelligent, judges thoroughly trained in their profession, and lawyers honorable, studious and learned, the conditions necessary to a scientific deduction from legal principles will not be found to exist.

It has been the good fortune of the English law that at no time, in its more modern history, have there been wanting great minds to aid in its development.[25]

We can almost trace the illustrious line, from father to son; the predecessor training, at all events, exercising a powerful influence over, his successors. Thus we see the chief justices mounting through every grade of their profession, to the attorney-generalship, and thence to the high seat of justice, which they do not abandon, except through infirmity or with their lives. Thoroughly familiar with every phase of legal practice, they bring all the multiform experience of the bar to a symmetrical result upon the bench. Having, previous to their elevation, practiced before men of the highest judicial cultivation, they became insensibly moulded after their pattern, so as to present a general likeness. "*Facies non omnibus una, nec diversa tamen.*" Said Lord Mansfield: "If I have had any success, it is owing to the great mind who presided in our highest court of judicature, the whole time I attended at the bar. It was impossible to attend him, to sit under him every day, without catching some beams of his light." In later days there has been a series of thorough jurists on the bench, so that even the side judges have been sometimes men of the most distinguished ability, as, for instance, Baron Parke, who has shed such a lustre upon the Court of Exchequer in our time, and whose name must be known to posterity as one of the ablest jurists of the age. To how many of these could Justice Buller's remark be applied—"that principles were explained and enlarged upon, until men were lost in amazement at the strength and the stretch of the human understanding?" In our own country, similar names can be mentioned of the illustrious dead, and of the no less illustrious living. Among the latter, without referring to any of our own citizens, I may be pardoned in alluding to an eminent judge, full of years and honors, who has achieved for the Supreme Judicial Court of Massachusetts what Baron Parke has accomplished for the Court of Exchequer in the mother country. Standing here, how could I forget one who once occupied the chair of jurisprudence in this venerable institution? It is not the least of its glories, to have numbered one of the principal authors of the Federalist among its students, and a great commentator on American law among its lecturers.

It is an interesting fact that in the development of this science, no jealousy or narrow-mindedness has been displayed by its expositors. The leading cases in our reports are cited in England with all the respect due to them, and not unfrequently influence the decision. The English Court of Exchequer recently abandoned a position previously taken by their own authorities, from a conviction of the unanswerable argument of one of our New York judges. Our own courts are quite in the habit of following recent English decisions in point, sometimes even without entire confidence in their soundness. This part of our subject may be fitly closed by the words of Hooker—"It is easier a great deal for men to be taught by law what they ought to do, than instructed how to judge as they should do of law; for the wisest are ready to acknowledge that soundly to judge of law is the weightiest thing a man can take upon him."

May we not hope that out of these various materials a code may arise, framed by profound lawyers, and submitted for suggestion and approval not to a despotic emperor, but to the best legal thinkers of an enlightened people; a code whose authors shall not assume to *originate* law, but are willing to perform the office of aggregation, selection and systematic arrangement, and who from the vast material will drop the overruled cases and will settle those that conflict; a code which shall include our personal rights, our domestic obligations, our rights of property, and, above all, those delicate rules of the criminal law, framed for the double purpose of protecting society and of preserving the rights of the prisoner; a code which, while no valuable line of the rugged common law is softened, and not a lot of its independence abated, is adorned with the jewels of the Roman law, and contains within itself all the best legal experience of the ages; a code which shall show the progress of judicial thought by a comprehensive sketch of the legal history of England and America, drawn by a master-hand. Thus, when the gold, the silver, the wood and the iron are gathered together, and the rubbish is burned, a fair and symmetrical temple may arise where Themis herself may sit and preside unseen, realizing in some measure the character given her by the ancients—the true daughter of heaven and earth.

But law is not to be understood merely as a *science*. It is also to be practiced as an *art*. The process of presenting a case to the judge and jury is very different from that of apprehending it when engaged in its study. You were then to be convinced yourself. You are now to convince others. You are to act the part of an expositor, of a teacher, with much suspicion as to the honesty of your motives. As far as you confine yourself to the truth, you combine those two points which are regarded in all other sciences as so difficult of combination—the character of an original thinker and investigator with that of an expositor. This exposition must often be made with all the clearness of expression and finish of rhetoric of which you are master; with coolness of judgment and versatility of action. You may have an antagonist sophistical in reasoning, ingenious m technicalities, and unscrupulous in the use of his advantages. You may have a judge prejudiced against you or your case, irritable in temper, discourteous in interruption, or impatient of argument. You may meet a jury incapable of appreciating your finespun reasoning, or even tampered with by the opposite party. The case which you had constructed, as you thought, so admirably, while in the seclusion of your office, falls to pieces under the batteries of your antagonist, or is blown away, like gossamer, and remorselessly by the judge. The cases on which you rested are overruled or doubted; they were decided in another State, and are not necessarily followed; or the law is good, but the judge thinks that they do not apply to the matter in hand; or the evidence on which you depended does not support your view of the cause. If the decision is rendered in your favor, you win it in the face of the most determined opposition. In the close hand-to-hand struggle at the bar you must have real muscle, flexibility of motion, and an unyielding will. You must anticipate sophisms, and kill them in the germ, and before they have time to grow. As was the test applied to the old knights in the days of chivalry, you can only prove your fitness for the work by parrying, though in the dark, all attacks, and meeting all surprises, from whatever quarter they may arise.

How shall such a profession, requiring for its successful practice such different qualities and training, be aquired? The full answer to this question is not altogether easy, and different minds may answer it in different modes. In general, this may be said, that, for the student, the acquisition of the principles of a science may safely precede its practice as an art. In the haste of office business, in the varied labors imposed upon a lawyer in full practice, in one of our large commercial cities, but little leisure will be found for the instruction of students. The carefully-drawn paper, which they are left to copy, is not understood. The work is done mechanically, and perhaps without more reflection than the press gives, which, in the opposite corner of the office, copies the letter unerringly for the employer. Let the student have gone over the principles of the science carefully and understandingly, with a full explanation of technical terms, and all the assistance and stimulus which a competent instructor can give, that, which before was dull and undesired, is then clothed with life and interest. On the other hand, the practice of gaining the whole of one's knowledge through the medium of copying and the details of office business, seems to invert the usual order of instruction used in the other sciences, and to place that first which ought to be placed last. Although some may have the power, from natural capacity, to rise to success through these difficulties, thousands drop by the way like untimely fruit, or lead only a sickly and a worthless life. It is certainly no argument in favor of a consumptive climate, that, though thousands may die, a few have lungs hardy enough to resist the malign influences of the atmosphere. The unhealthiness of any regimen is to be tested by the majority who die, and not by the minority who live.

This system seems to have been borrowed from England. Note what the poet Cowper says of it there. He was placed in an eminent solicitor's office, where by a legal fiction he was supposed to learn how actions were commenced and conducted, with the practice in law and equity. He says that he slept three years in the solicitor's house, but lived in the daytime in the society of the ladies, while he and a fellow student were employed in giggling and making others giggle instead of studying law. The legal knowledge thus gained is acquired by the process of insensible absorption. It is not unsafe to say that there are still in our country, though perhaps not in so busy a city as this, modes of studying law quite analogous. Some young men in England, of high purposes, in the last and one or two previous generations, perceiving the futility of this scheme, submitted themselves to the voluntary discipline of a special pleader's office, where, for a very large yearly fee, they received instruction. The well-known Mr. Tidd had four of his pupils sitting at one time in the House of Lords, as *Law Lords:* Lord Lyndhurst, Lord Denman, Lord Cottenham and Lord Campbell. The latter says: "To the unspeakable advantage of having been three years his pupil, I ascribe chiefly my success at the bar." Such coincidences as the above cannot be fortuitous.[26]

It is safe to say that the mass of young men, who engage in the study of law, commence their work with minds undisciplined to the nice distinctions and analysis required for its perfect mastery. It is also a growing complaint that the younger members of the profession are untrained in its principles, that they make the law a trade, a mere mechanical employment; that instead of being artists in their profession, they are content with being artisans. Perhaps we may yet have to carry out Lord Bacon's suggestion, that there should be a civil reprehension from the Bench of those advocates who bring to the case slight information, or are guilty of gross neglect, or who undertake an overbold defense. It is consolatory, however, to know that this class of men is not new to the profession, and that we are not so greatly degenerating. When old Lord Chancellor Hatton, some centuries ago, was addressing the bar on one occasion, he said: "I find that there are at the bar many unmeet young men, very raw and young men, negligent and careless, which truly, in my opinion, is a great sin and fault that we should commit our rights of goods and persons to such men."

It is unnecessary to say one word as to the evil inflicted upon the community by an ignorant bar. But it ought to be said that the leading members of the profession are themselves partly responsible for its existence. The standard of admission to practice has been placed too low. If, however, the recent rule of the Supreme Court is fully carried into effect, introduced, as I personally know, from the most praiseworthy motives, by one of the judges who longs for higher attainments among law students, and seconded, as it appears to have been, with earnestness by his brethren, much will be achieved. It introduces a new feature into many of our examinations, in that the student must be examined upon legal principles, and not merely upon practice.

It is at this point that law schools find their justification and found their claim to support. In my judgment, they ought, in this country, when fully organized, to combine both the gymnasium and the university. They should train the student and teach him how to study, and after the work is done, or while it is being done, communicate information on special topics by full courses of lectures. The period of study should be long enough to accomplish both results. The instruction should mainly be scientific; so far as it can at the same time be practical, it must be. While, on the one hand, a law school should not be a mere school of practice, on the other hand, it should not prepare its students to be mere lovers of the science of law. They should be lawyers, or, at least, their studies so shaped as not to give them a distaste for the practical side of the profession. It is our belief, then, that a mere system of lectures, which might, in a foreign country, be sufficient for a listener who had previously passed through a course of thorough preliminary study, is not applicable in a country where there is no path to the profession prescribed by law or public opinion, and where any adult male citizen, without such training, may claim its honors or degrade it by his unworthiness.[27]

We would not close this subject without stating our view, that at the foundation of all our law lies the doctrine of a true morality. The law, itself, is beneath all our constitutions, and without it no constitution is possible—at least, this law that the minority yield to the majority, with another equally important, that the majority hold their power only in trust for the general good. "Underneath our municipal law," says an old author, "is the law eternal, which ought to be always before our eyes, as being of principal force and moment to breed in human minds a dutiful estimation of all laws, because there can be no doubt that laws apparently good are copied out of the very tables of that high and everlasting law, not as if men did behold those tables, and accordingly frame those laws, but because it worketh in them, because it unfolds itself by them when the laws which they make are righteous." We are not exempted, as advocates, either, from the ethical rules which bind other men. On this point it is to be feared that the average public sentiment in the profession is too low. Men must not draw a nice distinction between *private* honor and *professional* honor. The one is as truly delicate as the other. Nor do we or the community feel sufficiently the close connection between the high character of the legal profession and the well-being of the State. The fact, that the laws are complete, is of no consequence, unless we have true men to administer them. The best laws, like machinery, are capable of having their power perverted. Law itself is inert; a mere abstract statement; as abstract as a mathematical proposition. It is but the major premiss of a syllogism. It is the advocate and judge who give it vitality and power. Both are ministers of justice. Each holds a high trust, to do no act which shall disturb the well-being of the Commonwealth. History and experience, alike, teach us that lawyers without principle may do unlimited harm. There have been those to whom Sallust's remark applied, that it was a great reward to them if they could only disturb those things which were previously quiet.[28]

Gentlemen of the Law Class, we invite you, then, to a course of study and of diligent labor. This science cannot be learned without study. We hope, however, to smooth the pathway to the subject, and to lighten, somewhat, the labors of the ascent. You may not reach the meaning of the principle at once. Be not discouraged, for, on a second perusal, or at some other time, it will become clear.

We would hope, in the language of Lord Coke, "that we may open some windows of the law, to let in more light to the student, by diligent search to see the secrets of the law, or to move him to doubt, and to enable him to inquire and to learn of the sages what the law, together with the true reason thereof, is, knowing, for certainty, that the law is unknown to him that knoweth not the reason thereof"—while we would extend to you, as a greeting, what he uttered as a farewell: "We wish unto you the gladsome light of jurisprudence, the loveliness of temperance, the stability of fortitude, and the solidity of justice."

NOTES

1. Hooker's Ecclesiastical Polity.

2. This point is still debated among law writers. If, however, any one will examine Bracton's very early work with care, comparing it closely with parallel passages in the Institutes of Justinian, he will be greatly impressed with the fact that the arrangement of subjects, collocation of passages, and the precise language of Justinian are reproduced by the later author. He will be almost persuaded that he is reading "The Institutes." How Lord Campbell (Lives of the Ch. Justices, vol. I., p. 63) can say that Bracton uses the civil law only for *illustration*, I cannot conceive. Although he was a civilian, yet he does not write as though his statements were new, but propounds them as accepted rules. However, Cooper, in his work on "The Public Records," vol. II., p. 401, says, that there are two distinct recensions of Bracton, in *one of which* many of the passages borrowed from the civil law do not appear. "The laws of all nations are, doubtless, raised out of the ashes of the civil law," per Lord Holt, 12 Mod. R., 482.

Still, it is fair to say, that the Germans, Anglo-Saxons and the English, in succession, have, in many instances, shown a spirit of hostility to the Roman law. Florus states, that when the Roman commander, Varus, had the control of the German provinces, he endeavored to govern barbarians by the civil law, which they regarded as harsher than his arms. And while he was citing them before his tribunals, they attacked his court and destroyed his legions. Having taken one of the lawyers a prisoner, after cutting out his tongue they sewed up his mouth, crying, "Now, viper, cease to hiss"—*vipera sibilare desiste.* Book IV., cap. 12.

When the Saxons first attacked England, they, like the other barbarians, had a great aversion to towns, and suffered those who were engaged in trade to carry on their employment undisturbed. In the country, however, they appear to have seized the whole of the land, and to have driven the former owners into exile, or to have reduced them into slavery. Their complete subjugation of the natives appears from the fact, that their *laws are written in their own language.* (See *Spence's Origin of Laws.*) Every reader of English history will remember that, after the Norman conquest, the people continually demanded the restoration of the old Anglo-Saxon laws. This feeling may have been carried too far, in some respects. See Bell's Commentaries, 1, 11. "That dread of the arbitrary maxims of the civil law, which has been the distinction and the boast of England, has perhaps produced a bad effect in matters of municipal regulation, though of invaluable benefit in the formation of the constitution."

3. "Questionless, the Saxons made a mixture of the British customs with their own."—*Selden's notes to Fortescue, de Laudibus legum Angliæ,* chap. 17.

4. Book 3d of Actions, chap. 9. Although Bracton admits this maxim, yet in a fine passage in the same connection he indicates the principles which ought to govern the conduct of the King. "The King ought," he says, "to exercise the power of law (which is the power of God), as if he were the vicar and minister of God on earth; the power of doing wrong belongs to the Devil, and not to God. Therefore, while he acts justly, he is the vicar of the Eternal King; but, when he turns aside to do wrong, he is the minister of the Devil. Nothing is so appropriate to imperial authority as to rule according to law, and to submit to the law is greater than it is to govern. He should pay a proper respect to the law, for it is that alone which made him King. He is no King whose will rules and not law. Let him be just as well as merciful, and let his eyes so precede his footsteps that his judgment shall not vacillate from want of knowledge, or his merciful nature be deceived from want of circumspection," &c., &c. The whole section is worthy of perusal. Still he furnishes no remedy for the King's wrong acts, for he says in another place, "As, however, no writ can be directed to him, his subjects can only petition that he will correct and change his evil course, which if he will not do, it is sufficient punishment that he will hereafter meet the Lord as his judge. Let no one presume to dispute his acts, much less to oppose him."

[Although Bracton, according to Lord Coke, lived when Magna Charta was granted, yet it is not much dwelt upon or recommended by him. Barrington on Statutes, p. 1. His work was published between 1262-7].

Fortescue, in his book "De Laudibus legum Angliæ," written in the reign of Henry VI. (1463), a book replete with noble thoughts, repudiated the civil law doctrine. In his assumed conversation with Prince Edward, he says, "Let it not trouble you, most noble prince, to know whether it is best for you to study the civil or common law, for the King of England *cannot* change or alter the laws of his nation at his pleasure. For he governeth his people by power not only royal, but also *politique.* The civil law says, what pleases the prince has the force of law. But this much differs from your power, for the people are ruled by such laws as they themselves desire. Rejoice, therefore, O Sovereign, and be glad that the law of the land is such." Old translation. He represents that many of the former kings of England were continually annoyed because they could not introduce this slavish principle into the English law. This view is confirmed by the existing formula of assent to a law passed by parilament—"le roi le vent."

5. I am aware that some writers explain these words differently. Mr. Hallam and Mr. Reeves are of opinion that the words "law of the land" refer to trial by combat or ordeal, while Mr. Forsyth, History of Trial by Jury, pages 108-12, insists that the words "judgment of his peers" do not refer to trial by jury. His main argument rests upon the use of the word *judgment.* He urges that the verdict of the jury cannot be called a *judgment,* and believes that the words refer to trial in county and manor courts. It seems incredible that the *barons* of *England* should have made this great State paper hinge on trial in manorial courts and on the law of combat and ordeal! Technical legal rules may be pressed too far in interpreting national documents. Trial by jury was originally a trial by witnesses from the vicinage, who informed the judge of what they themselves knew. It seems

probable that, while they relied mainly on their own knowledge, they also heard the statements of others. In the progress of jurisprudence, they were required to decide only on what was laid before them as evidence.

6. Savigny, History of Roman Law, vol. I., ch. 4. While admitting the above proposition, in regard to the jurisprudence of the middle ages, he regards the earlier Roman practice as quite similar to our own. In this he appears to have been mistaken. The Roman judex or juryman did not render a verdict for the court to act upon, but gave the *judgment.* This is a very important distinction, for, under this rule, the functions of the juryman were in the same danger of being absorbed by the judge, as in the middle ages.

7. Fortescue says, "that no other nation of the time could have a jury because of their condition. England had much pasture land and great numbers of cattle: in other countries men were mainly devoted to tilling the ground, which rural exercise engendereth rudeness of wit and mind." "England is so filled with landed men that a 'thorp' cannot be found so small where dwelleth not a Knight, or an Esquire, or a Franklein, or other freeholder, while there are many yeomen of substantial means to form a jury. In other countries the noblemen have small store of pasture and live far apart; so, as these cannot be assembled, the jury must be made up of poor men who are not ashamed of infamy, or are so blinded with rustic and brute rudeness as not to be able to behold the clear brightness of the truth." De Laudibus, 65, 69. His description of the England of his day is very attractive.

8. From 1791, when trial by jury was introduced into France, to 1848, the law concerning juries was changed no less than twelve times! Edinburgh Review, October, 1858. The author of the able article referred to favors the introduction into Scotland, in criminal cases, of our principle of an unanimous jury. See Forsyth, "Trial by Jury," for a full account of the European nations which have introduced the system, and the partial success which has attended its introduction. In Buckle's History of Civilization, chap. 9, are some very good remarks on the difference between individual development in England and in France, although, in pursuit of a favorite theory he does not give sufficient prominence to the Anglo-Saxon element in English character, nor to the training acquired by those who participate in jury trials.

9. "Rome, in her colonies, continually reproduced herself; every colony was but an image of the mother city, with like holy rites, like courts, like laws, temples and places of public commerce."—*Selden.* The early forms of the Roman law were rery technical. As the republic expanded its limits it became necessary to liberalize her jurisprudence. Savigny gives an account of the conflict between the old jurists, who strove to preserve the fixed forms of procedure, and the judges who wished to introduce broader principles to meet the exigencies of the case. The author shows, in a truly philosophical spirit, how all law must be treated as an index of a nation's development, and that the progress of legislation is not governed by chance, but is the expression of the very life of a people.

10. The jurisdiction of these courts is said to have been obtained by encroachment.

"The common law had cognizance in Edward First's time of things done upon the sea; however, afterwards it kept its limits within the body of the county, leaving the sea to the Admiralty." Selden's notes to Fortescue, chap. 32. He cites to the point of jurisdiction of the common law courts, a case in 25th year of Edward First's reign (fol. 82), with several other cases.

"The cognizance of wills and testaments does not belong by common right to the ecclesiastical courts, but to the temporal or civil jurisdiction, yet by the custom of England it pertains to the ecclesiastical judges." Hale's History of Common Law, p. 28. The jurisdiction was settled in Bracton's time. He says: "Si de testamento or latur contentlo, in *foro ecclesiastico* debet placitum terminari, quia de causa testamentariâ (sicut nec de causa matrimoniali) curia regia se non de causa intromittit." Book 2, p. 61. It is even recognized at an earlier period by Glanville. There is reason to believe with Dwarris (on Statutes, p. 759), that the jurisdiction of the ecclesiastical courts was not strictly usurped, but grew out of positive enactments by William the Conqueror. Bentham, vol. 2, p. 179, states forcibly the complexity of English procedure.

11. Ridgeway, P.C., 277.

12. Atkins' R., 379. There are some early decisions on this point in Coke's Reports. In King James First's reign, an effort was made to induce the Courts of ordinary jurisdiction to *prohibit* the ecclesiastical judge from hearing the case, on the ground that his decision might influence a jury, when the cause came before them. Commissioners appointed in the time of the Commonwealth recommended the abolition of this branch of the jurisdiction of the Ecclesiastical Courts.

13. The Roman code recognizes the necessity of an historical study of the previous law. Says Gaius, in a passage quoted: "Being about to interpret the laws, I must go back to the very origin of the city, not because I wish to make my commentaries verbose, but because I observe that I can only thus make my work symmetrical. For, if it is a shameful thing for an advocate to argue a cause before a judge, without making a preliminary statement of the facts, how much more disgraceful it is for one who pretends to interpret the law, to undertake the task without an historical examination of it, coming to the subject, as it were, with unwashed hands."

14. 36 English Law and Equity Reports, p. 526.

15. The mayor and aldermen of Bristol had become "judicial kidnappers of small rogues and vagabonds, whom they sent to America and sold." Jeffries appears to have treated these dignitaries with great severity. North, who was no friend to him, says, "that he delighted in such fair opportunities to rant." See a graphic account of the incident in North's Lives, vol. 2, p. 24-27.

16. This delay is not peculiar to English jurisprudence. (See *Fortescue de Laudibus,* 127.) He says: "While I was lately abiding in Paris, mine host showed me his process in writing, which, in the Court of Parliament, he has followed eight years, to recover eight pence sterling, and he was in no hope to obtain judgment in eight years more. I also knew other cases like unto these."—*Old Translation.*

17. 2 Campbell's Ch. Justices, p. 395.

18. See 17 Martin, Louisiana Rep., 583. As to the similar condition of the Roman law before the Justinian Code, see Savigny's

History of Roman Jurisprudence, vol. 1, page 8. He says: "The great Roman jurists entertained, on many subjects, very different opinions, and who possessed the power of reconciling these difference *by a judgment of higher authority?* The decision of lawsuits must have been exceedingly difficult, or unsteady and arbitrary. The Emporer Valentinian regulated the matter in the West by an imperial decree; the principle was afterwards adopted in the East by the Theodosian Code. By the rule then adopted, no treatises were to be cited except those of five jurists, who were named, viz.: Ulpian, Papinian, Paulus, Caius and Modestinus." A code is almost a necessary refuge where law is developed by mere thinkers; the idea of an *authoritative* exposition of principles must be carried out either by judicial decision or by legislation. The present very loose practice of reporting cases, both in this country and in England, threatens to introduce into the expositions of the common law the same vice of *uncertainty*. If reporting is not regulated by legislation, we shall be driven to a code.

19. This theory is as old as the law itself. Says Bracton, "If any new and unusual case arises, such an one as has not before arisen in the Kingdom, let it be adjudged according to analogous cases, if any exist, for it is good to proceed a similibus ad similia." Chap. 2.

20. 33 English Law and Equity Reports, p. 180.

21. See Report of Hon. S. B. Ruggles, 4 Bradford's Surrogate's Reports, 503.

22. 40 E. L. E., 581, Regina *vs.* Sharp.

23. "Es erben sich Gesetz und Rechte
Wie eine ew'ge Krankheit fort
Sie schleppen von Geschlecht sich zum Geschlechte
Und rücken sacht von Ort zu Ort."—*Goethe's Faust.*

24. Swanwick's Translation.

25. In the early history of England we find it said that foolish and unlearned persons ascended the seat of judgment before they had learned law. The old writer before quoted utters a solemn note of warning to this class of judges: "Let no silly and unlearned person dare to ascend the seat of judgment, which is like the throne of God, lest he shall put light for darkness and darkness for light; lest, with untaught hand, after the manner of a madman, he strike the innocent with the sword, and free the guilty, and lest he fall from his lofty seat as from the height of heaven, like one who began to fly before his wings were fledged; and let every judge beware how, in making a perverse and illegal judgment, obtained from him by entreaty or money, he may prepare for himself, instead of a slight temporal advantage, the sadness of an eternal mourning." Bracton, book 1, chap. 2. It is very noteworthy how closely this writer connects, in a variety of passages, human law with the "law eternal."

26. A historical account of the modes of legal education adopted in England, and under the Roman law, may not prove uninteresting. The later Roman Emperors required a study of the law for five years, commencing with the Institutes of Justinian, while certain other portions of the code were assigned to be studied during each year. There were well-known law schools established at Rome, Constantinople and Berytus; the one at Berytus was particularly famous for several centuries. The Emperor required a yearly account of the behavior and progress of the law students, in order that he might know what persons to employ in his service. It cannot be supposed, however, that all the lawyers in the Roman empire were educated in these law schools. They may have been especially established, for the training of those who were needed in public employments. Salaries, in some instances, were paid from the imperial treasury. During the middle ages, with a single exception, the study of the law was closely connected with its practice. If jurisprudence was studied at the seminaries, it was as a branch of general education. No separate schools existed. The exception was the school at Ravenna, in Italy, in the eleventh century, which was probably removed thither from Rome, and was afterwards transferred to Bologna, where it became famous. Thus we have strong reason to believe, that the Roman School of the empire has exerted, by this removal, a marked influence over the legal education of modern times. The university at Bologna deserves special notice. It was originally a simple unincorporated law school, which, by the excellence of its instructions, attracted crowds of scholars. The Emperor Frederick I., in 1158, granted peculiar privileges to foreign students, and, among others, the right to be tried in civil and criminal matters by their professors, or by the bishop of the province. This rule was copied from the enactment of Justinian, governing the law school at Berytus. At this time the scholars elected their own professors. Afterwards, students in the department of theology and medicine came thither, and the institution assumed the form of an university, with a rector. The law professors were of two classes: ordinary and extraordinary. The former read lectures upon certain authoritative books, at which all the students were expected to be present; the latter class lectured upon other treatises, and attendance is supposed to have been optional. Besides the formal lectures, there were full expositions of particular texts in the law, and questions were discussed, which had been previously announced to the disputants. As the school at Ravenna, at least, was in operation at the time of the Norman conquest, and was transferred to Bologna not long after, it is altogether probable that the ecclesiastics introduced into England, with the Roman Jurisprudence, this mode of studying law. The legal profession apparently had an ecclesiastical origin. (See Pearce's Inns of Court, p. 14.)

The common law of England, however, as far back as the middle of the thirteenth century, was studied in the Inns of Court, in a quiet retreat, between the City of London and Westminster. These Inns of Court were four in number, with preparatory schools called Inns of Chancery. These bodies well illustrate the character of the early Englishmen. They were voluntary associations, and unincorporated. They granted degrees in Municipal Law, and the barrister went to the bar without any authority except that granted by the heads of the Inn to which he belonged; the Judges had a private visitatorial power over the authorities in each Inn, probably because they were the chief men in the law, but they could not require the society to add any person to their number unless they saw fit, while no one could become a barrister in any other way than by belonging to one of these Inns, not even by letters patent. These four Inns stood on an equality, so as to form a kind of university. The Inns of Chancery, as has been mentioned, were preparatory schools, in which were taught the grounds and principles of law. Such men as Coke and Holt delivered lectures, while "mootings" and viva voce exercises occupied the students and prepared them for practice. Fortescue gives a pleasing account of these schools in his time. He says that "the students resorted thither in great numbers, to be taught as in common schools. Here was a school of commendable qualities. Here they learn to sing and to exercise themselves in all kinds of harmony. On the working days they study law, on the holy days Scripture, and their demeanor is like the behavior of such as are coupled together in perfect amity. There is no place where are found so many students past childhood as here." The labor of preparing lectures grew irksome after a time: the readers of lectures, on their appointments, were expected to give costly entertainments to the students, and the lectures, as a consequence, ceased to be read. Every advancement in the degrees of the students themselves "was attended with a position at the cupboard (a very desirable station), or with a garnish of wine."

Some curious details are given, by the authors cited below, of the masquerades and revelings at these Inns. In time, the requisitions for the preliminary admission became merely nominal. The students were examined in the classics, not to see whether they were scholars, but "to ascertain how they had spent their time before coming to the Inn, and whether they had the manners of gentlemen." The requisites for admission to practice, after becoming a student, mainly consisted in having eaten a certain number of dinners, in each year, for a fixed number of years, in the common hall. Latterly there has been a disposition to revive some part of the old plan of instruction. The present course is, to give lectures in the Inns, while those students, who wish to obtain position at the bar, employ a special pleader to teach them, in addition, and they also attend the discussions in the moot courts. The Lord Chancellor of Ireland, in a paper read before the Society for the Advancement of Social Science, reported in the *London Jurist*, of October 22d, 1858, after strongly insisting on the necessity of a more thorough classical and legal training among the members of the bar, predicts that the Inns of Court will soon adopt some effectual plan for increasing the attainments of law students. On the Continent, law schools arose in the fourteenth century, being formed on the plan of the Bolognese School. In Ger-many, for instance, all who are intrusted with legal business must receive their instruction under regular law professors. For full details of the school at Bologna, see "Savigny's Geschichte des Römischen Rechts," vol. 1, chap. 6; vol. 3d, pages 152, 272, and for English system, see "Pearce's Inns of Court," "Herbert's do.," "Duhigg's King's Inns, "Fortescue de Laudibus," &c., &c., &c.

27. Since the above was written, I have been gratified to meet with the following passage in a work on the study of the Roman law, by Prof. Veyrieres, law professor in Paris—he says: "In studying the civil law, it is necessary to present to the pupil its history, in order to show the connection of the different rules. It is also necessary to give exact definitions, whose precision shall be equal to their clearness—without the aid of good definitions, logical divisions, and recapitulations, succinct but accurate, which are as it were a species of definitions, and superior to them, the lectures of the professor *(I speak from experience)* are but idle words thrown out to the wind, while nothing, or next to nothing, is retained by the hearers."

28. The Roman jurist Ulpian had a high idea of the true dignity of his profession. He says: "We are properly called priests—we worship justice, profess the knowledge of good and evil, separating the just from the unjust, discerning the lawful from the unlawful, and, unless I am mistaken, desire a true and not a false philosophy."

Chapter 24

Municipal Law: Lecture Notes

1861-1871

Theodore W. Dwight

Theodore Dwight (July 18, 1822-June 29, 1892) was founder and professor in the law school of Hamilton College, and was Professor and Warden of Columbia Law School, from 1858 to 1891. His lectures and influence are described in chapter 1. See also his inaugural address in chapter 23. These notes are transcribed from a manuscript in the Treasure Room of the Columbia University School of Law.

Book I

Chapter I. Definitions and General Remarks

Municipal law is a rule of civil conduct, prescribed by the supreme power in the State. The rule that the law must be prescribed is peculiarly applicable to statutes. The common law is from time to time announced by the judges, and by a legal fiction is presumed to have been already known, on the principle that the law is a science and that the new rule is but a deduction from that previously known. It is an inference from the doctrine that the law must be prescribed that it should not go into effect until time enough has elapsed for those who are governed by it to became acquainted with its provisions. This principle, however, has often been violated. By a fiction of English law, the whole session of Parliament was counted as a single day. The result was that an act which was innocent when committed, might become criminal by a statute passed subsequently during the session. This severe rule is now repudiated and never prevailed in this country. It is a rule in New York that a statute does not go into effect until twenty days after its passage, unless there is some direction to the contrary in the act itself. It is important in this connection to point out the difference between a retrospective and an ex post facto law. The term retrospective is a general one and applies to all statutes of laws, which affect past transactions. An ex post facto law is that peculiar kind of retrospective legislation, which bears more severely upon an alleged criminal than the law did at the time the act was committed, either by increasing his punishment, or by rendering conviction more easy, or by changing the kind of punishment. When the punishment is diminished, the law is not ex post facto, though it may be retrospective. *Ex post facto* laws are forbidden by the U. S. Constitution and consequently void. Laws that are simply retrospective are not necessarily void. They may be so when they violate the rights of property. Sometimes, they are justified. When the law has been duly promulgated, the plea of ignorance cannot be received as an excuse for its violation. In this way a person might be criminally liable, who had done an act, which he honestly believed he had a right to do. The last part of our definition refers to the supreme power of the state. By this is meant according to American ideas,—the people, in whom the Supreme power resides. A distinction is thus taken between society and the government. Society limits the government by a written constitution. If its provisions are transcendent by the legislature, the law may be declared void. There is no such rule as this in England, and the Courts can not declare an act of Parliament, invalid. In analysing a law, it is important to regard the remedies which it provides and sanctions. By the term remedies is meant the redress given to every individual, whose right is violated. It is a legal maxim that where there is a right, there is a remedy. The remedy consists at law in giving an injured party damages in compensation for his injury. This, however, is not the universal rule, for, in some instances the wrong doer is prevented from doing an injurious act by an injunction, or he may be compelled to perform an act specifically. The vindicatory branch of the law, on the other hand, is the remedy given to society for the wrong, supposed to be done to public order. It thus happens that this twofold proceeding may exist in regard to the same act. One may be called a civil and the other a criminal proceeding. Thus if A. were wrongfully beaten, the civil action would be A versus B, and the damages recovered would belong to A. The criminal proceeding would be "The People versus B, and the wrong-doer might in this proceeding be punished by imprisonment or fine. The fine in such a case would belong to the government and not to A.

Chap. II. The Origin and Source of Municipal Law

Municipal Law in reference to its origin may be divided into common and statute law. The great difference between the two is that one is announced by the judges in the course of adjudication upon litigated causes, while the other is enacted by the legislature.

The common law of each State, except Louisiana is based upon the common law of England. Louisiana follows the Roman law. Sometimes the common law is adopted by constitutional provisions as in New York State, where it is provided in the Constitution that the common law of England, so far as it was in use in the colonies until April 19th, 1775, (Battle of Lexington) and not modified by any statute shall be the law of the State. Other States simply adopted the common law by legislative enactment. The common law is said to depend for its origin in England upon custom. Such custom is either of a general character or special and particular. It is only necessary now to consider the general customs. It must not be supposed that these are oral and handed down by tradition, but they are to be sought in books of reports and standard treatises. The principal sources of the law are the reports of cases. Legal principles are evolved by means of causes or actions. There must have been an actual controversy and it must have been necessary to announce the principle in order to dispose of the controversy. It is important to notice the difference between the records of the court and the reports of cases. A record has been defined to be an authentic statement formerly contained in rolls of parchment, but now written on paper and preserved in the court which is hence called a Court of Record. In the rolls are contained the judgment of the court on each case, and all the other papers such as the pleadings, &c. The records, therefore, forms a history of the case. A report, on the other hand, presents the principles set forth by the decision. It should contain the name of the case, the name of the Court in which the case originated, the mode in which the case was presented for judgment whether by demurrer on motion for a new trial, or upon an appeal; a sufficient statement of the facts to show the basis of the decision, sometimes the arguments of counsel, the opinion of the Court, and the final result. It is the duty of the reporter to prepare an abstract of the points decided, which is prefixed to his report. This is called a reporter's syllabus or headnote. It is a general rule of law, subject to important exceptions, that when a case has been once decided, and another case arises involving the same principles, a like decision should be made. The law is thus, a series of precedents. It is however, necessary to discriminate between reports, some being of much higher value than others. The following tests may be employed to determine the value of a decision and of a report.

1. Inquire where the case was decided, whether upon solemn argument before a full court or by a single judge in the haste and excitement of a trial. Decisions of the former kind are said to be rendered in banc

or in banco, i.e., by full bench; the latter are termed nisi prius decisions. They are in general of but little value, though the high character of a particular judge sometimes gives them authority. Nisi prius decisions are more frequently reported in England than in this country.

2. The second inquiry should be, was the case fully and ably argued by counsel. The value of a decision depends greatly upon the thoroughness of the argument. The court often in the press of business, confines its investigations to the briefs provided by counsel, so that the decision will be of no higher value than the argument. Many cases are overruled for this reason as a later and more thorough discussion shows the weakness of the reasons, on which the former decisions were made.

3. Inquire what judge held the court when the decision was rendered. Some judges have attained so great a reputation that their decisions gain weight from their reputation.

4. It is of some importance to notice whether the opinion of the court is composed by a particular judge who attaches his name to it or whether it is simply an expression of general views of the whole bench collectively. The latter is called an opinion per curiam, i.e., by the court, and is not of as great authority in general as the other. The reason is that in one case, no particular man is responsible, while in the other case, since a particular judge attaches his name, he would take care in order to preserve his reputation to give the subject careful study.

5. It is important to consider the grade of the court, whether an inferior tribunal or the court of last resort. It is plain that the decisions of the Appellate Court should in general have greater weight than those of a subordinate tribunal from which appeals are taken. Thus in New York State, the decisions of the Court of Appeals would be of the highest authority.

6. Regard the merits of the report itself. Consider whether the facts are fully stated and the points properly digested. It has already been said that it is the duty of the reporter to prepare a syllabus or headnote to be prefixed to the case. Sometimes the preparation of this note requires great legal ability and the reporter may err both in a defective statement of the points decided and in omitting to set forth the whole of a decision. Another source of error in the older reports grew out of the fact that the judges gave their decisions orally and the reporter took down, as well as he could, notes of what was said, and as the art of shorthand writing was either not understood, or known imperfectly, the ground of the decision is often badly stated. One means of correcting this is to consult contemporaneous reports, wherever that is possible, and it not infrequently happens that the same case is reported by a number of different men. There is an old book of great value, which enables us to find the contemporaneous reports of the same case. This is called the "Reportorium

14. Theodore W. Dwight (1822-1892), professor at Hamilton and Columbia. Dwight refined the dictated monologue lecture to nearly unheralded extremes, and he oversaw the growth of the dominant U.S. law school of the decade following the Civil War. (*Courtesy of Columbia University School of Law.*)

Juridicum." It is also to be remarked that a distinction must be taken between what is decided by the Court, or what is said by way of argument or illustration. Remarks of this kind are called dicta, sometimes, obiter dicta, things said, or things said by the way. These are not regarded as authority. When a reporter wishes to refer to dicta in his headnote he employs the words "it seems," and in the old reports the corresponding word is Semble. When a reporter wishes to indicate the very point decided in the cause, he used the word "Held." It has been remarked that a decision usually has the force of a precedent. Still, many cases have been overruled as being wrongly decided and having no authority. A large number are collected in Greenleaf's Overruled Cases, and also in the various Digests. A late work on the subject is Bigelow's Overruled Cases. At the present day, decisions are not slavishly followed, but those are adopted, which accord with the general analogies of the law. There is a technical distinction taken between cases considered as authority and those which are regarded as arguments. The difference would be, that if the case were authority, it must be followed while if it were regarded merely as argument, it might be rejected, if not consistent with general principles of law. As a general rule, English decisions made before the Revolution are regarded as authority. Since that time they are not technically authoritative, but are cited by way of argument. So decisions of the higher court of the state are authoritative upon the inferior tribunal and if a lower court refuses deliberately to follow them, it is a case of judicial insubordination, and would deserve censure. Decisions in the courts of sister States are cited, as arguments, and they should only be followed, when they have intrinsic merit, and in a like manner the decisions of the Supreme Court of the United States are authoritative in all State Courts on questions involving the construction of the United States Constitution but the decisions of that same court on other questions, such as commercial questions are not binding on State courts. There are some points in respect to which the decisions of the U.S. Supreme Court and New York Court of Appeals are in direct conflict. Reports of decisions are extremely numerous and an acquaintance with them a matter of special knowledge. An accurate list of reporters to 1860, may be found in last edition of Bouvier's Law Dictionary under "Reports." There is also a book on the subject of reports known as "Wallace on Reporters." The English reporters may be conveniently classified into the old and the new. Series of the old reports, under this classification would close at the American Revolution. The old reports are now consulted only occasionally. Many of the decisions in them have become obsolete. The most venerable of them is the collection known as "Year Books." There is a difficulty in consulting these books, arising from fact that they are written in an obsolete language, Norman-French, and with abbreviations, which it is now difficult to explain. Still they are sometimes resorted to in England and America in new and difficult cases. See 22 N. Y., 355. The Year Books were prepared by reporters appointed and paid by the government, but during the reign of Henry VIII, this system fell into disuse, and any one might report, who saw fit. In this way many worthless reports were published. Besides the reports, treatises, digests and abridgments are often resorted to for legal information. These should be regarded, in most cases, as a means of consulting the reports. As a general rule, when the treatise and report conflict, the report is to be preferred. There are of course instances where the writer of the treatise discusses a case and shows it to be unsound. In that case, the view of a treatise writer would prevail, not because it was authority, but by reason of its intrinsic merit.

Chapter 25

Legal Education in the Late Nineteenth Century, Through the Eyes of Theodore Roosevelt

1993

Robert B. Charles

Robert B. Charles is an attorney serving as committee counsel for the U.S. House of Representatives. This article first appeared in 37 *American Journal of Legal History* 233 (1993).

Far better it is to dare mighty things, to win glorious triumphs, even though checkered by failure, than to take rank with those poor spirits who neither enjoy much nor suffer much, because they live in the gray twilight that knows not victory or defeat.[1] —*Theodore Roosevelt*

The discovery of Theodore Roosevelt's law school notes adds measurably to what we know about legal education in late nineteenth century America. It also answers an historical question which has remained open for more than a century, whether Theodore Roosevelt ("TR") was, in fact, a trained lawyer.

I. Background: Legal Education in The Late Nineteenth Century

Between 1850 and 1900, America was swept into a wind tunnel of social, political and economic change. Driving forces included the Civil War and concomitant reconstruction; industrial, agricultural and governmental expansion; population and technology growth; and the proliferation of organizations, from the Grange and labor unions to corporate combines. Into this swirl came lawyers, to bring order. Lawyering became a "boom industry," and "law schools" followed.[2]

In 1850, according to Lawrence Friedman, there were only fifteen law schools on the entire North American continent. By 1900, one hundred and two law schools had thrown their doors "open for business."[3]

As TR's seven volumes of law school notes (the "Notes") illustrate, topics likely to be given attention by a late nineteenth century law student were: Federal Procedure, Bailments and Corporations, Municipal Law and related issues, Contracts, Bills and Notes, Insurance and Sales, Employee-Employer Relations (non-regulatory labor law), Criminal Law, Property, Intellectual Property (including Patents, Copyrights and Trademarks), Torts (especially Libel and Slander), and Family Law (Domestic Relations and the status of women).[5]

Notably absent from late nineteenth century law school curricula were: Administrative Law and Business Regulation (until creation of the Interstate Commerce Commission in 1887),[6] Antitrust Law (until the Sherman Act of 1890),[7] Income Taxation (until Grover Cleveland's "two percent tax" of 1894),[8] protective labor laws for children and women,[9] laws respecting workplace safety (until their enforcement in the 1890's)[10] and any serious discussion of the 13th, 14th or 15th Amendments, respectively outlawing slavery, guaranteeing "equal protection of the laws" and enfranchising America's Black population.[11]

The study of Procedure in the late nineteenth century invariably began with David Dudley Field's masterpiece, commonly known as "Field's Code." This 1848 Code of Civil Procedure was the first attempt to do away with what Jeremy Bentham termed the "ancestor-worship" of erratic common law procedure.[12]

By contrast, a law student's introduction to Property was uncodified and elementary. New York's statutory Land Law, while more developed than California's, was hardly the basis for a hornbook on New York Real Estate. In the American West at this time, the most riveting real property issue may have been identifying predicates for adverse possession; meanwhile, in the East, rights of adjoining land owners (for example, easements) and other plainly urban questions (for example, the nature of "fixtures") were becoming issues of popular contest.[13] Separately, the allocation of vast federal land grants influenced late nineteenth century public land law development. This area, too, changed markedly with "the death of the frontier" at the century's close.[14]

Intellectual Property law developed in the wake of the rush for patents in the last quarter of the century.[15] Meanwhile, trademarks began with "a few scattered judicial opinions," the first of which may have been an 1844 injunction to protect one possessive—and prescient—threadmaker.[16]

Tort law expanded, as did Corporation law, with the rise of Industrial America. Friedman notes that the post-Civil War era introduced "machines [which] had a marvelous capacity for smashing the human body," and thus advancing Tort law.[17] More specifically, judge-made Tort law galloped across the country in the unsettling dust of corporate negligence, particularly among the railroads.[18]

A major change in this area was the first case linking corporate negligence to insurability, *Ryan v. New York Central RR. Co.* (1866). In *Ryan*, a railroad fire consumed several homes. Damage was vast, and in the court's view, incalculable. However, far from penalizing the corporation, the *Ryan* court concluded that it could not find the railroad liable, since the damage was not insurable.

Ryan signals the beginning of a trend, namely judicial fortification of corporate defenses against tort liability. Judicial doctrines which evolved to serve this end included proximate cause, contributory negligence, assumption of risk and the fellow-servant rule.[19] Corporate lawyers gained tremendous influence during this period. The growth of Corporate Law contributed, in turn, to the flourishing of law schools. When Special Charter incorporation ended, unregulated private investment created an unprecedented period of corporate growth,[20] and of corporate indifference.[21] Lawyers, good and bad, were retained by corporations to advise, defend and order corporate growth.[22] A few lawyers were also retained to prosecute corporate excesses and negligence.[23] During the 1890's, the doctrine of *ultra vires* was viewed as an obstacle to progress, and withered. Corporations assumed the status of "persons" under the 14th Amendment. As Friedman recounts, "a striking series of cases turned the due-process clause into a kind of great wall against populist onslaughts."[24] Meanwhile, the Constitution's "Commerce Clause," eventually utilized by the federal government to regulate interstate commerce, remained relatively undiscovered.[25] Lawyers such as those serving John D. Rockefeller, began to consolidate corporate holdings in voting trusts, or simply "trusts." TR's presidential "trust-busting" aside, he appears to have learned early how corporate lawyers could achieve unfair advantages vis-a-vis labor, government and their corporate competitors.[26] TR later deplored what he viewed as "sharp practices," opportunism and amorality among the era's newly empowered corporate bar.[27]

Criminal Law experienced a similar expansion during the late nineteenth century. While the basic requirements of *actus reus* and *mens rea* were taught for each crime, standards were premised more upon the jury's state of mind than upon the offender's.[28] One example was the so-called M'Naughten Insanity Test, created in 1843.[29] Iowa Chief Justice John F. Dillon, later to become one of TR's professors, challenged the test in 1868, calling for an alternative "irresistible impulse" test. [30]

Finally, an area entitled Municipal Law was beginning to define the role of the "municipal corporation" and related topics. [31]

Of America's late nineteenth century law schools, we also know this. Three-quarters of them, in 1890, were attached to pre-existing colleges or universities. Formal law training was prestigious, but in many states not required. Law School admission requirements varied, but were high at Dwight's Columbia and Langdell's Harvard.[32] Two-year degrees were most common during the 1880's, although one-year degrees prevailed from 1850 to 1880. Finally, law schools taught not only legal principles, but the prevailing statutes and common law, as well as practical aspects of day-to-day lawyering.

TR's well-documented study of law in the late nineteenth century sharpens our understanding of what "the every student" of his day was studying, and adds valuable insight into our 26th president's legal training.

II. Theodore Roosevelt's Study of Law

Set against the backdrop of challenges by grizzlies, lions, czars, emperors, city bosses, bullets, bayonets, dedicated Democrats, and the Brazilian "River of Doubt,"[33] TR's study of law seems, at first glance, almost trite.

Unglorified by graduation or admission to a state bar, TR's legal training has long been relegated to the status of passing mention or elliptic footnote.[34]

After examining the seven surviving volumes of TR's previously unknown Law Notes (1880-1882), diary entries and personal correspondence from 1879 to 1883,[35] documentation from Columbia's Records Division,[36] information on his law school professors, and TR's subsequent addresses, publications and correspondence, a new conclusion emerges: TR's study of law, during the late nineteenth century, was serious and formative.

Below, the length, breadth, depth, and influence of TR's legal training is explored. First comes evidence from 1879 to 1883 that TR's legal studies were, despite his 1880 marriage to Alice Lee,[37] 1881 completion of *The Naval War of 1812*,[38] and incipient political activity,[39] pursued conscientiously.

For corroboration, TR's later writings are examined, including passages flickering with his keen understanding of key legal principles, rules, phraseology and methods.

Tracking TR's lawyerly illumination to its source, one arrives perforce at Columbia Law School, during the years 1880, 1881, and 1882.

III. TR's Late Nineteenth Century Law Studies

Black's Law Dictionary proclaims that a "lawyer" is no more or less than "[a] person learned in the law."[40] That definition would spark hot debate among those possessed of the license to practice.[41] Still, no less a legal authority than Sir Edward Coke (1552-1634) has admonished that "[reason is the life of the law,"[42] and even grudging practitioners must acknowledge that graduation from law school and admission to the bar confirms, rather than confers, the knowledge prerequisite to becoming a lawyer.

TR never received an LL.B. or a J.D.,[43] and never gained admission to a state bar.[44] On the other hand, TR's Notes reveal that, by the age of twenty-four, he had acquired a desk full, if not also a head full, of legal principles, rules, phrases and methods.

TR disclaimed his legal acumen in later life; but intellectual disclaimers were his way.[45] Edmond Morris has nimbly synthesized his extraordinary intellectual swath. TR was "equally comfortable with experts in naval strategy, forestry, Greek drama, cowpunching, metaphysics, protective coloration, and football techniques."[46] Zoology, ornithology, sociology and psychology could be added to that list.[47] Certainly, the discipline of law should be counted among his more serious intellectual pursuits.

Cursory historical reference to this topic notwithstanding, TR's study of law was neither short nor shallow. Indeed, he studied law for nearly two years. His academic courses criss-crossed subjects as diverse as Real Property, International Law, Criminal Law, Jurisprudence, and Municipal Law.[48]

The professors who taught TR were among the top legal minds of his day. TR's Notes are complete, neat and legally sound. His law texts are known to have been *Blackstone's Commentaries, Parsons on Contracts, Washburn on Real Property, Bishpham on Equity, Addison on Torts,* and *Greenleaf on Evidence.*[49]

While TR is best remembered for his political abilities, these abilities did not develop in a vacuum. Newly discovered and long forgotten boxes of brown, crumbling Notes, coupled with corroborating letters and diary entries, plead with modern historians not to forget that young TR was once determined to tackle a different discipline: The law.

A. Length of Study

We know, from TR's *Private Diary,* that his studies began at Columbia on Wednesday, November 17, 1880.[50] To matriculate, he had travelled to New York City, from Chestnut Hill, on October 3, 1880.[51] The choice of Columbia was, despite an undergraduate degree from Harvard, logical. Columbia, in the late nineteenth century, appears to have been the preeminent law school in the nation.[52] Moreover, by 1873, "Columbia College Law School was the largest law school in the United States."[53] In 1880, on the date that TR matriculated, the law school offered graduation in two years; Harvard insisted upon three.[54] The deciding factor, however, was probably convenience. Columbia was closer to TR's family, to New York's fertile job market, and to the social milieu into which he was expected to fit.

Externally, Columbia Law School was, in 1880, nothing more than a plain, portly, four-story building. Unannounced by sign, plaque, or inscription, it stood at 8 Great Jones Street, Manhattan.[55]

Confining as it appeared, it was nevertheless brimming with curious students and legal expertise. Socratic dialogue between professor and student was the rule of the day.

TR himself was known to have been an "energetic questioner of lectures."[56] His penchant for rigorous questioning, derided by one classmate as "interrupt[ion]," "obtrusive[ness]," and "egotism," may actually have been invited by his legal mentors. "True teaching . . . ," said Professor Dwight, "consisted not in formal lectures but in a combination of catechetical instruction and informal oral exposition, with free and ample opportunity for the students to ask questions, both in the classroom and in private."[57] Speaking of Dwight, a TR contemporary noted: "[W]e learned very much, too, by the questions which we asked of [Dwight] in the classroom, and which he, like another Socrates, freely encouraged."[58] Between classes, students were often boisterous and frequently discussed politics.[59]

TR's *Private Diary* shows "hard work" at the law from November, 1880 through December, 1881. Abruptly, on February 15, 1882, all entries end.[60] On January 1, 1883, they resume. While no mention is thereafter made of law school, TR did later reconsider private practice.[61]

The absence of any entries in the final nine months of 1882 complicates the task of rebutting charges that TR terminated his legal training in 1881 or early 1882.[62] However, available evidence now suggests a different conclusion. We know, for example, that on Thursday, October 6, 1881, following a vacation in Great Britain, France, and Switzerland,[63] TR observed to himself: "Began at the law."[64] We also know that the 1881-1882 academic year, scheduled to conclude on May 17, 1882, promised to culminate in TR's graduation.[65]

Further proof that TR studied law from November 1880 through late 1882 is, necessarily, a patchwork affair. Still, there is persuasive evidence suggesting that he did not put aside the study of law until at least late 1882. Among that evidence, TR's newly discovered Notes and correspondence, which offer substantial insight.

The last fully dated entry in TR's signed notebooks is December 7, 1881.[66] The quality and quantity of his signed, dated entries prior to December 7, 1881 imply considerable dedication. Beyond this, there are incompletely dated, undated, and unsigned TR Notes. These have recently been catalogued by Columbia as "Theodore Roosevelt's Class Notes." Most are indisputably in TR's handwriting.[67]

The surmise that TR studied until late 1882 is assisted by four corroborating facts. First, a group of the undated Notes pertaining to "Criminal Law" is twice boldly inscribed "Theodore Roosevelt."[68] Since most academic months between 1880 and 1881 are among TR's dated Notes,[69] and TR was inclined to date all Notes during 1880 and 1881, one may reasonably place these Notes in a different timeframe, for example after December 7, 1881.

Second, as late as September 1882, TR was writing to his sister identifying the practice of law as a leading reason for choosing not to settle outside New York City. Wrote TR on September 15, 1882:

> "The only, or at least the chief, drawback [to buying a farm in the country] is the distance from New York [City]. Still, if I were perfectly certain that I would go on in politics and literature I should buy the farm without hesitation; but *I consider the chances to be strongly favorable to my getting out of both—and if I intend to follow law or business I ought to stay in New York* [*City*]."[70] (emphasis added).

Thereupon, in October 1882, TR and Alice moved into their new home at 55 West 45th Street, New York City.[71]

Third, TR would have been, *after October 1882*, closer to all New York City commitments than he had been during the preceding Spring and Summer. During the latter period, TR was often in Albany.[72] The move would have allowed TR increased time, proximity and stability to focus on law; all three would have been valuable in approaching his comprehensive examination in law.[73]

Most powerful in corroborating TR's conscientious study of law through 1882 is the letter he wrote to his mother on July 5, 1882. In that letter he emphasized his commitment to the law, writing "I have decided to study law in John's office during three or four days a week for the rest of the summer."[74]

If TR studied the law as promised, he concluded his independent study near the 1882 date on which he wrote to his sister. At least on that date, he was still convinced that he would "follow law or business."[75] If TR studied law "three or four days a week" during Summer 1882, it is worth noting that he studied no fewer days per week than during an academic term. (See below.)

Several questions persist. Did TR take the two-year comprehensive examination which, at least on the date that he matriculated, would have entitled him to graduate and practice? If so, what were his results? If not, why did he not take the examination?

The answers to the first and second questions are frustratingly simple. There are no surviving records of TR's comprehensive examination.[76] Nor is there any record of TR's graduation from Columbia Law School. Indeed, the enormous 1932 Columbia University *Alumni Register* lists "Theodore Roosevelt" as a member of the Law Class of 1882, but not as a graduate.[77]

Why did TR choose not to take that examination, not to graduate, and not to enter private law practice? The answer to these questions, while speculative, may be more ascertainable than previously thought.

TR's interest in public service no doubt played a part in the decision not to enter private practice.[78] Practicing law in New York City at this time also appears to have offered little in the way of either adventure or moral gratification.[79] Indeed, TR's *Autobiography* vividly reconstructs the period, arguing that many private practitioners were ambivalent toward moral questions of the day.[80]

However, two other, potentially decisive, factors have been overlooked. Just as young TR was, in all likelihood, preparing himself to take Columbia's comprehensive examination in late 1882, New York's rules for entering private practice changed. Rather than two years of training and a successful score on Columbia's comprehensive examination, the aspiring lawyer had suddenly to complete a third year of legal training.[81]

Beyond that, Columbia graduates wishing to practice in New York were, in 1882, suddenly required to pass a state bar examination. Columbia's longstanding "diploma privilege," which had been in place when TR matriculated, was withdrawn.[82]

Even if young TR had felt prepared for a state bar examination, he is not likely to have concluded that a third year of law school was worth the additional costs—time away from political involvement, time away from Alice and his mother, time away from outdoor adventures, and another year's tuition.[83]

B. Breadth of Study

Based on the fully dated entries in TR's signed Notes, historians will reasonably conclude that he studied a variety of legal topics. These were grouped by TR under general headings, including "Municipal Law" (three notebooks), "Real Estate Lectures" (one notebook) and "Law" (one notebook). Beyond this, there are undated Notes twice bearing his name and focusing on "Criminal Law," as well as unsigned Notes and one volume not in TR's hand.

In 1880 and 1881, Municipal Law was a young, ubiquitous, fanning topic. In TR's "Municipal Law" notebook, one finds sections incorporating Family Law, Contracts, Copyright, Inheritance (i.e., Wills), Employer-Employee Relations, Procedure, Naturalization of Aliens (i.e., Immigration), Trusts, Evidence, Patents, Bills and Notes (i.e., Commercial Paper), Insurance, Corporations and elements of Torts (including Libel and Slander).[84]

Among areas appearing in the signed "Law" notebook, are Jurisprudence, Moral Law, International Law, Civil and Criminal Procedure, Constitutional Law, and a lengthy section entitled "Method of Preparing Case for Argument."[85]

TR's signed volume entitled "Real Estate Lectures" is the largest of the set. Dated 1881, this volume is signed on the inside, front cover and bears the inscription, in TR's hand, "Columbia Coll. Law School."

TR also chose to compete in optional[86] moot court competitions. His diary entry for Friday, January 21, 1881 reads, for example: "Argued case in moot court; successful."[87] According to an official Law School *Announcement* dated 1878-79, "[t]he design of these [moot courts] is to aid in training the student to discuss debatable questions of law. . . . These discussions are strongly recommended to students. They serve as a direct training for regular work in the profession."[88]

C. Depth of Study

The depth of TR's law study is documented by a constellation of simple but riveting facts:

(1) the volume of his Notes;
(2) the quality of his Notes;
(3) his attendance record;
(4) the eminence of his professors;
(5) periodic allusions to diligent law study in his *Private Diary*; and
(6) his personal correspondence from November 1880 to September 1882.

1. Volume of Notes

The sheer volume of Notes in TR's hand to which precise dates (i.e. month, day and year) are affixed, is impressive. No fewer than 738 pages of careful transcription are traceable to his hand. On average, TR wrote eight pages per day, including dictations.

Beyond this corpus, there lies a volume of signed, undated Notes totalling 224 pages. Within that volume, there is a set of undated "Criminal Law" Notes totalling 42 pages. This set, bearing TR's name and ending with "Professor Chase," may have been transcribed by Chase, but was likely used by TR for studying the subject.[89] Additionally, there is a set of dated, unsigned Notes totalling 53 pages.

Finally, there are two tightly packed volumes of undated, unsigned Notes, one of which is sandwiched between notebook covers identical to those signed by TR; these may not have been written by TR. The two undated, unsigned volumes contain 174 written pages. A reasonable surmise is that these Notes were treated as preparatory material by TR, as he approached the comprehensive examination. Collectively, TR's Notes fill two boxes and total 1,189 pages.

2. Quality of Notes

With the exception of several fascinating doodles, TR's Notes attest to a mind intent on learning the law.

His handwriting—in all legal subjects—is a steady, distinct cursive. Flowing across pages now brown and brittle, it betrays no weariness, no gaps in logic, no breaks in transcription, and no weakening of TR's determination to follow his respective mentor's reasoning.

The cogency of his writing confirms two accounts by persons who knew him at the time. John Burgess, who taught Public Law courses at Columbia during the period 1880 to 1882, is reported to have found TR "a student able to grasp everything instantly, who made notes rapidly and incessantly."[90] A classmate, George Thompson, left a similar account. One day, young TR apparently arrived in class covered with mud. Somehow, en route to the Law School, he had managed a spectacular fall. Thompson recalled, however, that TR's scholastic resolve was unshaken. "His face had a look of determination. . . . The students applauded his entrance, but he sat down at once on the little platform at Professor Dwight's feet and commenced to pay strict attention to business."[91] And so his neat and well-ordered Notes record.

On top of solid concentration, TR had a knack for getting the pithy best out of a lecture. He was a consummate practitioner of creative abbreviation. "Which" became "wh," "for" simply "4," "and" an ampersand; "equals" became "=," and the words "male" and "female" devolved into their respective signs (*i.e.*, "♂" and "♀").

In Property, TR's 1881 Notes are systematic and complete. All major areas of common law are covered. Intermittently, they become bold and faint, with the rise and fall of ink in his fountain pen. Occasionally, he switches to pencil. Now and then, he lays down a straight edge to square a chart, table or column. One such column is topped "common law." Beside it, a column reads "revised statutes." Down both columns, run the relevant legal authorities.

TR's attention to legal methods was as full as his attention to principles and rules. On October 7, 1881, he recorded a lesson which probably troubled him, and could have portended his eventual disillusionment with law study—if disillusionment it was. He writes: "We are concerned with [the] question of what law is, not what it ought to be."[92]

Elsewhere, the institutions of democracy and bases for their legitimacy occupied him. On October 8, 1881, he wrote: "[I]n [the] U.S. [,] supreme power is in [the] people; and some of it is parcelled out to Congress, some to States, and the residuary still remains with the people, in the shape of the Constitution."[93] Could he have possibly dreamed, as he wrote those words, that he would one day become the ultimate executor of the Constitution?[94]

The theoretical side of law was balanced against confidently penned directions to the potential litigator. On December 9, 1880, the day after his sister's coming-out party,[95] TR observed, for example, that a "Cross Action . . . should be set forth with some particularity as though it were an original cause of action. . . ." TR continued with twenty-three pages entitled "Method of Preparing Case for Argument." Do these Notes not strongly suggest that he was pondering private practice.?[96]

His Notes instruct: "1st thing to be done is to master leading principles applying to case." There follow several pages of discourse on legal "digests" and how to use them. TR continues:

> "After the reports have thus been considered [,] a suggestion of importance should be made, that a lawyer should not only study his own case but should examine all the authorities that can be cited by his opponent. He may thus be prepared to discredit his adversary's cases by showing that they have been overruled or [,] if not[,] that they conflict with well established principles."

Pages of litigation strategy follow, providing a prospective litigator with his essential trail-markers. Each marker is in TR's hand: "The next pt [sic] to be considered is the mode of preparing one's material for presentation to the Court. . . . The power to make points well must depend upon the power to reason correctly[,] which can be learned, however, from study of good examples." He meticulously records the mechanics of placing a case before the bench: "At head of first page appears name of the court in full then the names of the parties in brackets then the word points. If there is also a Statement of facts made these words should appear before the word pt [sic]. The paper used should be legal cap [sic] & all the papers referring to same should be fastened together. The document should then be signed by counsel & folded in 4 = folds. On back should be written Name of Court[;] 2d Names of parties in brackets[;] 3d the word points[;] & 4th the name of the counsel."

Would TR have gone to such lengths, recording the minutiae of legal practice, if he had not sincerely entertained the idea of utilizing such information?

Generally, TR's penmanship is steady. However, readers will stumble upon some choice doodles. Those familiar with parallel events in TR's life will find it hard to suppress a smile. They will recognize items relevant to TR, but oddly out of place in his law school Notes.

For example, on October 20, 1881, TR's attention appears to have slipped from Municipal Law (topics under discussion were "life insurance" and "negotiable bills").[97] Across the top of one page are ten carefully drawn arrowheads. Most boast "spear" shafts. Each is different in design. More arrowheads appear on the inside, front cover of Notebook "2" of Municipal Law.

Did these Indian arrowheads drift back to TR from his hunting and camping expeditions in the Indian territories of Maine? Afterall, in 1878, he had taken a college vacation to "the wilds of Aroostook County, in northern Maine."[98] In 1879, he had returned to Maine to climb Mount Katahdin, "the highest mountain in Maine, and . . . surrounded by some of the most intractable forest in the Northeast."[99] He undertook a second expedition in 1879, to "Munsungen Lakes" in a dugout canoe. And then a third, in which he covered more than 100 miles.[100] Perhaps TR recalled these arrowheads from his study of Natural History at Harvard.[101] In any case, such artistic specimens are curious additions to New York Municipal Law. No less curious are a cleverly drawn slingshot and feathered arrow in "Municipal Law 1881," Notebook "3."

On another day [likely in 1881], TR seems to have been daydreaming about his summer vacation in Europe. A classic British battle axe is neatly sketched.[102] Searching his *Private Diary*, one discovers that TR visited the medieval "Castle Blarney" in Ireland on May 22, 1881[103]; on June 2, 1881, he visited the "Tower [of London] crown jewels and armour," which he found "very interesting."[104] On yet another page, TR appears to have scrawled—with uncanny accuracy—two silhouette maps of France.[105]

Perhaps most predictable, and yet electrifying, are the strange, boat-shaped configurations on the inside, rear cover of "Municipal Law, 1881," Notebook "3." Gradually, the reader recognizes these famous "little ships." They are the ones TR drew whenever he had a spare minute.[106] These "little ships" at the rear of "Municipal Law, 1881" appear to be engaged in heavy crossfire, corroborating TR's contemporaneous labors on *The Naval War of 1812*, his seminal work on naval ballistics and ship movements during the War of 1812. That work was completed in December, 1881.[107]

TR further amused himself with scholarly and eccentric case references. Discussing criminal defenses, he concluded a section entitled "Want of Mental Capacity" with the addendum: "For an interesting case on monomania where a person was in the habit of stealing ladies shoes. [See] 2 Parker 43."[108]

Unpleasant topics were likewise addressed. On January 25, 1881, he writes: "Seduction accompanied with breach of promise of marriage is sometimes a crime. Thus by law of Congress when [a female] passenger is seduced by a [male] master of [a seafaring] vessel or other employee it is a crime. N.Y. statute refers solely to cases of breach of promise where [a female] is of chaste character. Conviction can not be had solely on testimony of [the female] seduced[,] and the subsequent intermarriage of parties is a bar to conviction." On the following day, he records the "rights of a bastard child"; on January 27, 1881, he discusses "inheritance" upon death.[109]

Lastly, his Notes reveal exceptional attention to the rights of women.[110]

Thus, while TR is reputed to have been an "energetic questioner of lectures,"[111] he was also a devoted listener, who obviously expended considerable effort in transcribing and understanding his lectures.

3. Record of Attendance

Although the record is incomplete, TR's attendance appears to have been high, averaging three to five class days per week. His classes formally lasted for one-and-a-half hours.[112]

Interpolating from the Notes, 1881 correspondence, and Columbia curricula for academic years 1880-81 and 1881-82, the total hours that TR spent in study was not far below New York's current annual requirements.[113] While many Notes are undated or unsigned, 738 pages are signed and identifiable by month, day, and year. That set breaks into eighty-two daily entries. These entries reveal a pattern of high, regular attendance during periods for which they exist.

The following table suggests the number of days per week that TR spent in class.

Theodore Roosevelt's Attendance Record Based on Law Notes

Year	Month	Fully Dated Entries	Comments	Average Days Per Recorded Week
1880	November	—	Dated but not signed	—
	December	9	Notes only after 12/9/1880	3
1881	January	16		4
	February	15		3.7
	March	20		5
	April	—	Dated notes missing	—
	May	—	Dated notes missing	—
	June-September	—	Summer Vacation	—
	October	11	Notes only after 10/7 1881 and before 10/21/1881	5.2
	November	7	Notes only after 11/15/1881	3.5
	December	4	Notes only before 12/7/1881	4
1882	January-September	—	Dated notes missing	—

The Nature of the Law Notes

	Entries	Signed
Total Pages Dated	53	738
Total Pages Undated	174	224

Assuming TR averaged only three classes per week,[114] attended class only from November 17, 1880 to December 7, 1881,[115] and prepared only one hour per class day,[116] he studied not less than 262 hours.[117]

More likely, TR was in attendance from November 17, 1880 to the end of the academic year, May 17, 1882,[118] prepared not less than two hours per class day, studied "three or four days a week" during the summer of 1882[119] (for perhaps two hours per day),[120] and had at least one two-hour legal commitment per class week (e.g., two moot courts per week.)[121] If these assumptions are correct, TR studied law for more than 500 hours.[122]

A full time student at Columbia Law School in 1989 was required by New York State law to study only 333.3[123] hours per academic year for graduation. Thus, TR's study during 1880-81 and 1881-82 may have involved a commitment on par with present standards.

4. Eminent Law Professors

TR studied law under at least three eminent Law Professors: Theodore W. Dwight, John W. Burgess, and George Chase.

Dwight taught Municipal Law in 1880 and 1881. At least three of TR's Municipal Law notebooks are from 1881. Burgess recorded his impressions of teaching TR. Chase is cited in TR's "Criminal Law" Notes. Based on TR's 1881 "Real Estate" Notes, he may also have been instructed by (Judge) John F. Dillon. Dillon was appointed Professor of Real Estate and Equity Jurisprudence at Columbia in 1879.[114] [Editor's note: Endnotes are numbered here as in the original, with note 114 beginning again here, following note 123.] Dillon resigned in Spring, 1881.[115]

Dwight, by all accounts, was the most famous. His forte was Municipal Law. His teaching method was renowned. The "Dwight Method" involved extensive preclass preparation by students, followed by in-class "recitations," "dictations," "oral interrogations" and lively classroom "colloquy."[116] A contemporary of Dwight's recalled: "[H]e never failed to recommend habits of hard work."[117] More specifically, "[h]e often declared that every successful lawyer must expect crises when the act of a moment must be the result of long periods of systematic preparation."[118]

Although TR's own reflections, after thirty-one years of public service, inpugn the absence of moral teaching in late nineteenth century law schools,[119] other students remember Dwight as a man who "pictured the law as a just and equitable science . . . based . . . upon principles of right and justice."[120] One student distinctly recalled: "It is not law that he taught . . . so much as justice. If a student had not discovered how a rule or axiom had its foundation somewhere in the distinctions of absolute right and wrong, new light was thrown upon the subject, new illustrations were drawn from an exhaustless treasury of wisdom, and ideal distinctions were sketched until it seemed that the speaker was in touch with the very fountains of equity."[121]

Nor was such praise limited to his former students. Speaking of Dwight, Columbia University President Barnard acknowledged: "[T]he success of this [law] school . . . is without parallel here or abroad; and in making this remark . . . it is but just to the eminent professor who has been its life and soul to ascribe to him the credit of having, by his splendid ability, his untiring energy, and his unequalled power of clear analysis and forcible illustration as a teacher and lecturer, been mainly instrumental in achieving this success."[122]

Foreign observers had similar respect for Dwight. One Englishman proclaimed: "[Columbia] possesses the best law school in the United States, and one quite unlike any insti-

15. Theodore Roosevelt (1858-1919). A fairly if not perfectly diligent student, Roosevelt in some ways typifies the law students of his age. Although he did not complete his studies, he did become New York Police Commissioner, as well as President of the United States. (*The Collection of Stephen Sheppard.*)

tution existing in England. At this school there are constant classes filled with pupils who are taught the elements of English law by one of the ablest professors that any school of law ever possessed . . . a man of genius who knows how to teach what his pupils need to learn. Professor Dwight . . . has a reputation . . . as the greatest living American teacher of law. . . ."[123]

Another Englishman, reviewing the American legal profession, declared: "[I]n New York, the institution called Columbia College is fortunate in possessing a professor of great legal ability and an extraordinary gift of exposition, whose classrooms . . . are crowded by large and highly intelligent audiences. Better law-teaching than Mr. Dwight's it is hardly possible to imagine; it would be worth an English student's while to cross the Atlantic to attend his course."[124]

John W. Burgess taught Constitutional History, International Law, Constitutional Law and Political Science. Burgess's memories of TR are succinct. "He entered our School of Law as a member of the class which would graduate in the summer of 1882. He registered however for all the courses in political history, public law, and political science and appeared to be more interested in these than in topics of municipal law. . . . He was very quick in comprehension, very accurate in examination, and the most rapid and voluminous reader of references in the school."[125]

Burgess' general recollections further illuminate TR's early attitude toward the law. Burgess wrote: "As my subjects in the law curriculum were optional, . . . and the only incentive to take them was the acquisition of the knowledge they represented, I had in my Law School class generally and almost exclusively the most intelligent and best prepared men coming from the best colleges in the land . . . my class consisted of about fifty out of the five hundred students of the Law School, and I could rely upon every one of them to prepare himself to recite each day on the lecture of the day before and on the references given."[126] Burgess is reputed "not [to have been] happy unless he had around him a circle of devoted and enthusiastic disciples. . . ."[127] TR appears to have been one such.

George Chase, Co-adjudicator of the Law School from 1874 to 1891, taught Criminal Law, Torts, and Procedure in 1878.[128] Valedictorian of his 1870 Yale College class and recipient of Columbia's 1873 award for top student, Chase appears to have possessed an exceptional mind. One historian has offered this snapshot: "As a teacher[,] Chase was distinguished for his powers of analysis and exposition, for his insistence upon accuracy of statement, and for his great patience with his students and kind sympathy for them."[129] That TR benefitted from Chase's instruction in Criminal Law can hardly be argued.

John F. Dillon taught Real Estate at Columbia from Autumn, 1879 to Spring, 1881.[130] TR's signed Real Estate Lectures bear the date 1881. While we will never know if Dillon instructed him, TR's discomfiture with what he later recalled as an absence of scruples among "many of the big corporation lawyers,"[131] may have originated with Dillon. Dillon, even while teaching, was General Counsel to the Union Pacific Railroad.[132]

5. Private Diary Entries

TR's study of law is charted in the portions of his *Private Diary* which survive. On Wednesday, November 17, 1880, TR recorded for the first time going "to the law school."[133] By November 24, 1880, he was writing to his *Diary*: "This law work is very interesting."[134] On Saturday, December 4, 1880, he concluded, "I like the law school work very much."[135] His interest in the law, at least prior to that date, may have been spurred by Municipal Law.[136] Another possibility is that Burgess' 1880-1881 political, constitutional, or international law courses gave rise to his interest.[137]

Returning from Christmas vacation, TR wrote on January 4, 1881: "Began work at Law School . . . ," adding, "Always walk up and down[,] to & from Law School."[138] During this period, TR was apparently walking from 6 West 57th Street to 8 Great Jones Street and back every day, "about 6 miles."[139] One could argue that such a regimen itself indicated a degree of dedication. On January 6, 1881, TR happily recorded, "Every moment of my time occupied."[140] On January 21, 1881 came this proud entry: "Argued case in moot court; successful."[141]

As February 24, 1881 rolled around, TR assured himself: "Am still working hard at the law school."[142] Five weeks later, on March 30, 1881, he wrote: "Am studying very hard at the law school."[143] One glance at TR's Notebook "4" reveals that March 1881 was heavily occupied with "Dictations in Municipal Law," including the study of topics such as "suits by stockholders [against corporations]," "personal property," "real property," and "debtor- creditor" relations.[144]

Suddenly, on April 13, 1881, TR got an opportunity to see legal theory in practice. TR confided to his *Diary*: "Came back to N.Y. Succeeded in arresting a swindler, had quite a struggle with him."[145] Six days later, on April 19, 1881, his determination produced results: "Had the swindler indicted by the Grand Jury." He adds, nonchalantly, "The weather is superb for driving."[146]

As TR grew closer to his summer 1881 vacation with Alice, he admitted on April 23, 1881: "Am working tolerably hard at my law."[147] On April 30, 1881, his personal involvement in enforcement of a criminal statute came to its zenith: "[H]ad the swindler put in the penitentiary for six months."[148] As Spring Term 1881 drew to a close, TR confessed: "Besides working pretty well at the law, I spend most of my spare time in the Astor Library on my 'Naval History.'"[149] His attention to law, nevertheless, appears to have been constant. Near the term's official end, May 11, 1881, TR completed his last class, proclaiming "My law school work is over."[150] He and Alice were off to Europe!

On his return from the summer abroad, TR dove again into the study of law on October 6, 1881. That day, he wrote: "Began at the Law."[151] On October 17, 1881, TR acknowledged two pressures specific to October, 1881—his campaign for a seat in the New York Assembly (part-time), and his publisher's December deadline for receipt of the *Naval History*. "Am working fairly at my law, hard at politics, and hardest of all at my book ('Naval History'), which I expect to publish this winter."[152]

While his fully-dated Notes document study through December 1881, and undated Notes and correspondence support study through late 1882, his *Private Diary* ends abruptly on February 15, 1882.[153]

6. 1881 Personal Correspondence

As noted earlier, a July 5, 1882 letter to TR's mother and a September 15, 1882 letter to his sister[154] indicate an enduring interest in law through late 1882. However, three 1881 letters further buttress that claim.

On March 29, 1881, TR began a letter to Alice this way: "Darling Baby, I have been studying hard all day—only drawing a few 'little boats'—and did not go out driving."[155]

On October 14, 1881, he again wrote to Alice, explaining his time commitments. These included work on the book, work on political primaries, and work at law. TR concluded: ". . . and the law is pretty hard."[156]

Finally, work in politics appears not to have subverted TR's resolve to complete law school. That is the message of a November 10, 1881 letter to Harvard classmate Charles Grenfill Washburn. In that letter, written after TR had already won his seat in the Assembly, TR wrote: "Finding it would not interfere much with my law[,] I accepted the nomination to the assembly, and was elected. . . . But don't think I am going to go into politics after this year, for I am not."[157]

IV. The Subtle Influence of TR's Legal Training

TR seldom made reference to his legal training. When speaking to licensed attorneys, he demurred, referring to himself as a "layman."[158] When addressing those without legal training, he wavered between disclosing his special knowledge and disclaiming it.[159] Disclosure added credibility to his attacks on unscrupulous private practitioners;[160] silence permitted him to appear untainted by association with the profession.[161]

Still, TR did not mince words when reviling those he deemed unworthy among "the great profession."[162] Speaking at Harvard in 1905, TR impaled the legal profession on a popular theme:

> We all know that, as things actually are, many of the most influential and most highly remunerated members of the bar . . . make it their special task to work out bold and ingenious schemes by which their very wealthy clients, individual or corporate, can evade the laws which are made to regulate[,] in the interest of the public[,] the use of great wealth.[163]

In his *Autobiography*, TR justifies the decision not to enter private practice this way: "[T]he big corporate lawyers, to whom the ordinary members of the bar then as now looked up, held certain standards which were difficult to recognize as compatible with the idealism I suppose every high-minded young man is apt to feel."[164] Did TR mean to suggest that he could not have upheld such moral standards? Or to suggest that lawyers serving big corporations were necessarily devoid of idealism? Certainly, the former is not true, and the latter is an overstatement. But then overstatement is no stranger to politics.

Elsewhere, TR lectured the private bar for permitting defendants' rights to obstruct the flow of retributive justice. In 1905, before an audience which included the President of the American Bar Association, TR propounded this thesis:

> "It is unfortunate that we have permitted practices that were necessary three hundred years ago for the protection of innocent people to be elaborated, or perverted, so that they become a means for allowing criminals to escape the punishment of their criminality."[165]

Still, as Putnam has acknowledged, "[TR's] position . . . was not precisely one of spurning the legal profession because of moral scruples."[166] TR himself stated that he would have "taken up the law or any other respectable occupation had he been compelled to earn all that he spent."[167] Putnam adds: "Some of his attitude [on 'big corporation lawyers'] here [in his Autobiographical memories of law school] was undoubtedly a carry-over from the experiences he was shortly to have with these men in political capacities."[168]

TR's deliberate underemphasis of law school may have been grounded in other facts. First, TR's intense legal study overlapped his entrance into politics; he may have consciously chosen to highlight political involvements. Second, TR was loathe to begin an undertaking without completing it; he may have felt perpetual unease at having never graduated from law school or gained admission to a state bar. Third, Cutright noted that he was "forever belittling his capacities as a student. . . ."[169]

Fourth, TR's law school training began in November 1880 and likely concluded in late 1882. He was married in October 1880 to Alice Lee. His memories of law school may well have been inextricably tied to his memories of Alice, who died of "Bright's disease" on February 14, 1884. That shock sent TR hurtling, in Edmond Morris' words, into "a state of cataleptic concentration on a task which now preoccupied him above all else. Like a lion obsessively trying to drag a spear from its flank, Roosevelt set about dislodging Alice Lee from his soul."[170] Morris effectively recreates TR's torment: "Nostalgia . . . if painful . . . must be suppressed, until the memory is too dead to throb."[171] While there is no corroboration from TR himself, one reasonable possibility is that his memories of law school summoned up other memories, about which TR would not let himself think. TR's solution: Suppress all but the essential memories; omit any references to this period, except as they give color to his political debut.

The private TR was not a legal layman, but a quiet practitioner. From 1881 through the publication of his *Autobiography* in 1913, he remained uncommonly facile with leading principles, idiosyncratic legal rules, legal phraseology, and the methods of a trained lawyer.

A. Legal Principles: Lifetime Touchstone

Somewhere near the time when TR acquired his political consciousness, he appears to have absorbed the central premise of political leadership, *Potentia non est nisi ad bonum*, "Power is not conferred but for the public good."

Defining "the public good" for TR, no less than for other historic conferees of public power, was difficult. On one hand, the law reflected America's collective will. On the other, TR possessed his own finely tuned sense of good and evil, or right and wrong. His own sense dictated that morality never be compromised in the service of "legalism," particularly on matters of "the public good." Thus, while legal principles gave life to TR's definition of the "public good," any clash of legal and moral principles ended with the latter prevailing.

Morality, then, was TR's chief touchstone; but legal principles were his second. He might have marvelled that a common law principle exists to accommodate this exception to "legalism," *Modus et conventio vincunt legum*, "an exception to the law is justified when to follow the law would be against public policy or morality."[172]

Documenting TR's reliance on legal principle is easier than establishing the causal connection between his reliance and two years of law school. Nevertheless, the inference—that but for his legal training he would not have arrived at a full understanding of such principles—is supported by logic and the written record.

Legal principles are generally instilled in one of two ways at law school: studying discreet legal cases from which an operative principle is drawn and studying the maxims themselves. TR seems to have familiarized himself with many cases during his two years of law study. In addition, his Notes contain express references to a number of legal maxims.

Not surprisingly, in describing Professor Dwight's method of teaching, one commentator observed that rules were often "crowned" by "one of those wonderful maxims of law he [Professor Dwight] was so fond of citing, which gave the very essence of the doctrine and fastened it, for all time, in the minds of his hearers."[173] The Dean who followed Dwight, Harlan Fiske Stone, explained why. "The law school, in carrying out its part of the educational process, must confine itself to general principles; the purpose of the law course is not so much the accumulation of knowledge of the technical details of law as acquaintance with its nature and its fundamental doctrines, and the development of capacity to use them."[174]

Below are a few examples of TR's uncommon knowledge of, and attention to, legal maxims or principles. These examples come from three areas of his later political interest: Criminal Law, International Law, and Equal Protection for Women and laborers.

1. Criminal Law

TR learned the foundations of "Criminal Law" from George Chase and perhaps Theodore Dwight.[175]

Criminal Law, more than any other legal terrain, is well-marked by guiding principles. Here and there, expressly and implicitly, TR relied on those principles.

For example: In Spring, 1889, TR was appointed Civil Service Commissioner by President Harrison, a post he held for six years.[176] Finding the political spoils system abhorrent to his notion of fair employment and efficient government, TR instituted and enforced a "merit hiring" system. To his great consternation, he "found at the beginning of [his] experiences [in enforcing the law] that there were many offices in which the execution of the law was a sham."[177] By 1885, TR was Police Commissioner. Soon thereafter, he became President of the Police Commission of New York.[178] His bete noire was the prevailing habit of not enforcing laws, including the so-called "blue" laws against public consumption of alcohol on Sundays. These laws had not been struck down, but their execution was a dead letter. TR would have none of it; he enforced them. Said he, on reflection, "as a matter of fact, I was only enforcing honestly a law that had hitherto been enforced dishonestly."[179]

Later, TR would publicly decry the reluctance of the Federal Executive to penalize the "abuses" of corporate monopolies. He recalled that, "[a]lthough under the decision of the courts the National Government had power over the railways, I found, when I became President, that this power was either not exercised at all or exercised with utter inefficiency."[180]

These are two examples of TR's lifetime faith, confirmed by word and deed, that *Parum est latam esse sententiam nisi mandetur executioni*, "The law is of little purpose unless it is executed."[181]

A similar principle, *Justitia non est neganda non differenda*, or "Justice must neither be denied nor delayed," animated TR's recurring ire at America's criminal bar and bench. While he clearly appreciated the importance of protecting the rights of an accused,[182] he gave powerful voice to the imperative that justice must not be delayed.

> "If some horrible crime is committed and the people feel that under the best circumstances there will be an indefinite delay in the punishment of the criminal . . . then a premium is put upon that kind of lawbreaking which more than any other is a menace to the law. Long delays of justice, abuses of pardoning power, the sluggishness with which either court or attorney

moves; all of those things count in bringing about the condition of affairs which produces lynch law."[183]

The Executive power to pardon and commute sentences, as employed by TR, bore signs of close attention to legal principle. Nor should such attention be surprising. TR's Notes of October 8th, 1881, for example, presage the power he would have: "[T]he Executive has pardoning power to alleviate punishment in certain exceptional cases."[184] Three decades later, TR reflected on how as Governor and President he would decide those "exceptional case[s]" which warranted the exercise of "power to alleviate punishment." He wrote:

> "One of the painful duties of the chief executive in States like New York, as well as in the Nation, is the refusing of pardons. Yet I can imagine nothing more necessary from the standpoint of good citizenship than the ability to steel one's heart in this matter of granting pardons. . . . As regards capital cases, the trouble is that emotional men and women always see only the individual whose fate is up at the moment, and neither his victim nor the many millions of unknown individuals who would in the long run be harmed."[185]

Thus, TR "steel[ed] himself" to serve a legal principle, *Justitia est duplex, viz; severe puniens et vere praeveniens*, "Justice is double; punishing severely and truly preventing."[186]

Nor did he flinch from following the counsel he gave. In the case of John W. Burley, for example, a man convicted of raping "a young negro girl, practically a child,"[187] he resolutely refused to commute "infliction of the death penalty." He recoiled at "the most hideous crime known to our laws," a "monstrous deed," "a crime so revolting that the criminal is not entitled to one particle of sympathy from any human being."[188] Again, TR was of the mind, as at common law, that *Peccata contra naturam sunt gravissima*, "crimes against nature are the most heinous."[189]

In exercising the Executive power to commute sentences, TR also kept a keen eye on questions of proportionality. In 1892, the time-honored legal edict that the punishment must fit the crime seemed destined for a home in the Eighth Amendment. That year, in a dissent, Supreme Court Justice Field condemned "all punishments which by their excessive length or severity are greatly disproportionate to the offenses charged."[190] Yet not until 1910, eighteen years later, did the majority of the Supreme Court agree to constitutional protection of this principle.[191] As elsewhere, TR was ahead of the Court. As he later recounted, "when President, I frequently commuted sentences . . . because the penalty was disproportionate to the crime. . . ."[192]

Nor did TR fail to pardon convicts on the principle of self-defense. TR's Notes recite, under the heading "Excusable Homicide," the operative New York rule: "[I]n cases of common assault, trespass and the like, . . . [the person threatened] must as the old phrase says 'retreat to the wall'; that is, retire and forebear as long as possible to kill his assailant. But in defense ofproperty[,] retreat is not necessary—the trespasser, however, must first be requested to leave a house, and cannot be killed unless in repelling an attack dangerous to the person."[193] As Governor of New York from 1898 to 1900, TR applied this learning. At one point, he received a pardon petition of a man convicted of second degree murder. The man, a watchman, had been attacked by a "gang . . . of roughs while on duty outside company property." "[T]o save his own life, he was obliged in self-defense to kill one of his assailants,"[199] wrote TR. "[H]e had simply been forced to fight for his life while loyally doing his duty. . . . I looked into the case . . . and gave the man a full pardon. . . ."[200]

Other examples of TR's familiarity with the principles of Criminal Law are legion. He appears, for example, to have possessed an understanding of legal concepts such as "moral turpitude,"[201] and the crimes of "rape, . . . the circulation of indecent literature, . . . 'white slave' traffic, . . . wife murder, . . . gross cruelty to women and children, . . . seduction and abandonment, . . . ," as well as others.[202]

2. International Law

During TR's study of International Law with Burgess,[203] he recorded the following lesson:

> "Law implies authority to sanction. International law depends upon universal consent of various nations; so progress is very slow. Some points are dictated by morals; in war no wells must be poisoned. Others are merely positive; do not depend on principle."[204]

This must have been one of TR's first exposures to the principles of public international law. The impact of that lesson is, of course, impossible to calculate. Certainly, his increasing exposure to the topic during later life added depth to his initial understanding of such principles. Still, one finds scintillating hints of his enduring memory.

As President, TR generally acted in accord with International Law, for example by signing treaties or, in one instance, persuading Mexico to bring "the first case ever . . . before the [International Court of Justice, or] Hague Court."[205] Most spectacularly, he "substitut[ed] friendly and judicial for violent methods"[206] in negotiating a peace between warring Russia and Japan.[207]

Only when International Law failed, in TR's view, to accommodate a moral imperative, did he depart from it—and then with acute awareness.

In 1903, TR intervened on behalf of Panamanian revolutionaries in Colombia's civil war. He dispatched an American warship to the region. That action facilitated Panama's independence from Colombia and, consequently, the start of work by the United States on what became the Panama Canal, an international waterway. TR defended this bloodless intervention on grounds not of International Law but of "international morality."

Looking back in 1905, he cogently explained the inadequacy of International Law. Sounding remarkably like Burgess, with a twist of Dwight's Municipal Law insight, he declared:

> "There is of course no analogy at present between international law and private or municipal law, because there is no sanction of force for the former, while there is for the latter. Inside our own nation [,] the law-abiding man does not have to arm himself against the lawless [,] simply because there is some armed force—the police, the sheriff's posse, the national guard, the regulars—which can be called out to enforce the laws. At present, there is no similar international force to call on. . . ."[208]

Similarly, in his *Autobiography*, TR explained his Panama action. "[T]he whole fabric of municipal law, of law within each nation, rests ultimately upon the judge and the policeman; and the complete absence of the policeman, and the almost complete absence of the judge, in international affairs, prevents there being as yet any real homology between municipal and international law."[209]

Is it so unthinkable that Burgess, or Dwight, planted the seeds of that understanding?

3. Equal Treatment for Women and "Wage-Workers"

While TR's attention to women's suffrage predates his time at Columbia,[210] the panoply of differences in treatment must have come into sharp focus at law school. His Notes abound with related subtopics. For example, in "Municipal Law," one finds sections devoted to the "Legal Consequences of the Marriage Relation," the "Rt. [sic] Husband acquires in property of wife," "wife's life estate," "maintenance of wife," "capacity of wife to make contracts," "woman's right to take patent for invention," and the rights of women generally.[211]

At the same time, his Notes are rife with detailed corporate prerogatives under New York law. Large sections are devoted to "[the] relationship between a corporation and its workers," *sub nomine* "master and servant." For example, on February 15, 1881, TR recorded that, under prevailing law, "[the] risk of injury . . . must be included in risks wh[ich] have to be considered in his [the worker's] wages."[212] His Notes then spell out a rule long since abandoned: "Thus[,] whenever employment in service of [a] R R Co[.] is such as necessarily to bring person accepting it into contact with traffic on the line[,] risk of injury from carelessness of those who manage traffic is one of risks necessarily & naturally incident to such employment & within rule."[213]

As history would have it, TR became a champion of both the rights of women and of workers. On ending his tenure as Civil Service Commissioner, he recalled: "I had grown to realize very keenly that the duty of the Government to protect women and children must be extended to include the protection of all the crushable elements of labor."[214]

The principle of "equal protection of the laws," which was enshrined in the Fourteenth Amendment in 1868, would not formally be extended to women until 1971.[215] Women's suffrage would not be embodied in the Nineteenth Amendment until August 18, 1920.[216] Yet, TR consistently pressed for state and federal legislation embodying the rights of women. As he noted in 1913:

> Much can be done by law towards putting women on a footing of complete and entire equal rights with man—including the right to vote, the right to hold and use property, and the right to enter any profession she desires on the same terms as the man.[217]

TR undertook parallel efforts to correct what he saw as an economic, social, and legal imbalance between "oppress[ed] wage-workers" and "the great law-defying corporations of immense wealth."[218] He blamed the "mighty industrial overlords," who "by means of . . . the giant corporations" created "a riot of individualistic materialism,"[219] but he also castigated the judiciary.

On the one hand, he sought enforcement and refinement of anti-monopoly and labor legislation[220] through the courts; on the other, he invoked a potent legal principle to attack the courts themselves. Saying "[i]t would be useless to enumerate all the suits we brought,"[221] he deplored the timidity and corruption of judges. On timidity, he said: "The courts . . . , to the grave detriment of the people and of their own standing, had for a quarter of a century been . . . the agents of reaction [to] . . . the great business combinations."[222] On corruption, he excoriated them:

> "It is difficult to speak about the judges, for it behooves us all to treat with the utmost respect the high office of judge. . . . [But] [a] judge who on the bench truckles to the mob or bows down before a corporation; or who, having left the bench to become a corporation lawyer,[223] seeks to aid his clients by denouncing as enemies of property all those who seek to stop the abuses of the criminal rich; such a man performs an even worse service to the body politic than the Legislator or Executive who goes wrong . . . the judge who by word or deed makes it plain that the corrupt corporation, the law-defying corporation, the law-defying rich man has in him a sure and trustworthy ally, the judge who by the misuse of the proceeds of injunction makes it plain that in him the wage-worker has a determined and unscrupulous enemy . . . these judges work as much evil as if they pandered to the mob, as if they shrank from sternly repressing violence and disorder."[224]

TR's sting came from understanding, and applying, one key principle of law, *Politiae legibus non leges politiis adaptandae*, "Politics are to be adapted to the laws, and not the laws to politics."[225]

TR practiced what he preached. As President of the Police Commission from 1895 to 1897, TR personally pursued those he suspected of corruption, including fellow Police Commissioner, Andrew D. Parker.[226] By the time TR had acceded in 1897 to Assistant Secretary of the Navy, he "had broken [the New York City Police Force's] connections with the underworld, toughened the police-trial system, and largely eliminated corruption in the ranks."[227] As Morris explains: "He had proved that it was possible to enforce an unpopular law, and, by enforcing it, had taught the doctrine of respect of the law."[228]

Seeking "just and effective laws" against corporate excess, TR deplored "judges whose one aim seems to be to construe such laws so that they cannot be executed."[229] One senses that TR felt, but did not pronounce, another legal truism, *non in legendo sed in intelligendo legis consistunt*, "the laws consist not in being read, but in being understood."[230] Elsewhere, he openly confessed his reliance on legal principle. For example, addressing the pursuit of "social and industrial justice," he wrote in 1913: "The principle to which we especially strove to give expression, through these laws and through executive action, was that a right is valueless unless reduced from the abstract to the concrete. This sounds like a truism. So far from being such, the effort practically to apply it was almost revolutionary, and gave rise to the bitterest denunciation of us by all the big lawyers. . . ."[231]

TR clearly enjoyed identifying persuasive principles and applying them. To a large extent, this is the practice of a lawyer. Moreover, many of the principles to which TR referred, or upon which he acted, were founded in the common law. Some became provisions of the United States Constitution; others are traceable to simple moral authority.

The areas enumerated above do not, by any measure, exhaust the range of actions on which TR sought justification by recourse to principle. Discussing his enormous legislative contribution to, or founding of, the conservation movement, for example, he wrote: "The principles thus formulated and applied may be summed up in the statement that the rights of the public to the natural resources outweigh private rights, and must be given its first consideration."[232] He continued: "One of the principles whose application was the source of much hostility was this: It is better for the Government to help a poor man to make a living for his family than to help a rich man make more profit for his company. . . . Another principle which led to the bitterest antagonism of all was this—whoever (except a bona-fide settler)[233] takes public property for private profit should pay for what he gets."[234]

Other principles of law with which TR was conversant included the doctrines of *caveat emptor*[235] and contractual "good faith."[236]

A. Legal Rules, Phraseology, and Habits: Lifetime Companion

TR's reliance on legal principles is only brought into sharper focus by his uncanny retention of legal rules, phrases, and habits.

1. Flashes of Special Knowledge: Obscure Legal Rules

Four examples of obscure legal rules later remembered (and cross-referenced in his Notes) illustrate TR's powers of recall. These include:

the legal defense of insanity to acts performed by an alcoholic;
the legal justification for terminating actual cohabitation between a wife and adulterous husband;
the prerogative of "peremptory" and "for cause" challenges during jury empaneling; and
the standard of "legal proof"

By the late 1880's, TR was painfully aware that his brother, Elliot, was a "confirmed alcoholic."[237] Elliot was married and had two children. TR was thoroughly shocked when, in 1891, he learned that "a servant girl named Katy Mann" was "with child," after having been seduced by Elliot. TR's instant reaction was to leap beyond alcoholism, to another explanation. Writing to his mother on the topic, TR pointedly concluded: "Of course he was insane when he did it."[238]

Later, in a wishful letter to his brother, dated June 14, 1891, TR attempted to convince Elliot (and perhaps himself) that, as a result of Elliot's alcoholism, "you were very sick, and for hours at a time were out of your head, and did not have any clear recollection of what you were doing. . . ." He warned his brother that Katy Mann "could get testimony that you were often wild and irresponsible, either from being out of your head or from the use of liquor or opiates."[239] Eventually, Mann appears to have received "hush money" of $4000 to $10,000, and thereafter "begins mysteriously to fade from history."[240]

But why did TR conclude that the seduction by his alcoholic brother was "[o]f course . . . insan[ity]"? This explanation, repeated whenever the affair was privately discussed or written about,[241] is unique, even odd.

One possibility is that TR recalled a lesson from law school, ten years prior. That recall could have been triggered by Katy Mann's threat of a "law suit."[242]

TR's 1881 Notes boldly state: "Drunkenness is, in general, no defense. . . . But insanity resulting from a continuous course of intemperance is entitled to the same consideration as insanity from any other cause."[243]

TR's awareness of the relevant law seems to have been keen. In writing his mother about Elliot's adultery and violence, and their effect on Elliot's wife, Anna, TR concludes: "Anna must be made to understand that it is both maudlin and criminal—I am choosing my words with scientific exactness—to continue living with Elliot. . . ."[244]

"Scientific" indeed. TR's Notes from 1881[245] describe the "common law" as based "on the principle that the law is a science and that . . . [each] new rule is a deduction from principles previously known."[246]

Still more on point, TR's Notes for December 20, 1880 unambiguously pronounce the acceptable basis for a divorce, if not also criminal charges: "[One party] must show such a continuous course of bad conduct as will satisfy [the] court that it is improper for [that party] with due exercise of [his or her] marital authority to cohabit with [the other party]."[247] Grounds for a divorce on the basis of "cruelty" existed if, for example, "[w]ords inflicting indignity or threatening pain [were] used," or a husband was proved to be "brandishing [his] fist in [his] wife's face in [a] menacing manner."[248] These grounds mesh well with reports of Elliot's behavior from Anna and TR's mother.

TR may have been concerned also, on Anna's behalf, with the legal effect of continuing cohabitation with Elliot. In his Notes, on December 9, 1880, he had carefully written: "A condoned charge of adultery causes [the] offense to be considered as though never committed."[249] Elsewhere, his Notes describe the legal procedures for proving whether an "adulterer" is "the father" of a child.[250]

Was TR's 1891 understanding of Anna's rights and Elliot's defenses based on a faint but gently pulsing recollection of these law school lessons? We will never know. Still, his 1891 references are unusually specific and, from a legal perspective, accurate.

Another legal rule not commonly drawn upon by laymen, but known to TR, pertained to the empaneling of a jury prior to trial. TR had specifically studied "trial by jury."[251] In most jurisdictions, each party has a right to challenge and remove a specified number of jurors in what is termed a "peremptory challenge" (for example, on the basis of age or gender). After peremptory challenges have been exhausted, the party may challenge the remaining jurors only "for cause," or by furnishing a legally satisfactory reason why a particular juror *ought* not be seated, for example bias. To win removal of a juror "for cause," a party must satisfy the trial judge that the reasons for removal are compelling.[252]

That being the rule, consider TR's account of challenges by Senators and Congressmen to his reforms at the Civil Service Commission: "[S]ometimes, to use a legal phrase, their hatred was for cause, and sometimes it was peremptory—that is, sometimes the Commission interfered with their most efficient, and incidentally most corrupt and unscrupulous supporters, and at other times, where there was no such interference, a man nevertheless had an innate dislike of anything that tended to decency in government."[253]

Similarly, TR never forgot that there are prerequisites for courtroom proof. "Legal proof" is the logically sufficient reason for assenting to the truth of a proposition advanced. "In its judicial sense, [proof] is a term of wide import, and comprehends everything that may be adduced at trial, within the legal rules, for the purpose of producing conviction in the mind of judge or jury, aside from mere argument."[254]

The definition of legal proof must have flashed through TR's mind when, in documenting corruption in New York's Legislature from 1882 to 1885, he said: "Of course[,] I never had anything in the nature of legal proof of corruption, and the figures I am about to give are merely approximate."[255]

2. Legal Phraseology

Another barometer of TR's proximity to law is his recurring use of terms with special legal meanings.

He makes innumerable references, for example, to "slander."[256] He often discussed the relationship between "rights" and "duties."[257] He took note of the difference between a law's "spirit" and "letter."[258] He understood the "theory" of constitutional law, as well as where he as Chief Executive fit into its practice.[259] He would commonly make references to the rules of evidence, such as the weakened influence which ought to be accorded "statements with no foundation in fact,"[260] "hearsay,"[261] "misrepresentation,"[262] or statements motivated by "malice."[263] Finally, there were the many legal terms he used in reference to legal "principles" or "rules."[264]

3. Legal Habits

Identifying and tracing lawyerly habits to law school is like nailing jello to the wall; the object and subject are unlikely to stay linked for long.

Still, if there is such a thing as a lawyer's penchant for cross-examination, for extensive preparation, for orderly thinking, or for thoughtful use of language, TR qualified by possession of these traits.

His skills as a cross-examiner, dating to law school, stood him in good stead as Civil Service Commissioner. More than once, he netted the unwary in a logical snare.[265] When he was attacked for investigating corruption like an English "star-chamber" and for asking "leading questions," he shot back like a nimble litigator: "[O]f course I used leading questions! I have always used them in examinations of this kind and always shall use them . . . to get at the truth."[266] Dwight had, after all, been known not only for teaching methods of practice but for "vigorously cross-examin[ing]" his students.[267]

As for extensive preparation, Morris explains that, "[u]nder maximum pressure Roosevelt was sunny, calm, and unnaturally clear." Making war preparations and facing a crisis as Acting Secretary of the Navy in February 1898, TR "was neither nervous nor spontaneous." His actions were "the logical result of ten months of strategic planning, at the Navy Department and at the Metropolitan Club, in his correspondence with Captain Mahan, and on his walks with Captain Wood."[268] Was this habit carried over from exposure to Dwight, who "often declared that every successful lawyer must expect crises when the act of the moment must be the result of long periods of systematic preparation"?[269]

TR publicly disdained disorderly thinking. He once dismissively remarked of a Postmaster-General, "I don't like him. . . . In the first place he has a very sloppy mind. . . ."[270]

Last, TR's thirty-seven orderly, original and detailed books evidence his rare and thoughtful use of language.

Conclusion

Between November 1880 and September 1882, Theodore Roosevelt listened to a minimum of eighty-two lectures on law. Each lecture lasted an hour and a half. Outside the classroom, TR methodically transcribed law treatises, participated in moot court competitions, and wrote to his friends and relatives of his priority on law. During the summer of 1882, TR was intent on studying law three or four days a week. In two years, TR wrote more than one thousand one hundred pages of law Notes. Those Notes provide new insight into the nature of law school in the late nineteenth century. They also indicate, when coupled with corroborating documents, that TR was a trained lawyer. Finally, the perceptible influence of TR's legal training on his later life suggests the formative nature of a late nineteenth century American legal education.

Notes

1. Speech before the Hamilton Club, Chicago (April 10, 1889).

2. Stevens, Robert, *The Law School: Legal Education in America from the 1850s to the 1980s* (Chapel Hill: Univ. of North Carolina Press 1983) (hereafter cited as "STEVENS"), at 22. Stevens reports that the number of lawyers in 1850 was 23,939; by 1880, that number had climbed to 64,137. See also, Gewalt, Gerard W., ed., *The New High Priests: Lawyers in Post Civil War America* (Westport, Connecticut: Greenwood Press 1984), at 97-123.

3. Friedman, Lawrence M., *A History of American Law* (New York: Touchstone 1973) (hereafter cited as "FRIEDMAN"), at 526.

4. TR's 1880-1882 Columbia Law School Class Notes consist of seven handwritten notebooks, collectively totalling 1,189 handwritten pages. These are preserved in the Special Collections Division of Columbia University Law School Library, New York, New York. The Notes have, until recently, been located in two boxes in the cellar of Columbia Law School. They have never been cited, quoted or referred to by any of TR's published biographers. Organized but crumbling and fading, they record TR's formal study of diverse legal subjects at Columbia. The Notes were acquired by Columbia in 1976 from Mary R. Pease (Trimble); the acquisition was formally announced in 1981. See *Columbia Law Alumni Observer*, Nov.-Dec. 1981, 10. In the announcement of the acquisition one reads: "[Mary R. Pease (Trimble)] . . . had acquired the books from her parents who had in turn received them from her father's brother, Walter Trimble, Roosevelt's Harvard College roommate. They [Roosevelt and Trimble] came to Columbia Law School together and though Trimble graduated, Roosevelt did not. Associate Dean Peter de L. Swords [Columbia Class of] [19]62, a family friend through whom the books were given, guesses that 'upon leaving law

school Roosevelt simply left behind the notebooks for the use of his friend Trimble.'" *Id.* The Alumni Observer indicates that these notebooks "give some insight into . . . the mind of the man who would become the nation's 26th President." *Id.*

5. See also STEVENS at 48, n.38, 39.

6. See FRIEDMAN at 384.

7. See *Id.* at 405.

8. *Id.* at 484-494.

9. While "[p]rotective labor legislation . . . grew from almost nothing before the Civil War to an impressive web of legislation by 1900," the sad truth was that "[c]hild-labor laws on the books were not the same as child-labor laws enforced." FRIEDMAN at 492. The minimal role of women in the legal profession during the late nineteenth century also contributed to a relative lack of emphasis on labor legislation protecting women. "Overall, the census reported 5 women lawyers in the United States in 1870. As of 1880, it listed 75 and, by 1900 there were 1,010." STEVENS at 83; see also, 435-440.

10. See FRIEDMAN at 484-494.

11. See *Id.* at 193; 299-302.

12. See *Id.* at 340-1; 351, quoting Bentham, Jeremy

13. See *Id.* at 359-61.

14. Until the close of the century, "[p]ublic property was looked upon as an inexhaustible treasure. Whether land was to be sold, or given away, used to create new centers of population, or to fund a school system, government's function was to divest itself of this primary form of wealth as soon and equitably as possible." FRIEDMAN at 365, see also, *id.*, at 361-367.

15. See, e.g., FRIEDMAN at 381-82.

16. *Id.* at 382.

17. *Id.* at 409.

18. See *Id.* at 409-11.

19. See, e.g., *Id.* at 411-12.

20. *Id.* at 449; see also Hofstadter, Richard, *The American Political Tradition* (Vintage Books: New York, 1974) (hereafter cited as "HOFSTADTER") at 230, 256, 291-94.

21. See, e.g., HOFSTADTER at 291-92; Gordon, Robert W. in Gewalt, *The New High Priests*, at 61.

22. Gordon has noted: "As intermediaries between corporate clients and powerful outsiders—investors, creditors, and stockholders as well as local national and foreign governments—and as cosmopolitans attuned to popular foreign public opinion, corporate lawyers were frequently in a position to tell their clients that some proposed action would have adverse long-run effects." Gordon, in Gewalt, *The New High Priests*, at 61. See also FRIEDMAN at 446-448.

23. See, e.g., HOFSTADTER at 293-95.

24. See FRIEDMAN at 455.

25. *Id.* at 455-59.

26. Roosevelt, Theodore, *Theodore Roosevelt: An Autobiography* (New York: MacMillan, 1913), at 165-66.

27. *Id.* at 55.

28. FRIEDMAN at 60-65.

29. *Id.* at 514.

30. *Id.* at 515.

31. See FRIEDMAN at 459-63; see also, STEVENS, *Law School*, at 48, n.39.

32. See *Id.* at 508.

33. In 1914, TR made a treacherous descent down Brazil's unexplored "Rio da Du'vida" or "River of Doubt." He became gravely ill. "Only his indomitable will kept Theodore from giving up in those days on the River of Doubt—now officially named Rio Teodoro by the Brazilian Government." Day, Donald, *The Hunting and Exploring Adventures of Theodore Roosevelt* (Dial Press, 1955) at 428. On grizzly bears, TR was "recognized as the world authority." Morris, Edmond, *The Rise of Theodore Roosevelt* (Ballantine, 1979) at 818, n.51. His personal encounters are riveting. See, e.g., Day, *Adventures*, at 85-87. No less exciting are TR's encounters with lions, including "a lion hunt with spears." See Day, *Adventures*, at 325; see also, Roosevelt, *Autobiography* at 36-37; see Roosevelt, Theodore, *African Game Trails* (Scribner's Sons, 1910) at 58-81. Czars and emperors were their own challenge, particularly as he negotiated the Russo-Japanese peace of 1905, for which he was awarded the Nobel Peace Prize. See, Einstein, Lewis, *Roosevelt: His Mind in Action* (Houghton Mifflin, 1930) at 141. The "absolute rule of the [city] boss" never ceased to stir TR's ire. See, e.g., Roosevelt, *Autobiography*, at 292-294. Bullets and bayonets were met, unflinchingly, by the "Rough Rider" in Cuba, during the Spanish-American War. See Morris, *Rise of Theodore Roosevelt*, at 643 (hereafter referred to as "MORRIS"). In 1912, TR was also shot by a would-be assassin. The account cannot be omitted: "The bullet lodged in his chest, broke a rib, and made a serious wound, which would have been fatal if its course had not been deflected by his iron spectacle case. . . . [H]e insisted on proceeding to the hall. . . . Nothing would stop him, and for one hour and a half he spoke, till [he weakened]. . . . On his way to the hospital he related to a friend that when he had left for the Cuban Campaign he had realized that he might be shot, but made up his mind that if he were . . . , he would go straight on no matter what happened to him afterward. . . ." See Einstein, *His Mind in Action*, at 214.

34. Edmond Morris, TR's Pulitzer Prize-winning biographer, devoted only two of seven hundred and forty-one pages of text to TR's study of law. See MORRIS, at 139-141. Morris maintained that TR did no more than "pay lip-service to the law" after October, 1881. See *id.*, at 772-3, n.68. Carlton Putnam devoted eight pages of his masterful biography to TR's study of law. See Putnam, *Theodore Roosevelt, Vol. I: The Formative Years, 1858-1886* (Scribner's 1958) at 216-221; 227-28. Einstein offered: "He took up law and dropped it. . . . [H]e was studying law and writing, a 'History of the Naval War of 1812'. . . . His interest in the

law had always been feeble." See Einstein, *His Mind in Action* at preface v, 33. Thayer, relying heavily on TR's *Autobiography*, provided a mere two paragraphs and this surprisingly hyperbolic conclusion: "His law studies seem to have absorbed him less than anything else that he undertook during all his life." Thayer, William Roscoe, *Theodore Roosevelt: An Intimate Biography* (Houghton Mifflin, 1919) at 32. Cutright offered only: "He [Theodore Roosevelt] studied law under his uncle, Robert Barnhill Roosevelt." Cutright, Paul Russell, *Theodore Roosevelt the Naturalist*, (Harper, 1956) at 33. Other biographies provide similar treatment of the topic. Bishop may have been most insightful. His short reference to law includes two rarely heard observations. First, TR "had at the time [when he was seated in the New York Assembly, January, 1882] no intention or expectation of abandoning the profession of law for a political career." Second, his learning on corporation law "made an impression upon young Roosevelt's mind which was never wholly effaced, but which deepened and strengthened as time went on [,] and found expression later in his action as president [,] in the direction of regulating and controlling the conduct of great corporations." Bishop, Joseph Backlin, *Theodore Roosevelt and His Time* (Scribner's Sons, 1920) at 6-7.

35. TR's *Private Diaries 1878- 1885*, as well as many pieces of original correspondence, are preserved in the Theodore Roosevelt Collection, Harvard College Library, Cambridge, Massachusetts. Also preserved there, and consulted for this paper, is his brittle *Harvard Scrapbook 1879- 80.*

36. The Records Division of Columbia University holds *The Junior Law Register 1880-1881* and *The Senior Law Register 1881-1882*, both of which record TR's name, address ("6 West 57th Street"), and registration during these academic years. *The Columbia University Alumni Register 1754-1931* (Col. U. Press, 1932) records that TR was a non-graduate of the Law Class of 1882. The "Columbiana Collection" records that TR received an honorary LL.D. in 1899.

37. TR married Alice Hathaway Lee, a native of Brookline, Massachusetts, on October 27, 1880, his birthday. His life seems marked by planned and unplanned coincidences. Among the intended, he announced his engagement to Alice on February 14, 1880, Saint Valentine's Day. Among the unintended, Alice died of a liver ailment called "Bright's disease" on February 14, 1884. As a double shock, his mother died on the same day of typhoid fever. See MORRIS at 123-5, 135, 241-44.

38. This volume, still definitive in the field, was begun at Harvard and largely researched and written during the summer of 1881. See MORRIS at 148-49. TR also completed, in March, 1881, an unpublished account of a sailing adventure with his brother. See *id.* at 771, n.20.

39. On October 28, 1881, TR accepted the nomination for Assemblyman of the Twenty First Assembly District in Manhattan, and collected his first political victory on November 9, 1881. See MORRIS at 151-53. TR's intent, however, was to maintain the priority on law, not politics. See, e.g., Letter to Charles Washburn, November 10, 1881, quoted in Morison, Elting E. and Blum, John, eds. *The Letters of Theodore Roosevelt*, vol. 1 (Harvard U. Press, 1954) at 85; see also, Bishop, *Theodore Roosevelt and His Time*, at 7.

40. H.C. Black, *Black's Law Dictionary* (West Publishing Co. 1891 5th Ed. 1979) at 363.

41. Each of the fifty States administers its own bar examination. Generally, persons wishing to practice before a State's courts must pass that State's bar examination.

42. Lord Edward Coke, *First Institute* (1628). Lord Coke memorialized four volumes of common law learning during the reign of Charles I.

43. The basic American law degree in the late nineteenth century was an LL.B. (Law Latin Bachelor), or Bachelor of laws. Today, the basic American law degree is a J.D., or juris doctor. The first honorary degree received by TR was awarded by Columbia University in 1899. That degree was an LL.D., or doctorate of laws. TR subsequently received twelve additional honorary degrees. These ranged from LL.D. (e.g., from Yale, 1901 and Harvard, 1902) to D.C.L. (Oxford U., 1910) and Ph.D. (U. of Berlin, 1910). See *Who Was Who in America*, vol. 1, 1897-1942, 5th Ed. at 1055.

44. "Bar admission [is the] [a]ct by which one is licensed to practice before courts of a particular state or jurisdiction after satisfying requirements such as bar examination, period of residency or admission on grounds of reciprocity after period of years as member of bar of another jurisdiction." *Black's Law Dictionary* at 135.

45. See, e.g., Roosevelt, *Autobiography* at 55. Einstein notes generally, that, "[a]fter he had achieved the highest honors a man can covet, he spoke disparagingly of his aptitudes in sport and intellect." Einstein, *His Mind in Action* at 14.

46. MORRIS at 23.

47. TR's "Ornithological studies," began at an early age. Cutright noted that, while TR was in Africa in 1909, "[o]rnithologists, too, were amazed at Roosevelt's knowledge of African birds, not being familiar at all with his escapades as a stripling of fourteen when he had stuffed plovers, cormorants, bee-eaters, and numerous other birds that had fallen to his gun along . . . the Nile from Cairo to Aswan." Cutright, *Theodore Roosevelt the Naturalist* at 200. His depth of zoological self-training and experience are evident in TR *African Game Trails, supra.* His well-developed understanding of human nature produced innumerable examples of expertise in practical sociology and psychology.

48. See *infra.*

49. See Putnam, *Theodore Roosevelt: The Formative Years*, 1858-1886 (hereafter cited as "PUTNAM") at 218; see also Goebel, Julius, Jr., and The Foundation For Research in Legal History, *A History of the School of Law: Columbia University* (Col. U. Press, 1955) (hereafter cited as "GOEBEL") at 80.

50. Theodore Roosevelt: *Private Diaries. 1878-1885*, November 17, 1880. Almost without exception, the entries in TR's *Private Diaries* during these years are short. Nevertheless, they provide insight into the content and progress of his thought.

51. See, e.g., Teague, Michael, "Theodore Roosevelt and Alice Hathaway Lee: A New Perspective," *Harv. Lib. Bull.* (Harv., Summer 1985) at 230.

52. Despite crowded quarters, Columbia Law School "was, nevertheless, the leading American law school of the time." PUTNAM at 218.

53. GOEBEL at 62.

54. *Id.* at 414, n.40.

55. See GOEBEL at 75; see also, *id.* at 415, n.56. Goebel indicates that, "[u]pon entering the Great Jones Street building, one found [Professor] Dwight's small cozy book-lined office upon one's left and the principal lecture room on the right. The latter was particularly notable for its lack of ventilation. The second floor was occupied by a second lecture room (later used for Burgess's classes) and the Trustee's room. On the third floor was the Law Library."

56. PUTNAM at 219, citing letter from Roosevelt's classmate Clayton Ryder.

57. GOEBEL at 95, quoting TR's Municipal Law Professor, Theodore Dwight.

58. *Id.* at 37.

59. See PUTNAM at 217, citing Taylor, "The Dwight Method" 7 *Harv. L. Rev.* 205 (1893).

60. TR's *Private Diary* entries for the period February 16, 1882 through December 31, 1882 appear not to have survived the intervening century.

61. Morris points out that, while TR was Vice President of the United States, then a uniquely unengaging occupation, he "asked Associate Justice [of the United States Supreme Court] Edward D. White for advice on resuming his long-abandoned legal studies in the fall [of 1901]." MORRIS at 37. Morris draws the conclusion that such inquiry was "a sure sign of confusion and pessimism about the future." *Id.* Other inferences might be that TR again sought a fruitful occupation for his additional time, wished for greater financial security, was acting upon his lifetime desire for a private career, or was simply uncertain about the future.

62. See, e.g., MORRIS at 139-41, 772-73, n.68.

63. See, *Theodore Roosevelt: Private Diaries*, May 12, 1881 through July, 1881.

64. *Theodore Roosevelt: Private Diaries*, October 6, 1881.

65. "[Generally,] [t]he Term commence[d] on the first Wednesday of October, and continue[d] until May 17th. The course of study embrace[d] two years." See Goebel, *History of the School of Law*, 61.

66. *Theodore Roosevelt: Private Diaries*, December 7, 1881.

67. These notebooks all have a gray, "beach pebbles" motif on their front and rear covers, and were all (apparently) purchased at "Joseph Laurier, Stationer, No. 1 Great Jones St., New York." See inside front covers. The handwriting matches that found in many of TR's authenticated documents housed in Harvard's Houghton Library.

68. This set of Notes also contains the name "Professor Chase" on its final page, but was certainly intended for TR's eyes. Professor George Chase taught Criminal Law at Columbia during 1880, 1881, and 1882. See, *infra*.

69. See *infra*, Chart, entitled "Theodore Roosevelt's Surviving Attendance Record Based on His Law Notes."

70. September 15, 1882 Letter from TR to sister, quoted in Morison, Elting E. and Blum, John, eds. *The Letters of Theodore Roosevelt*, vol. 1 (Harvard U. Press, 1956-57) at 56.

71. "[I]n October 1882, they [Theodore and Alice] at last moved into a home of their own at 55 West 45th Street [in Manhattan]." Teague, Harv. Lib. Bull., *supra* at 235.

72. TR was in Albany intermittently from January, 1882 until the New York Assembly adjourned on June 2, 1882. See MORRIS at 149-181.

73. He may have intended to take the examination late in 1882, or even 1883.

74. Letter from TR to his mother, quoted in Morison and Blum, *Letters* at 56.

75. Morison and Blum, *Letters* at 56.

76. Professor Burgess did recall that TR was "very accurate in examination," Burgess, *Reminiscences of an American Scholar* (N.Y. Col. U. Press, 1934) at 212-214, but none of the exams administered to TR by Burgess have survived. The Records Division at Columbia University does possess records of student grades for the period 1880-1883. However, these records are admittedly incomplete and unorganized. A comprehensive review reveals no recorded examination grades or course grades for TR.

77. See *Columbia University Alumni Register, 1754-1931*, Committee on General Catalogue (Col. U. Press, 1932) 743, col. 3, item 16.

78. TR always felt deep discontent on witnessing an act of patent immorality. His *Private Diary* throughout the Harvard years, coupled with correspondence with his father, reveal a powerful commitment to do "good" and to battle "against evil." See *Private Diaries*, e.g., March 15, 1878 ("Looked over his [father's] sweet, affectionate letters. They will always be to me a talisman against evil."); see also MORRIS at 144, citing Robinson, Corinne Roosevelt, *My Brother Theodore Roosevelt* (Scribner's, 1921) at 106.

79. See e.g., GOEBEL at 105. This historical treatise indicates, for example, that the "Association of the Bar of New York was organized to combat the prevailing demoralization of the legal profession" during the 1870's.

80. See Roosevelt, *Autobiography* at 55-56.

81. The third year could be spent in law school or "as a clerk in a law office." See GOEBEL at 104; see also *id.* at 433, n.144. Notably, in the 1870's, Dwight had opposed a third year of study because "he still doubted that young men would stay that long in a law school or attend a law school that required three years' study for a bachelor's degree." *Id.* at 74.

82. "As it happened, Professor Dwight's comprehensive final examination, thought by him as a test of the graduate's qualification for admission to the Bar, had also become anachronistic, for Columbia Law School graduates had now to submit to the regular court-controlled Bar examination just like any other candidates for admission. The class that was graduated in 1881 was the last group to be admitted to the New York Bar merely upon presentation of a diploma from the Columbia College Law School." GOEBEL at 104; see also *id.* at 53, 426, n.68.

83. TR explained his financial situation as follows: "[I]t happened that I had been left enough money by my father not to

make it necessary for me to think solely of earning bread. . . . [W]hile I must earn money, I could afford to make earning money the secondary instead of primary object of my career." Roosevelt, *Autobiography* at 56.

84. See Roosevelt, *Law Notes*, Municipal Law Notebooks "2," "3," "4" (1881), and 1880 Notebook entitled "Law." See also GOEBEL at 80; PUTNAM at 218.

85. See generally, Roosevelt, *Notes*.

86. Moot Court competitions were optional and judged by Professors Dwight, Chase, and Dillon. See GOEBEL at 80-81, 94.

87. Roosevelt, *Private Diary*, January 21, 1881.

88. GOEBEL at 418-19, n.95.

89. See *The Columbia Law Alumni Observer* at 10.

90. PUTNAM at 219.

91. *Id.*

92. Roosevelt, *Law Notes*, Notebook Entitled "Law," October 7, [1881].

93. *Id.* at October 8, [1881].

94. TR acceded to the Presidency of the United States in 1901, becoming that office's twenty-sixth holder, after the fatal shooting of President William McKinley on September 6, 1901.

95. See MORRIS at 141.

96. See Roosevelt, *Law Notes*, Notebook "2" in Municipal Law [1880]; Notebook "3" in Municipal Law [1881], "October 22."

97. See Roosevelt, *Law Notes*, Notebook "3" in Municipal Law, October 20, 1881.

98. MORRIS at 98.

99. *Id.* at 117.

100. *Id.* at 118. There are the cardboard envelopes affixed to one page in TR's "Harvard Scrapbook" entitled "Maine Woods [,] March 1879." Could these have contained arrowheads? See Theodore Roosevelt: *Harvard Scrapbook, 1879-80*, located in Theodore Roosevelt Collection, Harvard College Library, Cambridge, Massachusetts.

101. *Id.*

102. See Roosevelt, *Law Notes*, Notebook "3" in Municipal Law [1881].

103. Roosevelt, *Private Diaries*, May 22, 1881.

104. *Id.* at June 2, 1881.

105. See Roosevelt, *Law Notes*, Notebook "3" in Municipal Law [1881], January 24th.

106. TR, apparently, often sketched "little ships" during 1881, as he wrote his *The Naval War of 1812*. Putnam recounts that, "one can, with the help of Owen Wister, visualize him standing on one leg in front of a bookcase at 57th Street, the other leg crossed behind, toe touching floor, while he scribbles on a slide drawn out from the shelves, and Alice hurries in exclaiming, 'We're dining out in twenty minutes, and Teddy's drawing little ships.'" *Theodore Roosevelt: The Formative Years, 1858-1886*, 221.

Likewise, in a recently discovered and unpublished letter from TR to Alice on March 29, 1881, he writes: "Darling Baby, I have been studying hard all day—only drawing a few 'little boats'—and did not go out driving." *See* Letter to Alice Lee, March 29, 1881, Roosevelt. Collection, Harvard College Library.

107. MORRIS at 153-54.

108. Roosevelt, *Law Notes*, "Criminal Law" set.

109. Roosevelt, *Law Notes*, Notebook "3" in Municipal Law [1881], January 25, 26, and 27, 1881.

110. This interest represents a continuation of his college interest in women's rights; his 1880 senior thesis was entitled "Practicability of Giving Men and Women Equal Rights." See, e.g., MORRIS at 128. Putnam, *Theodore Roosevelt: The Formative Years, 1858-1886*, 219, quoting letter from Clayton Ryder to Carlton Putnam, dated July 17, 1952.

111. See GOEBEL at 61.

112. See *id.* at 61.

113. A "full-time" student of law, in October 1988, was required to have "1200 classroom periods of 50 minutes each, including examinations" over three years, in order to graduate. See New York State Court of Appeals, *Rules for the Admission of Attorneys and Counselors of Law*, Title 22, Chap. I, Sub-Chap. B, Section 502.3(c) (ii) (Oct., 1988). Thus, the annual classroom study requirement is one-thousand hours divided by three, or three hundred thirty- three hours. TR would appear to have studied somewhere between two hundred fifty and five hundred fifty hours.

114. Although Municipal Law was generally only taught 3 days a week, see GOEBEL at 61, TR's schedule during 1880, written in his own hand on the back flap of Notebook "2" of Municipal Law, appears as follows: "Wed. Even. 1, Thurs. Even. 1, Friday Even. 1, Sat. Even. 1, 8 P.M." Whether by altering his schedule or by taking other classes simultaneously, he also appears to have attended morning classes for some portion of the two academic years, 1880-81 and 1881-82. See MORRIS at 137 ("Theodore's first recitation was scheduled for 8:30 [a.m.]. . . .")

115. This period is the span of days for which there are either diary entries referring to law study, or law school notes, or both. Excluding the vacation period, May 18, 1881 to October 5, 1881, this period totals approximately 8.5 months or 35 weeks.

116. Dwight, for example, described the out-of-class requirements he imposed: "The student is assigned daily a certain portion of an approved text-book [sic] for his reading prior to listening to expositions of the subject involved. To make the assignment effective, he is asked questions upon the topic, mainly to make it certain that he has studied the subject and has in a measure comprehended it, and is thus in a position to listen with advantage to expositions, this is a prime element in legal as well as other instruction. . . ." GOEBEL at 36, quoting Dwight. One law student explained: "Our afternoons and evenings were fully occupied in a careful reading of the text for the next recitation, and the hours between early breakfast and recitation

were spent in reviewing what we had read the previous afternoon and evening." GOEBEL at 34-5, quoting Judge William J. Wallace, United States Circuit Court for the Second Circuit.

117. Three classes per week, for 35 weeks, at 1.5 hours per class, plus one hour per class in additional preparation, equals [(3 x 35 x 1.5) + (3 x 35 x 1) =], or 262.5 hours.

118. Although "[t]he Term commence[d] on the first Wednesday of October, and continue[d] until May 17th," see GOEBEL at 61, TR began his 1881 Fall Term one day late, since he "began at the Law," according to his *Private Diary*, on Thursday, October 6, 1881. Likewise, he appears to have begun study late in 1880. His first diary entry on law appears on Wednesday, November 17, 1880, when he notes "walked to the law school." This fits with the fact that he had married Alice on October 27, 1880, and thereafter they had enjoyed a "quiet fortnight together at Oyster Bay." See MORRIS at 137.

119. See *supra*.

120. This estimate is based on his seriousness of purpose during the 1880 and 1881 Terms, the volume of undated and unsigned Notes from which he may have studied, and the unlikelihood that he would consider "writing home" about a time commitment less significant than this.

121. The Board of Trustees of the Law School reported, for example, in 1864: "Two moot courts are held every week, at each of which a cause previously assigned is argued by four or more students selected from each class. The Counsel respectively prepares written points in the ordinary manner, supporting this position by citing legal authorities. The Court consists of the presiding Professor and the members of the Senior Class, who had acted as Counsel in the case previously argued. Associate judges deliver written opinions one week after the argument, and the cause is then concluded by the opinion delivered by the Professor." See GOEBEL at 61.

122. TR's actual class time probably consisted of roughly thirteen months. This estimate derives from evidence of his study from November 17, 1880 to the end of 1882 Spring Term, or May 17, 1882, excluding vacation or non-class periods, from May 18, 1881 to October 5, 1881 and beyond May 18, 1882. Thirteen academic months constitute approximately fifty-six weeks. His total number of classes would have been one hundred sixty-eight. If each class was 1.5 hours in length, and he prepared for two additional hours prior to each class, his total class and preparation hours would total four hundred twenty. If two additional hours are added per *week* (e.g., for non-class, non-preparation legal commitments, such as moot court or review of his notes), after fifty-six class weeks he would have studied an additional one hundred twelve hours. Finally, if he studied—as he promised his mother we would on July 5, 1882—from approximately July 5, 1882 until September 15, 1882 for only two hours per day, three days per week, over nine weeks, he would have studied an additional fifty-four hours. Together, the 420 class hours, 112 moot court and review hours, and 54 summer 1882 hours total 586 hours.

123. See *supra* at note 101. [Editor's note: Note numbering is preserved from the original, restarting at 114 following 123.]

114. See GOEBEL at 84.

115. *Id.* at 94.

116. *Id.* at 35-39.

117. *Id.* at 38, quoting Burgess.

118. *Id.*

119. In 1913, TR bemoaned a "teaching [which] . . . seemed to me against justice," the "repellent" doctrine of caveat emptor [or "buyers beware"], and the [absence of] "certain standards . . . compatible with the idealism I suppose every high-minded young man is apt to feel." See *Autobiography*, at 55.

120. GOEBEL at 39.

121. *Id.* at 39.

122. *Id.* at 63, quoting Barnard.

123. *Id.* at 63.

124. *Id.*

125. Burgess, J., *Reminiscences of an American Scholar* (1934).

126. GOEBEL at 85-86, quoting Burgess, *Reminiscences*, 181.

127. GOEBEL at 87. In 1881, Burgess became head of "Columbia's first non-professional graduate school," officially announced as "a School designed to prepare young men for the duties of Public Life [and] . . . entitled a School of Political Science." *Id.* at 89.

128. *Id.* at 83.

129. *Id.* at 79.

130. *Id.* at 85, 94.

131. Roosevelt, *Autobiography* at 55.

132. See GOEBEL at 85. Dillon's Columbia Law School salary was twice that of any non-Columbia professor, yet Dillon stated in 1881 that he was leaving Columbia for economic reasons; his salary "was much less than he could make in [private] practice." Dillon's instinct for ever increasing personal profit seems unlikely inspiration for lessons in public-spiritedness, professional morality or scruples. *Id.* at 94.

133. Roosevelt, *Private Diaries*, November 17, 1880.

134. *Id.*, November 24, 1880.

135. *Id.*, December 4, 1880.

136. Notebook "1" of Municipal Law is missing; Notebook "2" begins on December 9, 1881.

137. While the notebooks for these courses are missing, Professor Burgess, recalled TR registering for these courses in Autumn 1880. See *supra*, note 124.

138. Roosevelt, *Private Diaries*, January 4, 1881.
139. *Id.*, February 23, 1881.
140. *Id.*, January 6, 1881.
141. *Id.*, January 21, 1881.
142. *Id.*, February 24, 1881.
143. *Id.*, March 30, 1881.
144. See Roosevelt, *Law Notes*, Notebook "4" in Municipal Law, March 1881.
145. Roosevelt, *Private Diaries*, April 13, 1881.
146. *Id.*, April 19, 1881.
147. *Id.*, April 23, 1881.
148. *Id.*, April 30, 1881.
149. *Id.*, May 2, 1881 (emphasis added).
150. *Id.*, May 17, 1881.
151. *Id.*, October 6, 1881.
152. *Id.*, October 17, 1881.
153. See *supra*, note 36.
154. See *supra*.
155. Unpublished letter to Alice Lee, March 29, 1881, in Roosevelt Collection, Harvard Library. All Diary references to "study" or "studying" connote study of law; there is no reason, therefore, to believe that this reference in correspondence to "studying" does not also connote study of law. Drawing "little boats," is, of course, a reference to his diagrams of ship movements for the book. See also *supra*, note 93.
156. Unpublished letter to Alice Lee, October 14, 1881, Roosevelt Collection, Harvard Library.
157. Morison and Blum, *Letters* at 55.
158. See, e.g., *Roosevelt, Presidential Addresses and State Papers of Theodore Roosevelt* at 539, quoting Roosevelt, "At the Luncheon at Little Rock, Ark., October 25, 1905." (1905, reprint 1970).
159. See, e.g., Roosevelt, *Autobiography* at 55-56.
160. *Id.*; see also, Roosevelt, *Presidential Addresses*, 419-20, quoting address "At Harvard University, June 28, 1905."
161. See, e.g., Roosevelt, *Presidential Addresses*, 542-43, quoting address, "At the Luncheon . . . October 25, 1905."
162. *Id.*, at 539, quoting TR.
163. Roosevelt, *Presidential Addresses*, 419-20, quoting address "At Harvard University, June 28, 1905."
164. Roosevelt, *Autobiography* at 55.
165. Roosevelt, *Presidential Addresses*, 541 quoting address "At the Luncheon . . . October 25, 1905."
166. Putnam, *Theodore Roosevelt: The Formative Years, 1858-1886*, 220.
167. *Id.*; see also, Roosevelt, *Autobiography*, 55-56.
168. PUTNAM at 220, n.33.
169. Cutright, *The Naturalist*, 31.
170. MORRIS at 243.
171. *Id.*
172. See *Black's Law Dictionary*, 5th edition (West, 1979), 906.
173. GOEBEL at 37.
174. *Id.* at 227.
175. See *supra*.
176. Roosevelt, *Autobiography*, 132.
177. *Id.* at 137.
178. *Id.* at 172.
179. *Id.* at 196.
180. *Id.* at 448.
181. Literally, the Latin translates "It is to little that justice be given unless it is executed." *Black's Law Dictionary* at 1011.
182. Roosevelt, *Presidential Addresses*, 540 quoting Roosevelt, "At the Luncheon . . . October 25, 1905."
183. *Id.* at 543, quoting TR; see also, e.g., Roosevelt, *Autobiography*, 389-90.
184. TR, *Law Notes*, Notebook entitled "Law."
185. Roosevelt, *Autobiography* at 314.
186. *Black's Law Dictionary* at 778.
187. Roosevelt, *Autobiography* at 389.
188. Roosevelt, White House Pronouncement, August 8, 1904, quoted in *Autobiography*, 389-90.
189. *Black Law Dictionary* at 1017.
190. *O'Neil v. Vermont*, 144 U.S. 323, 340 (1892) (Field, J., dissenting). See also, *Howard v. Fleming*, 191 U.S. 126, 135-36 (1903) (proportionality principle defended).
191. See *Weems v. United States*, 217 U.S. 349 (1910).
192. Roosevelt, *Autobiography* at 316.
193. Roosevelt, *Law Notes*, "Criminal Law" set.
199. Roosevelt, *Autobiography* at 317.

200. *Id.*

201. TR defined "moral turpitude," a noticeably legal term, as "a literally astounding and horrifying indulgence . . . in wicked and depraved [behavior]. . . ." See Autobiography, 351. *Black's Law Dictionary*, at 910, defines this term as: "The act of baseness, vileness, or the depravity in private and social duties which man owes to his fellow man, or to Society in general, contrary to accepted and customary rule of right and duty between man and man."

202. TR, *Autobiography* at 314.

203. Burgess recalls TR being a student in his "public law" courses. See *supra.*

204. TR, *Law Notes*, October 8, 1881.

205. TR, *Autobiography* at 554.

206. Letter to TR from the Nobel Committee, January 1906, quoted in *Autobiography* at 559.

207. TR, *Autobiography* at 547-574.

208. *Id.* at 561, quoting Letter from TR to "Mr. Schurz," dated September 8, 1905.

209. TR, *Autobiography* at 548.

210. His senior thesis in college was entitled, "Practicability of Giving Men and Women Equal Rights." MORRIS at 128.

211. See, e.g., Roosevelt, *Law Notes*, Notebook "3" in Municipal Law [1881].

212. TR, *Law Notes*, Notebook "3" in Municipal Law, February 15, [1881].

213. *Id.*

214. TR, *Autobiography* at 162.

215. Two Supreme Court decisions in the early 1970's, *Reed v. Reed*, 404 U.S. 71 (1971), and *Eisenstadt v. Biard*, 405 U.S. 438, 447 n.7 (1972), were the first to hold that gender classifications in legislation could trigger a heightened level of judicial "scrutiny." The guiding principle of equal protection is that persons similarly situated are entitled to like treatment. Recently, the Supreme Court has applied what is called an "intermediate level of scrutiny" to statutes which classify persons by gender. This "intermediate" level of scrutiny theoretically lies between review under "strict scrutiny" (for statutes which make distinctions in treatment based on race) and review under a "rational basis" standard (for statutes which do not concern any group which has, historically, been subject to unjustified or invidious discrimination). Thus, today, a statutory gender classification must, in order to withstand constitutional challenge (on equal protection grounds), "serve important governmental objectives and must be substantially related to achievement of those objectives." *Craig v. Boren*, 429 U.S. 190, 197 (1976). If a gender-based statute does not pass this two-part test, it will be held unconstitutional.

216. The Nineteenth Amendment to the United States Constitution provides: SECTION 1. The right of the citizens of the United States to vote shall not be denied or abridged by the United States or by any State on account of sex. SECTION 2. Congress shall have power to enforce this article by appropriate legislation.

217. Roosevelt, *Autobiography* at 165.

218. Letter from TR to Attorney-General Bonaparte, January 2, 1908, quoted in *Autobiography* at 466.

219. Roosevelt, *Autobiography* at 437.

220. Among his achievements in this realm, TR signed legislation providing health and safety protection for factory employees, miners, and streetcar operators; signed child labor statutes and incorporated the National Child Labor Committee; established workmen's compensation for governmental employees; and signed legislation improving safety on the railways, and regulating the number of hours that could be required of railway laborers.

221. *Id.* at 458.

222. *Id.*

223. Recall, this is precisely what TR's likely professor of Real Estate, Judge John F. Dillon, did.

224. Roosevelt, *Autobiography* at 473.

225. See *Black's Law Dictionary* at 58.

226. MORRIS at 521-529.

227. *Id.* at 561.

228. *Id.*

229. Roosevelt, *Autobiography* at 469.

230. See *Black's Law Dictionary* at 951.

231. Roosevelt, *Autobiography* at 478.

232. *Id.* at 417.

233. A "bona-fide" possessor of property is "one who possesses as owner by virtue of an act sufficient in terms to transfer property, the defects of which he was ignorant. . . ." *Black's Law Dictionary* at 1048. Roosevelt seems to have understood this phrase as a legal term of art, and used it accordingly in its proper context.

234. Roosevelt, *Autobiography* at 417.

235. Literally, *caveat emptor* means "buyer beware." TR seems to have interpreted this principle, rather critically, as a suitable admonition for those who dealt with certain private practitioners of law. See, e.g., *Autobiography* at 55-56.

236. TR refers, for example, to the absence of "good faith of [particular] . . . corporations" in negotiations. He elaborates thus: "As soon as the change for which they had begged was inserted into the law, and the law was signed, they turned around and refused to pay taxes [i.e., reneged on their good faith promise]; and in the lawsuit that followed, they claimed that the law was unconstitutional, because it contained the very clause which they had so clamorously demanded." With a hint of quiet pride, he concludes: "The suit was carried through to the Supreme Court of the United States, which declared the law constitutional during the time I was President." *Autobiography* at 313-14, 397. See also *Id.* at 387.

237. MORRIS at 430.
238. Letter from TR to his mother, dated January 25, 1891, cited in MORRIS at 430, n.9.
239. Letter from TR to Elliot, his brother, dated June 14, 1891, quoted in MORRIS at 439.
240. MORRIS at 441.
241. TR eventually took measures to have Elliot declared legally "insane" from alcohol abuse. See *Id.* 442-43.
242. *Id.* at 439.
243. Roosevelt, *Law Notes,* Notebook including "Criminal Law" set.
244. MORRIS at 438.
245. See, Roosevelt, *Law Notes,* Notebook "3" in Municipal Law.
246. *Id.*
247. Roosevelt, *Law Notes,* Notebook "2" in Municipal Law, December 9, 1880.
248. *Id.*
249. *Id.*, December 9, 1880.
250. *Id.*, December 14, 1880.
251. Roosevelt, *Law Notes,* Notebook "3" in Municipal Law, October 26 [1881?].
252. *Black's Law Dictionary* at 769, 1023; see also *Fed. R. Crim. P. 24.*
253. Roosevelt, *Autobiography* at 138.
254. *Black's Law Dictionary* at 1094.
255. Roosevelt, *Autobiography* at 71.
256. *Id.*, at 160, 150, 139.
257. *Id.*, e.g., at 516, 373, 204, 166-67, 155.
258. *Id.*, e.g., at 576, 366.
259. *Id.* at, e.g., 292, 372, 314-317 (with respect to executive power), 440 (with respect to federal authority over corporations), 438 (with respect to states' rights and the judiciary), 403 (with respect to informal, constitutional precedent).
260. *Id.* at 142.
261. *Id.* at 158.
262. *Id.* at 139.
263. *Id.*
264. See *supra,* Section II, A. and B., for discussion of broad legal principles, and terms including self-defense, insanity, peremptory and for cause challenges at empaneling, legal proof, caveat emptor, contractual good faith, bonafide (possessor), and adultery.
265. See, e.g., Roosevelt, *Autobiography* at 140-142.
266. MORRIS at 449, quoting Roosevelt.
267. GOEBEL at 36.
268. MORRIS at 603.
269. GOEBEL at 38, quoting Burgess.
270. MORRIS at 444.

Chapter 26

The First Two Weeks of Term in Theodore Dwight's Municipal Law Lectures

Lecture Notes

1870

Theodore Roosevelt

Transcribed by Steve Sheppard. These notes are housed in the Columbia University Law Library as Theodore Roosevelt, Law School Notes, Treasure CU R68 Box 1 and Box 2.

[inside cover][1]
Theodore Roosevelt
Law
Law
[Stamp:] Joseph Laurier, Stationer, No. 1 Great Jones St. New York
[Page 1][2]
[The first week of class, October 1880]

Blackstone
Oct 7th[3]

Law; ambiguous. Law of nature; antecedent & congruent Our law denotes something imposed from without; implies a sovereign. In broad sen[se] means every rule; for humanity; too broad for us. Differentiate law as applied in courts; "a rule established by supreme pow[er] in state." contains an element of enforcement, always.; unlike a law of honor, because here sovereign power does not sancti[on] it. Moral laws can be: brought under domain of jurisprudence. Sovereign power = power able to carry out commands of society = essential element; we consider topics brought within control of state. Blackstone's def. does not cover International Law. Municipal L. however adopts it. "Our law is divided into

[Page 2]

two classes; one covers all ~~law~~ classes of rules between states considered as a family of nations; the other is only established in one and this we deal with. We need a rule: of civil conduct; & it must be prescribed. Is not a compact, is established, and so a sanction; it *must* be obeyed. Is civil; not religious &c. Prescribed so that a man can know about it in advance. No law here acts on a past action; no ex post facto law. Retrospective laws; generic; all that look back, that kind that affects a person criminally to his injury called ex post facto. Punishment can't be changed in kind; can be lessened in degree. So law must be made prospective. U.S. differ[s] from E. Main object of municipal law: to protect rights. We are concerned with question [illegible: of?] what law is;

[Page 3]

not what it ought to be. Civil law is subject of right & remedy. Ubi jus ibi remedium. Rights of persons; to things. Correlative is wrong; violation of right (criminal or civil. Wrong = tort. So we have 3 (1 rights of persons, (2 to things, 3 torts; violation of individual rights

crime " "public "'

A thing may be at once a tort & a crime. Sources of Law; 2.The decision or adjudication of court; is legislation. Judges profess or professed to ascertain customs, and if they were fair they were sanctioned. Only theoretically true in toto. Have followed some great maxims. "Let every man so use his own as not to injure another." "No one can allege his own turpitude." So a jurist has one great principle for a multitude of cases. Avoid being a case lawyer.

[Page 4]

Oct. 8th

Law implies authority & sanction. International law depends upon universal consent of various nations; so progress is very slow. Some points are dictated by morals; in war no wells must be poisoned. Others are merely positive; do not depend on principle. Constitutional law is a branch of municipal law which is divided thus into 2 branches.

Constitutional law v ~~common~~Common [superimposed] law proper. The former are a set of cases set apart; it is more than mere ordinary law, for it is binding on legislat[illegible: ive? ure? ion?] & c. ~~Nothin~~ Courts can overrule acts of legislature; very diff in England, as witness late tenant's eviction act of Ireland in Parliament. We do not study this.

p.10 Laws made for class; not for individuals; ~~f~~ but

[Page 5]

privileges can be granted to individuals as exceptions to laws.

11. Retrospective, generic li[illegible: mits?] include ex post facto, referring to crimes. Executive has pardoning power to alleviate punishment in certain exceptional cases; judiciary can not do this. In U.S. supreme power is in people and some of it is parceled out to Congress, some to states, and the residuary still remains with the people, in the shape of the constitution Sovereign power ultimately rests in 3/4 of State legislatures. When people have delegated a power to the legislature, the latter can not give it back.

p 22. Persons shall hold their rights. Ordinary word right means moral, legal right is a privilege to act without interference. Right & remedy are closely inter-related.

[Page 6]

Same act can be both remedial & vindicatory. Crime denotes violation of duty towards society. Tort is wrong done to individual, here remedy ~~comes~~ is given to individual; ~~bef~~ in crime to society. Same act may be both tort & crime.

25. Applies to legislature, not to judges.

30 Law originates 1) Common law; from Judicial Decisions; matter of reasons 2) Statute; from legislature; arbitrary.

34 maxim = generalization; states a universal application; not a mere rule. Is an abstract proposition.

38 Record; legally means a history of the case. Contains the papers called "pleadings" a judgment, &c. These altogether make a record. But judge also furnishes a *reason* of ruling

[Page 7]

why he thus decided; and these are made into Reports. A judge may sometimes over rule a former case; thus a supreme court does this, over a lower one. So reports are not infallible guide; we must get at principles.; must not be slavish.

These reports are of varying value. Certain tests; ~~w~~ 1) must be followed by courts 2) may be, Must take into account grade of court, in valuing case. Appellate court is far higher than decision of single judge. So "nisi prius" reports are of less value than cases made on appeal. *Man* has much to do with value of report. Fidelity of reporter. He puts head note or abstract at beginning; and he may blunder in this. And Remarks of judges are not the point decided. May be is discursive. ("Dicta") = [word lost to decay]

[Page 8]

And some ~~dis~~ cases are binding on courts; while others are not Some classes are authoritative, others are argumentative. So for 1st Appellate court on lower court. 2 Main court on N.Y. If Constitution gives Suprem[e] Court power in some case, State /court must follow it; but not if it is not constitutional. These books in England began very early, published in Norman-french year books.

[The Second week of Class]

[Page 9]

Oct 11th

p 43. ~~Has a thing been~~ Acquiescence for a sufficient length of time to show that it is not objected to.

44. Special customs if unreasonable can never be law.

Civil law is part of leges inscripta. Civil law is law simply by adoption. As far back as 1066 all business of I wills &administration of dec [superimposed] was managed by Bishop; also marriage & divorce. Archbishop & others had great lawyers to manage affairs of the ecclesiastical courts & lawyer was a surrogate (a deputy) ~~or~~. This court had roman law; even now surrogate's court has this law. Admiralty business here in U.S. is done by U.S. district courts; also Military. Se we have Probate, Admiralty & Courts Martial, all dependant on Roman law.

[Page 10]

Institutes are arranged like Blackstone, for students. Pandects; reference book for lawyers.

State's power to legislate is not derived from the states; its constitution has object to restrain power; while Congress confers. If Parliament can pass a law, so can State when it's constitution ~~7~~ restrains it. Congress can only be judged by its own constitution.

51. Declaratory statute isn't of so very much account. To find out meaning of statute. When law is addressed generally you must take popular sense; when to a class you must take special sense. When we have a statute or subject, we must look through whole course of legislation on

[Page 11]

it to find out its meaning. Foolish laws (*very* absurd / can not be executed. "Voluit sed non dixit." Palpable laws however, must be carried out. If states' courts change front U.S. courts will not; but will adopt first reading.

60 Right = liberty of acting without interference

66 Judgment of peers & C means in civil cases trial by jury. In criminal cases it means indictment by grand jury (23 men = 12 +12+1). Examine probability of guilt. Hear only complainant; could man be convicted of face of evidence? Majority rule. Petit jury (12); unanimity. Civil case needs no indictment; and in many cases (of equity) do not involve trial by jury. (Only money damages & land).

[Page 12]

Duress per minas [superimposed] can be pleaded only when threats are made such as would fright an ordinary man.

Libel; defamation is visible

slander: " audible.

Slander; only ~~remedy~~ remedy [superimposed] is by damages, but libel is far more heinous. Is more malicious and permanent. Habeas corpus does not relapse a man when regularly indicted; write is to see if regular form is observed

[Page 13]

Oct 12th

For write of habeas corpus to apply to some judge; formally only by a court / which sits only at certain intervals; called terms, and the judge also acts "at chambers" i.e. not during term time. So formerly these writs of habeas corpus would only be given by court; changed in Carl.IIth time. In some U.S. write of Hab. Corp. Comes before all other business), Man draws up his own petition or has it drawn; swears to it before notary; he endorsees it and judges sign name, which is called allowance of writ. Keeper must attend to it, he a penalty of attachment [superimposed] writes out a return; if untrue the prisoner "traverse[s] it; then judge acts. If held on paper Judge merely sees if papers are regular.

78. In N.Y. constitution we have clause

[Page 14]

saying private prop. Must be compensated for when used for public [illegible: ps.?] Legislature can not take property for private use. Right of eminent domain very diff. From taxation wherein man gets back nothing. In Em. Domain we take but one man's prop. In taxation, we take that of class.

86 Sheriffs main duties are ministerial. Ministerial officer is one whom the particular function is carrying out orders of another. Judge can not appoint deputy; ministerial office can. Sheriff must execute exact orders of Judges.

Doctrine of "Respondeat Superior," who has his remedy against subordinate. Sheriff has one class of civil duties growing out of fact that when we sue a man for uncertain damages (for slander c/ man put in no defense; then he admits his guilt but not the

[Page 15]

amount of damage. Nothing goes to court. Sher. Calls jury over which he presides to inquire into damages. This Sheriffs jury is held in afternoons to ascertain amt. Of damages when no reply is made.

Deodand was withdrawn from ordinary use. This was at first chief business of coroner. Coroner does not inquire into particular thing or man; arrests no one; inquires into cause of death; and only arrest at end of proceeding if jury so decide; in all other cases we arrest before trial. Coroner can be got any hour. Men of learning can assist the court; can

Undersheriff has more powers than deputy sheriffs; on demise of sheriff he takes his place; while deputies all disappear. In U.S. Justices of Peace are paid. Duties are both judicial and ministerial. Can arrest a man charged with any crime

[Page 16]

except homicide. He examines into case and commits him. He can try small matters.

Constable his right-hand man of Justice of Peace. A civil constable may be called marshals.

There are a class of state paupers, not all many county paupers.

A man born here is always an American citizen, may be a foreign citizen also. One class of cases is very difficult, as regards local allegiance. If a man in Canada kills a man in the U.S., offense is not complete in either country. What is the rule of criminal liability where (Adams vs People, 1st N.Y. Courts 173) crime is thus

[Page 17]

Dictation Exercise

Lectures on Municipal Law.

Book I Chap I

Definitions- General Remarks.

Municipal Law is a rule of civil conduct prescribed by supreme power in state. The rule that the law must be prescribed is peculiarly applicable to statutes. Common law is from time to time, announced by Judges and by a legal fiction is presumed to have been already known on the principle that the law is a science and that the new rule is a deduction from principles previously known. It is an inference from doctrine that law must be prescribed that it should not go into effect until time enough has elapsed to for those governed by it to become

[Page 118]

acquainted with its provisions. This principle however has often been violated by a fiction of English law that whole session of Parliament was counted as a single day. Result was that an act which was innocent when committed might become criminal by subsequent statute passed subsequently during the session. This severe rule is now repudiated and never prevailed in this country. In N.Y. it is a rule that a statute does not go into effect until 20 days after its passage unless there is some direction to contrary in act itself. It is important in this connection to point out difference between retrospective and

[Page 19]

an ex post facto law. The term retrospective is generic and applies to all statutes or laws which affect past transactions. An ex post facto law is that peculiar kind of retrospective legislation which bears more severely upon an alleged criminal than the law did at the time the act was committed either by increasing the punishment or by rendering conviction more easy or by changing kind of punishment. When punishment is diminished the law is not ex post facto though, it may be retrospective. Ex post facto laws forbidden by the U.S. Constitution and so are void. Thus simply retrospective not of necessity void. Maybe so when violating rights of property,

[Page 20]

sometimes are justified. When law has been duly promulgated plea of ignorance cannot not be received as an excuse. Thus a person might be criminally liable who had done an act which he honestly believed he had a right to do. The last part of our definition refers to supreme power of state; by this is meant (by Am. Ideas) the people in whom supreme power resides. A distinc is thus taken between society and the government. Society limits government by a written constitution; If its provisions are transcended by legislature the law may be declared void. There is no such rule as this in England and the courts can not declare an act of Parliament invalid.

[Page 21]

Oct 13th

Naturalization is exclusively ~~often~~ vested in Congress, yet state courts do all business, because it is deputed to them by Congress. But perjury is a violation of U.S. law. (When court has made a decision it is conclusive until it is directly canceled.)

An alien needs a special law to make him completely able to hold land. In West, Aliens can buy land; not so east. But a man by declaring his intentions to become a citizen may hold land. An alien gets no title whatever to land by descent. Titles only in one can descend by alien (dead men can be passed over if grandfather is [not] [superimposed] dead)

Slavery is created by law; service, by contract. Apprenticeship is also created by law; but object is very diff, being to educate apprentice; and it is temporary. Is often a compulsory relation. Apprentice is under power of master very largely but

[Page 22]

not entirely; this relation is created by rule of law. If master dies, executors support apprentice out of estate.

Servants are not distinguished in US except into slavery, apprenticeship and contract (No Menials vs. Labourers.)

134 [superimposed] Wages payable at end of year can not be recovered if servant leaves before. Entire contact.

2 Wages agreed to be paid at rate of so much a month Also entire contract.

3 Wages made payable monthly, then he must receive his wages every month.

If master discharges servant without cause during time of contract we should have same three cases.

In (1), if servant has worked specific time he can sue for wages; if he has not worked

[Page 23]

he sues for damages; because he has not been permitted to earn wages; and but one action can be for a contract. Damages = compensation. Where servant is wrongfully discharged from service before wages are actually earned, his proper course is not to sue for wages specifically but for damages. on ground that he has wrongfully been prevented from earning wages. This is an entire cause of action, only one can be brought.

Leading cases. Moody against Leverach, 4 Daly 401. Howard vs. Daly 61 N.Y. 367. Weed vs Burk 78 N.Y. 191. This rule is so far modified that it terms of contract. are of such a nature that wages are earned periodically and then wrongful discharge takes place after some periods have elapsed and before entire contract is completed, it [words disintegrated]

[Page 24]

Causes of Action, 1/ for wages actually earned 2 [erasure of "wages"] damages for not being permitted to perform residue of contract. There are many actions of this kind. Must not sue for too remote damages.

Acts of service often performed ~~b~~ not by servants. Contractors ~~a~~ do not [erasure] make master so liable. How is C. distinguished from Δ?-S has no independent employment; C result is stipulated for; but will S [C erased and S superimposed] result and mode of employment is stipulated for. With contractor there is no "Respondeat Superior."

[Page 25]

Dict.

In Analyzing a law it is important to regard remedies it provides & sanctions. By term remedies is meant redress given to every individual whose right is violated. It is a legal maxim that whenever there is a right there is a remedy; the remedy consists at law in giving an injured party damages; in compensation for his injury. This however is not the universal rule for in some instances the wrong doer is prevented from doing an injurious act by an injunction or he may be compelled to perform an act specifically. The vindicatory branch of the law on the other hand is remedy given to society for wrong supposed to be done in public order.

[Page 26]

It thus happens that this two fold proceeding may exist in regard to same act. 1 would be called a civil and 1a a criminal proceeding. Thus if A were wrongfully beaten the civil action would be A vs B, and the damages recovered would belong to A. Criminal proceedings would be People vs B. Wrongdoer might in this proceeding be punished be imprisonment or fine; which in such case would belong to Govt & not to A.

Chap II Origin vs source of Municipal Law. Mun Law in reference to origin may be divided into common and statute law. Great Diff. between two is that the one is announced by the Judge in course of adjudication

[Page 27]

upon litigated causes while the other is enacted by legislature. The Common law of each state (except L.) is based on Common Law of England. Louisiana follows Roman Law. Sometimes Common Law is adopted by constitutional provisions as in N.Y. where it is provided in Constitution that the Common Law of England as it was in use in the Colony until Apr 19th 1775 (Bat of Lexington) and not modified by any statute, shall be the law of the state. Other states simply adopted the Common law by a legislative enactment. Common law is said to depend for origin in England upon Custom. Such custom is either of general

[Page 28]

character or special & particular. Is now only necessary to consider general customs. It must not be considered that these are oral and handed down by tradition but are to be sought in books of reports and standard treatises. Principal sources of law are the reports of Cases. Legal principles are evolved by means of cases or actions. There must be an actual controversy and it must have been necessary to announce the principles in order to dispose of the controversy. It is important to note difference between records of Court vs reports of Cases.

[Page 29]

Oct 14th

There is no distinc between Ecclesiastical & Civil law. If a man married his ~~le~~ niece he would be held accountable by law, not be church.

143 If one party to contract is incapable, is contract void or voidable at election of weaker or incapacitated party/. Tendency in law is to voidability. If a sane man marries an idiot or lunatic; the woman alone can

raise question. So with marriage contracted by fraud or force. 4 voidable cases; insanity, idiocy, force or fraud.

House of Commons (6 lawyers, held that a priest was (or was not) necessary. undecided 3 vs 3. Common law varied from Statutes. And here we have no priest in English sense; Romanist or Episcopalian; so we are not like England. In Scotland Presbyterian. In N.Y. no statutes, here very easy to be married. Marriage can be made [illegible: in honest why? if honored by?] mere agreement.

[Page 30]

2 cases of Divorce. If cause existed from time of marriage is ~~l~~ void from beginning; is case of Nullity. If cause was subsequent; we get case of dissolution. If woman is innocent, she can only claim alimony in 2^{d} case. And in 2^{d} cases he gets her share of his property. In 1st case she sues him for damage, as a stranger, not as a husband. A fe[~~male~~?] [illegible: cotenant?] Can not make any contract. This is owing to the great rule of Impolicy This is undergoing transition; changes have to be introduced by statute; which only affects new transactions, not old ones. So 2 sets of cases. Husband acquires right over personal property; And over real estate, during the marriage. He would have use of its rents &c. Choses in action (notes, bonds, contracts e&c) as [illegible] there Husband shall have them if he gets them into possession; that is if he

[Page 31]

sues & collects them while the wife lives. After her death he is merely an administrator. Husband can not use anything except patience against his wife. She can go away whenever she wants to.

All states of Union do not adopt Testamentary Guardian. not by common law, as guardians by native vs socage. is statutory. Probate courts are local. Often ~~we~~ in important cases we of general jurisdiction, i.e., the chancery court in England, where Lord Chancellor superintends the property of all infants. So we have chancery [illegible: found?] in every state. Supreme Court here gives all power and ~~he~~ this court treats guardian as a trustee. Law does not regard any [illegible: fraction?] of a Day, so you can [illegible: see?]

[Page 32]

about a mans [illegible: voter?]; he can note 23 hours beforehand.

[Page 33]

Dict

A record has been defined to be an authentic statement formally contained in rules of parchment but now written on paper and preserved in the court. Which is hence called a court of record. In these roles are contained judgment of court in each case & all other papers such as the pleading.

Record, .:[therefore], forms a history of case. A Report, on the other hand, sets forth principles established by decision, it should contain name of case; name of court in which case originated, mode in which case was presented for decision, whether by demurrer, upon motion for a new trial, or upon appeal; A sufficient statement of facts to show basis of decision, sometimes the argument of counsel the opinion of court and

[Page 34]

the final result. It is duty of reporter to prepare an abstract of points decided which he prefixes to his report; this is called a reporters syllabus or head note it is a general rule of law, subject to important exceptions that when a case has been once decided and another case arises, involving the same principles a like decision should be made. Law is thus series of precedents; it is however, necessary to discriminate between reports. Some are of much higher value than others. The following test may be employed to determine value of decision as a report. 1st Inquire where case was decided; whether upon solemn argument before full court or by a single judge in the haste

[Page 35]

and excitement of a trial. Decisions of former kind are said to be rendered in banc or in banco, that is by the full bench; the latter are termed nisi prius decisions. Are in general but of little value through the high character of particular judges sometimes gives them authority. Nisi prius decisions are more frequently reported in England than here. 2. The 2^{d} inquiry should be, was case fully & ably argues by counsel. Value of Decision depends greatly upon thoroughness of argument; court often in press of business confines investigation to the briefs provided by counsel so that decision will be of no higher value than argument. Many cases are over ruled for this reason as a later & more

[Page 36]

discussion shows weakness of reasons upon which prior decision was made. 3^{d} Inquire what judges held court when decision was rendered. Some have attained so great distinction that there decisions gain weight from their reputation. 4th. It is of some importance to notice whether opinions of court is composed by particular judge who attaches his name to it, or whether it is simply an extension of the general views of whole bench collectively. The latter is called an opinion per curiam, that is by the court, and is not of as great authority in general as the other. Reason is that in one case no particular man is responsible while

[Page 37]

in other case, since a particular judge attaches his name he would take care to preserve his reputation to give the subject careful study. 5th It is important to consider the grade of the court; whether an inferior tribunal of the court of last resort; it is plan that the decisions of appellate court should in general have greater weight than those of a subordinate tribunal from which appeals are taken. Thus in N.Y. the decisions of court of appeals would be of highest authority. 6th Regard the merits of the report itself. Consider whether the facts are fully stated and the points properly digested, It has already been said that the duty of the reporter is to prepare a

[Page 38]

syllabus or head note to be prefixed to case. Sometimes the preparation of this note requires great legal ability & a reporter may err both in a defective statement of points decided and in omitting to set forth the whole of a decision. Another source of error in older reports grew out of fact that judges gave their decisions orally and the reporter took down as well as he could notes of what was said and as art of short-hand writing was either not understood or known imperfectly the ground of decision is often badly stated. One mode of correcting this fault is to consult contemporaneous reports whenever that is possible and it not in

[Page 39]

frequently happen that same case is reported by a number of different men.

[Page 40]

Oct 15th

[The first paragraph of this page has lightly penciled left parenthesis marks down the left margin, which are not reproduced here.]

If parent ~~attaches~~ sends off his son, sone may sum up bill, and tradesmen sue father. This is right in care of wife; but parent has no contract with child, so it is a little doubtful. And if child is made agent by parents. virtual consent- explicit or implicit) bill ~~can~~^{must} [superimposed] be paid.

If Father is dead. Mother must support child. Man ~~must~~ need not support stepchildren; but if he takes them into his family he can not send them bills. Court of Chancery, being custodian of all children, can make an allowance for any proper consideration. even if retrospective: All questions $^{\text{about children}}$ ultimately come up before some ~~chan~~ judge or court with chancery power. A man can not will away all his property to

[Page 41]

charitable institutions; This is to do good to his close relatives. Very rarely in general education made compulsory.

~~Parent~~ 3 rights that Father has over Child. 1 Custody. 2 to his services 3 Discipline. Custody, the mode of vindicating is twofold, one is ~~to~~ by writ of habeas corpus, ~~be~~ by ^{petition} court of chancery; & in the case idea is that child is falsely imprisoned; by refinement that child is only free when with Father. And court will not interfere if child is over 14. So writ of habeas corpus will recover any child under 14; but if over he can choose his own custody. By Statute or usage; if Father & Mother quarrel, then court takes into account interest of child.

If Father is dead Mother is entitled to childs services. This does not depend upon age of child if he is under 21.

[Page 42]

Father can punish child reasonably. Child can recover damages from father for injury. Child is guardian of his child's body but not of his estate. Father can delegate subject of discipline; & delegate is liable to double action.

Child must support parent or grandparent. ~~If~~

If husband had no access to wife child is illegitimate [te is superimposed over earlier inscription]. An ~~if~~ infant [sic] must support his own bastard. Bastard does not inherit, but even in states that do not make subsequent marriage legitimize bastard, yet statutes have made child able to inherit from its mother.

184 Corporation "one person" or "new person" established, differing from individuals; no such thing in partnership. Partnership must sue in their own names (giving Also the

[Page 43]

name of business; but a corporation sues under its own ~~hand~~ name. And so it company is sued, judgment is against Company and individual property can not be touched. while reverse is case in case of partnership, No ecclesiastical corporations in U.S.

Public (vs Private Corporations. Public is a municipal, city, village, town &c. Others are called private; are not mere instruments of Govt. Legislature may alter public charters, but cant change private charters. so with Dartmouth Col. vs Woodward, Legislature abrogated Charter of King; Trustees resisted; new treasurer was Woodward who took seal & the old College sued him. Supreme court held that old charter still held & legislature was unconstitutional

[Page 44]

If 20 years elapse presumption is that charter did exist. Kings Grant makes a charter, Here 3^{d} is main method to get charter is from legislatures; from Congress where they were exercizing the~~ir~~ power granted them by Congress.

And a Laying laying down from a general formula by legislative and allowing corporations ~~by~~ to organize themselves according to provisions of law. So in 1848 Legislature did this. If you wish to mine your file papers in a court. "Manufacturing Act of 1848." Corporation must have name which can only be changed by law. ~~Co~~ Individuals may speculate freely in land [illegible-c?]; but a corporation is organized for a particular purpose &

[Page 45]

it can not try anything else. Manhattan Company alone can do whatever it chooses. Doctrine of "ultra vires" what is effect of corporation gives beyond ~~wh~~ or transgresses it's powers; how far does it bind it.

[Page 46]

Dictation exercise

There is an old book of great value which enables us to find the contemporaneous reports of the same case; this is called the Reportorium Juridicum. It is also to be remarked that a distinction must be taken between what is decided by court and what is said by way of argument or illustration. Remarks of the last kind are all called dicta and sometimes obiter dicta, i.e. thing said or thing said by the way. These are not regarded as authority. When reporter wishes to refer to dicta in his head note he employs the words "it seems so and so" and in old reports the corresponding word is semble. When a reporter wishes to indicate the very point decided in the case he used word held. It has been

[Page 47]

remarked that a decision usually has the force of a precedent. Still many cases have been over ruled as being wrongly decided & having no authority. A large number are collected in Greenleafs Overruled Cases and also in various digests. A late work on subject is Bigelows overruled cases. At present day decision are not slavishly followed but those are adopted which accord with general analogies of the law. There is a technical distinction between cases considered as authority and those regarded as arguments. The diff would be that if case were authority it *must* be followed, while if regarded as argument merely it might be rejected if not consistent with reason and general principles

[Page 48]

of law. As general rule English decisions made before revolution are regarded as authority; Since then they are not technically authoritative but are cited by way of argument. So decisions of highest court of

State are authoritative upon inferior tribunals, and if a lower court refuses deliberately to follow them it is a case of judicial insubordination and would deserve censure. Decisions in courts of sister states are cited as arguments and they should only be followed when they have intrinsic merit. So decisions of supreme court of U.S are authoritative in all state courts upon questions involving construction of U.S. constitution; but decisions of that same court on other questions such as commercial

[Page 49]

questions are not binding on the State Courts. There are, for example, some points, in respect to which the decision of U.S supreme court vs of the N.Y. Court of Appeals are in direct conflict Reports of decisions are extremely numerous and an acquaintance with them is a matter of special knowledge an accurate list of reports to 1860 may be found in last editions of Bouviers Law Dictionary under head of reports. There is also a book on subject of reports known as Wallace on Reporters. The English reporters may be conveniently classified into old and new. The series of the old reports under this classification would close

[Page 50]

at American revolution. Old reports are now consulted only occasionally Many decisions contained in them have become obsolete. The most venerable of them is the collection known as the year books There is a difficulty in consulting these by reason of fact that they are written in an obsolete language the Norman-French, and with many abbreviations which it is now difficult to explain. Still they are sometimes resorted to both in England and in U.S particularly in new and difficult cases. See 22^{d} N.Y. 355. Year books were prepared by Reporters appointed & paid by Govt but during reign of Henry the 8th this system

[Page 51]

fell into disuse and any one might report who saw fit. In this way many worthless reports were published. Besides the reports, treatises, digests, and abridgements are often resorted to for legal information. These should be regarded in most cases as a means of consulting the reports. As a general rule where treatise and report conflict the report is to be preferred; there are of course instances where writer of treatise discusses a case and shows it to be unsound; in that case the view of a treatise writer would prevail not because it was authority but by reason of its intrinsic merit.

NOTES

1. Information in brackets is descriptive. Words or letters in brackets do not occur in the manuscript, although some words or letters are placed in brackets to represent likely original inscriptions that have been lost because the pages have been altered by decay. Roosevelt's spelling, punctuation, and abbreviations have been reproduced without change.

2. Pages refer to extant pages as of May 1, 1998. The pages do not have inscribed numbers.

3. The notebooks, in 1998, are terribly brittle and, despite great concern for conservation in recent decades, are now no longer completely intact. It is likely that Roosevelt's first day of class was October 6, and the notes for this day have been lost. Since the adoption of the law school's first statutes June 1863, Dwight had commenced his classes for the annual term on the first Wednesday of October. Trustees of Columbia College, Minutes, December 19, 1864; April 15, 1878. This would have been October 6 in 1880.

Chapter 27

Hints to Young Lawyers

1870

Thomas M. Cooley

Thomas McIntyre Cooley (January 6, 1824-September 12, 1898) was chief justice of the Michigan Supreme Court, a member of the Interstate Commerce Commission, and Dean and Professor of the University of Michigan School of Law, from 1859 to 1884. His influence is discussed in chapter 1. This lecture is reprinted from *Hints to Young Lawyers: An Address Delivered to the Senior Class of the Law Department of the University of Michigan by Hon. Thomas M. Cooley, Jay Professor of Law, Thursday, March 24, 1870* (Ann Arbor: Courier Steam Printing House, 1870).

Gentlemen of the Law Department:

The present is the last of my course of lectures to you for the year. We have gone together over many difficult and abstruse subjects, which I have endeavored to simplify and elucidate. If I have not always succeeded in this, my effort has nevertheless been received with the most courteous attention on your part, and as we separate I am able to look back over our intercourse without discovering the least occasion for unpleasant reflection. I recall on the other hand, invariable kindness, a general disposition to so receive the instruction of the professors as to make it of as much practical benefit as possible, and an entire absence of the careless disregard of the rights and feelings of professors and fellow students which sometimes makes the college career of a young man so far from agreeable to those with whom he is associated. I therefore can say with the utmost sincerity and heartiness, that as you depart from these walls to enter upon the duties of active life, you carry with you only kind regards, and most earnest wishes for your future prosperity and happiness. In my future years all the associations that will cluster about the recollections of the present college year will be in the highest degree agreeable, and I doubt not that the pleasure with which I shall recall them will be increased from year to year, as I receive reports of your subsequent life, and learn that you are pursuing the honorable course which your department here has so confidently promised. And what I say for myself I know I can say with the utmost confidence for my associates, whose diligent and faithful instruction has been satisfactorily rewarded by the corresponding effort you have made to render that instruction available. For them, therefore, as well as for myself, I bid you God-speed on your journey of life, hoping and trusting that in whatever of honorable aspiration you may now indulge, you are not to be hereafter disappointed, and that your future will be as abundant in fruition as your college course has been satisfactory in promise.

To those of you who are about to bear away from this institution the certificate of its approbation, I have a few words to say in response to what I understand to be your desire, that my last address should be devoted to such hints of a practical character as may be of service to you in your professional career. The transition from the life of a student to that of a practicing lawyer is so great that it is not possible for one to be too well prepared by such aid as he may obtain from the experience of others; but it cannot be expected that any one should give you in advance anything beyond the most general advice, and the young practitioner must make that applicable under the varying circumstances of his business life as best he may. I shall therefore proceed at once to my subject, not attempting to do more than to give a few general rules, with such hints as time may allow for their application.

Duty of the Lawyer to Himself

I shall begin what I have to say by calling your attention to duties you owe to yourselves, and which, though intimately connected with those you owe to others, are still of paramount importance, and may well be considered first. I do not refer now to the ordinary duties of christian morality and honesty, which every man is under obligations to observe and perform, but which I trust it is not needful for me to dwell upon in addressing a company of young men educated in an American community. If I supposed there was a man in the present class who was contemplating the practice of the law with a view to the advantages it gave him for dishonest practices, or who even failed to appreciate the strength which a pure life and an unsullied character would give him as a lawyer, I should desire to say to him here at the threshold of his career, that he had mistaken his calling, and would do better at once to seek an occupation in which the temptations were fewer, and the consequent risks of disgrace and dishonor less. But I have no such supposition, and therefore do not allow the possibility of such conduct to disturb me.

The duties which every lawyer owes to himself are of two classes: those which are due to himself as a man, and those which are due in his capacity as a lawyer. Of these the first are the highest and most important. It is of far more consequence that one should be thoroughly deserving of the respect and esteem of his fellows as a man than that he should be an eminent and successful lawyer. The one will carry with it a self respect for which no degree of success can be a satisfactory substitute, while eminence, if attained in unmanly ways, may annoy and embitter those years of one's life which need most the consolations of an approving conscience. At present, however, I do not desire to discriminate between the two classes of duties. I allude to the distinction only to say that first of all every person should strive to possess himself of those qualities and attainments which constitute the perfection of a manly character; and if having these he finds he lacks others which are essential to his success at the bar, he is not justified in regarding his life as a failure, but should cheerfully accept the fact, and turn his attention to some other occupation more suited to his peculiar abilities and disposition.

As a lawyer, every man owes it to himself to keep up after he enters practice a regular course of law reading. I know this is seldom done with system, but it is nevertheless true that where it is not done an important duty is neglected. You have endeavored while here to ground yourselves well in the general principles of the law; and now the temptation will be strong to look upon your student life as finished, and to consider yourselves as satisfying the demands of your profession if you carefully brief up for the successive cases you may becalled upon to conduct. It is impossible, however, for any man in two years to become a thorough lawyer; and if after that time he is disposed to rest contented with special investigations in reference to questions as they arise in practice, he will inevitably become a mere case lawyer, whose knowledge of legal principles will be limited and exceptional, and who, when required to act promptly on questions new to his practice, will be always hesitating, uncertain and unreliable. Systematic reading is essential to a steady advance in the law; and what is true of the student days, is true also of the lawyer's business life. The field upon which you enter now is so broad that if you would explore it all you must keep steadily and systematically employed, and if you fail in this, you will not only fail to become thorough and complete in legal attainments, but even when you make examinations with reference to particular cases, you will never be sure that you have not overlooked important principles which will have a controlling influence.

If I had time I might enlarge upon this point perhaps with usefulness, as not only a matter of duty, but of sound policy also. Of poor lawyers our country is full, but the number of those who are really able is comparatively small. He who enters the lower class finds always a sharp and persistent competition, not usually of the most honorable character; he who enters the higher will in any part of the land find a large field ready for his occupation, in which there will be employment at once honorable, lucrative and satisfactory. When one inquires whether there is room for more lawyers, the first point to be determined is the grade of the lawyer; there is always room for a good lawyer, while poor lawyers, who spend their time mainly in places of public resort, and neglect altogether anything like steady legal discipline, are superabundant everywhere.

The lawyer, also, ought to be well read in the political and constitutional history of his country and race. I need not remark to those who have read the law diligently, how largely that history enters into the law of this country. Our system of law has been a natural development, and we shall not fully catch its spirit until we understand how and under what circumstances it has grown to be what it is. Especially is this true of the principles of constitutional law, with which, as lawyers or legislators, we have so much occasion to deal. To familiarize yourselves with those principles many of you have made the literary societies of great service while you have been here, and you will do well if, wherever you go, you succeed in finding persons of kindred tastes with whom you can associate for purposes of mutual benefit in the fields of history and politics and indeed of general literature as well.

Duty of the Lawyer to the Court

The oath which the lawyer takes when admitted to the bar pledges him to faithfully perform his duty as attorney, solicitor and counsellor, with all due fidelity to the courts in which he may practice. I am very sorry to say that this oath is not always faithfully observed. I would not say this, however, without at the same time remarking that courts do not always treat the practitioners before them with the courtesy which is justly their due. The obligation here is reciprocal, and it is often forgotten on both sides. You may, possibly, at some time have been present in court when a judge has so grievously overlooked what was due to his position and to his profession, as to amuse himself with poor jokes to excite the laughter of the crowd at the expense of the bar. Perhaps he went farther, and treated the bar with ill-natured discourtesy, in the belief that he was thereby taking the side of the public against an unpopular profession, and elevating himself in public regard by lowering those from whose ranks he has but recently come. No man could make a greater mistake. The interests of the bench and of the bar are identical, and the lawyer who traduces the one, and the judge who rails at the other is equally guilty of a wrong against his own interests. The obligation to kindness, forbearance and uniform courtesy, is equally obligatory on both; and each should be ready at all times to defend the other against attacks. They are both pillars of one great legal system, and what assails or weakens the system at one point affects the whole structure. When a lawyer becomes unfit for courteous treatment from the bench, it is time to discipline him: when a judge has ceased to be worthy of professional confidence, it is time to attempt his removal: but until such time it is a mistake to reduce by detraction the influence of those upon whose support and assistance one's own standing must largely depend. The public will respect the bench and the bar if they mutually respect each other; and not otherwise.

When lawyer and judge design equally to deal fairly with each other, it is probable that the demand for kind forbearance is greatest upon the lawyer. The judge represents the public, and is endeavoring to hold the scales of justice equally; and without full knowledge of all the circumstances which induce counsel to manage the case as they do, he is often compelled to feel that time is uselessly wasted, that witnesses are unfairly treated, that the most skillful advocate is obtaining an advantage to the prejudice of justice; and it is not in human nature that he shall be uniformly kind, indulgent and courteous. If hasty and petulent remarks sometimes fall from a judge whose general deportment is unexceptionable, they are to be overlooked as having no bad motive for their cause, but as being the result rather of a sense of right, which from vexatious circumstances has expressed itself inopportunely or improperly.

The whole legal profession of this country has received a serious blow from the charges made and so generally believed, that a small portion of the judiciary of a certain state—whose bench is generally now, as it always has been, filled with able and most upright men—do sometimes so far forget what belongs to their positions as to allow personal considerations to affect their official action, and let friends approach them to discuss in private the cases they have in charge for decision. Among other things it is charged that certain lawyers are employed before these judges because of the influence they have with them as individuals, independent of any arguments they might bring to bear on legal grounds. We are not to suppose that these charges are well based, but they are made with a persistency of repetition which leads large numbers of people to accept them as true; and the baleful consequences to the cause of justice are almost as serious as if they were true beyond question. I need not say to you that it is disgraceful in a high degree for a judge to suffer himself to be approached out of court concerning the cases heard before him. Everyone understands and appreciates this; but everyone does not understand and appreciate so well that it is also disgraceful for a lawyer to be the tool of such judicial dishonor. Both are participants in corrupting the fountain of justice; and each, when clearly convicted, should equally be visited with the scorn and contempt of his professional brethren. If unfortunately a lawyer should discover that the judge before whom he practiced was open to improper influences, he would owe it to the cause of justice, to the honor of his profession, to a regard for his own manliness, not to become a participant in the judicial wrong and folly, but to abstain as scrupulously from secret and underhand courses as he would if the character of the judge rendered their success impossible. He owes it to the cause of justice to pay the judge the compliment of treating him in all their intercourse, as if his judicial character was unexceptionable, even if he knows it is not so.

Nor does the mistake the lawyer commits when he practices deceit upon the court require much comment. Aside from its injurious effect upon a man's own character, it is always in a business point of view bad policy. It is generally sacrificing the future to the present. Deceit in one case may win a cause, but it sows the seeds of distrust, and undermines the man's influence. And once successful, it is likely to be the beginning of a deceitful course of practice which will be followed through life. At the risk of becoming tedious, therefore, by the repetition of truisms, I desire to impress upon you the importance of always dealing frankly with the court, and avoiding all those little tricks which are almost sure in the end to be revealed, and which, besides their effect in blasting one's general reputation, will inevitably prevent his acquiring that just and proper influence with the court which the fair and candid counsel is always entitled to.

The Lawyer's Duty to His Client

But I must pass to the consideration of the dealings of the lawyer with his client. It is sometimes jocosely said that a lawyer's first duty is to obtain payment of a retainer; and the joke is not without a basis in truth. It is generally good policy for both lawyer and client that the fees should be paid as the services progress; and a good understanding between them is more likely to be perpetuated by that course than by postponing the application for payment until a bill can be presented in gross at the conclusion. The client will generally pay more cheerfully while the spirit of litigation is upon him than he will after it has passed away, and after the controversy has been disposed of either by voluntary adjustment for by the decision of the court. The extent of the labor performed for him will also be fresh to his mind at that time, and he will not be so likely to regard the charges as too high, as he will be a considerable time afterwards. Moreover, the lawyer who postpones application for payment until the immediate necessity for his services has passed, is in danger sometimes of being tempted to sue for his fees if his bill is disputed; and this, I think, he can very seldom afford to do. There may be cases of such manifest purpose on the part of his client to cheat him out of his dues as will warrant resort to the courts for redress; but if the client is honest, and from narrowness of mind or other cause has failed to appreciate the value of the services performed for him, it is better to

16. Thomas M. Cooley (1824-1898) was professor and dean at Michigan, building it into a national power in the late nineteenth century. (*Courtesy of Michael P. Cox, J.S.D., L.L.D.*)

sacrifice largely on the best compromise possible than to bring suit. It is almost impossible to prove satisfactorily the value of legal services, simply because it is impossible to present by evidence the facts which show precisely what those services were. How is a jury to be made to see and appreciate the value of the days, weeks, perhaps months of investigation and severe thought which have enabled a lawyer fitly and successfully to try a difficult and complicated suit at law? One must expect that reasonable fees in many cases will seem exorbitant to non-professional men, and he should be careful not to invite public criticism without strong necessity. I say therefore that the lawyer should avoid suits with his clients, and if he has failed to apply for his fees in due season and suffers loss in consequence, he should charge the loss in part at least to his own want of prudent foresight.

It may be well to examine in succession the several steps to be taken by the lawyer in the course of his duty for those who employ him in the conduct of causes. And,

1. *Of the client's preliminary statement of his case.* When litigation is contemplated, the lawyer should first of all take a full statement of his client's case, with all its particulars and circumstances. In a case of any complexity this ought to be taken in writing; and as it will be made by a party in his own favor, it cannot be criticised too closely. Insensibly a man will color his statements in his own favor; and however honest the client may be, every practicing lawyer knows that something must be allowed for the effect of passion, prejudice, hope and fear in coloring his communications. But unintentional deception is not the whole danger. Experience shows that men do not always deal candidly with their adviser; but that in their anxiety to justify themselves to him, they purposely keep back damaging facts, and leave them to be brought out on the trial when their effect may be fatal. You may say that when they do this, the counsel need not concern himself with the consequences; and while I agree that morally he is excusable for permitting the client to have his own way, I must still say that on grounds of policy he cannot afford it. His interest is, not to bring suits where there is no cause of action; and he ought therefore, when his client's statement is obtained, to proceed to cross-examine him upon it, and thereby bring out all the facts. Frequently it is as necessary to sift his client thoroughly by this process as it would be a hostile witness in court; and it is seldom that an observance of this precaution will be entirely without value.

Quintilian speaks particularly of this difficulty. The statements prepared for the advocate to act upon, he says, "add motives and coloring and inventions that do more harm than the plain truth; and most of our orators, when they receive these farragos think it wrong to make any change in them, but adhere to them as strictly as to cases proposed in the schools. The consequence is that they find themselves deceived, and learn the cause, which they would not learn from their own client, from the advocates of the opposite party." Again he says: "Frequently too the orator will find both the evil and the remedy in particulars which to the client appeared to have no weight on either side of the question." "In a word, the best advocate for learning the merits of a cause is he that is least credulous; for a client is often ready to promise everything; offering a cloud of witnesses and sealed documents quite ready, and averring that the adversary himself will not even offer opposition on certain points." And we may add to this that a principal reason why the lawyer is able to be of service to his client is, that he comes or should come to the case with an unbiassed mind, so that he is able to discover and perceive those important considerations bearing upon it which prejudice or passion blinds his client to.

2. *The preliminary investigation of the law.* When the statement is obtained, unless the case is a plain one, the lawyer ought to take time for investigation and reflection before expressing definite opinions upon it. Some lawyers think it important to appear ready at once to give opinions on the most difficult questions; but though they may thereby, for a time, excite the wonder of unthinking persons, the practice in the end will bring them into disrepute. Before the suit is brought is the time to investigate the law applicable to it; and counsel will then be prepared to give an opinion alike honest and intelligent.

3. *The preliminary advice to the client.* When he gives that opinion, be ought always to state frankly any doubts he may have, and call his client's attention to any thing that may tend to render his success uncertain. If authorities are conflicting, he should say so; if the case is one in which a slight variation in the proof might change the whole legal aspect, that also ought to be stated. At this stage the fullest disclosure of unfavorable circumstances is both most honorable and most politic. If the prospect is reasonable, it will not discourage the client from undertaking the litigation on which he will generally be found sufficiently determined, and if defeat results, the adviser is nevertheless justified, and will not lose the client's subsequent patronage.

4. *The preparation of pleadings.* If after the preliminary advice suit is directed to be brought, you will proceed to prepare the necessary papers. For common cases, printed blanks of declarations, complaints, bills in equity, etc., will be found at the law stationers, and it will be well to make use of them. For special cases these pleadings must be written out, and sometimes the process is long and tedious. But do not, in order to save labor, run the risk of a defective paper. Examine the books of forms; if you find one suited to the case, adopt it, even though it seems to be long and prolix: you may generally be sure that words which strike you as superabundant, are not without meaning and purpose. If you find no suitable form, make the best possible use of your judgment, and do not file a paper until you are satisfied of its sufficiency. Do not commit the mistake of putting on the files a pleading you are doubtful about, and leave your adversary to make public your blunders in court, where they cannot be otherwise than mortifying.

5. *Whether one should engage in an unjust cause.* It will perhaps be expected that I should say a word on a question that disturbs casuists somewhat, and in reference to which complaint is sometimes made of our profession. I allude to the question whether a lawyer may properly engage in a cause which he knows to be unjust, even though he thinks the law may be in his client's favor. The moralists say, no; and when the legal profession fails to follow the course which is pointed out by the abstract reasoning of these men, its members are charged with being mere mercenaries who are as ready for pay to do wrong as right, and who would deprive the widow of her mite, if they could do so by the forms of law, with as little compunction as they would enforce a just demand against a miser. Now the view which such men take is generally a very partial and imperfect one, and without any such knowledge of the general nature of litigation as entitles them to speak with the least authority. It is generally assumed by them that each case can have but one right side; but in truth, litigated cases are generally so circumstanced that whichever party the law and the evidence permit to succeed never finds his conscience reproach him with being guilty of a wrong. Frequently the parties have conflicting equities, and each is justified in sustaining his equitable right by the law if he can. This is generally the case in disputes about land titles. Nor do I think that where the law prescribes for the citizen a definite rule of action, as it does by the Statute of Frauds and the Statute of Limitations, that a lawyer need reproach himself for assisting to enforce it against a negligent party, even though that party loses a consciencious demand by reason thereof. These rules were prescribed because they were found necessary; and if beneficial statutes are allowed to remain a dead letter because they result in cases of individual hardship, the legislative authorities may well exclaim

> "Our decrees,
> Dead to infliction, to themselves are dead,
> And liberty plucks justice by the nose."

The sufferer must reproach his own negligence, and not the party who has insisted upon a salutary rule of law. There are cases, however, which no decent counsel would taint his reputation by meddling with. There are cases so contemptible for their pettiness that he will always frown upon them; cases of petty trespass, vexatious words which after all hurt nobody, debts so small that any suit for their recovery must necessarily cost a large sum. Let the pettifoggers have all such cases; or, if your regular clients desire to bring them, dissuade them if possible from so doing. I once knew a suit which was tried in two courts, and in which at the conclusion the only question in dispute was, whether one party should pay the other for six feet of rope he had borrowed. That rope cost the public hundreds of dollars, and you may be sure that it was impossible for the lawyers to make such charges as fully to compensate them for engaging in business so contemptible. But there are also cases of more magnitude which no man should touch. Some of these are frauds upon the law; such as the secret divorces which parties obtain on false allegations of residence, and on testimony which makes a false presentation of facts to the court. Others are cases where by fraud, accident or mistake, a party has obtained an unconscionable advantage which he may be able to sustain. I do not think the lawyer is to lay aside his conscience in these cases, and consider himself justified in acting as if the mere instrument of any one who sees fit to apply the proper motive power; he has his sense of justice and his own self respect to guard and protect: he is to bear in mind that he is the officer of justice, and he ought to treat with contempt all offers to employ him as the insensible machine is employed, which indifferently, when put in motion, cuts the golden harvest, or the limbs of the little child that chances to come before it.

The defence of criminal prosecutions stands on a different footing. You need not trouble yourselves with the sentiment sometimes uttered, that the lawyer should not lend his assistance to the atrocious offender. In the first place whether he is an atrocious offender or not is to be determined upon the evidence; and the jury, not the lawyer, are to judge of it. In the next place, if it belonged to him to judge, he would be subject to mistakes even in cases apparently the plainest. We are compelled constantly to take notice of the fact that confessions of guilt are unreliable; and that especially in cases of crimes which powerfully affect the public mind false confessions of guilt are frequently made, either because the parties who make them court the terrible notoriety, or because the excited imagination has dwelt upon the crime until it has overcome the mind with delusions. The lawyer would incur a terrible responsibility in many cases if because his client had confessed his guilt he was therefore to refuse him assistance. Insanity, however, is perhaps the principal agent which misleads the public in the case of apparent crime. This subtle deceiver succeeds often in concealing his presence so successfully as to defy all attempts to detect it; and many a man has gone to the scaffold amid general execration whose onlv crime was a disease inherited from his ancestors. The defence of insanity is an unpopular one, but in my opinion the number of insane persons who are ignorantly punished, is much greater than that of the sane who escape by setting up this defence. But whatever may be the case, a man accused of crime is entitled to a fair and full defence, and to be convicted, if at all, by the strict rules of law; and if he applies to you for aid, defend him; defend him fairly, defend him honorably, defend him with a due regard to your obligations to the public and to the court, but, observing these precautions, defend him to the very best of your ability.

6. *The necessity of system.* When you are retained in a case, you should enter it upon your Law Register; a book prepared for the purpose, and which should contain a condensed history of each case, giving the time when the several proceedings were had. Whenever any thing is done in a cause, the entry ought to be made at once in this book. The rules of court require that certain steps should be taken within a specified time; and unless the record is properly kept and frequently referred to, you will find yourself constantly forgetting important duties, and under the necessity of applying to the court to set aside your defaults and grant you other similar favors. A diary also, upon which you could note in advance any thing required to be done on any particular day, would also save you mistakes and losses. Bankers always keep something of this nature to inform them when paper needs attention, and lawyers with much business would find it

nearly as useful. Keep also in your office copies of all the important papers you put on file, or serve on the opposite party. You not only want them there for convenience of reference, but you want them in order to supply the place of the files in case they should be accidentally lost or destroyed Make neat copies, too, and not slovenly ones. The hand writing of many lawyers is atrocious, and their papers always blotched and blurred and dirty; and some persons seem to regard these things as signs of genius. As well might we look upon the slovenly habits of a dirty housekeeper as evidence of inherent loveliness. I do not believe that the best law is to be obtained in those offices where the floor is unswept, the tables are covered with dust, the windows with tobacco pipes, the stove with tobacco spittle; where the lawyer writes on dirty paper what nobody can read, and puts his document when finished where nobody, himself included, is likely to find it again. Slovenly habits of person are apt to accompany or to breed slovenly habits of mind; and in these little particulars we cannot be too careful to avoid them. A client, too, is entitled to require that the papers prepared for his use—the deeds, wills etc.,—shall be written neatly and legibly; and if a young lawyer at the beginning of his career has fallen into bad habits in this particular, he should set at once about correcting them. Haste is no excuse for bad writing; a good hand may be written as rapidly as any other; and indeed the very best penmen are frequently among the most rapid writers.

7. *Preparation for trial.* In preparing a case for trial, you ought to make out a full brief on the law and the evidence. This brief should contain the names of the witnesses, and what is expected to be proved by each. Wherever witnesses can be seen, it is desirable to ascertain in person just what they know, that you may not be surprised by their testimony on the trial. Anything of which you wish to be reminded in court, had better be mentioned in the brief, lest it may slip your mind at the time. Do not confine your brief on the law points to those you *know* will arise, but endeavor to anticipate any that may be raised by your adversary, and have the authorities noted so that they may be brought forward without delay. Fullness of preparation on collateral questions sometimes gives the party who has made it a controlling advantage over the other. Indeed I may say generally, that preparation goes vastly further as a general rule in ensuring success than any display of ability on the trial; and the lawyer, therefore, cannot afford to treat it as of little consequence.

8. *The trial.* A few hints regarding the management of a trial may be dropped here. One is, always to preserve in court complete control of the temper. Have no quarrel there with the court, or with the opposite counsel or party. A man is almost always put at a disadvantage when he gets angry, and the more he is subjected to annoyances, therefore, the more carefully should he cultivate the virtue of equanimity. It is not often a cause is aided by abusing a witness on the stand. Unless he is palpably dishonest, the abuse will give him the sympathy of the jury; and if he is dishonest, you will be more likely to make that fact apparent by your cross questioning, if you keep your own temper and do not put him upon his guard by your abuse. In ordinary cases avoid the temptation to flowery eloquence. It will not reach the heart of the jury. Beautiful figures of speech they are not likely to be much affected by, unless there is something in the case at the bar which renders their applicability peculiar and striking. It is very much better to talk in a straightforward way about the actualities of the case in hand, than to attempt to excite admiration of your oratorical attainments. Within proper bounds the graces of oratory are to be cultivated; but if an audience is to be moved by an address, the manner must be such that they forget the speaker while they become absorbed in what he says. Homer admirably portrays two styles of effective oratory:

> "When Atreus' son harangued the listening train,
> Just was his sense, and his expression plain,
> His word succinct, yet full, without a fault;
> He spoke no more than just the thing he ought.
> But when Ulysses rose, in thought profound,
> His modest eyes he fixed upon the ground;
> As one unskilled or dumb he seemed to stand,
> Nor raised his head, nor stretched his sceptered hand.
> But when he speaks, what elocution flows!
> Soft as the fleeces of descending snows,

The copious accents fall, with easy art;
Melting they fall, and sink into the heart."

The advocate should never allow himself to become tedious in a cause. The most persuasive speech will generally be short. He should choose the points that are most likely to be effective in his behalf, and press them earnestly upon the attention of the jury, giving less heed to those of minor importance. It will often be found that he who makes as many points as possible, and makes all equally prominent in his argument, will at the conclusion leave upon the minds of the jury the impression that his chief reliance was upon some point which they can plainly perceive was untenable; and they decide the case against him upon that, overlooking others which were sound. The same mistake is made in briefs sometimes; they convey a general impression of unsound law, because with one or two good propositions they combine others that the lawyer has not the least confidence in, but has inserted apparently under the impression that the value of a brief was to be estimated by the number of points made by it. The opposite is more nearly the general rule.

The advocate who presents his case as he ought, will seldom have occasion to complain of want of attention on the part of either court or jury. But he should always show himself sincere and earnest, and always keep his mind upon the case, and not upon himself. The success he should seek should be the success of his client, and not mere applause for his own effort. There are cases where the advocate, who prides himself upon his eloquence, so shapes his forensic display that while it may delight his audience, and elevate him in their eyes as a great orator, it nevertheless has a damaging effect upon the cause it was nominally designed to aid so that the client is sacrificed to the orator. This is especially the case when he allows himself to deal in invective, which even when applauded, will generally have an injurious effect upon his cause. Do not go into your final argument in a case tried upon the facts without a very full brief on the testimony which has been taken, if you have time to prepare one. Few men can fully trust their memory with the details of evidence on a long trial, and if they could, they would find their statements of it frequently disputed unless they were prepared to support them by reference to the minutes. This final brief in the case of a long trial is often fully as important as the one prepared to begin the trial upon; and though it must generally be prepared in the evening after the day's work in court is over, it is not to be overlooked on that account. Hard labor is the indispensible condition of success in all difficult cases. Even Demosthenes was unwilling to speak extempore, or before, as he expressed it, his argument had been *hewn into shape.*

9. *Fidelity to clients.* Throughout the trial and afterwards, adhere faithfully to the cause of the client, and allow no consideration of private advantage or of public clamor to influence you to do otherwise. This caution is specially important in criminal cases, where the public mind is greatly excited, and where a mob spirit prevails or threatens. Then if ever it is the lawyer's duty to stand unflinchingly by the accused. Then if ever he should face obloquy and detraction, trusting to the future to set him right. If temporarily he is affected in his standing with the public, and loses friends and business, it is better so than that he should sacrifice the interests of one who has confided life, liberty, reputation, property—one or more, and perhaps all—to his fidelity. The highest considerations of personal and professional honor demand of him that he do not undertake the trust and then betray it; and he does betray it in greater or less degree whenever he permits the clamor of others to relax his efforts on his client's behalf. The louder the clamor, the more imperative the duty on his part to face it and to defy it. His duty is to see that his client is tried by the law. He is not tried by the law if the public outcry secures the result. Any man who sees how a single sensational article in a newspaper, with the smallest possible share of reason for its basis, may be caught up and repeated and exaggerated and "worked up" until it seems as if the whole press of the country was uttering a settled conviction in the public mind that the person against whom the article was directed was the vilest of criminals, will appreciate how important it is that the judicial tribunals and the legal profession should be removed as far as possible from the influence of popular excitements, and that they should firmly set their faces against any attempt to coerce their judgment or control their action by any other than the legally appointed means. Popular excitements are as unreasoning as the winds; and they are as likely to demand immunity for a cold blooded murderer who is able to throw a glamour of romance about his case, or to cunningly appeal to some mawkish sentiment prevailing for the time being, as they are to seek the

punishment of the guilty. But whether they favor your case or oppose it, I say stand by your client; through the trial and after the trial; if he is unjustly convicted, do your best to secure him a new trial; if you fail in that, and he goes to prison or to the scaffold, let him feel to the last that his professional adviser has done his best to stand between him and outrage, and has never in any degree disappointed the confidence reposed in him. The public, when it recovers its senses, will respect such fidelity, and in the long run it will be fully rewarded. Mr. Webster has said that "a time-serving Judge is a spectacle to inspire abhorrence"; but a time-serving lawyer is only so in less degree, and the public in time will come to estimate him at his true value.

10. *General considerations.* Many considerations of a general nature press upon us as we consider this subject. One I will mention is the importance of making a thorough study of human nature. For this purpose a lawyer should keep his faculties of observation active wherever he goes. He needs to study the motives which influence all classes of people under all varieties of circumstances. To this end, however, it is not necessary to fall into bad habits, or to become the constant associate of vicious men. Nor does one necessarily make friends of even the vicious classes by these courses. On the contrary the very men who indulge in strong drinks, who spend their nights in unlawful games and their days in anything but steady labor, respect a man who has better control of his actions; and if they even have important business to transact, will be likely to seek aid from one who keeps a cool head, and never allows a vice or an idle habit to master his intellect. But to be able to judge well of the secret influences which move men is a great power, and one which can be wielded with wonderful effect in the courts. It is remarkable, sometimes, what slight touches of human nature in the speech of the advocate will control the action of the jury against the best efforts of the most polished orator. Little circumstances of the least possible apparent consequence will sometimes seem to the jury to characterize the whole case, and in their minds all the evidence will be colored by it, so as to seem to prove the opposite to what it did before this circumstance was brought forward. The appearance of a manifestly dishonest witness in a case may defeat the party who called him, notwithstanding his other evidence was abundant and unexceptionable. The manifest dishonesty of one affects with suspicion all the rest. One must have his eyes open to detect these damaging circumstances, and if they operate against him, he must be prudent and watchful in his endeavors to obviate their effect. If he knows men well, he may know precisely the chord to touch for that purpose; if he does not, he will be likely to blunder, and thereby deepen the effect already created against him. It was this knowledge, and not logic or learning that made Patrick Henry irresistable, and gave him the title of The Forest Demosthenes.

And here I will add a caution in regard to that portion of the lawyer's business which does not relate to litigation. I refer to the drawing of deeds, contracts, wills, and other private papers. These are often prepared without the least reflection, as if they were papers too simple to need thought or anything more than mechanical accuracy, when in fact the most serious study is often required to put them in the shape that will effectuate the intention of the parties. This is especially true of wills, which, except in the case of the most simple, ought never to be drawn in haste, nor without considering with the party very fully and in detail all the collateral consequence of what he proposes to do. It will sometimes be found, when this has been done, that if the will had been drawn according to first directions, it would have defeated, rather than effectuated, the testator's real desire. A lawyer does not discharge his duty in these cases by simply doing like a machine what is directed: he is applied to because of his superior knowledge and skill; and he should not allow the client to be led into error by a failure to employ those qualities.

Professional Courtesy

The obligation of courtesy to professional brethren has been indirectly hinted at, and it seems not necessary to do more. To preserve a good understanding it is important to avoid the occasions of dispute. With this in view, if for no other reason, it is well always to put stipulations between the counsel on opposite sides of a cause in writing. Oral understandings are too liable to be misunderstood, misinterpreted or forgotten. Besides, as they cannot generally be enforced, the party who relies upon them sometimes puts his client's legal rights at the mercy of his adversary; and this he cannot justify himself in doing. On all grounds, therefore, the written stipulation is the only one to receive or to offer to give.

If witnesses are to be treated courteously, it is still plainer that the opposite counsel is not to be made the target for abuse. How foolish is that lawyer who lays aside his dignity, descends to the position of blackguard, and attempts to benefit himself by ridiculing the personal peculiarities of his opponent, and by calling attention to unfortunate circumstances of person or life for which the other is not in fault, and which a gentleman will always avoid noticing! Men whose opinion is of value despise such behavior, and will not confide in the man guilty of it; the low and contemptible may applaud it, and among them such a lawyer must expect to find his congenial associates.

Chapter 28

Hastings Law Department of the University of California

Inaugural Address

1878

John Norton Pomeroy

John Norton Pomeroy (April 12, 1828-February 15, 1885) was a lawyer in Rochester, New York, professor at the University of the City of New York (now NYU), and professor at the University of California's Hastings College of Law in San Francisco, from 1887 to 1885. His influence is discussed in chapter 1. This lecture is reprinted from *Hastings Law Department of the University of California: Inaugural Address by John Norton Pomeroy, LL.D., Professor of Municipal Law, August 8, 1878* (San Francisco, Calif.: A. L. Bancroft & Company, 1878).

In this act of inaugurating the "Hastings Law Department of the University of California," it is proper for me to announce, in a public and formal manner, the views which are held by him to whom the function of instruction has for the present been intrusted, and which are approved and adopted by the founder through whose wise liberality the school has been established, and by the board of directors under whose supervision it has been placed. I shall, therefore, state in a brief and general manner those principles which I consider to be the foundation of a systematic education in the law of these Pacific commonwealths, which, more than any others, represent and embody the vital elements of American social life and civilization.

Any legal education which aims at completeness, which professes to prepare you young gentlemen for an immediate entrance upon the active duties of their calling, must be at once scientific and practical. In all our preliminary training two objects of paramount importance should steadily be kept in view—the laying a broad and firm foundation of principles and truths, upon which the student may in after times build, and complete the regular and harmonious superstructure of his knowledge; and the furnishing him with the means and facilities for applying his acquirements with ease and certainty in the daily routine of his profession. Should one of these objects be pursued to the exclusion of the other, the work of education would be but half done, and our duties to the student, to this institution, and to the State, would be but half performed. A familiarity with the details of practice alone would render the professional man an empiric; an acquaintance only with the science of the law would make him a theorist.

The structure of our government, the nature of our social and political institutions, and the customs of our bar, demand from the American lawyer a breadth of culture, an extent and diversity of learning, needed by his brethren of no other country. Witness for illustration the vast variety of questions which are constantly arising for decision by the Supreme Court of the United States, a tribunal which combines in itself the appellate functions, with few special exceptions, of all the English courts of common law, of equity, of admiralty, and of the privy council. That this culture and. learning are too often unattained and unsought, is a fact which I would not attempt to deny; but that they should always be aspired after by every student and by every instructor who is true to his own convictions, will not be questioned. There is with us little or nothing of that division of labor which renders the English barrister minutely skilled in the details of his own narrow field, while it permits him to be ignorant of the wide domain of jurisprudence lying beyond the range of his immediate vision. The young American lawyer rushes at once into the midst of the forum; he must hold himself ready to engage in any department of the national or the local legislation; he must be able to grapple with any question that may arise in the countless activities of the State, of society, or of business. He should combine the microscopic, pains-taking accuracy of the English counselor, with the broad generalizations and far-reaching range of the German jurist. The standard I am proposing may be considered an ideal one; but it is an ideal towards which every young man who enters upon the noble study and profession of the law should aspire; it is an ideal which many in our own and in former times have reached, and have thus offered themselves as masters to those disciples who would follow their examples.

A school established to give special training in the science and art of jurisprudence and legislation, should throw all the weight of its influence towards the promotion of these high aims and purposes among its students and among the members of the legal profession. While the needs of our country and society are such as I have described, the current of opinion, or rather of practice, is setting strongly in the opposite direction. This is an age of superficiality, and the tendency has confessedly invaded the bar, and is fast destroying its character as the great conserving element in our social and civil polity; although this destructive effect upon the legal profession has been felt to a less extent in California, I believe, than in some of the older commonwealths. It is the duty of this law school, a duty which it owes alike to the State, to the cause of a true and noble culture, and to the young men who may be its students, to resist and combat with all its energies this downward movement.

We shall have miserably failed in our vocation as instructors, if we do not succeed in turning some minds away from the heedless race after mere gain, to a love for truth, justice and equity as they are illustrated and embodied in the living jurisprudence of the state and nation; if we do not lead them to recognize that jurisprudence as the best exponent and stimulus of civilization; if we do not prompt them to labor for its improvement and perfection. What is required in the study of the law, I shall not attempt to describe in this inaugural address; but to meet these requirements within the period of time allotted for the course of instruction, will tax all our energies and call for the most constant application on the part both of student and instructor. Yet if we commence our labors with such motives and aspirations as should animate all who devote themselves to the noblest of sciences, we shall soon catch something of the spirit which the great jurists and legislators of another age have imparted to their work, and this will lead us on, by a quickened progress, to a complete success.

Of all the departments of knowledge, and of all the spheres of action, which have reference to the mortal life alone, none is so vast, so important, and so practical, as the Law. It presents itself in three aspects: To the student, as a science; to the lawyer, as an art and profession; to the citizen, as an element and means of civilization. As a science, it requires from its votary the highest exercise of the mental powers, and the most widely extended culture. As a profession, it demands from the practitioner unwearied labor, a keen perception of the motives and acts of men, and an unblemished integrity. As an element in the activities of life it meets the citizen at every moment, prescribes and directs his intercourse with his fellows and his relations with the State. By it all our temporal good is secured. Its improvement is the surest mark of a nation's progress from barbarism towards refinement. It is the clearest exponent of a civilization already attained; nay, it is more; as its development keeps pace with that of the State, it also reacts upon the people themselves, and is a constant stimulus to a further progress. The nations of ancient or modern times which have graven their character the most deeply into the world's history, which have the most profoundly influenced the movements of society, which have left a lasting impression upon the social ideas and forms of their contemporaries or their successors, are those which have possessed in the highest degree the organizing faculty, and have thereby brought their municipal law to a condition nearest perfection. The mere scholar loves to dwell upon Greece at her crowning period, as the best exemplar of a national advance. He sees in her literature, her art, her philosophy, and her politics, the evidence of a culture unequaled by that of any other people; he would describe her as heading the march of nations. But if civilization consists in that formative power which permanently elevates the human race, which opens to it the widest field of activity, which guards its interests and secures its rights, which reconciles force and liberty, so that mankind shall be freed from despotism on the one hand, and from license on the other, then the civilization of Rome was of a far higher type than that of Greece; her lessons to the world more of a far deeper import than those taught by Grecian poets and philosophers. In art, in literature, in politics, Rome was immeasurably the inferior. Her art was rude; her literature was an imitation; her politics was a fierce struggle between an oligarchy and a democracy until both became so corrupt that the iron rule of the empire was necessary to preserve the integrity of the State. But in her genius for organization, and in her law as the product of that genius, she rose superior to all other nations, and by it has prolonged her life to our own times. Through the edicts of her praetors and the constitutions of her emperors, she yet speaks in our own tribunals, and sways the actions of our own legislators.

It is upon a subject so interwoven with all the public and private interests of the citizen, so intimately blended with the history of the past, upon which the State rests for its security and maintenance, and which rests itself upon the sure foundation of right and duty, that we are about to commence the systematic study. The circumstances under which this work is inaugurated are peculiarly auspicious and promising, and seem to open for the "Hastings Law Department of the University of California" a career of influence and usefulness unlimited in its scope and extent, and unrivaled by that of any other similar institution in the country. Most of the American Law Schools are hampered and restricted by the necessities of their very organization, and are prevented from accomplishing all the results which their Faculties desire. Possessing little or no endowment, most of them are obliged to rely for their support in great measure upon the fees paid for tuition, and some of them are thus compelled to bid, as it were, for patronage, and thereby for income, by reducing the time required for attendance preliminary to graduation, and lowering the standard of attainment among the students. I do not make this statement by way of disparagement. The condition which I have described is not a fault of these institutions, but the necessary result of their circumstances, and is recognized and deplored by their Faculties. Through the far-sighted liberality of the founder, the Hastings Law Department is not dependent upon its students for its pecuniary support. On the contrary, it can open its doors and offer a legal education, virtually free, to all who come fitted by their previous training and culture to appreciate its benefits, and to profit by its advantages. It is thus enabled at the outset to establish a high standard both with respect to the scope and methods of its course of instruction, and to the nature and extent of the acquirements demanded from its students at their graduation. For no one thing connected with the institution, is its founder more deserving of credit and praise from the entire bar of the United States, in my opinion, than for the provision in the act of incorporation establishing the period of three years for the regular undergraduate course of study and instruction; a provision which places this school at once upon a position of proud eminence, which announces, in unmistakable language, the character of the work it intends to do, and which offers an example of progress that must exert a powerful influence upon legal education throughout the whole country.

Another fact of even greater magnitude is full of promise for the future importance and far-reaching influence of the institution whose session is this day inaugurated. The Hastings Law Department of the University of California will, as a matter of course, be a representative of the jurisprudence of California, both in respect to its subject-matter and its form, and will sympathize with the freedom of progress which has abandoned so many ancient dogmas, and has moulded to such an extent the legislation of the Pacific commonwealths. To any careful observer of public events in our own country and in England during the past twenty years, it is plain that California to-day stands absolutely the foremost in the promotion of legal reform among the communities whose jurisprudence has been based upon the English system of common law and equity. While other States, and England itself, have deliberated, and investigated, and even legislated to a partial extent, California has *acted*, and by one mighty stride has reached the point towards which the other commonwealths are tending with greater or less rapidity. She has accepted the principles of law reform, and reduced them to a practical operation. Blending the two opposing systems of law and equity into one harmonious and symmetrical whole, she has embodied the important and controlling doctrines and rules of her jurisprudence in the form of a scientific code; but a code which fundamentally differs from those of Austria, Prussia, and other European nations, since it retains all the elasticity, power of adaptation, and inherent capacity for further development, which are the distinguishing elements of the common law itself. The work which California has thus accomplished will certainly be imitated by other States. Her reformatory influence has already been felt in the legislation of neighboring communities; it will surely spread with ever increasing rapidity, until its effect shall be shown throughout the entire extent of our common country. I confidently believe that within a single generation the California type of jurisprudence will have been adopted by all the States of the American Union.

This law school is thus placed upon a vantage ground of power, influence, and future possibilities which is occupied by no other similar institution. Situated in such a state, untrammeled by any previous organization or by any obsolete and worn-out methods, it can take a leading part in the dissemination of the reformatory principles, which have already been accepted by the law-makers of this commonwealth. But it enjoys a still more important position of advantage. For the first time in the history of our legal education it has become possible in an organized and established institution to teach the *distinctive* principles and doctrines of the *American* law—those principles and doctrines which peculiarly belong to our American jurisprudence, which are the outgrowth of American institutions and civilization, and which the codes of California have expressed with so much clearness and emphasis. If I may be permitted to make a remark purely personal, I consider myself peculiarly fortunate in being connected with a law school which has no past history, and which from the very necessities of its geographical position affords an opportunity for giving that due prominence which they should have to American nations and the fundamental principles of American jurisprudence and legislation, in the regular course of legal instruction. It may be asked, What are these American notions? and how do they affect the work of legal education? This inquiry leads me to a few observations upon the true mode of studying our own law.

In the first place, I most profoundly believe that the law must be studied *historically*. History enters so largely into our jurisprudence that it may, without doing violence to language, be termed one of the component elements of that jurisprudence. The law of the present day is so intimately connected with the past, grows out of and derives its life from past epochs and stages of civilization, that its general doctrines and even its minuter rules cannot be fully understood unless they are studied from the historical point of view. The progress and development of doctrines must be traced, from their germs in early tribal customs or early civil institutions down through all their modifications, until they are found at present under a form so different that their origin can only be seen from such a mode of historical analysis. I cannot stop to give illustrations of this truth; they will readily suggest themselves to every member of the bar.

But while the historical method of study is thus absolutely essential, it is one thing to study the *present existing* law of the United States *historically*, and a very different thing, under the name of the historical method, to study only the law which existed and was in full operation in England a century ago. It is absolutely astonishing—it would be incredible in any other profession—how much time of students all over this vast country is wasted every year in learning doctrines and rules of the English law which are utterly obsolete, which were always arbitrary in their nature, and do not therefore aid in understanding the law of the present day—which must be forgotten and banished from the mind as soon as learned, and which only tend to interfere with and hinder a full and accurate comprehension of the rules which are now in active operation and are daily administered by our courts. It is not so in any other profession. A medical student is undoubtedly taught something of the history and progress of theories respecting diseases and their remedies; he is shown the gradual development of the various sciences which are the handmaids of his profession. But what would be thought of a medical school which should instruct its students only in the theory and practice of medicine as they existed a hundred years ago; which should occupy most of their time with a minute investigation of all the doctrines, methods and remedies in vogue during the last century, and should leave them to become familiar with the science as it is now established, after they were graduated and had begun the active practice of their profession. But this is exactly what is done to a very great extent in the preliminary professional instruction of law students throughout the whole United States.

I will illustrate this statement by a brief reference to some of the important doctrines of real property law. Every lawyer, of course, knows that the English real property law is an outgrowth of those peculiar institutions which are collectively known as the "Feudal System"; and that the ownership of land in England is feudal; that is, is based upon the principle of *tenure*. As a result of this conception, the English land law, even with all its modern improvements, is a mass of most highly artificial and arbitrary rules, unlike that of any other civilized country. Feudal property in land is utterly unlike, in its essence and in all its incidents, the property in a chattel. Partly as a consequence of common law principles, and partly as a result of statutory legislation, the English theory of property in land embraces two entirely distinct conceptions: 1. The legal *seisin*, which is partly a physical fact, and partly a legal right; and, 2. The *use*, which is an intangible right, more nearly answering to our notion of simple property or ownership. These two conceptions are entirely distinct. The seisin and the use may be united in the same person, but not necessarily. The seisin may be in one man, and does not include the idea of a real beneficial ownership; the use may be in another, who is treated as the true and beneficial owner. These two conflicting ideas of the seisin and of the use run through the entire system of the English real property law, and are the foundation of its numerous intricate and artificial dogmas and rules. I am not acquainted with a single text-writer who does not treat the American system of land law exactly as though it were based upon and embodied all these feudal theories and all these arbitrary but actually obsolete conceptions. It is certainly true that in studying our law of real estate, the *history* of these doctrines must be investigated, the progress which has been made through and out of them must be carefully traced and exactly understood. But it is a great mistake to represent all these theories and notions as now existing in this country, and as forming a part of our American law. In truth, the feudal foundation of our real property law has been utterly abandoned and abrogated in every State of the Union. By the State constitutions, or by statutes, land is everywhere declared to be allodial. Not a trace is left of the principle of tenure. The notion of a legal seisin and of a distinct and separate use is entirely banished from our jurisprudence, and only confusion of thought is produced by the continued employment of the words "seisin" and "seised." The American conception of the *property* in land is exactly the same in its essence as that of property in chattels. The entire system is therefore natural, simple, easy to be understood, and based upon principles wholly foreign to those feudal dogmas which underlie the English law of real estate—principles which have, in fact, a closer affiliation with the Roman law than with the ancient common law. It is true, that in many of the States, there are a few slight traces left of the effects of the feudal theory; as for example, in the doctrine that on the decease of the owner, his land descends immediately to his heirs, while his personal estate passes to his administrators. But even these slight traces are fast disappearing, and they have virtually been removed by the legislation of California, which gives executors and administrators the power to administer upon real estate as assets.

I have said enough, I hope, to explain my meaning. While the history of legal doctrines and rules should be carefully traced, the law as it now exists in our own country, should be presented in any properly arranged course of instruction with great prominence, and enforced with great emphasis. Time is now-a-days too valuable, life is too busy, to occupy years of the student's preliminary course of instruction in learning arbitrary doctrines which must be at once unlearned and forgotten as soon as he enters upon the active duties of his profession. It is in this very matter that the law school, properly conducted, can be of the greatest service to the student. The elementary or institutional text-writers which he reads are full of materials which would be misleading; they are all constructed upon the English law as it existed generations ago. It will be the duty of the instructor to guide the student in his reading; to point out what is real, active, present law; and what is obsolete or abrogated. In a word, it will be the aim of this law school to base its teaching upon the actual jurisprudence of the American States; to present to its classes the living principles and doctrines which are embodied in that jurisprudence, and thus to prepare them for entering at once upon the professional life for which they are obtaining a fitting preparation.

Having thus stated the principles which will govern our course of study, a few words may be proper with reference to the methods of instruction. In his address, pronounced on the occasion of the public organization of this law department, its founder announced, in my opinion, the grand central principle of all true education, whether professional or general. It is this: That the student must be something more than the mere recipient of information communicated to him. He must be taught and accustomed to *acquire* for himself. That knowledge will be found of little value, which the student has not actually acquired by his own mental processes, by his own investigation, study, and thought. The methods of instruction adopted in the Hastings Law Department are especially designed, and I believe fitted, to promote this object; to accustom the student to think and act for himself; to pursue independent courses of investigation; to rely, as far as practicable, upon his own efforts and his own judgment. To this end the whole course will be truly scientific in its classification and arrangement of subjects, but practical in its modes of study and work by the classes themselves. In many of our American law schools, even in some of those which stand among the foremost, the engagements of the professors as judges or as lawyers in extensive practice, prevent them from arranging their course of instruction, with any reference to scientific order, or the development of topics from the more fundamental and general to the more particular and practical. With us there is fortunately no such difficulty. The course of instruction is carefully planned, as the result of much study and thought given to the matter, and follows a natural and progressive order, both with respect to the subjects which are pursued, and the methods which are adopted for giving the instruction. It will be seen that the arrangement and classification of topics follows in its main features the principles and mode adopted by Roman jurists—by Gaius, in his Institutes, and by the Institutes of Justinian. Although this classification has been criticised by some modern theorists, with respect to some of its details, yet no other system has ever been suggested which combines so well a scientific accuracy and a practical adaptation to the needs both of students and instructors.

In the first or junior year the class will go over the fundamental or general principles and doctrines which constitute the framework of our jurisprudence in all of its most important departments of primary or substantive rights and duties; embracing the law as to persons, the primordial rights belonging to all persons, the classes and status of persons, the various relations which are grouped about the family as the vital unit of our social life; the law as to personal property; the law as to real property in all its branches, except certain more recondite and difficult heads which are postponed to the second year; and an outline of the law as to contracts, including the general doctrines and rules which are applicable to all contracts. The instruction during this year will be given by the means of particular text-books, definite portions being assigned for preliminary examination by the class, with an oral exercise upon such lessons, conducted by the professor in charge. This exercise will consist of exposition, questions and answers, free and full discussion with the class, and every other means which may tend to awaken the student's attention and promote a habit of independent investigation and thought on his part. In addition to the special text-books used, the class will be recommended to read, in connection with each subject under examination, other works which will from time to time be pointed out. Reference will also be made to leading judicial decisions, and to the statutory legislation of California, and of other States, so far as may be found necessary. Preliminary to this study, a short course of lectures will be given to the class upon the nature of and upon the true principles of classifying and arranging the subject-matter of our jurisprudence.

In the second or middle year, the branches of the law which form the subject matter of the course are, in the main, more advanced and practical than in the junior year; and the instruction will be more specific and detailed. The method of giving the instruction pursued during this year is especially fitted to throw the student upon his own resources, to accustom him to legal processes of thought and inquiry, and to familiarize him with the kind of work he will be called upon to perform after his admission to the bar. Having now obtained an outline of the general principles of the law, the student is no longer confined to particular text-books nor definite lessons. In commencing each important subject or department (e. g., corporations, or agency, or wills, etc.), the class will be furnished with a printed syllabus of the lectures to be given upon that subject. This syllabus states the doctrines and rules to be discussed in each lecture, and the various standard text-books, with a reference to the chapters or sections where the questions are treated. It also gives the "leading cases," English and American, in which the principles of the law have been formally announced, and also cites the subsequent most important decisions in which these principles and doctrines have been explained, extended, limited, modified, and applied. It is, in short, a skeleton of the law upon the particular branch under consideration, with a reference to the best sources and authorities, whether in the form of treatises or judicial decisions, by the aid of which the investigation of that branch may be pursued. The class is expected to study by the direction of this syllabus, to read some one or more of the treatises referred to, and especially to examine and master the judicial decisions which are cited. In this manner the class will be prepared for the oral examination and discussion of the professor in charge, which are based upon the outline contained in the syllabus. This oral discussion is not a formal lecture. It will aim at bringing out a full and free inquiry from the members of the class. Throughout the entire year the statutory legislation of the State concerning all the matters brought before the class, will be studied, so that the law as it actually exists, and is now administered by the courts, will be ascertained and impressed upon the student's memory. Among the topics which will form the course of study for this year, the following are the most important: a full treatment of the mercantile and commercial law, embracing corporations, agency, partnership, sale, bailments, negotiable instruments, suretyship, insurance, shipping contracts, etc.; certain heads of real property law, namely, remainders, trusts, and powers; the law of wills and of successions generally; the law as to torts, and equity jurisprudence.

In the senior year the course of study contemplates two distinct objects: *First.* The practical application of the substantive doctrines of the law which have been studied during the two former years; and, *Second.* The giving to the class a more complete, rounded and perfect acquaintance with all the departments of jurisprudence than is possible within a period limited to two academic years. In accomplishing the first of these objects, those branches will be taught which constitute the remedial portion of the law. In this department are included Pleading and Practice, according to the reformed system of procedure, which will be accompanied by so much instruction as may be necessary in the general theory of common law forms of action, and of common law and equity pleading; and the law of evidence. The second general purpose and object of this year's course will be attained by instruction in the following subjects, part of which, however, will probably be elective: Constitutional Law of the United States and of the State; International Law, both public and private; Medical Jurisprudence; the Principles of Morality and their application to the law and to its practice; the Roman Law and General Jurisprudence; Criminal Law; and, it is hoped, Admiralty Law and Patent Law. I design, when the course of the senior year is fully organized, to devote particular attention to Constitutional Law, International Law, and the Roman Civil Law. My limits of time do not allow me to enter upon the reasons for giving prominence to these branches. It is sufficient for me now to say, that the importance of constitutional law is self-evident; that questions involving the principles and doctrines of the private international law are constantly arising in the practice of the bar, growing out of the conflict between the legislation of different States; and that many of the rules of our own law, especially those established by modern statutes, are based upon the principles and doctrines of the Roman jurisprudence rather than upon the ancient common law of England. The law of real property, as it exists to-day in California and other States, bears a much greater resemblance to the Roman doctrines concerning ownership, than to the feudal principles which we are supposed to have inherited from our English ancestors.

I have thus stated, in a brief manner, an outline of the work which the Hastings Law Department of the University of California hopes to accomplish, of the high purposes which is has in view, of the lofty standard which it desires to establish, and of the methods which it intends to pursue. For my own part, as the Professor in charge, to whom the function of instruction has been entrusted, I pledge my best endeavors, and all the powers of body and mind with which I am endowed, to the carrying out of these noble objects, so that the institution may be an honor to the founder, to the legal profession, and to the State of California. May I not ask in return from the students who shall compose its classes, a corresponding devotion on their part; a diligence in attendance and in work, and a conscientious endeavor to improve all the advantages which may be here afforded to them? May I not ask from the legal profession of this city and of the State, their warm sympathy and hearty co-operation, in every practicable way, with this attempt to raise the standard, and to promote the cause, of legal education throughout the Pacific commonwealth? However faithful and diligently the authorities of the institution may labor, its future success must largely depend upon the favor which it meets with from the bar. And in conclusion, I do reverently ask the blessing of Almighty God upon this institution, and upon the work which is this day commenced.

Chapter 29

The Institutionalization of Legal Education in North Carolina, 1790-1920

1998

Thomas Hunter

Thomas Hunter is a sometime law professor and a doctoral candidate in history at The Johns Hopkins University.

Introduction

There can be little doubt that the greatest change in American legal education occurred over the course of the nineteenth century. The regimen pursued by those studying law in the early 1800s would be entirely foreign to today's law students. At that time, the vast majority of those aspiring to become attorneys individually "read" law in the office of an established practitioner. Such students would spend the majority of their time reading Blackstone and other legal treatises, observing their mentor in the courtroom, and copying various legal documents. By the early twentieth century, however, the majority of American law students were in programs that the law student of today would find quite familiar. Those students of nearly a century ago attended for at least two years a degree-granting law school that was but one department of a larger university. Such a student would be one of many in the school, all taking classes on subjects that are still the bedrock of American legal education. In addition, such courses were taught not by practicing attorneys or sitting judges, but, rather, by full-time instructors employed by the university; and in their instruction these men, seeing law as a science, would increasingly use the socratic method and casebook system.

Such a fundamental change, from individual instruction with an active practitioner to attendance of a university-based law school, did not happen overnight, nor was it a direct transformation. By the middle of the nineteenth century, many students were being taught in proprietary law schools which were formed and operated by some of the leading attorneys of the day, especially judges. The number of students attending such a school could range from a handful to nearly a hundred, and the timing of its sessions would necessarily depend upon the court schedules of the instructors. While most of these schools would cease functioning upon the retirement or death of their proprietor, some were incorporated into, and became the law departments of, major universities.

This article will examine the gradual yet drastic changes that occurred in legal education during the nineteenth century by focusing on legal training in one state, North Carolina. Besides adding to the somewhat meager literature on this important transformation,[1] this account should also help fill a gap in another neglected field, that of Southern legal history.

In a 1985 essay in the *North Carolina Law Review,* Paul Finkelman rightly decries the lack of attention scholars have bestowed upon the legal history of the South.[2] In the works of Grant Gilmore, Morton Horwitz, J. Willard Hurst, G. Edward White, and other lesser lights, legal cases, trends, and personages from below the Mason-Dixon line are almost totally ignored unless they involve the law of slavery.[3] Finkelman identifies eight "fruitful avenues in the search for a distinctive southern legal history," one of which is legal education.[4] He then unintentionally proves the point that Southern legal education is an unknown subject by stating that while the South initially led the nation in legal education, by the start of the Civil War "southern legal education no longer competed with that of the North." Finkelman posits that "the energies of leading southerners in the antebellum period were directed to politics and the defense of slavery. Law teaching was not a high priority for the leading legal minds of the South."[5] As shown below, all of these assumptions, at least for North Carolina, are highly questionable.

A reason for specifically choosing North Carolina for such a study is that despite scholarly neglect, the Old North State possesses a legal history as rich, varied, and impressive as any state's. A prime example of this is the talents and reputation of the North Carolina Supreme Court during the antebellum era. For nineteen years, the Chief Justice of this court was the estimable Thomas Ruffin (1787-1870), a Jeffersonian known for his stern manner and straightforward judicial opinions. Carl Swisher has written that Ruffin "as a state judge ranked in public estimation with Lemuel Shaw of Massachusetts and John G. Gibson of Pennsylvania," while Roscoe Pound has named Ruffin one of ten judges who rank first in American judicial history.[6]

For eleven years Ruffin was joined on the three-member court by William Gaston (1778-1844). Gaston was considered the most impressive Federalist in Congress during the War of 1812. By the time he reluctantly joined the court in 1833, Gaston was admired throughout the nation and his close friends included John Marshall and James Kent.[7]

The leading attorney to appear before Ruffin and Gaston was George Edmund Badger (1795-1866).[8] In the twenty-one years between leaving the Superior Court bench in 1825 and entering the United States Senate in 1846, Badger argued a staggering 739 cases before the state Supreme Court, which, excepting the June 1841 term when he was in the national cabinet, amounted to 30.7% of all cases heard by the court.[9]

Upon entering the Senate, Badger quickly became recognized as one of his nation's foremost legal authorities, especially on matters involving either the common law or the Constitution, and upon his death one out-of-state newspaper commented that "[a]s a constitutional lawyer we think it no exaggeration to say that Mr. Badger has never been surpassed."[10] Between 1849 and 1860, he argued forty-four cases before the U.S. Supreme Court, with Justice John McLean naming Badger as the ablest advocate then appearing before the Court.[11] Badger almost became a member of the U.S. Supreme Court himself in 1853, when President Millard Fillmore nominated him to replace the deceased Justice John McKinley.[12]

Before the North Carolina Supreme Court, Badger had at least two constitutional cases in which he convinced Ruffin, Gaston, and their fellow judge John J. Daniel to pronounce doctrines of law unique in American jurisprudence,[13] and of the 1,453 opinions written by Ruffin during his tenure on the court, he is chiefly remembered for these two cases as well as one which concerned the master-slave relationship.[14]

Besides its interesting and impressive legal history, North Carolina is also the best state to intricately study its nineteenth century legal education because of the recently completed six-volume *Dictionary of North Carolina Biography* ("*DNCB*"). During a twenty-five-year period, the dean of North Carolina historians William S. Powell convinced over 1,500 individuals to research and write detailed biographical sketches of those deceased individuals whom he considered the most notable residents of the Tarheel State. In all, 3,531 persons are profiled, and although the sketches vary somewhat in length and detail, the overall effect is to produce what is surely the most scholarly and inclusive biographical dictionary of any state.

For our purposes, it is extraordinarily fortunate that of those profiled, 610 (17.3%) were persons born between 1775 and 1899 who, while permanent residents of North Carolina, chose to study law, and of these, the sketches of 511 describe how the individual received his legal education. From a detailed analysis of the material recorded in these sketches much information can be gained about how, where, and with whom past North Carolinians studied law, and this in combination with other sources can enable one to develop a clear picture of legal education within nineteenth century North Carolina.[15]

I. 1790-1840: Age of Apprenticeship

Upon returning to his hometown of New Bern, North Carolina, after two years at Yale, sixteen-year-old George E. Badger on December 1, 1811, began the study of law under the direction of his first cousin John Stanly.[16] The thirty-seven-year-old Stanly was one of the South's leading Federalist politicians, having recently completed his second term in the United States House of Representatives. In addition, along with fellow townsmen William Gaston and Edward E. Graham, Stanly was one of eastern North Carolina's premier attorneys. In 1827, Chief Justice John Marshall wrote that "it was not possible to be in [Stanly's] company, without noticing and being struck with his general talent, and most especially his vivacity, his wit, and his promptness. He appeared to be eminently endowed with a ready elocution, and almost intuitive perception of the subjects of discussion."[17]

As was a custom during this period,[18] Badger kept a commonplace book while reading law, and from this something is known of his studies. He began his tutelage by reading Sir William Blackstone's four-volume *Commentaries on the Laws of England.* For a sixteen-year-old who was fond of novels, this must have been terribly dry reading; on January 9, 1812, Badger began the second volume of Blackstone, and he prayed to God that he "was done with it forever!!!"[19] This feeling likely did not improve, for he often copied into his commonplace book proverbs about studying harder.

Besides the four volumes of Blackstone, Badger's reading list included Cruise on *Real Property*, Comyn's *Contracts*, Tidd's *Personal Actions*, Espinasse's *Actions and Trials at Nisi Prius*, Kyd on *Bills*, Chitty on *Bills*, Peake's *Law of Evidence*, and Jones on *Bailments.* There were also two works specifically on North Carolina law, Haywood's *Manual of the Laws of North Carolina* and Martin on *Executors.*[20] While some law students of this period likely read more than Badger,[21] he at least received a passing acquaintance with the different areas of substantive common law, as well as learned about trial practice and various unique aspects of his own state's law.

In addition to reading about the law, Badger gained experience in legal drafting by copying various legal documents such as leases.[22] As was the custom, in his commonplace book he also compiled a fairly lengthy dictionary of legal definitions.[23] Not all of Badger's learning was in the law, however, for his interests in history, rhetoric, theology, and literature continued, and he undoubtedly read a great deal in these subjects as well.[24] In his commonplace book, Badger also drafted speeches on various subjects, in addition to copying the orations of others.[25]

By reading law under John Stanly, Badger at least vicariously became admitted into the highest legal and political circles in eastern North Carolina. He must have learned much from observing Stanly, Gaston, and Graham, both in the courtroom and out. In addition, Badger's Federalist ideology was strengthened by being Stanly's protegé, and because the latter was then serving in the North Carolina House of Commons, the young student was able to observe his state's political battles firsthand.

After two and one half years of study, Badger travelled to Raleigh in the summer of 1814 and, after questioning by Chief Justice John Louis Taylor, was licensed to practice before the county courts. As was the custom, after a year he was also licensed to appear before his state's then-highest court, the Superior Court.[26]

Years later, Badger mentioned to one of his own students that "he was forced through the want of property, to enter the bar with but very little legal knowledge—and had to acquire learning as he could afterwards."[27] Although he might have profited from additional study, once out in the real world Badger immediately began to prosper and make a name for himself. By 1816 he was arguing, and winning, cases against attorneys such as William Gaston, and that year he also won election, as a Federalist, to the North Carolina House of Commons. Four years later, in 1820, the twenty-five-year-old Badger became the youngest judge in state history when the General Assembly elected him to the state Superior Court.[28]

A. An Elite Bar

Although Badger's talents and his rapid rise into the state's highest legal and political circles were fairly unusual, his background was extraordinarily similar to that of the vast majority of those entering the legal profession in the early nineteenth century. Those who became attorneys were usually from North Carolina's most aristocratic families, especially the state's urban gentry, who hailed from such towns as Wilmington, Fayetteville, New Bern, Edenton, Halifax, Raleigh, Hillsborough, and Salisbury. The young men who chose to study law were already among the state's best educated, for of the 75 attorneys born between 1775 and 1799 who are listed in the *DNCB*, 57 (76%) attended a college for at least one term before beginning their legal studies; of these, forty attended the University of North Carolina, while ten ventured north to Princeton and four, including Badger, went to Yale.

Badger's political leanings were also common, for while the state after 1800 was dominated politically by the Jeffersonian Republicans, the majority of her lawyers appear to have been Federalists.[29] Although adherents of this party accounted for less than 40% of the membership of the state legislature in every session after 1800, one expert has estimated that of the eight Superior Court judges who served between 1800 and 1816, at least six were Federalists.[30] In addition, of those who represented North Carolina in the U.S. House of Representatives between 1795 and 1821, 71.4% of the Federalists were attorneys, as opposed to only 32.7% of the Republicans.[31]

B. Reading Law

Being well educated and coming from an urban, aristocratic, Federalist background made Badger quite typical of those who were then entering the legal profession. His method of legal study was also the overwhelming norm. Of the fifty individuals in the *DNCB* born between 1775 and 1799 whose legal education is known, 90.0% read law with a judge or private practitioner, while this figure slightly dips to 78.9% for the 114 would-be attorneys born between 1800 and 1824. Obviously, the vast majority of those studying law from the Revolution into the middle of the nineteenth century did so by apprenticing with an attorney.

Such education was in no way uniform, however, for some attorneys lavished attention on their charges, while others likely paid little attention to the young men in their offices. The amount of time one would spend reading law also varied greatly, from several months to several years. In short, the quality of one's legal education depended upon both the skill, and luck, involved in choosing a legal mentor and one's own efforts in mastering the subject matter.[32]

Like Badger, many aspiring attorneys were lucky in having a family member at the bar with whom they could study. The law was a profession that ran in families—Badger's father and uncle were attorneys, as were numerous first cousins, a son, three nephews, and three sons-in-law—so it is not surprising to find that of the 188 *DNCB* individuals who read law and whose preceptor is known, at least thirty-seven studied with a relative, usually a father or older brother.

That Badger was able to read law with one of the most prominent attorney-politicians in the state was also in no way unusual. Almost without exception, in antebellum North Carolina the men who were leaders of the state bar were also the state's most prominent politicians. In addition, contrary to the suggestion of Paul Finkelman,[33] most of these men were also quite concerned with educating the next generation of attorneys. From the Revolution until the Civil War, the legal training of the state's most promising youth would be a component in the legal practice of almost every notable attorney in the state—and those who would become prominent at the bar were the products of this system. For instance, François-Xavier Martin taught William Gaston, Archibald Henderson taught David F. Caldwell, William Richardson Davie instructed John J. Daniel, Duncan Cameron was the legal preceptor of Willie P. Mangum, and both James C. Dobbin and Duncan MacRae read law with Robert Strange.[34]

That one ably taught generation would find it a necessary obligation to properly prepare the following generation is quite evident, and one can easily diagram various educational chains or threads, whereby prominent attorney A taught B, who then instructed C, who was the legal mentor of D, etc.[35] One of the most impressive of these chains begins with William Duffy (d. 1810), who taught future Vice President William R.D. King as well as Archibald Debow Murphey, North Carolina's leading progressive politician in the early nineteenth century. Besides his plans for internal improvements, advances in education, and constitutional reform, Murphey (c. 1777-1832) was famous for instructing some of his state's leading attorneys, including Chief Justice Thomas Ruffin, Governors John Motley Morehead and Jonathan Worth, and Congressmen John A. Gilmer, James T. Morehead, and Bartlett Yancey. It was said that Murphey took a "deep interest" in his students, and that his influence on them was "profound and far-reaching." Interested in teaching more than basic legal principles, Murphey also attempted to instill in his charges a sense of public duty, and many of his pupils "became conspicuous advocates of his measures for public schools and internal improvements."[36]

Many of Murphey's students became noted law teachers in their own right, one of whom was Thomas Ruffin. Those who read law with Ruffin included Congressmen James Graham, Kenneth Rayner, Daniel Moreau Barringer, and Thomas S. Ashe, and Governor and U.S. Senator William A. Graham (1804-1875).[37] These Ruffin pupils also later prepared aspiring lawyers for the bar, with Governor Graham—who, ironically, was the Whig Vice Presidential candidate in 1852 in opposition to William R.D. King—teaching such leaders as Judge James W. Osborne and U.S. Senator Thomas L. Clingman.[38]

Along with Archibald D. Murphey, the attorney who became most noted for training young men for the bar was William Gaston. At times the famed New Bern Congressman and judge would have ten or more students in his office reading law,[39] and his most famous pupils included state Senator William B. Meares, Congressman David Outlaw, Confederate Congressman William Waightstill Avery, state Supreme Court Justice William B. Rodman, and nationally acclaimed humorist Ham Jones. While almost all of Murphey's students were from the Piedmont, Gaston attracted pupils from throughout the state, although a majority were from Down East.

In all, seventeen attorneys had three or more *DNCB* individuals read law in their offices. Table 1 lists these teachers and the number of *DNCB*-included attorneys each taught—the actual number of apprentices who read law with these individuals would, of course, be much greater.

TABLE 1: ATTORNEYS WITH WHOM THREE OR MORE *DNCB* INDIVIDUALS READ LAW

William Gaston	8
Archibald D. Murphey	8
Thomas Ruffin	7
Frederick Nash	6
William K. Ruffin	6
George E. Badger	4
William H. Battle	4
John A. Gilmer	4
William A. Graham	4
John Hall	4
David L. Swain	4
John H. Bryan	3
David F. Caldwell	3
William Eaton	3
Wm. H. Haywood Jr.	3
John Manning	3
Robert Strange	3

It is hazarding but little to say that these seventeen individuals were the most noted attorney-politicians in antebellum North Carolina. Gaston, Thomas Ruffin, Nash, Battle, and Hall served on the state Supreme Court, while Murphey, Badger, and Caldwell were judges on the Superior Court. Graham and Swain were Governors of the state, Badger, Graham, Haywood, and Strange served in the U.S. Senate, and Gaston, Gilmer, Bryan, and Manning were members of the U.S. House. In addition, Eaton was state Attorney General, while Swain, Battle, and Manning taught at the state university.

The only one who did not hold important legal or political office was Thomas Ruffin's son, William Kirkland Ruffin (1812-1880). The younger Ruffin was thought by some to possess greater legal ability than even his father,[40] but for various reasons he was never able to achieve greatness. When young he was "somewhat wild and dissipated," his demons being alcohol, drugs, gambling, and massive debt, not to mention the drunken shooting of a South Carolina innkeeper in 1838.[41] Sometime later the young Ruffin lost an entire leg, and because he was extremely heavy, it was only with extreme effort that he was able to leave his own bedroom. Thus, physically unsuited to active practice, the study, and teaching, of law became Ruffin's occupation, and he "so devoted himself to the study of Common Law, that he admired even its defects and its excrescences."[42]

C. Other Methods of Legal Instruction

While the vast majority of North Carolina attorneys born in the late eighteenth and early nineteenth centuries apprenticed in the offices of judges or private practitioners, this was never the only way to acquire a legal education. A few hardy souls attempted to read law on their own, two of whom, John Louis Taylor and Edwin G. Reade, sat on the state Supreme Court.[43] A handful of other young men read law at home while receiving occasional hints and instructions from distant attorneys.[44]

Before the Revolution, some young colonists traveled to England to study at the Inns of Court. Because a majority of these students were Southerners, and because George Wythe founded America's first university law school at William & Mary in 1779, Paul Finkelman has stated that the South initially led the nation in legal education.[45] Two hundred and twenty-five colonial and Revolutionary-era lawyers from below the Mason-Dixon line did study in the Inns of Court, yet while eighty-nine were from South Carolina and seventy-six were from Virginia, only eleven lived in North Carolina. In addition, many of the 225 were actually native Englishmen who only emigrated to the colonies once their legal education was complete, and of the eleven Inns of Court barristers who practiced in the Old North State, only four, Gabriel Cathcart, Henry Eustace McCulloh, Benjamin Smith, and Alexander White, were North Carolina residents who travelled to London for their legal education.[46] The vast majority of North Carolina attorneys in the eighteenth century, including the state's only U.S. Supreme Court Justices, James Iredell, Sr., and Alfred Moore, read law with individual practitioners.

1. Out-of-State Universities

As for university-based legal education, extraordinarily few North Carolinians crossed the Virginia border to study with George Wythe; of the 3,551 individuals in the *DNCB*, it appears that only Kemp Plummer studied with Wythe at William & Mary.[47] The school's reputation declined rapidly after the resignation of Wythe's successor St. George Tucker in 1804, although the hiring of Tucker's son Nathaniel Beverly Tucker in 1834 helped the school regain part of its former good name.[48] In the seven decades between Wythe's resignation in 1790 and the Civil War, only two North Carolinians included in the *DNCB* studied at William & Mary. Badger's brother-in-law Daniel Turner attended law classes in Williamsburg after graduating from West Point in 1814, while John H. Dillard studied under the younger Tucker around 1840.

After William & Mary's initial decline, there was not a prominent university-based law school in the nation until 1829, when Supreme Court Justice Joseph Story took over the struggling twelve-year-old program at Harvard. Under Story's leadership, Harvard quickly became the nation's premier law school, and its reputation, aided by national advertising campaigns, attracted students from around the nation.[49] In Story's first class at Harvard was North Carolinian Joseph Seawell "Shocco" Jones, who was later in the national eye when he orchestrated several notorious hoaxes.[50] Other North Carolinians soon followed, including Thomas L. Jones, William Rhodes, and Badger's son-in-law Montford McGehee.

Following in Harvard's footsteps, Yale established a law school in the late 1820s, and one of her early students was the Old North State's William N.H. Smith, who later served in Congress and was the state's sixth Chief Justice. Transylvania University advertised its legal department in the *Raleigh Register* in the 1830s and may have enticed some North Carolinians westward;[51] however, the only other university law school in which a *DNCB* individual studied before 1840 was the University of Virginia. The law department of Thomas Jefferson's University of Virginia enjoyed great success from its opening in 1826, and the fifty-year stewardship of John B. Minor would cement the school's reputation as the finest in the South.[52] After Minor began teaching in 1845, a steady stream of North Carolinians travelled to Charlottesville to attend his lectures, and U.Va. became the out-of-state school most frequently attended by those included in the *DNCB.*

2. Out-of-State Proprietary Schools

While only a small handful of those born before 1825 attended a university law school, slightly more received their legal education in a proprietary law school. By far, the nation's leading institution for law training during the first three decades of the nineteenth century was the Litchfield Law School in western Connecticut.

Operated between 1784 and 1833 by Tapping Reeve and James Gould, the school was in session almost year round, save for two breaks of four weeks apiece. Fourteen to eighteen months were usually required to complete the entire course, which consisted of a detailed examination of forty-eight different legal topics. An hour and a half lecture would be given each weekday, while students would spend the remainder of the day reading suggested works on the subjects under discussion. Detailed notes on both the lectures and readings were required to be taken, and the pupils were then to form their notes into what would essentially become a legal encyclopedia, which, when complete, would encompass five large volumes and serve as a handy reference guide in later years. In addition, there were weekly examinations on the lecture topics held on Saturday afternoons, and a Moot Court occupied the students' Monday evenings.

In the first three decades of the nineteenth century, Litchfield was clearly the most impressive law school in the nation, and students flocked to the school from every state in the Union. The school's largest class numbered fifty-five, and of the approximately 1,000 young men who studied under Reeve and Gould, around twenty percent were from below the Mason-Dixon line—of these, Georgia led the way with seventy, followed by South Carolina's forty-five. Many who studied at Litchfield became famous in later years, with alumni rolls boasting two Vice Presidents (Burr and Calhoun), three U.S. Supreme Court Justices, six Cabinet officers, fourteen Governors, twenty-eight U.S. Senators, and 101 members of the U.S. House.[53]

Although their numbers were not as great as those from the neighboring states to the south, twenty-three North Carolinians studied at Litchfield between 1811 and 1832.[54] One scholar has stated that of the Tarheels and Virginians who attended Litchfield, "not many were what are called big guns in after life," and this observation appears to be true.[55] Of the students from North Carolina, only six are given sketches in the very inclusive *DNCB.* The most notable of these was Francis L. Hawks, who also read law with both William Gaston and John Stanly, and then enjoyed a meteoric rise in the legal profession before abandoning it to become a famous educator and divine. Other prominent Litchfieldians included Thomas P. Devereux, who served for many years as the U.S. Attorney for North Carolina and Reporter of the state Supreme Court, Congressman Richard Hines, and Thomas G. Polk, an influential member of the General Assembly. On the whole, however, the majority of the North Carolinians trained at Litchfield, men whose legal education was presumably the best their nation had to offer, do not merit even a footnote in the state's legal or political history, and what this suggests about the connection between a first class legal education and future prominence is interesting to ponder.[56]

There were also other out-of-state proprietary law schools closer to home that attracted North Carolinians. Between the 1804 resignation of St. George Tucker from William & Mary and the 1826 founding of the law department of the University of Virginia, two famous proprietary schools were opened in the Old Dominion. The first of these was begun in Richmond in 1810 by Creed Taylor, who had earlier succeeded

George Wythe as Chancellor of the Richmond division of the High Court of Chancery. Taylor later reestablished the school at his Needham residence in Cumberland County, and for it he devised an intricate eighteen-month program which would take the pupil through three levels of readings and examinations, and six different moot courts. Highly successful, Taylor's program attracted up to nineteen pupils a year, and his students included future Secretary of State Abel P. Upshur, William Y. Gholson of the Ohio Supreme Court, Missouri Governor and Confederate General Sterling Price, and Congressmen Joseph W. Chinn and John Minor Botts.[57] Another student who later served in Congress, and who intensely praised his education under Taylor, was North Carolinian James Turner Morehead of Rockingham County.[58]

The second school was founded by another notable Virginia judge, St. George Tucker's eldest son, Henry St. George Tucker. In operation between 1824 and 1831, Tucker's school in Winchester attracted up to forty-four young men a year, including such notable Virginians as future U.S. Senator and Confederate Secretary of State Robert M.T. Hunter, Governor Henry A. Wise, U.S. Senator Isaac S. Pennybacker, Congressman and Minister to France Charles James Faulkner, Congressman William L. Goggin, and federal judge and law teacher John White Brockenbrough.[59] Like Taylor, Tucker was able to attract a fair number of out-of-state students to his school, including at least one North Carolinian, 1844 Democratic gubernatorial candidate Michael Hoke.

3. John Louis Taylor

While the early decades of the nineteenth century did not see a proprietary school in North Carolina to rival Creed Taylor's or Henry St. G. Tucker's, much less Litchfield, several schools were formed in the state during the 1820s. Historians have traditionally dated the state's first law school to 1822, when Chief Justice John Louis Taylor placed the following notice in the *Raleigh Register*:

> The Subscriber having lately, at the request of some of his old friends and pupils, undertaken the professional tuition of an additional number of Students, to whose improvement his constant residence at home enables him to pay more attention than heretofore, is encouraged to believe that his mode of instruction may be rendered more extensively useful by being made public.
>
> He is desirous of affording to the youth of the country an opportunity of acquiring a scientific knowledge of their own Laws without the inconvenience and expense of seeking it in other States, and of assisting them in a course of studies which even to those who are not destined to the profession, is of great importance in the ordinary affairs of social life, and seem necessary to the completion of an education adapted to the duties imposed by our free institutions.
>
> In addition to his present plan of weekly examinations, after a certain line of study, he proposes to commence in the last week in March, a Course of Lectures on the Common and Statute Law of the State as it now exists, incorporating into the text of the Common Law the modifications introduced by our acts of the Legislature, and refering the Student to the elementary books for the history and changes of British jurisprudence. This course, when completed, is intended to exhibit a systematic, though compendious view of our own law, so that there may be some one Work from which at least a general knowledge of it may be gathered. But the solid advantages offered to the Student, are frequent examinations and conversations on legal and literary topics, an extensive Law Library, the practice of drawing pleadings and discussing law questions; on all which subjects rules will be exhibited in the office and a more distinct notice hereinafter given.
>
> Board may be obtained within a few hundred yards of the office at $108 per annum, and more distant from it at $132; but at the latter house none but law students will be received.
>
> Feb. 14, 1822
>
> John Louis Taylor.[60]

Six months later, the Chief Justice placed an additional notice in the *Register* that the next session of his school would begin the following Monday, with lectures and examinations resuming on Friday. He then added, "It is recommended to Students of more than six months standing to furnish themselves with a set of Blackstone's *Commentaries*, for the purpose of making such annotations, indicative of the alteration of the Law as may be suggested in lecturing or in conversation on legal topics, and will be permanently useful to them."[61]

Taylor was a fifty-two-year-old native of London, who had attended William & Mary before studying law on his own. Despite his Federalism, he was elected to the Superior Court in 1798, and when the Supreme Court was formed in 1819, he was selected its first Chief Justice. A pioneer in both publishing his state's appellate opinions and revising its statutes, Taylor "brought learning, respectability, and prestige" to the courts during his thirty-one-year judicial career. The Chief Justice, who was married to William Gaston's sister, was a resident of New Bern for many years, although in 1813 his judicial duties forced him to relocate to Raleigh.[62]

Despite being considered the first proprietary law school in the state, very little is known about Taylor's Raleigh institution. While it is likely that the Chief Justice continued the school until his death in 1829, only two students are presently known: John H. Wheeler, an early historian who was also Minister to Nicaragua under Franklin Pierce, and David L. Swain, a three-term Governor who, for over thirty years, served as President of the University of North Carolina.

4. Leonard Henderson

The state's other major proprietary law school during this period was run by one of Taylor's fellow judges on the state Supreme Court, and his successor as Chief Justice, Leonard Henderson. Henderson (1772-1833) came from a family of noted attorneys, including his father Richard, a Superior Court judge and major land speculator who employed Daniel Boone to help settle the newly opened west, and his brother Archibald, a Federalist Congressman whom John Marshall thought "unquestionably" to be one of the finest lawyers in the nation. Like his father and brother, Leonard Henderson read law under his cousin Judge John Williams, and in 1808, he was elected to the Superior Court despite being an uncompromising Federalist. A decade later when the Supreme Court was established, Henderson, Taylor, and John Hall were chosen its first members, and in 1829 upon Taylor's death, Henderson became its second Chief Justice.[63]

Although Henderson began teaching law in 1808, if not earlier,[64] it was apparently only in 1826 that Henderson began advertising his school in the state press. On March 7 of that year, the *Raleigh Register* ran the following notice:

Law School

> I have four offices for the reception of Law Students, and shall have a fifth prepared in a short time.
>
> I shall not deliver formal lectures, but will give explanations whenever requested, examinations will be frequent, & conversations held on law and topics connected therewith occasionally, most usually at table after meals. Instruction and boarding, exclusive of washing and candles, at $225 a year.

L. Henderson

Near to Williamsborough, Granville Co. Feb. 25, 1826[65]

An advertisement Henderson placed in the same paper two years later noted, "My law offices continue open for the reception of Students." Henderson continued, "I shall occasionally deliver Lectures, but at no stated time; and will at all times give explanations, as far as I am able; and indulge in and invite free discussion and interchange of opinion upon legal subjects."[66]

The school was conducted out of Henderson's home, "Jonesboro," in Granville County, and it may have continued in operation until his death in 1833. In some ways the state's second Chief Justice should be considered the grandfather of modern legal education in North Carolina, for, as will be discussed below, two of his students became the most influential nineteenth century legal educators in the state: Richmond M. Pearson, who was Henderson's student for at least two years, later operated the state's most famous proprietary school, while William Horn Battle, who studied under Henderson for three years, founded the state's first university law school at the University of North Carolina. Other Henderson students included Governor Hutchins G. Burton, legislative leader Calvin Graves, and three state judges, Robert H. Burton, Robert B. Gilliam, and Anderson Mitchell.[67]

Thirty years after attending Henderson's school, Battle remembered:

> To the students who attended the law school which he established after he became a Judge of the supreme court, he was always kind, accessible and communicative. He did not deliver regular lectures, nor appoint stated hours for recitation, but directed the studies of his pupils, urged them to apply to him at all times for a solution of their difficulties, and was never better satisfied with them than when, by their frequent application to him for assistance, they showed that they were studying with diligence and attention.[68]

Although Henderson did not use the case method of instruction, "his pupils were well versed in concrete cases selected by [the instructor] from numerous volumes."[69] Robert P. Dick recalled that his fellow Supreme Court Justice Richmond Pearson spoke often "of Chief Justice Henderson in terms of high admiration and fond affection." Under Henderson, Pearson "acquired extensive legal learning with great accuracy," an example being that he once suggested to Dick that the answer to a tricky legal question could be found "in a note in Saunders' Reports, about the middle of the second volume, half-way down on the left-hand page." This information proved correct, and afterwards Pearson told his amazed colleague "that he remembered reading this note at the law school and had not seen it for more than forty years."[70]

It should come as no surprise that these schools, like almost every proprietary law school throughout North Carolina history, were operated by sitting judges.[71] In the nineteenth century, a North Carolina judgeship usually left one with two fairly large periods each year with no official duties; the state Supreme Court was in session from late December to February and June through July, while the judges of the Superior Court rode circuit from September to November and March through May. In the six or more months that their courts were not in session, the judges on both courts would be free to participate in almost any other activity, except, of course, the practice of law. These large periods of free time were coupled with the fact that judicial salaries were notoriously low; during the antebellum period, judges on the state Supreme Court made only $2,500 per annum,[72] while a leading attorney could make two or three times that amount.[73] Thus, by teaching aspiring attorneys, a North Carolina judge would find a quite worthy way to both occupy the months between court sessions and supplement his meager income—not to mention that his efforts would necessarily increase the quality of the arguments that he would hear over the rest of his judicial career.

Of course, not too much should be made of these early proprietary schools, for they were small affairs that in many ways appear little different from the offices of prominent attorneys such as William Gaston or Archibald D. Murphey, where numerous young men paid for the privilege of reading law and the teacher was actively involved in helping the students learn. In fact, Gaston's office, where upwards of ten persons would study at a time, might actually have been closer to a "school" than Taylor's or Henderson's, the latter of which had room for only five pupils. It is currently unknown to what extent Taylor's course of lectures and his "frequent examinations" made his legal instruction different from Gaston's, although the latter certainly also offered "conversations on legal and literary topics, an extensive Law Library, the practice of drawing pleadings and discussing law questions." Students of Thomas Ruffin even operated a weekly moot court.[74] Thus, the only major difference immediately noticeable between the office of a prominent attorney and one of the early proprietary schools is that Henderson and Taylor publicly advertised for students in the state press; and this raises an interesting question: had the two Supreme Court judges been as successful as Gaston in attracting students, presumably they would not have advertised, and, thus, without such advertising would anyone today credit them with developing the state's first proprietary schools?

The slender difference between reading law in a prominent attorney's office and studying in one of these early proprietary schools can be seen in the teaching career of Archibald D. Murphey. As has been detailed above, for many years Murphey was one of the leading attorneys under whom prospective students could read for the bar. No one has credited Murphey with leading a "school," however, before his actions of December 1831. Heavily in debt and in failing health, Murphey moved to Hillsborough, and in the December 16 edition of the Raleigh *Star* there appeared this simple notice: "A.D. Murphey having settled himself in Hillsborough Will receive a few Law Students."[75] Thus, based solely on this one-sentence notice, at least seven sources credit Murphey with having opened an "organized school," although there is no evidence that this endeavor differed in any way from his earlier teaching. Even if Murphey should be credited with operating a proprietary law school, however, the institution nevertheless had an extremely short life, for the noted progressive died only six weeks after the initial announcement.[76]

5. Richard T. Brumby

A final institution during this period that has been labeled a proprietary law school was operated by Richard Trapier Brumby (1804-1875) at Buffalo Shoal in Lincoln County.[77] In the December 14, 1829, edition of the *Raleigh Register,* Brumby advertised that he was an attorney who was unable to practice because of an "enfeebled constitution." Thus, he was building cabins near his house and was planning to open a school, where he and his brother would teach Latin, Greek, Mathematics, various types of Science, and, if necessary, "the elementary branches of an English education." Another subject would also be taught, for he added:

> I now have one Law Student, and am anxious to get a few more; to whose examination and instruction I would devote a sufficient portion of time to enable them to proceed with much greater ease than they generally do in lawyers' offices, in acquiring a knowledge of their profession; for it is a notorious fact that practicing lawyers have neither time nor inclination to direct the studies of their students, and that they do not examine them as often as once a month. Under such circumstances a young man must pursue his studies to great disadvantage; and often license to practice without a competent fund of practical information. I do not propose to deliver law lectures; but I will point out the authors, or the parts of them, which ought to be read; examine the young men daily upon them, converse with them upon the changes which have been made in the English law by the Constitution and laws of the United States, the Constitution and laws of this State, and by the decisions of the Supreme Court. I have a very good library of elementary law books; for the use of which, for instruction, and for boarding, including candles and washing, I will charge each student one hundred dollars per annum, twenty-five of which must be paid in advance.

As for references, Brumby listed "Judge Badger of Raleigh" and "Major Henderson of Lincolnton."[78]

Despite one writer's statement that "[l]ittle is known about this man,"[79] Brumby was one of the South's leading antebellum educators, although not in the law. Brumby was a native of Sumter District, South Carolina, who attended schools in Statesville and Lincolnton, North Carolina, before graduating at the head of his class from South Carolina College in 1824. He then returned home and read law under two prominent Sumter attorney-politicians, both of whom would later serve in the U.S. Senate: William C. Preston and Stephen D. Miller, who was also a South Carolina Governor and father of Civil War diarist Mary Chesnut. Upon being admitted to the South Carolina bar in 1825, Brumby formed a partnership with Preston; however, shortly thereafter poor health forced him to give up the active practice of law. After a tour of the west, Brumby settled in Lincolnton, and there married, in 1828, Mary Brevard, the daughter of a prominent family. The next year, the twenty-five-year-old Brumby was advertising his Buffalo Shoal school in the Raleigh papers, but it is unknown if he was able to attract any additional pupils.

Whether successful or not, the school had a short life, for two years later Brumby moved to Alabama, where he first edited a secessionist newspaper before being named, in 1834, the first Chair of Chemistry, Mineralogy, and Geology at the University of Alabama. Other subjects he taught included physiology, conchology, and agricultural chemistry, and Brumby held this chair for fifteen years before accepting a like position at his alma mater, South Carolina College. Poor health finally forced Brumby to retire from teaching in 1855, but not before he had gained a high reputation as a teacher of science and amassed and catalogued a collection of 30,000 minerals, rocks, fossils, and shells, which was considered the finest such collection in the South. Brumby spent his remaining years near Athens, Georgia, and a grandson, Richard B. Russell, was Chief Justice of Georgia, while the judge's son and namesake became one of the nation's most noted U.S. Senators.[80]

* * * * *

While he may have taught only one law student, Brumby should probably be listed with Taylor and Henderson as a conductor of an early proprietary law school in the Old North State. The problem of delineating exactly where the apprenticeship system stopped and where institutional legal education began, however, is difficult, for as is succinctly stated by historian Alfred Z. Reed, "A complete list of young practitioners or of elderly judges, who dignify their student classes by terming them 'schools,' cannot, in the nature of things, be compiled for any period in our history. The occasional office student merges into the institutional school by insensible gradations."[81]

Assuming that their advertisements can be taken at face value, Taylor, Henderson, and Brumby offered the young student a somewhat more systematic way to learn the law. Still, despite their efforts the vast majority of North Carolinians who studied law in the early 1800s did so by privately reading under a judge or practicing attorney. These early proprietary schools, like the handful of contemporary out-of-state private and university law schools, were important, however, for they were the first shots in a century-long effort to institutionalize the study of law. The apprenticeship system had its obvious disadvantages, especially if one unfortunately chose a disinterested or poorly trained mentor, and an attractive alternative for most North Carolinians would become available in the middle of the century, when the prevailing method of legal education was forever changed by the work of men such as William H. Battle, Richmond M. Pearson, and John L. Bailey.

II. 1840-1890: Rise of the Proprietaries

In the first week of January 1844, William Hooper Haigh of Fayetteville began reading law under George E. Badger in the latter's Raleigh law office. Haigh was an 1842 honors graduate of the University of North Carolina who, like his legal mentor, was interested in a wide array of intellectual topics. Luckily for the historian, Haigh kept a diary during his apprenticeship, and from this something is known of his legal studies.

Badger advised Haigh to "understand [the legal] profession thoroughly, before attempting to *obtain license.* He said that half the young men who entered the profession of law—went to the bar totally ignorant of legal matter—having acquired a smattering of technical phrases, and fancying themselves vastly learned." Before he was to apply for his county court license, Haigh was instructed to read Blackstone, Cruise, and Kent's *Commentaries* for instruction on real property, Stephen and Chitty for knowledge of pleading, and other authorities to thoroughly understand criminal law.[82]

Haigh would generally study in Badger's Edenton Street office during the mornings, and he made sure to be in the courthouse whenever his mentor was trying a major case. Badger would discuss these cases with his student and critique the arguments made by his opponents; in a slander case in April 1844 in which Badger represented the plaintiff who won a judgment for $500, the defendant's three lawyers proposed "very many ridiculous & untenable doctrines of law," and Badger told Haigh that "he would far rather have attacked [William] Pinkney in his palmiest days than his present antagonists—for he would have known where to have looked for the former."[83] Badger, who was quite the orator, would dissect his opponents' method of delivery as well, once telling Haigh that "the rock on which [attorney Duncan McRae] will be wrecked is his rhetorical flourishes. . . . [I]f he continues his present mode of speaking[,] he will some day be found vastly pathetic and elegant on a motion *to amend a writ.*"[84]

To have read law under Badger must have been a richly rewarding intellectual experience, for besides legal matters, he discussed such topics with his students as popular literature, politics, religion, current affairs, and society in general.[85] The pupils dined with Badger even when he entertained nationally important guests,[86] and they were "in constant association with him, and admitted to his family as one of its members";[87] two students, Haigh and Peter Mallett Hale, were literally admitted into the Badger family, for each married a Badger daughter.

Although it appears that Badger did not teach as many law students as some of his contemporaries, especially Gaston, Murphey, and Thomas Ruffin, all those known to have read law under the Raleigh attorney became noted civic leaders.[88] Badger obviously helped instill a sense of public duty in his pupils, and it is worth noting that during the 33rd Congress (1853-1855) when Badger was serving his final two years in the U.S. Senate, North Carolina's eight-man delegation at the other end of the Capitol in the U.S. House contained two former Badger pupils, Sion Hart Rogers and Thomas Ruffin (of Goldsboro).

Haigh's months with Badger clearly show the important advantages one could obtain by reading law under a prominent attorney. Unlike anything possible in modern legal education, the student, were he lucky enough to have the appropriate legal mentor, could form a close, personal relationship with a leading member of the bar that would last for many decades.[89] Without a doubt, the foremost attorneys in North Carolina history received their legal education through the apprenticeship system.

A. Disadvantages to Apprenticeship

There were many serious disadvantages to the system, however. Even in the best of offices, no lectures were offered; rather, the instructor would only suggest which books should be read. While the best office teachers might hold occasional conversations with their students to see what they had learned from such reading, there was no real way for the attorney to know if his student was mastering the material. There is no evidence that Badger or any of the other office teachers ever systematically examined their pupils to make sure that they were properly digesting the material, and, as shown above, this defect was prominently pointed out in the advertisements for the early proprietary schools. Chief Justice Taylor, for instance, planned to offer both a course of lectures and weekly examinations, while Leonard Henderson stated that his "examinations will be frequent." By far the teacher who was the strongest in denouncing this aspect of the prevailing system was Richard Brumby, who declared, "it is a notorious fact that practicing lawyers have neither time nor inclination to direct the studies of their students, and that they do not examine them as often as once a month." Thus, the Lincoln County attorney assured his prospective students that he "would devote a sufficient portion of time" to their instruction, including the holding of daily examinations, in order "to enable them to proceed with much greater ease than they generally do in lawyers' offices."

Even if an attorney were actively involved in the legal education of the young men in his office, the active practitioner, as well as the Superior Court judge, would by necessity have to be absent from home and office for many weeks a year. Badger, for example, would typically spend at least sixteen weeks a year attending the Superior Courts of neighboring counties, and he and his family would also vacation in the Virginia springs for two months every summer.[90] In addition, an attorney who did not live in Raleigh would have to spend additional weeks away from home were he a member of the legislature or involved in cases before the state Supreme Court; for example, before ascending the bench, William Gaston, who resided in New Bern, served eleven terms in the General Assembly, spent four years in Congress, and, along with Badger, was the leading attorney to appear before both the state Supreme Court and the United States Circuit Court for the District of North Carolina, which met twice a year in Raleigh. It is noteworthy that Gaston's brother-in-law, John L. Taylor, who with the formation of the state Supreme Court no longer had to ride circuit, and who had earlier moved to Raleigh, specifically mentioned in his notice that "his constant residence at home enables him to pay more attention than heretofore" to his students. Also, the first sentence of Brumby's advertisement stated that his poor health rendered "it impossible for me to take an extensive circuit in the practice of my profession as a Lawyer."

A further disadvantage to the apprenticeship system was that there were always some attorneys who would agree to take on students, and then completely ignore their education once they arrived at the office. Some students undoubtedly felt as if they were nothing more than errand boys and clerks, who were freely providing, or even paying for the privilege to provide, help in the most time-consuming yet least interesting chores of a law practice.

Harvard President Josiah Quincy at the 1832 dedication of Harvard's Dane Law College gave a fiery speech in which he denounced the prevailing apprenticeship system, stating that if a student read law with "one of the greater lights of the bar," his time would be spent doing the drudge work of a clerk: "What copying of contracts! What filling of writs! What preparing of pleas! How could the mind concentrate itself on principles amid the perpetual rotation of this machinery[?]" The student, unfortunately, would receive little in return for this effort, for "[b]ooks were recommended as they were asked for, without any inquiry concerning the knowledge attained from the books previously recommended and read. Regular instruction there was none; examinations as to progress in acquaintance with the law,—none; occasional lectures,—none; oversight as to general attention and conduct,—none." Thus, according to Quincy, "The student was left to his way by the lights of his own mind."[91] On these same grounds, an earlier critic of the apprenticeship system was Thomas Jefferson, who stated, "I have ever seen that the services expected in return have been more than the instructions have been worth";[92] Jefferson, of course, attempted to change the system by being the catalyst behind the formation of the law departments at both William & Mary and the University of Virginia.

B. A Changing Bar

While the disadvantages of the apprenticeship system had always been present in North Carolina, they became ever more pronounced when the state bar began to increase greatly in size. Although the early numbers are not available, it is quite apparent that over the course of the nineteenth century there was a tremendous increase in the number of lawyers in North Carolina, a trend that likely began around 1830 and increasingly escalated. While one source has listed only eighty-six attorneys who practiced in the state during the entire colonial period,[93] by 1850 there were 399 lawyers in North Carolina, and this figure had risen to 506 a decade later.[94] In 1880, the number of Tarheel lawyers had climbed another 52.6% to 772,[95] and the following two decades witnessed an additional 63.3% increase, so that there were 1,263 attorneys in North Carolina at the turn of the century.[96]

The constant and sharp increase in the number of attorneys likely began during the early Jacksonian period, when American society as a whole was becoming more democratic. Without a natural aristocracy, lawyers became the political and social leaders of the nation, for as was noted by that astute Frenchman Alexis de Tocqueville, "In America there are no nobles or literary men, and the people are apt to mistrust the wealthy; lawyers consequently form the highest political class and the most cultivated portion of society." He added, "If I were asked where I place the American aristocracy . . . it occupies the judicial bench and the bar."[97]

With a career in the law being the clearest way to achieve success in this new, undeveloped country,[98] a concomitant trait to Jacksonian democracy was that the legal profession increasingly appealed and became open to not just those of the upper class, but also the children of the more middling classes who aspired to increase their social, economic, and political status. That the law was the profession of choice for many young men is readily apparent from the statement of the *University of North Carolina Magazine* on the eve of the Civil War, which, while discussing the professions that the school's graduates would enter, stated: "Law stands first in respectability in the eyes of the young man, and consequently the greater number must choose that."[99] Two decades earlier, the *Raleigh Register* complained about the increasing number of young attorneys, most of whom had to struggle greatly to earn a sufficient living during their first few years at the bar. The editor opined: "There are . . . young Lawyers in this city, who, we venture to say, do not, each, earn three hundred dollars per annum. . . . [Y]et parents scorn to make their sons mechanics—but rather allow them to starve in professions. How injudicious!! If it was more fashionable to be a Carpenter than a Lawyer or Physician the difficulty would soon be overcome."[100]

The young men hoping to rise were helped greatly by the increasing emphasis North Carolinians were placing on higher education. Throughout the antebellum period, the state university in Chapel Hill grew and prospered, and the 1830s witnessed the founding of several important religious colleges, most notably Presbyterian Davidson College in 1837, Baptist Wake Forest College in 1834, Union Institute in Randolph County in 1838 (in the 1850s, acquired by the Methodists and renamed Trinity College, now Duke University), and in 1837 the Quaker institution that later became Guilford College.[101] Although collegiate training was not a prerequisite to legal study, most used it as a stepping stone; over 70% of those listed in the *DNCB* who received their legal education during the nineteenth century had earlier attended a college for at least one semester.

Another reason for the increasing attraction of the legal profession was that during the Jacksonian Era politics had become the national pastime, much like sporting events today, and the major players in the political process were, almost to a man, members of the bar. According to Tocqueville, it was only natural that politics and the law would become inextricably linked. The Frenchman held that "The government of democracy is favorable to the political power of lawyers; for when the wealthy, the noble, and the prince are excluded from the government, the lawyers take possession of it in their own right, as it were, since they are the only men of information and sagacity beyond the sphere of the people, who can be the object of the people's choice."[102]

There was also an extraordinarily practical reason why attorneys began to monopolize the political process. The Jacksonian period witnessed a new style of campaigning, wherein candidates and their backers actively courted the voters and asked for their support. Massive day-long rallies and barbecues with hours-long speeches became common, as did political clubs, torch-light parades, giant rolling balls, catchy songs and slogans, and much "treating" at the polls. The persons best suited for this type of campaigning would be the lawyers, who naturally had to rely on their powers of persuasion in order to earn a livelihood. In addition, on the county level almost every major political rally was held during one of the two weeks a year that the county's Superior Court was in session, for it was then that persons from the outlying areas of the county would gather at the county seat to conduct business, buy supplies, listen to interesting cases, trade gossip, etc. Of course it was also at this time that the prominent attorneys best suited for making the speeches at such rallies would be present.

The statistics strikingly show that the Jacksonian Era ushered in a system, which to a somewhat lesser extent still exists, whereby most leading officeholders were first members of the bar. Nationally, the 1830s was the first decade during which at least 60% of all new members of the House of Representatives were attorneys, a proposition which held true over the following eight decades. The trend was even more pronounced in the Old North State, for while only 40.9% of those who represented North Carolina in the U.S. House between 1795 and 1821 were attorneys, this figure almost doubled to 79.2% for those North Carolinians who served in the House from 1835 to 1861.[103] Thus, should one aspire to political office in the Age of Jackson or thereafter, one would almost necessarily have to first become a member of the bar. With the law as the surest means of attaining social and political advancement, it is no wonder that the bar saw such substantial growth during the last seven decades of the nineteenth century.

Not only were there more lawyers practicing in the state, but the number of those arguing in front of the most important North Carolina court, the state Supreme Court, also began to increase drastically around 1840. Earlier, a small, extremely elite bar centered around Raleigh had monopolized arguments in this court, and their abilities melded with very impressive judicial talent to create the court's "Golden Age" in the 1820s and 1830s. In the decades thereafter, the vast increase in the number of attorneys statewide coincided with a transportation revolution, brought on by the building of railroads, which made the court open to almost any attorney in the state who wished to make a quick trip to Raleigh to argue a case; especially by the 1850s, an advocate from almost any remote spot in North Carolina could travel to the capital in several days, unlike the week or more it might have taken several decades earlier. In addition, the Supreme Court did its own part to make the court more accessible by agreeing in the 1840s to hold yearly sessions in Morganton.

The best evidence of the vast increase in the number of lawyers appearing before the Supreme Court comes from the career of George E. Badger. Between the June 1825 and June 1834 terms of court, during which period Badger argued 320 cases, he appeared either with or against only twenty-nine different attorneys. By contrast, thirty years later, between June 1855 and June 1862, Badger appeared in a mere thirty-seven cases, yet the number of attorneys whom he faced or with whom he was associated was fifty-four.[104]

With the vast increase in the number of those wishing to become attorneys, and those who would be arguing the most important cases, there was no way that the old apprenticeship system could continue to produce the overall quality of lawyers that it had in the past, for there were not enough learned lawyers in the state to correctly train the growing numbers who aspired to practice. The state Supreme Court could have served as a mechanism to make sure that only those truly qualified would be admitted to the bar, for after 1818 all those wishing to be licensed had to be orally examined by at least two of the three judges on the high court. Such examination would usually be in two parts, with the petitioner first being questioned on property and estate law in order to gain a license to practice before the local County Courts. If successful, after a year's wait the applicant would then be examined on other subjects, after which he would be allowed to practice before the Superior and Supreme Courts. The only other requirements were that the applicant, through references, had to show that he was of good moral character, and he had to be at least twenty-one years of age.[105]

Although most, if not all, of the young men were nervous when going before the court for their examinations, the reality, according to one person who has studied the subject, was that "failure to pass the bar examination was an almost unheard of thing."[106] This appears to be the case, for in December 1859 only two of the approximately fifty applicants for licensure were found deficient.[107] This same authority has written that "the judges did not prepare extremely difficult examinations for the boys who came before them" because the "legal profession was not overcrowded." Whether this was the cause or not, during the latter half of the nineteenth century North Carolina did have, by far, the fewest number of attorneys per capita of any Southern or border state.[108]

During the examinations, some judges, especially John J. Daniel, asked questions about subjects that most would consider vastly unimportant. Daniel, who served on the Supreme Court from 1832 until his death in 1848, was clearly the least distinguished member on the court during the entire antebellum era, and he was also the only Supreme Court judge of the time not known for his efforts in advancing legal education. What Daniel was known for, however, was his knowledge of legal and historical trivia, and he almost always asked the applicants minutiae about feudal property law. In 1834, William Gaston instructed two of his students who were about to go before the court to be "prepared to tell Judge Daniel all about the *old feudal tenures*, when the Statute *de donis* was made, *when* and *how* lands became divisible, and what of the enactments and what the operation of the Statute of Uses."[109]

Interestingly, shortly after the deceased Daniel had been permanently replaced by Richmond M. Pearson, the Supreme Court, in 1849, published, for the first time, a list of books with which candidates for the bar should be familiar. These texts were:

For the County Courts.

Blackstone's Commentaries, 4 Vols. 2d Vol. *particularly*.
Coke on Littleton, or Cruise's Digest.
Fearne on Remainder and Executory Devises.
Saunders on Uses and Trusts.
Roper on Legacies, or Toller on Executors.
Revised Statutes, Chapter 37, Deeds and Conveyance; 38, Descendants; 121, Widows; 122, Wills and Testaments.

For the Superior Courts.

Third Book of Blackstone.
First volume of Chitty's Pleadings.
Stephens on Pleading.
Fonblanque's Equity.
Newland or Powell on Contracts.
Mitford or Cooper, Equity Pleading.
Fourth Book of Blackstone.
First volume Phillips, or Starkie on Evidence.
Revised Statutes, Chapter 31, Courts, County and Superior Chapter 34, Crimes and Punishments; Chapter 63, Lands of Deceased Debtors.
Selwyn's *Nisi Prius*.[110]

Thereafter, the court would make various changes to the list when it deemed other subjects important or when better titles became available; for example, the following year it replaced Fonblanque with Adams on Equity.[111]

These rules for licensure remained in place until 1868, when the General Assembly, under control of the radical Republicans, legislated that any male of age and of good moral character could become an attorney simply by paying a fee of twenty dollars; knowledge of the law was no longer a prerequisite. Such a rule did not long last, for two years later when the Conservatives regained the majority, examinations by the Supreme Court were again mandated.[112]

Except for minor changes in the reading list, the licensing rules remained the same until 1889, when the court, for the first time, mandated a time requirement for an applicant's studies. The idea of placing a minimum time on legal studies was not new, and as early as 1829 the *Raleigh Register*, responding to a proposal in the *Southern Review* that four or more years of study be required, stated that the legislature should take some sort of action.[113] Sixty years later, a time limit was finally provided, for the Supreme Court held that from then on one would have to study the law for at least twelve months before being licensed.[114] The court, however, did not specify where, or with whom, if anyone, one would have to do this studying.

While various litigants, as well as the public as a whole, suffered when a state's attorneys were poorly trained, the persons who would be in the best position to notice any shoddy work would be the state's judges, who heard the lawyers' arguments on a regular basis. Although members of the state judiciary did little at the licensing stage to make sure that all would-be attorneys were properly prepared, most were concerned about the subject; and instead of at licensing, the judges focused their attention earlier. In short, following in the footsteps of Chief Justices Taylor and Henderson, many of the state's judges, especially those on the Supreme Court, saw that the next generation of attorneys were properly prepared by conducting the legal education themselves, in both proprietary and university-based law schools. For example, as is detailed below, in the mid-1850s there were three excellent options within North Carolina for young men who wished to study law in an institutional setting, and all three were conducted by one of the three judges on the state Supreme Court: William H. Battle, Richmond M. Pearson, and Chief Justice Frederick Nash.

Through the efforts of these men, North Carolina witnessed an escalating institutionalization of her legal education over the half century between 1840 and 1890. It would be a mistake, however, to conclude that the old apprenticeship system was no longer an important method of legal instruction. Of the attorneys who are included in the *DNCB*, 51.4% of those born between 1825 and 1849 continued to read law in the office of a private practitioner, and this figure only decreased to 34.6% for those born between 1850 and 1874. In addition, because those profiled were, by definition, the "most prominent" North Carolinians of their time, the above figures might be somewhat higher for the bar as a whole. Thus, it is likely that it was in the 1880s when, for the first time, a majority of North Carolina law students were educated in an institutional setting.

C. University Law Schools

The form of legal education which eventually replaced the apprenticeship system, and which is the only method currently allowed for bar applicants in the state, is legal instruction within a university setting. While those Tarheels who wished to attend a university law school during the early decades of the nineteenth century were forced to attend an institution out of state, this changed when the University of North Carolina began teaching law in 1845. Two other state colleges, Trinity and Rutherford, also began to experiment with legal education during the Reconstruction Era, although by the mid-1880s U.N.C. was again the only college within the state where one could train for the bar. Still, by that time it was clear that attending a university-based law school was an increasingly popular way to receive one's legal education; although the numbers for the bar as a whole might be somewhat lower, 28.8% of those North Carolina attorneys profiled in the *DNCB* who were born between 1825 and 1849 received their legal education in this manner, and this number increased to 53.1% for those born between 1850 and 1874.

1. University of North Carolina

Although it would not be until the early 1890s that the University of North Carolina became the dominant institution within the state for legal education, the school began teaching the subject much earlier. The first mention of a law school came in 1824, when a graduating honor student, James W. Bryan of New Bern, used his commencement oration to ask whether the University should establish a professorship of law. Although the Board of Trustees did not immediately take up the idea, at some point thereafter the students on their own organized a Law Club.[115]

Further interest in the study of law was bestirred in 1835 when David L. Swain was named President of the University. Although only thirty-four years old, Swain (1801-1868) had already studied two years in Chief Justice Taylor's proprietary law school, gained a solid reputation practicing on the state's westernmost circuit, served five terms in the General Assembly, been elected to the Superior Court in 1830, and, starting in 1832, occupied the Governor's chair for three consecutive terms.[116]

In addition to serving as its President for the following thirty-three years, the University also named Swain its first Professor of National and Constitutional Law. Beginning in 1837, he taught to the senior class a second-semester course on English and American Constitutional history, covering topics that today, if taught at all, might be covered in upper-level undergraduate history and political science classes. According to the University's 1837 catalogue, Swain, using Chancellor Kent's *Commentaries on American Law* as his textbook, intended to present "an analytical review, in chronological order, of the *Magna Charta* . . . the Petition of Right; the Charters of Carolina; the Fundamental Constitutions of Carolina (by John Locke); the habeas Corpus Act; the Bill of [Rights]; the Declaration of Independence; the Articles of Confederation; the Treaty of Peace with Great Britain; and the Constitution of the United States."[117]

Zebulon Vance, while a student at Chapel Hill in 1851, enrolled in Swain's course, and later recalled:

> A single general question was asked and answered as to the subject in hand, and then [Swain] began to discourse of Chancellor Kent, whose treatise we were studying; from Kent he went to Story, from Story to Marshall, repeating anecdotes of the great Americans who had framed and interpreted our organic law; and touching upon the debate between Hayne and Webster. From there, he went back and back to the men and the times when the great seminal principles of Anglo-Saxon liberty were eliminated from feudal chaos, and placed one by one as stones polished by the genius of the wise, and cemented by the blood of the brave, in the walls of the temple of human freedom. He told us of the eloquence of Burke, of the genius of Chatham; he took us into the prison of Eliott and went with us to the death-bed of Hampden; into the closet with Coke and Sergeant Maynard; and to the Forum where Somers spoke; to the deck of the Brill where William, the deliverer, stood as he gazed upon the shores of England; to the scaffolds of Sydney and of our own glorious Raleigh. . . . [Swain's lectures] thrilled our souls like a song of the chief musician. A profound silence was evidence of the deep attention of the class, and the hour passed almost before we knew it had begun.[118]

Like modern undergraduate courses on constitutional law, Swain's course was meant not just for those who would pursue law as a profession, but for any and all students, for it was seen as a necessary element in a liberal education meant to prepare the leaders of the next generation. Most of the local county court justices as well as many legislators were not attorneys, yet in settling disputes, determining on minor criminal activity, and passing legislation, it was important that these men have a basic notion about the nation's constitutional system. Much different was the professional training necessary for the practice of law, and it was William H. Battle, not David L. Swain, who brought this form of education to the University of North Carolina.

William Horn Battle (1802-1879) was a native of Edgecombe County who graduated second in his class from the state university in 1820 and then studied law for three years at Judge Leonard Henderson's proprietary school near Williamsborough. This training made him so well prepared for the bar examination that he was not required to wait the customary year between admittance to the County courts and the Superior Court. Settling in Louisburg, for several years Battle was unsuccessful in gaining clients, and he also lost his first two elections for the state House. Showing the persistence which would be characteristic of his entire life, however, he eventually gained a number of clients as well as election to two terms in the House of Commons. In 1834, Battle was named co-reporter of the state Supreme Court, to assist Thomas P. Devereux, and upon Devereux's resignation in 1839, Battle moved to Raleigh to assume the sole responsibility of reporting. During the period he was associated with Devereux, Battle was also appointed to a three-man committee, with former Governor James Iredell, Jr., and Superior Court Judge Frederick Nash, to revise the state's statute law.

Battle's position as sole Reporter of the state Supreme Court was short-lived, for in 1840 the General Assembly elected him to the Superior Court. Although the latter position was "not particularly to his liking," he served on the court for the next eight years, until being given a temporary appointment by Governor Graham to the state Supreme Court in 1848. Later that year, the General Assembly selected someone else for the Supreme Court position, but the following session he was reelected to the Superior Court. In 1852 upon Thomas Ruffin's resignation, the legislature elected Battle to the Supreme Court, and he served there until the office was declared vacant by the 1868 Constitution. Battle was then forced to run for his old position in that year's general election, and as a former Whig who was running under the Conservative label, he was defeated in the Republican sweep.

In 1872, the General Assembly again appointed Battle to revise its statutes, this time by himself. The judge's necessary familiarity with his state's statute law was equalled by his knowledge of her case law. In the late 1860s, he produced a three-volume digest of the North Carolina Reports, in which he noted that he had "read over every case ever reported in North Carolina from the beginning to the end"; Chief Justice Walter Clark later stated that "Judge Battle was probably more thoroughly familiar with the case law of North Carolina than any other judge who ever sat on the bench." It is not surprising, then, that while on the high court, Battle was a conservative jurist who was strongly influenced by precedent: "His opinions were expressed in clear, simple language, without show or effect. He knew the precedents. He eschewed judicial legislation. He had no pet system or ideas to promote. He was eminently a safe judge."

Physically, "Judge Battle was rather below medium size," and was "an unusually handsome man, well-groomed, clean shaven, with fine regular features and the gentle eyes of a scholar." As for his personality, he has been described as "gentle and quiet in his demeanor," in addition to being "simple in his manners, cordial, and without affectation." Battle was also abstemious, eschewing the use of both alcohol and tobacco. In short, the Judge was conscientious and hard working, and he consistently earned the respect of his contemporaries, even if they might have found his personality less than stimulating.[119]

Shortly after being first elected to the Superior Court, Battle, in order to "add to his modest salary as judge, like many [North Carolina] judges, . . . found it best to open a law school."[120] In early April 1841, Battle and James Iredell, Jr., began advertising in the Raleigh papers that they would open a proprietary law school in Raleigh on June 1, "provided a sufficient number of students (eight at least) can be obtained to justify the undertaking." As for instruction, "the most approved course of studies will be adopted, and oral and written instruction will be given shewing the alteration of the law as laid down by Blackstone, arising from our Acts of Assembly and the decisions of our courts." In addition, "The students will be required to undergo frequent and stated examinations; and when they shall have become sufficiently advanced, it is proposed that they shall have a moot court, where they may argue legal questions, and be made acquainted with the forms of pleading and practice in the courts of this State." The proprietors envisioned that their entire course would last two years, although students could attend for a shorter period, and the tuition was set at $100 a year.[121]

James Iredell, Jr. (1788-1853), was undoubtedly associated with Battle for the months every spring and fall when the latter would be absent from home holding court. Although now less well known than his father, who was one of the first Justices of the United States Supreme Court, the younger Iredell was Thomas Ruffin's roommate at Princeton and then became one his state's finest attorneys. Entering politics, Iredell served as Speaker of the House of Commons, Governor, and U.S. Senator, although from the early 1830s he concentrated solely on the law. Settling in Raleigh in 1840, he replaced Battle as Reporter of the state Supreme Court, a position he held for twelve years.[122]

Whether eight or more young men responded to the Battle and Iredell notice, thus allowing the opening of the school, is unknown. If so, however, the institution was in existence for two years at the most, for in 1843 Battle removed to Chapel Hill. According to Walter Clark, there were two reasons for this move, to establish a law school and to enable Battle to educate his sons at the state university.[123] This first reason was in evidence on July 7, 1843, when Battle gave notice in the *Raleigh Register* that in eight days he would "open a LAW SCHOOL at the University, on the 15th of July next." David L. Swain would attend to the students while Battle was holding court, and a one-time tuition of $100 would be charged, with no extra charge "for those who may attend his instructions after completing a regular Course."[124]

Despite a large, bold caption reading "LAW SCHOOL, AT THE UNIVERSITY," and the fact that one of its instructors was the University's President, Battle's Chapel Hill institution was, at first, not officially associated with the University of North Carolina. Instead, it was held in "a small two-room building in the yard of [Battle's] home." Undoubtedly, however, the Judge intended for most, if not all, of his students to have recently attended the University, and there is also much reason to believe that he anticipated that his school would soon become associated with the University. Half a year earlier, on December 12, 1842, Battle's associate in the Raleigh institution, James Iredell, Jr., introduced and saw passed the following resolution at a meeting of the University's Board of Trustees: "Be it ordained . . . that the Executive Committee be & they are hereby authorized at their discretion to establish a Law Professorship and to prescribe such rules and regulations as to the duties and emoluments of such professorship, and also as to the class of Students who many attend instruction therein as may think proper."[125] Interestingly, one of the members of the Executive Committee authorized to establish the law program was William Horn Battle.[126]

In 1845, after only two years of independently operating his law school in Chapel Hill, Battle's school was officially incorporated into the University; on October 3, "President Swain attended the meeting of the [Executive] Committee and presented a program embracing a Law Professorship with the Hon. William Horn Battle at its head which with some modifications was approved."[127] Shortly thereafter, the University of North Carolina Catalogue for the academic year 1845-1846 described the new department:

> A department for the study of municipal Law has been recently established and placed under the charge of the Professor of Law. This department contains two Classes, of which, the first, called the Independent Class, will consist of such Students of Law as have no connexion with any of the College Classes; and the second, called the College Class, will consist of such irregular members of College as, with the permission of the Faculty, may be desirous of joining it.
>
> The plan of studies comprises Blackstone's Commentaries, Kent's Commentaries, Stephen on Pleading, Chitty on Pleading, Greenleaf on Evidence, Cruise's Digest of Real Property, and Williams on Executors, together with Lectures on municipal Laws of the State as modified by the Acts of the Legislature and decisions of the State Courts. A complete course will occupy two years for the Independent Class and two years and a half for the College Class, at the end of which the degree of Bachelor of Law will be conferred on such students as by their proficiency may be deemed to be entitled to it.
>
> The Independent Class will be called on for recitations three times a week. The recitations of the College Class will be only once a week, and will be so arranged as not to interfere with the ordinary studies of College.
>
> A Moot Court will be held occasionally by the Professor, for the discussion by the Students, of such legal questions as he may propose. The Students will also be required from time to time to draw pleadings and other legal instruments, and be instructed in the practice of the Courts.
>
> The Professor of Law receives no salary from the Trustees of the University, but is entitled to demand from each member of the Independent Class, fifty dollars per session for the two first sessions of the course, and twenty-five dollars per session afterwards; and from each member of the College Class twenty-five dollars per session. The sessions and vacations of this department will be same as those of College, but the Professor will give instruction during the vacations to such members of either Class as desire it without any extra charge.
>
> The Professor of Law and the members of the Independent Class will not be subject to any of the ordinary College regulations.[128]

In many ways, the University's new law school was little different from a proprietary school. The University was under no financial obligation for the institution, and those in the "Independent Class" were not subject to any of the University's regulations. In addition, all student fees would be paid directly to the instructor, and he could, and did, continue his employment outside of the university. For the students, however, there were advantages to attending a law school connected with the University. Most obvious was that if one satisfactorily completed the entire course, he would receive a university degree, an LL.B. In addition, those enrolled in the "College Class" could combine their law studies with a traditional college education.[129]

Battle began his law professorship "in one little room 16 by 18 feet, furnished with half [a] dozen split-bottom chairs." Over the following decade, the law department witnessed a haphazard yet substantial growth. During the 1847-1848 academic year, Battle taught eleven young men from the two different classes of students, and for several years the enrollment remained fairly stable, for there were twelve law students in 1854-1855. The following year saw a large increase, for twenty-two students were in the program, and the law department's largest class prior to the 1880s was in 1857-1858, when twenty-eight would-be attorneys prepared under Battle. While most of the students were from North Carolina, Battle's program attracted young men from throughout the South, including Virginia, Tennessee, Kentucky, Alabama, Mississippi, and Texas, as well as California.[130]

With a couple of minor alterations, the structure and curriculum of the law department as set out in the 1845 catalogue remained the same throughout Battle's long tenure. As mentioned above, in 1849 the state Supreme Court first published a reading list for bar applicants, and thereafter the books assigned by Battle mirrored those required by the high court. Thus, "[i]n 1854 Kent's *Commentaries* was dropped from the plan of studies; Smith on *Contracts* was substituted for Chitty; Iredell on *Executors* was substituted for Williams; and Selwyn's *Nisi Prius*, Fearne on *Remainders*, and Adams' *Doctrine of Equity* were added."[131] Of course Battle himself was on the Supreme Court from 1852 to 1868, so those students who had successfully completed the course at Chapel Hill had little to worry about when applying for license. A second, minor, change concerned tuition, for after 1858 each member of the College Class was charged $35 per session, although any student who initially paid $100 was allowed to attend for any length of time.[132]

As noted above, during his first twenty-three years at the University, Battle also continued to serve in the state judiciary. Thus, there would be several months every year when he necessarily would be absent holding court, and as at his two previous proprietary schools, another attorney would be needed to attend his classes. Undoubtedly David L. Swain continued to fill in for Battle during the first few years of the school, although by the late 1840s Battle was receiving help from a former student, Chapel Hill attorney Samuel Field Phillips.

Phillips (1824-1903) was the son of James Phillips, a longtime Professor of Mathematics at the University of North Carolina, and a brother to Charles Phillips, who was married to Battle's youngest sister and taught both mathematics and civil engineering at the state University and Davidson. Sam Phillips graduated from U.N.C. in 1841, sharing first honors with his brother Charles, and then studied law, first with President Swain and later in Battle's newly opened proprietary school in Chapel Hill. Opening a practice in his hometown, Phillips, who "possessed a brilliant, reflective mind and a dispassionate temperament," quickly gained success at the bar, and he began a political career by being elected to the state House in 1856.

During his first few years of practice, Phillips began filling in for Battle when the latter would be away from Chapel Hill fulfilling his judicial duties, and this teaching role later expanded, for university catalogues between 1854 and 1859 list Phillips as Assistant Professor of Law. During his tenure, the young Chapel Hill attorney was quite popular with his students, for Phillips "had a remarkable talent for imparting knowledge, as the Law students in the 50's . . . have always freely testified."

Phillips, however, is chiefly remembered not for his teaching abilities, but for the impressive legal career he enjoyed after he left Chapel Hill. During the 1860s, he served as state auditor, Speaker of the state House, and Supreme Court Reporter. He thereafter prosecuted several important Ku Klux Klan cases while serving as an Assistant U.S. Attorney, and this experience in part helped him garner an appointment in 1872 as Solicitor General of the United States. Phillips served in this position over the following twelve years, under Presidents Grant, Hayes, Garfield, and Arthur, and afterward he continued to live in

Washington and practice in front of the U.S. Supreme Court. While in private practice, Phillips' most famous case, which he and former North Carolina judge Albion W. Tourgée unfortunately lost, was *Plessy v. Ferguson.*[133]

The tremendous growth witnessed by both the state university and its law school during the 1850s was reversed early in the next decade when the vast majority of the state's young men went off to the field of battle.[134] Although it was much reduced in size, Battle continued teaching his law class throughout the Civil War, and during the first several years after peace was restored the school regained much of its strength, for in 1867-1868 Battle taught eighteen students in his class.

This effort at rebuilding was short-lived, however, for the 1868 Constitution, which deprived Battle of his seat on the Supreme Court, also radically restructured the University's Board of Trustees. The new Board, mainly consisting of radical Republicans, fired the entire faculty, and replaced them with highly inferior men. Upon his forced ouster, Battle moved to Raleigh, where he practiced law with two of his sons and occasionally had a student read law in his office. It appears that the new Board did not hire a replacement for the professor of law, and thus law instruction at the University ceased in 1868; as is mentioned above, it was also at this time that the Republican-controlled General Assembly legislated that one could become an attorney simply by paying a twenty-dollar fee. With a politicized, poorly trained faculty, and with scant resources, the entire university closed its doors in 1870.[135]

When the Conservatives regained control of the General Assembly, a new Board of Trustees was appointed, and after much effort the University reopened its doors in 1875. The new President was William H. Battle's son, Kemp Plummer Battle, who was able to have his father reappointed the school's Professor of Law. After being closed nearly nine years, in January 1877 the School of Law was reopened and the elder Battle, at age seventy-four, resumed his teaching career. The law school retained the structure it had possessed since its opening, with Battle teaching both the Independent Class and the College Class. One change, however, was that those in the Independent Class were now brought in closer contact with the University; although they were still responsible in their conduct only to the Professor of Law, these students were, for the first time, given access to the University's library and its literary societies, and they were allowed to attend other courses at the University "on easy terms."[136]

The reopened school got off to a slow start, for Battle taught only four students in 1878.[137] Worse still, the aged professor's health began to fail, which forced Battle to resign his position in January 1879, just two months before his death. Battle's son Kemp, who was trained as an attorney but was then the University's President, temporarily took charge of his father's classes, which he taught for the following year and a half.

During his long teaching career at the University, the elder Battle taught law to several hundred young men, twenty-three of whom are profiled in the *DNCB.* Of these, two served as North Carolina Governors, three as U.S. Senators, and three followed their teacher's example by becoming members of the state Supreme Court.

Unlike his chief competitor Richmond M. Pearson, little is known about Battle's teaching methods. Undoubtedly, he did not occupy the majority of his class time in giving lectures, for late in his tenure a university catalogue mentioned that "Lectures are given from time to time on such subjects as have been greatly modified by our statutes, such as Marriage, Descent, Wills, Limitations, &c."[138] Battle's son remembered that "Particular attention was directed to preparation for obtaining license to practice law, and it was sought in addition to give a broad general knowledge of the law."[139]

It is a routine assumption that with the advent of institutionalized legal education in the middle of the nineteenth century, the attention of law teachers turned from advising about the practical aspects of everyday legal practice to the teaching of legal theory and history.[140] While such an assumption contains much truth, it should not be overemphasized. Throughout history, there have been multiple goals to American legal education. First and foremost, all legal education is meant to teach the student inferential reasoning, or, as it is commonly termed, the ability to "think like a lawyer." Beyond that, there are other goals, some of which will necessarily have precedence over others depending on where, and with whom, one studies law.

At its most basic, legal education can consist of teaching about the procedural or "practical" elements of the law, such as how to draft and file legal documents, meet with clients, argue in court, etc. Turning to the substance of the law, another goal of legal education can be to teach the basic blackletter law, based on both statutes and cases. Finally, legal education can also involve legal "theory," touching such areas as how the law was originally formulated, how and why it has been changed, and the effects of having one law rather than another. These goals are not mutually exclusive, and most legal education will contain elements of all of the above, although some components will be more prevalent than others.

That the institutionalization of legal education within North Carolina necessarily brought with it the replacement of the "practical" aspects with the "theoretical" is not completely true. In fact, at any time in the past one has been able to find quite different types of legal instruction within the Old North State. Early in the nineteenth century, when the apprenticeship system was supposedly based on principally showing the student the day-to-day routine of a law practice, some of the best attorneys, such as Thomas Ruffin and later his son William, insisted that their students read the extraordinarily difficult, and highly "theoretical," Coke on Littleton.[141] Likewise, a century later when almost all legal education was university based, the education one received at one school could be completely different from that at another; for example, as is detailed below, at the same time that Samuel F. Mordecai at Trinity was intricately preparing his students over two years by using casebooks and the socratic method, a few miles away in Wake Forest Needham Y. Gulley in his summer course would prepare young men for the state bar exam through his ten-week lecture course on the state's blackletter law.[142]

A difference in emphasis was also noticeable between Battle and Richmond M. Pearson. As is discussed below, legal instruction under Pearson focused on legal reasoning and the theory behind the law, while the Chief Justice tended to downplay current blackletter law and completely ignored the practical aspects of a law practice. Such attitude carried over into his work on the bench, for Pearson had no qualms about overturning precedent should it be, in his opinion, wrongly decided. By contrast, his judicial colleague William H. Battle, both a former Supreme Court Reporter and two-time compiler of the state's statutes, was an eminently conservative judge, who knew the precedents and followed them religiously.

Thus, it is not surprising that legal education under Battle focused on blackletter law, especially North Carolina cases and statutes. The best example of this emphasis comes from the advice Battle gave his own son Kemp, after the latter had already attended his father's law class while also serving as an Assistant in Latin and Tutor in Mathematics at the state university. The younger Battle recalled that "[w]hen I consulted my father as to the propriety of spending a year at the Harvard Law School, he advised, as my intention was to live in North Carolina, that I should [instead] study diligently North Carolina Reports of cases decided by our Supreme Court."[143]

As for student opinion of the elder Battle, Chief Justice Clark later recalled that all of Battle's "students remember him with respect and affection."[144] Although complementary, such sentiments pale beside the glowing tributes of deep affection heaped by former students upon his contemporaries Pearson and John L. Bailey. Battle's temperament and knowledge of the law likely gained him the great respect of his students, yet the former might have also prevented them from becoming extraordinarily close to their teacher. Even in his homelife the ascetic Battle appears to have been more respected than deeply beloved, for his son Kemp remembered, "Father's duties as judge took him from home nearly half the time for many years, and when he was at home he was busy with his law students, or with his Reports, Digests, and Revisal. . . . We all loved and admired him to the utmost. But his professional cares prevented much association with his children."[145]

As noted above, when the dying Battle retired in January 1879, he was temporarily replaced by his son, University President Kemp Plummer Battle (1831-1919).[146] Following in the footsteps of David L. Swain, from 1876 until well into the 1900s President Battle taught the University's undergraduate course on International and Constitutional Law. A university catalogue stated that this course would be "conducted with the general view of imparting a clear understanding of the genius of our own government, State and National, and the relations between other countries and our own. For those who propose to pursue the legal profession, the course will constitute a valuable introduction to the general study of law."[147]

Undoubtedly, the duties of teaching this class and others in "political economy," in addition to serving as the University's President, left the younger Battle with little time for his father's law class, and in 1880 he reported to the Board of Trustees: "I have been compelled to take charge of the class in law. During the year I have had 13 pupils divided into two classes, five of whom are ready to apply for license to practice. It is much to be hoped that a suitable Professor of Law will be appointed as I find my duties quite onerous enough without this burden."[148] Such relief was not immediately forthcoming, for the following year Battle again asked the Trustees to appoint a permanent Professor of Law, adding, "I am not under any obligation to instruct in this department but keep it up for the benefit of the University, the fees being paid to the University except $100 which is retained to pay for clerical services."[149]

In 1881, the Board of Trustees finally appointed a Professor of Law, John Manning, Jr., of Pittsboro. Manning (1830-1899) graduated from the University in 1850 and then read law with his cousin John H. Haughton, one of the leading attorneys in eastern North Carolina; like many attorneys, Manning also had other familial connections to the bar, for his uncle was Chief Justice of Louisiana, while his wife was the granddaughter of John Hall, one of the first members of the North Carolina Supreme Court. In time, Manning became the leading attorney on his judicial circuit, and he also served in the Secession Convention, the Confederate Army, the 1875 Constitutional Convention, and both the North Carolina and United States Houses of Representatives. In the early 1880s, he was a member of a three-man panel appointed to revise the state's statutes, and later in his career Manning authored a volume analyzing both statutory and case law changes to the law as set out in the first volume of Blackstone's *Commentaries*.[150]

Once in Chapel Hill, Manning made minor alterations to the law program as taught by the Battles. The entire course of study continued to cover two years, but the new professor dispensed with the differentiation between the Independent Class and the College Class, and instead instituted two different, year-long courses. In the first year course, students would study the subjects and specific texts prescribed by the state Supreme Court as necessary for licensure.[151] While many would be satisfied with taking just this first year course, a second year course, after which one would be eligible for the LL.B. degree, would be offered for those who wished to gain a "broad and liberal knowledge of the law." Texts for the second year included Angel and Ames on Corporations, Pierce on American Railroad Law, May on Insurance, Darlington's Williams on Personal Property, Starkie or Stephens on Evidence, Russell or Washburn on Criminal Law, Pollock on Contracts, and Cooley's Constitutional Limitations.[152]

Manning's classes were open to those already attending the University as well as those wishing to study only law, and the school advertised that compared to other options for studying law, "the advantages offered by this school are: the use of the University and society libraries amounting in the aggregate to near 20,000 volumes . . . [and] the opportunities offered on easy terms of attending the lectures of the President and such other lectures as they may desire."[153] Of course such cross-pollination could cause difficulty in determining to whom a student was responsible for his conduct, so in 1884 the faculty ruled that a law student who either attended other university classes or roomed in the college was "subject to all the rules of the University touching the deportment, moral conduct, and habits of the students of the University." On the other hand, "A law student who is not a member of any other of the University classes, [and] who rooms in the village is [solely] under the control of the Prof. of law." The announcement further noted, however, that "No drunkenness or scandalous conduct will be tolerated nor will a law student be permitted to drink with a student of the University, or allow such student to drink in his room."[154]

Tuition for Manning's program would be $100 for the first-year course and the same for the second year, or $150 if a student desired to attend the full two years. It appears that Manning was allowed to keep $90 of the $100 student fee, with the remainder going to the university. Like William H. Battle, Manning continued to supplement this income by practicing law, and in June 1884 the visiting committee of the Board of Trustees recommended that the law professor should be made a regular member of the faculty with his fees supplemented by a regular salary from the university, in return for which he should devote his entire time to the law school. The next month the Trustees did not agree to such, although they did allow that "such fees as may be paid into the University by Professor Manning's law students shall be turned over to Professor Manning as an addition to his perquisites." This additional aid must have been deemed inadequate, for the following February President Battle reported to the Trustees that because of insufficient remuneration from the law school, Manning was "compelled to spend a large part of his time at the courts in the practice of his profession to the detriment of the school." Battle thus recommended that in return for Manning devoting all of his time to the school, he be given a salary of $1,000 in addition to his usual fees, and when the Board approved the plan in March 1885, the University's law professor, after forty years, at last became a regular member of the school's faculty.[155]

Manning was also able to add to his income when, in 1884, he instituted a summer law class at the University. For those unable to attend the regular sessions, instruction would be given from July 1 until the last Thursday in August on the same materials as studied in either, or both, of the regular year-long classes. Tuition was set at $30 for those studying the materials of the first year course, and $60 for those interested in the material taught to both classes.[156] Thus, it appears that in the mid-to-late 1880s, one may have had sufficient preparation for passing the state bar exam by taking only the nine-week, thirty-dollar, summer course at Chapel Hill. It is no wonder, then, that the Supreme Court in 1889 mandated that one would have to study law for at least one year before being allowed to take the bar exam.

Under Manning, the University's law school witnessed a steady growth. His first class in 1881-1882 numbered fourteen students, which increased to twenty-one the following year, and twenty-eight the year after—thus equalling Battle's largest class. This upward trend continued, so that by 1891-1892, Manning saw an enrollment of fifty-five young men.[157] Thus, despite the turbulence caused by the Civil War and Reconstruction, by 1890 the law school of the University of North Carolina was again firmly entrenched as a bastion of legal education within the state of North Carolina.

2. Trinity College (I)

While the University of North Carolina did not operate a law school from 1868 to 1877, this did not mean that during these years the state was bereft of a college or university at which students could train for the bar, for two additional colleges began teaching law during the Reconstruction Era. The first of these was Trinity College, which later, upon an infusion of tobacco money, was moved to Durham and became Duke University. Begun in the fields of northwestern Randolph County in 1838, and earlier called first Union Institute and then Normal College, by the late 1860s Trinity was a struggling, cash-strapped Methodist institution with an energetic President, Braxton Craven. Upon the firing of Battle in 1868, Craven saw the chance for his institution to become the state's only college to offer a law course, and he lost little time in seizing the opportunity.

Trinity's catalogue for 1868-1869 announced the opening of a school of law, explaining, "This school is organized to meet a growing demand. The instruction will be as thorough as possible and be given both by lecture and text-books." Among the latter, students would study Blackstone, Stephen on Pleading, Greenleaf's Evidence, Adams on Equity, Vattel on International Law, and a work on executors. As had been the case at the state university, classes would be composed of both students enrolled in other departments of the college and those who would be studying only law.

A problem was encountered, however, and one which shows the hasty nature of the school's opening, in finding enough funding to pay for a proper instructor. With no immediate funds available, Craven himself took on the duties of teaching the curriculum. The forty-six-year-old President was not trained in the law, yet he was widely recognized for his ability to teach almost any subject. Despite not having a trained attorney as its instructor, the school initially flourished, with thirty students studying law in 1869-1870, thirty-seven the following year, and twenty-seven the year after.

The Reverend Craven was quite concerned with establishing a reputable law school, and in 1870 he asked the college's trustees to fund a professorship in law "at the earliest practicable time." Again, the trustees could not come up with the means for such, and they informed Craven that he would either have to continue the teaching by himself or develop a suitable alternative. It seems almost incredible that Craven was able to teach the course without at least some aid from local attorneys or others trained in the law, yet there is no evidence of such help. It is also unknown why Craven did not adopt the method used at Chapel Hill and have the instructor's salary paid solely and directly out of student tuition.

During the 1872-1873 school year, Trinity at last hired a full-time instructor trained in the law. That year's catalogue listed Craven as "President and Professor of National and Constitutional Law," while an additional faculty member was "John W. Young, Esq., Instructor of Common and Statute Law." In addition, the catalogue noted that, "Complete instruction is given in daily lectures, examinations, etc. Students are fully prepared to obtain license. . . . Young men, who desire to study law, will find many advantages at

Trinity, not usually found at Law Schools." As for tuition, it was $20 a year for those students already enrolled in the college, and $60 per annum for those studying only law.

Young's connection with Trinity did not last long, for after 1874 it appears that Craven was again the only person teaching law at Trinity. Starting in 1875, college catalogues began listing a "Department of Law," rather than the previous "School of Law," although the importance of this change in nomenclature is unclear. Law training continued to be offered at Trinity until the early 1880s, although the number of students began to precipitously decline in the late 1870s. Undoubtedly the fact that Craven was not trained as an attorney hurt the program, as did the 1878 opening of the Dick & Dillard Law School in nearby Greensboro, discussed below, and the reopening of the law school in Chapel Hill. During the 1881-1882 academic year, only six students were enrolled in Craven's law class, and when the President died in November 1882, this experiment in law training at Trinity came to an end. In total, 150 students studied law under Craven and Young, five of whom are listed in the *DNCB*, including political boss and long-time U.S. Senator Furnifold M. Simmons.[158]

For some reason, those later involved with Duke University tend to downplay, if not totally ignore, this episode of law teaching, as well as a second, short-lived experiment, discussed below, in the early 1890s; instead, most date legal training at Trinity/Duke from 1904, when a law school became a permanent fixture on the Durham campus. Quite typical is a recent article about law teaching at Duke during the second quarter of the twentieth century which states, "Although Trinity had offered an undergraduate course in law as early as 1868 and there had been intermittent attention to instruction in law after that day, not until 1904 did Trinity establish a school of law."[159] As detailed above, this statement is, at best, misleading. All university legal education in the nineteenth century could be considered "undergraduate," in the sense that prior collegiate training was not a prerequisite, and students at Trinity, U.N.C., and other schools often mixed their law classes with a more traditional collegiate curriculum. The record is clear, however, that in the early 1870s, as well as the early 1890s, Trinity had a "School of Law" which was specifically preparing young men for the bar.[160]

3. Rutherford College

The other college during this period at which young men could prepare for the bar, although such training was not a part of its regular curriculum, was Rutherford College in Burke County. The school was founded in 1853 by the Reverend Robert L. Abernethy, who guided it over the following forty years. Originally known as the Owl Hollow Schoolhouse, it later became the Rutherford Academy, then Rutherford Seminary, and finally in 1871, when it was granted the right to confer degrees, Rutherford College. During the 1870s and 1880s, the school would typically have an enrollment of several hundred students, of both sexes, many of whom were given free tuition because of their impoverished backgrounds; in total Abernethy educated around four thousand students, with approximately fifteen hundred attending for free. The physical structure of the school was devastated by fire in the early 1890s, and even more damaging to the institution was Abernethy's death in 1893. Seven years later, Rutherford College was sold to the Methodist Church, which downgraded its status to a junior college. During the depths of the Depression, the denomination merged both Rutherford and Weaver Colleges with Brevard College, and in 1935 the Burke County campus, by that time surrounded by a town also known as Rutherford College, ceased its educative function.[161]

As for the school's connection with legal education, one knowledgeable source states that law was taught at Rutherford College from 1871 until 1884.[162] All evidence suggests, however, that this teaching was not part of the usual curriculum; rather, it was offered whenever such training was desired by one or more of the students. The school's catalogue for 1874 lists six different "schools" for male students, none of which directly concerned the law: Latin, Greek, Mathematical, English Literature & Rhetoric, Natural Science, and Mental & Moral Philosophy. A listing of the faculty, however, includes a Major Malone, who was the "Lecturer on Jurisprudence."[163]

More informative is an account of the school later written by one of Abernethy's daughters. In commenting on the contents of the 1880 catalogue, she states, "Col. G.N. Folk, the jurist, was secured as teacher of law for those who wished to take the Law Course; and prepared them to obtain license to practice.

This was not a regular course, but available when so desired, as Col. Folk lived at Lenoir, just ten miles from the school."[164] As detailed below, George Nathaniel Folk operated one of the state's leading proprietary law schools for thirty years starting in 1866, and, thus, by hiring Folk for this task, Rutherford College provided its students with the chance to obtain an excellent legal education. How many students took advantage of this opportunity is unknown, as are Folk's dates of service, although, as is noted above, Rutherford supposedly stopped offering legal instruction in 1884.

* * * * *

Through the efforts of U.N.C. and, to a lesser extent, Trinity and Rutherford, after 1845 any young white male in North Carolina with the finances and inclination could study law in a college setting without leaving the state. It was not until John Manning built up the program at Chapel Hill in the 1880s, however, that the overwhelming majority of such students would actually stay within the Old North State. For example, of the *DNCB* individuals born between 1825 and 1849 who attended a university law school, all of whom had the opportunity to study at such a law school within North Carolina, 47.1% chose to attend an institution outside the state. By far, the most popular of these out-of-state university law schools, and the leading institution in the South, was the University of Virginia.

Between 1845 and his death fifty years later, John B. Minor educated thousands of young men from throughout the South and west in his intricate two-year program featuring learned, comprehensive lectures on almost every legal subject, 8,000 pages of reading, and a finely honed set of moot courts.[165] The popularity of U.Va. among North Carolinians is witnessed by the fact that of those listed in the *DNCB* who were born in the forty years between 1820 and 1859, twenty-three chose to study law at the state university in Chapel Hill, while over half as many, twelve, ventured north to Charlottesville for the same purpose.

D. Proprietary Law Schools

While in the nineteenth century an increasing number of North Carolinians were educated in university law schools, the most notable aspect of the half century between 1840 and 1890 was the number of North Carolinians who received their legal educations at in-state proprietary law schools. For example, of those listed in the *DNCB* who were born between 1820 and 1859, forty young men studied at the three most popular university law schools, while fifty-four attended the three most favored proprietary schools. Thirty-nine of these young men were educated at the largest and longest-lived of these schools, operated for over forty years by Chief Justice Richmond M. Pearson, first in Mocksville and later at his Richmond Hill estate in what is now Yadkin County. In total, Pearson educated over 1,000 law students between the mid-1830s and his death in 1878, and it is hazarding but little to say that his proprietary school was the most important institution for legal education within North Carolina over the entire course of the nineteenth century.

1. Richmond M. Pearson

Richmond Mumford Pearson (1805-1878) was born in what is now Davie County, the son of Revolutionary veteran, state legislator, and large planter Richmond Pearson and his second wife, Elizabeth Mumford. The Pearson family was well connected in the highest political and social circles of western North Carolina, and two of Richmond M. Pearson's half-brothers, both nearly thirty years his senior, were Joseph Pearson, an attorney and "staunch and uncompromising Federalist" who served three terms in Congress, and Jesse A. Pearson, a major planter, militia general, and seven-term member of the General Assembly.[166]

The future Chief Justice was educated in Washington, D.C., while his brother was in Congress, and then at Mushat's Statesville Academy, and in 1823 he graduated first in his class from the University of North Carolina. While in college, "Pearson devoted but little time to the beauties of poetry and the elegances of polite literature," for he already possessed an overwhelming ambition for legal and political success, with his highest goal being the Chief Justiceship of the state.[167] Toward this end, after graduation he refused a tutorship at the University, and instead spent the following two or three years at Judge Leonard Henderson's proprietary law school in Granville County.

Settling in Salisbury upon his admission to the bar in 1826, Pearson's "preparation for the duties of his profession was so thorough and extensive that he did not have to undergo the melancholy period of long probation which many imperfectly prepared young lawyers ha[d] to endure before they achieve[d] success."[168] He quickly became one of the leading attorneys on his circuit, and following family tradition he also entered politics, serving in four consecutive terms in the House of Commons, from 1829 to 1832. In 1835, Pearson, as a nationalistic Whig, ran for his brother's former Congressional seat, but against two popular opponents he garnered only 21.6% of the vote.

In 1836, the General Assembly elected Pearson to the Superior Court, and thus began an unprecedented forty-two-year career in the state judiciary, which only ended upon Pearson's death in 1878. While on the Superior Court, one of Pearson's colleagues was William H. Battle, and the two became the leading contenders for a seat on the state Supreme Court when Judge John J. Daniel died in February of 1848. As the General Assembly was not then in session, Governor William A. Graham had the power to appoint, with the consent of the Council of State, a person to the court for the June session, although final approval would have to be voted by the legislature when it met in December. At the time, the Whig party was badly split by sectional divisions, for both eastern and western adherents loudly complained about a controlling "central clique" by pointing out that the Governor, both U.S. Senators, and the two remaining members of the Supreme Court were all from the neighboring counties of Orange and Wake. Battle, of course, was also from Orange, while Pearson was then residing in Surry county, so many westerners began contacting the Governor to champion the claims of the latter. In addition, Pearson did his own part in the campaigning, for shortly after Daniel's death he circulated a letter stating that he was the best candidate for the position. Despite the pressure brought to bear, Graham chose his friend Battle for the seat, and this only fanned the flames of sectional discontent.

Like the majority of North Carolina attorneys and judges, both Battle and Pearson were Whigs, but in the August 1848 legislative elections the party garnered only a one-vote margin on joint ballot, thus assuring that the Democrats would have a critical role in determining who would permanently replace Daniel. In December, the Democratic caucus chose former U.S. Senator Robert Strange to be its candidate, while the Whigs were badly split between Battle and Pearson, although the latter, through his own electioneering as well as that of his western adherents, appeared to be gaining ground. In the legislature, numerous inconclusive ballots were cast until the Whigs, sensing that Strange might have enough support to gain a majority, withdrew Battle's name, which eventually gave the election to Pearson. Several Whigs then joined with the Democrats to elect Rowan Democrat, and former Pearson student, John W. Ellis over Battle to fill the resulting vacancy on the Superior Court, a move which left the Chapel Hill law professor without a judicial position and likely caused much hard feeling.[169]

Pearson served on the high court the remainder of his life, and upon Frederick Nash's death in 1858 he became the state's fifth Chief Justice. During his thirty years on the Supreme Court, Pearson gained a reputation second only to Thomas Ruffin; Walter Clark, who in the early twentieth century surpassed Pearson as the longest serving member of the Supreme Court, opined that Pearson "was the equal of Ruffin, if not his superior, as a common law lawyer . . . [and] only fell behind Ruffin in his thorough grasp of the great principles which are applied in the administration of Equity."[170]

Unlike his longtime colleague Battle, Pearson was not the strongest worshiper at the temple of *stare decisis*. Clark recalled that his fellow Chief Justice "was not an idolator of other men's thought, and did not hesitate to overrule a precedent if he thought it wrong or in the progress of events had become an anachronism. He would say, 'You can't make an omelet without smashing an egg, nor clear a road through a forest without cutting down a tree.'"[171]

As is evident from the above quotation, Pearson "often used homely phrases and illustrations taken from everyday life, but they were always apt in elucidation of the matter discussed."[172] In his judicial opinions, "[h]e was not eloquent in words or imagery, but the clearness and precision with which he expressed himself, backed frequently by homely but forcible turns of expression, gave his opinions a vigor and a charm which are often lacking in more carefully prepared productions."[173]

Unfortunately for his later reputation, Pearson was involved in much controversy during the Civil War and Reconstruction. Like most North Carolina Whigs, Pearson had been a strong Unionist until Lincoln's call for troops, and during the War he "raised storms of protest in North Carolina and throughout the

South" by finding many persons exempt from military service and in issuing numerous writs of *habeas corpus* in order to free those unjustly held by the military authorities.[174]

Upon adoption of the 1868 Constitution, Pearson was forced to run publicly for the Chief Justiceship, but because he received the nominations of both parties, this caused little concern.[175] More trouble, however, was shortly at hand for the Chief Justice, in the form of the "Kirk-Holden War." In 1870, controversial Republican Governor William Woods Holden, in order to suppress the activity of the Ku Klux Klan, declared martial law in two North Carolina counties and called out the military. Holden's troops took over one hundred prisoners, and remembering Pearson's civil libertarianism during the Civil War, many of the military prisoners appealed to the Chief Justice for writs of *habeas corpus*.

Considering his oft-repeated Civil War principle of "Let justice be done though the heavens fall," Pearson proceeded to act very strangely. He held that Holden could not suspend the writ of *habeas corpus* and that the writs here should be issued. On the other hand, he also found that the military official in charge, former Union officer George W. Kirk, had good reason not to make returns to the writs, and that he would take no steps towards enforcing the writs, finding the power of the judiciary "exhausted." Many expressed outrage at this decision,[176] and shortly thereafter, in 1871, impeachment proceedings were brought against Governor Holden in 1871.

The presiding officer at the impeachment trial was the state's Chief Justice, and while Pearson presided over his friend's impeachment with outward impartiality, in private he gave advice to the Governor's five-attorney defense team. As most expected, Holden was convicted and removed from office, and for a while Pearson was "pathetically fearful" that he too would be impeached; the Chief Justice went so far as to engage counsel and prepare a written defense, which was sent to the state Senate but refused. In the end, however, Pearson's position proved safe, for "[w]hatever feeling there was against the Chief-Justice at the time was largely kept under by the influence of those who had studied law under him. They were numerous and influential, and to a man devoted to him."[177]

Pearson continued as Chief Justice until his death in 1878, and compared to the Civil War and Reconstruction, his last years on the bench were fairly tranquil, although the quality of his judicial opinions noticeably declined. In his latter years, reading and close study became "irksome" to the judge, and "his later opinions are often rather his conclusions than a statement of the reasons by which they were reached."[178] Nevertheless, his place as one of the state's greatest judges cannot be denied.

In temperament and habits, Pearson was almost the exact opposite of his colleague Battle. One of the state's foremost historians has described the Chief Justice as "plain and simple in manner, with a touch of the rough and uncouth, which many thought he cultivated. He had no high degree of culture, was cold and stern in temperament, inclined to be unforgiving in disposition, and was relentless in his determined ambition. For many years he drank to excess."[179]

Pearson dressed shabbily and indulged in "poor puns and worse jokes." Although learned in the law, he cared little about other intellectual subjects, and during the dark days of Reconstruction one disgruntled student opined, "I think he is narrow minded on all subjects except the law; being poorly informed—at least judging from his conversation—on questions of general interest & useful learning. I have heard that Bishop Atkinson calls him a narrow-minded barbarian—His manners & acts at home are certainly uncouth."[180] One of the Episcopal Bishop's complaints may have centered around Pearson's religious beliefs, for he was accused of being a skeptic.[181]

When young, Pearson "entered with much zest into the enjoyment of social life, and was remarkably fond of the society of ladies."[182] He married twice, his first wife, by whom he fathered ten children, being the daughter of U.S. Senator John Williams of Tennessee. As noted above, one part of the social life that Pearson continued to enjoy into his old age was alcohol, for throughout his public career there were comments about his public intoxication.

A friend once labelled Pearson's drinking his "chartered infirmity," and this description appears apt.[183] For example, when Governor Graham was deciding whom to appoint to the Supreme Court in 1848, one of Pearson's supporters wrote the Governor to refute the charge that the judge "drank too much," stating, "he, like all of us in the social intercourse may become lively, but never more than to be good, social company."[184] A decade later, Thomas S. Ashe reported to Thomas Ruffin that Pearson, "taking advantage of the physical weakness of our most excellent friend the Chief Justice [Nash], and the good, easy disposition of the Associate Judge [Battle,] has usurped the high prerogative of legislation and in the uncertain fitfulness of his mind declares what shall or shall not be law according to his drunken humors."[185] In addition, Pearson's defeat for the 1865 Constitutional Convention was partly accounted for by his "public drinking";[186] yet it was during the aftermath of the Kirk-Holden War that these accusations were most stridently aired in the public press. Shortly before Holden's impeachment trial, Josiah Turner in his Raleigh *Sentinel* informed his readers that "the Chief Justice had been maudlin drunk on the Bench," adding, "He has time after time been publicly drunk, as scores of witnesses can prove; and on more than one occasion he was publicly drunk at the Episcopal Church."[187]

Despite the drinking and his controversial actions during the Civil War and Reconstruction, there is little doubt about Richmond M. Pearson's place as the most important law teacher in North Carolina history. Over a nearly fifty-year period, more than a thousand young men received legal instruction from Pearson, almost all of whom attended the famous proprietary law school he operated, first in Mocksville and later at his Richmond Hill estate in what is now Yadkin County. Pearson's school received a national reputation such that Alfred Z. Reed has labelled it "the last example of the Litchfield type" of law school.[188]

Shortly after beginning his law practice in Salisbury, Pearson began instructing young men for the bar, with his first student being John Kerr, who was admitted to the bar in 1832 and later was a Congressman, Whig 1852 gubernatorial candidate, and one of the persons arrested during the Kirk-Holden War. Another of these early students was Jacob Thompson, who after his admission to the bar in 1835 moved to Mississippi, from where he served six terms in Congress and was Secretary of the Interior under James Buchanan.[189]

In 1835, Pearson moved to Mocksville, the county seat of Davie County, and the following year he was elected to the Superior Court. Following in the footsteps of his legal mentor Judge Leonard Henderson, shortly after ascending the bench Pearson began a proprietary law school in Mocksville, which would be in session during those times when he was not holding court.[190] An early advertisement, placed in the June 16, 1840, edition of the *Raleigh Register*, read:

> **Law School**
>
> I have opened a Law School at Mocksville, Davie County. The mode of instruction is that adopted by the late Chief-Justice Henderson, familiar conversation.
>
> No young gentleman will be recommended for License until he has studied one year; I advise two years as the term of preparation. The charge will be one hundred dollars, whether the student remains one year or two years. Students who have County Court License, may attend our conversations without charge.
>
> Books will be furnished.
>
> Mocksville is healthy, and offers but few temptations for dissipation and irregularity.
>
> The price of boarding in the Village $7.50 per month exclusive of washing, which will cost $1.00 per month.[191]

The school was conducted out of a small brick building on Gaither Street, and most of the students lived in a local hotel, the "White House."[192] One of the advantages of Mocksville was its "relatively low cost," and in March 1844 Lucy Battle wrote her husband William that a prospective student from Tarboro wished to study law at Battle's proprietary school in Chapel Hill, yet was going to study with Pearson in Mocksville because of the lower cost of living.[193]

The cost of living likely declined even more when Pearson, in 1846, moved his residence and school to that part of Surry County that was shortly thereafter formed into Yadkin County, purchasing an estate on the south bank of the Yadkin River. He named the property Richmond Hill, after his birthplace, and it was "a quiet, secluded spot, [with] the nearest point to the railroad [being] High Point, a distance of about forty miles."[194]

While the county seat of Rockford was only several miles away across the river, the entire area was quite inaccessible to the rest of the state, with one writer terming it "about as deep in the woods as [Pearson] could get without retreating to the mountains," and adding, "its isolation must have appealed to some dark side of his nature."[195] Pearson told one of his students that "he selected this place so he could get away from the whirl and excitement of society, so that his students could be quiet and have nothing to withdraw their minds from their books. He would jokingly say to his boys that it was a good place to wear their old clothes."[196]

Although they may have sometimes wished for more excitement, especially of the feminine variety, Pearson's students appear to have found Richmond Hill "an ideal place for a school. The climate was delightful, [and] the air invigorating, imparting the glow of health to the cheeks." To the north and west was the Blue Ridge, while Pilot Mountain was a dozen or so miles to the east. In addition, the Yadkin was "a clear, pure, limpid mountainous stream, as it meandered through the wooded hills and the blooming meadows," and in the never-ending woods "there was an abundance of hickory nuts, chinquapins and chestnuts."[197] When they were not studying, Pearson's students would hunt, fish, take excursions to Pilot Mountain, and even court Pearson's daughters, two of whom eventually married Richmond Hill alumni.[198]

After his election to the Supreme Court in 1848, Pearson would hold two sessions of his school every year, a spring session from mid-March to late May or early June, and a fall session from September to early December. The number of students each session would usually range from the upper teens into the thirties, and tuition remained the same throughout Pearson's four decades of teaching at $100 per year.[199] As for boarding, two students could live in the office-lecture room that Pearson built at the foot of the hill in front of his residence, while the others boarded with neighbors, including across the river in Rockford.[200] Because of the difficulties in finding suitable housing for all of his students, at some point Pearson erected "two rows of log buildings along the entrance" to his property.[201]

Pearson would hold "three lectures each week. Two of these were for the County Court students, which all of both classes were expected to attend. The other was for the Superior Court students only."[202] Pearson's classes were not "lectures" in the strictest sense, for most of the class time was devoted to orally questioning his students on their readings. One of America's first law teachers to use the socratic method of teaching, Pearson once opined that "his system was like manuring broadcast, while the other [lecture method] was like manuring in the hill."[203]

One student recalled that Pearson's "office was at the bottom of a hill, and before he would come in to lecture, he would walk around the hillside and he would break off a little twig from some favorite tree and come in chewing it and then he would take his seat and begin to ask questions."[204] Another remembered that "The Judge would come into his office and seat himself near the chimney corner, and the students usually about thirty, were ranged around the room in a sort of semi-circle. Usually a wooden box which held about 25 pounds of smoking tobacco occupied the middle of the floor." The tobacco box was there for a purpose, for Pearson "would bring his pipe and every student was at liberty to do the same, and sometimes the room would be filled with a cloud of tobacco smoke."[205]

Class sessions were "about two hours in length," and according to Council Wooten, Pearson, using the socratic method, "would take up some subject and exhaust it, and when he concluded the student was the master of the subject. He taught his students how to think and reason."[206] John W. Hayes recalled that under Pearson's socratic questioning, after a legal principle had been formulated, "Case after case was put to illustrate the application of [the] principle[], the student being required to make the application and to solve the legal problem involved." Pearson must have been quite a skilled teacher, for his students relished the chance to show their powers of legal reasoning under his close and careful questioning:

> Every student was kept upon his mettle. If he were selected for a special 'rushing' it was regarded as a compliment to his progress. If another student were pitted against him, it was a compliment to both. If they both failed, the question went around the class, and this was the new students['] opportunity. If a new man answered it correctly it brought him at once to the front. Sometimes the Judge would ply him with other questions as a further test of what was in him. Thus there was a constant stimulus to be on the alert, for no one knew when his opportunity might come. The bright and studious were not long in coming to the front, and indeed all were soon measured, weighed and appraised of their true worth.[207]

As for subject matter, the first term for the County Court students would begin with Pearson giving "a definition of law, and [describing] the gradual development of the system of common law. Then taking the analysis of the second book of Blackstone, as given in Chitty's edition, he would follow that book through to the end and would then take up the last five chapters of the first book." This would occupy the first two-and-a-half-month session, and it was followed by instruction on other material, for those studying for the County Court were "expected to read, as part of [Pearson's] prescribed course, Blackstone's Commentaries . . . , Coke on Littleton, Saunders on Uses and Trusts[,] Fearne on Contingent Remainders[,] and Toller on Executors." The Superior Court students were expected to be readily familiar with the above texts, as well as "to devote special attention to the third and fourth books of Blackstone and also to read Stephens on Pleading, Chitty on Pleading . . . , Adams Equity and Milford or Lulle on Equity Pleading, and Starkie on Evidence."[208]

While Pearson's "lectures were not delivered from manuscript, and were never put in writing by him . . . [t]he field of instruction travelled over by him in teaching each successive class was essentially the same." Thus, "from an early period the students began to note down the questions and answers of which these lectures consisted. The manuscripts thus prepared by one class became the heritage of the next, growing more complete from year to year through the additions made by diligent and painstaking students." Using this material, a former student, Benjamin F. Long, published a volume consisting of Pearson's lectures in 1879, a year after the judge's death.[209] This was the closest Pearson came to publishing a legal text, although early in his career he had begun to write a volume on equity jurisprudence, only to see Adams publish his comprehensive treatise on the subject shortly thereafter.[210]

As noted above, Pearson differed from Battle and many other contemporary teachers in the subject matter that he found important. Unlike Battle, he did not dwell on his state's current blackletter law and how it had changed from Blackstone's time. Teaching about the practical aspects of a law practice held even less interest, for "[h]e did not approve of moot courts nor did he care for his students to devote their time and attention to the practice of the courts. This, he thought, they would soon learn after entering upon actual practice." Instead, Pearson desired his students to become "thoroughly imbued" in "the first principles of the common law," and the principles and cases Pearson discussed in class "were taken from the antiquated black-letter law growing out of the feudal system and apparently of little value to the American lawyer of the present time."[211]

It is thus not surprising that Pearson's favorite legal author was Sir Edward Coke. In 1866, one student who had taken Cruise on Real Property to Richmond Hill soon learned the feelings of his instructor, writing home: "If I had a Coke at this moment, I would wade right through all this mud and would no doubt get into water where wading is impossible. But this aside, Coke is *the* book of the law." He then quoted Pearson as remarking, "If you want to drink out of the branch, read Cruise; but if you want to drink out of the *spring*, read Coke. It may be a little more trouble to get to the spring, but the water is so much better."[212]

Pearson did not confine his teaching to the lecture room, for he would discuss legal subjects with his students "whenever an opportunity was presented—at the table, on the path in the woods as they went to a neighbor's house, at the fishing place on the river, and in the Summer afternoons as they sat beneath the shades of the old oaks on the hill or down by the spring."[213] The judge also allowed his students ready access to his large law library, which consisted of at least 274 volumes in 1868 and approximately 700 by the time of his death.[214]

At the end of every term Pearson would throw a dinner party for all of his students, and many undoubtedly felt a touch of sadness when attending their last dinner deep in the woods of Yadkin. One authority who has closely studied the school at Richmond Hill has stated that "[a]lmost to a man, the students seem to have regarded their studies as challenging and Judge Pearson as a skilled and stimulating instructor."[215] Robert P. Dick, Pearson's one-time colleague on the high court and himself a noted law teacher, noted that the Chief Justice "had great skill in the art of communicating knowledge, and by his cheerful and paternal manner he won the respect, confidence and affection of 'his boys.'"[216] Mention has already been made of Chief Justice Clark's statement that Pearson likely would have been impeached in 1871 but for his former students, who were "numerous and influential, and to a man devoted to him."[217]

One of these students was Council S. Wooten, who later opined: "He was the greatest teacher that ever lived on the earth, and I don't believe that there will ever be such another."[218]

While the relations between Pearson and his students were almost always extraordinarily affectionate, the judge's actions during Reconstruction did cause a bit of friction at the school.[219] Things shortly settled down, however, and Richmond Hill remained the premier institution within the state for legal education until Pearson's death in 1878; in January 1877, thirteen of the twenty-four men licensed to practice law by the North Carolina Supreme Court were Pearson students.

Even those who completely disagreed with Pearson's politics had to admit his great prowess as a legal educator, and men who held Pearson the Judge in great contempt continued to send their sons to Richmond Hill to be educated in the law. The best example of this might be the state's most noted antebellum attorney, George E. Badger, who, of course, had trained young men for the bar himself. During a very important trial before the Northampton Superior Court in 1844, Pearson made a seemingly high-handed ruling which caused Badger to quit his participation in the trial and "ended . . . not only all social intercourse, but brought undisguised hostility between the two men." While there is no evidence that a reconciliation was ever made, in 1859 when Badger's talented son Richard graduated from the University of North Carolina, he was sent to Richmond Hill to learn the law under Pearson.[220]

Another of the many persons who found fault with Pearson was William H. Battle, and there is little doubt about the great rivalry between the law programs at Chapel Hill and Richmond Hill, with one observer noting the "sharp [but] honorable competition" between the two institutions.[221] In private, Battle was not above making disparaging, even catty, comments about both Pearson and his school, although such statements did not concern Pearson's ability as a teacher. One example is that the proper Battle was shocked that his colleague had married his second wife so soon after her husband's death.[222] Also, in a statement that obviously hinted at his strong disapproval of Pearson's drinking, Battle, while holding Superior Court across the river in Rockford in 1851, wrote his wife that "dissipation" was "very prevalent" in the area, adding, "There are quite a number of law students here, several of whom are preparing to practice at more bars than one."[223]

Battle had good reason to be jealous, for between 1840 and 1878, Pearson's school was clearly the dominant institution for legal education within North Carolina. Overall, Pearson instructed "more than a thousand law students," according to a statement he made to Robert P. Dick.[224] Unfortunately, unlike at Litchfield, Pearson did not keep a permanent roll of his students, so today only 178 of these young men can be positively identified.[225] Still, those known to have studied under Pearson made quite an impact on their state's legal and political institutions.

Twenty of the students later served on the state Superior Court, while six sat on the state Supreme Court, including three who were on the bench with their teacher and two who later followed him as Chief Justice. Nine former students were in the Secession Convention, and eight in the 1875 Constitutional Convention. In addition, Pearson taught at least sixty-seven members of the General Assembly, three North Carolina Governors, and fourteen men who would later serve in Congress, including four of North Carolina's nine man House delegation in the 49th Congress (1885-1887). In all, forty-three of Pearson's known charges are profiled in the *DNCB*, and of the over 800 as yet unidentified students, many likely settled in other states, where they undoubtedly made a positive difference. Without a doubt, through his teaching Richmond M. Pearson influenced both his state and nation well into the twentieth century.

2. John L. Bailey

It would be a mistake, however, to consider Richmond Hill the only important proprietary law school in North Carolina, either before or after the Civil War. Next to Pearson, the antebellum attorney best known for conducting a proprietary school in the state was John Lancaster Bailey.[226] Bailey (1795-1877), a native of Pasquotank County, graduated from the University of North Carolina in 1819 and then read law under James Iredell, Jr., in Edenton. After leaving Iredell's office, Bailey settled in Elizabeth City, and over the following fifteen years he represented Pasquotank in both houses of the General Assembly and the 1835 Constitutional Convention. His legal practice also prospered, and like almost every major attorney of the time, he began tutoring aspiring attorneys in his office.

In 1837, Bailey was elected to the Superior Court, and he served in this capacity for the following twenty-six years. At some point during his first years on the bench, Bailey moved nearly two hundred miles west to Hillsborough, and there in 1845 he established a proprietary law school. On May 30 of that year, Bailey announced in the *Raleigh Register*: "The Undersigned proposes to open a Law School in the Town of Hillsborough, on the first day of July next. To young gentlemen who are desirous of engaging in the study of the Law, he will give instruction during the time he is not necessarily attending his Courts."[227]

Shortly after forming this school, Bailey was able to persuade another Hillsborough judge, Frederick Nash, to join him in the endeavor. Although now not as well known as Ruffin or Gaston, Nash (1781-1858) was one of the state's most impressive antebellum judges. Born in New Bern, the son of a Governor and nephew of a martyred Revolutionary General, Nash graduated second in his class from Princeton in 1799, and then read law under Edward Harris. In 1807, he moved from New Bern to Hillsborough, and a successful legal and political career followed. Nash spent several terms in the General Assembly, and in 1818 the legislature elected him to the Superior Court, where he served until 1826, and again from 1836 to 1844. In the latter year, Nash was elected to the state Supreme Court to replace the deceased Gaston, after the Democrat-controlled Council of State refused, for purely political reasons, to confirm Governor John Motley Morehead's nomination of George E. Badger—Nash, like Badger, was a Whig, but he was much less partisan. Nash spent his last fourteen years on the Supreme Court serving with great distinction, and upon Ruffin's retirement in 1852 he became the state's fourth Chief Justice.[228]

In the decades before he ascended the Supreme Court bench, Nash tutored numerous young men for the bar, at least six of whom are included in the *DNCB*. While still on the Superior Court, Nash in 1841 formally turned this office teaching into a proprietary school by advertising his instruction in the state press. In a notice placed in the *Raleigh Register*, Nash stated that he and Hugh Waddell, should they receive as many as eight students, would open a law school in Hillsborough on January 1, 1842. While the legal reputations of these teachers would have been well known to all intelligent persons in the state, in their advertisement they made mention of "the advantages to be derived from pursuing such studies in the seclusion of a quiet Village, [and] those which spring from the *association* of minds engaged in the same pursuits." As for the method of study, Nash and Waddell would offer "the usual course of elementary instruction," with "written or oral instruction given as often as required." Examinations would be given monthly, and "by means of a Moot Court," they intended to give "some knowledge of the practice in the Courts of this State." As for costs, the notice cryptically stated that "[t]he usual fees for instruction will be required."[229]

Waddell (1799-1878), a grandson of Nash's uncle General Francis Nash, graduated in the same University of North Carolina class as James K. Polk and then read law. He became one of the state's leading attorneys as well as a noted Whig politician, serving in numerous sessions of the General Assembly.[230] Obviously, Nash wished to have his cousin associated with him in the school for the periods every spring and fall when the judge would be riding circuit to hold court. It is unknown if eight or more students responded to the advertisement and if the school was actually begun, although the partnership was necessarily fairly short, for Nash was teaching with Bailey by 1850.[231]

That Nash would become associated with Bailey seems only natural, and not only because both were noted judges and law teachers who resided in Hillsborough. Because they were on separate courts after 1844, Bailey on the Superior Court and Nash on the Supreme Court, the specific months that each would have to devote to judicial duties would not overlap, and, therefore, at least one of the two could always be present at the school in Hillsborough. This advantage was given prominent notice in the advertisements that they placed in the state press; for example a sentence in their January 1, 1851, notice in the *Raleigh Register* stated, "The one or the other of the instructors will have charge of the School nearly all the year, and during a portion of the time both will be here to give instruction." This advertisement also noted that the next session of the school would begin on January 15 and continue until June 7, and that students should plan to "attend at the first of the Session, so that they may be formed into the necessary classes." Tuition would be $100 a year, and textbooks were available at the prices charged by their supplier, *Fayetteville Observer* editor Edward J. Hale.[232] The following year, Nash and Bailey's advertisement included the additional information that "[a] Moot Court will be holden once in each week," and that "Board can be had in good families, in town and in the immediate neighborhood, upon reasonable terms."[233]

Bailey and Nash conducted their school in a two-room office which "housed the large and rich library which Judge Bailey had collected over a number of years." The students "were drawn from various parts of the South, even from as far as Louisiana; but the most of them were from North Carolina." One student from out of state was an Ogdan from New Orleans, who was a "great boxer," for "he is chiefly remembered, not for mastering Blackstone, but for beating everyone in Orange county who entered the ring with him."[234]

It is interesting to note that in the mid-1850s, a student who wished to study law in an institutional setting within the state had three excellent options: the law school at the state university operated by Battle and Phillips, Pearson's Richmond Hill establishment, and the Hillsborough school of Nash and Bailey. From 1852, the state Supreme Court consisted of Nash, Pearson, and Battle, and, thus, the state's three highest judges each operated one of the three institutions within the state for legal education.

Chief Justice Nash died in December 1858, and shortly thereafter Bailey moved another two hundred miles west, to Black Mountain. Settling on a "large tract of farm and mountain land," Bailey shortly thereafter advertised that he was opening a law school on March 1, 1859, at his residence "in Buncombe County on the North Fork of the Swannanoa." In this endeavor, he was to be joined by his son, William Henry Bailey (1831-1925).[235]

The younger Bailey must have inherited much legal talent from his father, for he was given a temporary, year-long appointment as state Attorney General in 1856 at the age of twenty-five. He has been described as "a brilliant advocate, a learned lawyer, and the author of a number of legal treatises." After serving in the Confederate Army, he practiced for many years with notable success, first in Salisbury and then Charlotte, before spending the final three decades of his long life in Houston, Texas.[236]

With his son off to war, John L. Bailey closed his Black Mountain school, and with his resignation from the Superior Court in 1863, he appeared to completely retire. At the end of the War, however, the seventy-year-old Bailey again moved west, to Asheville, where he began practicing law and reopened his school. Over the following decade, Bailey, teaching by himself, would again compete with Pearson for the privilege of tutoring the state's finest young minds for a life in the law. Many of his students were former Confederate soldiers, one of whom, Brigadier General James Green Martin, became Bailey's law partner.[237]

Throughout his long teaching career, Bailey was beloved by his students.[238] One later recalled that "The lessons were a delight, and we looked forward to the Conversations, as the lecture really was, as the pleasantest experience of the day. Nothing could equal the graciousness of the Judge's manner, nor the clearness with which the principles of law were enunciated." This source added, "His method was Socratic to an extent, but interspersed with a whimsical humor at times, when he would deal with specific cases that had come before him in the judicial capacity."

According to the description of another former pupil, Bailey possessed all the attributes of a great teacher, for the student recalled the judge's "unfailing patience, his gentle courtesy, his genial humor, . . . [and] his vast and profound range of knowledge of the law."[239] Bailey was also extraordinarily concerned with legal ethics. "He had almost a reverence for the law and a supreme contempt for the pettifogging lawyer. To him the law meant Justice, and he could not tolerate sharp practice from lawyers."

Thus, through his teaching "[t]he highest ideals were inculcated in his students, the utmost courtesy in handling a case, and a thorough study of the principles of law from the time of Coke and Littleton to the modern times."[240] From the 1820s into the mid-1870s, it is likely that hundreds of young men (ten of whom are profiled in the *DNCB*) were fortunate to learn the law from such a teacher, and as the proprietor of a private North Carolina law school Bailey should rank second only to Richmond M. Pearson.

3. Dick & Dillard

Bailey and Pearson died within seven months of each other and their deaths left a huge void in the structures for legal education within the state, one that the law school at the recently reopened state university could not hope to fill. Into this vacuum stepped two prominent judges, Robert P. Dick and John H. Dillard, and the school they created, known alternately as the Dick & Dillard Law School and the

Greensboro Law School, would be the leading institution for legal education within the state from 1878 into the 1890s.

Robert Paine Dick (1823-1898) was a native of Greensboro and son of John McClintock Dick, who served on the state Superior Court from 1835 until his death in 1861. The younger Dick graduated with distinction from the University of North Carolina in 1843, and then read law under both his father and noted Greensboro attorney George C. Mendenhall. Settling in his hometown, he became actively involved in Democratic politics, and in 1853 Franklin Pierce appointed him U.S. Attorney for North Carolina. In 1860-61 he was a Douglas supporter and Unionist, although like almost every Whig and Douglas Democrat he became a reluctant secessionist upon Lincoln's call for troops. By 1864, Dick was a strong supporter of peace, and at the end of the War he became a confidant of President Johnson and Governor Holden. A founder of the state Republican Party in 1867, the next year Dick was elected to the state Supreme Court. Once on the court, he became a close friend of Chief Justice Pearson, and undoubtedly the younger man learned much about the school at Richmond Hill.

Dick stayed on the Supreme Court only four years, for in 1872 President Grant named him the first U.S. District Judge for the Western District of North Carolina. He served on this court "with great distinction" for twenty-four years, resigning shortly before his death in 1898. A ruling elder in the First Presbyterian Church of Greensboro and a strong temperance advocate, Dick was cited by Chief Justice Walter Clark as "probably the best biblical scholar in the State." He was also especially known for his knowledge of history and literature.[241]

Judge Dick's partner John Henry Dillard was a native of Rockingham County. Dillard (1819-1896) attended the University of North Carolina for eighteen months before leaving because of poor health. He subsequently read law briefly with James T. Morehead, and then studied in the law school of the College of William & Mary under Nathaniel Beverley Tucker, where he received his LL.B. in 1840. First settling in Virginia, he returned home to Rockingham in 1846, and for the next fifteen years practiced law with Thomas Ruffin, Jr. During the War he served as a Captain in the Confederate Army, and in 1868, Dillard removed to Greensboro, where he again formed a partnership with Ruffin along with former Congressman John A. Gilmer. Dillard was elected to the state Supreme Court in 1878, but because of ill health and overwork, he only served three years, returning full-time to his practice and school in Greensboro in 1881.

Richmond Pearson found Dillard to be "an extremely able equity lawyer," while Judge Dick thought him "the best draftsman of legal papers and documents that I have ever known." Personally, Dillard has been described as "shy and reticent," and while he was a Whig before the War and a Democrat after, "he took little part in political affairs and was uninterested in social life." Like Dick he was a ruling elder in the Presbyterian Church, and one of his great passions in life was the growing of flowers; a memorialist recalled that during the months that his garden bloomed, "it was [Dillard's] custom seven days in the week to leave his home . . . with flowers in his hand for the young friends he was sure to meet on his way to his office or to his beloved church."[242]

Upon Chief Justice Pearson's death in early January 1878, Dick and Dillard quickly organized a proprietary law school in Greensboro to take the place of Richmond Hill. Their first student was Stephen A. Douglas, Jr., son of the famous Illinois Senator, who was admitted to the North Carolina bar in the Spring of 1878. Although it is unknown how many students attended the school during its first session, within two years the Greensboro Law School had seen such phenomenal growth that it had become the largest law program in the state to that time. The school year was divided into two sessions, which would typically begin on the second Mondays in January and August, and the two sessions in 1880 saw first fifty and then sixty-two pupils enroll. The numbers were even larger the following year, for seventy-four students attended the January 1881 session, and eighty-seven the following August.

As at Richmond Hill, tuition was set at $100, and the student was allowed to "remain as long as he may desire to do so"; several years later this was changed so that tuition was set at $50 a session, payable in advance. Room and board, of course, would cost extra, and it could be "obtained in private families at from $12 to $15 per month." The instructors announced to prospective students that three examinations and lectures would be given per week, and the course of study was fairly basic: "Blackstone's Commentaries, 2nd book, diligently. Coke, Cruise or other standard work on real property. Stephen and Chitty on

Pleading. Adams' Equity and 1st Greenleaf on Evidence. Some Standard Work on Executors and Administrators. Code of Civil Procedure." This list was later supplemented with Smith on Contracts, Bigelow on Torts, and the federal and state constitutions. Judge Dick was noted for the giving of eloquent lectures, and when some of these were later published, noted literary critic Archibald Henderson called them, "interesting and stimulating to the layman as well as to those learned in the law." His introductory lecture on the civil and common law systems, for example, was termed, "an admirable historical as well as legal document." On Sunday afternoons, Dick would give additional lectures on biblical literature for all those interested, and sixteen of these lectures were also published.

John H. Dillard was also an integral part of the law school during its first ten years, especially in the years after he left the Supreme Court in 1881. In late 1887, however, Judge Dillard decided to retire from the school, and this left Judge Dick as its only instructor. A notice advertising the first session of 1888 stated, "As Judge Dillard has retired from the Law School, there will be examinations six times a week, so that my occasional absence from home [to hold court] may not retard the progress of students." In addition, Dick announced that "There will be a review course and frequent extra examinations and lectures during the month that precedes each session of the Supreme Court," thereby helping to prepare all those who were planning to take the bar exam.[243]

It appears that Dick retired from teaching, and the Greensboro Law School closed its doors, after fifteen years of service in 1893.[244] In total, well over 300 law students were educated at Dick & Dillard, at least fourteen of whom are included in the *DNCB*. In 1881, a list of the first seventy-three pupils was published, and, as would be expected, the vast majority were from North Carolina.[245] In mapping the hometowns of these seventy-three, one finds that the students came from all corners of the state. While the counties around Greensboro were naturally well represented, so too were both the mountains and the coastal plain; the two areas which sent no aspiring attorneys to Greensboro were Charlotte-Mecklenburg and Orange County, the latter, of course, home of the other major law school within the state.[246]

Students from the Greensboro Law School compiled an amazing, near-perfect passage rate on the state bar exam, and many went on to future prominence. The class of 1885, for example, contained Thomas Settle, a future Congressman, noted author Thomas Dixon, Jr., and Stephen A. Douglas's other son, Robert Martin Douglas, who later served on the state Supreme Court. Robert M. Douglas had earlier married Dick's daughter Jessie, and their son Robert Dick Douglas was Attorney General of North Carolina at the turn of the century. R.D. Douglas was naturally close to his namesake grandfather, and he later recalled that "Judge Dick told me that during the life of the school it had sent to the Supreme Court more than 300 applicants for licenses, not one of whom had failed to pass; that a few of those from the school had failed to pass the bar examination, but all who failed had applied against his advice."[247]

With the entire population of Guilford County numbering only 23,585 in 1880, the eighty or more young men who arrived to attend Dick & Dillard must have made a large impact in the small town of Greensboro. Without a doubt, the interest in the visitors shown by the young females of the town stirred up much jealousy among the young native males, one of whom was William Sydney Porter, later known as the famous author O. Henry. In the early 1880s, Porter was working as a pharmacist's apprentice in his uncle's Greensboro drug store, and upon moving to Texas in 1882 he sent back to a friend a poem he had penned about "the dudes" who were attending the Greensboro Law School:

THE DUDES

See the city's lovely dudes—
Sidewalk dudes—
What a world of broken hearts
Their promenade precludes.
Clerks and students of the law,
Beauties all without a flaw,
Let us all get off the sidewalk for
the dudes.

Dudes, dudes, dudes,
For the lady killing, fascinating
dudes.

Look up there all in a row—
Gallery dudes—
With what grace can they assume all
Such enticing attitudes.
With their eyes, eyes, eyes,
And their sentimental sighs,
Oh, full rare and fragrant flowers
are the dudes
Are the dudes, dudes, dudes, dudes,
Dudes, dudes, dudes,
Are the Greensboro fair and radiant
dudes.[248]

4. G. N. Folk

While Dick & Dillard was the largest and best known proprietary law school formed in North Carolina after the Civil War, it was joined by several other ventures. The most notable of these was the school operated by Colonel G.N. Folk from 1866 until 1895. George Nathaniel Folk (1831-1896) was a native of Isle of Wight County, Virginia, who attended the College of William & Mary before moving to North Carolina and studying law in Charlotte. He initially settled in Boone, where he practiced law and, in the years before the Civil War, represented Watagua in the House of Commons as a Whig. During the War, Folk rose to become Colonel of the Sixty-fifth North Carolina, and while in service he was thrice wounded and, for six months, a Union prisoner of war. Afterwards, he settled in Lenoir and, in 1866, he opened a proprietary law school. The school was conducted out of Folk's residence, Cherry Hill, on North Main Street, and as would be expected the majority of his early students were Confederate veterans. Reentering politics, Folk became a state Senator in 1876, serving as chairman of the Judiciary Committee, and six years later he lost a bid to join the state Supreme Court. The year 1882 also saw Folk move his residence and law school out of the town of Lenoir and into Caldwell County, purchasing an estate known as Riverside.

Although Folk taught many students first at Cherry Hill, Lenoir, and then Riverside, he was equally known for travelling up the Blue Ridge every year and teaching, from 1867 to 1895, a summer law school held in either Boone or the nearby resort village of Blowing Rock. A report Folk filed in 1889 showed that he was then teaching nine students at his summer school in Boone, each of whom had paid $75 in tuition, thus suggesting that those studying in the mountains might have also been his students back at Riverside. In the report, Folk's library was listed as containing 600 volumes.

In addition to his schools in Caldwell and Watagua Counties, mention has already been made of Folk's law teaching at Rutherford College in Burke County. Overall, during his thirty year teaching career the Colonel likely instructed over a hundred pupils, at least five of whom became prominent enough to merit inclusion in the *DNCB*.[249]

5. Other Schools

Details about other proprietary law schools during this period are more sketchy, and only two can now be positively identified. For some time after 1876, a proprietary school was operated by Judge George Vaughn Strong in Raleigh. Strong (1827-1897), a native of Sampson County, graduated with highest honors from the University of North Carolina in 1845, and then read law under George W. Mordecai. Settling in Goldsboro in 1853, Strong began his career by both practicing law and editing the *Goldsboro Telegraph*, and during the Civil War he represented Wayne County in the Secession Convention before being named Confederate States Attorney for North Carolina. In 1871, Strong removed to Raleigh, where he practiced law with former Governor Thomas Bragg and future Chief Justice W.N.H. Smith, and represented Wake

County in the General Assembly. In 1876, Strong was elected judge of the Wake County Criminal Court, a post which he filled "with distinction for many years." While Strong was in this judicial capacity, he operated a proprietary law school in Raleigh. Unfortunately, little further information is available about this institution, although it was probably in operation into the 1890s. An obituary called Strong "one of the best known and ablest lawyers the State has produced," adding, "He was certainly one of the most learned members of the bar, and for years he gave instruction in law in this city."[250]

The other known proprietary school was started by Judge Edward P. Cantwell in Wilmington in 1878. Cantwell (1826-1891), a South Carolina native who was educated at Harvard, served in the Mexican War and was a Lieutenant Colonel in the Confederate Army. In 1868, he was elected to the New Hanover County Criminal Court, and six years later he represented New Hanover in the state Senate. Like many proprietary teachers, Cantwell was also something of a legal scholar, for he wrote *North Carolina Justice and Practice*.[251]

On August 21, 1878, the Wilmington *Morning Star* announced that at the request of a number of Wilmington citizens, Cantwell would begin a law school, with "the first of a series of lectures upon the theory and the practice of the law [to] be delivered at the Court room, on Tuesday evening next, at 8:30 o'clock." In addition, "A Moot Court will be held at the same place on the first Wednesday in September, when two of the students, previously appointed, will argue a case agreed upon before a jury to be selected from invited guests of the school. To this exhibition a limited number of invitations will be issued." The paper noted that it believed that "such an institution would pay as well here as anywhere else," and added, "We chronicle the establishment of this institution in our midst with great satisfaction."[252]

The school did not get off to an auspicious start, however, for a week later at the first lecture only four would-be students were in attendance. Cantwell, thus, adjourned the class until the following Tuesday, and the local paper noted that "if a sufficient number do not attend to effect the required organization, the scheme will be abandoned."[253] This did not happen, for the following week there was "a larger number in attendance," who "received with much satisfaction" Cantwell's "lecture about two hours in length on the nature of law in general, and explaining his method of instruction." The *Morning Star* also noted that "members of the bar in this city have evinced considerable interest in the success of the school and have agreed to assist the lectures," and that Cantwell was contemplating adding a business school, which would be taught by a Nathan Meyer.[254]

Cantwell's second and third lectures were given the following Friday and Tuesday evenings. At the latter meeting, plans were made for the first public moot court, which would see two students, Adam Empie and Addison G. Ricaud, try a criminal case before up to seventy-five invited guests, twelve of whom would be chosen to form a jury.[255]

Although the Wilmington *Morning Star* gave the school much free publicity, as well as encouragement, Cantwell, in the paper, also began placing advertisements for his school. The first noted that "[p]articular attention [was being] given to the preparation of Young Men for the Bar and Counting Room," including "Daily private instruction," supplemented by "[f]requent public lectures and Moot Courts." The entire course, which would be identical to that at Cantwell's *alma mater*, Harvard, would cover two years, although students would be "received at any time and for any period." Tuition would be "Twenty-five dollars per session of five months[,] Fifty dollars a year[, and] One hundred Dollars for the Whole Course," with board being available in Wilmington "at reasonable rates."[256] An advertisement placed several weeks later repeated the above information, while adding that, in addition to the private instruction, students could choose to attend Cantwell's two weekly lectures either in a day session, held Monday and Wednesday afternoons from 5 to 6 p.m., or Tuesday and Friday evenings, from 8 to 9 p.m. The giving of two sets of lectures suggests that enrollment had substantially increased, and Cantwell was also adding to his teaching repertoire, for he mentioned that for an extra charge he would give instruction in the "French, English, Latin and German Languages."[257]

Although Edward Cantwell's proprietary school appears to have eventually gotten off to a promising start, it is not known how long it continued in existence, nor how many students were taught; Cantwell died in 1891 at St. Simon's Island, Georgia. While many schools likely faced the initial problems that plagued Cantwell, what is especially noteworthy about his effort is both the impetus it received from the local legal community, and the support given it by both the press and public. At the time, Wilmington was fairly isolated from the rest of the state, and Wilmingtonians appear to have rallied around the new institution as a source of civic pride. As detailed below, twenty-two years after Cantwell's death, the coastal city would see a second, somewhat more successful, experiment in institutionalized legal education.

* * * * *

Although largely forgotten today, the efforts of such proprietary teachers as Cantwell, Strong, Folk, Dillard, Dick, Bailey, Nash, and Pearson changed forever the method of legal instruction within the Old North State. Starting around 1840, the vast increase in the number of young men wishing to study law made it imperative that an institutional form of legal education be found, one that could efficiently and effectively educate large numbers of students, and thus supplement, if not altogether replace, the prevalent apprenticeship system. Over the next half century, only one state college, the University of North Carolina, was strong enough to support a permanent law program, and, thus, it was left to a handful of far-sighted men, almost all of whom were sitting judges, to form the proprietary schools necessary to fill this demand.

One can divide most North Carolina proprietary teachers into three distinct generations. The first generation began teaching in the 1820s if not earlier, and was led by Chief Justices Taylor and Henderson; because of their advertisements, some might also include Murphey and Brumby. While these men taught few students, their influence, especially Henderson's, was far reaching. This era was short-lived, however, for it ended between 1829 and 1833, when Taylor, Henderson, and Murphey died and Brumby left the state.

The second generation of proprietary teachers was led by Pearson, Bailey, and Battle, men who began their teaching careers in the 1830s or early 1840s and who would teach hundreds of students over the next several decades. Under their direction, the institutionalization of legal education in North Carolina began in earnest, for by the 1850s twenty or more students might be studying law at the same time and place. Battle, of course, brought legal education to the state university, yet despite his efforts, there was not a dominant university law program within the state when these three died within twenty-two months of each other during 1877-1879.

The responsibilities for institutionalized legal education thus fell to a third generation of proprietary teachers, led by Dick, Dillard, Folk, and Strong. Although they were all gifted teachers, it was while these four were teaching that the state university under John Manning finally developed its potential to become the state's leading institution for legal education, shortly to be joined by Wake Forest in 1894 and Trinity in 1904. Much like the teachers of the earlier two generations, these four men all died within a short period, twenty-six months during 1896-1898, with Dillard and Folk dying on the same day. This time, however, because of the advances made by the in-state university law schools, there was no need for a fourth generation of proprietary teachers.

As stated by Alfred Z. Reed in 1921, in hindsight the eventual decline of the proprietary law school appears almost inevitable:

> In the absence of endowments and before the discovery that an independent law school might attract students by conferring the university degree of LL.B., a school of this type was entirely dependent for its success upon the personal force of its proprietor. When he died, or aged, or secured something better to do, there remained no definite asset upon which a successor might build. The significance of this group of schools in our educational development is that they served temporarily to bridge the gap between students who wished systematized instruction in law and the colleges that were not yet prepared to give it.[258]

Such inevitibility should not, however, diminish the importance of these schools in the state's legal history. Of the attorneys who are listed in the *DNCB*, at least 27.9% of those born between 1825 and 1849 received their legal education in proprietary schools, as did 23.1% of those born during the next quarter century. As impressive as these numbers are, for the bar as a whole they were likely higher, especially considering that over 1,000 students read with Pearson and at least 300 attended the Dick & Dillard Law School. Unfortunately, none of the state proprietary law schools kept a permanent roll of its students, so the true impact of these schools on the state bar will never be fully known.[259]

Even using the *DNCB* figures, however, it is clear that Pearson's school was the best attended and most important institution of legal education within the state from 1840 until his death in 1878, with the Dick & Dillard Law School holding this distinction from that date until at least the mid-to-late 1880s. Table 2, for example, lists those seven institutions where four or more of the *DNCB* individuals born between 1820 and 1859 received their legal education:

Table 2: Law Schools (proprietary and university) Attended by Four or More *DNCB* Attorneys Born between 1820 and 1859

R.M. Pearson (Richmond Hill)	39
University of North Carolina	23
University of Virginia	12
Harvard University	4
John L. Bailey	8
Dick & Dillard	7
Trinity College	5

It should also be noted that the state's one major university law school during this period, U.N.C., was itself the result of the incorporation of a proprietary law school, much like the law schools at other major universities, such as Yale, Georgia, Washington & Lee, and Cincinnati.

Thus, the half century between 1840 and 1890 is notable for the tremendous institutionalization of legal education within the state, a trend that owed its existence to the proprietary law school. After 1890, this institutionalization would continue through the efforts of the state's colleges, especially U.N.C., Wake Forest, and Trinity.

III. 1890-1920: Capture by the Universities

In 1890, twenty-two-year-old Lucius Polk McGehee began the study of law at the University of North Carolina. McGehee was a native of Person County and had earlier graduated from the University in 1887 as its valedictorian. After his undergraduate education, the young graduate taught school for three years in Asheville and Mebane; yet undoubtedly McGehee felt a strong pull towards the law. Such would be only natural, for he would be a fourth generation attorney in a family known for its legal prowess; his father Montford McGehee studied law at Harvard in the 1840s, while his maternal grandfather was George E. Badger.

After a year in Chapel Hill, McGehee was admitted to the bar, and his first few years of practice were spent in Raleigh and New York City. Unfortunately, McGehee was not destined to live an extraordinarily long life, for he died in 1923 at the age of fifty-five. During the three decades of his professional life, however, McGehee witnessed an extraordinary transformation in the way most North Carolinians received their legal education.

When Lucius McGehee was deciding upon a career path in the late 1880s, legal education in North Carolina had changed little over the past forty years. While there had been a gradual decline in the percentage of those reading law in private offices, nearly one-half of those studying for the bar still received their legal education in this manner. Many others still studied in proprietary law schools, with the state's leading institution for legal education at this time being the Dick & Dillard Law School in Greensboro. Finally, while some students travelled north to attend law classes at Harvard or Virginia, those wishing to study law in a university setting within the state had only one choice, the University of North Carolina. The rolls of those studying at Chapel Hill had grown to approximately forty students a year, but there remained only one professor, who relied on the lecture method to supplement the learning his young charges were absorbing through the reading of legal treatises.

Less than thirty-five years later upon McGehee's death, legal education in North Carolina had been revolutionized. By the early 1920s, very few North Carolinians were reading law in the offices of private practitioners, and there had not been a major proprietary law school within the state for almost three decades. Instead, the vast majority of those wishing to become attorneys attended a university law school. In 1923, the University of North Carolina employed five full-time law professors to train 123 young persons studying for the bar. Also, in these professors' classes the case method had become the norm, and one would have to spend three years at the school in order to earn a law degree. Chapel Hill was no longer the only choice for in-state university legal education, however, for over the past several decades two other major North Carolina colleges, Wake Forest and Trinity, had developed permanent law departments, not to mention a successful, degree-granting private law school in Wilmington. Thus, much had changed over a relatively short period of time, and McGehee had been not merely an observer of this transformation, but an active participant, for he served as Dean of the University of North Carolina School of Law from 1910 until his death thirteen years later.

A. A Restricted Bar

In the history of the American bar, the three decades between 1890 and 1920 are exceptionally noteworthy not only for the vast increase in the number of university law schools, but also in the tightening of requirements for admission to the bar. Like any institution, once the bar reached a certain size and strength its members monopolistically felt compelled to raise the standards for all those who would follow. Both state and national organizations were formed to help in this endeavor, including the American Bar Association and the Association of American Law Schools.[260]

The strengthening of bar requirements was much in evidence in North Carolina, and was helped greatly by the founding of the North Carolina Bar Association. Mention has already been made of the Supreme Court setting its first time requirement for legal studies, twelve months, in 1889. A decade later, a campaign was begun through the newly organized state bar association to increase the required time to two years, a movement which was spearheaded by University of North Carolina law professor J. Crawford Biggs. Interestingly, one of the persons opposing the measure was the other person then teaching law at the state university, law school Dean James C. MacRae, who asked, "What difference does it make how long a course is prescribed for a man, so that he is able to go before the Supreme Court and stand the examination?" An answer to this came from MacRae's own boss, university President Edward A. Alderman, who thought that only by adopting the two year requirement "can the [tendency] be checked to debase law schools from their high function into mere quizzing bees for obtaining license." Alderman was likely afraid that the law school's new-found prominence within the state could be lost to the upstart program at Wake Forest, where, according to its critics, Needham Gulley was teaching a "cram course" for the state bar exam.[261] After much debate, the state Supreme Court in 1901 agreed with the Biggs-Alderman position, finding that from then on one would have to study law for at least two years before admission to the bar.[262]

Three years later in 1904, the court also, for the first time, dictated with whom one would have to do this studying, for it mandated that applicants had to study "under the direction" of, or to the "knowledge and satisfaction" of, either a law school dean or an attorney licensed to practice before the state Supreme Court.[263] The new educational requirements were not the only major changes, for in 1898 the court also ruled that "in the future all examinations [for licensure] shall be in writing."[264] President Alderman felt that this too gave "new vigor to the [University's law] school, and . . . new dignity to the profession," although the small but increasing number of applicants who failed the new written exam likely disagreed.[265]

All of these new regulations had the desired effect of checking the heretofore vast increase in the number of persons flooding into the profession. While the state bar grew 63.6% during the final two decades of the nineteenth century, the first twenty years of the twentieth century witnessed only a 25.5% increase, to 1,585 attorneys in 1920. Still, it should be noted that such a gain was the second largest of any Southern or border state during this period, eclipsed only by Florida, and seven of these states, Alabama, Arkansas, Kentucky, Louisiana, Missouri, Tennessee, and Virginia, actually saw a decrease in the raw number of attorneys statewide between 1900 and 1920.[266]

B. Decline of the Traditional Methods

While the new regulations allowed for the continuation of the traditional apprenticeship system, provided that the supervising attorney was fully licensed and the studies lasted at least two years, by the turn of the century very few students were reading law in an attorney's office. The percentage of students who read for the bar had, of course, consistently declined throughout the nineteenth century, and of the attorneys in the *DNCB* who were born between 1875 and 1899, only 9.4% received any of their legal education in this manner.

The decades after 1890 were even more notable for the death of proprietary legal education, for none of the *DNCB* attorneys born in the last quarter of the nineteenth century were educated in such an institution. The success of North Carolina's proprietary schools over most of the century was predicated on three factors: a demand for institutionalized legal education, the availability of competent instructors, and little competition from the state's university law schools. While the demand for institutionalized legal education continued to increase, by the 1890s a position in the state judiciary was nearly full-time, thus precluding the active participation of such judges in proprietary schools. More importantly, the law school at Chapel Hill was increasingly growing stronger, and it would be joined shortly by successful programs at Wake Forest and Trinity. Thus, it is not surprising that 96.2% of the *DNCB* attorneys born in the last quarter of the nineteenth century attended a university law school.

The only known proprietary school begun after 1880 was started by Judge Alphonso Calhoun Avery in Morganton in 1897. Much like his predecessors in such endeavors, Avery (1835-1913) possessed sterling familial, educational, political, and judicial credentials. He was born into a very influential Burke County family, including a grandfather who served as the state's first Attorney General, and after graduating first in his class from the University of North Carolina in 1857, he studied law under Chief Justice Pearson at Richmond Hill. Shortly before the outbreak of the Civil War, Avery married a daughter of the Reverend Robert Hall Morrison, first President of Davidson College, thus making him the brother-in-law of three men who would shortly serve as Generals in the Confederate Army, including Thomas J. "Stonewall" Jackson.

During the War, Avery served as a Captain and was then on the staff of his brother-in-law D.H. Hill. After peace was restored, he attended Judge John White Brockenbrough's famous proprietary law school in Lexington, Virginia, before returning to his hometown of Morganton, from where he was elected to the state Senate in 1866. Avery also served in the 1875 Constitutional Convention, and three years later he was elected to the state Superior Court. Avery rode the circuits for ten years, and in 1888 he advanced to the state Supreme Court.

As will be discussed below, during his eight-year term on the high court Avery served for several years as the Dean of Trinity's second law school. After a reelection defeat during the Republican-Populist sweep of 1896, he returned to his law practice in Morganton, where he also began a proprietary law school. Other than the name of one student, John M. Mull, little is known about this school, and it may have been in existence for only several years, for one source states that Avery operated his school "before the turn of the century." While the details about this school are somewhat sketchy, Avery himself was quite impressive, both as a judge and scholar.[267]

In addition to operating the last proprietary school in the state, Avery should also be seen as one of the last of a dying breed of men who began teaching law during or after impressive political and judicial careers. Of the thirty-two men known to have taught law in an institutional setting in the state during the nineteenth century, twenty-seven were also at one time members of the state legislature, and sixteen served in the state judiciary. Even as late as 1894, four of the five members of the North Carolina Supreme Court would, at some point in their careers, teach law. This would shortly change, however, for starting around the turn of the century the ranks of the state's law professors would increasingly be filled by career teachers, men who began teaching after only a few years at the bar and who were not interested in political or judicial success.

The teaching methods employed by these new professors were also quite different from those of the earlier generations. The law was increasingly seen as a science, and the way to teach this science was through the "case method." Students would no longer read general treatises on the law, but instead they would study "casebooks" which almost exclusively contained edited appellate opinions on a particular subject. In class, the professors would closely examine their students on these cases by using the socratic method, and through this it was expected that the students would learn not only some blackletter law, but, more importantly, inferential reasoning, or as it is commonly termed, the ability to "think like a lawyer."

The case method was begun by Dean Christopher Columbus Langdell at Harvard in the 1870s, and despite great controversy over the next half century it was adopted by almost every leading American law school. Various elements of the system were not new to North Carolina, for example Chief Justice Pearson used the socratic method to teach legal reasoning at Richmond Hill; yet overall the new system was revolutionary, and, as will be seen below, it took many decades for it to be fully accepted by all law teachers in the Old North State.

Wishing to receive the most advanced legal education possible, ten percent of the *DNCB* attorneys born between 1875 and 1899 ventured north to Cambridge to study at the birthplace of the case method, thus causing Harvard to replace the University of Virginia as the out-of-state law school most favored by North Carolinians. In-state university law schools, however, continued to attract the bulk of those wishing to learn the law. As shown by Table 3, unlike the early and middle decades of the nineteenth century, from the 1880s into the 1920s almost three-quarters of those *DNCB* individuals who attended a university law school did so within North Carolina:

Table 3: Location of University Law Schools Attended By *DNCB* Attorneys

Year Born	*% In-State*	*% Out-of-State*
1775-1799	0.0	100.0
1800-1824	27.3	72.7
1825-1849	52.9	47.1
1850-1874	73.1	26.9
1875-1899	73.5	26.5

C. Growth of University Programs

1. *University of North Carolina*

As noted above, the only university law school in the state in the mid-1880s was the University of North Carolina, and while it would be shortly joined by several competing ventures, the Chapel Hill institution would retain its dominance into the twentieth century. The permanent growth of the University's law school had begun when John Manning assumed control of the program in 1881, and the steady enlargement seen throughout the 1880s continued over the following decade; Manning taught sixty-six students in 1893-1894, and eighty-seven in 1897-1898.[268]

By 1890, the U.N.C. law program had progressed to the point where a visiting committee of the Board of Trustees could report that "there is now no need for any young man to leave this State to fit himself for the practice of [law]," and two years later Manning was given permission to spend $100 advertising his program to young men in other states.[269] The progression of the program was also seen in 1897, when Manning felt secure enough to recommend to the Board of Trustees that age and prior education requirements be set for those applying for the LL.B. The Board approved this suggestion, although it reduced the requested age limit by one year, holding: "Applicants for the degree of Bachelor of Laws must be twenty years of age and must have completed an academic course equivalent to that of the Freshmen and Sophomore years in College."[270]

Manning also expanded the curriculum the students would face once they were in Chapel Hill. In 1893, the International and Constitutional Law course long taught by Kemp Plummer Battle became required for all those seeking the LL.B., and other courses in political economy, social science, anthropology, and sociology were also introduced into the curriculum.[271] By 1891, members of the first year class were required to attend "daily lectures and recitations," and all students desiring the LL.B. had to submit a written thesis.

In addition, the school began to offer "special lectures" by visiting practitioners, and the expanded Moot Court occupied the students' attention for three hours every Saturday evening. The students themselves also played a role in the law school's development, for they organized a "Blackstone Club."[272]

There were, however, disappointments for Manning and his students, one being a change in university policy regarding student discipline. Heretofore, all law students who did not attend other university classes and who did not room in the college were solely under the control of the professor of law. In 1893, however, University President George Tayloe Winston ruled that both law and medical students would be "subject to the same system of discipline" as all other university students. To this pronouncement, Manning filed an impassioned but futile dissent, stating:

> The students in this department are for the most part much older than the students in the other departments and should not be subjected in all respects to the discipline of the University and I therefore ask that these students be placed under my control except for such offenses as affect the *morals* of the young men such as drunkenness and the like. . . . If any other course is pursued with the special schools I feel sure that all of them will fall off in numbers for young men 23 or 24 years of age pursuing a post-graduate course will not subject themselves in all respects to the discipline necessary & proper for men of less mature years.[273]

Manning also battled with the University's administration over other matters, one of which was his own salary. In 1891, President Battle reported to the Trustees that the suggestion had been made to pay Manning $2,000 a year, but that "the payment of so large a sum directly out of the Treasury for the education of lawyers might not be agreeable to the taxpayer." Manning in reply, however, noted that the school was collecting over $2,000 a year in law student fees, and several years later on the recommendation of President Winston, the Trustees finally resolved that "after September 1st 1894 the Law Department be put upon the same footing with the other Chairs of the Institution, and that the Professor be paid a salary of $2,000 from the Treasury and the fees of his Department belong to the University as the other fees paid by students."[274]

Once he had his salary raised, Manning began a campaign for the hiring of an assistant professor. Although the Board again for several years refused to heed his suggestion, after a visiting committee in 1897 "reported him ill from overwork," the President and Trustees agreed that an Instructor in Law could be appointed at a salary of $500 a year. The first person to hold this position was Thomas Davis Warren in 1897-1898, who resigned after a year and was replaced by James Crawford Biggs, later Solicitor General of the United States under Franklin Roosevelt. Manning was also able to persuade the Trustees to allow $100 a year of student fees to be spent on purchasing books for a law school library.[275]

Throughout the 1890s, Manning continued to teach the summer law course which he had instituted in 1884, and which typically ran from the first of July into late September. To help him in this endeavor, Manning in 1891 recruited Justice James E. Shepherd of the North Carolina Supreme Court, who taught for eight summers. The Manning-Shepherd program was quite successful, for it usually attracted around forty students; in fact, it may have been too successful, for in 1896 the University's Board of Trustees placed some of the blame for a temporary decline in student enrollment in the regular program to the "superior advantages and lower cost of our Summer Law School as compared with the regular sessions of the law school." Because it appears as if Manning and Shepherd were able to keep all of the student tuition from the summer course, the Trustees may have seen the venture as cheating the University out of student tuition that it otherwise would have had. This was changed several months after Manning's death, when, in August 1899, the Trustees incorporated the summer law program into the University, declaring that its teachers would be paid $250 a month. Thus, after fifty-four years the law school was at last fully integrated within the University of North Carolina.[276]

When John Manning died in February 1899, he left an extraordinarily strong legacy. During his eighteen-year teaching career, the law school at Chapel Hill had grown from fourteen students to at least eighty-seven, and he had become the state's first full-time law professor, with an assistant professor as well. In addition, Manning must have been a highly effective teacher, for in 1894 the University's Alumni

Quarterly proudly stated that "[t]he excellence of the school . . . is shown by the fact that no student holding its certificate has been rejected after examination by the Supreme Court for license to become a member of the bar."[277]

To replace Manning as Dean, the Trustees chose James Cameron MacRae of Raleigh. MacRae (1838-1909) was a native of Fayetteville and the younger half-brother of noted lawyer and 1858 gubernatorial candidate Duncan McRae, the young attorney whom George E. Badger noted might "some day be found vastly pathetic and elegant on a motion *to amend a writ.*" MacRae, who for some reason added an "a" to his last name, did not attend college, but studied law on his own and in his brother's office before starting a practice in his hometown. He later served in the Confederate Army and in the 1874 General Assembly, and from 1882 until 1890 he was a member of the Superior Court. MacRae advanced to the state Supreme Court in 1892, although two years later he was defeated for reelection by Republican David Furches. Remaining in Raleigh, MacRae opened a private law practice and became the attorney of a leading railroad.[278]

Accepting the University's offer of the Deanship of its law school, MacRae moved to Chapel Hill, where he would successfully spend the last decade of his life. As Dean, MacRae was immensely popular, for he "immediately endeared himself to his students and always retained their affection. He was a man of rare charm, with a fund of anecdote and humor for every appropriate occasion." The Dean was also known for his hospitality, for "[h]is 'possum suppers tendered to his law students—'possum, taters and simmon beer,' to say nothing of a further generous menu—became annual events, and many . . . recall[ed] his introductions of the students to his daughters as his prospective sons-in-law."[279]

During MacRae's tenure, the number of law students appears to have remained nearly equal to Manning's largest class, for there were eighty-two pupils in 1909, although the decade did see, in 1907, the addition of a third professorship. While the two lower professorships initially witnessed much turnover, with six men, James Crawford Biggs, Thomas Ruffin (III), Lucius Polk McGehee, Patrick Henry Winston, James C. MacRae, Jr., and Edgar D. Broadhurst, all teaching under Dean MacRae, by 1910 these posts were starting to be seen as permanent, long-term positions.[280]

In addition to the expanding faculty, the physical structure of the law school was also greatly enlarged during MacRae's Deanship. When MacRae was appointed, the school was confined to one room in the Old West Building that could seat approximately fifty pupils, although the next year it was allowed the use of a much larger room in the South Building. Several years later, around 1904, the law department was at last given the use of its own building, the fairly small Smith Building.[281] MacRae's tenure also saw the school's law library more than double in size, to 3,000 volumes, and in 1909 the Trustees agreed to spend $1,000 annually for the purchase of law books.[282] In addition, MacRae himself helped add to the amount of legal literature, for he edited one of the first law journals in the state, the *North Carolina Journal of Law*, which unfortunately lasted only two years.[283]

As for the prerequisites and curriculum of the school, they remained much the same as during Manning's latter years. The 1907-1908 catalogue noted that "[a] good English education is essential to success at the Bar, and the completion of a full collegiate course before beginning the study of law is urged in all possible cases." The Trustees, however, did not set any specific prerequisites for admission into the program, although one continued to need two years of collegiate training in order to be eligible for the LL.B. While the classes and teaching methods remained as before, during MacRae's tenure the number of "special lectures" by members of the bar greatly increased, and the Moot Court was expanded and divided into civil and criminal divisions. The summer law course also expanded, for in 1906 fifty-seven men were in attendance.[284] Overall, the young attorney Thomas Ruffin (III), who taught at Chapel Hill over most of this decade, later stated that it was during MacRae's Deanship that the law school "began to burst its swaddling clothes."[285]

As noted above, upon MacRae's death he was replaced by Lucius Polk McGehee, who served as Dean until his own death in 1923. The University's law school witnessed many important changes during McGehee's thirteen-year stewardship, not the least of which was the introduction of the case method. During his first year, McGehee oversaw the transition from textbooks to casebooks in thirteen of the school's twenty courses, the rest of which were changed over the following decade. While some professors continued to lecture rather than use the socratic method, a noticeable change occurred in 1919, when the school hired its first faculty member trained at Harvard, Oscar Ogburn Efird. Thus, while not entirely universal, by the time of McGehee's death the casebook and its partner the socratic method were at least well established in Chapel Hill.[286]

Another major change was that for the first time entrance requirements were set for those wishing admittance into the law school. In 1910, it was held that "graduation from a good high school" was a necessary prerequisite for admission into the program, while this was raised in 1923 to one year of college, and two years of college were required after 1925.[287] Dean McGehee also oversaw the addition of a third year to the law program for those interested in attaining the LL.B. This was a high priority for McGehee, who was concerned that many of his students, "regard[ing] the bar examination and not the law as the object and end of their studies," did not even complete the two year course.[288] In 1918, he wrote:

> We are too much inclined to regard the law course solely as a means of imparting enough knowledge to students to enable them to pass the bar examination of the State. The University should provide for a more extended study of law both as a theoretical and as a practical science. The student should be made to feel, not that law consists of a certain number of dead propositions contained in 'law books,' but that it is a living, growing thing, with roots indeed deep in the past, but in vital relation with every phase of contemporary life.
>
> Some day there will be at the University a school which will not only ground the student fully in the fundamental elements of technical law studies, but will also guide him in courses suggesting the place of law in history and its relations to philosophy, society, and the state. With the greater demands which North Carolina is learning to make of its University, we will one day be called upon to realize such an ideal. For the present we must be content with gradual improvement. To that end I earnestly urge at this time the extension of the course to three years and the employment of an additional instructor.[289]

McGehee's persistence paid off, for in 1919 the Trustees agreed to add an additional year to the law program, and to aid him in this endeavor the faculty was increased to four that year, and five in 1921.[290] As would be expected, various new subjects were added to the curriculum, including courses on Public Service Corporations, Legal History, Statute Drafting, Administrative Law, and Legal Ethics.[291] In addition, in 1922 the law school hired its first secretary and full-time law librarian, Wilbur Stout, and this same year witnessed the founding of the *North Carolina Law Review*.[292]

One of McGehee's largest legacies was the planning and construction of a new law school building, which opened in the fall of 1923 and was named for John Manning. During its first semester in Manning Hall, the law school witnessed its largest enrollment to that time, 123 students, all but eight of whom were from North Carolina. Of the 123, sixty-three were first year students, forty-three were in their second year, and seventeen were there for a third year; forty-three of the total planned to stay all three years to receive the LL.B. As for their academic backgrounds, twenty were college graduates, an additional sixty had at least two years of college, twenty-nine had attended a college for one year, and fourteen had no collegiate training.[293]

The death of McGehee in the fall of 1923 sparked a wide-ranging discussion among the University's President, Trustees, and alumni as to the future direction of the law school. President Harry Woodburn Chase, a psychologist originally from Massachusetts, felt that the school was at a crossroads, for it could choose either to be "a coaching school for the bar examination" that "prepare[d] an inferior brand of lawyers for law as a trade," or it could become "a real professional law school in the modern sense" that "prepare[d] men for practice and leadership in law as a profession." Chase, of course, desired the latter course, and after a tour of Harvard, Columbia, and the University of Chicago, he delineated five changes that should be made: entrance requirements should be toughened; a larger percentage of students needed to take the entire three year course; the faculty should be larger and better paid; academic requirements should be stiffened with the case method universally employed; and the summer law school, "a coaching class for the bar examination," needed to be eliminated.[294]

Chase's proposals led to much discussion, especially on three subjects: entrance requirements, the method of instruction, and the type of person who should be chosen as the new Dean. Chase had his critics, including the state's Governor Cameron Morrison, who decried the further toughening of entrance requirements; Morrison was one of Robert P. Dick's last students at the Greensboro Law School and had himself not attended college. In addition, a number of Trustees wished to continue the practice of hiring a leading North Carolina attorney as the law school's Dean, in opposition to Chase, who wanted a nationally recognized legal educator and administrator. The President did have his supporters, however, including one alumnus who wrote:

> The University Law Department has been hide-bound for 100 years by aristocratic and family and political ties. Because someone's grandfather has been Chief Justice, or a member of the Cabinet or a distinguished North Carolinian, such men have been put into positions where they taught well but where they missed the vision necessary in preparing the students for the different business eras in the growth of this country. We have graduated political lawyers.[295]

In the end, Chase was able to win on all three issues, and the man he saw appointed as Dean was apparently the first non-North Carolinian to teach law within the state, former George Washington University Law School Dean Merton Leroy Ferson.[296] According to some, it was at this point that the "modern law school" of the University of North Carolina emerged.[297]

While some credit must go to Chase's far-sighted, non-parochial view, in hindsight his vision actually appears to be the continuation and natural consequence of the four decades of constant growth and strengthening of the law program under the watchful eyes of Deans Manning, MacRae, and McGehee. While it would grow significantly over the following seventy-five years, the law school McGehee bequeathed to future generations would be quite recognizable to those currently studying in Chapel Hill.

One of the reasons why President Chase was so concerned about strengthening the University's law program was that it no longer had a monopoly on legal education within the state. By the 1920s, Wake Forest and Trinity/Duke both had flourishing law programs, and there was also a notable private law school in Wilmington. This great growth in university legal education started between 1888 and 1894, when three colleges within the state began to teach law.

2. Shaw University

The first of these law programs, at Shaw University in Raleigh, was unique, for it was the first attempt to provide institutionalized legal education for members of the state's large black population. Shaw University itself was the first institution of higher education in the South for African Americans, having been established in December 1865 by the American Baptist Home Missionary Society. The school's founder was Henry Martin Tupper, a Baptist minister and Union Army veteran from Massachusetts who decided to remain in the South to help educate the newly emancipated freedmen. While the institution was initially established to train young men for the ministry, within twenty years it grew to contain six different schools or departments: college, scientific, normal, theological, medical, and industrial. The medical school, whose "faculty include[d] some of the most eminent members of the medical profession in [North Carolina]," graduated 134 physicians during its thirty-eight years in existence, 1881-1918.[298]

In 1888, Tupper determined that his institution also needed a law school, in order to give "good legal help to colored people who . . . were being taken advantage of."[299] During the antebellum era, it was common to find many of the state's finest attorneys such as George E. Badger successfully defending slaves and free blacks before the state's highest courts, even on charges of raping white women, and compared to other courts and the population in general, the North Carolina Supreme Court was especially noted for its liberality in cases involving black litigants.[300] This legal protection may have changed somewhat in the decades after emancipation, when black citizens were able to aspire to legal and political equality, including the election of black Congressmen and state legislators. When the Republican party, with its many black voters, fused with the Populists to overthrow the Democrats' dominance of the state in 1894 and 1896, it created a tremendous racial backlash that led not only to a period of extreme violence but also to the virtual disfranchisement of the black population. Obviously, the Reverend Tupper as early as the late 1880s could feel the tremors of this approaching storm, for in establishing the law school he told the Home Missionary Society Board: "From the circumstances in which the colored people are placed they are compelled to act upon the defensive, and it is highly important that they not only in legal affairs, but in all matters, social and political . . . have trained minds. The South will be much more secure to have such a class of men as leaders."[301]

While the faculty of Shaw's medical school included some of the finest white doctors in the state, Tupper, either by choice or necessity, chose an African American to lead his law school—John S. Leary, an attorney who had represented Cumberland County in two sessions of the General Assembly in the late 1860s. In 1893, Leary was joined on the faculty by the school's first graduate, Edward A. Johnson.

Born into slavery in Wake County, Johnson (1860-1944) graduated from Atlanta University in the early 1880s and later returned home to Raleigh to serve as principal of the Washington School. While in this position, he wrote the first of his several histories and also studied law at Shaw, graduating in 1891. Two years later, Johnson became a member of the faculty, and at some point he replaced Leary as Dean of the school. During his fourteen years at Shaw, Johnson was also extraordinarily busy in other activities, including serving as a Raleigh Alderman, delegate to the Republican National Convention, and Assistant United States Attorney for the Eastern District of North Carolina, arguing, and winning, many cases before the state Supreme Court, and helping found both a cotton mill and what became the world's largest black insurance company. In 1907, Johnson, upset with the deteriorating social and political conditions for blacks within the state, moved to Harlem, where a decade later he became the first African American member of the New York legislature.[302] Thus, there is little doubt that the students at Shaw, at least during Johnson's tenure, received a fine legal education.

It appears as if Shaw was the first law school in the state to have a three-year program, and in addition to the usual subjects and a moot court, the students were required to take courses in short-hand and typing, for the administration believed that "the young lawyer who can write short-hand or operate a typewriter can find many openings [since] many legal firms will employ a young lawyer who [has these skills] as an office assistant in preference to one who does not." In total, the school graduated fifty-four students between 1888 and 1914, and as late as the 1930s the majority of black lawyers in both North and South Carolina were Shaw graduates.[303]

In February 1914, Shaw's Board of Trustees voted to close the school. Although no official reason was given, it appears as if the move was made not because of any pressure from the white community but, rather, because of problems with student discipline. Shaw's "law students were in the forefront of a 1913 student [protest] against the rather strict [university] rules . . . [which] required that all students, including those in the professional schools and those who roomed off-campus, observe early curfews and eat all meals in the campus cafeteria." Finding such regulations intolerable, the law students "led a student strike objecting to these rules during the first semester of the 1913 school year," and shortly thereafter the Board, supposedly as a result, voted to disband the law program.[304] In hindsight, the wisdom of such a move is highly debatable; it would be a quarter of a century before the state's second black law school, at North Carolina Central University in Durham, was established.

3. Trinity College (II)

The second law school to be started between 1888 and 1894 was the revival of the law program at Trinity College. As discussed above, law was taught at Trinity from 1868 until 1882, although the program was not well financed and eventually died because of a lack of interest coupled with the death of President Craven. In 1887, the school through its history department began to offer a course on elementary law, which was required of all graduating seniors. A description of this course in the college catalogue noted: "Every liberally educated young man should, whether he expects to make law a profession or not, know the principles and definitions of our common law."[305]

In the early 1890s, the Trustees of Trinity, with the financial backing of the newly wealthy Duke family, decided to move the college from Randolph County seventy miles east to Durham. It was also determined that once in Durham, the college would reestablish its School of Law, and to train Trinity students for the bar Justice Alphonso C. Avery of the North Carolina Supreme Court was hired as the law school's Dean.

While Trinity initially planned to be in Durham by 1891, complications arose which delayed the move for a year, and because Justice Avery's judicial duties required him to remain in Raleigh, he could not offer the law course during the 1891-1892 academic year. The school, however, was able to find a substitute, for at the close of the year the college announced: "The regular law course, as presented by Judge A.C. Avery, Dean of the Law School, was not offered this year on account of having to open college in our old buildings at Trinity, Randolph Co., N.C., but in the absence of Judge Avery, the above special course was offered by the instructor in law." This "special course" "covered the Supreme Court requirements for the bar examination," and its instructor was Blake Baker Nicholson of Washington, N.C., a young man who graduated from Trinity in 1890 and then studied law under John B. Minor at the University of Virginia.[306]

When Trinity moved to Durham in 1892, Avery, as Dean of the law school, began "teaching a law class for two hours . . . twice a week, in addition to carrying on his other duties"; it is not clear, however, whether this teaching was in Durham or in Raleigh. While Avery's teaching was highly praised, Trinity's second attempt at legal education was even more short-lived than its first, for the law school was closed in 1894. As for the reason, a 1916 article in the *Trinity Alumni Register* stated that Avery "was an exceedingly efficient and conscientious instructor, and it was only the financial weakness of the College at the time that closed the school."[307] As described below, these financial difficulties would finally be overcome a decade later, when Trinity's third attempt at legal education proved successful.

4. Wake Forest College

The final law school begun between 1888 and 1894, and the only one to prove permanent, was an institution started at Wake Forest College, a well respected, sixty-year-old Baptist institution situated seventeen miles north-northeast of Raleigh in the town of Wake Forest. There had been talk of establishing a law school at Wake Forest as early as 1872, when the pastor of the First Baptist Church of Raleigh, Thomas H. Pritchard, noted in the Baptist state newspaper, the *Biblical Recorder*, that "one of the pressing wants of Wake Forest College is a Law Professorship." Six years later, Pritchard became President of Wake Forest, and it was likely because of his influence that the Board of Trustees in June 1879 resolved that "a law class be established in connection with Wake Forest College at as early a day as possible." Pritchard, however, soon assumed a pastorate in Kentucky, and no action was taken in regard to the resolution.[308]

In 1892, school President Charles E. Taylor mentioned to the Trustees that the college should establish a law school, and the following year he stated that a law school "now seems to be a necessity, and I hope the Board will discover some way to establish such a school, either at the College or in Raleigh, [but] without spending any of the income of the College therefore." The Trustees in their June 1893 meeting agreed with Taylor's recommendation and appointed a three-man committee to oversee the immediate establishment of such a school. This committee worked quickly, for shortly thereafter they secured a strong faculty, the members of which then decided upon the curriculum, printed an attractive announcement, and set an opening date of September 6, 1893.

The announcement stated that the faculty would consist of three lawyers, the first listed being state Supreme Court Justice Walter Clark, who was named "Professor of Common and Statute Law." Although Clark would later become the state's most impressive Chief Justice of the twentieth century, at the time he may have been somewhat overshadowed in the world of legal education by the school's "Professor of Equity and Pleading," George V. Strong, the noted Raleigh judge who for many years operated an important proprietary law school. The third attorney, named "Professor of Elementary Law," was the least known of the three, Needham Y. Gulley of Franklinton, who had been on the Trustees' committee to oversee the school's establishment. In addition, President Taylor and E.W. Sikes, a soon-to-be Johns Hopkins Ph.D. and future President of Clemson College, were named "Professors of Constitutional Government, Political Economy and Political History."

The school's curriculum would cover "two sessions of forty weeks each," with students attending five recitations per week. In the first year, students would study the course prescribed by the state Supreme

Court for licensure, while the readings for the second year were: "Beach on Corporations, Public and Private, Destey's Federal Procedure, May on Insurance, Smith's Mercantile Law, Benjamin on Sales, Schouler on Domestic Relations, Devlin on Deeds, Jarman on Wills, Jones on Mortgages, Pierce's American Railroad Law, [and] Bishop's Criminal Law." Second-year students were also given the option of studying political science.

As for the methods of instruction, the students would be "required to familiarize themselves with the text-books, and in addition to this to make a careful study of cases." Lectures would supplement the students' readings, and both civil and criminal moot courts would be held. In addition, "[f]rom time to time students will be required to write opinions in cases taken from the Docket of the Supreme Court," and there would also be instruction in the drafting of "pleadings, contracts, deeds, mortgages, wills, deeds of assignment, etc."

Tuition, including two small university fees, would be $100 a year, or $170 for both years. Board could be had from local private families "at from $2.00 to $2.50 per week [, or] in clubs, at from $1.50 to $1.75 per week. Unfurnished rooms in the College building are rented for $12.00 per session of forty weeks, one-half to be paid by each occupant." As for student discipline, the announcement stated: "The Law School is a part of the College, and its students are subject to the same restrictions and entitled to the same privileges of Literary Societies, Library, Reading-room, etc., as other students." The brochure then closed by stating that for further information one should contact Taylor, Clark, Gulley, or Strong.[309]

On paper, the Clark-Strong-Gulley program looked as strong as, if not stronger than, both the Chapel Hill program taught by Manning, and Avery's law class at Trinity. When Gulley travelled with "pen in hand" to Wake Forest in early September, however, not one student registered for the program. A combination of factors likely caused this, one being the strong competition from Chapel Hill and, to a much lesser extent, Trinity. Also, while $100 had been the standard tuition charged by North Carolina law schools since the 1820s, this amount was double the regular Wake Forest tuition, and because the nation was then experiencing a severe economic recession, if not depression, such an amount would have been even harder to come by than usual. Finally, the most important reason likely was that the course was new, and the time for its advertisement had necessarily been extremely short.[310]

Thus, the planned law course was stillborn, and Judges Clark and Strong would never have the opportunity to teach law at Wake Forest. One man, however, did not give up the idea of establishing a law program at Wake, for Gulley, putting aside his "trifling shade of discouragement," decided to travel the ten miles from Franklinton "once a week in a buggy pulled by a sorrel nag to give free lectures on [various] points of law, thereby hoping to interest enough students in the program to start a law school the next year." Such a plan eventually proved wise, the first evidence of which was the surprising number of students who began to attend these free lectures.[311]

Needham Yancey Gulley (1855-1945) was a native of Johnston County who graduated as valedictorian of Wake Forest in 1879. He then served as the principal of several schools in addition to reading law under E.W. Pou (Sr.) Settling in Franklinton, Gulley in 1883 began to practice law and edit a weekly newspaper, and two years later he was elected to a term in the state House. In May 1893, Gulley became a Trustee of his *alma mater*, having earlier married the daughter of a former President, and, as is mentioned above, the next month he was appointed a member of the committee to oversee the establishment of a law school.[312]

After giving the free lectures during the 1893-1894 school year, Gulley determined to offer a summer law course at Wake Forest in 1894, and this time two students, Stephen McIntyre and R.O. Fry, decided to register. Fry quickly quit the program, but McIntyre, the principal of a school in Louisburg, stayed the entire summer, and a visitor to Wake Forest recalled seeing Gulley and his one student holding class while seated on a bench under a campus tree.[313]

Building on these small successes, Gulley was able to persuade the Trustees to again attempt the start-up of a law school in 1894-1895, this time with the Franklinton attorney as its only instructor. Gulley agreed to a salary of $750 for the year, in return for which he would travel to Wake Forest three days a week and teach all of the law courses, as well as classes in Government and Political Economy.

The Wake Forest *Bulletin* for that year noted that the law program would cover two years, with the work of the first, or Junior, year covering "the course prescribed by the Supreme Court of North Carolina for applicants for license to practice law." This work was divided into two separate courses, both of which would meet for three hours a week. In the first of these courses, which could also be used as an elective for those seeking a Bachelor of Arts degree, the students would read Blackstone, Adams' Equity, and the first volume of Greenleaf on Evidence, along with the state code and leading cases from the state Supreme Court. The second course covered the other readings required by the Supreme Court, including specific treatises on Real Property, Contracts, Torts, Criminal Law, Domestic Relations, Corporations, Executors, Constitutional Law, Pleading, and Civil Procedure. In addition, this course would see "practical work in drawing pleadings and other papers, and in preparing briefs."

The second, or Senior, year consisted of one course, which would meet for five hours each week. There were no preassigned readings for this course, but students were "required to consult the best writers" on various subjects, including "the law of Railways, Public and Private Corporations, Insurance, Wills, Evidence, Code Pleading, Negotiable Instruments, and Criminal Law." In addition, Gulley would lead his charges through a "careful study of cases from the Supreme Court Reports of North Carolina and other states, and of the United States."

As for Gulley's method of instruction, the students were "required to study carefully the subjects assigned," and their work would be "supplemented by lectures, recitations, quizzes, moot-courts, and special lectures by prominent members of the Bar." A moot court would be held "every Friday afternoon, and students are required to participate in the trial of cases, and thus become familiar with all the details of actions, both criminal and civil, from the issuing of process to final judgment." To be eligible for the LL.B., a student was required to complete both the Junior and Senior law courses, take additional classes in History, Political Economy, and Constitutional Government, and prepare a written thesis on a subject selected by Gulley.

The *Bulletin* also noted that a summer law course would begin on the first Monday in July and continue for ten weeks. The subjects covered would be "as nearly as possible, the same as those of the regular College session," with particular attention given to preparing the students for the state bar exam.[314]

In the fall of 1894, Gulley's efforts finally began to show dividends, for twelve students enrolled in his law courses. Even more were in attendance the following semester, and seeing this success the Board of Trustees, in June 1895, named Gulley Professor of Law and Political Science, with a salary of $1,350. Accordingly, Gulley quit his practice, moved to Wake Forest, and became the state's second full-time law instructor. He would live in the quiet, 2,000-person Wake County village for the final fifty years of his life, during forty-four of which he taught at the law school he had single-handedly founded.[315]

Throughout his career, Gulley was a master teacher who was adored by his students. Although he taught as late as 1942, Gulley never adopted the case method, nor did he harshly question his students using the socratic method. Near the end of his career, he partially explained his system to a critic:

> In my class work I followed very much the method I would have followed if I had been writing a book or a lecture on the same subject. I made a careful analysis of the subject under discussion, dividing and subdividing as far as I deemed necessary. I then selected cases to illustrate or modify these general statements. These cases were chiefly, though not exclusively, from North Carolina decisions, for then as now nearly all our students were from North Carolina and intended to remain in this State. These divisions and sub-divisions, with cases cited, were written upon the blackboard so that the attention of the student need not be distracted during class periods by making notes of citations.[316]

With this outline on the blackboard, Gulley then conducted a lively class discussion on the law. His classes "from the earliest days to the last, infused life, meaning, and essence into legal education," causing him to earn a reputation as a "showman." He knew his students well, and explained the law in terms and images that they could readily understand, using everything from his own farm animals to the newspaper comics. Not one to "hide the ball," Gulley once stated, "I try to make what I teach so obvious that my men can't miss it."[317]

Gulley's insistence on teaching substantive blackletter law caused critics over four decades to charge that he was teaching a "cram course" for the state bar examination. By 1935, the nearly eighty year old Gulley had finally heard enough of this criticism, for he exploded in a letter to the President of the Association of American Law Schools:

> Yes, I have attempted to "cram." I have been present at over thirty thousand class periods, [and] if there has been a single one of them in which I have not attempted to "cram" something into the student I now regret it. My chief object has been to "cram" into their minds some knowledge of the principle of law under discussion and particularly I have attempted to "cram" obedience to law and respect for authority into their behavior. I have attempted to "cram" into their hearts respect for the rights of every human being. Into their souls I have attempted to "cram" a deep and abiding love of God.[318]

Despite harsh criticism from the ever increasing number of disciples of the case method, no one could deny the great success of Gulley's program at Wake Forest. Starting with twelve students in 1894, a decade later Gulley was teaching an average of seventy-five pupils in his program, and this rose to 140 by 1915. The majority of these students were from rural or small-town North Carolina, and most of them were also Baptist. While such students might have felt more comfortable at Wake Forest than Chapel Hill, another advantage was that starting from his first class in the fall of 1894, the tuition charged by Gulley was not the traditional $100 for legal education, but, rather, the significantly lower amount paid by all other Wake Forest students.[319]

During his tenure, there was a great amount of cross-pollination between the law school and the college. Most of Gulley's students took college classes in such subjects as History, Political Science, and English, while approximately three-fourths of the college's undergraduates took at least one law class as an elective. Because Gulley was disinclined to give any student a failing grade, it was said that "the classes of the Law School were long made catchalls for students, especially athletes who were hardly prepared for any of the academic classes."[320]

While Gulley's classes saw many undergraduates enroll, most of those attending were there to prepare for the practice of law. Over the first decade sixty young men completed the entire two year course and earned the LL.B., and they were but a small percentage of all those studying to be lawyers at Wake Forest. By 1905, the law program was producing 40% of all those licensed to practice law by the state Supreme Court, and three years later it was noted that 280 Wake Forest students were practicing law within the state.[321] This number included those who only attended Gulley's summer course, which, because of its $20 tuition, was quite popular; for example, eighteen students attended in 1895 and twenty-three in 1900. Whether a student attended his classes during the regular academic year or just in the summer, Gulley considered them all to be Wake Forest men, and he was extremely proud of their record on the state bar examination. Only one Gulley student failed the exam during the years when it was given orally by the state Supreme Court, and these good results continued when the Supreme Court adopted the written exam in 1898; in 1907 Gulley told the Trustees: "We have had four men to fail in the last seven examinations, a record unsurpassed in the State."[322]

In 1905, the Board of Trustees named Gulley Dean of the law school, a position which he would hold for the following thirty years, although the change in nomenclature meant little until the following year, when the school hired a second full-time faculty member. Gulley had already seen some assistance in his teaching, however, for between 1900 and 1904 noted Raleigh attorney and legal author Samuel Fox Mordecai traveled to Wake Forest twice a week to lecture on the common law, statutes, and equity. Mordecai would arrive on the morning train about noon and leave three hours later on the afternoon train, between which he would give lectures which any student could attend, and where no class rolls were kept nor grades given. In 1904, Mordecai's connection with Wake Forest ended when he was named Dean of Trinity's third law school.[323]

The full-time faculty member hired by Wake Forest in 1906 was Edward Walker Timberlake, the son of a former state Superior Court judge. The younger Timberlake followed his father's footsteps by earning a Bachelor of Arts degree from Wake Forest, in 1901, and then studying law at the University of Virginia, where he received his LL.B. in 1905. After this, Timberlake prepared for the state bar exam by studying under Gulley in the fall of 1905, and he was admitted to practice the following February. Beginning his teaching career in the fall of 1906, Timberlake would teach at Wake Forest until his retirement in 1954. In class, he presented dry, formal lectures, and although his students "respected his knowledge of the law and his effectiveness in teaching them," they also "spoke of difficulties in trying to stay awake in his classes."[324]

When Timberlake joined the faculty, Gulley was able to expand the course for the LL.B. to three years, something which was not done in Chapel Hill for thirteen years. The third year was initially called the "Practice Course," although its contents appear to have been a combination of readings on procedure as well as those on more obscure substantive topics. A 1916 admissions brochure noted that in the first year students were assigned readings on Domestic Relations, Personal Property, Wills, Executors, Criminal Law, Negotiable Instruments, Sales, Constitutional Law, Contracts, Torts, and Bailments. During the second year, the subjects were Equity, Common Law and Equity Pleading, Civil Procedure, Evidence, Real Property, Corporations, and Partnership. Finally, the third year saw assignments and instruction on Criminal Procedure, Code Pleading, Federal Procedure, Guaranty and Suretyship, Bankruptcy, Damages, Conflict of Laws, International Law, Admiralty, Civil Law, Insurance, Banking, and Legal Ethics.[325]

Law students continued to pay "the same tuition and matriculation fees as other students in the College," which in 1916 was $44 per term, and they could also "without additional charge, take work in any school of the college with the exception of the School of Medicine." Such other work, in fact, continued to be required for those seeking the LL.B., for in 1909 two years of "physical culture" was required for a law degree, and this was joined in 1913 by freshman English.[326]

While the LL.B. was a three year course after 1906, many of the students were able to complete the requirements in two years and a summer. This was indicative of Gulley's "flexible attitude toward meeting what he perceived to be the educational needs of [his] students," whether these needs were to earn a law degree or just to gain admission to the state bar. In the 1910 college *Bulletin*, Gulley wrote that "[t]he courses of instruction are arranged to meet the wants of students." Specifically, there were "six courses each extending over a year with daily lectures[,] and a seventh class daily from September to February." For those who only wanted to pass the state bar exam, "Courses 1 and 2 embrace the subjects prescribed by the Supreme Court," and a student could take these courses over separate years or, if he wished to spend only one year at Wake Forest, he could take both courses simultaneously. In addition, there was even a way for a student to spend only half a year at the school, for during the fall semester he could take both Courses 1 and 2 and the extra, September to February, class to prepare for the February examination, or, if he wished to take the August exam, a semester of Courses 1 and 2 plus the summer law class would be sufficient. In replying to his critics, Gulley ended his description by stating: "In these different courses each subject is fully and comprehensively taught; the method is not a mere cram for the examination."[327]

Gulley was also extremely flexible in his admissions criteria for the program. In the 1904-1905 *Bulletin*, he noted that "every young man intending to study law should take as thorough and complete collegiate course as his circumstances will allow." Gulley, however, knew that many of his students could not afford college, so he did not set any specific prerequisites for his law program, only stating that those who could "not take a college course must be proficient in the elements of an ordinary English education. No lawyer can succeed who can not write and speak well, and is not familiar with elementary mathematics."[328]

The 1916 admissions brochure noted that students who had not completed four years of high school would not be eligible for the LL.B., although they could, "in the discretion of the Faculty, be admitted to the Law School as special students." In defending his refusal to accept any specific admissions criteria, Gulley told the Board of Trustees that "schools are made for men and not men for schools, and it does not seem wise to say that a man who has not opportunities such as his more fortunate neighbor has, shall be cut off entirely."[329]

The flexibility of Gulley's program paid off handsomely, for in the decade between 1906 and 1915 he and Timberlake taught an average of 140 students a year, making it, by far, the largest law program in the state to that time. This decade also saw an additional 124 LL.B. degrees granted, and by 1916 the school could boast 635 attendees then practicing within the Old North State.[330]

As for the summer course, it continued to grow and prosper, witnessing forty-three students in 1910 and fifty-one in 1916. Many of the summer students were graduates of other law schools who were attracted to the Wake Forest program by the "low tuition and living expenses and the success rate of Gulley's students on the bar examination"; for example, eighteen of the forty-three 1910 attendees were alumni of other law schools. Tuition for the summer program remained at $20, although because all of this amount went to Gulley and his teachers, the college added a five dollar matriculation fee in 1914. The law school's admission brochure for 1916 noted that the summer school would begin on the first Monday in June and continue until the bar examination in August, and it was estimated that books for the course would cost about $25, while "good board" could be found for $15 a month, and rooms from two to six dollars per month. In addition, obviously anticipating the United States' entry into the war then tearing apart Europe, the brochure also announced that a summer course in either German or French was available from the college for an additional $10.[331]

As suggested above, during this period the school continued its great success on the state bar exam, for the 1916 admissions brochure noted that ten Wake Forest Law classes had posted a perfect passage rate, while "[a] number" of other classes had witnessed only one failure. There were exceptions, however, the most notable being the exceptionally hard August 1914 exam, when only twenty-four of thirty-eight Wake Forest men passed. Gulley was also concerned about the three failures (out of twenty-one applicants) on the August 1908 exam, followed by two failures (out of fifteen) the next February. He told the Trustees: "These failures were probably due to [the] want of ability to write and spell as anything else. I mention this by way of explanation, not apology, for we have done as well before the Court as any others represented there." It is interesting to note that shortly thereafter Gulley required all of his degree candidates to pass freshman English.[332]

Despite the great success of Gulley's program, it was not strongly supported by the Wake Forest Board of Trustees. The law school had been inaugurated with the understanding that it would be self-sustaining, causing no expense to the larger college, and by 1916 the Trustees had spent only $2,200 on the school, for equipment and books. The library was in especially poor shape, for while the Chapel Hill Trustees were allowing $1,000 a year for the purchase of law books, their counterparts in Wake County were spending an average of $42.96 a year for the same purpose during the first decade of the twentieth century, and $87.00 per annum over the 1910s.

Gulley was also undoubtedly discouraged that the law school was allowed the use of only one small thirty-by-forty foot room in the Heck-Williams Building, and one-third of this meager space had to be partitioned off to hold the law library. After years of petitioning the Trustees for an improvement, Gulley in 1911 was given permission to raise funds for a new building, but he then ran into opposition from both others at the college and the Baptist denomination generally, and it was only after fifteen years that an extension was added onto the Heck-Williams Building.[333]

Gulley, however, did achieve some success with the Board of Trustees, including the permission to hire a third full-time law professor in 1916—thus allowing Wake Forest to equal Chapel Hill and Trinity in the size of its faculty. The new hire, Robert Bruce White, graduated from Wake Forest in 1891 and was then a member of Gulley's second law class. He thereafter practiced law for twenty years in Franklinton and Louisburg, and also represented Franklin County for two terms in the state Senate, where he "drafted the bill which brought prohibition to North Carolina." Gulley, Timberlake, and White, the "Great Triumvirate" of the Wake Forest law school, would continue to be the institution's only instructors until 1928.[334]

The addition of White, who was quite popular with the students, allowed the school to offer a strong three-year program for the LL.B. After White joined the faculty in 1916, a candidate for the LL.B. was required to pass forty hours of classes in law and twenty-four hours in various college subjects. In 1921, the course of study for those without any college education who wished to earn the law degree expanded to four years, with the first year consisting entirely of "regular college courses in English, Mathematics, Science, and a foreign language." Then, during years two through four, the student would take the complete law course in addition to "History in the second year, Economics in the third year, [and] Government and a second course in Social Science in the fourth." These requirements were again toughened in 1924, when the law school held that two years of college work would be required for those seeking the LL.B.[335]

Despite these escalating requirements, the percentage of law students earning the LL.B. continued its steady rise, for 175 young men achieved this distinction in the ten years between 1916 and 1925;[336] still, into the 1930s a majority of Wake Forest law students chose not to pursue a degree. In the decade after White's arrival, the law school taught approximately 150 students a year, and these students continued to perform well on the state bar exam; of the fifty-four exams given by the state Supreme Court between 1895 and 1922, eighteen saw every Wake Forest student pass.[337]

Needham Y. Gulley would continue as Dean of the Wake Forest Law School until June 1935. In total, between 1,600 and 1,700 of his students were licensed to practice law, 523 of whom earned the LL.B.; by 1931, Gulley could report to the Trustees that approximately half of all North Carolina attorneys had studied law at Wake Forest.[338] Despite this great success, in 1935 Gulley, who was then eighty years old yet showing no diminution in his capacities, was unceremoniously forced to resign his Deanship in what is one of the saddest episodes in North Carolina legal history.

Wake Forest College had been attempting to gain full accreditation from the Southern Association of Secondary Schools and Colleges ("SASSC"), and for this it was required that the law school become a member of the Association of American Law Schools ("AALS"). Trinity had become the South's second member of the AALS in 1906 and the University of North Carolina followed in 1925, however over these years Gulley had been little concerned about attaining an outside agency's mark of approval. Under pressure from the SASSC, Wake Forest finally applied for AALS membership in 1931 and was rejected for numerous reasons. Thereafter, the Trustees helped Gulley correct many of these "faults" by hiring additional faculty and purchasing a number of books for the law library. After a December 1934 inspection, however, the President of the AALS indicated that membership would not be given until Gulley was forced out as Dean. The crux of the matter was that despite Timberlake's 1929 introduction of a casebook into two of his courses, Gulley and those who taught under him continued to shun the case method by assigning textbooks and then lecturing in class. In addition, Gulley, Timberlake, and White also failed very few of their students.

Desperate for AALS membership, and thus full accreditation by the SASSC, the school's administration forced Gulley to resign the Deanship in June 1935. Even this did not fully placate the AALS, however, for when the school contemplated naming a leading alumnus to the position, the Association let it be known that a necessary prerequisite for Wake Forest's membership was the hiring of a Dean trained in the "modern" methods of legal education. Thus, buckling under to this pressure, the school hired Dean Dale Foster Stansbury of Mercer University.[339]

As for Gulley, he taught half-time for three years and then completely retired in 1938 to raise cattle. Over his tenure, Gulley had been active in numerous outside activities, including teaching a Sunday School class and serving as both a North Carolina Code Commissioner and Chairman of the Wake County Board of Education, and in his retirement he also remained quite busy. Gulley's final connection with the law school occurred in 1942 when, at the age of eighty-seven, he completed teaching a course on Civil Procedure for an instructor pulled away by World War II.[340]

In the annals of legal history, Needham Y. Gulley should be remembered not as the octogenarian who was forced to abandon his lifetime's calling; but, rather, as the younger man whose forceful, far-sighted efforts gave birth to and then nurtured the Wake Forest law program. Within a decade, Gulley went from seeing not one person enroll in his law classes to leading a program that equalled Chapel Hill in the number of North Carolina attorneys it was producing. Gulley's program was especially valuable in providing a legal education to a class of persons who generally did not attend Chapel Hill: young men from rural or small town North Carolina who were, more often than not, both middle class and Baptist. As is witnessed by Table 4, which lists the law schools attended by four or more of the attorneys included in the *DNCB* who were born in the last quarter of the nineteenth century, the law students who trained at Wake Forest did not, on the whole, become as prominent as those who studied at Chapel Hill. Nevertheless, this in no way lessens the impact Gulley and his Wake Forest students had on the legal profession in North Carolina.

Table 4: Law Schools Attended by Four or More *DNCB* Attorneys Born Between 1875 and 1899

University of North Carolina	53
Wake Forest	20
Harvard	11
Trinity (Duke)	7
University of Virginia	5
Columbia	4

5. Trinity College (III)

Table 4 also shows that there was one in-state law program which could produce, per capita, as many, if not more, distinguished North Carolinians as Chapel Hill, the law school at Trinity. Gulley's first law class in 1894 coincided with the closing of Trinity's second attempt at a law school; however, a decade later the Durham college again determined to start offering legal education. The instigator behind this third attempt was Trinity's President John Carlisle Kilgo, who in 1902 suggested that such a school at Trinity "would stimulate undergraduate admissions, and . . . provide a badly needed improvement in the profession." Obviously not impressed by the programs in nearby Chapel Hill and Wake Forest, Kilgo thought that another college needed to assume the responsibility for proper legal education within the state. For such to happen at Trinity, he suggested that a $100,000 endowment be secured as well as a strong five-member faculty.[341]

Kilgo was unable to secure the six-figure endowment, however in 1904 he was able to persuade the school's two major benefactors, the brothers Benjamin N. and James Buchanan Duke, to pledge $6,000 a year for a school of law. The President then set about laying the foundation of what, for North Carolina, would be a uniquely rigorous law program. Kilgo wanted to hire "a faculty of professional lawyers" who would also be "strong teachers," and "whose work would be supplemented by instruction in history and economics."[342]

The man he chose as Dean of the new school was Samuel Fox Mordecai of Raleigh, who for the past four years had given lectures on the law at Wake Forest. Mordecai (1852-1927) was the scion of a very impressive Jewish family with ties to both North Carolina and Virginia. A grandfather, Moses Mordecai, was one of Raleigh's most impressive attorneys, as was Moses's younger half-brother George W. Mordecai, who was also Samuel's guardian.

Samuel Mordecai attended the University of Virginia and was licensed to practice law by the North Carolina Supreme Court in 1875. Settling in Raleigh, he formed a partnership with William H. Battle's son R.H. which lasted for thirty years. It was said that during those years, "No lawyer in the state was more successful than he, and no lawyer had more completely devoted his life to the scientific study of the science and profession." In 1897 Mordecai published his first legal treatise, *Mechanic's Liens*, followed two years later by *Negotiable Instruments Law in North Carolina*.[343]

A serious student of the law with two legal treatises to his name as well as four years of teaching and a highly successful thirty-year practice, Mordecai appeared to be an ideal fit for Trinity. One potential problem, however, was his religion, for he came from Jewish forebears who had converted to Episcopalianism in the nineteenth century. Mordecai was "not much given to formal religion" and laughingly called himself an "Episcopal Jew," yet he also realized that Trinity was a staunch Methodist institution. At some point during the interview process, Mordecai raised the question of his religion, and President Kilgo to his great credit responded, "I am not hunting for a churchman, but for a lawyer." Thus reassured, Mordecai agreed to the Deanship, and he would later describe himself, referencing both the Wake Forest and Trinity positions, as a "Methodist, Episcopal, Baptist Jew."[344]

As this self-description suggests, Mordecai was a first-class character; one person has described the new Dean as "a punster, a collector of dogs, an untidy dresser, and the composer of execrable doggerel." The white bearded Mordecai could at times be quite profane, and he "delighted in writing clever prose and mediocre poetry." As for the dogs, the most celebrated was "a dachshund named Pompey Ducklegs, who could allegedly chew tobacco with the aplomb of his master." All in all, Mordecai's "personal charm and learned discourses endeared him to the college community."[345]

Although Trinity's new Dean was "perhaps as famous for his wit and erudition as for his legal ability," it was because of the latter that he was chosen for the position. Mordecai possessed a "cutting mind" with a "near-encyclopedic" knowledge of the law, and he was "always reading and discovering new things in the law and . . . continually working on some subject." During his twenty-three years in Durham, Mordecai continued to publish scholarly works, including a casebook on Remedies (with McIntosh), works on Real Property and Second Blackstone, his *Law Notes*, "a resumé of all the law covered in the various case books taught at Trinity," and Mordecai's *Law Lectures*, an invaluable thirteen-hundred-page reference book "of North Carolina Law with the cases of authority cited." In 1916, one commentator wrote that "Mr. Mordecai has perhaps written and published more law books than any North Carolina author."[346]

While no one could deny that Mordecai was "a first-rate legal scholar," he was also exceptionally valuable to Trinity because he "loved to teach." One former student remembered him as a "thoroughbred teacher" who knew "how to approach the student, how to excite his interest, and how to command the preparation of his work." While Mordecai's "dynamic lectures . . . provided the basis of [Trinity's] growing reputation," his actions towards his students outside of the classroom were also admirable. An alumnus wrote that the Dean's "chief asset" was the personal interest he showed "in every law student. He talks with the students, walks with them, and frequently invites them to dine with him. One of the most pleasant things about the course in law at Trinity College is that of having the dean visit the students, and in turn the students visit the dean, and discuss such matters as are of common interest."[347] In all, a better choice for heading Trinity's third attempt at starting a law school could not have been made.

Although President Kilgo initially wished to hire four full-time instructors to teach under the new Dean, economic considerations reduced this number to two, both of whom were practicing law within North Carolina when they were hired. For one of these positions, Kilgo and Mordecai chose Atwell Campbell McIntosh, a forty-five-year-old attorney from Taylorsville who had graduated from Davidson in 1881, taught school in several states, and then read law under Judge David Schenck and B.C. Cobb. Following his Dean's lead, while teaching at Trinity McIntosh showed an interest in legal scholarship, publishing casebooks on Remedies (with Mordecai) and Contracts. In 1910 he left Trinity to accept a like position at Chapel Hill, where he would teach until his retirement in 1934. At Trinity, he was replaced by an R.G. Anderson.[348]

The second hire was R.P. Roade, a "brilliant young lawyer of Durham" who had received an LL.B. from the University of Michigan. Like the subordinate positions at Chapel Hill, the two Assistant Professorships at Trinity must not have been seen, at least at first, as long-term positions—either that, or Mordecai was a hard man for whom to work—for by 1916 Roade and Anderson had left Trinity, and been replaced by W.S. Lockhart and H.G. Hedrick, both of whom had received their undergraduate and legal training at Trinity in addition to studying law at Harvard.[349]

After assembling his first faculty in 1904, Mordecai travelled north to visit some of the nation's major law schools, principally to gain information on whether to use the case method or the older treatise-lecture method. He returned to Durham with the decided and firm conviction that the case method ought to be employed, even though he recognized that it was "hard on the dull student, required better prepared teachers, and took more time." In return, however, the Dean felt that by use of the case method "a bright man would be[come] a better lawyer."[350]

The use of the case method evinced Mordecai's determination to form the Trinity law program into one of the nation's most rigorous. This was also seen in the admissions standard Mordecai set of two years of prior college work, a uniquely high requirement for a Southern law program. In addition, Mordecai saw that the law school's library was well stocked, and in 1906 Trinity became only the second Southern institution to gain admittance into the AALS.

Mordecai's "course was designed primarily to prepare men in two years for the state bar," and this it did extraordinarily well, for in 1916 it was reported that Trinity had yet to see one of its men fail the North Carolina bar examination. Of course it should be noted that not only were those coming out of Trinity the products of at least four years of higher education, but they were also many fewer in number than those coming from both Chapel Hill and Wake Forest. From the start, Mordecai and his professors showed "a preoccupation with high standards and an indifference to numbers." Seven men, all from North Carolina, were in the first Trinity class, which studied at Durham from 1904 to 1906, and by 1910 the total enrollment had risen to only seventeen. Such small numbers continued over the following decade, for between 1910 and 1918 Trinity averaged nineteen students a year. While most of these students stayed the entire two years, Mordecai and Trinity required three years of legal study for a student to earn an LL.B.—an odd requirement considering that the Durham school offered only the two year course. It is not surprising, therefore, that from its opening in 1904 until Trinity College became Duke University in 1924, only two men were awarded a Trinity LL.B., both of whom studied for a third year at Harvard.[351]

While its enrollment may have been quite small, Trinity set the pace for North Carolina law schools in a number of areas, including setting high admissions standards, employing the case method, and encouraging, if not demanding, faculty scholarship. Unlike Trinity's previous attempts, with the proper financial backing and the guiding hand of Samuel F. Mordecai, the college's third attempt at legal education proved permanent, and its proud descendant is now the Duke University School of Law.

6. A Hybrid in Wilmington

In many ways Trinity's law school was vastly different from anything ever seen in the North Carolina, as was the other institution formed in the early decades of the twentieth century, the Wilmington Law School. On July 3, 1913, three young Wilmington attorneys, William F. Jones (President), Henry E. Rodgers (Vice President), and Walter C. Benson (Secretary-Treasurer), incorporated such an institution, stating that its purpose was "not solely to prepare candidates for bar examinations, but to teach the law as a practical science to all who desire[] instruction therein, whether intending to practice law or not." The first class was held on September 10, 1913, and the school initially had only one instructor, its Vice President and Dean, Henry Edmund Rodgers.

Rodgers (1885-1969) was a twenty-eight-year-old native of Ohio who graduated from Denison University in 1909 and received an LL.B. from the University of Pennsylvania in 1913. The law program he taught was initially "a two-year course of 40 weeks each," although a third year of studies was added sometime thereafter. "Classes were held on Monday and Thursday evenings for three hours, with no vacation and no holidays except Thanksgiving and Christmas days. The tuition was $12 monthly with a $5 diploma fee."

As for the curriculum, it was quite standard, for after the school expanded to three years the first-year students would study "Blackstone, wills, administration, contracts, agency, bailments and carriers, partnership, torts, sales and personal property." This was followed the next year by instruction on "real property, mortgages, equity, trusts, criminal law and procedure, civil procedure, North Carolina cases and statutes, corporations, and domestic relations." Finally, the third-year students would study "constitutional law and [the] federal Constitution, legal ethics, bankruptcy, insurance, evidence, [the] North Carolina Constitution, guaranty and surety, conflict of laws and negotiable instruments."

During its twenty-nine-year existence, the school was held in three Wilmington locations: the Masonic Temple (1913-1917), the Garrell Building (1917-1928), and the Murchison Building (1928-1941). Rodgers used a combination of textbooks and casebooks to teach his students, and "[a]s each subject was completed, thorough written examinations were held[;] at the end of the term an examination was given on the work of the entire term." Such instruction must have proved successful, for the school's 1926-1927 brochure boasted that "the Wilmington Law School has the distinction of having had all of its graduates pass the examination before the [North Carolina] Supreme Court." It is unknown how many students eventually attended the school, although one person has compiled a list of sixty alumni who later practiced in Wilmington, including forty-four who earned the institution's LL.B.[352]

In many ways the Wilmington Law School harkened back to North Carolina's strong proprietary tradition, for it was not affiliated with any larger institution and the most instructors it had at any given time was two. In several other ways, however, the school was quite unlike the earlier proprietary institutions; it was a corporation with a set of officers, it had the right to confer degrees, the school's Dean was northern born and educated, and classes were held at night, thus allowing its attendees to hold daytime employment.

In addition, the Wilmington Law School was far ahead of the state's university law schools in that it was co-educational.

At the time of the school's opening, there was only one female lawyer within the entire state of North Carolina. The first woman licensed to practice law within the Old North State had been Tabitha Anne Holton (1854-1886), who studied law alongside her brothers and then surprised the state when she appeared before the North Carolina Supreme Court in 1878 seeking admission to the bar. This action caused great consternation, yet despite the decided opposition of William Horn Battle the court agreed to test Holton, who supposedly answered every question correctly. A Raleigh paper commented at the time: "we certainly admire this noble little woman's pluck, if we can't say so much for her judgment." Although she had initially planned to immigrate to Kansas, Holton stayed within the state and conducted an office practice before dying of tuberculosis at the age of thirty-two.[353]

Despite Holton's licensure, it was thirty-three years before another North Carolina woman would attempt to gain admittance to the state bar. This second attorney was Lilian Rowe Fry, who was licensed in 1911 after being the first woman to study law at Chapel Hill. Three years later, Fry was joined at the bar by Julia McGehee Alexander, a Congressman's daughter who studied law at Columbia, the University of Michigan, and the University of North Carolina, where she was the President of her class. The first woman to earn an LL.B. from Chapel Hill was Margaret Berry Street, who attained this distinction in 1915. Thus, the state university allowed women to study at, and graduate from, its law school as early as the 1910s; however, well into the 1930s most of the school's classes contained no female law students, and there were only five female LL.B.s through 1935.[354]

As for the state's other two university law schools, they were even slower than Chapel Hill in admitting women. The Wake Forest Board of Trustees in 1915 voted not to admit women, although two non-enrolled women, who were wives of students, attended that year's summer course. The following year, Needham Gulley told the Trustees: "It would be wiser for most women to keep out of the profession, but they are coming in. The Baptists have no school in which they can be taught. It seems to me that [admitting women to Wake Forest's law school] demands serious consideration." While this plea did not change the opinion of the Board, over the following decade Gulley continued to allow a handful of non-enrolled women to attend his lectures, two of whom passed the state bar exam in 1927. That June, the Wake Trustees finally allowed women to enroll in the law school, and the following year saw the school's first female LL.B. As for Trinity/Duke, it was even slower than Wake Forest, for the school did not admit its first woman until 1927, and Duke's first female graduate was in the class of 1935.[355]

As noted above, unlike the state's three university law schools, the Wilmington Law School had no qualms about admitting women, and its first female graduate, and the second woman to earn an LL.B. within North Carolina, was Rodgers's wife, Lillian Morton Baugh Rodgers. Lillian Rodgers (1870-1960) was the daughter of a Governor of Pennsylvania, and she was also fifteen years her husband's senior. The most notable aspect of her life, however, was that after graduating from the Wilmington Law School in 1918, she joined her husband on the school's faculty, thus becoming the state's first female law professor, decades before the hiring of a female instructor was even contemplated at the state's other law schools.[356]

The Rodgerses, who were also law partners, conducted the Wilmington Law School until 1941, when the school closed its doors because of declining enrollment, many prospective students having been lured away by World War II.[357] Because it did not survive, few people now have ever heard of the Wilmington Law School, yet the school should be remembered within the state's legal community, both as a unique institution in twentieth century North Carolina, and for its role in promoting women in the practice and teaching of law.

* * * * *

Two years before the Wilmington Law School closed its doors, in 1939, the state witnessed the founding of a fifth law school, at the predominantly black North Carolina Central University in Durham. In many ways the school at Central was a descendant of the law program at Shaw, and it proved quite valuable to the state's African American community, especially in the years before the state's other law schools were fully integrated. The final North Carolina law school to be established was at Campbell University in Buies Creek, in 1975. If North Carolina Central harkened back to Shaw, the law school at Campbell in many ways reminds one of the early Wake Forest program, especially in its Baptist affiliation and its emphasis on teaching North Carolina law.

In addition to the founding of law schools at North Carolina Central and Campbell, the final eight decades of the twentieth century witnessed a large expansion of the law programs at the University of North Carolina, Wake Forest, and Duke. Recent figures show that the state's five law schools collectively employ 216 full-time faculty members to teach 2,471 students. This legal education is no longer the sole province of white males, for 46.1% of these students are female, and 21.2% are minorities. The state's programs, especially its "Big Three," have grown not only in size, but also reputation, for the latest *U.S. News and World Report* rankings of the nation's 174 accredited law programs show Duke (#11), the University of North Carolina (#25), and Wake Forest (#34) all well within the nation's "first tier" of law schools.[358]

While such growth has been both substantial and impressive, the actual structure of legal education within North Carolina has changed very little since 1920. This is especially true when compared to the revolutionary structural changes which occurred over the eight decades leading up to that date. If Lucius Polk McGehee could visit North Carolina today, he would instantly recognize the law program at Chapel Hill as the fruition of the small program he nurtured seventy-five years ago. By contrast, his grandfather's legal mentor, John Stanly, might have some difficulty in immediately comprehending what has transpired in North Carolina legal education in the 165 years since his death.

Conclusion: Trends

As was noted in the introduction and referenced throughout this article, the sketches in the *Dictionary of North Carolina Biography* of the 610 attorneys who were born between 1775 and 1899 are an excellent source for tracking the vast changes in North Carolina legal education over the nineteenth century. While the numbers extracted may not exactly match those for the bar as a whole,[359] they are the best approximation currently available, and they readily show the profound transformations that happened over the course of the century.

For purposes of comparison, one can divide the 1775-1899 period into five twenty-five-year blocks, and Table 5 lists how many of the 610 attorneys were born within each of these periods, and how many of these attorneys attended a college for at least one term before beginning their legal studies. Most importantly, the table also quantifies, within each period, how many of the attorneys received their legal education by each of the three basic methods: reading law in a private law office, studying at a proprietary law school, and attending a university law school (note that some individuals received their legal education by more than one method).

Table 5: Undergraduate and Legal Education of the *DNCB* Attorneys

Year Born	*#*	*# College (%)*	*Legal Education*	*# Read*	*# Prop LS*	*# Univ LS*
1775-1799	75	57 (76.0%)	45	5	1	25
1800-1824	146	107 (73.3%)	90	21	11	32
1825-1849	135	94 (69.6%)	57	31	32	24
1850-1874	140	101 (72.1%)	45	30	69	10
1875-1899	114	92 (80.7%)	10	0	102	8
Total	610	451 (73.9%)	247	87	215	99

Although the percentages might be slightly lower for the bar as a whole, the *DNCB* numbers show that throughout the nineteenth century the majority of North Carolina attorneys received at least some college education before beginning their legal instruction. While it would be expected that members of the bar would be among a state's best educated, the figures also show a subtler, more interesting, trend—one that might run counter to common wisdom. Because of the great strides made in higher education over the nineteenth century, one might expect that the percentage of those attending college would successively increase during each twenty-five year period. Such is not the case, however, for the percentages decrease in the second and third periods, only to reverse course and increase in the final two—with only the percentage for those born in the last quarter of the nineteenth century eclipsing the percentage for those born in the last twenty-five years of the eighteenth century.

The reason for this undulation appears to be that in the first few decades of the nineteenth century the bar was the province of the upper class, and these young men would almost invariably attend the state university, if not Princeton or Yale, before heading to a well respected lawyer's office to read for the bar. As the century progressed, a greater number of young men were attracted to the law, especially those of the middle class who wished to gain social, economic, and political success. These were men who may not have been able to afford college and who definitely valued an education more practical than classical. Thus, as the bar became larger, the percentage of attorneys with college educations decreased. Of course, the antebellum period also saw the founding of several important private colleges, institutions which, like the state university, enlarged and strengthened in the final three decades of the nineteenth century. Thus, the overall number of persons attending college increased steadily after Reconstruction, and during this time university legal education was also coming to the fore, thus allowing an increasing number of young men to receive their collegiate and legal educations at the same institution. It is, therefore, no surprise that the number of attorneys with college educations increased in the late nineteenth and early twentieth centuries.

As for where these *DNCB* attorneys received their undergraduate instruction, Table 6 lists the nine institutions attended by five or more of these individuals. As would be expected, Chapel Hill was by far the most popular choice, distantly followed by the state's three leading private colleges, Wake Forest, Trinity, and Davidson, and three noted institutions to the north, Princeton, Yale, and the University of Virginia.

TABLE 6: UNDERGRADUATE COLLEGES ATTENDED BY THE *DNCB* ATTORNEYS (5 OR MORE ATTENDEES)

North Carolina	278
Wake Forest	40
Trinity (Duke)	22
Princeton	22
Davidson	16
Yale	9
Virginia	8
Trinity (Conn.)	7
West Point	6

For our purposes, however, the most important figures from Table 5 do not concern the collegiate education of the *DNCB* attorneys, but, rather, how they received their legal education. Using information from the *DNCB* as well as other sources,[360] one can divine how 511 of the 610 attorneys received their legal education. This information has been quantified in Table 5, and using the number of attorneys whose method of legal instruction is known as the denominator, one can calculate the percentage of *DNCB* attorneys within each period who received their education by each of the three methods. This information is shown in Table 7, which is, by far, this study's most vivid indicator of the gradual yet drastic changes which occurred in North Carolina legal education from 1800 until the early decades of the twentieth century. (Again, note that the cumulative percentages for each time period will be slightly more than 100%, since a few attorneys used more than one method to learn the law.)

Table 7: Legal Education of the *DNCB* Attorneys Whose Schooling Is Known

Year Born	*% Read Law*	*% Prop LS*	*% Univ LS*
1775-1799	90.0	10.0	2.0
1800-1824	78.9	18.4	9.6
1825-1849	51.4	27.9	28.8
1850-1874	34.6	23.1	53.1
1875-1899	9.4	0.0	96.2

These figures strikingly show that the apprenticeship system was almost universally employed at the start of the nineteenth century, only to steadily decrease in popularity until fewer than ten percent of would-be attorneys were reading law a century later. By contrast, university legal education went from being nearly nonexistent in 1800 to being the overwhelming norm in the first decades of the twentieth century. The figures also show that proprietary legal education was the most popular form of institutional legal education over the first half of this period, thus suggesting that the proprietary schools were more important than the universities in establishing the institutionalization; although they were eventually supplanted by university law schools, the proprietary schools remained important until the last decade of the century.

As for the actual university and proprietary law schools attended by the *DNCB* attorneys, these are listed in Table 8. Again, as would be expected the state university was, by far, the most popular university law school, followed by Wake Forest, Virginia, and Harvard. It is also no surprise that Richmond Hill was the most popular proprietary institution.

Table 8: Institutions Where the *DNCB* Attorneys Studied Law

University Law Schools	
North Carolina	122
Wake Forest	24
Virginia	21
Harvard	19
Trinity (Duke)	13
Columbia	10
Geo. Washington	3
Michigan	3
Yale	2
William & Mary	2
Oxford	2
South Carolina	2
Shaw	2
Cumberland	2
Howard	1
Georgia	1
Georgetown	1
Louisville	1
Kentucky	1
Wash. & Lee	1
Texas	1
Pennsylvania	1
Vanderbilt	1
Minnesota	1
Proprietary Law Schools	
R. M. Pearson (Richmond Hill)	43
Dick & Dillard (Greensboro)	14
John L. Bailey	10
Litchfield	6
Leonard Henderson	5
G. N. Folk	5
George V. Strong	2
William H. Battle	2
John Louis Taylor	2
Winchester (Tucker)	1
Lexington (Brockenbro')	1

While the basic themes of the North Carolina transformation are easy to describe, it remains to be seen whether this pattern was similar to what transpired in other states. At first blush, it appears that the North Carolina experience fits nicely within the overall national pattern, yet full confirmation of this will have to wait until many additional studies are written, both on the transformation within the nation as a whole and on what happened within various states.

As for what the North Carolina experience adds to Southern legal history, this too is difficult to gauge absent detailed studies of legal education in at least several of the other states. The transformation in the Tarheel State, however, does cast at least some doubt on the assumptions Paul Finkelman has made concerning Southern legal education—that the South initially led the nation in legal education only to fall behind the North by the time of the Civil War, and that "the energies of leading southerners in the antebellum period were directed to politics and the defense of slavery[; l]aw teaching was not a high priority for the leading legal minds of the South."[361]

While America's first university law school was at William & Mary, apparently only one North Carolinian ventured north to Williamsburg to learn at the feet of George Wythe, and such institutionalization did not in any way find its way south for many decades. Thus, far from being a trend setter, North Carolina legal education at the turn of the nineteenth century appears about on par with that in most of the nation. Sixty years later, however, it is at least arguable that the legal education available in the Old North State, especially at the various schools conducted by the judges of the state Supreme Court, was actually somewhat in advance of that available in many other states.[362]

In addition, it is clear that during the secession crisis the large majority of the state's leading attorneys and judges were strong Unionists, at least until Lincoln's call for troops, and unlike law teachers from the Deep South such as Georgia's Thomas R.R. Cobb, the state's foremost legal educators, most notably Pearson, Battle, and Bailey, invested their energy in teaching the law, not in precipitating a sectional crisis.

While this might suggest that during the late antebellum period there was a difference in the type of men who conducted the legal education in the upper South vis-à-vis the lower South, mirroring the regions' different views on secession, what evidence there is suggests that even states within the same subregion had quite different experiences in legal education. By far the most thorough history of legal education of any one state is the work produced by W. Hamilton Bryson on the developments in Virginia from 1779 to 1979,[363] and even a cursory glance through this impressive 774-page volume makes it clear that the development of institutional legal education took a far different path in the Old Dominion than it did in her sister state to the south.

As noted above, America's first university law school was formed at William & Mary in 1779, and in 1826 it was joined by the law program at the University of Virginia, which soon became recognized as the South's premier institution for legal education. In addition, the Commonwealth was home to six major proprietary law schools, all but one of which were formed in the years between St. George Tucker's resignation at William & Mary in 1804 and the 1845 hiring of John B. Minor at the University of Virginia; the other proprietary school was operated by Judge John White Brockenbrough in Lexington from 1849 until it became incorporated into Washington & Lee University shortly after the Civil War.

Thus, Virginia's first university law program was opened sixty-six years before William Horn Battle began teaching at the University of North Carolina, by which time the Commonwealth boasted yet another university law school. In Virginia, the institutionalization of legal education was led by the universities, not the proprietary schools, yet when the universities failed in their mission to provide superior legal instruction, various leading attorneys, most of whom were judges, stepped forward to form the necessary proprietary institutions. At the time, these schools were both more numerous and much larger than their counterparts in North Carolina; for example thirty to forty students were studying with Henry St. George Tucker in Winchester in the late 1820s, at a time when the leading North Carolina proprietary teacher, Leonard Henderson, had room for only five pupils at his Granville County school. North Carolina eventually developed a strong proprietary tradition, yet by the time of its full flowering in the 1870s, all of Virginia's institutional legal education was again conducted by her universities. Thus, compared to North Carolina, institutionalization happened both much earlier and in an entirely different manner in the Commonwealth of Virginia.

Other differences between North Carolina and her neighbors are also apparent, for example in the colonial era eighty-nine South Carolinians and seventy-six Virginians studied at the Inns of Court in London, compared to only eleven North Carolinians. A generation later when seventy Georgians and

TABLE 9: NORTH CAROLINA LAW SCHOOLS (PROPRIETARY AND UNIVERSITY)

Name/proprietor	*Location*	*Date Started*	*Date Closed*
Leonard Henderson	Granville Co.	1808(?)	1833(?)
John Louis Taylor	Raleigh	1822	1829(?)
Richard T. Brumby	Lincoln Co.	1829	1831
Archibald D. Murphey	Hillsborough	1831	1832
Richmond M. Pearson	Mocksville/Richmond Hill, Yadkin Co.	1836(?)	1878
William H. Battle & James Iredell, Jr.	Raleigh	1841	1843
Frederick Nash & Hugh Waddell	Hillsborough	1842	1845(?)
William H. Battle & David L. Swain	Chapel Hill	1843	1845
John L. Bailey & Frederick Nash	Hillsborough	1845	1858(?)
University of North Carolina	Chapel Hill	1845	1868
John L. Bailey & William H. Bailey	Black Mountain	1859	1861(?)
John L. Bailey	Asheville	1865	1877(?)
George N. Folk	Lenoir/Caldwell Co./ Boone/Blowing Rock	1866	1895
Trinity College/Duke University	Randolph Co.	1868	1882
Trinity College/Duke University	Randolph Co./Raleigh(?)	1891	1894
Duke University	Durham	1904	open
Rutherford College	Burke Co.	1871	1884
George V. Strong	Raleigh	1876(?)	1890s(?)
University of North Carolina	Chapel Hill	1877	open
Dick & Dillard/ Greensboro Law School	Greensboro	1878	1893
Edward P. Cantwell	Wilmington	1878	(?)
Shaw University	Raleigh	1888	1914
Wake Forest College/University	Wake Forest/Winston-Salem	1894	open
Alphonso C. Avery	Morganton	1897	(?)
Wilmington Law School	Wilmington	1913	1941
North Carolina Central University	Durham	1939	open
Campbell University	Buies Creek	1975	open

forty-five young men from South Carolina received the nation's best legal education at the Litchfield Law School, they were joined by only twenty-three residents of the Old North State. The reasons for such disparities will be left for future scholars, although it is worth noting that North Carolina has always been perceived as possessing a society less aristocratic than its immediate neighbors to the north and south—"a vale of humility between two mountains of conceit," according to one popular saying.

While the Virginia bench and bar were clearly superior to North Carolina's in the colonial, Revolutionary, and early Federal periods, this was not the case in the decades leading up to the Civil War; in some ways the antebellum North Carolina bar could even be seen as superior to Virginia's, for after the 1830s the Old Dominion could not claim a jurist as renowned as Thomas Ruffin, nor an advocate as learned and skilled as George E. Badger. Why the Virginia bar was unable to maintain its superiority is an interesting question that will also be left for the future.

For now, it is enough to note the efforts of the disparate men who spent countless hours educating the attorneys who would follow, whether it was in discussing the law one-on-one with an apprentice in a small rural law office, supervising the reading of a handful of students in a proprietary school, or lecturing to 100 students in a university classroom. Table 9 lists all known institutions in North Carolina history which could possibly be labeled as law schools, and one person's "top ten" list of all North Carolina law teachers, whether in an institutional setting or not, might read, in rough chronological order: William Gaston, Archibald D. Murphey, Leonard Henderson, Richmond M. Pearson, William H. Battle, John L. Bailey, Robert P. Dick, John Manning, Needham Y. Gulley, and Samuel F. Mordecai. All ten, as well as many others, were far-sighted individuals who cared deeply about legal education within the Old North State. Each built upon his predecessors' accomplishments, and this has continued to the present day such that students now come from every state in the union to receive their legal education in North Carolina.

NOTES

1. See, e.g., Alfred Zantzinger Reed, *Training for the Public Profession of the Law* (1921); Anton-Hermann Chroust, *The Rise of the Legal Profession in America* (1965); William R. Johnson, *Schooled Lawyers: A Study in the Clash of Professional Cultures* (1978), specifically on developments in Wisconsin; Robert B. Stevens, *Law School: Legal Education in America from the 1850s to the 1980s* (1983), focusing on Harvard; W. Hamilton Bryson, *Legal Education in Virginia, 1779-1979: A Biographical Approach* (1982). One scholar has recently stated, "One of the striking facts about the literature of American history is the scarcity of works on . . . legal education." She adds that "[l]ittle work" has been published on the apprenticeship system, and "the role of the private law school is virtually a *terra incognita*." Merian C. McKenna, *Tapping Reeve and The Litchfield Law School* (1986), ix.

2. Paul Finkelman, "Essay: Exploring Southern Legal History," 64 *N.C. L. Rev.* 77 (1985).

3. *Id.* at 78-84.

4. *Id.* at 116.

5. *Id.* at 111-13.

6. Carl B. Swisher, *The Taney Period: 1836-64*, Vol. V of the Oliver Wendell Holmes Devise History of the Supreme Court of the United States (1974), 241; Roscoe Pound, *The Formative Era of American Law* (1938), 3, 4, 30. The definitive biography of Ruffin, who served on the court from 1829 to 1852 and 1858 to 1859, has yet to be written, although early this century his papers were collected and published in four volumes. *The Papers of Thomas Ruffin*, ed. J.G. deRoulhac Hamilton (1918-1920). See also Blackwell P. Robinson, "Thomas Ruffin," *Dictionary of North Carolina Biography* (1979-1996), V, 266-68 (hereafter referred to as *DNCB*). For a good overview of his court's views on slavery, see Julius Yanuck, "Thomas Ruffin and the North Carolina Slave Law," 21 *J. S. Hist.* 456 (1955).

7. On Gaston, see Robert D.W. Connor, *William Gaston: A Southern Federalist of the Old School and His Yankee Friends* (1934); J. Herman Schauinger, *William Gaston, Carolinian* (1949); Charles H. Bowman, Jr., "William Joseph Gaston," *DNCB, supra* note 6, at II, 283-85; and the William Gaston Papers, Southern Historical Collection, University of North Carolina, including John Marshall to Gaston, November 9, 1831, and July 22, 1832, and James Kent to Gaston, February 3, and June 12, 1834.

8. The author is currently completing the first full-scale biography of Badger. See also William A. Graham, *Discourse in Memory of the Life and Character of the Hon. Geo. E. Badger* (1866), reprinted in *The Papers of William Alexander Graham*, eds. J.G. deRoulhac Hamilton, Max R. Williams, et al. (1957-1992), VII, 161-79; Lawrence Foushee London, "The Public Career of George Edmund Badger" (unpublished doctoral dissertation, University of North Carolina, 1936), and "George Edmund Badger," *DNCB, supra* note 6, at I, 79-80; Thomas Rogers Hunter, "George Edmund Badger, 1795-1866: A North Carolinian's Life in Politics and the Law" (unpublished master's thesis, University of Virginia, 1990).

9. Author's analysis of the *North Carolina Reports* from 1825 until 1863: 10 N.C. (3 Hawks) through 59 N.C. (6 Jones Eq.). After 1846, when Badger was serving in the United States Senate and then concentrating his practice before the U.S. Supreme Court, he nevertheless argued an additional forty-nine cases before the North Carolina Supreme Court, with his last case coming during the June 1862 term.

10. *Vicksburg Herald*, May 1866, quoted in the Raleigh *Sentinel*, June 1, 1866. For just a few of the many comments made by his colleagues in Congress concerning Badger's great legal ability, see *Congressional Globe*, 30 Cong., 1 Sess., 91, App. 862, 31 Cong., 1 Sess., App. 1595, 2 Sess., 517, 32 Cong., 1 Sess., 1340, 2183, 33 Cong., 1 Sess., 316, App. 290, 2 Sess., 326, 621. Thomas Hart Benton considered Badger the nation's foremost authority on the common law. Kemp Plummer Battle, *Memories of an Old-Time Tar Heel* (1945), 141. In addition, in a letter of introduction to Justice Joseph Story, Daniel Webster wrote that Badger was Story's legal equal and Webster's superior. Raleigh *Intelligencer*, April 15, 1891; New York *Watchman*, date unknown, in Scrapbook of Badger Material, North Carolina Collection, University of North Carolina, 17.

11. New York *Tribune*, January 8, 1853; *Vicksburg Whig*, February 10, 1853.

12. Although no one could deny Badger's qualifications for the U.S. Supreme Court, a number of political factors weighed against his confirmation, the most important being that Fillmore was a lame duck Whig president who would be replaced by Democrat Franklin Pierce in less than two months, Badger was a highly partisan Whig at a time when the Democrats controlled the Senate by thirteen votes, Badger's ardent nationalism concerned many Southern Democrats, and Badger was not a resident of the judicial circuit in which he would have to hold federal circuit court—as was a tradition. After a month of debate, the

nomination was "postponed" by a one-vote margin; to this day, Badger is the only sitting U.S. senator ever to have been rejected by the Senate for a seat upon the high court. On the nomination, see Hunter, "Badger," *supra* note 8, at 314-46.

13. The first of these was *Hoke v. Henderson*, 15 N.C. (4 Dev.) 1 (1834), wherein Ruffin held that a public official possesses a property interest in his job, and thus under the state constitution cannot be deprived of the position without use of the law of the land. For an excellent discussion of *Hoke*, although it does not mention the role of the attorneys in the case, see Walter F. Pratt, Jr., "The Struggle for Judicial Independence in Antebellum North Carolina: The Story of Two Judges," 4 *Law & Hist. Rev.* 129 (1986).

Hoke "received the high encomium of [James] Kent and other authors on constitutional law," and it was the main authority Reverdy Johnson used in his argument before the Supreme Court in *Ex parte Garland*, 71 U.S. (4 Wall.) 333 (1867), against the constitutionality of Congress' test oath designed to exclude those who had served the Confederacy from arguing cases before the U.S. Supreme Court. William A. Graham, *Life and Character of the Hon. Thomas Ruffin, Late Chief Justice of North Carolina* (1871), reprinted in *Ruffin Papers*, *supra* note 6, at I, 29. Kent specifically noted that *Hoke* was "replete with sound constitutional doctrine." James Kent, *Commentaries on American Law*, ed. Charles M. Barnes (13 ed. 1884), II, 13 n.(b), see also *id.* at III, 454 n.(c), 457 n.(a).

On the other hand, *Hoke* was never followed by another state, and one nineteenth-century court held that the decision "stands out in strong contrast . . . to every published decision and opinion on the subject which we have seen," *Conner v. Mayor of New York*, 2 Sandf. 355, 373 (N.Y. Super. Ct. 1849), *aff'd* 5 N.Y. 285 (1851), quoted in Pratt, "Struggle for Judicial Independence," at 149 n.110, while another described the doctrine as being "without support of reason or authority." *Alexander v. McKenzie*, 2 S.C. 81, 92 (1870). In North Carolina, the use of *Hoke* by the state Supreme Court to preserve the offices of various Republicans and Populists after the Democrats regained control of the state government in 1898 caused much controversy, and the case was finally overturned in an acrimonious three-to-two decision in *Mial v. Ellington*, 134 N.C. 131 (1903). On *Hoke*, see also Edward S. Corwin, *Liberty Against Government* (1948), 94-95, and "The Doctrine of Due Process of Law Before the Civil War," 24 *Harv. L. Rev.* 366, 383-84 (1911); Harold M. Hyman and William C. Wiecek, *Equal Justice Under Law: Constitutional Developments, 1835-1875* (1982), 23.

The second case was *Raleigh and Gaston Rail Road Company v. Davis*, 19 N.C. (2 Dev. & Bat.) 451 (1837), wherein Ruffin for the court agreed with Badger that, under the North Carolina constitution, the state government could use its powers of eminent domain to take land from private citizens for the use of a private corporation, should the corporation, in this case a railroad, be formed to provide a public benefit.

14. The other case was *State v. Mann*, which attracted international attention. In *Mann*, Ruffin held that in terms of punishment, "[t]he power of the master must be absolute to render the submission of the slave perfect. . . . [However,] as a principle of moral right every person in his retirement must repudiate it." 13 N.C. (2 Dev.) 263, 266 (1829). J.G. deRoulhac Hamilton in his sketch of Ruffin for the *Dictionary of American Biography* mentions only *Hoke*, *Davis*, and *Mann*, as does Blackwell P. Robinson in his Ruffin sketch for the *Dictionary of North Carolina Biography*. "Thomas Ruffin," *Dictionary of American Biography*, eds. Allen Johnson, Dumas Malone, et al. (1929-1936), XVI, 217; Robinson, "Thomas Ruffin," *DNCB*, *supra* note 6, at V, 267. Also, the only Ruffin opinion specifically mentioned by William A. Graham in his Ruffin eulogy was *Hoke*. *Ruffin Papers*, *supra* note 6, at I, 29.

15. While the sketches in the *DNCB* do a generally good job of including where a person received his legal education, they are necessarily incomplete, and when available, this information has been supplemented by other sources, including Samuel H. Fisher, *Litchfield Law School, 1774-1833: Biographical Catalogue of Students* (1946), showing that three additional *DNCB* individuals studied at Litchfield; Wilson Angley, *Richmond M. Pearson and the Richmond Hill Law School* (Historical Research Report for the North Carolina State Archives, 1978), six additional Richmond Hill students among those listed in the *DNCB*; Archibald Henderson, "John Bailey, Teacher of Law," and "Private Law Schools in North Carolina," Raleigh *News and Observer*, June 17, and July 1, 1928; John Gilchrist McCormick, *Personnel of the Convention of 1861* (1900).

In addition, the reader is cautioned that the legal education of those included in the *DNCB* might not be entirely representative of the legal education of all North Carolina attorneys of the time, for those included were, by definition, the most "prominent" North Carolinians, and it is possible that they benefitted by having a better legal education. Of course the reason why most of the 611 were included was not because of their legal careers but because they were notable for other activities, usually politics and public service but also war, business, the ministry, education, and philanthropy—and one need not have received the best legal education in order to succeed in these other activities. Despite its great inclusiveness, not a few of the state's finest attorneys and judges of the nineteenth century were not included in the *DNCB*, including Edward E. Graham, John L. Bailey, John M. Dick, Robert B. Gilliam, Patrick H. Winston (of Rockingham and Anson), Wright C. Stanly, Augustus Moore, John Paxton, James Martin (of Rowan), Atlas Jones, Robert H. Burton, James F. Taylor (Sr.), George C. Mendenhall, Charles R. Kinney, George W. Haywood, Priestly H. Mangum, Henry W. Miller, Robert R. Heath, Richard C. Badger, and William K. Ruffin. In addition, just because one received a first-class legal education did not necessarily mean that one would become prominent—in later years or in the eyes of history—for example, as is detailed below, of the twenty-three North Carolinians who studied at the prestigious Litchfield Law School, only six are included in the *DNCB*. After closely studying the matter, it appears that for those born in the late eighteenth and early nineteenth centuries, and who thus studied law when the bar was small and the province of the upper classes, it is likely that the *DNCB* numbers are representative of the bar as a whole. Later in the nineteenth century as the bar grew, it is fairly probable that more would-be attorneys read law or attended proprietary law schools than the *DNCB* numbers would suggest. Also, the percentage of law students who had earlier attended college might be somewhat overestimated. Nevertheless, it is important to remember that the *DNCB* numbers used below are not meant to show the legal education of the bar as a whole, but only to show the general statewide trends—and this they do extraordinarily well.

16. George Edmund Badger's Commonplace Book, 1807-1815, Perkins Library, Duke University, 50.

17. John Marshall to Archibald Debow Murphey, October 6, 1827, *The Papers of Archibald D. Murphey*, ed. William Henry Hoyt (1914), I, 365. On Stanly, see also Gertrude S. Carraway, *The Stanly (Stanley) Family and the Historic John Wright Stanley House* (1969), 23-28; Norman D. Brown, *Edward Stanly: Whiggery's Tarheel "Conqueror"* (1974), 6-28; and "John Stanly," *DNCB, supra* note 6, at V, 424-26.

18. See, e.g., Bryson, *Legal Education in Virginia, supra* note 1, at 6; Jean Edward Smith, *John Marshall: Definer of a Nation* (1996), 80, 555 n.69.

19. Commonplace Book, *supra* note 16, at 50.

20. *Id., passim*, listing: William Cruise, *A Digest of the Law Respecting Real Property*; Samuel Comyn, *A Treatise of the Law Relative to Contracts and Agreements Not Under Seal*; William Tidd, *The Practice of the Court of King's Bench, in Personal Actions: With References to Cases of Practice in the Court of Common Pleas*; Isaac Espinasse, *A Digest of the Law of Actions and Trials at Nisi Prius*; Stewart Kyd, *A Treatise on the Law of Bills of Exchange and Promissory Notes*; Joseph Chitty, *A Practical Treatise on Bills of Exchange, Checks on Bankers, Promissory Notes, Bankers' Cash Notes, and Bank Notes*; Thomas Peake, *A Compendium of the Law of Evidence*; Sir William Jones, *An Essay on the Law of Bailments*; John Haywood, *A Manual of the Laws of North Carolina*; Francois Xavier Martin, *Martin's Treatise on the Powers and Duties of Executors and Administrators, According to the Law of North Carolina*. It is unknown which editions of these works were read by Badger.

21. For sample reading lists of Virginia law students, see Bryson, *Legal Education in Virginia, supra* note 1, at 25-31. It is interesting to note that although Badger became known as a superb equity lawyer, none of his specific reading was on this side of the bar. Governor Graham recalled that although Badger's "learning in his profession was profound and necessarily the fruit of much study," he did not spend his spare moments poring over general treatises on the law. Rather, "whenever in his practice . . . his curiosity became excited on any topic, he pursued it until he had mastered it in all its ramifications,—a habit of mind, which he was accustomed to apply to other subjects, historical, literary, or scientific, to which his attention might be attracted." It helped greatly that he was an extraordinarily quick reader with an almost photographic memory. Fellow attorney Henry Seawell stated that when reading a legal text he would have to stop at the end of each sentence to make sure that he fully understood the author, but Badger could read a dense legal work "like a novel, and by the time he gets to the bottom of a page or the end of the treatise, he has in mind not only all that the author has taught, but a great deal that the author never knew." Graham, *Badger*, in *Graham Papers, supra* note 8, at VII, 167, 169.

22. See, e.g., Commonplace Book, *supra* note 16, at 85.

23. *Id.* at 200-300.

24. See, e.g., Thomas P. Devereux to William A. Graham, June 1, 1866, *Graham Papers, supra* note 8, at VII, 119-22; Graham, *Badger*, in *Graham Papers*, at VII, 165.

25. See, e.g., Commonplace Book, *supra* note 16, at 107.

26. At the time of his licensure, Badger was only nineteen years of age, two years under the required age of twenty-one. The waiving of the age requirement was almost unique in North Carolina legal history, and when asked about the decision, Judge John Louis Taylor "replied that if the clients and people who knew him best chose to trust him with their business, he saw no reason why he should interpose to prevent them." In addition, Taylor found Badger to be "a youth of great promise, [who] was poor and anxious to do something for a widowed mother and sisters." Raleigh *Sentinel*, May 15, 1866; Graham, *Badger*, in *Graham Papers, supra* note 8, at VII, 164. See also Fannie Memory Farmer, "The Bar Examination and Beginning Years of Legal Practice in North Carolina," 29 *N.C. Hist. Rev.* 159, 163-64 (1952).

27. William Hooper Haigh diary, January 5, 1844, Southern Historical Collection, University of North Carolina.

28. Badger's success was in contrast to the vast majority of young attorneys, including his father Thomas Badger, who, when he attended his first court week in the late 1780s, found himself without any clients and as "he was too poor to buy a dinner, was compelled by hunger to eat green apples from an orchard." Edward Stanly to William A. Graham, November 23, 1866, *Graham Papers, supra* note 8, at VII, 229. That a lawyer, no matter his talents, would struggle for business during his first few years of practice appears to be the norm during this period. See, e.g., Farmer, "The Bar Examination," *supra* note 26, at 168-70.

29. See James Brousard, *The Southern Federalists, 1800-1816* (1978), 379.

30. *Id.* at 295, 222. One problem with this statement is that there were more than eight men who served on the court during this time. See *North Carolina Government: 1585-1979*, ed. John L. Cheney (1981), 360.

31. Taken from analyzing the *DNCB* sketches of the sixty-five men who served during the Fourth through the Sixteenth Congresses. In addition, during the First Party System almost every leading Federalist in the state was an attorney, e.g., William Richardson Davie, William Barry Grove, Archibald Henderson, William Gaston, and John Stanly. By contrast, the leading Republican, Speaker of the U.S. House and U.S. Senator Nathaniel Macon, as well as many of the leaders of his dominant Warren Junto, such as Badger's first father-in-law Governor and U.S. Senator James Turner, were major planters, not lawyers.

32. See section II, below, for a full description of both the advantages and disadvantages of the apprenticeship system. Also, for various experiences in reading law, see Fannie Memory Farmer, "Legal Education in North Carolina, 1820-1860," 28 *N.C. Hist. Rev.* 271 (1951).

33. See note 5, *supra*.

34. Unless otherwise noted, these relationships as well as those listed below can be found in the various biographical sketches in the *DNCB, supra* note 6.

35. The reader, of course, is cautioned that just because one is at the end of an impressive educational chain, one will not

necessarily be the beneficiary of the collected wisdom of one's learned predecessors. While in elementary school, the author had a piano teacher who liked to draw for him a chart showing that he, as a music pupil, was a direct descendant of—about seven steps removed from—Ludwig van Beethoven. Unfortunately, such a distinguished teaching pedigree did nothing to help the author's own wretched piano playing.

36. Albert Coates, "A Century of Legal Education," 24 *N.C. L. Rev.* 307, 322 (1946). Murphey's far-ranging advice also attempted "to correct the foibles and follies of young men entering life ambitious of notoriety and the promptings of vanity," for he gave Paul C. Cameron "an earnest entreaty never to be seen wearing a ring, or walking with a gold-headed cane, or riding a pony." *Id.* at 322. On Murphey, see *The Papers of Archibald D. Murphey*, ed. William Henry Hoyt (1914); Herbert Snipes Turner, *The Dreamer: Archibald Debow Murphey, 1777-1832* (1971); H.G. Jones, "Archibald Debow Murphey," *DNCB, supra* note 6, at IV, 345-56; William S. Powell, *North Carolina Through Four Centuries* (1989), 253-66.

37. See the *Ruffin Papers, supra* note 6, for numerous references to students reading law under Ruffin.

38. Another impressive thread begins with Chief Justice John Louis Taylor, who in his office "school" taught Governor and longtime University of North Carolina President David Lowry Swain. Swain, in turn, was the legal preceptor of state senator Nicholas W. Woodfin, who afterwards instructed the most acclaimed North Carolinian of all, Governor and U.S. Senator Zebulon Vance. Other legal training chains take ironic twists; for example, among the students of George E. Badger was Henry W. Miller, who later taught William Woods Holden. Holden, who would receive great notoriety during Reconstruction as the only North Carolina governor ever impeached and convicted, was, before the war, the vituperative editor of the Democratic Raleigh *North Carolina Standard.* In this position, one of Holden's major targets was Whig U.S. Senator Badger, and for many years the men hated each other with a passion. On the extraordinarily controversial Holden, see Edgar E. Folk and Bynum Shaw, *W.W. Holden: A Political Biography* (1982); Horace W. Raper, *William W. Holden: North Carolina's Political Enigma* (1985); William G. Harris, *William Woods Holden: Firebrand of North Carolina Politics* (1987).

39. When Ham Jones began to read law with Gaston in 1819, he joined "about ten other students." Richard Walser, "Hamilton Chamberlain Jones," *DNCB, supra* note 6, at III, 318. According to Gaston's biographer, "To all his pupils Gaston devoted himself unsparingly and patiently, giving each his earnest attention and courteous consideration." He advised William B. Meares, for example, that even after beginning a law practice he should "devote much time to study, knowledge being evanescent. He must acquire a thorough knowledge of legal science, a facility in expressing thoughts clearly, correctly, and agreeably and so arrange them as to illustrate, convince, and persuade; he must give an unremitted attention to the interests of his clients and finally have an incorruptible integrity. Gaston advised him to make plain, short briefs at first, and always to go to original sources. He must read the classics to aid his style. Finally, he warned him that the most dangerous pest of society was the wicked unprincipled lawyer, whose reason was a slave to his appetite, whose honor was but a fashionable honor, whose religion was pride, revenge, and sensuality. He felt that vice and its temptations held out more than usual allure to lawyers." Schauinger, *Gaston, supra* note 7, at 35-36.

40. Joseph Blount Cheshire, *Nonnulla: Memories, Stories, Traditions, More or Less Authentic* (1930), 123, 130.

41. *Id.* at 124; Jean Bradley Anderson, *The Kirklands of Ayr Mount* (1991), 56-57, 140.

42. Cheshire, *Nonulla, supra* note 40, at 131. Joseph Blount Cheshire, later an Episcopal bishop, read with Ruffin for several months, specifically concentrating on Second Blackstone and Cruise on Real Property. Before Cheshire departed to read for three additional months with Judge George Howard, Ruffin extracted a promise from the student to read the entire Coke on Littleton, which Ruffin considered the greatest of all legal works. Cheshire, who was given specific instructions to purchase not another man's arrangement, but "Coke on Littleton in an old edition, just as Coke published it," eventually found, in a used bookstore in Baltimore, a suitable copy that had originally been owned by U.S. Supreme Court Justice Gabriel Duvall when he was a law student in the 1770s. Cheshire later recalled that there was "an immense mass of commentary in those 789 large folio pages, difficult to read in the small black-letter characters, and very trying on the eyes." Nevertheless, he "waded conscientiously through it all, Law-French, Latin, and black-letter," and after much inquiry over the following years, Cheshire came to the conclusion that he was "the last lawyer in North Carolina who thus read Coke on Littleton from beginning to end." As for the results, he added, "There may remain in my mind some unconscious legal erudition from the months devoted to this wearisome task, though it did not make me a great lawyer." *Id.* at 131-33.

43. Coates, "Century of Legal Education," *supra* note 36, at 315; Farmer, "Legal Education in North Carolina," *supra* note 32, at 272-73. Before reading law on his own, Taylor had, in the 1780s, attended William & Mary, and although his education there has been described as "classical," it is conceivable that he attended the law lectures of George Wythe.

44. See, e.g., James M. Williamson to Thomas Ruffin, March 19, 1834, *Ruffin Papers, supra* note 6, at II, 114. Chief Justice Ruffin, like his eldest son William, thought highly of law students reading Coke on Littleton, and young James Williamson had the same opinion of this work as Joseph Blount Cheshire forty years later. See note 42 above. Williamson wrote the Chief Justice: "I have succeeded in *wading* through it now almost for the second time. I cannot say however that I have *touched bottom* in all places. I feel greatly discouraged at the very small proficiency I have made. Indeed I find that the three volumes of Coke and his commentators contain such a *mass* of curious and cunning and I might add valuable learning, that I find it as yet utterly impossible to keep up any thing like a connected view of the whole."

45. Finkelman, "Exploring Southern Legal History," *supra* note 2, at 111-12.

46. J.G. deRoulhac Hamilton, "Southern Members of the Inns of Court," 10 *N.C. Hist. Rev.* 274 (1933). On the legal education function of the Inns of Court, see Bryson, *Legal Education in Virginia, supra* note 1, at 1.

47. Daniel M. McFarland, "Kemp Plummer," *DNCB, supra* note 6, at V, 104. As noted above, Chief Justice John Louis Taylor also attended William & Mary at this time, although it is unknown if he studied with Wythe.

48. Bryson, *Legal Education in Virginia, supra* note 1, at 24-25, 37-38, 40-41.

49. On Story's success at Harvard, see R. Kent Newmyer, *Supreme Court Justice Joseph Story: Statesman of the Old Republic* (1985), 237-70. On the development of modern university legal education, see Steve Sheppard, "Casebooks, Commentaries, and Curmudgeons: An Introductory History of Law in the Lecture Hall," 82 *Iowa L. Rev.* 547 (1997). Between Tucker's resignation at William & Mary and Story's success at Harvard, the nation's leading university law school was Kentucky's Transylvania University, although David Hoffman designed an impressive law program for the University of Maryland that unfortunately never came to full fruition. See *id.* at 568-72.

50. On Jones, see Edwin A. Miles, "Joseph Seawell Jones," *DNCB, supra* note 6, at III, 322-23.

51. Cited in Farmer, "Legal Education in North Carolina," *supra* note 32, at 284. On early university legal education generally, see Paul D. Carrington, "The Revolutionary Idea of University Legal Education," 31 *Wm. & Mary L. Rev.* 527 (1990). Unlike most commentators, Carrington opines that from 1818 until its closure in 1858, the nation's "most important university law program" was at Transylvania. *Id.* at 537-38.

52. Bryson, *Legal Education in Virginia, supra* note 1, at 38-42, 417-30.

53. Samuel H. Fisher, *The Litchfield Law School, 1775-1833* (1933); McKenna, *Reeve and Litchfield, supra* note 1.

54. Nineteen North Carolina attendees are listed in A.J. Morrison, "Virginia and North Carolina at the Litchfield Law School," 2 *Tyler's Qtly.* 157-58 (1921). In addition, Samuel H. Fisher, *Litchfield Catalogue, supra* note 15, lists these nineteen plus three additional students who were definitely from North Carolina, Richard Hines, Charles George Spaight, and Josiah Collins, Jr. (III), and one who likely was, an Abraham Maer (Mayer), who was born in Bertie County in 1795 and attended the University of North Carolina for four years. In addition, a John W. Cardwell might have been from the Old North State, for Fisher states that he was of Connecticut ancestry, was "probably" born in North Carolina, and died in Georgia. Fisher's evidence also raises the possibility that one of the nineteen listed by Morrison, Arthur O'Hara, might have actually been from South Carolina, for nothing connecting him to North Carolina is listed, but he attended South Carolina College and was married in Charleston.

55. Morrison, *North Carolina at Litchfield, supra* note 54, at 157. Morrison's following statement is, "We may fancy that most of them were Federalists." *Id.* It is unclear if Morrison was thus suggesting that their politics doomed these students to second-class careers. Such an assumption would be far from the truth, for many former Federalists, including William Gaston, Willie P. Mangum, George E. Badger, and Thomas P. Devereux, enjoyed great political and legal success during the Second American party system.

56. Samuel H. Fisher has identified, and written biographical sketches of, 903 of the approximately 1,000 students who studied at Litchfield. Fisher, *Litchfield Catalogue, supra* note 15. For seventy-five of these he could find no information save for their names, years of attendance, and, usually, states of residence. The vast majority of these seventy-five were from the South, including six from North Carolina; that the Old North State had a disproportionate share of these obscure Litchfieldians is seen by the fact that while Fisher was able to find at least one additional piece of information about 92.2% of the students from other states, of the North Carolinians he could find information on only 73.9%.

Of the seventeen students from North Carolina for whom there is some additional information, six graduated from Yale while ten attended the University of North Carolina. Besides Polk, three others served in the General Assembly. It is also interesting to note that there were apparently four sets of North Carolina brothers at Litchfield, from the Devereux, Hawks, Wilkins, and Pickett families. As stated above, six of the seventeen are given sketches in the *DNCB*, and it appears that many of the remaining eleven did not become as prominent in North Carolina because they either died young or moved to other states; at least six of the eleven died before reaching their forty-third birthdays. Also, some, such as Thomas P. Devereux's brother George, chose a planter's life rather than practice law or engage in any other type of public service.

57. Bryson, *Legal Education in Virginia, supra* note 1, at 30-31, 589-95, 762-63.

58. *Id.* at 593, 763. Morehead also read law with Archibald D. Murphey. Coates, "Century of Legal Education," *supra* note 36, at 322.

59. Bryson, *Legal Education in Virginia, supra* note 1, at 32-33, 601-13, 763-66.

60. *Raleigh Register*, February 15, 1822. Charles L. Coon, in his pioneering *North Carolina Schools and Academies: 1790-1840* (1915), xliv, states that "[t]he first law school in this state seems to have been conducted by Judge John L. Taylor at Raleigh in 1822," and with the exception of Joseph Lacy Seawell, this has been accepted as fact by all other writers since. See, e.g., Farmer, "Legal Education in North Carolina," *supra* note 32, at 278; Gertrude S. Carraway, "John Louis Taylor," *DNCB, supra* note 6, at VI, 11. As detailed below, while Taylor was the first North Carolinian to advertise his school in the press, it seems certain that the first proprietary school in the state belonged to his fellow judge on the state Supreme Court, Leonard Henderson.

61. *Raleigh Register*, August 2, 1822.

62. "John Louis Taylor," *DAB, supra* note 14, at XVIII, 334-35; Gertrude S. Carraway, "John Louis Taylor," *DNCB, supra* note 6, at VI, 11-12; Walter Clark, "The Supreme Court of North Carolina," 4 *The Green Bag* 457, 461-62 (1892).

63. Lucy B. Royster, "Leonard Henderson," *DNCB, supra* note 6, at III, 103; "Leonard Henderson," *DAB, supra* note 14, at VIII, 529; Clark, "Supreme Court of North Carolina," *supra* note 62, at 462-64.

64. The 1808 date, which comes from Lucy B. Royster, "Leonard Henderson," *DNCB, supra* note 6, at III, 103, would be too late for Henderson to teach the Burton cousins in his "school." The sketch of Henderson in the *Dictionary of American Biography* states that "[f]or thirty years he conducted a law school in connection with his law office," which would place the beginning of the school earlier, around 1803. *DAB, supra* note 14, at VIII, 529. A third source states that while the exact date that Henderson opened his school is unknown, and possibly before 1810, it was "the first law school ever established in the State." Joseph Lacy Seawell, *Law Tales for Laymen* (1925), 302-03. This seems correct, although Taylor was the first to advertise his school.

65. *Raleigh Register*, March 7, 1826.

66. *Id.*, March 3, 1828. For further notices, see also *id.*, March 2 and 4, 1827, and June 10, 1828. Henderson supposedly had

local attorney and clerk of the Supreme Court William Robards assist him in conducting the school. Farmer, "Legal Education in North Carolina," *supra* note 32, at 279 n.50.

67. Lucy B. Royster, "Leonard Henderson," *DNCB, supra* note 6, at III, 103.

68. William H. Battle, "Memoir of Leonard Henderson, Late Chief Justice of the Supreme Court of North Carolina," 9 *N.C. Univ. Mag.* 200 (1859), quoted in Farmer, "Legal Education in North Carolina," *supra* note 32, at 289.

69. *Id.*

70. Robert P. Dick, "Richmond M. Pearson," *Biographical History of North Carolina*, eds. Samuel A. Ashe and Stephen B. Weeks (1908), V, 295, 297. This sketch is a shortened version of a memorial address Dick delivered upon Pearson's death.

71. Almost every important proprietary teacher in North Carolina, including Taylor, Henderson, Pearson, Battle, Frederick Nash, John L. Bailey, Robert P. Dick, John H. Dillard, and George V. Strong, sat on the bench while teaching. The same was true in Virginia, with such judges as Creed Taylor, Henry St. George Tucker, and John W. Brockenbrough operating schools.

72. Kemp Plummer Battle, *An Address on the History of the Supreme Court* (1889), 44. Numerous noted judges on the Superior Court resigned because of the low pay, including Ruffin, Badger, and Frederick Nash. See, for example, an editorial on the subject in the *Raleigh Register*, July 21, 1826. Because of the low pay, it was only with great difficulty that William Gaston was convinced to accept a seat on the Supreme Court in 1833. Still, some thought that even these low salaries were too high. In the state House of Commons in 1828, the controversial Robert Potter moved to reduce the Supreme Court salary from $2,500 to $1,500, and Badger wrote Ruffin in disgust: "If measures such as these shall open the road to popular favor, how can we rationally expect any permanent good or enviable fame for the State." George E. Badger to Thomas Ruffin, November 18, 1828, *Ruffin Papers, supra* note 6, at I, 455.

73. During the 1830s, George E. Badger would typically earn between $200 and $500 during each of his eighteen Superior Court weeks, in addition to a good amount more for the forty or so state Supreme Court cases he would argue every year and his two weeks yearly before the local federal Circuit Court.

74. On the Ruffin moot court, see William A. Graham to Thomas Ruffin, October 5, 1825, *Ruffin Papers, supra* note 6, at I, 332. That there was little difference between reading law and studying in a proprietary school is a point made by Anton-Hermann Chroust, who states that the "private local law schools, which stressed the practical side of legal training, in essence were nothing more than systematized 'extensions' or 'enlargements' of the old and time-honored apprenticeship method, available to a much larger group of students than the traditional 'private law office' could possibly accommodate." He later adds, "Any lawyer who had a permanent office and perhaps a handful of lawbooks could, if he wished to do so, establish a law school of his own, advertise this fact in a local newspaper, and admit whatever students would care to show up. . . . [I]n many instances [these schools] differed from the traditional 'office apprenticeship' only in that he choose [sic] to call it by the honorific name of 'law school.'" Chroust, *Rise of the Legal Profession, supra* note 1, at II, 210, 220.

75. Raleigh *Star*, December 16, 1831.

76. Coon, *North Carolina Schools, supra* note 60, at xliv, cites this notice for the proposition that Murphey operated a law school, as does Chroust, *Rise of the Legal Profession, supra* note 1, at II, 217; Reed, *Training for the Public Profession of the Law, supra* note 1, at 432; Ruth Blackwelder, *The Age of Orange: Political and Intellectual Leadership in North Carolina, 1752-1861* (1961), 135; Guion Griffis Johnson, *Ante-Bellum North Carolina: A Social History* (1937), 288; Ethel Stephens Arnett, *Greensboro North Carolina* (1955), 57 (who states that "most of Guilford's early lawyers were trained" in Murphey's Hillsborough "law school"); and Farmer, "Legal Education in North Carolina," *supra* note 32, at 280 (who states that the sentence in the *Star* was Murphey's "first notice of an organized school"). Farmer's next sentence states that because of the great number of public matters that concerned Murphey, "one may doubt that his law students received much attention," yet as has been shown above, Murphey was known for lavishing attention on his students.

77. Coon, *supra* note 60, at xliv, Chroust, *Rise of the Legal Profession, supra* note 1, at II, 215-16, and Farmer, "Legal Education in North Carolina," *supra* note 32, at 279-80, all credit Brumby with having operated a proprietary law school. Buffalo Shoal is now in eastern Catawba County, with the nearest town being Statesville, about ten miles away.

78. *Raleigh Register*, December 14, 1829. Brumby's advertisement continued in this paper until at least February 22, 1830.

79. Farmer, "Legal Education in North Carolina," *supra* note 32, at 279.

80. William L. Sherrill, *Annals of Lincoln County North Carolina* (1937), 101; Thomas McAdory Owen, *History of Alabama and Dictionary of Alabama Biography* (1921), III, 240. Mary Chesnut, who was about three when Brumby was studying under her father, visited the Professor while both were staying in Lincolnton in early 1865 attempting to avoid Sherman's destructive path. At one point she confided to her diary that she had successfully humored Brumby by patiently listening to various stories, all the while being mainly interested in having him sell her some leather with which a pair of shoes could be made. *Mary Chesnut's Civil War*, ed. C. Vann Woodward (1981), 749.

81. Reed, *Training for the Public Profession of the Law, supra* note 1, at 132.

82. William Hooper Haigh diary, January 5, 1844, Southern Historical Collection, University of North Carolina.

83. *Id.*, April 4, 1844. Interestingly, one of Badger's opponents in the case was his former student Henry W. Miller.

84. *Id.*, January 9, 1844.

85. See, e.g., *id.*, January 5, 9, 10, and 22, 1844.

86. See, e.g., *id.*, July 12, 1844.

87. *Id.*, January 17, 1844.

88. The six persons known to have read law under Badger are William Hooper Haigh, Peter Mallett Hale, Willie P. Mangum, Jr., Henry W. Miller, Sion Hart Rogers, and Thomas Ruffin (of Goldsboro). Mangum, a noted diplomat, was the nephew of his namesake the U.S. senator, while Ruffin was apparently not related to the great judge.

89. In many ways, the closest experience to this today is serving as a law clerk to a prominent, and accessible, judge.

90. On Badger's schedule, see various letters in the Polk, Badger, and McGehee Papers, Southern Historical Collection, University of North Carolina. A lawyer's travelling was certainly disheartening to his family. For example, shortly after their marriage, Badger's second wife, Mary, wrote him, "I do not know what I shall do when you go off to stay four weeks, to become accustomed to your absence, now, appears impossible, however I hope to conquer th[ese] dejected feelings as becomes a Lawyer's Wife." Mary Polk Badger to George E. Badger, February 12, 1827, in *id.*

91. Quoted in Chroust, *Rise of the Legal Profession, supra* note 1, at 221.

92. Quoted in McKenna, *Reeve and Litchfield, supra* note 1, at 14.

93. Coates, "Century of Legal Education," *supra* note 36, at 308-09.

94. Farmer, "Legal Education in North Carolina," *supra* note 32, at 271; *Eighth United States Census (1860)*, 363 (500 lawyers and six judges).

95. *Tenth United States Census (1880), Population*, I, 733.

96. *Twelfth United States Census (1900), Special Reports: Occupations*, 352-53.

97. Alexis de Tocqueville, *Democracy in America* (Bradly ed., 1945), I, 278.

98. In 1841, Henry St. George Tucker in his introductory lecture as law professor at the University of Virginia stated, "the profession of law is the most successful path, not only to affluence and comfort, but to all the distinguished and elevated stations in a free government." Quoted in E. Lee Shepard, "Breaking into the Profession: Establishing a Law Practice in Antebellum Virginia," 48 *J. S. Hist.* 393, 393 (1982).

99. Quoted in Farmer, "Legal Education in North Carolina," *supra* note 32, at 271. Even as early as 1820, the sons of the gentry were complaining about "persons of inferior rank enter[ing] the learned professions in an attempt to elevate their social positions." For example, that year, John Y. Mason, a young Virginian who had recently graduated from the University of North Carolina and who would later serve in the national cabinet, wrote Tarheel John H. Bryan: "The profession of Law is become daily fashionable. It is, the dernier resort, in this State of every s-o-b-, who fails in every other attempt at subsistence—the profession has lost much of that dignity and elevation of character which in former times was the passport to honorable reputation and which united the most distinguished and most virtuous into its ranks." Johnson, *Ante-Bellum North Carolina, supra* note 76, at 60-61. For the great increase in the number of Virginia attorneys, see Shepard, "Breaking into the Profession," *supra* note 98, at 404-05.

100. *Raleigh Register*, May 31, 1836.

101. For general histories of higher education in North Carolina, see Charles Lee Smith, *The History of Education in North Carolina* (1888); William S. Powell, *Higher Education in North Carolina* (1964).

102. Tocqueville, *Democracy in America, supra* note 97, at I, 275.

103. Nationally, 45% of those who entered the U.S. House in the final decade of the eighteenth century were attorneys, and except for the following decade (42%), this percentage steadily increased (1810s, 55%; 1820s, 57%; 1830s, 64%) until in both the 1840s and the 1850s 67% of those entering the House were members of the bar. Since then, the percentage has slipped back into the 50s. Mark C. Miller, *The High Priests of American Politics: The Role of Lawyers in American Political Institutions* (1995), 58.

Traditionally, a higher percentage of members of Congress from the South have been attorneys, *id.* at 57, and this is especially true for North Carolina. Over the course of the Second Party System, the number of North Carolina congressmen who were attorneys constantly rose, so that at the start of the Civil War, seventeen of the last eighteen Democrats elected to the U.S. House, as well as eighteen of the last twenty Whigs (including Americans) were members of the bar. The tremendous increase in the number of attorneys serving North Carolina in the U.S. House during the Second Party System can also be seen in the percentage of congressional elections by decade where an attorney was elected (1800s, 39.3%; 1810s, 41.7%; 1820s, 44.1%; 1830s, 53.0%; 1840s, 90.0%; 1850s, 88.1%).

104. During this period, there was also a vast increase in the number of attorneys appearing before the Virginia Supreme Court of Appeals. See Shepard, "Breaking into the Profession," *supra* note 98, at 405.

105. Farmer, "Bar Examination," *supra* note 26, at 160-63. See also Albert Coates, "Standards of the Bar," 6 *N.C. L. Rev.* 34 (1927).

106. Farmer, "Bar Examination," *supra* note 26, at 163.

107. Angley, *Pearson and Richmond Hill, supra* note 15, at 35-36.

108. In 1860, for example, North Carolina had one lawyer for every 1,962 residents, compared to (with the number of persons per attorney in parentheses): South Carolina (1,533), Mississippi (1,225), Alabama (1,201), Virginia (1,169), Maryland (1,115), Tennessee (1,042), Missouri (986), Louisiana (983), Kentucky (937), Arkansas (919), Georgia (890), Florida (776), and Texas (656). See the 1860 United States census, *supra* note 96. In 1880, when the Old North State contained one attorney for every 1,813 citizens, the state still had the fewest lawyers per person of any Southern or border state, and even today in the 1990s, North Carolina is second in the nation in the fewest number of attorneys per capita.

109. William Gaston to Eliza Gaston, July 3, 1834, William Gaston Papers, Southern Historical Collection, University of North Carolina (emphasis in original). Gaston had thought Daniel "wholly unqualified" for a seat on the high court, and upon Daniel's election he exclaimed, "My country—O my country!" Gaston to Hannah Gaston Manly, December 31, 1832, in *id.* Likewise, their colleague Thomas Ruffin found it "impossible to depict the pain and mortification" which he experienced in serving with Daniel. When Chief Justice Henderson died in 1833, Ruffin wrote Gaston that he would retire from the Supreme Court "unless the member now to be placed on the Bench be a man differing in almost all respects from" Daniel; in short, Ruffin wanted someone who was "*able, honest,* possessed of and entitled to the confidence of the good and intelligent citizens

of the country; one for whose understanding and acquirements I can entertain respect and of whose integrity I shall feel no doubt." Ruffin to Gaston, August 21, 1833, in *id.* (emphasis in original). Ruffin, of course, got his wish, for Gaston himself replaced Henderson on the court. For a fascinating description of Daniel by George E. Badger, see Badger to Ruffin, March 10, 1818, *Ruffin Papers, supra* note 6, at I, 202-05.

110. 32 N.C. at 437, 607 (1849). See also Coates, "Standards of the Bar," *supra* note 105, at 40.

111. 33 N.C. at 452 (1850).

112. Coates, "Standards of the Bar," *supra* note 105, at 39.

113. Farmer, "Legal Education in North Carolina," *supra* note 32, at 296-97.

114. Coates, "Standards of the Bar," *supra* note 105, at 35, 39.

115. Coates, "Century of Legal Education," *supra* note 36, at 326-27.

116. On Swain, see Carolyn A. Wallace, "David Lowry Swain," *DNCB, supra* note 6, at V, 483-86.

117. Quoted in Coates, "Century of Legal Education," *supra* note 36, at 327.

118. Quoted in *id.* at 327-28.

119. Clark, "Supreme Court of North Carolina," *supra* note 62, at 531-35; W. Conard Gass, "William Horn Battle," *DNCB, supra* note 6, at I, 118; Battle, *Old-Time Tar Heel, supra* note 10, at 12-14; Edward W. Phifer, *Saga of a Burke County Family*, 39 N.C. Hist. Rev. (1962) 305, 309.

120. Clark, "Supreme Court of North Carolina," *supra* note 62, at 532.

121. Raleigh *Star*, April 7, 1841.

122. A good biographical sketch of Iredell has yet to be written. For now, see Beth Crabtree, "James Iredell, Jr.," *DNCB, supra* note 6, at III, 255.

123. Clark, "Supreme Court of North Carolina," *supra* note 62, at 532.

124. *Raleigh Register*, July 7, 1843.

125. Quoted in Coates, "Century of Legal Education," *supra* note 36, at 328.

126. *Id.* at 328.

127. *Id.* at 329, quoting the Trustee Executive Committee minutes.

128. Quoted in *id.* at 329-30.

129. See, e.g., *id.* at 331.

130. *Id.* at 330; Farmer, "Legal Education in North Carolina," *supra* note 32, at 283.

131. Coates, "Century of Legal Education," *supra* note 36, at 330.

132. Farmer, "Legal Education in North Carolina," *supra* note 32, at 286.

133. Coates, "Century of Legal Education," *supra* note 36, at 332; Allen W. Trelease, "Samuel Field Phillips," *DNCB, supra* note 6, at V, 93. Two sources, Thomas Ruffin, "Early Days of the Law School—Reminiscences 1900-1910," 24 *N.C. L. Rev.* 414, 414 (1946), and Farmer, "Legal Education in North Carolina," *supra* note 32, at 283, suggest that Phillips assisted Battle well before he was named Assistant Professor in 1854, and this appears to be the case, for several earlier students listed in the *DNCB*, including George Howard, Jr., who attended U.N.C. in 1849-1850, studied under both Battle and Phillips. See, e.g., Mary Ferebee Howard, "George Howard, Jr.," *DNCB, supra* note 6, at II, 213-14.

134. The entire student body of the University of North Carolina numbered 230 in 1850, 456 in 1858, 376 in 1860, 129 in 1861, and only 60 in 1864. Coates, "Century of Legal Education," *supra* note 36, at 390.

135. The standard history of the University of North Carolina, from its inception until 1912, is Kemp Plummer Battle's two-volume *History of the University of North Carolina* (1907, 1912).

136. Coates, "Century of Legal Education," *supra* note 36, at 337.

137. *Id.* at 391.

138. Quoted in *id.* at 334.

139. Battle, *History of the University of North Carolina, supra* note 135, at II, 126.

140. Fannie M. Farmer, in her history of legal education in North Carolina from 1820 to 1860, for example, mentions that reading law, where one's education was "grounded in the actual practice of law" gave the student "a practical education. . . . About the middle of the nineteenth century the emphasis began to shift and the history of law and jurisprudence was presented to the pupils." Twenty pages later, she makes the same point, stating, "Toward the middle of the nineteenth century . . . law schools began emphasizing theory rather than practice." Teachers "taught accurate principles and fastened the history of law in the minds of the students. . . . Less attention was paid to the routine aspects of practice. . . . [The student] was thoroughly soaked in the theory and the history of law." Farmer, "Legal Education in North Carolina," *supra* note 32, at 276, 296.

141. On Coke, see Bryson, *Legal Education in Virginia, supra* note 1, at 7-8, 19, as well as notes 47 and 49, above.

142. On Mordecai and Gulley, see section III below. Even today, there is a noticeable difference in how the law is taught, depending upon where one receives one's legal education.

143. Battle, *Old-Time Tar Heel, supra* note 10, at 81.

144. Clark, "Supreme Court of North Carolina," *supra* note 62, at 532.

145. Battle, *Old-Time Tar Heel, supra* note 10, at 13.

146. On Battle, see *id.*, as well as W. Conard Gass, "Kemp Plummer Battle," *DNCB, supra* note 6, at I, 114-15.

147. Quoted in Coates, "Century of Legal Education," *supra* note 36, at 336-37.

148. Quoted in *id.* at 332.

149. Quoted in *id.* at 333.

150. Elizabeth W. Manning, "John Manning, Jr.," *DNCB, supra* note 6, at IV, 213-14; Coates, "Century of Legal Education," *supra* note 36, at 333.

151. At this time, the texts were "Blackstone's Commentaries, four books, Stephen on Pleading, Smith on Contracts, Bigelow on Torts, Washburn or Williams on Real Property, Greenleaf on Evidence, first volume[,] Schouler on Executors, Adams' Equity, the Constitutions of the United States and of North Carolina, [and] the Code of North Carolina, particularly the Code of Civil Procedure." Battle, *History of the University of North Carolina, supra* note 135, at II, 239; see also Coates, "Century of Legal Education," *supra* note 36, at 333.

152. Battle, *History of the University of North Carolina supra* note 135, at II, 239; Coates, "Century of Legal Education," *supra* note 36, at 333.

153. Quoted in Coates, "Century of Legal Education," *supra* note 36, at 390.

154. Quoted in *id.* at 337-38.

155. *Id.* at 338-39; Battle, *History of the University of North Carolina, supra* note 135, at II, 240.

156. Coates, "Century of Legal Education," *supra* note 36, at 336; Battle, *History of the University of North Carolina, supra* note 135, at II, 239-40.

157. Coates, "Century of Legal Education," *supra* note 36, at 335, 391.

158. Walter G. Sheppard, "The Trinity College Law School," 1 *Trinity Alumni Register* (1916), 264, 264-67; Nora C. Chaffin, *Trinity College, 1839-1892, The Beginnings of Duke University* (1950), 299-300. On Craven, see Mattie U. Russell, "Braxton Craven," *DNCB, supra* note 6, at 455-56.

159. Robert F. Durden, "The Rebuilding of Duke University's School of Law," 66 *N.C. Hist. Rev.* (1989), 321, 321.

160. In addition, in his 1921 listing of all known university law schools, past and present, Alfred Z. Reed listed Trinity as teaching law from 1868 until 1881 in Randolph County, from 1890 until 1894 in Raleigh, and after 1904 in Durham. Reed, *Training for the Public Profession of the Law, supra* note 1, at 424.

161. On the school, see Powell, *Higher Education in North Carolina, supra* note 101, at 75-76, and, for more detail, a series of newspaper articles collectively entitled "Love Story of Rutherford College," by Abernethy's daughter, Mrs. P.M. Rutherford, which appeared in the Morganton *News-Herald* during the fall of 1935.

162. Reed, *Training for the Public Profession of the Law, supra* note 1, at 425.

163. *Catalogue of The Rutherford College* (1874).

164. Morganton *News-Herald,* November 5, 1935.

165. See Holly B. Fitzsimmons, "John Barbee Minor," in Bryson, *Legal Education in Virginia, supra* note 1, at 417-30. See also *id.* at 38-42.

166. On the Pearson family, see George Raynor, *Piedmont Passages: V—Famous Families of 19th-Century Rowan County* (1991), 1-25; James W. Wall, "Jesse A. Pearson," and "Joseph Pearson," *DNCB, supra* note 6, at V, 47-48. Unless otherwise noted, information on Pearson's career is from Dick, "Pearson," *BHNC, supra* note 70, at V, 295-319; Clark, "Supreme Court of North Carolina," *supra* note 62, at 535-39; Angley, *Pearson and Richmond Hill, supra* note 15; "Richmond Mumford Pearson," *DAB, supra* note 14, at XIV, 360-61; and Memory F. Mitchell, "Richmond Mumford Pearson," *DNCB, supra* note 6, at V, 49-51.

167. Dick, "Pearson," *BHNC, supra* note 70, at V, 296-97.

168. *Id.* at V, 297.

169. See, e.g., Max R. Williams, "William A. Graham, North Carolina Whig Party Leader, 1804-1849" (unpublished doctoral dissertation, University of North Carolina, 1965), 261-62; Marc W. Kruman, "Thomas L. Clingman and the Whig Party: A Reconsideration," 64 *N.C. Hist. Rev.* 1, 10-11 (1987). One of the reasons the handful of Whigs supported Ellis was that the Salisbury Democrat promised if elected to abstain in the upcoming election for U.S. senator, a move that was one of the reasons why George E. Badger was able to win a very uncertain reelection on the fifth ballot. See David Outlaw to Emily Outlaw, December 17, 1848, David Outlaw Papers, Southern Historical Collection, University of North Carolina; George E. Badger to John J. Crittenden, January 13, 1849, Crittenden Papers, Library of Congress; and Brian G. Walton, "Elections to the United States Senate in North Carolina, 1835-1861," 53 *N.C. Hist. Rev.* 168, 182-84. The following year, Battle was reelected to the Superior Court, and in 1852 upon Thomas Ruffin's resignation, he joined Pearson on the high court.

170. Clark, "Supreme Court of North Carolina," *supra* note 62, at 535. Clark also stated: "Few will deny Ruffin's rank as our greatest judge. None will deny Pearson's claim to the second place, except those who claim him the first." *Id.* In the hundred years since making that statement, nothing has changed except that one would have to also include Clark himself in discussing the state's greatest judges. For similar sentiments to Clark's, see also "Richmond Mumford Pearson," *DAB, supra* note 14, at XIV, 361.

171. Clark, "Supreme Court of North Carolina," *supra* note 62, at 539.

172. Dick, "Pearson," *BHNC, supra* note 70, at V, 300.

173. Clark, "Supreme Court of North Carolina," *supra* note 62, at 539.

174. When, in 1864, the Confederacy suspended the writ, Pearson found the action unconstitutional and continued releasing individuals, which infuriated Confederate officials and likely played a part in Pearson's defeat when he ran for the 1865 Constitutional Convention. See Mitchell, "Pearson," *supra* note 166, at V, 50.

175. More troubling was Pearson's public endorsement later that year of U.S. Grant for the presidency, which combined with other political acts to precipitate "the sole occasion in the history of the State when there has been antagonism between the bench and bar." Fearing that the judiciary was becoming intolerably politicized in favor of the Republican party, in the spring of 1869 the "father of the bar" B.F. Moore authored a formal protest, which was then signed by 107 prominent attorneys, including five future Supreme Court justices, two former and three future governors, and two men who would later serve in

the U.S. Senate. Pearson overreacted and had the court issue an order barring the 108 protesters from practicing before the high court, and it was only after tempers had cooled, and the attorneys had stated that they did not hold the court in contempt, that the order was rescinded. See *id.* at V, 50; Clark, "Supreme Court of North Carolina," *supra* note 62, at 539; Memory F. Mitchell, "Bartholomew Figures Moore," *DNCB*, *supra* note 6, at IV, 294-95.

176. According to Chief Justice Clark, "a wave of disappointment swept over the State, like that which a nation feels, when one who 'Might have lighted up and led his age[,] Falls back in night.'" Clark, "Supreme Court of North Carolina," *supra* note 62, at 536. See also Mitchell, "Pearson," *supra* note 166, at V, 50; Richard L. Zuber, *North Carolina During Reconstruction* (1969), 28-41. The men were finally freed when a federal judge, George W. Brooks, took the actions refused by Pearson and the Grant Administration failed to support Holden.

177. Clark, "Supreme Court of North Carolina," *supra* note 62, at 536-37; Mitchell, "Pearson," *supra* note 166, at V, 50-51; "Richmond Mumford Pearson," *DAB*, *supra* note 14, at XIV, 361.

178. Clark, "Supreme Court of North Carolina," *supra* note 62, at 535; Angley, *Pearson and Richmond Hill*, *supra* note 15, at 86.

179. "Richmond Mumford Pearson," *DAB*, *supra* note 14, at XIV, 360-61. The author of this sketch was J.G. deRoulhac Hamilton.

180. Angley, *Pearson and Richmond Hill*, *supra* note 15, at 56, quoting Lewin Barringer to Daniel Moreau Barringer, April 18, 1872.

181. Mitchell, "Pearson," *supra* note 166, at V, 51.

182. Dick, "Pearson," *supra* note 70, at V, 51.

183. Raynor, *Piedmont Passages*, *supra* note 166, at 24.

184. Joseph Allison to William A. Graham, March 5, 1848, *Graham Papers*, *supra* note 8, at III, 215.

185. Thomas S. Ashe to Thomas Ruffin, October 24, 1858, *Ruffin Papers*, *supra* note 6, at II, 613.

186. Angley, *Pearson and Richmond Hill*, *supra* note 15, at 80.

187. *Id.* at 84, quoting the Raleigh *Sentinel*, January 16, 1871. It is somewhat ironic that Pearson refused his daughter Eliza's request to marry a Dr. Waddle because of the doctor's "serious drinking problem." *Id.* at 18-19.

188. Reed, *Training for the Public Profession of the Law*, *supra* note 1, at 133.

189. Council S. Wooten, "A Famous Old Time North Carolina Law School," 2 *N.C. J. of Law* (1905) 465, 465-66. Thompson also read under John M. Dick, while Kerr supposedly studied in Richmond as well.

190. J.G. deRoulhac Hamilton, "Pearson," *DAB*, *supra* note 14, at XIV, 360, places the school's opening "[i]n 1836"; Memory F. Mitchell, "Pearson," *supra* note 166 at V, 49, states that it was "about 1836"; and Wilson Angley, *Pearson and Richmond Hill*, *supra* note 15, at 8, dates the opening between 1836 and 1840.

191. Quoted in Angley, *Pearson and Richmond Hill*, *supra* note 15, at 9.

192. *Id.* at 9; Raynor, *Piedmont Passages*, *supra* note 166, at 23.

193. Angley, *Pearson and Richmond Hill*, *supra* note 15, at 9-10.

194. Wooten, "Famous Old Time Law School," *supra* note 189, at 465. Several authors have confused Pearson's Richmond Hill estate in Yadkin County with the large house of the same name near Asheville, which was built by his son Congressman Richmond M. Pearson, Jr., and is now a noted inn.

195. Raynor, *Piedmont Passages*, *supra* note 166, at 23. While this isolation seemed to bother neither Pearson nor his students, his first wife Margaret became increasingly insane before dying at an early age, and an attending physician "placed at least some of the blame . . . [on] the isolated and rustic life at Richmond Hill." Angley, *Pearson and Richmond Hill*, *supra* note 15, at 16-18.

196. Wooten, "Famous Old Time Law School," *supra* note 189, at 465.

197. *Id.* at 465.

198. Angley, *Pearson and Richmond Hill*, *supra* note 15, at 52-53, 55.

199. *Id.* at 39-40, 43.

200. *Id.* at 44-45.

201. Raynor, *Piedmont Passages*, *supra* note 166, at 23. It is unknown if such structures were why the area was also known as "Logtown." In August 1859, a Francis D. Koonce was unsuccessful in obtaining board and lodging in the Richmond Hill area, despite having already attended the school for a session. He was also unsuccessful in finding lodgings in Chapel Hill, so he wrote Thomas Ruffin to ascertain if the elderly judge would be willing to take on one law student. Ruffin's answer is unknown. Francis D. Koonce to Thomas Ruffin, August 17, 1859, Ruffin Papers, *supra* note 6, at III, 41-42.

202. Angley, *Pearson and Richmond Hill*, *supra* note 15, at 41, quoting student John W. Hayes.

203. Wooten, "Famous Old Time Law School," *supra* note 189, at 466. Especially when confronted with a harsh or ineffectual user, many law students over the past century would agree that the Socratic method was indeed akin to "manuring broadcast."

204. *Id.* at 466.

205. Angley, *Pearson and Richmond Hill*, *supra* note 15, at 38, 41, quoting John W. Hayes.

206. Wooten, "Famous Old Time Law School," *supra* note 189, at 466.

207. Quoted in Angley, *Pearson and Richmond Hill*, *supra* note 15, at 41.

208. *Id.* at 41-42, quoting John W. Hayes.

209. *Id.* at 42, quoting *The Law Lectures of the Late Chief Justice Richmond M. Pearson*, ed. Benjamin F. Long (1879). The handing down from year to year of student outlines of a specific professor's class is still a custom at some law schools, especially if the professor has been teaching the same material for a number of years.

210. Dick, "Pearson," *supra* note 70, at V, 298.

211. Angley, *Pearson and Richmond Hill*, *supra* note 15, at 41-42, quoting John W. Hayes. Thus, there is good reason why Pearson wished every student "to have a tolerable acquaintance with the history of England" before beginning his course. *Id.* at 41.

212. *Id.* at 43 (emphasis in original), quoting John Steele Henderson to his mother, March 2, 1866.

213. Dick, "Pearson," *supra* note 70, at V, 309.

214. Angley, *Pearson and Richmond Hill*, *supra* note 15, at 43.

215. *Id.* at 50.

216. Dick, "Pearson," *supra* note 70, at V, 308.

217. Clark, "Supreme Court of North Carolina," *supra* note 62, at 537.

218. Wooten, "Famous Old Time Law School," *supra* note 189, at 466.

219. Angley, *Pearson and Richmond Hill*, *supra* note 15, at 83-84.

220. The case was *State v. Rives* and involved the state of North Carolina suing for damages noted Virginia railroad promoter Francis Rives for tearing up part of the Petersburg railroad in Northampton County. Badger, representing the defendant, in the midst of a "great argument" before the jury began a sentence, "The law in this case[,] gentlemen of the jury," was immediately interrupted by Judge Pearson before he could complete the sentence. Pearson "rapped with his knife on the bench, and quietly, but pointedly said, 'Mr. Badger, the court will instruct the jury upon the law in the case, you need not trouble yourself, sir, further to do so.'" Upon hearing this, Badger "gazed fixedly for a moment at the judge, then defiantly turned, took his seat, and uttered not another word in the case," which, of course, "produced quite a sensation."

In 1891, historian Pulaski Cowper stated that this confrontation "ended, certainly for a long time not only all social intercourse, but brought about undisguised hostility between the two men, and I am not prepared to attest that any reconciliation [was] ever . . . effected." Raleigh *Intelligencer*, April 15, 1891. At this time, William H. Bailey also remembered that when he was Badger's protégé in the mid-to-late 1850s, the great lawyer "hated [Pearson] with the bitterness of a Calvin." Elizabeth City *Economist-Falcon*, May 12, 1891.

Badger appealed the *Rives* case, and the state supreme court found his client liable for only nominal damages. 27 N.C. (5 Ired.) 297 (1844). He also drafted and had his friends introduce in the General Assembly "a Bill concerning Jury Trials" which, among other provisions "authorizes Counsel to argue the whole case, as well Law as fact, *to the Jury*, but with the express authority to the Judge (except in State cases) to lay down authoritatively the Law to the Jury." Hugh Waddell told William A. Graham that while some lawyers were fearful of retaliation from the judiciary, "generally the bar stands up," adding, "When properly understood it is no more than a Declaratory Statute of what the profession has always considered the settled Law of this State." Waddell to Graham, December 5, 1844, *Graham Papers*, *supra* note 8, at II, 530. Undoubtedly the assembly must have agreed, for it enacted the legislation. *Id.* at II, 530 n.47, 534; Raleigh *Intelligencer*, April 15, 1891. As for Badger's son Richard Cogdell Badger attending Richmond Hill, see the Raleigh *News & Observer*, April 23, 1882.

221. [James C. MacRae,] "The North Carolina Bar," 1 *N.C. J. of Law* 1, 2 (1904).

222. Angley, *Pearson and Richmond Hill*, *supra* note 15, at 24.

223. *Id.* at 52, quoting William H. Battle to Lucy M. Battle, March 11, 1851.

224. Dick, "Pearson," *supra* note 70, at V, 308.

225. Wilson Angley, *Pearson and Richmond Hill*, *supra* note 15, identifies 178 students in his Appendix A, although a couple of his included names, Edwin G. Reade and David S. Reid, are highly questionable. Those known to have attended Richmond Hill who are not listed include Leonidas J. Merritt and Richard C. Badger. While Angley's material is highly accurate, the same cannot be said of another manuscript housed in the North Carolina Division of Archives and History, Lewis Shore Brumfield's *Chief Justice Pearson and His Students* (1992).

226. Unless otherwise noted, information on Bailey and his teaching is from Henderson, "John Bailey," *supra* note 15.

227. *Raleigh Register*, May 30, 1845.

228. Jaquelin Drane Nash, "Frederick Nash," *DNCB*, *supra* note 6, at IV, 359-60.

229. *Raleigh Register*, November 9, 1841.

230. Mary R. Keating, "Hugh Waddell," *DNCB*, *supra* note 6, at VI, 105-06.

231. Blackwelder, *Age of Orange*, *supra* note 76, at 135.

232. *Raleigh Register*, January 1, 1851.

233. *Id.*, January 21, 1852.

234. Henderson, "John Bailey," *supra* note 15.

235. *Raleigh Register*, February 16, 1859. Immediately above this notice was an additional advertisement Bailey placed, offering for sale his Hillsborough residence.

236. Henderson, "John Bailey," *supra* note 15; Suzy Maynard, "William Henry Bailey," *DNCB*, *supra* note 6, at I, 85-86.

237. Half a century later, Archibald Henderson in his article "John Bailey, Teacher of Law," *supra* note 15, listed twenty-two noted students who studied under Bailey at either Black Mountain or Asheville.

238. General Theodore F. Davidson, a Bailey student and later state attorney general, recalled, "he was the ideal Southern gentleman, a learned lawyer, a safe counsellor and unusually distinguished for his loyalty to friend and principle. In the last particular I have always thought he was the greatest man I ever knew; and I never pass his grave without raising my hat to his transcendent virtues." Likewise, another student later wrote, "I believe it no exaggeration to say that no man of whatever position who has lived and served in high or low places in North Carolina in any period was more respected and loved by all classes than Judge Bailey." This student continued, "Many of the young gentlemen who enjoyed his lectures and came under

the influence of his sweet personality afterward attained great distinction in their profession and in other ways; many are yet living blessing his memory and lovingly recall his unfailing patience, his gentle courtesy, his genial humor, his scholarly accomplishments, his vast and profound range of knowledge of the law as a great system, and that moral and spiritual elevation which so strongly marked [h]im as the perfect citizen, the ideal lawyer a[n]d genuine Christian." Both quoted in *id.*

239. *Id.*

240. *Id.*

241. Horace W. Raper, "Robert Paine Dick," *DNCB, supra* note 6, at II, 63; Clark, "Supreme Court of North Carolina," *supra* note 62, at 574.

242. William S. Powell, "John Henry Dillard," *DNCB, supra* note 6, at II, 69; Henderson, "Private Law Schools," *supra* note 15; Clark, "Supreme Court of North Carolina," *supra* note 62, at 585-86. Chief Justice Clark described Dillard as "[a] large fine-looking man, with a large brain and kindly heart, [who] looks more like a bishop than a layman." Clark continued that the "unostentatious" Dillard was "the only lawyer in North Carolina who does not appreciate how great a lawyer Judge Dillard is."

243. The source for all of the information in the above four paragraphs is Henderson, "Private Law Schools," *supra* note 15.

244. The closing date of 1893 may not be exact, for it is extrapolated from Levi M. Scott's 1907 address before the Guilford Historical Association in honor of John H. Dillard, in which he states that the Dick and Dillard Law School was conducted for fifteen years. Bettie D. Caldwell, ed., *Founders and Builders of Greensboro, 1808-1908* (1925), 160. A recent search by the Greensboro Historical Museum could not uncover when the school closed its doors. Francis D. Pitts III to the author, December 16, 1997.

245. A list of these seventy-three, as well as information as to the total number of students, can be found in Henderson, "Private Law Schools," *supra* note 15.

246. Twenty-two students were from Guilford and its bordering counties, while fifteen were from the western Piedmont and mountain sections (roughly the area west of a line from Winston-Salem to Charlotte), and twenty-two travelled from Raleigh and points east.

247. Henderson, "Private Law Schools," *supra* note 15. On the Douglas connection, see Lindley S. Butler, "Robert Martin Douglas," *DNCB, supra* note 6, at II, 98-99. Stephen A. Douglas's first wife was from Rockingham County, North Carolina.

248. Quoted in Henderson, "Private Law Schools," *supra* note 15.

249. On Folk and his school, see Kimberly P. Barger and Richard D. Howe, "George Nathaniel Folk," *DNCB, supra* note 6, at II, 215-16.

250. Raleigh *Press-Visitor*, October 11, 1897. Two additional sources, [MacRae,] "The North Carolina Bar," *supra* note 221, at 5, and McCormick, *Personnel of the Convention of 1861, supra* note 15, at 81, credit Strong with operating a proprietary school, with the latter stating that it was while he was on the bench. Unfortunately, Claiborne T. Smith, Jr.'s sketch of Strong for the *DNCB, supra* note 6, at V, 466-67, while presenting much information about the subject, does not mention the teaching.

Details about the possible teaching activities of a Quinton Holton (1818-1890) are even fewer. He was the father of Alfred Eugene Holton, chairman of the state Republican party when it and the Populists controlled state politics for several years in the 1890s, and later U.S. Attorney for the Western District of North Carolina. In the sketch of A. Eugene Holton in the *DNCB*, it is stated that his "early legal training came from his grandfather, Jesse Holton, and his father. According to family tradition, Quinton Holton trained aspiring lawyers and several hundred young men read under his direction. The Holton children were reputed to have walked around with copies of Blackstone under their arms. Four of them became lawyers: A. Eugene, Samuel, John Q., and their sister Tabitha—the first woman licensed to practice law in North Carolina." While this might suggest that Quinton Holton operated some form of proprietary law school, the sketch lists his occupation not as attorney, but as "farmer and Methodist Protestant minister," and it is stated that Eugene also read law with Judge Albion W. Tourgée. *Id.* at III, 192. Further muddling the matter is that Memory F. Mitchell's sketch of Tabitha Anne Holton for the *DNCB* also describes her father as a minister, and states that she "studied law by reading books lent her by members of the Greensboro bar, and had occasionally been examined by these lawyers as she had had 'no regular preceptor.'" *Id.* at III, 193.

251. Crockette W. Hewlett and Leora H. McEachern, *Attorneys of New Hanover County, 1724-1978* (1979), 29; Wilmington *Morning Star*, April 17, 1891.

252. Wilmington *Morning Star*, August 21, 1878.

253. *Id.*, August 28, 1878.

254. *Id.*, September 5, 1878.

255. *Id.*, September 6 and 11, 1878; Hewlett and McEachern, *Attorneys of New Hanover County, supra* note 251, at 182. Cantwell's second lecture was on "Foreign Treaties, Consuls, and Ambassadors," while the third described "the various steps of the passage of law through the Legislature, mode of authentication, constitutional provisions, laws required to be passed, particular limitations on legislative authority in the National and State Constitutions, and general rules of interpretation."

256. Wilmington *Morning Star*, September 13, 1878.

257. *Id.*, October 1, 1878.

258. Reed, *Training for the Public Profession of the Law, supra* note 1, at 133.

259. In addition to there being no permanent rolls, it seems certain that descendants several generations removed would be more likely to recall if their ancestors had attended a college or university, especially one that was still in operation, as opposed to recalling if the ancestor had read law with a now- forgotten state judge in his proprietary school.

260. See, e.g., Johnson, *Schooled Lawyers, supra* note 1; Stevens, *Law School, supra* note 1.

261. For a full description of Gulley's course, see below, section III-C-4.

262. Coates, "Century of Legal Education," *supra* note 36, at 346-48; Coates, "Standards of the Bar," *supra* note 105, at 35, 39.

263. Coates, "Standards of the Bar," *supra* note 105, at 41.

264. *Id.* at 41.

265. Coates, "Century of Legal Education," *supra* note 36, at 348.

266. Figures taken from the *Tenth United States Census (1880), supra* note 95; *Twelfth United States Census (1900), supra* note 102; and *Fourteenth United States Census (1920), Population: Occupations*, 988. Between 1880 and 1900, the South broadly defined (the eleven states of the Confederacy plus Maryland, Kentucky, and Missouri) saw a 75.5% increase in the number of attorneys, while these same fourteen states witnessed a 1.0% decrease in lawyers from 1900 to 1920.

267. Isaac Thomas Avery, Jr., "Alphonso Calhoun Avery," *DNCB, supra* note 6, at I, 66-67; Edward William Phifer, Jr., *Burke: The History of a North Carolina County, 1777-1920* (rev. ed. 1982), 147; Bryson, *Legal Education in Virginia, supra* note 1, at 773; Phifer, *Burke County Family, supra* note 119, at 333-37. Avery was also know for his absentmindedness, for it was said that "[l]ike a great many people of large intellectual attainment, Judge Avery was inclined to be preoccupied and frequently he was oblivious of the ordinary matters that clutter the mind of the average person." *Id.* at 337.

268. Battle, *History of the University of North Carolina, supra* note 135, at II, 505; Elizabeth W. Manning, "John Manning, Jr.," *DNCB, supra* note 6, at IV, 213-14.

269. Coates, "Century of Legal Education," *supra* note 36, at 335.

270. *Id.* at 334-35.

271. *Id.* at 337, 390.

272. *Id.* at 334.

273. *Id.* at 338. Not only the law students were upset with "the iron hand with which Winston led the student body," for during his tenure "disgruntled students painted in bright red letters two feet high 'Winston's Military Academy'" on the college chapel. Neil Fulghum, "George Tayloe Winston," *DNCB, supra* note 6, at VI, 245-46.

274. Coates, "Century of Legal Education," *supra* note 36, at 339.

275. *Id.* at 335-36.

276. *Id.* at 336, 339.

277. Quoted in Battle, *History of the University of North Carolina, supra* note 135, at II, 505.

278. Linda Mylan, "James Cameron MacRae," *DNCB, supra* note 6, at IV, 192; Coates, "Century of Legal Education," *supra* note 36, at 339-42. When starting the study of law, MacRae received some very good advice from his brother Duncan:

> The first book to study is the 'Bible.' Study it well. It is the earliest history of the world. It contains the first rudiments of the Law, the best reductions of logic, the loftiest flights of eloquence, the purest touches of imagination. Master the Bible and you are at once skilled in that knowledge of Human Nature, so essential a weapon with the Lawyer. After the Bible, ancient history, Plutarch, Gibbon, Hallam, Sismondi, the history of Germany and France, Hume and its continuations. It is in these soils of the feudal times deep down, that you find the roots of that tree of legal science whose branches have overspread the world, bearing ripe principles for the benefit of Man. Most young men neglect all this. I tell you the profound study of history before commencing that of Law, is all essential to enable you to grasp the science, and now is your time for this. Of course the history of your own country is not to be omitted.
>
> Conventional and Legislative Debates, the orations and speeches of eminent men—and in this connection Blair's Lectures, The Speeches of Mr. Barker, Lord Chatham, Mr. Webster. Some work as Hedge on Logic, to frame the mind and reasoning, to the conception of ideas and their proper clothing in tasteful and persuasive language. Nor should you fail to cultivate the fancy, with a tight rein for it is a mettlesome and unruly steed, but capable of excellent service if held with a curb and directed with a skillful hand and a sure rein—read poetry sacred and profane. Milton, Pope, Allenside, Shakespeare, Campbell, Scott, Byron . . . abound with instructive teaching—and may be studied with profit. When you come to the study of the Law, take up the severest masters and never let them go till you have thoroughly read and comprehended them. Coke's Commentaries contain the whole science of the law and the man who knows and understands them is [at] once a lawyer.
>
> [Fearne] on Contingent Remainders, Saunders on Deeds and Trusts, Chitty on Pleading are elementary studies of first importance, and your time to master these studies is before you come to the bar. The human mind has in its employ a variety of employees. You study a book. Nothing occurs perhaps on your first reading to strike you. You take it up again and you discover a treasure. So it is especially with the severe law authors. At every reading you will find that some employee of the mind has taken up and stored away a thought unconsciously oftimes to yourself which comes to serve you at a most useful juncture.
>
> You must also study *Man.* Mix with all classes. Study their tastes, their modes of reasoning; their means of arriving at conclusions, their language, their phrases, their prejudices & their affections. Important causes have been gained by the use of the juror's ideas. I am sure that I saved the life of some soldiers in Wilmington who were tried for murder by a well timed allusion to 'temperance societies' in which I adopted the sentiments of a leading juror whom these institutions in that particular way were a hobby. And last of all after a proper use of the means I have pointed, success at the bar is to be gained only by patience, by diligence, energy, devotion to duty, fidelity and *Strict honesty* & truth.

Quoted in *id.* at 340-41.

279. Ruffin, "Early Days of the Law School," *supra* note 133, at 417-18.

280. Coates, "Century of Legal Education," *supra* note 36, at 344-45.

281. Ruffin, "Early Days of the Law School," *supra* note 133, at 419.

282. Coates, "Century of Legal Education," *supra* note 36, at 345.
283. *Id.* at 349-52.
284. *Id.* at 342-43.
285. Ruffin, "Early Days of the Law School," *supra* note 133, at 418.
286. Coates, "Century of Legal Education," *supra* note 36, at 353-55; Frank P. Caudle, "Oscar Ogburn Efird," *DNCB, supra* note 6, at II, 143.
287. Coates, "Century of Legal Education," *supra* note 36, at 357.
288. *Id.* at 355.
289. *Id.* at 356-57.
290. *Id.* at 357, 361.
291. *Id.* at 353.
292. *Id.* at 359, 379-81.
293. *Id.* at 360.
294. *Id.* at 361-64.
295. *Id.* at 368.
296. *Id.* at 369. Ferson stayed in Chapel Hill only two years.
297. *Id.*
298. Harold R. Washington, "History and Role of Black Law Schools," 5 *N.C. Cent. L.J.* 158, 165 (1974); Smith, *History of Education in North Carolina, supra* note 101, at 157-58; Powell, *Higher Education in North Carolina, supra* note 101, at 49.
299. Washington, "Black Law Schools," *supra* note 298, at 165.
300. See, e.g., Hunter, "Badger," *supra* note 8, at 40-47, 70-71; John Hope Franklin, *The Free Negro in North Carolina, 1790-1860* (1943), 81-101.
301. Washington, "Black Law Schools," *supra* note 298, at 165-66.
302. Willard B. Gatewood, Jr., "Edward Austin Johnson," *DNCB, supra* note 6, at III, 288-89. A contemporary, noting Johnson's success at the bar, remarked, "no man stands higher in the esteem of the substantial people of the old North State than Mr. Johnson." *Id.*
303. Washington, "Black Law Schools," *supra* note 298, at 166. It is interesting to note, however, that despite the efforts at Shaw, the percentage of black North Carolina attorneys actually declined between 1900 (25 of 1,263) and 1920 (27 of 1,564).
304. *Id.* at 166.
305. Sheppard, "Trinity College Law School," *supra* note 158, at 267.
306. *Id.* at 267; Chaffin, *Trinity College, 1839-1892, supra* note 158, at 462.
307. Phifer, *Burke County Family, supra* note 119, at 336; Sheppard, "Trinity College Law School," *supra* note 158, at 267-68. The reason for the uncertainty over where Avery held his class is that Alfred Z. Reed's listing of law schools, a very reliable source, shows Trinity's second attempt at a law school as occurring in Raleigh. Reed, *Training for the Public Profession of the Law, supra* note 1, at 424.
308. J. Edwin Hendricks, *Wake Forest University School of Law: One Hundred Years of Legal Education, 1894-1994* (1994), 9.
309. *Id.*, picturing a copy of the 1893 announcement.
310. *Id.* at 10; John R. Woodard, "Needham Yancey Gulley," *DNCB, supra* note 6, at II, 384-85.
311. Woodard, "Gulley," *supra* note 310, at II, 385; Hendricks, *Wake Forest School of Law, supra* note 308, at 10, 12.
312. Woodard, "Gulley," *supra* note 310, at II, 384; Hendricks, *Wake Forest School of Law, supra* note 308, at 11-12. Hendricks misidentifies Gulley's legal preceptor, for he states that it was E.W. Pou (Jr.) who served three decades in Congress in the early twentieth century. The younger Pou, however, had yet to even enter college during the period when Gulley was studying law.
It is ironic that when they founded their respective law programs at Chapel Hill and Wake Forest, both William H. Battle and Needham Y. Gulley not only were honors graduates of their college and members of its board of trustees but also were members of special committees appointed to establish law programs.
313. Hendricks, *Wake Forest School of Law, supra* note 308, at 12-13; George Washington Paschall, *History of Wake Forest College* (1943), III, 307.
314. Hendricks, *Wake Forest School of Law, supra* note 308, at 13, 131-32; Paschal, *Wake Forest College, supra* note 313, at III, 304, 312.
315. Hendricks, *Wake Forest School of Law, supra* note 308, at 13.
316. *Id.* at 21.
317. *Id.* at 21, 23, 25; Woodard, "Gulley," *supra* note 310, at II, 385.
318. Hendricks, *Wake Forest School of Law, supra* note 308, at 21.
319. On Gulley's program generally, see Hendricks, *Wake Forest School of Law, supra* note 308, at 9-42.
320. *Id.* at 14, 26; Paschal, *History of Wake Forest, supra* note 313, at 311 n.12, 315.
321. Stevens, *Law School, supra* note 1, at 78; Hendricks, *Wake Forest School of Law, supra* note 308, at 15, 19. Stevens mistakingly states that by 1904 40% of *all* North Carolina attorneys had studied at Wake Forest, rather than 40% of those entering the bar.
322. Hendricks, *Wake Forest School of Law, supra* note 308, at 15.
323. *Id.* at 14.
324. *Id.* at 23-24. Hendricks styles Timberlake, "E.W. Timberlake, Jr.," although this appears to be wrong, for he was *Edward* Walter Timberlake, while his father the judge was *Edwin* Walter Timberlake. See John R. Woodard, "Edwin Walter Timberlake," *DNCB, supra* note 6, at VI, 36.

325. Hendricks, *Wake Forest School of Law, supra* note 308, at 26, 31-32.
326. *Id.* at 26, 32.
327. *Id.* at 20, 26.
328. *Id.* at 14.
329. *Id.* at 32; Paschall, *Wake Forest College, supra* note 313, at III, 306 n.5.
330. Hendricks, *Wake Forest School of Law, supra* note 308, at 29, 31; Paschall, *Wake Forest College, supra* note 313, at III, 315.
331. Hendricks, *Wake Forest School of Law, supra* note 308, at 29-32. The summer programs at Wake Forest and Chapel Hill were in many ways the forerunners of the bar review courses offered today.
332. *Id.* at 31-32.
333. Paschall, *Wake Forest College, supra* note 313, at III, 305; Hendricks, *Wake Forest School of Law, supra* note 308, at 33-34.
334. Hendricks, *Wake Forest School of Law, supra* note 308, at 24-25.
335. *Id.* at 26-27.
336. Paschall, *Wake Forest College, supra* note 313, at III, 315.
337. *Id.* at 309-10; Hendricks, *Wake Forest School of Law, supra* note 308, at 29.
338. Hendricks, *Wake Forest School of Law, supra* note 311, at 19, 27, 31, 40.
339. Hendricks, *Wake Forest School of Law, supra* note 308, at 39-42.
340. *Id.* at 19, 42; Woodard, "Gulley," *supra* note 310, at II, 384-85.
341. Earl W. Porter, *Trinity and Duke, 1892-1924: Foundations of Duke University* (1964), 91-92, 143.
342. *Id.* at 143-44.
343. Mark C. Stauder, "Samuel Fox Mordecai II," *DNCB, supra* note 6, at IV, 318-19; Sheppard, "Trinity College Law School," *supra* note 158, at 268.
344. Stauder, "Mordecai," *supra* note 343, at IV, 318-19; Porter, *Trinity and Duke, supra* note 341, at 144.
345. Stauder, "Mordecai," *supra* note 343, at IV, 318-19; Porter, *Trinity and Duke, supra* note 341, at 144.
346. Stauder, "Mordecai," *supra* note 343, at IV, 319; Porter, *Trinity and Duke, supra* note 341, at 144; Sheppard, "Trinity College Law School," *supra* note 158, at 270-71.
347. Porter, *Trinity and Duke, supra* note 341, at 144; Stauder, "Mordecai," *supra* note 343, at IV, 319; Sheppard, "Trinity College Law School," *supra* note 158, at 269.
348. Sheppard, "Trinity College Law School," *supra* note 158, at 268, 271; Coates, "Century of Legal Education," *supra* note 36, at 352-53.
349. Sheppard, "Trinity College Law School," *supra* note 158, at 268, 271.
350. Porter, *Trinity and Duke, supra* note 341, at 145.
351. *Id.* at 143-46; Sheppard, "Trinity College Law School," *supra* note 158, at 268-71.
352. Bill Reaves, "Inside Old Wilmington," Wilmington *Morning Star*, January 16, 1975, p.11-C; Hewlett and McEachern, *Attorneys of New Hanover County, supra* note 251, at 128, 182-84; Wilmington *Morning Star*, October 27, 1969 (Rodgers obituary).
353. Memory F. Mitchell, "Tabitha Anne Holton," *DNCB, supra* note 6, at III, 193.
354. Laura N. Gasaway and Judith W. Wegner, "Women at UNC and in the Practice of Law," 73 *N.C. L. Rev.* 705, 706-07 (1995).
355. Hendricks, *Wake Forest School of Law, supra* note 308, at 33. In 1920, there were twenty-one (out of 1,585) female attorneys within North Carolina. *14th U.S. Census, supra* note 266.
356. Reaves, "Inside Old Wilmington," *supra* note 352; Hewlett and McEachern, *Attorneys of New Hanover County, supra* note 251, at 128, 183; Wilmington *Morning Star*, April 11, 1960 (Lillian Rodgers obituary).
357. Hewlett and McEachern, *Attorneys of New Hanover County, supra* note 251, at 183; Reaves, "Inside Old Wilmington," *supra* note 355.
358. U.S. News and World Report, *America's Best Graduate Schools* (1998).
359. See note 15, above.
360. See note 15, above.
361. Finkelman, "Exploring Southern Legal History," *supra* note 2, at 111-13.
362. The different interpretations are because Finkelman bases his conclusions on where the nation's foremost legal education was being taught at a given time, and clearly George Wythe at William & Mary offered the nation's best institutional legal education in the 1780s, a distinction which shortly passed on first to Connecticut's Litchfield Law School and later to Harvard University. It appears better, however, to compare what the average legal education was like at a certain time, and under this comparison it is unclear whether the South outperformed the north in the 1780s, or vice versa in the 1850s.
363. Bryson, *Legal Education in Virginia, supra* note 1.

D. Study in a Nineteenth-Century Law Office

Chapter 30

Notes for a Law Lecture

1850?

Abraham Lincoln

Abraham Lincoln (February 12, 1809-April 15, 1865) was a successful lawyer in Illinois before becoming the sixteenth President of the United States. This fragment was reprinted by Rutgers University Press in Volume 2 of *The Collected Works of Abraham Lincoln* (Springfield, Ill.: Abraham Lincoln Assoc., 1953). A note appended to the fragment reads: "The date assigned to this piece by Nicolay and Hay has been retained in the absence of satisfactory evidence to the contrary, but it seems probable that Lincoln wrote these observations on the legal profession several years later."

[July 1, 1850?]

I am not an accomplished lawyer. I find quite as much material for a lecture in those points wherein I have failed, as in those wherein I have been moderately successful. The leading rule for the lawyer, as for the man of every other calling, is diligence. Leave nothing for to-morrow which can be done to-day. Never let your correspondence fall behind. Whatever piece of business you have in hand, before stopping, do all the labor pertaining to it which can then be done. When you bring a common-law suit, if you have the facts for doing so, write the declaration at once. If a law point be involved, examine the books, and note the authority you rely on upon the declaration itself, where you are sure to find it when wanted. The same of defenses and pleas. In business not likely to be litigated,—ordinary collection cases, foreclosures, partitions, and the like,—make all examinations of titles, and note them, and even draft orders and decrees in advance. This course has a triple advantage; it avoids omissions and neglect, saves your labor when once done, performs the labor out of court when you have leisure, rather than in court when you have not. Extemporaneous speaking should be practiced and cultivated. It is the lawyer's avenue to the public. However able and faithful he may be in other respects, people are slow to bring him business if he cannot make a speech. And yet there is not a more fatal error to young lawyers than relying too much on speech-making. If any one, upon his rare powers of speaking, shall claim an exemption from the drudgery of the law, his case is a failure in advance.

Discourage litigation. Persuade your neighbors to compromise whenever you can. Point out to them how the nominal winner is often a real loser—in fees, expenses, and waste of time. As a peace-maker the lawyer has a superior opportunity of being a good man. There will still be business enough.

17. Abraham Lincoln (1809-1865), here shown in the earliest known photograph of him, was a successful attorney in practice from 1836 to 1847 before entering into a political career. He was the sixteenth President of the United States. (*Courtesy of Art & Visual Materials, Special Collections Department, Harvard Law School Library.*)

Never stir up litigation. A worse man can scarcely be found than one who does this. Who can be more nearly a fiend than he who habitually overhauls the register of deeds in search of defects in titles, whereon to stir up strife, and put money in his pocket? A moral tone ought to be infused into the profession which should drive such men out of it.

The matter of fees is important, far beyond the mere question of bread and butter involved. Properly attended to, fuller justice is done to both lawyer and client. An exorbitant fee should never be claimed. As a general rule never take your whole fee in advance, nor any more than a small retainer. When fully paid beforehand, you are more than a common mortal if you can feel the same interest in the case, as if something was still in prospect for you, as well as for your client. And when you lack interest in the case the job will very likely lack skill and diligence in the performance. Settle the amount of fee and take a note in advance. Then you will feel that you are working for something, and you are sure to do your work faithfully and well. Never sell a fee note—at least not before the consideration service is performed. It leads to negligence and dishonesty—negligence by losing interest in the case, and dishonesty in refusing to refund when you have allowed the consideration to fail.

There is a vague popular belief that lawyers are necessarily dishonest. I say vague, because when we consider to what extent confidence and honors are reposed in and conferred upon lawyers by the people, it appears improbable that their impression of dishonesty is very distinct and vivid. Yet the impression is common, almost universal. Let no young man choosing the law for a calling for a moment yield to the popular belief—resolve to be honest at all events; and if in your own judgment you cannot be an honest lawyer, resolve to be honest without being a lawyer. Choose some other occupation, rather than one in the choosing of which you do, in advance, consent to be a knave.

Chapter 31

Lincoln and His Law Clerks

1892

William H. Herndon

William Herndon (December 25, 1818-March 18, 1891) was Abraham Lincoln's law partner. This excerpt is from *Herndon's Lincoln: The True Story of a Great Life* (New York: D. Appleton & Co., 1892).

How Lincoln appeared and acted in the law office has been graphically and, I must confess, truthfully told by a gentleman now in New York, who was for several years a student in our office. I beg to quote a few lines from him: "My brother met Mr. Lincoln in Ottawa, Ill.,[1] one day, and said to him: 'I have a brother who I would very much like to have enter your office as a student.' 'All right!' was his reply; 'send him down and we will take a look at him.' I was then studying law at Grand Rapids, Mich., and on hearing from my brother I immediately packed up and started for Springfield. I arrived there on Saturday night. On Sunday Mr. Lincoln was pointed out to me. I well remember this first sight of him. He was striding along, holding little Tad, then about six years old, by the hand, who could with the greatest difficulty keep up with his father. In the morning I applied at the office of Lincoln and Herndon for admission as a student. The office was on the second floor of a brick building on the public square, opposite the court-house. You went up one flight of stairs and then passed along a hallway to the rear office, which was a medium sized room. There was one long table in the center of the room, and a shorter one running in the opposite direction, forming a T, and both were covered with green baize. There were two windows which looked into the back yard. In one corner was an old-fashioned secretary with pigeon-holes and a drawer, and here Mr. Lincoln and his partner kept their law papers. There was also a book-case containing about 200 volumes of law as well as miscellaneous books. The morning I entered the office Mr. Lincoln and his partner, Mr. Herndon, were both present. Mr. Lincoln addressed his partner thus: 'Billy, this is the young man of whom I spoke to you. Whatever arrangement you make with him will be satisfactory to me.' Then, turning to me, he said, 'I hope you will not become so enthusiastic in your studies of Blackstone and Kent as did two young men whom we had here. Do you see that spot over there?' pointing to a large ink stain on the wall. 'Well, one of these young men got so enthusiastic in his pursuit of legal lore that he fired an inkstand at the other one's head, and that is the mark he made.' I immediately began to clean up about the office a little. Mr. Lincoln had been in Congress and had the usual amount of seeds to distribute to the farmers. These were sent out with Free Soil and Republican documents. In my efforts to clean up, I found that some of the seeds had sprouted in the dirt that had collected in the office. Judge Logan and Milton Hay occupied the front offices on the same floor with Lincoln and Herndon, and one day Mr. Hay came in and said with apparent astonishment: 'What's happened here?' 'Oh, nothing,' replied Lincoln, pointing to me, 'only this young man has been cleaning up a little.' One of Lincoln's striking characteristics was his simplicity, and nowhere was this trait more strikingly exhibited than in his willingness to receive instruction from anybody and everybody. One day he came into the office and addressing his partner, said: 'Billy, what's the meaning of antithesis?' Mr. Herndon gave him the definition of the word, and I said: 'Mr. Lincoln, if you will allow me, I will give you an example.' 'All right, John, go ahead,' said Mr. Lincoln in his hearty manner. 'Phillips says, in his essay on Napoleon, "A pretended patriot, he impoverished the country; a professed Catholic, he imprisoned the Pope,"' etc. Mr. Lincoln thanked me and seemed very much pleased. Returning from off the circuit once he said to Mr. Herndon: 'Billy, I heard a good story while I was up in the country. Judge D was complimenting the landlord on the excellence of his beef. "I am surprised," he said, "that you have such good beef. You must have to kill a whole critter when you want any." "Yes," said the landlord, "we never kill less than a whole critter."'

NOTE

1. John H. Littlefield, *Brooklyn Eagle*, October 16, 1887.

E. Nineteenth-Century Legal Scientists

Chapter 32

Tracing the Roots of American Legal Education

A Nineteenth-Century German Connection

1987

David S. Clark

David Clark is Professor at the University of Tulsa School of Law. This article first appeared at 51 *Rabels Zeitschrift* 313 (1987).

A summary of this paper was presented at the Association of American Law Schools annual meeting (January 1987) for the comparative law section's panel: "German Influence on Nineteenth- and Twentieth-Century American Law." I wish to thank my colleagues *Paul Aliferis, Gerhard Dilcher, Judith Finn, Donald H. Gjerdingen, Michael H. Hoeflich, John H. Langbein, Mathias W. Reimann, John Henry Schlegel, Peter Stein,* and *Jürgen Thieme* for valuable comments useful in preparing this article. I am indebted, in addition, to the Max-Planck-Institut für ausländisches und internationales Privatrecht and its staff—especially Co-Director *Hein Kötz* and, in the Library, *Jürgen Gödan*—for accommodating me during my stay in Hamburg during the academic year 1984/85 and the summer of 1986 and for facilitating research in their outstanding institution, as well as to the Alexander von Humboldt-Stiftung for awarding me the Max Rheinstein Senior Research Fellowship and to The University of Tulsa for a sabbatical leave.

Literature cited in abbreviated form: Edgar Bodenheimer, Jurisprudence, The Philosophy and Method of the Law^2 (1974); *Anthony Chase,* The Birth of the Modern Law School: Am. J. Leg. Hist. 23 (1979) 329-348; *John P. Dawson,* The Oracles of the Law (1968); *Thomas C. Grey,* Langdell's Orthodoxy: U. Pitt. L. Rev. 45 (1983/84) 1-53; *Jürgen Herbst,* The German Historical School in American Scholarship, A Study in the Transfer of Culture (Ithaca, N.Y. 1965); American Higher Education, A Documentary History, ed. by *Richard Hofstadter/Wilson Smith,* II (1961) (cited: American Higher Education); *Henry James,* Charles W. Eliot, President of Harvard University, 1869-1909, I-II (1930); *Charles E. McClelland,* State, Society, and University in Germany, 1700-1914 (1980); *Edwin W. Patterson,* Jurisprudence, Men and Ideas of the Law

(1953); *Alfred Z. Reed,* Training for the Public Profession of the Law, Historical Development and Principal Contemporary Problems of Legal Education in the United States with Some Account of Conditions in England and Canada (1921) (Carnegie Foundation for the Advancement of Teaching, Bulletin 15); *Joel Seligman,* The High Citadel, The Influence of Harvard Law School (1978); *Robert Stevens,* Law School, Legal Education in America from the 1850s to the 1980s (1983); *Arthur E. Sutherland,* The Law at Harvard, A History of Ideas and Men, 1817-1967 (1967); *Charles F. Thwing,* The American and the German University, One Hundred Years of History (1928); *Charles A. Warren,* History of the Harvard Law School and of Early Legal Conditions in America I/II (1908, repr. 1970); *Franz Wieacker,* Privatrechtsgeschichte der Neuzeit, Unter besonderer Berücksichtigung der deutschen Entwicklung[2] (1967).

Questions of "comparative intellectual history of law" (vergleichende Geschichte der Rechtswissenschaft) are seldom discussed in the law journals of the United States or Germany[1]. Nevertheless, both countries in the twentieth century have become leading proponents and exporters of legal rules and institutions from their own distinct, competing legal traditions. In this respect the United States and Germany are somewhat more insular in their legal systems than nations that are net importers or borrowers of ideas about law[2]. It was not always so; in earlier eras, Germany and the United States "received" the major ideas that made them respectively a civil law and a common law country[3].

I. Introduction

American law schools, today predominantly affiliated with public and private universities, can partially trace their roots to medieval European university experience[4]. This European genesis occurred in the twelfth and thirteenth centuries, when two universities distinguished themselves in developing and transmitting knowledge to such a degree that they attracted students from throughout Europe. The University of Bologna became famous for its instruction in Roman and canon law, while the University of Paris, renown for its schools of theology and liberal arts, influenced subsequent universities in their organizational structure[5].

In a quest for the origins of modern American legal education, the path back into such distant periods is crisscrossed by many promising trails. Nevertheless, I believe it is possible to get from Cambridge on the Charles River to Bologna. I can only signal, going back in time, a few of the major milestones: Harvard University in 1870, the German universities at Berlin in 1809, Göttingen in 1737, Halle in 1694, and the university founded by Emperor Charles IV in Prague in 1348[6].

I contend that modern legal education in the United States has been derived in significant respects from the experience of university law faculties in continental Europe; it is not wholly an indigenous development, nor is it largely an import from England as part of our Anglo-American common law tradition.

Even if one favors the view that American legal education comes from England, English reform of legal education in the 1860s, in fact, was substantially affected by German ideas[7]. John Austin (1790-1859), in his "Lectures on Jurisprudence"[8], first published in 1832, borrowed heavily on his experience for two years at the University of Bonn and on his reading of German law treatises and encyclopedias of Roman and civil law[9]. Austin wrote:

> "Turning from the study of the English to the study of Roman law, you escape from the empire of chaos and darkness, to a world which seems by comparison the region of order and light."[10]

A demand for systematic treatment of law in new English university law schools was met partly by original textbooks based on Austinian ideas and partly by translations of German Pandectists' treatises and textbooks. One of the most influential English books based on the Pandectist model, designed for a new university law course, was "Elements of Law"[11] by William Markby (1829-1914). He asserted that law must be studied

> "as a science . . . a collection of principles capable of being systematically arranged, and resting, not on bare authority, but on sound logical deduction."[12]

By the end of the nineteenth century, American university law schools had also adopted important elements related to the goals, method, structure, and ceremony of European—and especially German—legal education[13]. There was even some minor Roman and civil law influence on the content of American legal instruction[14]. Prior to World War I, for example, the German emperor funded at Columbia Law School the Kaiser Wilhelm chair for visiting civilians. Rudolf Leonhard (1851-1921), a law professor from the University of Breslau, occupied the chair during the academic year 1907-1908. He later published an article based on his Columbia lectures in which he asserted that Roman law texts remained an important bond between Germany and America. America's common law, he argued, shared a cultural past with European nations that should be further developed in "New Europe"[15].

American law training, therefore, can be better understood as part of a long and rich tradition now more than nine centuries old[16]. The claim that German legal education had a significant impact on American law schools (infra, III-V) centers on the reform at Harvard University after Charles Eliot (1834-1926) became president in 1869, during the tenure between 1870 and 1895 of Christopher Columbus Langdell (1826-1906), the law school's first dean. Harvard Law School's influence on the rest of legal education in America during the twentieth century is unequivocal; according to Robert Stevens, Harvard decreed the structure and content and set the style[17].

II. English Influence Prior to the American Civil War

Prior to 1865, the intellectual origins of American legal training were predominantly English[18]. Most attorneys in the nineteenth century learned law through the English apprenticeship approach. William Blackstone (1723-1780) had established a place for student and practitioner use of legal treatises with his four-volume "Commentaries on the Laws of England"[19], which was widely used in American editions and emulated in commentaries on American law[20]. Henry St. George Tucker (1780-1848), a professor at William and Mary College, for instance, published an edition of Blackstone's "Commentaries" in 1803 with copious notes adapting it to American usage[21]. James Kent (1763-1847), a lecturer in law and also chancellor of New York, began publishing his four-volume "Commentaries on American Law" in 1826[22]. Joseph Story (1779-1845), United States Supreme Court justice and professor at Harvard, published nine "Commentaries" on various aspects of American law between 1832 and 1845[23]. He frequently cited Roman and civil law sources[24].

If we focus on the Litchfield Law School, which operated from 1784 to 1833, or the 20 other law-office-type schools patterned on it, English influence seems clear. Tapping Reeve (1744-1823), Litchfield's founder, administered the school like a law practice. Students drafted pleadings and conveyances. This practical education was then supplemented with lectures roughly following Blackstone's "Commentaries" and with periodic examinations[25].

Two additional currents beyond the English influence were also significant. First, Jacksonian Democracy after 1820 belittled the need for formal education, putting fledging law schools and universities under economic pressure. The judiciary in many states was made subject to popular election; some states abolished or reduced apprenticeship requirements for bar membership. Formal education fell into disrespect[26]. Second, civil law doctrines and methods were trumpeted as a supplement to, if not a substitute for, those of the common law. Law professors and lecturers preached the civilian virtues of reason and order; European treatises were translated into English, and law journals emphasizing civil law themes were published[27].

III. Harvard University and Charles Eliot

Instruction at Harvard Law School, opened in 1817, was only slightly more intellectual than instruction at a Litchfield-type law school. Professors used, in addition to lectures, a textbook or recitation method, for which students had to memorize assigned portions of textbooks. During recitation sessions, a teacher explained the text and quizzed students to determine how accurately they had memorized their assignments. By 1869, the Law School curriculum had been reduced to 18 months, examinations had been abolished, and less than half the students graduating in law possessed college degrees[28].

In October 1869, three professors constituting the law faculty signed a report stating that "the condition of the School at the present time is eminently satsifactory"[29]. A committee from the Harvard Board of Overseers, however, disagreed and called for an investigation, prompting one professor to resign. In fact, the Law School, like Tapping Reeve's Litchfield, was conducted like a large office of attorneys. A student's annual tuition was 100 dollars, the same amount an apprentice usually paid in a law office, where textbooks were provided to study. Naturally, when Professor Asahel Stearns (1774-1839) at the Law School placed his private library at the students' disposal, he collected and kept their tuition payments[30].

Harvard Law School's rise to prominence is attributable primarily to the appointment of Eliot as university president in 1869 and Langdell to the newly created post of law school dean in 1870. Of the two men, Charles Eliot was easily the more important. He actively initiated and supported reform throughout the university, especially in the undergraduate science curriculum and in the law and medical schools[31]. Eliot presided over most law school faculty meetings and pushed for the appointment of professors who lacked a background of professional practice. He fought for the school in the Harvard Corporation and in the Board of Overseers, and defended its policies before alumni and the community[32].

Where did Eliot's ideas on educational reform originate? As an assistant professor of mathematics and chemistry at Harvard College in 1858 and head of the Lawrence Scientific School laboratory at Harvard University in 1861, he had already demonstrated a preference for laboratory instruction. However, when he failed to secure academic promotion to professor or acceptance of his proposal to reorganize the Lawrence Scientific School, he left Harvard in 1863. For two years he traveled through Europe, exhaustively studying French and German educational systems, including stops at Paris, Karlsruhe, Heidelberg, Hohenheim, Marburg, Stuttgart, and Tübingen. Upon his return in 1865, he accepted a faculty position at the new Massachusetts Institute of Technology (M.I.T.) and began designing an industrial and teaching laboratory[33].

IV. German Universities as a Model for American Higher Education

1. American Students in Germany

Charles Eliot was not the only American academic to set sail for Europe and to enter the lecture halls, research institutes, seminars, and laboratories of German universities[34]. During the hundred years beginning in 1815, some 9,000 Americans made the long ocean voyage to Europe and matriculated in German universities. Many of them returned home with a doctoral degree at a time when American graduate schools could scarcely compete. United States universities and colleges in 1876, for instance, awarded only 44 doctorates[35]. The most popular German university was Berlin, with fifty percent of the American matriculation. Leipzig and Heidelberg each accounted for about ten percent, while the remainder enrolled mainly at Bonn, Göttingen, Halle, and Munich and to a lesser extent at Breslau, Marburg, and Würzburg[36].

Jürgen Herbst, in his study of the transfer of culture between 1876 and 1914, concludes:

> ". . . the returning scholars made possible the rapid growth of American graduate education in the 1880's and 1890's, and to a very large extent were responsible for training the professions. As teachers they introduced German ideals into undergraduate education."[37]

Americans were not the only conduit for the importation of German ideas; between 1815 and World War I, about 300 Germans took up residence in the United States as teachers and leaders in higher education[38].

2. The Importance of Legal Studies

Up to 1880, law was the second most popular subject for Americans to study in Germany[39]. After that time, when American matriculation increased dramatically, the relative importance of law for American students declined to about nine percent at Heidelberg and to six percent at Berlin and at Leipzig[40]. Of the German students enrolled in universities, in contrast, approximately one quarter studied law. In 1892 there were 6,900 law students at 20 law faculties, three of which—Berlin, Leipzig, and Munich—each had over 1,000 law students. Berlin, the largest law faculty, had 27 teachers (of whom 11 were full professors). But even the smallest law faculties with fewer than 100 students had at least five full professors in residence[41].

Nineteenth-century German legal education, after the successful innovations at Berlin University, aimed toward humanistically and scientifically training public civil servants in Kantian concepts of duty[42]. From an American perspective, even though the curriculum consisted of German law as well as Roman and canon law, it was attractive both as general education and as the best professional preparation for a gentleman lawyer[43]. Most American law students before 1850, using Göttingen University as an example, came from the South. Americans from southern states found the idea of the gentleman lawyer congenial. They sought out professors from the historical school of jurisprudence, such as Barthold Niebuhr (1776-1831) and Friedrich Carl von Savigny (1779-1861) who opposed Enlightenment concepts of natural law and natural rights, thus providing support for their interest in slavery[44].

Americans also engaged in the German tradition of switching universities. They went to hear Heinrich Zachariae (1806-1875) at Göttingen lecture on criminal procedure, to listen to Rudolf von Gneist (1816-1895) on English constitutional and administrative law at Berlin, and to study international law at Heidelberg with Johann Caspar Bluntschli (1808-1881)[45].

3. Science and Romanticism

German universities in the nineteenth century were the world's most acclaimed and emulated. The ideal of systematic knowledge and "science" (Wissenschaft) inaugurated at innovative universities such as Berlin became the leading principle at other German universities after 1840.[46] "Romanticism" (Romantik) transcended the realm of literature and art to condition a new scientific research ethic and to color almost every area of thought, including law. Theodor Birt (1852-1933) saw the dualism as science and "fatherland" (Vaterland):

> "German science in our century signifies a triumph of the German spirit over the rest of the world. It is our title of honor. And its workplace is in our German universities."[47]

Romanticism, fatherland, and neohumanism inspired fields as disparate as law, natural science, language, and history—utilizing concepts like the "soul of the people" (Volksseele)[48].

Friedrich Carl von Savigny, for instance, fostered the idea that law was determined by the peculiar character of a "people's spirit" (Volksgeist).[49] Correct law, according to Savigny, is identical with the opinion and practices of the people in matters of right and justice. It is the product of gradual and organic growth, not arbitrary and deliberate actions. Law becomes valid as part of an historical process, not through mere legislative acts. As civilization proceeds, a distinct class of jurists emerges that represents people for the more technical questions of law. At this stage of development, there are thus two types of law: popular law, which is intelligible to the masses and continues as part of a people's organic life, and technical law, which enters the domain of jurists representing the people[50].

Savigny's background also helps to explain his resistance to legislation and codification, and especially why he sought to prevent in Germany the enactment of codes similar to the Code Napoléon. First, he was a conservative nobleman who rejected the equalitarian rationalism of the French Revolution. Even though he fought against many Enlightenment ideas and embraced the Prussian restoration, the consensus of scholars is that Savigny was a reform conservative; he chose a middle path between contemporary political extremes. Second, he was a German nationalist—before Germany had achieved statehood—promoting national codification as a goal for legal scholarship. He opposed not only the revolutionary but also the imperial implications of the French-supported school of natural law, which contended that fundamental legal principles were the same everywhere and for all time.[51] In addition, Savigny's marriage to Kunigunde Brentano, sister of the poet—Clemens Brentano, provided him entrance into important romanticist literary circles[52].

Americans studying in Germany during the late nineteenth century were caught up in this intellectual excitement. German professors, in probing the secrets of the past—secrets of language, law, or the material universe—believed that new and exciting discoveries could be made by an individual mind if properly trained. Bold acts of intelligence and will were all that was required[53].

The German historical school led a reaction against speculative philosophy and natural law in favor of empirical investigation, verification, and inductive logic. A scientific spirit shaped Germans' concept of Wissenschaft, tempered with a concern for human motive and purpose embodied in the critical analysis of philology, of biblical scholarship, or of research at law faculties inquiring historically into Justinian's "Digesta"[54].

Savigny and his romanticist followers saw history and "legal science" (Rechtswissenschaft) as two sides of the same coin[55]. Savigny was drawn to classical Roman law because he believed as an organicist in historical continuity (evidenced ideologically by the German Holy Roman Empire) and as the scientist that he could find in the classical jurists a rational system of legal principles[56]. Law professors and judges, trained in legal science, became representatives of the Volksgeist; they were thus competent to develop the law in its technical aspects[57].

German romanticism eroded the faith that eighteenth-century Enlightenment scholars had held in a natural order—an elegantly simple reality based on certain principles of liberty and equality that were eternal postulates of reason and justice. Romanticism, alternatively, stressed individuality (the right of a superior individual to realize his potential), organicism (an infinite evolving essence of the universe), and, most importantly, relativism. Enlightenment rationalists looked to the future with an optimistic belief in progress. German romantics venerated the past; they were fascinated by history and preferred the fullness and incoherence of life to the mathematical order of the French "philosophes"[58].

The institutionalization of Wissenschaft occurred outside the traditional German lecture hall. It flowered in the expansion of seminars, laboratories, institutes, and practical classes with their assigned "written exercises" (Übungen). Some seminars became significant organizations with their own directors, libraries, meeting rooms, and budgets. A small number of students typically participated in seminar classes to interpret difficult texts, undertake and report on independent research assignments, and receive comments from the professor and fellow students[59]. Practical exercise classes used a problem method of instruction. In these courses, the professor gave law students a statement of facts for solution at home. Each student prepared a research paper with his solution for the case, which was corrected by the instructor and discussed at subsequent class meetings. Students received grades that, although they had no effect on their state bar examination, gave them welcome feedback on their educational progress[60].

The suitability of university students for this rigorous curriculum was fostered by training and examination in the classical German secondary school (Gymnasium), which led to the "Abitur" or "Matura", required for matriculation at a university. Once enrolled, the desirability of entering a liberal profession or the civil service stimulated students to prepare themselves for the difficult and mandatory state examinations[61].

V. Educational Reform at Harvard University After 1869

1. Charles Eliot as President

Charles Eliot, after the publication of his views on educational organization by "Atlantic Monthly"[62], was selected in 1869 as president of Harvard University. The institutional and instructional reforms Eliot proposed or implemented at Harvard College, the Lawrence Scientific School, and at M.I.T. during the 1860s included four elements that also bore some resemblance to German and French educational practice, which he continued to support as president[63].

First, Eliot favored a classroom laboratory method, with its inductive reasoning process, to replace the lecture and recitation methods of instruction[64]. Instructors and students were to work together in developing general principles from concrete cases. Eliot and a colleague prepared in 1867 the first laboratory manual—a compilation of materials—ever used in an American classroom[65]. Second, Eliot established written entrance examinations, which functioned as a kind of Abitur. Third, he set up a definite curriculum to be satisfied for a degree, gradually phasing in electives for upperclassmen. Eliot also considered final examinations essential to upgrading educational standards[66]. Germans, alternatively, received specific feedback on their progress only in seminars and Übungen, prior to the state examination[67]. Finally, Eliot intended that Harvard should become a great seat of learning, attracting mature scholars as did the best European universities[68].

2. Christopher Langdell as Law Dean

Eliot brought Christopher Columbus Langdell to the Law School to be its first dean in 1870, in spite of some misgivings from members of the university's Corporation and the Board of Overseers[69]. The initial 15 years of Langdell's deanship institutionalized five important changes. Langdell, with the help of Eliot's leadership, established: first, a law school entrance examination; second, initially a two-year and then a three-year progressive curriculum, leading to an undergraduate bachelor of laws degree (LL.B.); third, requisite annual examinations before students could proceed on to the next year's subjects[70]; and fourth, Langdell began to institutionalize a research function at the Law School similar to that existing in German universities[71]. Langdell contended that he was by example trying to put American law faculties on a level with universities in continental Europe[72].

Langdell's most significant innovation, however, was the introduction of an instructional method utilizing Socratic dialogue to discuss appellate court cases. Justified as a scientific process to elaborate general, organic principles of the common law, it supplanted lecturing and recitation based on treatises. Professors and students, the idea ran, should together work through questions and answers to discover common law principles, aided by classroom research manuals called casebooks[73]. Langdell explained:

> "Law, considered as a science, consists of certain principles or doctrines . . . Each of these doctrines has arrived at its present state by slow degrees; in other words, it is a growth, extending in many cases through centuries . . . [T]he only way of mastering the doctrine effectually is by studying the cases in which it is embodied. But the cases which are useful and necessary for this purpose at the present day bear an exceedingly small proportion to all that have been reported."[74]

Eliot later observed:

> "Professor Langdell's method resembled the laboratory method of teaching physical science, although he believed that the only laboratory the Law School needed was a library of printed books."[75]

3. Similarities Between the German Historical School and Langdell's Legal Science

Langdell's theory of legal science and organic development was similar to that of Savigny[76]. Josef Redlich (1869-1936), a law professor at the University of Vienna who was first brought to the United States in 1913 by the Carnegie Foundation to study the case method of instruction, made the comparison regarding legal science:

> "For Anglo-American law just as much as for the common German law of the nineteenth century, the birth and powerful influence of the new historical method marks the turning-point at which the inheritance of the Middle Ages—legal craftsmanship and practical expertness in law—becomes converted into legal science. What Savigny and his pupils and the entire legal-historical school of Germany accomplished for the common law of Germany has been performed in no less admirable fashion in the last half-century for the English common law by such men as Thayer, Langdell, Ames, and Bigelow in America."[77]

The process of transforming legal craftsmanship into legal science convinced Savigny and Langdell that the job belonged in the university. In this sense, both men desired to keep legal theory and practice separate[78].

Under Savigny's organic theory, the object of legal history was

> "to trace every established system to its root, and thus discover an organic principle, whereby that which still has life, may be separated from that which is lifeless."[79]

Langdell's similar organicism, which saw legal doctrine as "a growth, extending in many cases through centuries"[80] should also be viewed in the context of Charles Darwin's "The Origin of Species"[81]. The idea that a species can originate by evolution parallels the notion that laws are not immutable, but alterable and contingent[82].

The connection between the German historical school of jurisprudence—with its members' concern for legal science and organicism—and Harvard Law School did not first begin with Langdell[83]. Georg Friedrich Puchta (1798-1846), a disciple of Savigny and his successor at the University of Berlin, saw "customary law" (Gewohnheitsrecht) as the most genuine expression of a people's common convictions. Custom was, for this reason, superior to legislation, which could be useful only in so far as it embodied prevailing national sentiments and usages[84]. In 1848 Luther Cushing (1803-1856) began lecturing at Harvard Law School, sympathetically expounding doctrines of the German historical school[85]. Cushing had earlier translated Savigny's "The Law of Possession"[86]. One of Cushing's students, James Carter (1827-1905), became a leading member of the bar, a supporter of Langdell, and an advocate for the theories of Savigny and Puchta[87]. Carter was appointed to give a series of lectures at Harvard in 1904-1905 entitled "The Origin, Growth and Function of Law"[88] where he said that custom furnishes the rules governing human conduct and that judicial precedent is in reality authenticated custom. A judicial decision, therefore, puts the stamp of public approval on custom. This settles a problem of right or wrong and evidences the genuineness of its resolution. Courts do not make law; they discover it[89].

Just as the influence of German ideas at Harvard did not begin with Eliot and Langdell, it did not end with them. As dean, Langdell recruited James Barr Ames (1846-1910) as an assistant professor in 1873. Ames was a new breed of academic lawyer, with limited experience in practice, who was appointed with Eliot's blessing for his scholarly and teaching potential. Ames had studied for more than a year at German universities. He became a popular instructor, using Langdell's Socratic method, and produced many casebooks that were widely used in American law schools[90]. The "Harvard Law Review", furthermore, between its founding in 1887 and 1930, published twenty articles on topics dealing with Roman and civil law[91].

VI. Conclusion

Langdell began his life's work at Harvard within this cultural milieu[92]. Robert Stevens observes:

> "Intellectually, in the period after 1870, the law schools had attempted to embrace a kind of Germanic 'scientism' while retaining an Anglophilic and Anglophonic facade."[93]

Legal science promised a complete and orderly system of norms; it offered determinate answers in an increasingly complex world[94]. The "American Bar Association Committee on Legal Education and Admissions to the Bar" accepted this model in 1879[95].

While Germans might have looked to professors to ascertain the true content of law, Americans could turn to judges, assisted of course by the professorate. Legal science, Thomas Grey concludes,

> "built a bridge between lawyers' urge to feel that they practiced a learned profession, and the need of the new universities for an alliance with the rich and influential bar."[96]

Legal science—bringing order, system, and prestige—made sense.

There were some American law professors near the end of the nineteenth century, such as Christopher Tiedeman (1857-1903), who had attended Rudolf von Ihering's (1818-1892) classes at Göttingen. Tiedeman wanted to borrow more heavily from German legal education[97]. He wrote:

> "If I were called upon to establish a course of legal instruction, I would follow the German methods as nearly as the situation and public opinion in America would allow."[98]

Many leading practitioners, such as members of the American Bar Association's Committee on Legal Education and Admissions to the Bar, in their 1892 Report, agreed that continental law teaching methods, including a comprehensive survey of the legal order and emphasis on the historical school's search for organic development, were preferable to Langdell's case method[99]. The Committee recommended

> "the abandonment of the present method of teaching the law mainly by distinct topics, at least during the first year of the course, and the substitution for it of a careful and systematic study of the [legal] system as a whole after the European method."[100]

Ernst Freund (1864-1932), who earned his law degree at Heidelberg, pushed for such a curriculum after his arrival as professor of political science at the University of Chicago in 1894. When the university trustees decided to establish a law school, President William Harper in 1902 authorized Freund to draft a curriculum for the new school. Public law and jurisprudence were to play a more prominent role than at Harvard. In addition, the case method was to be used only to the extent that it did not impede students' ability to learn the subject under study systematically. However, after Harper's negotiations with the Harvard administration led Professor Joseph Beale (1861-1943) to accept the Chicago deanship, Freund's ideas were dropped and the Harvard plan implemented[101].

The flow of people between Germany and the United States continued unabated into the twentieth century, until World War I. In 1902 Prince Henry of Prussia visited Harvard to present a collection of art from his brother the emperor to the University's new Germanic Museum. The governing boards voted to confer an honorary doctorate of laws upon the prince. Although President Eliot would have preferred that Germany were a republic, in his remarks at the first Harvard presentation ceremony to honor a foreign prince, he acknowledged Germany's contribution to America's universities[102].

To reciprocate, the German government conferred the Royal Order of the Prussian Crown upon Eliot in 1909[103]. In that same year, Eugen Kühnemann (1868-1946), professor of philosophy at the University of Breslau and twice, during the academic years 1906-1907 and 1908-1909, holder of the German interchange professorship at Harvard, wrote an essay as "an homage of Germany to President Eliot on his retirement from office"[104]. Kühnemann traced the development of Harvard during Eliot's tenure, incidentally pointing out resemblances to the German educational system. He indicated that from 1869 to 1909, the number of professors at the Law School had increased from three to sixteen[105]. Kühnemann felt that:

> "Nowhere have President Eliot's courageous reforms met with a finer reward than in the development of the Law School; . . . he has accomplished the evolution of Harvard into a genuine university in the European sense."[106]

Amid paeans of mutual admiration between Germans and Americans, few foresaw the gathering clouds of 1914. Once the storm hit, it would not be until the 1930s, and then under very different circumstances, that Germans would once again significantly influence legal education in the United States[107]. Ernst Rabel, the founder of this Journal, was one of them[108].

NOTES

1. An exception to this observation is *Ernst Rabel*, Deutsches und amerikanisches Recht: RabelsZ 16 (1951) 340-359. See also Bernhard Groβfeld, Probleme der Rechtsvergleichung im Verältnis Vereinigte Staaten von Amerika—Deutschland: *ibid.* 39 (1975) 5-27; *Jürgen Thieme*, Einführung [Ernst Rabel (1874-1955), Schriften aus dem Nachlaβ, "Vorträge—Unprinted Lectures"]: *ibid.* 50 (1986) 251-281.

2. See generally *Alan Watson*, Legal Transplants, An Approach to Comparative Law (1974).

3. See *Helmut Coing*, Die Bedeutung der europäischen Rechtsgeschichte für die Rechtsvereinheitlichung: RabelsZ 32 (1968) 1-21; *Elisabeth Gaspar-Brown*, British Statutes in American Law 1776-1836 (1964) (reviewed by *Kurt Siehr*, RabelsZ 32 [1968] 563-565).

4. See *Charles Homer Haskins*, The Rise of Universities (1957, first published 1923) 21, and see *id.* 3: ". . . the university of the twentieth century is the lineal descendant of mediaeval Paris and Bologna."

5. *Heinrich Denifle*, Die Entstehung der Universitäten des Mittelalters bis 1400 (1885) 746f.; *David S. Clark*, The Medieval Origins of Modern Legal Education, Between Church and State: Am. J. Comp. L. 35 (1987) (in press).

6. This article grew out of research I am conducting for a book on the history of German legal education (see *supra* n. 5 and accompanying text). In that investigation, I examine the relationship in society between university legal education and dominating spheres of influence, such as church, state, and market. It is a premise of this model that at different times in the history of cultures a particular organizing influence comes to prevail in these relationships, although one or both of the other spheres may also be significant in promoting its own political or economic interests. An imperative of each type of order—whether it be church, state, or market—aims to control and thereby to benefit from universities and legal education.

7. *David Sugarman*, Legal Theory, the Common Law Mind and the Making of the Textbook Tradition, in: Legal Theory and Common Law, ed. by *William Twining* (1986) 26-61 (30f., 44f.).

8. *John Austin*, Lectures on Jurisprudence[5], ed. by *Robert Campbell* (1885).

9. *M.[ichael] H. Hoeflich*, John Austin and Joseph Story, Two Nineteenth Century Perspectives on the Utility of the Civil Law for the Common Lawyer: Am. J. Leg. Hist. 29 (1985) 36-77 (38-41, 47-52, 72f.); see very recently *id.*, Transatlantic Friendships and the German Influence on American Law in the First Half of the Nineteenth Century: Am. J. Comp. L. 35 (1987) 599-611 (published after this article went to press).

10. *Austin* (*supra* n. 8) 58.

11. *William Markby*, Elements of Law Considered with Reference to Principles of General Jurisprudence (1871, microfiche 1986); *Peter Stein*, Continental Influences on English Legal Thought, 1600-1900, in: La formazione storica del diritto moderno in Europa (1977) III 1105-1125 (1119-1121); *A.[lfred] W.[illiam] B.[rian] Simpson*, Innovation in Nineteenth Century Contract Law: L. Q. Rev. 91 (1975) 247-278 (256 and 259); see also *Enid Campbell*, German Influences in English Legal Education and Jurisprudence in the 19th Century: U. W. Austr. L. Rev. 4 (1957-59) 357-390 (358-363); *Andreas B. Schwarz*, John Austin and the German Jurisprudence of His Time: Politica 1 (1934-35) 178-199 (186-197).

12. *Markby* (*supra* n. 11) p. X.

13. Charles Thwing (1853-1937), President of Western Reserve University, traced the history of foreign influence on American higher education back to the English university. He maintained that the English tradition could be seen at places like Harvard College and William and Mary College both in academic government and in the methods and content of instruction. It continued until the outbreak of the Revolutionary War, when French influence took over through men such as Thomas Jefferson, who founded the University of Virginia. The final fall of Napoleon caused French importance to wane just as German significance was beginning; *Thwing* 3-7.

14. *Hoeflich*, Roman and Civil Law in American Legal Education and Research Prior to 1930, A Preliminary Survey: U. Ill. L. Rev. 1984, 719-737 (728-733, 736).

15. *Rudolf Leonhard*, The Vocation of America for the Science of Roman Law: Harv. L. Rev. 26 (1912/13) 389-415 (390, 414f.); see *id.*, Methods Followed in Germany by the Historical School of Law: Colum. L. Rev. 7 (1907) 573-581 (578) (address delivered at the law school's opening exercises), and see *Hoeflich* (*supra* n. 14) 722f., 735f.

16. *Harold J. Berman*, Law and Revolution, The Formation of the Western Legal Tradition (1983) 163; *id.*, The Origins of Western Legal Science: Harv. L. Rev. 90 (1976/77) 894-943 (941). Berman argues that between the years 1075 to 1300 a revolutionary transformation in the nature of Western law occurred. The growth of university law teaching, the rediscovery of Roman law texts, and a new dialectical method of interrelating cases and concepts—harmonizing contradictory authori-

ties—resulted in a European legal science accepted in many respects up to this century; *Berman*, Law and Revolution (supra) ch. 3.

17. *Stevens* ch. 3 and 4. See also *Seligman* and *Chase* (*supra* n. *).

18. *Reed* 11-24, 29-35; *Seligman* 21; *Robert W. Gordon*, Legal Thought and Legal Practice in the Age of American Enterprise, 1870-1920, in: Professions and Professional Ideologies in America, ed. by *Gerald L. Geison* (1983) 70-139 (82-87).

19. *William Blackstone*, Commentaries on the Laws of England I-IV (1765-1769, repr. 1966). Blackstone's "Commentaries" resulted from his attempt to reform legal education with a series of lectures on English law delivered at Oxford beginning in 1753. He was, as were so many others, unsuccessful in persuading the English legal community that law would be best taught in universities; *J. H. Baker*, An Introduction to English Legal History[2] (1979) 148.

20. *Reed* 107-112; *Sutherland* 18-24, 31; *Robert Stevens*, Two Cheers for 1870, The American Law School, in: Law in American History, ed. by *Donald Fleming/Bernard Bailyn* (1971) 403-548 (410-412).

21. *Henry St. George Tucker*, Blackstone's Commentaries, With Notes of Reference to the Constitution and Laws of the Federal Government of the United States, and the Commonwealth of Virginia (1803, repr. 1969); see *Lawrence M. Friedman*, A History of American Law (1973) 280.

22. *James Kent*, Commentaries on American Law I-IV (1826-1830); see *Seligman* 22-25.

23. See, e.g., *Joseph Story*, Commentaries on the Conflict of Laws, Foreign and Domestic, in Regard to Contracts, Rights, and Remedies, and Especially in Regard to Marriages, Divorces, Wills, Successions, and Judgments[1] (1834).

24. See *Seligman* 22-25; *Hoeflich* (*supra* n. 9) 57-71, 74-76; *Gerhard Kegel*, Joseph Story: RabelsZ 43 (1979) 609-631 (617-621).

25. *Reed* 128-133; *Seligman* 21 f.; *Sutherland* 27-29.

26. *Stevens* 5-10.

27. *Peter Stein*, The Attraction of the Civil Law in Post-Revolutionary America: Va. L. Rev. 52 (1966) 403-434 (404, 407-427).

28. *James* I 267f., 293, II 64; *Josef Redlich*, The Common Law and the Case Method in American University Law Schools (1914) 7f. (Carnegie Foundation for the Advancement of Teaching, Bulletin 8); *Reed* 137-140; *Seligman* 27f.

29. *James* I 266.

30. *James* I 266f.

31. *Stevens* 36; *Chase* 336, 342f.; see *Warren* II ch. 51 (the early relationship between Eliot and Langdell).

32. *James* II 62f.

33. *James* I 69, 88f., 94f., 98-103, 107-112, 113-116, 121-123, 134-138, 152, 160-162; *Warren* II 354f.; *Chase* 334. Eliot took a second European trip from June 1866 until the spring of 1867; *James* 1172 f. For a somewhat critical evaluation of Eliot's European experiences, see the view expressed by the German exchange professor Kühnemann, *infra* n. 106.

34. To illustrate, around 1815 two Massachusetts students matriculated at Göttingen and later earned German university degrees. George Ticknor (1791-1871), who became Charles Eliot's uncle, tried in the 1820s as Harvard College professor of belles lettres to introduce an elective system and to reform the college in the direction of German universities; *James* I 29,106, 221; *Thwing* 18, 21, 37f. Edward Everett (1794-1865) returned to the United States as professor of Greek and later became president at Harvard College, where he tried but failed to implement the type of student life and organizations he had seen at Göttingen. Everett was also governor of Massachusetts and a United States senator; *Thwing* 19, 26.

35. *Herbst* 1f.; *Thwing* 18, 40 (estimate of 10,000); *C. John Walton*, Graduate Study in Universities and Colleges in the United States (1934) 19f.; see *Laurence R. Veysey*, The Emergence of the American University (1965) 125-133. By 1900 the number of American doctoral degrees had risen to 342; *Walton* (*supra*) 19f.

36. *Thwing* 40f.

37. *Herbst* 24, see p. X; *Reed* 331, 334f. A much smaller number of American students enrolled at French and English universities. In 1895, for example, there were 30 Americans enrolled at the Sorbonne compared to more than 200 at Berlin. English universities suffered from a poor reputation, since most science and learning were conducted outside their walls; *Herbst* 8-13.

38. *Thwing* 103.

39. *Herbst* 6f. James Hart (1839-1916), for example, earned a law degree at the University of Göttingen and later wrote a popular book about his experience; *James Morgan Hart*, German Universities, A Narrative of Personal Experience, Together with Recent Statistical Information, Practical Suggestions, and a Comparison of the German, English and American Systems of Higher Education (1874), excerpted in: American Higher Education 569-583. Hart stressed the progressivism in the German ideas of: "Wissenschaft" ("knowledge in the most exalted sense of the term, namely, the ardent, methodical, independent search after truth in any and all of its forms, but wholly irrespective of utilitarian application") (571); "Lehrfreiheit" (a teacher's freedom "to teach what he chooses, as he chooses") (loc. cit.); and "Lernfreiheit" (a student's "emancipation . . . from Schulzwang, compulsory drill by recitation") (572).

Most students were drawn to Germany to study medicine and the supporting natural sciences, given the deplorable condition of American medical training. Their numbers declined when reforms were introduced at Chicago, at Harvard under Eliot's reorganization of the medical faculty (infra n. 68), and at Johns Hopkins; *Herbst* 6.

40. *Thwing* 41f.

41. Rechtsforschung und Rechtsunterricht auf den Deutschen Universitäten, ed. by *Otto Fischer* (1893) Anhang, 133-142 (140).

42. *Wieacker* 438-449; see *Immanuel Kant*, Grundlegung zur Metaphysik der Sitten (1785) = *id.*, Groundwork of the Metaphysic of Morals, transl. by *Herbert James Paton* (1964) 89-91.

43. *Herbst* 7. The following lecture courses, to illustrate, were offered at Breslau University during 1892-1893: introduction

to legal science; history of Roman law; Roman law Institutes; Roman law Pandects (Digest); German legal history; German private law; commercial law; canon law; German constitutional law; German criminal law; German civil procedure; German criminal procedure; European international law; legal philosophy; Prussian state law; German administrative law; political economy; and macroeconomics; see *Fischer*, Rechtsforschung und Rechtsstudium im Allgemeinen, in: Rechtsforschung und Rechtsunterricht (*supra* n. 41) 1-20 (16f.).

44. *Herbst* 7.

45. *Herbst* 15-18; *Gerd Kleinheyer/Jan Schröder*, Deutsche Juristen aus funf Jahrhunderten, Eine biographische Einführung in die Geschichte der Rechtswissenschaft[2] (1983) 42, 99, 356.

46. *McClelland* 2, 152f. The German word "Wissenschaft," usually translated as "science", has a broader connotation—meaning also organized knowledge or learning—than the current American term science. Science in the United States typically refers to "empirical science" (Erfahrungswissenschaft); *Ralf Dahrendorf*, Gesellschaft und Demokratie in Deutschland[1] (1965) 178.

47. *Theodor Birt*, Deutsche Wissenschaft im 19. Jahrhundert, Eine Rede zur Jahrhundertwende (1900) 8, excerpted in: *Thomas Ellwein*, Die deutsche Universität, Vom Mittelalter bis zur Gegenwart (1985) 195-197 (195).

48. *McClelland* 172.

49. *Friedrich Carl von Savigny*, System des heutigen römischen Rechts I (1840) 14, see also 13-21. Savigny had earlier used the phrase » die gemeinsame Überzeugung des Volkes«; *id.*, Vom Beruf unserer Zeit für Gesetzgebung und Rechtswissenschaft (1814) 8 (in: Thibaut und Savigny, Ein programmatischer Rechtsstreit auf Grund ihrer Schriften . . . , ed. by *Jaques Stern* [1914, repr. 1959] 69-166 [126]) = *id.*, Of the Vocation of Our Age for Legislation and Jurisprudence, transl. by *Abraham Hayward* (1831, repr. 1975) 24: "the common conviction of the people" (I will hereinafter cite to the English translation of Savigny's "Vocation," which had a larger readership in America than the German original).

50. *Savigny*, Vocation (*supra* n. 49) 24, 27-30.

51. *Bodenheimer* 71-73; *Hans Hattenhauer*, Die geistesgeschichtlichen Grundlagen des deutschen Rechts[3] (1983) 114-119; *Joachim Rückert*, Idealismus, Jurisprudenz und Politik bei Friedrich Carl von Savigny (1984) 43-55, 178, 187, 192, 208f., 227-229, 386 (Abhandlungen zur rechtswissenschaftlichen Grundlagenforschung, 58); *Horst Schröder*, Friedrich Karl von Savigny, Geschichte und Rechtsdenken beim Übergang vom Feudalismus zum Kapitalismus in Deutschland (1984) 34-48 (Rechtshistorische Reihe, 36); *Peter Stein*, Legal Evolution, The Story of an Idea (1980) 56-65; *Wieacker* 381-399.

Germanists such as Jacob Grimm (1785-1863), and Georg Beseler (1809-1888), and also Otto von Gierke (1841-1921), who also promoted the historical school of law, were more systematically nationalistic than Savigny and his colleagues in the Romanist branch of the historical school; *Wieacker* 377, 405-410, 453 f.

52. See *Kleinheyer/Schröder* (*supra* n. 45) 229. Clemens Brentano (1778-1842) and Achim von Arnim (1781-1831) collaborated on romanticism's great collection of folk songs, *"Des Knaben Wunderhorn, . . ."* (1806); see *Eugen Wohlhaupter*, Friedrich Karl von Savigny und Achim von Arnim, in: *id.*, Dichterjuristen, ed. by *H.[orst] G.[erhard] Seifert* (1953) 97-119 (102).

53. *McClelland* 172f.

54. *Dawson* 450; *Herbst* 53.

55. *Ruckert* (*supra* n. 51) 331-334; *Savigny*, Vocation (*supra* n. 49) 64f.

56. *Dawson* 454f. Roman law, according to Savigny, was received in Germany due to internal necessity. The nomadic character of Germanic tribes deprived their customs of a territorial focus; *Stein* (*supra* n. 51) 62.

The idea of Rechtswissenschaft was supported at the beginning of Justinian's Institutes (I, 1, 1): "Iurisprudentia est divinarum atque humanarum rerum notitia, iusti atque iniusti scientia"; Corpus Iuris Civilis, ed. by *Ioann. L. G. Beck*, I (1829) 1. This translated in nineteenth-century German: » Rechtsgelahrtheit ist die Kenntniss der göttlichen und menschlichen Dinge, die Wissenschaft des Rechten und des Unrechten«; Das Corpus Juris Civilis, ed. by *Carl E. Otto/Bruno Schilling/Carl F.F. Sintenis*, I (1830) 1. In English this translates: "Jurisprudence is the knowledge of matters divine and human, and the comprehension of what is just and what is unjust"; The Civil Law, ed. by *Samuel P. Scott*, II (1932) 5. Taking "comprehension" as a synonym for "science," "iusti scientia" had come to mean by the nineteenth century "Rechrswissenschaft" or "legal science"; see *Stefan Riesenfeld*, A Comparison of Continental and American Legal Education: Mich. L. Rev. 36 (1937/38) 31-55 (51f.).

57. *Patterson* 411 f; *Wieacker* 399 f.

58. *Gordon A. Craig*, The Germans (1982) 190-192; *McClelland* 172.

59. *McClelland* 174-181, 195; *Fischer* (*supra* n. 41) 17-20; *Ernest C. Lorenzen*, Seminary Methods of Legal Instruction in the German Universities, in: Law and Jurisprudence Series I (1905) 15-33 (19, 24f., 28-33).

60. *Lorenzen* (*supra* n. 59) 17; *Max Rheinstein*, Law Faculties and Law Schools, A Comparison of Legal Education in the United States and Germany: Wisc. L. Rev. 1938, 5-42 (21-23).

61. *McClelland* 193f., 248-251. Eliot discussed his view of the relationship between Gymnasien, American secondary schools, and the American bachelor of laws degree in his 1869 inaugural address as president of Harvard; in: *Eliot*, Educational Reform, Essays and Addresses (1898) 1-38, excerpted in: American Higher Education 601-624 (606 f.).

62. *Eliot*, The New Education: Atlantic Monthly 23 (Febr., March 1869) 203-220 and 358-367, excerpted in: American Higher Education 624-641.

63. *Herbst* 35f., 50; *James* I 69, 94-96, 264; *Warren* II 355; Chase 336.

Eliot, however, had emphasized that his European ideas should not be slavishly imitated in America:

"When the American university appears, it will not be a copy of foreign institutions, or a hot-bed plant, but the slow and natural outgrowth of American social and political habits"; *Eliot* (*supra* n. 62) 637.

James reports:

"People have said—usually those who were opposed to his policies—that Eliot's ideal for Harvard resembled too much the pattern of a German university, and have assumed that what he saw while in Germany was what won him to a belief in some such ideal";

James I 136.

Although James recognizes that Eliot's "ideal was something more like the Continental system than like that of Oxford and Cambridge" (*James* loc. cit.) he does not find any direct evidence for a German connection from Eliot's letters which he wrote while he spent the winter of 1864-1865 at the University of Marburg) (*James* loc. cit.).

64. *James* I 98 and 246; *Chase* 334. Eliot had said that teachers and students should be encouraged in "making their own observations without imitating or copying, then describing accurately what they saw, and lastly, drawing the right inference from what they had themselves done and seen"; *James* I 162.

65. *James* I 162-165.

66. *James* I 244-246, 260, 265; *Chase* 334 f., 340.

67. See *supra*, text at n. 60.

68. *James* I 260. After Eliot had assumed the presidency, he totally revamped the Harvard Medical School. He initiated clinical and laboratory instruction, stiff entrance requirements, a progressive three-year curriculum, and written examinations that had to be passed at the end of each academic year; *id.* I 263, 281 and 291; Chase 334f., 340.

69. *James* I 256. Eliot had described an early meeting with Langdell:

"He told me that law was a science: I was quite prepared to believe it. He told me that the way to study a science was to go to the original sources. I knew that was true, for I had been brought up in the science of chemistry myself"; *Eliot*, quoted in: *Warren* II 361.

70. *James* I 269 f., 291, 300 f.; *Seligman* 32 f.; *Chase* 332. Langdell wanted legal study to be a graduate program, since American secondary school students were so ill-prepared for academic work. In 1875 the Law School adopted a regulation that required future students to be either college graduates or to pass an entrance test that asked applicants to translate certain classical Latin passages. The German Abitur for Gymnasium students, by comparison, which was a prerequisite for matriculation in a German university, required extensive knowledge of Latin and Greek. The Harvard Board of Overseers rescinded this new admission standard, however, concerned inter alia that Abraham Lincoln would not have qualified to study law at Harvard since he neither graduated from college nor read Latin. The admissions requirement of graduation from college was not finally achieved at Harvard until 1909; *Seligman* 38f.; *Warren* II 387, 394-398; *Stevens* (*supra* n. 20) 427.

71. *Sutherland* 188.

72. In an 1886 speech celebrating the 250th anniversary of Harvard College's founding, Langdell said:

". . . in all the rest of Christendom law has always been taught and studied in universities; . . . the true interests of legal education in this country required that, in this respect, we should not follow longer in the footsteps of England, but should bring ourselves into harmony with the rest of the civilized world. . . . I have tried to do my part towards making the teaching and study of law [at Harvard] worthy of a university, . . . toward placing the law school, as far as differences of circumstances would permit, in the position occupied by the law faculties in the universities of continental Europe"; *Christopher C. Langdell*, The Harvard Law School: L. Q. Rev. 3 (1887) 118-125 (123 f.).

73. *Redlich* (*supra* n. 28) 17; *Warren* II 495-502; *Chase* 332; see *Langdell*, A Selection of Cases on the Law of Contracts, With References and Citations[1] (1871), [2](1879). Nevertheless, it is likely that in many instances the case method ranged from rhetorical questioning by a professor to recitation by students without achieving the desired dialogue.

74. *Langdell*[2] (*supra* n. 73) p. VIII. The term "science" in 1870 was commonly used in a broad sense to describe an organized body of knowledge (Wissenschaft) as well as in a narrower sense related to empiricism; see also *supra* n. 46. Langdell was confusing on this point, since he used the term in both its senses. Analogous to the natural sciences, for instance, he contended that materials for legal science are contained in printed books, so a library should be the legal scientist's laboratory; *Sutherland* 175f. See also chapter 74 of this book.

75. *Eliot*, A Late Harvest, Miscellaneous Papers Written Between Eighty and Ninety (1924) 54. See also chapter 33.

76. *Patterson* 419 n. 61; *Sugarman* (*supra* n. 7) 32, regarding Albert Dicey's comparison, in England, of Savigny and Langdell (see *Albert V. Dicey*, Can English Law Be Taught at the Universities? [1883] 24). Savigny's legal science was a kind of juristic geometry:

"In every triangle, namely, there are certain data, from the relations of which all the rest are necessarily deducible: thus, given two sides and the included angle, the whole triangle is given. In like manner, every part of our law has points by which the rest may be given: these may be termed the leading axioms. To distinguish these, and deduce from them the internal connection, and the precise degree of affinity which subsist between all juridical notions and rules, is amongst the most difficult of the problems of jurisprudence. Indeed, it is peculiarly this which gives our labours the scientific character"; *Savigny*, Vocation (*supra* n. 49) 38f. (see also 45).

Eliot had favored a notion of organicism similar to that of Langdell:

". . . the universe, as science teaches, [is] an organism which has by slow degrees grown to its form of to-day on its way to its form of to-morrow, with slowly formed habits which we call laws, and a general health which we call the harmony of nature"; *Eliot*, in a manuscript from the 1870s, quoted in: *James* I 318.

77. *Redlich* (*supra* n. 28) 43.

78. *Hattenhauer* (*supra* n. 51) 117; see *supra* text at nn. 69 to 74.

79. *Savigny*, Vocation (*supra* n. 49) 137.

80. *Langdell*[2] (*supra* n. 73) p. VIII; see *supra* text at n. 74.

81. *Charles Darwin*, On the Origin of Species by Means of Natural Selection, or, The Preservation of Favoured Races in the Struggle for Life (1859).

82. *Marcia Speziale*, Langdell's Concept of Law as Science, The Beginning of Anti-Formalism in American Legal Theory: Vermont L. Rev. 5 (1980) 1-37 (3, 13, 19-24, 34).

83. *Stein* (*supra* n. 27) 424f., 432f. Charles Follen (1796-1840), born in Germany and educated at universities in Gießen and Jena, taught a course in civil law at the Law School in 1834. Nine of the school's 44 students attended; *Thwing* 84-89; *Warren* I 493.

84. *Bodenheimer* 72 f.; *Wieacker* 400 f.

85. *Bodenheimer* 76.

86. *Savigny*, Das Recht des Besitzes, Eine civilistische Abhandlung[1] (1803) = *id.*, The Law of Possession, transl. by *Luther S. Cushing* (1838).

87. *James Coolidge Carter*, Law—Its Origin, Growth, and Function, Being a Course of Lectures Prepared for Delivery Before the Law School of Harvard University (1907) 59; see *Bodenheimer* 76f.; *Grey* 30; *Warren* II 126, 132 and 185.

Just as Savigny had crusaded against German codification based on the French Code civil and its natural law underpinnings, Carter battled David Dudley Field's proposed civil code for New York on the ground that it would impede the growth of law; *Carter*, The Proposed Codification of Our Common Law (1883); see *Patterson* 421-424.

88. *Carter*, Law—. . . (*supra* n. 87); see *Warren* II 478.

89. *Carter*, Law—. . . (*supra* n. 87) 65, 84-86, 118-120; see *Bodenheimer* 76 f.; *Patterson* 424.

90. *Patterson* 419 f.; *Stevens* 38. Langdell said:

"What qualifies a person, . . . , to teach law, is not experience in the work of a lawyer's office, . . . but experience in learning law; not the experience of the Roman advocate, . . . but the experience of the Roman jurisconsult"; *Langdell* (*supra* n. 72) 124.

91. See *Hoeflich* (*supra* n. 14) 733. A favorable discussion of Savigny's ideas on legal science and the organic development of law took place within the American Bar Association (ABA); see "Report of the Committee on Legal Education and Admissions to the Bar": Am. Bar Ass. Rep. 15 (1892) 313-393 (333-337).

92. *Stevens* 51-53, 156. Oliver Wendell Holmes, Jr. (1841-1935) too recognized the German legal science influence on Harvard Law professors; *Oliver Wendell Holmes*, The Use of Law Schools, in: *id.*, Collected Legal Papers (1920) 35-48 (41-43) (a speech in 1886 before the Harvard Law School Association); see *Stevens* 122f.

93. *Stevens* 134.

94. *Grey* 30f., 36.

95. *Stevens* 93; see "Report of the Committee: Am. Bar Ass. Rep. 2 (1879) 209-236 (212-222).

96. *Grey* 37f.

97. *Christopher C. Tiedeman*, Methods of Legal Education (III): Yale L. J. 1 (1891/92) 150-158 (151).

98. *Tiedeman* (*supra* n. 97) 158.

99. "Report of the Committee . . . " (*supra* n. 91) 330, 340-354 and 362. In this Report it is also said that

". . . the historical method commends itself for elementary teaching because it shows the law neither in the form of mere abstractions nor in that of individual cases, but illustrates at every step the process by which it rises from the mere evidential fact to the highest generalization" (344). ". . . So long as the books used in our schools are mere collections of . . . the cases in which each point is sustained, without a word to show how one rule is connected with another, how the points owe their genesis to principles, the evil will remain. It is absurd to expect that a class of beginners will strike out a scientific method for themselves in a mass of such 'practical' rubbish, merely because we deafen them with praises of the logical consistency and scientific character of the law" (350).

See also the earlier "Report of the Committee . . .": Am. Bar Ass. Rep. 14 (1891) 301-360 (349f.); see also *Anthony Chase*, The American Law School and the Rise of Administrative Government (1982) 47.

100. "Report of the Committee . . ." (*supra* n. 91) 360.

101. *Chase* (*supra* n. 99) 47f., 51-59.

102. *James* II 137-140, 142.

103. *James* II 141. Eliot received an honorary Ph.D. from the University of Breslau in 1911; *id.* II 359.

104. *Eugen Kuehnemann* [Kühnemann], Charles W. Eliot, President of Harvard University (May 19, 1869—May 29, 1909) (1909) Prefatory Note, where he also stated that the German original of his essay appeared in the "Deutsche Rundschau" (Berlin) 1909, May and June issues.

105. *Kuehnemann* (*supra* n. 104) 5, 7, 13, 23-25, 30f.

106. *Kuehnemann* (*supra* n. 104) 21, 84. Although Kühnemann believed that from his travels Eliot had received an accurate impression of German intellectual life, especially the strictly scientific sphere, he felt, however, that Eliot was not well informed about Goethe's ideas and that his view of Kant was a "spirit of rigid Protestantism which connects Kant with Puritanism"; *id.* 73. See also *supra*, at n. 33.

107. See *Laura Fermi*, Illustrious Immigrants, The Intellectual Migration from Europe, 1930-41 (1968) 352f. Nevertheless, German legal thinking continued to have an influence on certain American scholars in the 1920s; *James E. Herget/Stephen Wallace*, The German Free Law Movement as the Source of American Legal Realism: Va. L. Rev. 73 (1987) 399-455 (422-434).

108. See *Max Rheinstein*, Einführung in die Rechtsvergleichung[1], ed. by *Reimer von Borries* (1974) 58-63; *Thieme* (*supra* n. 1) 260, 266-268.

Chapter 33

Langdell and the Law School

1895

Charles W. Eliot

Charles W. Eliot (March 20, 1834-August 22, 1926) was President of Harvard University from 1869 to 1909 and hired Langdell to be Dean. See chapter 1. This speech was first published at 9 *Harvard Law Review* 518 (1895).

When, in conversation, I first proposed to Mr. C. C. Langdell of the New York Bar that he become the Dane Professor in the Harvard Law School, I saw that the proposal attracted him strongly. He apparently wished to teach law rather than practice it, but to teach it in a new way. He called my attention to the obvious fact that he was a new kind of candidate for a professorship in the Harvard Law School, and expressed a good deal of doubt as to whether he could be elected. He was right in both respects; but clearly he had in mind some reform in legal education, some reconstruction of the Law School which I much wished to hear about, having some visions of my own about educational reform. He was distinctly attracted by the fact that it was the Dane professorship that was vacant, the professorship which Nathan Dane, eminent lawyer, legal author, and politician had founded by the gift of ten thousand dollars in 1829, and which Joseph Story had held for sixteen years thereafter. It was Dane, too, who in 1832 provided the growing school with an adequate building for the accommodation of its students and its library. When Dane founded his professorship, he provided that the lectures delivered on the foundation should be published. This provision Langdell thought a very wise one; and it accorded with his own purposes and anticipations. On the whole, my proposal fell in with Langdell's views of life, and he soon accepted the risks of the unusual candidature.

The Corporation consented, though with some reluctance, to elect Mr. Langdell Dane Professor, probably out of some general purpose to support their young President—all the members of the Board were old enough to be my father—whom they had placed in a difficult position in spite of much public and private criticism. The Board of Overseers in their turn consented to the election, but with even more reluctance, which was overcome mainly by the testimony of James C. Carter and Joseph H. Choate of the New York Bar to the effect that Langdell was a man of prodigious learning in the law and of remarkable industry, and that he had a legal mind of extraordinary acumen and sagacity.

The next step was to make him Dean of the School. A new statute required that the Faculty of each professional school should select from among its members a dean, whose duty it should be to keep the records of the Faculty and prepare its business. At the Faculty meeting called for this purpose there were present President Eliot, Professor Washburn, who had been for fourteen years one of the three professors who really managed the School, Professor Nathaniel Holmes, who had been a professor in the School for only two years and had never taken any active part in its administration, and the new Dane Professor. So far as can now be ascertained, there never had been any Faculty meeting in the Law School with a record of proceedings. Professor Washburn testified that he had never heard of one. The intervention of the President in any Law School proceedings was also unexampled. A few months after I entered on the duties of President, I stepped into Professor Washburn's office in Dane Hall to ask him some question about the state of the School. At sight of me Professor Washburn held up both hands and exclaimed, "This is the first time I have ever seen a President of the University in this building." Presidents Kirkland and Quincy took some interest in the Law School because of their warm friendship for Judge Story; but no subsequent President and no earlier one had manifested an interest in the School. The meeting was rather an awkward one. The President stated its object—to elect a Dean. Now deans were rather recent creations in Harvard University. The Medical School had had a Dean since 1864; but his chief function was friendly and charitable intercourse with the students. Professor Gurney had just been appointed Dean of the College Faculty; but the nature of his functions and influence was not yet visible. Whether the functions of the Dean of the Law School were to be chiefly clerical and eleemosynary or not was not clear to Professors Washburn and Holmes; but at any rate neither of them desired the office. The only candidate seemed to he Professor Langdell, who had only just come to the School; but Professor Langdell himself said nothing. Professor Washburn, after explaining his complete ignorance of such matters, moved that Professor Langdell be elected Dean. This motion was carried by the votes of Professors Washburn and Holmes, Professor Langdell not voting. Then began in 1870 a process of conservative experimentation and construction in the Law School which is not yet finished. The phrase in the new statute that the Dean should prepare the business of the Faculty gave the new Dean all the powers he needed.

The first subject Dean Langdell was called upon to deal with was the construction of a new curriculum for the School, divided into first and second year courses. To fill out this new programme required some additional courses, which the President and the Dean coöperated to procure. A similar reform was going on in the Medical School for like reasons. For three years the needed enlargement was procured by appointing eminent lawyers at the bar or on the bench to give instruction on special subjects in relatively short courses. Eight such lecturers were appointed during the first three years of the new regime, of whom three, Messrs. Bradley, Gray, and O. W. Holmes afterward became regular professors. Professor Langdell was distrustful of this method of increasing the instruction in the School; because he held that the fact that a man had become a distinguished lawyer or a respected judge did not prove that he knew how to teach law, or indeed that he could learn to teach law. He was inclined to believe that success at the Bar or on the Bench was, in all probability, a disqualification for the functions of a professor of law. He cordially assented, however, to the appointment of Messrs. Gray and Holmes; because he thought them genuine scholars in the law, capable both of discriminating research and of accurate exposition. President Eliot had seen at the Medical School that a distinguished practitioner of medicine or surgery might easily prove to be a poor teacher; although he might continuously interest medical students as an example of professional success. In the Law School he thought it prudent to provide for a few years the best possible examples of the old-fashioned method of teaching law, partly to break the force of the flood of criticism which was pouring in from members of the American Bar, but chiefly that the good students in the School might have the best possible opportunity to compare the old method with the new.

Professor Langdell's views concerning teachers of law received a striking illustration when in 1873-74 James Barr Ames, a recent graduate of the School, who had had no experience in practice, was appointed Assistant Professor of Law. Both the Corporation and the Overseers consented to this appointment with reluctance; and in all probability their consent was given only because the appointment was one limited by statute to a term of five years. The President was prepared to support Dean Langdell in this bold adventure; because he had already seen that there were parts of professional teaching which young men could do better than old men, even though the young men had had but little professional experience.

Before the expiration of the five years Mr. Ames was appointed full Professor of Law with general approbation, so conspicuous was his success.

As soon as Dean Langdell had completed his reorganization of the courses of study in the Law School, and put into operation his progressive programme covering two years, he turned his attention to the condition of the School's library, and set about, first, providing protection and safe management for the library, and, secondly, enlarging it. Langdell knew well the lack of supervision of the library before 1870. He had been himself its student librarian for several years. He had himself used the books of the library with complete freedom, especially in the preparation of his valuable notes to Parsons on Contracts. He knew what extensive losses and damages the library had suffered because of the lack of supervision and the carelessness of the students. He regarded a well-selected, well-kept, and ample library as the one essential piece of apparatus for any law school, and especially for the Harvard Law School he hoped for. It had been the practice of the School to supply all the students gratuitously with copies of the textbooks they used. To abolish this costly practice was one of Langdell's first measures. He soon procured the services of a permanent librarian, who should be in constant attendance in the library. These measures for the protection and better ordering of the library were taken within a few months of Langdell's becoming Dean; but it was not till 1873, when Mr. John Hines Arnold became librarian, that the future of the Law School library conducted on Langdell's principles was assured.

As the case system came into use, another principle with regard to the conduct of the library had to be often applied. Duplicates had to be supplied of reports and other books which were in frequent demand. With a special appropriation made by the Corporation much was done during the year 1870-71 to improve the fittings of the room occupied by the library, to repair the bindings, and fill the numerous gaps in the series of important reports which the School had acquired during its first fifty years. When Mr. Arnold become librarian in 1873 the librarian and the Dean worked together in perfect harmony, and indeed in the same spirit; and both lived to see the library increase greatly in number of volumes, serviceableness to the students and teachers, and pecuniary value.

To Professor Langdell books had a kind of sacrosanct character. They were to be handled carefully, preserved from dust and heat, and never defaced by pencil marks or words written on the margins of the pages. Mr. Arnold shared these sentiments of the Dean, especially in

18. Charles W. Eliot (1834-1926), an unusually energetic president of Harvard, not only hired Langdell to be Dean but supported him unto his eventual triumph, even though Langdell's changes were deeply unpopular and enrollment drained. (*Courtesy of Art & Visual Materials, Special Collections Department, Harvard Law School Library.*)

regard to books which had been obtained at high cost and could not certainly be replaced. These feelings were very much injured when certain teachers in the Law School, who were writing books, contracted the habit of sending books direct from the School library to one of the Cambridge printing offices, in order that the type might be set directly from the printed book, instead of from copies of the passages the authors proposed to use. Inevitably the books came back to the library with some of their pages defaced with black finger-marks and other smooches, and in some instances with pages torn. This state of things reported by the librarian to the Dean, the Dean made some mild suggestions that the offending authors do as he had done,— have passages they wished to quote copied. When he found that this proposition was regarded by the offenders as unreasonable and was wholly ineffectual, he came to the President's office one morning with a grave aspect indeed, and in his official capacity requested my aid. He regretted the necessity of asking me to intervene; but the evil was intolerable. I had some difficulty in convincing the offenders that the Dean was right, and that his request should be respected. This is the only instance I can recall in which Dean Langdell procured the enforcement of his wishes by an exercise of the President's authority. In general, he eagerly desired to convince his associates and his students by argument that his way of looking at measures or doctrines was right or sound.

The instructive story of the success of Professor Langdell's method of teaching law has been well told by competent witnesses in the Centennial History of the Harvard Law School. Professor Langdell and I waited patiently, but anxiously, for the verdict. The number of students declined more than either of us had expected, and the demonstration of success achieved in prominent law offices and in practice by graduates of the School, who had enjoyed Langdell's system and thoroughly utilized it, came more slowly than we had anticipated. On the other hand, that demonstration, when it came, was accepted by the legal profession with surprising readiness.

Other restrictive measures, such as the requirement for admission to the School of the degree of Bachelor of Arts or its equivalent, had to be postponed somewhat, but not for long. Dean Langdell thought that English and American law should be studied by itself without admixture of other subjects, such as government, economics, international law, or Roman law; but he also wanted every law student to have had a preliminary training in a good secondary school and a good college. When Professor Ames wished to include in the purchases for the library many books on Roman law, Dean Langdell acquiesced reluctantly, but was ultimately convinced that a great law library should include even that somewhat remote or detached subject.

During this long struggle with adverse circumstances, and especially with severe criticism of the case method and its results, Dean Langdell never cared to defend himself in print or by public speech. He knew that there was only one way to refute criticism, namely, to exhibit the professional success of his disciples. His silence did not mean lack of confidence in his method; far from it. Even when the failure of his eyesight compelled him to modify his method in his own classroom, he remained sure of the superiority of his original case method to any other, although he could no longer use it successfully himself.

Professor Langdell had, I think, no acquaintance with the educational theories or practices of Froebel, Pestalozzi, Seguin, and Montessori; yet his method of teaching was a direct application to intelligent and well-trained adults of some of their methods for children and detectives. He tried to make his students use their own minds logically on given facts, and then to state their reasoning and conclusions correctly in the classroom. He led them to exact reasoning and exposition by first setting an example himself, and then giving them abundant opportunities for putting their own minds into vigorous action, in order, first, that they might gain mental power, and, secondly, that they might hold firmly the information or knowledge they had acquired. It was a strong case of education by drawing out from each individual student mental activity of a very strenuous and informing kind. The elementary and secondary schools of the United States are only just beginning to adopt on a large scale this method of education,—a method which is not passive but intensely active, not mainly an absorption from either book or teacher but primarily a constant giving-forth. Professor Langdell's method resembled the laboratory method of teaching physical science, although he believed that the only laboratory the Law School needed was a library of printed books. His case system has been widely applied in this country to the teaching of clinical medicine and surgery, as a useful addition to the ordinary practice of teaching those subjects at the bedside of actual patients. The combination he used of the lecture and the recitation is capable of wide application in both primary and secondary schools and in colleges and universities. Indeed, the conference method used with small advanced groups in universities is an earlier example of his method, the merits of which have been recognized for at least a century wherever such groups have existed.

Langdell's disposition or character was singularly honest, just, candid, and serene; although he was also capable of indignation, quick and evanescent, or slow-gathering and persistent. He was a curious mixture of the conservative and the radical, having the merits of both. His relation to his wife, who was much younger than himself, and to her mother was so delicate and tender that it was a high privilege to witness it. About his own affairs he was reticent or reserved. Cut off in youth and manhood from the amusements and relaxations of most educated men, he took pleasure in the careful investment of his savings, as soon as he could make any. I was one of the few persons with whom he sometimes discussed investments; although he soon learned that, compared with him, I knew little about the subject. I heard from him something about farm mortgages in Iowa and other fertile western states. I found he held strong opinions about the security of the mortgage bonds of certain western railroads, and the insecurity of others, and that he enjoyed the careful researches which led him to these opinions. Such studies, however, were only the by-play of his mind. He was as successful there as he was in his other mental work; so that he left an estate whose amount surprised all his friends. He was as sagacious and far-seeing in this his sport as he was in his serious labors.

A striking characteristic of Professor Langdell was courage, both physical and moral. His moral courage was perfectly illustrated by his acceptance of the Dane professorship and his whole conduct as Dean of the Law School. His physical courage was illustrated by his going about alone on foot by day and by night in the streets of Cambridge, when he could see hardly anything, especially in the glare of bright sunshine. His daily walks between Austin Hall and his house were terrifying to onlookers, particularly after the advent of the automobile, but never to him. He would wait to cross the streets till his ears assured him that no horse or horse vehicle was very near; but his ears could not warn him in time of the rapid approach of a quiet automobile. Then he had to trust that the chauffeurs would see that a blind man was crossing the broad street. For several years he was quite unable to go alone on an unfamiliar path. This helplessness was a great trial to a man who had always been self-reliant in high degree; but he bore the calamity with unfaltering patience. As a teacher, Langdell was a great benefactor of the legal profession, and hence of every free and orderly community. As a man, he was worthy of all love and reverence.

Charles W. Eliot.

Cambridge, Mass.

Chapter 34

Teaching Law as a Science

1886

Christopher C. Langdell

Christopher Columbus Langdell (May 22, 1826-July 6, 1906) was Dane Professor and Dean of the Harvard Law School from 1870 to 1900. His influence on instruction and his casebooks are described in chapter 1. This address was delivered to the newly formed alumni association at "Law Day" in 1886 and printed in *Harvard University 1636-1886: A Record of the Commemoration, November Fifth to Eighth, 1886 on the Two Hundred and Fiftieth Anniversary of the Founding of Harvard College* (Cambridge: John Wilson and Son, 1887).

Gentlemen of the Harvard Law School Association:

I am very grateful for this unexpected greeting. You will be surprised to learn that this is the second time that your President has called upon me to speak for the Harvard Law School. The first time was nearly seventeen years ago, when I was about to assume the duties of Dane professor. And I do not know that I can do better than begin now where I left off then. On that occasion I called attention to the anomalous condition of legal education in English-speaking countries, — the anomaly consisting in the fact that in those countries a knowledge of law had been acquired, as a rule, only by or in connection with its practice and administration, while in all the rest of Christendom law has always been taught and studied in universities. And I ventured to express the opinion, that the true interests of legal education in this country required that in this respect we should not follow longer in the footsteps of England, but should bring ourselves into harmony with the rest of the civilized world.

Since that time I have not concerned myself with legal education outside of the Harvard Law School; but I have tried to do my part towards making the teaching and the study of law in that School worthy of a university; towards making the venerable institution of which we are celebrating the two hundred and fiftieth anniversary a true university, and the Law School not the least creditable of its departments; in short, towards placing the Law School, so far as differences of circumstances would permit, in the position occupied by the Law Faculties in the universities of continental Europe. And what I say of myself in this respect I may, with at least equal truth, say of all my associates.

To accomplish these objects, so far as they depended upon the Law School, it was indispensable to establish at least two things: first, that law is a science; secondly, that all the available materials of that science are contained in printed books. If law be not a science, a university will best consult its own dignity in declining to teach it. If it be not a science, it is a species of handicraft, and may best be learned by serving an apprenticeship to one who practises it. If it be a science, it will scarcely be disputed that it is one of the greatest and most difficult of sciences, and that it needs all the light that the most enlightened seat of learning can throw upon it. Again, law can only be learned and taught in a university by means of printed books. If, therefore, there are other and better means of teaching and learning law than printed books, or if printed books can only be used to the best advantage in connection with other means, — for instance, the work of a lawyer's office, or attendance upon the proceedings of courts of justice, — it must be confessed that such means cannot be provided by a university. But if printed books are the ultimate sources of all legal knowledge; if every student who would obtain any mastery of law as a science must resort to these ultimate sources; and if the only assistance which it is possible for the learner to receive is such as can be afforded by teachers who have travelled the same road before him, — then a university, and a university alone, can furnish every possible facility for teaching and learning law. I wish to emphasize the fact that a teacher of law should be a person who accompanies his pupils on a road which is new to them, but with which he is well acquainted from having often travelled it before. What qualifies a person, therefore, to teach law is not experience in the work of a lawyer's office, not experience in dealing with men, not experience in the trial or argument of causes, — not experience, in short, in using law, but experience in learning law; not the experience of the Roman advocate or of the Roman prætor, still less of the Roman procurator, but the experience of the Roman juris-consult.

My associates and myself, therefore, have constantly acted upon the view that law is a science, and that it must be learned from books. Accordingly, the Law Library has been the object of our greatest and most constant solicitude. We have not done for it all that we should have been glad to do, but we have done much. Indeed, in the library of to-day one would find it difficult to recognize the library of seventeen years ago. We have also constantly inculcated the idea that the library is the proper workshop of professors and students alike; that it is to us all that the laboratories of the university are to the chemists and physicists, all that the museum of natural history is to the zoölogists, all that the botanical garden is to the botanists.

From what I have already said it easily follows, first, that a good academic training, especially in the study of language, is a necessary qualification for the successful study of law; secondly, that the study of law should be regular, systematic, and earnest, not intermittent, desultory, or perfunctory; thirdly, that the study should be prosecuted for a length of time bearing some reasonable proportion to the magnitude and difficulty of the subject. Accordingly, to secure the first of these objects, we have established an examination for admission for such as are not graduates. To secure the third, we have made three years of study necessary in all cases for a degree. To secure the second, we have done several things. First, we have established a course of study which we require to be pursued in the prescribed order. Secondly, we have established annual examinations to be held at the end of each year in the work of that year. Thirdly, we require every candidate for a degree to pass his examinations in the studies of the first year at the end of his first year as a condition of being admitted into the second year, and in the studies of the second year as a condition of being admitted into the third year; and we do not permit any one to pass his examinations in the studies of any year unless he has been regularly admitted into that year at the beginning of the year. In other words, we do not permit any one to pass examinations in any studies except those of the year to which he belongs. Fourthly, we have increased the amount of instruction, in the last seventeen years, from ten hours a week to thirty-six hours a week. This enables us to give the whole of the three years' course every year, thus giving to each class its appropriate instruction.

The result of all these measures is that the School is strictly divided into three classes, each class doing the work which belongs to its year, and every man having the strongest possible inducements to do his work *as* it should be done and *when* it should be done.

Let it not be supposed that we are unmindful of the work of our predecessors; we should indeed be ungrateful if we were. We do not forget that they began with nothing, while we have enjoyed the fruits of all their labors. We do not wish to disguise the fact that we could not have done our work, had we not had the labors of our predecessors to build upon as a foundation.

Nor are we unmindful of the support and encouragement which we have constantly received from the

President of the University. He has never hesitated, wavered, or faltered when any responsibility was to be assumed or work to be done.

Lastly, we are not unmindful of the support we have received from the students of the School, both while they were in the School and since they have left it. Without their support and co-operation, the various measures to which I have referred (many of which could not have been expected to be popular measures) could never have been maintained. It has been in a great degree the eagerness with which they have always encountered difficulties, the ability with which they have followed the subtlest lines of reasoning, and detected the slightest flaws or sophistries in argument, and the persistence with which they have refused to be satisfied so long as any doubt remained in their minds to be cleared up, that has given to the instructors such success as they have achieved. Finally, it is almost wholly to their testimony, both while in the School and after leaving it, that the School is indebted for such public recognition as it has received.

Chapter 35

The Harvard Law School, 1869-1894

1894

Christopher C. Langdell

Christopher Columbus Langdell (May 22, 1826-July 6, 1906) was Dane Professor and Dean of the Harvard Law School from 1870 to 1900. His influence on instruction and his casebooks are described in Chapter 1. This article was one of four by various authors devoted to the presidency of Charles Eliot and was printed in 2 *The Harvard Graduates' Magazine* 490 (1894).

The history of the Law School may be divided into four periods, the first extending from the original establishment of the School (May 14, 1817) to the appointment of Judge Story as Dane Professor (June 3, 1829); the second extending from the latter event to the death of Judge Story[1]; the third extending from the death of Judge Story (Sept. 10, 1845) to the election of Charles W. Eliot as President of the University (May 19, 1869); and the fourth extending from the latter event to the present time.

During the whole of the first period, the School was small and feeble, and gave little promise of what it has since become. It had no home of its own,[2] not a dollar of endowment, only a meagre library,[3] and only one professor. The professor had no salary, but received as his compensation the tuition fees paid by the students. The whole number of different students who entered the School during the period was 103, being an average of about 8.5 in each year. How small the School was at the close of this period may be judged by the fact that only five students entered during the last year, and that the first year of the second period opened with only two students who had entered during the first period.

The second period was one of great prosperity, and of constant and rapid growth. From the beginning of it, there were two professors, namely, the Dane Professor,[4] and the Royall Professor,[5] and an endowment of $17,943.63.[6] In the first year of the period, the number of students whose names appeared on the annual catalogue was 24, all but two of whom were then members of the School for the first time; the number of students who entered during the year was 38, and the tuition fees for the year amounted to $3,000. In the last year the number of students whose names appeared on the annual catalogue was 154, the number who entered during the year was 133, and the tuition fees for the year amounted to $13,985. During this period, Dane Hall was erected, the older part in 1832, and the newer part in 1845, and the library attained such magnitude and perfection that it was very generally believed to be the largest and best law library in the United States. According to the report of a committee[7] of the Board of Overseers, dated February 7, 1850, the tuition fees during Judge Story's time amounted in the aggregate to $105,000, of which $47,800 were applied to the payment of current expenses, $29,000 were expended upon the library, $12,700 in the erection of Dane Hall, and the remaining $15,500 stood to the credit of the School as a surplus on the books of the Treasurer.

At the beginning of the second period, an important change took place in the aim and object of the School, — a change which has ever since been steadily adhered to. During the first period, the School was *local*; since the beginning of the second period, it has been *national*; and this change appears to have been due in part to Nathan Dane, and in part to Judge Story.

During the third period, the School failed to hold its own. In the last year of that period, the number of students whose names appeared on the annual catalogue was 138, being less by 16 than in the last year of the preceding period; the number who entered during the year was 95, being less by 43 than in the last year of the preceding period, and the tuition fees for the year amounted to $11,537.50, being less by $2,457.50 than in the last year of the preceding period. Though there was no increase in the "plant" of the School during this period, unless the books purchased for the library be deemed an increase of "plant," yet the surplus of $15,500, accumulated during the second period, had become at the end of the third period a deficit of $1,670.12.[8] At the end of the period, the library, as compared with its condition at the end of the preceding period, was almost a wreck. After the resignation of Professor Greenleaf, there was no professor in the School who took a strong personal interest in the library, nor any one who apparently had an adequate conception of the requirements of such a library. The purchase of books was limited almost wholly to such books as were sent to the library by the booksellers with whom the School dealt; and very little attention was given to the important subject of the binding and repairing of books. Moreover, there was a degree of freedom from restraint in the use or abuse of the library, which, if persisted in, was sure to ruin it first or last. It was kept open constantly from 9 A. M. to 9 P. M.; and yet there was no one to exercise any supervision or control over those who might choose to resort to it. The librarian was always a student in the School, and his chief duties related to the text-books kept for the use of the students, and which constituted in effect a circulating library. If the professors had taken a strong and active interest in the care and preservation of the books, the evil day might have been deferred; but, as it was, the condition of the library had come to be so ruinous, at the close of the third period, that some radical change in its administration was imperatively called for.

Of legislation during the third period, whether by the Corporation or by the Faculty of the School, there was almost none. How little there was, any one may easily see by comparing the annual catalogue for 1868-69 with that for 1844-45.

Apart from the particulars already adverted to, the Law School underwent little substantial change prior to the time of President Eliot. It was originally established upon the model of a lawyer's office, and a lawyer's office it remained, in substance, to the end. It was for this reason that the tuition fee was always $100 a year, that being the sum which students who studied in offices had to pay; and as students who studied in offices did not have to purchase any books, so the Law School adopted and continued the practice of furnishing every student with a copy of the text-books which he had occasion to study. It was, perhaps, in accordance with the same idea that Professor Stearns placed his own law library at the service of the students,[9] the tuition fees paid by them going to him.

The Faculty of the School, as such, had never had more than a nominal existence. The President had always left the management of the School entirely to the professors, and the latter, when they acted together, did so without any of the forms of legislation. So far as is known, no recorded meeting of the Faculty had ever been held.

According to the annual catalogues, the students in the School were divided into three classes from 1831 down, but this division had no reference to the instruction given, nor even to the length of time that the students respectively had been in the School, but was based solely upon the length of time that they had studied law, either in the School or elsewhere; and the only effect that it had was upon the appointment of the students as counsel in moot court cases. In respect to instruction, there was no division of the School into classes. There was always, indeed, one course which was specially designed for beginners, but, with that exception, all the instruction given was intended for the whole School.

There never had been any attempt by means of legislation to raise the standard of education at the

School, nor to discriminate between the capable and the incapable, the diligent and the idle. It had always been deemed a prime object to attract students to the School, and with that view as little as possible was required of them. Students were admitted to the School without any evidence of *academic* acquirements, and they were sent from it, with a degree, without any evidence of *legal* acquirements. The degree of LL.B. was conferred solely upon evidence that the student had been nominally a member of the School for a certain length of time, and had paid his tuition fees, the longest time required being one and one half years.

President Eliot assumed the duties of his office at the beginning of the academic year 1869-70. In the latter part of that year, a circular was issued for the year 1870-71, which announced a new course of study, and that the degree would thereafter be conferred only upon examination.

During the summer vacation in 1870, the room in which the library was kept was completely renovated, and divided into two compartments, one of which was converted into a "stack" or repository for books, and the other into a reading-room for the students. Such of the books in the library as were in constant use were placed in the reading-room, and the gaps thus made in the general library were filled by new purchases. At the same time, a permanent librarian was appointed, whose whole time was to be devoted to the duties of his office, and who was to have such assistants as should be found necessary for the efficient administration of the library. Such was the origin of the system which is now in operation, and which formed the basis of the architect's plans for the second story of Austin Hall.

In the beginning of 1870-71, a change was made, in one course,[10] in the method of study and instruction, the essence of which consisted in substituting a selection of cases as the text-book instead of a treatise. This change was gradually extended to other courses, until it became, and now is, universal. It has also had, and is still having, a powerful influence upon legal education throughout the country.

On September 27, 1870, the first recorded Faculty meeting was held. Since that date, inclusive, 198 such meetings have been held, at all but five of which the President has presided.

In the circular for 1871-72, it was announced that the tuition fee would thereafter be $150 for the first year, $100 for the second year, and $50 a year thereafter. One object of this was to increase the revenues of the School, while another object was to induce students to remain longer in the School.

By the same circular, it was announced that thereafter every candidate for a degree would be required to pass his examination in the studies of the first year at the end of his first year, and of the second year at the end of his second year; and that no student would be admitted to the second year, until he had first passed his examinations in the studies of the first year. The policy thus begun has since been steadily adhered to.

On June 2, 1873, a wholly new step was taken by the Corporation in appointing a young man (J. B. Ames, '68) who was still a student in the School, as assistant professor of law for five years; and this was followed up by promoting him to a full professorship before the expiration of his term. Since then, this mode of recruiting the teaching force, and of filling professors' chairs, has become the settled policy of the School.

In the circular for 1878-79, it was announced that thereafter the honor degree of LL.B. *cum laude* would be conferred upon such students as passed examinations of distinguished excellence, and complied with certain other conditions. This was the origin of the present distinction between the ordinary degree and the honor degree.

At the beginning of 1877-78, the course of study was extended, as to all students then or thereafter entering the School, from two years to three years, and an examination for admission was also established for all candidates for a degree who were not graduates of colleges. At the same time, the tuition fee was fixed at the uniform rate of $150 a year. The year before these changes were made, the number of students whose names appeared on the annual catalogue had risen to 187, the number who entered during the year had risen to 128, the tuition fees for the year had risen to $26,683.34, and there was a surplus of $8,909.44 standing to the credit of the School on the Treasurer's books. In 1882-83, the number of students whose names appeared on the annual catalogue had fallen to 131, the number who entered during the year had fallen to 84, the tuition fees for the year had fallen to $19,375, and the surplus had fallen to $6,751.89. From this time, the recovery from the effect of these changes began, and continued without interruption.

19. Christopher Columbus Langdell (1826-1906), the "bearded prophet of Austin Hall," whose lecture method and case pamphlets inspired the universal legal pedagogy in the twentieth century. (*Courtesy of Art & Visual Materials, Special Collections Department, Harvard Law School Library.*)

In 1883, Austin Hall was completed, at a cost of over $140,000, and during the summer vacation of that year the School moved into it. For this fine building, the School was wholly indebted to the munificence of Mr. Edward Austin.

In 1886, on the occasion of the celebration of the 250th anniversary of the founding of the College, the Harvard Law School Association was formed. This Association now numbers 1,684 members, and has exerted an incalculable influence in promoting the prosperity of the School.

Within a few months after the establishment of the Law School Association, the *Harvard Law Review* was established. This now has 902 paying subscribers, and has accumulated a fund of $2,000.

In 1888, a complete catalogue was issued of the past members of the School, giving, so far as possible, the full address of all such as were living, and the precise time and place of the death of all such as were dead. This was followed, in 1890, by a second catalogue, on the same plan as the first, but much more complete and perfect; and, as this was intended to be followed by a new catalogue every five years, it was called a quinquennial catalogue. These two catalogues cost the School in money over $4,000; and yet the largest element in their cost was the time and labor expended in their preparation.

At the beginning of the year 1893-94, the requirements of the examination for admission were increased by the addition of another language; and all persons then or thereafter entering the School, other than graduates of colleges, were required to pass the examination, whether candidates for a degree or not.

It was also announced in the circular for 1893-94 that, after the year 1895-96, only graduates of some one of 108 colleges, of which a list was given, and persons qualified to enter the Senior Class of Harvard College, would be admitted to the School as candidates for a degree.

At the beginning of President's Eliot's administration, the instruction in the School was given by three professors, and consisted of ten lectures and one moot court in each week. In 1892-93, 51 lectures were given in each week by six professors, two assistant professors, and two lecturers.

The number of students whose names appeared on the annual catalogue, in 1892-93, was 394, the number who entered during the year was 223, the tuition fees for the year amounted to $57,950, the surplus for the year amounted to $13,818.56, and the total surplus to the credit of the School on the books of the Treasurer at the end of the year amounted to $76,301.20.[11] Moreover, this large surplus was accumulated in spite of the fact that, between the years 1869-70 and 1892-93, there was an expenditure upon Dane Hall and Austin Hall, including the furnishing of each, of over $37,000, — an expenditure which was caused largely by the growth of the School.

During President Eliot's administration, 22,374 volumes of books have been purchased, at an expense of $67,224.29, and $14,328.02 have been expended in the binding and repairing of books; and the sum of $9,447.09 was expended for these purposes in the year 1892-93. The library now contains upward of 33,000 volumes, including at least three copies of all important English and American reports.

Prior to President Eliot's time, the teaching of law as a career was a thing unknown in this country, as it has always been a thing unknown in England. Now, however, a very different state of things exists, at least so far as this School and its graduates are concerned. Of the eight professors and assistant professors now in the School, the four youngest received their legal education in this School since President Eliot's administration began, and all of them deliberately chose the teaching of law as a career in preference to the practice of it. Many of the recent graduates of the School are also now actively engaged in teaching law in other institutions, and the number so engaged is rapidly increasing. Indeed, many institutions now habitually look to the recent graduates of this School for their supply of teachers. The School may, therefore, fairly claim, not only that it has succeeded in inspiring its students with enthusiasm for the cultivation of law as a science and for a professorial life, but also that its students have shown a degree of aptitude and capacity for teaching law which has caused their services to be sought for, not only by their *Alma Mater*, but by sister institutions as well.

NOTES

1. The second period is precisely coeval with the administration of President Quincy. The latter was inaugurated June 2, 1829, and the appointment of Judge Story was made on the following day. President Quincy resigned his office August 27, 1845, and Judge Story died September 10, 1845.

2. Until the erection of the older part of Dane Hall in 1832, the Law School occupied two rooms, in an "old, low-studded wooden building which had been long inhabited by the college students," and which stood about where Mr. Huntington's shop now is. See Story's *Life*, ii, 39.

3. The size and contents of the library in 1826 appear from a catalogue printed in that year.

4. The Dane Professorship was established June 2, 1829, the day before the appointment of Judge Story.

5. The Royall Professorship was established September 4, 1815, but it was established as a College professorship. The duties of the first Royall Professor (Chief Justice Isaac Parker) were merely those of a non-resident lecturer. His lectures (a single course of not less than fifteen lectures in each year) were for the benefit of the Senior Class in College, and of resident graduates, and attendance at them was regarded as a part of a general (not of a professional) education. Even when the professorship became vacant, November 15, 1827, there seems to have been no thought of conferring it upon Professor Stearns. When, however, John Hooker Ashmun was appointed Royall Professor, June 11, 1829 (just eight days after the appointment of Judge Story), the duties of the professorship were entirely changed, and were transferred to the Law School; and in this way the Law School obtained the benefit of the Royall endowment.

6. Namely, the Dane endowment of $10,000, and the Royall endowment of $7,943.63. In 1835-36, Mr. Dane increased his endowment to $15,000.

7. This report was written by Charles Sumner. See Sumner's *Works*, ii, 377, 388.

8. After the receipt by the Corporation of the Bussey estate, in May, 1861, as the income of the School from endowments was largely increased, and as the annual amount of such income fluctuated widely, the questions, whether a surplus or a deficit appeared on the Treasurer's books at the end of any particular year, and what was the amount of either, ceased to have much significance for purposes of comparison.

9. That he did so, appears from the catalogue of the library before referred to.

10. It need hardly be said that this was the course given by Professor Langdell himself, who was appointed Dean of the Law School in 1870. —*Editor.* [Editor's note in 1998: This note placed by the editor in 1884.]

11. A comparison of these figures with those already given for the year 1868-69 will show the growth of the School since President Eliot's administration began.

Chapter 36

Langdell, Gray, Thayer and Ames

Their Contribution to the Study and Teaching of Law

1931

Joseph H. Beale

Joseph H. Beale (October 12, 1861-January 20, 1943) was a founder of the *Harvard Law Review* (see chapter 71) and Royal Professor of Law in the Harvard Law School from 1890 to 1937. This article first appeared in 8 *New York University Law Quarterly Review* 385 (1931).

From the year 1870 to the end of the nineteenth century the Harvard Law School became a place where students worked enthusiastically, studied law by a new method, and by their success as lawyers induced schools over the whole country to accept the same method which had proved satisfactory. Success in any school of law must be determined by the effect of the instruction upon the minds and actions of the students. Success in teaching must be judged by the enthusiastic response of those who are taught. What was accomplished in thirty years in the Harvard Law School must accordingly be ascribed to the influence upon the students of the faculty at the time. It was, indeed, a wonderful body of men. Four men, different in every respect, in age, in early experience, in abilities, in methods; in short, in every way in which teachers can differ from one another these four men differed. They did, however, all possess this one quality of arousing enthusiasm in their students.

I. Christopher Columbus Langdell

Christopher Columbus Langdell found himself in the late sixties of the nineteenth century wishing he were back in the time of the Plantagenets. His sober and austere spirit, his detached mind, his natural shyness in the face of modern ways suited with that careful plodding investigation, thoroughness of search, reliance upon mental processes rather than experience which were characteristics of the Year-Book worthies.

In his life in New York, although a useful member of a busy firm, he lived in a little room above his office; climbing up or down his winding iron stair as he needed sleep or a book. Was such a recluse able to change the whole course of legal education and of legal thought in the Anglo-American world?

He became first Dean of the Harvard Law School; and at once dealt with the problem before him as he dealt with a legal problem. Experience was nothing to him; otherwise following experience, he would have stayed in the rut in which the school had run for twenty-five years, since Story's death. In full reliance upon the result of his own mental processes, he worked out his novel plans and put them into effect; soberly, carefully and thoroughly, turned aside neither by ridicule nor criticism.

Up to this time the method of learning, even in the universities, had been by the student hearing or reading the knowledge of a teacher, didactically expressed. But Langdell, engaged while in the school on the notes to *Parsons on Contracts*, knew that information received fourth-hand does not take possession of one like information one gains for himself, first hand, from the sources. The impression may not be as formally correct as that received from a master; but it is one's own, living, ready when self-corrected to become a part of his mental fiber. Having a course on Contracts to teach, Langdell placed in the hands of each student the decisions on the subject under discussion, chiefly English, which he wished them to read; and the change in method was made. His predecessor had placed in the hands of each of his students his own *Treatise on Contracts*, for which Langdell had made the notes.

20. Joseph H. Beale (1861-1943), professor at Harvard and dean at Chicago, a leading proselytizer for the Langdellian movement. (*Courtesy of Art & Visual Materials, Special Collections Department, Harvard Law School Library.*)

Langdell proved to be a thinker, an inventor, an administrator, but never a teacher. At first his teaching method was to question his students in order to make sure they had read their cases. Later, as his sight became dim, he lectured, criticising and explaining the cases. But it is to be remembered that Langdell never claimed to have discovered a method of teaching, but a method of study; teaching to him was relatively unimportant. The technique of modern American law teaching derives from Ames.

But while he invented a method of study which has become the standard in law schools, he had also the task of administering the school. He found it a school with no requirements for admission, no graded curriculum, no examinations, no tradition of scholarship, no requirements for the degree. The highest praise a loyal student could give the school of the fifties and sixties was that those who chose to work might do so. Before Langdell ceased to be Dean the school required for admission a college degree, offered a progressive three-year curriculum with a stiff examination of the problem type (his invention) in each course; and the school aroused in the minds of the students a spirit of industry and an enthusiasm for the work, seldom equalled in an institution of learning.

Throughout his service as Dean the school was poor. There was very little income except from the tuition fees of the students. The library at the beginning was almost worthless: it had to be provided. A medieval-minded recluse does not promise to become a financial genius; but Langdell so carefully husbanded the income of the school as to provide a larger faculty, a first-rate library, and before his death a monumental building for the school, bearing his name, and erected and equipped from the accumulated surplus earned by the school.

In his own affairs he was equally successful. Marrying late in life, he had saved a considerable amount from his salary, which he invested wisely, but characteristically. He never, I believe, took advice on investments. When he contemplated an investment he secured a small library of books on the subject, studying a whole industry, and then a few particular concerns. After at least a year spent in this study (which so far as I know never included a personal inspection), he would buy largely, if at all; his investment ordinarily amounted to at least twenty-five thousand dollars. If he did not have enough uninvested cash on hand, he borrowed from a savings bank with the investment as security. His wife survived him only a short time; and when the estate was finally settled there was no investment which did not pay its interest or dividends during the bad times of 1907.

By the time I knew him, Langdell was a heavily built, white-haired man with very dim eyes, a rather helpless-looking figure as he stood at a crossing, calling to his venturesome little dog, his constant companion; but he never had any trouble in getting about, in that day of the horse-drawn vehicle. He was always a cold man in appearance, as a result of his combination of austerity and shyness; but he meant to be cordial, and was never repellant. His law, like himself, seemed medieval until one used it in court, when it proved sound and modern.

As one of the editors for the first volume of the Harvard Law Review I had charge of the short-lived department of Lecture Notes. I wrote up my notes on one of his best lectures in Equity Jurisdiction and went to him for leave to print. He hum'd and ha'd a while, then decided he would write it out for himself. The result was a long series of articles on the subject. He had a weakness for his own legal ideas, and rather resented having any one else express them.[1]

II. John Chipman Gray

Very different from Langdell was John Chipman Gray. They were both big, strong men; but while Langdell had been a poor boy and earned not merely his education but his bread with his own hands, Gray had been born and reared in the comfortable life of the old commercial class in eastern Massachusetts. After graduation from college he had been a staff officer in the Civil War. His letters to his friend Ropes, lately published, show the pose and self-reliance of a young man of his birth and education, though the judgment they show was less than he later acquired. Returning after the war, he formed a partnership with his friend Ropes which became the leading legal firm east of New York. He always had the ear of the court, and usually won his cases; when he lost, he properly disciplined the court by writing a book about it. Though in active practice all his life, he was only one day a week in his office, the rest of his working time being spent in the school, which he loved. For the first twenty years of his teaching he lectured and his lectures were delightful. Taken in long-hand, they read like a well-written book. The students regarded his careful sentences as oracles of the law. As a younger colleague said of him, he was a rock of trust. As in the school, so in practice, great estates were entrusted to him, and he was consulted in great affairs.

Personally he was kind and approachable to his students, always accessible, sympathetic and friendly. To his younger colleagues he was a delightful link to an older and more courtly generation—not that he was in any way pompous or unctuous, for a simpler man never showed himself in all ways the gentleman. His quality of swearing on occasion in a most satisfying way he doubtless learned in the army. He detested reading examination books, and he always had a lot of them to read. One who passed the door of his office in Langdell Hall could see him struggling with a book, groaning and occasionally swearing—all in a most gentlemanly way. He was the only one of us who didn't turn back the cover of each book before reading it. He said it lightened the tedium to know the student's name. "Richardson—he has a very pretty sister. Prescott—what a harum-scarum his father used to be in college. Jones—his uncle, poor fellow, was in my regiment, killed at Newburn. Jackson—I must see what the fellow says on question 4; he was well muddled about it in class."

Gray got tired of teaching Property, and after Thayer's death took up Evidence and Constitutional Law; but his mind was not as well adapted to those subjects, and after a few years he went back to Property. He was the first of the great faculty to begin teaching, back in 1868, and he continued the last of them all. In his last year of teaching he had become feeble, and it was a grief to us to see our beloved colleague, formerly so strong and confident, a war-horse rejoicing in his strength, creeping about the stack, an old man at last after three score and fifteen years of lusty life. He gave up teaching in February, 1913, and lived only a few months longer.

Gray was above all a man; a unique combination, a man of the world and a man of the schools. He had the respect of the Boston Bar, and was a useful liaison officer between that Bar and the School. The Boston Bar had been deeply shocked by Langdell's novelties, and remained unreconciled long after New York had fully accepted the new regime; but with Gray on our side we could not quite be sent to Coventry. He was a sound and clear, if not an inspired, thinker; and he was full of the democracy of scholarship. I was greatly flattered, as I was sitting in the reading-room of Austin Hall at the end of the examination period in my second year, to have him sit on the table beside me and share a great joke with me. One of the poorest men in my class had made a mistake in answering the second question on his paper that led him to find a point in the question that neither Gray nor any of the other students had noticed. We laughed about it as heartily and socially as if I had already been his colleague. Dean Pound tells a story illustrating the same quality in him. In the Christmas holidays of his first year, Dean Pound was reading an elementary book on Roman law in the Austin reading room. Gray, as he passed, glanced at the book, then reached down and took it. "Don't read that," he said, "it isn't worth it." In a few minutes he returned with another book on Roman law, a translation from the German. "Read that," he said, and dropped it on the table.[2]

III. James Bradley Thayer

James Bradley Thayer, second of the quartet in point of age, was a scholar made lawyer instead of (like Gray) a lawyer made scholar. He had the benign austerity of the Brahmin caste of New England, to use Holmes' expression. He gave the impression of "plain living and high thinking," of peace and goodwill to men, of success; in short, unqualified if not tremendous, in any enterprise of scholarship or of philanthropy to which he might devote himself. For nearly twenty years he was the law member of a successful law firm in Boston, having as a younger colleague Oliver Wendell Holmes, Jr. Then he was called to a chair in the Harvard Law School. If there had been a chair in the department of English or of History he might as well have been called to that. He was a scholar of mankind, whether humanity flowered in language, in literature, in history, in philosophy or in law. His philanthropic urge colored everything from the local charities to the American Indian, his downtrodden hero through the best years of his life, and later the Filipino. But for his declination, forced on him by advancing years, he would have been a member of the first Philippine Commission.

Like all men who come to teaching late in life, Thayer was some time finding himself as a teacher. Subjects to which he was early assigned, Criminal Law, Trusts, Sales, seemed not to appeal to him. His course in Sales I found stupid and unfruitful. His Criminal Law was fine in parts, but scrappy. One would have expected him to develop fundamental and, for the time, modern theories of crimes; instead he worked out thoughtful suggestions in detail. Not *M'Naghten's Case*, but *Middleton's* exercised his best powers.

Two courses, however, he made his own; and in each his work became the foundation of later thought on the subject. His lectures in Evidence in my time were, for the best students, great intellectual treats. Those who went to the lectures without preparation floundered despondently; for his work has been well characterized as "commentaries on an undelivered lecture." He was last and greatest of the Glossators.

One who read the cases which he gave out in advance, or after he published casebooks, one who read his cases from the book, found his lectures absorbingly interesting. When in preparation for the final examination one rearranged his lectures in the form of a short treatise, it proved to be such a fully reasoned commentary as, if published, would have been far the best in the field on the subject.

But his work in Constitutional Law seemed to him and to his pupils the acme of his scholarship. There, where to do so was hardest, he developed fundamental principles, important and original, which since his time have been generally accepted. His two main theses, of the presumption in favor of the constitutionality of a statute, and of interpretation of the Constitution to fit reasonable requirements of the time, were first invented, I believe, by him. He began to teach the subject just as the first cases under the Fourteenth Amendment were coming up; and his teaching was authoritative and statesmanlike.

His stern New England conscience made him overfastidious as to his own work. After ten years or thereabouts of teaching Evidence he prepared a short treatise on the subject which, the story goes, was actually put in type; but doubts assailed him, and the type was distributed. When the *Harvard Law Review* appeared and he was urged to write, he began a series of very carefully written articles on the history of Evidence, and on certain discriminatory omissions from the subject, such as presumptions and burden of proof. These articles were gathered into a *Preliminary Treatise in Evidence*, and had a marvellous success throughout the country. He became best generally known of the faculty, and on the foundation of the Association of American Law Schools, in 1901, he was made its president. Great regret was expressed in all quarters at his inability to be present at the first regular meeting in Denver in 1902; I, his substitute from the faculty, distinctly felt the odium of his absence. His constructive work in the law was ended; all too soon because of his overfastidiousness. In a few months his sudden death occurred; and this pathetic memorandum was found on his work desk. "Next year I must finish Evidence, the year after, Constitutional Law; and then the end."

So much for Thayer the scholar; but one cannot leave so very human a subject without considering Thayer the man. Tall, straight, spare and ascetically beautiful, he was charming to every one. His students adored him. Every year he entertained the third-year class (not then a class of four hundred) at his house, inviting distinguished judges and lawyers to meet them. It was at his house that I first met two judges of the present Supreme Court; and at his table I met a grave, shy young fellow of the University of Pennsylvania, now Dean Mikell. We were two grave, shy, youngsters together; but that was more than thirty years ago. We have been on jesting terms since.

His family life was beautiful. His two gifted sons became, one dean of his own school, the other a leading member of the faculty of the leading American medical school, and a distinguished surgeon; his grandson is a member of the faculty to which he belonged. The students adored him as his colleagues did. He died suddenly in the middle of winter, without warning and without losing a lecture. He was buried in a driving snow-storm, the worst of the season; but seven hundred students lined the road along which his body was carried from the college chapel to the gate of the yard, bareheaded in the driving snow; and then, as a guard of honor, marched through the drifts a mile and a half to Mount Auburn, and his grave. To Ames alone, of all who have taught in the schools, would the students have shown such uncomfortable honors: to Thayer and Ames and the School they did so much to make.[3]

IV. James Barr Ames

James Barr Ames was captain of the Harvard Baseball team in the sixty's. While in college his health became poor, and he spent a year on a farm in southern New Hampshire. He learned human nature at work and at play. After graduation from college, and a year in Europe, he became a tutor in French and in History. While still a tutor he entered the Law School as a member of Langdell's first class in Contracts, and at once became the leader of "Kit's Freshmen," as Langdell's enthusiastic disciples were called. After three years of study he was named as Assistant Professor of Law.

At once a storm of opposition broke out. True, he was an experienced teacher, and a distinguished student of law; but he had had no experience at the bar or on the bench. Not ability to teach, but reputation at the bar had always been the criterion for a professor of law. Langdell the bar had swallowed, on President Eliot's assurance that he had been in successful practice in New York; but this man—. After a hard fight Ames was confirmed by the Overseers, expressly on the understanding that it was an experiment.

The experiment succeeded. Ames proved an exceedingly good teacher, suggestive, inspiring, a master of the Socratic method, which he made his own. The Langdell method of studying cases before coming into class, joined with the Socratic method of teaching, developed in pupils an independent, self-reliant mind, a skill in argument, and an instinct for the solution of legal problems which no other method, yet invented, has equalled. Lawyers so trained were useful in every department of office practice—in resourceful consultation, in looking up a case, in dealing with clients, in discovering the salient points of a problem. The test of practice put a seal of approval on the method, and slowly gave the school a standing.

As a lawyer and teacher, Ames stood for continuity and completeness in the law, and for the discovery of fundamental principles by legal reasoning. To him the law was a seamless web long before Maitland discovered and stated the fact. To this mental attitude was due Ames' ability to teach any course with small preparation. He had his method of approach; after reading and pondering a hundred well-selected cases he had discovered the fundamental principle of the subject. He always built up his successful courses around some fundamental principle. Thus in Torts he stressed the need of a sufficient excuse for doing harm to another; in Partnership he built his whole thought around the real entity of the firm; in Trusts he never lost sight of the duty of a trustee to act in all things for another, not for himself.

He was certainly, to use a current phrase, a conceptualist; yet he had one quality in common with the behaviorists. He gave little heed to the language of the court, particularly in the early American cases. Such cases he always cited for their decisions, not for their reasoning. But he was so good a lawyer that his students took no harm. His instinct as a master of the common law and his instinct as a teacher combined to keep him from false principles and from faddy teaching.

Not only was Ames a remarkable teacher and a sound lawyer; he became a great scholar. Early in his career he bought the folio yearbooks, read them through, and took copious notes. From these he constructed his *Lectures on Legal History*. Being a trained historian, he could properly appraise and assemble his material; and much of his work was discovery. From the old law he traced legal principles through the seventeenth and nineteenth centuries; and when, in 1887, the *Law Review* was founded he was able to supply a series of scholarly articles upon which, and upon Thayer's articles on Evidence, the early success of the *Review* was based. Until a few years ago his work stood as the last word in historical study of our law.

Thus in the first twenty years of his teaching Ames had come to be known as a successful teacher and a promising legal scholar. In 1895 Langdell resigned as Dean, and Ames was appointed his successor. From that time his productive scholarship was practically at an end. The dean of a large modern law school may continue to be a good teacher, but his work as a productive scholar is done. From this time Ames devoted his life to his students. He taught them law, he helped them in all their troubles, he became their dear friend and their model of honor and uprightness. Probably not one of his pupils has failed to think, in one of the moral crises that come to everybody: "What would James Barr Ames say to this?" They called him "The good Dean," and they loved him as few teachers have been loved. To this day I can hardly speak of him without a tremor in my voice. He must have realized that this devotion to the students meant his own failure to gain lasting distinction as a scholar and yet, instead of furthering his own fame, he preferred to rouse to flame the minds of many students.

The School prospered under him. In numbers it doubled in the fifteen years of his deanship. Such excellence as it had reached in 1895 it retained intact in 1910. The character of the student body remained high, and the faculty remained almost as it was; Thayer's death and Brannan's appointment were the only changes of importance. Two men appointed in Langdell's deanship are still teaching, but none who joined the faculty in Ames' time. So matters remained, successful and enthusiastic, until Ames' sudden death in January, 1910.[4]

Four men, greatly different in every way united to create that intangible state of thought and of character which is the Harvard Law School. They worked in various ways; the recluse, the man of affairs, the scholar, the friend. But they all used the same method, after all. They reached minds, they touched them with fire, they re-created them; they took young men, thinking the thoughts of their kind, and they turned them out lawyers, thinking the thoughts of lawyers, full of the dignity of their profession, eager for the service of their fellow men.

NOTES

1. For fuller accounts of Langdell, see 8 LEWIS, GREAT AMERICAN LAWYERS (1909) 465; (1906) 20 HARV. L. REV. 1, 5, 7, 9, 12.

2. For a fuller account of Gray, see (1915) 28 HARV. L. REV. 539, 544, 548.

3. For a fuller account of Thayer, see LEWIS, *op. cit. supra* note 1, at 343.

4. For a fuller account of Ames, see AMES, LECTURES ON LEGAL HISTORY 1; (1910) 23 HARV. L. REV. 321, 325, 330, 336.

Chapter 37

Methods of Legal Education

1892

These essays were originally published at 1 *Yale Law Journal* 139 (1892).

I. By Hon. Edward J. Phelps, Professor of Law in Yale University

My opinion is asked in respect to the methods of legal instruction. I am not an authority upon that subject. My connection with it has been too limited and too brief to entitle any conclusions of mine to be placed in comparison with those of gentlemen who by long and honourable service have attained a distinguished reputation in that important field. Such views as I have, are not derived from consideration of systems of study, but from observation of their results. I have paid little attention to the processes of culture, but have had large opportunities to observe the harvest, for my acquaintance with the profession in all its grades has been long and wide.

Men of exceptional intellectual power, or specially qualified by the character of their minds to deal with legal principles, will reach distinction, if they devote themselves to that pursuit, in spite of all disadvantages of education. Some great lawyers have had no more fortunate beginning than the study of a tattered Blackstone by the light of a pine-knot fire. There is another class of students, unfortunately, to whom no facilities of instruction, however excellent, will prove useful. They are either those who are lacking in mental capacity, or in natural adaptation to the study of law—for capacity is more frequently adaptation to the work in hand than is always remembered—or they are those who cannot or will not bring themselves to perform the necessary labour. Some young men are disposed to regard the profession of the law as a genteel way of getting a living without work, or as a convenient introduction to that highest of American ambitions, the holding of some sort of public office. In the latter expectation they may perhaps succeed, as it does not usually much depend upon intellectual qualities; in the former they will not fail to find out their mistake, perhaps after it is too late. But the man of fair abilities, sufficient to have insured him a satisfactory if not a brilliant success, and willing to do the work that is necessary in order to make the most of himself, not infrequently fails to achieve much at the bar. And it has seemed to me that the reason is generally to be found in the lack of the mental discipline and the true foundation of legal knowledge, which must be acquired, if at all, in early life and in educational studies. The want of these is rarely overcome. He who sets out in the wrong direction, is likely to get further away from his course the longer he travels. The building that is erected upon an incomplete and insecure foundation, however it may be elaborated and wrought over in its upper storeys, is never strong or permanent. When the rains descend and the floods come, it will be seen to be founded upon the sand.

The very first and indispensable requisite in legal education, without which there can be none that is worthy of the name, is the acquisition of a clear and accurate perception, a complete knowledge, a strong, tenacious grasp of those unchangeable principles of the common law which underlie and permeate its whole structure, and which control all its details, its consequences, its application to human affairs. That should be the work of the law school, to the student who is happy enough to enjoy its privileges. If it does that for him, it does quite enough, and all there is time for. If it fails to do that,. it does nothing that is really worth while. If the student goes out from it with hazy and uncertain conceptions, and vague and indefinite knowledge, if he is enriched only by a vast and varied misinformation, and a widely extended misunderstanding; he had better address himself to almost any other profession for which he is disqualified, than to the profession of the law. And it is certain that his mental habits will be of the same character as his acquirements.

If I were to venture upon any criticism of the system of instruction that is now, so far as I know, universally in vogue in these institutions, because universally demanded, I should say that they attempt too much for the time at their disposal, and the capacity of their average students. In establishing their standard they fix their eyes rather upon what should be accomplished at the end of a lawyer's career than at its beginning. They cover too much ground; they burden the student with too much reading, too much instruction, too many topics. They cram him with more than he can digest; they load him with more than he can carry. The culture he receives is too wide to be deep. The mental discipline, without which knowledge is only an encumbrance, is sacrificed or impaired in the overstrained effort at accumulation. Learning is made to take the place of knowledge, and knowledge outruns strength. No man, certainly, can evolve a mastery of the law out of his own inner consciousness; it must be obtained by study, and the real lawyer must be a student in earnest, all the days of his life. But on the other hand, mere learning can never make a lawyer. The faculties of acute and accurate perception, of seeing things just as they are, of strong logical reasoning, and of a high and clear sense of justice, must be formed and trained and incorporated into the mind, as legal knowledge is acquired. The process therefore, cannot with most men be very rapid. Excellence will be found a plant of slow growth. Study should consist not merely in reading and hearing, but in reflection; so that what is received may be thoroughly mastered. The unhappy tendency of our time, not merely in schools but to a considerable degree in the profession and in the courts, is to encumber the law with much that is called learning, sought to be deduced from millions of heterogeneous, often irreconcilable, and sometimes incomprehensible cases, each of which, instead of being a decision upon the point involved, is a dissertation upon the general law of the subject. The terse clear and logical judgments that are found in the earlier English and American reports, in which conclusions are deduced from principles, instead of from other conclusions, are not now much in fashion. It is easy to find single opinions in which more authorities are cited than were mentioned by Marshall in the whole thirty years of his unexampled judicial life, and briefs that contain more cases than Webster referred to, in all the arguments he ever delivered. To plunge a student into this chaos, with his powers untried and imperfect, and his knowledge of principles incomplete, to grope his way through it as best he may, and to triangulate from case to case, supposing that he is getting forward when he is only going astray, is not to educate him, but tends rather to make him proof against education. If the time comes when he can encounter it with the discrimination that is born only of a lucid conception of legal principles, he may be more safely trusted in a great law library, without danger of being conducted "by learned reasons to absurd decrees." He will then see how cases may illustrate the application of principles which they do justice and cannot destroy; that the law is, after all, the science of justice, as far as justice can be made effectual by general and established rules; and that its warrant and its eulogy are only to be found in "the good justice that is done in the land."

If I were to frame a law school upon my own old-fashioned idea of what it should be, it would attract no students. It would be like the common school by the side of the academy. The slenderness of its library—small but well selected, rich principally in what it did not contain, and jealous of new accessions—the simplicity of its curriculum, the moderation of its speed, the apparent modesty of its extent of attainment, would be likely to excite derision. Such was the school which I had the advantage of attending in the happy days of my youth. Out of such schools and from the same system of instruction outside of them, have come a large proportion of the greatest lawyers I have ever seen, or ever expect to see. What was taught there was only fundamental, but it was taught effectually. It sank into the student's mind, and wrought itself into his ideas and his modes of thought. The habit of reasoning from principles to conclusions gave him, if he was capable of attaining it, the large comprehension and strong logical power which are the characteristics of the sound lawyer, and the true weapons of the advocate. On the foundation thus formed, the superstructure can be rapidly built in after life. To a mind so trained, no legal propositions however new will be difficult; no complication of facts however unusual will embarrass the application of the rules of law, or put justice out of court. Beware of the man of one book, is an old proverb. Beware of the lawyer of few books, wisely chosen and entirely understood, is a good adaptation of the proverb to the matter in hand. Asking lately the leader of the Connecticut Bar, how it came to pass that the lawyers who framed the United States Constitution had obtained such a mastery of legal principles and such a clearness in the expression of them as are there displayed, he replied, "Why, they had so few books!"

I would confine therefore, the business of the law school, were it left to me, chiefly to the groundwork of the law. This I would try to have taught with extreme thoroughness. *Multa non multis* should be the motto. And I would regard mental discipline, habits of thought, and the learning how to think clearly, accurately, and with the confidence that can only come from the consciousness of a sure foundation, as far more important than the premature accumulation of much knowledge. This would leave a good deal for future acquisition, it is true, but, as it seems to me, the deficiency would be more than compensated by the enlarged faculty of acquisition, and the effectual planting, broad and strong, of the foundations upon which alone can learning and scholarship usefully repose in practical life.

I have felt less hesitation in expressing these antiquated views, because there is no danger of their being adopted. Institutions must meet the demands of their time, right or wrong, or they will soon cease to be institutions, for the lack of disciples. Public opinion in these times upon any subject that much attracts public attention, flows in currents which sweep everything before them. It is idle to try to go against the stream; one must go with it or be left behind. Education in all its departments, nowadays, is the business of rapidly imparting universal knowledge to all mankind. The end sought is acquirement rather than strength, accumulation at the expense of understanding, quantity instead of quality. This can only be corrected, if it needs correction, by the experience which perhaps may disclose that such is not the way to make strong men.

I may well enough terminate these observations, in the language of a worthy and honest justice of the peace in the State of Vermont, who in rendering judgment in an action that had been sharply contested before him, concluded by saying, "These are my views in respect to this case; I have no doubt about it; very likely I am wrong; I am generally wrong."

II. By Prof. William A. Keener, Dean of Columbia College Law School

In complying with a request for a statement of the method of instruction in the Columbia College Law School, I must state at the outset that there is no uniform method of instruction, if these words are used as indicating a method which one is expected as a member of the Law Faculty to follow. At Columbia a professor is selected because he is supposed to be qualified for his work, and the method of doing it rests entirely with himself.

What I shall describe is the method pursued in most of the courses because it is thought to be productive of the best results. That method is, with the modification hereinafter described, the case system as introduced at Harvard. In describing this system I shall state in the first place what *it is not.*

1. It does not consist in the study of isolated propositions of law.
2. It does not proceed on the theory that the law consists of an aggregation of cases.
3. It does not proceed on the theory that to learn law one must *memorize cases.*
4. It does not proceed on the theory that law is to be taught or learned in a law school by the reading of cases merely.
5. It does not leave the student to deduce the principles of law from the cases *by himself.*

What then is the case system? What is the theory on which it is based? What is the use made of the cases?

The case system consists in putting into the hands of the student a number of cases on any given subject, taken not at haphazard but selected by the professor with a view to developing the law on that subject. The theory on which this proceeds is that it is only by regarding law as a science that one can justify its being taught in a university, and regarding it as a science, the student should not only be encouraged to investigate the law in its original sources, but should be distinctly discouraged from regarding as law, what is, in fact, simply the conclusions of writers whose opinions are based upon the material to which the student can he given access.

The case system then proceeds on the theory that law is a science and, as a science, should be studied in the original sources, and that the original sources are the adjudged cases and not the opinions of text writers, based upon the adjudged cases. But the law is an applied science and therefore to appreciate thoroughly the principle involved in a given topic the student should deal with it in its application, and as he learns these principles in their application they are not a mere abstraction, but have assumed to him a concrete form, and he is prepared to apply them in mastering new problems. Instead of reading about principles he is studying and investigating the principles themselves. Under this system the student is taught to look upon law as a science consisting of a body of principles to be found in the adjudged cases, the cases being to him what the specimen is to the mineralogist. It should be remembered that the student is not simply given the specimen and asked to find out as best he can what it is, but each specimen is accompanied by an elaborate explanation and classification.

In comparing the system of teaching by cases with the ordinary text-book system, it should not be forgotten that the decision of the Court is not simply a judgment for the plaintiff or for the defendant upon a given statement of facts, but that the reasons therefor are given at length, and the opinion of the court giving the reasons for the conclusion reached, is really the only authoritative treatise which we have in our law.

In explanation of the use made of the cases, I shall quote from a statement made by me on another occasion for the purpose of showing that one of the strongest arguments in favor of the system of teaching by cases is the fact that it is so extremely practical:

> "A system in which principles are studied in their application to facts would seem to combine in the highest possible degree the theoretical and practical. In no other way can a student so thoroughly acquaint himself with the methods used by judges in applying principles of law to the facts before them. It must be borne in mind that this method of teaching does not consist in lectures by the instructor, with references to cases in support of the proposition stated by him. The exercises in the lecture room consist in a statement and discussion by the students of the cases studied by them in advance. This discussion is under the direction of the instructor who makes such suggestions and expresses such opinions as seem necessary. The student is required to analyze each case, discriminating between the relevant and the irrelevant, between the actual and possible grounds of decision. And having thus discussed the case, he is prepared and required to deal with it in its relation to other cases. In other words, the student is practically doing as a student what he will be constantly doing as a lawyer By this method the student's reasoning powers are constantly developed, and while he is gaining the power of legal analysis and synthesis, he is also gaining the other object of legal education, namely, a knowledge of what the law actually is."

I might add that the power which this practice gives him of analyzing the complicated facts of a case, and of clearly and concisely stating them, is what in no small degree distinguishes the good lawyer from the poor or indifferent lawyer.

It is evident that the system which I have described is not the system which is described by Mr. J. Bleecker Miller in the December number of the *Counsellor* as follows:

> "Of course, teaching by 'case law' is the furthest possible remove from this German system; teaching by 'case law' went out of use on the Continent over a hundred years ago. To use again our comparison between law and composition, what would we think of a system of teaching the

> latter which consisted in impressing on the memory of the pupil a number of correctly expressed sentences, from approved authors, and then expecting that the pupil should be able to judge whether a given sentence is rightly or wrongly expressed by comparing it with one of these approved sentences? That is teaching by 'case law.'"

That is not the case system as the phrase is used at Columbia, and I heartily concur with Mr. Miller in his condemnation of such a system. There is no reason for supposing that Mr. Miller had in mind, in making the above statement, the method of instruction herein described, though the statement represents a notion very generally entertained about it.

From my explanation of the system it is evident:

1. That it is not open to the charge of regarding the law as a mere aggregation of cases. Indeed, the system rests on the fundamental doctrine that while the adjudged cases are numerous, the principles controlling them are comparatively few, and can and should be thoroughly mastered.

2. That it does not proceed on the theory of learning law by the reading of cases only, as the student has the constant help of the instructor by way of suggestion, criticism, and the formal statement of propositions of law.

3. That the system, if not open to the objection just mentioned, cannot be open to the objection that the student is required to deduce the principles from the cases *by himself*. Even before the discussions and suggestions of the class room he has the benefit of the opinion of the court in every case, and of the argument of counsel in many cases to aid him in reaching his first impressions.

4. That instead of involving the memorizing of a lot of cases, the danger to guard against is that the student may not have a sufficient regard for decisions which in his opinion are not based on principle. Judge Story's attitude when presiding at a moot court is very much the attitude of the professor and his class in the lecture room. Judge Story is quoted as saying when presiding at a moot court, "Gentlemen, this is the High Court of Errors and Appeals from all other courts in the world. Tell me not of the last cited case having overruled any great principle,—not at all. Give me the *principle*, even if you find it laid down in the Institutes of Hindu law."

5. That as the cases are selected to develop a particular branch of law, nothing is more erroneous than to suppose that the system consists of the study of isolated propositions. To say that the study of cases is only the study of isolated propositions is to deny that the law has been developed through the cases.

It will doubtless interest your readers to know what men other than those engaged in teaching under this system, think of it. I will, with your permission, quote from three or four such persons, whose opinions ought to have weight. In an address delivered on the two hundred and fiftieth Anniversary of Harvard College, Mr. James C. Carter, who, if not the leader of the New York Bar, is certainly second to none, expressed himself as follows:

> "What is it that a student goes to a Law School to learn? What is it to begin the study of what we call 'the law'? What is this thing which we call 'law,' and with the administration of which we have to deal? Where is it found? How are we to know it? It is not found in that code which was proclaimed amid the thunders of Sinai! It is not immediately and directly found in the precepts of the gospel. It is not found in the teachings of Socrates or Plato, or Bacon. It is alone found in those adjudications, those judgments which from time to time, its ministers and its magistrates are called upon to make in determining the actual rights of men.
>
> "What was our former method of acquiring it? Going primarily to those judgments? No, for the most part the basis of these investigations was in the study of text books, the authors of which if they had acquired any knowledge of law for themselves, must have obtained it by resorting to those original sources. We, therefore, got it at second-hand. I think the result of all investigations concerning the method by which any science may be acquired and cultivated, has been to teach us to go to the original sources, and not to take anything at second-hand.
>
> "Now, is this method open to the objections that the study of cases is apt to make the student a mere case lawyer? Not at all. The purpose is to study the great and principal cases in which

are the real sources of the law, and to extract from them the rules which, when discovered, are found to be superior to all cases.

* * * * *

"This method of studying law, by going to its original sources, is no royal road, no primrose path. It is full of difficulties. It requires struggle. If there is anything which is calculated to try the human faculties in the highest degree it is to take up the complicated facts of different cases; to separate the material from the immaterial, the relevant from the irrelevant; to assign to each element its due weight and limitation and to give to different competing principles and rules of law their due place in the conclusion that is to be formed, and I know on the other hand of no greater intellectual gratification than those which follow from the solution in this way of the great problems of the law as they successively present themselves."

In April 1889, Sir Frederick Pollock in the fifth volume of the *Law Quarterly Review*, at page 228, expressed himself as follows:

"Not many English lawyers have seen a Harvard class at work. Those who have, will agree, we think, with Mr. Fisher that the system is a thoroughly sound and practical one. One of the first and greatest fallacies besetting law students is to suppose that law can be learned by reading *about* the authorities. Professor Langdell's method (for it should justly bear the name of the inventor) strikes at the root of this."[1]

Mr. Dicey in the second volume of the *Law Quarterly Review*, at page 88, in reviewing Finch's Cases on Contracts, says:

"To master the rules of English law you must study these rules as applied to the affairs of life. They are maxims which derive their full real force from their application to cases. As Paulus excellently said of Roman law, confuting by anticipation the pretentious and shallow writers who fancied that Roman lawyers were less practical than English ones, '*Non ex regula ius sumatur, sed ex iure quod est regula fiat.*' Judicial decisions are legal experiments; reports are the record of such experiments, our evidence of '*ius quod est.*' The lawyer or student who really enters into the results of a line of leading cases learns more than a few verbal maxims which may be committed to memory. He sees what is the true meaning of legal doctrines when applied to facts; he 'becomes,' as Mr. Finch well expresses it, 'familiar with the tone of thought, the attitude of mind, which prevail in our courts, he gets a touch of the genius of English law; I may venture to add of the English race.' He learns in short, by the only method by which it can be learned, the notion of justice which the lawyers and judges of England have developed by labors extending over centuries, and have impressed upon the minds of English people."[2]

I said at the beginning of this article that the case system was with a slight modification followed by the members of the Columbia Law Faculty. Some of us have thought that if one who had never studied law could first be made familiar with the outlines of certain topics before taking up the principles in their application as illustrated by the cases, the ground would be as effectually covered and his mind would better grasp the principles involved, than if, being an entire stranger to the subject of law, he were immediately put at work upon cases. Accordingly Professor Burdick has published a selection of cases upon Torts to be used in connection with Pollock on Torts, and I have published "Selections on Contracts," consisting of selections from Leake's Elements of the Law of Contracts, and Finch's Cases on Contracts, the text of Leake on a given topic preceding the cases from Finch and being discussed and criticised in the class room before the cases on that topic are taken up.

I was induced by my experience at Harvard to try the effect of such a modification. The experience of the last five months justifies me in saying that its effect is to remove an objection to case system which I have always considered a forcible one, namely, that to plunge a beginner, unacquainted with technical terms and expressions, and with legal modes of thought, into a mass of conflicting authorities, must produce great confusion of thought, resulting in discouragement on the part of the student, and causing a loss of valuable time without a sufficient compensation for its loss. The result has, in my opinion, justified the experiment. The student having had the benefit of some preliminary instruction, reads the cases more intelligently and as a consequence grasps the principles involved more quickly and quite as firmly as if his study had been confined to the study of cases. And yet while the student *thinks* quite as freely and as independently in dealing with the cases, he certainly *guesses* less than when he studies the cases without the aid of any preliminary instruction.

This modification is intended to be limited to the first year, and to certain branches of the law. My own experience has convinced me that a student who is not able after a year of such drill, to deal with legal problems as involved in the study of cases, is not intellectually fitted to pursue the study of law.

It must be admitted that this system is not the "short cut" to the law. It takes time, but in three years one can under this system very thoroughly cover the field of law.

It must also be admitted that this system does not proceed on the idea of "the law made easy." Its advocates believe the law to be a difficult science which can only be made easy at the expense of thoroughness, and therefore at the expense of the student.

In conclusion I would say: 1. The cardinal difference between the method which I have attempted to describe, and any other method of instruction by which law is taught as a science, is that the student is required to deal with the original sources of the law, and does not take his law at second hand. The method instead of being a set system, is so flexible that two men might use it as a basis of instruction, and the teaching of the one hardly suggest the teaching of the other. It is distinctly a method for the development of individuality in teaching.

2. I think that time can be saved without the sacrifice of substantial benefit *in the first year*, by discussing in some subjects the elementary principles as stated by text writers before discussing the cases on a given topic. This simply for the purpose of acquainting the student with legal modes of thought and expression.

3. In his subsequent study I would eliminate the use of text books, except for purposes of reference and comparison, and would have the student learn his law by the statement, analysis and discussion of cases under the direction and guidance of a competent instructor.

III. By Prof. Christopher G. Tiedeman, of the Law Department of the University of the City of New York

The question of legal education is receiving more attention in this country than it has ever before had given to it. This great manifestation of interest in discussions over the merits of different methods of instruction cannot fail to be productive of great good by the detection of whatever is faulty in each of the so-called methods of instruction, and the possible construction of a new system, composed of whatever is found to be good in the several prevalent methods. But the caution must be observed that, after all, no iron-cast method of instruction can be successful in actual application, however flawless it may seem to be in theory. The individuality of the teacher must not be paralyzed by any fixed system of instruction. For the native talent of the professor for teaching counts for a great deal more than the peculiarities of his method of instruction. And very often the strong personality of the teacher will successfully conceal the defects of the methods which he employs. But after due allowance has been made for the full play of the teacher's individuality, methods of instruction may be made to conform to general principles, and may be improved or made worse according to the correctness of the fundamental principles upon which they are established. Bearing in mind that a very poor and fundamentally faulty method of instruction may be made to produce satisfactory results by the indefinable and immeasurable influence of a truly great teacher and eliminating, as far as possible, this personal equation from the criticism of different methods of instruction, there is but one way to ascertain with any reliability their respective merits and demerits, and that is, by a criticism of the soundness or unsoundness of the fundamental conceptions of the law upon which they are based.

In the first place, a distinction should be made between the relative merits of methods of instruction and of the materials used in imparting instruction. If I have not entirely misconceived the character of the discussions which have been provoked by recent events, and by the active interference of the American Bar Association, they principally relate to the character of the materials employed in giving instruction, and not to rival methods of instruction. There are but two essentially different methods of legal instruction in use in this country, viz.: the European system of formal lectures with or without the collateral aid of the seminarium, and on the other hand, instruction by a combination of recitations and informal discussions of questions and principles of law in proportions varying with the individuality of the teacher. In many of the law schools, probably in the great majority of them, both methods are employed to some extent, but only two prominent law schools employ the first method more or less exclusively. If I have not been misinformed, the other prominent law schools of the country, as well as the great majority of the smaller schools, employ in the main the latter method of instruction, *i.e.*, by recitation and informal discussion by teacher and student. If the law students of any one school were composed entirely of college-bred men, and therefore possessed of more or less well-trained minds, the former method of instruction is in my judgment unquestionably superior to the latter. For if the duty of the teacher is to explain and discuss the principles and rules of law, he can do so more effectively and can accomplish more in a given time, if he is not obliged to take up his time with catechising the students, and listening to their opinions, which even in the case of college-bred men must be the immature reflections of a tyro. And that method of instruction would be brought to a state of comparative perfection, if the lecturer were to place in the hands of his hearers an elementary treatise on the subject of of his instruction, whose treatment and analysis he follows in his lectures so that the student can come to the class-room already possessed of information concerning the elementary principles, sufficient to enable the professor to proceed directly to the more profound discussions of the subject, and to the practical application of these principles to the variety of cases, which the teacher can best draw from the adjudications of the courts. This is the system which I learned to admire while sitting under the skillful instruction of the celebrated von Ihering of the University of Goettingen.

But the formal lecture is not suited for the ordinary American law school, for the reason that the average law student does not come to the law school with such a trained mind as a college course generally insures. I cannot think there is much doubt that as long as the law schools are obliged, in the consideration of the highest interests of the legal profession, to accommodate themselves to the needs of students who come to them with untrained minds, the latter method of instruction, *i.e.*, of recitation and informal colloquies, is the best adapted to our present needs. I believe that the legal profession generally entertain the same opinion. At any rate, with very few exceptions,—and the most prominent law schools do not constitute these exceptions,—the common method of instruction is the one described as a combination of recitations and colloquy.

The most serious discussion relates not so much to methods of instruction, in the sense in which I employ the terms here, as to the materials used in giving the instruction. The important inquiry, to which I understand myself to have been invited to principally direct myself, in the present instance, is concerning the relative value of the use of text-books or treatises or, of leading adjudicated cases, in giving legal instruction. As I understand it, both parties to this controversy substantially agree that the instruction in the class-room should generally assume the informal character of a recitation and colloquy, their point of difference being the materials from which the student is to recite, and about which the colloquy is to be had.

The relative value of text-books and of adjudicated cases in giving legal instruction can only be determined, as I stated above, by a criticism of the conceptions of law which underlie the contention, and the aims held in view in providing for legal instruction.

There are four things to be attained by systematic legal instruction, and no system is complete which does not make provision for the attainment of all of them, viz: to teach (1) what is the law; (2) how law is evolved or made; (3) how to extract the ruling principle of law from an adjudicated case; (4) how to apply known principles of law to new cases as they arise.

No one would deny that the study of actual cases will alone satisfy the third and fourth requirements of legal education, as just set forth. Nor can there be much doubt that a student cannot learn how law is made, unless he studies adjudicated cases, even where the particular matter is regulated by statute. For the statute does not always contain the true living rule of conduct. The true rule or rules, which are produced by the enactment of a statute, are not to be found in the letter of the statute, but in the construction placed upon it by the courts. The law student cannot find in the Statute of Frauds all that is necessary for him to determine when a writing is necessary to the validity of a contract. He must look for an accurate answer to his inquiry to the thousands of cases in which the provisions of the statute of frauds have been construed and modified in their application to particular cases, or he must go to some reliable treatise on the subject, whose author has made the investigation for him. The student should be made to understand that the edicts of the legislature are not in themselves necessarily living law, except so far as they reflect the prevalent sense of right, but that the real rule of civil conduct is to be extracted from the cases, in which the statutory rule finds in its application to individual litigation the more or less serious modification which is necessary to bring it into conformity with the popular sense of right.

The second and third aims of legal education, as here differentiated, only serve to teach the student how to discover for himself what is the law, while the fourth gives him an opportunity to learn how to make a practical use of his legal knowledge. Legal educators may differ as to the amount of time which should be devoted in a law school course to the attainment of these three elements of professional education; but they cannot seriously deny that the study of cases is the only method by which this instruction may be imparted. Nor can there be much cause for doubt or dispute that the major part of a law school course must be devoted, not to teaching how law is evolved, or how to extract the law from adjudicated cases, or how to apply it to new cases important as these things are, but to teaching what is the law, what are the principles, general and special, which give logical shape to all systems of jurisprudence. And it is at this point in the discussion of educational methods, that there is the greatest cause for contention.

There is very little room for doubt that, at least in the Anglo-Saxon world, the adjudicated cases are the great reservoir of legal learning, and that the original investigator must go to these cases for the materials out of which he may construct our jurisprudence, or satisfy the more modest desire of ascertaining what is the law of the land on a particular subject. But he would use the cases not for the purpose of learning directly from them what is the law, but to discover, as the scientific investigator hopes by his experiments with the forces of nature, the fundamental principles underlying the concrete manifestations of their influence. If the chemist or physicist, or biologist, wants to learn what is already known about their respective sciences, he goes to the treatises in which are recorded the results of the investigations of others. He does not open the book of nature, and expect to find therein the principles set forth in such intelligible terms as that he who runs may read. He goes to his library, instead of to his laboratory.

The adjudicated cases constitute nothing more than materials out of which the scientific jurist is to construct a science of jurisprudence. They are not law in themselves, they are but applications of the law to particular cases. Law is not *made* by the courts, at the most only promulgated by them. Any one who believes that judges are free agents in the rendition of decrees and judgments, may be inclined to question the soundness of the last proposition. But he who is fully persuaded that law is not the independent creation of the judicial mind, but is the resultant of the social forces reflecting the popular sense of right, will readily give his assent. The judge is but an instrument for the promulgation of this popular sense of right in its particular application to the cause at issue. When I first met with the proposition, which is so often enunciated by legal writers, as a proper and satisfying explanation of the relation of statutory law and "judge-made" law, as Bentham contemptuously calls it, that the judge, in rendering a decision on a novel question, or in modifying a principle of law which has been previously enunciated, does not make law but only declares what was the pre-existing, although perhaps as yet unexpressed, law—I was inclined to repudiate the doctrine altogether as a fiction, and to give my approval to Bentham's criticism of this judicial liberty. But when I looked deeper into the origin of the law, and satisfied myself that all law, so far as it constituted a living rule of civil conduct, whether it takes the form of statute or of judicial decision, is but an expression of the popular sense of right through the popular agents, the legislator or the judge as the case may be—then a new light was thrown upon what I was inclined to pronounce an unwarrantable fiction, and I believed all the more firmly that neither the judge nor the legislator makes living law, but only declares that to be the law, which has been forced upon them, whether consciously or unconsciously, by the pressure of the popular sense of right, that popular sense of right being itself but the resultant of the social forces which are at play in every organized society.

If this be the true conception of the origin and development of law, then it must be conceded that learning what principles of law have been given birth or have been more or less modified in a particular decision or set of decisions is not an elementary work which may be entrusted to beginners, or which law students, at least in the earlier stages of their professional training, may be expected to do satisfactorily to themselves and to their teachers. In the first place, the whole law or any appreciable part of it, on a particular subject, cannot be learned from the study of a few leading cases, but only from a very large number of cases. For example, in order to learn the law in relation to the requirements of the statute of frauds, one would have to read not a few cases, but thousands of cases. To teach law by cases,—granting for the present that it is possible to teach law as a science by cases alone,—it would require an incredible length of time to teach even the elementary law.

But apart from the physical impossibility of reading enough cases in order to enable the student to learn the law in the time to which the exigencies of American life require a law school course to be limited, the legal tyro is not mentally capable of extracting the principles of the law from adjudicated cases, even though he be a college bred man, and possessed of more than the average of ability and industry. A few men of extraordinary mental powers may be able to collect together and formulate correctly, by the study of cases alone, the principles upon which the adjudications rest, but the average student will, by such a system of instruction, if pursued exclusively, be impressed with the great weight of judicial precedent, and he will become, what is so generally deprecated, a case-lawyer, who thinks the whole business of advocacy consists of persuading the court that the cases he cites in support of his side of the controversy, are to be followed, not because they enunciate a profound scientific truth, but merely because they have given judgment for the plaintiff or defendant on a similar statement of facts. The higher aim of their instructors to make of them conspicuously original investigators in the law is lost on the average law students. Law students, in the present state of public opinion, are inclined to consider rules of law, as they are enunciated by the court, as distinct and independent propositions, which may be strung together in a digest in some more or less orderly manner, but which have no logical connection, leading up to the formation of a compact scientific system of jurisprudence. And it strikes me that this evil, so far at least as the average student is concerned, will be intensified by telling him that he must learn the law from the cases alone. The average student will not do the necessary work in order to be able to construct for himself, out of the mass of judicial decisions, an orderly and logical presentation of the fundamental principles, which are the groundwork of every system of jurisprudence, and a knowledge of which is absolutely essential to any scientific conception of the law as a whole, or in the detailed application to special cases in actual practice.

If it taxes the mental energies of the most experienced and skillful of our law writers to present accurately and logically the law on a given subject, so as to guide and not to mislead the active practitioner and judge in the winning and settlement of judicial contests, we certainly cannot expect the student to do this work satisfactorily or accurately. One of the most successful of our American legal authors once observed in my presence that he often found it impossible to discover the common principle by which conflicting decisions, even of the same court, may be reconciled. He did not refer to cases in which there was a direct repudiation of a prior decision, but to those cases in which there was an express or implied confirmation of the prior decision, but with so great a departure in practical results, as to force one at least to the conclusion, that the later decision imposes a serious modification of the rule of law as laid down in the prior decision. To present in a clear light the rule of law, as it emerges in a modified form, from the clashing interests represented by two or more decisions requires the skill and leisure of the experienced legal author. The busy practitioner has not the time, and the tyro has not the skill or experience to enable him to escape the confusion of ideas which the reading of conflicting decisions occasions.

But even if the student is capable of doing this work from which old practitioners shrink, why should he be forced to learn the law exclusively in this laborious and difficult manner? Must he be denied the privilege, which the students of medicine, chemistry and the other sciences enjoy, of learning at the outset of his study from treatises what other original investigators have discovered? Like the student of the different sciences, the law student must learn how to make original investigations for himself, and diagnose, so to speak, the principles of law from the cases in actual litigation. But no reason can be given why he must learn the whole science of the law by his own investigations in the undigested mass of raw material in the shape of adjudicated cases. No medical school can pretend to give a complete course of instruction at the present day, without introducing into its curriculum a comprehensive course of clinics. Nor does the professor of physics or chemistry teach these sciences exclusively by the use of the text-books and pictorial representations of the various experiments as was once the practice. But the instructors of these sciences have not discarded the treatise; they have only supplemented the use of the treatise with the resort to the laboratory and operating room.

The difficulty in reaching a common agreement in the present discussion over methods and means of legal instruction is the difficulty which is often experienced in finding the middle and true ground of a controversy. Impressed by the defects of the older systems of instruction, in which the law student was presented with more or less abstract propositions of law, with the aid of text-books, which often were either nothing more than digests of the cases, and put together in an illogical and disorderly manner, or whose statements of the law were so loose and inaccurate as to prove misleading; and more impressed with the necessity of "legal clinics" in the course of instruction in the law school instead of being left for acquisition in the law office, the advocates of instruction by cases have gone to the opposite extreme of placing too high a value upon the study of cases, and of unduly depreciating the value of the study of theoretic law, apart from learning it through the medium of practical law. But notwithstanding their undue appreciation of the study of cases, they tacitly concede its inefficiency as a sole means of learning the law, by accompanying the study of the cases with a glossary or commentary of that part of the law, which is treated in the cases. The cases are therefore used merely as illustrations of the law which is set forth in the commentary, which is either given to the student in printed form or imparted by the professor in his class-room instruction. If the commentary consists of a scientific and logical treatment of the branch of law selected, corresponding to the methods adopted by the better legal treatises of modern times, the instruction by cases differs only from the instruction with the aid of the best text books, in that the illustrations of the law constitute the text, while the law is put into foot notes, and has the disadvantage of misleading the student as to what is, and what is not the nature of the law. If the glossary or commentary is nothing more than a digest of the cases for which space could not be found in the text, then the employment of such a book in a class-room instruction will not avoid many of the evils which were complained of under the older *regime.*

The advocates of instruction by the use of cases have effected an important reform in legal education by arousing the law schools of the country to the importance of infusing more life into their instruction, and of introducing into their curricula what I would call "legal clinics," and for this great good the legal profession should be grateful to them. But the great danger of driving out of the schools all scientific study of the fundamentals of the law in the unchecked study from the cases of isolated propositions of the law, ought not to be lost sight of. I think we may, in this connection consider with profit the order of legal instruction pursued at the German universities. In the first half of their three years' course, the student gets nothing but theoretic and relatively elementary law, which he gleans from the lectures of the professor and from treatises, corresponding to the English and American text-book. The same course of instruction is maintained to the end of the university course, except that the seminarium is added, in which the student gets his first insight into practical law, and where the method of instruction is practically a study of law by cases, except that the cases are in the main hypothetical. When the student receives his doctorate, he is enrolled among the officials of the court as a *referendar,* performing duties as an assistant to the judges, which are calculated to give him the practical experience which is aimed at by the law in many of the American States in requiring of candidates for the bar an apprenticeship or clerkship in a practicing lawyer's office.

If I were called upon to establish a course of legal instruction, I would follow the German methods as nearly as the situation and public opinion in America would allow. I would make the course in the law school three years. During the first year, I would confine the student to the study of the fundamental principles of the law with the aid of the most approved treatises, and without any resort to cases, except by the instructor, who would use them in the class-room for the purpose of illustrating the text. The second year would be in the main similar to the course of instruction of the first year, with a partial introduction of "legal clinics" and of the seminary methods. In the third year the instruction would largely consist of the study of cases, and of practice and pleading.

During the entire course in the law school I would place the ban upon the resort of the student to the law office. His clerkship in the law office should begin upon his graduation from the law school.

Although the views here presented, reflect no one's opinions but my own I desire to say in conclusion that, in the University of the City of New York, of whose faculty I am a member, no one method of instruction is followed exclusively: all methods are in turn adopted so far as they seem to serve the purpose of making lawyers out of the young men who come to us; and each professor is permitted to adopt whatever methods will enable him to give the best expression to his own individuality.

IV. The Following Was Originally Part of a Letter from Prof. J. C. Gray of the Harvard Law School to the Editors

In all law schools, I suppose, the students learn from text books, cases, and oral instruction. At any rate they do so here. Each teacher is free to use these means as he pleases. The different professors do actually use them in different ways and proportions, and so does each professor, as he is dealing with different topics. But, while in most law schools, the text book is the basis of instruction, and the lecture and sometimes a reported case is employed to explain or illustrate (or it may be, contradict) the text book, with us the *predominant* mode of study is to make reported cases the basis of instruction and to use oral instruction and the consultation of texts books as aids in drawing out, formulating and classifying the principles involved in the decisions.

Therefore on any topic, in most of the courses, the students are referred to cases in chronological order, which are largely collected into volumes, so that each student may have for himself a small library of selected authorities. These cases having been read by the students before each (so called) lecture, they are there asked to state them, to deduce the principles which govern them, to discuss them, to suggest distinctions, and to formulate results, the professor directing and controlling.

Among the reasons why this practice has been so generally adopted here, are the following:

a.—It accustoms the student to consider the law not merely as a series of propositions having, like a succession of problems in geometry, only a logical interdependence, but as a living thing, with a continuous history, sloughing off the old, taking on the new. The acquisition of this attitude towards the law is likely to be deemed of fundamental importance according as a professor is a believer in the common law. We are all here firm believers in it. We desire that the students may be filled with its spirit.

b.—The reading of text books on a subject of which one as yet knows nothing is dreary work; a student is apt to come from it into lecture with practically an empty mind. But we find that students, in reading cases, whether they approve, or disapprove, or are in doubt, or perplexity, yet come into lecture interested, and eager to express their views, or to have their doubts determined, or their perplexities removed.

It is well to study a question and puzzle over it before one gets the formulated answer.

I think a professor sometimes fails to realize how very dull a text book is to students. He himself knows a good deal about the subject, the leading authorities are familiar to him, he is aware of the difficult and doubtful points, he probably has had a case involving them in practice, very likely he has lost his case, and perhaps his temper too; it is all very real to him, and so he takes up the text book, eager to see what the author has to say; whether he agrees with it or not, it is *interesting*. But to the students this background is wanting. The professor thinks "what an admirable, exact and lucid statement of these difficult and complicated topics, it is just the book for students; they cannot help finding it delightful." But the students, not having had any experience of the difficulties and complications, cannot appreciate the merits of the book; they are not delighted with it at all. They find it hard to keep awake over it.

c.—To extract law from facts is *the* thing that a lawyer has to do all his life; to do it well makes the successful lawyer; to do it pre-eminently well makes the great lawyer; a student cannot begin it too early.

d.—Lectures and questions on lectures are apt to be, and perhaps necessarily must be, adapted to the students of slower apprehensions. To the quicker witted they are a bore and a waste of time. But to tackle a tough bit of pleading, or the detail of an involved business transaction, or the provisions of a complicated will, to make oneself rapidly a master of them, and to be able to give a neat oral statement of the facts and the precise point of law involved, and to show how the decision has extended or modified the law as previously held, will give full occupation to all the faculties of the cleverest man. Our experience has been that the greater the legal ability of a student, the more readily does he take to, and the more thoroughly enjoy this mode of study.

e.—Many bright young men in school and college develop an extraordinary capacity for having other people's ideas pumped into them, and win rank and reputation thereby, but they have never intellectually "labored" in their lives. Our mode of study is a sharp break in their habits and traditions. The result is at first perturbing, often amusingly so, but it is invariably salutary.

f.—This dealing with actual cases is an effectual corrective to unreal and fantastic speculation, which is the most dangerous tendency of academic education.

I will take the liberty of referring you to a short article I wrote on "Cases and Treatises," 22 Am. L. Rev. 756.

I have no love and scant respect for *a priori* dogmatism in legal education. When I talk myself or hear others talk of the "case system" or the "Harvard system" or any other "system," I feel a slight instinctive disgust; it is not entirely reasonable I admit, but it has some justification. A man who has much to say about "systems" is sailing perilously near the shoals of cant. Not by their systems but by their fruits shall ye know them.

If a school is filled with hard and enthusiastic workers of a superior intellectual training, if its graduates, all with credit, and many with brilliancy, have passed repeated searching examinations on the fundamental doctrines of law and equity and their practical applications, and if its past members look back on its works and ways with strong feelings of approval and gratitude, such feelings being the strongest in those whose success and ability in the profession have been the most marked, then, "system" or no "system," that school, wherever it may be, is not far from the kingdom.

NOTES

1. I have assumed Sir Frederick Pollock to be the author of the above statement for the reason that it appears in the editorial notes of the *Law Quarterly Review*, of which he is the able and learned editor.

2. This review is written over the initials "A. V. D." which is my reason for attributing it to Mr. Dicey.

Chapter 38

Courses of Study in Law Schools in 1891

1893

American Bar Association and U.S. Bureau of Education

From the *Report on Legal Education, Prepared by a Committee of the American Bar Association and the U.S. Bureau of Education.* Washington: Government Printing Office, 1893. pp. 44-63. The ABA Committee on Legal Education presented this report in 1892. Over its life from 1890 to 1893, when the report was being prepared, that committee comprised William G. Hammond, George M. Sharp, Henry Wade Rogers, George O. Shattuck, and J. Hubley Ashton. Samuel Williston joined the committee in 1893. The survey here reproduced was chapter one, section two, of the largely comparative and occasionally sketchy report and was prepared by Wellford Addis for the committee. The reader is cautioned not to consider this list exhuastive of the law schools in America during this time.

STATISTICS, SUBJECTS TAUGHT, TEXT-BOOKS USED, AND TIME ALLOTTED, AS FAR AS REPORTED IN THE CATALOGUES OF THE INSTITUTIONS; WITH SOME REMARKS CONCERNING THEIR ORGANIZATION AND METHODS OF INSTRUCTION.

1. *Albany Law School (Union University)*, Albany, N. Y., Lewis B. Hall, dean. Twelve instructors, 41 students, 18 having degrees in letters or science, 36 graduates, 38 weeks in school year 1891-'92. Students must attend one course of three full terms.

2. *Law Department of Allen University*, Columbia, S. C. One instructor, 11 students, 32 weeks in school year. Has a course of 2 years.

3. *Law School of Indiana University*, Bloomington, Ind., David D. Banta, dean. Two instructors, 61 students, 5 having degrees in letters or science, 16 graduates, 32 weeks in school year.

Course of study: First year.—Elementary law (Robinson's, with notes and collateral reading), 39 hours; constitutional law (Cooley's, and study of leading cases), 26 hours; contracts (Anson, with notes, and study of cases), 65 hours; contracts (Recitation in Parsons; with notes and cases), 50 hours; personal property,

60 hours; international law, 10 hours; domestic relations, 30 hours; notes and bills, 2 hours; criminal law, 10 hours.

Second year.—Jurisdiction and procedure in equity (Bispham's Principles and Lube's Equity Pleading), 65 hours; common-law pleading (Stephens'), code pleading, 65 hours; real property (Tiedeman, with notes and cases, and practice in the examination of titles), 50 hours; wills and administration, 10 hours; evidence (Stephens'), 30 hours; pleading and practice, 20 hours; corporations (Morawetz) 50 hours; torts, 30 hours; pleading and practice, 20 hours.

Organization and methods of instruction.—Examinations for admission are not technical, but are intended to test applicant's knowledge of the common-school branches, and especially his ability to write the English language easily and correctly. Instruction is given by text-books, lectures, and study of leading cases. The last feature is especially emphasized, the object being to acquaint the student with the leading cases in each of the more important branches of the law.

4. *Boston University School of Law*, Boston, Mass. Edmund H. Bennett, dean. Twenty-five instructors; 210 students, 50 having degree in letters or science; 62 graduates; 35 weeks in school year.

Course of study: First year.—Contracts (required), 125 hours; torts (required) 120 hours; sales (required), 30 hours; agency (required), 20 hours; criminal law (required), 25 hours; development of law, 25 hours; history of the common law, 10 hours.

Recommended: Benjamin, Bishop, Metcalf, Anson, or Smith on contracts; Bigelow, Cooley, or Pollock on torts, or Bishop on noncontracts; Benjamin on sales; May or McClain on criminal law; Meechem or Story on agency.

Second year.—Bailments (required), 20 hours; bills and notes (required), 75 hours; domestic relations, 10 hours; insurance, 15 hours; landlord and tenant (required), 10 hours; Massachusetts conveyancing, 10 hours; partnership (required), 10 hours; real property (required), 140 hours. Books used: Williams, Washburn, or Tiedeman on Real Property; Schouler, Bailments, Chalmer's Digest (Benj. edition) on Bills, Bigelow's Leading Cases or Bills and Notes; Story on Partnership, Schouler's Domestic Relations; Taylor's Landlord and Tenant.

Third year.—Equity jurisprudence, including trusts (required), 100 hours; equity pleading (required), 20 hours; evidence (required), 70 hours, jurisdiction and practice of the United States courts (required), 15 hours; law of railroads, 20 hours; pleading and practice at common law (required), 50 hours: wills (required), 10 [?] hours. In addition to the studies above-mentioned, lectures are given before the senior class each year on several of the following topics: Admiralty and shipping, 10 hours; conflict of law, 15 hours; constitutional law, 10 hours; constitutional legislation, 10 hours; corporations, 10 hours damages, 10 hours; law of elections, 6 hours; medical jurisprudence, 10 hours; Massachusetts practice, 12 hours; American statute law, 20 hours; patent law, 10 hours; parliamentary law, 10 hours. Books used: Bispham or Bigelow's Equity, Vol. 1, Greenleaf's Evidence; Stephen's Digest (Chase's edition); Stephen's or Gould's Pleading; Best's Evidence (Chamberlayne's edition); Story's Equity Pleadings; Curtis's Jurisdiction of the United States Courts.

Methods of instruction.—The course of instruction includes the regular oral text-book exposition and recitation, free and written lectures, reviews, examinations, exercises in drafting contracts, conveyances, pleadings, indictments, and other legal papers, the criticism of briefs, and arguments in moot courts, courses of reading, etc. The importance of the study of judicial authority, especially the cases referred to in the lectures and recitations, is urged.

5. *Buffalo Law School of the University of Buffalo*, Buffalo, N.Y. Charles Daniels, dean.—Twenty-two instructors; 60 students, 13 having degrees in letters or science; 21 graduated; 33 weeks in school year.

Course of study: First year.—Elementary law and contracts, criminal law and procedure, torts, practice in civil actions, marriage and divorce, domestic relations, transmission of estates.

Second year.—Law of property, evidence, equity jurisprudence, and pleading, sales, agency and partnership, corporations, negotiable bills and notes, medical jurisprudence, maritime and admiralty law, constitutional law, legal ethics, trial actions, special proceedings, manufacturing corporations, wills and estates of deceased persons.

Methods of instruction.—Instruction is given by means of lectures, recitations, and especially by the study of leading cases. Moot courts are held.

6. *Law Department of General Tennessee College*, Nashville, Tenn.—Three instructors, 8 students, 4 graduates, 36 weeks in school year. Has a course of two years.

7. *Law School of Cincinnati College*, Cincinnati, Ohio. Jacob D. Cox, dean.—Six instructors; 161 students, 33 having degrees in letters or science; 83 graduates; 33 weeks in school year.

Course of study: First year.—Elementary law, contracts, real property, Blackstone's commentaries, Anson's contracts, Bliss on code pleading.

Second year.—Pleadings and civil procedure, torts, real property; equity jurisprudence, mercantile law and contracts, evidence, court law, criminal law, corporations, statute law. Books used: Stephen's Pleading, Bliss's Code Pleading, Bigelow's Torts, Williams' Real Property, Bispham's Equity, Kent's Commentaries, Greenleaf's Evidence, Stephen's Evidence, Cooley's Constitutional Law, May's Criminal Law.

Methods of Instruction.—The daily exercises consist of lectures and recitations from standard text-books. Leading cases and collateral authorities on the subject under consideration are referred to by the professor, and at the succeeding recitation the class will be examined upon the whole matter of text and comment. Moot courts are held each week during the year.

8. *School of Law of Columbia College, New York, N. Y.* Theodore W. Dwight, dean to June, 1891.—Nine instructors, 625 students, 63 graduates, 32 weeks in school year.

Course of study, 1891-92: First Year.—Required: Contracts, 102 hours (Keen's); real and personal property, 68 hours (Gray's cases); torts, 48 hours. (Burdick's cases); criminal law and procedure, 54 hours (Chaplin's cases); law of persons and domestic relations, 32 hours (Ewell's cases, students' edition); common law pleading and procedure, 36 hours (Ames's cases); elements of jurisprudence, 10 hours. Optional: Constitutional history of Europe and the United States, 136 hours; constitutional history of England, 68 hours; institutes of Roman law, 34. In the first year the required work for a degree is 310 hours, i.e., 10 hours a week.

Second year.—Contracts and quasi-contracts, 102 hours (Keener's selections on contract and cases on quasi contracts); administrative law, 68 hours; bailments, 68 hours; equity jurisprudence, 68 hours, (Ames's cases on trusts); history of European law, 68 hours; real and personal property, 68 hours (Gray's cases); agency, 36 hours; code practice, comparative constitutional law, 72 hours, (Burgess's political science and constitutional law); equity pleading and procedure, 40 hours; insurance, 36 hours (Richard's treatise and select cases); sales of personal property, 40 hours, (Benjamin's sales). Optional: Medical jurisprudence. The courses of the second year are elective. The required work for the degree during the year is 408 hours.

Third year.—Code pleading and practice, 68 hours; private corporations, 68 hours (Cummings's cases); equity jurisprudence, 68 hours (Langdell's cases); evidence, 68 hours (Thayer's cases); international law, 68 hours; negotiable paper, 68 hours (Ames's cases on bills and notes); partnership, 68 hours (Ames's cases); suretyship and mortgage, 68 hours; systematic jurisprudence, 68 hours; wills and administration, 68 hours (Gray's cases on property); admiralty and shipping, 36 hours; conflict of private law, 40 hours; municipal corporations, 40 hours; law of taxation, 36 hours. Optional: Conflict of criminal law, extradition and nationality, 36 hours. The courses in the third are elective. The work required for the year is 340 hours.

Admission and methods of instruction.—Applicants for admission must have received a good academic education, including a knowledge of the Latin language as is required for admission to the freshman class of the school of arts. The examination to ascertain this is waived in the case of graduates of literary colleges. Moot courts are held each week.

9. *Law Department of Cornell University*, Ithaca, N. Y., Douglass Boardman, dean.— Fourteen instructors; 152 students, 3 having degrees in letters or science; 37 graduates; 35 weeks in school year.

Course of study: First year.—Elementary law (Blackstone), contracts, agency, criminal law and procedure, torts, domestic relations, law of real property, evidence, bailments, common law pleading and practice in cases at law, civil procedure under the code, English constitutional history. The regular class instruction of the schools is at no time less than 15 hours a week for each class.

Second year.—Private and municipal corporations, wills and administration, mercantile evidence, real property, equity jurisprudence, equity pleading and procedure in State and United States courts, civil procedure under the codes, chattel mortgages, mechanics' liens, assignments for the benefit of creditors, practical suggestions concerning the preparation, trial, and argument of causes, Roman law, international law, American constitutional history, American constitutional law. The regular class instruction is at no time less than 15 hours a week for each class.

Note: Course of special lectures is given apparently during the two years as follows: The statute of frauds and fraudulent conveyances (two courses), constitutional law (two courses), shipping and admiralty, patent laws of the United States, medical jurisprudence, law of insurance, extradition. Opportunities are given to students for instruction in elocution and oratory.

Admission and methods of instruction.—There is an examination for admission as required by the law of the State of New York.

The instruction is carried on by lectures and examinations, by oral text-book exposition and recitations, and by the study of selected cases. Instruction to the more advanced students by means of the study of cases is made a special feature of the school. A session of the university court is held, as a rule, each week during the school year.

10. *School of Law of Chaddock College*, Quincy, Ill. Thomas R. Petrie, secretary.— Four instructors; 12 students, 1 having degree in letters or science; 1 graduate; 36 weeks in school year.

Course of study: First year.—Criminal law, torts, real estate, equity, contracts, constitutional law.

Second year.—Common law, pleading and practice, mercantile law, evidence, corporations.

Admission and methods of instruction.—Applicant for admission is examined if unable to present a college diploma from an institution of collegiate or academic grade. The instruction is given by lecture and recitation. Moot courts are held at convenient times.

11. *Law School of the Columbian University*, Washington, D. C., H. G. Hodgkins, registrar. Twelve instructors, 383 students, 63 having degrees in letters or science, 160 graduates; 35 weeks in school year.

Course of study: First year.—Real and personal property, contracts, crimes and misdemeanors, three times a week. Blackstone, Kent, Parson's Contracts, Byles on Bills. Also lectures on domestic relations, commercial paper and torts.

Second year.—Pleading, evidence, equity jurisprudence, pleading and practice, partnership, with lectures on ejectments, quo warranto, etc., three times a week. Also a course of lectures on constitutional law, law of corporations, international law, civil law, patents. These are open to students of first year. The lectures on constitutional law are given every Saturday. Books used: Stephen's Pleading (Tyler's edition), Greenleaf's Evidence, Smith's Manual of Equity, and Mitford and Tyler's Pleading and Practice in Equity.

Third year.—(Graduate course in practice) Cox's Exercises for Law Students, Archbold's Law of Nisi Prius, Mitford's and Tyler's Equity Pleading and Practice. Also lectures on jurisdiction, practice and peculiar jurisprudence of the courts of the United States, and also on criminal law, legal bibliography, practical commercial law, and the history of law. The last three courses are open to all classes of the school.

Organization and methods of instruction.—The school has three classes, to wit, junior, senior, and graduate classes in practice. In the junior class a lesson is assigned in the text-book which forms the subject of the professor's lecture. In lecture the professor brings out the points of the text, and then quizzes the class upon both text and lecture. In the senior class the method is the same with the exception that the quizzing occurs at the meeting following that upon which the lecture was given. This method of course does not apply to the lectures on constitutional law, civil law, etc., In the graduate class for more than half the time the exercises are those of a nisi prius moot court.

12. *Law School of Cumberland University*, Lebanon, Tenn., N. Green, dean. Three instructors, 71 students, 52 graduates, 40 weeks in school year.

Course of study: First, year—Caruther's History of a Lawsuit, Kent's Commentaries, Vols. I, II, III, Field's Corporations, Cooley's Torts, Greenleaf's Evidence, Vol. I, Stephen's Pleading.

Second year—Kent's Commentaries, Vol. IV, Barton's Suit in Equity, Strong's Equity Jurisprudence, Parson's Contracts, Wharton's Criminal Law. (This course, as given for two years, may be completed in ten months).

Method of instruction.—Moot courts are held.

13. *School of Law of De Pauw University*, Greencastle, Ind., Augustus L. Mason, dean. Seven instructors, 48 students, 9 having degree in letters and science, 19 graduates, 38 weeks in school year.

Course of study: First year.—Elementary law, sources of law and philosophy of legal history, domestic relations, personal property, contracts, agency, bailments, partnership, negotiable instruments, torts, pleading and practice, statutory construction, international law. Each student needs the statutes of his own State. Juniors entering at the beginning of the junior year need Blackstone's Commentaries.

Second year.—Law of real property, equity jurisprudence, constitutional jurisprudence of the United States, wills and decedents, estates, evidence, criminal law, pleading, practice and advocacy, mercantile guaranty and suretyship, patents and copyrights, private corporations, railroads, express and telegraph companies, banks, building associations, insurance companies, municipal corporations. Seniors are expected to attend junior lectures.

Methods of instruction—The work is largely conducted by lecture. Moot courts are held, during a large part of the course, by the dean.

14. *School of Law, Georgetown University*, Washington, D. C., Martin F. Morris, dean. Ten instructors, 268 students, 132 graduates, 34 weeks in school year.

Course of study: First year.—Personal property, tort, domestic relations, criminal laws, real estate, contracts, bills and notes, 4 times a week during school year. Books used: Blackstone's Commentaries, Schouler's Personal Property, Vol. I, Bishop's Contracts, Byles' Bills, Cooley's Tort's, Williams' Real Property, Browne's Domestic Relations. To relieve the embarrassment of those who find a knowledge of the Latin language essential to the study of law, a course in Latin has been established in the law school by the classical department of the university.

Second year.—Real estate, contracts, bills, and notes. Twice a week during the year. Pleading, practice evidence, equity pleading and practice, moot court three times a week during year. Books used: Stephen's Pleading, Cox's Practice, Greenleaf's Evidence, Vol. I, Adams's Equity, Barton's Suit in Equity.

Third year (post-graduate course).—Pleading, practice, evidence, equity, equity pleading and practice, moot courts, three times a week during year. Partnership, corporations, constitutional and international law, admiralty and comparative jurisprudence, conveyancing, office practice, etc., twice a week during year. Special lectures: Statutory law, testamentary law, once a week during year. Books used: Sedgwick's Statutory and Constitutional Law, Paschal's Annotated Constitution, Story's Partnership, Boone's Corporations.

Organization and methods of instruction.—School has a junior, senior, and post-graduate course of study. The system of instruction is as follows.: A lesson averaging from thirty to forty pages of the text-book is assigned in advance, which the student is expected to master. During the recitation hour the lecturer goes over this ground and then quizzes the class. Thus, the student has three opportunities of becoming familiar theoretically and practically with each topic treated in the course. The moot court is divided into a circuit court and a court of appeals, the former holding two regular sessions weekly, the latter sits once a month.

15. *Law School of Harvard University*, Cambridge, Mass., C. C. Langdell, Dean. Nine instructors, 363 students, 44 graduates, 38 weeks in school year.

Course of study: First year.—Contracts, 108 hours; criminal law and procedure, 72 hours; property, 72 hours; torts, 72 hours; civil procedure at common law, 36 hours. Books used: Langdell's Cases on Contracts; Chaphin's Cases on Criminal Law; Gray's Cases on Property, Vols. 1 and 2; Ames's Cases on Torts; Ames's Cases on Pleading.

Second year.—Agency, 72 hours; bills of exchange and promissory notes, 72 hours; law of carriers, 72 hours; contracts, 72 hours; evidence, 72 hours; jurisdiction and procedure in equity, 72 hours; property, 72 hours; sales of personal property, 72 hours; trusts, 72 hours. Books used: Ames's Cases on Bills and Notes, Kener's Cases on Quasi-Contracts, Langdell's Cases in Equity Pleadings, Grey's Cases in Property, Vols. 3 and 4, Langdell's Cases on Sales, Ames's Cases on Trusts.

Third year.—Constitutional law, 72 hours; corporations, 72 hours; jurisdiction and procedure in equity, 72 hours; partnership, 72 hours; property, 72 hours; surety and mortgage, 72 hours. Books used: Ames's Cases on Partnership, Gray's Cases on Property, Vols. 5 and 6.

Extra courses.—Patent law, 10 lectures; peculiarities of Massachusetts law and practice, 2 hours a week.

Admission and methods of instruction.—Applicants for admission not graduates of a college are examined in Latin (Cæsar, Cicero), Blackstone's Commentaries. The character of the instruction is shown in a general way by the text-books used. Every student who has been in the school one year or more has an opportunity each year of arguing in a case before one of the professors in a moot court.

16. *Hastings College of the Law*, University of California, San Francisco, Cal. C. F. Dio Hastings, dean. Six instructors, 92 students, 15 graduates, 39 weeks in a school year.

Course of study: First year.—Persons and personal rights, during a portion of the year; real property, during a portion of the year; contracts, during a portion of the year. Books used: Pomeroy's Municipal Law, Blackstone's Commentaries, Kent's Commentaries, Cooley's Torts, Schouler's Domestic Relations, Bishop's Contracts, Tiedeman's Real Property.

Second year.—Mercantile law, 5 times a week (lectures and recitations) during a greater portion of the year, wills and decedents' estates, lectures and recitations during portion of the year. Books used: Benjamin's Sales, Schouler's Bailments, Tiedeman's Commercial Paper, May's Insurance, Story's Agency, Bates's Partnership, Morawitz's Corporations, Schouler's Wills, Code of Civil Procedure, Title Proceedings in the Probate Court.

Third year.—Equity jurisprudence, recitation twice a week during a portion of the year; evidence, recitations twice a week during a portion of the year; pleading and practice, recitations, discussions, and practical exercises three times a week throughout the year; constitutional law, recitations twice a week during a portion of the year; legal ethics, 8 or 10 lectures to class. Books used: Stephens on Pleading, Lube's Equity Pleading, Bliss on Code Pleading, Code of Civil Procedure, Greenleaf's Evidence, Pomeroy's Equity Jurisprudence and Constitutional Law. Lectures on special subjects are given and leading cases are constantly referred to and are required to be studied.

Admission and methods of instruction.—Applicants must pass an examination in English, arithmetic, algebra, plane geometry, history and geography, Cæsar (Books I-IV). There is a moot court upon which the second and third year students are required to attend.

17. *Law Department of Howard University*, Washington, D. C., B. F. Leighton, dean. Six instructors, 74 students, 33 graduates, 32 weeks in school year.

Course of study: First year.—Blackstone's Commentaries, William's Real Property, Browne's Domestic Relations, Boone's Real Property, Parsons Contracts, Byler's Bills.

Second year.—Stephen's Pleading, Cox's Criminal Law Practice, Adams's Equity Jurisprudence, Bishops' Criminal Law.

18. *Little Rock Law Class in connection with Little Rock University*, Little Rock, Ark. Three instructors, 30 students, 1 graduate, 12 weeks in school year. Course of study two years.

19. *Law Department of McKendree College*, Lebanon, Ill. W. W. Edwards, dean. One instructor, 25 students, 3 graduates, 36 weeks in school year.

Course of study: First year.—Blackstone's Commentaries, books 1 and 2; Lectures on Constitutional History, English and American, 13 weeks. Blackstone's Commentaries, books 3 and 4; Washburn's Criminal Law; Lectures on American Constitutional Law 11 weeks. Walker's American Law, Gould's Pleading, General Review of Blackstone, 10 weeks.

Second year.—Bishops' Contracts; Kent's Commentaries, Parts I-IV, lectures on pleadings, 13 weeks. Tiedeman's Real Property, Kent's Commentaries, Parts I-IV; Lectures on International Law, 11 weeks. Cooley's Torts, Greenleaf's Evidence, Story's Equity Jurisprudence, 10 weeks.

Organization and methods of instruction.—Applicants for admission to the Junior Class must pass a satisfactory examination in the studies required for admission to the Freshman Class in the Scientific Department of the college. Daily recitations are had and the lectures are an important feature of the work. A complete system of moot courts is maintained.

20. *Law Department of the National University*, Washington, D. C. Eugene D. Carusi, dean. Eight Instructors, 115 students, 32 weeks in school year.

Course of study: First year.—Real and personal property, contracts, negotiable instruments, criminal law, constitutional law, bailments, domestic relations. Blackstone's Commentaries, Williams's Real Property (with references to Kent), Smith's Contracts (with references to Anson), Ralston's Discharge of Contracts, Benjamin Chalmer's Digest of the Law of Bills and Notes (with references to Byles).

Second year.—Equity jurisprudence, pleading, torts, constitutional law, Federal jurisprudence and practice. The members of this class are also expected to attend the exercises of the class of the first year. There is also a special course in patent law and one in practice, open to all students in the school. Moot court optional. Cooley's Torts, Stephen's Pleadings, Greenleaf's Evidence, Vol. I, Adams's Equity, Walker's Patent Law.

Third year.—(Post-graduate course.)—Mercantile law, criminal law, applied evidence, constitutional law, practice in moot court. The members of this class are required to attend the exercises of the senior class. Smith's Mercantile Law Greenleaf's Evidence, second and third volumes, Paschal's American Constitution, Cox's Practice.

Organization and methods of instruction.—The school has junior, senior, and post-graduate classes. Each class is provided with a professor who devotes himself exclusively to its instruction, maintaining a constant system of oral examinations. The students pursue a regular course of reading and are called upon to note the substance of what they have read. What is deemed of peculiar advantage in this law school is the method of teaching, "which is entirely Socratic." Two moot courts are held each week, one for motions, etc., and the other for the arguments of the questions of law and trials of fictitious suits. There is also a court of appeals.

21. *Law Department of the State University of Iowa*, Iowa City, Iowa. Nine instructors, 174 students, 32 having degrees in letters or science, 73 graduates, 36 weeks in school year.

Course of study: First year.—Legal study and ethics, 1 week; elementary law, 9 weeks; contracts, 10 weeks; pleading, 5 weeks; study of cases, 4 weeks; criminal law, 3½ weeks (McClain's outlines), torts 9 weeks, (Cooley's); domestic relations, 3 weeks; trial and judgment, 4½ weeks; evidence, 2 weeks; evidence, 5 weeks (Vol. I, Greenleaf's); sales, bailments, and pledges, 5½ weeks; negotiable instruments, 5 weeks; Benjamin's Chalmers's bills, notes, and checks; probate law and procedure, 4½ weeks.

Second year.—Real property, 10 weeks (Tiedeman's); insurance, 4 weeks; chattel mortgages, 4 weeks; carriers, 4 weeks; damages, 4 weeks; patents, 2 weeks; equity and equity pleading, 11 weeks (Bispham); corporations, 3 weeks; medical jurisprudence, 2½ weeks; appellate proceedings, 1 week; agency, 1 week; criminal procedure, 3½ weeks (McClain's outline); partnership, 4½ weeks; Federal jurisprudence and admiralty, 2 weeks; constitutional law, 7½ weeks (Cooley's); constitutional limitations, 1 week; attachment, garnishment, and execution, 3 weeks; justice practice.

Third year.—Note to the course of two years: If the faculty permit, the student may take the following courses: Roman Law (given during 1892-'93), History of Constitutional Law in the United States (not given during 1891-'92), State Law (open to seniors only when three or more apply for a course in the law of a particular State.)

Organization and methods of instruction.—Applicants not graduates of a higher or secondary institution, or not possessed of a teacher's certificate, must pass an examination in English language and history, and American history. Instruction is given by means of lecture, text-books, and the study of cases. Two moot courts are conducted in curriculum with the exercises of the school.

22. *St. Louis Law School of Washington University*, St. Louis, Mo. William G. Hammond, dean. Eight instructors, 81 students, 23 having degrees in letters or science, 21 graduates; 34 weeks in school year.

Course of study: First year.—Real property, personal property (including sales and bailments), personal property and obligations arising from torts, contracts, causes of action between tort and contract, negotiable contracts in their simple forms. A daily course of lessons upon elementary law, both civil and criminal, until Christmas vacation. There are also two recitations in Bishop on Contracts. Pleading is taught in its code form with weekly exercises in the pleading of cases in the moot court. After the vacation pleading is continued, and Greenleaf's Evidence, Vol. I, taken up. Contracts as dealing with bills and notes is continued, and Cooley's Torts taken up, as also Tiedeman's Real Property, Benjamin's Sales, and Schouler's Bailments.

Second year.—Common law pleading, equity pleading, corporations, domestic relations, agency, partnership, negotiable paper, insurance, surety and guaranty, special forms of tort, equity and equitable estates, real property and mortgage, constitutional law and limitations, the law of decedent's estates.

Before Christmas vacation the class studies Tiedeman's Real Property, and Stephen's Common Law Pleading, and attends a course of lectures on agency. After the vacation the class studies Bispham's Equity, Parson's Partnership, Taylor's Corporations, May's Insurance, Woerner's Administration, Cooley's Constitutional Limitations, and attends lectures on domestic relations, law of successions, and the history of the common law, and pursues a course of instruction in the practice of the Federal courts.

Third year (advanced class).—Chapters III and IV of Pommeroy's Remedies and Remedial Rights in connection with practical exercises in pleading, until the class has gone over the entire field of actions. Washburn's Easements, Dillon's Municipal Corporations, Best's Evidence, and Story's Conflict of Laws. Moot courts. Room is left for special subjects, such as the Elements of Roman Law.

Admission and methods of instruction .—An examination for admission is held. This is directed chiefly to the fundamental elements of education. The course is of two years with the option of a post-graduate course. The method of instruction is by lecture and recitation from text-books. A moot court is held weekly.

23. *Law Department of the University of Notre Dame,* Notre Dame, Ind. William Haynes, dean. Thirteen instructors, 35 students, 7 having degree in letters or science, 10 graduates, 40 weeks in school year. No course of study given.

Organization and methods of instruction.—A preliminary examination is held to ascertain that the applicant has a fair general education and can accurately write the English language. There are two courses in the school, one of three the other of two years duration, which practically are the same, though the shorter course is for more mature students. The chief methods of instruction consist in the delivery, daily, of two lectures, the taking of notes by the students, the subsequent reading by them of the decisions cited in the notes, the study of standard elementary text-books, the analysis and recitations in substance of the most important leading cases, oral examinations daily, and written examinations, weekly, the trial of actions at law and suits in equity in the moot court, and debates and exercises in public speaking at least once a week.

24. *Law Department of the Tulane University of Louisiana,* New Orleans, La. Henry Carleton Miller, dean. Six instructors, 49 students, 26 weeks in school year.

Books used: First year.—Kent's Commentaries; Woolsey's International Law; Wheaton's International Law; Conklin's United States Admiralty; Civil Code of Louisiana and Code of Practice; Cooper's Justinian; Laurent's Cours de Droit Civil; Marcadé on the French Code, or Mourlon's Répétitions Ecrites; Blackstone's Commentaries; Story's Equity Jurisprudence; Smith's Manual of Equity; Smith's Mercantile Law; Story's Bills of Exchange and Promissory Notes; Abbot on Shipping; Arnould on Insurance, and Greenleaf on Evidence.

Remarks: The degree will be conferred on those students only who shall have attended two full courses of lectures, or one full course after having pursued their studies for the term of twelve months under a respectable counselor at law. The provisions of the code of Louisiana having been mainly derived from the civil law, the study of this law becomes necessary.

25. *Northwestern University Law School* (Union College of Law), Chicago, Ill. Henry W. Blodgett, dean. Thirty-four instructors, 264 students, 74 graduates, 36 weeks in school year.

Course of study: First year.—Practice in cases at law, contracts, bailments, agency; criminal law and procedure; personal property; real estate (fixtures and easements); code practice; private corporations and trials; law of express, telegraph, and telephone companies ; English constitutional history. In addition to lectures on the foregoing, instruction is given by the use of text-books, as follows: Blackstone's Commentaries; Stephen's Common Law Pleading; Bispham's Equity; Cook's Private Corporations; Tiedeman's Commercial Paper; Anson on Contracts; Edwards' Bailments; Tiedeman's Sales. For text-book work the junior class is divided into two sections, the first reciting from 9 till 10 a. m. on Monday, Tuesday, Wednesday, Thursday, and Friday, the second from 7:30 till 8:30 p. m. on the same days. Lectures to the junior class are given from 4 till 5 p. m.

Second year.—United States constitutional law; Federal jurisprudence; administration and distribution of estates of deceased persons, wills; municipal corporations; constitutional history of the United States;

general principles of equity jurisprudence; statute law; practice at law; practice in equity; trusts. In addition to lectures on the foregoing, instruction is given by the use of text-books, as follows: Chitty's Pleadings; Greenleaf's Evidence; Story's Equity Pleadings; Bigelow's Torts; Lindley's Partnership; Bliss's Code Pleading; Tiedeman's Real Property. For text-book work this class is divided into two sections also, the first reciting from 8 till 9 p. m. on Monday, Tuesday, Wednesday, Thursday, and Friday, the second from 8:30 till 9:30 p. m. on the same days. Lectures to the seniors are given from 5 till 6 and from 7:30 till 8:30 p. m.

Third year (post-graduate course)—Comparative constitutional law; public international law; private international law: history of English law; medical jurisprudence; railway law; proceedings in rem; insurance; Roman law; patent law; law of waters; trade-marks and copyrights; interstate commerce. Candidates for the degree of masters of laws must, in addition to the foregoing requirements, make themselves thoroughly familiar with Austin's Jurisprudence, High's Extraordinary Legal Remedies, and Cooley's Constitutional Limitations. Furthermore, they are required to prepare a thesis. Instruction in this course is given on Monday, Wednesday, and Friday at 4:30 p. m.

Organization and methods of instruction.—Candidates for admission not graduates of a college or a high school are required to pass examinations in the common school branches, including English history. Students are required to make a careful study of cases and original investigations, the classes being divided into sections for seminary work. Special attention is given to matters pertaining to practice. A common-law practice court is held during the junior and senior years and a chancery practice court in the senior year.

26. *Law School of the University of Alabama,* University post-office. Richard C. Jones, dean (1890-'91). Three Instructors, 19 students, 3 graduates, 36 weeks in school year.

Course of study: First year—International and constitutional law, one lecture a week with special reference to the United States, eleven weeks; Cooley's Principles; Kent's Commentaries; Cooley's Constitutional Limitations; Calhoun's works; Woolsey's Introduction; Wheaton's International Law; Vattel; Wharton's Constitutional Law. Common and statutory law: Walker's American Law; Kent's Commentaries; Stephen's Pleading; Greenleaf's Evidence; selected portions of Blackstone's Commentaries; Bishop's Contracts; Bigelow on Torts; Byles on Bills; Clark's Manual of Criminal Law; Code of Alabama; May's Criminal Law; Bliss' Code Practice; Equity Jurisprudence; Adam's Equity; Mitford's and Tyler's Pleadings and Practice; Code of Alabama; Bigelow's Equity; Langdell's Equity Pleading.

Organization and methods of instruction.—The school has three departments: (1) the school of international and constitutional law; (2) the school of common and statute law; (3) the school of equity jurisprudence.

Lectures are delivered during the course by the professors upon the various branches of the law, in addition to the oral examinations of the classes upon the text-books. Moot courts are presided over by one of the professors of the department with an occasional substitution of some eminent attorney in full practice and of proper legal acquirements. The academic schools are open to the law students and they are urged to avail themselves of the course in English language and literature as well as in ancient and modern languages offered there.[1]

27. *Law School of the University of Georgia,* Athens, Ga. Andrew J. Cobb, dean. Nine instructors, 14 students, 8 having degrees in letters or science, 13 graduates, 40 weeks in school year.

Course of study: First year.—Blackstone's Commentaries; Brown's Commentaries (contracts and torts); Constitution of the United States; Constitution of Georgia; Part I of Georgia Code (political organization of the State); Georgia Penal Code; Ewell's Medical Jurisprudence (12 weeks); principles of pleading, evidence, equity, equity practice, commercial law, civil code, and code of practice of Georgia (23 weeks); also lectures on medical jurisprudence delivered twice a week.

Method of instruction.—Lessons are assigned in the text-books and the students recite what they have memorized, the professor illustrating and illuminating the text.

28. *Law Department of Emory College,* Oxford, Ga. Two instructors, other items not reported.

Course of study: First Year.—Blackstone's and Brown's Commentaries; Robinson's Elementary Law (12 weeks); Chitty's Pleadings; Greenleaf's Evidence; Adam's Equity; Bishop's Criminal Law; Code of Georgia.

29. *School of Law of the University of Kansas,* Lawrence, Kans. J. W. Green, dean. Six instructors, 79 students, 5 having degrees in letters and science, 29 graduates, 40 weeks in school year.

Course of study: First year.—Kent's and Blackstone's Commentaries; Cooley's Constitutional Law; Schouler's Domestic Relations; Bishop's Contracts; Story's Agency; Story's Bailments; Tiedeman's Commercial Paper; Parson's Partnership; Story's Sales; Davis's International Law; Schuyler's American Diplomacy.

Second year—Bigelow's Torts; Morawetz's Corporations; Tiedeman's Real Property; Washburn's Real Property; Greenleaf's Evidence; Bliss's and Gould's Pleading; Story's Equity Pleading; Bispham's Equity Jurisprudence; Bishop's Criminal Law.

Organization and methods.—Applicants for admission to the school are examined in English language, in American and general history. Graduates of colleges and other secondary institutions are exempt from this examination, as are also those presenting first and second grade teachers' certificates. The instruction is given by daily recitations upon assigned portions of text-books, the drill of the recitation room being supplemented by lectures.

30. *Law School of the University of Louisville,* Louisville, Ky. W. O. Harris, dean. Three instructors, 40 students, 17 graduates, 28 weeks in school year.

Course of study: First year.—Institutes and elementary law; real property; pleading, contracts, bills of exchange, and promissory notes; criminal law; domestic relations; torts. Books used: Blackstone's Commentaries, Smith's Contracts, Story's Bills of Exchange, Bigelow's Torts, Smith's Mercantile Law.

Second year.—Pleadings and civil procedure, evidence, equity jurisprudence, commercial law, real property, criminal law (continued). Books used: Stephen's Pleadings.; Greenleaf's Evidence; Blackstone's Commentaries; Bispham's Equity; Smith's Mercantile Law; Bliss's Pleading.

Method's used.—Students are required to take notes on the lecture and read the leading cases referred to, and every afternoon in the week they are closely examined on the lectures and cases already gone over. In the moot court students are required to collect the authorities on important questions, and to make oral and written arguments.

31. *Law School of the University of Maryland,* Baltimore, Md. George William Dobbin, dean. Seven instructors, 100 students, 16 having degrees of letters or science, 22 graduates, 34 weeks in school year.

Course of study: First year.—Elementary common law; personal property and domestic relations (16 weeks); real property, contracts, 16 weeks.

Second year.—Criminal law, executors and administrators, pleading, torts, (16 weeks); real property (titles); commercial law, bills and notes, corporation, pleadings (16 weeks).

Third year.—Practice, evidence, international law, and admiralty (16 weeks); equity jurisprudence and procedure, constitutional and statute law (16 weeks).

Remarks.—The course extends over three years. The faculty being satisfied that students who have made considerable progress in the study of law do themselves and their school an injury by attempting to graduate after a shorter period. The methods of instruction is by lectures, reading, and catechising.

32. *Baltimore University School of Law,* Baltimore, Md. Just organized; 25 weeks in school year.

Course of study: First year.—Common law, domestic relations, pleading and practice, evidence, real property, equity, testamentary law, torts, crimes, and punishments, corporations, contracts, commercial law (except bills and notes). Eight lectures a week in the course.

Second year.—Domestic relations (continued), extraordinary remedies, bills and notes, insurance, medical jurisprudence, statutory crimes, criminal procedure, and evidence; constitutional law, international law, railroad law, admiralty. The moot court meets once a week during the session.

33. *Law School of the University of Mississippi,* University P. O., Miss. Albert Hall Whitefield, dean. Five instructors, 21 students, 2 having degrees in letters or science, 13 graduates; 40 weeks in school year.

Course of study: First year—Political and legal constitution of England, public and domestic relations of individuals, real estate, personal property, organization and jurisdiction of courts, pleading and practice, law of evidence, maritime law, bills of exchange and promissory notes, principal and agent, partnership, principal and surety, bailments, insurance, corporations, criminal law, criminal pleading and practice, medical jurisprudence.—Books used: Chase's Blackstone, Stephen's Pleading Evidence, first volume, Bishop's Criminal Law, Bishop's Criminal Procedure.

Second year.—Contract, torts, equity including testaments and administration, equity pleading and practice, including probate and minor's business, public international law, American Constitutional law, including taxation; Federal jurisprudence and procedure, railways and common carriers, real estate, code study. Books used: Smith's Contracts, Bigelow's Torts, Adams's Equity, Bispham's Equity Jurisprudence, Barton's Suit in Equity, Davis's International Law, Cooley's Constitutional Limitations, Foster's Federal Practice, Constitution of the United States, and of Mississippi, Pierce's Railroads, Tiedeman's Real Estate, Mississippi Code.

Methods of instruction.—Text-books are the chief means of instruction in this school and lectures are not informally read to the classes. Moot courts are held from time to time during the term.

34. *Law Department of the University of Michigan*, Ann Arbor, Mich. Gerome C. Knowlton, dean. Twenty-eight instructors; 648 students, 68 having degree in letters or science; 290 graduates, 36 weeks in school year.

Course of study: First year.—Lectures. Pleading and practice, personal property and title thereto, fixtures and easements, equity pleading and practice, bailments and carriers' contracts, domestic relations, torts, agency. Partnerships.—Text-book instruction: Cooley's Blackstone, Book 2, Anson's Contracts, Stephen's Pleading, Lube's Equity Pleading; Benjamin's Chalmer's Bills and Notes. The members of this class are required to make a study of leading cases. Elocutionary exercises are given as an option.

Second year.—Lectures: Jurisprudence of the United States, evidence, real property, criminal law, wills, probate, corporations. Constitutional law.—Text-book instruction: Heard's Criminal Pleading and (for those coming from code States) Bliss on Code Pleading. Study of forensic orators and oratory and oral discussions are optional.

Third year (post-graduate course).—Public international law; history of treaties; history of real property law (based on Digby); law of railroads; science of jurisprudence (Holland's work); railroad problem; corporative constitutional law; advanced course in constitutional law and history; writs of mandamus quo warranto, etc.; High's Extraordinary Legal Remedies; the interstate commerce act; admiralty law; insurance; medical jurisprudence; code pleading and practice; injunction and receivers; toxicology and its legal relations; mining law; legal microsopy; patent law; history of the common law.

Admission and methods of instruction.—An examination as to general education is required of applicants for admission. The examination embraces arithmetic, geography, composition, English and American history, portions of books 1 and 2 of Blackstone and all of book 4. Instruction is given by lectures and recitations. The members of both the regular classes are examined daily throughout the year on the lectures delivered. In addition to this work the classes are divided into sections and are required to recite daily upon the lectures after the manner adopted in the text-book instruction. Moot courts are held from time to time during the year.

35. *College of Law of the University of Wisconsin*, Madison, Wis. Edwin E. Bryant, dean.—Twelve instructors, 126 students, 2 having degree in letters or science, 53 graduates, 37 weeks in school year.

Course of study: First year: Elementary law, contracts, agency, domestic relations, real property, personal property, common law, pleading and practice (14½ weeks), real property, contracts, partnership, equity pleading and practice, criminal law, private corporations (12 weeks), contracts, bailments, real property, criminal law, and practice, public corporations, practice and pleading under code (10½ weeks), Bishop's Contracts, and Noncontract Law, Bishop's Criminal Law, Benjamin's Sales, Dillon on Municipal Corporations, Morawetz's Private Corporations, Parson's Contracts, Stephen's Pleading, Story's Agency and Partnership, Tiedeman's Real Property and Sales, etc.

Second year.—Contracts, bills of exchange and promissory notes, evidence, wills, real property, uses and trusts, common carriers, taxation, practice and pleading under code (14½ weeks), constitutional law, real property, eminent domain, bills of exchange and promissory notes, evidence, equity jurisprudence, practice after judgment, special proceedings, special actions, railway law, damages, estoppel (12 weeks), constitutional law, equity jurisprudence, torts and remedies therefor, evidence, railroad law, administration of estates, negligence, practice in special actions and proceedings, Cooley's Torts, Edward's Bills of Exchange and Promissory Notes, Greenleaf's Evidence, Langdell's Equity Pleading, Lewis's Eminent Domain, Mecham's Agency, Mills's Eminent Domain, Pomeroy's Equity Jurisprudence, Pomeroy's Remedies and Remedial Rights, Redfield's Wills.

Admission and methods of instruction.—Candidates for admission not graduates of higher or secondary schools are required to pass an examination in the English language and literature, in American and general History, and in the Constitution of the United States. The instruction is imparted by means of lectures in which student is referred to leading cases, and study of text-books with recitations. Moot courts are held.

36. *College of Law, University of Minnesota,* Minneapolis, Minn., William C. Paultee, dean. Sixteen instructors; 242 students, 20 having degrees in letters or science; 56 graduates; 36 weeks in school year.

Course of study: First year.—Contracts, torts, criminal law and procedure, real property, equity jurisdiction and procedure, domestic relations, suretyship and mortgage, partnership, common law and code pleading, evidence.

Second year.—Contracts, corporations, fire and life insurance, wills and administration, taxation, international law, conflict of laws, admiralty laws, medical jurisprudence, and practice of United States courts.

Third year.—For the benefit of those who desire further instruction a third-year course has been established. It is concerned with equity, civil and criminal procedure, and such other branches as may be desired. Special attention, however, is given to Minnesota law and practice, general jurisprudence, international and constitutional law, constitutional history of the United States.

Methods of instruction.—The method of instruction is not confined either to lectures or to recitations, but a combination of both is adopted. Reports are used to familiarize the student with the leading cases upon the various subjects in which he receives instruction. A moot court is organized at the beginning of each year and continues during the three terms. There is also a system of moot courts corresponding to the justice, the district, and the supreme courts of Minnesota.

37. *Department of Law of the University of the City of New York,* New York City. Austin Abbott, dean. Ten instructors, 342 students, 35 having degree in letters or science, 91 graduates, 32 weeks in school year.

Course of study: First year—Elementary law, Roman law, persons, property, elements of torts, corporations, criminal law, 3:45 to 4:30 p. m.; contracts and relations of contracting parties, corporations, 4:30 to 5:15 p. m.; negotiable paper, sales, torts, and civil remedies, 5:15 to 6 p. m.

Second year.—Principles of pleading, equity jurisprudence, evidence, short illustrative exposition of applied law, 3:45 to 5:15 p. m.; real property, 5:15 to 6 p. m.; wills and administration.

Methods of instruction.—The instruction is by lectures by the regular professors and special lectures and by the study of text-books, cases, and statutes (select titles), recitations, moot courts, etc.

38. *Law School of the University of North Carolina,* Chapel Hill, N. C., John Manning, professor. Three Instructors, 55 students, 20 having degree in letters or science, 7 graduates, 40 weeks in school year.

Course of study: First year.—Blackstone's Commentaries, Washburn's Real Property, Schouler's Executors, Stephen's Pleading, Chitty's Pleading, Adams's or Bispham's Equity, Vol. I of Greenleaf's Evidence, Smith's Contracts, Addison or Bigelow's Torts, Constitution of the United States and of North Carolina, Code of North Carolina, particularly the Code of Civil Procedure. For the degree course: Pollock's Contracts, Pierce's American Railroad Law, Angell and Ames's or Dillon's Corporation, Pomeroy's Equity Jurisprudence, Cooley's Constitutional Limitations, Wharton's Criminal Law, Best's Principles of Evidence, Cooley's Taxation, May's Insurance.

Second year.—(The course for a degree may be completed in one year, but ordinarily requires two years.)

Remarks—The plan of study comprises, first, the course prescribed for applicants for license by the Supreme Court of the State; second, a course of study for those desiring to compete for the degree of Bachelor of Laws. To complete the entire course would ordinarily require two years.

39. *School of Law of the University of Oregon,* Portland, Oregon. Richard H. Thornton, dean. Four instructors, 55 students, 5 having degree in letters or science, 19 graduates, 30 weeks in school year.

Course of study: First year.—Blackstone's Commentaries, Kent's Commentaries, Parson's Contracts.

Second year.—Gould's Pleading, Stephen's Evidence, Pomeroy's Equity, Constitutional Limitations, General Laws of Oregon.

40. *Law Department of the University of Pennsylvania*, Philadelphia, Pa., C. Stuart Patterson, dean. Seven instructors, 176 students, 2 having degree in letters or science, 50 graduates, 29 weeks in school year.

Course of study: First year.—Real property, elementary equity, contracts, torts, pleading.—Books used: Bispham's Equity, Williams's Real Property, Mitchell's Lectures upon Real Estate and Conveyancing in Pennsylvania, Pollock's Contracts, Anson's Contracts, Hare's Contracts, Pollock's Torts, Bigelow's Torts, Ames's Cases, Stephen's Pleading.

Second year.—Real property and conveyancing, partnerships, equity, contracts, evidence. Books used: Stephen's Evidence, Parson's Partnership, in addition to those mentioned under first year.

Third year.—Constitutional law, wills and administration, commercial law, practice and pleading in equity, contracts, criminal law, practice. Books used: Russell's Crime, Stephen's History of the Criminal Law, Story's Constitution, Hare's Constitution, Patterson's Federal Restraints on State Action.

Admission and methods of instruction.—Examination in high-school studies imposed upon those applicants for admission who are not Bachelors of Arts or of Sciences. The instruction is given by lectures and by frequent examinations, and the students are required to read leading cases illustrating the subjects of instruction. Moot courts are held once a week, at which questions prepared by the professor are argued.

41. *Department of Law of the University of Texas*, Austin, Tex.—Two instructors, 76 students,—having degree in letters or science, 26 graduates, 32 weeks in school year.

Course of study: First year.—Personal rights, domestic relations, estates in and titles to property, both real and personal; torts, criminal law, contract, sales, agency, pleading, practice and evidence. Books used: Blackstone's Commentaries, Anson's Contract, Tiedeman's Sales, Sayle's and Bassett's Texas Pleading and Practice, Robert's Elements of Texas Pleading, Bishop's Non-Contract Law; Greenleaf's Evidence, Vol. I.

Second year. —Government of the United States and of Texas, with judicial system of each; international law, constitutional law, equity, suretyship and guaranty, negotiable instruments, partnerships, private corporations, legal ethics. Books used: Revised Statutes of Texas, containing Constitution of United States and of Texas; Kent's Commentaries, vol. I, Peeler's Law and Equity in the United States Courts, Bispham's Equity, Taylor's Private Corporations.

Remarks: The methods of instruction contemplate the use of text-books, with daily examinations and oral explanations, and also contemplate throughout the entire course occasional lectures, supplementing the text-books and developing the peculiar features of Texas jurisprudence. Moot courts are held.

42. *Law Department of the University of Virginia*, University P. O., Va. John B. Minor, sr., professor.—Three instructors, 134 students, 30 having degree in letters or science,—graduates, 39 weeks in school year.

Course of study: First year.—Minor's Institutes of Common and Statute Law, Vol. I of Rights, which relate to the person; Vol. II of Rights, which relate to real property; Minor's Synopsis of Criminal Law, Blackstone's Commentaries. Lectures Monday, Wednesday, and Friday, from 11 a. m. to 12:30 p. m. Books used: Vattel's International Law, with lectures; Lectures on Government; Federalist; Gilmore's Notes on Vattel and the Constitution. Lectures Thursday and Saturday, 12:30 p. m. to 2 p. m.

Second year.—Minor's Institutes; Vol. IV of the Practice of Law in Civil Cases, including pleading; Vol. III of the Rights which relate to Personal Property, Stephen's Pleading. Lectures Tuesday, Thursday, and Saturday, from 11 a. m. to 12:30 p. m. Books used: Smith's Mercantile Law, Greenleaf's Evidence, Adams's Equity, with lectures and notes. Lectures Monday, Wednesday, and Friday, 12:30 p. m.

Remarks.—The course is intended for two years, but may be completed in one. The department is divided into two schools, known, respectively, as the School of Common and Statute Law and the School of Constitutional and International Law, Mercantile Law, Evidence, and Equity.[2]

43. *Law Department of West Virginia University*, Morgantown, W. Va. Two instructors [number illegible] students, 3 having degree in letters or sciences, 19 graduates, 30 weeks in school year.

Course of study: First year.—Rights of persons and things, Blackstone, international law, common law, pleading, contracts, negotiable instruments, equity pleading, evidence, 14 weeks; constitutional law, international law, Blackstone, first and second books continued and third and fourth books begun, agency, partnership, surety and guaranty, practice in the courts, equity, evidence, 12 weeks; constitutional law continued, Blackstone, third and fourth books continued, real property, bailments, corporations, practice in the courts, insurance, equity.

Books used: Blackstone's Commentaries, Stephen's Pleading, Brooke's Notes on Common Law Pleading and Practice in West Virginia, Williams's Real Property. Federalist and Cooley's Constitutional Law, Woolsey's Introduction to International Law.

Second year: The course as given in preceding paragraph may be spread over 2 years.

Organization and methods of instruction.—In many cases students take two or three branches of the academic course in connection with the studies of the law department. Such students divide the law course into 2 years. The methods of instruction consist of lectures and examinations from approved text-books read in course, the drawing of various legal papers requisite in the ordinance practice of the law, and moot courts.

44. *Law Department of Vanderbilt University*, Nashville, Tenn. Thomas H. Malone, dean. Four instructors, 37 students, 5 having degree in letters or science, 18 graduates, 40 weeks in school year.

Course of study: First year.—Bishop's Contracts, Schouler's Domestic Relations, Agency, Tyler's Partnership, Heard's Civil Pleading, Lubé's Equity Pleading, 18 weeks; Taylor's Corporations, bailment, Cooley's Torts, Washburn's Crimes, Reynolds's Evidence, moot court, 17 weeks.

Second year.—Daniel's Negotiable Instruments, Tiedeman's Real Property, Reynolds's Evidence, moot court, 18 weeks; Bispham's Equity Jurisprudence, Cooley's Constitutional Limitations, Lubé's Equity Pleading; admiralty proceedings, moot court. (The student may finish the course as given for two years in one year.)

Remarks.—The daily exercises consist of recitations from the text-books, accompanied with rigid oral questioning and full illustrations and lectures on kindred topics. Moot courts are held.

45. *School of Law of the Washington and Lee University*, Lexington, Va. G. W. C. Lee, dean. Two instructors, 63 students, 2 having degree in letters or science, 2[?] graduates; 36 weeks in school year.

Course of study: First year.—Junior class: Natural law and international law, 77 hours; Constitutional law, 89 hours; Contract. and carriers, 68 hours; real and personal property, 93 hours; Anson's Contracts, Hutchinson on Carrier's, Tiedeman's Real Property, Blackstone's Commentaries, book 2; printed lectures on real property; Schouler's Personal Property, Vol. 2; Blackstone's Commentaries, book 1, with lectures on natural law; Woolsey's International Law, with lectures; Cooley's Constitutional Law, with lectures; negotiable paper and corporations, 53 hours; equity, domestic relations, and the conflict of laws, 148 hours; torts and crimes, 77 hours; pleading and evidence, 89 hours; Bigelow's Torts; May's Criminal Law; Blackstone's Commentaries, books 3 and 4; Gould's Pleading (Heard's edition); Greenleaf's Evidence, Vol. 1; printed lectures on negotiable paper; printed lectures on corporations; Bispham's Equity; Schouler's Domestic Relations; lectures on partnership; insurance; shipping and admiralty; printed lectures on the conflict of laws.

Second year.—The course may be pursued so that its completion will require 2 years.

Remarks.—The course is so arranged as to render possible its completion in one session of 9 months. Students are advised, however, to devote 2 years to the study of law. The basis of instruction is the study of the text-book, with frequent oral examinations. Lectures are delivered by the professors to supplement the text. Two moot courts are organized.

46. *College of Law of Willamette University*, Salem, Oregon. William Ramsey, dean. Twelve instructors, 5 students, 1 graduate; 36 weeks in school year.

Course of study: First year.—General commentaries upon municipal laws, contracts, real estate, commercial law. Books used: Blackstone's Commentaries, Tiedeman's Real Property, Kent's Commentaries, Parson's Contracts.

Second year.—Equity jurisprudence, torts, criminal law, evidence. pleading, and practice. Books used: Cooley's Torts, Bispham's Equity, Wharton's Criminal Law, Greenleaf's Evidence, Chitty's Pleadings, Vol. 1, Bliss's Code Pleading, Daniel's Negotiable Instruments.

Organization and methods of instruction.—There is an examination for admission. The daily exercises consist of lectures and recitations from standard text-books, the latter being accompanied by oral explanations. Moot courts are held regularly.

47. *Law Department of Yale University*, New Haven, Conn. Francis Wayland, dean. Five professors, 2 assistant

professors, 26 instructors and lecturers, 171 students, of whom 15 have degrees, 44 graduates; 33 weeks in school year.

Course of study: First year.—English constitutional law, bailments, evidence, international law, elementary law, pleading, evidence, mercantile law, nature and history of American law, wills (or Roman law), contracts, torts, forensic elocution.

Second year.—Evidence, equity, real property, medical jurisprudence, domestic relations, forensic oratory, criminal law, mercantile law, American constitutional law, public and private corporations, wills (or Roman law), practice, contracts, torts, international law, patents, attachments, judgments and executions, corporate trusts, transfer of monetary securities, insurance, the beginning of practice.

Third year.—(First year of graduate course.) Patents, taxation, railroad law, practice in U.S. courts, admiralty law, sales, municipal corporations, statute law, Federal jurisprudence, international law, mortgages, political science and history, English constitutional history, railway management.

(Second year of graduate course.) Early history of real property, canon law, comparative jurisprudence, code Napoleon, English constitutional law, political and social science, Roman law, economics of transportation, public finance.

Organization and methods of instruction.— The courses of the school are: An undergraduate, a graduate, and two special courses, each of two years, except the first special course, which is of one year. The first and second years of the graduate course have no direct connection. Indeed, the first year of the graduate course is considered as a fitting conclusion to the studies of the undergraduate course. Neither of the special courses is professional. The method of instruction is mainly that of recitation. Hence, although certain subjects are taught by lectures, care is taken that the same topic is covered by recitation work in connection with the wider branches of the law to which they belong. Leading cases are constantly referred to and studied in connection with the various subjects. Public moot courts, besides those in the class quiz-clubs, are regularly held, one of the professors presiding. The requirements for admission are that the applicant must be 18 years of age or over, and must have passed an examination in American and English history on the text of the Constitution.

48. *College of Law of Illinois Wesleyan University*, Bloomington, Ill., Owen T. Reeves, dean. Eight instructors, 44 students, 17 graduates, 36 weeks in school year.

Course of study: First year.—Elementary law (Robinson), 26 hours; American law (Walker), 65 hours; torts (Bigelow), 26 hours; civil procedure, 13 hours; English common law (Blackstone, books 1 and 2), 24 hours; contracts (Benjamin and Parsons), 106 hours; pleading (Stephen and Gould), 42 hours; English common law (Blackstone, books 3 and 4), 18 hours; civil procedure (Moore's Civil Practice), 34 hours.

Second year.—Common law (Kent, Parts I to V), 26 hours; real property (Tiedeman), 50 hours; evidence (Greenleaf and Chase), 34 hours; pleading (Chitty), 50 hours; practice (Illinois Practice Act), 25 hours; common law (Kent, part V), 24 hours; equity jurisprudence (Bispham), 24 hours; common law (Kent, part VI), 18 hours; criminal law (Harris), 18 hours; torts (Cooley), 18 hours; equity pleading (Heard), 9 hours; practice (Illinois Chancery Code), 9 hours.

Methods of instruction—The method adopted is mainly that of daily recitation from text-books, during which the text is illuminated by examples easily comprehended by the student. Moot courts are held throughout the course.

49. *Department of Law of the University of Tennessee*, Knoxville, Tenn. Henry H. Ingersoll, dean. Eight instructors, 10 students, 3 having degree in letters or science, 6 graduates, 40 weeks in school year.

Course of study: First year.—Robinson's Elementary Law, May's Criminal law, Bigelow's Torts, Bishop's Contracts, Schouler's Domestic Relations, Tiedeman's Real Property, Smith's Commercial Law, History of a Law Suit.

Second Year.—Cooley's Constitutional Law, Boone's Corporations, Stephen's Pleading, Greenleaf's Evidence, Vol. 1; Ram's Legal Judgment, Bispham's Equity, Gibson's Suits in Chancery. (The course may be completed in one year by earnest application and sole attention to the law.)

Methods of instruction.—The methods employed are text-book study, with daily recitation and colloquial instruction, weekly moot courts and lectures.

50. *Department of Law of the University of South Carolina,* Columbia, S. C. Thomas A. Saxon, dean. One instructor, 20 students, 4 graduates, 32 weeks in school year.

Course of study: First year.—Organization and jurisdiction of courts of the United States and South Carolina, sources of municipal law, domestic relations, personal property, and title to same, administration, wills, contracts, bailments, bills and notes, principal and agent, corporations, criminal law and herein of torts and nuisance, public and private, evidence. Class meets five times a week during session. Constitution of United States and the Judiciary Acts, Vol. 1; Kent's Commentaries, Constitution of South Carolina, organization of judiciary, acts, etc., bearing on organization of judiciary, Kent's Short Chapters on Domestic Relations, Reeve's Domestic Relations, Kent's Personal Property and Statutes of South Carolina, Blackstone's Commentaries (book 4), May's Criminal Law and South Carolina Criminal Law.

Second year.—Pleading and practice, real property, equity jurisprudence, conveyancing, trial of title to lands, maritime law and law of nations, statute law of the State on subjects not read in connection with the text and lectures of the course—deeds, recording, habeas corpus, etc. Class meets five times a week during session.

Boone's Code Pleading, the South Carolina Code, Kent's Commentaries, Vol. 4; Blackstone's Commentaries (selections); Washburn's Real Property, Vol. 2, Adams's Equity, Story's Equity, White and Tudor's Leading Cases in Equity, Martindail's Conveyancing, Sedgwick and Walt's Ejectment.

Methods of instruction.—Instruction is given by lectures and text-books. Moot courts are held once a week.

51. *The Dickinson School of Law,* Carlisle, Pa. William Trickett, dean. Twelve instructors, 31 students, 7 having degree in letters or science, 13 graduates, 34 weeks in school year.

Course of study not given.

52. *School of Law of Ohio State University,* Columbus, Ohio. Marshall J. Williams, dean. Nineteen instructors, 63 students, 17 graduates, 36 weeks in school year.

Course of study: First year.—Elementary law, criminal law, domestic relations, torts, evidence, contracts, common law pleading.

Second year.—Agency, partnership, sales, bailment., bills and notes, and commercial law, municipal corporations, private corporations, mortgages and liens, equity jurisprudence, real property, constitutional law (elective), equity and code pleading and practice, insurance, medical jurisprudence (elective), legal microscopy (elective).

Organization and methods of instruction.— Those not able to give satisfactory evidence of scholastic attainments must undergo an examination equivalent to that required of applicants for admission to one of the four-year courses of the university. The system of instruction is by lectures, text-books, and recitations. Moot courts are held. "For those who complete the course in law, but have not had the required amount of general education necessary for the degree of LL.B., a certificate of having completed the course in law is provided." —(H. L. Wilgers, esq., in reply to inquiry from Bureau of Education.)

53. *Law Department of the Missouri State University,* Columbia, Mo. Alexander Martin, dean. Seven instructors, 75 students, 15 having degree in letters or science, 25 graduates, 36 weeks in school year.

Course of study: First year.—Elementary law, criminal law, torts, bailments, contracts, law of sales, commercial paper, partnership, domestic relations. Books used: Robinson's Elementary Law, Bishop's Contracts, Cooley's Torts, Schouler's Domestic Relations and Bailments, Tiedeman's Sales, Pollock's Partnership, Tiedeman's Commercial Paper, Criminal Code of Missouri.

Second year.—Law of real property, constitutional law, interpretation and construction of statutes, pleading and practice, equity jurisprudence, admiralty, insurance, law of corporations, international law, law of evidence. Books used: Tiedeman's Real Property, Bispham's Equity Jurisprudence, Greenleaf's Evidence, Vol. 1; Boon's Corporations, Cooley's Principles of Constitutional Law, Woolsey's International Law, May's or Flanders's Insurance, Bliss's Code Pleading, Deshy's Shipping and Admiralty and Federal Procedure.

Third year (graduate course).—Constitutional law, corporations, insurance, trusts, patents, law of homicide. The student in this course is allowed to select any special subject in law for extended examination and study, to be presented concurrently with the subjects embraced in the course.

Organization and methods of instruction.—The course is of two years, but to provide the intending practitioner with a more extended and practical knowledge of the most important subjects embraced in modern law a post-graduate course was established in April, 1891. The faculty are more and more satisfied that the highest results can not be reached by lectures alone, however clear and thorough they may be, and that the study of text-books and leading cases is also necessary. A moot court is held every Friday.

54. *Iowa College of Law*, Des Moines, Iowa, Josiah Given, dean. Six instructors, 37 students, 12 graduates, 32 weeks in school year.

Course of study: First year.—Elementary law (Walker's American Law), contracts (Bishop's), torts (Bishop's Noncontract Law), pleading and practice (Stephen's Work and Boone's Code Pleading), review and general discussion (once in two weeks), 10 weeks; criminal Law (Wharton's), partnership (Story), agency (Meechem's), bills and notes (Tiedeman's), pleading and practice, review and general discussion (once every two weeks), 11 weeks; bailment. and common carriers, (Schouler's), domestic relations, Browne's Real Property (Tiedeman), pleading and practice (Kinne's), review and general discussion (once every two weeks), 10 weeks.

Second year.—Elementary law (Blackstone's Commentaries), personal property (Brantley's), evidence (Greenleaf's, vol. 1), sales and chattel mortgages (Tiedeman's), pleading and practice (Kinne's), review and general discussion (once every two weeks), 10 weeks; elementary law (Blackstone's Commentaries), equity jurisprudence (Bispham's), corporations (Boone's), insurance (May's), pleading and practice, (Kinne's), review and discussion (once every two weeks), 11 weeks; elementary law (Blackstone's Commentaries), corporations, constitutional and international law, civil law, pleading, and practice, review and general discussion.

Organization and methods of instruction. —Lectures and text-book recitations upon lessons previously announced are combined. Topics are assigned to students, who are required to present them orally and often without notes to the class. Moot courts are organized immediately after the opening of the full term. An admissions examination is held for those not having been educated in a college or secondary school. The subjects of examination are arithmetic, history, orthography, English grammar, and composition.

55. *Law School of Mercer University*, Macon, Ga. —Three instructors.

Beyond the course of the school (which is not given), lectures are given during the year on special topics, such as pleading and evidence, commercial law, law of ejectment, equity, professional ethics, etc.

56. *Law School of the University of Colorado*, Boulder, Col. Moses Hallett, dean. Fourteen instructors; 36 weeks in school year.

The school having been organized in May, 1892, it is not desirable to present statistics until it fairly enters upon its work in September, 1892.

Course of study: First year.—American constitutional law, Roman law, contracts, real property, criminal law and procedure, torts and personal rights, bailments, common law and code, pleadings, domestic relations, personal property, private corporations, agency, wills.

Second year.—Federal jurisprudence, sales of personal property, evidence, equity jurisprudence, pleading and practice, trusts, executors and administrators, suretyship and mortgages, bills of exchange and promissory notes, partnership, damages, carriers, peculiarities of Colorado law and practice; special lectures will be delivered.

Organization and methods of instruction.—Although the method of instruction is mainly that of lectures, the same subject matter will be covered by recitation work. Moot courts will be held each week. "Those who are not graduates of colleges or high schools are required to undergo a written examination in respect to general education."

Summary of statistics of law schools in the United States.

Number of law schools	56
Number of instructors	453
Number of students	6,106

The number of students who had, previous to their engaging in the study of law, obtained a degree in letters or science, either from a college or some other institution conferring literary or scientific degree, is unknown. Many colleges take no record of such facts; others again may be apprehensive that invidious distinctions may be drawn against themselves, if the facts in their case be known. Under these conditions there is but one method to follow, that is, to take the total number of students in the schools that report the fact in question and to compare that total with the total number of students reported as having previously obtained a bachelor degree in arts or science. This has been the method followed by the specialist who has prepared the chapter on professional schools in the Annual Report of the Bureau of Education, when preparing the diagrams illustrating the increase of attendance at the various professional institutions in Germany, France, and particularly in the United States. Adopting this method of procedure then, it appears that the—

Number of schools reporting the fact was	26
Number of students in them	3,261
Number of students having a degree	498

To put the matter briefly, 15 in every 100 students in 26 schools had obtained a degree in some institution not giving professional instruction, or, more technically expressed, had obtained a degree in letters or science.

The length of the course is two years. Of 54 schools reporting 40 have a two years' courses, 7 have a course of 1 year which in several instances may be spread over two, 7 schools have a three years' course. Of the 40 schools with two years' courses, several permit the student to take it in one year, and 7 schools, on the contrary, offer a post-graduate course. In Washington, D. C., this is called a "post-graduate course in practice." Yale Law School has an undergraduate course of two years and a post-graduate course also of two, but one (the last) of which need not be taken.

NOTES

1. Editor's note: See also Remarks for entry 42, for UVA.
2. Editor's note: See also Remarks for entry 26, for Alabama.

Chapter 39

The Use of Law Schools

1886

Oliver Wendell Holmes, Jr.

Oliver Wendell Holmes, Jr. (March 8, 1841-March 6, 1935) was a professor at Harvard Law School, chief justice of the Massachusetts supreme judicial court, and Associate Justice of the United States from 1902 to 1932. This address to the Harvard Law School Association on the 250th anniversary of Harvard University was printed in Oliver Wendell Holmes, Jr., *Speeches* (Boston: Little, Brown, 1913).

It is not wonderful that the graduates of the Law School of Harvard College should wish to keep alive their connection with it. About three quarters of a century ago it began with a Chief Justice of the Supreme Court of Massachusetts for its Royall Professor. A little later, one of the most illustrious judges who ever sat on the United States Supreme Bench—Mr. Justice Story—accepted a professorship in it created for him by Nathan Dane. And from that time to this it has had the services of great and famous lawyers; it has been the source of a large part of the most important legal literature which the country has produced; it has furnished a world-renowned model in its modes of instruction; and it has had among its students future chief justices and justices, and leaders of state bars and of the national bar too numerous for me to thrill you with the mention of their names.

It has not taught great lawyers only. Many who have won fame in other fields began their studies here. Sumner and Phillips were among the Bachelors of 1834. The orator whom we shall hear in a day or two appears in the list of 1840 alongside of William Story, of the Chief Justice of this State, and of one of the Associate Justices, who is himself not less known as a soldier and as an orator than he is as a judge. Perhaps, without revealing family secrets, I may whisper that next Monday's poet also tasted our masculine diet before seeking more easily digested, if not more nutritious, food elsewhere.[1] Enough. Of course we are proud of the Harvard Law School. Of course we love every limb of Harvard College. Of course we rejoice to manifest our brotherhood by the symbol of this Association.

I will say no more for the reasons of our coming together. But by your leave I will say a few words about the use and meaning of law schools, especially of our law school, and about its methods of instruction, as they appear to one who has had some occasion to consider them.

A law school does not undertake to teach success. That combination of tact and will which gives a man immediate prominence among his fellows comes from nature, not from instruction; and if it can be helped at all by advice, such advice is not offered here. It might be expected that I should say, by way of natural antithesis, that what a law school does undertake to teach is law. But I am not ready to say even that, without a qualification. It seems to me that nearly all the education which men can get from others is moral, not intellectual. The main part of intellectual education is not the acquisition of facts, but learning how to make facts live. Culture, in the sense of fruitless knowledge, I for one abhor. The mark of a master is, that facts which before lay scattered in an inorganic mass, when he shoots through them the magnetic current of his thought, leap into an organic order, and live and bear fruit. But you cannot make a master by teaching. He makes himself by aid of his natural gifts.

Education, other than self-education, lies mainly in the shaping of men's interests and aims. If you convince a man that another way of looking at things is more profound, another form of pleasure more subtile than that to which he has been accustomed—if you make him really see it—the very nature of man is such that he will desire the profounder thought and the subtiler joy. So I say the business of a law school is not sufficiently described when you merely say that it is to teach law, or to make lawyers. It is to teach law in the grand manner, and to make great lawyers.

Our country needs such teaching very much. I think we should all agree that the passion for equality has passed far beyond the political or even the social sphere. We are not only unwilling to admit that any class or society is better than that in which we move, but our customary attitude towards every one in authority of any kind is that he is only the lucky recipient of honor or salary above the average, which any average man might as well receive as he. When the effervescence of democratic negation extends its workings beyond the abolition of external distinctions of rank to spiritual things—when the passion for equality is not content with founding social intercourse upon universal human sympathy, and a community of interests in which all may share, but attacks the lines of Nature which establish orders and degrees among the souls of men—they are not only wrong, but ignobly wrong. Modesty and reverence are no less virtues of freemen than the democratic feeling which will submit neither to arrogance nor to servility.

To inculcate those virtues, to correct the ignoble excess of a noble feeling to which I have referred, I know of no teachers so powerful and persuasive as the little army of specialists. They carry no banners, they beat no drums; but where they are, men learn that bustle and push are not the equals of quiet genius and serene mastery. They compel others who need their help, or who are enlightened by their teaching, to obedience and respect. They set the examples themselves; for they furnish in the intellectual world a perfect type of the union of democracy with discipline. They bow to no one who seeks to impose his authority by foreign aid; they hold that science like courage is never beyond the necessity of proof, but must always be ready to prove itself against all challengers. But to one who has shown himself a master, they pay the proud reverence of men who know what valiant combat means, and who reserve the right to combat against their leader even, if he should seem to waver in the service of Truth, their only queen.

In the army of which I speak, the lawyers are not the least important corps. For all lawyers are specialists. Not in the narrow sense in which we sometimes use the word in the profession—of persons who confine themselves to a particular branch of practice, such as conveyancing or patents—but specialists who have taken all law to be their province; specialists because they have undertaken to master a special branch of human knowledge—a branch, I may add, which is more immediately connected with all the highest interests of man than any other which deals with practical affairs.

Lawyers, too, were among the first specialists to be needed and to appear in America. And I believe it would be hard to exaggerate the goodness of their influence in favor of sane and orderly thinking. But lawyers feel the spirit of the times like other people. They, like others, are forever trying to discover cheap and agreeable substitutes for real things. I fear that the bar has done its full share to exalt that most hateful of American words and ideals, "smartness," as against dignity of moral feeling and profundity of knowledge. It is from within the bar, not from outside, that I have heard the new gospel that learning is out of date, and that the man for the times is no longer the thinker and the scholar, but the smart man, unencumbered with other artillery than the latest edition of the Digest and the latest revision of the Statutes.

The aim of a law school should be, the aim of the Harvard Law School has been, not to make men smart, but to make them wise in their calling—to start them on a road which will lead them to the abode of the masters. A law school should be at once the workshop and the nursery of specialists in the sense which I have explained. It should obtain for teachers men in each generation who are producing the best work of that generation. Teaching should not stop, but rather should foster, production. The "enthusiasm of the lecture-room," the contagious interest of companionship, should make the students partners in their teachers' work. The ferment of genius in its creative moment is quickly imparted. If a man is great, he makes others believe in greatness; he makes them incapable of mean ideals and easy self-satisfaction. His pupils will accept no substitute for realities; but at the same time they learn that the only coin with which realities can be bought is life.

Our School has been such a workshop and such a nursery as I describe. What men it has turned out I have hinted already, and do not need to say; what works it has produced is known to all the world. From ardent coöperation of student and teacher have sprung Greenleaf on Evidence, and Stearns on Real Actions, and Story's epoch-making Commentaries, and Parsons on Contracts, and Washburn on Real Property; and, marking a later epoch, Langdell on Contracts and on Equity Pleading, and Ames on Bills and Notes, and Gray on Perpetuities, and I hope we soon may add Thayer on Evidence. You will notice that these books are very different in character from one another, but you will notice also how many of them have this in common—that they have marked and largely made an epoch.

There are plenty of men nowadays of not a hundredth part of Story's power who could write as good statements of the law as his, or better. And when some mediocre fluent book has been printed, how often have we heard it proclaimed, "Lo, here is a greater than Story!" But if you consider the state of legal literature when Story began to write, and from what wells of learning the discursive streams of his speech were fed, I think you will be inclined to agree with me that he has done more than any other English-speaking man in this century to make the law luminous and easy to understand.

But Story's simple philosophizing has ceased to satisfy men's minds. I think it might be said with safety, that no man of his or of the succeeding generation could have stated the law in a form that deserved to abide, because neither his nor the succeeding generation possessed or could have possessed the historical knowledge, had made or could have made the analyses of principles, which are necessary before the cardinal doctrines of the law can be known and understood in their precise contours and in their innermost meanings.

The new work is now being done. Under the influence of Germany, science is gradually drawing legal history into its sphere. The facts are being scrutinized by eyes microscopic in intensity and panoramic in scope. At the same time, under the influence of our revived interest in philosophical speculation, a thousand heads are analyzing and generalizing the rules of law and the grounds on which they stand. The law has got to be stated over again; and I venture to say that in fifty years we shall have it in a form of which no man could have dreamed fifty years ago. And now I venture to add my hope and my belief, that, when the day comes which I predict, the Professors of the Harvard Law School will be found to have had a hand in the change not less important than that which Story has had in determining the form of the textbooks of the last half-century.

Corresponding to the change which I say is taking place, there has been another change in the mode of teaching. How far the correspondence is conscious, I do not stop to inquire. For whatever reason, the Professors of this School have said to themselves more definitely than ever before, We will not be contented to send forth students with nothing but a rag-bag full of general principles—a throng of glittering generalities, like a swarm of little bodiless cherubs fluttering at the top of one of Correggio's pictures. They have said that to make a general principle worth anything you must give it a body; you must show in what way and how far it would be applied actually in an actual system; you must show how it has gradually emerged as the felt reconciliation of concrete instances no one of which established it in terms. Finally, you must show its historic relations to other principles, often of very different date and origin, and thus set it in the perspective without which its proportions will never be truly judged.

In pursuance of these views there have been substituted for text-books more and more, so far as practicable, those books of cases which were received at first by many with a somewhat contemptuous smile and pitying contrast of good old days, but which now, after fifteen years, bid fair to revolutionize the teaching both of this country and of England.

I pause for a moment to say what I hope it is scarcely necessary for me to say—that in thus giving in my adhesion to the present methods of instructions I am not wanting in grateful and appreciative recollection (alas! it can be only recollection now) of the earlier teachers under whom I studied. In my day the Dean of this School was Professor Parker, the ex-Chief Justice of New Hampshire, who I think was one of the greatest of American judges, and who showed in the chair the same qualities that had made him famous on the bench. His associates were Parsons, almost if not quite a man of genius, and gifted with a power of impressive statement which I do not know that I have ever seen equalled; and Washburn, who taught us all to realize the meaning of the phrase which I already have quoted from Vangerow, the "enthusiasm of the lecture-room." He did more for me than the learning of Coke and the logic of Fearne could have done without his kindly ardor.

To return, and to say a word more about the theory on which these books of cases are used. It long has seemed to me a striking circumstance, that the ablest of the agitators for codification, Sir James Stephen, and the originator of the present mode of teaching, Mr. Langdell, start from the same premises to reach seemingly opposite conclusions. The number of legal principles is small, says in effect Sir James Stephen, therefore codify them; the number of legal principles is small, says Mr. Langdell, therefore they may be taught through the cases which have developed and established them. Well, I think there is much force in Sir James Stephen's argument, if you can find competent men and get them to undertake the task; and at any rate I am not now going to express an opinion that he is wrong. But I am certain from my own experience that Mr. Langdell is right; I am certain that when your object is not to make a bouquet of the law for the public, nor to prune and graft it by legislation, but to plant its roots where they will grow, in minds devoted henceforth to that one end, there is no way to be compared to Mr. Langdell's way. Why, look at it simply in the light of human nature. Does not a man remember a concrete instance more vividly than a general principle? And is not a principle more exactly and intimately grasped as the unexpressed major premise of the half-dozen examples which mark its extent and its limits than it can be in any abstract form of words? Expressed or unexpressed, is it not better known when you have studied its embryology and the lines of its growth than when you merely see it lying dead before you on the printed page?

I have referred to my own experience. During the short time that I had the honor of teaching in the School, it fell to me, among other things, to instruct the first-year men in Torts. With some misgivings I plunged a class of beginners straight into Mr. Ames's collection of cases, and we began to discuss them together in Mr. Langdell's method. The result was better than I even hoped it would be. After a week or two, when the first confusing novelty was over, I found that my class examined the questions proposed with an accuracy of view which they never could have learned from text-books, and which often exceeded that to be found in the text-books. I at least, if no one else, gained a good deal from our daily encounters.

My experience as a judge has confirmed the belief I formed as a professor. Of course a young man cannot try or argue a case as well as one who has had years of experience. Most of you also would probably agree with me that no teaching which a man receives from others at all approaches in importance what he does for himself, and that one who simply has been a docile pupil has got but a very little way. But I do think that in the thoroughness of their training, and in the systematic character of their knowledge, the young men of the present day start better equipped when they begin their practical experience than it was possible for their predecessors to have been. And although no school can boast a monopoly of promising young men, Cambridge, of course, has its full proportion of them at our bar; and I do think that the methods of teaching here bear fruits in their work.

I sometimes hear a wish expressed by the impatient, that the teaching here should be more practical. I remember that a very wise and able man said to a friend of mine when he was beginning his professional life, "Don't know too much law," and I think we all can imagine cases where the warning would be useful. But a far more useful thing is what was said to me as a student by one no less wise and able—afterwards my partner and always my friend—when I was talking as young men do about seeing practice, and all the other things which seemed practical to my inexperience, "The business of a lawyer is to know law." The professors of this Law School mean to make their students know law. They think the most practical teaching is that which takes their students to the bottom of what they seek to know. They therefore mean to make them master the common law and equity as working systems, and think that when that is accomplished they will have no trouble with the improvements of the last half-century. I believe they are entirely right, not only in the end they aim at, but in the way they take to reach that end.

Yes, this School has been, is, and I hope will be, a centre where great lawyers perfect their achievements, and from which young men, even more inspired by their example than instructed by their teaching, go forth in their turn, not to imitate what their masters have done, but to live their own lives more freely for the ferment imparted to them here. The men trained in this School may not always be the most knowing in the ways of getting on. The noblest of them must often feel that they are committed to lives of proud dependence—the dependence of men who command no factitious aids to success, but rely upon unadvertised knowledge and silent devotion; dependence upon finding an appreciation which they cannot seek, but dependence proud in the conviction that the knowledge to which their lives are consecrated is of things which it concerns the world to know. It is the dependence of abstract thought, of science, of beauty, of poetry and art, of every flower of civilization, upon finding a soil generous enough to support it. If it does not, it must die. But the world needs the flower more than the flower needs life.

I said that a law school ought to teach law in the grand manner; that it had something more to do than simply to teach law. I think we may claim for our School that it has not been wanting in greatness. I once heard a Russian say that in the middle class of Russia there were many specialists; in the upper class there were civilized men. Perhaps in America, for reasons which I have mentioned, we need specialists even more than we do civilized men. Civilized men who are nothing else are a little apt to think that they cannot breathe the American atmosphere. But if a man is a specialist, it is most desirable that he should also be civilized; that he should have laid in the outline of the other sciences, as well as the light and shade of his own; that he should be reasonable, and see things in their proportion. Nay, more, that he should be passionate, as well as reasonable—that he should be able not only to explain, but to feel; that the ardors of intellectual pursuit should be relieved by the charms of art, should be succeeded by the joy of life become an end in itself.

At Harvard College is realized in some degree the palpitating manifoldness of a truly civilized life. Its aspirations are concealed because they are chastened and instructed; but I believe in my soul that they are not the less noble that they are silent. The golden light of the University is not confined to the undergraduate department; it is shed over all the schools. He who has once seen it becomes other than he was, forevermore. I have said that the best part of our education is moral. It is the crowning glory of this Law School that it has kindled in many a heart an inextinguishable fire.

NOTE

1. The orator referred to above was James Russell Lowell; the poet was Oliver Wendell Holmes.

Chapter 40

The Study of Cases

1894

Eugene Wambaugh

Eugene Wambaugh (1856-1940) was professor at the State University of Iowa and at Harvard. This excerpt is taken from his book, *The Study of Cases: A Course of Instruction in Reading and Stating Reported Cases, Composing Head-notes and Briefs, Criticising and Comparing Authorities, and Compiling Digests* (2nd ed. Boston: Little, Brown, and Co., 1894).

Preface to the First Edition

The aim of this volume is to teach students the methods by which lawyers detect *dicta* and determine the pertinence and weight of reported cases. The most important points as to those methods are explained in the general view with which the volume opens. As the methods cannot be mastered without practice, the remainder of the volume is devoted to cases for study. The intention is that the student shall state the cases, discover the doctrines of law established by them, compose head-notes, point out *dicta*, make all possible comments as to the weight of the decisions, and compile a digest. Simple cases have been placed near the beginning of the volume, and an attempt has been made to lead the student by easy steps to the rather difficult cases with which the volume closes. Without material departure from that plan, the cases on related points of law have been placed together and have been arranged chronologically; and thus the student has been aided to compare cases and to trace the growth of law.

January 15, 1892.

Preface to the Second Edition

In the preface to the first edition it was explained that the aim of the volume is to teach students the methods by which lawyers detect *dicta* and determine the pertinence and weight of reported cases, and that the plan includes both a general statement of the methods pursued by lawyers and a collection of cases intended to serve as material for experiments by the student. In the second edition that aim is retained, and the same plan of combining a theoretical statement with practice is pursued; but to the original plan is now added an attempt to teach by example. Accordingly, an attempt is now made to present for study cases that not only afford suitable material for the beginner's experiments in detecting *dicta*, framing head-notes, and comparing and criticizing authorities, but also afford, in the arguments of counsel or in the opinions of the judges, suggestive illustrations of the way in which skilled persons perform this same work. Further, in the theoretical chapters the text is now illustrated by inserting in the foot-notes quotations, ancient and modern, showing the point of view from which English and American lawyers have always regarded precedent.

For use in a more extended course, a companion volume has been prepared, entitled Cases for Analysis, which contains nothing but cases, and presents among many others the cases given in the first edition of The Study of Cases. To prevent possible confusion, it seems necessary to explain the respective fields of the two volumes. The Study of Cases is intended solely to give training in the methods of using authorities; and in preparing the introductory text and in selecting and annotating the cases, no attempt has been made to give prominence to the doctrines of any one branch of law. Cases for Analysis, on the other hand, though having for its principal purpose training in the methods of using authorities, is composed of cases selected and annotated in such a manner as to serve, if so desired, as helps in a course of study partly devoted to the mastery of elementary topics in Contracts or in Torts. Thus the volumes differ in detail; and yet each of them is intended to aid the beginner to lay a foundation for thorough knowledge of the ways in which reported cases are to be discovered, summarized, combined, attacked, supported, and otherwise utilized for the purposes of the practical lawyer. Each volume is complete in itself. If both volumes are used, it is practicable to use them simultaneously or to cause either one of them to precede the other; but it is preferable to begin with Cases for Analysis, especially if the student has an instructor's aid, for the use of that collection will give the beginner the greater amount of actual practice with cases and will tend to prevent his laying too great stress upon the mere reading of the theoretical and didactic matter that necessarily finds place in the first book of The Study of Cases.

October 31, 1894

Chapter I: Preliminary Topics

§ 1. The Purpose of the Volume: Law and Fact: Reports as distinguished from Trials.

This volume is intended to be used by law students as a means of learning by practice, rather than by precept, how reported cases should be read, digested, criticized, and compared. By actually studying cases, and not by reading about the proper way of studying them, one best learns how they ought to be treated. Hence the student is urged to plunge promptly into the cases printed in the second book, or into some other collection of cases for students.[1] The only part of the volume intended to be read by the student before he studies his first case is this preliminary chapter.

Undoubtedly the beginner well knows that a volume of law reports gives accounts of actual litigation, but he may not know why a volume of law reports differs so vastly from accounts of the same litigation contained in newspapers. The difference between these two sorts of accounts results largely from the distinction between law and fact,—a distinction not always easy to take, but nevertheless in the main obvious enough. A question of fact asks whether certain events have happened.[2] A question of law asks whether from the happening of certain events there result rights which a court will recognize or enforce.[3] A law, in short, is a rule to the effect that when facts of a certain nature exist the courts will recognize or enforce certain rights and liabilities.

Further, a fact, an event, occurs but once; but a law, a rule, reappears upon innumerable occasions. That an event has happened is slight indication that a similar event will happen again; and if a similar event does happen, still it is merely a similar event, and not the same one. On the other hand, that a rule of law has been applied once is an indication both that there is such a rule, and that when similar facts arise the same rule, not a somewhat similar one, will be applied.

To the public, the minute details of the facts shown by the evidence, even the very words and appearance of witnesses, and of counsel and of judges, may be of interest, because strange or dramatic; and to this public interest the newspapers appeal. To lawyers, however, at least after the case is decided, almost the sole interest of the case resides in the points of law, the facts ceasing to be important save in so far as they present problems for the application of rules; and therefore the law reports give simply such an account of litigation as will indicate what problems of law arose and what rules were applied.[4] Sometimes, it is true, the facts of a case are so novel and interesting as to cause it to become a *cause célèbre*, or the examination of witnesses is conducted with peculiar skill, or the addresses of counsel are extraordinarily striking; and then even lawyers wish a permanent account similar to the one contained in a newspaper, the result being an account termed a trial, usually containing a transcript, word for word, of the questions addressed to witnesses, their answers, the addresses by counsel, and the judge's charge to the jury; but the volumes of trials are comparatively few and are seldom used.[5]

21. Eugene Wambaugh (1856-1940), a professor at Iowa and Harvard, was responsible for many decanal appointments for case-method adherents. (*Courtesy of Art & Visual Materials, Special Collections Department, Harvard Law School Library.*)

A report of a case usually consists of six parts: (1) the title of the case, which title usually contains the names of the parties;[6] (2) a head-note or syllabus, in which the reporter, or sometimes a judge of the court, indicates the point of law for which the case is by him considered to be an authority;[7] (3) a statement, usually by the reporter, but sometimes by a judge, of the nature of the litigation and the manner in which the case reached the court whose action is reported, including as elaborate an account of the pleadings and of the evidence as may be necessary in order to show what question was presented to that court;[8] (4) an abstract of the arguments of counsel;[9] (5) the opinions of the judges;[10] (6) a memorandum of the disposition made of the case in that court.[11]

§ 2. The Purpose of the General View or Summary.

Although many rules of pleading and procedure attempt to bring about a separation of questions of law from questions of fact,[12] and although the opinions of the judges and the labors of the reporter give great assistance in determining the point of law decided, it must not be inferred that it is always easy to discover the proposition of law for which a reported case is authority, nor the weight of the case. Many reported cases are difficult to analyze, and all must be examined with care. The method of determining the doctrine and the weight of a case may appear easy when mastered; but it cannot be mastered without attentive study, and hence this volume has been prepared as an aid. The first book gives a general view of the subject. The student may find it to his advantage to refer to the first book from time to time, but he will do well to postpone the consecutive reading of it until he has studied the cases, for by studying the cases with the aid of a competent teacher he will most easily and most thoroughly master the principles of which the first book is a mere summary.

§ 3. The Way to use the Cases. Reading and Stating Cases: Writing Head-Notes: Comparing Cases: Compiling a Digest.

The student should begin by reading the first case rather rapidly from end to end, his purpose being to get a general idea of the purport of the case. He should then read the case again, looking up in a law dictionary or elsewhere the meaning of all abbreviations, technical words, and obscure expressions, and not stopping until he is sure that he understands the whole case. This does not mean that the student is to stop upon each sentence until he understands it. It is not necessary or right to attempt to understand each sentence by itself. Sentences are not written in that way. Each sentence lies in the writer's mind as part of a context; and as the writer views each sentence in connection with what goes before and after, the reader should do likewise. By taking sentences in their natural connection with one another and by keeping in mind the subject under discussion, the case can be mastered even though there remain an obscure sentence here and there. The chief things the student seeks are the points presented to the court whose opinion is reported, and the propositions of law for which the decision is authority. Having made up his mind as to these matters, the student should next, with the book open before him, make a brief oral statement of the case, omitting none of those facts as to the pleadings, the evidence, or the procedure, which may be necessary to show what the points were and how they came before the court whose opinion is reported, and in conclusion he should give the result and the reasons upon which the court relied. He should then write a head-note containing the points of law for which the decision is authority, omitting *dicta*.[13] He should test the accuracy of his head-note in every possible way, attacking it as an enemy might.[14] Finally, he should consider whether the decision is right, and whether it conflicts with other decisions to which he has access.

After treating all the cases in this way, the student will be in a position to systematize his knowledge regarding the study of cases by reading the first book.

Last of all, the student should make a digest of the cases.[15]

Notes

1. The cases in the second book are chiefly cases in which the topics found in the first book are discussed by counsel or the court. In a companion volume, entitled Cases for Analysis, are gathered cases turning chiefly on points in Contracts or in Torts, and giving occasion to put into practice the matter of this volume. With Cases for Analysis, rather than with the cases in the

second book of this volume, should begin the work of the student who intends to pursue the study of cases thoroughly, or who wishes the study of cases to supplement a text-book course in Contracts or in Torts.

2. Facts include both physical and mental phenomena. Physical phenomena, e.g. the presence, color, and size of objects, are cognizable by the sense; but mental phenomena, e.g. knowledge or intention, are directly cognizable by consciousness only, and hence by persons not experiencing them must be indirectly inferred from reasoning upon physical phenomena conceived to be causes, accompaniments, or effects of such mental phenomena. Even some physical phenomena are not actually perceived by the senses, but are inferred from other physical phenomena. For example, when X says that he saw Y kill Z, X really means that he saw Y point a gun towards Z, and that he heard a discharge, and that he saw Z fall dead, and that Y's acts were the only apparent cause of Z's death, and that consequently X believes Y killed Z; and that this is not perception but is inference is obvious enough when one reflects that a person ignorant of firearms would give a very different account of the transaction. So, too, when the question is whether certain conduct is negligent, the standard assumed for comparison, the case taken by a man of ordinary prudence, is obviously an intricate conception not derived from one perception of phenomena. Vaughan v. Menlove, 3 Bing. N.C. 468, 475 (1837), *per* Tindal, C.J.; Commonwealth v. Pierce, 138 Mass. 165, 176 (1884), *per* Holmes, J; Holland's Jurisprudence (6th ed.), 98-101. Negligence, it should be noticed, is not a mental state, save in a negative sense, the sense, namely, in which it is conceived as excluding an active intention to do a wrongful act. Holland's Jurisprudence (6th ed.), 97-101; Markby's Elements of Law, §§ 225-230, 680-685.

3. J.B. Thayer, "Law and Fact," 4 Harvard Law Rev. 147 (1890); largely reprinted in Thayer's Cases on Evidence, 143-154.

4. See § 99.

5. The most famous collection of trials is the series containing English trials for treason and the like, entitled Howell's State Trials.

6. See § 101. When a title is written or printed, the usual form is—(the plaintiff) v.—(the defendant). This is usually read as—against—.

7. See §§ 27-33, 102.

8. See § 103.

9. See § 104.

10. See §§ 105-107.

11. See § 108. This memorandum is usually printed in italics at the very end of the case.

12. In procedure at law, as distinguished from procedure in equity, the most usual methods of originally raising questions of law and separating them from questions of fact are these:—

(1) Demurrer.

(2) Objections to the admissibility of evidence.

(3) Motion for a nonsuit; or demurrer to the evidence; or motion to take the case from the jury by means of a peremptory instruction to find for one party or for the other. Smith's Action at Law, (12th ed.) 137-139; 2 Thompson on Trials, §§ 2245-2274.

(4) Objections to the charge.

(5) Special verdict. 3 Bl. Com. 377.

(6) Agreed statement of facts.

(7) Motion for new trial.

(8) Motion for judgment *non obstante veredicto*, or motion in arrest of judgment.

(9) Writ of error. 3 Bl. Com. 406-411.

The third, sixth, and seventh methods do not always prevent discussions as to weight of evidence and, indeed, the first, eighth, and ninth methods are the only ones that invariably present merely questions of law. By adopting the appropriate procedure, a question of law raised by any method may be taken to a higher court.

13. See §§ 28-33.

"The student would find it an admirable exercise to endeavor to frame his own marginal abstract of a case, and then compare it with that of the report. A little practice of this kind would soon enable him to detect the points of a case,—to seize upon its true bearings; and this . . . is one of the most distinguishing characteristics of what may be termed a legal or judicial mind." Warren's Law Studies (3d ed). 1307. See also Sir Matthew Hale's preface to Rolle's Abridgment; Bishop's First Book of the Law, § 392; Reed's American Law Studies. § 246.

"An uncodified system of law can be mastered only by the student whose scientific equipment enables him to cut a path for himself through the tangled growth of enactment and precedent, and so to codify for his own purposes." Holland's Jurisprudence, (6th ed.) I.

14. See §§ 4-33.

15. See §§ 34, 114-118.

Chapter 41

A Comparison of the Use of Treatises and the Use of Case-Books in the Study of Law

1912

George Chase

George Chase (December 29, 1849-January 8, 1924) was Professor at Columbia Law School and the founding Dean of New York Law School in 1891. This article first appeared at 3 *American Law School Review* 81 (1912).

Surprise is sometimes expressed that law schools pursuing the "Dwight method" of instruction should profess to cover a larger field of study in a given time than those following the "case method." The explanation, however, is simple, as an illustration will make clearly manifest. One of the standard volumes of selected cases is that of "Cases on Evidence," by Prof. James B. Thayer, who was, until his death a few years since, professor of this important subject at the Harvard University Law School. If a comparison be made between this work and a text-book like Greenleaf on Evidence, as regards the treatment of a particular topic, as, e.g., the "Presumption of the Continuance of Life," the result is as follows:

Greenleaf on Evidence (16th edition) vol 1, sec. 41.
The statement of the law, as here made, is as follows:

"Where the issue is upon the life or death of a person, once shown to be living, the burden of proof lies upon the party who asserts his death. But after the lapse of seven years, without intelligence concerning the person, the presumption of life ceases, and the burden of proof is devolved on the other party; this period was inserted upon great deliberation, in the statute of bigamy, and the statute concerning leases for lives, and has since been adopted from analogy, in other cases; it is not necessary that the party be proved to be absent from the United States; it is sufficient if it appears that he has been absent for seven years from the particular State of his residence, without having been beard from. The presumption in such cases is, that the person is dead; but not that he died at the end of the seven years, nor at any other particular time. The time of the death is to be inferred by the jury from the circumstances."

Thayer's Cases on Evidence (2d edition, page 52).

The first case given on this this topic is *Doe v. Jesson*, an English decision of the year 1805. It reads as follows:

"This was an ejectment (brought in 1804) for a house and a small parcel of land, which was tried before Rooke, J., at the last assizes at Northampton; and the principal question was whether the action were brought in time within the second clause of exceptions in the statute of limitations, 21 Jac. 1, c. 16. The person last seized of the premises from whom the lessors of the plaintiff claimed, was one Thomas Jesson, on whose death in the year 1777, David, his elder brother, took possession of them, and transmitted the possession to the defendant, his grandson. Thomas Jesson left a son John and a daughter Frances him surviving. John was baptized in 1767, and after the death of his father, being then about ten years of age, was put out apprentice to the sea service by the parish, and was seen by a witness on his return from his first voyage about a year after the father's death; soon after which he went to sea again, and had not been heard of since, and was believed to be dead. Frances, the daughter, one of the lessors of the plaintiff, was baptized on the 21st of May, 1771, and afterwards married George, the other lessor. It was contended at the trial by the defendant's counsel that the ejectment was out of time; for it was uncertain when John, the son of Thomas, the ancestor last seized, died, and that the twenty years given by the statute began to run immediately on the death of Thomas in 1777, and consequently expired in 1797; or that, if the statute favored Frances, the daughter, till ten years after the disability of her infancy was removed, at any rate as she was of full age in 1792, she ought to have brought her ejectment in 1802, and consequently this ejectment, brought in 1804 was too late," etc., etc.

After additional matter in Thayer's Cases, equal in length to that above quoted, the decision of the court is reached, which is as follows:

"The time allowed by the statute for making an entry might be indefinitely extended if the construction contended for by the plaintiff were to be admitted. As to the period when the brother might be supposed to have died, according to the statute 19 Car. II, c. 6, with respect to leases dependent on lives, and also according to the statute of bigamy (1 Jac. I, c. II), the presumption of the duration of life, with respect to persons of whom no account can be given, ends at the expiration of seven years from the time when they were last known to be living. Therefore, in the absence of all other evidence to show that he was living at a later period, there was fair ground for the jury to presume that he was dead at the end of seven years from the time when he went to sea on his second voyage, whioch seems to be the last account of him. That was about the year 1778, which would carry his death to about 1785."

The next case in Thayer's Cases supports the rule stated in the last two sentences quoted from Greenleaf. The two cases together contain more than ten times as much reading matter as the quotation from Greenleaf, and even then they say nothing about the rule in Greenleaf that "it is not necessary" in this country "that the party be proved to be absent from the United States."

It thus appears that case-books take a good deal more space to set forth the law on a given subject than do text-books, and even then they may not do this with satisfactory completeness. Even in reading such entertaining books as Dickens' novels, it takes a good deal more time to read a two-volume work like David Copperfield than a single volume like Oliver Twist, and in reading law-books where careful attention and concentration of mind are necessary, the same truth is even more conspicuously evident. Thayer's Cases on Evidence is a volume of 1255 pages and its large pages contain so many words that a careful estimate has shown that this single volume has as much reading matter as 3½ volumes of the size of Greenleaf's treatise. And, notwithstanding this, there are various important matters for which Greenleaf finds space, which Thayer does not treat at all.

Another well-known case-book is "Keener's Cases on Quasi-Contracts," by Prof. Keener, formerly professor in Harvard University Law School, and later dean of the Columbia University Law School. This is an extensive work in two large volumes, with pages of unusually large size. Prof. Keener afterwards wrote a text-book on the same subject, but his case-book would make about 4½ volumes of the size of his text-book.

In view of these facts, therefore, it will not seem surprising that a law school using treatises as the fundamental basis of its instruction can cover the same field of legal knowledge in a shorter time than schools which confine themselves to case-books. The case-books can print but a few cases on each topic, and, even so, are oftentimes very voluminous. The text-books extract the pith from many cases and state it in compact systematic form, so that a moderate-sized volume may contain the substance of thousands of cases. Thayer's Cases on Evidence contains about 800 cases, while Greenleaf's treatise sets forth the law extracted from 14,600 cases as is shown by the list of cited cases in its latest edition. Another advantage results from this, viz., that when the law on any subject differs in different states, the treatise writer, with his compact form of statement, can find room to set forth the diverse doctrines, while the author of a case-book cannot print as many cases from the different states as would be necessary to show this, without enlarging his book beyond all reasonable bounds. At a meeting of the American Bar Association a few years since, a lawyer practicing in a Western state, but who had been educated in the East at a school following the case method, complained that the case-books on the law of real property which he had used at the law school had been of little use in preparing him for his practice in the West. A law school using a comprehensive treatise may therefore most effectually prepare its students for practice in different states of the country. It may also readily combine with the study of the text-book the reading of a moderate number of cases, to illustrate the practical application of the legal rules and principles which the text-book sets forth.

Chapter 42

Adapting the Case-Book to the Needs of Professional Training

1908

Henry Winthrop Ballantine

Henry Ballantine (1880-1951) was Professor at Wisconsin from 1913 to 1916, dean at Illinois from 1916 to 1920, professor at Minnesota from 1920 to 1924, and professor at the University of California, Berkeley, to 1951. This article first appeared in 4 *The American Law School Review* 114 (1916). This article first appeared in 2 *American Law School Review* 135 (1908). See also chapter 55.

There are many who have long felt that the present Harvard Law School case-books, while giving an excellent foundation for a future career on the bench or in theoretical teaching, fall far short in fitting lawyers for the actual work of their profession. This is strikingly manifest in comparison with the training given by medical and engineering schools.

In his article, "The Next Step in the Evolution of the Case-Book," 21 Harvard Law Review, p. 92, Professor Albert Martin Kales has grappled frankly and honestly with the pre-natal plight in which the graduates of our best law schools find themselves in the practical world. He demonstrates by concrete example how unfitted the graduate is to take up the work of his profession, even along the lines upon which the law school attempts to prepare him.

With all honor to the case system, if the case-books are inadequate, if they do not represent perfection of education and professional training for all time to come, what is to be the direction of their evolution? It is submitted that Professor Kales' proposition to retain the case-book along its present lines, but to alter the selection of cases, in order to make it display a true picture of the present state of the law in the particular jurisdiction in which it is studied, fails to point out the true path of evolution, or indicate the next step to be taken.

Evolution is universal, and consists in the adaptation of means to meet the requirements of actual conditions. Law, as the practitioner actually encounters it, may be regarded in two aspects, as a science and as an art. The problem of legal science is what the rule of law is, which comes down to what a particular court will or may be persuaded to decide on a given proposition. The practitioner's art consists in executing legal operations, either in safeguarding his client in business and corporate dealings, or in the skillful handling of the various phases of litigation.

Law schools, rightly or wrongly, do not attempt to inculcate legal art, the ability to execute legal operations, the power to do legal business, but leave that to be acquired in the office. Let us, then, take them on their own ground and see how their means, namely casebooks, are adapted to the needs of professional training in legal science.

On the very day that the graduate leaves the school and enters an office (besides being commissioned to check his chief's trunk or buy theater tickets for his wife), he will probably be requested to look up the law on some technical and undecided point in his own state. There is nothing in his case-books or notes to help him, and he is turned loose in the maze of codes, statute books, compilations and revisions of statutes annotated, of digests, abridgments, treatises, and encyclopedias. After disheartening hours of labor, struggle, and despondence he finds very little or nothing; perhaps the chief clerk then takes pity on him, and goes for the shelves himself, seizing now the encyclopedias, now the Century Digest, running his eye rapidly through the Annuals, and in less than half an hour has a list of cases covering the point. The graduate, never having settled a legal proposition by finding cases for himself, watches with amazement the chief clerk, who has never been to law school, drag up cases from the reservoirs of the law. He seems to know instinctively under what heading or within the scope of what subject he should find a grouping of similar cases. He exhausts all the labyrinthine approaches to legal knowledge with the greatest possible ease and precision.

Probably the graduate, like the clerk, will gradually learn how to determine the law for himself, after a fashion, in the office; but, as Mr. Frank B. Gilbert, Librarian New York State Library, says (2 Am. Law School Review, p. 90), the best time to acquire this power is during his student days, and the best place is the law school, having as part of its equipment a complete law library, with competent assistants, whose business it is to teach by actual demonstration how all these books are to be used. It is unreasonable to leave this fundamental matter to chance or inflict it on the overworked lawyer. This practice should be carried to greater or less extent in connection with all courses. Permanent scholarly habits cannot be acquired, or the methods of using the mechanism of a great law library inculcated, by a few lectures, moot court cases, or even a course in brief-making and the use of law-books. Most lawyers are guilty of anything but system, and fall into the most slack and slovenly methods of investigation. They have no conception of the way to use every available law tool. What is to be expected of the young graduates who become their clerks and depend upon them for example and training?

The fact that law librarians, who come in daily contact with experienced practitioners, are frequently astonished at their ineptitude in their using digests, tables of cases, and other devices, is pointed out by Mr. Gilbert in the article cited. This ineptitude is a serious handicap to the lawyer, whose time is money both to himself and to his client. Although principles and not precedents are of first importance, nevertheless it is the case which is sought for. The science of how to find the law is, says Mr. Gilbert, a concomitant part of the science of the law itself. It is the way in which the problem of legal science actually presents itself. The thing to do is to find the case, and to recognize it and use it when you have found it.

In this aspect of legal science our present "case-book system," and the modification suggested by Professor Kales, give little preparation or assistance.

If the object of the three-years course is to equip the graduate for the actual work of his profession, why not substitute for books of pre-selected opinions, books of concrete facts or skeleton cases raising the important and crucial issues of the different topics of the law. Let the student attack these problems on his own initiative, and then verify his conclusions by a search for cases in point, particularly with reference to his own jurisdiction. The student will then see the bearing of his work, and will be afforded an exercise in the application of principles drawn from every source. This will be found far more interesting and instructive, and better calculated to develop his working knowledge and powers of reasoning, of analyzing, distinguishing, and applying cases, than a mechanical dawdling over or underlining of pre-selected case-books, whether they contain the opinions of local or English judges. The way to learn is to do. This would seem indeed a logical carrying out of the Langdell idea, which has already produced splendid results at Harvard and other law schools, and which will be further advanced by forcing the student to go to the sources themselves, by training him to search for the law and use the original authorities as he will have to do in actual practice. Let us illustrate by examples:

STATEMENTS OF FACTS, WITH PRACTICAL HINTS ON THE PROPER WAY TO LOOK UP THE LAW.

Contractor vs. Owner. (From "Brief Making and the Use of Law Books," p. 326-1906.)

A contractor agreed to build a house in accordance with plans and specifications furnished by an architect and to the satisfaction of the architect. The materials furnished and services rendered by the contractor were in substantial compliance with the contract, but by mistake slightly wider clapboards were used in the gables of the house than were specified, and some of the boards used in the floors were wider than those called for. The usefulness and value of the house were not diminished thereby, and the difference in cost was less than $50. The last payment, amounting to $1,525, due under the contract, was not made. Can the contractor recover that payment?

11th Century Digest: topic, Contracts; V. Performance or Breach: (J) Substantial Performance: section 1353, Building Contracts; column 1619.

American Digests for 1897 and subsequent years: topic, Contracts: V. Performance or Breach. Bimonthly Advance Sheets, American Digest, issued since publication of last Annual Digest, same topic and subdivision.

9 Cyclopedia of Law and Procedure: topic, Contracts: IX. Discharge: Discharge by Performance: 3, Strict and Substantial Performance: page 601.

Text-books on Contracts, chapters or subdivisions on performance or discharge, and cases cited.

Householder vs. Executor of Plumber. (From Pamphlet "How to Find Cases in Point." p. S—West Publishing Co.)

In this case A. sued a plumber for so improperly repairing the plumbing in A.'s house that the sewer gas injured his health and poisoned his five children, of whom three died, after protracted illness, subjecting A. to expense. After issue was joined in the suit, defendant died. Did the suit survive as to the claim for damages for expense occasioned by the illness of A.'s children?

Landowner vs. Purchaser from Finder. (From Pamphlet "How to Find Cases in Point." p. 11-West Publishing Co.)

Goddard was the owner of a certain tract of land in W. county, Iowa, which in the year 1890 was leased to E. On May 2, 1890, an aërolite passed over northern and northwestern Iowa, a fragment of which, weighing about 60 pounds, fell on Goddard's land, burying itself in the ground to a depth of about three feet.

The fall of the aërolite was noticed by a member of the family of H. H., the day after the fall, went to the land and dug out the fragment in the presence of the tenant and took it to his house, claiming to own it, for the reason that he had found it and dug it up.

On May 5th H. sold the aërolite to Winchell, who at once took possession thereof.

Goddard brings replevin. Can he maintain the action?

The value for teaching purposes and the study of law of such problems is demonstrated by "Law in Daily Life," a collection of legal questions connected with the ordinary events of every day life by the eminent jurist, Rud. Von Ihering, which has passed through more than twelve editions. The questions were framed for students at German Universities and based mainly upon the Roman law, but are capable of being answered by English law, and have been translated into Italian, Hungarian, modern Greek, and recently into English by Mr. Henry Goudy. (Oxford Clarendon Press, 1904.) The questions are of the most practical and interesting character, and require the student to reflect and apply accurately legal principles to concrete problems. No references or solutions are given.

LAW IN DAILY LIFE

"Believing that a passing tramear is going to the South Station, I get into one for the West Station. Is the mistake here an essential one, and the contract consequently void? Must I pay the fare, supposing that, having immediately discovered the mistake, I get out? Must I pay if I travel with the car to its destination?"

"How, if the conductor gave an affirmative answer to my question—'Is this car for the South Station?' Must I even then pay the fare, or have I not a right on my side to claim damages from him or his employers, and by what action? I can still manage by taking a cab to reach the South Station before the train starts, provided the driver goes very rapidly, and accordingly I promise him double fare if he arrives in time; must the tramway company make good to me this last-mentioned payment, or can it refuse on the plea that no one need pay double fare? Can the cab driver keep this extra payment for himself or must he hand it over to his employer? Does it stand on the same footing as a tip promised to him without any such proposal or bargain?"

"If the conductor, in answering my question as above, intended to play a practical joke on me, may there be yet another kind of action against him, apart from that arising out of the contract? May actions arise out of jokes? Can this question be answered without regard to the personal relations of the parties to each other? Does a joke played upon a stranger stand on the same footing with that upon an acquaintance? Is the conductor, to whom I am ready to pay the fare, bound to give me change for a five-pound note because I have no small change? What happens when he either cannot or will not do so? May I get off without having paid? Is it enough that I assure him I will return when I have got change? Is a banker again, to whom I have to make a payment, not obliged to give me change? Would his refusal to accept payment for the reason above stated involve him in any consequent liability?"

"I am making my way on foot to the station, and, in ignorance whether the train has already started, I ask some one I meet if it has, and upon his answering in the affirmative I turn back. Assuming that the train had not yet started, and that I should have been in time to catch it, can I sue my informant to make good any damage thereby sustained (for example, loss of my ticket already purchased for me by a porter sent on ahead with the luggage)? How, if my informant is free from fault—say he absent-mindedly answered 'Yes,' instead of 'No'? How, if he deliberately told an untruth? Does anything turn on the point whether he knew that I should sustain damage?"

Excellent use has been made of original questions and problems by the late E. W. Huffcut in his book "The Elements of Business Law." Students often take up this method on their own initiative, voluntarily going over together old examination papers, as the best means to test their knowledge.

This method, which might be called the "Fact" or "Briefing System," to contrast it with the "Case-Book System," would seem to meet the need to which Professor Kales calls attention. By giving in case-books skeleton cases and practical material the student could learn law at a national law school at the feet of the greatest masters, and yet become familiar with the law in terms of cases of his particular jurisdiction. He could study general law with a definite point of view. It is sufficient that the student be put in touch with local law in the ordinary professional channels, if he make it a regular and systematic study. No doubt it is useful for scholars to compile their digests, text-books, and abridgments of different branches for professional use, but this is not the function of case-books.

The idea of making the case-book display a true picture of the law in itself seems a reversion to the text book idea. The value of the cases lies in the concrete problems of fact which they present to the student for solution, not in the answers given in the opinions. It would seem to the writer a very dubious thing, in our present system, that we obviate the necessity of solving the problems by providing ready-made answers. How many students consider the facts independently before reading the opinion? What we have in fact in our excellent case-books is a text-book method, merely supplemented by illustrations and by quiz in class; it is not a case system.

In his comment upon Professor Kales' article in the Harvard Law Review, Professor Wambaugh seems satisfied with our present system. He agrees that unquestionably "the successful practitioner must be acquainted with local law." He asserts, however, that the student's systematic work with local statutes and local decisions should be undertaken merely by way of a comprehensive review of the whole law just before or just after admission to the bar.

Our working knowledge, then, is to be picked up as best we may, when the years set apart for quiet study and preparation have gone by and we are in the struggle of professional work, or else incidentally and hastily at examination time, or when each topic is completed in class, without any regular provision therefor in the law school regime. Professor Kales has demonstrated that in certain subjects this cannot be done; at any rate experience indicates that in large part it practically goes undone. Moreover, we cannot agree with Professor Wambaugh that the majority of students cannot predict where they will spend their professional life, or that they will be dealing largely in business in all parts of the United States. We believe, with Professor Kales, that there are few recent case-book graduates who would not exchange their present incapacity and inferiority in the offices and courts of the jurisdiction where they begin to practice for efficiency and knowledge gained by a systematic study under special supervision of the reports of their own state.

Since the subject-matter of the law and the issues arising thereon are everywhere the same, these could be presented by skeleton cases, adaptable to every law school and every jurisdiction and a knowledge of the rules actually enforced in a particular jurisdiction might be acquired, even in national law schools, by systematic study from a definite point of view in the regular professional channels. What is proposed, then, is that experts prepare books of abstracts of fact, problems, and points for briefing, so arranged as properly to develop and unfold the various branches of the law, with the proper infusion of references, citations, and other aids such as the needs of the student may dictate.

This method of the "Briefing System" would have many advantages over the "Case-Book" System, beside that of giving opportunity to study the actual rules of law in force in any particular jurisdiction; it would impart the power to go to the bottom of legal problems independently; it would save the time now wasted by the statement in class of cases which all have read and to which none pay attention; it would compel clear statements, better attention, and quick comprehension; it would enable the casebook to cover a broader field and give a truer idea of the scope and relations of different subjects; it would give free range to the powers and originality of the different students.

Difficulties will arise in evolving a new method, which study and experience alone can solve. Will the beginner have sufficient knowledge of legal principles to enable him to look up the law for himself? No doubt the beginner would have to go slowly and receive much assistance from the instructor, as well as actual demonstration from the law librarian and his assistants, as to the use of the law library.

A more serious problem is time. Impossible, it may be objected, that the student should find his own cases, the straw with which to make his bricks! It may be replied that it does not take the initiated long to determine the law on a problem for one's own state, or even the weight of authority, with modern appliances. Sufficient aids, such as notes and citations, could be given. Collections of cases might still be useful adjuncts for reference, combining with the new the merits of the old pre-selected system. Concrete problems and skeleton cases would not require exhaustive examination of all the authorities on a given point in every instance. There is no reason why one should repeat, day after day, case after case, the same process; why all case-books should be mechanically constructed along the same lines, or why all topics should be treated alike and with the same emphasis.

In conclusion, it may be noted that science, the systematic knowledge of the law, is not the aim and end of most law graduates. Theirs is not the academical attitude which looks upon knowledge as something existing in and for itself, without regard to its usefulness to man, its correlation to real life. The worth of the science to them consists in its power to guide action and the conduct of legal business. The scientific side, ascertaining and forecasting the law, is but one feature of the lawyer's work. If the proper aim of the law school is to turn out lawyers well equipped for practice, or who will become so on brief apprenticeship, is the law school doing its duty in the matter of imparting the practitioner's art? Why are there practically no attempts to provide any courses whatsoever in applied law, in the handicraft of practice?

The answer, given by Prof. Chas. F. Carusi, Dean of the National University Law School (2 Am. Law School Review, p. 92), is that the nonpracticing faculty of our "Schools of Jurisprudence" believe that the knowledge of the science in which they are skilled is of more fundamental importance to the student than a training in an art of which they are ignorant. Since there is no time for both elaborating all their theories and also for teaching the application of law, training in the "soulless unsatisfying handicraft" of practice, is entirely relegated to a post-graduate apprenticeship in the law office.

The result is that the graduate enters practice entirely untrained and unfitted for the actual work of his profession, either on its scientific or operative side, either for knowing or doing law. Is there not, then, an unreasonable burden thrown by the law school on the law office? Practicing lawyers are too busy to teach students nowadays. It is entirely a matter of favor or chance whether the post-graduate obtains any systematic training, except such crumbs of the practitioner's art as he is capable of picking up for himself. In view of the fact that the office is so essential a department of legal education, will not some philanthropist establish subsidized law offices throughout the country, where graduates of our "schools of jurisprudence," by right and not merely by good luck and favor, may find a clinic or laboratory for operations in the subject-matter of law practice and become as completely equipped for their work as the graduates of engineering and medical schools? If not, let professors of law consider well what is to be the next step in the evolution of their case-books.

Chapter 43

Weaknesses of the "Case Method" in American Law Schools

Suggestions Looking Toward Improved Instruction

1910

Josef Redlich

Josef Redlich (1869-1936) was an Austrian professor of history, law, and government. This article first appeared in 4 *American Law School Review* 1 (1910). It consists of a chapter taken from a report made by Dr. Josef Redlich to the Carnegie Foundation for Advancement of Teaching, subsequent to an investigation and study on the part of Dr. Redlich of methods pursued and the results obtained in a number of our representative law schools. The full report, consisting of some 75 pages, was published in pamphlet form in December, 1914, by the Carnegie Foundation, under the title "The Common Law and the Case Method in American University Law Schools." Two important conclusions reached by Dr. Redlich looking toward improved instruction in schools using the case method are set forth in the article. Briefly stated, these are: First, before the student enters upon the case method of study, he ought to have a certain foundation upon which to build, which should give him a prospectus and should acquaint him with the elementary ideas and the fundamental concepts common to all branches of the law. Similarly, at the end of the term of study, an effort should be made to give the student a comprehensive view of the law as a whole, and of its relation to the administration of justice. Second, the law school course should be lengthened to cover a period of four years.

Herein we find the strength, but herein also the weaknesses, of the case method. These weaknesses, to sum up the writer's opinion in a word, lie on the scientific side of American legal instruction in its present form. In this connection we may distinguish between, first, the influence exerted by the case method upon the scientific comprehension of law by the students, that is to say, upon legal instruction proper; and, secondly, its reaction upon the scientific elaboration of law in general, that important function of law faculties which we must consider apart from their purely pedagogic aims.

With respect to the first point, it seems to me that the following consideration is of some importance. It is characteristic of the case method that where it has thoroughly established itself, legal education has assumed the form of instruction almost exclusively through analysis of separate cases.[1] The result of this is that the students never obtain a general picture of the law as a whole, not even a picture which includes only its main features. This is, in my opinion, however, just as important for the study of Anglo-American law as for the codified continental systems, and is a task which should also be accomplished by the law courses in the universities. To this end, the following seems to me above all things requisite:

First, as an introduction to the entire curriculum, care should be taken to introduce to the students, in elementary fashion, the fundamental concepts and legal ideas that are common to all divisions of the common law. Or, to express it in a word current in European pedagogy, the beginners in American law schools should be given a legal Propädeutik, or preparatory course, which in simple yet scientific manner shall set forth the elements of the common law—shall furnish, that is to say, a comprehensive view of the permanent underlying concepts, forms, and principles, not forgetting the elementary postulates of law and legal relationships in general. The more rigorously casuistic the case method of instruction which then follows necessarily has to be, the more important it seems to me it is to make clear to the students at the very beginning certain fundamental facts and guideposts of the law which are removed from all casuistry and theoretical controversy. Only in this way will their future studies rest upon a solid and scientifically grounded foundation.

Classical Roman law at its height developed, as is well known, a special literary type, the Institutes. This was a comprehensive presentation of the elements of law, intended to introduce and facilitate the regular course of study, and the fact that Justinian retained it as an introduction to his Code shows what importance was attached to it. Now when, at the beginning of the nineteenth century in Germany, thanks to the work of Savigny, modern teaching of the so-called German common law came to be developed, the real foundation for this new teaching was the reception of the Roman law; and so, naturally enough, the name and form of the Institutes were taken over for the introductory legal instruction. In all the German law faculties it became the invariable practice to begin legal instruction with a so-called "Institutes-course" (Institutionenvorlesung), which usually comprised, first, a general elementary discussion of the relation between law and the state; next, some account of the external history of the Roman law; and, finally, a description of the fundamental institutions and main principles of the Roman private law in its important divisions, such as the law of persons, of property, of liens, of inheritance, of obligations, etc., in connection with which the main events of the inner legal history, that is to say, the development of the most important concepts and doctrines, were also presented. When, later, codification began in the great German provinces, scientific instruction in the law (the Codes again being in large part founded upon Roman legal thought) very soon recovered from the error, which it originally committed, of immediately beginning to teach these new law codes dogmatically. The faculties returned rather to the practice of introducing scientific instruction in law by thoroughly inculcating the fundamentals of the historic Roman law, and so again, at the very forefront of this instruction, stood an Institutionenvorlesung. This can be traced with especial clearness in the history of legal education in the Austrian universities, where, about the middle of the nineteenth century, the reforms connected with the name of Josef Unger occurred in the manner described. In the German Empire, too, although the Civil Code, since its introduction, as a matter of course constitutes the core and the main substance of legal instruction, the custom of prefacing an "Institutes-course" has continued.

Similarly, in my opinion, in American university law schools the students ought to be given an introductory lecture course, which should present, so to speak, "Institutes" of the common law. Every department into which the American law is divided, whether as common law or equity, employs certain common elementary ideas and fundamental legal concepts which the student ought to be made to understand before he is introduced into the difficult analysis of cases. Concepts such as choses in action, person and property within the meaning of the law, complaint and plea, title and stipulation, liability and surety, good faith and fraud, should, in these introductory lectures, be given to American students in connection with a system of the law, even although this should include only the general fundamental features. They should not, as usually occurs to-day, come to the students unsystematically and unscientifically, as scraps of knowledge more or less assimilated out of law dictionaries and indiscriminate reading of text-books.

And there is a second consideration which must be taken into account as bearing upon this question of the comprehension of law as a whole. The current common law of England and America is an essentially historical law. Many of its current concepts and doctrines go back through a development of centuries, and can be comprehended only on the basis of a fundamental historical explanation. For Anglo-American law just as much as for the common German law of the nineteenth century, the birth and powerful influence of the new historical method marks the turning point at which the inheritance of the Middle Ages—legal craftsmanship and practical expertness in law—becomes converted into legal science. What Savigny and his pupils and the entire legal-historical school of Germany accomplished for the common law of Germany has been performed in no less admirable fashion in the last half-century for the English common law by such men as Thayer, Langdell, Ames, and Bigelow in America, and in England by that incomparable genius, F. W. Maitland.

The task which now in our time confronts scientific legal instruction in America, the task of teaching the historical development of the separate doctrines and principles of the common law, is already in part being most excellently performed in those schools where the necessary casebooks have been provided, and where the case method is so handled as to lay proper emphasis, in the analysis of the separate cases, upon the historical point of view. But here, also, it seems to me that the historical scaffolding of the English common law, as a general introduction to the analytical study of Anglo-American law, is extremely desirable and of the greatest importance. A scientifically constructed survey of the main sources of the common law and of their relation to one another; of the concepts of customary and positive law; a short external history of the law, which should include the origin and development of the English courts of justice; a brief exposition and development of the nature and extent of the concept of equity; a description of that institution so important for Anglo-American law, the Reports, and of the concept of precedent; finally, also, a glance at the phenomenon of statutory law (legislation) and its nature and forms—all these things and much else connected with them ought to be furnished the students at the beginning of their studies, before their introduction to the analytical study of the cases. The fact that this ground can be covered only in elementary and summary fashion need not prevent the presentation from being thorough and scientific.

This, then, would be another task to be accomplished by an "Institutes-course" in the English common law. A further service would be the introduction of the students from the beginning into the atmosphere peculiar to legal science, through direct lecturing on the part of a living teacher. I attach very great importance to the direct lectures of a legal scholar who has been trained in a thoroughly scientific manner. It is simply doctrinaire exaggeration on the part of many contemporary law teachers in American universities, when, in order to preserve the exclusiveness of the case method as a unique, hermetically sealed system of teaching, they reject every lecture a limine as a means of instruction; when they describe such lectures as mediaeval and therefore obsolete; when they declare that lectures to-day do not easily arouse, and still less easily hold, the interest and attention of the students. In the same way that the students put down in their notebooks the main points which are brought out by discussion in the pure case method exercises, so they can just as well jot down the train of thought of a series of such lectures, in which, the elementary concepts of the law and the most important details of legal terminology are explained to them. Such a course of preliminary lectures, whose nature throughout should be that of talks to beginners, would, in my opinion, with great profit, take the place of the now customary, unscientific introduction to the law, through law dictionaries and discursive reading.

The course of lectures on Institutes, which I here recommend to serve as authoritative introduction to the study of law, would naturally divide itself along the two lines of approach already indicated. First would come a sort of "general part," an exposition of an essentially dogmatic kind, in which the main legal concepts, forms, and fundamental institutions, corresponding to the examples I have already cited, should be systematically set forth, while the second part should give a beginners' course in the sources of the law, and a historical survey of the main events in its development. Such a course of lectures, which should be given for about three or four hours a week, would doubtless extend over a part of the first year of study, at least the first third or the first half. On the other hand, there is no reason why a part of the case method exercises which are now conducted during the first year in separate fields of the common law should not also go on simultaneously. If, however, during the first few weeks of study, the main task of the pupils

22. Joseph Redlich (1869-1936). Although an Austrian, Redlich's report for the Carnegie Foundation was instrumental in consolidating the position of the case method as the national method of instruction, as well as the ABA style of law school organization as the national model. (*Courtesy of Art & Visual Materials, Special Collections Department, Harvard Law School Library.*)

consisted in a course of "Institutional Lectures," then, in my opinion, we should essentially shorten and diminish that confusion and obscurity which—as is admitted by even the most zealous advocates of the exclusive case method—troubles most of the young men at present during a large part of their first year in their attempts to analyze the cases. They would enter upon the analysis with a certain amount of definite knowledge, and certainly with a better understanding of the sense of the entire machinery of the law. They would learn more quickly to group under several general heads the particulars with which the study of the cases supplies them, and thus from the beginning would introduce a certain orderly arrangement into their growing knowledge of the law. In other words, the accumulation of the material of legal thought, taking place daily through the analytical exercises, would from the beginning take place systematically and with a certain consciousness of purpose.

Such an introduction to the law, effected by means of a scientifically systematized course of lectures, would in my opinion enhance those great advantages which subsequent instruction under the case method undoubtedly possesses for the students. Particularly would this be true for those who by mental aptitude incline more to the dogmatic or synthetic method of thought than to the analytic, a distinction which is given by nature, and to which far too little importance is attached by the advocates of an exclusively analytic method.

An introductory course of lectures, then, upon the Institutes of the common law seems to me extremely desirable, in order that before the student enters upon the casuistic study of law—lasting several years and of necessity splitting the topic up into fragments—he may be given a general survey of legal organization, and may thus be made to see the system of law as a living whole, the product of centuries of development. I go farther than this, however. It seems to me very advisable to add also at the end of the course lectures which shall furnish the American law student once more, before he steps out directly into practical legal life, a certain general summing up and survey of the law. If the student has mastered all essential institutions and doctrines of the common law during his three years' course, through the analysis of countless cases, he will certainly now be sufficiently matured to undertake, with full understanding, two important tasks. First, he should be able to grasp the general scientific theory of the law as one of the great dominating phenomena of human civilization and human thought. Secondly, he should now be fully prepared to cast to great advantage a comparative glance at that second mighty system of law which has shaped the history of humanity, namely the Roman law.

The first mentioned task corresponds pretty closely to what has for a long time been designated by English and American teachers of law by the term "Jurisprudence," and is taught as such in several universities. By this is understood, broadly speaking, a presentation of the leading fundamental principles that are more or less common to the modern law of every civilized people, considered both as products of a developing positive law and as influenced and perfected by the theories and ideas of legal philosophy. Historical, philosophical, and sociological aspects of the law have here to be bound together in harmony with one another, in order to help erect a theory of the fundamental principles of law which shall rest upon the surest possible foundations. The concept of law in general, the concept of sovereignty, of law as an objective norm on the one side, as subjective authority on the other; the various classifications and divisions of the law—public, private, and international; the various manifestations of the law—customary, written, and judge-made; in connection with this, moreover, a general theory of the sources of law; further, the philosophic basis of the great legal institutions of possession, of property, of inheritance, of contract, and of damages; in connection with this the theory of the will in law; and, finally, the great basic forms and fundamental principles of the safeguard of law, of procedure; these, and many other fundamental theoretical problems besides, could be presented to the mature students in such a course of lectures, under the head of Jurisprudence, to their great advantage.

The second course of lectures, on the other hand, those dealing with Roman law, would also, of course, be primarily so planned as to bring the outlines of this system of law into comparison with the common law, already familiar to American students at this stage. The analogies and the differences which are brought out sharply by the comparative method would go far to make the features and characteristics of the native law still clearer to the students, and to deepen their understanding of their own law through their insight into that of other peoples.

Now, it is perfectly true that through both of these additions—the institutional lectures at the beginning and the two encyclopedic courses at the close of the course of study—the curriculum, already very comprehensive and with difficulty to be covered in a three years' course, would be very appreciably enlarged. Indeed, the subdivision of the three original departments of the law—common law, equity, and procedure—has now been pushed so far and the number of specialized courses has thereby become so great, that three years appears entirely too short for a legal education, pursued with the earnestness and thoroughness which characterize the leading university law schools of America at present. A glance at the annexed curriculum offered at Harvard brings this fact out unmistakably.

First Year: Agency; Civil Procedure at Common Law; Contracts; Criminal Law and Procedure; Property; Torts.
Second Year: Bills of Exchange and Promissory Notes; Equity; Evidence; Insurance; Property; Public Service Companies; Sales of Personal Property; Trusts; Damages; Law of Persons.
Third Year: Conflict of Laws; Constitutional Law; Corporations; Partnership; Property; Suretyship and Mortgage; Bankruptcy; Equity; Municipal Corporations; Quasi-Contracts; Admiralty.

Harvard, realizing this fact, and at the same time desirous to take a step forward in the development of legal scientific studies, introduced several years ago an optional fourth year, open, of course, only to graduates. As appears from the list given below,[2] there are offered in this fourth year, besides legal philosophy, general jurisprudence, and Roman law, a number of special courses which from their very nature can avail themselves of the analytical case method only in part. Assuredly, then, if an obligatory fourth year should be added to the American university law curriculum, enough time would be gained to find place not only for the courses here suggested, but also for special lectures, and for special practical analytic exercises conducted by the case method; so, in particular, in international law and American administrative law. There would also be time for lectures upon legal reform, designed to give the students, even before they go out into practice, some critical guidance in the problems of the lex ferenda. In general this lengthening of the period of law study would undoubtedly permit a deepening in various directions of the students' theoretical knowledge of the law, and this, again, would act as a powerful stimulus to many, after they have left the school, to continue their scientific studies.

It is not as though lengthening of the legal curriculum necessarily means any loss of time; this need not be the case if the year be taken away from the place where, at present, it is spent to the least advantage, namely, from the college. It would lead me too far, and I ought not to venture on the basis of my own very insufficient personal experiences, to say here anything definite in regard to the efficiency of the present-day American college. The question is too difficult, and involves too many important considerations. But much that I have heard and read of the college and of its success in its present form, much that I could observe for myself, leads me with all caution to the conclusion that in those very institutions in which college work is taken as a preliminary to law, the benefits of the college training could easily be secured to future law school students by setting a more rigorous pace in a period of time shortened by a year. The gain of this full year would undoubtedly, however, be a good thing for the law school and hence for legal education.

NOTES

1. Judge Baldwin (14 Harv. Law Rev. 258) replies to the question, What is a case-book? in the following words: "It is in substance a series of fragmentary discussions of particular topics, interspersed with fragmentary portions of opinions from reported cases. * * * No science can be learned purely from particulars. The universals must be studied, to discover what the particulars mean and whence they sprang."

2. *Graduate Courses*: Roman Law and the Principles of the Civil Law Modern Code as developments thereof; Criminal Procedure and Procedural Reform; Administrative Law; History of the Common Law; International Law as administered by the Courts; Introduction to the Year Books; Jurisprudence.